The New Zealand Bed and Breakfast Book

Homestays • Farmstays • B&B Inns

Complimentary Copy from
Cor Reutel

Moonshine Press

Copyright ©2000. Moonshine Press

Published by Moonshine Press,
56 Mortimer Terrace
Wellington, New Zealand
Telephone: 04-385 2615, Fax: 04-385 2694
Website: http://www.bnb.co.nz

ISBN 0-473-06252-6

All information in this guidebook has been supplied by the hosts. The publishers endeavour to verify information supplied, but will not be liable for any inaccuracies.

Cover photo: "Kawatea" Okains Bay, Banks Peninsula

The NZ B&B Book
Schedule of Standards
All properties have been inspected

General
Local tourism and transport information available to guests
Property appearance neat and tidy, internally and externally
Absolute cleanliness of the home in all areas used by the guests
Absolute cleanliness of kitchen, refrigerator and food storage areas
Roadside identification of property
Smoke alarms
Hosts accept responsibility to comply with local body bylaws
Pets & children must be mentioned in *NZ B&B Book* listing
Host will be present to welcome and farewell guests

Bedrooms
Each bedroom solely dedicated to guests with -
Bed heating
Heating
Light controlled from the bed
Wardrobe space with variety of hangers
Drawers
Mirror
Power point
Waste paper basket
Drinking glasses
Night light or torch for guidance to w.c. if not adjacent to bedroom
Opaque blinds or curtains on all windows where appropriate
Good quality mattresses in sound condition on a sound base
Clean bedding appropriate to the climate, with extra available
Clean pillows with additional available

Bathroom & toilet facilities
At least one bathroom adequately ventilated and equipped with -
Bath or shower
Wash handbasin and mirror
Wastebasket in bathroom
Lock on bathroom and toilet doors
Electric razor point if bedrooms are without a suitable power point
Soap, towels, bathmat, facecloths, fresh for each new guest
Towels changed or dried daily for guests staying more than one night
Sufficient toilet and bathroom facilities to serve family and guests adequately
Towel rail per guest in the bathroom or bedroom

Meals
Beverages: water, milk, tea, coffee should be offered
If fruit juice is offered it must be 100% pure juice
Breakfast: A generous breakfast must be provided

New Zealand

Northland

Great Barrier Island

Auckland

Coromandel

Waikato, King Country

Bay of Plenty

Gisborne

Taranaki, Wanganui

Hawkes Bay

Manawatu, Horowhenua

Wairarapa

Wellington

Nelson, Golden Bay

Marlborough

West Coast

Canterbury

Chatham Islands →

South Canterbury, North Otago

Otago

Southland

Stewart Island

Contents

Tips for easier B&B travel

Ensuite and private bathrooms are for your use exclusively,
Guests share bathroom means you may be sharing with other guests,
Family share bathroom means you will be sharing with the family.

In the tariff section of each listing 'continental' breakfast consists of fruit, cereal, toast, tea/coffee; 'full' breakfast is the same with an additional cooked course; 'special' breakfast has something special.

Do not try to travel too far in one day. Take time to enjoy the company of your hosts and other locals.

Book your B&B. It is a nuisance for you if you arrive to find the accommodation has been taken. And besides hosts need a little time to prepare.

The most suitable time to arrive is late afternoon, and to leave is before 10 in the morning.

If you would like dinner please give your host sufficient notice to prepare.

If you are unsure of anything ask your hosts about it. They will give you a direct answer.

Most of our B&Bs are able to accept credit cards.

If you have made your reservations from overseas, check that your dates are correct. You might cross the dateline to come to New Zealand.

Please let your hosts know if you have to cancel. They will have spent time preparing for you.

Make your Cook Strait Ferry reservation in advance.

If you need to use a public phone, use the first one you see. It may be hours before you see another.

Carry a B&B phone card. Most public phones do not take coins. Free Phone cards can be obtained from any of our hosts.

New Zealand road signs are getting better, but your best directions come from asking a local.

Some listings show hosts accept vouchers. The only vouchers accepted are The New Zealand Bed & Breakfast Book vouchers.

A week's free B&B

**FILL IN A COMMENT FORM AND
YOU WILL BE IN THE DRAW FOR
A WEEKS FREE B&B FOR TWO**

• At most B&Bs you will find comment forms. **There is also a comment form at the back of the book**. Simply fill in a comment form and return it to us, and you will be in the draw for **a week's free B&B.**

• Every comment form you send in will increase your chances of winning the **week's free B&B**, so complete a form for each place you stay.

• We suggest you save your comment forms in one envelope, and send them in together at the end of your trip.

• Each person staying can complete a comment form - a couple can complete two separate forms.

• Entries will be drawn on 21 December 2000 and the winner will be notified by mail immediately.

The Prize
• The prizewinner will be given vouchers entitling them and a partner to 7 nights B&B at any B&B accepting vouchers in *The New Zealand Bed and Breakfast Book*.

• The stays can be any time in 2001. They need not be consecutive.

———————————————

Introduction

The popularity of B&B in New Zealand has increased each year since we first published *The New Zealand Bed and Breakfast Book*. The reason for this amazing growth is quite simply that the hosts are such wonderful people. Most hosts who are listed here are homeowners who want to share their love of the country with travellers. Each listing has been written by the host, and you will discover their warmth and personality is obvious in their writing. Ours is not simply an accommodation guide but an introduction to a uniquely New Zealand holiday experience.

Any holiday is remembered primarily by the people one meets. How many of us have loved a country simply because of one or two especially memorable individuals encountered there? Bed and Breakfast offers the traveller who wants to experience the feel of the real country and get to know the people to do just that. Bed and Breakfast in New Zealand means a warm welcome into someone's home. Most of the places listed are homes, with a sprinkling of private hotels and guesthouses. Remember that Bed and Breakfast hosts cannot offer hotel facilities. Therefore please telephone ahead to book your accommodation and give ample notice if you require dinner.

Guarantee of Standards - All properties inspected
All B&Bs which are newly listed are inspected to ensure that they meet our required standard. We expect that all B&Bs in *The New Zealand Bed and Breakfast Book* will offer excellent hospitality. **Please fill in our comment forms so that our high standard can be maintained.**

Tariff
The prices listed will apply until 31st December 2000 unless otherwise stated. Prices are in New Zealand dollars, and include Goods and Services Tax. There will be no extra costs to pay unless a surcharge is indicated with vouchers, or you request extra services. Some offer a reduction for children. Unless otherwise stated this applies to age 12 and under.

Breakfast
Breakfast is included in the tariff. Some homes offer a continental breakfast which includes fruit, cereal, toast and tea or coffee. Others offer a full breakfast indicated by (full) in the listing, which includes a cooked course as well.   Some offer a special breakfast, indicated by (special) which includes some specialties of the house.

Vouchers
Some hosts have indicated in their listings that they will accept vouchers. The vouchers referred to are *The New Zealand Bed & Breakfast Book* vouchers which can be obtained from Bookin (see page 8). *Vouchers accepted* refers only to The Bed & Breakfast Book vouchers.

Self-contained accommodation
Many homes in towns and on farms can offer separate self-contained accommodation. In almost every case linen and food will be provided if required. The tariff will vary depending on your requirements, so check when booking.

Campervans

For those who get to know the country by camping or motor-home, Bed and Breakfast offers wonderful advantages. You will see in many listings the word 'campervans'. These homes have suitable facilities available such as laundry, bathroom, electricity and sometimes meals by arrangement. The charge, usually for up to four people, is modest and is shown in each listing.

Finding your way around - Using the New Zealand B&B Book

A satisfying part of compiling *The New Zealand Bed and Breakfast Book* is that we have been able to change an irritating aspect of most New Zealand guide books. Usually towns are listed alphabetically so that we hop about the country from such places as Akaroa to Auckland to Blenheim for example. This is infuriating to reasonably well-travelled natives like ourselves, so we imagine the despair of a visitor unfamiliar with place names and local geography.

New Zealand is long and narrow. It makes more sense to us to travel southwards down the islands listing the homes as we come to them.

We have divided New Zealand into geographical regions and have included a map of each region. We have simply listed the homes as they occur on our southward journey.

In areas such as Southland where we travel across more than down, the route we have taken should be obvious.

Whether you are from overseas or a fellow New Zealander, please take the opportunity to stay with New Zealanders in their homes. Chat with your hosts. Enjoy their company. Each host will be your additional personal travel agent and guide. We wish you an enjoyable holiday and welcome comments from guests.

Please write with comments or suggestions to:

> *The New Zealand Bed and Breakfast Book*
> Moonshine Press
> 56 Mortimer Terrace
> Wellington
> New Zealand

Happy travelling

Moonshine Press

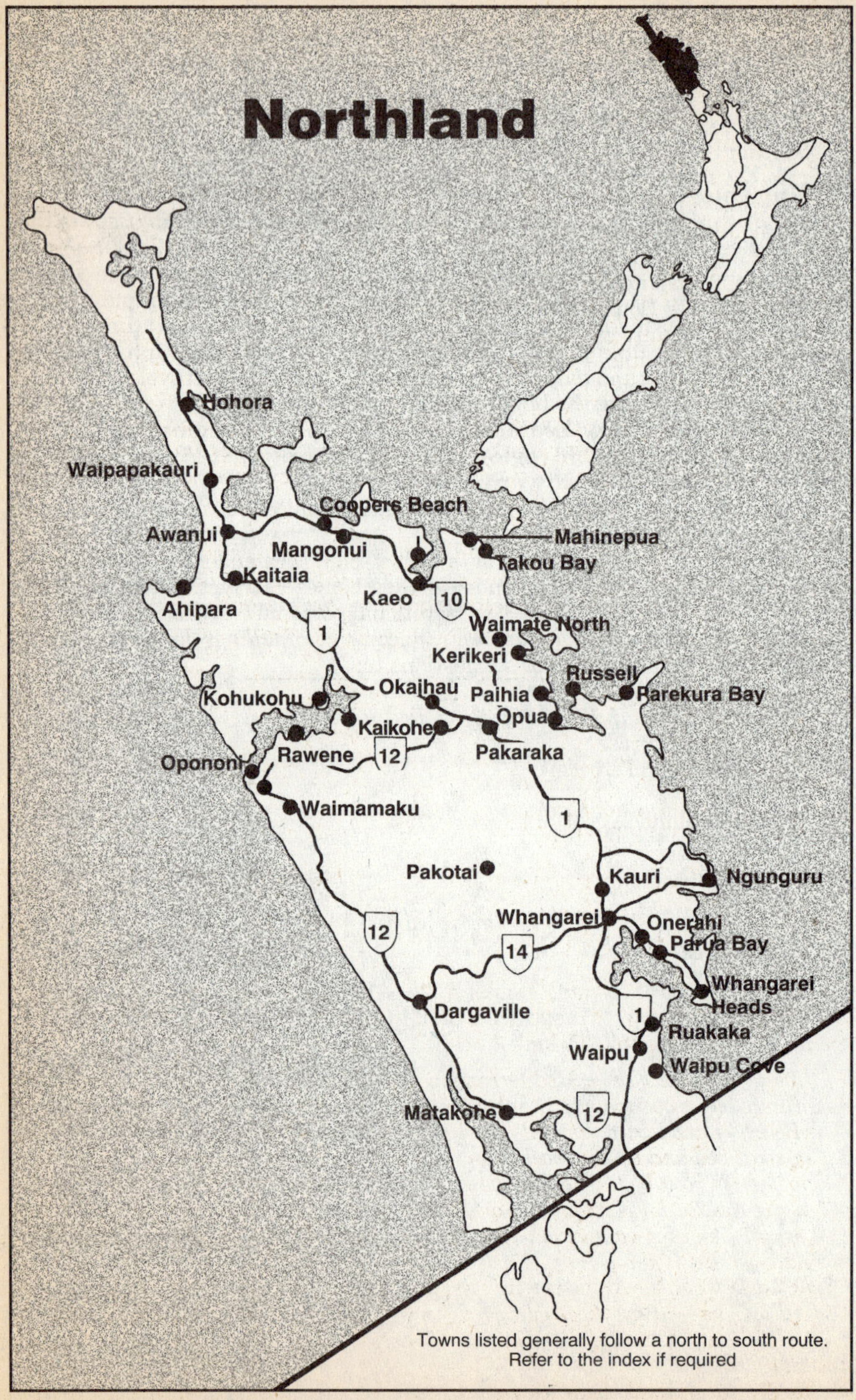

Northland

Hohora

Waipapakauri

Coopers Beach

Awanui

Mangonui

Mahinepua

Kaitaia

Takou Bay

Kaeo

10

Ahipara

1

Waimate North

Kerikeri

Kohukohu

Okaihau

Russell

Paihia

Parekura Bay

Opua

Opononi

Kaikohe

Rawene

12

Pakaraka

Waimamaku

1

Pakotai

Kauri

Ngunguru

Whangarei

Onerahi

Parua Bay

14

Whangarei Heads

Dargaville

1

Ruakaka

Waipu

Matakohe

12

Waipu Cove

Towns listed generally follow a north to south route.
Refer to the index if required

Houhora
Homestay
Address: Far North Road, Houhora,
700m North of BP station opposite Houhora Fire Station.
Name: Bruce & Jacqui Malcolm
Telephone: (09) 409 7884
Fax: (09) 409 7884
Mobile: (025) 926 992
Email: houhora.homestay@xtra.co.nz
Beds: 3 King (or 6 Single), (3 bedrooms)
Bathroom: 2 Ensuite, 1 Private
Tariff: B&B (full) Double $90, Single $70, Dinner $25.
Credit cards. Enquire about seasonal specials.
Nearest Town: Kaitaia - we are 44km north.

We have fled our largest city to live here in paradise on the shores of the Houhora Harbour, and are ideally situated to cater for your Far North expeditions.
If you are visiting Cape Reinga, take time out to enjoy the beautiful beaches and the other attractions that are within easy commuting distance. We can arrange four wheel drive trips, line or deep sea fishing excursions, and are close to two golf courses and offer you relaxed and quality accommodation on your return from your days outing. We'll supply you with a continental or full breakfast. The bread is home-made, the food on our table comes from our developing 3 1/2 acre garden or is purchased locally. Fresh fish when Bruce has time to get out and catch them. Lunches and evening meals can be provided as an extra by arrangement. Clothes washing, E-mail, Internet and fax facilities available.

Ahipara – Kaitaia
Guest House
Address: "Siesta Luxury Guest Lodge",
P.O. Box 30, Ahipara, Northland
Name: Carole and Alan Harding
Telephone: (09) 409 2011
Fax: (09) 409 2011
Mobile: (025) 2939 665
Email: ninetymile@xtra.co.nz
Beds: 2 Queen (2 bedrooms)
Bathroom: 2 Ensuite
Tariff: B&B (full/continental) Double $135,
Single $100, Dinner by arrangement. Credit Cards.
Nearest Town: Kaitaia 15 km

We live in a large sunny Mediterranean style home set in private grounds with panoramic views overlooking the sheltered Ahipara Bay and the magnificent Ninety Mile Beach. Each luxurious well-appointed room has a private balcony, comfortable queen-sized bed and ensuite bathroom. Sleep to the sound of the sea and wake up to seaviews from your bed. The most beautiful beaches and hidden treasures are close-by. Horse trekking, 4 WD bike hire or simply walk and discover your own wilderness. Fish, game-fish, surf-cast, scuba dive, surf or swim on our safe local beach. Travel on local air-conditioned buses up Ninety Mile Beach to the Cape.
Directions: *Take the Ahipara road west and drive past Ahipara School, turning left toward Shipwreck Bay. Keep going a kilometre until you get to the beach. Opposite, on the left, you will see Tasman Heights. Follow the road up the hill and you will see the "Siesta" signs.*
Home Page: www.ahipara.co.nz/siesta

Ahipara - Ninety Mile Beach. Kaitaia
2 fully self-contained Beach Front Units on Waters edge
Address: "Foreshore Lodge",
Ninety Mile Beach,
269 Foreshore Road, Ahipara,
RD1 Kaitaia.
Name: Maire & Selwyn Parker
Telephone: (09) 409 4860
Fax: (09) 409 4860
Beds: Family Unit: 1 King, 2 Single
(2 bedrooms/lounge, 2 double bedsettees)
Studio Unit: 1 Super King, 1 Foldaway Bed.
Bathroom: 1 Private, 1 Ensuite
Tariff: B&B (continental) Double $84-$104 (2 people),
seasonal. Single $74. Price negotiable for longer stays.
Children very welcome. No pets. Credit Cards welcome.
Nearest Town: Kaitaia17km (15 mins)

Foreshore Lodge is situated right on the waters edge in Ahipara Bay, at the sheltered southern end of Ninety Mile Beach facing north. Perfect setting. Our unpolluted water and beach is very safe for fishing, surfing, swimming or walking. Relax and enjoy lovely seaviews from the comfort of your unit or sheltered terrace with BBQ.
Golf course 3 km, Take-away's and dairies 2 km, restaurant 1 km. All tours to Cape Reinga, Around Reef point over gumfields, 4 WD fishing tours and Quad hire - all from our front door. Our family unit has access for a small manual wheelchair inside, and easy walking for everyone across road onto the lovely sandy beach.
Directions: *Take the road to West Coast from Kaitaia to Ahipara 15km. Drive straight past school to the beach along Foreshore Road 2km till you see our sign, Foreshore Lodge. Come relax and enjoy all year round.*

Ahipara
Bed & Breakfast
Address: 72 Foreshore road, Ahipara
Name: Marie and Brian Veza
Telephone: (09) 409 4819
Beds: 2 Single (1 Bedroom)
Bathroom: 1 Ensuite
Tariff: B&B (Special/Continental) Double $70,
Single $40, Children half price, Dinner $20.
Campervan facilities $12.
NZ B&B Vouchers accepted $10 surcharge.
Nearest Town: Kaitaia 15 min (16 km)

We invite you to share our comfortable home with modern private bedroom with ensuite. Relax and enjoy our sea views, the rolling surf and beautiful sunsets, walk for miles and explore or if more energetic, swimming, surfing, quad hire, horse riding, deep sea fishing and our 18 hole golf course is just around the Bay. We are both keen golfers and have a beef farm at Herikino, for those who are keen on farming can visit.
Directions: *Take road to Ahipara from Kaitaia, turn left at Ahipara School, follow road around corner, 3rd house on beach side.*

Awanui, Ninety-Mile-Beach – Kaitaia

Farmstay
Address: Beach Road, Awanui R.D. 1,
Northland
Name: Tony & Helen Dunn
Telephone: (09) 406 7494
Beds: 2 Double (2 bedrooms)
Bathroom: 1 Guests share
Tariff: B&B (special) Double $90, Single $45,
Children (under 10 yrs) 1/2 price, Dinner $25.
Nearest Town: Awanui 9 kms, Kaitaia 16 km

We have a comfortable, modern home, built for the sun and view, on a hill overlooking the farm, the Aupouri Pine Forest and the Ninety Mile Beach. "Ninety Mile Angoras" is a property of 40 hectares of rolling sand hill country, presently carrying cattle, sheep and goats. Ninety Mile Beach, noted for its fishing, is one minute drive away to the West, while a feast of East Coast Beaches lie within thirty minutes easy drive. All have beautiful golden sands and unpolluted waters. This home is an excellent central point to fully explore the North of New Zealand. Cape tour buses collect and deliver passengers from the farm gate. Mohair products for sale. Horse treks arranged.
Directions: *From Awanui, drive North approximately 6 kms. Turn left at signs to The park Ninety Mile Beach. Our farm is on the right, approximately 3 km after turn off, the last farm before the forestry and beach.*

Kaitaia

Homestay B&B
Address: Historic Wireless Rd
Bed & Breakfast, RD 2, Kaitaia,
Far North.

Name: Clive and Cherie Johnston
Telephone: (09) 408 1929 **Mobile**: 025 268 1353
Beds: 1 Queen, 1 Double, 1 Single (3 Bedrooms)
Bathroom: 1 Guests Share
Tariff: B&B (Full/Continental) Double $70,
Single $40, Children under 12 years half price.
Nearest Town: Kaitaia 4km, Mangonui 20 minutes.

Enjoy a completely relaxing stay in our recently renovated grand 86 year old Kauri villa. Set on 5 acres in a semi-rural setting, we are surprisingly close to over 30 beautiful beaches and great fishing. We can organise an exciting trip along the famous 90 Mile beach to the lighthouse to Cape Reinga or a horse trek along 90 Mile beach. Relax in a beautiful appointed room or one of the spacious lounges.
Wireless Rd was once the site of a ship to shore radio station, commissioned December 18th, 1913, an important link with allied ships during World War 1. This house was built to accommodate the radio staff.
We have two children, Elaine 12 and Leigh 10, two cats and a dog.
Directions: *From Awanui 6km south Wireless Rd is on the right opposite the Collard tavern. From Kaitaia 4km north Wireless Rd on the left.*

Coopers Beach
Homestay
Address: 104 State Highway 10,
Coopers Beach
Name: Mac'n'Mo's
Telephone: (09) 406 0538
Fax: (09) 406 1539
Email: MacNMo@xtra.co.nz
Beds: 1 Queen, 2 Double,
2 Single (4 bedrooms)
Bathroom: 2 Ensuite, 2 Guests share
Tariff: B&B (continental) Ensuite $75, Double $65, Single $40,
Dinner $25. NZ B&B Vouchers accepted $15 surcharge ensuite.
Nearest Town: Mangonui/Coopers Beach 3 kms

Mac 'n' Mo's has sparkling views over Doubtless Bay with Coopers Beach just across the road and down some steps. Enjoy your breakfast overlooking the bay in our "slice of paradise", you may even see dolphins. We have secure off street parking with a private guest entrance and two into separate en suite units which are $75.00. Refrigerators and tea and coffee making facilities are available for all guests. The tour bus to Cape Reinga stops at our gate, you may like to visit a glow worm grotto, kiwi house, go on a craft or wine trail, swim with the dolphins, visit a Kauri forest, go fishing, diving or just relax on our unpolluted uncrowded beaches. We have several fine restaurants and world famous fish and chips close by. All this can be done from Mac 'n' Mo's. and they will take good care of you. Special winter and long stay rates

---

Coopers Beach
Guest House + B&B.
Address: Doubtless Bay Lodge,
33 Cable Bay Block Rd, Coopers Beach,
Mangonui 0557
Name: Harry and Berwyn Porten
Telephone: (09) 406 1661
Fax: (09) 406 1662
Mobile: (025) 275 2144
Beds: 3 Queen, 2 Single (4 bedrooms)
Bathroom: 4 Ensuite
Tariff: B&B (full) Double $90, Single $55,
Children $20, Dinner $25, Credit Cards.
NZ B&B Vouchers accepted $20 surcharge
Nearest Town: Mangonui 3.5 km south.

*Our purpose built guest house is 800 metres north of the Coopers Beach shops.
We are about an hours drive north of Paihia and 35 minutes south of Kaitaia on State Highway 10.
Our children are grown up and off our hands. We are enjoying the sun and the sand, the fishing and the walking. We enjoy the rural and sea views of this lovely place.
We have left traffic and hassles of Auckland behind us and invite our guests to do the same!
Each room has ensuite and Cable TV (with Sky sport), fridge and tea and coffee facilities. Home style evening meals are provided by arrangement.
Cape trips, dolphin watching and fishing arranged.*

Mangonui

Homestay B&B
Address: Corner of Beach Road (The Loop)
and Grey St west ext, Mangonui fishing village.
Name: Heaven Dessent, "Frankly Heaven"
Telephone: (09) 406 1068
Beds: 3 Double, 2 Single (3 bedrooms)
Bathroom: 2 Ensuite, 1 Family share
Tariff: B&B (full) Double $65, Single $35, Dinner $20pp,
Full breakfast. NZ B&B Vouchers accepted
Nearest Town: Mangonui - Kerikeri & Kaitaia 3/4 hour away.

Welcome to Frankly Heaven's exciting Bed & Breakfast with a difference. Awaken to the panoramic vista of the beautiful "Mill Bay" with its anchorage of sailing and fishing boats, sparkling crystal waters and a necklace of luscious green vegetation upon gently sloping hills. A leisurely stroll to the picturesque Mangonui wharf could see you catching a John Dory or Kingfish - "What a way to spend a day". Our comfortable guest rooms open onto a sunny decking where you can savour our home style country meals that we take particular pride in. We offer our guests a warm and inviting home of old world charm and memorabilia. Dress up in the romantic ballgowns of yesterday. Sing your hearts out around the pianola or enjoy a friendly game of pool. At the end of day indulge yourself in the romance of a candle lit dinner and leave with unforgettable memories to treasure forever.

Mangonui, Kaeo

Homestay, Farmstay
Address: Taratara Rock Farmstay,
Otangaroa Road, RD2, Kaeo
Name: Jan Tagart and Steve Cottis
Telephone: 09-405 0092
Beds: 1 King, 2 Single (2 bedrooms)
Bathroom: 1 Private
Tariff: B&B (continental) Double $60,
Single $30, Dinner $20.
Children under 12 half price.
Credit cards accepted.
Nearest Town: Kaeo is 16 km south, Mangonui is 18 km north.

Our old wooden home is 4 kms from SH 10. A little bit off the beaten track, set in farmland and native bush. Very beautiful, very peaceful. We offer a warm welcome, home cooking, country amusements: - walks, farm animals, pets.
Conveniently located for boating and fishing (Whangaroa Harbour), day-trips to Cape Reinga, Doubtless Bay beaches and Kerikeri history and shopping.
We have two children, aged four and nineteen. Our (outdoor) dog is called Emma. We request that guests do not smoke inside the house.
Directions: *Please phone for directions*

Takou Bay, Kerikeri
2 Self Contained Flats
Address: Te Ra Road,
Takou Bay, Kerikeri RD2
Name: Sandra Thornburgh
Telephone: (09) 407 7617
Beds: 1 Queen, 1 Double,
2 Single (3 bedrooms)
Bathroom: 1 Ensuite, 1 Private
Tariff: B&B (continental) Double $70,
Single $45 NZ B&B Vouchers accepted Except major holidays.
Nearest Town: Kerikeri

Situated between the Bay of Islands and Matauri Bay, Takou Bay is one of Northland's best kept secrets. Twenty minutes north of Kerikeri off SH10, it is an ideal base to explore all the sights of the Far North right up to Cape Reinga. Or stay close to home and enjoy the quiet, unspoilt beauty of Takou Bay Surf Beach.
My house sits a top the hill overlooking the sea, with panoramic views of the beach, river and Cavalli Islands which meet the rolling green hills of Northland. With my sister, I have a 50 acre life style farm carrying goats and horses. Americans by birth, we are Kiwis at heart and love the rural lifestyle.
Accommodation consists of two self-contained flats in my warm, two storey house. Both flats offer spectacular seaviews from every window and each have their own kitchen and private bathroom. The upstairs unit has two bedrooms and lounge while the downstairs is a double bedsit with cozy fireplace. Breakfast is provided in the flats to be taken when desired. **Directions**: *Please phone or write.*

Te Ngaere Bay, Kaeo
Self-contained Accommodation
Address: Te Ngaere Bay, R.D. 1, Kaeo
Name: Mrs June Sale
Telephone: (09) 405 0523
Fax: (09) 405 0604
Mobile: (025) 903 861
Email: snowcloud@xtra.co.nz
Beds: 2 Single (1 bedroom + 1 combined lounge-kitchen)
Bathroom: 1 Ensuite
Tariff: $60 Dec/March per night inclusive up to 2 people, $20 per extra person; $50 all other times per night inclusive up to 2 people, $15 per extra person. Credit cards (VISA/MC/BC). Breakfast not applicable. NZ B&B Vouchers accepted
Nearest Town: Kerikeri, 35km south of Te Ngaere

Our home is situated on the beach at Te Ngaere Bay, a safe and sheltered bay on one of New Zealand's finest stretches of coastline, in the Far North near Matauri Bay. The drive out gives you spectacular views of the beautiful Cavalli Islands and many other secluded bays and islands along the coast. There is much to do in the area: kauri forests to visit, sailing, fishing, big-game fishing, horse riding, coastal walks, swimming, snorkelling and diving are but a few activities, or visit the 'Rainbow Warrior' Memorial at Matauri Bay. We personally run 'Snow Cloud', a skippered charter yacht from Whangaroa, doing day trips and longer. There are excellent licensed restaurants in the area. It is a good central base from which to explore the North, or, you might like to beachcomb or just sit on the beach. "Smokey" and friends are our pet cats. Looking forward to having you to stay.
Directions: *Please phone for bookings and details of how to find us. Bookings are essential.*
Home Page: www.kerikeri.net/snowcloud

Mahinepua, Kaeo

Homestay
Address: Waiwurrie, Mahinepua Bay,
RD 1, Kaeo, Northland
Name: Rodger and Vickie
Telephone: (09) 405 0840
Fax: (09) 405 0854
Beds: 1 Queen (1 bedroom)
Bathroom: 1 Ensuite
Tariff: B&B (full) Double $175, Single $125,
Dinner $35 pp. Mastercard & VISA accepted.
Nearest Town: Kaeo (22 kms), Kerikeri (40kms)

Imagine waking up to the sound of waves lapping on the beach front, the birds chirping in the trees, fresh air and sunshine. Bliss.
We would like to welcome guests to our wonderful part of the world and let you enjoy what we have to offer.
Reasonably central to Cape Reinga, Whangaroa Harbour, Cavailli Islands, Kerikeri and Bay of Islands, guests may sightsee to the Cape, deep sea fish, dive the "Rainbow Warrior", fish, swim, play golf, visit the Bay or just lie on the beach.
Don't worry about dinner because we will provide it; the nearest restaurant is 10kms away.
Our home is three years old, surrounded by forest, farmland and the Pacific Ocean. We have two boys; also Benson the dog and Moppet the cat.
We love to entertain and would enjoy meeting you.
For more information please phone us.

Kerikeri

Farmstay-Homestay
Address: 'Aspley House', Waimate North,
Kerikeri R.D.3, Bay of Islands, Northland
Name: Atkinson, Joy
Telephone: (09) 405 9509
Fax: (09) 407-7403
Beds: 1 Double, 2 Single (2 bedrooms)
Bathroom: 1 Ensuite, 1 Private
Tariff: B&B (of your choice)
Double $120, Dinner $30. NZ B&B Vouchers accepted Surcharge $30
Nearest Town: Kerikeri 10 mins, Paihia 10 mins, Airport 10 mins

"ASPLEY HOUSE" with its old-world charm offers a relaxing and comfortable stay and is ideally situated in picturesque rural surrounds of the Atkinson family farms and citrus property. Two large, well-appointed guestrooms open on to a wide veran- dah, with views of landscaped gardens, over-looking a small lake and beyond to rolling farmland where sheep and cattle graze. Being descendants of pioneer families we have a good knowledge of local history as well as being widely travelled. Over the past 18 years we have hosted guests from all over the world. Family antiques contribute to the atmosphere of this stately, attractive, colonial-styled home. The three-course evening meals feature home-grown fresh produce and New Zealand wines. Summer-time guests can enjoy the inviting kidney-shaped pool. "Aspley House", with its central location is an excellent base from which to explore the many tourist attractions of the Historic Bay of Islands and the far North. Kiwi listening can be arranged, weather permitting. We offer quality accommodation and look forward to your visit. Pets: Jake, a Jack Russell and Mr. Cat.
Directions: *West of SH 10 at Puketona Junction then 3kms up Te Ahuahu Road, on left.*

Kerikeri

Homestay
Address: Matariki Orchard,
Pa Road, Kerikeri
Name: David & Alison Bridgman
Telephone: (09) 407 7577
Fax: (09) 407 7593
Mobile: (025) 278 2423
Beds: 1 Queen, 2 Single (2 bedrooms)
Bathroom: 1 Guests share
Tariff: B&B (full) Double $100, Single $50,
Children $20, Dinner $30. Credit cards.
NZ B&B Vouchers accepted $10 surcharge
Nearest Town: Kerikeri (4 mins), Paihia (20 mins)

New Zealand
Association
FARM & HOME
HOSTS

We welcome guests to our home surrounded by a citrus orchard, large garden and swimming pool. It is a pleasant walk to the Stone Store, historic area and 3-4 mins by car to township, clubs and craft outlets. David, previously a sheep farmer, is now involved with local tours. We can help arrange your tours and activities whilst in the Bay of Islands. We are 5th generation New Zealanders, have travelled extensively within New Zealand and other countries. We love to help with "where to go & what to do", and are interested in sharing travel experiences. Our family of 4 have left home. We love to provide a 3 course dinner of locally grown foods, lamb, beef, seafood and wine. If this is not required, restaurants are available. We are happy to meet plane or coach at no cost. Members of NZ Association Farmer & Home Hosts.
Directions: *Turn off Highway 10 into Kerikeri township. Turn right at the roundabout into Hobson Rd, continue on at intersection, now Cobham Road, which runs into Inlet Road. Pa Road is first on the left. We are the 3rd house on right. Please phone.*

Okaihau, Kerikeri

Farmstay
Address: Wiroa Road, R.D. 1, Okaihau
Name: Neville & Shennett Clotworthy
Telephone: (09) 401 9371
Fax: (09) 401 9371
Beds: 1 double, 4 Single (3 bedrooms)
Bathroom: 1 Guests share
Tariff: B&B (full) Double $70, Single $35,
Dinner $25. NZ B&B Vouchers accepted
Surcharge $10
Nearest Town: Kerikeri 10 minutes, Okaihau 6 minutes.

We have sheep, cattle and horses on our 280 acre farm. Our native bush has resident Kiwis and there are fantastic views of the Bay of Islands area from our home which is 1,000 feet above sea level. Puketi Kauri Forest, historic Hokianga, Kerikeri and Paihia are close by. 7km to the Kerikeri Airport.
We are both descended from Northland families that settled in the 1840's and our special interests are travel, tramping, farming, genealogy, Northland history, dog-trialling and equestrian activities. We have an extensive library on Northland history and families.
Directions: *West of State Highway 10. Take Wiroa/Airport Road at the Kerikeri intersection and we are 9km on the right. OR East of State Highway 1. Take the Kerikeri Road, 500 metres South of Okaihau, and we are the 4th house on the left, past the golf course. (8 kms)*

Kerikeri

Farmstay
Address: 'Kilernan', State Highway 10, Kerikeri, RD2.
Name: Heather & Bruce Manson
Telephone: (09) 407 8582
Fax: (09) 407 8317
Mobile: (025) 790 216
Email: manson@igrin.co.nz
Beds: 1 Queen, 2 Single (2 bedrooms)
Bathroom: 2 Ensuites
Tariff: B&B (full) Double $100, Single $65, Dinner $30, Not suitable for children. Credit Cards (VISA/MC).
NZ B&B Vouchers accepted with surcharge $30
Nearest Town: Kerikeri 9 km, Airport 10km.

KILERNAN ORCHARD offers superior accommodation approx. 9km from Kerikeri and an easy drive - 30 km to Paihia in the Bay of Islands.
Set in 45 acres well removed from the highway our home has been specially designed for guest accommodation. You have the choice of double or twin room with your own ensuite for complete privacy.
Enjoy a full breakfast indoors or on our sunny spacious deck which overlooks stream, pasture and native bush. For your evening meal we offer the best of local fare including New Zealand wine and preceded by complimentary sundowners.
We share our property with "Monty" our pedigree boxer and some cattle and our orchard grows mandarins and persimmons which are picked in May/June.
If you are arriving by air we provide pick up from Kerikeri airport.
Directions given at the time of booking which is recommended.

Kerikeri

Country Homestay
Address: 'Stoneybroke' Edmonds Road, Kerikeri
Name: Vaughan & Gillian
Telephone: (09) 407 7371
Beds: 1 Double, 2 Single (2 bdrms)
Bathroom: 1 Guests share
Tariff: B&B (full) Double $75, Single $40, Dinner $25.
NZ B&B Vouchers accepted. Credit cards accepted with 5% surcharge: Visa/MC
Nearest Town: 11 1/2km east of Kerikeri

Vaughan and Gillian welcome guests to their modern timbered home in its tranquil rural setting, overlooking Kerikeri inlet. Your hosts are experienced travellers and enjoy exchanging travel tales and introducing visitors to the varied delights of the region - historic sites, golf courses, country walks, boat charters and art and craft galleries abound. Interests include history, travel, gardening and painting. Weary travellers may prefer to relax in our pleasant garden and read from our extensive book collection, while sampling life on a typical NZ small holding. We grow macadamia nuts and almonds and run cattle, but have no household pets. Your accommodation consists of one double-room with inlet and garden views, one twin-bedded room and guests own bathroom/toilet. Twin-bedded "sleepout" accommodation is sometimes available - all smoke free. Dinner is an optional extra featuring home grown vegetables, preserves and homemade bread, accompanied by complimentary wine. Please telephone in advance.

21

Kerikeri
Farmstay
Address: Inlet Road, RD 3 Kerikeri
Name: Kerikeri Inlet View
Telephone: (09) 407 7477
Fax: (09) 407 7478
Mobile: (025) 934 317
Beds: 1 Queen, 2 Double, 2 Single (3 bdrms).
Bathroom: 2 Ensuite, 1 Guests share
Tariff: B&B (full) Double $70, Single $45, Dinner $18.
Children under 12 years $10, Children over 12 years $15.
NZ B&B Vouchers accepted
Nearest Town: Kerikeri - 8 mins

Would you like some good old Kiwi hospitality?
Our seven bedroom home has superb views, not only of the Inlet, but of Cape Brett and Russell. Our 1100 acre sheep and beef farm borders the Waitangi Forest. It has two lakes and many species of timber trees and natives which we have planted. Enjoy a full breakfast consisting of free-range chook eggs and our own sausages before exploring the many attractions Kerikeri has to offer. We have three very gentle horses for horse treks also.
Note: Please phone first for bookings, detailed direction or if you need to be picked up.
Directions: *At Kerikeri township turn right into Cobham or Hobson Street which turns into Inlet Road. About 8 km on seal look out for white B&B sign on right. Follow arrows.*

Kerikeri
Homestay
Address: Highway 10 Orchard,
S.H.10, Waipapa, Keri Keiri
P.O. Box 516 Kerikeri
Name: Nan & Malcolm Laurenson
Telephone: (09) 407 7489
Fax: (09) 407 7483
Beds: 1 Double, 1 Single (1 bedroom)
Bathroom: 1 Ensuite
Tariff: B&B (full) Double $75, Single $50,
Children under 12 half price, Dinner $25.
NZ B&B Vouchers accepted
Nearest Town: Kerikeri 7.3km

Waipapa

**HOMESTAY
ACCOMMODATION**

We Would Love To Meet You

Bay Of Islands

Easy to find, we are minutes north of Keri Keri on the main highway.
Our traditional style home, surrounded by lawns and shrubs, is on a flat citrus orchard, with swimming pool.
Your well appointed bedroom with ensuite, has its own entrance.
Nan will prepare the breakfast of your choice which you may eat in our dining room or in your room if you prefer.
We are central to sightseeing in the North, a bus pickup point for the Cape Reinga tour is just five minutes walk from your room.
Relax here with our genuine friendly attention and in a quiet and relaxed atmosphere. Our cat wont disturb you, she sleeps all the time.
Directions: *Please phone where possible.*

Okaihau

Farmstay
Address: 'Lewood Park', Mangataraire Road,
R.D.1, Okaihau, Bay of Islands
Name: Ron & Pat Lewis
Telephone: (09) 401 9290
Private: (09) 401 9941
Fax: (09) 401 9290
Mobile: (025) 277 7305
Beds: 2 Double, 1 Single (2 bedrooms)
Bathroom: 1 Guest share
Tariff: B&B (continental) Double $75,
Single $40, Dinner $25, Campervans $25,
Credit Cards. NZ B&B Vouchers accepted
Nearest Town: Okaihau 15 mins, Kerikeri 30 mins, Paihia 40 mins.

Welcome to the hidden Valley of Utakura. Originally purchased from the Crown in 1896 by three Lewis brothers, it has remained in the family ever since. We are central to both Bay of Islands and historic Hokianga. Visit Mangungu Mission House, site of the largest signing of the Treaty of Waitangi. We farm sheep, beef and forestry on 1000 acres of land. Our home is furnished with family heirlooms. The guest area is private and opens onto a patio. Stroll through our garden with exotic trees from around the world. After dinner Ron will take you to visit our glow worm display. Pat has a small cottage industry making speciality preserves. We specialise in home grown meats and game food. We are NZKC registered breeders of Blue Heeler Dogs. Your generous continental breakfast is served on antique china. Tea / coffee available from the tea wagon. Pet sheep called Daffodil.
Directions: *Please phone, sign at Cooks corner and Mangataraire Road.*

Kerikeri

Homestay
Address: 'Fairway View',
6 Wentworth Terrace, Kerikeri
Name: Betty & Rex Mitchell
Telephone: (09) 407 5001
Fax: (09) 407 5001
Mobile: 025 711306
Beds: 1 Queen, 2 Single (2+ bedrooms)
Bathroom: 1 Ensuite, 1 Family share
Tariff: B&B (special) Double $75, Single $60,
Dinner $30, Credit Cards. NZ B&B Vouchers accepted $15 surcharge
Nearest Town: Kerikeri 300 metres

Guests are assured of warm and generous hospitality. Fairway View, in a quiet cul-de-sac, is definitely Kerikeri's prime central location, with memorable panorama of the local championship golf course (one of New Zealand's best!)
Principal guest accommodation is large and well equipped with ensuite, queen size bed, bed settee, table and chairs, refrigerator, television, wardrobe, baggage rack, laundry and ironing facility, hair dryer, plus an adjoining single bedroom.
A twin room with family share bathroom is also offered.
Breakfasts are "never less than special". Local restaurants are within easy walking distance. We also offer dinner, with New Zealand wine, by arrangement to suit all tastes and diets. Extensive use is made of fresh local produce for all meals. Our knowledge of the region enables us to assist guests in planning sight seeing tours. We are a retired couple with varied interests including golf. We have no pets.

Kerikeri
Orchard Stay
Address: Puriri Park Orchard,
SH10, Kerikeri
Name: Puriri Park
Telephone: (09) 407 9818
Fax: (09) 407 9498
Email: puriri @xtra.co.nz
Beds: 1 Double, 1 Single (1 bedroom)
Bathroom: 1 Private
Tariff: B&B (full) Double $75, Single $55,
Children $10; Dinner $25. NZ B&B Vouchers accepted
Nearest Town: Kerikeri 8 Kms

Puriri Park has long been known for the warmth of its hospitality to travellers in the Far North. We have a large, rambling house set in beautiful grounds with mature trees and gardens. We have an orchard of export-quality kiwifruit and another of oranges which provide freshly-squeezed juice for breakfast. We have five acres of bird-filled native bush, mostly totara and puriri. Guests are welcome to wander around our garden, sit by the lilypond, feed the white fantail pigeons or swim in the large swimming pool. However, if they wish to explore the Far North, we are in an excellent situation for day trips to Cape Reinga and sailing or cruising around the lovely Bay of Islands. Kerikeri itself has a fascinating history and we are only a few minutes from the Stone Store and the Inlet. We can arrange trips for you or pick you up from the airport. Pets: one Persian cat.

Kerikeri
Self-contained Accommodation
Address: Inlet Road, P.O. Box 230, Kerikeri
Name: Villa-Maria Petit Hotel
Telephone: (09) 407 9311
Fax: (09) 407 9311
Email: VillaMaria@compuserve.com
Beds: 3 Large Villas with each 2 separate bedrooms
(Queen and Twins), 1 smaller bungalow,
All fully self contained.
Bathroom: 4 Private
Tariff: Double from $175-$300 depending villa.
Single from $95-$150 depending villa.
Studio double $130 incl breakfast. Continental - cooked breakfast $15.
Four adults from $250 - $350 depending villa. Smoking designated areas.
Little angels welcome. Completely renovated.
Nearest Town: Kerikeri 4km

The Villa-Maria Residence - is famous for peace and tranquillity, and personal attention. Four luxurious spacious villas with sea view are set in a subtropical park. Three Mediterranean villas have 2 separate bedrooms, very large lounge, fully equipped kitchen, ironing facilities, tiled bathroom, private indoor garage and terraces. 7000 acres of forest surround the residence and to complete this idyllic picture you can enjoy breathtaking sea views or refresh in our Italian style swimming pool. Your hosts also speak German, French, Italian and Flemish. We advise to book in advance. You will recommend it. Minimum stay 2 nights.
Home Page: http://www.friars.co.nz/hosts/vilamaria.html

Kerikeri
Homestay
Address: "Sunrise Homestay" B&B,
Skudders Road, Skudders Beach, Kerikeri
Name: Judy & Les
Telephone: (09) 407 5447
Fax: (09) 407 5447
Mobile: (025) 774941
Beds: 1 Double, 4 Single (3 bedrooms)
Bathroom: 1 Ensuite, Guests share
Tariff: B&B (full) Double $80, Single $50, Dinner $30pp,
Major credit cards welcome. Credit cards.
NZ B&B Vouchers accepted Surcharge 1st Dec to 1st Feb: $10.
Nearest Town: Kerikeri 7Kms.

A warm welcome awaits you at our restful homestay overlooking the Kerikeri Inlet. A magnificent sunrise, we think the best in the world. The Bay of Islands has a wonderful range of things to do and see, we would only be to pleased to help arrange these with you. We are 7 mins from town by car.
Laundry facilities available. Tea or coffee available at all times. By prior arrangements Judy and Les offer you meals inc. special diets or you may choose one of our many excellent restaurants.
We consider ourselves very lucky to own one of the best locations in Kerikeri, do come and share it with us. Courtesy pick up from town or airport. Please phone or fax for your bookings or leave your number on our answer phone and we will call you.
Not suitable for young children.
We will endeavour to make your stay in Kerikeri, Bay of Islands an enjoyable as possible. Happy holidays and travelling.
Directions: *Please phone.*

Kerikeri
Homestay
Address: "Ironbark Lodge",
Ironbark Road, Kerikeri
Name: Rangi & Dail
Telephone: (09) 407 9302
Fax: (09) 407 9302
Beds: 2 Queen, 1 Single (3 bedrooms)
Bathroom: 3 Ensuite
Tariff: B&B (full) Double $95, Single $45, Credit Cards (VISA/MC/BC).
NZ B&B Vouchers accepted $20 surcharge Dec 1st to March 31st
Nearest Town: Kerikeri

Your holiday, a special time to have as many adventures as you can, or simply a wonderful opportunity to relax and spoil yourself. Whatever your holiday dream we can help you achieve it.
Ironbark Lodge, set in a 20 acre farmlet with tennis court, close to a Kauri forest, and surrounded by imposing eucalypt trees is the perfect base from which to explore. Each bedroom has a private ensuite. You'll love the comfy beds, and a substantial breakfast will ensure a perfect start to every day. Join us for an evening meal by arrangement ($25pp). Kerikeri restaurants 15 minutes away, Paihia 30 minutes.
Pets: 1 cat, 1 dog.
A holiday at Ironbark Lodge will never be quite long enough.
Directions: *Please phone.*

Kerikeri
Homestay
Address: "Glenfalloch", Landing Road,
PO Box 477, Kerikeri
Name: Evalyn & Rick
Telephone: (09) 407 5471
Fax: (09) 407 5471
Mobile: (025) 280 0661
Beds: 1 King, 1 Queen, 1 Double,
1 Single (3 bedrooms)
Bathroom: 1 Ensuite, 1 Guests share
Tariff: B&B (full) Double $75-$85, Single $55,
Children $15, Dinner $25p.p., Credit Cards.
NZ B&B Vouchers accepted
Nearest Town: Kerikeri - 2.6km

Venture down Glenfalloch's tree lined driveway to our peaceful garden paradise which we share with an abundance of bird life including tui, wood pigeon, kingfisher and pheasant. On arrival Evalyn and Rick welcome guests with refreshments which may be enjoyed in one of the lounges or outdoors on one of the decks. You are welcome to wander about the garden, use the pool, tennis court and the golf putting course, or just relax on the decks or in the lounges.
Breakfast can be enjoyed at your leisure and weather permitting this can be served outdoors. Children welcome. Laundry facilities available. Smoking outdoors.
Directions: *Travel North 0.6km from the Stone Store corner and we are the second drive on left after Dept of Conservation sign.*

Kerikeri
Bed & Breakfast
Address: "Graleen", Kerikeri Road,
RD3, Kerikeri
Name: Graeme & Colleen Wattam
Telephone: (09) 407 9047
Fax: (09) 407 9047
Mobile: (025) 940 845
Email: graleen@xtra.co.nz
Beds: 1 Queen, 1 Double, 2 Single (3 bedrooms)
Bathroom: 3 Ensuite

Tariff: B&B Double $70, Single $40, Credit Cards. NZ B&B Vouchers accepted
Nearest Town: Kerikeri 3 mins, Paihia and Waitangi 20 mins.

After extensive travel all over the UK and having experienced and enjoyed the company and hospitality of so many people in their own homes, we decided we would like to do the same in our home town.
We designed and built a new home with guest accommodation and comfort in mind. All bedrooms have ensuites and TV with direct access to our lovely sheltered veranda where you may relax and enjoy tea or coffee.
We serve a continental breakfast (cooked on request) in our large guest lounge.
Kerikeri is a lovely rural town surrounded by orchards and farms and is centrally situated to all Bay of Islands and Northlands many tourist attractions.
We are only 20 mins from historic Waitangi and Paihia. "Graleen" is only 3 mins from the township, restaurants, RSA Club, bowling club, golf course, and many craft galleries.
Home Page: www.kerikeri.co.nz/graleen

Kerikeri
Homestay
Address: Pukanui, Kerikeri Road, Kerikeri
Name: Bill and Elaine Conaghan
Telephone: (09) 407 7003
Fax: (09) 407 7003
Mobile: (025) 771 569
Email: pukanui@igrin.co.nz
Beds: 2 Queen, 1 Twin (3 bedrooms)
Bathroom: 3 Ensuites
Tariff: B&B (continental) Double $90-$110,
Single $45-$65, Dinner $30 pp. Not suitable for children.
Visa/Bankcard/Mastercard. Off season rates avaialble.
Nearest Town: Kerikeri - 5 minutes stroll

Elaine and Bill invite you to stay in their home set in private park-like grounds and citrus orchard, Kerikeri, with its restaurants, cafe's, craft shops and movie theatre is an ideal location to base your holiday activities in Northland. Our large home offers three spacious guest bedrooms with ensuite and tea and coffee making facilities in a well appointed non-smoking environment. Each has its own patio for breakfast in the sun.
Should you wish to "eat in" we are happy to provide an evening meal by prior arrangement. For your enjoyment there is a large inground swimming pool, petanque court, and lawn for putting practice before visiting the many golf courses in the region. Also of interest are wineries potteries and craft shops. We can also arrange your tours to various points of interest. Pixie the elusive cat also resides here only to appear when hungry. Complimentary airport transfers.

Kerikeri
Homestay, Bed & Breakfast
Address: Blacks Road, Kerikeri
Name: Jane and Tony Holmes
Telephone: (09) 407 7500
Fax: (09) 407 7500
Email: tony_holmes@xtra.co.nz
Beds: 1 Queen, 2 Single (2 bedrooms)
+ 1 Bed settee in guest lounge.
Bathroom: 1 Private, 1 Family share
Tariff: B&B (continental) Double $70,
Single $45, Dinner $20. Credit Cards accepted.
Nearest Town: Kerikeri (3 1/2 kms)

Just 3 1/2 kilometres from town overlooking Kerikeri Inlet you enjoy superb water and country views. Sheep munch next door and we have two pet calves. Bird life is abundant.
We warmly welcome guests to our large, comfortable smoke-free bungalow, set amidst delightful shrubs and trees. Relax in the spa, perhaps join us for a bbq at sunset on the deck. Having travelled extensively and lived in many places, we now enjoy sailing and walking. Our yacht is close by. We can show you Kerikeri's bush walks, arrange night kiwi walks and fishing.
Directions: *At Kerikeri roundabout turn right into Hobson Ave. At 1.1 km turn left into Inlet Rd. At 3.4 km (NB 65 km sign left) turn left into Blacks Rd. We are halfway down hill on left*

Kerikeri
Homestay
Address: 100 Riverview Road,
Kerikeri, Bay of Islands
Name: Tracy Norris and Robbie Burton
Telephone: (09) 407 6786.
Reservations: 0800 936 786
Fax: (09) 407 6786
Email: pescador@xtra.co.nz
Beds: 5 Queen, 2 Double, 2 Single, (6 bedrooms)
Bathroom: 5 Ensuites
Tariff: B&B (full) Double $110-$130, Single $90-$110, Dinner $25 pp.
Apartment $150 (does not include meal). Credit Cards: Visa/Mastercard.
NZ B&B Vouchers accepted $40-$55 surcharge
Nearest Town: Kerikeri 4 km

Restore & rejuvenate yourself in the peace & tranquillity which pervades our comfortable, spacious homestay. Escape & be pampered in style with a choice of bedrooms to suit your needs (all with ensuites) plus a two bedroom self-contained apartment. Soak up the sun around the pool in summer or be welcomed by a warm cosy open fire in winter. Enjoy a delicious breakfast of fresh orange juice, muffins and fresh bread baked that morning plus fresh fruit and a mouthwatering cooked breakfast at the dining table or relax in the warming sun on the balcony while enjoying breathtaking sea view up Kerikeri inlet to Cape Brett and the famous "Hole-in-the-Rock". You are welcome to stay and enjoy a delicious homecooked dinner with us as well. Join our family - Robbie & Tracy, our young daughter Rebecca and our cat Sylvester. We'd love to see you soon. Our property is totally smokefree.
Home Page: www.kerikeri.net.nz/pescador/

Kerikeri, Bay of Islands
Bed & Breakfast/Self Contained Accommodation
Address: The Summer House, Kerikeri Road, Kerikeri
Name: Rod and Christine Brown
Telephone: (09) 407 4294
Fax: (09) 407 4297
Email: summerhouse@xtra.co.nz
Beds: Main House: 1 Queen, 1 Double (antique).
Self Contained: 1 Superking/twin option (3 bedrooms). Guest lounge
Bathroom: 3 Ensuites
Tariff: B&B (Special) Double $115-$125, Single $100.
Special winter and long stay rates. Credit cards. Picnic lunches by arrangement.
Nearest Town: Kerikeri Town Centre 1.5 km.

The setting is idyllic; over one hectare of citrus orchard and sub-tropical gardens sheltered by towering trees. Inspired by French Provincial architecture, The Summer House is professionally designed and luxuriously appointed to meet guests' every need; for comfort, warm hospitality, gourmet cuisine, private amenities, peace and quiet, conviviality and such leisurely pursuits as petanque. To stay at The Summer House is to share in Rod and Christine's dream of creating quality guest accommodation based on the very best of their experiences in Europe, Australia and New Zealand. Bountiful breakfasts are served in the dining room or on the patio and could include such dishes as corn and kumara fritters with ham and spiced mandarin. Rod and Christine's interests include gardens, native forests and sailing. Resident cat, Duchess, may grace you with her presence. Pick-up from the airport would be a pleasure. Some French and German spoken. Smoke-free. Not suitable for children.
Directions: *1.7 km along Kerikeri Road from SH 10.*

Kerikeri

Coastal Homestay
Address: 'Oversley", Doves Bay Road,
RD 1 Kerikeri.
Name: Maire and Tone Coyte
Telephone: (09) 407 8744
Fax: (09) 407 4487
Mobile: (025) 959 207
Email: e.milne@xtra.co.nz
Beds: 1 King, 1 Queen, 2 Single (3 Bedrooms)
Bathroom: 2 Ensuites, 1 Private
Tariff: B&B (Full/Continental) Double $120, Single $90,
Dinner $30 pp. Credit Cards: Visa/Mastercard/Bankcard.
Nearest Town: Kerikeri 15 mins.

Share our paradise in the north. We are a retired couple and 'Oversley' is our 15 acre secluded property situated on the Kerikeri Inlet, 12 kms east of Kerikeri. Enjoy our magnificent panoramic water views and often spectacular sunsets, sweeping lawns and private native bush walk to the water. Our spacious, comfortable home offers a friendly relaxed atmosphere with quality accommodation and laundry facilities. We are an easy going couple who have travelled extensively. We enjoy all sports, sailing and fishing on our 13 meter yacht, golfing on Kerikeri's first class course (15 minutes away), like good food and wine and are animal lovers. Enjoy a continental or full breakfast, alfresco or chatting around the breakfast bar. If you would care to join us for dinner and share a bottle of wine, we welcome your company. Our home is your home - please enjoy.
Directions: *Please phone for detailed directions.*

Kerikeri

Bed & Breakfast Inn
Address: Kerikeri Village Inn - Fine Accommodation,
165 Kerikeri Road, Kerikeri
Name: Peter and Jackie
Telephone: (09) 407 4666
Fax: (09) 407 4408
Mobile: (021) 215 1446
Email: kerikeri.village.inn@xtra.co.nz
Beds: 3 Queen, 1 Single (3 Bedrooms)
Bathroom: 3 Ensuite
Tariff: B&B (Special) Double $125,
Single $90, Credit Cards Accepted.
NZ B&B Vouchers accepted $50 surcharge
Nearest Town: Kerikeri, short walk.

Relax, unwind, and sample gracious hospitality, delicious breakfasts and panoramic views of the countryside! Our warm, comfortable masonry villa with its antiques and outdoor living has three queen bedrooms with private ensuites, pretty linens, fresh flowers and special chocolates. Enjoy gourmet breakfasts, served overlooking the view, with fresh orange juice and fruit, home-made muesli and muffins, plus your choice of salmon'n'eggs, Eggs Benedict, blueberry pancakes, or bacon & eggs. Fresh coffee, selection of teas, and biscuits, always available. We're on the main Kerikeri Road, a short walk to shops, restaurants and the historic Stone Store river basin with early colonial buildings. Kerikeri's balmy weather, central Bay of Islands location, arts and crafts, and abundance of outdoor activities make this perfect for a memorable holiday - we'll help with planning and reservations.
PS: Fax and email available and cocker spaniels to cuddle if you wish. Please reserve - see you soon! **Home Page**: www.kerikerivillageinn.co.nz

Bay of Islands, Pakaraka
Farmstay and B&B
Address: "Bay of Islands Farmstay",
Highland Farm, Pakaraka SH1
R.D.2, Kaikohe 0400
Name: Ken & Glenis Mackintosh
Telephone: (09) 404 1040 or (09) 404 0430
Fax: (09) 404 1040 **Mobile**: (025) 249 8296
Beds: 1 Double, 3 Single (2 bedrooms) 1 Foldaway.
Bathroom: 2 Ensuite
Tariff: B&B (full) Double $75, Single $50,
Children (school age) half price, Cot/Highchair no charge.
Dinner: 3 course $28, including drinks,
Credit cards (VISA/MC/BC). NZ B&B Vouchers accepted
Nearest Town: Kawakawa or Paihia

Beautiful 51 acre property with historic stone walls, Barbery Hedges, sheep, cattle, pigs. Ken trains pups and dogs morning and evenings. You may enjoy watching and help shift the sheep and cattle, try your hand at shearing. Take farm walks and view the historic Pouerua Mountain, sit on or photograph with "Mr. Angus" our lovable pet steer. Our cats are named "Monkey" and "Governor Grey" you will understand why when you meet them. Summertime: Swim in pool. A cosy home in winter. TV, video, pooltable, hairdrier. We book tours and horse rides. (Skin-care lip colours sun screen. Inhome shopping:) Environmentally safe products. Only 15 minutes drive to Paihia, Kerikeri, Kaikohe. Golf, bowls, beaches, shopping, tours, Ngapha Springs, Kawakawa Vintage Train Rides. A good base, very central. only 1 hour to Whangarei or Kaitaia. Book early or take pot luck! Visa, Mastercard, Bankcard. On SH 1., (10 minutes north Kawakawa) 1km south (Pakaraka Junction). Welcome to the Bay of Islands! Enjoy your holiday. Be our guests!

Paihia
Bed & Breakfast
Address: "Waitangi Bed & Breakfast"
48 Tahuna Road, Paihia
Name: Laraine & Syd Dyer
Telephone: (09) 402 8551
Fax: (09) 402 8551
Email: larained@ihug.co.nz
Beds: 1 Queen, 2 Single (3 bedrooms)
Bathroom: 1 Family share
Tariff: B&B (continental) Double $65, Single $40,
NZ B&B Vouchers accepted
Nearest Town: Paihia

We invite you to stay with us and relax in our home, only minutes walking distance to the beach. Enjoy the beauty of the bay with its golf course, bush walks and historic places all close by. On arrival a warm welcome awaits you , along with a cup of tea or coffee and a chance to unwind. Should you need assistance with your itinerary we are only to happy to help with the arrangements. Together with Bessie (our aged dog) we look forward to the pleasure of your company, and ensuring your stay is as comfortable and memorable as possible. Our courtesy car will meet you should you be travelling by bus.

Central Paihia

Hilltop Bed & Breakfast
Address: 'The Totaras', 6 School Road,
Paihia, Bay of Islands
Name: Frank & Christine Habicht
Telephone: (09) 402 8238
Fax: (09) 402 8238
Beds: Self Contained Studio:
1 Queen, 1 Single
Bathroom: 1 Ensuite
Tariff: B&B (special) Double $165,
Single reduction, Dinner $30. Off season rates. Credit cards Visa.
Nearest Town: Central Paihia

. . . For the sophisticated traveller . . . luxury with charm and unsurpassed views. Enjoy Paihia's best and central location from a hill top residency. Watch the sunrise from your spacious and well appointed apartment with ensuite and your private sundeck overlooking the harbour, Waitangi, Russell, the islands and the endless horizon.
Why not start your day with delicious Austrian pancakes in your scenic conservatory or one of the sundecks. A short track will lead you to the village, wharf (ferry ride to Russell 15 minutes), restaurants and beaches. A leisurely beach stroll will take you to historic Waitangi. Christine has a degree in Hotel Management and Frank is an international photographer. One of his latest books depicts the beauty of the Bay. Australia's "Weekend Away and Holiday Guide" highlighted "The Totaras" amongst their favoured ten Getaways in New Zealand. Wir sprechen auch Deutsch. Try to book in advance. Minimum stay 2 nights.
PS: Please no smoking inside.

Paihia

Countrystay
Address: "Puketona Lodge",
Puketona Road,
R D 1, Paihia 0252
Name: Heather & Maurice Pickup
Telephone: (09) 402 8152
Fax: (09) 402 8152
Mobile: (025) 260 7058
Email: puketona@voyager.co.nz
Beds: 1 King/Twin (2 Single), 1 Double, (2 bedrooms)
Bathroom: 1 Ensuite, 1 Private
Tariff: B&B (full) King/Twin $110, Double $100, Single $80, Children not suitable, Credit Cards (MC/VISA). 10% discount for 3 nights or longer.
NZ B&B Vouchers accepted Not between Dec 20-Jan 7. $25 Surcharge
Nearest Town: Paihia 8 kms

Heather and Maurice invite you to visit us in our modern home, built of native timbers, by Maurice. Originally from England, we also lived in the United States. Our home is situated in quiet countryside with many native birds in our large garden. Our bedrooms are large with private facilities and both open onto the outside deck. We are close to Haruru Falls, Waitangi, beaches and walks. We can book cruises and tours, or drop you off on a walk thru the bush. Breakfast is your choice, cooked or continental featuring home made breads and preserves. Complimentary refreshments are provided on arrival. We have 2 friendly dogs and one small cat.
Heather has taught ceramics for 30 years, and enjoys showing guests thru her studio.
We are on the main road from Paihia, 8km from the beach.
Please phone for reservations, and directions. We are a smoke free home.

Paihia
Countrystay
Address: Lily Pond Orchard, Puketona Rd,
Paihia, Bay of Islands
Name: Allwyn & Graeme Sutherland
Telephone: (09) 402 7041
Beds: 1 Double, 1 Twin, 1 Single (3 bedrooms)
Bathroom: 1 Guests share, Separate toilet.
Tariff: B&B (full) $40 per person.
NZ B&B Vouchers accepted $10 surcharge
Nearest Town: Paihia 7km

Drive in through an avenue of mature liquid amber trees to our comfortable timber home with sloping lawns down to a small lake, refuge for wild duck and home for our black swans and goldfish. Set in 10 acres of park-like grounds the atmosphere is quiet, peaceful and conveniently situated 8 min drive from Paihia.
The guest wing accommodation has views of the fountain and lake with the double and twin rooms having private access from your verandah.
We graze a few sheep and have 500 assorted fruit trees. Freshly squeezed orange juice, fruit and homemade jams are served at breakfast.
We are born N.Zers, have a wide variety of interests, Graeme having won local awards for his traditional Maori beef bone-carving. We have travelled extensively throughout our country and have sailed thousands of miles living aboard our 50ft yacht in the Pacific. We invite you to share the tranquillity of our small piece of paradise in the beautiful Bay of Islands.
Directions: *We can be found on the Paihia – Kerikeri road and the "Lily Pond Orchard" sign is at our gate.*

Central Paihia
Homestay + Self contained Accom.
Address: 5 Sullivan's Road, Paihia,
Bay of Islands
Name: The Cedar Suite, Jo & Peter Nisbet
Telephone: (09) 402 8516
Fax: (09) 402 8555 **Mobile**: (025) 969 281
Email: Cdr.Swt@xtra.co.nz
Beds: 3 Queen, 1 Single (3 bedrooms)
Bathroom: SC studio: 1 Queen with ensuite,
 SC Apartment: 1 Queen + 1 Single with ensuite. 1 Queen with ensuite
Tariff: B&B (continental) Double $95-$125, Single $85-$115,
(Studio + apartment with spa pool available self-catering $78-$110).
Credit cards (MC/VISA) on direct bookings only.
NZ B&B Vouchers accepted 1 May to 30 September with surcharge $24 to $53.
Nearest Town: Paihia - 1km to wharf

New Zealand Association
FARM & HOME HOSTS

For a homestay with a difference 'The Cedar Suite' offers you friendliness, atmosphere and fun, while you relax in our modern cedar home amid beautiful mature native bush. Suites are separate, with their own superior ensuite bathroom or shower. Peter has a career background with the New Zealand Symphony Orchestra, and he also very much enjoys cooking. Jo's interests range from photography through fashion to interior design. Both of us enjoy music and gardening, and our use of fresh produce from the Bay makes breakfasts an enticing delight of special homemade creations, which include crunchy muesli, yoghurt and freshly brewed espresso coffee and herb teas. Guests have private parking, TV, quality appointments and particularly comfortable beds; all within easy walking distance of the Bay, Paihia shops and tours. Laundry service available at small extra charge, and in all cases we suggest you book in advance.

Paihia Waterfront

Bed & Breakfast
Address: Te Haumi House,
12 Seaview Road, Paihia
Name: Enid & Ernie Walker
Telephone: (09) 402 8046
Fax: (09) 402 8046
Beds: 1 Queen, 2 Single (2 bedrooms)
Bathroom: 1 Guests share
Tariff: B&B (continental) Double $70, Single $45,
Children under 12 yrs half price. Visa?MC accepted.
NZ B&B Vouchers accepted
Nearest Town: Paihia 2km

We have a well established home on the waterfront in Te Haumi Bay with fantastic seaviews of the inner harbour.
Location: 3 minutes north of the Opua turn off and 1 minute south of Paihia township and opposite the Beachcomber Motel.
Our interests since retiring, are gardening, floral art and involvement in the Masonic Lodge. We enjoy meeting people from all walks of life and are very proud to share our wonderful area with you and to make your stay as memorable as possible.
Guest pick-up from Paihia is available.
P.S. Please no smoking inside, but outside is fine.

Central Paihia

Self-Contained Accommodation
Address: 49 Kings Road,
Paihia, Bay of Islands
Postal: P.O. Box 15, Paihia, Bay of Islands
Name: Anne Corbett & Garth Craig
Telephone: (09) 402 7882
Fax: (09) 402 7883
Beds: Garden Room: 1 Super King
or 2 Singles (1 bdrm),
Tree House: 1 Super King (1 bdrm)
Bathroom: Garden Suite: Ensuite and Laundry, Tree House: Ensuite
Tariff: Accommodation only: Garden Room: Double $95, Tree House: Double $95,
Optional continental breakfasts available at $7.50pp, Credit cards.
NZ B&B Vouchers accepted
Nearest Town: Central Paihia.

Welcome to Craicor Accommodation where the trees almost hug you and the native birds visit. The perfect spot for those seeking a quiet, sunny, central location. Discover the Garden Suite and Tree House. Two self contained modern units nestled in a garden setting with sea views. Each unit has ensuite bathroom, fully equipped kitchen for self catering, super king-size double bed, TV, insect screens, and is tastefully decorated to reflect the natural colours of the bush and garden.
We offer optional continental breakfast which you can enjoy at your leisure either indoors or on the deck of your unit.
Both units have safe off street parking. The wharf, restaurants and shopping centre are a five minute stroll down the waterfront.
Your hosts have lived in Paihia since 1978, and have a wealth of local knowledge on the B.O.I. area which they will gladly share.
Home Page: http://nz.com/webnz/bbnz/craicor.htm

Paihia
Self-contained Accommodation
Address: PO Box 126, Paihia
(Postal) 29 Bay View Road, Paihia
Name: Iona's Lodge
Malcolm & Mary Sinclair
Telephone: (09) 402 8072
Fax: (09) 402 8072
Email: Bay of Islands
Beds: 2 Double, 1 Single (2 bedrooms)
Bathroom: 2 Ensuite
Tariff: B&B (continental) Double $75-$95, Single $60.
Credit Cards. NZ B&B Vouchers accepted
Nearest Town: In central Paihia

*We live in Bay View Road, which is a quiet street with one of the best views in Paihia.
We overlook the town and wharf with magnificent sea views across the bay and out to
Russell. Centrally situated and within walking distance of all booking offices, Post
Office, shops, restaurants and the beach.*
*One unit is one bedroomed with a double bed and single bed. Upstairs are the bathroom
with shower, toilet and washing machine, a lounge area with TV and fold out double
sofa and kitchen.*
*The studio unit has double bed, kitchen, TV and ensuite. Both are well equipped and
comfortable. Each unit has their own deck area. There is a gas BBQ and ample
parking.*
*I supply a generous breakfast tray in your fridge for you to enjoy at your leisure.
We enjoy welcoming new friends from all over the world.*

Paihia, Bay of Islands
Homestay
Address: "Fairlight River Lodge",
107B Yorke Road, Haruru Falls, Paihia,
Bay of Islands.
Name: Anna & Michael
Telephone: (09) 402 8004
Fax: (09) 402 8048
Mobile: (025) 281 9999
Email: fairlight@bay-of-islands.co.nz
Beds: 3 King, 3 Double, 3 Single, (3 bedrooms)
Bathroom: 2 Ensuites, 1 Guests share
Tariff: B&B (continental) Double $110-$130, Single $70-$90.
Nearest Town: Paihia 5 mins, Kerikeri 20 mins

*Anna, Michael and family welcome you to our RIVERSIDE RETREAT set on the banks of
the Waitangi River. A peaceful and tranquil haven surrounded by beautiful native bush, home
to over 24 species of birdlife. A "BIRD WATCHER'S PARADISE!" Single / twin, double
rooms / ensuites with magnificent river, bush and garden views with all day sun. Enjoy
spacious grounds with an evening stroll on the rivers edge. Kayakers and bush walkers pass
by to nearby "FALLS". Ducks, herons and shags settle in for the night. Sounds of KIWI, owls
and fish splashing take over. Onto swimming with DOLPHINS, deep sea FISHING,
ISLAND HOPPING or the famous 'Cream Trip", Historical Waitangi Treaty houses,
Waimate Mission house, Russell, Ninety Mile Beach, MAORI CULTURE, diving ....restau-
rants / entertainment. We are 3 1/2 hours drive north or a 40 minute flight from Auckland.
Please phone for reservations and directions.*
Home Page: http://www.bay-of-islands co.nz/accomm/fairlite.htm

34

Central Paihia
Self Contained Accommodation and B&B
Address: "Chalet Romantica", 6 Bedggood Close, Paihia
Name: Inge & Edi Amsler
Telephone: (09) 402 8270
Fax: (09) 402 8278
Mobile: (025) 285 5600
Email: babs.co.nz/romantica
Beds: SC Mini-Suite with King-size bed
or 2 singles. Two room with Queen-size beds.
Bathroom: 2 Ensuites, 1 Private
Tariff: Accommodtion only: Queen-size rooms $75-$140 depending on season.
Mini-suite: $110-$175 depending on season. Optional Swiss-style breakfast $10.50 pp.
Credit Cards: Visa/Mastercard. Special rates from Dec 26 - Jan 4th.
Nearest Town: We are in Paihia

CHALET ROMANTICA is the perfect destination for the discerning traveller who is looking for a special, quiet place in a great location with fantastic seaviews over the Bay of Islands. Located on two acres in the heart of Paihia, only a stroll from shops, cafes and the beach. Beautifully appointed rooms / suites with comfortable beds, telephone, Sky TV, radio, fridge, tea / coffee making, bathrooms with hairdryers, heated towel rails and more, are offered to our valuable guests. Everyone gets it's own private, sunny balcony or patio with awesome views. Also available is a fully self-contained Mini-suite (Honeymoon suite) with kitchenette in the real Chalet type atmosphere. Superb comments! AN INDOOR HEATED LAP POOL, HOT SPA AND GYM ARE THERE FOR THE PLEASURE OF ALL GUESTS. For more Info visit our pictorial Webpage on the Internet or give us a call. Wir sprechen deutch, on parle francais and we speak english. Pre-bookings are advisable! **Directions**: *Find Kings road, turn left into Mc.Murray road, opposite the tennis courts turn into Bedggood Close, follow to the top.*
Home Page: http://babs.co.nz/romantica

Central Paihia
Self-contained Accommodation
Address: "A Paradise View"
34 Selwyn Road, Paihia, Bay of Islands
Name: Iris Bartlett
Telephone: (09) 402 8458 **Fax**: (09) 402 8457
Mobile: (021) 684 580
Beds: Paradise Glory: 1 Double, 6 Single
Paradise View: 1 Double, 3 Single + fold out settee.
Bathroom: Private bathroom with comfortable bath, separate shower units.
Tariff: B&B (continental) Double $95, Single $59. (High season surcharge)
NZ B&B Vouchers accepted $25 surcharge
Nearest Town: Paihia 100 metres (very central)

Welcome to Paradise Glory / Paradise View - 2 fully self contained and separate stand alone units, nestled in virgin native forest with million dollar views over the beautiful Bay of Islands. My husband's family have lived in Paihia since the 1940's. Being early residents, we were able to secure Premium Sites. Paradise Glory - nestled tranquilly on its own, a Romantic Hideaway, an attraction for those wishing to unwind and get away from it all. Balcony at tree top level, gives the best views imaginable while you soak up that warm sun. Paradise View - 1 minute walk to Paihia Village, outdoor gazebo for relaxing. Both units - fully equipped kitchens, microwaves, refrigerators. Laundry has automatic washing machines. Linen, electric blankets, duvets supplied for your comfort. Continental breakfast to have at your leisure. You'll love these idyllic spots with birds singing, golf course, beach for swimming, fishing, bush walks, boating, spectacular ocean views.

Paihia Bay of Islands
Homestay+Self-contained Accom.
Address: 168 Marsden Road, Paihia
Name: "Windermere"
Telephone: (09) 402 7943
Fax: (09) 402 7943
Mobile: (025) 798 367
Beds: 3 queen (3 bedrooms)
Bathroom: 1 Ensuite, 1 Guests share
Tariff: B&B (continental) Double $90/$100, Single $60.
Credit Cards. NZ B&B Vouchers accepted $12 surcharge
Nearest Town: Paihia

Welcome to historic Paihia and the home hospitality in our large spacious modern home. We have magnificent panoramic views of the Paihia Harbour, islands and historic Russell. We are 10 minutes walk to the centre of Paihia township full of good restaurants and a short ferry ride to Russell.

We overlook Waitangi Reserve and the world famous golf course. A short drive away is Kerikeri famous for its citrus orchards and its arts and crafts. Our residence is directly above a safe swimming beach. The self contained unit has its own terrace for you to enjoy the wonderful views.

Bill and Molly enjoy meeting people. They own their own yacht and enjoy sailing. We are happy for you to stay as long as you like. Please no smoking inside, outside OK.
Directions: *Please phone.*

Paihia
B&B, also Self Contained
Address: 2 McMurray Road, Paihia
Name: Admiral's view Lodge.
Robyn and Peter Rhodes
Telephone: (09) 402 6236
Fax: (09) 402 6237
Beds: 4 double, 6 Single (5 bedrooms)
Bathroom: 4 Private
Tariff: B&B (full/continental)
Double $76-$95.
Dinner $20. Credit Cards accepted.
NZ B&B Vouchers accepted $15 surcharge
(March till November)
Nearest Town: Paihia 500 metres

Admiral's View Lodge is in a quiet central location overlooking the Bay with spectacular sea views yet only 100 m walk to beach and a leisurely stroll to town centre, wharf and restaurants. Meals are served on our sunny sheltered deck. We have two bedrooms with private bathrooms, tea & coffee facilities, fridge, TV, own patios, seaviews. One twin/double room fully self contained with private bathroom, own patio. Also a 2-bedroom unit with two double, two single, own bathroom bath/shower, lounge/dining, bay window seat, fridge, toaster, microwave, tea & coffee facilities, seaviews. all units serviced daily to a high standard. Laundry facilities. Off-street parking. Residing in the Bay since 1975 we trust we understand Travellers' needs as we have travelled extensively ourselves and enjoy meeting people. Our interests are gardening, golf, fishing, square dancing. We have two very friendly cats, Cleo and Levi.

Paihia
Bed & Breakfast
Address: 30 Puketiro Place,
Te Haumi, Paihia, Bay of Islands
Name: Glenys and Steven Rossell
Telephone: 09 402 8492
Mobile: 025 277 2239
Beds: 1 Double, 1 Single (1 Bedroom)
Bathroom: 1 Ensuite
Tariff: B&B (continental) Double $80,
Single $40-$50, Children (5-12 years) $20.
NZ B&B Vouchers accepted $10 Surcharge
Nearest Town: Paihia approx 1 km.

Welcome to our home. Relax and Enjoy.
Your spacious guest room sleeps 3, but to accommodate extra family members it also has a comfortable bed settee.
Start your day with breakfast served in your room, to enjoy at your leisure. Tea and coffee always available.
For guests without transport we are happy to collect from, or deliver to, Paihia or Opua. For guests with transport, safe off road parking is provided.
We have two children, Dean and Claire and also a cat called Five, so children are most welcome.
We have a variety of interests and are quite well travelled. We look forward to helping to make your stay memorable. Would smokers please refrain from smoking inside.
Directions: *When heading into Paihia from Opua, turn left into Te Haumi Drive. Turn 1st right into Puketiro Place.*

Paihia
Bed & Breakfast
Address: 15 Bayview Road,
Paihia, Bay of Islands
Name: Marlin House Fishing Lodge
Telephone: (09) 402 8550
Fax: (09) 402 6770
Mobile: (025) 487 937
Email: chrisgh@voyager.co.nz
Beds: 1 Queen, 2 Single (2 Bedrooms)
Bathroom: 2 Ensuites
Tariff: B&B (Special/Continental) Double $85-$125, Single $70.
Nearest Town: Paihia

Situated in a quiet tree clad spot overlooking the Paihia basin, the lodge is only three minutes walk to the village. The building has been recently extended and tastefully modernised in the colonial style with off-road parking.
The accommodation is for four persons in two suites. One is a twin-bedded with a large sitting room and dining area and has a luxury en-suite shower. The other room has a queen bed with an en-suite bath and sitting area, TV & fridge in both rooms. The beds are luxury class. Both suites have private sitting-out decks.
A self drive eight metre fishing launch with marine toilet, full safety equipment, communication, GPS and fish-finder is owned by the Lodge and is available with a guide. For a reasonable charge we have access to the very best fishing charter boats in the Bay and will be pleased to tailor your fishing preferences to your own particular requirements.

Paihia
Homestay/Self Contained Accommodation
Address: 18 Goffe Drive, Haruru Falls, Paihia
Name: Villa Casablanca
Telephone: (09) 402 6980
Fax: (09) 402 6980
Mobile: (021) 666 567
Email: derek@bestprice.co.nz
Beds: 3 King/Queen, 6 Single (6 Bedrooms)
Bathroom: 4 Ensuites, 2 Private, shower/toilets
Tariff: B&B (Full) Guest Wing: Double $160, Single $140.
Garden Apartments 2br $160, 1br $120 (available from September 1999). Dinner $30 pp.
Credit Cards: Amex, Visa, Mastercard. NZ B&B Vouchers accepted $60 surcharge
Nearest Town: Paihia 4 km

*Villa Casablanca is a private hilltop guesthouse enjoying spectacular views of Waitangi and
the Bay of Islands. Although only 4km from central Paihia, it provides a secluded retreat
amidst a garden of flowering shrubs and native bush. Casablanca is smokefree and
unsuitable for young children. The villa is modelled on a Spanish hacienda and has been
recently upgraded to the highest standards. We offer a choice of traditional homestay in our
guest wing or the privacy of self-contained accommodation in our garden apartments.*
*The guest wing includes the Baywatch Room (King/Twin with private shower/toilet), the
Champagne Room (Queen, en-suite, double spa) and the Falls room (Twin, guest share), a TV
lounge with wood fire and Library/Breakfast Room where house guests enjoy a traditional
cooked breakfast before the day's activities. Garden Apartments are available with either one
or two bedrooms. Each has private shower/toilet and cooking facilities with continental
breakfast provided.* **Home Page**: bestprice.co.nz/casablanca

Opua, Paihia
Homestay
Address: 'Rose Cottage',
Oromahoe Road,
Opua, Bay of Islands
Name: Pat & Don Jansen
Telephone: (09) 402 8099
Fax: (09) 402 8099
Beds: 1 Double,
1 Twin/King, (2 bedrooms)
Bathroom: 1 Private (only 1 party taken at a time)
Tariff: B&B (continental) $40 pp.
NZ B&B Vouchers accepted $10 surcharge Dec-March incl
Nearest Town: Paihia 5km

*Rose Cottage enjoys a tranquil bush garden site with spectacular sea, bush and rural
views of the Upper Harbour area. Private wing with private entrance and deck sleeps
4. Tea, coffee, microwave and fridge facilities. TV. Enjoy breakfast of home-made
bread and jams, cereals, fruit, juice, tea/coffee and eggs any fashion with your hosts.
Pat is a retired nurse and Don a retired carpenter. Our interests include sailing,
walking, reading, fishing, gardening, kauri woodwork, local history, and helping our
guests enjoy their stay. Russell car ferry 1 km, Russell passenger ferry 5 km. Home
hosting has been an enjoyable part of our lives for 12 years.*
*We have made many friends and look forward to continuing to welcome guests into our
home. Non smokers preferred.* **Directions**: *Please phone.*

38

Opua, Paihia

Homestay+Self-contained Accom.
Address: 7 Franklin Street, Opua
Name: Margaret Sinclair
Telephone: (09) 402 8285
Fax: (09) 402 8285
Beds: 1 Double, 2 Single (2 bedrooms)
Bathroom: 1 Family share.
Self-cont. Accom: 1 Double, 2 Single,
separate toilet & shower.
Tariff: B&B (full) Double $65, Single $40.
Self-cont. Accom: Double $60, $10 each extra guest.
NZ B&B Vouchers accepted
Nearest Town: Paihia

You are welcome to stay in my lovely home above the harbour at Opua sharing the facilities with just myself.
Enjoy panoramic views of the water where there is much boating activity - there always seems to be something happening.
You are handy to all the tourist activities of this area and there is a large heated spa pool to relax in on your return from your day's outing. You may like to wander in my garden which is my big interest.
Downstairs there is a large 2 roomed fully self-contained unit with separate shower and toilet and a large private deck with the same stunning views.
To find my home, take the road to Paihia from Whangarei. Turn right where the sign indicates the Opua-Russell ferry - this is Franklin St. My house is clearly visible on the left, on the seaward side of Franklin Street. I can meet bus arrivals at Paihia.

Opua, Paihia

Homestay+Self-contained Accom.
Address: "Seascape", 17 English Bay Rd,
Opua, Bay of Islands
Name: Frank & Vanessa Leadley
Telephone: (09) 402 7650
Fax: (09) 402-7650
Email: frankleadley@xtra.co.nz
Beds: 1 Double, 2 Single (2 Bedrooms)
Bathroom: 1 Ensuite, 1 Family share
Tariff: B&B (continental) Self Contained Flat: Double $80, with Breakfast $90.
Guest Room: Double $80, B&B Single $50. NZ B&B Vouchers accepted
Nearest Town: Paihia 5 km. Russell ferry 2 mins.

"Seascape" has a tranquil setting on a bush-clad ridge. Enjoy spectacular views over the inner Bay of Islands, stroll 100m. through bush to the coastal walkway, enjoy our beautifully landscaped garden, experience the many activities the Bay offers, or relax on your private deck listening to the sounds of water and birds.
We invite you to share our home, and will welcome you with complimentary afternoon tea on arrival. We are very willing to help you plan your time in NZ. We are keen travellers, and our other interests include music, boating, fishing, gardening, Rotary, and floral art. And we enjoy life to the full!
Our fully self-contained flat has double bed, divan in lounge, TV, laundry, own entrance and deck. You can join us for breakfast and chat, or look after yourselves. Guest room with shared facilities also available. We love it here, and so will you.
Directions: *Phone or fax, or guest pick-up from Paihia.*

39

Opua, Paihia

Homestay + Self Contained
Address: 10 Franklin St, Opua
Name: Florence Morrison
Telephone: (09) 402 7488
Fax: (09) 402 7488
Beds: 1 Queen, 2 Single (2 bedrooms).
Bathroom: 1 Guest share
(Separate toilet & shower), + 1 Family share
Tariff: B&B (continental or full on request)
Double $65, Single $40, Dinner $20 pp,
Children under 12 half price. Credit Cards accepted.
Laundry facilities. NZ B&B Vouchers accepted
Nearest Town: Paihia 5km.

New Zealand Association FARM & HOME HOSTS

The front of my home overlooks the beautiful and busy Port of Opua, and the back the tranquil reaches of Kawakawa River, alongside which the Bay of Islands vintage railway travels. Native bush nearby attracts many birds.
You are handy to all tourist attractions, bush and coastal walks. Opua has Boat Charters, yacht club, a restaurant on the water, or just relax on my deck to watch the boats.
I am a local, now retired, with plenty to do, gardening, the local theatre group, family and simply enjoying the Bay. Buses to Cape Reinga pass the door. Guest pick up from Paihia.
Directions: *Whangarei / Paihia Rd - turn right at Opua (as for Ferry to Russell). No 10 Franklin St will welcome you.*

Russell

Homestay
Address: 67 Wellington Street
Russell
Name: Kay's Place
Telephone: (09) 403 7843
Fax: (09) 403 7843
Mobile: 025 2723 672
Beds: 1 Twin, 2 Double, 1 Single (4 bedrooms)
Bathroom: 1 Private, 1 Guests share
Tariff: B&B (full) Double $100, Single $50
NZ B&B Vouchers accepted $20 surcharge per person.
Nearest Town: Whangarei

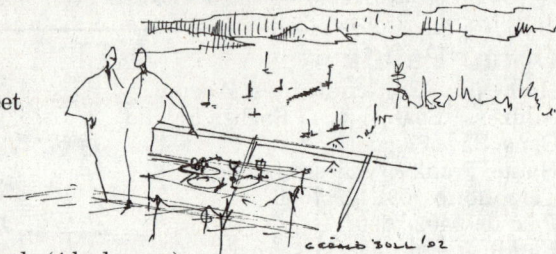

My home overlooks Russell Bay with magnificent water and bush views. Born and bred in Northland I take great pride in showing my guests NZ's first capital. I love every type of fishing and frequently escort my guests out game fishing. I am a national doll collector and I love the world coming to stay with me. Meals are usually served on the terrace. I have found my guests like to explore and sample the different fish restaurants that abound in Russell. We have several lovely walks handy, as well as golf, bowls, diving, cruises and yacht charters. I belong to Russell RSA, bowling, gamefishing, yachting clubs, if my guests wish to meet our locals I take them to whichever club interests them. All I ask of my guests is to completely relax and use my home as theirs.
Directions: *By car - take Opua car ferry to Russell, through Russell, on left Wellington St., a no exit road and we are just up the hill on the right - letter box signed. I do have an elevator.*

Russell, Matakaraka Beach
Homestay
Address: Major Bridge Drive,
R.D.1, Russell
Name: Eva Brown
Telephone: (09) 403 7431
Fax: (09) 403 7431
Email: evabrown@voyager.co.nz
Beds: 1 Double, 1 Single (2 Bedrooms)
Bathroom: 1 Private
Tariff: B&B (full) Double $75, Single $50.
Dinner: Pasta or pizza and salad $16 per person.
Credit cards. NZ B&B Vouchers accepted $10 surcharge
Nearest Town: Russell, 7 km by car or 20 minutes rowing by our rowboat

Our wooden house is near a quiet beach in a sheltered bay. We recommend walking shoes to our guests because parking is on the top of the hill and our house is by the water. A footpath leads down through a tunnel of native fern, kanuka and manuka. We provide a dinghy free for fishing or crossing to Russell, the historic first capital of New Zealand. Beach walks start at our door. Guests may swim right off our beach or take a sailing trip to the islands. Historic places, Maori pa sites, kauri trees, golf, diving, dolphin watching and kayaking are all nearby. Breakfasts range from fresh fruit, muesli and yoghurt to wholemeal toast with homemade jams, marmalade and bacon and eggs. Please phone ahead for direction. We gladly meet guests at the ferry.

Russell
Homestay+Self-Contained Accom.
Address: 2 Robertson Road, Russell
(PO Box 203)
Name: 'Te Manaaki'
Sharyn & Dudley Smith
Telephone: (09) 403 7200
Fax: (09) 403 7537
Mobile: (025) 972 177
Email: triple.b@xtra.co.nz
Beds: Self-Contained Villa: 1 Superking (1 bedroom)
Homestay Unit: 1 Superking or 2 Singles (1 bedroom)
Bathroom: 2 Ensuite
Tariff: B&B (full) Villa: Double/Single $150, Homestay: Double/Single $110,
Extra persons $15, Credit Cards. Discounts for extended stays.
NZ B&B Vouchers accepted Vouchers accepted for Homestay unit, $40 surcharge
Nearest Town: Central Russell

We have been welcoming B&B guests to 'Te Manaaki' for twelve years. Our property is centrally situated on an elevated section overlooking the historic town and harbour of Russell - a two minute stroll from the village shops, restaurants, and wharf. Opportunities for Island Cruising and Fishing aboard our charter boat "Triple B". Garden spa is available for guests use. We have two choices of accommodation: An attractively appointed sunny spacious de luxe self-contained Villa with its own private entrance, garden, sundeck and terrace. The Villa enjoys magnificent sea and village views, has a Super-King size bed and tasteful ensuite. Kitchen facilities, TV and BBQ. Breakfast available on request. Our new modern home has a large ground-floor, self contained unit with private ensuite facilities, TV, refrigerator, tea/coffee making. A cosy Bay-Window in which to relax and enjoy the fine Harbour views. Off street parking adjacent to the unit. Breakfast is included in the tariff.
Home Page: http://nz.com/webnz/bbnz/smith.htm

Russell - Waipiro Bay

Homestay

Address: 'Gasthaus Waipiro Bay',
PO Box 224, Russell
Name: Beate & Thomas Lauterbach
Telephone: (09) 403 7095
Fax: (09) 403 7095
Email: lauterbach@igrin.co.nz
Beds: 2 Queen, 1 Single (2 bedrooms)
Bathroom: 1 Ensuite, 1 Private
Tariff: B&B (special) Double $135/$150,
Reduction for singles, Dinner $45, Credit cards.
Nearest Town: 15km east of Russell on the coastal scenic drive

Dream of a place, an artist's home above a bay, the Pacific Ocean on the horizon, islands to explore, fish to catch, beaches and forests to roam, nature at your doorstep. This world of space and light has inspired artist Thomas Lauterbach to paint strong images of land, sea and the Maori people.
We offer our guests a warm and imaginative home of timber and stone, comfortable bedrooms with spectacular views. Enjoy the spacious private living-room, the open fire place and works of art.
Relax on verandas amidst the beautiful garden or follow a romantic path to the beach. Explore the islands on a local boat - bring home your own fish.
We love to cook gourmet meals with flavours from Italy to the South Pacific.
For a taste of heaven on earth - come and let us spoil you a little.

Russell

Homestay

Address: 'Treetops', 6 Pinetree Lane,
Te Wahapu Rd, Russell, Bay of Islands
Name: John & Vivienne Nathan
Telephone: (09) 403 7475
Fax: (09) 403 7475
Mobile: (025) 272 8881
Beds: 1 King, 1 Double (2 bedrooms)
Bathroom: 1 guests share
Tariff: B&B (full) Double $85,
Single $65, Dinner $30 (incl. wine),
Credit cards. NZ B&B Vouchers accepted
Nearest Town: Russell 7km.

Our home is situated at the end of Te Wahapu Peninsula, 2.5km from the Main Russell-Opua Road. We are surrounded by native bush, and Tuis and Fantails are our constant companions. Kiwis are often heard during the night.
Both upstairs bedrooms have beautiful sea views from your bed; one room has colour TV. The guest bathroom is also upstairs. Guests are welcome to sit in the spa pool and watch the sun set over Paihia across the bay.
A track through the bush leads down to the beach where you are welcome to use our dinghy for fishing or a pleasant row out to Torretorre Island for a picnic. Guest barbecue available.
Historic Russell is a mere ten minute drive and offers a unique charm.
Cooked or continental breakfasts are available and you are welcome to join us for dinner. Please phone in advance. Major credit cards accepted.

Russell

Homestay+Self-contained Accom.
Address: 'Inn-The-Pink' B&B,
1 Oneroa Road, Russell
Name: Mary & Kent MacLachlan
Telephone: (09) 403 7347
Fax: (09) 403 7347
Mobile: (025) 289 3652
Email: mary&kent@xtra.co.nz
Beds: Self-contained unit: 1 Queen.
Homestay: 1 Queen or 3 Singles (2 Bdrms)
Bathroom: 1 Ensuite, 1 Private
Tariff: B&B (full/continental) Self contained unit: $140.
Homestay: Double $100, Single $60. No dinner.
Children under 12 years half price. Discounts for extended stays.
Nearest Town: Central Russell

A warm and friendly welcome awaits you at Inn-the-Pink. Enjoy our unique location with magnificent harbour views overlooking Russell and across the bay to historic Waitangi. Our house sits nestled amongst beautiful gardens, just a few minutes stroll from the picturesque waterfront of downtown Russell. We have two choices of accommodation. Our separate self contained unit has a queen-sized bed, bathroom, fridge, TV, microwave, and coffee/tea making facilities. Relax on your own private deck and enjoy incredible sunsets over the bay. Our smoke-free home has two comfortable bedrooms with a private bathroom. Join us for a hearty breakfast which includes fresh orange juice, fresh fruit salad, home-made muesli, yoghurt, muffins and a variety of delicious cooked breakfasts. We are a Kiwi/Canadian couple who enjoy sailing, fishing, gardening and tennis. We spend July & August cruising Lake Ontario.
Home Page: http://www.bay-of-islands.co.nz/inthepnk

Russell

Homestay
Address: 21 Titore Way,
Russell (last house on right)
Name: Michael & Robin Watson
Telephone: (09) 403 7458
Fax: (09) 403 7458
Mobile: 025 765 459
Email: mikerobe@igrin.co.nz
Beds: Guest wing with 2 double bedrooms
(one Queen, one 2 Singles), with bathroom and separate toilet.
Bathroom: 1 Private
(We cater for one couple only or 4 people in the same party, usually)
Tariff: B&B (full) Double $140, Single $100, Credit Card (VISA).
Nearest Town: Russell 2 minute drive or 10 minute walk

Tokouru, our home is a modern natural timber house with magnificent bush and sea view and large sunny decks, tranquil and relaxing. Bush walks to Russell Village, Flagstaff Hill and a private beach begin at our property.
We are keen cruising yachties with our own 40 foot yacht. The use of a tennis court is available. Historic Russell has many tourist attractions and daily trips.
Predominantly Bed & Breakfast, dinner is supplied only by arrangement. There are excellent local restaurants open nightly or a 10 minutes ferry trip to Paihia can be enjoyed for an evening meal. We have one friendly black Labrador - Ben.

43

Russell

Historic Guest House + S.C. Cottage
Address: 'Ounuwhao' Matauwhi Bay, Russell, Bay of Islands.
Name: Marilyn & Allan Nicklin
Telephone: (09) 403 7310
Fax: (09) 403 8310
Email: thenicklins@xtra.co.nz
Beds: 4 Queen, 2 Single (4 bedrooms)
Bathroom: 3 Ensuite, 1 Private
Tariff: B&B (special, full) Double $120-$150 with ensuite, Single $100-$120.
Children under 12yrs half price (if sharing with adults).
S/C Cottage: 1 Queen, 1 Twin, $150-$200 p/night. Credit Cards (MC/VISA)
Nearest Town: 1km from Russell Village

Welcome to historic Russell; take a step-back into a bygone era and spend some time with us in our delightful, nostalgic, immaculately restored Victorian Villa (Circa 1894). Enjoy your own large guest lounge; tea / coffee and biscuits always available, with open fire in the cooler months, and wrap-around verandahs for you to relax and take-in the warm sea breezes, in the summer
Each of our four double rooms have traditional wallpapers and paintwork, with handmade patchwork quilts and fresh flowers to create a lovingly detailed, traditional romantic interior.
Breakfast is served in our farmhouse kitchen around the large kauri dining table or al-fresco on the verandah if you wish. It is an all homemade affair; from the freshly baked fruit and nut bread, to the yummy daily special and the jam conserves.
Our self-contained cottage is set in park-like grounds for your privacy and enjoyment: with two double bedrooms, it is ideal for a family or two couples travelling together. It has a large lounge overlooking the reserve and out into the bay, a sun-room and fully self-contained kitchen. Wonderful for people looking for that special place for peace and time-out. Breakfast is available if required.
Complimentary afternoon tea on arrival. Laundry service available. We look forward to meeting you soon. Our homes are SMOKE-FREE.
We are closed June and July. We are a member of NZ Heritage Inns Group.
EXPERIENCE OUR HISTORIC B&B. ENJOY A WORLD OF DIFFERENCE.
Home Page: http://nz.com/heritageinns/ounuwhao

Russell
Homestay/Studio Unit.
Address: 6 Ashby Street, Russell
Name: "Brown Lodge"
Telephone: (09) 403 7693
Fax: (09) 403 7683
Email: brown.lodge@xtra.co.nz
Beds: 3 Queen, 1 Single (3 Bedrooms)
Bathroom: 3 Ensuite
Tariff: B&B (continental) Double $160,-$195, Single $160-$195.
Extra person in room $60. Credit Cards (VISA/MC).   Rates may change from 1st
October 2000. NZ B&B Vouchers accepted $100 surcharge
Nearest Town: Russell 3 mins walk

Quite central position with fine sea views over Russell and the Bay. One of the interesting new homes architecturally designed in keeping with the historic nature of Russell. An all timber construction featuring New Zealand Kauri, Rimu, Douglas Fir and Pine. A special place to stay and share an intimate glimpse of a Russell life style. A look at craftsmanship of today with old world atmosphere combined with modern private facilities and true home comforts. Friendly and personal attention is assured. Breakfast at our antique Kauri table amongst Rimu wood panelling, old bricks and over 100 years old re-sited arched windows. Furnished with antiques, Persian carpets throughout and examples of Roly's Kauri furniture and cabinetry Air conditioning and heating for all year round comfort. Two private spacious suites, each with their own entrance from the main foyer,both have sea views, queen size beds, ensuites, TV, fridge and tea / coffee making facilities. Studio unit with private entrance and own verandah to enjoy the view over Russel and the Bay. Air conditioning, queen bed and one large single, fridge, TV, large ensuite. Russell township is easy 3 minute walk to restaurants, shops, wharf. Relax on the front veranda with peaceful sea views to Waitangi and Paihia. We can advise and book restaurants, boat cruises around the Bay and bus trips to Cape Reinga etc. Smoke free home, safe off street parking, no wheel chair access. Please phone or fax ahead to avoid disappointment.
Home Page: http://nz.com/webnz/bbnz/brownI.htm or
                   http://www.friars.co.nz/hosts/brown.html

Russell

Homestay
Address: 1 Pomare Rd, Russell
Name: Lesley's
Telephone: (09) 403 7099
Email: three.gs@xtra.co.nz
Beds: 1 Double, 1 Single (1 bedroom)
Bathroom: 1 Private
Tariff: B&B (special) Double $95, Single $60,
Children half price, Dinner $20pp.
NZ B&B Vouchers accepted $25 surcharge
Nearest Town: Russell 1 Km

My home is in a quiet cul-de-sac and the design inspired by Greece where I once lived. When the weather is fine you can breakfast on the verandah and look out to Matauwhi Bay and Russell Boat Club otherwise relax in the glassed in breezeway with fresh waffles and maple syrup. Or you may like a traditional English breakfast using fresh eggs from our chickens. The guest room has its own entrance and large bathroom featuring an antique bath set in a sun window. Sometimes our guests feel like 'staying at home' for dinner and as a family we enjoy sharing a meal with people from other parts. My two children are comfortable mixing with people from other cultures. Our combined interests include travelling, music, gardening and art (I did the sketch) and our cat Mudge. It is a ten minute walk to Historic Russell.
Check out this website http://www.bayofislands.co.nz.
Directions: *Please phone.*
Home Page: http://www.bayofislands.co.nz.

Russell - Okiato

Homestay B&B/Self Contained
Address: Aimeo Cottage, Okiato Point Road, R.D.1 Russell
Name: Annie & Helmuth Hörmann
Telephone: (09) 403 7494 **Fax**: (09) 403 7494
Mobile: 025-272 2393 **Email**: aimeo-cottage.nz@xtra.co.nz
Beds: 1 Super King, 1 Double, 1 Single (2 Bedrooms)
Bathroom: 2 Private
Tariff: B&B (special) Double $105, Single $85, Children (3-12 yrs) $15.
First night $105, following nights $95. Dinner available on request. Off season rates,
Credit cards. NZ B&B Vouchers accepted $30 Surcharge : 1 Dec to 30 April
Nearest Town: 9km eastw. to Russell

New Zealand Association FARM & HOME HOSTS

Aimeo Cottage "a quiet place to relax" Your hosts Annie and Helmuth Hörmann sailed half way around the world to find this beautiful quiet place in the heart of the Bay of Islands. We would be happy to share this with you for a while. We can communicate in English, French, German and some Spanish. Aimeo Cottage is built on the hill of Okiato Point, a secluded peninsula overlooking the Bay. Only a stone throw from the site of the country's first Government House and just across the Bay, where the British and the Maori leaders signed the historic Treaty of Waitangi in 1840. Your accommodation is a comfortable, private self-contained studio, or a double beded room with private bathroom and separate entrance. We serve continental or cooked breakfast in our spacious living room or on your own porch. Dinner is available on request. Rates are very moderate. In 10 minutes you are in historic Russell, the site of many historic buildings, and interesting museum and art galleries. There are bushwalks right from the door; we provide advice for sightseeing or local tours. Beaches are close by. Ask for off-season rates.
Directions: *You find us 200 m behind the car ferry, first road on the left.*
Home Page: http://www.bay-of-islands.co.nz/aimeo/index.html.

Russell - Te Wahapu

Homestay+Self-contained Accom.
Address: Te Wahapu Road, Russell, R.D. 1
Name: Heino & Brigitte Sass 'BRISA COTTAGE'
Telephone: (09) 403 7757 **Fax**: (09) 403 7757
Email: brisa@xtra.co.nz
Beds: Self-contained Cottage: 1 Queen (1 bdrm);
Self-contained Aptm: 1 Double (1 bdrm)
Bathroom: 2 Ensuite
Tariff: B&B (continental) High season
(Labour Weekend to Easter Holidays): Cottage: Double $115, Single $105.
Apartment: Double $95, Single $85. Low Season (after Easter Holidays to Labour
Weekend) Cottage: $95, Single $85. Apartment: Double $75, Single $65.
Extra Person $20. NZ B&B Vouchers accepted $35/$20 surcharge for Cottage.
$25/$10 surcharge for Apartment
Nearest Town: Russell 7 Kms

*BRISA COTTAGE is situated on Te Wahapu Peninsula, tucked away in an idyllic position,
lush native bush, bird life, own beach, views over Orongo Bay. 1 studio-style cottage (separate),
and 1 Apartment (attached to our house) available. Cottage and Apartment are as new, with
Ensuite, kitchen facilities, cosy and comfortably furnished, TV/Radio. Equipped with
comfortable slate-bed, Duvet & Patchwork Quilt for a restful sleep. We serve a wholesome
breakfast in our house. We share our 1 acre waterfront property with our friendly dog, cat and
some chickens. Dinghy, fishing gear and BBQ for guest use. A snug hideaway, yet only 10
minutes drive to historic Russell, which offers several excellent restaurants, craft shops, and
an Art Gallery. We sailed from Germany on our yacht BRISA in the early 70s and believe we
found just the right spot. Come, enjoy this private and tranquil place with us for a while.
Non smokers preferred.*
Home Page: www.bay-of-islands.co.nz/accomm/brisa.html

Parekura Bay, Russell

Self-contained Accommodation
Address: "Carpe Diem", Parekura Bay,
Rawhiti Road, Russell
Name: Martin & Jewel Collett
Telephone: (09) 403 8015
Fax: (09) 403 8015
Beds: 1 Double, 2 Single (2 bedrooms)
Bathroom: 1 Private, 1 Family share
Tariff: B&B (full) Double $75 (share), $95 (private).
Single $45 (share), $50 (private). Dinner $35.
NZ B&B Vouchers accepted 1st May to 31st October
Nearest Town: Russell

*Our house is an upstairs-downstairs, we offer guests our downstairs unit, which is
fully self-contained. The view is beautiful. Be part of the Bay of Islands, you relax and
enjoy, we will do our best to make your stay memorable.*
*We are situated 20km east of Russell - walk to the beach, walk a track and experience
the magic of the Bay of Islands, or just sit and enjoy the view.*
*Historic Russell is always worth a visit, hop a ferry, large or small, across to Paihia,
or the vehicular ferry to Opua, from there you can visit the Treaty House at Waitangi
- or drive to Kerikeri - take a bus to the Ninety Mile Beach, or a "Quick-Cat" to the hole
in the rock - we will arrange for you any activity you may wish to do. - See you soon.
- We also rent on a weekly basis, we supply linen, you cook for yourself. - Rates on request
- Boat ramp - Mooring when available.*

Russell

Homestay+Self-contained Accom.
Address: "Mako Lodge & Fishing Charters",
Te Wahapu Road, Russell
Name: Graeme & Jean McIntosh
Telephone: (09) 403 7770 or Toll free:0800 625669
Fax: (09) 403 7770 **Mobile**: 025 739 787
Email: mako.lodge_charters@xtra.co.nz
Beds: Homestay: 1 Double (1 bedroom)
Lodge: 1 King, 2 Single, 1 Bedsettee (double).
Studio: 4 Single bunk beds
Bathroom: 1 Private in each
Tariff: B&B (full) Double/Single $95, Dinner $35pp. Lodge: High season $170 Double, addit persons $25, Low season $140 Double, addit persons $25. Studio: High Season, Double $100 extras $20, Low Season, $80 extras $20. (Breakfasts and dinners are optional extras). Tariff concessions for stays longer than 7 days. Credit Cards (MC/VISA).
Nearest Town: Russell 7km

Mako Lodge is set in quiet seclusion on the shores of Orongo Bay on the beautiful Te Wahapu Peninsula. We are just 3km on towards Russell from the car ferry. B&B guests amenities include own bathroom, toilet, shower, TV, refrigerator, tea/coffee making, verandah, plus garden and water views from your bedroom. Our adjacent luxury lodge can sleep up to 6, has full kitchen facilities, TV, video, laundry and BBQ. Additional accommodation also available in our studio - sleeps 4 singles. Whichever accommodation you choose, you are welcome to amble down the bush path to the waterfront lawn where dinghies are available to explore the sheltered waters of the inner Bay. Perhaps catch your own Flounder or John Dory which we will prepare for your breakfast, or embark on one of our famous light tackle fishing charters on "MAKO" our 28' fast, modern diesel launch and experience the wonderful fishing or sightseeing of the Bay of Islands. We have a very friendly golden labrador called Tessa.
Home Page: htpp://www.bay-of-islands.co.nz/mako

Russell

Homestay
Address: 11 Gould Street, Russell
Name: Danielle & Dino Fossi
Telephone: (09) 403 8299
Fax: (09) 403 8299
Beds: 4 Double, 2 Single (5 bedrooms)
Bathroom: 1 Private, 1 Guests share, 1 Ensuite
Tariff: B&B (continental) Double $95-$130,
Children $25, Dinner $45pp, Credit Cards (VISA/MC).
NZ B&B Vouchers accepted Surcharge $30
Nearest Town: Russell 0.5km

Enjoy our mix of traditional European culture (food) in the midst of the beautiful Bay of Islands, historic heartland of New Zealand. La Veduta is the perfect pied-a-terre for your Northland holiday. Only few minutes walk from the township, sandy beach, bush walks. Relax, or we can arrange a wide range of activities. Deep sea fishing, sailing, diving, kayaking etc... Restaurants and ferry are handy. Transport is available for arrivals and departures Kerikeri/Whangarei Airport. We offer our guests a warm welcome and personalised service. By arrangement you may wish to share a 5 course meal with your hosts. English, French, Italian spoken. A large garden for our black poodle, Gaston, a balcony for sunset lovers, TV room, billiard room, laundry.
Home Page: www.KiwihomeCo.NZ/veduta

Russell

Self Contained Accommodation
Address: 4 Russell Heights Road,
Russell, Bay of Islands
Name: Eldon and Gill Jackson
Telephone: (09) 403 7109
Fax: (09) 403 7159 **Mobile**: (025) 276 2870
Email: paws.for.thought@xtra.co.nz
Beds: 1 Double (1 bedroom)
Bathroom: 1 Private
Tariff: S/C Double $100 ($20 each additional person). Not suitable for children.
Nearest Town: Russell 10 minutes walk to village, 5 mins walk to Long Beach.

Our self-contained apartment / unit is adjacent to our home with magnificent seaviews and a beautiful garden for you to enjoy, and is located in a quiet no-exit street, just 5 minutes drive from the village and beautiful Long Beach.
The unit has one double bedroom, plus a double sofa / settee in the lounge for extra guests. The fully equipped kitchen adjoins a lounge and dining area, which opens onto a sunny outdoor deck where you can watch the spectacular sunsets that Russell is famous for. Tea / coffee / milk are provided but the unit is self catering.
We have lived in Russell for 13 years and would love to share the history and scenic attractions of the region with you. Eldon loves boating and fishing, Gill is a keen gardener. We share our home with a cat and a small friendly dog.
Friendly hospitality awaits you.
Home Page: http://www.bay-of-islands.co.nz/paws

Kohukohu

Homestay/Guest House
Address: Rakautapu Rd,
Kohukohu, Northland
Name: 'Harbour Views Guest House'
Jacky & Bill
Telephone: (09) 405 5815
Fax: (09) 405 5865
Beds: 1 Queen, 2 Single
(2 bedrooms/2nd bedroom is twin)
Bathroom: 1 Private
(We only take one party at a time)
Tariff: B&B (full/continental) Double $80, Single $40, Dinner $18.
NZ B&B Vouchers accepted
Nearest Town: Kerikeri, Kaitaia and Kaikohe

Harbour Views Guest House is situated in historic Kohukohu, on the north side of the Hokianga Harbour. Our fully and beautifully restored kauri home is set in two acres of gardens and trees and commands a spectacular view of the upper harbour. Our guest rooms, opening out onto a private and sunny verandah, and with their own luxurious bathroom, are in a private wing of the house, but our guests are encouraged to feel part of the family and to use our living areas. Evening meals are prepared using home grown produce in season.
We have lived in this area for twenty years and are interested in and knowledgeable about its history and geography. Kohukohu, once the hub of Northland's kauri timber industry, is now a friendly and charming village. Apart from exploring the village, day trips to the rugged West Coast, Cape Reinga, Bay of Islands and Opononi are all possibilities. Laundry facilities available.

Hokianga

Guest House
Address: Riverhead Guest House
Main Road, Horeke
Name: Dick and Lila Holdaway
Telephone: (09) 401 9610
Fax: (09) 401 9610
Beds: 3 Double, 4 Single (4 bedrooms)
Bathroom: 1 Guests share, 1 Family share
Tariff: B&B (full) Double $65-$75, Single $35-$52, School children half price,
Dinner $25.   NZ B&B Vouchers accepted. Credit cards.
Nearest Town: Kaikohe or Keri Keri

Riverhead is a fine 1870's Kauri farmhouse which has been beautifully restored by your hosts, and now offers Victorian elegance and style with 20th century convenience. Dick and Lila are retired folk who will make you welcome and comfortable in true country style sharing with you their wide knowledge of the North. Riverhead overlooks Horeke Village and the head of the Hokianga Harbour, an area rich in history and homeland of the powerful Ngapuhi tribe and the focus of much at NZ's early history with numerous pa sites and quaint old pioneer towns like Kohukohu and Rawene. Its central location makes it a superb base for exploration, within easy reach of Bay of Islands, Whangaroa and Mangonui, Kaitaia and the Ninety Mile Beach, and the Waipoua forest / Opononi area. Marine charters are available on the harbour and horse treks, bushwalks, etc are available locally. The relaxed and hospitable style of the community make a stay in Horeke a memorable experience.
No facilities for pets.

Rawene

Homestay
Address: 'Hokingamai', P.O. Box 105, Gundry Street, Rawene
Name: David & Gillian McGrath
Telephone: (09) 405 7782
Email: david.gill@xtra.co.nz
Beds: 1 Double, 2 Single (2 bedrooms)
Bathroom: 1 Private (we only host one group at a time)
Tariff: B&B (continental) Double $70, Single $35, Children $25.
Credit cards. NZ B&B Vouchers accepted
Nearest Town: Kaikohe 43km

Rawene is NZ's third oldest settlement, and "Hokingamai" is situated on the shores of the Hokianga Harbour. Enjoy glorious harbour views, sunsets, peace and tranquillity. It is a 5 min walk to village, local pub, ferry, restaurant, library etc.
Your hosts have lived and travelled extensively in the South Pacific and Europe, and enjoy meeting people, being of service, and sharing the history of the Hokianga. Our home is sunny, warm and comfortable and it is our pleasure to make your stay enjoyable and memorable. Golf course and clubs for hire.
Laundry facilities available.
We are 1 hour from Bay of Islands and 3/4 hour from Waipoua forest.
Turn left at the Fire Station Rawene, into Gundry Street (B & B sign on corner) drive down to waters edge. Afternoon tea and supper included.
We have a Labrador X dog and a cat (both friendly!)

Rawene
Homestay
Address: 'Searell's', Nimmo Street, Rawene
(Postal: PO Box 100, Rawene 0452)
Name: Wally & Nellie Searell
Telephone: (09) 405 7835
Fax: (09) 405 7835
Beds: 1 Double, 2 Single (2 Bedrooms)
Bathroom: 1 Private (we only host one group at a time).
Tariff: B&B (continental) Double $65, Single $35, Dinner on request $20 p.p
Full Breakfast $5 pp. NZ B&B Vouchers accepted
Nearest Town: Kaikohe 43 km east on Highway 12

We are retired couple who enjoy sharing our comfortable home and magnificent panoramic views of Hokianga Harbour and surrounding hills with all who visit. The sunsets are breathtaking.
Our 1 acre garden includes many native trees and tropical fruit trees. Fresh fruit can be picked almost every day.
Wally is an ex-navalman and member of R.S.A. Our interests are many including gardening, wine making, photography and exploring New Zealand.
Rawene is on Highway 12, where the vehicular ferry crosses Hokianga Harbour then it's approx 1 hour to Kaitaia - Waipoua Kauri Forest is 3/4 hour south and Bay of Islands 1 hour east.
Service station, hotel, restaurants, shops, musical toilets, ferry and historic Clendon House, Mangrove walk, only 1km.
Turn off main road, motor camp sign over hill veer left. At Nimmo St. turn left to top of hill, flat easy parking area, house on right, easy access.

Opononi
Self Contained Accommodation
Address: 62 Fairlie Crescent, Opononi (PO Box 82, Opononi)
Name: Ruth and Jesse Dawn
Telephone: 09-405 8241 Freephone 0800 468397
Fax: 09-405 8773
Email: a.dawn@xtra.co.nz
Beds: 3 Superking/Twin in 2 Bedrooms and Lounge
Bathroom: 1 Private
Tariff: B&B (continental) Double $95, Single $60, $35 for each extra person.
Children under 12 years half price. Weekly rate reduced by 20%.
Visa/Mastercard.
Nearest Town: Opononi

Opononi is an enchanting place reminiscent of a Mediterranean village, yet with surprising diversity allows you within minutes to be in the wilderness of subtropical rainforest, climbing soaring desert dunes or alone on a thundering ocean beach - Magical places to discover.
We invite you to stay a while in this small community and enjoy our new self contained apartment with magnificent views over the Hokianga harbour. Complete with full kitchen, laundry, phone/fax, TV and video; you can be totally comfortable for an extended period. Breakfast makings include fresh fruits, real coffee, cereals and farm-fresh eggs to prepare at your leisure.
Just a short walk to the beach and pub, you can sit and yarn with the locals or enjoy a meal of the freshest fish possible. Other attractions locally include a rich history and world-class artists and crafts people.
Come and see for yourself - we think you'll be enchanted.

Opononi
Homestay
Address: Koutu Lodge
RD Kaikohe
Name: Tony and Sylvia Stockman
Telephone: (09) 405 8882
Fax: (09) 405 8332
Mobile: (025) 220 6020
Beds: 1 King, 1 Queen, 1 Double, 1 Single (3 Bedrooms)
Bathroom: 2 Ensuite, 1 Private
Tariff: B&B (Continental) Double $80 - $90, Single $45, Children negotiable.
Dinner $25. NZ B&B Vouchers accepted $15 surcharge
Nearest Town: Opononi 5 kms, Kaikohe 51 kms.

Situated on Koutu Point overlooking the beautiful Hokianga Harbour, our home has views both rural and sea. Two bedrooms have private decks. We provide a games room with pool table, dartboard and piano. A video and CD library is also available for your pleasure and entertainment. Our interests include gardening, fishing and meeting people.
Opononi and local areas offer horse treks, interesting walkways, sand boarding, fishing charters, or bring your own boat. Koutu Lodge is 1 1/2 hours from Kerikeri and the Bay of Islands. We are a Kiwi couple, and our aim is to provide you with a memorable stay, peaceful or as active as you wish. Opononi is a spectacular area to visit, clean and green, world famous sand dunes, giant Kauri forests, restaurants and hotels. We have a friendly staffy who lives outside.
Directions: *Koutu Loop Rd is 3 kms north of Opononi, then left 2.4 kms on tarseal to Lodge.*

Omapere
Bed & Breakfast
Address: Signal Station Road,
Omapere, Hokianga
Name: Alexa & Owen Whaley
Telephone: (09) 405 8641
Fax: (09) 405 8643
Beds: 1 Queen, 3 Single (2 bedrooms)
Bathroom: 1 Ensuite, 1 Family Share
Tariff: B&B (full) Double $70, Single $35,
Children half price. NZ B&B Vouchers accepted
Nearest Town: 60km west of Kaikohe on SH 12; 20km north of Waipoua Forest.

Our 10 year-old home nestles into the hillside overlooking the historic Hokianga Harbour, its unique sandhills and bar-bound harbour entrance - just a short drive up from Omapere village. So we have magnificent views which we feel should be shared. We are a retired couple, our family off our hands, and we are enjoying our escape from city living with tree-planting, gardening, and taming our hilly 5 acres with sheep, goats, chickens and ducks. Two friendly dogs and a marmalade cat help us.
We offer a restful stay for travellers - peaceful surroundings, comfortable sunny rooms with good beds, fresh home-grown produce for breakfast. Restaurants in easy walking distance, as are the ocean and harbour beaches, favourite lookout points and village shops. Kauri forests, bushwalks, spectacular waterfalls are a short drive away.
Directions: *Our name is by the gate and we are exactly 200m west of SH 12 on the Waipoua Forest side of Omapere village.*

Omapere

Bed & Breakfast
Address: Harbourside Bed & Breakfast
State Highway 12,
Omapere, Hokianga
Name: Joy & Garth Coulter
Telephone: (09) 405 8246
Beds: 1 Queen, 2 single (2 Bedrooms)
Bathroom: 2 Ensuites
Tariff: B&B (Continental) Double $75, Single $45.
NZ B&B Vouchers accepted $5 surcharge
Nearest Town: 60 km west of Kaikohe on SH12; 20 km north of Waipoua Forest

Our new two storey beachfront home is situated on State Highway 12 and Pioneer Walk at the Western end of Omapere overlooking the Hokianga Harbour. The beach is just 30 metres away. Take a walk, go fishing or have a swim.
We are within easy walking distance of restaurants and bar as well as other retail outlets.
Both rooms have ensuites, refrigerators, tea making facilities and TV with separate entrances opening on to decking that you can relax and enjoy superb views from. This is a comfortable, convenient and central location to stay when travelling through or exploring the district in full. The Waipoua Forest, Wild West Coast beaches, harbour entrance, sand hills or historic Rawene are all within 20 km.
With a lifetime involvement in Hokianga farming, forestry and education we would be delighted to share this history with you.

Waipoua Forest

Homestay
Address: Solitaire Historic Homestay,
SH12, Waimamaku, South Hokianga
Name: Jenny & Les Read
Telephone: (09) 405 4891   **Fax**: (09) 4054891
Email: lesjen.read.@clear.net.nz
Beds: 3 Double, 2 Single (4 bedrooms)
Bathroom: 2 Guests share
Tariff: B&B (continental) Double $90, Single $50, Dinner $25pp.
Credit Cards (VISA/MC). NZ B&B Vouchers accepted $20 Surcharge
Nearest Town: 70 km West of Kaikohe; 6 km North of the Waipoua Forest.

Visit our restored Kauri homestead just north of the enchanting Waipoua Kauri forest. You'll have no trouble finding us, we're adjacent to State Highway 12 in the sheltered Waimamaku Valley.
An ideal base to visit the giant Kauri trees, the Hokianga harbour and the West Coast beaches. Solitaire homestay is flanked by two rivers, with 30 acres of farm land abounding with bird life. Peace and tranquillity are guaranteed. We have neither pets or children.
Security doors with fly screens are fitted to all guest rooms. Each bedroom opens out onto a covered verandah.
Waimamaku, a place of ancient Maori and European settlement is surrounded by splendid forest and coastal walks. Come and experience the hospitality of the Hokianga region.

Dargaville
Farmstay, Bed & Breakfast Inn
Address: 'Kauri House Lodge',
Bowen Street,
PO Box 382 Dargaville
Name: Doug Blaxall
Telephone: (09) 439 8082
Fax: (09) 439 8082
Email: kauri@infomace.co.nz
Beds: 2 King,
1 Twin (3 bedrooms)
Bathroom: 3 Ensuites
Tariff: B&B (full) Double $140-$160.
Nearest Town: Dargaville 1 1/2 kms.

We are high on a hill overlooking the town. No highway noise or smells. The only thing to disturb the peace and tranquillity here, are the birds. Our guests enjoy: - Antiques, Kingsize very firm beds with superior line, own ensuites and large fluffy towels. Fly screened windows for your summer comfort. Our home is around 6000 sq. ft. Built by craftsmen early this century, with unique use of native timbers in panelling, ceilings and doors. It took 4 years to build. Billiards room with log fire in winter. Library with thousands of books. Drawing room with unusual Rimu dresser. Fully Kauri panelled dining-room. We are set in 8 acres of grounds and large swimming pool (summer only). Activities nearby include horse treks, river cruises, beaches, lakes, walking tracks and local restaurants. Our farm is separate. Bring good walking shoes to go exploring our beautiful mature native bush with Doug. Outside animals: - Dogs, cats, donkeys, cows. Smoke-free.

Dargaville
Self-contained Accommodation
Address: Awakino Point Lodge,
State Highway 14, Dargaville,
Postal: PO Box 168, Dargaville
Telephone: (09) 439 7870
Fax: (09) 439 7870
Mobile: 025-519 474
Email: apl.j.hyde@xtra.co.nz
Beds: 3 Units with Queen and Twin.
Bathroom: Each unit has ensuite facilities.
Tariff: B&B (continental) Double $75-$85 (seasonal), $15 each extra person.
Credit Cards. NZ B&B Vouchers accepted surcharge
Nearest Town: Dargaville 2km

S/H 12 To North   S/H 14 To Whangarei

← 1.5kms to Dargaville | S/H 12 | 1.5kms to Lodge →

Auckland

This unique country lodge is situated in a peaceful rural setting on a five acre farmlet surrounded by attractive gardens, orchard and aviary. It's just two minutes drive from the small township of Dargaville less than 2 km along state highway 14. There are two 2 bedroom suites and one 1 bedroom suite. The best features of the New Zealand Motel system and the Bed and Breakfast scheme have been amalgamated to create the best of both worlds. You will enjoy your own private self contained suite with private bathroom combined with friendly personal service and a good breakfast most of which is home produced. Pottery, painting, gardening and making wine from various fruits are just a few of the hobbies pursued, and after 15 years of hosting would say meeting people is yet another hobby. There are plenty of good restaurants in Dargaville reasonably priced but should you wish to have dinner at the lodge please arrange in advance. Credit cards accepted, but cash or travellers cheque would be much preferred. No smoking indoors, please.

Baylys Beach, Dargaville

Self-contained Accommodation
Address: Oceanview Bed & Breakfast,
7 Oceanview Terrace, Baylys Beach, Dargaville
Name: Paula and John Powell
Telephone: (09) 439 6256
Mobile: (025) 268 7255
Beds: 1 Double, 1 Single, 1 camp bed (1 Bedroom)
Bathroom: 1 Ensuite
Tariff: B&B (Continental) Double $70, Single $40, $20 per extra person.
Children under 5 yrs (no charge), under 12yrs ($10). NZ B&B Vouchers accepted
Nearest Town: 12 kms west of Dargaville off SH12

2 1/2 hours north of Auckland, just off Highway 12 you will find Baylys Beach. Sometimes wild, always wonderful, the west coast is an ideal spot to take time out. The beach is 200m from our property - go swimming, fishing, surfing, gather shellfish, hike cliff paths or simply stroll the beach to refresh body and soul. Golf, horse-riding and beach tours are available locally. The Kai Iwi Lakes and Waipoua Forest are 1/2 and 1 hour away.

We enjoy a relaxed lifestyle with our two young children and two cats. The children delight in our visitors, however your privacy is assured as your accommodation is independent of our family home. With sea views from the lawn area, the cottage is sunny and comfortable and furnished with TV, radio, refrigerator, tea / coffee facilities and ensuite bathroom with a great shower. Take breakfast at your leisure as this is provided in the cottage for you.

Directions: *Please phone for directions.*

Dargaville

Homestay, Farmstay, Bed & Breakfast, dinner optional
Address: 'Kauri Ridge', R.D.2, Dargaville
Name: Agnes & Wallace Bennett
Telephone: (09) 439 5163
Beds: 2 Double, 2 Single (3 bedrooms)
Bathroom: 1 Guests share, 1 Family share
Tariff: B&B (continental) Double $60,
Single $30, Dinner $20, Campervan
facilities available, $12 per couple - meals available.
Credit Cards accepted. NZ B&B Vouchers accepted
Nearest Town: Dargaville 28km.

Real Country - 28km from the hustle and bustle and restaurants. Agnes offers a three course meal - complimentary wine etc. We have 30 acres including native bush, kauris and a variety of birds. A dog for the sheep work and a sociable cat.
50km to Whangarei, 50km to Kai Iwi lakes, a little further to the Kauri Forests. There are long tramps or short walks in the district. Wallace is involved with Free Masonry and Agnes joins him in 60s up Movement. We retired from farming and Wallace spent six years with IHC and Agnes with a retirement home. This is our 5th year meeting strangers who become friends.
Bedrooms are upstairs but we enjoy your company downstairs. Our home is smoke free and please no dogs.
We look forward to meeting you and offer complimentary tea or coffee.
Directions: *12km from Dargarville on Whangarei Road (large B&B sign). Take Tangowahine Valley Rd after 15km turn right into Karaka Road. 1 km right into Somerville Road and 300 yards to our home.*

Matakohe

Farmstay
Address: Tinopai Road, R.D.1, Matakohe
Name: "Maramarie" Elinor & Tom Beazley
Telephone: (09) 431 6911
Email: maramarie@xtra.co.nz
Beds: 1 Double (1 bedroom -
extra beds available for children)
Bathroom: 1 Private
Tariff: B&B (continental) Double $75,
Single $40, Children half price, Dinner $17.50.
NZ B&B Vouchers accepted
Nearest Town: Matakohe 4km, Paparoa 10km

"Maramarie" is a secluded kauri homestead 4km from the unique Matakohe Kauri Museum. A visit to the museum is a great introduction to Northlands Kauri history. Kauri forests and the west coast with its endless beaches are not far away.
Beautiful farming country and views over the Kaipara Harbour will welcome you to Matakohe.
Our sheep and beef farm is gently rolling and invites you to stretch your legs.
Your room has a verandah overlooking the harbour and the mature garden.
I am Swedish and Tom is a New Zealander. We have three schoolage children. There are two dogs that help with the stockwork and one lazy cat.
Come and visit our family and relax on our farm.
Please phone for reservation and direction. Pick up from regular bus services to Matakohe available.

Kauri, Whangarei

Homestay
Address: Karamea House, Apotu Road,
Kamo, Whangarei
Name: Tony and Cherry Hopkins
Telephone: (09) 435 3401
Fax: (09) 435 3495
Mobile: (025) 276 4096
Email: tonyhopkins@clear.net.nz
Beds: 3 Queen, 1 Single (3 Bedrooms)
Bathroom: 1 Guests share, 1 Family share
Tariff: B&B (Full) Double $95-$135, Single $90,
Dinner $30. Children half price. Credit cards accepted.
Single party bookings only.
Nearest Town: Whangarei

Welcome to Karamea House. This magnificent colonial homestead is set in total privacy but is only ten minutes north of Whangarei and just 2 kms off State Highway 1. It is ideally positioned to visit the beautiful East Coast Bays and 40 minutes from the Bay of Islands.
Although conveniently located, we offer peace and quiet in a rural setting surrounded by beautiful grounds and paddocks with pet lambs and horses. Excellent amenities include an all weather astroturf tennis court, swimming pool and outdoor spa pool. The two story house features open fire places as well as central heating, a formal dining room, two lounges, a study and a huge country style kitchen. Guests enjoy exclusive use of the first floor. Dinner is available and, of course, a generous breakfast is provided.
Our policy of single party bookings only ensures complete privacy for our guests.
Home Page: www.karamea.co.nz

Ngunguru
Homestay
Address: 'Glengarry',
45 Te Maika Road,
Ngunguru, R.D.3. Whangarei
Name: Bet & Noel Glengarry
Telephone: (09) 434 3646
Beds: 2 Single (1 bedroom)
Bathroom: 1 Ensuite
Tariff: B&B (full) Double $65,
Single $40.
NZ B&B Vouchers accepted
Nearest Town: Whangarei 25 km

We are a retired couple with a Siamese cat whose cottage style home, set in half acre of tranquil gardens, is situated on the beautiful Tutukaka Coast. The sunny guest room, with ensuite, has its own entrance and tea / coffee making facilities. We grow our own fruit and vegetables and keep hens to provide fresh eggs and home made preserves for your breakfast. There are several excellent restaurants within five minutes drive where you can dine. We are two minutes walk from beautiful beaches and five minutes drive from Tutukaka for diving, Big Game fishing, or sightseeing trips to the world renowned Poor Knights Islands. We aim to make your stay as comfortable and enjoyable as possible and are always happy to help with bookings for dives, cruises etc.
Directions: *From Whangarei follow Tutukaka Coast Road for 25km. Travel through Ngunguru and turn right into Te Maika Road. Please phone ahead.*

Whangarei
Farmstay
Address: 'Parua House', Parua Bay,
Whangarei Heads Road, R.D.4, Whangarei
Name: Pat & Peter Heaslip
Telephone: (09) 436 5855
Fax: (09) 436 5855
Email: paruahomestay@clear.net.nz
Beds: 1 Queen, 5 Single (4 bedrooms)
Bathroom: 2 Ensuite, 1 Private
Tariff: B&B (full) Double $90-$100,
Single $50, Dinner $30, Children half price. NZ B&B Vouchers accepted $10 surcharge
Nearest Town: Whangarei 17km

Parua House is a classical colonial house built in 1883, comfortably restored and occupying an elevated site with panoramic views of Parua Bay and the Whangarei Harbour. The property covers 29 hectares of farmland including two protected native reserves which are rich in native trees (including kauri) and birds. Guests are to welcome to explore the farm and bush, milk the Jersey house cow, explore the olive grove and sub-tropical orchard or just relax in the spa-pool or on the verandah. A safe swimming beach adjoins the farm, with a short walk to the fishing jetty. Two marinas and a golf course are nearby. We have travelled extensively and our wide interests include photography, patchwork-quilting and horticulture. The house is attractively appointed with antique furniture and a rare collection of spinning wheels. Home-grown produce is used where possible. Vegetarian food is provided if requested. A warm welcome awaits you. Featured on TV's "Ansett NZ Time of Your Life" and "Corbans Taste NZ".

Whangarei
Homestay
Address: 477 Whangarei Heads Road,
Waikaraka, R.D.4, Whangarei
Name: Waikaraka Harbour View
(Marrion & John Beck)
Telephone: (09) 436 2549
Beds: 2 Single (1 bedroom)
Bathroom: 1 Ensuite
Tariff: B&B (continental)
Double $65, Single $40.
(reductions for long stays & winter)
NZ B&B Vouchers accepted
Nearest Town: Whangarei 10 km

Welcome to our self-contained studio built new in 1996 (twin beds, en-suite, tea/coffee facilities, TV, radio, Refrigerator, tables, chairs and adjoining decks). Enjoy the spectacular harbour and landscape views, fishing, beaches, walks, golf, gardens and the many other attractions in the Whangarei area. We retired here in 1990 after 25 years in the area. We enjoy travel, the outdoor life and hope we can help you to find similar enjoyment. Laundry facilities available. Smoking outdoors or on the decks please.

Directions: *From the "Town Basin" (Whangarei city centre) head east for Onerahi (5 kilometres) - 150 metres past the Onerahi shopping centre, turn left onto the Whangarei Heads Road - 4.77 kilometres to Waikaraka Harbourview B&B. (sign on left).*

Whangarei City
Bed & Breakfast
Address: "Chelsea House"
83 Hatea Drive, Whangarei
Name: Mel & Cathy Clarke
Telephone: 0508 243 573
(0508 CHELSEA) (Free call)
Mobile: (025) 379 976
Email: mel.clarke@clear.net.nz
Beds: 1 Queen, 2 Single (2 Bedrooms)
Bathroom: 2 Ensuites.
Tariff: B&B (full) Double $70-$90,
Single $40, Children welcome $20,
Credit Cards accepted.
NZ B&B Vouchers accepted $20 surcharge on double room.
Nearest Town: Whangarei cit y easy 10 min walk.

Welcome to Chelsea House, the most convenient B&B in Whangarei. Our home is a double gable villa built in 1910 and very close to the central city, Town Basin, restaurants and heated pools. Just across the road is the entrance to Mair Park which features walkways through beautiful native bush to the summit of Parahaki, the site of the largest Maori pa in NZ. Let us drive you to the top for spectacular views and a leisurely walk back down to Chelsea House. We have two rooms available; the double room ($90) is self contained wit h a fully equipped kitchen and ensuite bathroom. The twin room ($70) has tea and coffee making facilities and ensuite bathroom. Our two school age children have two cats, and Peanut (a Jack Russell). A cooked breakfast of your choice can be served in our family kitchen or outside in the delightful cottage garden. Laundry available.
Directions: *Please phone.*

Onerahi, Whangarei
Self-contained Suites
Address: "Channel Vista",
254 Beach Rd., Onerahi, Whangarei
Name: Murray & Jenny Tancred
Telephone: (09) 436 5529
Fax: (09) 436 5529 **Mobile**: (025) 973 083
Email: tancred@igrin.co.nz
Beds: 2 Queen (2 fully self-contained suites,
own lounge, TV, kitchen), also 1 Twin, 1 Queen (separate bedrooms in house).
Bathroom: 2 Ensuite + 1 guest share (in house)
Tariff: B&B (full) Double $90-$110, in house bedrooms $80,
Dinner 2 course $25pp (with wine), Credit Cards: Visa/Mastercard.
Nearest Town: Onerahi suburb, Whangarei city 9km

Murray & Jenny welcome you to "Channel Vista" situated right on the shore of the Whangarei Harbour and only 10 minutes from the city centre. Many sports facilities within 15 minutes (eg. 4 golf clubs, game fishing, heated pool, bowls etc). Our home is custom built to accommodate you in a degree of luxury we trust will help you to really enjoy your stay in Northland 'The Jewel of New Zealand'. Fantastic panorama of Whangarei Harbour with all boating passing in front of you. 20 metres to lovely little beach, boat and outboard for hire. Tours, fishing, airport pick ups etc. easily arranged. 1st class restaurant handy and only 9km to central Whangarei with the choice of restaurants, cafes, top retail outlets and many tourist attractions. Attractive scenic walks, drives, beautiful beaches - all reached in day trips from our homestay. Complimentary beverage in your unit. We provide a smoke free environment for you but outdoor smokers are welcome. Complimentary laundry, drier and ironing facilities available, also fax. We have a dog and a cat. Phone ahead to ensure your booking, directions and book meal if wanted at this new and popular venue.

Whangarei
Homestay/Farmstay
Address: "Gardner Homestead",
Clapham Rd, Whangarei
Name: Margaret Gardner
Telephone: (09) 437 3611
Fax: (09) 437 3611
Beds: 1 Double,
2 Single (2 bedrooms)
Bathroom: 1 Ensuite
Tariff: B&B (full) Double $70,
Children $20, Dinner $25.
Nearest Town: Whangarei 4km

Enjoy the peace and quiet of the countryside while only five minutes from Whangarei city centre. Our quaint old kauri homestead (the original home of Clapham Clocks) with its large garden and fish ponds lies in thirty acres of bush and paddocks which we share with three very friendly dogs, a cat, chooks, sheep, cattle and two horses (riding by arrangement). We offer a pleasant walk through our bush down to the Hatea River with its idyllic swimming hole. Reed Park with its kauri trees is only short walk away. Close by are Parahaki, Abbey Caves and Whangarei Falls.
The large upstairs guest suite has an ensuite and a smaller adjacent bedroom with two single beds and has television, radio, microwave, tea & coffee, reading matter and heating. We will be happy to meet you at airport or bus depot.

Whangarei
Homestay
Address: "Koinonia Manor",
260 Ngunguru Road,
RD 3, Whangarei
Name: Allan & Adele Kimber
Telephone: (09) 437 5961
Beds: 2 Double,
3 Single (4 bedrooms)
Bathroom: Guests share, Family share
Tariff: B&B (special) Double $70,
 Single $40, Children half price,
Dinner $20. Also charming 2 bedroom cottage tariff negotiable.
Nearest Town: Whangarei 8km

Welcome to Koinonia Manor, our lovingly restored historic homestead in Glenbervie built by Lord and Lady Douglas in 1880. Comfortably furnished with antiques and collectables, it is surrounded by cottage gardens and a macadamia nut orchard through which guests can wander. Three kilometres beyond Whangarei Falls, we are situated enroute to beautiful beaches where a playground of coastal adventures abound. Golfing greens and enticements of the town basin are also nearby.
Whether you are touring NZ, honeymooning, holidaying or here on business, it is our pleasure to assist you to make your stay memorable. Specialities by arrangement include dining al fresco, relaxing with a barbecue or by intimate candlelight.
Guests thoroughly enjoy the charm of yesteryear, warm hospitality, peaceful surroundings, the call of birds and wide verandahs. Bookings by letter are welcome, phoning at mealtimes or evenings is appreciated.

Whangarei
Bed & Breakfast
Address: Graelyn Villa,
166 Kiripaka Road, Whangarei
Name: Grace Green &
Linda McGrogan
Telephone: (09) 437 7532
Fax: (09) 437 7533
Email: graelyn@xtra.co.nz
Beds: 2 Queen,
2 Single (3 bedrooms)
Bathroom: 3 Ensuite
Tariff: B&B (continental) Double $70-$80, Single $55, Children $15, Dinner $25, Credit Cards (VISA/AMEX/DINERS/MC).NZ B&B Vouchers accepted
Nearest Town: Whangarei (4.5km to city centre)

A very warm welcome awaits you at Graelyn Villa. Beautifully presented in a tranquil garden setting, "Graelyn" is a turn-of-the-century villa that has been lovingly restored to offer comfort and luxury. Mother and daughter team, Grace and Linda, offer you friendly personal service. Breakfast is served on the verandah in summer, or by the cosy pot belly fire on colder days. A hearty cooked breakfast is available for a small extra charge, other meals by arrangement. Our rooms offer superbly comfortable beds, TV, tea and coffee, heaters and electric blankets. We are ideally situated, being only five minutes from the city centre, with a variety of top class restaurants, handy to the spectacular Whangarei Falls, also golf, bush walks, a 20 minute drive to beaches, game fishing and diving on the Tutukaka Coast, local shops nearby. We have a dog and cat, your pets welcome. Smoking on the verandah please. Laundry facilities available.

Whangarei
Homestay
Address: "Taraire Grove",
Tatton Road, RD 9, Whangarei
Name: Jan & Brian Newman
Telephone: (09) 434 7279
Fax: (09) 434 7679
Email: cooper@irgrin.co.nz
Beds: 1 Queen, 2 Single (2 bedrooms)
Bathroom: 1 Guests share
Tariff: B&B (full) Double $75,
Single $45, Dinner $12- $20.
Visa/Mastercards accepted.
Vouchers accepted 1 May to 31 August
Nearest Town: Whangarei 15 mins, Dargaville 30 mins

We welcome you to our charming country residence situated at Maungatapere, and within easy driving distances to East and West coast beaches to enjoy swimming, fishing and picnicking. Sightseeing and good shopping in Whangarei city.
We are a semi-retired couple and having travelled overseas using B&Bs, we welcome the opportunity to return hospitality that we have experienced. We have a cat (Joe) and Jack Russell (Max). Our home has lots of decking and overlooks a stream. We are gradually developing the 3 1/2 acres into lawns, gardens and ponds. The guest wing is private and has a TV room with tea & coffee making facilities. Our laundry is available for your use. No smoking indoors please. Evening meals - Whangarei has excellent restaurants, or you can choose to relax and dine with us. Ring or fax for reservations and directions.
Home Page: http://nz.com/webnz/bbnz/taraire.htm

Whangarei
Homestay
Address: The Wright Place,
2 Memorial Drive,
Riverside, Whangarei
Name: Selwyn and Margaret Wright
Telephone: (09) 438 7441
Fax: (09) 438 7441
Mobile: (025) 245 4177
Email: wright.place@clear.net.nz.
Beds: 1 Queen, 1 Double,
2 Single (3 bedrooms)
Bathroom: 1 Ensuite, 1 Family share
Tariff: B&B (full) Double $70-$80, Single $50.
NZ B&B Vouchers accepted $10 surcharge
Nearest Town: Whangarei 2.3km

Welcome to our quiet, centrally situated home with lovely views overlooking Whangarei City and the Hatea River. Stroll to the Town Basin and City Centre, Let us recommend a restaurant or cafe. We are handy to the Airport, Golf Links and Ocean Beaches or a comfortable drive to the Bay of Island. Our home has a swimming pool and lovely gardens for your enjoyment. Choose between a cosy detached bedroom with ensuite or Guest bedrooms upstairs. A quiet lounge with TV is provided but guests may share our family/living room. We share our home with "Storm" our cat. Quiet location. Privacy assured.

Whangarei
Homestay
Address: "City Lights",
40A Vale Road, Riverside,
Whangarei, Norhtland
Name: Kevin and Doug
Telephone: (09) 438 2390
Fax: (09) 438 2390
Mobile: (025) 958 243
Beds: 1 Queen,
2 Single (2 bedrooms)
Bathroom: 1 Guests share
Tariff: B&B (full/continental)
Double $70, Single $40.
Nearest Town: Whangarei Post Office 1.2 km

Our comfortable elevated home is only 1.2 km from the town centre and Post Office with views over the Hatea River to the Western Hills with magnificent views over the city. Walking distance to town basin, restaurants, cafes and bars, heated swimming pool. Forum North and Whangarei Area Hospital. We have a lovely walk at the end of our street along the Hatea River and up into Mair Park. An easy drive to many fine beaches and 4 golf courses. Unfortunately our place is not suitable for children. We have two lovable Boxer dogs, Cara and Cass also P4 the cat. We are non smokers but outdoor smokers are welcome. Pick up from downtown and the airport provided. We look forward to meeting you sometime in the future.
Directions: *Please phone ahead to ensure a booking and directions.*

Whangarei
Bed & Breakfast
Address: State Highway 14,
RD 9, Whangarei
Name: Errol and Sharon Grace
Telephone: (09) 438 9967
Fax: (09) 438 9967
Beds: 1 Double (1 Bedroom)
S/C Unit: 1 Queen,
2 Single, (2 Bedrooms)
Bathroom: 2 Ensuite

Tariff: B&b (Special/Full) Double $80, Single $55.
Dinner on request. Concession rates for childen. Credt Cards accepted.
Nearest Town: Whangarei 6 km

Our home is 6 km from central Whangarei on Highway 14 from Whangarei to Dargarville, and was built four years ago by Errol, a builder. Olde English styled with attic rooms, leadlight windows, New Zealand native floors with cedar joinery, sited on 1 1/2 acres next to native bush reserve, cedar trees line the driveway to a cottage garden featuring a spit roast waterwheel. Sharon handcrafts fabric animals and teddy bears and displays dried flowers in her studio. Bush walkways next door head to Whangarei Museum, Bird Recovery Centre, Kiwi House and Barge Park which hosts national horse events and local shows; walk ways over acres of bush and grasslands. Sherwood Part Golf course is 2.5 km away. Self contained unit, large deck, fridge, stove, pot belly, sleeping four persons. In house double bed, private bathroom.
You are welcome in this peaceful rural setting. Laundry, barbecue available. Breakfast menu, ordered evening meals, sometimes fresh seafood as Errol loves diving and fishing.

Whangarei

Homestay
Address: 2 Cairnfield Road
Kensington, Whangarei
Name: The Immigrant Leprechaun
Telephone: (09) 437 7991
Freephone: 0800 367 474
Mobile: (025) 294 1263
Email: lacollecutt@xtra.co.nz
Beds: 1 Queen, 7 Single (4 Bedrooms)
Bathroom: 2 Guests share
Tariff: B&B (Special) Double $65,
Single $45, Dinner $20 by prior arrangement.
Cooked breakfast small extra. Children special rates. Credit cards: Visa/Mastercard.
Nearest Town: Whangarei (we are central)

The Immigrant Leprechaun, Hosted accommodation, Bed and Breakfast. 2 Cairnfield Road,
Kensington, WHANGAREI. Freephone 0800 FOR IRISH (367 474) Bookings only.
(09) 437 7991 anytime. Mobile 025-294 1263 A warm Irish welcome awaits you at our 1898
Kauri Villa. 20 mins big game fishing and diving centre of the North. Minutes only from city
centre, town basin, restaurants, river, bush walks, Abbey caves, Whangarei falls and 10 mins
to local airport. Our delightfully appointed villa has separate guest lounge with TV or you may
join us in our lounge for a cuppa and a chat. Rooms 1 Twin; 1 Queen with extra single bed;
Family room with 2 full sized single bunks plus single bed, one single room.
Two guest share bathrooms, tea and coffee facilities 24 hours. Off street parking, fully fenced
section. Pets welcome. Special rates for children.
Home Page: http://mysite.xtra.co.nz/~immlep

Whangarei

Self Contained Accommodation
Address:
Country Garden Tearoom & B&B
526 Ngunguru Road,
Glenbervie, Whangarei
Name: John and Margaret Pool
Telephone: (09) 437 5127
Mobile: (025) 519 476
Beds: 2 Queen, plus double
Danske bed settee (2 Bedrooms)
Bathroom: 2 Ensuite
Tariff: B&B (Full) Double $65,
Single $40, Dinner $20. Campervans $10. Laundry available.
Nearest Town: Whangarei 10 kms.

Enjoy a warm friendly welcome. We have three acres of beautiful trees, many varied
shrubs, bulb, iris, perennials and succulents, plus much, much more. We are
surrounded by stone walls which are a feature of the area. There is also an abundant
bird life including Tuis, quail, wood pigeon, friendly fantails and many more.
Guests have own entry to spacious self contained unit with fridge, microwave, tea
making facilities. Home made cookies included. Enjoy full country breakfast in our
dining room overlooking the garden (or on a sunny verandah). We also operate a
Devonshire tea-room Friday to Sunday. We are 10 km from Whangarei CBA on the
Ngunguru, Tutukaka Coast Road. Five minutes from Whangarei Falls. 15 minutes
to beautiful coastal beaches, restaurants, deep sea diving, fishing and golf courses.

Whangarei

Fine Country Accommodation
Address: Mulryan's, Crane Road, RD 1, Kamo
Name: Val and Kevin Ryan
Telephone: (09) 435 0945
Fax: (09) 435 5146
Email: info@mulryans.co.nz
Beds: 2 Queen (2 Bedrooms)
Bathroom: 1 Ensuite, 1 Private.
Tariff: B&B (Special) Double ensuite $150, Double private $130, Dinner $45 pp.
Not suitable for children. Credit cards accepted.
Nearest Town: Whangarei

Stay awhile in a restored and renovated kauri villa which has been tastefully redecorated but still retains its earlier charm and character. Situated 5 minutes north of Kamo, Whangarei, Mulryan's is nestled within a large garden with established trees, including some magnificent magnolias, beautiful old fashioned roses, natives and exotics. After a refreshing nights sleep awake to the aroma of baked muffins or brioche. Enjoy a special breakfast of fruit juice, fruit salad or winter compote, home-made jams and marmalades, muesli and yoghurt. Choose also from a variety of egg dishes, using free range eggs. Dine alfresco on the verandah overlooking the pond, or in the sunny country kitchen. During winter enjoy the dining room with its warm cosy fire. Dinner and brunch can be arranged to suit your requirements. Summer picnic hampers are also available for day excursions. Enjoy a game of lawn tennis, or try a relaxing game of petanque, take a leisurely stroll amongst the gardens, soak in a warm spa, or take a refreshing dip in the pool. Others may choose the thrill of big game fishing or experience a variety of other aquatic activities available within the area. Play a round of golf, or two, with a choice of three courses within 10 minutes drive. For the gardener discover some of Whangarei's glorious gardens or explore the many other natural attractions that Whangarei has to offer. Fax and email facilities are available. Regrettably, Mulryan's facilities are not suitable for children. Smokefree. We share our home with a cat and dog.
Mulryan's is a member of the Heritage Inns of New Zealand group and assures you of a warm friendly welcome, tranquil country setting and excellent service.
Home Page: http://www.mulryans.co.nz

Whangarei

Homestay
Address: "Owaitokamotu",
727 Otaika Valley Road,
Whangarei
Name: Minnie and George Whitehead
Telephone: (09) 434 7554
Beds: 2 Queen, 2 Single (3 Bedrooms)
Bathroom: 1 Guests share
Tariff: B&B (Full) Double $75,
Single $40, Dinner $25,
Children $1 per year of age
up to 12 years. Campervans $10
for 2 people, $14 for 4 people.
Nearest Town: Whangarei 12 km.

Come and enjoy the absolute tranquillity of "Owaitokamotu" a place of water, magnificent rocks of all shapes and sizes, and pristine native bush awaiting your rambling walks, all set on 10 1/2 acres of easy contour and newly created gardens. Our home is newly built and is wheelchair friendly. Bedrooms have private access from exterior. TV, tea, coffee and cookies. A wide verandah offers pleasant relaxation. Smoking outside only please. Laundry facilities available.
Please phone or write.

Parua Bay, Whangarei

Address: Pen-Y-Bryn, Headland Farm Park,
Parua Bay, R.D.4, Whangarei
Name: Tina & Wayne Butler
Telephone: (09) 436 1941
Fax: (09) 436 1946
Mobile: (025) 932 578
Email: wayne.home@michaelhill.co.nz
Beds: 1 Double (1 bedroom)
Studio: 1 Queen with ensuite
Bathroom: 1 Private
Tariff: B&B (full) Double $90-$115,
Single $80. Dinner $30,
Credit Cards (VISA/MC).
Nearest Town: Whangarei 15km

ENJOY OUR MILLION DOLLAR VIEWS.
Our spacious modern home and self contained studio are located on a ridge in Headland Farm Park, a unique 300 acre farming / housing concept overlooking Parua Bay and Whangarei Harbour. The Farm runs Deer, Sheep and Cattle, and has a safe swimming beach, orchard and security gates. Adjacent is "The Pines" golf course, which welcomes visitors. We have lovely walks through the Park and a Spa Pool, Dinghy and Kayaks for use. Other activities in the area include horse trekking, fishing, tramping, tennis, harbour and ocean beaches. Enjoy a leisurely breakfast with home made treats. Dinner is by arrangement and served with New Zealand wine. We have a friendly, small house dog, and our varied interests include our garden landscaped with rocks, sports, craft / patchwork, genealogy. We have travelled extensively and lived in the Solomons and the UK. We request NO SMOKING inside. Phone for directions and gate code.
See our Website at: www.pen-y-bryn.co.nz

Whangarei Heads
Homestay/Self-contained accommodation
Address: Manaia Gardens,
R.D.4, Whangarei
Name: Audrey & Colin Arnold
Telephone: (09) 434 0797
Beds: 2 Queen, 1 Double,
1 Single (3 bedrooms)
Bathroom: 2 Private
Tariff: B&B (special)
Double $65
($60 second and
subsequent nights),
Single $50, Extra people $15 pp.
Self catering: Double $50, Extras $10. Credit cards (Bank). Vouchers accepted
Nearest Town: Whangarei

A stone's throw from your cabin to the beach, bush behind. Two quaint 60 year old cabins in the garden offer privacy and peace. Around us are beaches, both ocean and harbour, and over 400 hectares of Conservation land. Dinghy, laundry and barbecue, a nearby shop, artists galleries. We have a small farm and a large garden, and one cat. Breakfast includes home-made bread and free-range eggs. NB: Both cabins have two rooms, own bathroom, TV, microwave, fridge, toaster, tea/coffee, plates and cutlery, linen. RATA: double bed + single available, kitchenette. POHUTUKAWA; Queen bed, 1 single, 1 double day bed.
Directions: *Take the Whangarei Heads Road. We are 31km from the Whangarei Yacht Basin bridge and 1.7km past the Taurikura store. We are the only buildings in the bay. Rock wall in front, red mailbox 2487*

___

Whangarei Heads
Homestay
Address: 'Bantry', Little Munro Bay,
R.D.4, Whangarei
Name: Robin & Karel Lieffering
Telephone: (09) 434 0751
Fax: (09) 434 0754
Email: lieffrng@igrin.co.nz
Beds: 1 Queen, 2 bunks (2 bedrooms)
Bathroom: 1 Guests
Tariff: B&B (full) Double $95, Single $50,
Children under 12 half price. Dinner $25.
Only one party booked at a time. Campervans welcome.
NZ B&B Vouchers accepted $20 surcharge. Same day restrictions Nov - March.
Nearest Town: 28km Whangarei

We are a semi-retired couple (plus an outside dog), in our late 50's. Between us we speak English, Dutch, French, German and Japanese and like to laugh. We have travelled extensively and enjoy overseas guests. Our unusual home with rocks being part of the interior walls is at the edge of a safe-swimming be2ach. We have wonderful views of coastal "mountains", bays and sea. On our doorstep is one of several bush reserves with walking tracks. Photographically a fascinating area. Nearby is a golf course, tennis courts, horse-riding, several beaches and three popular on-shore fishing spots within five minutes walk or you can use our dinghy. Guests have their own entrance and sitting room if they wish to be alone and all rooms have sea views. We prefer guests not to smoke inside. Robin likes to cook and dinner includes good New Zealand wine.
Directions: *Phone, fax or email for reservations, and we will fax/email you a description*

Ruakaka

Farmstay/Self-contained Accomm
Address: Doctor's Hill Road, Ruakaka.
Postal: Dr's Hill Rd., RD 2 Waipu
Name: Vince & Joyce Roberts
Telephone: (09) 432 7842
Fax: (09) 432 7842
Mobile: 025 419 585
Email: robertsb.b@xtra.co.nz
Beds: 2 Queen, 2 Single (3 bedrooms)
Bathroom: 1 Private, 1 Family share
Tariff: B&B (full) Double $70, Single $40, Dinner $20 (includes wine),
Credit cards. Winter rates & Pensioner discount. NZ B&B Vouchers accepted
Nearest Town: Ruakaka - approx 2 hrs north of Auckland - 2 hrs south Bay of
Islands.

Magnificent views, peace and quiet greet you at our home.
Your accommodation is a two room bedsitter with its own bathroom, kitchenette and fridge,
a ranchslider leads onto deck with views of the entrance to Bream Bay, Mt Mania and
surrounding Islands.
FREE bush and scenic drive over our 150 acre dry stock farm can be arranged. Our wetland
area is home to the rare brown bitten. Beautiful beaches, squash courts, golf course, racetrack
where Vince trains our racehorses and good restaurants are a short drive from our home.
Reserve time to see the FREE refinery Video and model at Marsden Pt, Claphams Clock in
Whangarei and the Matakohe Kauri Museum an hours drive west.
As Ex dairy farmers with a grown family of four children, we have enjoyed doing B&B for the
past nine years, other interests include gardening, golf and travel.
As we spend a lot of time outdoors, we suggest you phone in the evening for bookings, however
passing callers are welcome. **Homepage**: www.roberts_joyce@hotmail.com

http://www.bnb.co.nz

take a look

Ruakaka
Homestay/Self-contained Accom.
Address: 15 Camellia Ave, Ruakaka
Name: Belle-vue
Telephone: (09) 432 8977
Fax: (09) 432 8994
Beds: 1 Queen, 1 Double, 2 Single (3 bedrooms)
Bathroom: 1 Private, 1 Family share
Tariff: Homestay (full) $60 Dbl, $40 Sgl.
Self Contained Unit (continental) $60 Dbl, $50 Sgl, $20 each extra adult.
Credit cards. NZ B&B Vouchers accepted
Nearest Town: Ruakaka (scenic route) 32 kms south of Whangarei

Our 2 storey home is situated on the ridge 2 minutes drive from the beautiful Ruakaka surf beach. The 1100 sqft self contained unit on the ground level has its own cooking facilities, TV and video. Upstairs has 1 Queen (1 bedroom) with shared household facilities. Both are serviced daily so you may relax and enjoy your stay with us. Your hosts have many years involvement in the tourist industry welcoming both overseas and local visitors. Our interests include boating, horse racing, golf, music and your company. We are handy to Waipu Golf Course, Ruakaka Racecourse (where the Turf meets the Surf) and the Marsden Point Oil Refinery with video and display model a must see. We are happy to share with you our wide knowledge of Northland's attractions to make your stay with us more memorable.
Directions: *Turn off SH1 at Ruakaka into Marsden Point Road, 1st right into Beach Road, 1st left into Camellia Ave.*

Waipu
Farmstay+Self-Contained Accom.
Address: Cove Road, Waipu Cove
Name: Andre & Robin La Bonte
Telephone: (09) 432 0645
Fax: (09) 432 0645
Email: labonte@xtra.co.nz
Beds: 1 King, 2 Double, 2 Single (3 bedrooms)
Bathroom: 2 Private
Tariff: B&B (continental) Double $80, Single $50,
Dinner $20. NZ B&B Vouchers accepted
Nearest Town: 10km sth of Waipu on Cove Rd, 50km sth of Whangarei via SH1.

My wife and I are Americans who became residents of New Zealand in 1985. Our modern home with separate guest accommodation is situated by the edge of the sea on 36 acres including a 2.5 acre freshwater lake. Sleep to the sound of the ocean in either the separate efficiency apartment or in the guest bedrooms, with double or two single beds and private bathroom. No smoking please. enjoy expansive views of the Pacific Ocean and offshore islands. Explore our 850 ft of shoreline with limestone rock formations or just sit and relax under the mature pohutukawa trees that grace our shoreline. The beach at Waipu Cove is a ten minute walk along the shoreline. We are a licensed fish farm raising fish for food and aquatic weed control. We graze cattle and have flea free cats. Glow worm caves, deep-sea fishing, scuba diving and golf are all available locally.
Directions: *Please phone. Bookings recommended.*

Waipu

Seaside farm stay + Self-contained Accom.
Address: Cove Road, Waipu
Name: The Stone House
Telephone: (09) 432 0432
Fax: (09) 432 0432
Beds: 2 Queen, 2 Double,
3 Single (4 bedrooms)
Bathroom: 1 Ensuite, 3 Private
Tariff: B&B (full) Double $80-$100 (seasonal), Single $60,
Children plus Extra Adults $20 pp, Dinner $20. Credit Cards
NZ B&B Vouchers accepted $20 surcharge on some rooms
Nearest Town: 35km south of Whangarei, then 6km from Waipu on Cove Road
(Scenic Route)

Relax in a charming self-contained stone cottage by the sea, or if you prefer stay with your hosts Gillian and John in their unique Stone House. We offer a touch of Cornwall complete with cosy log fires in the winterless North!
The House and cottage are set in picturesque rock gardens with croquet lawn and sheltered patios. This extends to the green pastures of our farmlet, a jetty and lagoon. Use our dinghys or canoes (at no extra charge) to explore an extensive bird sanctuary, sand dunes and unspoilt ocean beach adjoining the property.
Fishing including surfcasting, deep sea fishing and boat trips, swimming, horseriding, scenic bush walks, glowworm caves, golf, tennis, talented art / crafts are all at hand. Our specialties include both Kiwi and German cuisine.
• Over 3000 beautiful orchids in season • Genuine NZ hospitality • Colour TV, video, coffee / tea facilities • German spoken.

Waipu

Guest House
Address: "Wychwood Lodge",
Cove Road, Langs Beach,
RD 2, Waipu
Name: Barry & Jan Dyer
Telephone: (09) 432 0757
Fax: (09) 432 0760
Mobile: (025) 277 4440
Beds: 3 King, 1 Double (4 bedrooms)
Bathroom: 3 Ensuite, 1 Private
Tariff: B&B (full) Double $135-$195, Credit Cards (VISA/AMEX/ DINERS).
Nearest Town: Waipu 10 Kms

A very special place. A pastoral and coastal paradise set in 11 acres with native bush, stream and waterfall. We have unsurpassed views across Bream Bay and we are walking distance to two of NZ's most beautiful white sand beaches. All rooms have private bathrooms and balconies. Edwardian style conservatory for breakfast. Two restaurants a few minutes away for dinner. Large guest lounge with log fire. Two golf links nearby. Fishing and diving arranged. Hiking trails and bush walks. Our aim is to give you luxury with friendly informality. Two cats in residence. Our interests include art, design, international travel and we are passionate gardeners. Italian spoken. **Directions**: *Less than two hours drive from Auckland, midway to the Bay of Islands. Take Mangawhai turnoff on SH1 past Te Hana. This is the scenic "Coastal Route North" (sealed roads) Wychwood Lodge is 30 mins from here through Mangawhai, alternatively take the Waipu turnoff from SH1, 10 mins to Langs Beach from here through Waipu Cove.*

Waipu Cove
Self-contained Accommodation
Address: 53 St Anne Road, Waipu Cove, RD 2, Waipu
Name: Flower Haven
Telephone: (09) 432 0421
Mobile: (025) 287 2418
Email: flowerhaven@xtra.co.nz
Beds: 2 Double (2 bedrooms)
Bathroom: 1 Private
Tariff: B&B (continental) Double $90 (Dec-Feb, Easter & Labour weekend)
or $70 (Mar-Nov), Non smokers only. No pets.
NZ B&B Vouchers accepted $20 Surcharge summer rates
Nearest Town: 8km south of Waipu, off Cove Road

At Flower Haven we enjoy an elevated position with panoramic views of the sweep of Bream Bay and off shore islands. We are retired with interests in genealogy, meeting people and gardening, and are developing the quarter acre grounds as a garden retreat.

Our accommodation is a fully self-contained downstairs two bedroomed flat with separate access, fridge/freezer, stove, microwave, washing machine, radio and TV. Linen, duvets, blankets and bath towels are provided. Reduced tariff applies if continental breakfast is not required. We are a 5 minute walk to the shop, sandy surf beach and rocks. Restaurants are handy and we are near many places of interest such as bird sanctuary, museums, golf courses, horse riding treks, chartered fishing trips, limestone caves, walking tracks, Marsden Point Oil Refinery visitors centre, with Auckland 1 1/2 hours away.

Directions: *Last house on left of St Anne Road (off Cove Road).*

Waipu
Homestay
Address: Cove Road, Langs Beach, Waipu
Name: Lochalsh
Telephone: 09-432 0053
Fax: 09-432 0053
Email: langs@xtra.co.nz
Beds: 1 King, 2 Single (2 bedrooms)
Bathroom: 2 Ensuite
Tariff: B&B (full) Double $70-$100 (depending on season),
Single $65, Dinner $20. Credit Cards accepted
Nearest Town: 1hr 40 mins north of Auckland, 10mins south Waipu.

Our great-grandfather settled this area in 1853. Our home is the old Lang homestead and it is right beside this beautiful white sandy surf beach which is lined with pohutukawa trees and is safe for swimming. Sit on the long warm sunny verandah and look out over Bream Bay and the Hen and Chicken Islands.

Both bedrooms have ensuites and there is a cosy guest lounge with small kitchen, fridge/freezer and microwave, plus dishes and cutlery. Several restaurants are a short drive away or you can dine in.

There is wonderful coast walks on private beaches with lovely shells, fishing is good, or just sit on the sand and dream.

Being less than two hours from Auckland you can make us your first night stop on your Northland tour. Many of our guests just don't want to move on! Graham and Billie and cat Rug look forward to your company.

http://www.bnb.co.nz

take a look

Auckland

Mangawai Heads

Te Hana
Wellsford
Leigh

Sandspit
Snells Beach
Warkworth
Kawau Island
Algies Bay

1

Puhoi

16
Orewa
Silverdale
Whangaparaoa
Kaukapakapa
Okura

Helensville
Albany
North Shore
Waiheke Island

Huapai

Kumeu
Devonport
Howick
Beachlands
Maraetai
Waitakere
Bucklands Beach
Bethells Beach
Auckland City
Swanson
Whitford
Clevedon
Piha
Mangere
Manukau City
Manurewa

Papakura
Kaiaua
Hunua
Drury
Awarimu
1
Waiuku
Bombay
Pukekohe
2
Pokeno
Mercer

22

Port Waikato

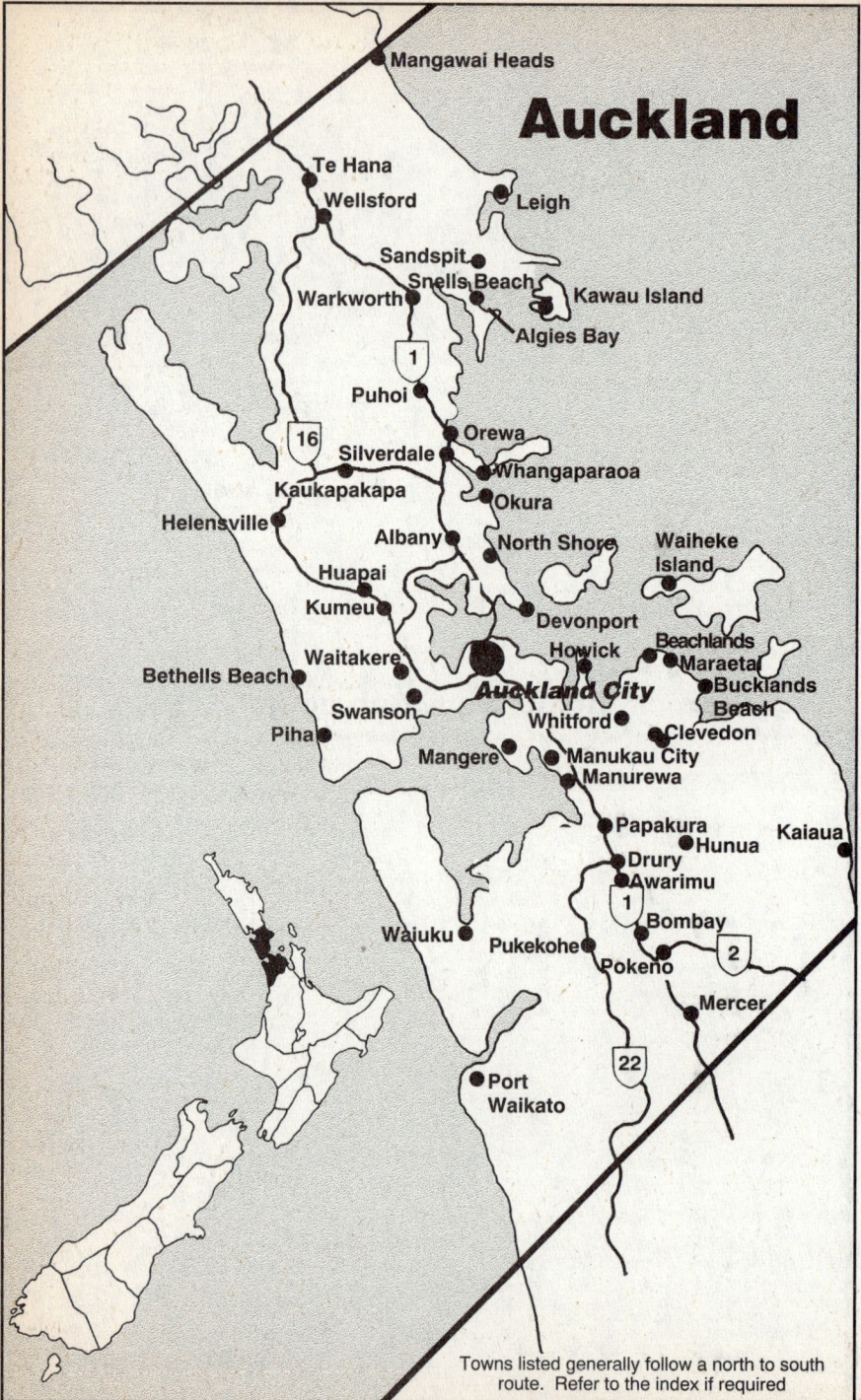

Towns listed generally follow a north to south
route. Refer to the index if required

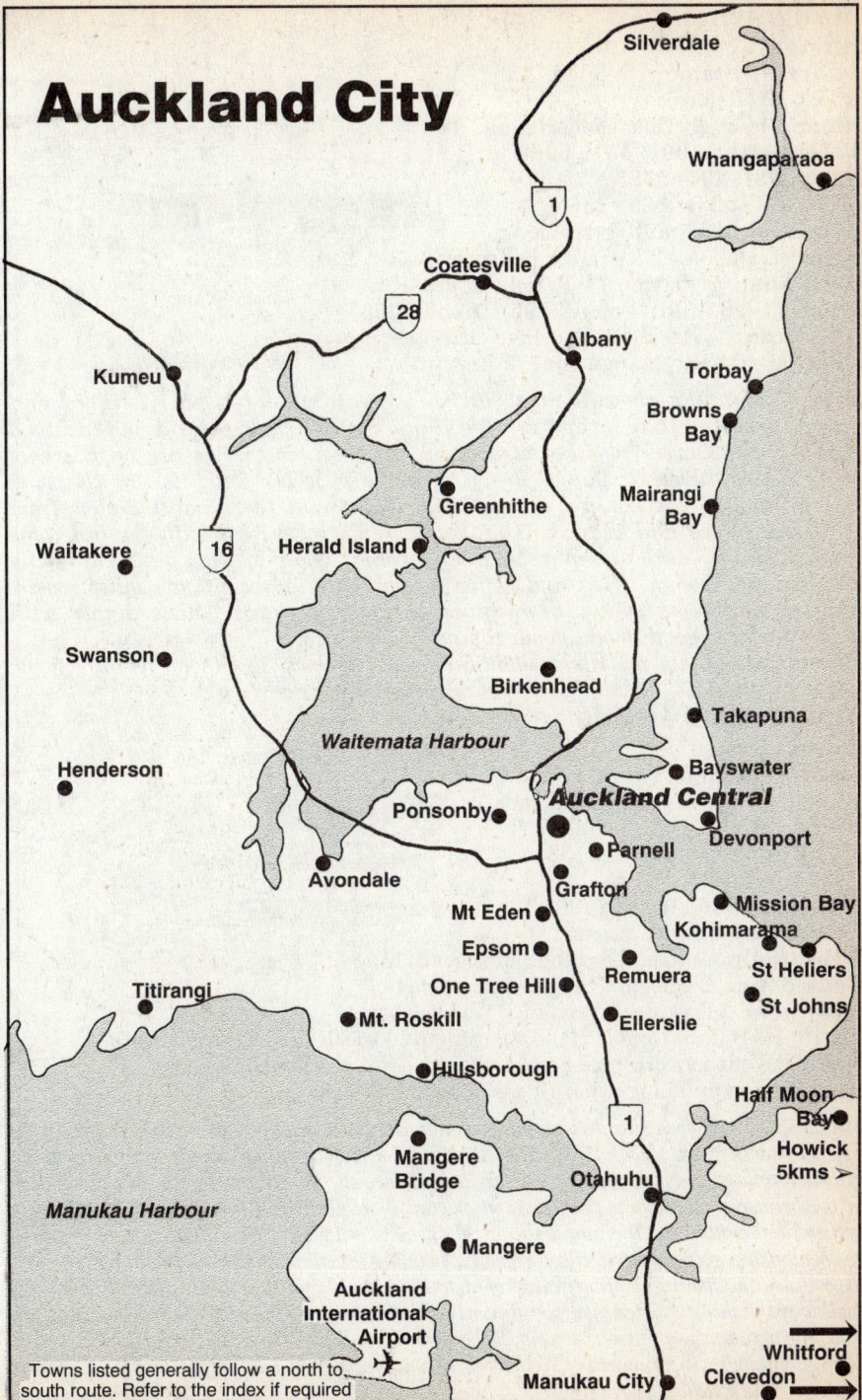

Auckland City

Silverdale

Whangaparaoa

1

Coatesville

28

Albany

Kumeu

Torbay

Browns
Bay

Mairangi
Bay

Greenhithe

16

Herald Island

Waitakere

Swanson

Birkenhead

Waitemata Harbour

Takapuna

Henderson

Bayswater

Ponsonby

Auckland Central

Devonport

Parnell

Avondale

Grafton

Mission Bay

Mt Eden

Kohimarama

Epsom

One Tree Hill

Remuera

St Heliers

Titirangi

Mt. Roskill

Ellerslie

St Johns

Hillsborough

Half Moon
Bay

1

Howick
5kms ➤

Mangere
Bridge

Otahuhu

Manukau Harbour

Mangere

Auckland
International
Airport

Whitford

Clevedon

Towns listed generally follow a north to
south route. Refer to the index if required

Manukau City

73

Mangawhai
Homestay
Address: Staniforth Road,
R.D.5, Wellsford
Name: Jean & Don Goldschmidt
Telephone: (09) 431 5096
Fax: (09) 431 5063
Mobile: (025) 829 736
Email: goldschmidt@xtra.co.nz
Beds: 1 Queen, 1 Twin (2 bedrooms)
Bathroom: 1 Private, 1 Family share
Tariff: B&B (full) Double $95, Dinner $25.
Credit cards   NZ B&B Vouchers accepted
Nearest Town: Mangawhai 7 km

High on the hills above Mangawhai on the east coast between Wellsford and Whangarei lies our property. 90 mins north of Auckland makes it a convenient stopover from the airport on the road north. We are on a scenic route which takes in Langs Beach and Waipu. Our delights are the long empty beaches, the fishing, the golf, the walks and the expansive view from the house of sea and islands. Our house is ideal for B&B with the bedrooms in two wings, with a separate sitting room, good heating and charming architectural design. Tea and coffee is available in the private quiet rooms. Sharing our home with visitors gives us great pleasure. Have dinner with us and enjoy good food, good company and fun.
Directions: *13km on Mangawhai Rd from Highway 1. Phone for directions.*

Mangawhai Heads
Guest House
Address: "Mangawhai Lodge",
4 Heather St, Mangawhai Heads
Name: Mangawhai Lodge
Telephone: (09) 431 5311
Fax: (09) 431 5312
Mobile: (025) 271 2790
Email: the.lodge@xtra.co.nz
Website:http://nz.com/webnz/bbnz/mangawhai.htm
Beds: 3 King, 2 Queen, 7 Single (5 bedrooms)
Bathroom: 2 Ensuite, 1 Private, 2 Guests share
Tariff: B&B (full) Double $90-$130, Single $60-$80. Credit cards.
NZ B&B Vouchers accepted $30 surcharge. (Not accepted Jan/Feb)
Nearest Town: Mangawhai Heads - 5 minute walk.

Mangawhai Lodge is situated at Mangawhai Heads, a scenic water lovers paradise 90 minutes north of Auckland. This elevated colonial-style lodge offers spectacular views of the harbour, white sandy beaches and outer island of the gulf. This makes for an idyllic stop-over or weekend retreat. Rooms furnished in elegant Northland Pacifica style open onto wide verandahs, enhancing the ambience of this gracious house. Being opposite an 18 hole championship golf course, licensed cafe and bowling green makes Mangawhai Lodge ideal for couples and fishing / golfing groups of up to 10 guests. Enjoy the white sandy surf beaches, walkways, fishing charters, golf, crafts and cafes or lounge on the veranda reading the wide selection of magazines, just watching the boats sail by. **Directions**: *From Auckland turn R Mangawhai sign (6 km north of Wellsford). From North turn L at Waipu and follow scenic coastal route south.*
Bookings recommended. Please telephone.

Te Hana, Wellsford
Historic Farmhouse

Address: 'The Retreat', Te Hana,
R.D.5, Wellsford
Name: Tony & Colleen Moore
Telephone: (09) 423 8547
Email: theretreat@xtra.co.nz
Beds: 1 Queen, 1 Double, 1 Single (2 bedrooms)
Bathroom: 1 Guests share
Tariff: B&B (full) Double $85, Single $50, Dinner $25,
Credit cards. NZ B&B Vouchers accepted Surcharge $10
Nearest Town: Wellsford (6km)

"The Retreat" is a historic kauri homestead built in 1867 for a family with 12 children. The house is set back from the road overlooking farmland, including our eight acres where we graze black and white sheep. The pet sheep enjoy being hand fed. Colleen is a spinner and weaver producing handcrafts from the wool, and the finished articles are available for sale. An acre of landscaped garden compliments the house, including a large herb garden, fish pond garden, and perennial borders leading to the summer house. Enjoy a game of croquet on a summer's evening or relax in front of the log fire in cooler months. Fresh vegetables from the garden and fruit from our orchard are on the menu in season. We have travelled extensively overseas and in New Zealand and are keen to promote our scenic and historic places - especially local ones.
Directions: *"The Retreat" is on the left 6km north of Wellsford on State Highway 1 and 13km south of Kaiwaka. You will see the "Weaving Studio" sign at our entrance.*

Leigh, North Auckland
Homestay

Address: 10 Ferndale Avenue, Leigh
Name: Joan & Ken Helliwell
Telephone: (09) 422 6099
Fax: (09) 422 6099
Beds: 1 Double, 4 Single
(2/3 bedrooms. Guest living room
with TV and tea making equipment)
Bathroom: 1 Guests share
Tariff: B&B (full) Double $65,
Single $45, Dinner $20pp. Vouchers accepted
Nearest Town: Warkworth 23km

Leigh is a seaside fishing village 70-80 minutes drive North of Auckland, situated on the cliffs above the Leigh Cove. It offers facilities for boating, including a ramp and anchorage within the small harbour. The village community has a church, a hotel, a garage, a general store, "take-away" cafe and dairy. Some good restaurants are also in the vicinity. Within 5 minutes car travel are sandy swimming beaches; a good surfing beach; tidal flats as well as deep water and rocky shore coastline; coastal and country walks and the Goat Island Marine Reserve where underwater diving is welcomed, and where the Glassbottom Boat goes exploring. Our home is in the village. We are retired school teachers living in the family home. We have travelled overseas extensively, enjoy other people's hospitality, and would be glad to offer a warm "Kiwi" welcome to our guests. We have no pets or children.

Warkworth
Farmstay
Address: 'Blue Hayes Farmstay',
44 Martins Bay Road,
13 km east Warkworth
Name: Rod & Rosalie Miller
Telephone: (09) 425 5612
Fax: 09 4255612
Mobile: 025 776 873
Beds: 4 Single (2 bedroom)
Bathroom: 1 Family share, 1 Ensuite
Tariff: B&B (full) Double with ensuite $75, Double share $65, Single $40, Children 1/2 price, Dinner $20, Credit cards. NZ B&B Vouchers accepted
Nearest Town: Warkworth 13 Kms

We live on a 314 acre coastal farm overlooking Kawau Bay, Mahurangi Heads and river in the Hauraki Gulf, approximately 80 km north of Auckland. We farm sheep, poultry, deer and cattle. You are welcome to participate in daily farming activities including hand feeding deer. We live in a private setting with plenty of open space, close to good safe beaches and seaside shopping centre, 13 km from Warkworth on sealed road. Our family home is 50 years old, comfortable, warm and relaxed with open fireplace, woodstove and beautiful views. Farm walks and natural bush reserves on property with tracks to view N.Z. flora including restored old school. Rod is a commercial pilot and flying instructor. Scenic flights both local and Hauraki Gulf available. Local area attractions include craft centres, Goat Island Marine Reserve and historic Kawau Island. Rod and Rosalie welcome you to share their hositality before a 3 course dinner. **Directions**: *Please phone.*

Warkworth
B&B+Self-contained Accom.
Address: 'Homewood Cottage',
17 View Rd., Warkworth
Name: 'Homewood'
Ina & Trevor Shaw
Telephone: (09) 425 8667
Fax: (09) 425 9610
Mobile: 025 2357469
Beds: 1 Double, 2 Single (2 bedrooms)
Bathroom: 2 Ensuite
Tariff: B&B (continental) Double $70, Single $60, Extra bed $20 each
NZ B&B Vouchers accepted Double room only. Credit Cards: Visa/Mastercard.
Nearest Town: Warkworth 0.5km - Auckland 1 hour - SH1

Our home is a peaceful, quiet place with its cottage garden and views of Warkworth and the hills. We like sharing it with guests. The bed-sitter style rooms are a good size. Each, privately situated has its own entrance, views, ensuite, tea-making, TV, patio and car park; no cooking facilities. The comfortable, warm beds, electric blankets. Many use our home to visit family locally. We understand many enjoy the privacy of the rooms but feel free to use the lounge and chat. The choice is yours. The laundry, small fridge, hair dryer are available. Breakfast is substantial continental - with choice of cereals, preserves, fruits and lovely local breads. Ina is an artist. Trevor has had a lifetime in journalism. We enjoy golf, walking, the theatre and our guests. Our home is Smoke free.
Directions: *At traffic lights, left up Hill St, 2nd left View Rd.*

Snells Beach, Warkworth

Homestay/Farmstay
Address: 416 Mahurangi East Road,
Snells Beach, Warkworth
Name: Mahurangi Lodge
Telephone: (09) 425 5465
Fax: (09) 425 5465
Beds: 3 Double, 5 Single, (4 bedrooms + 1 Family Room)
Bathroom: 2 Ensuite, 1 Guests share, 1 Family share
Tariff: B&B (continental) Double $50-$80, Single $25-$45, Children half price, Dinner $20 by prior arrangement, Discounts apply, please ask. Credit Cards (VISA/MC/BC). Campervans welcome. BBQ area.
NZ B&B Vouchers accepted $10 surcharge for ensuite room (Discounts apply)
Nearest Town: Warkworth 9km

Welcome to our colonial-style homestay just 1 hour from Auckland (1 1/2 from Airport) on a 30 acre farmlet overlooking Kawau Bay, Great Barrier, Little Barrier, Coromandel and the Mahurangi River. Our upstairs bedrooms are spacious, clean and with superb seaviews in a relaxed friendly smokefree atmosphere, with a Manx cat and native birds around. Your needs are our top priority with some local attractions offering our guests special discounts. A complimentary Kawau Island cruise included in longer stays. Enjoy a welcome 'cuppa' on arrival with everything available anytime you want another. Let us help you maximise your sightseeing of the numerous nearby attractions or further afield. There are several restaurants nearby and in Warkworth. Recommended by Jane King's 'N.Z. Handbook'. At Warkworth traffic lights follow Snells Beach signposts, straight ahead at Roundabout 1 1/2 km right on the hilltop. We have travelled overseas and throughout NZ and love to learn about your area.

Warkworth Sandspit

Homestay
Address: 38 Kanuka Rd,
R.D. 2, Warkworth
Name: Belvedere Homestay.
Margaret & Ron Everett
Telephone: (09) 425 7201
Fax: (09) 425 7201
Mobile: (025) 284 4771
Beds: 2 Queen, 1 Twin (3 bedrooms)
Bathroom: 1 Ensuite, 1 Private
Tariff: B&B (continental) Queen with Ensuite $90. Queen & Twin $90, Single $50, Dinner $30pp. NZ B&B Vouchers accepted $20 surcharge
Nearest Town: Warkworth 7km

Set in 11 acres, overlooking the Spit where the ferries leave for 'Kawau Island' with a 360 degree view from countryside to 'Little Barrier'. We have bush and pastures for our cows and native birds. For your relaxing and pleasure there is fishing from the beach or boat, golf, tennis and town within 7km. With ever increasing vineyards being planted and cafes. We have air conditioning and central heating, games room with pool table, relaxing spa, conservatory, outside terrace and deck plus a sunken rose garden barbeque area. Continental breakfast is included in the price which is mainly home produced (Full breakfast on request) Margaret's flair with cooking is a great way to relax over pre-dinner drinks and wine with your 3 course meal. Warkworth has many attractions, well worth a visit. Our house, Nicky our friendly dog look forward to making your stay a memorable one. Smoking on terrace and decks.

Warkworth - Algies Bay
Homestay
Address: 'Ceri', 56 Mera Road,
Algies Bay, Warkworth
Name: Ngaire Miller
Telephone: (09) 425 5603
Mobile: (025) 977 941
Email: nmiller@maxnet.co.nz
Beds: 3 Single, 1 Double (Double and Single bedroom/1 Family room - 2 single)
Bathroom: 1 Private
Tariff: B&B (full) Double $70, Single $40, Children half price. Dinner $20.
Packed lunch by arrangement, Vegetarian meals on request.
Credit Cards   NZ B&B Vouchers accepted
Nearest Town: 10km from Warkworth, 1 hour drive from Auckland.
Mahurangi shopping area 2km.

A warm welcome awaits you to share this spacious well appointed home in restful garden surroundings with bush backdrop and two happy cats. It offers panoramic sea views of Kawau Bay. From here you can explore many bays, parks and historical sites including Mansion House on Kawau Island. The area also has arts, crafts, wineries and a selection of restaurants, plus golf, tennis and bowls. Two minutes walk to safe swimming beach, ramp for boating and picnic area. Waken to the sounds of native birds and the smell of fresh home baked bread. TV, fridge, tea and coffee making facilities. Privacy. As a VIC volunteer Ngaire is well equipped to assist you maximise your stay in this beautiful area. Come and unwind in this quiet, relaxing smokefree environment. Ngaire is a registered nurse and offers therapeutic massages. Only one set of guests accommodated at a time. Telephone or call at Information Centre, Warkworth for directions.

Warkworth
Guest House
Address: 'Kowhai Lodge',
348 Kaipara Flats Rd, R.D.1, Warkworth
Name: Christina & Barrie Ellison
Telephone: (09) 425 9193
Fax: (09) 425 9193
Mobile: (025) 241 3783
Email: kowhai.lodge@xtra.co.nz
Beds: 2 Double, 2 Twin (4 bedrooms)
Bathroom: 1 Guest share
Tariff: B&B (special) Double $90, single $50, Dinner $30. Children over 12 years only. Credit Cards accepted. NZ B&B Vouchers accepted $20 surcharge Mon-Thur
Nearest Town: Warkworth 6km

Kowhai Lodge is a beautifully restored 1920's bungalow in a rural location minutes from Warkworth. The bedrooms are furnished in different woods, the doubles are oak or kauri and the twin, rimu or mahogany. Jodie our house dog will make you most welcome as will Chevis our Persian cat. Refreshments are readily available. We take great pride in our special breakfasts. All baking is home-made as are jams and relishes. A hearty meal can be prepared especially for you by prior arrangement, or you can enjoy dinner at one of our local restaurants. We hope your stay with us will be memorable as we do our best to "make you feel special". We welcome you into our home as guests and trust that you will leave as friends. We are a non-smoking household.
Directions: *Sign posted form SH1.*

Sandspit, Warkworth

Bed & Breakfast
Address: The Saltings Guest House,
Sandspit Rd, R.D.2, Warkworth
Name: Jean Mason
Telephone: (09) 425 9670
Fax: (09) 425 9674
Mobile: (021) 675 425
Email: salting@wk.planet.gen.nz
Beds: 2 King, 1 Queen, 1 Double, 4 Single (4 bedrooms)
Bathroom: 3 Ensuite, 1 Private
Tariff: B&B (full) Double $110-$140, Single $90-$120.
Credit Cards. NZ B&B Vouchers accepted $40 surcharge
Nearest Town: Warkworth 6km.

GUEST HOUSE

Situated on the Sandspit Rd, this is a Bed & Breakfast with a difference. The house has been renovated to give a French provincial feeling, with the added comfort of Kiwi hospitality making it ideal for couples who want to get away from it all and enjoy a clean fresh environment, with plenty of outdoor activities in the area. The Saltings Guest House sits on six acres of elevated farmland overlooking the beautiful estuaries of Sandspit and surrounding farmland. Just one hour drive north of Auckland city, and five minutes from the delightful village of Warkworth, plus we are within walking distance to the ferry where many cruises are available, including a visit to Kawau Island and the historic Mansion House. The four well appointed guest bedrooms are beautifully decorated with comfort in mind. Myself and friends Tess (Dalmatian dog), Pipi and Tom (cats) look forward to meeting you, and making your stay a memorable one. Young adults welcome.
Directions: *Please phone for directions.*
Home Page: http://nz.com/webnz/bbnz/salting.htm.

Warkworth

Homestay+Self-contained   Accom.
Address: 541 Woodcocks Road,
Warkworth
Name: Willow Lodgee"
Telephone: (09) 425 7676
Fax: (09) 425 7676
Mobile: (025) 940 885
Beds: 1 Queen, 2 Double, 4 Single (4 bedrooms)
Bathroom: 2 Ensuite, 1 Private
Tariff: B&B (full) Double $80-$100, Single $60, Children $20,
Dinner $30. NZ B&B Vouchers accepted
Nearest Town: Warkworth 5 kms.

Your hosts John and Paddy have more than 30 years experience in the hospitality field and have lived in Warkworth for the past 26 years. Our wealth of local knowledge will help ensure your stay at Willow Lodge is both memorable and enjoyable. Willow Lodge boasts tranquil rural views over rolling farmland and is set in two acres of landscaped gardens. We offer luxury self-contained units which open onto a private courtyard. Should you prefer, acommodation in the form of a double bedroom with private bathroom is available within our home. We provide continental or cooked breakfasts and mouth-watering evening meals by arrangement. We are a comfortable one-hour scenic drive from downtown Auckland, and therefore well situated for guests arriving via Auckland Airport. P.S. We are more than happy to arrange transport and trips.

Warkworth

Homestay/Self-contained   Accommodation
Address: "Omaha Orchards",
282 Point Wells Rd, R.D. 6, Warkworth
Name: John & Barbara Maltby
Telephone: (09) 422 7415
Fax: (09) 4227 419
Beds: Self Contained Unit: 1 Queen in bedroom, 1 Double bed settee in
lounge. Homestay: 1 Queen, 1 Super King/Twin (2 Bedrooms)
Bathroom: Self Contained Unit: 1 Private. Homestay: 1 Private.
Tariff: Self Contained Unit: Double $75, $12 per extra person.
Homestay: B&B (Continental) Double $75, Single $40, Children $20.
Dinner with hosts available by arrangement $15-$20. Discounts for 2
nights or more. Weekly rates on request. Winter rate May-Sept $50 dbl.
NZ B&B Vouchers accepted
Nearest Town: Warkworth 13kms

*Our home and new (1999) semi detached self contained unit is set on 11 acres,
and nestles on the shores of the Whangateau Harbour. Enjoy genuine Kiwi
hospitality in the peace and tranquility of this setting, relax in the extensive
gardens, swim in the beautifully appointed pool, play petanque, and walk the
shores of the harbour. For your added enjoyment we have bikes and canoes
available for a small extra charge. Two minutes away is Omaha ocean beach, golf
course and tennis courts. Also close by are an interesting variety of restaurants,
art and craft studios, pottery works, museum, sheep world, honey centre, and
ferries to Kawau Island. This is some of the prettiest coastline in New Zealand. John
and Barbara, together with Buddy the dog and Abby the cat, look forward to
sharing their little slice of paradise with you. Smoking outside only.*

Warkworth

Country Homestay, Bed & Breakfast
Address: "Bellgrove",
346 Woodcocks Road, RD 1, Warkworth
Name: John & Julie Bell
Telephone: (09) 425 9770
Fax: (09) 425 9770
Email: bellgrove@xtra.co.nz
Beds: 1 King, 1 Queen, 2 single (3 bedrooms)
Bathroom: 1 Ensuite, 1 Private
Tariff: B&B (full) Double $80, Single $50, Children half price,
Dinner $25, Credit Cards.
Nearest Town: Warkworth 4km

BELLGROVE

*Nestled in a valley beside the Mahurangi stream with a bush backdrop, Bellgrove is
a tasteful country home and farmlet only 3 km on a sealed road from Highway 1. Our
extensive decks overlook the large in-ground swimming pool, manicured gardens, and
paddocks of sheep. Stroll amongst the farm animals or through the adjacent native
tree reserve. Relax with a book from our extensive library or tickle the ivories on the
baby grand piano. We are both in our forties with a 9 year old daughter, Jessica. John
has been involved in the tourism industry for 10 years and has travelled extensively.
Julie's interests include cooking and entertaining. We enjoy fine food, good wine and
music in a casual atmosphere. Guests private accommodation is upstairs and separate
from the family with ensuite or own private bathroom. We invite you to share our
smoke-free home and enjoy the many attractions of the greater Warkworth area.*

Warkworth

Homestay/2 Self-contained Accommodations
Address: "Island Bay Retreat",
105 Ridge Road, Scott's Landing,
RD 2 Warkworth
Name: Joyce and Bill Malofy
Telephone: (09) 425 4269
Fax: (09) 425 4265
Mobile: (025) 262 8358
Email: islandbay@noworries.com
Internet: islandbay.noworries.com
Beds: 2 Queen,
2 Singles (3 bedrooms).
Bathroom: 2 Ensuites
Tariff: B&B (special continental), optional,
if not required then reduced tariff of
$15 per night applies. SC Loft Double $115.
SC Deluxe Garden 3 room suite: Double $130. Not suitable for children
Nearest Town: Snells Beach Shopping Complex 5 mins, Warkworth 15 mins drive. Auckland 1 hr.

ISLAND BAY GUEST HOME is a peaceful retreat that is an idyllic setting, a slice of paradise whatever the season or weather, this place is magic and will captivate you with its fabulous sea and rural views that just oozes with romanticism. A perfect secluded hideaway for a weekend or extended stays. We are on the scenic Mahurangi Peninsula surrounded by water on both sides, an exciting place to explore for nature's enthusiasts. Scotts Landing is at the tip of our road, it has a boat ramp and also leads to regional parks abundant with native birdlife and many sheltered bays. Our new brick and cedar home is nestled on nearly 2 acres of landscaped gardens overlooking our beautiful Island Bay. Amble down our garden path to the water's edge, swim, explore or join us for a spot of fishing on our boat.

* We have two self-contained suites that are in a separate wing, private from your hosts - own entrances, parking for car and boat.
* Both suites have panoramic sea and rural views.
* Both fully equipped kitchens are provided for self catering, you can cook your own meals or dine out at our nearby restaurants and cafes.
* Upstairs studio loft is a spacious open plan with rimu wood ceilings - glass double doors open on to your own veranda.
* The large garden level unit has 3 rooms, kitchen with wide ranchsliders opening on to your patio and BBQ area, spacious bedroom with lounge area, dressing room and quality bathroom.
* Whatever you choose both are tastefully decorated and have quality new beds and linen, electric blankets, heated towel rails, fans, heaters, clock radio and TV.
* We provide a scrumptious breakfast that is brought to your suite at your convenience, it is optional and if not required then reduced charges apply.
* There are many local attractions so whatever your interests are, tramping, deep sea fishing, scuba diving, swimming, golfing, tennis, island cruises or just relaxation, it's all here on the Kowhai Coast which offers an unspoiled pristine environment.
We Joyce and Bill were born in Canada and have lived in NZ for many years, we and our little dog "Toby" and "Mertle" the turtle look forward to meeting you and making your stay an unforgettable one.

Matakana, Warkworth
Homestay+Self-contained Suite+B&B
Address: "Hurstmere House",
Tongue Farm Road, Matakana
Name: Anne & Bob Moir
Telephone: (09) 422 9220
Fax: (09) 422 9220
Mobile: (025) 820 336
Email: hurstmere@hotmail.com
Beds: 3 Queen, 2 Single
(4 bedrooms/1 S.C. Suite with Queen bed)
Bathroom: 4 Ensuite
Tariff: B&B (full) Double $150, Single $100, Dinner $40pp BYO wine. Pre-dinner drinks provided, Self-contained Suite: $175 per couple. Credit Cards (VISA/MC/American Express).
Nearest Town: Warkworth 10km, Matakana Village 3 minutes

Hurstmere House overlooks picturesque Matakana valley farmland. This gracious two storey homestead is only one hour North of Auckland, 10 minutes from Warkworth, and within coo-ee of the beaches and islands of the golden Kowhai Coast. The charm of the restored old home with rimu timber panelling and staircase blends with the new architecturally designed French Provincial farmhouse kitchen and dining room extensions. Your hosts Anne and Bob offer you genuine North Auckland hospitality and sumptuous dinners with wine and flowers and gourmet or continental style breakfasts. When refreshed you can venture to two golf courses, village crafts markets, walk, fish, play tennis, swim, visit vineyards or Morris & James pottery works. Three restaurants within 3 minutes. Visit nearby Leigh, Goat Island marine reserve, Tawharanui Regional Park, or catch a boat to Mansion House on Kawhau Island. This is heaven on earth - the best of countryside and seaside all rolled into one. Who could ask for anything more? **Directions**: *Please ask when booking.*
Home Page: http://www.kiwihome.co.n.z./stay/b-b/auckland/matakana.html#top

http://www.bnb.co.nz

take a look

Warkworth
Farmstay
Address: "Ryme Intrinseca",
121 Perry Road, RD3, Warkworth
Name: Elizabeth & Cam Mitchell
Telephone: (09) 425 9448
Fax: (09) 425 9458
Beds: 2 Queen, 1 Double, 1 Single
(3 bedrooms: 1 Queen + 1 Single -1 room, 1 Queen -1 room, 1 double -1room)
Bathroom: 1 Guests share
Tariff: B&B (full) Double $85, Single $50, Children half price, Dinner
$25. NZ B&B Vouchers accepted $15 surcharge
Nearest Town: Warkworth 6 km

*Our 110 acre beef and sheep farm is ideally situated for travellers on their way
to the Bay of Islands as it is an easy hours drive from Auckland, just 1km off SH1
and 6km south of the attractive rural town of Warkworth.*
*Our spacious cedar and kauri home is set in a secluded valley overlooking native
bush and surrounded by gardens and a croquet lawn. Join in farm activities or
just relax. We offer comfortable farm house accommodation and the upstairs
bedrooms with their extensive farm views open into a large guest sitting room
with TV, and tea/coffee making facilities. Evening meals, if requested, feature
home-grown produce. Local sightseeing attractions include historic Kawau
Island, the Mahurangi Harbour, Regional Parks and many lovely beaches.*
*Our interests include gardening, reading, sailing and caring for our farm and
animals including our Jack Russell terrier. We are widely travelled within NZ and
overseas and warmly welcome visitors to our home.*

Sandspit, Warkworth
Homestay, Self Contained Accommodation
Address: Jacaranda Cottage
1186 Sandspit Road, RD2 Warkworth
Name: Rhondda and Les Sweetman
Telephone: (09) 425 9441
Fax: (09) 425 9451
Mobile: (025) 816 341
Email: Rhondda@xtra.co.nz
Beds: 1 Queen, 1 Double,
2 Single (3 Bedrooms)
Bathroom: 1 Ensuite, 1 Guests Share.
Tariff: B&B (Full) Double $80-$110,
Single $50-$60, Dinner $30,
Children welcome. Credit Cards accepted.
Nearest Town: Warkworth 6 km.

*Welcome to Jacaranda Cottage, our new architecturally designed home a few metres from the
Sandspit estuary. The views are magnificent and so close that you will feel part of the
panorama. Sandspit is 6km from Warkworth, a picturesque town, one hour north of
Auckland. The local area provides opportunities for sightseeing and relaxation, including
restaurants, vineyards, art galleries etc. We are a few minutes walk from the Sandspit wharf
where boats leave for Kawau Island. There are bush walks and the swimming is great. We
have a fully, self-contained unit with a Queen-sized bed. Our other rooms are a double
bedroom and one with two single beds. We have a border collie dog, Jess. In front of our house
is moored our 9 metre launch. We will take you fishing or sightseeing by arrangement (possibly
to view the America's Cup).*

Puhoi

'Farmstay - the gentle way'
Address: 'Our Farm-Park',
RD3 Kaukapakapa, Auckland 1250
Name: Peter & Nichola(s) Rodgers
Telephone: (09)422 0626
Fax: (09)422 0626
Email: ofp@friends.co.nz
Beds: 1 Queen bedroom,
1 Twin bedroom with child's window-seat bed
(2 bedrooms)

Boundary almost 5km - long and interesting walk with streams, waterfalls, rock pools, farm animals, birds, trees, amazing views; choose to go by foot or horse.....

Bathroom: 1 Private
Tariff: B&B only, $95 double (single from $80), Dinner $25pp.
All meals available. Children (with parents) under 5 free; 5-12 $10; 13-17 $20.
Additional adults $40. Ask about "Three night family holiday" rates. Credit cards accepted. Prices firm to 1 October 2000. NZ B&B Vouchers accepted
Nearest Town: Puhoi 4.5km, between Orewa & Warkworth; on fast new motorway, 50km north cntral Auckland, International Airport 70km.

KIA ORA. Share with us our 110-acre organic property high in the hills, beautiful panoramic views, fresh air, and clean water. Very comfortable beds. Delicious meals (vegetarian if you ask) based on taste-filled, GE Free, organic fruit and vegetables; fresh baking. NO-ONE SMOKES HERE. We farm with kindness. There are touchable sheep, spring lambs, beautiful Belted Galloway cows in family groupings with calves at foot; horses; ducks; poultry running free; providing farm milk, butter, yoghurt, ice-cream, cheeses..... There are 30 restaurants in the district. Go canoeing, visit Hot Pools, beaches (wild surf or child safe), bush walks, bird sancturies, Island trips, Marine Reserves, snorkelling, diving, fishing, Honey Centre, Historic sites, Crafts, etc. The new motorway to Auckland provides easy shopping, zoo, evening events, etc. Sleep off "jet-lag"; talk and share knowledge over dinner, see the unusual home we are building ourselves; share our love for Taha Maori, environment, flora, fauna; and use our library, or go for long walks in the hills through trees we have planted, adding to the views and streams and secluded private places (See map). Arohanui Peter and Nicola(s)

'Farmstay - the active way' *organic farming at Puhoi. Come and touch lives with us for a longer stay. We can be your base for family contact on your NZ tour.*
Learn about organic farming and/or horticulture *with hands on experience - ride our 4 -wheeler; plant trees, make fences, do some building, handle the animals (milk a cow, check cattle on horseback), learn safety with firearms, use our business facilities, including computer - we schedule our work to fit your interests. And relax with "farm golf", Petanque.....Receive a COFCAL merit certificate on completion.*
Learn "Conversational English" *as well. You will work with Peter (qualified teacher, psychologist) using a method called "Total Immersion". Only you from your country here in the first 10 days. Over 100 hours in one burst! Students from Japan, Germany, Korea, Switzerland and Vanuata have found this a very effective way to learn to speak English quickly. For information write or fax or send blank email to english@friends.co.nz.*
Gain real stress relief *talking with Peter, psychologist specialising in relationship counselling. Private, relaxed and unhurried. To the world, you appear only a guest.*
Tariff: From additional $30 (per family). More information on internet www.friends.co.nz or write, fax or email us. (see above). Certain conditions apply and activities are subject to weather etc. Please check.
Home Page: www.friends.co.nz. Japanese site: www.friends.co.nz/japan

Puhoi
Homestay
Address: Westwell Ho,
Saleyards Rd, Puhoi, Warkworth
Name: Fae and David England
Telephone: (09) 422 0064
Fax: (09) 422 0064
Mobile: (025) 280 5795
Beds: 1 Queen, 1 Double,
1 Single (2 Bedrooms)
Bathroom: 1 Ensuite, 1 Private
Tariff: B&B (Full) Double $90,
Single $50, Dinner $25 pp,
Children $25.   NZ B&B Vouchers accepted
Nearest Town: Orewa/Warkworth. Auckland 40 mins.

The tree lined drive welcomes you to our sunny colonial style home in the lovely Puhoi Valley. There are wide verandahs where we breakfast in summer, or in the evening sit listening to the birds or playing croquet.
The small historic village of Puhoi is one of the most beautiful and interesting in New Zealand. There's a historic pub full of memorabilia from the early settler days, a General Store, old church, Bohemian Museum, and the famous Puhoi Valley Cheese Factory. There are hire canoes for you to paddle down the winding Puhoi River to Wenderholm, a lovely beach resort on the coast (but only 5 minutes by car). Nearby are the Waiwera Thermal Pools and lots of beaches and restaurants within 10 mins drive.
We live on a small road up behind the pub (2 mins walk) and only 2 mins west of the Main North Highway by car.

Orewa
Homestay
Address: 54 Walton Street,
Red Beach, Orewa
Name: Helen and Sonny
Telephone: (09) 426 6963
Beds: 1 Double. 1 Double,
1 Single in detached loft room
Bathroom: 2 Private
Tariff: B&B (continental)
Double $60, Single $35;
Dinner $20.
NZ B&B Vouchers accepted
Nearest Town: Orewa 5 km

This is a pleasant place 2km from State Highway 1 and 100 metres from a good beach which we enjoy very much. We have had many guests here, on their way or returning from the North, or simply to enjoy what this area has to offer, the pleasant town of Orewa 5km, Waiwera Thermal Pools 10km, the Whangaparaoa Peninsula with its many Bays, and Auckland 30km. A warm welcome is assured, comfortable beds and a breakfast to suit your taste. There is a resident cat. Approximately 1 hour from airport.

Orewa
Lodge
Address: Moontide Lodge,
19 Ocean View Road, Orewa - Hatfields Beach
Name: Monika and Jurgen Resch
Telephone: (09) 426 2374
Fax: (09) 426 2398
Mobile: (025) 263 0102
Email: moontde@nznet.gen.nz
Beds: 4 Queen (4 bedrooms)
Bathroom: 3 Ensuite, 1 Private
Tariff: B&B (full) Double $150-$180,
single $130-$160, Dinner $40, Visa/Mastercard/Diners Club/American Express.
Nearest Town: Orewa (2 minutes north by car)

Overlooking the native bush and the sheltered bay of beautiful Hatfields Beach Moontide Lodge offers a high standard of "boutique" accommodation. We are situated on a cliff with access to the beach. Each of our four luxuriously appointed bedrooms features ensuite or private bathroom and breathtaking seaviews. All rooms in European style with writing desk, chairs and table, telephone, TV/video on request, clock/radio, hair dryer, heater and tea/coffee facilities. Enjoy your complimentary tea/coffee and sherry in our elegant guest lounge with open fireplace. Breakfast and dinner (by appointment) is served in our formal dining room or al fresco on the verandah during the summer. Excursions in our comfortable mini bus to the nearby Tourist attractions can be arranged. Small conference venue. German and French spoken. We are a smoke-free Lodge. Timmy, the resident dog, is a friendly extra.

Silverdale, Auckland
Bed & Breakfast
Address: 'The Ambers', 146 Pine Valley Road,
Silverdale, Auckland 1462
Name: Diane & Gerard Zwier
Telephone: (09) 426 5354 **Fax**: (09) 426 3287
Email: gzwier@xtra.co.nz
Beds: 2 Double, 2 Twin/Double (4 bedrooms)
Bathroom: 3 Ensuites, 1 Family share
Tariff: B&B (full) Double $110-$120, Single $65-$85,
Credit Cards (DC/AMEX only, Visa/MC not accepted).
NZ B&B Vouchers accepted $50 surcharge
Nearest Town: 2 km south of Silverdale on State Highway 1,
Auckland City 30 mins, Albany University 15 mins.

If you think romanticism is dead.....think again. Come and stay at "The Ambers", set on 14 picturesque acres, and enjoy the old world charm and luxury. Share our tranquil country atmosphere and warm hospitality. Relax with complimentary pre-dinner drinks in our elegant guest lounge with French doors into the garden or venture into our woodland area with stream. Both of us have travelled extensively and have interests in Art, Design and Philosophy. We have 3 German shepherd dogs which are very friendly but are restricted from guest areas. Guest rooms are individually decorated. Enjoy our attic suites with sloping ceilings or relax in our European style rooms with wonderfully comfortable beds and finest bed linen. Breakfast on the terrace or in our formal dining room with delicious country style breakfasts. Auckland is only 35 minutes away and we are minutes from beaches, restaurants and shops. Please phone for reservations/directions. **Home Page**: www.the-ambers.co.nz

Whangaparaoa Peninsula
Homestay
Address: Cedar Farm Bed & Breakfast,
39 Cedar Tce,
Stanmore Bay, Whangaparaoa
Name: Maureen and Alan Fullerton
Telephone: (09) 424 3133
Fax: (09) 424 3134
Mobile: (025) 281 3868
Beds: 1 Queen, 1 Twin,
1 Single (3 bedrooms)
Bathroom: 1 Ensuite, 1 Guests share
Tariff: B&B (continental) Queen $105, Twin $90, Single $50, Dinner $25pp.
Credit cards. NZ B&B Vouchers accepted $20 surcharge
Nearest Town: Whangaparaoa 1 Km, Orewa 6 Km

We are retired dairy farmers who enjoy having guests. Our home is on a 10 acre lifestyle block, grazing horses. Access is flat and easy and our house has a quiet tranquil setting, only minutes from local amenities. Breakfast is served by our courtyard pool - the energetic can swim, or play table-tennis in our games room, others may like a relaxing walk in our gardens. Whangaparaoa has lovely beaches, golf courses, Shakespeare Park for bush walks and bird watching. We are in an excellent position for you to go to Tiritiri Matangi Island bird sanctuary, a wonderful excursion. Ferries leave from Gulf Harbour Marina for the Island, and also to Auckland for city touring. We will happily help you plan activities.
Cedar Farm is a relaxing home, ideal distance on your way to/from Auckland Airport, 30 minutes drive north of Auckland Harbour Bridge.
Directions: *Please phone for reservations and easy directions.*

Gulf Harbour, Whangaparaoa
Apartment Stay
Address: Gulf Harbour,
Whangaparaoa, Hibiscus Coast.
Name: Paul and Jenny Steele
Telephone: (09) 428 1400
Fax: (09) 428 1400
Email: paul/jenny@xtra.co.nz
Beds: 1 King/Queen, 1 Double or 2 Single (2 bedrooms)
Bathroom: 2 Ensuites
Tariff: B&B (full) $120-$250 (depending on room and season).
Dinner $30 pp.
Nearest Town: Whangaparaoa Town Centre 6.5kms. Auckland city 50kms.

A stunning Mediterranean retreat situated above the boat laden canal of Gulf Harbour is truly a GOLFING and AQUATIC paradise. From our comfortably appointed and spacious high-rise apartment there are panoramic views of Sky Tower, the North Shore, Kawau Island and the Gulf Harbour Country Club (venue for the 1998 World Cup of Golf). Play can be arranged mostly at discounted rates. Restaurants within strolling distance or easy driving. New Zealand style dinners cooked by arrangement after first night. We offer a complimentary tour of local highlights including many ferry/cruise options. Safe swimming beaches nearby. Two double ensuite bedrooms ensure privacy. Sauna available. Airport pick up available. Please phone for further information and tariff.
Home Page: http://www.nzhomestay.co.nz/steele.htm

Whangaparaoa

Homestay/Self Contained Accommodation/Bed & Breakfast
Address: "Hibiscus Homestay",
895 Whangaparaoa Road, Little Manly,
Whangaparaoa
Name: David and Judy Turnbull
Telephone: 09-424 7507
Fax: 09-424 7517
Mobile: 025-273 9851
Email: djjg.turnbull@xtra.co.nz
Beds: 1 Double (1 bedroom)
Bathroom: 1 Ensuite
Tariff: B&B (continental)
Double $100, Single $60.
Nearest Town: Whangaparaoa 10 km, Auckland 50 kms

Whether kiwis or overseas visitors, we welcome you to join us (and our cat) at our home and spacious grounds overlooking Little Manly beach. Members of our family have lived here since 1925, each generation being captivated by the bay. Whatever the weather, this place is magic. Our interests are sailing, fishing, gardening. Dinghy available for you to try your luck or join fishing/sailing charters at Gulf Harbour Marina. The area offers many other interesting activities, cafes, bars, golf courses, excursions to Tiri Island Bird Sanctuary, coach tours, regional park tramping tracks and the clean, safe swimming beaches the Peninsular is renown for. Self contained with own cooking facilities for long stay (self catering rates available); Continental breakfast for B&B.
Directions: *Phone, fax or write for reservations and directions.*

Whangaparaoa

Homestay/Bed & Breakfast
Address: "Southridge", 2b Arkles Drive,
Arkles Bay, Whangaparaoa Peninsula,
Hibiscus Coast
Name: Bruce and Cheryl Cade
Telephone: (09) 424 0380
Fax: (09) 424 0380   **Mobile**: (025) 936 121
Email: southridge@hibiscuscoast.co.nz
Beds: 1 Superking or 2 Singles, 1 Queen (2 Bdrms)
Bathroom: 1 Guests Share
Tariff: B&B (Full) Double $85-$100, Single $50.
Dinner N/A, Children N/A. Credit Cards: Visa and Mastercard.
Nearest Town: Whangaparaoa Town Centre, 2 mins walk.
Auckland City, 30 mins drive

Bruce and Cheryl welcome you to experience genuine kiwi hospitality in their new modern home overlooking the restful views of Arkles Bay, Rangitoto Island and the City Sky Tower. Relax and watch the boats leisurely cruising the inner Hauraki Gulf or the yachts on the Americas Cup Race Course. A short drive to Gulf Harbour Village and Marina, Sailing and Fishing Charters, 3 Golf Courses, Hot springs, Leisure Centre and Regional Parks. Ferry Service to Tiritiri Island Bird Sanctuary, Kawau Island and Auckland City. The Whangaparaoa Peninsula is reknown for it numerous safe swimming beaches. We are only two minutes walk to the shops, restaurants/cafes, banks, postshop, doctors and cinema complex. Our home is a smoke free environment. Not suitable for children.
Directions: *Take Whangaparaoa Road off SH1 north of Silverdale. Arkles Drive second on right after Whangaparaoa Shopping Centre.*
Home Page: www.hibiscuscoast.co.nz/soutridge

Whangaparaoa Peninsula

Homestay/B&B
Address: 1 Beach Road, Manly,
Whangaparaoa, Hibiscus Coast
Name: Bayview Manly Quality Homestay/B&B
Telephone/Fax: (09) 428 0990
Web: http://babs.co.nz/bayview
Email: BAYVIEWMANLY@xtra.co.nz
Beds: 1 Queen, 1 Double, 2 Single (3 Bedrooms)
Bathroom: 2 Ensuites, 1 Private
Tariff: B&B (full) Double $100 - $145.
Not suitable for children. Visa/Mastercard.
Nearest Town: Whangaparaoa 2 km, Orewa 10 km.

Directions

Silverdale (Factory Shops)   Orewa
From Auckland (30 mins)   SH1 → North
Cinemas   Whangaparaoa Rd
Pacific Plaza   Manly Village
          Beach Road
To Gulf Harbour   WE ARE HERE
(Tiritiri Matangi Island Ferry)   Beach

* *The Ultimate in "Home Away from Home" Accommodation for the discerning traveller. *
*Mediterranean style house - All rooms lockable and with private facilities. *Comfortable beds.
Heated towel rails. Clock radios. Hair driers.*
* *Queen and twin rooms have balconies and sea views.*
* *Guest lounge-with TV, video and sunny deck. Tea, coffee making facilities.*
* *Super Breakfast-cooked, continental or both.*
* *Adjacent Manly Village Restaurants and Shops. Stroll to Sandy Beaches.*
* *4Km to Gulf Harbour Complex for Golf, Fishing, Diving and Sailing.*
* *Short drive to Shopping Plaza, Factory Shops, Cinemas, Regional parks.*
* *Bookings arranged for Ferry to Tiritiri Matangi Island Bird Sanctuary.*
* *Our home is yours to enjoy, we live "next door" in the attached apartment.*
* *Complementary laundry. Fridge/freezer space available. Luggage stored.*
* *Local & Tourist information if required. Airport pick up can be arranged.*
* *Personal attention and hospitality assured. Honeymooners welcome.*

Kaukapakapa

Farmstay+Self-contained   Accom.
Address: Kereru Lodge, Arone Farm,
Makarau Road, R.D. 3,
Kaukapakapa
Name: Betty Headford
Telephone: (09) 420 5223
Fax: (09) 420 5223
Mobile: (025) 297 5523
Beds: 2 Queen, 2 Double,
1 Single (3 bedrooms)
Bathroom: 1 Ensuite, 1 Guests share, 1 Family share
Tariff: B&B (full) Double $65, Single $45, Children $15, Dinner $20, Campervans
$25. Self-contained cottage: price on application.
Credit cards. NZ B&B Vouchers accepted
Nearest Town: Kaukapakapa 9 mins

Kereru Lodge

*Relax. Be pampered. Come to our quiet rural valley and enjoy the peaceful tranquillity. The
Homestead is large and modern, designed for relaxed indoor/outdoor living. Wander in our
garden, over the farm or through our native bush. You may play pool, petanque and croquet
or have drinks in the summer house and listen to the birds sing. There are several local bush
walks and the Kaipara Harbour for fishing, kayaking or watching the Godwits and other
migrating birds. Play tennis or go golfing at one of the many surrounding golf courses. You
can be sure of a friendly welcome whether passing by for one night or staying for serveral days
to unwind. The Homestead is B&B or fully catered if required. We have many varied interests
and love having a house full of people. We are non smokers. Please phone, fax or write.*

89

Kaukapakapa
Bed & Breakfast
Address: "Willowbrook Farm",
Stoney Creek Road, Kaukapakapa
Name: June & Don Lamont
Telephone: (09) 420-5909
Fax: (09) 420-5909
Mobile: (025) 389 675
Beds: 1 Queen
Bathroom: 1 Ensuite
Tariff: B&B (Special) Double $80, Single $65, Dinner $25 each (by arrangement), Not suitable for children. NZ B&B Vouchers accepted $20 surcharge
Nearest Town: Helensville 12 km, Orewa 20 km

Willowbrook is a character 2-storey timber farmhouse. It is set in an attractive 50-acre valley on which we run cattle. Your spacious, sunny suite is well appointed, has its own entranceway and is located on the upper wing of the house. This includes lounge / dining area, TV, tea / coffee making facilities and ensuite shower and toilet. You can enjoy the gardens and relax on the warm and sheltered verandah. Beside the cattle, we share our farm with "Barney", a well-behaved Golden Retriever; a few friendly chickens; and a small aviary of budgies.
We offer a substantial continental breakfast, including fruit, freshly baked bread and muffins. Break your journey with a relaxed and memorable stay with us at Willowbrook Farm, conveniently located close to State Highway 16.
Our home is smoke free.
Directions: *Willowbrook is located 2.5km along Stoney Creek Road which runs directly off State Highway 16 at Kaukapakapa.*

Helensville/Parakai
Homestay

KAIPARA HOUSE

Address: Cnr Hwy 16 & Parkhurst Rd,
Parakai/Helensville
Name: John & Diane Barrett
Telephone: (09) 420 7462
Fax: (09) 420 7458
Mobile: (025) 814 617
Email: www.helensville.co.nz
Beds: 1 Queen, 1 King or 2 single, 2 single (3 Bedrooms)
Bathroom: 1 Ensuite, 1 Family share
Tariff: B&B (full) Double $70-$90, Single 45, Children negotiable.
Nearest Town: Helensville 1/2km, Auckland city 35 mins.

Our 106 yr old Villa has been lovingly restored with skill and adorned with yester-years furniture and todays modern lovely rich colours that enhance the enchanting structure of the older homes. We are set on nearly an acre with gardens being seasonal. We offer your Edwardian or Victorian room with morning sun and comfort through our home and the open fire in winter. Breakfast optional, in bed or in front of the old coal-range with home made jams and bottled fruit. We are in our 40's, young at heart, have a scotty dog and two cats and have enjoyed quite some travel throughout New Zealand and abroad. Being on the Northland Tourist Route, we can advise you on local activities, ie visiting antique shops, soaking in hot pools or spa's 2 minutes away, horse-riding, parachuting, Kaipara boat cruises along with the local cafes, restaurants, crafts and historical sights. Now do you see why we choose a conspicuous place to meet people?

Helensville

Bed & Breakfast, + Self Contained Accom

Address: "Malolo House" 110 Commercial Rd, Helensville
Name: Andrea & Michael Mullin
Telephone: (09) 420 7262 Toll free 0800 28 6060
Fax: (09) 420 7262 **Mobile**: (021) 216 4994
Email: malolo@xtra.co.nz
Beds: 2 Queen, 4 Double, 6 Single (8 bedrooms)
Bathroom: 2 Ensuite, 1 Private, 2 Guests Share
Tariff: B&B (special) Double $68-$110,
Single $42-$80, Children $10, Credit Cards. NZ B&B Vouchers accepted
Nearest Town: Helensville - 50m, Auckland 46km

A former cottage hospital, our turn-of-the-century kauri villa has old world charm with modern conveniences. In the heart of historic Helensville, we're far from Auckland's hustle and bustle, on the scenic Twin Coast Dicovery route. Steps from first class restaurants, cafes, pioneer museum and shops, we are listed on the heritage walk. Enjoy stunning views of the Kaipara River Valley from our guest lounge and multi-level sun-drenched deck. Relax in our hot tub / spa after a day visiting vineyards, wild West Coast beaches, Muriwai's Gannet colony, mineral hot springs, river cruises, horse treks, fishing, and great golf. Polished kauri floors, tasteful, heated guest rooms with incredibly comfortable queen sized beds, feather duvets and luxurious modern bathrooms all contribute to a fabulous stay. Our spacious guest lounge with library and cosy fire offers 24 hour tea, coffee and port. Lavish Kiwi-Canadian breakfasts include freshly ground coffee, home baked muffins, fresh fruit and Eggs Kaipara. Our self-contained studio sleeps 4.
Home Page: www.helensville.co.nz/malolo.htm

Helensville

Self Contained Accommodation, Bed & Breakfast

Address: 2191 State Highway 16, Helensville
Name: Dianne and Richard Kidd
Telephone: (09) 420 8007
or toll free 0800 755 433
Fax: (09) 420 7966
Email: kidd.home@xtra.co.nz
Beds: 1 Queen (1 bedroom)
Bathroom: 1 Ensuite
Tariff: B&B (ful) Double $95, Single $60.
Not suitable for children. Credit Cards accepted.
Discount for two or more nights. Vouchers accepted $25 surcharge
Nearest Town: Helensville and Parakai 4 kms

"Rose Cottage" offers comfort and privacy set within the gardens of the beautifully restored Whenuanui Homestead (Kauri villa circa 1908). Whenuanui is a 320 ha Helensville sheep and beef farm providing magnificent farm walks. We also have thoroughbred horses and farm forestry. The family homestead and gardens have panoramic views over Helensville and the Kaipara Valley. Comfortable and relaxing accommodation includes ensuite, TV and kitchenette . Smoking outdoors appreciated. Whenuanui is located on SH 16 (Northland Tourist Route) 35 minutes north west of Downtown Auckland. It provides an authentic and convenient NZ rural stopover either to or from Northland, or a base to explore the attractions in West Auckland including Kumeu wine trails, fishing / cruises on the Kaipara Harbour, Muriwai gannet colony and thermal pools at Parakai. Other local activities include: horse-riding, 4 wheel motorbike trails, a selection of four golf courses, parachuting and a variety of local restaurants and cafes.

Huapai - Kumeu
Homestay/Farmstay

Address: 45 Trigg Rd,
Huapai, Auckland
Name: Andrea & Jim Hawkless
Telephone: (09) 412 8862
Fax: (09) 412 8869
Email: hawkless@ww.co.nz
Beds: 2 Queen,
3 Single (3 bedrooms)
Bathroom: 1 Guests share
Tariff: B&B (full) Double $70, Single $50,
Children half price, Dinner $20, Credit cards.
NZ B&B Vouchers accepted
Nearest Town: Auckland 30 minutes drive.

Foremost Fruits is surrounded by several top NZ wineries on a small orchard specialising in hot house table grapes. You will be warmly welcomed by experienced hosts who provide comfort and relaxation plus swimming and spa pool. Guests have the upstairs to themselves with 2 large bedrooms each with Queensize and one single bed plus another single room. Guests share their bathroom and toilet. Breakfast is of choice with homemade bread and jams. There are top restaurants in the area plus casual and take-aways. We provide details on local attractions which include wineries, beaches, golf, gannet colony, balloon rides, horse riding and canoeing. Smoking permitted outside.

Directions: *From Auckland take Northwestern Motorway to end. Turn left to Kumeu (8k) past Garden Centre over railway line to Trigg Rd (left before 100K sign). No 45 on left.*

http://www.bnb.co.nz

take a look

Kumeu

Countrystay

Address: Nor-West Greenlands,
303 Riverhead Road, R.D.2, Kumeu
Name: Kerry and Kay Hamilton
Telephone: (09) 412 8167
Fax: (09) 412 8167
Mobile: (025) 286 6064
Email: bed@farm-stay.co.nz
Beds: 2 Double, 2 Single (3 bedrooms)
Bathroom: 1 private, 1 Guests share
Tariff: B&B (Full) $115 Double, $80 Single, Dinner $30; Children negotiable,
Credit cards (Mastercard/Visa). NZ B&B Vouchers accepted
Nearest Town: Kumeu 3 1/2 km, Auckland city 26 km south.

Kerry and Kay of Nor-West Greenlands extend a warm welcome to you to join them on their 15 acre farm which is situated 25 minutes north of Auckland midway between the east and west coast beaches. Our two storied home with private guest bathrooms, and guest lounge, is set in secluded gardens with a swimming pool and bush walks. Our sheep are tame and can be hand fed. They are part of the family together with Minstrel the Dalmatian dog and three black and white cats. Ranging from summer barbecues to a three course dinner, all meals are available with prior notice. Local attractions; wineries, beaches, gannet colony at Muriwai, surfing, craft shops, orchards, golf, horse-riding, kayaking, parachuting, bush walks, and hot pools. **Directions**: *From Auckland city via North Western Motorway on to SH 16, 5 km north, right into Coatsville / Riverhead Highway (H28), Riverhead Road is the second on the left. Our home is the second one down a long drive.* **Home Page**: http://homepages.ihug.co.nz/~kk4bb

Auckland

Homestay, Self Contained Accommodaiton

Address: 81 Penguin Drive, Murrays Bay, Auckland
Name: Greg and Sue Sweeney
Telephone: (09) 479 3581
Fax: (09) 479 3532
Mobile: (025) 479 3581
Email: g.sweeney@xtra.co.nz
Beds: 1 Double, 2 Single (2 Bedrooms)
Bathroom: 1 Private
Tariff: B&B (Continental) Double $120, Single $60, Dinner $20 by
arrangement. Children $15. Stay 7 nights and the next night is free.
Nearest Town: Auckland

Our new home at the top of Murrays Bay is a stroll to local cafes, restaurants and safe swimming beaches. We have views over the Hauraki Gulf and Rangitoto Island (venue for the Americas Cup), and our local native bush reserve. Adjacent Mairangi Bay shopping centre has all community facilities including Post Office, banking and Supermarket. Enjoy the privacy of your self-contained guest wing complete with kitchen and sunny courtyard. We have two large bedrooms with sea views, one double and the other twin sharing a bathroom with a shower and laundry. The sunny lounge has TV and a kitchen with fridge and microwave and breakfast bar. After a night in comfortable warm bedding, you will be served a breakfast of cereal, fruit and toast with juice, and tea or coffee. You will find us friendly, informative and helpful, well travelled and we enjoy hospitality. Our accomodation is accessible by wheelchair. Children are welcome. We have no pets. Murrays Bay is 10 mins. North of the Harbour Bridge. Phone for directions.

Bethell's Beach, West Auckland
Self-contained Accommodation

Address: 'Turehu Cottage' & 'Te Koinga Cottage'
P O Box 95057, Swanson, Auckland. (Bethells Beach)
Name: Trude & John Bethell-Paice
Telephone: (09) 810 9581 **Fax**: (09) 810 8677
Beds: "Turehu Cottage" 1 Queen, 1 Double Bed/Sofa. "Te Koinga Cottage" 1 Queen, 3 Single & 1 Double Divan
Bathroom: 2 Private
Tariff: "Turehu cottage": $150 + $10 bed/sofa per day, suitable for couple and 1 child or 2 friends. "Te Koinga cottage": 2 people $235 and $20 pp thereafter. Suitable for 2 couples or a family.
Meals: Breakfast $20 pp. Dinner $35 pp. Meals by prior arrangement (tariffs inclusive GST). Visa and Mastercard facility (5% surcharge).
Company workshop days - functions and weddings quoted on individual basis.
Nearest Town: Swanson 20 minutes, Auckland 40 minutes

Drive 40 minutes from Auckland city to one of the most unique parts of the West coast. The Bethell's settled this area 6 generations ago and Trude and John continue the long family tradition of hospitality. They have created two magic cottages in this spectacular place where the best sunsets and seaviews are to be experienced. Both cottages have a sunny north facing aspect and are surrounded by 200 year old pohutukawa's (NZ Christmas tree). Each one is totally separate, private and has a large brick barbecue. The vast front lawn is ideal for games and the gardens are thoughtfully designed for relaxation. The cottages are made up with your holiday in mind - not only are beds made and towels / linen put out, but Trude and John have attended to too many details to mention and laundry facilities are available. Even the dog and cat will welcome you. As seen in Vogue Australia 1998. Life / The Observer (Great Britain 1998) - 'one of twenty great world wide destinations'. British TV Travel Show 1998. She magazine (February 1999) - 'one of the 10 most romantic places to stay in NZ'. North and South magazine (January 1999) - 'one of the 14 best Bed and Breakfasts in NZ'.

'TUREHU' COTTAGE has a studio atmosphere with double bi-folding doors from the conservatory. For outdoor dining sit under a pohutukawa tree at your own bench and table on the hillside with views over the beach and Bethell's valley. Cork floor in the kitchen, TV and bedroom area, gentle cream walls and white trim. Warm slate floors in the conservatory with lounge, dining table and bathroom (shower and toilet). Kitchen has microwave, large fridge / freezer, stove and coffee plunger, with all kitchen and dining amenities.

*'TE KOINGA' COTTAGE, this superb home away from home is 80sq m and has 2 bi-folding doors onto a 35sq m wooden deck for outdoor dining and relaxation in this sun trap. Set under the shade of a magnificent spralling pohutukawa tree and surrounded by garden. A fireplace for winter warmth and sixteen seater dining table. The two bedrooms have carpet and terracotta tiles expand to the dining, kitchen, bathroom and toilet. Wood panelled and cream / tan rag rolled walls for a relaxing atmosphere. The bathroom offers a bath and shower. Kitchen has microwave, large fridge / freezer, stove, dishwasher and coffee maker, with bar and open planned. Trude is a marriage celebrant and Trude and John specialise in weddings, private functions and company workshops. A local professional chef is available for these occasions. LOCAL ADVENTURES - Bethell's beach is a short half a minutes drive or walk. Pack a picnic lunch and discover Lake Wainamu for fresh water swimming and expansive sand dunes or go on a bush walk with excellent examples of New Zealand native flora. If you head in the direction of the beach you may enjoy exploring the caves (at night the magic of glow worms and phosphorescence in the shallows), or go surfing or fishing. You are close to many world class Vineyards and restaurants / cafes. You may fancy a game of golf - two courses within 10-20 minutes drive from your cottage. Many more activities in a short driving distance. Magnificent coastal walk. **Directions**: Directions given when you book.*

Bethells Valley, West Auckland
Farm/Self-contained   Accommodation
Address: Greenmead Farm, 115 Bethells Road,
R.D.1, Henderson, Auckland
Name: Averil & Jonathan Bateman
Telephone: (09) 810 9363
Fax: (09) 810 9122 **Email**: jabat@magic.gen.nz
Beds: 4 Single (2 bedrooms). Fold-out double bed on request.
Bathroom: 1 Private
Tariff: (accommodation only) Self-contained cottage: Double $90 + $20
for each extra guest; Continental Breakfast optional extra. NZ B&B
Vouchers accepted Accommodation only. 50% surcharge.
Nearest Town: Henderson 15 mins,   Downtown Auckland 30 mins.

*Our property is situated in a rural valley in the Waitakere Ranges, only 30 minutes
drive NW of Auckland City. Gardens and orchard surround the homestead and
guest cottage including an extensive organic vegetable garden and a herb garden
featuring culinary and medicinal plants. Swings for children. We handmilk a
house cow, keep cattle, bees, two working dogs, some hens but no cats. Visitors
have sole use of the cottage which is fully self contained. There is a well equipped
kitchen/dining room, parlour (TV), a bathroom and two bedrooms each with two
single beds (linen provided). Usually guests prefer to cater for themselves but
breakfast can be provided by prior arrangement.   Longer stays welcomed. A
network of walking tracks through spectacular scenery link bush, beach and lake.
Wine can be sampled at vineyards in Henderson or Kumeu.   The cottage offers
comfort and privacy in a tranquil setting close to Auckland city.*
Directions: *Please phone.* **Home Page**: babs.co.nz/greenmead

Herald Island, Waitakere City
Homestay
Address: 84 The Terrace, Herald Island,
Waitakere City, Auckland
Name: Harbour View Homestay
Telephone: (09) 416 7553
Fax: (09) 416 7553 **Mobile**: (025) 289 6112
Beds: 1 Queen, 6 Single (4 bedrooms)
Bathroom: 1 Private, 1 Family share
Tariff: B&B (full) Double $80-$95, Single $50-$65, Children under 12
yrs half price, Dinner from $15, Credit Cards. Vouchers accepted
Nearest Town: Glenfield 15km, Henderson 20km, Auckland city 26km.

*Your hosts Bev & Les have a two storey home with superb accommodation, right on waters
edge. Upstairs has 2 bedrooms, 1 Double, 1 Twin, each with its own sundeck overlooking the
upper reaches of the Waitemata Harbour. Own lounge, bathroom and tea and coffee making
facilities. Downstairs, 2 Twin share facilities. Very homely, easy access. Within 20 mins
radius, wine tasting, horse riding, golf course, bush walks, cinema and vintage car museum.
We also have a boat for fishing or a leisurely cruise. Bev serves a hearty home cooked dinner,
or lunch if required. Rooms serviced daily and laundry facilities available at no extra. We
have 1 dog Emma, 1 cat Tiger, both very friendly. Finalist Bank of New Zealand Waitakere
Eco City Business Awards.*
Directions: *Take North-Western (Helensville) Motorway to end. Turn right at
traffic lights into Hobsonville Road. 2nd on left Brigham Creek Road. (Liquor store
on corner) 1st on right Kauri Road. Continue along until Kingsway Road on right
(Herald Island sign). 1st road on left over causeway, The Terrace.*

Swanson

Homestay
Address: 1194 Scenic Drive North,
Swanson, Auckland
Name: Janice & Fleur, 'Unser Schön Chalet'
Telephone: (09) 833 4288
Fax: (09) 833 4288
Mobile: (025) 786788
Beds: 2 Queen, 1 Twin (3 bedrooms)
Bathroom: 1 Ensuite, 2 Family share
Tariff: B&B (full) Double $95-$120, Single $60-$75, Children under 12 half price, Dinner $25. Credit cards. Vouchers accepted $20 surcharge
Nearest Town: Henderson 10 mins, Auckland City 25 mins

Unser Schön Chalet is situated in the Waitakere Ranges on 17 1/2 acres of native bush and pasture. Our romantic chalet is of Austrian influence and its setting is truly that of peace and tranquillity. Great for honeymooners. We offer you comfy beds, feather duvets, plump pillows and fluffy towels. After a restful night's sleep you will be offered a delicious full breakfast served on your own balcony overlooking the Waitakere Ranges and onto Rangitoto Island, or served with our family. Tea and coffee facilities with plenty of home baking are available any time. Guests are welcome to join in the family barbecue and enjoy our outdoor entertaining area, relax in the spa pool. Our family pet is a large ginger cat, Antony is his name. We request no smoking indoors. Tourist features of the area - scenic drive at the base of the Waitakeres, Western beaches, bush walks, West Auckland vineyards, golf courses, restaurants and cafes. We enjoy having guests and promise them a happy stay. **Directions**: *Please phone.*

Swanson, Waitakere City

Bed & Breakfast/Guesthouse
Address: "Panorama Heights",
42 Kitewaho Road, Swanson,
Waitakere City, Auckland
Name: Paul and Allison Ingram
Telephone: (09) 832 4777
Fax: (09) 833 7773
Mobile: (025) 272 8811
Beds: 2 Queen, 1 Double, 2 Single (4 Bedrooms)
Bathroom: 2 Ensuite, 1 Guests share
Tariff: B&B (Special) Double $110, Single $65, Credit Cards (Visa/M.C.) Children under 12 half price. Dinner by request. Self contained rates available.
Nearest Town: Henderson 10 mins. Auckland City 35 mins.

The panoramic views are breathtaking from our guesthouse located high in the Waitakere Ranges northwest of Auckland in a quiet cul de sac street adjacent to the Scenic Drive. Watch the sun rising across native kauri trees, bush and Auckland city as you spot native birds from our large deck and enjoy a sumptuous breakfast prepared by your host. At the gateway to New Zealand's first Eco-City we are within easy access to over 200 km of walking tracks through 17,000 hectares of native rainforest. West coast beaches with their unique black iron sands are only 10-15 mins away. Attractions nearby:
* Wineries and Wine Trails * Artists and Artisans Trail
* Gannet Colony at Muriwai * Two scenic Golf courses on our doorstep
* Restaurants and Cafes * Day Tours can be arranged.
Paul & Allison extend a warm welcome to you.
Directions: *Airport pickup can be arranged. Please phone for bookings & directions*

Henderson
Detached B&B
Address: 295 Swanson Road,
Henderson, Waitakere City, Auckland
Name: Rod & Alma Mackay - The GARRETT
Telephone: (09) 833 6018
Fax: (09) 833 6018
Beds: 1 King, 2 Single (2 bedroom)
Bathroom: 1 Ensuite
Tariff: B&B (continental) Double $75,
Single $45, Children $22, under 5 years free, Campervans $20. NZ B&B
Vouchers accepted
Nearest Town: Henderson 5 min - 15 min. Downtown Auckland

Just 15 minutes from Auckland City and 5 minutes from historical Henderson The Garrett offers, Villa style accommodation complete with an ensuite and private terrace, twin beds (or King size if you prefer) We are able to accommodate extra guests with folding beds available on request. High ceilings and period furnishings create an atmosphere of Old in this delightful Self Contained Homestay just minutes away from Waitakere City's leading attractions which include - Wine Trails, Art Out West Trail - including Lopdell House Gallery, Waitakere Ranges Bush Walks, Aratiki Heritage and Environment Centre, World renowned Golf Courses, West City Shopping Centre, Lynn mall and St Lukes. The Garrett is situated in the vacinity of local train and bus routes and within an easy drive of all the main West Coast Beaches including Muriwai and the Gannet Colony, Karekare and Piha.
Directions: *Please telephone.*

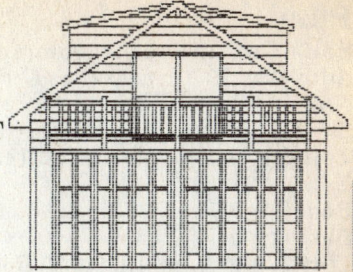

Henderson
Self-Contained Accom
Address: Please phone.
Name: Amethyst Gardens,
Len & Svargo
Telephone: (09) 836-3698
Fax: (09) 813 3710
Mobile: (021) 61-99-52
Email: amfoods@ihug.co.nz
Beds: 1 Queen, 1 Bedroom
Bathroom: 1 Ensuite
Tariff: B&B (continental) Double $100
Nearest Town: Henderson 1km

Amethyst Gardens is a 2 1/2 acre property adjacent to Henderson, gateway to the vineyard district. The cottage is newly refurbished and fully self contained. It has it's own modern bathroom, kitchen area and a cosy breakfast nook with window seats. A comfortable lounge area and private deck lead onto the cottage garden. The cottage has wonderful views of the Waitakere hills and local vineyards. It is west facing and known for spectacular sunsets. The main garden area is under development with wildflower beds being prepared at the time of writing. We are 3 minutes drive from Henderson, with restaurants, shopping malls and all amenities, and about 20 minutes from central Auckland. We are non-smokers and prefer guests not to smoke in our home. Phone, fax and e-mail facilities are available for those who need to keep in touch. Yours hosts Len and Svargo look forward to meeting you.

Piha

Self Contained Accommodation
Address: 79 Glenesk Road, Piha
Name: Piha Cottage,
Steve and Tracey Skidmore
Telephone: (09) 812 8514
Fax: (09) 812 8514
Beds: 1 Double, 1 Single (1 Bedroom)
Bathroom: 1 Private
Tariff: B&B (continental) Double $85.
Extra person over double $15.   Children welcome.
Nearest Town: 20 km West of Henderson, Piha is 45 mins drive West
from Auckland

Piha Cottage is a secluded fully self contained cottage in quiet bush surrounds near beach and walking tracks. This open plan home incorporates a compact kitchen, dining area, living area and bed in the open area. A private bathroom is attached. We have a young child, Asha. Inside the cottage is smoke free. Our cat, Floyd, enjoys guests' company. Piha is located 45 minutes west of Auckland on the rugged West Coast, nestled into native forest. The beach is world renown for surfing and is patrolled for swimmers in summer. There is a network of bushwalks to choose from: through lush native forest, along spectacular cliff tops and beaches, beside idyllic streams or to a dramatic water fall. We can provide maps and advise on the tracks which we know intimately. The cottage is an ideal home to return to after a day in the city or exploring the Waitakere forest or rugged West Coast.
Directions: *Please phone for bookings and directions.*

Piha

Self Contained Accommodation/Homestay
Address: 117 Piha Road, Piha
Name: Piha Adventure Homestay
Telephone: (09) 812 8595
Fax: (09) 812 8583
Email: pihaadventurehomestay@xtra.co.nz
Beds: Ocean Unit: 1 Queen, 1 Double,
1 Single (2 Rooms).   Surf Unit: 1 Queen, 1 Double bed/sofa (2 Rooms)
Bathroom: 2 Private
Tariff: B&B (Deluxe continental) Ocean $120. Surf: $120. $15 each extra
person. Credit Cards accepted.
Nearest Town: Henderson, Titirangi Village. Auckland City 40 mins.

Comments from our guests .....
"Thanks for letting us share your little corner of paradise".
"Great place to get away and recharge the batteries, we will be back".
"Perfect setting for a great family occasion".
To visit Piha is an adventure into some of nature's best ideas. Situated in the sub-tropical rainforest of the Waitakere Ranges and on the wild West Coast, Piha has one of New Zealand's top surf beaches and magnificent sunsets that are legendary. Enjoy the many bush walks, climb Lion Rock, visit the fairytale Kitekite Falls or relax in our fully fenced, solar heated swimming pool, hot Jacuzzi spa, or games room.   We offer quality accommodation in a secure, private setting with stunning panoramic sea and bush views. Meals by request. Gas barbecues and laundry facilities available.   Our 2 very friendly little Bichon dogs are kept separate from the units. Nearby: vineyards, golf course, arts & crafts.

Okura - North Shore City

Homestay
Address: "Okura B&B",
20 Valerie Crescent, Okura RD2 Albany
Name: Judie and Ian Greig
Telephone: (09) 473 0792
Fax: (09) 473 1072
Email: ibgreig@clear.net.nz
Beds: 1 Queen, 3 Single (3 bedrooms)
Bathroom: 2 Guests share
Tariff: B&B (full/continental) Double $80, Single $65
NZ B&B Vouchers accepted $20 surcharge
Nearest Town: Browns Bay 8km. Auckland City 23km, Albany 6km.

Situated at the "top" of Auckland's North Shore City, Okura is a small settlement bounded by farmland and the Okura River, an estuary edged with native bush. We have travelled both in NZ and internationally, and look forward to welcoming you, sharing our home with you and to hearing of your travels. We offer you off street parking, your own spacious living-room with TV, dining area, coffee and tea making facilities and fridge. There is one double bedroom, one single bedroom, own bathroom, plus a further two single beds in the house guest room with own bathroom. Nearby are a wide variety of cafes, restaurants and shops, Browns Bay and Long Bay Reserve, bush and cliff walks, North Shore Stadium, Massey University, Browns Bay RSA, and golf courses. Stay and relax. No smoking inside, please. We have no pets or children.
Directions: *Directions on request.*

Albany - Coatesville

Farmstay
Address: 'Camperdown', -
455 Coatesville/Riverhead Highway,
R.D.3 Albany, Auckland
Name: Chris & David Hempleman
Telephone: (09) 415 9009
Fax: (09) 415 9023 **Mobile**: 025 727-108
Beds: 1 King/Twin, 1 Queen, 2 Double, 3 Single, 1 Cot (4 bedrooms)
Bathroom: 2 Guests share
Tariff: B&B (full) Double $95, Single $60, Children Neg., Dinner $30.
NZ B&B Vouchers accepted $25 Surcharge
Nearest Town: Albany 7km

*We are only 20 minutes from Auckland City. Relax in secluded tranquillity in a park like rural setting, on our 18 acre farmlet running cattle, sheep, and pet lamb. Our large Tudor home opens into lovely cottage gardens native bush and stream, offering the best of hospitality and a friendly relaxed atmosphere. Our guest areas are spacious and well appointed consisting of queen and twins bedrooms, guest bathrooms and delightful sitting room with television and coffee/tea making facilities. Evening meals are available by arrangement. 'Camperdown' is situated in the beautiful Coatesville Valley, just 4km from Highway 1. Nearby activities include orchards, wineries, restaurants, horseriding, river kayaking, hot air ballooning and the Gannet Colony. Guests are also most welcome to play tennis on Camperdown's new tennis court; or have a game of snooker and table tennis in our games room.   **Directions**: From Auckland city travel north on Highway 1 through Albany - turn left into Coatesville/Riverhead Highway. Transfers are available.   **Home Page**: babs.com.au/nz/camperdown.htm*

Albany-Coatesville
Country Stay
Address: 'Hedingham',
446 Coatesville Riverhead Highway,
R.D.3, Albany.
Name: John & Angelika de Vere
Telephone: (09) 415 9292
Fax: (09) 415 7757
Mobile: (021) 459 292
Email: devere@kcbbs.gen.nz
Beds: 1 Queen, 2 Single (2 bedrooms)
Bathroom: 1 Guests share
Tariff: B&B (full) Double $105, Single $65, Children under 12 half price. Dinner $35pp. Prior booking essential.
Nearest Town: Auckland

No road noise. Fresh air, peace and tranquillity. This is "Hedingham". A large stately house on 22 acres in the picturesque Coatesville valley, one of the closest rural areas to Auckland Central, only 20 minutes drive. Guests have their own bathroom and lounge. Your bedrooms are tastefully decorated; comfortable beds with feather duvet. Wake up to freshly brewed coffee and enjoy a delicious country breakfast. John (4th generation Kiwi) and Angelika (a native German) are well travelled and enjoy exchanging stories, always happy for a chat and keen to assist you with your NZ travel plans. During your stay you might like to feed our pet sheep or just take a stroll in the bush by our river. We are handy to the main tourist route North, and only 40 minutes to Auckland Airport. Dinner is by arrangement as is lunch. Children are welcome, as we have 3 sons. Our smoking "room" is outside.

Homepage: www.hedingham.co.nz

http://www.bnb.co.nz

take a look

Albany, Auckland
Country Home
Address: Albany Country Home: "Birethanti",
57 Ngarahana Ave, Albany
Name: Bruce & Patricia Fordham
Telephone: (09) 413 9580
Fax: (09) 413 9583
Mobile: (025) 745 898
Email: fordham@nznet.gen.nz
Beds: 1 Queen, 1 Double (2 bedrooms)
Bathroom: 1 Ensuite, 1 Private
Tariff: B&B (special) Double $100-$120, Single $80-$100. Dinner by arrangement. Credit Cards. NZ B&B Vouchers accepted $25 surcharge
Nearest Town: Albany - 7 minutes off SH 1

We absolutely guarantee you will enjoy your stay! If you are not absolutely delighted you can renegotiate!
When you arrive to awesome river views you will be greeted to a warm welcome, be offered tea, coffee or juice with freshly baked muffins or slice.
You will sleep in luxurious linen, have plenty of soft fluffy towels and all the little extras that will make your stay special! You will awake to birdsong, the smell of freshly baked bread, you could amble down to the jetty before breakfasting on fresh tropical fruit, your choice of oaty pancakes, French toast and bacon, poached egg with smoked salmon, English or continental breakfast.
"We never think of staying anywhere else " say Barry and Dorothy of Cambridge England (after their third stay).
We are 7 minutes from Albany, North Harbour stadium and university, 19 minutes from Auckland and ideal stopover before heading North or South. We look forward to sharing our home with you!
Chester our friendly springer Spaniel is housed separately from the guest area.
Directions: *Turn opposite the "Albany Inn" into the Avenue. Travel 7km then turn left into Attwood Road. 1 km left into Ngarahana Avenue. 1km to cul-de-sac, 2nd house on right, down private road. White colonial house.*

Albany-Coatesville

Country Homestay
Address: Te Harinui 102 Coatesville Highway,
RD 3, Albany, Auckland
Name: Mike & Sue Blanchard
Telephone: (09) 415 9295
Fax: (09) 415 9261
Email: sueblanchard@xtra.co.nz
Beds: 1 Queen, 2 Single (2 Bedrooms)
Bathroom: 1 Guests share.
Tariff: B&B (Full) Double $75-80, Single $60,
Dinner $25, Children negotiable.
NZ B&B Vouchers accepted
Nearest Town: Albany 3km

A kauri bungalow ringed by bush with views over the country. Guests have the use of the lounge with television and stereo, and swimming pool in summer, there is also a pool table in the garage. Sue speaks conversational French and is learning Mandarin. Visitors may walk over the paddocks and feed our horse, goat and pet coloured sheep. Our two dogs and cat are also extremely friendly. Local attractions include horseriding, beaches, hot pools and nearby stadium, buses are ten minutes walk. We can provide outings to West Coast beaches and the gannet colony. Dinner is served as requested, we are happy to cater for special needs. Coffee and teas are available at all times. We have wheelchair access and welcome less able visitors. Situated fifteen minutes north of Auckland, let us start or continue your holiday with a relaxed break. We will meet travellers at the airport.

Albany

Country Homestay
Address: Albany Grove,
34 Top Road, RD2 Albany
Name: Patricia and Gregory
Telephone: (09) 415 8945
Fax: (09) 415 1285
Email: gvans@voyager.co.nz
Beds: 1 Queen, 2 Single (3 Bedrooms)
Bathroom: 1 Private Bathroom, 1 Guests Share
Tariff: B&B (Full) Double $95, Single $55. Not suitable for children. Credit Cards accepted.
Nearest Town: Albany 11km, Auckland City 27km

Come and enjoy our hospitality and the comforts of home less than 20 minutes north of Auckland City. Walk amongst the trees, shrubs and flowers in our 10 acre garden or cool off in the salt water swimming pool. At 'Albany Grove' separate from the main house we offer a private spacious double room (plus private bathroom) which is connected to the house via a covered walkway. In the house there are two single rooms with shared bathroom. All rooms have extensive rural views. Nearby are beaches, bushwalks, thermal pools and golf courses. Breakfast is served in the family room where we also enjoy a pre-dinner drink with our guests. There are many good restaurants and cafes within 10 minutes driving. If you are en route to or from the Far North we are an ideal stopover, within easy 50 minutes drive of Auckland International Airport.
Directions: *Phone/Fax for directions.*
Home Page: http://www.informate.co.nz/~albany

Greenhithe
Homestay
Address: 'Waiata Tui Lodge',
177 Upper Harbour Drive,
Greenhithe, Auckland
Name: Therese & Ned Jujnovich
Telephone: (09) 413 9270
Fax: (09) 413 9270
Beds: 2 Queen, 2 Single
(3 bedrooms)
Bathroom: 1 Private, 1 Guest share
Tariff: B&B (special) Double $85-$95, Single $65,
Dinner $25, Credit Cards. NZ B&B Vouchers accepted $20 surcharge
Nearest Town: Auckland city 15 minutes, Albany Centre and Statium 7
minutes.

You are assured of a warm welcome to Waiata-Tui Lodge. Situated on 9 acres of pasture and native forest down to the waters edge, it is so peaceful yet only 15 minutes from Auckland city. Nestled among century old Kauri's our home overlooks the upper harbour and the more distant Waitakere Ranges. An ideal place to relax, swim in the pool, bird watch or bush walk, yet close enough to explore the sights of Auckland city, the beaches, the gannet sanctuary and wineries. Ten minutes to East Coast Bays. Local sightseeing easily arranged, including balloon safaris, fishing trips or horse riding. Greenhithe is a handy starting-off place for Bay of Islands. Therese is a keen wine maker and spinner. We have both travelled extensively in New Zealand and overseas. A smoke-free home. **Directions**: *From Auckland - over the Harbour Bridge - exit left at Upper Harbour Highway - left at next 2 intersections - turn right at next lights into Upper Harbour Drive. Travel 2km. 177 is on left at the end of right of way.*

Torbay
Bed & Breakfast
Address: 161 Deep Creek Road, Torbay,
North Shore City.
Name: Pauline and Geoff Ockleston
Telephone: 09-473 0643
Beds: 1 Queen (1 bedroom)
Bathroom: 1 Private
Tariff: B&B (continental) Double $75
NZ B&B Vouchers accepted $10 surcharge
Nearest Town: Auckland City 20 mins, Browns Bay 5 mins, Takapuna
15 mins.

Torbay is a marine suburb in Auckland's North Shore City. We are one minute's walk from the local village shopping centre, where there are restaurants, take away food outlets, hairdressers, bakeries, Post Office and other shops. We are within walking distance of two of Auckland's most popular beaches, Long Bay and Waiake. There are other cafes and restaurants nearby as well.
Our property has pleasant views over Hauraki Gulf and Waitemata harbour, off road parking is available.
Directions: *Please phone for directions.*

Browns Bay

Bed & Breakfast
Address: 'Amoritz House',
730 East Coast Rd.,
Browns Bay, Auckland
Name: Gary & Carol Moffatt
Telephone: (09) 479 6338
Fax: (09) 479 6338
Mobile: 025 806958
Beds: 1 King/Twin, 1 Double (2 bedrooms)
Bathroom: 2 Ensuite
Tariff: B&B (full) Double $90-$110, Single $75-$95,
Dinner by arrangement: $10, $20, $30 pp.
Nearest Town: Browns Bay 1.5km, Downtown Auckland City (south 12 mins by car)

We are a friendly well travelled couple who invite you to stay with us. Spend a peaceful night in our quiet guest bedrooms with garden and rural outlooks, followed by a hearty Kiwi breakfast to prepare you for your day ahead. Each lockable bedroom is provided with electric blankets, heater, fan, clock/radio, colour/sky TV. A separate guest entrance leads into a kitchenette with 24hr tea and coffee making facilities, fridge, microwave and washing machine, with a guest lounge beyond. Dinners arranged with prior notice. Breakfast includes fruit juice, cereals, fresh fruit, yoghurt, tea, coffee, toast etc, as well as a cooked breakfast. We overlook North Harbour Stadium and are minutes to a variety of restaurants, cafes, beaches, shopping and Auckland City Centre with all its attractions. Off street parking, 2 minutes to motorway. Non-smoking. Barrier Free Trust accredited.

Mairangi Bay

Homestay
Address: 12 Marigold Place,
Mairangi Bay, Auckland 10
Name: Anthony & Julie Lewis
Telephone: (09) 479 6392
Beds: 2 Queen (2 bedrooms)
Bathroom: 1 Ensuite, 1 Private
Tariff: B&B (full)
Double $80, Single $50.
NZ B&B Vouchers accepted surcharge $10
Nearest Town: Browns Bay 4km, Takapuna 8kms, Auckland 13km

We are an English couple who enjoy sharing our home and spending time with travellers to Auckland. Our home has a lovely view to the ocean and Rangitoto Island. We have two guest bedrooms both equipped with Queensize beds and tea and coffee making facilities. There is a comfortable guest lounge complete with Sky TV and stereo should you require privacy. The beach and local shops are an easy ten to fifteen minute stroll away - as well as restaurants and a number of pleasant cafes. You can be sure of a special welcome. We can introduce you to the many local beaches and cliff top walks that Auckland's North Shore has to offer. House rule - No smoking indoors. 2 car garage available.
Directions: *Please phone.*

Takapuna

Homestay
Address: 89 Stanaway St,
Auckland 10
Name: Pat & John Heerdegen
Telephone: (09) 419 0731
Fax: (09) 419 0731
Email: pat&johnh@xtra.co.nz
Beds: 1 Double, 1 Twin
Bathroom: 1 Ensuite, 1 bathroom shower
Tariff: B&B (full) Double $100, Single $65,
Dinner $25pp. Credit cards. NZ B&B Vouchers accepted $20 Surcharge
Nearest Town: Takapuna 4km

Considering a New Zealand holiday? John will greet you on your arrival at Auckland, with the promise of warm hospitality for your vacation as you travel across Auckland to our North Shore home which offers expansive views of our city and harbour. We provide lunch, dinner, breakfast and drop off to your next departure point. Double NZ$250, Single NZ$150.
Enjoy our Home Comfort Holiday plan visiting with fellow home hosts, partake of their friendship, hospitality and advice on attractions you should visit. This holiday plan includes accommodation, meals, a Travel Pass for transport by coach, ferry, train and plane, so you may enjoy a hassle free as possible vacation of New Zealand.
Excellent references. Non smoking residence.
Home Page: www.visitnz.pl.net

Midway Takapuna/Devonport

Homestay
Address: 9B Elderwood Lane,
Takapuna
Name: Jim & Val Laidlaw
Telephone: (09) 489 5420
Fax: (09) 489 5420
Beds: 3 Single
(2 bedrooms)
Bathroom: 1 Ensuite, 1 Family share
Tariff: B&B (continental)
Double $85, Single $55,
Dinner $15. NZ B&B Vouchers accepted
Nearest Town: Takapuna and Devonport 10 mins, Auckland City 15 mins.

Our house is in a very peaceful and central location with good off street parking and ready access to shops, buses, ferries and motorways. Main accommodation is downstairs with twin bedroom, bathroom and separate lounge area with TV and radio. Ranch sliders from the lounge lead to a private garden patio, while upstairs is a single bedroom with family share facilities. Tea, coffee and laundry facilities are available to all. We have travelled extensively, both at home and overseas, and offer warm comfortable accommodation with a homely atmosphere. All our family have left home, we have no pets, so you can be assured of a quiet time, with all the attention from us that you ask for. Our interests include Probus, U3A, art, aviation, music, walking and petanque. Our area abounds in restaurants and food halls and we are close to bus routes. We will happily help with any travel arrangements. We request that guests do not smoke in our home.
Directions: *Please phone for directions.*

Bayswater

Homestay
Address: 27 Norwood Road, Bayswater
Name: Bayswater Point Lodge
Telephone: (09) 445 7163
Fax: (09) 445 7166
Mobile: (025) 994 295
Email: titchener@xtra.co.nz
Beds: 4 Queen (4 bedrooms)
Bathroom: 4 Ensuites
Tariff: B&B (Full) Double $165-$195
Nearest Town: Takapuna/Devonport

Bayswater Point Lodge is situated on the northern shores of the Auckland Harbour, overlooking downtown Auckland. It has a 180 degree view, which extends from Rangitoto Island to the Auckland Harbour Bridge. There is a ferry service from Bayswater to downtown Auckland and this takes 5 minutes. The Lodge offers luxury accommodation and is a blend between the old world splendour to the spacious charm of the Cape Cod tradition. Your hosts are Prue and Paul, who have lived in their home for 35 years, and when the children left home we decided to turn it into a quality Bed and Breakfast. We spent many months doing the renovations and are very pleased with the end result. Prue and Paul love to entertain their guests and Paul will gladly take them on a tour of historic Devonport. Paul is a former Mayor of North Shore city and local historian.

Home Page: http://nz.com/webnz/bbnz/baylodge.htm

Devonport

Homestay
Address: "Cheltenham-By-The-Sea", 2 Grove Road, Devonport, Auckland
Name: J & H Mossman
Telephone: (09) 445 9437
Fax: (09) 445 9432
Email: mossman.@clear.net.nz
Beds: 1 Queen with Ensuite, 1 Double, 1 Twin, 2 Single (5 bedrooms)
Bathroom: 1 Ensuite, 1 Private, 1 Guests share
Tariff: B&B (continental) Queen/Ensuite $100-$130, Single $75; Children under 12 yrs $15. Transport available by 'Super' Shuttle Bus direct from airport. NZ B&B Vouchers accepted $40 surcharge
Nearest Town: Devonport Auckland

Cheltenham By The Sea

Adjacent to lovely Cheltenham Beach with safe swimming and pleasant walks in unique area. 45 mins from International Airport or 12 mins from downtown Auckland Ferry across Waitemata Harbour. Contemporary spacious home in quiet area with spacious lawn, shade trees and secluded patio. Several restaurants handy. An escort service by private car for business, sightseeing, pleasure and places of interest is available at reasonable rates. Two minutes walk to bus stops and shops. Short walk to golf course, bowling and croquet clubs, tennis and squash courts. Our interests are people, travel, family, swimming, camping, fishing and gardening. There is no other marine suburb which offers so much in such a small picturesque area. We have enjoyed 18 years of home hosting, and a warm welcome is assured by your hosts. Reservations are advisable to avoid disappointment. Children are welcome,

Devonport

B & B + Self-contained Cottage
Address: 'Karin's Garden Villa',
14 Sinclair St, Devonport, Auckland 9
Name: Karin Loesch
Telephone: (09) 445 8689
Fax: (09) 445 8689 **Email**: karins@ihug.co.nz
Beds: 2 Double, 3 Single (4 bedrooms)
Bathroom: 1 Ensuite (shower+bath), 1 Private, 1 Guests share
Tariff: B&B (continental) Double $125-$155, Single $85-$105, Children negotiable, (cot available). Credit cards Visa/mastercard/Amex. Winter and longstay rates available. NZ B&B Vouchers accepted $75 surcharge
Nearest Town: Auckland - 15 mins by ferry or car.

Tucked away at the end of a quiet cul-de-sac, Karin's Garden Villa offers REAL home comfort with its light cosy rooms, easy relaxed atmosphere and the warmest of welcome from Karin and her family. A beautifully restored spacious Victorian villa surrounded by large lawns and old fruit trees. It is the ideal retreat for your year-2000 holiday. Karin's Garden Villa has also been featured on NZ and Australian television advertising for its relaxed, peaceful setting. Just 5 minutes stroll from tree-lined Cheltenham Beach, sailing, golf, tennis, shops and restaurants and only a short drive or pleasant 10 minute walk past extinct volcanoes to the picturesque Devonport centre with its many attractions. Your comfortable room offers separate private access through French doors, opening onto a wide verandah and cottage garden. And for those visitors wanting ultimate comfort and privacy, there is even a self-contained studio cottage with balcony and full kitchen facilities to rent (min. 3 days). Sit down to a nutritious breakfast in the sunny dining room with its large bay windows overlooking everflowering purple lavender and native gardens. Guests are welcome to join the family barbecue and relax on our large lawn. We welcome longer stays and can arrange favourable discounts accordingly. Help yourself to tea and German-style coffee and biscuits anytime and feel free to use the kitchen and laundry. Karin comes from Germany and she and her family have lived in Indonesia for a number of years. We have seen a lot of the world and enjoy meeting other travellers. Always happy to help you arrange island cruises, rental cars and tours. Children welcome! "See you soon - bis bald - à bientôt"
Directions: *Airport Shuttle Bus to our doorstep or to Downtown Ferry Terminal. Courtesy pick-up from Devonport Wharf. By Car: After crossing Harbour Bridge, take Takapuna-Devonport turnoff. Right at T-junction, follow Lake Road to end, left into Albert, Vauxhall Road and then Sinclair Street.*
Home Page: http://homepages.ihug.co.nz/~karins

Devonport
B&B Inn

Address: Luxury B&B Inn,
46 Tainui Road,
Devonport, Auckland
Name: Devonport Villa Inn
Telephone: (09) 445 8397
Fax: (09) 445 9766
Email: dvilla@ihug.co.nz
Beds: 2 King,2 Queen, 2 Single (5 bedrooms)
Bathroom: 5 Private
Tariff: B&B (full) Double $175-$210,
Credit cards (VISA/Amex/MC)
NZ B&B Vouchers accepted $120 surcharge
Nearest Town: Auckland - 15 minutes by car or ferry . Shuttle bus
from airport - 24 km

Devonport Villa Inn, winner of the NZ Tourism Awards for hosted accommodation, is in the heart of Devonport, 2 minutes walk from Auckland's best kept secret, sandy and safe Cheltenham Beach. There is something special about every aspect of this exquisite historic home build in 1903 by a wealthy retired English doctor. Edwardian elegance, spacious individual rooms with king and queen beds, extensive guest library, rich woollen carpets, restored colonial furniture, outstanding stained glass windows and the guest lounge with its amazing vaulted ceiling and polished native timber floor. Choose from the unique upstairs Turret Room, the romantic and sunny Rangitoto Suite with its private balcony, the colonial style Beaconsfield Suite with antique clawfoot bath and four-poster king bed or the Oxford and Gold rooms. Each cosy room is individually decorated with delightful handmade patchwork quilts, firm beds, soft woollen blankets, fresh bouquets of flowers from the garden, plump pillows and crisp white linen. And in the morning you will be cooked a delicious full breakfast, including freshly squeezed juice, natural yoghurt, nutritious muesli, muffins baked daily, Belgian waffles, double smoked bacon with eggs and preserves.....join other guests in the dining room overlooking the garden, or if you like we can serve breakfast in some rooms at a time to suit. Please ask when booking.
Sit in the sunny shell courtyard overlooking the Edwardian style garden with lavender hedges, old roses and spacious lawns.
Enjoy a moonlit stroll along the beach to North Head and dinner at a nearby restaurant. Devonport Villa is within easy walking distance of the major wedding reception venues and the historic sights of Devonport. Let us help you to make your stay in Devonport relaxing, pleasant and unique. Fax and E-mail available. Smoking is not permitted in the house.
Home Page: http://www.DevonportVillaInn.co.nz

Devonport
Luxury Accommodation
Address: Hyland House - fine accommodation,
4 Flagstaff Terrace, Devonport, Auckland
Name: Carol and Bruce Hyland
Telephone: (09) 445 9917
Fax: (09) 445 9927
Mobile: (021) 986 221
Email: hyland@voyager.co.nz
Beds: 2 Queen (2 bedroom)
Bathroom: 2 Ensuite
Tariff: B&B (special) Double $225 to $275, Single $190 to $225. All major credit cards. NZ B&B Vouchers accepted $100-$175 surcharge
Nearest Town: Auckland - 15 minutes by ferry or car.

Hyland house is an elegant Victorian residence on the waterfront in the seaside village of Devonport, a 10 minute ferry trip from Auckland City, providing the very best in private accommodation for discerning travellers. Original architectural detailing has been retained in this stunning two storey brick home, with French country style interior design. Hyland House offers two sumptuous suites, the 'Atea Suite', Maori for "a place close to heaven", comprising a carved four-poster bed and large ensuite with antique clawfoot bathtub; as well as the 'Provence Room' with French sleighbed and ensuite. Guests are served a complimentary three course gourmet breakfast in the conservatory, or alfresco by the swimming pool - Eggs Benedict, French Baked Eggs, Smoked Salmon Scrambles etc. Fax and email available. Smokefree inside. Restaurants, galleries, beaches, ferry - 2 minutes walk away. Hyland House is a wonderful location from which to explore the whole of Auckland. **Home Page**: www.hyland.co.nz

Devonport
Self-contained Garden Room B&B + Villa Room
Address: 'The Garden Room',
23 Cheltenham Road, Devonport, Auckland 9
Name: Perrine & Bryan Hall
Telephone: (09) 445 2472
Fax: (09) 445 2472 **Mobile**: (025) 989 643
Email: b.hall@clear.net.nz
Beds: 2 Double, 1 Single (Rollaway) (2 bedrooms)
Bathroom: 1 Ensuite, 1 Private
Tariff: B&B (full) Double $135-$150, Single $110-$120 Children welcome. NZ B&B Vouchers accepted $85 surcharge peak season
Nearest Town: Auckland 15 mins by car or ferr.

Within our garden is a private sunny hideaway. Large french doors open onto a tranquil villa garden where you may enjoy your breakfast in the sunny courtyard or served in the privacy of your room. Enjoy a swim before breakfast at Cheltenham Beach, a few steps from our door or a walk up North Head for great harbour views. Breakfast includes fresh juices, tropical fruits served with our own muesli and home-made yoghurt, croissants, breads, muffins, free range eggs, bacon with good coffee or tea. Enjoy too, the luxury of crisp cotton sheets, bathrobes, fresh flowers, chocolates, complimentary port.The Garden Room also offers all facilities for complete independence including ensuite, TV, tea / coffee, refrigerator etc. Phone, fax or email available in the villa where one bedroom also offered. Off-street parking and private entrance to Garden Room. McHughs reception lounge opposite. Short stroll to Devonport, ferry, restaurants and Duders.We have both travelled widely, and have knowledge of French and Spanish. **Directions**: *A Super shuttle bus brings you from the airport to our door.*
Homepage: http://members.tripod.com/GardenRoom/

Devonport, Auckland
Bed & Breakfast Inn

Address: 'Villa Cambria Bed & Breakfast Inn ',
71 Vauxhall Road, Devonport, Auckland
Name: Clive & Kate Sinclair
Telephone: (09) 445 7899 **Fax**: (09) 446 0508
Mobile: (025) 843 826 **Email**: villacambria@xtra.co.nz
Beds: 3 Queen, 1 Double, 1 Twin, (5 bedrooms)
Bathroom: 5 Ensuite
Tariff: B&B (full) Double $150-$200, Single $120-$150, Children over 12yrs, Dinner by arrangement. Credit cards (VISA/MC/AMEX). NZ B&B Vouchers accepted $75 Surcharge may apply
Nearest Town: Auckland 15 minutes by car or ferry

Villa Cambria is an historic Victorian Villa featuring Nineteenth Century architecture and ambience with amenities styled for todays living. Private and extensive treed grounds attract a variety of birds, and provide a relaxing and private location with quiet nooks, shaded verandahs, sundecks, barbecue and patios.

In our home there are four double bedrooms with ensuite and private bath facilities for our guests, whilst in the garden there is the lovely 'Loft' which is self-contained with its own balcony and extensive views over the surrounding landscape.

The villa's guest sitting room looks out onto the garden and the adjacent ante room houses a large collection of books for your enjoyment. The excellent breakfast (try the homemade bread) can be enjoyed on the verandah, patio or in your room, or at the old kauri table with the other guests.

For those who enjoy golf, why not join your host for a round of golf at the Waitemata Golf Course, only 5 minutes walk away. If you enjoy shopping or simply dining out Devonport Village offers gourmet restaurants and sidewalk cafes where you can savour the art studios, museums, antique shops and the delightful harbour walks. It is a 2 minutes walk to Cheltenham Beach.

A 20 minute walk will enable you to enjoy the sights from the extinct volcanic peaks of North Head or Mt Victoria, with their unsurpassed views of the city and the harbour. Having looked after hundreds of visitors from all over the world your hosts Clive and Kate take particular care to make you feel at home.

So why not escape and enjoy being in the peace and tranquillity of Devonport only 12 minutes by ferry from the heart of Auckland.

Directions: *From Airport: Shuttle Bus door to door service. By car: Travelling north, cross Auckland Harbour Bridge, 1.5km north take Devonport/Takapuna exit from motorway. Follow signs to Devonport along Lake Road. At roundabout turn left into Albert Road. At "T" junction turn left into Vauxhall Road, Villa Cambria is on the corner behind the trees.*

HomePage: www.villacambria.co.nz

Devonport
Bed & Breakfast
Address: 'Top of the Drive',
15c King Edward Parade,
Devonport, Auckland
Name: Viv & Ray Huckle
Telephone: (09) 445 3362
Fax: (09) 445 9636
Beds: 1 King, 1 Queen, 1 Single.
Extra single bed available (3 bedrooms)
Bathroom: 2 Ensuite, 1 Private (1 toilet & vanity), 1 Family share
Tariff: B&B (full) Double $110-$140, Single $70-$100
Nearest Town: Auckland 15 mins by ferry or car

We are situated along Devonport's lovely waterfront, only a delightful 5 minute stroll to our local historic seaside village with its shops, cinema, wide variety of restaurants, cafes and ferry service to Auckland City. (Also very close to Duders and McHugh's reception venues). We have a quiet and private location being back from the road, away from traffic, with good off street parking. We offer 3 spacious bedsitting rooms with ensuite/private bathrooms. All rooms have firm comfortable beds (King, Queen, Single), armchairs, TV, tea/coffee and pleasant view. There is also a guest lounge opening onto a sunny garden. Enjoy a leisurely breakfast in the dining room. We provide lots of fresh fruit, orange juice, a selection of cereals and breads, yoghurt, tea, fresh coffee and a full cooked breakfast. Non smoking - laundry facilities. We look froward to meeting you, looking after you and making your stay an enjoyable one.

Devonport
Homestay
Address: "Amberley Bed & Breakfast",
3 Ewen Alison Ave., Devonport, Auckland 1309
Name: Mary and Michael Burnett
Telephone: (09) 446 0506
Fax: (09) 446 0506 **Email**: amberley@xtra.co.nz
Beds: 3 Queen, 2 Single (4 bedrooms)
Bathroom: 2 Guests share (one wih double spa bath)
Tariff: B&B (special) Double $100-$130, Single $70-$100. Credit cards (VISA/MC/AMEX). NZ B&B Vouchers accepted $50 surcharge
Nearest Town: Auckland -10 min. ferry ride. Shuttle available from airport.

Nestled at the base of Mt Victoria, our family home is a charming colonial villa within easy walking distance of Devonport's numerous cafés, shops, safe swimming beaches, golf course, and ferry terminal. Spectaclular panoramic views can be enjoyed from the summit of Mt Victoria. Our bedrooms are spacious and charmingly furnished with exceedingly comfortable beds! The guest bathrooms with beautiful stainedglass windows, are not ensuite, but bathrobes are provided. Our large guest lounge has Sky TV, complimentary tea/coffee making facilities, guest frig and homebaking. Early a.m. flight guests are welcome. Door to door shuttle service from airport. Laundry facilities are available. A delicious breakfast is served in our spacious diningroom with city views. Relax sitting in the sun in our private bricked courtyard. We have travelled extensively both here and overseas and we look forward to meeting you and making your stay in our beautiful country an enjoyable experience.
Directions: *Turn right at Mt Victoria roundabout, 200 mtrs, first right at Victoria Superette corner. Off-street parking.*

Devonport
Bed & Breakfast
Address: 'The Rainbow Villa',
17 Rattray Street, Devonport, Auckland 9
Name: Judy McGrath
Telephone: (09) 445 3597 **Fax**: (09) 445 4597 **Email**: rainbowvilla@xtra.co.nz
Beds: 1 King, 1 Queen, 2 Single (3 bedrooms)
Bathroom: 3 Ensuites
Tariff: B&B (full) Double $130-$160, Single $95-$120.
Credit Cards (VISA/MC/AMEX).
Nearest Town: Auckland; 15 mins by car or ferry.

I look forward to welcoming you to my home. The Rainbow Villa, a beautiful and historic Victorian villa, built out of kauri in 1885, which I refurbished and restored in December 1996. Your home away from home in charming Devonport is nestled on the lower slopes of scenic Mount Victoria in a quiet cul-de-sac filled with historic homes. Despite the peace and quiet, it is just a two minute stroll from Devonport's main street with its delightful cafes, fine restaurants, unique art and craft shops, a safe swimming beach, peaceful parks and fascinating museums and art galleries, where there is always plenty to see and enjoy. If you are feeling energetic the climb up Mount Victoria produces magnificent 360 degree views of the glorious Waitemata Harbour and the city beyond. Or, if you are looking for more action, then downtown Auckland with its casino, nightclubs, bars and shopping malls is just a 10 minute ferry trip away. Before setting off to enjoy all that Devonport and Auckland have to offer enjoy a leisurely breakfast in the garden dining room. My breakfasts feature freshly squeezed orange juice, fresh fruit in season, organic muesli, homemade yoghurt, free range eggs, lean bacon, tomatoes, plus all the tea, coffee or herb tea you want. At the end of the day relax in your own room or you can rest in the guest lounge's cosy armchairs, wander outside to the garden chairs where you can soak up the sun or even enjoy a relaxing soak in the hot spa pool to refresh you for your next day's exploration. The Rainbow Villa has three spacious rooms, each with a private ensuite, comfortable beds, Sky TV and heating. All rooms are lockable and the villa is smoke free. As a sixth generation New Zealander, I have taken great care to preserve the villa's historic appearance and comfortable atmosphere and I am sure you will enjoy staying here as much as I do. Welcome. Complimentary tea, coffee and sherry are available whenever required and herb teas are also available.
Directions: *Rattray Street is the first on the left going down the hill, past the picture theatre.*

Devonport

Homestay
Address: 'Duck's Crossing Cottage',
58 Seabreeze Road,
Devonport, Auckland 9
Name: Peter & Gwenda Mark-Woods
Telephone: (09) 445 8102
Fax: (09) 445 8102
Beds: 1 Queen, 1 Double,
2 Single (3 bedrooms)
Bathroom: 1 Ensuite, 2 Private
Tariff: B&B (full) Double $85-$100, Single $65.
Special winter rates, special long stay rates. NZ B&B Vouchers accepted $20 surcharge
Nearest Town: Devonport - 3 mins by car.

Welcome to our charming, modern home built 1994, surrounded by cottage gardens. Peaceful with attractive decor, spacious and sunny. Two bedrooms open on to balconies and a third through French doors to the garden. All bedrooms have TV's. Comfortable warm bedding with patchwork quilts. Delicious home cooking, fresh garden produce. Tea and coffee facilities. Summer breakfasts available on the sheltered terrace. Stroll to Narrow Neck Beach alongside the beautiful Waitemata Golf Course. Swim, sail, walk or explore Devonport Village and sample the many lovely cafés and restaurants. Hosts are friendly, informative and helpful, well travelled and enjoy hospitality.
Directions: *From the Airport, take Super Shuttle to our door. If driving take Route 26, into Seabreeze Road, 1st house on left. Offstreet parking. (Courtesy pick ups to and from ferry, on request)*

Devonport, Auckland

Quality Accommodation
Address: "Badgers of Devonport",
30 Summer Street, Devonport, Auckland
Name: Heather & Badger Miller
Telephone: (09) 445 2099
Fax: (09) 445 0231
Mobile: (025) 720 336 **Email**: badgers@clear.net.nz
Beds: 4 Double, 2 Single (4 bedrooms)
Bathroom: 3 Ensuite, 1 Private
Tariff: B&B (special) Double $119-$135, Single $95, Dinner $25 (2 course) pp. Credit Cards Visa/Amex. M/C. Vouchers accepted $30 surcharge
Nearest Town: Auckland 10 mins by ferry or 15 mins by car.

Welcome to our home. Let us pamper you in our quiet, sunny Villa furnished with antiques, oriental carpets and memorabilia from our extensive travels. On arrival relax with complimentary drinks on the verandah. Indulge in chocolates whilst lazing on your Victorian brass bed or soak in our original antique bath. All bedrooms have en-suites, bathrobes, toiletries, flowers, TVs and resident teddy bears to cuddle. Enjoy the privacy of your self-contained guest wing complete with kitchen. Laundry, airport transfers available. Off-street parking. Sumptuous beakfast for vegetarians and meat lovers. Stroll to the beach or enjoy Devonports restaurants, cafes, art galleries, shops and museums.
Directions: *From airport take shuttle direct. By car follow Devonport directions down Lake Road to Mt Victoria roundabout, turn right, take the 4th right turn into Calliope Road, Summer Street is 6th road on right. (Courtesy pick up from ferry upon request.)* **HomePage**:/www.badger.co.nz

Devonport

Exclusive Accommodation

Address: 6 Flagstaff Terrace, Devonport, Auckland

Name: 'The Peace & Plenty Inn'

Telephone: (09) 445 2925

Fax: (09) 445 2901

Email: peaceandplenty@xtra.co.nz

Beds: 5 Queen, 2 Single (5 bedrooms)

Bathroom: 5 Ensuite

Tariff: B&B (full) Double $230, Single $200, Dinner N/A, All Credit Cards. NZ B&B Vouchers accepted Surcharge $170

Nearest Town: Auckland - 10 minutes by ferry

HERITAGE INNS of New Zealand

A MEMBER OF

Australia & New Zealand's Finest B&B's

& Rural Retreats

Recommended by the New York Times, leading tourist guide books and International Interior Design magazines, The Peace & Plenty Inn offers a world of graciousness, romance, comfort, fine food and hospitality. Situated in an unbeatable location from which to explore all of the Auckland area, The Peace & Plenty Inn is on the waterfront in the seaside village of Devonport, and steps away from many fine restaurants, shopping, museums, galleries, the beach, and the ferry to central Auckland. Built in 1888, The Peace & Plenty Inn has been impeccably restored with five individual Queen guest rooms in French Country Style with feather duvets, fine linens, plump pillows, oriental carpets, antiques, fine art, fireplaces, all bedrooms with private ensuite bathrooms. Enter a world of comfort with French Marcellas, Belgian chocolates, Italian toiletries, and bouquets of fresh flowers everywhere. Relax in a private lounge with complimentary Port, Teas, Coffee and cookies. Select from our gourmet breakfast menu - your choice of Eggs Benedict; French Baked Eggs with Brie and Avocado; Waffles; Eggs Devonport with smoked salmon; double-smoked bacon and eggs any way you like them - freshly squeezed orange juice, scrumptious muffins baked daily, homemade yoghurt and fresh tropical fruits. Proud to be a member of the Heritage Inns of New Zealand and The Small Hotel Company.

Home Page: http://nz.com/heritageinns/peace&plenty

Mt Victoria, Devonport

Self-contained B&B
Address: 'Albertine', 45 Church Street,
Devonport, Auckland 9
Name: Moira & Ross Taylor
Telephone: (09) 445 6443 **Mobile**: (025) 924 420
Beds: 1 Double, 2 Single (foldaways) (1+ bedroom)
Bathroom: 1 Ensuite
Tariff: B&B (full) Double $130, Single $110, Children welcome.
NZ B&B Vouchers accepted $65 surcharge peak season
Nearest Town: Auckland 15 mins by car or ferry. Airport super shuttle will
bring you to our door.

*Albertine is a gracious farmhouse built in 1860 on the North Eastern slopes of Mt
Victoria. Enjoy lovely views over harbour and suburb and a tranquil garden
setting. Open the gate to Flagstaff Lane and take a stroll around Mt Victoria or
climb to the summit then down for a swim at nearby Torpedo Bay. Devonport's
artist studios, delicious cafés and restaurants, bar and shops are within easy
walking distance as are Duder's and McHugh's reception lounges. A delicious
breakfast of tropical fresh fruit, and juices, homemade muesli, yoghurt and
muffins, croissants and breads with a variety of spreads, bacon and free range
eggs can be served in your own sitting room or outside on the verandah in the
morning sun. Albertine offers a peaceful and private environment, a romantic
old fashioned bedroom and ensuite, your own separate entrance and adjoining
sitting room. Tea/fresh coffee/TV available. A warm welcome awaits you at
'Albertine' from Moira, Ross and family.*

Devonport, Auckland

Self Contained Apartment B&B
Address: 82B Wairoa Road,
Devonport, Auckland
Name: Ivanhoe
Telephone: (09) 445 1900
Fax: (09) 446 0039
Email: gbarton@xtra.co,nz
Beds: 1 Queen, 1 Single Rollaway (1 bedroom)
Bathroom: 1 Ensuite
Tariff: B&B (continental) Double $120, Single $80, Children $20. From
Nov-April, Double $150, Single $120, Children $20.
Weekly rates negotiable. Visa/Mastercard
Nearest Town: Devonport 5 mins

*IVANHOE, our fully furnished private apartment, looks out upon the sparkling
waters of the Waitemata harbour off Narrow Neck; the venue for the America's
Cup. Situated on the ground floor, this light and airy apartment includes a lounge
with TV and private phone; both the bedroom and tiled bathroom are spacious;
kitchenette with full cooking facilities. Complementary continental breakfast
available includes: juice, home-made muesli and yoghurt, fruit, toast or muffins,
jam and honey. Within easy access, across the road by the beach is a park, with
a golf course, public tennis courts, gym and squash courts all only minutes away.
A 5 minute drive to historic Devonport enables you to enjoy a variety of shops
and restaurants. A ferry sails to downtown Auckland every half hour where boat
trips depart daily to the many islands in the gulf. Off-street parking is available.
Courtesy pick-up from Devonport Wharf. We look forward to meeting you and
making your stay enjoyable.*

Devonport, Auckland
Fully self contained cottage B&B
Address: 3a Cambridge Terrace,
Devonport, Auckland
Name: Devonport Sea Cottage
Telephone: (09) 445 7117
Fax: (09) 445 7117 **Email**: lethabys@ihug.co.nz
Beds: 1 Queen, single also available (1 bedroom)
Bathroom: 1 Ensuite
Tariff: Double $120, Single $100, Children welcome. Breakfast optional extra.
Weekly rates. Vouchers accepted $40 surcharge in peak season
Nearest Town: Auckland city 15 mins by car or ferry. Airport Super
Shuttle Bus directly to our door.

A unique, beautifully appointed cottage in our garden, exclusively yours and only metres to the sea. Charming and private. The interior has a variety of living spaces including ensuite, kitchen, dining room and private verandah. Light and airy with a delightful serene atmosphere. The perfect location in Devonport, ideally situated mid way between lovely Cheltenham Beach historic North Head in one direction and Devonport village and the ferry in the other. Step out of the cottage and cross the road to the park and sea. A short stroll takes you along the waterfront to Duders or McHughs reception lounges. Our cottage has full facilities or we can provide a delicious home cooked breakfast. We are very suitable for longer stays or a short term. Tea / coffee and TV provided. John, Michele and family (including two small cuddly pets) look forward to meeting you. We warmly welcome you to our home.

Devonport
B&B + Self Contained Cottage
Address: Englishmans Retreat
36 Stanley Point Road,
Devonport, Auckland.
Name: Judith and Peter Machin
Telephone: (09) 445 6549
Fax: (09) 445 6549
Email: P_J_Machin@xtra.co.nz
Beds: 2 King, 1 Queen (3 Bedrooms)
Bathroom: 3 Ensuites, 1 Guests share
Tariff: B&B (Full/Continental)
Double $130-$160, Single $110-$140, Children under 12 years free.
Nearest Town: Devonport

The lavender and rose fronted Englishmans Retreat is located on the picturesque Stanley Point, 2 km from the village of Devonport. The only noise you will hear is the bird song in our beautiful gardens. Enjoy a 2 min. stroll to the nearby beach, reserve or ferry point which can take you within 10 mins to Auckland City. Take advantage of our private sunny verandah and enjoy complimentary beverages or a welcoming glass of NZ wine. Alternatively relax in the evening in front of our log fire with a book from our wide selection. Our breakfast is specially prepared fresh fruits, juices, muesli, croissants, muffins, or organic Devonport breads, combined with your choice of Englishmans breakfast. 5 minute drive to Waitemata Golf Course. Airport transfers can be arranged. We can advise on travel plant throughout New Zealand, as we have travelled extensively both here and overseas. E-mail and fax service also available.

Waiheke Island
Homestay+Self-contained   Accom.
Address: 'Gulf Haven', 49 Great Barrier Road,
Enclosure Bay, Waiheke Island
Name: Alan Ramsbottom & Lois Baucke
Telephone: (09) 372 6629
Fax: (09) 3728558 **Email**: gulfhavn@ihug.co.nz
Beds: Homestay: 1 Queen, 1 Double (2 bedrooms). 2 Self-Contained
Studio Apartments: 1 Queen, 1 Super King/Twin option
Bathroom: Homestay: 1 Guests share. Studios: both with ensuites.
Tariff: Dec 1st 99 to Nov 30th 00. Homestay: B&B (continental) Double
$85, Queen $100, Single (double bed) $75. SC Studio Apartments:
Double $165. Continental breakfast option extra. Credit cards (VISA/
MC) NZ B&B Vouchers accepted Homestay only with surcharge $25
Nearest Town: Auckland

*Waiheke Island is different. A unique lifestyle, superb scenery, yet only 35
minutes from downtown Auckland.*
*Our home and studio apartments sit on a low ridge in 2 acres of garden
running down to the sea. A path takes you via a dramatic deck to secluded
rock pools and clear deep water. Our modern interesting indoor/outdoor
home takes advantage of the dramatic views of the Northern Coast of
Waiheke Island with Coromandel Peninsula and Great Barrier Island beyond.
Friendly home hospitality or luxury self-contained studio apartments for two people
with private decks, both offer an exclusive location to relax and unwind. Have
breakfast on the deck, overlooking the sea; savour the Island's cafes and restaurants.
Tea and coffee is always available. Lois and I enjoy the outdoors and Arts and are non-
smokers. We have a Burmese cat, Misty. Regretably Gulf Haven's facilities are not
suitable for children. Explore the Island (we have 2 bicycles) acclaimed for its beaches
and fine wines or just relax. We can arrange tours, kayaking, horseriding, golf etc. We
enjoy our Island hideaway and its mild climate and welcome you to experience it with
us.*
Directions: *Shuttle bus from Auckland Airport then passenger ferry from
Ferry Building, Downtown Auckland, approx. every 1 to 2 hours. Also
vehicular ferry and plane charter service. We will meet you from most
ferries, but please phone first.*
Home Page: http://nz.com/webnz/bbnz/haven.htm

Waiheke Island

Homestay Bed & Breakfast and Self Contained Apartments
Address: "Punga Lodge",
223 Ocean View Rd, Little Oneroa, Waiheke Island
Name: Dyan Sharland & Rob Johnston
Telephone: (09) 372 6675 **Fax**: (09) 372 6675
Beds: Lodge - 3 ensuite Double, 1 Double garden ensuite,
1 Queen garden ensuite. Apartments - 4 Double or
Queen plus Singles. **Bathroom**: All with private bathrooms.
Tariff: B&B (continental) Double $110-$145,
Apartments $95-$200. Transfers included. $15 to $20 for extra adults. Children
welcome in apartments. Off season and midweek rates available. Visa/MC accepted.
Vouchers accepted Only for Homestay with a $30 Surcharge
Nearest Town: Auckland - 35 mins by ferry

*Escape to Waiheke Island where Punga Lodge provides an informal, relaxed
atmosphere in a native bush setting just 150 metres from a safe swimming beach and a 12
minute walk to cafes and restaurants in the main town of Oneroa. All guest suites and
apartments have private bathrooms and TVs and open onto sunny private verandahs
overlooking gardens, native bush and birdlife. Complimentary home cooked afternoon teas
are a B&B speciality and breakfasts include home-made muffins. Tours, horse riding,
kayaking etc organised for guests. We specialise in group bookings - for fun get togethers or
conferences with a separate fully equipped conference facility for groups of up to 15 people. We
take all the hassle out of the planning because we'll do it for you, tailor-made to meet your needs
or interests. Minimum two night weekend bookings on most accommodation. We have two
children and two cats. **Directions**: Ferry from downtown Auckland. Complimentary
transfer from Waiheke wharf.*
Home Page: www.ki-wi.co.nz/punga.htm

Waiheke Island

Bed & Breakfast
Address: "Blue Horizon",
41 Coromandel Road, Sandy Bay,
Waiheke Island
Name: David & Marion Aim
Telephone: (09) 372 5632
Beds: 2 Queen (2 bedrooms)
Bathroom: 1 Ensuite, 1 Family share
Tariff: B&B (continental) Double $70-$85, Single $55-$70, Dinner on
request. NZ B&B Vouchers accepted $25 surcharge ensuite
Nearest Town: Auckland

*We live above Sandy Bay which is 2-3 mins walk away with spectacular views of
the Hauraki Gulf and its many islands, from Rangitoto around to Coromandel
Peninsula. Our home is modest and we are very proud of the new guest wing
Marion and I built with help from our neighbours. All the rooms in our home face
due north catching the sun all day, ideal for our spoilt cat. After farming while
our 4 children were growing up and owning a garden centre, we really enjoy the
lifestyle of Waiheke Island with its lovely bush walks, sandy beaches and rock
pools to explore. Waiheke caters for adventuring, dining out or just relaxing on
one of our decks. The thing most of our guests enjoy about staying with us is our
friendliness and the panoramic views from wherever you are in the house. Most
days we can see the Americas Cup boats practicing in the distance.
Directions: Ferry from downtown Auckland. Approx every 2 hrs. Complimentary ferry transfers. We look forward to sharing our beautiful island with you.*

118

GIVERNY

HERITAGE INNS OF

NEW ZEALAND

Oneroa Waiheke Island

Self Contained Accommodation, B&B

Address: Giverny,
44 Queens Drive, Oneroa,
Waiheke Island
Name: Giverny Inn
Telephone: (09) 372 2200
Fax: (09) 372 2204
Mobile: (025) 949 062
Email: giverny@pop.ihug.co.nz
Beds: 2 Queen, 2 Singles (2 bedrooms)
Bathroom: 1 Ensuite,
1 Private in cottage
Tariff: B&B (special) Double from $155,
Single from $120, Dinner $65 pp.
Children $40 (cotttage only).
Credit Cards accepted.
Nearest Town: Oneroa

Giverny Inn on Waiheke Island welcomes you to Paradise. Waiheke is a magical island of wine, olives, lavender, and emerald edged beaches. We are only 35 minutes form Down Town Auckland by ferry. BACCHUS COTTAGE. You can choose to stay in Bacchus cottage, a restored historic cottage furnished in elegant simplicity. Self service or hosted service, and a balcony to sit and enjoy stunning views. VENUS SUITE. A romantic suite (sitting room and B/R) from where you can gaze out to sea views or sit on the balcony with a drink to contemplate. Venus Suite is furnished with antiques, Persian rugs and chandeliers. Both Bacchus Cottage and Venus Suite have fine linens, goosedown comforters, port, chocolates, fresh fruit and flowers. Oscar our cat welcomes guests also. Stunning walks are nearby, as are restaurants, beaches, golf, vineyards, including the famous Stoney Ridge, scenic flights and fishing. Louisa and Cliff enjoy cooking Waiheke fish for breakfast and also will provide dinner from $65 per person. While eating you can gaze at the moon and Oneroa's twinkling lights from the harbour and town.
Home Page: www.waiheke.co.nz/giverny.htm

119

Waiheke Island
B&B
Address: "Signal Hill", 66 Cory Road,
Palm Beach, Waiheke Island
Name: Barry Kirkwood PhD
Telephone: (09) 372 5161
Fax: (09) 372 5161   **Email**: bjk@ihug.co.nz
Beds: 3 Queen (3 bedrooms)
Bathroom: 3 Ensuite (1 with bath)
Tariff: B&B (full) Double $100,
Single (queen bed) $70.
Off-season, Longer stay, day, group and conference rates negotiable.
Candlelit dinner $20-$30. Lunches, brunches, picnics, barbecues,
paella parties by arrangement. Credit cards: Visa/Mastercard.
Nearest Town: Auckland - 35 mins by ferry.

*A Mediterranean style house and garden above an unspoiled cove, enjoying dramatic views
over Hauraki Gulf, Signal Hill is dedicated to the comfort and welfare of adult couples and
singles. Separate sleeping and living wings give choice of socialising or seclusion. Guest rooms
have queen size beds and tiled ensuite bathrooms. All rooms display New Zealand art, and
open to patios. The open plan living area has a kauri banqueting / conference table, library
and sound system (bring your favourite CD). Candlelit dinners and other meals a specialty.
We (Barry and two Burmese cats) favour locally sourced organically grown foods. Your host:
Retired academic with interests including: food, wine, travel, arts, literature, amateur radio
(ZLIDD), sailing, aviation. Smokefree Signal Hill is centrally situated in easy reach of
beaches, bush walks, restaurants, vineyards. Laundry and Office facilities. Courtesy pickup
from wharf / airfield.* **Home Page**: www.waiheke.co.nz/signal.htm

---

Waiheke Island, Auckland
Self Contained Accommodation/Vineyard Stay
Address: 44 Donald Bruce Road, Surfdale,
Waiheke Island
Name: Susan and Neal
Telephone: (09) 372 5600
Fax: (09) 372 6205
Email: sunsethill@ihug.co.nz
Beds: 2 Queen, 2 Single (3 Bedrooms)
Bathroom: 1 Ensuite, 1 Private
Tariff: B&B (continental) Double $150
(2 persons) per night,
Single $150 (1 person, per night).
House $275 per night (6 persons). Credit Cards accepted.
Nearest Town: Auckland (35 min by ferry)

*Our vineyard guest house, set overlooking one of the oldest and largest stands of pohutukawa
trees on the island, has stunning sea views back to Auckland and Rangitoto. The house has
complete privacy and is only a short stroll in any direction to one of many secluded swimming
bays and is a 20 minute walk to Surfdale. For wine lovers staying on a vineyard offers an
intimate glimpse of the vineyard process and a taste of the wine (if available at the time of your
stay). The beautifully furnished house includes three bedrooms and two baths and can be
rented in smaller units, e.g. one bedroom w / ensuite and kitchen or two bedrooms, lounge with
a mini-bar and private bath. The house is equipped with TV, VCR, stereo, wood burning fire,
and laundry facilities.*
Home Page: http://members.xoom.com/kennedy point

Auckland Central

Self Contained Accommodation + Guest House

Address: Freeman's B&B Hotel & Apartments,
65 Wellington Street,
Freemans Bay, Auckland 1
Name: Fiona & Dan Perratt
Telephone: (09) 376 5046 Freephone: 0800 437 336
Fax: (09) 376 4052 **Mobile**: (025) 239 8026
Email: freemansbb@xtra.co.nz
Beds: 1 Triple, 9 Double, 4 Single
(12 Bedrooms + 4 Apartments)
Bathroom: 4 Ensuites, 1 Private, 2 Guests share
Tariff: B&b (Continental) Double $95, Single $65,
Children $15.   Credit cards accepted.   Breakfast optional extra.
Nearest Town: Auckland City

Freeman's is a friendly Bed & Breakfast Hotel located within ten to fifteen minutes walk of Auckland City, Victoria Park Markets, Ponsonby and harbour. Five minutes walk to Casino. Shuttles provide a 24 hour two-way service between the Airport and Freeman's. Our guest lounge provides complimentary tea, coffee and chocolate. A fridge, television and telephone are available for our guests' convenience. The lounge opens onto a secluded garden with a conservatory. We also have laundry facilities. Our healthy breakfast caters especially for the need of our energetic travellers. Our coffee is the best in New Zealand. We provide a friendly relaxed atmosphere and are always available to assist you in planning your stay in Auckland and New Zealand. Ask about car rentals, tours and all other travel arrangements. Freeman's the friendly guest house welcomes you to "your home away from home".

Home Page: www.freemansbandb.co.nz *or* www.outandabout.co.nz

Ponsonby

Self-Contained Cottage

Address: 43 Douglas Street,
Ponsonby, Auckland 2
Name: Ponsonby Potager
Telephone: (09) 378 7237
Fax: (09) 378 7267
Mobile: 025-272 7310
Email: raywarby@compusereve.com
Beds: 2 Double (2 bedrooms)
Bathroom: 1 Private
Tariff: B&B (special) Double $120, Single $90
Nearest Town: Auckland.   You're there! "Downtown" 2 Kms away.

Prepare to be pampered at the "Ponsonby Potager". Enjoy a "self-help" breakfast served in the garden room, or throw open the french doors and relax on the decks. We respect your privacy but are here to help.
The Potager is divided in two; you have your own entrance, bathroom, lounge and fully equipped kitchen. It is peaceful here but only 3 minutes walk to the shops, cafes and bars of Ponsonby or 5 minutes drive to the casino and city centre.   Your bedrooms have the finest linen, bathrobes, plenty of towels, fresh flowers and TV.   Fresh fruit always available. Complimentary laundry service.   Don't forget to pack your favourite CDs and tapes as you have your own entertainment centre as well as fax facilities, a small library of books and videos and Sky TV.

Ponsonby, Auckland Central
Homestay B&B
Address: 35 Clarence Street,
Ponsonby, Auckland City
Name: Colonial Cottage
Telephone: (09) 360 2820
Fax: 09 360 3436
Beds: 1 King, 1 Queen,
1 Single (3 bedrooms)
Bathroom: 1 Guests share
Tariff: B&B (special) Double from $100, Single from $80,
Dinner $25. Single party occupancy available; tariff from $200 depending on
number.
Nearest Town: Auckland city centre

Relax in the hospitable atmosphere of this turn-of-the-century Kauri villa offering delightful olde-worlde charm with modern amenities.
• Quiet inner-city location with green outlook.
• Short walk to Herne Bay, the Ponsonby Cafe Mile and quality restaurants.
• Handy to public transport including the City Link bus service to Downtown, Newmarket and Parnell.
• Easy distance to City attractions and motorways.
• Airport shuttle service available door-to-door.
• Smokefree Indoors.
• Health foods and special dietary requirements readily catered for with an emphasis on fresh seasonal produce, organic where possible.
• Radionics treatment and therapeutic massage available.
A ready welcome day or night. Please phone first.

Parnell, Auckland
Bed & Breakfast
Address: 34 Awatea Rd,
Parnell, Auckland
Name: Eleanor Manning
Telephone: (09) 379 4100
Beds: 2 Queen, 1 Double
(3 bedrooms)
Bathroom: 2 Guests share
Tariff: B&B (continental)
Double $90-$120,
Dinner $35. NZ B&B Vouchers accepted
Summer top Price Surcharge on vouchers
Nearest Town: (Centre) Auckland

Peaceful Parnell. Seaviews. Walking distance of Parnell shops and restaurants.
Seaside walks to waterfront via St Stephens Ave and overbridge.
Your hosts are keen to meet people from overseas and fellow Kiwis.
Directions available to places of interest.
Comfortable warm beds and good food.
Dinner on request.
Door to door shuttle.

122

Parnell, Auckland City

Guest House, Small Hotel
Address: 36 St. Stephens Avenue,
Parnell, Auckland 1
Name: Ascot Parnell
Telephone: (09) 309 9012
Fax: (09) 3093-729
Email: AscotParnell@compuserve.com
Beds: 9 Queen/Twin, 2 Single
(11 bedrooms, all with phone, private facilities and heating)
Bathroom: 10 Ensuite, 1 Private
Tariff: B&B (full) Double/Twin $145, Single $95, Superior $165-$185.
Cooked breakfast included. Parking available. All credit cards accepted.
Nearest Town: Auckland city centre 1 mile, Parnell Village 400m.

The ASCOT PARNELL - an elegant mansion in a subtropical garden - "is one of Auckland's most pleasant and atmospheric inns." (FROMMERS GUIDE NZ). All 11 charming guestrooms have bathrooms, telephones, heating and electric blankets. The intimacy of the ASCOT PARNELL makes it possible for the guests to enjoy a friendly service and personal attention. A delightful breakfast is served in a dining room which shows the beauty of this lovely home. Throughout the day tea, coffee and juice is served in the lounge. The airport shuttle stops in front of the house. Bus to all parts of the city every 10 minutes. We will help you to book tours, find reasonable priced rental cars and recommend shops and restaurants. Our house is a peaceful place to stay, very close to the city centre and within walking distance to many tourist attractions such as PARNELL VILLAGE, Auckland Museum and rose gardens. We also speak Flemish/Dutch, French and German.
We advise to book well in advance, you will recommend it.
Your hosts: Bart & Therese Blommaert.
Home Page: http://nz.com/HeritageInns/AscotParnell

THE REDWOOD
• CHARMING BED & BREAKFAST •

Parnell, Auckland City
Redwood Bed & Breakfast
Address: 11 Judges Bay Rd,
Parnell, Auckland
Name: Sherrie and Alan
Telephone: (09) 373 4903
Fax: (09) 373 4903
Mobile: (025) 758 996
Email: kotuku@wave.co.nz
Beds: 2 Queen, 4 Single (3 bedrooms)
Bathroom: 2 Ensuite, 1 Family share
Tariff: B&B (special) Double $100-$165, Single $75-$120, Extra adult $40, Children $25. Credit Cards: Visa/Mastercard. Off-street parking. NZ B&B Vouchers accepted $30-$50 surcharge (Oct-May)
Nearest Town: Auckland city centre 2km

The Redwood offers an eclectic ambience; our comfortable home is at your disposal. Stroll through our peaceful inner-city native garden and you will find a stand of tree ferns, Nikau palms and cabbage trees. Native birds frequent the garden and as we do you shall enjoy their evensong.

We invite you to use the lounge and deck from where you will experience our everchanging view of pleasure craft and shipping over the Waitemata harbour to Devonport and Mt Victoria. You will also breakfast with views of the harbour and have a choice of fresh fruit, yoghurt, cereals, daily baked muffins, breads and pastries, including an extensive cooked breakfast menu. We are located close to many popular attractions, including Parnell Village and its restaurants, the Auckland domain and museum, Kelly Tarlton's Underwater World and the salt water Parnell pools. If you are enjoying a day of sightseeing picnic hampers can be supplied on request. We are a one stop bus ride from the city centre and waterfront where you will enjoy the cinemas, theatre and many more restaurants. Door to door shuttle buses are available and the Airport bus stops close by. We are happy to advise and assist you with onward travel. Our rooms are comfortable and have queen or single beds with all the conveniences you would expect. A snack menu is available for our early arrivals or late departures. Sherrie offers a pre or post jet-lag therapeutic massage and other beauty therapy treatments. Alan is an interior designer and his company represents some of the top British and French furnishing and textile houses. English born, he visits Great Britain and Europe every few years. You will find us well-travelled and conversant on many topics of interest. We share our home with a liver Dalmatian NZ.CH. Kashflow of Kalesha, Kash to his friends. Sherrie has worked as an international flight attendant for more than a decade, she understands the needs of the discerning traveller and the service we offer is 'first class'. Fax and office facilities available. French and German spoken.

Home Page: http://www.cyberlink.com.au/bedbreakfast/Redwood

Parnell, Auckland City

Bed & Breakfast/Guest House
Address: 43 St Georges Bay Road,
Parnell, Auckland 1
Name: St Georges Bay Lodge
Telephone: (09) 303 1050
Fax: (09) 303 1055
Mobile: (021) 613 501 or (021) 613 105
Email: enquiry@stgeorge.co.nz
Beds: 2 King, 1 Queen, 1 Twin,
(4 bedrooms)
Bathroom: 3 Ensuite, 1 Private
Tariff: B&B (full) Double $185 or $225,
Single $165 or $185, Credit Cards (VISA/MC/Amex)
Tariffs are reviewed annually at 1st October.
Nearest Town: Auckland city centre 1.5km

St Georges Bay Lodge is an elegant Victorian Villa which has the charm of a by-gone era, with the comfort of modern amenities.
There is no better location for your stay in Auckland City. We are minutes from: picturesque PARNELL VILLAGE, designer boutiques and speciality stores, great cafes, restaurants, and night club life, health centres, swimming pools, gardens, parks, and the Museum in Auckland Domain and Holy Trinity Cathedral. Also within comfortable walking distance: Newmarket and the Central City business district the Casino, yet more restaurants and City night life, the University of Auckland, Waitemata Harbour, watersports, island destinations, ferry tours, and beaches in the City of Sails. At our back door, the Railway Station, buses and the motorway systems.
We have four refined guest rooms, each with central heating, tastefully and comfortably decorated. Relax in the many open living spaces from the beautiful lounge, to the light and airy conservatory, balcony and verandah. Start your day with a bountiful and healthy breakfast where every offering is fresh and natural - eggs, fruit, juices, yoghurt, muesli, croissants and muffins. We are sure you will appreciate the little extras we like to provide, such as speciality teas and coffee, alfresco mornings on the balcony ... and complimentary New Zealand port.
"We look forward to sharing our house with you. We like to offer service with style and are welcoming to all" - Alan and Wendy your hosts.

Parnell, Auckland
Bed & Breakfast

Address: 41 Birdwood Crescent, Parnell, Auckland
Name: Birdwood House.
Barbara Bell-Williams
Telephone: (09) 306 5900
Fax: (09) 306 5909
Mobile: (025) 777 722
Email: info@birdwood.co.nz
Beds: 4 KIng/Twin (4 bedrooms)
Bathroom: 3 Ensuites, 1 Private
Tariff: B&B (Special/Full) Double $155-$175,
Single $130-$150.
Not suitable for children.   Visa/Mastercard
NZ B&B Vouchers accepted Winter only, $60 surcharge.
Nearest Town: Auckland City 1.5 km

VERY CENTRAL SPECIAL BREAKFAST*
UNIQUELY AUCKLAND THEMED ROOMS*

Birdwood House is located adjacent to Auckland's exclusive PARNELL boutiques, 5 minutes by car from Auckland's central CBD, 4 minutes by car or a 10 minute flat stroll from Auckland's trendy fashion centre NEW MARKET, the AUCKLAND HOSPITAL, the DOMAIN, and the MUSEUM, ... we are VERY, VERY CENTRAL. A regular bus service links Parnell, the CBD, Auckland Hospital and New Market. The airport shuttle operates a 24 hour service to our front door (20 minute ride). Motorway access to Auckland's Southern, Western and Northern suburbs is only minutes away. Enjoy with us our 1914 NEWLY RESTORED, 'Arts and Crafts' Edwardian style character bungalow. We stand majestically in the prestigious suburb of PARNELL, overlooking Auckland city and the sky tower. Our elevated back view takes in the Auckland MUSEUM and the luxurious BOTANICAL GARDENS of the DOMAIN. Parnell village with its range of AWARD winning RESTAURANTS, ART galleries and BOUTIQUE shops is virtually on our doorstep. Birdwood House is located on the Parnell Historic Walk in amongst historic houses/buildings. The NEW MARKET business district is to the south and has a large selection of designer and speciality shops, cinemas and swimming pool and gymnasium. WAITEMATA HARBOUR with its sandy beaches, water sports and Kelly Tarltons Aquarium is close by. We can enhance your stay by arranging tours or by suggesting 'unique' Auckland things to do. At Birdwood House we embody Edwardian quality and hospitality. A HOME AWAY FROM HOME Birdwood House's original features include a beautiful KAURI staircase, delightful stained LEADLIGHT windows and a mesmerising inglenook FIREPLACE. Every bedroom in the house is decorated on a sumptuous theme such as the museum room which overlooks the Auckland's museum and the Cathedral room which reflects Parnell's newly renovated Holy Trinity Cathedral. After a comfortable nights sleep enjoy our healthy SPECIAL BREAKFAST with an emphasis on FRESH and in season produce. You can enjoy breakfast in bed if you are feeling decadent. Business facilities are available should you require to hold a meeting we have a separate lounge to accommodate your guests. You may encounter our cat "Chutney" and our small dog "Mandy", but they are confined to a separate living area. OUR AIM is to make your stay in Auckland memorable and cater for your individual needs. When we first saw this house it beckoned us to enjoy it, we invite you to join us and help us do the same. **Home Page**: www.birdwood.co.nz

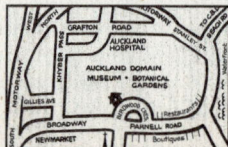

Amersham House

Parnell, Auckland
Bed & Breakfast
Address: Amersham House,
Corner of Gladstone Road and Canterbury Place,
Parnell, Auckland
Name: Jill and Robin Stirling
Telephone: 09-303 0321
Fax: 09-303 0621
Email: info@amershamhouse.co.nz
Beds: 1Super KingTwin, 1 King, 1 Queen, 1 Double (4 bedrooms)
Bathroom: 4 Ensuites
Tariff: B&B (full gourmet breakfast) $380, $280, $230.
Off peak and longstay rates available.
Nearest Town: Downtown Auckland (1 mile),
Parnell Village (1/2 mile)

Our guests enjoy Amersham House as much as we do. "Just like home",
"Absolutely exceeded all our expectations".
Elegant, Romantic and Relaxing, all our bedrooms are sunny and spacious
with Sky TV, phone, free in room internet and email service, and office
facilities. All en suites are unique and stylish. Perhaps select a room that
has an en suite with spa bath and double shower or choose one with a
private sauna. They all have great views, original art and top quality beds
and linen.
Our "oasis in the city" has a gas heated 10 metre pool surrounded by marble
and illuminated palms and orchids as well as an outdoor spa. Indoors, the
guest lounge and library has 180 degrees city to harbour views.
Your hosts have travelled extensively and live in a separate part of the home
with their two children . You can take our gourmet breakfast with fresh local
produce "al fresco" by the garden or pool, privately in our formal dining
room, or informally with your New Zealand born hosts.
Amersham House is a short easy walk to the restaurants and boutique shops
of Parnell and a little further to the Newmarket malls or to the museum,
Winter gardens and parks of the Domain.
Drive to downtown Auckland in 5 minutes or catch the hop-on hop-off
tourist bus.
Home Page: http://amershamhouse.co.nz

Parnell, Auckland
Bed & Breakfast Hotel
Address: Chalet Chevron,
14 Brighton Road,
Parnell, Auckland
Name: Brett and Jennie Boyce
Telephone: (09) 309 0290
Fax: (09) 373 5754
Email: chaletchevron@xtra.co.nz
Beds: 1 Queen, 5 Double, 2 King
16 Single (14 Bedrooms)
Bathroom: All ensuites.
Tariff: B&B (Full) Double/twin $108-$150, Single $78-$90, Children
$25. All credit cards accepted. Vouchers accepted surcharge may apply.
Nearest Town: Auckland city centre 2 kms

Chalet Chevron is a small hotel with old-world charm and extensive sea views, situated in fascinating Parnell, with its historic houses, interesting streets, shops and many restaurants. We are close to the Cathedral, Museum, Parnell Rose Gardens, Parks and Beaches and you'll find bustling Newmarket nearby. Hop on the handy cityloop bus into downtown Auckland and visit the Sky Tower and casino if you dare! We offer warm friendly Kiwi hospitality and will be pleased to help with tours, hire cars, sightseeing and shopping suggestions. Airport shuttles come to the door. Our comfortable bedrooms have direct dial phones, own bathrooms, electric blankets and heating. Enjoy breakfast in our sunny dining room while looking out at the sparkling Waitemata Harbour. You will love staying in Parnell, and we'll love having you here!

Grafton, Auckland City
Homestay
Address: 17A Carlton Gore Road,
Grafton, Auckland 1
Name: George & Janette Welanyk
Telephone: (09) 377 4319
Fax: (09) 377 4319
Mobile: (021) 377 431
Beds: 1 Twin, 1 Single (2 bedrooms)
Bathroom: 1 Guests share
Tariff: B&B (full or continental)
Twin $80, Single $60.
NZ B&B Vouchers accepted $7.50 Surcharge
Nearest Town: Auckland City centre 1km

From our home it is a ten minute walk to the centre of the city, Newmarket and the Museum. The university, hospital and Parnell Village are nearby. My wife and I invite you to stay with us, the house was built in 1925, is large and comfortable with excellent facilities.
Facilities for guests include a private sitting room with colour television, tea/coffee making and use of fax. Your hosts have travelled extensively overseas and welcome visitors. Private facilities - bathroom and sitting room by arrangement. We offer a discount for a stay of over 3 nights.
Directions: *From the Airport take the door to door shuttle minibus. Please telephone.*

Grafton
Bed & Breakfast Homestay

Address: Please 'phone
Name: "Farm Cottage"
Telephone: (09) 366 4669
Fax: (09) 366 4415
Beds: 2 Twin, 1 Single
(2-3 bedrooms)
Bathroom: 1 Guests share
Tariff: B&B (fresh and healthy continental style) $70-$150.
Nearest Town: Auckland central 2 1/2km

This turn-of-the century colonial cottage which started life as the farmer's dwelling reflects the personality and simplicity from that era. Nestled now in the central inner city environment of Grafton.
Comfortable and reassuringly homely in its style yet a reflection of a quieter time. A warm welcome awaits, created by rich red carpets, open fires and afternoon-sun verandah. Your accommodation will be an intimate TV lounge for your personal use adjoining little twin room and single room. Guest quarters include cottage's washing machine/drier. Suitable for one, two or three, plus two in a small upstairs attic. Private entrance for returning from your day's activities or nearby City, Parnell and Newmarket restaurants. Everything's a stroll away, but so is the Link-bus which is faster round these locations. Continental breakfast, your New Zealand host works too, but traditional home-style fare may be by special arrangement. Non-smokers please.
Directions: *Motorway exits - Khyber Pass, Gillies Avenue and Grafton.*

Mt. Eden, Auckland City
Bed & Breakfast

Address: "811 Bed & Breakfast"
811 Dominion Road,
Mt. Eden, Auckland 4
Name: David Fitchew & Bryan Condon
Telephone: (09) 620 4284
Fax: (09) 620 4286 **Mobile**: 025 289 8863
Beds: 2 Double, 1 Twin (3 bedrooms sharing 2 guest bathrooms).
Bedrooms with hot and cold hand basins.
Tariff: B&B (Full) Double $65 Single $45 includes cooked breakfast, home-made muffins etc. Tea & coffee always available. NZ B&B Vouchers accepted
Nearest Town: Auckland

All are welcome at 811 Bed and Breakfast. Your hosts Bryan and David, Pfeni and their Irish Water Spaniels welcome you to their turn of the century home. Our home reflects years of collecting and living overseas. Centrally located on Dominion Road (which is an extension of Queen Street city centre). The bus stop at the door, only 10 minutes to city and 20 minutes to airport, shuttle bus from airport. Easy walking to Balmoral shopping area (banks, excellent restaurants). We have operated a bed and breakfast on a farm in Digby County, Nova Scotia, Canada. The nicest compliment we can receive is when Guests tell us, it's like visiting friends when they stay with us. Our breakfast gives you a Beaut start to your day in a layed back atmosphere.
Directions: *From north-south motorway, Greenlane off ramp, continue on Greenlane, to Dominion Road. Turn left and we are 7 blocks on your right to 811 (between Lambeth and Invermay and across from Landscape Road).*

Mt Eden, Auckland City
Small Hotel
Address: 83 Valley Road,
Mt. Eden, Auckland 3
Name: Bavaria B&B Hotel
Telephone: (09) 638 9641
Fax: (09) 638 9665
Email: bavaria@xtra.co.nz
Beds: 5 King/Queen, 2 Double, 4 Single (11 bedrooms)
Bathroom: 11 Ensuite
Tariff: Delightful Breakfast Buffet, Double $120, Single $80, Children $12.50:
valid till 30.9.2000 Reduced rates in winter, Major Credit cards accepted. NZ
B&B Vouchers accepted $16 Surcharge/person.
Nearest Town: Auckland city centre 2km

*We invite you to stay at Bavaria B&B Hotel, a small professionally run hotel,
situated in the heart of Mt Eden, a quiet century-old suburb only 2km from the
city centre. All our 11 non-smoker rooms are furnished with private bathrooms,
telephones, suitcase racks, clock radios, heating and electric blankets. The 80-
year-old, completely renovated kauri villa is designed generously, the decor is
fresh and friendly and maintained immaculately. Enjoy sitting in our large sunny
lounge and meet other travellers or sunbathe on our private deck looking on to
an exotic small garden. Off-street parking available, city bus stop close-by. All
the necessary amenities and many fine restaurants in walking distance. We speak
English and German, offer first-class service and personal attention and are
happy to assist you with your travel plans i.e. recommend tours or inexpensive
rental vehicles.* **Home Page**: http://nz.com/webnz/bbnz/bavaria.htm

Mt Eden, Auckland
Bed & Breakfast Hotel
Address: 22 Pentland Avenue, Mt Eden, Auckland
Name: Pentlands Bed & Breakfast Hotel
Telephone: (09) 638 7031 **Fax**: (09) 638 7031
Mobile: (025) 339 928 **Email**: hoppy.pentland@xtra.co.nz
Beds: 2 Family, 5 Double, 3 Twin, 5 Single (15 bedrooms)
Bathroom: 4 guests share, 5 toilets.
Tariff: B&B (continental) Double/Twin $79-$99, Single $49-$59, Additional Adults $25/
night, Children $20/night. Credit Cards Vouchers accepted $10 surcharge pp
Nearest Town: Auckland

*Tourists, holiday makers, business people, families, sporting or cultural groups
are all welcome at Pentlands which is located in a quiet cul-de-sac in the heart of
Auckland. Pentlands is a stately villa, set in spacious, sunny grounds with
elevated views, native trees, a tennis court and picnic tables. The hotel has a large
guest lounge with TV (including Sky) and an open fire. It offers ample off-street
parking, laundry facilities, cooking facilities, guest phone, luggage storage plus
internet and fax facilities. 24 hour tea and coffee is included in the tariff.
Pentlands is a short walk from buses, supermarket, restaurants, cafes, shops,
banks, post office and Eden Park. Your hosts are friendly and helpful and are only
too pleased to assist you with car hire, travel and sightseeing arrangements.*
Directions: *From airport: Shuttle bus to the door. From city terminals: Phone
for directions. From south: Exit at Symonds Street from motorway SH1, turn left continue left
into Mt Eden Road, right turn into Valley Rd at Mt Eden Village. Third left into Pentland
Avenue. From the North: Exit at Gillies Ave; right into Owens Rd; right into mt Eden Rd; left
into Valley Rd. Pentland Ave is 3rd on the left.* **Home Page**: www.pentlands.co.nz

Epsom, Auckland City

Homestay
Address: 10 Ngaroma Road,
Epsom, Auckland 3
Name: Janet & Jim Millar
Telephone: (09) 625 7336
Fax: (09) 625 7336
Email: jmillar@xtra.co.nz
Beds: 1 King, 1 Queen, 2 Single (3 bedrooms)
Bathroom: 1 Ensuite, 2 Private
Tariff: B&B (full) Double $80-$90,
Single $60-$70, Children $15; Dinner $30.
Credit cards (VISA/Mastercard).
NZ B&B Vouchers accepted $15 surcharge
Nearest Town: Auckland - 5 km to City centre

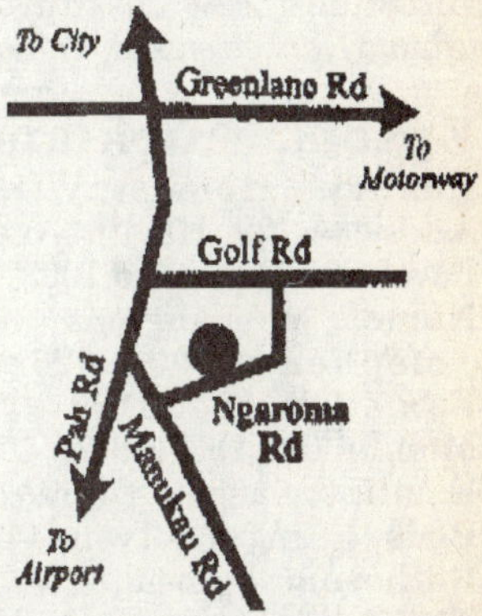

Our home, built of heart timber in 1919, is located in the middle of the isthmus, and on the lower slopes of One Tree Hill. We are within easy walking distance to its Domain, Cornwall Park, one of Auckland's loveliest parks with glorious views. Greenwoods Corner Village is at the end of our street and contains wonderful restaurants, P.O., the bus stop into the city, banking facilities and a magnificent china shop with many of Auckland's antique shops nearby. Our upstairs guest bedroom (Kingsize bed) has its own en-suite. The downstairs Garden Suite has a double bedroom and a large sun lounge complete with desk, twin beds (enabling us to cater for families), its own bathroom, refrigerator, and a laundry is available. It takes 10 minutes by car to downtown. We have three grown-up married children (one living in Finland), and six grandchildren. We enjoy meeting people and making them feel at home. We've travelled extensively overseas and in N.Z. and we enjoy exchanging experiences. No smoking indoors please.
Homepage: www.nz-travel.co.nz/brochure_rack/millars/homestay.htm

131

Epsom, Auckland

Homestay
Address: 2/7 Tahuri Rd,
Epsom 3, Auckland
Name: Kathy & Roger Hey
Telephone: (09) 520 0154
Fax: (09) 520 0184
Mobile: 021 642 652
Email: R.K.Hey@xtra.Co.NZ
Beds: 1 Super King size Double, 2 Single (2 bedrooms)
Bathroom: 1 Guests share
Tariff: B&B (continental) Double $80, Single $50, Children concessions, Dinner $20 by prior arrangement. Vouchers accepted March-Oct
Nearest Town: 4km from central city

In 1993 we built this lovely spacious 4 bedroom house, with ideal features for homestay. All comforts, and bedrooms offer views of One Tree Hill, Mt St John and Mt Hobson. Epsom is a very quiet garden suburb, with parks, restaurants, showgrounds, hospitals, postal facilities, banks and shops around us, one minute from the motorway. The Airport is 15 minutes away on door to door shuttle bus service. Excellent bus service two minutes walk away. We are extensive travellers, both in NZ and overseas, enjoy meeting people, swopping tales and helping guests feel at home. We will collect guests from the railway station, and can suggest a variety of Auckland attractions. Laundry facilities, off-street parking, juice, tea and coffee always available. Family groups welcome. We ask no smoking indoors.
Directions: *Leave Motorway at Market Road, travel west, cross over Great South Road, first left into Dunkerron Ave. Tahuri Road is 2nd left, we're at the end of the cul-de-sac.*

Epsom, Auckland

Luxury Homestay/Inn
Address: 29 Haydn Avenue,
Royal Oak, Auckland 1003
Name: The Langtons
Telephone: (09) 625 7520
Fax: (09) 624 3122
Mobile: 025 285 4493
Email: thelangtons@xtra.co.nz
Beds: 4 King or 4 Twin (4 bedrooms)
Bathroom: 4 Ensuite
Tariff: B&B (special) Double/Twin $185-$225,
Dinner Special $40-$50. Credit Cards (VISA/MC/AMEX/DINERS) accepted.
Nearest Town: Auckland City 5kms

Luxury accommodation with personal service and attention to your every need is what George and Sandra Langton offer you in their comfortable smoke free, tudor home. We are sited on the slopes of One Tree Hill bordering 450 acres of parkland with wonderful city views, just 10 minutes from central Auckland. The upstairs bedrooms are luxuriously appointed with ensuites, superior beds, bedding and furnishings. The main lounges, dining room and conservatory open onto large decks overlooking the swimming pool and garden. Food and wine are our special passion, with Sandra's knowledge of New Zealand wines, and George's experience in the hospitality industry we are able to offer an interesting blend of gourmet delights or even a picnic in the park. Our home is complimented by a collection of New Zealand works of art, and we also have two pets. Situated 10 minutes from the airport, our meet and greet service is available to all guests.
Home Page: www.thelangtons.co.nz

Epsom, Auckland
Guest House
Address: 18 Epsom Avenue,
Epsom, Auckland
Name: Cloudy
Telephone: (09) 630 7710
Fax: (09) 630 7710
Email: TYCHEN@ihug.co.nz
Beds: 3 Queen, 1 Double,
1 single (5 Bedrooms)
Bathroom: 1 Ensuite, 2 Guests share
Tariff: B&B (Full/Continental) Double $79-$99,
Single $65-$79. Credit Cards Visa/Mastercard
Nearest Town: Newmarket - Auckland City.

Taurima is a beautiful restored 70 year old villa in the residential part of Epsom. We are situated between Gillies Avenue and Manukau Road within 3 minutes of both northern and southern motorways and just 15 minutes from Auckland International Airport. The locality abounds with cafes and restaurants and Newmarket shopping, Mt Eden, Epsom Show Grounds and Alexandra Park Raceway are all within easy walking distance. Auckland City shopping and business centre and the world's most beautiful harbour is a 5 minutes drive. Taurima also features a fully self-contained four room Garden Cottage comprising bedroom, bathroom, kitchen and lounge. Tariff $90 per night double. Breakfast is not included in the Garden cottage. Extra adult $10. Children under 16 years stay free.

One Tree Hill, Auckland
Homestay+Self-contained   Accom.
Address: 39 B Konini Road,
One Tree Hill, Auckland 5
Name: Ron & Doreen Curreen
Telephone: (09) 579 9531
Fax: (09) 579 9531
Beds: Self cont. 1 King, (1 bedroom),
1 Sofa bed in lounge. Homestay: 1 Queen, 1 Double (2 bedrooms)
Bathroom: 1 Ensuite Homestay: 1Guest share
Tariff: B&B (Continental) King $75, Queen $65, Double $65, Single $45, Children $15, Dinner $25pp. Credit Cards.
NZ B&B Vouchers accepted -surcharge applies
Nearest Town: Newmarket

A warm friendly welcome awaits you at 39b.
Situated 15 mintes from the airport and city centre, our large contemporary home in a secluded garden setting on private right of way offers pleasant views and peaceful surroundings. We are close to Ellerslie Racecourse, One Tree Hill Domain, Alexandra Park, Epsom Showgrounds and Ericsson Stadium. Restaurants, antique shops, supermarket and bus service are a short distance away. Our spacious self contained unit has a large bedroom with king-sized bed, ensuite, lounge with TV, kitchenette, microwave, washing machine and extras. As an extaxi driver Ron can take you on sightseeing tours. Arrive as a guest - depart as a friend.
Directions: *Take Ellerslie-Pensrose exit on Motorway (1) North, or South to Great South Road. North to traffic lights, left into Rockfield, first right into Konini Road.*

One Tree Hill, Auckland City
Homestay
Address: 21 Atarangi Rd, Greenlane, Auckland 5
Name: Clare Ross & Winston Dickey
Telephone: (09) 523 3419,
Freephone 0800 254 419
Fax: (09) 524 8506
Email: homestay@xtra.co.nz
Beds: 2 Queen, 3 Single (4 bedrooms)
Bathroom: 1 Ensuite, 1 Guests share, 1 Family share.
Tariff: B&B (full) DoubleTwin $65-$85, Single $40-$60,
Dinner $15, Children one only.
Credit Cards NZ B&B Vouchers
Nearest Town: Newmarket - 3km North, Downtown Auckland 6km

Our comfortable non-smoking home has modern facilities and is situated on the lower northern slopes of One Tree Hill and this extinct volcano can be accessed through lovely Cornwall Park at the end of our short street. We have five restaurants within few minutes walk including European, Chinese, Nepalese and McDonalds. Downtown Auckland is 10 minutes away, Airport 20 minutes. Close by- Ellerslie races, Epsom trotting, NZ Expo, Ascot Hospital, Greenlane Hospital. Tea, coffee facilities and TV at all times. Off-street parking. We have one cat. We encourage guests to have the freedom of our home and grounds.
Directions: *Exit State Highway 1 motorway at Greenlane, head west - then left at traffic lights, then second right (Atarangi Road).*
Directions: *Ex Airport toward Auckland, exit motorway at Queenstown Road, follow route 12, 3.3km, turn right into Greenlane (Route 9). After passing the park turn first right then first left (Atarangi Road).*

Remuera
Homestay
Address: 'Lakeside',
18 Darwin Lane,
Remuera, Auckland 5
Name: Tony & Joanna Greenhough
Telephone: (09) 524 6281
Fax: (09) 524 6281
Email: lakeside.homestay@xtra.co.nz
Mobile: 025-272 9035
Beds: 1 Queen, 2 Single (2 bedrooms)
Bathroom: 1 Private, 1 Guests share
Tariff: B&B (full) Double $95, Single $75,
Double with private bathroom and lounge $140.
Nearest Town: Auckland City Centre 5km

Come and enjoy this unique location with its magnificent views to green hills right in the heart of the city, where all rooms overlook the water at the bottom of our peaceful garden. You can walk to local restaurants, or Lakeside is only minutes by car from the waterfront beaches and cafés, Parnell / Newmarket with its wider selection of restaurants and excellent shopping, the Museum, and many other visitor attractions.   Our house is interesting and thoroughly comfortable. Guest accommodation is in one wing with large bedrooms, spacious modern bathroom, sittingroom with television and coffee / tea making facility. There is plenty of off-street parking. We look forward to meeting you, and know you will enjoy your stay. **Directions**: *Door to door shuttle from the airport; by car take the Greenlane exit from the motorway.*

134

Remuera, Auckland City

Homestay

Address: 'Woodlands', 18 Waiatarua Rd,
Remuera, Auckland 1005
Name: Judi & Roger Harwood
Telephone: (09) 524 6990
Fax: (09) 524 6993
Mobile: (025) 270 6378
Email: woodlands@ake.quik.co.nz
Beds: 1 King, 1 Double, 1 Single (2 bedrooms)
Bathroom: 1 Ensuite, 1 Private
Tariff: B&B (special) Double $110-120, Single $90, Dinner $45pp, Children not suitable. Credit cards (VISA/MC).
NZ B&B Vouchers accepted Surcharge $30
Nearest Town: Auckland city centre 10km

Our two guest bedrooms overlook the pool and lush native greenery. The ensuite bedroom is larger and has french windows opening out to a private sunny Conservatory. The "Pink Room" has a private bathroom. Each room has tea/coffee making facilities, heated towel rails, coloured TV's and electric blankets. Both rooms are very quiet and private. There is safe off-street car parking. Central heating in the winter. Our breakfasts are special. Individual platters of seasonal fruits, homemade jams, yoghurts, choice of teas, or percolated coffee, then a full cooked breakfast of your choice. In the evening, join us for a candlelit Advanced Cordon Bleu dinner. We delight in serving NZ produce. Bookings essential. Guest book comments - "superb hospitality with delectable food", "Divine breakfasts", "Incredible dinners - wow". We are close to Motorways, Shopping Centres, Ericsson Stadium, Racecourses, Restaurants, Showgrounds, Hospitals, beaches and Downtown. No pets, one pet teenager! **Directions**: *Telephone, fax or write.*

Remuera

Bed & Breakfast

Address: 54 Seaview Road,
Remuera, Auckland
Name: The Brooks, Longwood
Telephone: (09) 523 3746
Fax: (09) 523 3746
Mobile: (025) 744 035
Email: longwood@ihug.co.nz
Beds: 1 Queen, 2 Single
(2 bedrooms)
Bathroom: 2 Ensuite
Tariff: B&B (full/continental) $80-$130.
Nearest Town: Parnell/Newmarket.

Longwood is a fully restored farmhouse, built in the 1880's. We have two guest rooms, each with ensuite and our spacious home features sunny verandahs overlooking the gardens and pool. Breakfast to suit - healthy or indulgent or a little of both. We are superbly located close to the shops, galleries, theatres and parks of Auckland City, Parnell, Newmarket and Remuera. We ask no smoking please indoors. We have a friendly cat.
Directions: *The airport shuttle will bring you to our door, or phone for easy directions.*
Home Page: http://homepages.ihug.co.nz/longwood/

Remuera, Auckland
Boutique Hotel
Address: 39 Market Road, Remuera, Auckland 5
Name: Aachen House
Telephone: (09) 520 2329 Freephone: 0800 AACHEN
Fax: (09) 524 2898
Email: info@aachenhouse.co.nz
Beds: 3 Californian King, 2 Super King, 2 King/Twin, 2 Twin (9 bedrooms)
Bathroom: 9 Ensuite, 1 Powder Room
Tariff: B&B (full) Suites $225-$310, Super King $203, King Single/Twin $170-$203. Children 16 years and over. Credit Cards.
Nearest Town: Auckland - 4 km from central city

Enter a timeless world where the qualities of excellence welcome you. Where each step is one into an era where graciousness abounds. Each stay is a further return to a hotel that recognises your appreciation of elegance, and attention to every small detail. This is a grand residence, truly a quality Bed & Breakfast Boutique Hotel for the selective traveller. This immaculately presented residence provides nine spacious guest rooms, each superbly decorated in period style. All rooms feature a luxuriously appointed ensuite bathroom and either Californian king, super king and king twin or twin beds. Guests rooms are complete with direct dial telephones, hairdryer, bathrobes and toiletries while four rooms have direct access to a private balcony. Disabled person facilities are provided in one of the king twin rooms. For the comfort and safety of guests, Aachen House is centrally heated and complies with modern international fire safety standards. Smoking is limited to outdoor areas.
Restaurants, parks, antique shops and public transport are within easy walking distance with major attractions, the airport, city centre and Auckland's renown harbour just ten minutes away by car. Easily located by leaving the main north / south motorway at the Market Road exit and following sign posting 300 metres to Aachen House. Guests arriving from the airport will find taxis or the airport shuttle bus readily available.
Home Page: www.aachenhouse.co.nz

Remuera
Homestay/Self-contained   Accom.
Address: 11B Kitirawa Road,
Remuera, Auckland
Name: Colleen Lea
Telephone: (09) 524 2325
Beds: 1 Queen (1 bedroom)
Bathroom: 1 Ensuite
Tariff: B&B (continental)
Double $70, Single $60. NZ B&B Vouchers accepted $10 Surcharge
Nearest Town: Downtown Auckland 7 km

Our home, set in one of Auckland most central suburbs, is situated up a short driveway in a quiet treed garden with spacious lawns, which we think, creates a feeling of tranquillity. We are only minutes from major shopping areas and many good restaurants. Should you feel you would rather go by bus the bus stop is a minutes walk around the corner and will take you to Remuera, Newmarket and Auckland city. You are assured of a relaxing stay in our "East Wing", modern self-contained accommodation with TV, lying to the sun and an outside deck to enjoy your breakfast on if you so wish. We will be pleased to direct you to Auckland's major attractions which are many and varied. We wish you to enjoy your stay in our city and our country. Smoking outside please.
Directions: *The airport shuttle bus will bring you to the door.*

Remuera
Homestay/B&B
Address: "Omahu House", 35 Omahu Rd,
Remuera, Auckland
Name: Omahu House
Telephone: (09) 524 9697
Fax: (09) 524 9997
Mobile: (025) 208 0469
Email: omahu@voyager.co.nz
Beds: 3 King/Twin, 1 Single (4 bedrooms)
Bathroom: 3 Ensuite, 1 Private
Tariff: B&B (full) Double $160, Single $120/$140, Dinner $40,
Children by arrangement. Credit Cards (VISA/MC).
Nearest Town: Auckland city, Newmarket, Remuera

"Omahu House", (Maori translation, quiet retreat) character bungalow in peaceful Remuera with off-street parking, minutes from city attractions, bus routes. Omahu House offers friendly personal care, comfort and complete privacy for visitors, - cool in summer (the pool is well used), central heating, fires in winter. Spacious rooms with ensuites, newly decorated, King, Twin beds, quality linens and furnishings, laundry facilities. Evening meals by arrangement, Shirley is Cordon Bleu certificated, breakfast served in / outdoors as light or hearty as desired. Smoking is a permitted outdoor activity, our cat provides company. Keith's speciality, NZ motor bike touring, his legendary tours made famous for their "off the beaten track" content. Keith's NZ touring knowledge is extensive. Omahu House, located by Market Rd Motorway off-ramps, travel to Remuera Rd, at Kings Junior School, turn into Omahu Rd - No. 35. We specialise in comfort with convenience, welcoming new and previous guests to our new venture Omahu House. **Home Page**: http:www//friars.co.nz/hosts/omahu.html or http://www.nz-travel.co.nz/brochure_rackomahu/house.htm www.home-farmstay-auck.co.nz

Remuera, Auckland
Bed & Breakfast
Address: 186 Upland Road,
Remuera, Auckland
Name: Gordon and Jo Thompson
Telephone: (09) 524 2666
Fax: (09) 524 6435
Mobile: (025) 272 7725
Beds: 3 Single (2 Bedrooms)
Bathroom: 1 Private,
Tariff: B&B (Full) Double $80, Single $60,
Not suitable for young children.
Nearest Town: Remuera

Jo and Gordon invite you to relax in our pleasant modern, smoke free home overlooking the Orakei Basin and only minutes from Parnell, Newmarket, the Central City and Ellerslie Racecourse.
Refreshments available in your own TV lounge with modern fire place. Telephone, fax, laundry, hairdrier available. Off street parking. Exclusive guest bathroom. We are keen on the Arts, music, gardening and have travelled extensively. We look forward to sharing our home with you. We have a Siamese cat.

Ellerslie
Bed & Breakfast
Address: 1/33 Roberts Street,
Ellerslie, Auckland.
Name: John & Mary Keir
Telephone: (09) 580 1022 or 0800 363 036
Mobile: (025) 289 9311
Email: http://nz.com/webnz/kotuku/
Beds: 1 King, 1 Queen (2 Bedrooms)
Bathroom: 2 Ensuite
Tariff: B&B (full or continental)
Double $90-$150, Credit Cards (VISA/MC)
Vouchers accepted Surcharge $30
Nearest Town: Thames 45km

WE ARE HERE
TO CITY
ELLERSLIE RACECOURSE
OFF-RAMP
STHN MOTORWAY
TO ROTORUA

LUXURY AT AFFORDABLE PRICES
Our comfortable home is very central being:
1 minute to Ellerslie racecourse, Function Centre, C/T club and corporate houses. 3 minutes to Alexander Park Showgrounds, Greenlane Hospital, Cornwall Park, Newmarket and Ericson Stadium. 6 minutes to Museum, city downtown, Casino and waterfront. 1 minute to Ellerslie motorway ramp and 3 minutes flat walk shops and restaurants. Our modern home has large bedrooms each with their own ensuite, hairdryer, TV, heater, and coffee making facilities. Each bed has been especially selected for a good nights rest. We are a friendly retired couple who have been in the hospitality sector for several years and having travelled extensively both within New Zealand and overseas feel we have something to offer the discerning visitor. Email office and laundry services are available. There is ample off street parking. Rental cars can be arranged and we offer free pick up and return to the airport. **Home Page**: john.keir@xtra.co.nz

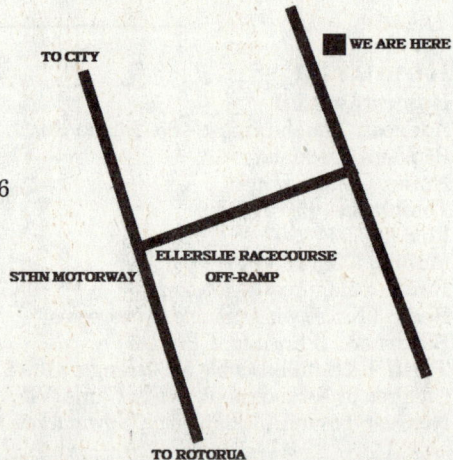

Ellerslie, Auckland

Homestay
Address: 'Taimihinga', 16 Malabar Drive, Ellerslie, Auckland 5
Name: Marjorie Love
Telephone: (09) 579 7796 **Fax**: (09) 579 7796
Beds: 1 Double, 3 Single (3 bedrooms)
Bathroom: 1 Ensuite, 1 Host share
Tariff: B&B (continental) Double Ensuite $80, Single $60. Downstairs
(family share) Double $70, Single $50. Dinner $25pp by arrangement,
Full breakfast on request, Credit Cards. NZ B&B Vouchers accepted
Nearest Town: 8km to city centre (12 mins on Motorway), 5 mins to
Newmarket and Remuera. Ellerslie, short walk.

Taimihinga = softly calling o'er the ocean. Answer the call - enjoy the welcome!
Ellerslie has LOCATION, LOCATION, LOCATION! This convenient, comfortable,
indoor-outdoor home and garden is situated in a quiet cul-de-sac with a pleasant
northerly outlook. A special pleasure is sharing Auckland's particular attractions
with travellers and business people from overseas and other parts of New
Zealand. The motorway is close - 1km - and Ellerslie affords ready access to most
places of interest around Auckland. Nearby are Ellerslie and Alexandra Park
Racing, Showgrounds/Expo Centre, several conference venues, Central Park
Business area, all the hospitals, One Tree Hill Domain, Ericsson Stadium. Also local
parks, sports, gymnasiums, cinemas and restaurants. Public transport -train and
bus- to city. Interests: Family now in faraway places, people, travel, the Arts,
church (Anglican), Probus, gardening, tennis. Tea, coffee and cookies in rooms,
hairdryer, bath robes, laundry, fax. A smoke-free home. Convenient shuttle service available
at airport. **Directions**: *Please phone, fax or write.*

St Johns Park, Remuera, Auckland

Homestay
Address: 47 Norman Lesser Drive,
St Johns Park, Remuera, Auckland 1005
Name: Jean & Neville Taylor
Telephone: (09) 521 1827
Fax: (09) 521 1863
Email: jean.neville.taylor@xtra.co.nz
Beds: 3 Single (2 bedrooms)
Bathroom: 1 Guests share
Tariff: B&B (full) Double $90, Single $45.
NZ B&B Vouchers accepted $20 Surcharge on twin
Nearest Town: Downtown Auckland 8 kms

Relax with tea, coffee or cold drink in our conservatory, comfortable lounge or
courtyard garden on arrival. Our smoke free home with off street parking is warm
and comfortable in a quiet residential area which surrounds Remuera Golf
Course. All beds have electric blankets, cosy duvets and patchwork quilts.
Laundry and ironing facilities are available and we have smoke alarms installed
in bedrooms. We are a retired couple who have travelled extensively in Europe,
UK, USA and New Zealand. Choosing to stay in B&B accommodation ourselves
we understand your needs, and can cater for them. Our interests include Travel,
Quilting and Patchwork, Gardening and Probus. There is a range of restaurants
nearby. Bus stop to and from Auckland City at gate. We are handy to Tamaki
University Campus, Adventist and Ascot Hospitals. **Directions**: *Greenlane Exit*
from Motorway. Shuttle Bus from Auckland Airport. Phone for directions;

Orakei, Auckland

Homestay
Address: "Sealladh"
2/9 Rewiti Street, Orakei,
Auckland 1005
Name: Heather and Bill Nicholson
Telephone: (09) 522 2836
Mobile: (025) 211 7186
Fax: (09) 522 9666
Email: sealladh@xtra.co.nz
Beds: 1 King, 2 Single (Twin)
Bathroom: 1 Ensuite for King, 1 Private for Twin
Tariff: B&B (Full) Double $120-$150, Single $90, Dinner $30.   NZ B&B Vouchers accepted $45 surcharge
Nearest Town: Auckland City Centre 5 mins

Welcome to our modern sunny and spacious home. Enjoy the views from the King bedroom and exclusive guest lounge which has stereo, TV, video, piano, library and mini kitchen including complimentary tea and coffee. A full breakfast is served in the sunny dining room or "al fresco". We have plenty of secure off street parking and laundry facilities are available. Close to amenities in a quiet residential area we are 5 minutes to restaurants, cafes, theatres, CBD and casino. Five minutes to beaches, Kelly Tarlton's Underwater World, harbour cruises and many other tourist attractions. 10 minutes to racecourses and northern and southern motorways. Enjoy many local scenic walks, a short stroll to post office and bus stop. Warm and friendly hospitality is assured. We have travelled extensively in New Zealand and overseas. No smoking indoors please.
Directions: *Airport Shuttle to door.   Phone/fax.*

Mission Bay, Auckland

Homestay
Address: 41 Nihill Crescent,
Mission Bay, Auckland
Name: Jean and Bryan
Telephone: (09) 528 3809
Beds: 1 Double (1 bedroom)
Bathroom: 1 Private
Tariff: B&B (full) Double $80, single $60,
Dinner $25 pp.   Credit Cards accpeted.
NZ B&B Vouchers accepted $12 surcharge
Nearest Town: Auckland (10 mins drive)

We warmly welcome you to our modern split level home. The upper level is for your exclusive use featuring sunny north facing patio, double bedroom, fully equipped bathroom and private lounge if preferred. Only 5 minutes walk to Mission Bay beach - cafes and restaurants. The stunning waterfront with its ever changing vista of yachts, marine activities and the unsurpassable islands on the Gulf.
The water front is a walkers' paradise (host to the world famous "Round the Bays Run"). Or should you prefer we are only 10 minutes scenic bus or car ride to downtown Auckland and the ferry terminal, harbour and islands in the Gulf. We are retired and have enjoyed living and visiting in many parts of the world. We look forward to sharing our special part of Auckland with you. Airport shuttle bus to our door, please no smoking, please phone for directions.

Kohimarama Beach, Auckland City

Homestay

Chalet on the Park

Address: Chalet-on-the-Park,
19 Baddeley Avenue,
Kohimarama Beach, Auckland
Name: Trish and Keith Janes
Telephone: (09) 521 2544.
Freephone 0800 360 544 **Fax**: (09) 521 2542
Mobile: (025) 397 116 **Email**: chalet@bigfoot.com
Beds: 2 Queen (2 Bedrooms)
Bathroom: 1 Private, 1 Family share
Tariff: B&B (Special/Full) Double $90, Single $70, Dinner $25 pp, Children $25. Credit cards: Visa/MC/Diners/Amex. Vouchers accepted $15 surcharge
Nearest Town: Auckland downtown 8 km.

Kohimarama Beach is a marine suburb central to all Auckland activities. We have travelled all over New Zealand and extensively overseas. Stayed in B&B and delight in showing guests our city. Our child-free chalet overlooks a park and is a short flat walk to three beaches for swimming, shopping, banking and fifty restaurants. All year we offer complimentary sailing on the worlds finest harbour and gulf, and bicycles for cycling around the bays. Picnic hampers are a speciality $8 p.p. Guests occupy entire top floor (Keith will carry your bags). Guest lounge and sunny deck. Laundry facilities available and tea / coffee anytime. Special breakfast menu choice. Traditional 3 course dinner (roast lamb) $25 pp with prior notice. No smoking indoors please. Our interests include travel, other cultures, hospitality and yachting. Shamus is our Irish Setter. Only one group at a time. Free use of e-mail. **Directions**: *Take airport shuttle to our door, or Freephone 0800 360 544 for directions.*

St Heliers, Auckland

Self-contained Accommodation

Address: 51 Cliff Road,
St Heliers, Auckland
Name: Jill Mathew
Telephone: (09) 575 4052
Fax: (09) 575 4051
Mobile: 025 769405
Beds: 1 King (1 bedroom)
Bathroom: 1 Ensuite
Tariff: B&B (continental) Double/Single $195.
Nearest Town: St Heliers 200 metres, Auckland 8km (5 miles)

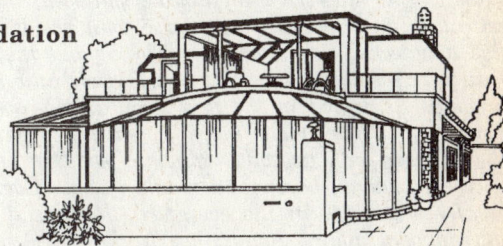

For those who would like to enjoy breathtaking views from sheer cliffs high above a succession of some of Auckland's most famous beaches, Mission Bay, St Heliers, Kohimarama, pleasure yachts silently gliding by their windows, cruise ships, ocean liners and harbour ferries leaving and entering the harbour day and night, this may be where you would like to stay for two nights (minimum) or more that four nights (at discount rates). Just across the road you can make your way down an easy winding track to Ladies Bay, always secluded often deserted, to bathe or fish in the "Sparkling Waters" of the Waitemata Harbour or you may just indulge yourself, rise late enjoy a bountiful continental breakfast while you survey the whole inner harbour, much of the Hauraki Gulf and some of the inner islands from this exclusive guests apartment in a prestage area surrounded by top quality executive homes.

St. Heliers
Boutique Bed & Breakfast

Address: "Seaview Heights",
23A Glover Road,
St. Heliers Bay, Auckland 5
Name: Anthea & John Delugar
Telephone: (09) 575 8159
or 0800 398 902
Fax: (09) 575 8155
Mobile: (025) 854 659 **Email**: seaview@seaview.co.nz
Beds: 2 Super King/Queen, 2 King Single (3 bedrooms)
Bathroom: 2 Ensuites, 2 Guests share
Tariff: B&B (full) Room rate Double $130-$260,
Single from $110. Children are welcome. Credit Cards (VISA/MC/BC).
Nearest Town: Auckland central 15 mins St Heliers 2 mins Airport 35 mins

TELECOM/TOURISM AUCKLAND "SPECIALITY ACCOMMODATION" FINALIST
Ich spreche Deutsch/Je parle français/Hablo español/Parlo italiano
Seaview Heights is set high on a hill, 250 metres back from the cliffs at St. Heliers Bay, and backs onto a tranquil park, the crater of an extinct volcano. There are extensive sea views from many rooms, overlooking yachts and pleasure boats enjoying Auckland's beautiful Waitemata Harbour. Close to the city, yet very peaceful, with no traffic noise. Only a 2 minute drive or a 5/10 minutes stroll past the park, down Cliff Road to the beach, restaurants, cafes at St. Heliers Bay, or to a bird sanctuary nearby with many native birds. The house comprises three levels and has a majestic quality and feeling of grace and space. An impressive spiral staircase leads up to the guest bedrooms on the top floor. The Bay View Suite has a king-size bed, double spa-bath, and balcony - a perfect honeymoon retreat. The Park View suite, also with ensuite bathroom, overlooks the Park and has a balcony with seaviews. Throughout the house fine antiques and Mediterranean decor contribute to the stylish and restful atmosphere. A delicious breakfast is served in the first floor dining-room overlooking the Bay: fresh fruit platter; hot home-made muffins; muesli; yoghurt and choice of cooked breakfast dishes (eggs with avocado, salmon; egg benedict; herb omelette; french toast with slices of banana, bacon and maple syrup. Courtesy car available to drive you to local restaurants in the evening. John is a lawyer. He is very interested in international affairs. Anthea has worked in Germany, Switzerland and Spain. She is an interpreter of German, French, Spanish and Italian and has been a tour-guide throughout New Zealand. They have a son Andrew, aged 26 and a daughter, Charlotte, aged 23. They all promise you a warm welcome. They have a cat, Tui, and a Golden Retriever dog, Amber. Sorry, our house is smoke-free. Fax and e-mail available. **Directions**: *From City, take Tamaki Drive to St. Heliers, halfway up Cliff Road, turn into Springcombe, then Glover Rd. OR from Motorway: Green Lane exit; Remuera Rd; St. Johns Rd; then St. Heliers Bay Rd. to seafront, then Cliff Rd, Springcombe, Glover Rd. Shuttle bus/taxis always available at airport.* **Home Page**: http://www.friars.co.nz/hosts/seaview.html
http:nz.com/webnz/bbnz/seaview.htm

St Heliers Bay
B&B Homestay
Address: "The Totara", 1/17 Glover Road,
St Heliers Bay, Auckland
Name: Peter & Jeanne Maxwell
Telephone: (09) 575 3514
Fax: (09) 575 3582
Mobile: (025) 284 0172
Email: maxwell.totara@clear.net.nz
Beds: 1 Queen, 1 Twin (2 bedrooms)
Bathroom: 1 Guests Exclusive
Tariff: B&B (full) Double or Twin $120.00, Single $90.00.
Sorry, not suitable for children. Credit Cards accepted.
Nearest Town: St Heliers Bay 2 mins, Auckland C.B.D15 mins

*St Heliers Bay, one of Auckland's premier waterfront beaches only 15 minutes drive from the central city following the 'waterfront drive' - **don't miss it.** Come and stay with us in our modern home overlooking picturesque Glover Park 5 / 10 minutes walk from the beach, cafes, restaurants, shopping and banking / postal facilities. Enjoy a latte or meal overlooking the harbour. Start the day with our hearty cooked breakfast - take a bus to the city - Kelly Tarlton's Antarctic & Underwater World - cruise the Waitemata Harbour and visit the islands in the gulf and much much more. We are happy to assist with your sightseeing and travel plans. Our bedrooms with tv are warm and sunny with your comfort in mind - relax with tea / coffee in our guest lounge overlooking the park. Peter and I together with Sophie (our lucky black cat) **look forward to your stay.** Please no smoking indoors.*
Directions/ Bookings: *Phone-fax-email.*
Home Page: http://www.nzhomestay.co.nz/totara.htm

St Heliers, Auckland
Bed & Breakfast
Address: 102 Maskell Street,
St Heliers, Auckland
Name: Jill and Ron McPherson
Telephone: (09) 575 9738
Fax: (09) 575 0051
Email: ron&jill_mcpherson@xtra.co.nz
Beds: 1 Queen, 2 single (2 bedrooms)
Bathroom: 1 Private
Tariff: B&B (continental) Double $110,
Single $65. Not suitable for children/pets.
NZ B&B Vouchers accepted $20 surcharge
Nearest Town: Auckland city (12 mins drive)

We welcome you to our modern home with off street parking in a smoke free environment. Only one group of guests are accommodated at a time. Having travelled extensively ourselves both in New Zealand and overseas we are fully aware of tourists' needs. Only 8 minutes walk to St Heliers Bay beach, shops, restaurants, cafes, banks and post office. A picturesque 12 minute drive along the Auckland waterfront past Kelly Tarlton's Antarctic Encounter and Underwater World to Downtown Auckland. Our grown up family have left home and are now living in various parts of the world and are left at home with Tabitha the cat. Our interests including all sports, gardening and Jill is a keen cross stitch embroiderer.

St Heliers, Auckland

Homestay, Bed & Breakfast
Address: 15 Tuhimata Street,
St Heliers, Auckland
Name: Pippi's Bed and Breakfast
Telephone: (09) 575 6057
Fax: (09) 575 6055
Mobile: (021) 989 643
Email: pswells@xtra.co.nz
Beds: 1 Queen, 1 Double (2 Bedrooms)
Bathroom: 1 Ensuite, 1 Private
Tariff: B&B (Continental or Full) Double $135, Single $110.
NZ B&B Vouchers accepted $90 surcharge. Credit Cards accepted.
Nearest Town: St Heliers Village 400 metres, Auckland city 15 mins by car along scenic Tamaki Dr, 10 mins drive to motorways.

Our character home with picturesque peaceful cottage garden offers guests a sunny, restful retreat. The spacious bedroom has level access with TV, stereo, tea/coffee making facilities, and Italian tiled ensuite bathroom. A delicious breakfast of fresh fruit, home-made bread, muesli etc.., and/or full breakfast, juice, espresso coffee or tea, is served in our dining room, or on the garden deck. Winter evenings are warmed by cosy fire and gas heating, and beds have electric blankets. Telephone, fax, email, hairdryer, laundry facilities and off street parking available. We are a short walk from St Heliers beautiful harbour beach, shops and restaurants. Bus stops are handy, and nearby is Mission Bay with cafes and restaurants, 4 cinemas, Kelly Tarlton's Underwater World and outdoor activities. We have a gentle golden retriever, a toy poodle and dainty pussycat. Our home is smoke free. We look forward to offering you a warm welcome.
Home Page: http://mysite.xtra.co.nz/~OooPippisBedAndB/index.html

---

Mt Roskill, Auckland

Homestay
Address: 29 Maioro Street,
Mt Roskill, Auckland
Name: Helen & Des Doyle
Telephone: (09) 626 4195
Fax: (09) 626 3013
Beds: 1 Double, 2 Single (2 bedrooms)
Bathroom: 1 Guest share
Tariff: B&B (full) Double $65,
Single $40, Children $15, Dinner $20
Nearest Town: Auckland City Centre 20 minutes.

We invite you to share our home which is very central to most locations in Auckland and is also on a main bus route. We enjoy meeting people from far and near and look forward to making your stay an enjoyable one. A full cooked breakfast is provided and we welcome you to join us for dinner by arrangement. Off street parking is available for guests with their own transport. Non smokers and no pets preferred. We are 20 minutes from Downtown Auckland and 10 minutes from two major shopping centres, St Lukes and Lynmall.
Directions: *Shuttle bus to and from Auckland Airport. Please phone ahead for other directions.*

Titirangi, Auckland
Homestay
Address: "Kaurigrove",
120 Konini Rd,
Titirangi, Auckland 7
Name: Gaby & Peter
Telephone: (09) 817 5608
Mobile: 025-275 0574
Beds: 1 Double,
1 Single (2 bedrooms)
Bathroom: 1 Guests share
Tariff: B&B (special) Double $85,
Single $45, Children negotiable.
Credit cards (VISA/MC).
NZ B&B Vouchers accepted $20 surcharge
Nearest Town: Auckland, 20 minutes to Downtown by car.

Welcome to our home! Situated at Titirangi, the gateway of the Waitakere Ranges and Auckland's historic West Coast with its magnificent beaches and vast native bush areas!
Nearby are other attractions such as the Titirangi Golf course, cafes, restaurants and walking tracks. Gaby and Peter, your hosts of German descent, are keen trampers themselves and are happy to introduce you to the highlights of Auckland and its surrounding areas.
P.S. Non smoking inside residence.

Avondale, Auckland
Christian Community
Address: 31b, Cradock Street, Avondale,
West Auckland. ,
Postal: P O Box 19404, Avondale
Name: Kodesh Christian
Community(Sue or Gayle)
Telephone: (09) 828 5672
Booking essential
Fax: (09) 828 5684
Email: kodesh@xtra.co.nz
Beds: 1 Double, 1Double/single,
2 Single (4 bedrooms)
Bathroom: 2 Guests share + 2 toilets
Tariff: B&B (continental) Double $45, Single $30 Dinner $8. NZ B&B Vouchers accepted $5 surcharge for 1 night stay.
Nearest Town: Auckland 11Kms

Kodesh is an ecumenical (interchurch) Christian community situated in a quiet cul-de-sac in Avondale, West Auckland - 8 minutes by car from downtown and on good bus and train routes. Most members of the community go out to work each day and are actively involved in various churches and parishes around Auckland. The average number of residents is 25, including families and singles. Our guest rooms are situated in a large modern home and cooking facilities are available. An evening meal is served in the communal dining room weekdays and guests are welcome, bookings are essential by midday. The atmosphere is casual and relaxed and guests can amalgamate into the life of the community as much or as little as they desire. Longer term accommodation is available by negotiation.

145

Hillsborough, Auckland
Homestay, Self Contained Accommodation
Address: 'Hillsborough Heights Homestay",
434a Hillsborough Road,
Hillsborough, Auckland
Name: Sandra and Ian Burrow
Telephone: (09) 626 7609
Fax: (09) 626 7609
Mobile: (021) 626 760
Beds: 2 Queen, 2 Double (2 Bedrooms)
Bathroom: 2 Ensuites
Tariff: B&B (Full) Homestay Double$100, Single $70.
Self Contained $100 Double, Dinner $25, Children by arrangement. Credit cards accepted. Vouchers accepted $30 surcharge for self contained (Double)
Nearest Town: Auckland city 15 mins; Manukau city 15 mins, by car.

A warm welcome to our beautifully appointed new Mediterranean-style home and garden overlooking the Manukau Harbour, 12 minutes from Auckland airport. City buses stop at our gate. Stay in our delightful upstairs room (private TV room, luxury bathroom with spa bath) or in our downstairs self-contained apartment (bedroom, bathroom, lounge including sofa-bed, kitchen, dining, TV). Laundry available. Relax on your own; socialise with us; experience our home theatre system. Golf courses, swimming pool, gym within 5 minutes; major shopping centres within 10 minutes, or we can direct you to Auckland's many attractions. Breakfast alfresco in the garden, sunny kitchen conservatory, or ask for room service. Barbecue available. 3-course dinner available on request. Nearest restaurant 200 metres. Smoking outside please. Ian is an architect, and our interests include travel, garden (20 plus hanging baskets), sport, music, antiques (extensive collection of blue and white china). **Directions**: *Please phone for reservations and directions.*

Auckland Airport - Mangere
Homestay
Address: 288 Kirkbride Rd., Mangere
Name: May Pepperell
Telephone: (09) 275 6777
Mobile: 025 289 8200
Beds: 3 Single plus single fold-away bed (2 bedrooms)
Bathroom: 1 Guests share
Tariff: B&B (continental) Double $60, Single $40, Children negotiable, Dinner $15. NZ B&B Vouchers accepted
Nearest Town: Papatoetoe 5km

My clean comfortable home is only five minutes from the airport but not on the flight path so there is no aircraft noise. Ten minutes from five large shopping centres and Rainbow's End amusement park. Within walking distance to our local centre, restaurants and take-away bars. Lakeside Convention Centre is three minutes away, also Villa Maria Winery. The Aviation Golf Course is situated near the airport and green fee players are welcome. My interests are golf, travelling, meeting people and Ladies Probus, and I am involved in voluntary work. An evening meal can be provided by arrangement. Beds have woollen underlays and electric blankets. There is a sunny terrace and fenced swimming pool. Courtesy car to/from airport at reasonable hour. On bus route to city. Vehicles may be left while you are away from $1 per day.

Mangere Bridge, Auckland
Homestay
Address: 146 Coronation Rd, Mangere Bridge
Name: Carol O'Connor & Brian Thomas
Telephone: (09) 636 6346
Fax: (09) 636 6345
Beds: 2 Double, 2 Single (3 Bedrooms)
Bathroom: 1 Guests share, 1 Family share
Tariff: B&B (full) Double $60, Single $40, Children half price, Dinner $15. NZ B&B Vouchers accepted
Nearest Town: Auckland City 14km, Manukau City 14km

We invite you to share our home which is within 10 mins of Auckland Airport an ideal location for your arrival or departure of New Zealand. We enjoy meeting people from far and near and look forward to making your stay an enjoyable one. A full cooked breakfast is provided and we welcome you to join us for dinner by arrangement. We provide a courtesy car to and from airport, bus and rail depots. Off street parking is available for guests with own transport. If you smoke we ask that you do so outdoors. We request no pets. Inspection welcomed.
Directions: *Please phone.*

Auckland Airport, Mangere Bridge
Homestay, Self Contained Accommodation
Address: 34 Andes Avenue,
Mangere Bridge, Auckland
Name: Bob and Helen Lindsay
Telephone: (09) 634 2132
Fax: (09) 634 2132 Mobile: 025 288 3640
Beds: 1 Queen. 1 Bed Settee (1 Bedroom)
Bathroom: 1 Ensuite
Tariff: B&B (Full) Double $80 (Self contained), Single $40, Dinner $15, Children $15. NZ B&B Vouchers accepted $20 surcharge, Credit Cards accepted.
Nearest Town: Auckland 16 km, Manukau 16 km, Mangere Bridge Town 2 km.

Our home is a few steps on to Kiwi Esplanade and next to a Regional park with sheep, cows and lots of native birds, and beautiful views of the Manukau. We share our home with one teenage daughter and a small dog, a parrot and a cat. BBQ facilities are available or restaurant and take-away bars are close by.
We are 10 minutes form Auckland airport and can offer you a peaceful location for your arrival or departure from New Zealand or relax with a long cool swim in outdoor pool in summer or leisurely cycle along Kiwi Esplanade. Parking available for guests with own transport, otherwise taxi or shuttle bus can be arranged.
Directions: *Please phone, fax or write.*

Mangere Bridge
Homestay, Self Contained Accommodation
Address: 5 Feltwell Place,
Mangere Bridge, Auckland.
Name: Kathleen and Jack Longair
Telephone: (09) 634 8377
Mobile: (025) 206 5927 **Fax**: (09) 634 8377
Email: magicp@xtra.co.nz
Beds: 1 Queen, 1 Double, 2 Single (3 Bedrooms)
Bathroom: 1 Private, 1 Family share
Tariff: B&B (Full/Continental) Queen $90. Double $70, Single $40,
Dinner $25, Children $15.
Credit cards accepted. NZ B&B Vouchers accepted $20 surcharge.
Nearest Town: Auckland City 16 km. Manuka City 16 km. Mangere
Bridge 2 km.

We offer you a taste of the Irish cum Kiwi experience. Minutes walk from Kiwi Esplanade in a quiet cul-de-sac is our "Garden of Eden" complete with fully fenced swimming pool, luscious trees and BBQ area. Take a walk through Ambury Regional Park/Farm, explore the dormant volcano which is Mangere Mountain. Enjoy a round of golf or a game of tennis at The Aviation Club. Sample the wines at Villa Maria Winery.
Continental breakfast provided (or full breakfast at extra charge). Dinner provided by prior arrangement at extra cost. No smoking or pets please. We are only 10 mins from Auckland airport. Guest wing with separate entrance and parking, with wheelchair entry.
Directions: *Please phone, fax or write.*

http://www.bnb.co.nz

take a look

Otahuhu, Auckland City

Homestay
Address: 70 Mangere Road, Otahuhu, Auckland
Name: Gerard & Jerrine Fecteau
Telephone: (09) 276 9335
Fax: (09) 276 9235
Beds: 1 Queen, 1 Double, 2 Single (3 Bedrooms)
Bathroom: 2 Guests share
Tariff: B&B (full) Double $60, Single $40, Children half price, Dinner $20. Credit cards. NZ B&B Vouchers accepted
Nearest Town: Auckland 20 mins

Gerard and Jerrine offer you Canuck-Kiwi hospitality in their comfortable home in the most central location in Auckland, Otahuhu. The motorways and trains are just minutes away and the airport simply 10 minutes down the road. If you begin your Kiwi holiday and want to plan your route or rent a bargain rental car - we can help you. If you want to rest before the long flights "home" - #70 is the rest stop and handy for the early morning flights. Washing facilities available.
We are collectors of amazing things and have an interesting variety of many cactus, coins of the world, coloured depression glass tableware, native Canadian art, brass, glass birds and a cat called Alice.
In addition to breakfast you are invited to join us for lunch and dinner by arrangement.
Please phone, fax or write to reserve. Our courtesy van to pick you up at the airport, train or bus.

Chapel Heights - Manukau City

Homestay
Address: "Tanglewood",
5 Inchinnam Rd,
Chapel Heights, Manukau City
Name: Roseanne & Ian Devereux
Telephone: (09) 274 8280
Fax: (09) 634 6896
Email: rocklabs@clear.net.nz
Beds: 1 Queen, 1 Double,
2 Single (3 bedrooms)
Bathroom: 1 Ensuite, 1 Guests share
Tariff: B&B (full) Double $80, Single $60, Children $10, Dinner $20,
Credit Cards: Visa. NZ B&B Vouchers accepted
Nearest Town: Manukau City 6.5km, Howick 5km

We welcome you to 'Tanglewood'. Our cottage with its 2 acres is in a country setting, but close to the international airport. The Garden Loft is separate from the house and overlooks the garden and pond. It has an ensuite, TV, fridge, and table and chairs. We have accommodation inside the house, with own bathroom. We are 2 minutes from beautiful bush walks, 25 minutes from downtown Auckland, close to Regional Botanic Gardens, beaches, and golf courses. We have travelled extensively and enjoy meeting people. Delicious home cooked breakfast including eggs from our free range hens. You can join us for dinner, or by candlelight by the fire, or served on our terrace on a summer evening. There are several good restaurants close by. We have a swimming pool, large peaceful gardens, and a friendly Labrador dog, Daisy. We are non-smoking. Booking is essential, please. **Directions**: *For directions: please phone*

Half Moon Bay, Auckland

Homestay
Address: "Endymion Lodge",
21 Endymion Place, Half Moon Bay
Name: Dave & Helen Jeffery
Telephone: (09) 535 8930
Fax: (09) 535 8042
Mobile: (025) 951 038
Email: helenj@xtra.co.nz
Beds: 1 Queen, 1 Single (2 bedrooms)
Bathroom: 2 Private
Tariff: B&B (full) Double $90, Single $55, Dinner by arrangement $30.
Most credit cards accepted.Vouchers accepted $30 surcharge applies
Nearest Town: Howick 10 mins, Pakuranga 10 mins

Endymion Lodge is situated in a cul-de-sac on a sunny, north facing rise above Half Moon Bay marina with views to Rangitoto Island and Bucklands Beach. You will find us on the eastern side of Auckland, within walking distance of local buses or a fast ferry ride to Downtown Auckland. Our area offers nice beaches, great walks, excellent golf courses, good shopping, theatres, cafes and the historic Howick Colonial Village. Join us in our lounge or enjoy the privacy of your own self contained area comprising bedroom, own bathroom facilities, lounge, kitchenette plus tea and coffee making facilities. We also run sailing charters on our 40ft yacht and offer day sails or extended cruising on the glorious Hauraki Gulf. Laundry facilities available for use. **Directions**: *Pick up from airport can be arranged. Please phone for reservations and directions.*
Home Page: http://www.sailingholiday.co nz

Manurewa, Auckland

Homestay
Address: 16 Collie Street,
Manurewa, Auckland 1702
Name: Graham & Katrine Paton
Telephone: (09) 267 6847
Fax: (09) 267 6847
Mobile: (021) 215 7974
Beds: 1 Double, 3 Single (3 bedrooms)
Bathroom: 1 Ensuite, 1 Guests share
Tariff: B&B (full) Double $70, Single $45, Children half price. Dinner $15. Credit cards NZ B&B Vouchers accepted
Nearest Town: Manukau City, 5 minutes north

Our sunny, spacious home is in Hillpark, a pleasant suburb of Manurewa. We are 15 minutes from Auckland Airport, 20 minutes from Auckland City Centre, by motorway, gateway to the route south and Pacific Coast Highway. We warmly welcome you to our home, assuring you of a comfortable stay. We have a Tonkinese cat. Beds have electric blankets and fleecy wool underlays. Within 2 kilometres is the Manukau City Shopping Centre, Rainbow's End Adventure Park, restaurants, Cinemas, factory and souvenir shops, Nathan Homestead Community Arts Centre, Regional Botanic Gardens (Ellerslie Flowershow), Totara Park, and bush walks. Golf courses, scenic country drives and beaches are in the area. Graham is Fund-raising Co-ordinator for the Red Cross, while Katrine is a part-time Primary School teacher. Our interests include painting, pottery, gardening, classical music, Christian interests, photography, reading, woodwork and travel. Laundry facilities available. We're a smoke-free home. **Directions**: *Please phone.*

Manurewa, Auckland

Country Homestay

Address: "Top of the Hill Homestay", Fitzpatrick Road, Brookby, Manurewa, Auckland

Name: Trevor & Pat Simpson

Telephone: (09) 530 8576

Fax: (09) 530 8576

Mobile: (025) 288 0835

Email: topofthehill@nzhomestay.co.nz

Beds: 2 Queen, 4 Single (4 bedrooms)

Bathroom: 4 Ensuite

Tariff: B&B (full) Double $110, Single $75, Dinner $30 pp. Sorry, not suitable for children. Credit Cards (VISA/MC).

Nearest Town: Manukau City 15 mins. Auckland city/Airport 25mins.

"Brookby-Auckland's best kept secret". Gateway to the Pacific Coast Highway, this beautiful valley is just over the hill from Clevedon Village and offers guests a unique, relaxing environment. Our spacious new home, designed and built by Trevor, has all the comforts to make your stay with us a special one. The luxurious guest wing containing four large bay windowed bedrooms with tiled ensuites all command awe-inspiring landscape and sea views.The guest lounge has panorama windows where you can sit in comfort just enjoying the view, or wander over our 42 acres. Visit friendly farm animals, take a bush walk at night with Trevor to see the glow worms. Enjoy Pat's tasty home cooking, try a summer BBQ under the "Southern Cross". Jessie our friendly dog, as we do, greatly looks forward to welcoming you. **Directions**: *Follow the Pacific Coast Highway signs from Manurewa to Brookby, sign posted "Homestay" from Alfriston School.*

Home Page: http://ww.nzhomestay.co.nz/simpson.htm

Manurewa, Auckland

Homestay

Address: "Manuka House", 176 Hill Road, Manurewa, Auckland 1792

Name: Margrit and Joe Fullemann

Telephone: (09) 267 8159

Mobile: (021) 216 2630

Email: mf.jm@xtra.co.nz

Beds: 1 King, 2 Double, 1 Twin (4 bedrooms upstairs)

Bathroom: King has ensuite, 2 Guests share

Tariff: B&B (Full) King $100, Double $80, Single $50.

Credit cards: Visa/Mastercard.

Nearest Town: Manukau City 5 mins north, 25 mins to Downtown Auckland, 15 mins. to Airport.

Relaxed comfort awaits you in our spacious, sunny and quiet home. The Regional Botanic Garden and Totara Park are within walking distance.
Margrit your host (original from Switzerland) is a trained beauty therapist and Homeopath and runs a clinic from home. So as well as quality comfort in our well appointed home you can avail yourself to a range of treatments that will pamper the body and soul as you enjoy your stay.Joe & Margrit look forward to making your time with us as memorable and enjoyable as you would wish. Our interests are gardening, cooking, painting and meeting people in our smoke-free home. **Directions**: *Take Manurewa motoway off ramp, turn left into Hill Rd. Bookings essential.*

Howick, Auckland

Homestay

Address: The Fishers, 'Above the Beach',
141 Mellons Bay Road, Howick, Auckland
Name: Marjorie and Max Fisher
Telephone: (09) 534 2245
Fax: (09) 534 2245
Email: kea.nz@ibm.net
Beds: 1 Queen, 1 Double, 2 Single (4 bedrooms)
Bathroom: 1 Ensuite, 1 Private, 1 Guests Share.
Tariff: B&B (Continental) Double $80-$100, Single $55. Dinner by request.
Credit cards (Visa/Bankcard/MC) Vouchers accepted $15 surcharge
Nearest Town: Howick 1/2 kilometer. Pakuranga

Relax with us in our comfortable home 50 metres "Above the Beach". Kauri trees growing through our decks and lovely sea views to Rangitoto and Waiheke Island. We are 20-25 minutes from the airport, 16 kilometers to Auckland by road and just a 35 minute ferry ride to and from the city. Howick is a delightful village on the east coast, with at least 14 restaurants, an historic church, colonial village, 6 beaches, 2 golf courses - and the Auckland ferry all within a 2 mile radius. Our double rooms have feather duvets, electric blankets, heaters, and individual decks looking on to bush and see. Easy chairs, lounge suite, fridge and TV's for your convenience. Tea and coffee complimentary. We can advise on places of interest, rental cars etc. We offer -A Home Away From Home- and super breakfasts. We look forward to meeting you - Marjorie and Max.
Directions: *Shuttle from airport. Please phone ahead for more directions. Please no smoking indoors.*

Howick (Auckland)

Homestay

Address: "Cockle Bay Homestay",
81 Pah Road, Cockle Bay, Howick, Auckland
Name: Jill & Richard Paxman
Telephone: (09) 535 0120
Fax: (09) 535 0120
Mobile: (021) 685 638 **Email**: cocklebay.homestay@clear.net.nz
Beds: 1 Queen, 1 Twin/King (2 bedrooms)
Bathroom: 1 Ensuite, 1 Private
Tariff: B&B (continental/full) Double $85-$110, Single $70-$100,
Dinner by arrangement $30pp. Credit Cards Visa/Mastercard.
Vouchers accepted $30 surcharge for Queen Room. No surcharge for Twin/King.
Nearest Town: Howick 3km

Welcome to "Cockle Bay Homestay". Situated in a quiet location at the gateway to "Pacific Coast Highway and the Seabird Coast, and 20 minutes from Auckland airport / City. Howick is one of the oldest settlements in New Zealand being one of the original four settlements established around 1847, many of the original buildings still exist. As our home is elevated we have panoramic sea views looking towards Little Barrier Island, Waiheke Island and many other islands of the Hauraki Gulf. Experience the sun rises over the Coromandel. Five minute walk will take you to the beach and historic Windross Restaurant. A ferry ride from Howick to the City - a delightful way to see the harbour, use the bus at end of driveway to City. Guest rooms are spacious and comfortable with sea views. Our small dog wins the hearts of all our guests. Off street parking and laundry facilities available. **Directions**: *Transport to / from the airport can be arranged. Please telephone for directions. Non smokers.*

Bucklands Beach

Bed and Breakfast
Address: "Hattaway House",
42 Hattaway Avenue,
Bucklands Beach, Auckland
Name: Sue and Bernie Drumm
Telephone: (09) 534 4592
Fax: (09) 534 4592 **Mobile**: (021) 653 443
Email: bernie.drumm@xtra.co.nz
Beds: 2 Queen, 1 Single (3 Bedrooms)
Bathroom: 1 Ensuite, 1 Guests share
Tariff: B&B (Continental) Double $100-$120, Single $80.
Not suitable for children.
Nearest Town: Howick 10 mins, Pakuranga 10 mins

Sue, Bernie and Charlotte (aged 9) welcome you to "Hattaway House" one of Bucklands Beach's original homes, elegantly restored and extended in 1991 offering you complete comfort and privacy with "olde worlde charm". Our guestrooms provide a quiet and restful atmosphere to help make your stay a peaceful and memorable one! A substantial continental breakfast is offered. Each room is tastefully decorated and has heating, robes, TV, tea and coffee making facilities, comfortable warm beds, iron and ironing board. A guest lounge is available for your leisure, an open fire will welcome you in winter - choose a good book and relax. Or in summer, lounge in our spacious summerhouse or cool off in the pool. Enjoy a stroll along the beach - golf, boating, fishing, restaurants all within 5 minutes walk, bus 2 mins walk, and ferry to the city from nearby Halfmoon Bay.
Directions: *Shuttle bus from the Airport or phone for directions.*

Beachlands

Homestay
Address: 51 Wakelin Road,
Beachlands 1705
Name: Enid and Terry Cripps
Telephone: (09) 536 5546
Fax: (09) 536 5546
Beds: 1 Queen (1 Bedroom)
Bathroom: 1 Private
Tariff: B&B (Full/Continental)
Double $80, Single $50, Dinner $25 pp by arrangement. Credit cards:
Visa/Bankcard/Mastercard. NZ B&B Vouchers accepted $10 surcharge
Nearest Town: Howick 25 km

Enid and Terry offer you a warm welcome to the Marine Garden suburb of Beachlands which is situated on the East Coast, 40 km South East of Auckland City. Our converted cottage is only 3 minutes walk form the beach at Sunkist Bay, local shops and licensed restaurant. The Formosa Auckland Golf Course and Pine Harbour marina are 5 minutes drive away.
We are both in our early 60's, have travelled widely and share our home with a shy cat. Guest accommodation is a large upstairs bedroom with sitting area, TV and a shaded balcony facing the sea. You are welcome to share the downstairs lounge with us or relax in your own room as you please.
Directions: *Shuttle bus from the Airport or phone for directions.*

Whitford
Farmstay
Address: Springhill, Polo Lane, Whitford, Auckland, (Postal: R.D. Manurewa)
Name: Derek & Judy Stubbs
Telephone: (09) 530 8674
Fax: (09) 530 8274
Beds: 2 Queen, 2 Single (3 bedrooms)
Bathroom: 2 Ensuite
Tariff: B&B (full) Double $75, Single $50, Children $25, Dinner $25pp by arrangement. NZ B&B Vouchers accepted
Nearest Town: Auckland 30 km, Howick, 12 km

Springhill is a 16 hectare farm situated in Whitford, an attractive rural area approximately 30km south east of Auckland, and 12km from Howick, a village suburb rich in early European settler history. We are only 2km from a beautiful golf course and 10km from Hauraki Gulf beaches. Most of the farm is planted in pine trees. We breed Angora goats and have some sheep, assorted bantams, two cats and two dogs. We have a large comfortable home and spacious garden, BBQs being a specialty during the summer. We enjoy travelling and Derek is a keen sailor. Our guest accommodation is one double bedroom with ensuite and a large area above the garage, comprising one double room, bathroom and a room with 2 single beds and seating. Ideal for families with children. Both rooms have TV and tea and coffee making facilities. We welcome guests to join us for dinner by arrangement.
Directions: *Left off Whitford Park Road 1km past golf course or please phone.*

Clevedon
Countrystay, Self contained Accomodation.
Address: 816 North Road, PO Box 72, Clevedon
Name: A. Hodge
Telephone: (09) 292 8707
Fax: (09) 292 9266
Mobile: (025) 984 102
Email: hodgebb@wave.co.nz
Beds: 1 Twin, 2 Single (3 bedrooms)
Bathroom: 1 guests share
Tariff: B&B (full) Double $70, Single $40, Children half price, Dinner $20; Campervans welcome. Self-contained 2 bedroom unit, sleeps 5, one ensuite unit sleeps 3. Credit cards accepted. NZ B&B Vouchers accepted.
Nearest Town: 40 km from Auckland, 23 km from Papakura

Relax in a peaceful environment, 35 minutes from Auckland International Airport in a rural community that has a wide range of farming activities. Views from our comfortable home include the lower reaches of the Wairoa River Valley from Clevedon, Waiheke and other small islands in the Hauraki Gulf to the distant Coromandels. We offer a range of guest accommodation, B&B with own bathroom, 2 self contained motel style units, 1 sleeps 5 with full cooking facilities, 1 sleeps 3 with tea and coffee. Meals, BBQ and games room are available. Activities that are available with hosts or nearby include fishing boat trips, sheep shearing, bush, farm, beach walks, horse riding, dairy and orchard farm visits. We are available by prior arrangement to greet you at plane, train or coach. Kitty, the cat resides somewhere in the garden. **Directions**: *Clevedon is 14 km east of Papakura. Our home is on the left on North Road, 9 km from Clevedon.*

Clevedon
Country Homestay
Address: 'Willowgrove', Clevedon, Kawakawa Bay Road, RD 5, Papakura
Name: Brian & Eileen Wallace
Telephone: (09) 292 8456
Fax: (09) 533 1136
Mobile: (025) 954 605
Email: ciwallace@clear.net.nz
Beds: 1 Double, 2 Single (2 bedrooms)
Bathroom: 2 Ensuite
Tariff: B&B (full) Double $90, Single $50,
Children half price. Dinner $25. NZ B&B Vouchers accepted
Nearest Town: Clevedon 10 mins, Papakura 20 mins, Auckland 40 mins.

We are situated near the beginning of the Pacific Coast Highway, the gateway to the Coromandel, Bay of Plenty, Eastland and Hawkes Bay. Clevedon is a rural village with restaurants, craft shops, all services and a range of rural activities. On our property of about 11 acres we raise cattle and sheep and grow all our own vegetables. The house is set in a large garden which has a very restful atmosphere. We have hosted guests from many countries over the last 10 years and look forward to meeting you. Our main guest room is a large upstairs room with its own lounge area, TV and an ensuite. The second bedroom is on the ground floor with twin beds and also has an ensuite. You may share our family room and lounge or relax in your room.
Directions: *Please phone. If required we can collect from airport or public transport.*

Clevedon
Country Home Stay
Address: 'Fairfield',
Kawakawa Road,
Clevedon,
R.D. 5, Papakura
Name: Christopher & Paddy Carl
Telephone: (09) 292 8852
Fax: (09) 292 8631
Email: carl.fairfield@xtra.co.nz
Beds: 1 Queen (1 bedroom)
Bathroom: 1 Ensuite
Tariff: B&B (full) Double $110,
Single $80, Dinner from $40 pp by arrangement. Credit Card - Visa.
Nearest Town: Clevedon 10 mins, Papakura 20 mins, Auckland 40 mins

Our Ranch Style house is on a hill, set in 14 acres with extensive rural views and a glimpse of the sea. Mangere airport and Auckland city are 40 minutes away, and there are many lovely beaches nearby leading to the pretty scenic route to the Coromandel. We offer a self-contained bed-sitting room with ensuite and own private courtyard. The room has a television and coffee and tea making facilities. Local activities such as fishing, golf and horse riding can be arranged. We are both well travelled; Paddy is involved in the fashion industry and Chris retired after 35 years as a Naval Officer with the New Zealand Navy. We welcome you to join us in our comfortable spacious home.
Directions: *7kms from the roundabout at Clevedon down the Kawakawa Road or please telephone.*

Clevedon - Auckland

Heritage Inn
Address: 'Birchwood', R.D. 3,
Clevedon, Auckland
Name: Birchwood. Ann & Mike Davies
Telephone: (09) 292 8729
Fax: (09) 292 8555
Email: birchwood@xtra.co.nz
Beds: 1 King, 1 Queen (2 bedrooms)
Bathroom: 1 Ensuite, 1 Private
Tariff: B&B (special) King $195,
Queen $180.
Credit cards (VISA/MC/AMEX).
Nearest Town: Clevedon 5 mins, Manukau 10 mins, Auckland City/
International Airport 20 mins.

"Birchwood"

Enjoy the gracious and relaxing atmosphere of this lovingly restored country house (circa 1887). We have 2 guest rooms offering the ultimate in away from home comfort - fine linens, fresh flowers, robes and toiletries.
Breakfast to suit - healthy or indulgent or a little of both, served in the large farmhouse kitchen or al fresco by the pool. We are located 20 minutes from Auckland Airport / central city, in the picturesque Clevedon Valley (on Pacific Coast Highway). Minutes from restaurants, golf courses, polo grounds, Botanical Gardens, beaches and tourist trails. A great central location. No smoking indoors. Enjoy Birchwoods 'old-worlde' charm and warm hospitality.
Directions: *Please phone - bookings advisable.*
Home Page: http://nz.com/HeritageInns/Birchwood.htm

Kaiaua, 'Seabird Coast'

Homestay
Address: 'Corovista', 1841B East Coast Road,
Waharau, Kaiaua R.D.3, Pokeno, Auckland
Name: Bob & Julia Bissett
Telephone: (09) 232 2842
Fax: (09) 232 2862 **Mobile**: (025) 245 5269
Beds: 1 Super King/2 Singles, 1 Double (2 bedrooms)
Bathroom: 1 Guests share, 1 Family share
Tariff: B&B (full) Main Bedroom Super King/2 Single: $90, Single $50.
Double Bedroom: $65, Single $40, Dinner (3 course) $30 pp includes freshly caught fish in season. Credit Cards. Vouchers accepted $25 surcharge
Nearest Town: Thames 53 km, Pukekohe 55 km, Manukau City 72 km

Our home "COROVISTA", is so named because of its commanding and panoramic views of the Coromandel Ranges which rise above a foreground of the Hauraki Gulf and sparkling waters of the Firth of Thames. Surrounded by a delightful garden, the home's elevated position with its full length deck designed for the view has a private guest wing. The added advantage of this locality, is its placement upon the recommended scenic route south of Auckland through Clevedon, and its near proximity to the Hunua Parklands, an internationally recognised bird sanctuary and thermal hot springs at Miranda, with fishing, tramping and picnicking also available. We, your hosts, are widely travelled and offer warm hospitality to local and overseas guests. We retired within easy reach of the city, to a peaceful rural area, and our desire is to share it with those who travel this beautiful country. We have a small terrier that lives outdoors. Our interests are varied and include golf, arts, crafts, music and the pleasure of a comfortable smoke free home. **Directions**: *Please phone.*

Kaiaua
Homestay
Address: "Kaiaua Seaside Lodge",
1336 Pacific Coast Highway, Kaiaua
Name: Fran Joseph and Denis Martinovich
Telephone: (09) 232 2696
Fax: (09) 232 2699
Mobile: (025) 274 0534
Email: Kaiaua_lodge@xtra.co.nz
Beds: 2 Queen, 1 Double, 3 Single (5 bedrooms)
Bathroom: 2 Ensuite, 1 Guests share
Tariff: B&B (special/full)   Double $85-$105,
Single $55.   Dinner by arrange ment.
Nearest Town: Thames 30 minutes, Auckland Airport 55 minutes

Kaiaua Lodge is situated right on the water's edge with panoramic views of the Coromandel across the Firth of Thames.   The Seabird Coast is renowned for its birdlife, Miranda thermal pools and nearby Regional Parks.   Kaiaua Lodge is also ideally positioned for visitors who enjoy a leisurely stroll along the seashore or a more active tramp through the Hunua Ranges.   Boating and fishing facilities are available and Fran is happy to cook your catch for you.   Breakfast includes flounder or snapper, in season.   A range of accommodation is available from 2 large bedrooms with ensuites to other bedrooms furnished with double or single beds.   There is a separate guest lounge with television and a fridge.   The Lodge is easily found on the Pacific Coast Highway (scenic route), one hour south of Auckland and 3 km north of Kaiaua township, famous for "the best fish n chips in New Zealand".

Papakura
Homestay
Address: "Hunua Gorge Country House"
482 Hunua Road, Papakura
Name: Joy, Ben & Amy Calway
Telephone: (09) 299 9922
Fax: (09) 299 6932
Mobile: (021) 669922
Email: hunua-lodge@xtra.co.nz
Beds: 1 King suite, 1 Queen room, 1 Twin room,
1 Single, 2 Bunks (5 bedrooms)
Bathroom: 1 Ensuite, 1 Private, 1 Family share (wheelchair)
Tariff: B&B (full) King $120, Queen & Twin $90, Single $80, incl. afternoon tea & full breakfast. 3 Course dinner with NZ wines on request $45.   Credit Cards (VISA/MC).
Nearest Town: Papakura 5 mins, Auckland airport 25 mins, Auckland city 25 mins.

Welcome to our beautiful wilderness on the doorstep of Auckland City.   A great place to start and end your New Zealand holiday.   Peace, tranquillity, great food, magic sunsets, wild scenery, leafy greenery, views from all rooms.   Large comfortable newly decorated home, verandahs, lawns, garden, bush and rural setting on 50 acres with sheep, ponies and cattle, birdlife ponds and stream.   Stay a few days and discover the wonders of Auckland or learn to ride a horse.   We can arrange anything from wine or farm tours to horse and trap rides or scenic flights, airport transfer not a problem.   We are well travelled 40's interested in food and design, travel and wine, sport and people from all walks of life.   Fresh food, fresh air, comfortable beds, guaranteed.   Please phone

Papakura

Homestay
Address: Campbell Clan House,
57 Rushgreen Avenue, Papakura
Name: Colin and Anna Mieke Campbell
Telephone: (09) 298 8231
Fax: (09) 298 7792
Mobile: (025) 967 754
Email: colam@pl.net
Beds: 1 Queen, 2 Single (2 Bedrooms)
Bathroom: 1 Guests share
Tariff: B&B (Full) Double/Twin $90, Single $50,
Dinner $25 pp, Children half price. Credit Cards accepted.
Nearest Town: Papakura 2 mins; Airport 15 mins; Auckland CBD 25 mins.

Colin and Anna Mieke welcome you to their Mediterranean styled family home which is 2 minutes from the Southern Motorway. Our north facing bedrooms and large guest lounge (with TV, library and tea / coffee making facilities) open onto an upstairs balcony overlooking Pahurehure reserve and estuary. Guests can choose whether to have meals privately upstairs or join us in our family living area downstairs. Anna Mieke specialises in Mediterranean and Asian cooking but particularly enjoys outdoor entertaining and BBQ meals throughout the summer months. Having travelled extensively, mainly Britain and Europe, we welcome overseas guests and are happy to help with holiday arrangement, airport transport, rental vehicles etc. We operate a business from our home office and can offer fax and internet facilities by arrangement. Guests may use our laundry. A 15 minute walk to Papakura will find restaurants, shopping, swimming pool, sports facilities and Regional and Intercity buses and trains. **Directions**: *Please phone*

Drury

Country B&B
Address: "Briardale", 23 Maxted Rd, Ramarama, RD3 Drury.
Name: Archie and Sue McPherson
Telephone: (09) 294 7417
Fax: (09) 238 7592
Mobile: (025) 736 313
Email: sue.mcpherson@icn.co.nz
Beds: 1 Queen, 2 Single/King
(2 Bedrooms)
Bathroom: 2 Guests Share
Tariff: B&B (Full) Double $100, Single $50.
Dinner by arrangement. Children negotiable.
Nearest Town: Papakura and Pukekohe 10mins. Auckland 30 mins. Airport 20 mins.

Briardale Bed and Breakfast

Briardale offers warm country hospitality in a delightful rural setting, just a minute from the Southern Motorway. Guests can mingle with the hens, ducks, doves and friendly sheep on the 2.5 hectare hobby farm at Auckland's southern gateway. A stand of native trees attracts a variety of native birds including tui, blue heron, fantails, wood pigeon and kingfishers. A flock of cheeky rosella parakeets also visits the picturesque property. Accommodation is limited to two guest rooms to ensure a restful and private visit. Guests are welcome to stroll through the large garden, enjoy the spa pool (Jacuzzi) or a game of petanque or lawn croquet. Archie and Sue have travelled extensively and have worked in the food and media industries for more than 30 years. They will greet you as enthusiastically as Oscar the schnauzer and Katie the west highland terrier. No smoking in the house please. **Directions**: *Take Ramarama on / off ramp from Southern Motorway, Maxted Rd is 3rd right on Ararimu side of Motorway.*

Drury

Homestay In The Country
Address: 'Tuhimata Park',
697B Runciman Road, R.D.2, Drury
Name: Pat & Susan Baker
Telephone: (09) 294 8748
Fax: (09) 294 8749
Email: tuhimata@iprolink.co.nz
Beds: 2 Double, 2 single (3 bedrooms)
Bathrooms: 1 Ensuite, 1 Guests share
Tariff: B&B (full) Double with Ensuite $110 - Single $70; Other Double $100 - Single $60: Twin $90 - Single $55: Children - special discount, Dinner by arrangement $25-$30pp; Campervans $15pp including breakfast. VISA & Mastercards accepted. NZ B&B Vouchers accepted Surcharge $25
Nearest Town: Papakura & Pukekohe 10 mins, Auckland 30 mins, Airport 20 mins.

An ideal place to start or finish a New Zealand holiday. A large, comfortable, family home in a setting of giant oak trees and an expansive lawn, in the country but close to the city, only 20 minutes from the Airport and 3 minutes from the Southern Motorway. Also available are: tennis court, spa pool (hot tub), billiard/pool table, table tennis, swimming pool, indoor BBQ, TV in all bedrooms, and lovely wide covered verandahs, large comfortable lounge, and a huge conservatory with an indoor garden. Guests can relax in the spacious setting which overlooks pretty green countryside. Pat and Susan have travelled widely and have entertained overseas visitors for many years. As well as 35 years of dairy farming behind them they have been extensively involved in NZ politics and education. We have a family cat. Laundry facilities available. **Directions**: *Please phone for directions.*

Hunua

Homestay
Address: Nairns Road,
RD 3, Papakura, Auckland
Name: Bonami House
Telephone: (09) 292 4191
Fax: (09) 292 4291
Beds: 2 Double, 2x1 Single (4 bedrooms)
Bathroom: 1 Private, 2 Guests share
Tariff: B&B (full) Double $80,
Single $60, Children $15, Dinner $25.
Nearest Town: Papakura 10 minutes / Clevedon 15 minutes

A large comfortable home set on a elevated position surrounded by 15 green gentle sloping acres.
With decks taking in the views of the Hunua Ranges. Hunua is best known for its many bush walks. The Hunua Falls, the Cossey, Wairoa and Mangatangi dams. Relax in our beautiful garden or just take in the magical views and tranquillity of the property. At night enjoy a soak in the spa.
Our overseas guests comment to our hospitality which we are proud of as Bonami means friends forever. Hearty cooked dinner on request.
Directions: *Take southern motorway turn off at Ramarama, turn left signposted to Ararimu, continue for 8 minutes turn left at Ararimu Rd, continue until road changes to Gelling Rd, follow road until you come to Nairns Rd which is on the right Bonami House is at end of road and is signposted. On route to Rotorua and Coromandel.*

Hunua - Paparimu

Homestay - Self Contained Accommodation

Address: 10 Wilson Road,
Paparimu, RD 3, Papakura
Name: Rob and Gillian Wakelin
Telephone: (09) 292 5062
Mobile: (025) 289 6919
Fax: (09) 292 5062
Email: gillrob@voyager.co.nz
Beds: Self contained cottage: 1 queensize upstairs,
1 comfortable double bed/settee downstairs. Extra single and cot available.
Bathroom: 1 Private in cottage,
Tariff: B&B (Full) Cottage Double $95 + $20 each extra guest. Children reduced rate. .
Dinner $30 pp by prior arrangement. Self-catering option. Credit cards accepted.
Nearest Town: Papakura 15 mins. Auckland International Airport 35 mins.

On clear nights the stars are quite incredibly bright because there are no city lights here, yet we are within easy distance of the Airport, Auckland city, beaches, some lovely gardens and nurseries, Miranda Hotpools and walking in the Hunua Ranges. We are handy to State Highway 2 for travel South or to Coromandel Peninsula. Our attractive one bedroom cottage nestles peacefully amongst mature trees and you will awaken to the sounds and sights of the country. Guineafowl and bantams wander freely in our ever-evolving 2 acre garden, along with Balinese cats which we breed. Cows, sheep and sometimes horses graze the surrounding 23 acres. We are busy restoring our 80 year old farmhouse. Whether you choose to enjoy our country meals and summertime BBQ's or self-cater helped by herbs and vegetables from our garden, you will be made welcome. **Directions**: *Leave Motorway at Ramarama, or State Highway 2 via Lyons Road, Mangatawhiri.*

Waiuku

Homestay + Riding School

Address: "Totara Downs",
Bald Hill Road,
RD 1, Waiuku, South Auckland
Name: Janet & Christopher deTracy-Gould
Telephone: (09) 235 8505
Fax: (09) 235 8504
Email:totaradw@ihug.co.nz
Beds: 1 Queen, 2 Single (2 bedrooms)
Bathroom: 1 Ensuite, 1 Private
Tariff: B&B (full) with ensuite $100,
with private bathroom $90, Single $70, Children half price. Credit cards.
Nearest Town: Waiuku 5 minutes, Pukekohe 10 minutes

Just 50 minutes drive south from Auckland Airport "Totara Downs" is found on a back country road, in large country house gardens on 10 acres of farm land, offering spectacular rural views. Our bedrooms offer electric blankets, quality linen, feather duvets and tea/coffee making facilities in each room. Waiuku offers wild west coast or quiet peninsula beaches, sailing the Manukau Harbour, aboard Scow Jane Gifford, farm or bush walks. During summer enjoy a game of croquet, or relax beside the pool, in winter around the open fire in the sitting room. Our Riding school offers sand arena with qualified B.H.S.A.I. instructor, horses/ponies provided, extra charge. Stables and boxes available. With our teenage daughter and son plus family cats, Fifi, Turbo and Flora our West Highland terrier we look forward to your company. No smoking in the house please. For directions please telephone or fax.

Pukekohe - Auckland
Farmstay
Address: 'Woodside', 195 Ostrich Farm Road,
R.D.1, Pukekohe
Name: Evelyn & Les Atkinson
Telephone: (09) 238 7864
Beds: 5 Single (3 bedrooms)
Bathroom: 1 Guests share
Tariff: B&B (full) Double $75,
Single $40, Children half price;
Dinner $17.50 per person. NZ B&B Vouchers accepted
Nearest Town: Pukekohe 6 kms, Auckland 48 kms

Pukekohe is a thriving farm and vegetable growing area situated 48 km south of Auckland. Our 10 acre farm is mostly beef fattening with a few sheep, geese, cats (2), a dog called Buddy, ducks and hens. We are 5 mins away from an excellent golf course and 10 mins to the famous Glenbrook vintage railway. The wild west coast of NZ is a pleasant 20 mins drive. Auckland, our wonderful "City of Sails" is only a 40 mins drive, making it close enough for our visitors to view all of its magnificent attractions. Over the years, Les and I have been fortunate to enjoy travelling throughout NZ and overseas to the UK, Continent and Australia. We love meeting people and can offer warm Kiwi hospitality - we also enjoyed 'farm stays' on our trips abroad. Our guests are very welcome to dine with us, or in their own dining / lounge area.
Directions: *Southern motorway to Drury off-ramp - follow signs to Pukekohe-Waiuku (6 kms). Right turn at Golf Course - first left to Ostrich Road, then left into Ostrich Farm Rd. "Woodside" 2 km down road on right.*

Pukekohe

Homestay+Self-contained Accom.
Address: "Deveron",
Sommerville Rd, Glenbrook.
(Postal: PO Box 146, Patumahoe)
Name: Tony & Sally McWilliams
Telephone: (09) 236 3673
Fax: (09) 236 3631
Email: marcus@ww.co.nz
Beds: Homestay: 1 Queen, 2 Single
(2 bedrooms)
Self-contained Accom: 1 Queen, 2 Single
Bathroom: Homestay: 1 Guests share   Self-contained Accom: 1 Private
Tariff: B&B (full) Double $85, Single $60, Self-contained Accom: $125 per night or weekly by arrangement, Credit Cards. NZ B&B Vouchers accepted $12 surcharge
Nearest Town: Pukekohe 10 mins

We welcome you most warmly to "Deveron", our country home which nestles in beautiful native bush. Location: Franklin County - 45 minutes south of Auckland. Tranquil, park-like surroundings provide the ultimate in peaceful relaxation. Sunny comfortable rooms overlook the bush and garden which attract prolific bird life. Our guests are free to use either their private sitting area (with tea and coffee making facilities) or join us. We also have a self-contained, fully-furnished apartment with 2 double bedrooms above our barn, where Tony makes woodcrafts. Orcharding and landscaping are other interests, while Sally is a keen gardener and tramper. Attractions in the area include west coast beaches, several golf courses, the Glenbrook Vintage Railway, cruises on the Manukau Harbour on the old scow the "Jane Gifford" plus garden and farm visits. Airport shuttle available. **Directions**: *Please phone. Non smokers please.*

Pukekohe East - Sth Auckland

Country House

Address: "Holyrood Farm", 308 Runciman Road, Pukekohe East. Postal: P O Box 48, Bombay, South Auckland

Name: Marie &Jack Watson

Telephone: (09) 238 2925

Fax: (09) 238 1516

Mobile: (025) 315 102

Beds: 1 Queen, 2 Single (2 bedrooms)

Bathroom: 2 Ensuite

Tariff: B&B (full) Double $85, Single $50, Children half price, Dinner $30, Credit Cards (VISA/MC). NZ B&B Vouchers accepted

Nearest Town: Pukekohe 6km

We are situated within 5 minutes of the Southern Motorway exit at Bombay (handy to Auckland International Airport and Auckland City). Our home is surrounded by peaceful and beautiful countryside. We offer a warmly hospitable alternative to a hotel or motel at the start or close of your visit to northern New Zealand. We can meet you at the Airport, and arrange rental cars and horse riding. The attractions of Franklin District, including golf course and Glenbrook Vintage Railway are close. Our large house was designed to accommodate guests, extended family, 2 friendly cats, and an elderly miniature dachshund who is a well-known personality world-wide! We've travelled widely, and welcome both overseas and New Zealand guests. No smoking in the house, please.

Directions: *Exit Southern Motorway at Bombay, towards Pukekohe. Right into Runciman Road (3 kilometers). "Holyrood Farm" then 3 kilometres, on right.*

Bombay

Country Homestay

Address: "Brookfield Lodge", State Highway 1, 2114, RD Bombay, South Auckland

Name: Noreen and Ray Lee

Telephone: (09) 236 0775

Mobile: (025) 292 1422

Beds: 1 Double, 2 Single (2 bedrooms)

Bathroom: 1 Guests share.

Tariff: B&B (full) Double $110, Single $70, Dinner $30 pp by arrangement, Children special rate.

Nearest Town: Pukekohe and Papakura 10 mins. Auckland 30 mins. Airport 25 mins.

Situated on the North-South Highway a mature tree lined driveway leads to the spacious country home. Secluded in one and a half acres of lovely garden this is perfect for your relaxation and enjoyment and makes an ideal place to start or finish your holiday. We are surrounded by beautiful countryside and close to coastal drives, tourist trails and thermal hot pools. The twenty acre property with resident cat and Labrador grazes and trains thoroughbred racehorses. This may interest guests. Attractive bedrooms consist of a double room with patio or a twin bedroom, both with adjacent indoor spa room opening onto a sunny deck. A three course dinner is available by arrangement and your day begins with a generous breakfast. Filter coffee, tea and homebaking always available. Restaurants nearby. We offer modern elegance, tranquillity and warm hospitality. Airport Pickup - nominal charge.

Directions: *From North: Southern Motorway - Take Pukekohe-Bombay off ramp. Turn right to Pukekohe. After 50 metres turn left into BP Service Centre. Brookfield Lodge private access Rd is beside McDonalds carpark: 2 mins. From South: 1 km from Beaver Rd on left.*

Mercer
Farmstay / Separate Accom
Address: RD 2, Mercer, 233 Koheroa Road, Mercer
Name: Alan & Dorothy McIntyre
Telephone: (09) 232 6837
Fax: (09) 232 6837
Beds: 1 Queen, 1 Double (2 bedrooms)
Bathroom: 1 Private
Tariff: B&B (full) Double $75, Single $40, Children negotiable; Dinner $20, Campervans welcome. NZ B&B Vouchers accepted
Nearest Town: Pukekohe 24km

We live on a cattle farm with a modern brick home which has a separate unit with private bathroom and tea & coffee making facilities. We have a large swimming pool surrounded by one acre of interesting garden which guests are welcome to wander through and enjoy. We are 3 km off the main Auckland-Hamilton highway. Our house site gives wide panoramic views of the countryside from Bombay to Thames. We have no children or pets. We are very happy to provide dinner. There are also numerous eating facilities in the area. The farm provides ample opportunity for taking walks and viewing farm animals plus turkeys, pheasants, ducks and quail. As we are only 30-40 minutes from Auckland Airport, this is an ideal first or last night in New Zealand.
Directions: *Travel State Highway 1 to Mercer. On reaching Mercer do not enter Mercer Mobile Service Centre - travelling from north turn left across railway line-travelling from south turn right across railway line, travel 3 km up Koheroa Road, house is on left at Kellyville Road junction. Name clearly visible.*

Port Waikato - Sunset Beach
Homestay
Address: 31 Oceanview Road, Sunset Beach, Port Waikato.
Postal: R.D 5, Tuakau.
Name: Cabana Costena
Telephone: (09) 232 9665
Fax: (09) 232 9965
Mobile: (025) 988 487
Beds: 1 Queen, 1 Double, 1 Single (3 Bedrooms)
Bathroom: 1 Ensuite, 1 Guests share
Tariff: B&b (Full) Queen $90, Double $75, Single $50, Dinner $20. Children under 12 years half price.
Nearest Town: Pukekohe

CABANA Costena
BED & BREAKFAST

Sunset Beach - Auckland's undiscovered gem. Magnificent sunsets, incredible black sand dunes, awesome surf, the historic Waikato River. Uncrowded beaches. One hour from Auckland. Nature at its best. Christine and Tim invite you to share their hacienda on the Beach. Kick back and relax by the large salt water swimming pool or for the more energetic, wonderful beach or bush walks, tennis, fishing (river or surf) whitebait and duck shooting in season, limestone caves. Onewhero Golf Course nearby. Dine by candlelight in the courtyard or by the cosy fire during winter. (Dinner extra by arrangement). Excellent local cafe - dine overlooking the Waikato River (seasonal). Special occasion or pampered weekend escape? A suite overlooking beach, ensuite, lounge area, private deck looking down the river. Also available one double room on courtyard - one twin room. Share bathroom. Pick up from Auckland by arrangement. Nominal charge. We have two small social dogs.

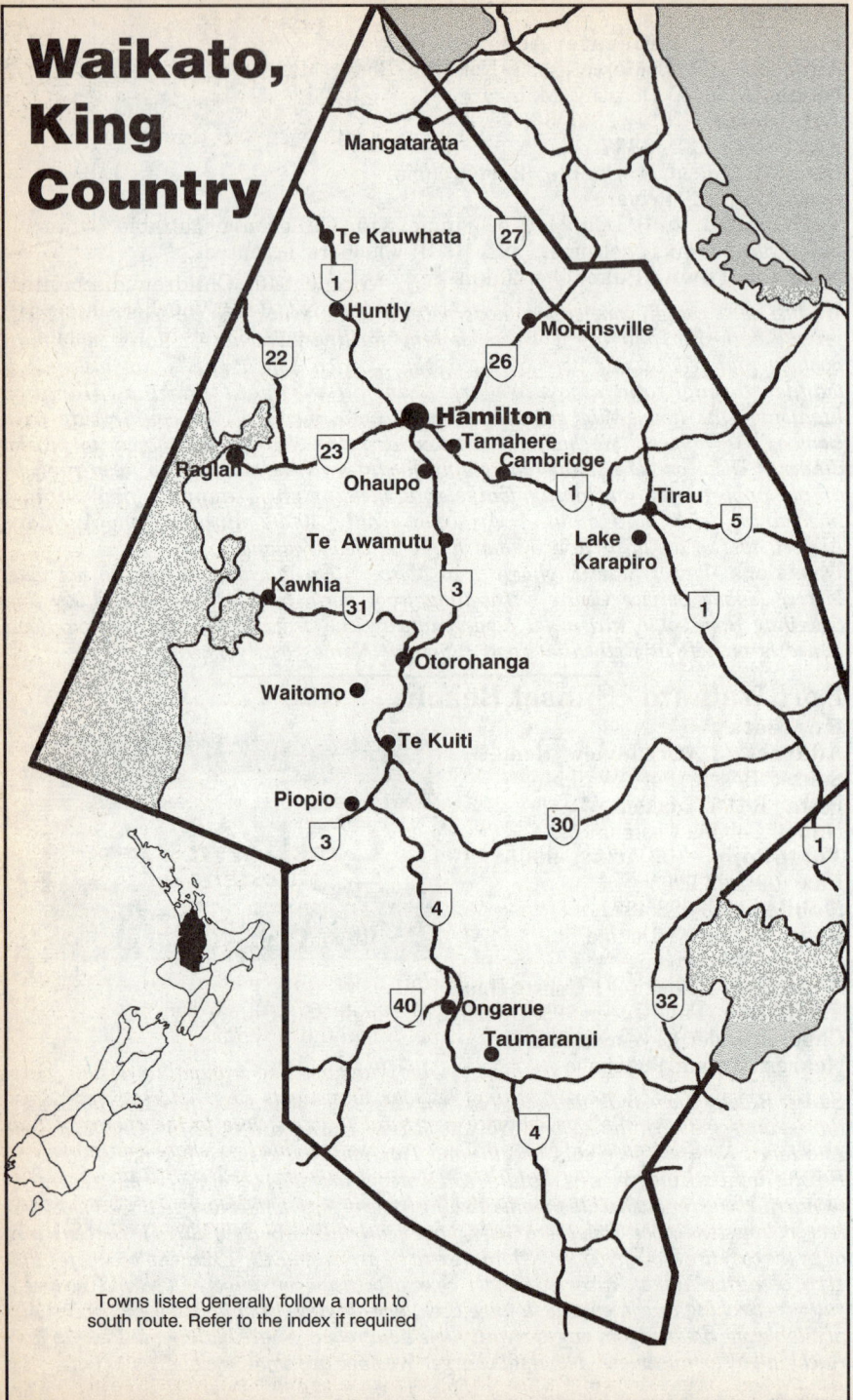

Waikato, King Country

Mangatarata

Te Kauwhata

27

1

Huntly

Morrinsville

22

26

Hamilton

Tamahere

23

Cambridge

Raglan

Ohaupo

1

Tirau

Te Awamutu

5

Lake Karapiro

Kawhia

3

1

31

Otorohanga

Waitomo

Te Kuiti

Piopio

30

3

1

4

40

Ongarue

32

Taumaranui

4

Towns listed generally follow a north to
south route. Refer to the index if required

Mangatarata

Farmstay

Address: Clark's Country Touch,
209 H/way 27,
Mangatarata, Thames R.D.6
Name: Betty & Murray Clark
Telephone/Fax: (07) 867 3070
Mobile: (021) 808 992
Beds: 1 King or 2 Single (1 bedroom)
Bathroom: 1 Family share
Tariff: B&B (continental) Double $65, Single $40, Children discounted.
Dinner $15. Campervans facilities available. NZ B&B Vouchers accepted
Nearest Town: Ngatea 13km to the east, Thames 33km to the east.

*Welcome to our beef farm and summer fruit orchard. Our home has lovely
views of rolling pastures and bush, and a short walk over the farm gives
fabulous views to the Firth of Thames and Coromandel ranges. Our
guestroom is sunny and comfortable with TV, tea/coffee/cookies and is
opposite the bathroom. We are 2 minutes south of the Hauraki Golf Course/
Bowling Club, 8 minutes takes you to Ngatea township and gemstone
factory, 15 minutes to Miranda Hot Springs and seabird coast, 25 minutes
to Thames and beaches, 50 minutes to Auckland, Hamilton and 90 minutes
to Rotorua, Tauranga. We have a friendly dog Becky, who lives outside, and
a cat called Watson! We are aged '50ish', and enjoy sharing our home and
local knowledge. Our varied interests include 4 wheel driving, vintage
machinery, handcrafts and gardening. We assure you of a very warm
welcome. Non-smokers preferred.*

Te Kauwhata

Farmstay

Address: "Herons Ridge Farmstay & Stud"
1131 Waikare Road, RD1, Te Kauwhata
Name: David
Telephone: (07) 826 4646
Fax: (07) 826 4646
Email: herons_ridge@xtra.co.nz
Beds: 2 Queen, 1 Double, 1 Single (3 bedrooms)
Bathroom: 1 Private, 1 Ensuite
Tariff: B&B (Full): Double $80. Studio $120, Single $50, Dinner $25,
Children Discount. NZ B&B Vouchers accepted $12 or $39 surcharge
Nearest Town: Te Kauwhata 7 Kms Auckland 1 hour.

*Welcome to Herons Ridge your home in the Waikato. The tranquillity of our Farm
and Horse Stud is the perfect setting for your first nights stay. Horses, Live Stock,
Pets, Ponds and Pine Woods enhance our rural location close to the shores of Lake
Waikare. Whilst respecting your privacy we are delighted to share our home and
hospitality with you. Our quality air conditioned Garden Studio gives the
opportunity for self catering. Breakfast and Dinner are served in our dining room.
Continental breakfast optional; discounts are available for longer stays. French/
Spanish spoken. Herons Ridge your choice for peace and quiet, country walks,
Honeymoon Suite, Golfing holidays, Horse Riding, Natural Hot springs close by
or our pool. Herons Ridge is a KiwiHost business, a commitment to quality service.*
Directions: *SH1 Turn off to Te Kauwhata. Pass through town. 6 km along
Waerenga Road signpost for Waikare Road and Farm Stay. 1 km on right gate
number 1131.* **Home Page**: http://www.nz.com/webnz/bbnz/heron.htm

Huntly
Farmstay
Address: "Parnassus Farm & Garden",
191 Te Ohaki Road, RD 1, Huntly
Name: David & Sharon Payne
Telephone: (07) 828 8781
Fax: (07) 828 8781
Email: parnassus@xtra.co.nz
Beds: 2 Double, 4 Single (3 bedrooms)
Bathroom: 1 Guests share, 1 Family share, 1 Private
Tariff: B&B (full) Double $80, Single $45, Children according to age.
Family concessions available. Dinner and lunches by arrangement,
Campervans $20. Credit cards.
NZ B&B Vouchers accepted $10 surcharge
Nearest Town: 4km west of Huntly

*Parnassus offers you all the calm and beauty of the New Zealand countryside only
minutes off SH1 and wonderful farmhouse meals using garden fresh produce. We
are a successful farming venture combining dairying, forestry, sheep and beef
and have an extensive garden incorporating formal rose beds, woodland area,
orchard, berry-fruit courtyard and kitchen gardens. We have both a swimming
pool and heated spa. Children enjoy our delightful range of birds and small
animals. Auckland, Raglan, Hamilton, the Coromandel, Waitomo, Rotorua and
Taupo are all easy day trip destinations. Courtesy pick-up is available from
Huntly bus or rail. We offer a delicious cooked breakfast and picnics, luncheon
and dinners are available by arrangement. Be assured of a warm country
welcome at Parnassus.*

Morrinsville
Country Stay
Address: 102 Horrell Road, Morrinsville
Name: Farrand's B&B
Telephone: (07) 889 5843
Fax: (07) 889 5843
Mobile: (025) 847 688 or (025) 222 2606
Beds: 1 Queen, 2 single (2 bedrooms)
Bathroom: 1 Guests share
Tariff: B&B (full/continental) Double $80, Single $40. Dinner $20,
Children $ negotiable.
Nearest Town: Morrinsville 2 kms NE (1 km from SH 26)

*Welcome to Morrinsville, a friendly central Waikato town. We offer a peaceful
retreat on 5 acres. We have no children but we have a "people loving" horse, 2
cats and sheep. Your accommodation is in the form of a cosy, private wing
attached to our modern home. Although this allows you more privacy we enjoy
meeting new faces and hope you make yourselves at home with us. We hope you
enjoy the new furnishings and bedding which include Queen and King single
beds. Laundry facilities available. If only two guests staying we offer the option
of converting the second bedroom into a comfortable lounge. For those who wish
to be totally private, we offer a continental breakfast, including home made
muesli and jams in your room. Honeymoon/Anniversary Suite - total privacy,
extras including champagne, nibbles, chocolates, and breakfast in your suite
(already set up) $95. Indulge in a little luxury at an affordable price.*
Directions: *Horrell Rd branches off SH26, just East of Morrinsville. Well sign
posted.*

Raglan

Farmstay + Self-Contained Accommodation
Address: 'Matawha', R.D.2, Raglan, No. 61
Name: Peter & Jenny Thomson
Telephone: (07) 825 6709 **Fax**: (07) 825 6715
Beds: 1 Double & 2 Single or 3 Single (1 Bedroom)
Bathroom: 1 Private
Tariff: B&B (special) Double $55, Single $25, Children half price,
Dinner $15; Lunch $10, Campervans $20 (laundry and bathroom
facilities available) Meals $15 per person.   NZ B&B Vouchers accepted
Nearest Town: Raglan 30 minutes, Hamilton 1 hour, Auckland 2 1/2

*We are a family with two boys aged 23 and 20 years and we are fortunate to have
a farm right on the West coast with panoramic views of the Tasman Sea. Our beach
is very private with good fishing, hang gliding, surfing and paragliding. Our farm
has been in the family for over 100 years and we've taken great pride in breeding
top class Romney sheep, and stud and commercial Hereford cattle. We also do
some riding and have a large flower garden. Most of the vegetables and meat are
supplied by a large vegetable garden and by the farm. We also have 3 lovely cats.
We have excellent scenic drives and bush walks plus of course our own beach. We
enjoy having visitors from all over the world and they enjoy participating in all
our farm activities.* **Directions**: *Take Hamilton—Raglan road (route 23) Travelling approx 30 minutes – through Te Uku, take the Kauroa and Te Mata Bridal
Veil Falls (signposted) turning left. Take the first turn to the right at Te mata
School - Ruapuke Rd for 9 1/2 kms to the Tutu Rimu Road - turn Left into this road
travelling another 1 1/2 kms to the T junction (signposted "Matawha Rd No Exit,
Tutu Rimu Rd, Ruapuke Beach Access, Te Mata 11 kms").   No. 61 on cattlestop.*

Te Mata/ Raglan

Farmstay/Self Contained House
Address: 334 Houchen Rd,
Te Mata, R.D.1 Raglan
Name: Marcus and Jan-Maree Vernon
(& daughter Cleo)
Telephone: (07) 825 6892
Fax: (07) 825 6896
Mobile: (025) 756 276
Beds: 1 Queen, 2 Double, 2 Single (2 bedrooms)
Bathroom: 1 Private
Tariff: B&B (full) Double $80, Single $50, Children $25, Dinner $20,
Campervans welcome. Dogs outside, kennel provided. Vouchers accepted
Nearest Town: Raglan - 20 mins.

MAGIC MOUNTAIN

FARMStays & HORSE Trekking
TE MATA, RAGLAN, NZ

New Zealand Association
FARM & HOME HOSTS

*Our farm is the only one in the world where you can see 3 harbours (Aotea, Raglan
and Kawhia) and 4 volcanoes (Mounts Karioi, Pirongia, Taranaki and Ruapehu).
At 328 metres above sea level the views are magical. The farm has 380 acres of
rolling pastures and native bush. We have sheep, cattle and pigs grazing and also
keep dogs, horses, turtles, cats, all tame and friendly. We welcome you to ride our
beautiful horses around the farm, daylight or moonlight. We also horse trek to
the Bridal Veil Falls (55 metres high). For the adventurous we offer fishing and
hunting trips (fish, pigs, rabbits, goats and possums). Join in our daily farm
activities or simply relax amongst the tranquil surroundings, soaking up the views from your
balcony, couples or families with children. We offer warm country hospitality. Within a 30
minute drive visit Raglan's cafes, beaches, bushwalks, harbour cruise or swim at Waingaro
Hot Springs. This distination is perfect for either couples or familes with children.*

Hamilton

Homestay/Self Contained Accom.
Address: 2 Ruakiwi Road,
Hamilton
Name: Richard & Sue Harington
Telephone: (07) 838 2328
Beds: 1 Double, 2 Single
(2 bedrooms).
1 Double (self contained accommodation
Bathroom: 1 Ensuite, 1 Private
Tariff: B&B (continental)
Double $70, Single $45.
No Credit Cards. NZ B&B Vouchers accepted
Nearest Town: Hamilton 1km central city

Our spacious, modern home is within 1km from transport terminals and the inner city with its numerous restaurants and cafés. On a fine morning take a stroll through the Hamilton Lake Domain, and breakfast on our roof-top garden and enjoy the views across the city. We would particularly like to welcome you to our home as we have travelled widely using B&Bs ourselves wherever possible. We know it's a wonderful way to get to know a country, its people and the lifestyle.
Richard belongs to Lions and is a keen woodworker. We both enjoy music, travel, the outdoors and caravaning. We have a cat. Hamilton is a university city astride the Waikato River and is surrounded by magnificent farming country. We will be happy to show you around or help plan an itinerary. Laundry facilities are available.
Two single beds convert to one Kingsize. A child's bed is also available.

Hamilton

Homestay
Address: 7 Delamare Road,
Bryant Park, Hamilton
Name: Esther Kelly
Telephone: (07) 849 2070
Mobile: (025) 263 9442
Email: esther@enlighten.co.nz
Beds: 1 Double, 2 Single
(2 Bedrooms)
Bathroom: 1 Ensuite, 1 Private.
Tariff: B&B (continental)
Double with ensuite $85, Twin $75, `Single $55, Dinner $20. Credit cards.
NZ B&B Vouchers accepted $15 surcharge ensuite, $7 surcharge twin.
Nearest Town: Hamilton 3 Kms

I have travelled in many countries and would welcome tourists and would be happy to advise you on travel in New Zealand. I live in the suburb of Bryant Park, close to the Waikato River with its tranquil river walks and I am within walking distance of St Andrews Golf Course. Hamilton is a picturesque city with rose gardens, Museum, Ruakura Animal Research Farm and an agricultural museum called "Farmworld". Hamilton is in the centre of the dairy industry. My interests are cooking, gardening, tramping, boating, trout fishing, playing golf, art and also Mah Jong. I look forward to offering you friendly hospitality.
Directions: *Approaching from Auckland. Leave main highway half way down Te Rapa Straight (4 lane highway entering Hamilton) by turning left at round intersection into Bryant Road. At end of Bryant Road turn left into Sandwich Road. Delamare Road is 2nd street on right.*

Hamilton

Homestay
Address: 530 Grey Street,
Hamilton East
Name: Frances & Norman Wills
Telephone: (07) 838 2120
Fax: (07) 838 3042
Beds: 1 Twin pr, 2 Single (3 bedrooms)
Bathroom: 1 Private, 1 Guest share
Tariff: B&B (full) Double $65, Single $40,
Children under 10 half price. Credit cards. NZ B&B Vouchers accepted
Nearest Town: Hamilton 1/2km City Centre.

WAIKATO

*Spacious nicely renovated family home away from traffic noise but only 3
minutes from CPO and central shopping. Secluded offstreet parking.*
*We have travelled overseas and are accustomed to entertaining visitors –
American, Asian and European. We can assist with local and district sightseeing
information. Comfort guaranteed.*
Directions: *From South, follow Highway One and watch for the sign "Hamilton
East. Grey Street" on right opposite Hamilton Gardens.*
*From North, from roundabout at Te Rapa where Highway 1 diverges follow signs
to City Centre and continue on south end of main street, turn left on to Victoria
Bridge. From Highway 3, turn right at Normandy Avenue roundabout, follow
"City Centre" then "Hamilton East" signs to Bridge Street, proceed straight down
Bridge Street and across the bridge. At top of Bridge Street (facing St. Mary's
Church) turn left into Grey Street. No. 530 is less than 100m along, down
driveway on right - tall trees at entrance.*

Hamilton

Homestay
Address: 24 Pearson Ave,
Claudelands, Hamilton
Name: Matthews B&B
Telephone: (07) 855 4269
Fax: (07) 855 4269
Mobile: (025) 747 758
Email: mgm@xtra.co.nz
Beds: 3 Single (2 bedrooms)
Bathroom: 1 Guests share, 1 family share
Tariff: B&B (Full) Double $60, Single $40, Children 1/2 price, Dinner
$20, Campervans $20 (up to 4 persons). NZ B&B Vouchers accepted
Nearest Town: Hamilton, 120 km south of Auckland.

*We would like to welcome you to our home situated 2 seconds off the city
by-pass on Route 9 & 7 through the city in the Five Crossroads area.
Adjacent to the showgrounds and only 5 minutes from the inner city, it is
a comfortable walk if you wish to shop. Ruakura, the world famous
agricultural research station is just two blocks from our home, if farming
is your interest. Our home is a 'lived-in' comfortable home, warm in winter
and cool in summer with an in-ground swimming pool for your use. Our
four children have left home and we and our cat enjoy spending time with
guests from both NZ and overseas. We have hosted people from many parts
of the world and for seven years Maureen taught conversational English to
Japanese students. We have travelled extensively and therefore are able
to help you plan your holiday.*

Hamilton
Homestay
Address: 162 Beerescourt Rd, Hamilton City
Name: John & Glenys Ebbett
Telephone: (07) 849 2005
Fax: (07) 849 8405
Beds: 2 Single (1 bedroom)
Bathroom: 1 Private
Tariff: B&B (full)
Double $75 Single $55,
Dinner $20.
NZ B&B Vouchers accepted $7 Surcharge
Nearest Town: Hamilton, 7 minutes drive city centre

Having travelled extensively ourselves, we enjoy visitors to our home which was built in 1990 and commands a spectacular view of New Zealand's longest river. You are welcome to share travel anecdotes with us, or just enjoy the privacy of your own bedroom-bathroom-shower-ensuite (own tea making facility). Only minutes from town centre, river walks, swimming complex, St Andrews Golf Course, and excellent restaurants. Auckland International Airport is less than one and a half hours drive. This appeals to many tourists just arriving to or leaving the country. We treat home hosting as a way of reciprocating the pleasure we have had meeting people in other parts of the world, and we have very much enjoyed the 6 years we have been involved. One request - non smokers please. We don't have any animal pets, or young children.

Hamilton
Homestay
Address: 164 Clyde Street, Hamilton
Name: Val Wood
Telephone: (07) 856 0337
Fax: (07) 856 0337
Email: VAL.AND.COLIN.WOOD@xtra.co.nz
Beds: 1 Double, 2 Single (3 bedrooms)
Bathroom: 1 Guests share
Tariff: B&B (continental) Double $65, Single $40, Children $15, Dinner by arrangement $20. NZ B&B Vouchers accepted
Nearest Town: Central Hamilton 2km.

Our home is five minutes drive from the centre of Hamilton and further along Clyde Street is the Waikato University. In daylight hours we are happy to meet you at the Hamilton train or bus station if required. Our guest accommodation has television and tea making facilities and we endeavour to make you feel at home. We encourage people to stay in Hamilton while visiting the tourist areas of the Waikato and Rotorua and return each night to sleep in the same bed without the hassles of packing and unpacking. Hamilton is ideal for this type of holiday as it is within one and a half hours of most places of interest and has many delightful places to visit in the city itself.
Our home is a no smoking zone and we have off street parking. We look forward to having you visit us. No Smoking

Hamilton

First Class Manor Accom. & Luxury Cottage
Address: 'Anlaby Manor',
91 Newell Road, R.D.3, Hamilton
Name: Halina & Pryme Footner
Telephone: (07) 856 7264
Fax: (07) 856 5323
Email: anlaby.manor@xtra.co.nz
Website: www.anlabymanor.co.nz
Beds: Manor: 3 Queen (3 bedrooms)
Cottage: 1 Queen, 2 Single (1 bedroom).
Bathroom: Manor: 2 Ensuite, 1 Guests share. Cottage: 1 Own Private.
Tariff: B&B (full) Double $180, Single $120, Children under 12 years half price,
Dinner $60. Credit cards. Vouchers accepted $102 surcharge
Nearest Town: Hamilton 5 minutes. Airport 5 minutes.

*Anlaby Manor has been built as a replica Yorkshire stately home after a Sir Edwin Lutyens'
design. The original design was established and built in Yorkshire in the 19th century. It
features a huge grand central staircase replicated from that of "Gone with the wind". A formal
English garden of 2.5 acres is planted round a century-old pin oak with neo-roman statuary,
fountains, box hedging and roses. Leadlight windows are complemented by antique furniture,
heirloom china and English style oil paintings. A very spacious luxury 2 storey cottage fully
self contained is also available for honeymooners and families or guests may prefer to stay in
ensuite bedrooms in the Manor. There is a swimming pool, tennis court, sauna and billiard
room. Complimentary hors d'oeuvres and pre-dinner wine is served from an outstanding
cellar. We both enjoy travel, gardening and meeting our guests. We prefer no smoking.
Brochures available.*

Hamilton

Country Retreat
Address: 'The Monastery',
212B Newell Road, R.D.3, Hamilton
Name: Diana & Robert Scott
Telephone: (07) 856 9587
Fax: (07) 856 9512
Beds: 2 Double 4 Single (4 bedrooms)
Bathroom: 2 Ensuite, 1 Guests share
Tariff: B&B (full) Double $150, Single $120,
Children half price, Dinner $55. Credit cards.
Nearest Town: 3km south of Hamilton boundary, Airport 6km

*This Historic Home offers the atmosphere and elegance of the Edwardian era.
Built in 1907, the private residence later became the Passionist Monastery.
Relocated on a peaceful ten acre rural setting near the Waikato River and lovingly
restored, it features stained glass windows, pressed steel ceilings, ornately carved
panelled doors, verandahs and antiques. All bedrooms offer comfortable beds,
electric blankets, quilts, heaters and attractive garden views. Two peaceful
spacious lounges have fireplaces and sunny bay windows. Three course dinners
with wine (by arrangement) and special breakfasts are served in our formal
dining room. Complimentary pre-dinner drinks, hors d'oeuvres and afternoon
teas. Enjoy our large attractive garden, relaxing beach walk, warm hospitality and
friendly animals. Robert is a landscape designer. Our interests include gardening,
antiques and equestrian pursuits. Central to Hamilton gardens and airport,
Mystery Creek and Cambridge. 1 1/2 hr drive to Waitomo Caves, Rotorua and
Auckland. No smoking. **Directions**: Please phone.*

Hamilton
Homestay

Address: 11 Tamihana Ave, Hamilton
Name: Des & Marion Slaney
Telephone: (07) 855 3426
Fax: (07) 855 3426
Mobile: 025 815 404
Email: slaney.dm@xtra.co.nz
Beds: 1 Double, 1 Single (2 bedrooms)
Bathroom: 1 Guests share
Tariff: B&B (continental) Double $70, Single $40.
NZ B&B Vouchers accepted
Nearest Town: Hamilton 1 Km from main street.

Guest accommodation is in spacious studio loft separate from house and overlooking our cottage garden with patio and summer house. Both rooms, double and single, have colour TV, and the upstairs double room has a balcony and a small kitchen with fridge and microwave. We are within walking distance of Hamilton's main street and the Waikato River with its lovely walkways. With relaxation and privacy in mind we supply a continental breakfast in your studio to have at your leisure. Maps are provided showing Hamilton's main attractions, restaurants etc. For those interested in exploring Hamilton's countryside, you are welcome to our walking and cycling maps.
Directions: *Cross Whitiora Bridge at the northern end of Hamilton's main street, - Victoria Street, turn left off the bridge into Casey Avenue and first left again into Tamihana Avenue. We are third house on right. Transfers and pick ups provided. Off street parking available.*

Hamilton
Country B&B

Address: "Twelve Oaks" Tamahere, Hamilton
Name: Ezra & Craig Campbell
Telephone: (07) 856 2030 **Fax**: (07) 856 2089
Beds: 1 Queen in "Stable Wing", 1 Double or 2 Single in Loft.
Bathroom: 1 Ensuite, 1 Private
Tariff: B&B (special) Double $130, Single $100, Children half price.
Dinner/Picnic Hamper $40 includes wine.
Nearest Town: Hamilton and Cambridge 5 mins drive. Airport 6 km.

"Twelve Oaks" blends privacy and luxury with tranquillity and charm. Twelve ancient oaks line the driveway to our Homestead. Nestled amongst trees, expansive gardens and walkways on the rise of the historic 1865 Tamahane peace site, we look across leading horse stud countryside, Mt Pirongia to the west, on our eastern boundary a Department of Conservation Reserve, a rare remnant of pre-pioneering forest. Craig enjoys off duty time developing wood lots and gardens. Ezra, a sculptor and designer, has a historic, old studio, visited via a garden stroll. Guests enjoy their own private entrance, charming sitting room, reading room, bathroom and luxurious bedroom with all the comforts of home ..... stable doors opening onto delightful courtyard and salt-water pool. Unwind swimming, playing croquet, patting the ponies or the nearby activities of golf, tennis, antique shopping, wineries, museums, galleries, bush walks, mineral spas. Horse stud visits, scenic flights, fishing and jet boating can be arranged or simply relax over a quiet drink by the pool. Discerning travellers will find a little style, a lot of warmth, discreet hospitality, comfort, a good breakfast and sound local knowledge. **Directions**: *Please phone/fax for bookings and directions.*

Hamilton
Homestay
Address: 50A Queenwood Avenue, Chartwell, Hamilton
Name: Judy & Brian Dixon
Telephone: (07) 855 7324
Email: jdixon@voyager.co.nz
Beds: 2 Single (1 bedroom)
Bathroom: 1 Private
Tariff: B&B (continental) Double $65, Single $45. NZ B&B Vouchers accepted
Nearest Town: Hamilton

Haere mai - Welcome. Our homestay home is a comfortable smoke free, homely Lockwood nestled within a quiet garden. Travellers have sole access to their bathroom and bedroom. Our aim is to provide a warm environment where guests may relax and enjoy themselves. We are within a 100 metres of the popular restaurants Cafe en Q, the Platter Place and within walking distance of Chartwell Square. Waikato River walks are close by. We have a beach home with guest facilities and magnificent sea views on the East Coast near Opotiki which is also available if requested. Judy is in Education and Brian is retired and always willing to make and share in a cuppa and help with maps and directions. We share our home with a friendly cat named Zapper.
Directions: *Please phone first. From Auckland turn left at Taupiri and proceed through Gordonton to Thomas Road on right. Turn left into Hukanui, right at Glenn Lynn and left into River Road. Queenwood Avenue is first on left. From South follow River Road North to Queenwood Avenue on right.*

Hamilton
Country Home & Garden Stay
Address: "The Poplars", 402 Matangi Road, RD 4, Hamilton
Name: Lesley & Peter Ramsay
Telephone: (07) 829 5551
Email: ramsay@waikato.ac.nz
Beds: 1 Double, 2 Single (2 bedrooms)
Bathroom: 1 Guests share
Tariff: B&B (full) Double $90, Single $65, Children 10 and under half price, Dinner $25pp. Credit Cards accepted.
Nearest Town: 4km south of Hamilton city boundary, airport 12km

Just fifteen minutes drive from Hamilton, Mystery Creek and Cambridge, the Poplars offers a relaxed haven of peace and quiet.
Feed the donkeys, ducks and geese, take a row on the lake, recline by the solar heated pool and spa pool, or stroll around the 3 acre garden with its many different rooms. A garden for all seasons with special emphasis on internationally acclaimed Daffodils which herald spring followed by over 600 roses. The Poplars has featured on national TV, in NZ Gardener and Next Magazines. It is a garden of surprises. Each comfortable guest room has tea and coffee making facilities, electric blankets and TV. Hosts Peter and Lesley offer you the charms of country living along with great Kiwi hospitality. Seasoned travellers they know the difference a warm welcome can make especially when shared with their friendly pets. A unique and special stay awaits you at The Poplars.
Directions: *Please phone.*

Tamahere, Hamilton
Homestay/Farmlet
Address: Pencarrow Road,
RD 3, Hamilton
Name: Pat & Roger Williams
Telephone: (07) 856 2499
Fax: (07) 856 2499
Mobile: (025) 261 1959
Email: port.williams@clear.net.nz
Beds: 1 Queen, 1 Double, 2 Single (2 bedrooms)
Bathroom: 2 Ensuites, 1 Guest share spa bath
Tariff: B&B (continental) Double $75, Twin $80,
Single $50, Credit Cards.
Nearest Town: Hamilton 6km

Come and join us in our Mediterranean style villa. We are a friendly couple and now our family have left home we are happy to share our new surroundings. Having travelled extensively we understand the importance of hospitality. We are non-smokers and have many arts and craft interests. On a 5 acre farmlet in the country we are conveniently 3kms from the Hamilton Airport and also the National Fieldays site. Just off State Highway 1, we are 6kms from Hamilton and 11kms from Cambridge.
Our tranquil views are over the Narrows Golf Course, the Waikato River Valley and West to Mt Pirongia and glorious sunsets. The house is placed for maximum sunshine in a landscaped garden on a ridge, with a farmed gully below, in which goats and sheep graze. Our dogs live outdoors.
Directions: *For reservations and directions please phone.*

Lake Rotokauri, Hamilton
Country Garden Stay, Self Contained
Address: Exelby Rd, Hamilton.
Please phone for directions
Name: David and Cathy Dewes
Telephone: (07) 849 9020
Mobile: (021) 896 674
Beds: 1 Queen (1 bedroom)
Bathroom: 1 Ensuite
Tariff: B&B (special/continental) Double $110, Single $80.
Credit Cards accepted. NZ B&B Vouchers accepted $40 surcharge
Nearest Town: 5 mins north/west of Hamilton. 1.5 hours to Auckland

"The sun sets over the Hakarimata Ranges. It lights the sky with inspiring colours and patterns, mirrored in lake Rotokauri. Mt Pirongia becomes a silhouette and the surrounding farmland is quiet". *Soak up this view from our upstairs self-contained bed and sitting room. It fills with sunshine during the day and is warm, quiet and private. Detailed attention has been made for your comfort. The queen-size bed is very comfortable. Dressers, arranged with fresh flowers, and chairs are from yesteryear. Our special self-serve breakfast is full of home-made treats. A separate guest entrance and balcony overlooks the garden - 3 acres of native bush and woodlands waiting to be explored. A spa with adjacent swimming pool, is fun to unwind in. We, with our children, are keen outdoors people and can direct you to local attractions ..... the Hamilton zoo is just 2 minutes away with its famous 'free flight' sanctuary. We are 'smoke free' and have 1 cat. Professional therapeutic massage is available by appointment to complete your stay.*
Directions: *Please phone for reservations and directions.*

Hamilton
Homestay
Address: "Magnolia House",
28B Nixon Street, Hamilton East
Name: Karin and Neil Kitney
Telephone: 07-856 5392
Beds: 4 Single (2 bedrooms)
Bathroom: 1 Guest share
Tariff: B&B (continental - cooked b/f extra availalable on request)
Double $70, Single $40, dinner by arrangement.
Not suitable for children.
NZ B&B Vouchers accepted $10 surcharge
Nearest Town: Hamilton (1.5 km to city centre)

WAIKATO

We welcome you to our home at the end of a long drive way (off street parking) only 100 metres from SH1 near Hamilton Gardens. We are surrounded by trees, so it is peaceful. Located conveniently to Hamilton Gardens, Waikato University and only minutes from Hamilton East shopping centre and the city centre, bus stop just one block away. We have travelled widely in New Zealand and overseas and enjoy meeting people and have many tourist tips to help you explore the local region's places of interest, many of which are within one and one half hours drive of Hamilton.
Karin was born in Germany, speaks German fluently and we have found this helpful in our travels.
We thank you for not smoking in our home and look forward to your visit.

Hamilton
Homestay B&B
Address: "Hillcrest Heights",
54 Hillcrest Road,
Hillcrest, Hamilton
Name: Barbara and Tony
Telephone: (07) 856 4818
Mobile: (025) 226 7386
Beds: 2 Queen, 1 Double,
3 Single (3 Bedrooms)
Bathroom: 1 Ensuite, 1 Guests share
Tariff: B&B (Continental) Double $75-$85, Single $55, Dinner $25.
Nearest Town: Central City 5 minutes

Our home is spacious, clean and comfortable. All facilities are upstairs to enable you to enjoy the views over Hamilton city. Our aim is to provide guests with good quality accommodation in a friendly, relaxed environment. We offer plenty of off street parking, complimentary tea and coffee, laundry facilities, exercise room and swimming pool with barbecue area. A great breakfast is guaranteed and dinner can also be provided by prior arrangement. On city bus route but free transport can be provided to and from the local airport, bus and train stations. Waikato University is 2 minutes walk away. Beautiful Hamilton Gardens and river walks are nearby. We are central to Ruakura Agricultural Research Centre and Hamilton cafes, restaurants and museum. Tennis, badminton and squash centres are minutes away. We extend a warm welcome to all our visitors. Our children have flown the nest but Turbo the cat remains. Please phone for directions.

Ohaupo, Hamilton

B&B Homestay
Address: 15 Main Rd, Ohaupo 2452
Name: Ridge House
Telephone: (07) 823 6555
Fax: (07) 823 6555
Beds: 1 Double, 2 Single (2 bedrooms)
Bathroom: 1 Guest's (share)
Tariff: B&B (continental) Double/Twin $60, Single $40, Dinner $15pp, Full breakfast $5pp extra. Credit Cards.
Nearest Town: Hamilton 15km north on SH3 - Te Awamutu 12km sth

A warm welcome awaits you at "Ridge House". Enjoy ever-changing views of Mt Pirongia, Lake Rotomanuka opposite and beyond, our lush Waikato pastures. John, a retired New Zealand Railways Locomotive Engineer, enjoys photography, videoing and American Model Railroading (Life Member NMRA). Kay, homemaking, her roses and garden, sceniking John's railroad and, last but not least, a lovely puss named 'Chessie". We are an ideal base - 6 minutes to Hamilton International Airport (courtesy car) and Mystery Creek, the home of Fieldays and Farmworld - 15 minutes to CENTRAL Hamilton and Cambridge - 30 minutes Waitomo Caves - approx.1 hour Rotorua - Tauranga, and, boast 6 golf courses within a 12km radius! Relaxed country-style breakfast and dinners. COMPLIMENTARY laundry service, home-baking and hot drinks (always available). EXTRA-warm muffins with breakfast. We look forward to your company and sharing with you our 'smoke free' home, our table and our lovely countryside. Happy travelling - Kay and John.

Hamilton

Homestay/B&B
Address: "Green Gables of Rukuhia", 35 Rukuhia Road, RD 2, Ohaupo
Name: Earl & Judi McWhirter
Telephone: (07) 843 8511
Fax: (07) 843 8514
Mobile: (021) 848 030
Beds: 2 Double, 3 Single (3 bedrooms)
Bathroom: 1 Guests share
Tariff: B&B (continental) Double $75, Single $45, Dinner $20, Special tariff for Field Days, Credit Cards.
Nearest Town: Hamilton 4km SH3

Warm, comfortable home surrounded with garden, in a quiet rural setting. Two storeyed house, guest rooms, lounge downstairs; dining, hosts upstairs. Only 4km south of Hamilton, just off SH3, 5 minutes from airport. Viligrad Winery just down the road, Gostiona Restaurant 2 minutes walk. Ideally situated for Field Days. Free pick up/delivery, airport, bus, train terminal just part of friendly service. With breakfast we include homebaked bread, selection of plunged coffee to suit your taste. Judi lectures in statistics, University of Waikato. Earl is "retired" school teacher. Both enjoy country music, dancing, outdoors. Earl hires out as a guide on Whanganui River, is a kayak instructor, and masseur. One daughter still lives at home. We ask that guests do not smoke on the property. Thank you. We look forward to your company, if we can't provide it, we'll help find someone who can.

176

Cambridge
Bed & Breakfast

Address: 'Park House',
70 Queen St, Cambridge
Name: Bill & Pat Hargreaves
Telephone: (07) 827 6368
Fax: (07) 827 4094
Email: Park.House@xtra.co.nz
Beds: 1 Queen, 1 Double, 1 Super King/Twin
Bathroom: 2 Ensuite, 1 Private.
Tariff: B&B (full) Double $120-$130, Single $100, Credit cards (VISA/MC/Amex). NZ B&B Vouchers accepted $55 surcharge
Nearest Town: Cambridge - 1 block

WAIKATO

Step back into a time warp of gracious living at Park House. Built in the 1920's as an Inn, Park House is centrally situated overlooking the tree-lined village green and has been beautifully restored as a private residence. For more than 10 years we have offered this superb setting for guests who appreciate the finer comforts of life. Throughout this large home are antiques, comfortable traditional furniture, patchworks, stained-glass windows all creating an elegant and restful atmosphere for your enjoyment. The lounge features an elaborately carved fireplace, board and batten-work ceiling, fine-art, library, TV and complimentary sherry. The bedrooms, in a separate guest wing, provide every comfort and privacy. In keeping with the Inn of yesteryear, an ample breakfast is served in the Formal Dining Room. A selection of excellent Restaurants, Antique, Craft and Shops are within easy walking distance.

Cambridge
Farmhouse

Address: 'Birches', Maungatautari Rd., Pukekura, Postal: PO Box 194, Cambridge
Name: Sheri & Hugh Jellie
Telephone: (07) 827 6556
Fax: (07) 827 3552
Email: hugh@plade.co.nz
Beds: 1 Queen, 1 Double, 1 Single (2 bedrooms)
Bathroom: 1 Ensuite, 1 Private
Tariff: B&B (full) Double $90, Single $60, Dinner $28 (GST inclusive), Credit cards. NZ B&B Vouchers accepted $20 Surcharge on double.
Nearest Town: Cambridge 4km

Our 1930s character farmhouse offers comfort from open fires in winter to tennis and swimming pool in summer. The beautiful countryside surrounding our small acreage and rambling cottage garden, is amongst leading horse studs. Hugh, a veterinarian, specialises in dairy cow reproduction. With Lake Karapiro only 2 minutes away we can offer waterskiing or a base for rowing supporters. Picturesque Cambridge, "Town of Trees", and with its many antique shops and restaurants is only 5 minutes away. We are within an hour of Waitomo, Rotorua, Mt Maunganui beach and several top golf courses. We are both extensively travelled and with our one daughter and her pets at home are keen water/snow skiers. Guests have a choice of twin with guest bathroom and spabath, or a quaint garden cottage, queen with ensuite, both with tea making facilities. Dinner by arrangement and we serve countrystyle breakfast in our formal dining room or in the sunshine. **Directions**: *Please phone for directions.*

Cambridge
Homestay
Address: 7 Marlowe Drive,
Cambridge
Name: Paul and Diane White
Telephone: (07) 823 2142 **Fax**: (07) 823 2143
Mobile: (025) 963 224
Beds: 2 Queen, 1 Double (3 bedrooms)
Bathroom: 1 Ensuite, 1 Guests share
Tariff: B&B (special) Double $70-$75, Single $40,
Dinner by arrangement. Credit Cards accepted. NZ B&B Vouchers accepted
Nearest Town: Cambridge

We look forward to welcoming you to our comfortable spacious home beside the river. An easy 5 minute stroll will take you into the town centre where you'll find nationally recognised award winning restaurants, local crafts, a myriad of antique outlets, parks and gardens and of course the many hundreds of old majestic trees that give Cambridge its unique identity. Lake Karapiro is just a few minutes drive away, Mystery Creek and Waitomo Caves nearby, Rotorua less than an hours drive. All guest rooms have quality bed linens, TV, ensuite or guest bathroom facilities and total privacy.
Both of us are ex Restaurateurs so we guarantee you a lavish breakfast to set you up for the day. No smoking indoors please. laundry facilities available.
Directions: *Cross bridge at south end of the main street (Victoria Street), turn right off bridge, Marlowe Drive is first on right.*

Cambridge
Bed & Breakfast
Address: 58 Hamilton Road and Cnr of Bryce St. -
Also known as SH1 Cambridge
Name: Hansel & Gretel Bed & Breakfast
Telephone: (07) 827 8476
Fax: (07) 827 8476
Mobile: 025 537 928
Beds: 1 King/Queen, 1 Double, 2 Single
(3 bedrooms) (only 2 rooms at any one time)
Bathroom: 2 Private
Tariff: B&B (continental) Double $75, Single $65,
Credit Cards. NZ B&B Vouchers accepted
Nearest Town: Cambridge - 5 mins walk to centre of town

When you are wanting home comfort and privacy or want to chat you will find it here. Having spent most of our lives on sheep and dairy cow farms we bring country into our town home. In 5 minutes you can walk into Cambridge. We are near restaurants only 5 minutes walk. We have a Cairns terrier dog. There are many horse studs in our area. We have operated motor hotels and enjoy the many and varied people that visit and stay with us. The Waikato region provides visitors easy daily leisurely drives to Waitomo Caves 40 mins - Rotorua 55 mins, Hamilton Fieldays 15 mins - Lake Karapiro 10 mins and a host of other nearby interesting drives and walks. We can arrange visits to horse studs and horse trekking. We have testing golf course but easy walking.
Directions: *SH1 nearby Landmark Large White Anglican Church. Please phone and bookings are recommended.*

178

Cambridge
Homestay Bed and Breakfast
Address: 6 Curnow Place,
Leamington, Cambridge
Name: "Glenelg"
Ken & Shirley Geary
Telephone: (07) 823 0084 **Fax**: (07) 823 4279
Beds: 2 Queen, 1 Double, 1 Single (4 bedrooms)
Bathroom: 2 Ensuite, 1 Guests share
Tariff: B&B (full) Double $100, Single $65, Children $15, Dinner $15. NZ B&B
Vouchers accepted Surcharge
Nearest Town: Cambridge 2km

Glenelg welcomes you to Cambridge to a new home with quality spacious accommodation - warm quiet and private overlooking beautiful Waikato Farmland, with plenty of off street parking. Dinner meals available on request. A spa bath available for all guests. Beds have electric blankets and woolrests. Therapeutic massage available on request. Lake Karapiro is only 5 minutes away and we can offer accommodation for Rowers and all water sports. Mystery Creek where the NZ National Field Days and many other functions are held is only 15 mins away. Hamilton Airport is 20 mins away. Tours are also available to Waitomo Caves, Rotorua, Tauranga, Mt Maunganui, Auckland, Taupo, Coromandel Peninsula, Cambridge Horse Studs and Farm Tours. Courtesy vehicle available from Hamilton Airport, Cambridge Bus Depot, Hamilton Bus Depot. Small charge for Auckland Airport. Sky TV, laundry facilities available. Non smokers preferred - Smoking area provided. Pets welcome. For a brochure and directions, please phone.

Cambridge
Homestay
Address: "Riverlands", 7 Pope Tce, Cambridge
Name: Dave Lamb and Gemma McGarry
Telephone: (07) 827 6730
Mobile: (025) 578 718
Email: riverlands@amcom.co.nz
Beds: 1 Queen, 2 Single (2 bedrooms)
Bathroom: 1 Guests share
Tariff: B&B (special) Double $70, Single $40, Children $15, Dinner $20.
Credit cards. NZ B&B Vouchers accepted Surcharge $10
Nearest Town: Cambridge 1 Km to town centre

We are energetic young people, keen to meet new people and offer a warm friendly welcome. The home is a cosy modern 4 bedroom brick house nestled amongst the trees with the Waikato River flowing nearby with its picturesque bush walks. Cambridge town is only a short walk away with an excellent selection of restaurants, arts and crafts and antique stores. Bedrooms are comfortable with electric blankets, heating and tea/coffee making facilities. Breakfasts are hearty with a choice of cooked or continental and evening dinners are available on request. Laundry facilities and off street parking also available. The local region offers plenty to do with tramping, equestrian tours, horse riding and golf courses. Lake Karapiro is only minutes away for boating, fishing and we cater especially for water skiing, lake kayaking, mountain biking and trout fly fishing. All gear available. Mystery Creek Pavilion/Fieldays and Hamilton airport are only 10 mins away. We request no smoking indoors. We look forward to sharing the home and one cat with you and making your stay an enjoyable one. **Directions**: *Please phone for bookings and directions.*

Cambridge

B&B Country Stay
Address: 'Dunfarmin',
55 Gorton Road, RD 2, Cambridge
Name: Jackie and Bob Clarke
Telephone: (07) 827 7727
Fax: (07) 823 3357
Mobile: (025) 862 500
Beds: 1 Queen, 1 Double, 3 Single (3 bedrooms)
Bathroom: 1 Ensuite, 1 Guests share
Tariff: B&B (full) Double $90, Single $50, Dinner $25.
Nearest Town: Cambridge 9 kms

Welcome to our country home. Dunfarmin is situated 9 kms south of Cambridge just off state highway one, positioned on a commanding knoll, 20 acres sheltered by mature trees which offers the weary traveller peace and tranquillity. The outlook from the spacious home with in-ground swimming pool provides panoramic views of the surrounding Waikato country side. Further amenities include a floodlit tennis court and access to spa bath. Within easy reach of cafes, restaurants, antique and craft shops. Also Lake Karapiro famous for water skiing, rowing and boating. Enjoy your breakfast or other meals by prior arrangement in pleasant surroundings. We delight in meeting people and, having travelled ourselves, we appreciate the needs of the traveller.
Please feel at home with us plus Murdoch the old dog and Possum the cat. Being non smokers, we appreciate no smoking in the house.

Tirau

Farmstay
Address: 357 Rotorua Road,
R D 2, Tirau 2372
Name: Lin & Joy Cathcart
Telephone: (07) 883 1471
Beds: 1 King, 1 Double,
1 Single (3 bedrooms)
Bathroom: 1 Ensuite, 1 Family share
Tariff: B&B (full) Double $70, Single $45,
Dinner $22. NZ B&B Vouchers accepted $5 surcharge
Nearest Town: Tirau 5kms

Our 250 cow dairy farm is an easy 2 1/2 hour drive south from Auckland International Airport. We welcome visitors to our attractive property over which you may wander at leisure, fish our two trout streams or Lin will give you a tour in his "ute". All beds have electric blankets and complimentary tea/coffee are always available. Our family are adult and away from home - however we do have a cat. Hobbies include gardening, golf, patchwork, bridge and travel. By car we are central to Rotorua, Taupo, Waitomo Caves, Tauranga and Hamilton. Our home is "smoke free", and sorry no children under 12 years.
Directions: *Follow SH1 south from Tirau 2 km. Then take SH5 left to Rotorua for 3 km, cross Waihou River Bridge, and 200 metres on left is our gate - name on mailbox.*

Lake Karapiro/Tirau
Bed & Breakfast/Homestay
Address: 'Riversong', 213 Horahora Rd, RD1, Tirau. South Waikato 2372
Name: Maureen and Tony Jones
Telephone: (07) 883 1477
Fax: (07) 883 1477
Email:riversong.bb@xtra.co.nz
Beds: 2 Double, 2 Single (3 Bedrooms)
Bathroom: 1 Ensuite, 2 Private
Tariff: B&B (Full) Double Ensuite $80, Double $75, Single $45, Dinner $20 (by prior arrangement). Vouchers accepted $15 surcharge.
Nearest Town: Tirau

'Riversong' is situated alongside Lake Karapiro in the heart of the beautiful South Waikato set on an acre with lake views. Maureen and Tony are proud to offer a relaxed, smoke-free environment (indoors). We welcome overseas and local tourists as well as those just seeking a quiet retreat. Enjoy our log fire in winter. The lake offers water skiing, rowing, boating and fishing. Other amenities close by include golf, bowls, stud and farm tours. Private boat parking available. Also laundry facilities. We are 15 minutes south of the beautiful 'Tree Town' of Cambridge and 7 minutes north of Tirau, both with their arts, crafts and fascinating antique shops and eateries. We are very central with Rotorua Thermal Wonderland, Taupo, Waitomo Caves, Tauranga, Mount Maunganui and Hamilton all within an hours drive. We are 2 hours south of Auckland Airport. Both Tony and Maureen have travelled extensively and would love you to come and experience honest NZ hospitality at 'Riversong". **Directions**: *Heading south turn right off SH 1, half a km south of Route 29 (Tauranga), Riversong is 2.13 kms on left opposite lake, right hand driveway.*

Te Awamutu
Farmstay/Guest House
Address: Storey Road, Te Awamutu
Name: Regula Bleskie
Telephone: (07) 871 3301
Beds: 1 Double, 8 Single (5 bedrooms)
Bathroom: 1 Ensuite, 1 Guests share, 1 Family share
Tariff: B&B (full) Double $90, Single $50, Children $25, Dinner $25, Campervans welcome.
Nearest Town: Te Awamutu 4.5km

The 85 acre farm is situated in beautiful rolling countryside with cattle, horses, pigs, poultry, sheep, goats and pets. A spacious home with large living area, swimming pool and tennis court (racquets available) in a well planned garden. It welcomes you in winter with underfloor heating and a huge open fireplace. Large guest rooms, all with doors to the garden, some with lofts.
Specials: horsebackriding for beginners and experts long or short trips only $10.
Gigrides are available too, for children and adults. Blueberry, Raspberry and Persimen picking in season. Access to the milking of 450 dairy cows.
Directions: *100m after signpost Cambridge turn left into Te Rahu Rd, follow 3.5 km - come into Woodstock Rd, follow 1 km - Storey Rd. 1st driveway on your left (it's a long driveway).*

Te Awamutu

Farmstay
Address: Leger Farm,
114 St Leger Road,
Te Awamutu
Name: Peter & Beverley Bryant
Telephone: (07) 871 6676
Fax: (07) 871 6679
Mobile: (025) 364 419
Beds: 1 Double, 3 Single (3 bedrooms)
Bathroom: 1 Ensuite, 1 Private, 1 Guests share
Tariff: B&B (special/continental) Double $115, Single $60, Dinner $25.
NZ B&B Vouchers accepted $35 surcharge
Nearest Town: Te Awamutu 2km

'Leger Farm' offers country living at its finest. Panoramic views of the surrounding countryside are seen from every aspect of our home which is built of 'old' red bricks and redwood timber. The stunning architecturally designed home is tastefully decorated and nestled on 40 acres of some of NZ's best grazing land. Garden vistas overlook Mount Pirongia and Kakepuka. Grazing sheep, beef and deer can be seen close by, on our property. All bedrooms offer views, comfortable beds, electric blankets, quilts, flowers, reading material and balconies. We share interests of music, drama, gardening, tramping, travel, antiques, Lions Club and BPW. NZ meals of lamb and venison are our specialty. Leger Farm is located 2km south of Te Awamutu, off SH3. Te Awamutu, renowned world wide for its beautiful rose gardens is centrally situated, 30 mins north of Waitomo, famous 'Black Water' rafting and extensive limestone grotto. One hour to Rotorua thermal area, golf course 1km. Hamilton 30 mns.
Directions: *Please phone or fax for reservations and directions.*

Te Awamutu

Homestay
Address: 10 Brill Road,
RD 5, Te Awamutu
Name: Morton Homestay
Telephone: (07) 871 8814
Fax: (07) 871-8865
Beds: 1 Double, 2 Single
(2 bedrooms)
Bathroom: 1 Guest share
Tariff: B&B (full) Double $70,
Single $40, Dinner $20, Credit Cards Accepted. Campervans welcome.
NZ B&B Vouchers accepted $10 Surcharge
Nearest Town: Te Awamutu 8 mins

We welcome visitors to enjoy our hospitality and views of Mount Pirongia from our smoke-free home near Te Awamutu. Famed for its Rose Gardens, Te Awamutu is situated on State Highway 3, 2 hours drive south of Auckland. The Waitomo Caves, Rotorua and Lake Taupo are within easy driving distance from here. Hamilton airport is approx. 15 minutes away. Te Awamutu is an excellent base for bush walkers, golfers, fishermen (or should I say fisherpersons) and the field day site is only a short distance away. Marg & Dick are a very young middle aged couple whose sons have left home. We enjoy our garden travelling and other interest included philately music and woodturning. You are welcome to join us for dinner if you so wish or dine in Te Awamutu which has a good cross section of eating establishments.
Directions: *Please phone or fax for reservations and directions.*

Kawhia

Homestay
Address: Rosamond Tce, Kawhia
Name: "Rosamond House"
Mike Annette & Jessica Warrender
Telephone: (07) 871 0681
Fax: (07) 871 0681
Beds: 1 King (or 2 Single), 2 Double,
2 Single (4 bedrooms)
Bathroom: 1 Guests share
Tariff: B&B (full) Double $65, Single $45,
Children half price, Dinner $15.
Nearest Town: Te Awamutu 50 mins and 1 hour 10 mins from
Waitomo Caves SH31

If you are wanting to step back in time, then read on.
Our specialty is hospitality, peace and tranquillity. We want you to enjoy the comfort of our beautiful 96 year old solid kauri villa, which has a million dollar view, overlooking the Kawhia Harbour and township. Features we can offer you: Swimming pool, sauna, mountain bike riding, kayaking, caving, abseiling. Other attractions, hot pools, tennis courts, golf course, sports club, walks etc. I also operate Annie's Cafe/Restaurant in the main street. Kawhia which has an "a la carte" menu, come sit and relax over a wine or ale and enjoy the spectacular views of the Kawhia Harbour - open 7 days in summer. Winter hours changeable. Whether you are touring New Zealand on holiday or just seeking a quiet and peaceful retreat from daily life, we welcome you into our home and cafe. **Directions**: *Please phone.*

Otorohanga - Waitomo District

Homestay+ Self-contained Accom
Address: 'Brake's B&B', 147 Main North Road, (SH3), Otorohanga
Name: Ernest & Ann Brake
Telephone: (07) 873 7734 **Mobile**: (025) 845 419
Beds: 2 Single (1 bedroom)
Bathroom: 1 Family share.
SELF-CONTAINED UNIT: 1 Queensize, 1 single, plus rollaway bed.
Tariff: B&B (continental) Double $70, Single $47.50;
In SELF-CONTAINED UNIT: Double $60, Single $42.50, Third person $17, each extra $12, Children $1 per year of age minimum $5, Cot available; Breakfast optional and extra (continental $5, full $8 each). Discounts for 3 or more nights' stay. Vouchers accepted
Nearest Town: Otorohanga 2.5 km, Waitomo Caves 18 km

We are a retired farming couple with an adult family and have travelled overseas. Our home is on the northern outskirts of Otorohanga and we enjoy extensive views of the countryside from our elevated position. The self-contained unit is a quaint little garden cottage tastefully furnished with walls of natural timber panelling, quiet, private and comfortable. It has tea/coffee making facilities, toaster, fridge, TV; laundry facilities available. Evening meals are available at several restaurants in Otorohanga, while we invite you to enjoy breakfast with us. Otorohanga is an interesting rural town with its native bird park featuring a Kiwi house and aviary. It is the nearest town to Waitomo Glow-worm Caves and numerous bush walks, Waitomo Golf Course and the Waipa River, a good trout fishing stream. **Directions**: *From Otorohanga town centre take the main road (SH3 north and find us on the left approx 2.5km from town.*

183

Otorohanga - Waitomo District
Self-contained Accommodation

Address: Crofthill, R.D. 3, Otorohanga
Name: Jim & Jennifer Beveridge
Telephone: (07) 873 8232
Fax: (07) 873 8232
Mobile: (025) 501732
Email: crofthill@xtra.co.nz
Beds: 4 Single
(2 Bedrooms - each with 2 beds)
Bathroom: 1 Private
Tariff: B&B (full) Double $80, Single $50, Dinner $25 with pre-dinner drink available. Credit Cards. NZ B&B Vouchers accepted
Nearest Town: Otorohanga (6kms)

Crofthill is set in a large rural garden near Otorohanga with panoramic views from Mt Pirongia to Mt Ruapehu. The modern unit, connected to the house by a walkway, has 2 large twin bedrooms, shower, separate toilet, sitting room with television, books etc. and kitchen area with fridge and tea/coffee facilities. You are welcome to relax there and join us when you wish - perhaps for dinner (with a little notice, please). We retain an interest in farming through our son who farms in the heart of the King Country. We are ideally situated for visiting the Kiwi House, Waitomo Caves and other areas of interest. The Fieldays site is approximately 30-40 minutes away. We have a friendly cat by accident, inherited when our daughter went flatting. **Directions**: *Turn on to SH31 at the Southern end of Otorohanga - road to Kawhia. We are 6 kms from Otorohanga on the left hand side at the top of the first hill.*

Otorohanga, Waitomo District
Rural/Main Road B&B

Address: 'Kiwi Country B&B', cnr. SH3
& Mangaorongo Rd, North of Otorohanga
(Postal: PO Box 16, Otorohanga)
Name: Edsel & Marg Forde, Sons Rory & Paddy
Telephone: (07) 873 8173
Beds: 2 Double, 1 Single (2 bedrooms)
Bathroom: 1 Private
Tariff: B&B (continental) One person $38, Two people $70, Three people $100, Four people $130, Five people $150. Children negotiable. Pets negotiable. Cooked breakfast negotiable. Vouchers accepted
Nearest Town: Otorohanga 3km

A warm welcome awaits travellers at our comfortable modern home near NZ's Kiwi town, Otorohanga, closest town to the famous Waitomo Caves. We sampled, and enjoyed, B&B hospitality countless times on our travels of NZ and many parts of the world. Now, we appreciate any chance to offer the same at our home, which is handily located just off the main highway north of Otorohanga, set amongst trees and rolling green paddocks. Otorohanga's Kiwi House Complex is five minutes drive, Waitomo Caves approx 15 mins. Our home is smoke-free but for those who must, both bedrooms and the guest lounge/dining room have their own sunny decks. The lounge offers books, magazines, TV and hot drink making facilities. Our guest bathroom has internal access from both bedrooms so we have ensuite capacity. We offer comprehensive information on our region and NZ, with brochures and based on our own wide personal experience. Cot available. We look forward to meeting you.

Otorohanga - Waitomo
Farmstay+Self-contained   Accom.
Address: Meadowland B&B   746 SH 31, R.D.3, Otorohanga
Name: Tony & Jill Webber
Telephone: (07) 873 7729   **Fax**: (07) 873 7719
Beds: 1 Queen, 3 Double, 2 Single plus bunks (5 bedrooms)
Bathroom: 1 Private, 1 Guests share
Tariff: B&B (full) Double $75, Single $50, Children$20.   In self contained unit: Double $65, Single $45, Extra adult $20, Children $15.
Breakfast $5 pp extra (optional). Credit cards. Vouchers accepted
Nearest Town: Otorohanga 8 km

Welcome to Meadowland. Our farm is 8 km north of Otorohanga on State Highway 31. Places to visit in our area include: Kiwi House and bird aviary, Waitomo Caves, black water rafting, abseiling, natural bridge, bush walks, Marakopa Falls etc. We can arrange a visit to a nearby rotary cowshed; or carnation houses next door; or perhaps take you old time dancing or indoor bowling. We have swimming pool, tennis court, magnificent panoramic views of farmland, Pirongia and Kakepuka mountains and weather permitting Mt Ruapehu. Our accommodation is: three double bedrooms in our house with guest shared separate bathroom and toilet; or our self-contained cabin, can sleep up to six, with bunk beds and double bedsettee in one room and double bed in separate room. Own shower/toilet, washing machine, fridge, small stove, microwave, TV, electric blankets, heaters etc., breakfast optional. Non-smokers preferred. We have travelled overseas and enjoy meeting and talking with people.
Directions: *Turn on to SH31 at the South end of Otorohanga (between Price Cutter and the Holden Garage), we are 8 km from Otorohanga on the right hand side at the top of the second hill.*

Otorohanga
Homestay, Farmstay
Address: Mt Heslington Stud, 1375 Main North Road, RD 4, Otorohanga
Name: Jean and Philip Newman
Telephone: (07) 873 1873
Fax: (07) 873 7622
Mobile: (025) 490 817
Beds: 1 Double, 4 Single (2 bedrooms)
Bathroom: 1 Private
Tariff: B&B (special/full) Double $80, Single $50, Children $15, Dinner $25 pp (by arrangement). NZ B&B Vouchers accepted
Nearest Town: Otorohanga 12 km, Te Awamutu 18 km.

Guests are very welcome in our comfortable home where our aim is your comfort and guests are treated as friends. We are centrally situated on Straight Highway 3, 20 minutes from Te Awamutu, 20 minutes from Waitomo glow worm caves with the picturesque Waitomo golf course past Otorohanga with its wonderful large kiwi house. Our large home is surrounded by dairy farms and on our main highway property we have an Angus cattle stud and thoroughbred race horses. The horses continue to win in New Zealand, Australia and Asia. We offer a warm welcome and good hospitality, relax around the swimming pool, partake in farm activities, our pool table for evening entertainment. Warmth in our beds and our home is our criteria. Our vegetables, fruit and meat are all home grown.

Otorohanga - Waitomo District

Farmstay/Self Contained Cottage
Address: Waitomo Big Bird Bed & Breakfast,
17 Waitomo Caves Road (SH37), RD 7, Otorohanga
Name: Ann and Ross Barnes
Telephone: (07) 873 7459 or
0800 733 244 (see big birds)
Beds: Homestead: 2 Queen, 1 Single (2 Bedrooms).
Cottage: 1 Queen, 2 Double, 2 Single (3 Bedrooms)
Bathroom: 1 Guests share, 1 Family share
Tariff: B&b (Full or Continental) Double $65, Single $40, Dinner $20,
Children $10. Family $80. Credit cards accepted.
Nearest Town: Waitomo 8 kms, Otorohanga 8 km, Te Kuiti 10 km.

Relax and enjoy Waitomo Country Living visiting the first farm on Waitomo Caves Road. Ideally situated, just over 5 minutes to Waitomo, Otorohanga, Te Kuiti and 2 minutes to two highly recommended restaurants and golf course. We raise Ostrich, Emu and Cattle. A 15 minute farm walk provides panoramic views of this region. Free tour and Ostrich and Emu products for sale when available. Our setting - typical early NZ Homestead, spacious guest rooms opening onto veranda / garden area. Our self-contained cottage is perfect for families or groups. We have enjoyed being involved in the Tourist Industry here for 27 years, from guiding and developing caves to building walkways with DOC. We also own a Craft and Souvenir Shop "Baraka Crafts" in Otorohanga. The attraction here is "The World's Largest Spinning Wheel" and guests are offered 10% discounts. We also have a cat and dog. Common comments from visitors: "Friendly hospitality - a home away from home". Come as guests and leave as friends.

Waitomo Caves - Waitomo District

Farmstay
Address: Glenview Station,
R.D. 8, Te Kuiti
Name: Cindy & Warren Clayton-Greene
Telephone: (07) 878 7705
Fax: (07) 878 5066
Beds: 2 Double, 1 set of bunks (2 bedrooms).
Bathroom: 1 Ensuite. Private Lounge
with tea and coffee facilities and TV.
Tariff: B&B (full) Double $80, Single $50,
Children $25, Dinner (by prior arrangement) $20. NZ B&B Vouchers accepted
$20 surcharge
Nearest Town: Waitomo (5 km), Te Kuiti (23 km), Otorohanga (20km

You're invited to stay on a scenic New Zealand sheep and cattle station. A 2,200 acre station with 6000 sheep and 700 beef cattle. Enjoy the quiet and hospitality of rural life in New Zealand. Relax amongst the beautiful native bush, trout streams and unique limestone formations. Our guests enjoy hiking on the farm, or taking a drive out to the trout streams or relax in the conservatory. We have two school age children, so private lounge is available with tea/coffee facilities and television, or enjoy the evening with the family in the main lounge. We have a large attractive home set in beautiful gardens. You'll find us nestled in the hills above the Waitomo Caves with panoramic views. We are non smokers. **Directions:** *5km from Waitomo Caves: carry on past the Waitomo Caves going west towards Marakopa straight ahead at the round-about: we are on the tar seal road. Look on the right for the "Glenview" sign and our name and sign on the mail box. Please phone.*

186

Waitomo Village
Self-contained Accommodation
Address: Waitomo Caves Village
Name: Andree & Peter Dalziel
Telephone: (07) 878 7641
Fax: 07 8787466
Beds: 3 King/Queen, 1 Double,
2 Single, (5 Bedrooms)
Bathroom: 5 Ensuite
Tariff: B&B (continental)
Double $70,
Single $50. NZ B&B Vouchers accepted
Nearest Town: Waitomo Village, 100 metres

WAIKATO

Our home is only 100 metres from the Museum of Caves information office in the centre of the village and a few hundred metres from the Glow Worm Caves.
Our detached double and twin rooms with their individual ensuite toilet and shower facilities are of the highest standard.
With a variety of cave adventure trips - Black Water Rafting, Lost World, horse riding, excellent bush walks, a top golf course and a selection of the country's best gardens to visit, all within a short distance - we recommend that you allocate at least two days to spend with us.
We will arrange your meals.
If you cannot reach us by phone, just arrive - you will find a place with warm and friendly hospitality.

Te Kuiti - Waitomo District
Homestay
Address: 5 Grey St, Te Kuiti
Name: Pauline Blackmore
Telephone: (07) 878 6686
Email: pblackmorebb@hotmail.com
Beds: 2 Queen, 2 Single (3 bedrooms)
Bathroom: 2 Ensuite, 1 Private
Tariff: B&B (full) Double $60 - $70,
Single $40, Children $20, Credit Cards. NZ B&B Vouchers accepted
Nearest Town: Te Kuiti 1km.

We live in a comfortable old bungalow only 50 metres off Highway 3 where you will be greeted with warmth and invited to share a cup of tea or percolated coffee and homemade biscuits. All bedrooms have private toilet facilities and all beds are firm and comfortable with electric blankets, winter or summer duvets and a choice of pillows. There are electric heaters and teamaking facilities in the bedrooms. Fred the ginger cat shares the house with us. The atmosphere is relaxed and guests are welcome to chat or watch TV in the comfortable lounge. Breakfast is timed to suit you and includes fruit juice, cereals and fruit, followed by the full English breakfast. Tea or coffee of course. Waitomo Caves Village is 18 km north. Attractions there include White and Black water rafting in addition to the Waitomo Glowworm Cave and the Caves Museum.

Te Kuiti - Waitomo District

Farmstay

Address: 'Tapanui', 1714 Oparure Road, R.D. 5, Te Kuiti
Name: Mark & Sue Perry
Telephone: (07) 877 8549   **Fax**: (07) 877 8541   **Mobile**: (025) 949 873
Email: tapanui@xtra.co.nz
Beds: (Sleepyhead Elite)3 Super-King/twin zipper,1 Single (3 bedrooms)
Bathroom: 1 Ensuite, 1 Guests share or Private, Bathrobes for private bathroom.   Toiletries in both bathrooms.
Tariff: B&B (full) Double $110-$150, Single 100-$140, Dinner $35, Not suitable for children.   Visa/Mastercard.   NZ B&B Vouchers accepted $39-$75 surcharge Double/$30-$66 surcharge Single
Nearest Town: Te Kuiti 20km, Otorohanga 32km, 17km from SH 3.

"A Note From Two Fellow Travellers"
"This is New Zealand at its very best: an extraordinary scenic drive on a sealed road through endless green hills brings you to "Tapanui", not far from Waitomo Caves. You feel genuinely welcome in this magnificent home owned by an active farming couple with wide ranging interests in gardening, fishing and travel.   "Take part in the farm work or watch their day unfold while you lazily tend to the pet sheep, donkeys, and Charlotte the kune kune pig. Then, enjoy knowledgeable conversation about the farm and about the world.   "The homestead is wonderful, very large and with tremendous privacy. One separate guest wing includes a spacious bedroom, a super-king bed, a single bed and ensuite. Just out the huge windows are vistas of green, everywhere. And, your own patio!   "Other rooms include either comfortable and cosy twin or super-king beds (your choice) with a bathroom. Again, the view is from a story book, the hospitality warm and heartfelt.   "Everything has been thought of from feather duvets and electric blankets to heated towels rails, fly screens and central heating. The home cooked meals alone are worth the visit.   "Over 3000 Romney sheep and 700 head of cattle roam the hillsides. Most happily, it all gives you those very special moments that cameras and memories capture. Forever you will treasure your trip to "Tapanui".   "We came as guests and left as friends."
Rick Antonson and Janice Sapergia, Vancouver, Canada
Directions: *Please email, phone, fax or write for reservations and directions. Our home is smoke free. Web sites:*
http://nz.com/webnz/bbnz/tapa.htm
http://www.friars.co.nz/hosts/tapanui.html
http://www.ginz.com/accomm/tapanui.htm
Home Page: http://nz.com/webnz/bbnz/tapa.htm

Te Kuiti - Waitomo District
Homestay
Address: Gadsby Road, Te Kuiti
Name: Margaret & Graeme Churstain
Telephone: (07) 878 8191
Beds: 1 Queen, 3 Single (3 Bedrooms).
Unit: 1 Double, 3 Single.
Bathroom: Ensuite Unit - Guests share upstairs.
Tariff: B&B (continental) Double $60, Single $30, Dinner (with prior notice) $15pp, Campervans facilities available $20pp. NZ B&B Vouchers accepted
Nearest Town: Te Kuiti 3kms - Waitomo District

Our B&B is on a farmlet on Gadsby Road, signposted on S.H.3 at the Northern end of Te Kuiti. We have enjoyed accommodating visitors from all over the world and New Zealand for some years now, offering a relaxed and comfortable homestay. To sit on the deck we guarantee rural views you would find hard to forget, with aerial topdressing and farming activity common scenes from all round views. In one of New Zealand's best sheep and cattle producing areas and boasting the "Shearing Capital of the World" and a statue to match Te Kuiti and surrounding areas offer many leisure activities with the famous Waitomo Caves only 10 minutes away. Warm comfortable beds we can provide with guests share bathroom or if you prefer, our downstairs unit is available with private bathroom, ideal for families. Laundry facilities are available at a small charge. Our dog and cat welcome yours.

Waitomo Caves
Farmstay
Address: 'Forest Hills', Boddies' Rd, RD 1, Te Kuiti
Name: Jocelyn and Peter Boddie
Telephone: (07) 878 8764
Fax: (07) 878 8764
Email: jocpetbod@xtra.co.nz
Beds: 1 Double (1 bedroom)
Bathroom: 1 Private
Tariff: B&B (continental) Double $85, Single $60, Dinner $25 pp.
Nearest Town: Waitomo Caves 8km, Te Kuiti 13km

New Zealand Association FARM & HOME HOSTS

Joss and Peter Boddie invite you to stay,
Enjoy country living down Waitomo way.
In our hilltop residence, Ruapehu the view,
500 hectares of farmland and near the caves too.
Midwife and farmer with interests abounding,
Art, music, gardens in a rural surrounding.
The four kids we had have largely all flown,
Just cats Fred and Presto to call us their own.
A smokefree environment we do highly treasure,
Our large family home now awaits your pleasure.
You're welcome where able to fit in on the farm,
Go for walks, enjoy peace and discover rural charm.
There's a spa on the deck to rest and unwind,
Please phone for directions - we're easy to find.
Forget city life, stress, phone and fax,
Enjoy drinks by the fire at days end to relax.

Te Kuiti
Farmstay/B&B
Address: "Panorama Farm",
Carter Road,
RD 2, Te Kuiti
Name: Michael & Raema Warriner
Telephone: (07) 878 5104
Fax: (07) 878 8104
Beds: 1 Double, 3 Single
(2 bedrooms)
Bathroom: 1 Guests share
Tariff: B&B (full) Double $66, Single $35,
Children half price, Dinner $20.
Credit Cards. NZ B&B Vouchers accepted
Nearest Town: Te Kuiti 6km

Welcome to Panorama Farm 72 acres of lush pasture producing prime beef and lamb. Our home is a large renovated house with modern facilities. A verandah shades two sides providing a panoramic view of bush-clad hills, fertile valleys and distant peaks with golden dawns and spectacular sunsets.

Situated 6km east of Te Kuiti we provide easy access to many attractions, the famous Waitomo Glowworm Caves, Lost World, Blackwater rafting and other adventures are only 25 mins away. Within 2 hours are Rotorua, Taupo, Whakapapa skifields and Tauranga, Auckland Airport 2 1/4 hours. But why not relax with a farm walk or garden stroll or just read a good book. Be our guest. We have lived in this area for 40 years and know and appreciate its points of interest which we would love to share with you. Phone or fax for directions. Resident cat.

Piopio - Waitomo District
Farmstay
Address: Puke-Kohatu,
Aria Road, Piopio,
Te Kuiti
Name: Maurice & Jennifer Kearns
Telephone: (07) 877 7801
Fax: (07) 877 7801
Beds: 4 Single (2 bedrooms)
Bathroom: 1 Private
Tariff: B&B (full) Double $80,
Single $40, Children negotiable,
Dinner $20pp. Credit Cards accepted.
NZ B&B Vouchers accepted
Nearest Town: Piopio 8 km, Te Kuiti 30 km

Would you like to share our home with us for a night - or longer?
We have 2 twin rooms with snug beds, feather duvets, electric blankets and heaters. All rooms have garden outlooks. No steps. We accept only one booking (1-4 persons) per night. Gardening is our special interest and our home is nestled amongst natural limestone outcrops and mature trees, interspersed with perennial plantings. A working waterwheel, rock formations and small caves add interest, and contribute to an atmosphere of peace and tranquillity. Retired, but still living on our farm, we enjoy sharing our time and our environment with visitors.
Directions: *Travelling south on SH3, turn left at crossroads in centre of Piopio. Proceed for 8 km. We are first home on right after passing the Paekaka Road (which turns off to right). Name on mailbox.*

Pio Pio - Waitomo District

Farmstay
Address: Carmel Farm, Main Road, Box 93 Pio Pio
Name: Leo & Barbara Anselmi
Telephone: (07) 877 8130 **Fax**: (07) 877 8130
Email: Carmelfarms@xtra.co.nz
Beds: 8 Single or 2 Super-king, 4 single (4 bedrooms)
Bathroom: Ensuite family unit, 1 Guests share upstairs.
Tariff: B&B (full) Double $100, Single $50, Dinner $25pp (with complimantary wine). Credit Cards Visa/Mastercard.
Nearest Town: Te Kuiti 19 kms

Barbara and Leo Anselmi own and operate a 1200 acre sheep, beef and dairy farm. You will be welcomed into a 3000 square feet modern home set in picturesque gardens, in a lovely limestone valley. You will be treated to delicious home cooked meals and the warmth of our friendship. Whether enjoying the excitement of mustering mobs of cattle and sheep, viewing the milking of 500 cows, driving around the rolling hills on the four-wheeled farm-bike, relaxing as you bask in the sun by the pool or wandering through the gardens, you will experience unforgettable memories of breathtaking scenery, a clean green environment. We have farm pets who love the attention of our guests. The donkeys are waiting to be fed. We look over a beautiful 18 hole golf course which welcomes visitors. The property is a short distance from Black Water Rafting and canoeing activities, The Lost World Cavern, and the famous Waitomo Caves. Nearby are bush walks and the home of the rare Kokako bird. We can help to arrange activities for people of all ages & interests including garden visits and horse riding. Please let us know your preference. We are 140 kms from Rotorua/Taupo.
Directions: *Travel 19 kms South of Te Kuiti on SH3 towards Piopio. Carmel Farm is on the right. We can arrange to pick up from Otorohanga, Te Kuiti or Waitomo, if required.*

Piopio - Waitomo District

Country Homestay
Address: 'Bracken Ridge'
Aria Road, Piopio
Name: Rob & Susan Hallam
Telephone: (07) 877 8384
Email: rhallam@piopio.school.nz
Beds: 4 Single (2 Bedrooms)
Bathroom: 1 Private
Tariff: B&B (full) Double $70, Single $40,
Children under 12 years $20. Dinner $20pp.
NZ B&B Vouchers accepted
Nearest Town: Te Kuiti 24km, Piopio 1km

Please join us and enjoy a peaceful, relaxing time at our large, modern family home set in attractive, landscaped gardens on a 10 acre sheep and cattle farmlet. Our elevated site provides panoramic views of the beautiful King Country's green pastures, trees and limestone rocks. We are happy to share our knowledge of local attractions including bush walks, waterfalls, scenic drives, trout fishing, golf and museum. Private guest facilities on a separate level offer spacious rooms with comfortable beds and electric blankets. Please do not smoke inside nor bring pets. Our interests range from music and gardening to boating and we enjoy meeting people from all over the world.
Visit the world famous Waitomo Caves just 30 minutes away.
Directions: *Travelling south on SH 3 turn left at centre of Piopio village and proceed 1 kilometre. Look for our name at gate on right past 100km sign. Please phone ahead for reservations.*

Ongarue, Taumarunui

Farmstay
Address: 'Foxley Station', RD Ongarue
Name: Tony & Kitrena Fullerton-Smith
Telephone: (07) 896 6104
Fax: (07) 896-6919
Beds: 1 Queen, 2 Single
(2 bedrooms)
Bathroom: 1 Private
(only 1 party of guests taken at a time).
Tariff: B&B (continental, Full on request)
Double $85, Single $50, Dinner from $25 (with complimentary wine and pre dinner drink). NZ B&B Vouchers accepted
Nearest Town: 25km north of Taumarunui on SH 40.

'Foxley Station' is a 3500 acre hill country farm situated in the heart of the King Country, running sheep, cattle and deer. The 'Homestead' is set in a lovely country garden with tennis court and swimming pool. We welcome people to observe or participate in our farm life. Go walking through our Native Bush Reserve or just relax. Enjoy home cooked meals or for something special try our 'Game Menu' (trout, duck, venison). Nearby attractions all within one hour of us: Lake Taupo, Wanganui River, Tongariro National Parks, Scenic Flights, Waitomo Caves, Ski Fields, Local Gardens and Golf Course. We are in our 40's. Our children, Sarah and Andrew are away at University. We invite you to experience our friendly and relaxed farm life and country living. Looking forward to entertaining you in our home. **Directions**: *Please phone, fax or write for reservations and directions. Our home is smoke free*

Taumarunui
Farmstay
Address: Eastward Road, Waituhi,
R.D.4, Taumarunui
Name: Yvonne & Eric Walker
Telephone: (07) 896 6041
Fax: (07) 896 6040
Beds: 1 Double, 2 Single (2 bedrooms)
Bathroom: 1 Family share
Tariff: B&B (full) Double $60, Single $35,
Children half price, Dinner $15, Campervans accepted.
NZ B&B Vouchers accepted
Nearest Town: 25km east of Taumarunui off SH 41

Our home is large and comfortable, with a spacious living area, overlooking garden and swimming pool. It is set in pleasant surroundings in a peaceful valley only 20 minutes from the rural township of Taumarunui.

Taumarunui offers Jetboat tours down the Wanganui River, canoeing and trout fishing, as well as a golf course with an excellent reputation which welcomes visitors.

Our farm is a 45 minute drive from Tongariro National Park where seasonal activities such as skiing and tramping are available.

For those keen on exploring a genuine NZ farm, we have 360 hectares, 60 of which are in native bush. We farm sheep, cattle, deer and have various other animals such as pigs, dogs, a cat and also horses suitable for riding.

Please phone for directions.

Taumarunui
Farmstay
Address: Orangi Road, RD 4,
Taumarunui
Name: Gayle and Dave Richardson
Telephone: (07) 896 6035
Fax: (07) 896 6035
Beds: 1 Double, 3 Single
(2 bedrooms)
Bathroom: 1 Family Share
Tariff: B&B (full) Double $70,
Single $35, Children under 12 half price, Dinner $15 per person, Campervans welcome $20 max 4 people, Backpackers welcome. NZ B&B Vouchers accepted
Nearest Town: 10 km East of Taumarunui on SH 41.

Welcome to Orangi.

Come and relax in our lovely old homestead, with plenty of room for children, while ensuring quiet and privacy for those without.

Our guestrooms are spacious and comfortable, with electric blankets and comfy duvets. Go trout fishing at the backdoor, or just stroll along the riverbank. Toby and Jana aged 10 and 11 complete our family, they are well mannered and well behaved children, who enjoy company.

Our outside dog and our cats are very friendly.

We love meeting and entertaining people, and look forward to enjoying your company in our spacious home. We hope you will join us for dinner, for a good country meal, or feel free to just come for bed and breakfast. Our laundry is always available for use.

193

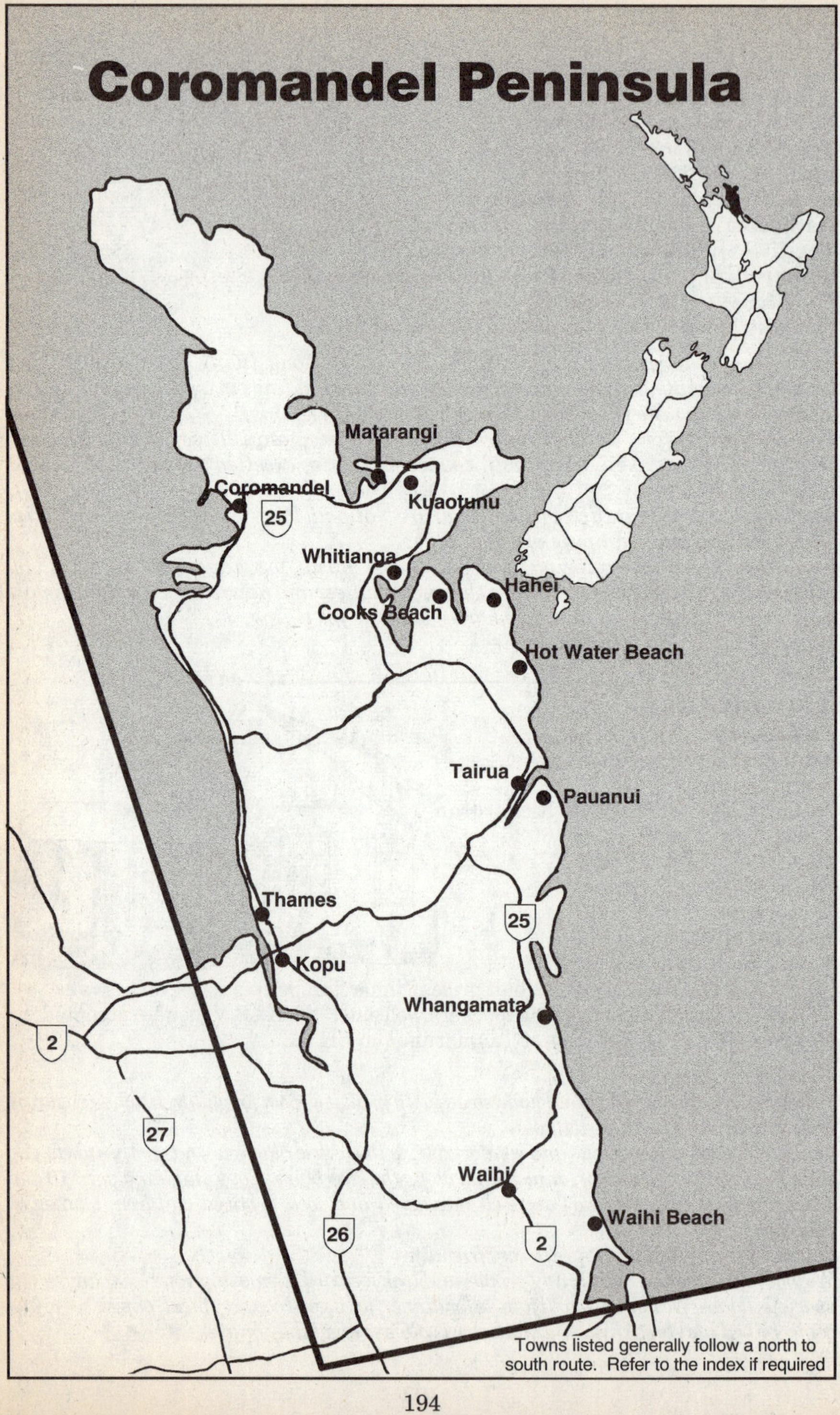

Coromandel Peninsula

Matarangi

Coromandel

25

Kuaotunu

Whitianga

Hahei

Cooks Beach

Hot Water Beach

Tairua

Pauanui

Thames

25

Kopu

2

Whangamata

27

Waihi

26

2

Waihi Beach

Towns listed generally follow a north to
south route. Refer to the index if required

194

Thames

Homestay
Address: Please phone
Name: Russell Rutherford
Telephone: (07) 868 7788
Fax: (07) 868 7788
Mobile: (025) 737 993
Email: rrutherford@xtra.co.nz
Beds: 1 Double, 3 Single (2 bedrooms)
Bathroom: 1 Private, 1 Family share
Tariff: B&B (continental) Double $70, Single $45, Children 1/2 price;
Dinner $20.   NZ B&B Vouchers accepted
Nearest Town: Thames - 5 mins walk

Glenys and Russell are NZ born and enjoy their comfortable and spacious home overlooking the Firth of Thames. Our interests include, golf, music, gardening, travel and geneology. Our guest accommodation has a private lounge, TV, a selection of books, self service tea and coffee. The garden provides fruit for preserves and breakfast which includes a selection of cereals, muffins, toast, tea and freshly ground coffee. Being an historic goldmining settlement, gold prospecting diggings are of particular interest. Due to its natural beauty the Coromandel has attracted many painters and potters. Their galleries can be visited on a scenic day trip up the coast to Coromandel village, returning back through the beach resorts of Whitianga, Hot Water Beach and Pauanui. The rugged hills and native bush appeal to hikers and nature lovers. Take time to relax in comfort and enjoy Kiwi hospitality. We welcome your visit. Safe off-street parking.

Thames

Farmstay+Self-contained Garden Apartment.
Address: 'Thorold', Kopu,
R.D.1, Thames
Name: Helen & Tony Smith
Telephone: (07) 868 8480
Fax: (07) 868 8480
Mobile: 025-941 286
Beds: 1 Queen, 1 Double,
 4 Single (4 bedrooms)
Bathroom: 2 Private
Tariff: B&B (continental)

New Zealand
Association
FARM & HOME
HOSTS

Apartment $70pp x 2, $50pp x 4 ($200), Double $140, Single $80, Children $40,
Dinner $45 with comp drinks and wine. Vouchers accepted $40 surcharge
Nearest Town: Thames - 5 Kms

'Thorold' is perfectly situated for visitors to the Coromandel Peninsular - 5 minutes from Thames in a private, peaceful farm setting. The garden apartment is deluxe, spacious, beautifully appointed and totally private. Two bedrooms - 1 Queen, 1 Twin with bathroom adjoining. Kitchen, sitting room with TV and Billiard table. All rooms open to a large verandah and swimming pool. In our home we have a Double or Twin bedroom with TV and private bathroom. Only one group of visitors at any one time in apartment or our home. We have a beef farm at Coromandel and Tony has a Livestock Company based at home and is usually available to enjoy breakfast with our visitors in the dining room. Our interests include tramping, fishing, building, gardening, trees and forestry. We are 4th generation New Zealanders and can assure you of a memorable stay at Thorold.
Directions: *Please phone.*

Thames Coast
Country Homestay

Address: 29 Eames Crescent,
Te Mata Bay,
Thames Coast.
Please phone for directions.
Name: Helen & Charlie Burgess
Telephone: (07) 868 4754
Fax: (07) 868 4757
Mobile: (025) 233 0656
Email: temata.hstay@xtra.co.nz
Beds: 1 Queen, 1 Double, 2 Single (3 bedrooms)
Bathroom: 1 Guests share + shower room + separate toilet.
Tariff: B&B (full) Double $80, Single $40, Dinner $25.
Nearest Town: Thames 23km, Coromandel 34km

Come and stay with us at Te Mata Bay, any day of the year. You won't be disappointed! Good beds, excellent home cooked meals, great company too! Enjoy the peace, the wonderful sea and mountain views from the balcony which surrounds our large comfortable home. Guests Bedrooms are pleasantly furnished and have sea and mountain views. We have a pianola and pool table for your enjoyment. Also a comfortable lounge with a log fire. Visit our local water garden and square Kauri 15 min drive or Coromandels Driving Creek Railway 35 min away or the famous Hot Water Beach 50 min by car. Hot bread, croissants, cappucino and fresh perculated coffee along with fresh eggs from our chickens and a large choice of cereals and fruit are offered for breakfast. Make our day come and stay. WE ARE A NON SMOKING FAMILY.
Directions: *Please phone for directions.*

Thames
Farmstay+Self-contained Accom.

Address: 'Wharfedale Farmstay',
R.D.1, Thames
Name: Rosemary & Chris Burks
Telephone: (07) 868 8929
Fax: (07) 868 8926
Beds: 1 Double, 2 Single (2 bedrooms)
Bathroom: 2 Private
Tariff: B&B (full, special or continental)
Double $100-$120, Single $80.
Nearest Town: Thames.
We are situated 8km South East of Thames on SH 25A

For 10 years we have enjoyed offering hospitality to guests from around the world and have featured in Air New Zealand "Pacific Way" and Japan's "My Country" magazines. We cordially invite you to share our idyllic lifestyle set in 9 acres of paddocks and gardens surrounded by lovely native bush. Meander across the lawn to the riverwalk, picking perhaps peaches or citrus fruits and enjoy in total privacy natures swimming pools whilst kingfisher and rosella swoop overhead. Our gardens reflect our interests in old roses, no dig organic cultivation. We enjoy wholefoods and home produced meat. Our goat herd allows us to share their lives and milk. We are 75 minutes from Auckland and 10 minutes from Thames. Close proximity to beautiful Coromandel beaches. Wharfedale offers double room or self-contained flat both with private bathrooms. Cosy log fires and electric blankets in winter and cool shade in summer. We have no children or indoor animals. We look forward to meeting you.

Thames
Self-contained Accommodation
Address: 304 Grafton Road,
Thames
Name: David & Ferne Tee
Telephone: (07) 868 9971
Fax: (07) 868 3075
Mobile: (025) 835 402
Beds: 1 Queen, 4 Double,
2 Single (6 bedrooms)
Bathroom: 6 Ensuite
Tariff: B&B (continental) Double $110-$150,
Single $90. Visa/Master
Nearest Town: Thames

Grafton cottage is nestled in the foothills of the Coromandel Peninsula overlooking the Historic gold and timber town of Thames. The tree lined property offers rest and privacy for the romantic weekend away while being central to the many Restaurants, Arts and Crafts centres, Museums and old gold workings. Being just 1 hour from Auckland International Airport, Thames is the ideal base to explore the Peninsula and is away from the hustle and bustle of the city. The Peninsula boasts extensive bush reserves covering rugged mountainous ranges. To the east are world renowned Pacific beaches, while in the west are the calmer waters of the Firth.
Directions: *Turn right at Toyota factory (Bank St) follow to end, turn right into Parawai Road, 4th on left is Grafton Road. Go to the top of road.*

Thames
Homestay
Address: Brunton House,
210 Parawai Rd, Thames
Name: Albert & Yvonne Sturgess
Telephone: (07) 868 5160
Fax: (07) 868 5160
Mobile: (025) 235 2449
Email: BruntonHouse@xtra.Co.Nz
Beds: 1 Queen, 2 Double, 2 Single (3 bedrooms)
Bathroom: 1 Guests share, 1 Family share
Tariff: B&B (full) Double $85, Single $50, Dinner $25pp by prior
arrangement. NZ B&B Vouchers accepted $15 surcharge
Nearest Town: Thames 1 mile

We invite you to share the grace and charm of our lovely Victorian home. Built in 1869 it is spacious but also homely, comfortable and smoke-free.
In summer excellent indoor outdoor living, BBQ area, tennis court and swimming pool make this a great place to relax. In winter with fires and good heating, comfortable beds with electric blankets and fluffy quilts our home is cosy and warm. Self service tea and coffee always available. In the evening enjoy the use of our billiard table, read and relax with a book from our comprehensive library, watch TV or sit and chat in the comfortable lounge. Our interests include travel, steamtrains, embroidery, square dancing, reading, gardening. We have a cat and a dog. Thames is the gateway to the Coromandel Peninsula for you to explore and enjoy the whole of the Coromandel.
Directions: *Opposite Toyota turn into Banks St, turn right into Parawai Rd. After Brunton Cres look for us on the left.*

197

Thames
Homestay
Address: 'Huia Lodge',
589 Kauaeranga Valley Rd,
R.D.2, Thames
Name: Val & Steve Barnes
Telephone: (07) 868 6557
Fax: (07) 868 6557
Beds: 2 Queen, 2 Single (3 bedrooms)
Bathroom: 2 Ensuite
Tariff: B&B (full) Double $75, Single $40, Children $15,
Dinner $20 - by arrangement. Credit cards. Vouchers accepted $10 surcharge
Nearest Town: Thames 10 mins, Auckland City 1 hr 40 mins.

Your choice of 2 Units:
Upstairs - one large room has queen and single bed and ensuite. Downstairs one single room plus double (queen) room with ensuite. Both units have tea / coffee facilities. Stay with us and enjoy the peace and tranquillity of Kauaeranga Valley, just 10 minutes from Thames. We grow our own fruit and vegetables and enjoy the rural lifestyle with Bart the cat on our 4 acre property. We're in our early 50's and both enjoy meeting travellers. You'll be free to relax in your Unit or to share our living rooms and deck with us. We'll be happy to suggest outings such as local attractions in Thames, a gentle native bush walk in the nearby Forest Park or a more energetic hike to the spectacular Pinnacles - 2500 ft. Guests have found Huia Lodge to be an ideal base to explore the whole Peninsula from.
Directions: *Turn into Banks St at the BP Petrol Station at the south end of Thames. Banks St becomes Parawai Rd which leads you to the Valley. You'll find our Huia Lodge sign 8 kms from the Petrol Station.*

Thames
Country Stay+Self-contained Accom
Address: "Kauaeranga Country",
446 Kauaeranga Valley Rd,
Pakaraka, Thames
Name: Lyn and Dave Lee
Telephone: (07) 868 6895
Fax: (07) 868 6895
Beds: 1 Queen, 2 Single
(2 bedrooms)
Bathroom: 1 Private
Tariff: B&B (full) Double $90, Single $50, Children $20 by arrangement. Credit cards. NZ B&B Vouchers accepted May to September
Nearest Town: Thames 6 kms

Our country-stay offers you:
- *A spacious private guest wing.*
- *Peaceful surroundings on the banks of a stream.*
- *Close proximity to bush walks and Dept. of Conservation.*
- *Kayaks for fun in the water.*
- *Safe private swimming in Stoney bottomed stream.*
- *Closeness to beautiful Coromandel beaches.*
- *Only one group of guests at a time.*
Dave and I are a Kiwi couple who have lived most of our lives in Thames, and enjoy gardening, horse riding and local history. Dave has a forge where he shoes our horses and is more than happy to give you a "demo". Arrive as strangers and leave as friends.

Thames
Homestay
Address: 'Mountain Top Bed & Breakfast',
452 Kauaeranga Valley Rd,
R.D.2, Thames
Name: Elizabeth McCracken & Allan Berry
Telephone: (07) 868 9662
Fax: (07) 868 9662
Beds: 1 Queen, 1 Single,
1 Double (2 Bedrooms).
Bathroom: 1 Guest share
Tariff: B&B (full) Double $85,
Single $45, Children discounted, Dinner $20-$25. Credit cards.
NZ B&B Vouchers accepted between 1 February - 24 December.
Nearest Town: Thames

Allan and I grow mandarins, olives and raise coloured sheep on a small organic farm. Our house and dining room overlook river and ranges. The guest wing comprising two bedrooms, decks overlooking the river, shared bathroom, lounge with fridge, TV and extensive library, is well suited to four or spacious for two. Our families are grown up, leaving us time to entertain and cook for guests mostly from home grown produce. Coromandel Forest Park with superb walking tracks,is 15 minutes away. From home we can arrange walks over neighbouring farmland through bush or swimming in forest pools. In our relaxed garden we raise native trees, teach our grand children about the forest or entertain our friends with our Jack Russell Bob and cat Mehitabel. Sometimes we go yachting but above all we like meeting people. Come and let us look after you.

Thames
Bed & Breakfast
Address: Acorn Lodge,
161 Kauaeranga Valley,
RD2, Thames
Name: Dennis and Pat
Telephone: (07) 868 8723
Fax: (07) 868 8713
Mobile: (025) 239 3858
Beds: 1 Queen, 1 Double,
1 Single (3 Bedrooms)
Bathroom: 2 Guests share

Tariff: B&B (Full/Continental) Double $85, Single $50, Dinner $20 by arrangement. Credit Cards accepted. NZ B&B Vouchers accepted $15 surcharge
Nearest Town: Thames 5 mins. Auckland airport 1 hour.

Relax and enjoy the tranquillity of rural and bush views from our large comfortable, smoke-free home, set in 2 acres of park-like grounds. You will be welcomed with a pot of tea or coffee and hot muffins. Our large guest lounge features an atrium with a cascading waterfall, where you can be pampered or watch TV. The queen size guest room opens onto its own private sunny patio. For the more energetic, the Kauaeranga Forest park offers a wide range of tramping tracks, mountain biking, horse trekking and swimming in the many deep pools. One of these pools is only 2 mins walk from Acorn Lodge, and at night you can see the glow worms. We have a large vegetable garden, fruit trees, a friendly German shepherd (dog), cat, goat and 10 sheep. We look forward to making your stay special.

Coromandel

Coromandel Homestay
Address: 74, Kowhai Drive,
Te Kouma Bay, Coromandel
Name: Hilary & Vic Matthews
Telephone: (07) 866 8046
Fax: (07) 866 8046
Beds: 2 Double, 1 Single (2 bedrooms)
Bathroom: 1 Ensuite, 1 Private
Tariff: B&B (continental) Double $80, Single $50, Dinner with wine by prior arrangement $30. Credit cards, Vouchers accepted $15 surcharge.
Nearest Town: Coromandel 11km, Thames 60km, Auckland 2.5 hours. Ferry service to Auckland. On most days. Docks in Te Kouma Bay.

Our modern pole house is situated 740 metres from a safe, sandy beach on the southern side of the Coromandel Harbour. We have a bush setting and beautiful views. Vic is a professional furniture designer and maker. Our home is full of beautiful hand made furniture. Hilary weaves, spins and enjoys gardening and woodturning. We travel widely and have many interests. We feel that due to open stairs and balconies, the house is unsuitable for toddlers. We have a pet cat and a smoke free home. Coromandel area offers beaches, swimming, fishing and walking. **Directions**: *Travel north from Thames (SH 25) for about 60 minutes, down a steep hill to Coromandel Harbour, turn very sharply left into Te Kouma Road. Drive around the Harbour's edge, past a big boat ramp for about 3km. Turn left into, Kowhai Drive. Our house is up the steep hill. There is a large wooden sign on the right giving our name.*

Coromandel

Homestay/Countrystay
Address: 'Jacaranda' Lodge,
3195 Tiki Rd, Coromandel
Name: Gary & Gayle Bowler
Telephone: (07) 866 8002 **Fax**: (07) 866 8002
Email: jacarandaCOROMANDEL@xtra.co.nz
Beds: 3 Queen, 1 Double, 1 Twin (5 Bedrooms)
Bathroom: 2 Ensuite, 1 Private, 1 Guests share.
Tariff: B&B (continental) Double $75-$120, Single $45-$60, Dinner $30, Children negotiable. Credit Cards.   NZ B&B Vouchers accepted $30 surcharge for ensuite/private bathroom.
Nearest Town: Coromandel 3km, Thames 50km,

Welcome to Jacaranda, a warm, relaxing and comfortable home set on 6 acres of peaceful farmland and landscaped gardens featuring roses and natives. Enjoy our spacious bedrooms and gracious lounge enhanced by family paintings, crafts and handwork. We offer ample verandahs, separate TV lounge and kitchen facilities for guests. We both enjoy gardening. Gayle loves tramping the many wonderful local trails. Gary loves tennis, golf and fishing. Games can be arranged and equipment is available. Other activities include craft and garden trails and great beaches. Whenever possible breakfast is served outside overlooking the rose garden. Homemade bread or muffins and preserves are features of our continental breakfast as are organic meat and vegetables or seafood of our dinners. Jacaranda is an excellent base for your Coromandel holiday. Perfect for small groups. Negotiable off season rates. One lovely outside dog. Self contained unit available by arrangement and beach house at beautiful Whangapoua **Directions**: *On Pacific Coast Highway, (SH25). We look forward to meeting you.*

Coromandel

Homestay Bed & Breakfast-"Huntington Lodge"
Address: SH 25.
1745 Tiki Road, Coromandel
Name: Judy and Bill
Telephone: (07) 866 7499
Fax: (07) 866 7499
Beds: 1 King, 1 Queen, 1 Single (2 bedrooms)
Bathroom: 1 Guests share
Tariff: B&B (continental) Double $75, Single $50, Dinner $30, Children negotiable. Full breakfast $5 pp extra. Laundry facilities available. NZ B&B Vouchers accepted $8 surcharge
Nearest Town: Coromandel 1 1/2 km north. 55 km Thames, Auckland 2 1/2 hours. Ferry pick up passes gate.

We invite you to share our recently renovated comfortable home on 1 1/2 acres of rural land with views of surrounding farm land and bush clad hills. The bedrooms are warm and inviting, one with a king-size and single bed plus adjoining toilet. A long shady verandah provides an opportunity to just sit a while or enjoy breakfast (which includes hot, home-made bread) outdoors. Barbecue available for guests' uses. Dinner is available (by arrangement) with three courses and includes New Zealand wines, home grown produce, our own lamb and local seafood. Guests have the opportunity to talk to our sheep (we have a few), make acquaintance with George our cat, explore the Coromandel Peninsula with is varied tourist attractions, beautiful beaches or just let us pamper you.
We are available by prior arrangement to meet ferry, bus or plane.
Directions: *Easy to find on SH 25 1 1/2 km south of Coromandel town.*

Coromandel

Self Contained Accommodation B&B
Address: "Country Touch",
39 Whangapoua Road,
Coromandel
Name: Colleen and Geoff Innis
Telephone: (07) 866 8310
Fax: (07) 866 8310
Mobile: (025) 971 196
Beds: 2 Queen, 4 Single (4 bedrooms)
Bathroom: 4 Ensuites
Tariff: B&B (continental) Double $85, Single $50, Children negotiable.
NZ B&B Vouchers accepted &10 Surcharge. Laundry facilities available.
Nearest Town: Coromandel 0.5 km

Geoff and I are a retired couple who enjoy meeting people to share local knowledge and invite you to a restful holiday in a country setting of 4 acres with a modern home. Newly established trees and gardens, roses becoming a speciality. You have the independence of 4 units (sleep 2-4 people) situated slightly apart from our home. Two Queen. Four twins with disabled ensuite access, both with fold out sofas, TV, fridge, tea and coffee making facilities. Your choice of continental or cooked breakfast. You have a country touch feeling with just a 10 minute stroll to Coromandel township where you can enjoy our local arts and crafts, restaurants and shops. We can arrange chartered tours or fishing trips. Train rides or anything else you feel you would enjoy.
Directions: *Cost Road from Thames to Coromandel, turn right on Whangapoua Rd, State Highway 25, approximately 300 metres first on left.*

Coromandel
Bed & Breakfast

Address: The Green House,
505 Tiki Road, Coromandel
Name: Ross and Estelle Cashmore
Telephone: (07) 866 7303
Email: rosstelle@xtra.co.nz
Beds: 2 Queen, 2 Single (3 Bedrooms)
Bathroom: 1 Ensuite, 1 Guests Share.
Tariff: B&B (Continental) Double $75-$85, Single $45-$55. Children negotiable. NZ B&B Vouchers accepted $10 surcharge. Credit cards: Visa/MC.
Nearest Town: Coromandel 0.5 kms. Thames 55 kms.

Welcome to our newly redecorated Coromandel home. We have three guest bedrooms. Upstairs there is one room with a queen bed and one room with twin beds. There is also a guest lounge and complementary tea and coffee making facilities. Upstairs guests share a bathroom. The view to the east is of bush clad hills and to the west seaviews and spectacular sunsets. Downstairs we have one guestroom with queen bed and ensuite. Breakfast is served outdoors in the developing garden if weather permits. BBQ available for guests' use. Web/Internet available. Historic Coromandel Township with lovely craft shops and restaurants is five minutes walk. We have travelled extensively in England, Europe, Canada, America, the Caribbean, Australia and New Zealand and look forward to returning some of the wonderful hospitality we experienced as travellers.
Directions: *Highway 25, 2 minutes south of Coromandel Town.*

Matarangi Beach
Homestay

Address: 'Pinekatz', 108 Matarangi Drive,
Matarangi Beach, R.D.2, Whitianga
Name: Glenys & Trevor Lewis
Telephone: (07) 866 2103
Fax: (07) 866 2103
Email: pinekatz@wave.co.nz
Beds: 1 Queen, 2 Single (2 Bedrooms)
Bathroom: 1 Guest share
Tariff: B&B (full) Double $75, Single $45, Dinner $20pp, by arrangement. Credit Cards (Visa/MC) NZ B&B Vouchers accepted
Nearest Town: Coromandel 24km, Whitianga 24km

We invite you to share with us the unique unspoilt natural beauty and peaceful tranquillity that is Matarangi Beach. A sun and sea paradise providing an escape from the rigours of today's busy lifestyles. Between its dazzling 5km long ocean beach on one side and the calm sheltered Whangapoua Harbour on the other lies a splendid variety of activities to satisfy all ages. Activities include swimming, diving, snorkelling, boating/fishing (trips by arrangement), tennis, beach and bush walks and a 9 hole golf course designed by Bob Charles (further 9 holes under development), power cycles available for hire. Our family of 4 adults have been replaced by 3 cats who own us. The guest bedrooms are upstairs and are warm and inviting, served by their own bathroom. We look forward to the pleasure of your company and ensuring your stay is a memorable one.
Directions: *24km north of Whitianga or 24km east of Coromandel (1km off SH25).*

Kuaotunu
Bed & Breakfast
Address: The Kaeppeli's, Grays Ave,
Kuaotunu, R.D.2, Whitianga
Name: The Kaeppeli's.
Jill and Robert Kaeppeli
Telephone: (07) 866 2445
Mobile: (025) 287 3598
Beds: 2 comfortable Kingsize, 4 Single, 1 cot, 1 childs bed (4 Bedrooms)
Bathroom: 2 Ensuite, 1 Guests share
Tariff: B&B (full) Double $70-$120, Single $45-$70, Children 6-12yrs half price, Dinner by arrangement $25   NZ B&B Vouchers accepted $10-$50 Surcharge
Nearest Town: 17km north of Whitianga on SH25

We are a Swiss/Kiwi family who have had restaurants in Switzerland for years. We now enjoy sharing with our guests, the peace and tranquillity of Kuaotunu, in our newly built home and garden "suite", on our 5 1/2 hectare property, with its tremendous views out over the bay. Evening meals by arrangement. Robert is an excellent Swiss Chef who takes pride in preparing our guests meals, using home produce and our wood-fired oven. Meals can be enjoyed in the guests dining-room or in the garden enjoying the views. Children are welcome and can make acquaintance with our daughter and animals. Walk to clean, safe, white sandy beaches, handy to many other beautiful spots and an ideal starting point for exploring other parts of Coromandel Peninsula or for bush walks, fishing, horse trekking, water-sports, golf, tennis or just relaxing.   Look forward to welcoming you at "The Kaeppeli's".

Kuaotunu
Homestay
Address: "Blue Penguin", 11 Cuvier Cres,
Kuaotunu, RD 2, Whitianga
Name: Glenda Mawhinney and Barb Meredith
Telephone: (07) 866 2222
Freephone (0800) Penguin
Fax: (07) 866 0228 **Email**: blue.penguin@xtra.co.nz
Beds: 1 Queen, 2 Double, 2 Single (2 bedrooms)
Bathroom: 1 Guests share
Tariff: B&B (continental) $5 surcharge for full B&B. Main Guestroom: $95 (single or couple), Family Guestroom: $75 Double, Children under 12 years $25, Single $55. NZ B&B Vouchers accepted $25 Surcharge.
Visa/Mastercard accepted.
Nearest Town: 17km north of Whitianga on State Highway 25

We offer you the upper leve of our architecturally designed home that takes good advantage of spectacular views out to the Mercury Islands and Great Barrier. With just two minutes down to the white, sandy beach, this is a magic spot. A rimu staircase leads you upstairs, the master (or mistress) guest room has a queen sized bed, window seats and a small balcony. A modern bathroom is nestled between this and a large family bedroom which contains two double and two single beds, a TV and video. This room is ideal for your children (complete with rainbow on the ceiling and plenty of toys and games) or for your travelling companions. We are two professional women (ex wine industry and theatre nursing) and we also run a Private Beach House Rental business with over 70 homes available for rent. We enjoy the lifestyle with our Jack Russell, Poodle and Retriever. WELCOME!
Directions: *Please Phone.* **Home Page**: www.bluepenguin.co.nz

Kuaotunu
Homestay

Address: Kuaotunu Bay Lodge, State Highway 25, Kuaotunu, RD 2, Whitianga
Name: Bill and Lorraine Muir
Telephone: (07) 866 4396
Fax: (07) 866 4396
Beds: 2 Queen, 2 Single (3 bedrooms)
Bathroom: 2 Ensuite, 1 Private.
Tariff: (B&B) full Double $130-$150, Single $95, Dinner $35.
Credit Cards accepted: Visa/Mastercard.
Nearest Town: Whitianga

Situated on the coast on SH25, 18 km north of Whitianga , our new home has been purpose built for guests, with ensuites, under floor heating and private decks. Enjoy breakfast in the sunny conservatory or a private dinner on your deck, listening to the waves and watching the sun set over Moehau mountain. The very safe beach is just a short walk through the garden. Ideal for all sea activities, fishing by arrangement or bring your own boat. Close to Matarangi airfield and golf course, a car will pick you up from the airfield - 15min flight from Auckland.
Whitianga with its restaurants and tourist activities is just a 20 min drive. Close to bush walks and local art and craft. We also have a self contained unit suitable for four people. Our 10 acre property has a small bush reserve, hens sheep and a friendly dog.

Whitianga - Mercury Bay
Bed & Breakfast

Address: 'Cosy Cat Cottage', 41 South Highway, Whitianga
Name: Gordon Pearce
Telephone: (07) 866 4488
Fax: (07) 866 4488
Beds: 2 Queen, 1 Double, 1 Single (3 bedrooms/Queens with ensuites)
Bathroom: 2 Ensuite, 1 Private
Tariff: B&B (special) Double $80-$95, Single $50-$60, Credit cards (Visa/MC). NZ B&B Vouchers accepted $20 Surcharge
Nearest Town: Whitianga 1 km south of Post Office

Welcome to our picturesque two storied cottage, filled with feline memorabilia. Relax with complimentary tea or coffee any time, served on the verandah, in the garden or in the guest lounge which has a library, TV and board games for your use.   Enjoy a good night's rest in comfortable beds. Choose a variety of treats from our breakfast menu - fresh fruit salad, semi-roasted muesli, honey from our own bees, and hot dishes prepared the way you like them. Special diets catered for. You will probably like to meet our two playful Tonkinese cats or just be amused by the unique feline ambience.   Whitianga enjoys a pleasant climate and relaxed way of life, with magnificent scenery and safe sandy beaches. Our excellent restaurants and other amenities make it an ideal base for your Coromandel Peninsula exploration.   Friendly, helpful service is assured at Cosy Cat Cottage. See you soon!
Home Page: http://nz.com/webnz/bbnz/cosycat.htm.

Whitianga - Coromandel

Homestay

Address: 119 Albert St.,
Whitianga
Name: Anne's Haven.
Anne and Bob
Telephone: (07) 866 5550
Beds: 1 Double, 2 Single (2 bedrooms)
Bathroom: 1 Family share
Tariff: B&B (full) Double $65,
Single $35, Children $20, Dinner $20.
NZ B&B Vouchers accepted $5 surcharge
Nearest Town: Whitianga 400m

A warm welcome awaits you along with a cup of tea or coffee. Relax in our modern spacious home and enjoy the cottage garden. We are ordinary Kiwis who like sharing our home with you. Bob enjoys making and sailing model boats and flying model planes. Anne makes pottery, gardens, line dances and knits. We are in our early 50's. The shower, toilet and bathroom are each separate rooms for easy access. After a good nights sleep in comfortable beds with electric blankets you can enjoy a light and healthy breakfast of fruit and muesli or good hearty bacon and eggs, or both, followed by toast and homemade jams. We are 400 metres from the shopping centre and restaurants, six beautiful beaches within strolling distance, golf course and bush walks nearby. One night or one week let us make your stay a memorable one. Our courtesy car will meet you from the bus or plane.

Whitianga

Homestay

Address: Whitianga Bed & Breakfast
12 Cook Drive, Whitianga
Name: Pat and Bill Carse
Telephone: (07) 866 5547
Fax: (07) 866 5547
Mobile: (025) 383 379
Email: bcarse@altavista.net
Beds: 1 Double, 2 Single
(2 bedrooms)
Bathroom: 2 Family share
Tariff: B&B (full) Double $60,
Single $45. Credit cards
NZ B&B Vouchers accepted
Nearest Town: Whitianga 500m

We are a retired couple originally from Scotland and have enjoyed home hosting for the past 13 years. Our comfortable modern home is away from busy main street traffic. Guests share the family lounge / TV room. Tea or coffee is available at any time. Free pick up from bus station or airfield. We offer a friendly homely atmosphere and a relaxed base from which to explore the many unspoiled features of Mercury Bay. We are always ready to supply local information to make your stay more interesting. Bill is retired from a career in agricultural research. Pat is a legal secretary, and is a volunteer ambulance officer.
Home Page: www.geocities.com/Heartland/Meadows/5845/index.html

Whitianga
Bed & Breakfast Homestay
Address: Camellia Lodge - Cnr Golf Road
& South Highway, R.D.1 Whitianga
Name: John & Pat Lilley
Telephone: (07) 866 2253
Fax: (07) 866 2253
Mobile: 021-662 538
Email: www.whitianga.co.nz/camellia-lodge
Beds: 1 Queen, 2 Twin, 2 Double (4 bedrooms)
Bathroom: 2 Ensuite, 2 Guests share
Tariff: B&B (full) Double $80/$95, Single $65, Children under 12 half price, under 5 free, Dinner $25.   Credit cards.
NZ B&B Vouchers accepted sucharge $20
Nearest Town: Whitianga 4km south of Whitianga SH 25

Kia ora. Welcome to our friendly home, surrounded by 73 camellia bushes. Our home is nestled at the rear of a spacious parklike garden, which includes kauri, rimu, totara trees, also we offer for your enjoyment the use of a spa, swimming pool and lots of lovely gardens to relax in. You may like to have a round of golf or a scenic flight. We would be glad to arrange this for you. You would normally be woken up to the tune of the bellbirds singing in the trees, then you settle into a hearty breakfast which will set you up for the day. We are situated approx 4km south of Whitianga in a quiet rural area, but not to far a bushwalk, swimming, fishing or any of the lovely attraction Whitianga has to offer. We can assure you of a warm friendly welcome and a comfortable stay.
Home Page: http://www.mercurybay.co.nz/Camellia.html

Whitianga - Coromandel
Bed & Breakfast
Address: 252 Cook Drive,
Whitianga
Name: Benny's Rest
Telephone: (07) 866 5464
Fax: (07) 866 0446
Beds: 1 Double, 2 Single (1 bedroom)
Bathroom: 1 Private (shared with laundry)
Tariff: B&B (full) Double $70-80,
Single $35, Twin $60-70, Children half price. (Flat: 1 bedroom - 1 double & 2 single beds, own bathroom, Upstairs: twin bedroom family share bathroom).   NZ B&B Vouchers accepted
Nearest Town: Whitianga 2km.

A very warm welcome to you when you stay with us in our comfy home in the holiday mecca of Whitianga in semi-tropical Mercury Bay. An appetising breakfast of your choice on the deck outside will start the day of sightseeing and activities. Trevor operates a Coast Guard receiving station and Barbara has lots of hobbies including swimming and knitting. We are armchair travellers who really enjoy chatting with our guests. Downstairs you can relax, make a tea or coffee and watch TV or wander 3 minutes to the beach for a refreshing swim or to catch a glimpse of the birds in the bird sanctuary. We have a small friendly dog and cat. As Kiwi Hosts we strive to make you welcome and your stay with us a highlight of your holiday. Your satisfaction is our pleasure. We have a smoke free home. Children welcome.

Whitianga - Coromandel

Homestay + B&B
Address: No 1 Golf Road, Whitianga
Name: "A Hi-Way Haven" Joan & Nevin Paton
Telephone: 64-07- 866 2427
Fax: 64-07-866 2424
Email: enquiries@whitianga.co.nz
Beds: 1 Double, 2 Single, 1 Queen,
& 1 large Bedsitting room King or Twin, with Quadraplegic ensuite (4 rooms)
Bathroom: 1 Ensuite, 1 Guests share.
Tariff: Per couple: Twin, Double & Queen (B&B continental) $60, (B&B cooked) $70. Quadraplegic Ensuite with King or Twin (B&B continental) $80, (B&B cooked) $90. Single (per person) (B&B continental) $40, (B&B cooked) $45. NZ B&B Vouchers accepted $10 surcharge
Nearest Town: Whitianga (3.2km south of Whitianga)

Looking for peaceful, quiet, comfortable, friendly, homely, affordable and excellent accommodation, then we are your answer. We are situated approximately 3.2 km from the beautiful town of Whitianga. A hearty cooked breakfast will keep you going all day. A picturesque 18 hole golf course where hire clubs are available set amidst parklike surroundings is adjacent. Only a three minute drive to Whitianga township with many excellent restaurants and your hosts or the Information Centre will be only too happy to arrange all your holiday wishes, which have to be seen to be believed. Guests own lounge with TV is available as is tea/coffee making facilities and filtered cold drinking water, also laundry facilities. Plenty of off-street parking and a courtesty car available for meeting buses, planes etc. We also have a friendly dog and cat. We at 'Our World' Hi-Way Haven know that you will come as a visitor and depart as a friend.

Whitianga

Homestay
Address: "The Peacheys" Homestay, Centennial Drive, Whitianga
Name: Dale and Yvonne
Telephone: (07) 866 5290
Fax: (07) 866 5290
Email: DYPeachey@xtra.co.nz
Beds: 1 King, 1 Double, 2 Single (2 bedrooms)
Bathroom: 1 Private, 1 Ensuite
Tariff: B&B (Special) King $120, Double $90, Single $60, Dinner $25pp, Credit Cards Visa
Nearest Town: Whitianga 4km

FRIENDLY HOSTS, MODERN HOME, BUSH & SEAVIEWS, QUIET LOCATION.
Stay with us and we will ensure your time spent in Whitianga is a real "Kiwi Experience". Start with afternoon tea on the deck taking in the view of our lovely Buffalo Beach, a 4 minute walk away. Our home, your home away from home, was designed and built for us 12 years ago, and has drawn many favourable comments on the style and the great views it commands from every room. Being open plan, on different levels it is a people friendly house. Muffin the cat (part owner) will be there to meet you. SMOKEFREE INDOORS. We really enjoy meeting and chatting with our guests around the table over dinner, which we can prepare if you require (seafood if available). Dale enjoys fishing, hunting and rugby, while I enjoy my garden and walking. **Directions**: *Please phone for directions.*

Whitianga - Mercury Bay

Bed & Breakfast

Address: The Beach House,
38 Buffalo Beach Road,
PO Box 162, Whitianga
Name: Helen & Allan Watson
Telephone: (07) 866 5647
Fax: (07) 866 5647
Mobile: (025) 284 7240 or (025) 834 766
Email: swatson@ww.co.nz
Beds: 1 SuperKing/2 Single, 1 Queen, 3 Single (3 bedrooms)
Bathroom: 2 Ensuite, 1 Private
Tariff: B&B (special) Double $70-$150, Single $50-$120. Seasonal rates.
Credit Cards (VISA/MC).
Nearest Town: Whitianga 1km

Our BEACHFRONT location with a 180 degree sea view from your room is unequalled. A 5 minute level stroll to beachfront restaurants, cafes, wharf, passenger ferry and shopping village. Our spacious upstairs rooms offer superior accommodation with individual tea/coffee making facilities, TV, refrigerator, reading lights, fan, heaters, table and chairs, etc. Photograph the sunrise over the horizon from your balcony and watch the fishing, sailing and pleasure craft plying our sparkling clean bay. Safe swimming, sunbathing and surfcasting is just across the road, guests own entrance, off street parking and secure bedroom doors allow total privacy when required, honeymooners welcome. We are fortunate to have lived in this captivating area for nearly 40 years, and enjoy sharing our love of the Peninsula and our home with our guests. Courtesy transport to local bus/airfield. Smoke free indoors.

Whitianga

Homestay, Bed & Breakfast

Address: "Raven-Owl House",
4 Harbour Lights Terrace,
 RD 2, Whitianga
Name: Rosemary & Jim Grant
Telephone: (07) 866 2957
Fax: (07) 866 2957
Mobile: (025) 299 8869
Beds: 1 Queen, 2 Single (2 bedrooms)
Bathroom: 1 Guests share + extra toilet
Tariff: B&B (full) Queen $90, Twin $85 , Single $50, Credit Cards
(VISA/MC). NZ B&B Vouchers accepted $10 surcharge
Nearest Town: 5km north of Whitianga town centre

Rosemary and Jim offer friendly homestay hospitality in a quiet location with panoramic views of Mercury Bay and Whitianga township. After dark the harbour lights are an added bonus. Raven-Owl House is close to beaches and a 5 minute drive to town centre and restaurants. Whitianga is an excellent base from which to explore the Coromandel and is the nearest town to Hot Water Beach and Cathedral Cove. We can assist with local knowledge. Comfortable beds are a priority - one room with a Queen 'Dreambed' has its own deck overlooking the bay. The twin room has rural views and opens to the garden. Guests are welcome to share our lounge. Another priority is a homestyle breakfast (continental or cooked) with fresh fruit always available and served outside when weather permits. Tea & Coffee making facilities. TV available. Smoke-free indoors.

Whitianga
Homestay
Address: LynNZ Inn B&B and Cybercafe 25 Arthur Street, Whitianga
Name: "PJ " & "DK" Lynn
Telephone: (07) 866 2880
Fax: (07) 866 2960
Mobile: (025) 275 1538
Email: LynNZInn@MercuryBay.co.NZ
Beds: 1 Private 2 bedroom suite with bath (perfect for families).
1 Queen with pull out sofabed. 1 Double (2 bedrooms)
Bathroom: 1 Guests share (solar heated bath w/spa tub & shower)
Tariff: B&B (special) Queen $ 85, Double $80, Single $75/70. $20 pp extra,
Dinner $25, Credit Cards: Visa/ MC
Nearest Town: Whitianga town centre a short 1.3km north

Our home, vintage 1930s, is newly renovated yet still retains its "old world" charm with polished wood floors, sliding doors and flyscreens throughout. Located one block from the estuary, we have a beautiful view of the surrounding mountains. Upon arrival, relax on our deck to watch a spectacular sunset and listen to our varied CD collection. We also provide a lounge with a 31" screen TV and 300+ videos. PJ's breakfast includes cappuccino, homemade yoghurt, muffins and waffles. DK's cybercafe offers complimentary e-mail service and web browsing during your stay. We have 3 bicycles, one a racing tandem, which you may use to explore the varied attractions of Mercury Bay. Visit the area's beaches, hiking trails, Kiwi conservation block, and town centre shops as well as the local potters, knitters and other artisans. Our friendly "Black Magic" Lab answers to "Maggie". **Directions**: *Before Whitianga on S/H 25, turn right on Arthur Street, just past Sarah Ave.*
Home Page: http://www.mercurybay.co.nz/Lynnzinn.html

Whitianga
Bed & Breakfast (Homestay)
Address: The White House,
129 Albert Street, Whitianga
Name: Jessie and Murray Thompson
Telephone: (07) 866 5116
Fax: (07) 866 5116
Mobile: (025) 341 029
Beds: 1 King/2 Single, 1 Queen,
1 Queen/double (3 bedrooms)
Bathroom: 1 Ensuite, 1 Guests share
Tariff: B&B (Full) Double $90-$120, Single $70-$80. Dinner by arrangement.
Credit cards: Visa/Mastercard.
NZ B&B Vouchers accepted $35-$45 surcharge.
Nearest Town: Whitianga - 500 metres.

"When only the best will do". We are committed to looking after guests in a comfortable friendly environment. Relax, sightsee , and holiday for a few days on arrival in NZ or before departure. We are 2 1/4 hours from Auckland International Airport. Murray offers a personalised tour of historic Whitianga/Mercury Bay. For breakfast enjoy traditional, continental or special seafood delicacy. Shops and fine dining are within walking distance. Explore a whole range of activities in the Whitianga, Mercury Bay, Coromandel area from a central point. Visit Hot Water Beach, Cathedral Cove, and beautiful beaches. We can arrange small intimate weddings for couples planning to be married while holidaying in New Zealand. We believe that Mercury Bay is a special place and has something to offer all visitors. We make a promise that all our guests will enjoy their stay in Whitianga.

Whitianga-Coromandel

Travellers Accommodation

Address: 14 Parkland Place,
Brophys Beach, Whitianga
Name: At Parkland Place
Telephone: (07) 866 4987
Fax: (07) 866 4946
Mobile: (025) 291 7495
Email: parklandplace@wave.co.nz
Beds: 1 King, 1 Queen,
1 King or 2 Singles (3 Bedrooms)
Bathroom: 1 Ensuite, 1 Guests only, share
Tariff: B&B (full) Double $100-$120, Single $70-$80, Dinner $25, Children $15,
Credit Cards accepted.
Nearest Town: Whitianga

Enjoy European Hospitality at Parkland Place. Maria, a ship's chef from Poland and New Zealand husband Guy will make your stay a memorable experience in our new spacious luxurious house. Large rooms with TV, radio and writing desk, guest lounge/dining room and a sunny outdoor area with spa pool and BBQ, superb breakfast and meals. Laundry, email and fax available. Situated next to reserve and farmland ensures peace and quiet. A two minute stroll to Brophys Beach or five minute drive to Whitianga township where you can explore local arts and craft shops or wine and dine at fine restaurants and cafés. Seafood is a local speciality, coming in daily from local fishing boats. A modern Marina berths many charter boats offering scenic, fishing and diving trips in picturesque waters. Other activities include golf, windsurfing, surfing, horse riding and scenic bush walks. You will not regret coming.

Whitianga

Homestay & Self Contained Accommodation

Address: 11 Monk Street,
Whitianga
Name: Central Homestay and B&B
Telephone: (07) 866 4589
Fax: (07) 866 4587
Beds: 2 Queen, 2 Single (3 Bedrooms)
Bathroom: 1 Private, 1 Guests share
Tariff: B&B (Continental) Double $100,
Single $70, Dinner by arrangement.
Children under 12 years half price.
Credit Cards accepted. NZ B&B Vouchers accepted $30 surcharge for double
Nearest Town: Whitianga

Your hosts George and Joanne Harding (retired business and deer farming couple) have created a modern spacious two storey apartment above shops in Central Whitianga, to form a base for your Coromandel experience.
A few minutes stroll to unspoilt beaches, marina wharf and ferry and 10 licensed restaurants and clubs. Downstairs to shops. 50m to bus. Courtesy car to local airport. Overnight off-street parking. We offer billiard room, large patio for outside dining, complimentary tea or coffee any time in our comfortable lounge. Our interests include meeting people, travel, good food and wine, fishing - we have a roomy launch on the marina for salt water fly fishing and we enjoy other leisure pursuits. The town offers golf, horse riding, kayaking, bush walks and surfing among many other activities. We will try to make your stay a memorable one. We have no pets. We thank you for not smoking in the house.

Whitianga
Homestay
Address: 365 Mill Creek Road, RD1, Whitianga 2856
Name: Hisae and David Lynch
Telephone: (07) 866 0166
Fax: (07) 866 5399
Mobile: (025) 846 873
Email: hisae@aikido.co.nz
Beds: 1 Large Caravan, 1 Twin, 1 Single (2 Bedrooms)
Bathroom: 1 Guest share, 1 Sauna
Tariff: B&B (Full) Double $90, Single $60, Dinner $30. Credit Cards: Visa, Mastercard.
Nearest Town: Whitianga

Spacious seven year old home plus large Caravan provide clean accommodation for non smokers. We are located in a tranquil valley and have a 16 acre sheep and cattle farm and organic orchard with 65 acre bush block attached. Beautiful nature all around, including waterfalls and kauri trees.Refresh your spirit in one of the most beautiful parts of the country. Coromandel activities including horse riding, boating, trekking can be easily arranged. David Lynch was manager of the New Zealand Government Tourist Office in Japan for 15 years. He and his Japanese wife Hisae are consultants on Tourism and Trade. David is also a 6th-dan instructor in aikido, the Japanese martial "way of harmony' and Hisae's interests include meditation and ikebana (flower arrangement). International and domestic guests will be given a warm welcome.
Home Page: http://www.aikido.co.nz/

Whitianga
Self Contained Accommodation
Address: 309 Road, RD1, Whitianga
Name: Maree and Richard
Telephone: (07) 866 5155
Fax: (07) 866 5155
Email: retreat@xtra.co.nz
Beds: 1 Double (1 Bedroom)
Bathroom: 1 Private
Tariff: B&B (Continental)
Double $120 per night, Single $120.
Nearest Town: Whitianga 10 mins drive SH25

You are invited to share our Riverside Retreat, on the edge of the waters which run through the beautiful Mahakirau valley. At the end of the maple-lined driveway your private cottage awaits you, nestled amongst native trees in 3 acres of landscaped gardens. The cottage has full kitchen, sunny lounge, private bathroom and upstairs mezzanine floor with double bed and views over the gardens and river. You can fly-fish for trout in the river, or after a generous breakfast provided, take a fresh-water swim, or bush walk, or just relax on your private beach by the river with a good book. The perfect place to unwind, and leave the world behind. Whitianga's shops, restaurants, and beaches are just 10 mins away from the Riverside Retreat. So secluded yet so close. Your hosts and our moggy "Woz" look forward to making your stay a memorable one.
Directions: *Homepage or fax/phone.*
Home Page: http://www.nz.com.webnz/bbnz/retreat.htm

Cooks Beach
Rural Homestay
Address: Mercury Orchard,
141 Purangi Road, RD1, Whitianga
Name: Heather and Barry Scott
Telephone: (07) 866 3119
Fax: (07) 866 3115
Mobile: (025) 283 0176
Beds: 2 Queen (2 Bedrooms)
Bathroom: 1 Ensuite, 1 Family share
Tariff: B&B (Full) Double $90, Single $55,
Dinner by arrangement. NZ B&B Vouchers accepted $20 surcharge
Nearest Town: Tairua 17km, Whitianga 31km.

Mercury Orchard is 5 acres of country garden and organic orchard situated on the road to Cooks Beach and in close proximity to Hahei, Cathedral Cove, Hot Water Beach and Ferry Landing, where a 5 minute ferry ride will take you to Whitianga. We invite you to share a complimentary glass of wine with us before dining at one of the local restaurants. Our large guest room opens through French doors to a private garden area, has tea and coffee making facilities, crisp cotton bed linen and ensuite bathroom. An adjoining bedroom with Queen bed is also available. We cater for only one party at a time. After a country style breakfast feel free to either relax by the pool or in the garden or enjoy the local attractions. We share our home with two small dogs and a cat and we look forward to making your Coromandel experience a memorable one. Our home is smokefree.

http://www.bnb.co.nz

take a look

Hahei Beach, Whitianga

Homestay

Address: 'Spellbound Homestay/Bed & Breakfast',
77 Grange Road, Hahei Beach, R.D.1, Whitianga
Name: Barbara & Alan Lucas
Telephone: (07) 866 3543
Fax: (07) 866 3003
Mobile: (025) 720 407
Beds: 3 Queen, 1Super King/2 Single (4 bedrooms)
Bathroom: 3 Ensuite, 1 Private
Tariff: B&B (Special continental) Double $100-$125, Single $60-$85,
Dinner $25, Children negotiable. Credit cards: VISA/MC/Eftpos.
Nearest Town: Tairua 36 km, Whitianga 38 km

Barbara and I live overlooking the sea with panoramic views from the Alderman Islands to the Mercury Islands.

We are five minutes from Hahei Beach and are on the road to Cathedral Cove and its beaches, a must when visiting this area. Hot Water Beach is just a short distance away where you can enjoy a warm soak at any time of the year.

The area offers bush walks, surf beaches, fishing and spectacular views for photography. "The Paradise Coast".

Most rooms have sea views with ensuites/private bathrooms, all beds have electric blankets and insect screens are fitted to most windows.

We have tea/coffee making facilities and a refrigerator for the use of all guests.

We can assure you of excellent meals. My wife is a first class cook, at least, I think so. Weather permitting, our generous continental breakfast is served on our front deck.

We thank you for not smoking in the house. We have no animals.

Please give us a telephone call when you wish to come and we can promise you a most enjoyable stay.

Directions: *Turn off at Whenuakite (Highway 25). Grange Road is on left by Hahei Store. We are on left near top of hill. Look for 'Spellbound' signs, follow Service Road. Street numbers not consecutive.*

Home Page: http://nzcom/webnz/bbnz/spell.htm

Hahei Beach
Bed & Breakfast with Restaurant

Address: THE CHURCH,
87 Beach Road, Hahei
Name: Karen Blair & Richard Agnew
Telephone: (07) 866 3533
Fax: (07) 866 3055
Mobile: 025-596 877
Email: www.whitianga.co.nz
Beds: 7 Queen (7 bedrooms)
Bathroom: 7 Ensuite
Tariff: B&B (full) Double $80-$120, Winter rates: Easter - Labour weekend
Off peak: Labour weekend to Xmas.
Single $75-85, Children by arrangement.
Dinner according to menu, Major Credit Cards.
Nearest Town: Whitianga 38km, Tairua 36km

First on the right, entering Hahei, The Church, built in 1913 has been moved and lovingly rebuilt to provide a character dining room for our delicious breakfasts and evening meals. Set in native bush and gardens we can accommodate 14 people in cosy wooden cottages, and rooms, all with ensuites, tea and coffee making facilities and fridges. (3 with TV.) Much of our food is produced on site and our interests include cooking, gardening, fishing, diving and socialising. We emphasise a relaxed homely atmosphere and live here with our 8 year old daughter and dog. Enjoy our warm hospitality, and the beauty of Hahei, Cathedral Cove and Hot Water Beach. Children accommodated by arrangement. Smoking outside only. Pets are unable to be accommodated.
Directions: *Please telephone for directions.*

Hahei Beach Whitianga
Homestay

Address: "Cedar Lodge",
36 Beach Road,
Hahei, R.D.1, Whitianga
Name: John & Jenny Graham
Telephone: (07) 866 3789
Fax: (07) 866 3978
Beds: 1 Queen, 1 Single
(1 bedroom)
Bathroom: 1 Private
Tariff: B&B (full) Double $80, Single $50,
Major Credit Cards. NZ B&B Vouchers accepted $10 surcharge
Nearest Town: Whitianga 38km, Tairua 36km

Come and unwind in our comfortable private upstairs studio apartment and enjoy the sea views and relaxing atmosphere.
Take a 200m stroll to the beautiful beach and experience the magic of Hahei. Scenic boat and fishing trips can be easily arranged with local operators. The Cathedral Cove Walkway is 3 minutes drive from the house, and Hot Water Beach where you can dig your own hot pool in the sand when the tide is low, is nearby. We can recommend the local 9 hole golf course, tennis courts and the various bush walks in the area.
We have an adult family scattered around the world and two friendly cats who live in the family part of our home. We thank you for not smoking indoors. We enjoy an active retired lifestyle, so please phone ahead for bookings and directions.

Hahei

Homestay - Cottage
Address: Bon Appetit Hahei,
Orchard Road, Hahei,
RD1, Whitianga
Name: Andy and Monika Schuerch
Telephone: (07) 866 3116
Fax: (07) 866 3117
Mobile: (025) 293 0929
Email: schuerch@wave.co.nz
Beds: 1 Queen (1 Bedroom)
Bathroom: 1 Private
Tariff: B&B (Full) Double $85.   Portacot available.
Nearest Town: Whitianga and Tairua

Relax and enjoy the breathtaking views and the absolute privacy of our Bed and Breakfast. Having Cathedral Cove and Hot Water Beach just 5 minutes away, we are perfectly situated for your stay in Hahei.
We offer you a warm, homely stay with excellent breakfast. Our cottage, surrounded by native bush, contains ensuite, tea and coffee making facilities and fridge. Feel free to use our laundry and barbecue terrace. Portacot available. We have two children and a friendly cat.
Directions: *Coming into Hahei, drive down Pa Road (first on the right), after the little bridge on Pa Road, take the gravel road to the right. This is a dead-end road, we are the last house on this road.*

Hot Water Beach

2 Self-contained units
Address: Auntie Dawns Place
15 Radar Road, Hot Water Beach,
R.D.1 Whitianga
Name: Dawn and Joe Nelmes
Telephone: (07) 866 3707
Fax: (07) 866 3701
Beds: Queen + Double,
Queen + Single, (2 bedrooms)
Bathroom: 2 Private
Tariff: B&B (continental)
Double $70/$80, Single $40, Children $15.   Credit cards.   NZ B&B
Vouchers accepted $7 and $8 surcharge
Nearest Town: Whitianga 32km, Tairua 30km

New Zealand Association
FARM & HOME
HOSTS

Hot Water Beach is a beautiful surf beach. At low tide hot water bubbles up at a particular place in the sand and you can dig yourself a "hot-pool" to bathe in. Your hosts "Auntie Dawn" (and Joe) enjoy gardening and relaxing on 1 hectare. Set amongst giant Pohutukawa trees. (And Joe likes making home-brew beer.) We have a small dog.   Our home is only 150 metres from the sea.
We provide comfortable bedrooms, private bathrooms, private lounges, TVs, cooking and laundry facilities. Juice, tea, coffee, cereal, bread, butter, jam   are in units and guests prepare their own breakfast preferred time.
Nearest cafe and restaurant 10 mins drive away.
Directions: *Turn right into Radar Road 200m before Hot Water Beach shop. A phone call would be appreciated 07-866 3707.*

Hot Water Beach

Homestay/B&B
Address: 48 Pye Place,
Hot Water Beach, RD 1, Whitianga
Name: Gail and Trevor Knight
Telephone: (07) 866 3991
Fax: (07) 866 3291
Mobile: (025) 799 620   **Email**: TKnight@xtra.co.nz
Beds: 1 Queen, 1 King/Twin (zip together) (2 Bedrooms)
Bathroom: 2 Ensuites
Tariff: B&B (Full) Double $100-$125, Single $75-$90, Dinner $25 pp on request, Children under 12 years half price.   Children under 5 years free (port-a-cot and highchair available). Major Credit Cards accepted.
Nearest Town: Whitianga 32km, Tairua 30km

We have a spacious elevated home a stones throw from the beach with sweeping, panoramic sea and beach views. Relax on our extensive decks, enjoy the spa pool or play on our full sized billiard table. Join us, if you wish, for a home cooked meal or alternatively we can transport you to one of several restaurants at the adjacent beach. A generous breakfast will be served at your leisure with freshly brewed coffee. Trevor has spent 10 years in the NZ tour industry and is happy to advise on sightseeing or leisure activities. These include bushwalks, kayaking, fishing, horse riding, golf, scuba diving, surfing, swimming and beachcombing. We have a cat and a friendly Boxer dog. Smoking is outside only, thank you. So why not come and enjoy some time in the natural hot springs on our beach. We provide the spades!!
Directions: *Please phone (07) 866 3991*
Home page: http://www.hotwaterbedandbreakfast.co.nz

http://www.bnb.co.nz

take a look

Tairua

Self-contained Apartment
Address: 18 The Esplanade,
Tairua 2853 via Thames.

We are here

Name: The Esplanade Holiday Apartment
Telephone: (07) 864 8997
Fax: (07) 864 8997 **Email**: jcharlton@wave.co.nz
Beds: 1 Queen, 2 Single (1 bedroom + sleeping area in lounge)
Bathroom: 1 Ensuite (private toilet facilities)
Tariff: B&B Continental (on request) $65-$95 (seasonal variation) for up to 4
persons., Credit Cards. Vouchers accepted Low season only
Nearest Town: Tairua 1km

*Beautiful quiet harbour location with sunbathing beach and safe swimming on
the doorstep. Homely hospitality or if desired 'just leave you to it'. Your own
private garden area with table and chairs overlooks numerous harbour activities.
The apartment is self contained and fully equipped, includes laundry, washing
machine, drier, TV, radio, microwave, B/top oven, hair drier, fridge/freezer,
private shower, toilet facilities and garage for your car. Ideal for self catering and offers
discerning private comfort for up to four persons. A double bedroom with two single beds and
an additional queen settee bed in the lounge. High standard accommodation with long stay
tariff negotiable, ideal short or long stay. Boat launching location and wharf fishing nearby.
This is our paradise which we invite you to share for a while. Your stay will be one to remember.
Continental breakfast (on request) included in tariff. Not one disappointed guest.*
Directions: *Over one way bridge, follow Manaia Rd around the harbour to The Esplanade
waterfront at the base of Mt Paku.*
Home Page: http://nz-coromandel.com/tairua/esplanade.html*

Tairua

Bed & Breakfast
Address: The Dunes,
106 Ocean Beach Rd., Tairua
Name: "The Dunes B&B"
Hosts: Tony & Carol
Telephone: (07) 864 7475
Fax: (07) 864 9495
Mobile: (025) 281 3809
Email: manu.tours@xtra.co.nz
Beds: 1 Queen, 1 Double (2 bedrooms)
Bathroom: 2 Ensuite
Tariff: B&B (continental) Double $100, Single $75. NZ B&B Vouchers accepted
$30 surcharge
Nearest Town: Tairua, Thames 50km

*Be lulled to sleep by waves breaking on the beach, wake to a spectacular sunrise over off-shore
islands and the smell of home made bread and muffins. Our tastefully decorated guest rooms
are upstairs and a feature of your stay may be breakfast on the balcony overlooking the
sparkling Pacific Ocean. At our backdoor is Tairua's beautiful white sandy beach. Relax with
a book on the balcony, engage in the many activities Tairua has to offer or use us as a base for
exploring the Coromandel's many attractions, including Hot Water Beach and Cathedral
Cove. We have travelled extensively and enjoy most things to do with the great outdoors. As
well as our homestay we run scenic and nature tours which you are welcome to join. Come
and enjoy our smokefree home that we share with our children Ayden and Shaan and outside
dogs Punta and Tip. Warm hospitality is assured.*

Tairua

Bed & Breakfast
Address: "Kotuku Lodge",
179 Main Road, Tairua
Name: Dawn & Alan
Telephone: (07) 864 7040
Fax: (07) 864 7040 **Email**: kotuku@wave.co.nz
Beds: 1 King, 1 Queen, 1 Double plus single (3 bedrooms)
Bathroom: 3 Ensuite
Tariff: B&B (special) Double $90-$115, Single $65-$75, Children $25.
Credit Cards accepted VISA/Mastercard.
NZ B&B Vouchers accepted $30 surcharge Sept to April
Nearest Town: Thames 45km

Just 2 hours from Auckland on the beautiful Coromandel Peninsula KOTUKU LODGE offers rest and relaxation for that "get-away" break. Tairua is a great base for exploring the rest of the Coromandel, known for its natural wilderness, lush native bush plus giant Kauri trees. Breakfasts are a house speciality! So start your day with our delicious continental choices served in the dining room where you will experience the ever-changing view of Tairua harbour and Paku Mountain. Our bedrooms each with their own ensuite and balcony have comfortable King, Queen or single beds, hairdryer, fridge, plus tea and coffee making facilities. The guest TV lounge opens onto a BBQ area, swimming pool and a tranquil garden setting which makes it a lovely spot for relaxing, at any time of the day. Allow time to spend at CATHEDRAL COVE and HOT WATER BEACH, where you can dig your own HOT TUB in the sand beside the sea. The area offers beautiful beaches for swimming and surfing. If you are enjoying a day of sightseeing, picnic hampers can be supplied on request. There are some outstanding bush walks including going through a GLOW WORM tunnel to old goldmine workings. Stop to enjoy a walk along a bush clad river and watch the trout rising in the evening. Trout licenses are available. For the sea fishing and diving enthusiasts, this is one of the MECCAS of NZ, for those who want to go out to the off shore Islands there are fishing and diving trips available most days as well as charter and hire boats. All fishing and diving equipment can be hired. Take a stroll around our golf course and for the enthusiasts there are several others close by. Several restaurants are a 5-10 minutes level walk away or short drive to others. We enjoy most things to do with the Great Outdoors and Alan as well as a dedicated fisherman and photographer is also a wood carver. We have two friendly black Labradors. Having travelled extensively within NZ and overseas, we understand your needs, and aim to provide you with a home away from home with every effort being made to ensure your stay is a pleasant and enjoyable one. Email and office facilities available.
Home Page: http://nz.com/webnz/kotuku/

Pauanui Beach

Tourist accommodation
Address: 7 Brodie Lane,
(off Dunlop Drive),
Pauanui Beach
Name: Pauanui Pacific Holidays:
Hosts Kevin & Kay
Telephone: (07) 864 8933
Fax: (07) 864-8253
Mobile: 025 971 305
Beds: 1 Queen, 2 Double,
4 Single (4 bedrooms)
Bathroom: 4 Ensuite
Tariff: B&B (self help) Double $100-$115,
Single $80-$115, Credit cards accepted.
Nearest Town: Thames 40 min

Pauanui is on the east coast of the Coromandel Peninsula and one of the most magnificently planned resorts in this area with red chip roads to add to the landscape. Activities are catered for by 9 and 10 hole golf courses, 4 tennis complexes each with 4 courts, mini-putt, restaurants. Self help continental breakfast is provided, we have ideal self catering facilites. We have 4 units, each with ensuites, TV, fridge and tea/coffeee facilities. Games room/lounge, cooking facilities, large BBQ area, sauna, spa and swimming pool. Included in tariff are bikes, canoes and windsurfers. We also cater for fishing trips and scenic tours. Nearest town Thames 40 mins, Hot water beach 1 hr, Tairua 20 mins (5 min by ferry). Auckland 2 hrs. Transport to and from airports arranged. Ask about our free tour of Pauanui.

Pauanui Beach

Bed & Breakfast
Address: Ash-Leigh Cottage,
11 Golden Hills Drive,
Pauanui Beach
Name: Alan & Joan Parker
Telephone: (07) 864 8103
Fax: (07) 864 8752
Email: ashleighp@wave.co.nz
Beds: 2 Single (1 bedroom)
Bathroom: 1 Ensuite
Tariff: B&B (continental) Double $90
Nearest Town: 50km east of Thames

Our home, with off-street parking, is set in a quiet cul-de-sac close to the Tairua Harbour and walking distance to the ocean beach.
Your sunny room has twin beds, a cosy dining area, tea/coffee making facilities, TV, and ensuite. French doors open into the garden.
Breakfast is served in the sunroom or can be delivered to your room.
At Pauanui you can be as active or relaxed as you desire. Play golf, bowls, tennis, go swimming, or tramping or just laze on the golden sands or under the trees. There is a choice of licensed restaurants within a few minutes walk or drive. Pauanui is an ideal base for exploring the rest of the Coromandel Peninsula. We, together with Misty, our little dog, look forward to welcoming you to our smoke-free home and making your stay an enjoyable experience.

219

Whangamata
Homestay

Address: Fairway Homestay,
130 Kiwi Road -
PO Box 22, Whangamata
Name: Elsa & Snow Jenkins
Telephone: (07) 865 7018
Fax: (07) 865 7685
Mobile: (025) 829 943
Email: fairway.jenkins@xtra.co.nz
Beds: 1 Double & 1 Single,
2 Single (2 bedrooms)
Bathroom: 1 Guests share. Laundry facilities available.
Tariff: B&B (continental) Double $95, Triple $120, Single $70, Dinner by arrangement $25 per person. Children by arrangement. Tariff current to September2000. Credit cards NZ B&B Vouchers accepted $20 Surcharge
Nearest Town: Waihi 31km South, Thames 55k West.

Come and share our comfortable home after your exciting day around the Coromandel Peninsula. Stay a day or two and experience our superb beach, walking tracks or play a little Golf. Our back gate is on the eighth fairway of Whangamata's 9 Hole Golf Course with a magnificent 18 Hole Course a short drive away. A short walk across the course and down Lowe Street will lead you to our other magnificent feature - our Surf Beach.
Each room has its own exit to decking with seating set at various places along the sunny side of the house. On a sunny day this is where you may find one or both or our cats. Sometimes they hide among our garden shrubs.

Whangamata
Guest Lodge

Address: Brenton Lodge,
Cnr Brenton Place, SH 25,
Whangamata. , P O Box 216, Whangamata
Name: Jan & Paul Campbell
Telephone: (07) 865 8400
Fax: (07) 865 8400 **Mobile**: (025) 780 134
Email: brentonlodge@xtra.co.nz
Beds: 2 Queen (1 bedroom + sofa sleeper)
Bathroom: 2 Ensuite
Tariff: B&B (special) Double $220, Single $200. Valid until 30 September 2000. Credit cards. Non smoking.
Nearest Town: Whangamata

Peace, Privacy and Pampering. Charming Guest Cottages. Set in one acre of lovely gardens, with mature trees, aviary and swimming pool. Panoramic views of Whangamata, with seaviews to Mayor Island, 1.5km to surf beach and village. Relax in your separate upstairs guest chalet, which overlooks both the garden and seaviews. Tastefully furnished country cottage style, with extra touches, crisp white cotton sheets, fresh flowers, french doors, own balcony, add to the character. Open plan with its own bathroom, tea/coffee facilities, TV, sofa, table/ chairs. Non smoking. Liquor licence. Delicious special breakfast is served in the privacy of your cottage or alfresco on your balcony. Hosts have a luxury 6 metre boat available for guest charter. Experience - fishing, sightseeing with a gourmet lunch. Escape, and enjoy our peaceful tranquil setting, where the choice of privacy or company is yours. **Home Page**: www.brentonlodge.co.nz

Whangamata
Country Retreat & Gourmet Restaurant
Address: "Bushland Park Lodge & Nickel Strausse",
Wentworth Valley Road, Whangamata
Name: Reinhard & Petra Nickel
Telephone: (07) 865 7468 **Fax**: (07) 865 7486
Email: bushparklodge@xtra.co.nz
Beds: 3 Queen, 1 King-Zip (2 bedrooms, 2 Suites)
Bathroom: 4 Ensuites
Tariff: B&B (special) Double $145-$225, Single $125-$185, Dinner at
Gourmet Restaurant, Credit Cards (Amex, Diners, Visa, M/C), Private
outdoor sauna $15 per person, Hydrotherapeutic spa pool $10 per person,
Massage, Yoga, beauty treatment please enquire.
Nearest Town: Whangamata (Thames 49km, Waihi 30km)

*Just 5km off the Pacific Coast Highway (turn into Wentworth Valley Road at the
18 hole golf course south of Whangamata) you will find, after crossing a river ford,
Bushland Park Lodge & Nickel Strausse, the award winning country retreat
combined with the unique German Black Forest winery style restaurant offering
gourmet cuisine. The colonial style buildings provide 2 comfortable bedrooms
with balcony and 2 spacious suites with private decks set in 2 hectares of native
rainforest and park grounds, close to Wentworth Falls rainforest walkway, golf
courses and perfect beaches. With 1-2 hours from Auckland the ideal venue for
overcoming your jetlag, get relaxed and ready for your overseas trip, celebrate
your honeymoon, anniversary or birthday - or to surprise your partner with a
romantic escape! No TV reception gives you ample time to stroll around the water
lily pond, sit under the twin kauri trees, discover the secret Nikau palm glow worm grotto, relax
in the outdoor bush sauna or spa pool or melt away during a massage. Bush and Beach at
its best!* **Home Page**: http://www.wellness.co.nz

Whangamata
Homestay
Address: Il Casa Moratti, 313 Mary Road, Whangamata
Name: Bev and George Moratti
Telephone: 07 865 6164 **Fax**: 07 865 6164
Email: moratti@thepeninsula.co.nz
Mobile: (021) 685 027
Beds: 1 Double, 2 Single (2 bedrooms)
Bathroom: 1 Guests share
Tariff: B&B (full) Double $95, Single $70, Dinner $25
(by arrangement). Credit Cards accepted. Special winter rates.
NZ B&B Vouchers accepted $25 surcharge
Nearest Town: Whangamata - 1 km to township

*Your hosts Bev and George welcome you to their comfortable, clean, modern smoke-free home,
only minutes away from our magnificent surf beach. Handy to town, park and surf club.
Guests have their own lounge with TV, tea and coffee making facilities, microwave and fridge.
We have travelled extensively and enjoy swapping experiences with fellow travellers. Our other
interests are gardening, sport, fishing, tramping and conservation. Whangamata has plenty
to offer visitors - surfing, swimming, boating, fishing and tramping through beautiful native
bush. the area abounds with history of kauri gum digging, gold mining and kauri timber
milling. We have one very friendly Boxer dog named Alice. Dinner by arrangement.*
Directions: *Please phone for bookings and directions.*
Home Page: http://www.the peninsula.co.nz/moratti

Whangamata

Homestay
Address: Waireka Lodge, 108 Waireka Place, Whangamata.
Name: Gail and Dick Wilson
Telephone: 07-865 8859
Fax: 07-865 8859
Email: waireka@whangamata.co.nz
Beds: 1 Queen, 2 Single (2 bedrooms)
Bathroom: 1 Private
Tariff: B&B (full) Double $95, Single $70, Dinner by arrangement $25 pp, Credit Cards accepted. Off season discounts.
NZ B&B Vouchers accepted $25 surcharge
Nearest Town: Whangamata 1km

Extra touches. Something Special.
*Just two hour's drive from Auckland or Rotorua our Homestay provides an ideal base from which to explore the Coromandel Peninsula. Take time to discover Whangamata's superb beaches, seascapes and bushwalks. Waireka Lodge is in a beautiful garden setting bordering a harbour reserve featuring native trees - just perfect for walks. We invite you to share our relaxed beach lifestyle in our charming new smokefree home. Enjoy quality cuisine with produce from our garden. Your party will be our only guests as we limit bookings to one group. Through our interests we can provide or arrange a variety of activities including: golf, boating or fishing, swimming, guest kayak, petanque, floral art, kiteflying. We love sharing our knowledge to help plan your holiday. As licensed tour operators we provide individualised tours by large airconditioned car throughout the upper North Island. Free Whangamata orientation tour. We have a cat.***Home Page**: http://www.thepeninsula.co.nz/waireka

Whangamata (Rural)

Bed & Breakfast
Address: Copsefield Bed & Breakfast, 1055 Tairua Road, RD1, Whangamata
Name: Trish and Richard Davison
Telephone: (07) 865 9555
Fax: (07) 865 9555
Mobile: (025) 289 0131
Email: copsefield@xtra.co.nz
Beds: 2 Queen, 2 Single (3 Bedrooms)
Bathroom: 3 Ensuites
Tariff: B&B (Full) Double $125, Single $90, Children under 5 years free. Credit Cards: Visa/Mastercard.
Nearest Town: 8km north of Whangamata on SH25.

Copsefield is architecturally designed for your comfort and is situated at the Southern end of the stunning Coromandel Peninsula.Our home is surrounded by 3 acres of orchard and mature trees, and is bounded by a river and views of native bush and peaceful countryside.Two beaches are within a few minutes of our home. The whole vista and pleasure of the Coromandel Peninsula is an easy drive north. This includes the famous Hot Water beach. Relax in one of our tastefully furnished Queen bedrooms or twin room, all en-suited, with verandahs accessed through french doors. Each room has a different outlook. All rooms are non smoking.Tea and coffee facilities and TV are available in the guest lounge, which leads to a large deck. A full breakfast is served with home grown eggs and fresh fruit. Your hosts offer you a warm and friendly welcome and personal attention.
Home Page: http://nz.com/webnz/bbnz/copsefield.htm

Waihi

Homestay
Address: Westwind Gradens , 22   Roycroft Street, Waihi
Name: Josie & Bob French
Telephone: (07) 863 7208
Beds: 4 Single (2 bedrooms)
Bathroom: 1 Guests share
Tariff: B&B (continental) Double $65, Single $35, Children under 12 years 1/2 price), Dinner $15. 10% discount for 3 days or more. Credit Cards. NZ B&B Vouchers accepted
Nearest Town: Waihi (1km from Post Office or Bus Depot)

We welcome you and offer a friendly restful stay at "West Wind Gardens" our modern comfortable home with new beds and electric blankets. Enjoy our lovely 3/4 acre terraced garden which was selected for the New Zealand Open Garden Scheme. Waihi is the gateway to both the Coromandel Peninsula with its beautiful beaches and the Bay of Plenty the Kiwifruit centre of New Zealand.
It is a historic town with a vintage railway running between Waihi and Waikino, a working mine discovered in 1878, worked as an underground mine until 1952, re-opened in 1989 as an open cast mine. Free mine tours available. Beaches 10 minutes away, beautiful native bush walks, golf courses and trout fishing. Enjoy a 3 course home cooked meal or sample our local restaurants. Our interests are gardening, dancing and travel. Smoking outdoors only.
Directions: *Roycroft St is off the Whangamata Road opposite Eastend Supererette.*
Home Page: babs.com.au/nz/westwind.htm

Waihi

"Country House" fine accommodation.
Address: 'The French Provincial Country House',
Golden Valley, Trig Road North, R.D. 1, Waihi
Name: Margaret & Johannes van Duyvenbooden
Telephone: (07) 863 7339
Mobile: (025) 488 845 **Fax**: (07) 863 7330
Beds: 1 Super King, 1 Queen, 1 Double (3 bedrooms)
Bathroom: 1 Luxurious Ensuite,1 Private with
2 person spa bath,1 Guests share
Tariff: B&B (continental special) Super King Ensuite "Bridal Suite" $225, Queen Private 2 person spa bath + shower $165, One Double bed available, extra, as one party booking. Credit Card (VISA), Non smoking. Not suitable for children. Tariff current until 30th Sept 2000. Closed during July/August.
Nearest Town: Waihi 5km, Auckland airport 2 hours.

We warmly welcome you to the French Provincial Country House, set in a pretty farming valley, only 5km from Waihi's historic township. A great central location to the Coromandel and Bay of Plenty. Our charming 2 storey smokefree home is spacious and elegant. In summer colourful gardens, large shade trees and swimming pool for your leisure. Our 3 delightful guest bedrooms have individual decor and all modern quality comforts. Privately upstairs a large luxurious "Bridal Suite" where the decor is soft in colour, lavish and romantic. Two private balconies for your use only. A generous breakfast is served in a formal dining area or in the garden room. There's a variety of restaurants, wineries and cafés, beautiful safe beaches, easy bush walks, golf courses, summer gardens, steam train rides. We personally assure your stay will be relaxing and a memorable one. One night in this area is not long enough. **Directions**: *Please phone for Reservations saves disappointment.*   **Home Page**: http://www.friars.co.nz/hosts/french.html>

Waihi Beach

Homestay
Address: 12 Mayor View Tce,
Waihi Beach
Name: Seaview, D M Cooper
Telephone: (07) 863 5041
Mobile: 025 277 2381
Beds: 1 King/Queen,
2 Single + 1 Foldaway (2 bedrooms)
Bathroom: 1 Guests Share
Tariff: B&B (full) Double $85,
Single $60, Children under 13 half price, Dinner $25.
NZ B&B Vouchers accepted Surcharge $15
Nearest Town: Waihi - distance 10km

Welcome to my home overlooking Waihi Beach a true living leisure treasure. Breathtaking seaviews from three level brick home in beautiful Bay of Plenty set in cottage and tropical gardens. Bathroom is spacious with separate toilet and shower. Also guests lounge, dining room with TV and tea making facilities. Guests will be provided with continental or cooked breakfast as desired. Dinner by arrangement. We have very good eating places at beach or Waihi. There is a short walk to our beach (about 8km of rippling while sand) lovely bush walk, 9 and 18 golf courses, and gardens to visit. We have a large goldmine in our area. There are tours organised. Waihi Beach is truly the centre of a visitors paradise. My interests are tennis, badminton, gardening and providing for you.
Please phone or write for directions.

Waihi Beach

Homestay
Address: 17 The Esplanade,
Waihi Beach
Name: John & Kay Morgan
Telephone: (07) 863 4342
Fax: (07) 863 4342
Mobile: (025) 287 1104
Email: k.morgan@xtra.co.nz
Beds: 1 King/Queen, 1 Double,
1-2 Single (2 bedrooms)
Bathroom: 1 Private
Tariff: B&B (continental) Double $90, $10 per extra persons,
Flat let as self contained unit. Credit Cards.
NZ B&B Vouchers accepted (with surcharge)
Nearest Town: Waihi 11km

Waterfront Homestay
Fully self contained two double bedrooms plus single bed. Very suitable for two couples or small family group. Unit on lower floor of family home. Situated on waterfront of beautiful uncrowded ocean beach. Walk from front door directly onto sandy beach. Safe ocean swimming, surfcasting, surfing and coastal walks. 9 hole golf course with club hire in township, 18 hole golf course 11km away. Restaurant within walking distance of accommodation or use facilities provided with accommodation. Tariff $90 per couple bed & breakfast, $10 per extra persons. Off season rates available. Hosts John & Kay Morgan

http://www.bnb.co.nz

take a look

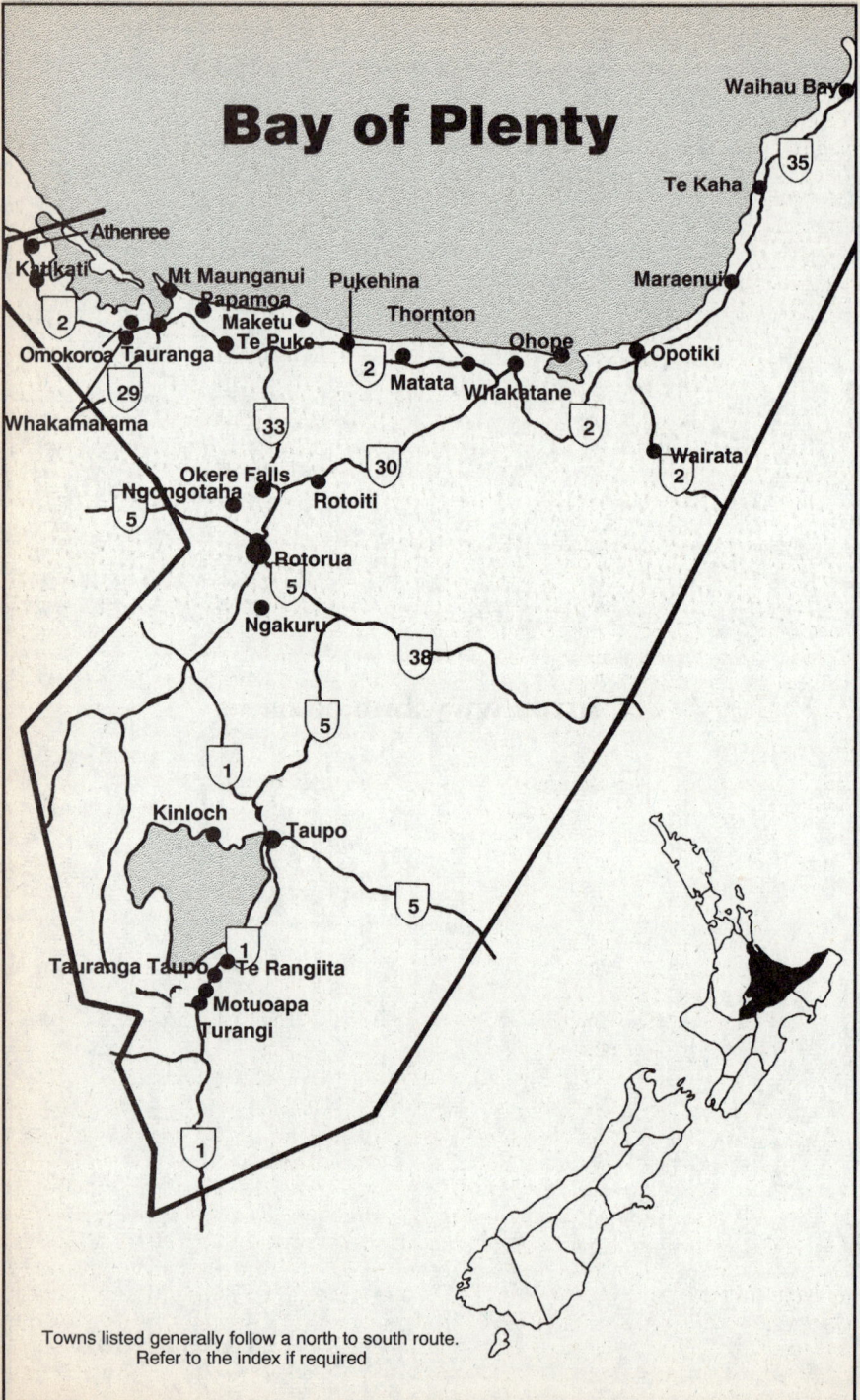

Bay of Plenty

Waihau Bay

Te Kaha

35

Maraenui

Athenree

Katikati

Mt Maunganui
Papamoa

Pukehina

Thornton

Opotiki

2

Maketu

Ohope

Omokoroa Tauranga

Te Puke

Whakatane

29

2

Matata

2

Whakamarama

Wairata

33

2

30

Okere Falls

Ngongotaha

Rotoiti

5

Rotorua

5

Ngakuru

38

5

1

Kinloch

Taupo

5

1

Tauranga Taupo

Te Rangiita

Motuoapa

Turangi

1

Towns listed generally follow a north to south route.
Refer to the index if required

Katikati

Farmstay+Self-Contained Accom.
Address: Jacaranda Cottage, 230 Thompson's Track, RD2, Katikati
Name: Lynlie & Rick Watson
Telephone/Fax: (07) 549 0616 **Mobile**: (025) 272 8710
Email: jacaranda.cottage@clear.net.nz
Beds: House: 1 Queen, 2 Single (2 bedrooms)
SC Cottage: 1 Double, 1 Single (1 bedroom) + fold-out divan in lounge
Bathroom: House: 1 Guests share. SC Cottage: 1 Ensuite
Tariff: B&B: (Full) House: Double $65, Single $40, Dinner by arrangement $18,
Children discounted. Campervans $25, Cyclists/backpackers' budget accommodation
$15. SC Cottage: Double $70, $25 each extra adult, weekly rate discounted, minimum
stay 2 nights. Credit cards. NZ B&B Vouchers accepted
Nearest Town: 30 km north of Tauranga, 8 km south of Katikati

*A warm welcome awaits you at Jacaranda Cottage, a 5-acre farmlet enjoying magnificent 360
degree views - from sea to mountains, from rolling farmlands and orchards to native forests.
We offer you a taste of simple country life - generous hospitality; wholesome farmhouse food;
and clean, warm accommodation in either the main house or in the fully-equipped hillside
cottage (no smoking inside, please). Children enjoy the friendly animals on our farmlet and
are welcome to help with smallfarm activities. Swim, horseride, search for glowworms at
night. Experience the nearby native forests by tramping to Twin Falls, old Eliza Mine, or the
Sentinel Kauri Tree. Visit the unspoilt beaches, hot pools, birdgardens, arts and crafts, winery
and good restaurants. See Katikati's many colourful murals depicting scenes from the area's
past. Horse treks, guided tramps and local tours available. Good base for Bay of Plenty or
Coromandel sightseeing, or simply relax in the tranquil surroundings of Jacaranda Cottage.*
Directions: *Thompson's Track is 6 km south of Katikati, on the Tauranga side of the Forta
Leza Restaurant. Jacaranda Cottage is 2.3 km up Thompson's Track, on the right.*

Katikati

Self-contained Apartment
Address: Pahoia Road, R.D. 2, Tauranga
Name: Trevor & Thora Jones
Telephone: (07) 548 0661
Fax: (07) 548 0661
Beds: 1 Queen (1 bedroom)
1 convertible divan in lounge,
1 cot. Additional beds available in main house.
Bathroom: 1 Private

HARBOURVIEW

Tariff: B&B (Deluxe continental) Double $70, Single $45, Children $15. Credit Cards
Accepted NZ B&B Vouchers accepted
Nearest Town: 20km south of Katikati, 23km north of Tauranga

*We have retired to this pleasant rural region of the Bay of Plenty, on a horticultural lifestyle
property. The modern, self-contained apartment is furnished with all amenities including
laundry. For a larger family group, additional beds (and additional guests bathroom) are
available in the main house. For breakfast a variety of cereals, orchard and home-made
produce, farm eggs and hot bread are provided for self-service. We look northward across the
Tauranga Harbour (water's edge 200 metres away) and westward to the Kaimai Ranges with
their striking sunsets. Available for guests' use are BBQ, dinghy, grass court and games rooms
for billiards, table tennis etc. Attractions in the area include hot pools, beaches, and walking
opportunities in the Kaimai Range. We have special interests in gardening, tramping, the bush
and mountains. For the less energetic, this is a peaceful place to relax, listen to the birds and
contemplate the spectacular scenery.* **Directions**: *Out on Pahoia peninsula, 3km from State
Highway 2. Please phone for bookings and directions.*

227

Katikati
Farmstay
Address: 'Aberfeldy'
164 Lindemann Road, R.D.1, Katikati
Name: Mary Ann & Rod Calver
Telephone: (07) 549 0363
Fax: (07) 549 0363 **Mobile**: 025 909 710
Email: aberfeldy@xtra.co.nz
Beds: 1 Double, 3 Single (2 bedrooms, triple & twin, also private lounge)
Bathroom: 1 Guests only
Tariff: B&B (full) Double $85, Single $50, Children half price, Dinner $25
3 course. We have only one party at a time in the guest accomodation.
NZ B&B Vouchers accepted. Credit Cards accepted.
Nearest Town: Katikati 3km

Aberfeldy is on Lindemann Road off State Highway 2, 3kms north of Katikati, the unique murals town. Your hosts have a sheep and cattle farm with a stoney bottomed stream, and 100 year old trees. They also operate a high producing kiwifruit orchard nearby. There are panoramic views of farmland, bushclad hills and the Tauranga Harbour. Mary Ann and Rod have travelled extensively and love people, gardening, horseriding, tramping, music, reading and cooking. Activities can include bush and farm walks, swimming and meeting the various tame animals, including Sue our Kunekune pig. A golf course is nearby and we are close to the ocean beach. The comfortable attractive home is set in an extensive garden with the private guest accommodation opening to their own patio. The guests have their own bathroom and sunny lounge with tea and coffee making facilities and TV. Jax, our Australian terier will welcome you. A warm welcome is assured and we can pick guests up from Katikati at no extra charge.

Katikati
Country **Homestay+Self-contained**
Address: 'Hammond House', 195 Beach Road, Katikati
Name: Jan & John Nicoll
Telephone: (07) 549 1377
Fax: (07) 549 2217 **Email**: jnicoll@xtra.co.nz
Beds: Self Contained Cottage 1 Queen,
2 Single (2 bedrooms) **Bathroom**: 1 Private.
Tariff: B&B (full) Double $120, Single $80.
Nearest Town: Katikati 2 km

"Hammond House" is an elegant and spacious two storey Tudor style home set in 5 acres of trees, cottage gardens and a kiwifruit orchard. We offer guests self-contained accommodation in a two level Tudor style garden cottage a few metres from the main homestead. The cottage has kitchenette, bathroom, a Queen size French bed downstairs and two single beds upstairs all with electric blankets and feather duvets. We provide television, gas heating, fresh fruit from our orchard, guests can read the latest magazines on the balcony and enjoy a glass of port, whilst enjoying the peace and tranquillity. Enjoy a leisurely breakfast in our conservatory. Breakfast may feature fruit juice, fresh fruit and home made yoghurt, cereals, a variety of egg dishes, venison sausages, bacon, tomatoes, mushrooms, home baked bread and freshly ground coffee. Attractions within 15 minutes drive are ocean beaches, beautiful native bush walks, golf, bird gardens, hot mineral springs, a winery and a selection of restaurants. Katikati (the town of murals) is on the main route between Rotorua and Coromandel and two hours from Auckland. We have a Golden Cairn Terrier "Molly" and two Burmese cats - brothers "Eton" and "Harvard".We look forward to meeting you.

Katikati
Bed & Breakfast/Homestay
Address: Waterford House Bed & Breakfast,
15 Crossley Street, Katikati
Name: Alan & Helen Cook
Telephone: (07) 549 0757
Beds: 1 Queen, 1 Double,
5 Single (2 Twin/1 Single) (5 bedrooms)
Bathroom: 3 Guests share
Tariff: B&B (full) Double $65, Single $40, Children discounted, Dinner
$15-$20. Credit Cards. Cot and highchair available.
NZ B&B Vouchers accepted
Nearest Town: Katikati 1km; 37km north of Tauranga on SH2, 26km
south of Waihi on SH2

Waterford House provides spacious accommodation with wheelchair access throughout. A large comfortable guest lounge with TV, stereo, radio, fridge/ freezer, microwave, and tea/coffee making facilities. Local attractions include historic Twickenham Cafe and Antiques, Morton Estate Winery, Katikati Bird Gardens, Ballantyne Golf Course and Cafe, Sapphire Springs Hot Pools, Kaimai bush walks, Uretara River walkway, pottery and craft workshops, gardens, and of course Katikati "The Mural Town" and "Best Kept Small Town" with more than 25 historic murals and sculptures. Alan and Helen have travelled extensively in New Zealand and overseas, and have gained first-hand experience on how to cater for their guests. Waterford House is situated in a quiet semi-rural area, one kilometre north of Katikati Post Office, just off SH2, opposite the Uretara Domain. We have a cat called 'Matilda'.

Katikati
Rural Homestay
Address: Cotswold Lodge,
183 Ongare Pt Road, Katikati
Name: Jan & Graham Taylor
Telephone: (07) 549 2110
Fax: (07) 549 2110
Beds: 2 Double, 2 Single (3 bedrooms)
Bathroom: 3 Ensuite
Tariff: B&B (full) Double $105, Single
$65, Dinner $25pp. Credit card (VISA/MC).
NZ B&B Vouchers accepted $30 Surcharge
Nearest Town: 7km north of Katikati

Welcome to Cotswold Lodge - as the name suggests we originate from the Cotswolds in England. On arrival in New Zealand we fell in love with the colonial architecture and have built our large, comfortable home on those lines complete with facilities for disabled and elderly people. It is set in peaceful gardens with beautiful views to the Kaimai Ranges and just a short stroll to the beach and harbour. Come and stay awhile and unwind from the hurly burly of everyday life. Graham restores antiques from his workshop on the premises while Jan spins, paints and potters in her garden, with the help of her friendly Labrador. Katikati, the Mural town of New Zealand, is ideally situated to explore the beautiful Bay of Plenty and the Coromandel Peninsula with their varied attractions. We would be happy to arrange tours or transport for you - otherwise just relax and enjoy yourselves.

Katikati

Orchard Stay + Private Suite
Address: Peaceful Panorama Lodge, 901 Main Road North, (SH2), RD1, Katikati
Name: Heather & Bernie Wills
Telephone: (07) 549 1882
Fax: (07) 549 1882
Email: wills@bopis.co.nz
Beds: 2 Double, 3 Single (3 bedrooms)
Bathroom: 1 Ensuite, 1 Guests share
Tariff: B&B (full/special) Double $75, Single $45. Private Double suite $95 (lounge, bathroom, bedroom) Extra adult in suite $25, Children $20. Hearty NZ style dinner $20, Light dinner $10-$15. Credit Cards (VISA/MC/AMEX). NZ B&B Vouchers accepted $20 surcharge for private suite
Nearest Town: Katikati 9km. Auckland 1 3/4 hours, Tauranga 35 minutes.

*Comfortable, casual & friendly.......enjoy the tranquillity of Peaceful Panorama.......
Sea-views from every room. 10 acres are yours to explore with : gardens, pool, birds, pet cows, hens, emus, kiwifruit and avocado orchard. Only minutes to the harbour or ocean beach. No animals or smoking indoors, guest/family lounge, pianola, laundry service, complimentary "cuppas" anytime. **Nearby**: Bush-walks, horse-riding, scenic flights, murals, golf, hot pools, ocean beach, gardens, fishing. - **Interests**: Vintage cars, musical memorabilia, photography, winemaking, spinning, gardening. - **Home-made Breakfast:** Freshly squeezed juice, fruit, cereal selection, new laid eggs, pancakes, croissants, muffins, gingerbread, jams, filtered coffee, teas or chocolate. - **Dinner**: Hearty NZ style main & desert, or a light meal. Special Diets if required. - **Rooms**: Double, Twin or Private Suite, all with sea-views, comfortable beds, wool duvets, electric blankets, clock radios etc. **Directions**: 901 State Highway 2. Yellow letter box. 9km North of Katikati, 16 km South of Waihi.*

Omokoroa, Tauranga

Homestay/Cottage
Address: 'Walnut Cottage'
309 Station Rd, Omokoroa,
R.D. 2, Tauranga
Name: Ken & Betty Curreen
Telephone: (07) 548 0692
Fax: (07) 548 1764
Email: homestay@cybersurf.co.nz
Beds: Cottage: 1 Queen. House: 1 Double ("Kowhai Suite")
Bathroom: Cottage: 1 Ensuite House: 1 Ensuite
Tariff: B&B (continental) Double $60, Single $40, Dinner $15, NZ B&B Vouchers accepted
Nearest Town: 15 minutes north Tauranga on SH2

Walnut Cottage is situated on scenic Plummers Point Peninsular and we overlook beautiful Tauranga Harbour. We are a semi-retired couple who invite our guests to enjoy the tranquillity our "little-corner-of-the-world" has to offer. Both the cottage and Kowhai Suite are clean and comfortable with ensuites, T.V and tea/coffee making facilities. Relaxing mineral hot pools are a 5 minute walk away and a 2 minute stroll takes you to the waters edge where you can enjoy the peace of the estuary or fish from the jetty. Our breakfasts feature freshly squeezed orange juice (in season) homemade jams, muesli, yoghurt and eggs, a good start to see local sights and activities including water gardens, horseriding, golf, bowls and tramping. Our semi-rural retreat is close to Tauranga city, popular for its shopping, fishing trips and sightseeing.
Directions: *Station Rd is opposite Whakamarama Service Station on SH2. We are 3km along Station Rd.* **Home Page**: *www.cybersurf.co.nz/curreen*

Omokoroa Peninsula
Homestay
Address: Armadale,
296 Omokoroa Rd.,
R.D.2, Tauranga
Name: Shirley & Graeme Macdonald
Telephone: (07) 548 1944
Fax: (07) 548 1944
Beds: 1 Double, 2 Single (2 bedrooms)
Bathroom: 1 Guests share
Tariff: B&B (full) Double $70,
Single $35, Children 12 & under half price, Dinner $20pp.
Nearest Town: City of Tauranga - 17km

Shirley and Graeme Macdonald welcome guests to our home and property, currently being developed into gardens, home orchard, horticulture and a simple pitch and putt course. Visitors may take advantage of the wide range of activities offered in the Omokoroa area. These include - safe swimming, hot pools, horse riding, golf, bowls, sophisticated or casual dining, children's playground, and a ferry service to Matakana Island. There are some excellent open gardens and scenic walks. We have one friendly cat and a family of fantail pigeons. Our particular interests include trout and sea fishing, gardening, golf and hosting guests.

Omokoroa Peninsula, Tauranga
Homestay and B&B
Address: 81 Kayelene Place,
RD2, Omokoroa,
Tauranga
Name: Gordon and Diana Stone
Telephone: (07) 548 1270
Fax: (07) 548 1278
Mobile: (025) 289 9331
Email: gdstone@wave.co.nz
Beds: 1 Queen, 2 Single (2 Bedrooms)
Bathroom: 1 Guests share
Tariff: B&B (Full) Double $70, Single $40,
Dinner $20 pp (by arrangement), Campervans welcome.
NZ B&B Vouchers accepted. Credit cards accepted.
Nearest Town: Tauranga 18 km (Katikati: approx equidistant)

We welcome you to our home situated in a peaceful garden setting overlooking the golf links. You may relax or enjoy a walk to the estuary beach with its abundance of birds or the harbour beaches. There are many local attractions - golf, bowls, tennis, swimming, and hot pools. The boat ramp and jetty are 5 minutes away for fishing or a scenic trip to Matakana Island. Nearby, there is kayaking, horse riding, bush walking, and mountain biking. Wineries, and both formal and informal dining, are available within close proximity. We have two resident cats and visiting doves. We enjoy fishing, gardening, golf, music when time from our orchid business allows us. Our home is smokefree.
Directions: *Please ring for directions.*

Whakamarama
Homestay
Address: 'Highlands',
89 Whakamarama Rd,
R.D.6, Tauranga
Name: Shirley & John Whiteman
Telephone: (07) 552 5275
Fax: (07) 552 5770
Beds: 1 Queen, 2 Single
(2 bedrooms)
Bathroom: 1 Guest share
Tariff: B&B (full) Double $75, Single $45, Children under 12 half price, Dinner
$20. Credit Cards NZ B&B Vouchers accepted
Nearest Town: Tauranga 14km north on S.H.2 (15 mins)

Our home is situated in a quiet rural area with spectacular views of Mayor Island, Mt Maunganui and Tauranga Harbour.
You are very welcome to dine with us, alternatively there is a selection of good restaurants within 5 mins drive. We offer 2 bedrooms, a lounge and kitchen (with fridge) for your use, all opening to garden, catching morning sun and panoramic views. Laundry facilities available.
We are handy to golf links, bowling green, horse riding, hot pools, bush walks and good boat launching.
Directions: *Highlands is 2km off state highway two on Whakamarama road (no89) which turns right at Whakamarama shops when travelling south. 15 mins from Tauranga. Signposted on main Highway. Please phone if possible.*

Tauranga
B&B Homestay
Address: 8A Vale Street,
Bureta, Tauranga
Name: Christine & Gordon Ross
Telephone: (07) 576 8895
Email: rossvale@xtra.co.nz
Beds: 2 Single (1 bedroom)
Bathroom: 1 Private
Tariff: B&B (special) Double $70, Single $40.
NZ B&B Vouchers accepted $10 Surcharge
Nearest Town: Tauranga

Welcome to our home, an attractive new townhouse, at a new location. We are easily located close to town (2 kms), with a golf course and licensed restaurant nearby and a park opposite. There is lots to do and see in Tauranga for all age groups.
Our guest room has every comfort and a large private bathroom and you can enjoy our spacious lounge and sunny balcony or take a short stroll to the Harbour edge.
Your hostess, Christine, is an enthusiastic miniaturist, makes porcelain dolls and has travelled extensively; we are both retired.
We offer breakfast of your choice, off street parking, and we will meet public transport.

Tauranga
Homestay
Address: 'Bolney Gate',
20 Esmeralda Street,
Welcome Bay, Tauranga
Name: Jack & Joyce Ingram
Telephone: (07) 544 3228
Fax: (07) 544 3228 **Mobile**: (025) 277 5387
Beds: 1 Twin room, Family room (1 Queen, 2 Singles)
Bathroom: 1 Family share
Tariff: B&B (continental - special available)
Double $60, Single $35, Children under 10 $15, under 16 $20, Dinner $20,
Campervans 2, Credit cards (VISA/MC). NZ B&B Vouchers accepted
Nearest Town: Tauranga - 6 mins by bus or taxi

*Bolney Gate is interesting and spacious, overlooking a park dotted with a variety
of mature trees. The park has activities for both old and young. Practice golf,
jogging, jungle gyms, swings & slides, trolley riding, kite flying or just walking.
The view is varied from quiet residential homes set on the hills around the park
to restful rural views. We have both indoor and outdoor living. An enclosed and
secluded pool with an elevated wooden deck at one end as a leisure area for
reading, writing, eating out or just sharing. We live in the very heart of the Bay
of Plenty and Welcome Bay is just a few minutes drive from downtown Tauranga
and Mount Maunganui - 15 to 20 minutes from the horticultural centre of Te Puke
or 40 minutes to the delightful small rural town of Katikati, known as the Mural
town of New Zealand, offering Kiwi orchards, art in every form, rural and bush
walks. We have both travelled widely in N.Z. and many countries of the world and
enjoy people from all walks of life. We have Sky TV.*

Tauranga
Heritage Bed & Breakfast Inn
Address: 'Taiparoro House 1882',
11, 5th Avenue, Tauranga
Name: Kevin & Lois Kelly
Telephone: (07) 577 9607
Fax: (07) 577 9264
Mobile: (025) 223 5675
Email: kl.kelly@clear.net.nz
Beds: 3 Queen, 1 Double, 2 Single (5 bedrooms) **Bathroom**: 5 Ensuite
Tariff: B&B (special) Double $150-$210, Single $105, Credit cards.
Nearest Town: Tauranga 100 metres

*Enjoy a taste of the past in one of Tauranga's oldest and most beautiful historic
homes. Taiparoro's five guest rooms, all have ensuites and telephone, and a
lounge/conservatory exclusively for guests. The historic theme is evident with all
rooms furnished in keeping with the colonial era. For a special occasion, or just
to pamper yourself, stay in the lovely Harbour View Suite and soak in the original
claw foot bath. Breakfast is delightful with fresh fruits, homemade muesli,
organic yoghurts, fresh baked croissants, home made bread, brewed coffee plus
choose from a selection of cooked meals. An assortment of teas and coffee are
available at any time. Go for a stroll, relax in the English Conservatory, in front
of the fire, or enjoy the stunning view of Tauranga harbour from the garden.
Situated in tranquil surroundings, Taiparoro is only 10 minute stroll to the city
centre, excellent restaurants, cafes, bars and quality shopping.*
Home Page: http://www.heritageinns.co.nz/taiparoro

Tauranga
Country Homestay+Self Contained Accom.
Address: 322 Oropi Road,
R.D. 3, Tauranga
Name: 'Baumgarten Lodge', Henri & Colleen Limacher
Telephone: (07) 543 2799
Fax: (07) 543 2799
Beds: 1 King (TV in room), 1 Queen, 2 Single (3 bedrooms)
Bathroom: 1 Guests share.
Tariff: B&B (full) Double $70, Single $45. NZ B&B Vouchers accepted
Nearest Town: Tauranga City Centre 9 minutes.

Baumgarten Country Lodge and Self Contained Accommodation, both clean and comfortable is semi rural, 2km off Highway 29. The lodge is a large spacious single storied home with indoor spa room. Situated on a 5 acre farmlet, nestled amidst our avocado orchard, various fruit trees and gardens. We graze a few calves and have one outdoor dog and a cat called Sammy. Semi-retired we enjoy meeting visitors. Henri, Swiss born speaks German. The outdoor swimming pool and 9 pin bowling ally are features to be enjoyed. The comfortable detached, self contained and fully furnished accommodation sleeps 5-6 persons. Only minutes from Greerton Village, restaurants, golf club, racecourse, R.S.A and heated pool. Short drive to Mt. Maunganui Beach, plus easy day excursions to Waitomo Caves, Rotorua, volcanic White Island and more. We request no smoking in the house.

Matua, Tauranga
Bed and Breakfast
Address: 210 Levers Road,
Matua, Tauranga
Name: John & Heather Christiansen
Telephone: (07) 576 6835
Fax: (07) 576 6464
Beds: 1 Queen, 2 Single (2 Bedrooms)
Bathroom: 1 Guests share
Tariff: B&B (full) Double $80, Single $50, Credit Cards.
NZ B&B Vouchers accepted $12 surcharge
Nearest Town: Tauranga city centre 6km

Our home is in the pleasant suburb of Matua, enhanced by a garden of New Zealand native trees, shrubs and ferns. The guest wing is quiet and comfortable. Please join us in our lounge, read our books and listen to our music. Our other interests include the performing arts, growing New Zealand native plants, collecting antiques and motorcycling. Our home is smoke-free. Breakfast - see our menu of special choices when you arrive. We can cater for people with food allergies. We are close to harbour beaches and parks; seven minutes drive to Tauranga city centre and fifteen minutes to Mount Maunganui's Ocean Beach. We have a broad knowledge of the Bay of Plenty and its attractions. A gift of home grown citrus fruit can be provided, in season, when you depart. Best to call or phone before 9.00am or after 5.30pm.

Te Puna, Tauranga

Homestay
Address: 'Taurima',
186 Minden Road,
R.D.6 Te Puna, Tauranga
Name: Ursula Kassin & Judith Simpson
Telephone: (07) 552 5800
Fax: (07) 552 5800
Mobile: 021-703 260
Email: TaurimaBOP@xtra.co.nz
Beds: 1 Queen, 2 Single (2 bedrooms)
Bathroom: 1 Guest private
Tariff: B&B (full) Double $80, Single $45. NZ B&B Vouchers accepted
Nearest Town: Tauranga 15 mins

Your private and personal holiday choice in the Bay of Plenty. Share our home nestled into the hillside with 360 degrees sea, bush and farmland views. This is the ideal stopover for exploring the many natural gifts of the Bay of Plenty. Stride out along our beaches, soak in hot pools, delight in beautiful gardens, visit the thermal wonderland of Rotorua, tempt your taste buds at the wineries and restaurants. We came to New Zealand 5 years ago from London. Ursula is originally from Vienna, Judith is New Zealand born. Prior to leaving London we spent 2 years working on Menorca (Balearic Islands, Spain). Chocolate the Burmese completes the household.
Welcoming, fun loving and ever adaptable, we look forward to meeting you.
Directions: *Please phone.*

Oropi, Tauranga

Homestay/Farmstay
Address: 'Grenofen',
Castles Road, Oropi, R.D.3, Tauranga
Name: Jennie & Norm Reeve
Telephone: (07) 543 3953
Fax: (07) 543 3951
Email: n.reeve@wave.co.nz
Beds: 1 King, 2 Single (2 Bedrooms)
Bathroom: 2 Ensuite
Tariff: B&B (full) Double $90, Single $60, Dinner 3 course incl. complimentary wine $30pp, by arrangement.
NZ B&B Vouchers accepted $20 surcharge
Nearest Town: Tauranga

We invite you to stay with us in our spacious home overlooking the undulating countryside, with the sea, Tauranga city, and Mount Maunganui in the background. Our property is a sheltered 3 1/2 acres sloping to the north with trees, gardens, lawns and two friendly donkeys. You may wish to relax in total privacy, enjoy the spa or swim in our pool. A short drive takes you to Tauranga racecourse, golf courses, beaches, and historic places, or you may like to sample the excellent shopping facilities available. Guests may choose double bedroom, with King size bed or twin bedroom, each with ensuite, electric blankets, TV, comfortable chairs and rural views. Tea/coffee making facility with fridge in guest area - laundry can be done overnight if required. We have travelled extensively and enjoy the company of local and overseas travellers. Our interests include skiing, cycling, golf, gardening, walking and travel. Be sure of a warm welcome.

Tauranga

Homestay
Address: Ohauiti
R.D.3, Tauranga
Name: Bernie & Alison Rowe
Telephone: (07) 544 0966
Fax: (07) 544 0916
Mobile: (025) 945 785
Email: Rowesdale.xtra.co.nz
Beds: 1 Queen, 1 Double,
2 Single (3 Bedrooms)
Bathroom: 1 Private, 1 Guests share
Tariff: B&B (continental) Double $80, Single $50, Children $25.
NZ B&B Vouchers accepted $12 Surcharge
Nearest Town: Tauranga 8km.

Alison and Bernie welcome you to Tauranga and to our home which is surrounded by beautiful trees, gardens, a tennis court and swimming pool. Tennis racquets available. Guests have own bathroom. Two bedrooms have adjacent private lounge, suitable families.
We are only 10 mins drive from centre of city and a great selection of very good restaurants. Very handy to beautiful golf courses, beaches, diving, deep sea fishing and tramping. Alison and Bernie enjoy entertaining and meeting new people and are happy for you to stay as long as you like. Please no smoking within the house, outside is fine.
Directions: *Please phone.*

Te Puna, Tauranga

Homestay
Address: 310 Snodgrass Road,
R.D.2, Tauranga
Name: Diana & Alastair Melvin
Telephone: (07) 552 5313
Mobile: 025 589 443
Beds: 2 Double, 2 Single
(3 bedrooms)
Bathroom: 1 Ensuite, 1 Guests share
Tariff: B&B (continental) Double $70,
Single $35, Children under 15 half price. Dinner $20 (by arrangement).
Nearest Town: Tauranga 10km south Highway 2

We are an outgoing couple with a grown family who live away from home. Our comfortable single storey home is set amongst mature trees. We have a guest wing with all services, including electric blankets and heaters. We are an easy twelve minutes drive from Tauranga, and twenty five minutes from Mt Maunganui beach, in the midst of orchards and lush farmland. A two kilometre drive takes you to a tidal inner-harbour beach with a good boat ramp. A leisurely continental breakfast is included. A home cooked dinner with complimentary wine is available by prior arrangement. Guests are welcome to see our two acres of fruit trees and garden. Our home is smoke free. Our interests include gardening, walking, weaving, craftwork. You will be only minutes away from hot pools, golf course, deep sea fishing, diving, superior shopping, winery and award winning restaurants.
Directions: *Please phone after 5.30pm.*

Tauranga
Superior Bed & Breakfast Inn

Address: Hollies, Westridge Drive,
Bethlehem, Tauranga
Name: Shirley & Michael Creak
Telephone: (07) 577 9678
Fax: (07) 579 1678
Email: stay@hollies.co.nz
Beds: 1 Queen, 2 Single, 1 King/twin
Bathroom: 2 Private, 1 Ensuite
Tariff: B&B (full) Double $110 to $150, Single from $75, Dinner $30pp.
Visa/Mastercard. NZ B&B Vouchers accepted Surcharge $40 to $75
Nearest Town: Tauranga 5km

Hollies is an elegant sophisticated modern country house set in an acre of gardens. Large luxuriously appointed guest rooms have panoramic views of gardens and rolling hills. The spacious suite has super king (or twin) bed, ensuite, lounge & TV, kitchenette, alternative private entrance and balcony. Perfect for longer visits. The queen and twin rooms have private bathrooms with hairdryers, bathrobes and toiletries. Fresh flowers, chocolates and crisp linen and every attention to detail combine to ensure your stay is truly memorable. On arrival, complimentary tea/coffee is served in the guest lounge. Landscaped gardens with roses, camellias, a gazebo, swimming pool with waterfall. Enjoy petanque, croquet. Breakfast, healthy of indulgent, home-made bread, muffins and muesli, fresh fruit and tempting cooked dishes. Hollies is a smoke free complex, not suitable for young children. Laundry available. Complimentary golf at Ballantyne Golf Country Club. Award winning restaurants, winery and hot mineral pools two minutes away. **Home Page**: www.hollies.co.nz

Tauranga
Homestay

Address: Pukemapu Homestead
208 Pukemapu Road,
RD 3 Oropi, Tauranga
Name: Jill and John Mitchinson
Telephone: (07) 543 3502
Fax: (07) 543 3512
Mobile: (025) 992 148
Beds: 2 Queen, 2 Single (3 bedrooms)
Bathroom: 1 Ensuite, 1 Guests share
Tariff: B&B (full) Double $95, Single $65, Dinner $25pp, Credit Cards (MC/VISA).
Nearest Town: Tauranga, 11Kms from C.B.D.

Genuine Kiwi hospitality is assured when you stay with John and Jill in their beautiful new and spacious home. Enjoying the peace of country living, Pukemapu Homestead is located just minutes from Greeerton village at the southern end of Tauranga city. Slightly elevated the property provides expansive views of the city, Mt Maunganui and the Kaimai Ranges. The one hectare mandarin orchard is close to the Tauranga racecourse, 18 hole golf course, hot pools and a variety of activities within the Oropi area ranging from mountain bike riding to beautiful gardens and nurseries. It is only 15 minutes to one of New Zealands finest beaches at Mt Maunganui. Tea and coffee making, laundry and car washing facilities are available. The home is smoke free but guests are welcome to smoke outside. The children have left home and there are no pets apart from an aviary of finches. A warm welcome awaits you.

Tauranga
Orchard Homestay
Address: "Ripo Moana",
69 Asher Road,
Welcome Bay, RD 5, Tauranga
Name: Rei Preston-Thomas
Telephone: (07) 544 2184
Beds: 2 Single (1 bedroom)
S.C. Cottage: 2 Single (1 bedroom)
Bathroom: 1 Private   S.C. Cottage: 1 Private
Tariff: B&B (continental) Double $70, Single $40.
NZ B&B Vouchers accepted
Nearest Town: Tauranga 13km

What could be more restful than staying in a cottage overlooking the harbour on an avocado orchard. The cottage is joined to the house by an attractive walkway, and naturally guests are welcome in the house, and usually prefer to come over for breakfast. There is also a double bedroom with private bathroom in the house. "Ripo-Moana" is a six acre orchard growing avocados and mandarins. It is situated on the edge of the inner harbour with the front lawn extending down to the water. It offers a very warm welcome, the peace and tranquillity of the countryside, and yet is only twelve minutes drive to downtown Tauranga or Mount Maunganui, and fifty minutes to Rotorua. Your host has travelled widely and lived and worked in several countries.
Directions: *Approximately 5km along Welcome Bay Road from the Maungatapu roundabout, but it is suggested you ring for detailed instructions.*

Tauranga
Homestay
Address: Matua Homestay,
34 Tainui Street, Matua, Tauranga
Name: Peter & Anne Seaton
Telephone: (07) 576 8083
Mobile: 025 915566
Email: pa.seaton@clear.net.nz
Beds: 1 Double, 2 Single (2 bedrooms)
Bathroom: 1 Guests share
Tariff: B&B (continental) Double $70,
Single $40, Children half price
NZ B&B Vouchers accepted $10 surcharge
Nearest Town: Tauranga - 8 mins drive

We welcome you to Tauranga and offer friendly Kiwi hospitality in our modern comfortable one level home, situated in the peaceful suburb of Matua. We invite you to relax and make yourself at home. You won't be disappointed. Take a 200 metre stroll to Fergusson Park to see spectacular views of estuary and Mount Maunganui, or a pleasant 5 minute walk to Matua Shopping Centre, enjoying modern homes and picturesque gardens enroute. Enjoy a good nights sleep in our comfortable beds and tastefully furnished guest rooms. Breakfast may be served indoors or outdoors in our sunny private garden area. Tea, coffee and milo are available at any time. We have enjoyed travelling in NZ and overseas and look forward to sharing your company. We would be happy to help you plan visits to any local places of interest. Laundry facilities available. Smoke free inside.

Tauranga
Orchard Homestay
Address: 26 Station Road,
Omokoroa, RD 2, Tauranga
Name: Bronwen and Alan
Telephone: (07) 548 1936
Beds: 1 Queen, 2 Single (2 bedrooms)
Bathroom: 2 Private
Tariff: B&B (continental)
Double $75-$85, Single $50, Dinner $25,
Children half price. No Credit Cards.
Nearest Town: Tauranga, 15 kms South

Montrose set among a one acre garden overlooking our avocado orchard, across farmland to the sea and city lights. The upper storey of our home is solely for guests' use, has 2 balconies, tea/coffee making facilities and pool table/lounge room. The bedroom has two single beds and private bathroom. Downstairs we have a bedroom with Queen bed and private bathroom. Take a stroll in our garden or walk to the local water gardens. Browse through our New Zealand books, some containing our son's work - a talented landscape photographer. Relax in the local hot pools. Enjoy home made bread and home grown fruit and juices. Our interests include bowls, gardening and our beautiful country. We have two sons and a daughter pursuing careers away from home. Holly our Cairn Terrier loves visitors. Boris our ginger cat is more shy. We look forward to your company. Station road off SH2 opposite Whakamaramara Service Station 200 m on right.

Tauranga
Bed & Breakfast/Homestay
Address: Harbinger House,
209 Fraser Street, Tauranga
Name: Helen and Doug Fisher
Telephone: (07) 578 8801
Fax: (07) 578 8801
Mobile: (025) 583 049
Email: d-h.fisher@xtra.co.nz
Beds: 2 Queen, 2 Single (3 bedrooms)
Bathroom: 1 Guests share
Tariff: B&B (special) Double $70-$90, Single $55-$75, dinner $25 pp.
Credit Cards accepted. Vouchers accepted $10 surcharge can apply
Nearest Town: Tauranga (2 km to CBD or 30 mins walk)

Welcome to Harbinger House. Our upstairs has been renovated with your comfort a top priority. The two queen rooms have vanity units and private balconies. All rooms have quality furnishings, tea and coffee making facilities and tourist information. A guest telephone is installed for your use. Laundry facilities are available. Our house is centrally located being close to the hospital, conference facilities, shops and beaches. We have a lovely garden which you are welcome to use. Breakfast is a gourmet event with fresh juice, local fruits where possible, yoghurt, muesli, freshly baked bread and a cooked dish. Packed picnic lunches are a speciality as is dinner - both by prior arrangement. Complimentary pick up from airport and bus station. Off street parking. We are a well travelled couple who enjoy having guests to stay. Helen is a keen cook, loves gardening and crafts. Our house is smoke free inside. **Home Page**: www.harbinger.co.nz

Tauranga
Homestay, Self Contained Accommodation
Address: 98E Boscabel Drive,
Ohauiti, Tauranga
Name: Lutz and Lydia Heutmann
Telephone: (07) 544 0219
or (07) 578 9113
Fax: (07) 544 0215
Email: Lutzh@ihug.co.nz
Beds: 2 Queen, 1 Double (3 bedrooms)
Bathroom: 3 Ensuite
Tariff: B&B (full) Double $80, Single $60,
Dinner $20.   NZ B&B Vouchers accepted
Nearest Town: Tauranga (10 minutes)

We have recently built our dream home in Boscabel, an exclusive rural residential subdivision in Tauranga. Our large home includes two self-contained studio apartments with kitchenettes and one large double ensuite bedroom, all with central video system. The house is set on a landscaped 1 3/4 acre section with extensive views and a large picturesque pond. Breakfast and dinner and bar-b-que facilities are available by arrangement as Lydia loves cooking. The use of our ozone swimming pool in a tranquil garden setting is available during the summer months. We are located only 10 minutes from the Tauranga city centre and 13 minutes form the Ocean Beach at Mount Maunganui. We are a recently-retired German couple in our early fifties and would love to welcome Kiwi and overseas visitors to this beautiful part of the Bay of Plenty with its excellent beaches, fishing and four 18-hole golf courses.

Tauranga
Homestay
Address: "Birch Haven",
Welcome Bay Road, RD5,
Tauranga
(adjacent Welcome Bay Hotpools)
Name: Judy and George McConnell
Telephone: 07-544 2499
Mobile: 025-414 289
Beds: 1 Super King/Twin,
1 Queen (2 bedrooms). Campervan for hire.
Bathroom: 1 Guests share
Tariff: B&B (full) Double $80, Single $50, Dinner $25, Children under 12 years $25. NZ B&B Vouchers accepted $12 surcharge
Nearest Town: Mt Maunganui. Tauranga (15 mins drive).

Have you been travelling or sight-seeing for hours? How about a 'cuppa' once you've settled into our peaceful one-level home on 3 acres amongst lovely trees. In summer perhaps a swim in the pool, a typical New Zealand barbecue or in winter a spa and dinner by the open fire. Sky/TV, music or our company are all evening options but within 15 minutes drive are numerous good restaurants (nearest 1 km) and entertainment. We love walking and can recommend several good walks nearby. We are happy to help you see and do as much or as little as you wish. Travel, good food and wine, gardening, reading and sport interest us and Blackie our cat will join us if he chooses. We offer courtesy pick-up from Tauranga terminals and want to make your stay a happy memory.
No smoking inside please. **Directions**: *Please phone if possible.*

Te Puna, Tauranga
Orchard Bed & Breakfast

Address: 63 Snodgrass Road,
RD 2, Te Puna, Tauranga
Name: Maple Lodge
Telephone: (07) 552 4050
Fax: (07) 552 4050
Mobile: (025) 279 4121
Beds: 1 Double, 2 Single (2 bedrooms)
Bathroom: 1 Guests share
Tariff: B&B (continental) Double $75, Single $45.
NZ B&B Vouchers accepted
Nearest Town: Tauranga 10 km South S/H 2.

We invite you to come and experience our character home overlooking a mixed orchard of citrus, avocados and nashis. You can relax beside the pool, ramble through the mature gardens and orchard then relax on the deck and enjoy the sunset. A short drive takes you to a variety of restaurants and cafes. Harbour beaches are only minutes away as are wonderful garden centres, craft shops, hot pools or the city lights. Breakfast is served using fresh fruit from the orchard or local, with a choice of cereal and toast or croissants. Gordon works full time on the orchard, is interested in classic cars and plays electric piano. Robyn is a Natural Therapy Practitioner and has a home clinic specialising in herbal remedies, flower essences and supplements. Homer our three legged cat joins with us to make your stay a really enjoyable one. We are smoke free. No children at home. **Directions**: *Please phone.*

Tauranga
Homestay

Address: "Bayview Homestead",
Pahoia, R. D. 6 Tauranga
Name: Verna and Bill
Telephone: (07) 548 1551
Fax: (07) 548 1551
Mobile: (025) 464 488
Email: bayviewhomestead@xtra.co.nz
Beds: 1 Queen, 2 Single (2 bedrooms)
Bathroom: 1 Guests share
Tariff: B&B (special) Double $130, Single $100, Dinner $30. Credit Cards accepted. Not suitable for children under 12.
Nearest Town: 20 km North of Tauranga

Beauty, peace and tranquillity will be yours while you stay with us. Our three acre property has sweeping lawns, attractive developing gardens and petanque court, with panoramic views of rolling farmland, the Bay of Plenty and the Kaimai Ranges. Our spacious, smoke free home has generous guest bedrooms with a large bathroom and separate toilet for guest use. You also have full use of a formal lounge/dining area with log fireplace, open kitchen/family area and billiard room. Meals may be taken inside or on the deck. Enjoy home-made cakes and cookies with your tea or coffee. Freshly made bread, muffins, pancakes, eggs Benedict or a traditional cooked breakfast are available. Located mid-way between Katikati and Tauranga, local attractions include river, coastal and bush walks, golf, hot pools, restaurants and mural town. Children over 12 welcome. Fluent French and basic German spoken.
Directions: *Please phone*

Bethlehem-Tauranga

Homestay and B&B
Address: 172 Crawford Road,
R.D.1, Tauranga.
Name: Crawford House
Telephone: (07) 552 5404
Mobile: (025) 243 6297
Email: craig.madsen@xtra.co.nz
Beds: 1 Double, 2 Single (2 Bedrooms).
Bathroom: 1 Guests share
Tariff: B&B (continental) Double $70,   Single $40,
Dinner $20 pp by arrangement.
Nearest Town: Tauranga

Crawford House is situated four kms off State Highway 2 up Wairoa Rd (turn at bridge) to Crawford Road - just 10 mins out of Tauranga.

A warm welcome awaits you on a 5 acre farmlet enjoying wonderful views of Mt Maunganui and Omokoroa Harbour. Guests quarters are provided with deck and outdoor area. A generous breakfast of freshly squeezed juice, fruit, home-made muesli, or selected cereals, toast, croissants and brewed coffee is served in the hosts dining area, and there are numerous restaurants in Bethlehem or Tauranga for dining out. Crawford House is just minutes away from quality shops, cafes, garden centres, restaurants, wineries, beaches and bush walks. Your hostess Maureen is an ex Home Economics teacher whose hobbies now include quilting, papertole, cooking, gardening, photography and travel. Please phone or email for reservations and directions. You are assured of a warm welcome in our smoke free house.

http://www.bnb.co.nz

take a look

Tauranga
Homestay, Farmstay
Address: 70 Gargan Road,
RD1, Tauranga
Name: Sue Phillips & John Speirs
Telephone: (07) 543 0454
Fax: (07) 543 0454
Email: s.phillips@clear.net.nz
Beds: 1 Queen (1 Bedroom)
Bathroom: 1 Private
Tariff: B&B (Full) Double $85, Single $65, Dinner $25.
NZ B&B Vouchers accepted $20 surcharge
Nearest Town: Tauranga

Our comfortable country-style home, which is set on 5 acres, has a warm relaxed atmosphere. We invite you to share our home and enjoy one of the Bay's finest gardens with rural valley views. Pick seasonal fruit and garden produce, feed the pigeons, collect the eggs or sit and enjoy the tranquillity on the verandah. Our family includes two boys plus two cats and one dog, all of which are very friendly. We really enjoy hosting guests and making you comfortable. We also offer tennis (rackets available), swimming in our large pool during summer months, putting green, petanque, cycling, walking, listening to music or reading. Enjoy an open fire during the winter.

Your spacious room is complete with refreshments, crisp white linen, TV, stereo and comfortable furniture. A full or continental breakfast can be served alfresco style or indoors as with dinner which is optional. Our handy location allows you to enjoy many and varied amenities and attractions.

Tauranga (harbour's edge)
Self Contained Accommodation
Address: 75 Forrester Drive,
Welcome Bay, Tauranga
Name: Dale and Alan Withy
Telephone: 64 - 7 - 544 4973
Fax: 64 - 7 - 544 4711
Email: alanwithy@clear.net.nz
Beds: 1 Queen, 1 Single (1 bedroom)
plus foldout double bed in living room
Bathroom: 1 Private
Tariff: B&B (Continental self service) Double $90, Single $60, Children $15 each. Credit cards accepted. Vouchers accepted $10 surcharge
Nearest Town: Tauranga, 10 mins drive

Our modern self-contained unit is off a quiet no-exit-street and on the shore of beautiful Tauranga Harbour - you may drive to the door. It is fully furnished with microwave, television, telephone, linen and crockery. It includes a bedroom with walk-in wardrobe, living/dining room, kitchenette, bathroom, spa-bath and laundry. We have canoes, spa pool and barbecue that you may use. You can be totally private, but when you choose, you will be welcome to mix with our family. Our home and unit are smoke-free. We are within 10 minutes drive of Tauranga and Mount Maunganui (arguably the best surf beach in the country). Both have numerous cafes and restaurants. There are a variety of pleasant walks within 10-30 minutes drive - in bush, around the harbour, on the beach and around the Mount. Rotorua is an hours drive away, and various other popular tourist destinations are within easy reach.

243

Mt Maunganui

Homestay+Self-contained   Accom.

Address: 'Homestay On The Beach'
85c Oceanbeach Road, Mt Maunganui
Name: Larraine & Bernie Cotter
Telephone: (07) 575 4879
Fax: (07) 575 4828
Mobile: (025) 766 799
Beds: 2 Queen, 1 Single (2 bedrooms).
Self contained unit.   Double Hydabed in lounge.
Bathroom: 1 Ensuite, 1 Private.   Hair Dryer.
Tariff: B&B (continental) Double $120, Single $70. Children under 12 years $15 or up to 16 years half price. Laundry facilities.   Non Smoking. NZ B&B Vouchers accepted May 1st until October 31st. $30 surcharge
Nearest Town: Mt Maunganui 4km, Tauranga 4km

Welcome to our modern home on the beach, with superb seaviews and 25 kms of sand to enjoy leisurely walks. We have one queen sized bedroom with ensuite, one room with queen and single bed and bathroom. A guest lounge with kitchenette for tea and coffee facilities, microwave, fridge, TV etc, opening onto a large sundeck to relax and take in the sun and surf. You may choose to rent the self contained unit on its own, sleeping up to 4 guests at $180 per night or $130 per night for 2 guests, including continental breakfast with eggs any style. Close by are golf courses, bowling green and hot mineral pools. A 45 minute walk around the base of the Mount is fantastic. An easy 2 1/2 hour scenic drive from Auckland and one hour from Rotorua. There is off-street parking. Look forward to having you stay, and sharing our many trips overseas.

Mt Maunganui

Bed & Breakfast plus Holiday Flats

Address: 463 Maunganui Rd, Mt Maunganui
Name: Fitzgerald's Irish Inn Hosts: Bill, Edna + Kelly
Telephone: (07) 575 4013 **Fax**: (07) 575 4013
Mobile: 025 794 555 **Email**: fitzgeraldsinn@hotmail>com
Beds: 4 Double (4 bedrooms),
plus 2 Self Contained Holiday Flats
Bathroom: 2 Guests share
Tariff: B&B (full) Double $75-$85 (seasonal), Single $55,
Dinner $15, Credit Cards. NZ B&B Vouchers accepted $25 surcharge
Nearest Town: Tauranga 5 kms, Mt Maunganui 1Km

Cead Mile Failte

Are you looking for a relaxed, friendly atmosphere? The 'Fitzgerald Irish Inn' offers real hospitality at affordable prices, including warm comfortable rooms with TV's. Billiard and games room with tea and coffee available at all times. We provide supper and a good hearty breakfast (home made muesli or cereal, fruit, toast and home-made marmalade), followed by the favourite bacon and egg. Our Irish Inn is situated close to colourful downtown Phoenix shopping centre, featuring new restaurants and cafes, beautiful harbour and ocean beaches for swimming or strolling, Blake park Sports Centre, golf, RSA, cosmopolitan club, and have you experienced the pleasures of our famous hot salt water pools at the base of Mt Maunganui, which are soooo relaxing after a walk around the base of the Mount or a walk to the top if you so desire. We are warm and caring hosts ensuring every guest enjoys a memorable stay. If you desire a longer and more relaxing time in lovely Mt Maunganui, please enquire about our 2 fully self contained holiday flats. Cead mile failte (A hundred thousand welcomes).

Omanu Beach, Mt Maunganui
Homestay
Address: Please phone
Name: Judy & David Hawkins
Telephone: (07) 575 0677
Email: j.hawkins@xtra.co.nz
Beds: 2 Single (1 bedroom)
Bathroom: 1 Private
Tariff: B&B (continental) Double $70, Single $40, Dinner $15pp.
Nearest Town: Tauranga/Mt Maunganui - both 5 kms.

We are a retired farming couple who invite you to share our quiet and comfortable home just 60 seconds off one of the country's finest beaches, where you can just relax and enjoy our sea view, or if more energetic there is plenty of good swimming, surfing and walking available or even climb up "The Mount" for a 360 degree view of the Bay. Hot salt water pools (great for tired limbs), the golf course and bowling greens are all just a few minutes away as is the Bayfair Shopping Complex. A twin bedded room with bathroom for guests is available and a home cooked dinner by prior arrangement. Homemade jams and preserves are served for breakfast. An excellent place for visitors to stop and unwind for a day or two between Auckland and Rotorua. We enjoy meeting people and would like to share your travel experiences over supper each evening. A smoke, pet and child free home.
Directions: *Please phone for directions.*

Mount Maunganui
Homestay
Address: 28a Sunbrae Grove, Mt Maunganui
Name: Barbara Marsh
Telephone: (07) 575 5592
Mobile: (021) 707 243
Beds: 1 Queen, 2 Single (2 bedrooms)
Bathroom: 1 Guests share
Tariff: B&B (full) Double $95 Single $60, Dinner $25 pp. Credit cards. NZ B&B Vouchers accepted $15 Surcharge
Nearest Town: Mt Maunganui and Tauranga 9km

We invite you to stay with us and relax, while enjoying stunning ocean views from our lovely home, on the shores of beautiful Mount Maunganui. You may choose to be a Homestay guest or, alternatively, rent the self-contained accommodation (at a separate rate), allowing you to be independent.
Sunbrae Grove is a quiet cul de sac at the end of Oceanbeach Road, and we offer undercover, off-street parking for guests. Dinner is available by prior arrangement please. Laundry facilities. Your well-travelled hostess shares her smoke-free home with Bella, a very sociable Balinese cat. We are 10 minutes from the hot salt pools at the foot of the Mount itself, and a similar distance from Tauranga. Bayfair Shopping Centre is only minutes away. We welcome your inquiries and look forward to meeting you.
Directions: *Please feel free to phone for directions.*

Mount Maunganui
Homestay/Self-contained   Accom.
Address: "Fairways",
170 Ocean Beach Rd., Mt. Maunganui
Name: John & Philippa Davies
Telephone: (07) 575 5325
or Bus. (07) 578 5899
Fax: (07) 578 2362
Email: pipjohn@clear.net.nz
Beds: 1 Queen, 1 Double (2 bedrooms)
Bathroom: 1 Ensuite, 1 Family share.
Tariff: B&B (full) Double $90, Single $60,
Dinner by arrangement including wines $35pp.
Nearest Town: Mt Maunganui 3 kms

A Golfer's Paradise! Step from our garden onto the 8th fairway, and enjoy a bonus lesson from John, a former scratch golfer. Work up an appetite with a swim in the surf, a mere 50 meters away, and, in winter, relax in our ozone filtered spa! Whatever the weather, enjoy with us our relaxed and comfortable smoke free home, with interesting food, wine, company, music and conversation. Take time out, unwind and discover the beauty of the Bay of Plenty, with its street cafes, stylish restaurants, hot salt water pools, mountain walks and excellent shopping. Pippa is a registered nurse enthusiastically involved in a natural health clinic; John is a retired solicitor and teacher. Our dinners are leisurely, fun occasions - John loves sharing his interest in wine, and his desserts are legendary. We both enjoy meeting people, are well travelled, and experienced hosts. We look forward to welcoming you. **Home Page**: www.bigfoot.com/~homestay

Mount Maunganui
Homestay
Address: "Pembroke House",
12 Santa Fe Key,
Royal Palm Beach,
Papamoa, Mt Maunganui
Name: Cathy & Graham Burgess
Telephone: (07) 572 1000
Email: PEMBROKEHOUSE@XTRA.CO.NZ
Beds: 2 Queen, 2 Single (3 bedrooms)
Bathroom: 1 Ensuite, 1 Guests share
Tariff: B&B (full) Double $80, Single $50, Children under 13 yrs $25. Credit cards. NZ B&B Vouchers accepted $15 surcharge
Nearest Town: Mt Maunganui 9km, Tauranga 9km,
Rotorua 50 minutes.

Welcome to our modern smoke-free home, with unrestricted seaview. Cross the road to the ocean beach, where you can enjoy swimming, surfing and beach walks. Near Palm Beach Shopping Plaza. One room has queen size bed and ensuite. Two other bedrooms, one queen size and one twin, share a separate guest bathroom. Separate guest lounge with TV and tea making facilities. Laundry available. Cathy is a primary school teacher and Graham semi-retired - your host. We are widely travelled and both enjoy meeting people. Our home is shared with two precious cats - Twinkle and Crystal. We all look forward to welcoming you. (Not suitable for children under five years)
Directions: *Please phone ahead for reservations and directions.*

Papamoa Beach

Homestay
Address: 'Markbeech Homestay', 274 Dickson Road, Papamoa, BOP.
Name: Joan & Jim Francis
Telephone: (07) 542 0815 or 0800 168 791
Fax: (07) 542 0815
Mobile: (025) 318132
Beds: 1 Queen, 3 Single (3 bedrooms)
Bathroom: 1 Guests share
Tariff: B&B (full) Double $65, Single $35, Children half price; Dinner by arrangement $18. Breakfast full.
NZ B&B Vouchers accepted. Credit cards accepted.
Nearest Town: Mount Maunganui or Te Puke 11 km each on SH 2

Retired, in our 60's, we have hosted guests for ten years. With family and friends in many countries, our interests are gardening, travel, tourism. Our home, in a quiet road, is full of books, antiques and warm welcome! A high level of pesonal service in surroundings which we hope will make you feel relaxed and comfortable. We offer electric blankets, full size bath as well as shower, free laundry, cot and high chair. Short stroll to the pleasures of a safe swimming / fishing beach with surf casting rods available. 15-20 minutes drive to local tourist attractions all featured on the Pacific Coast Highway route. Children welcome. We will happily meet public transport and take you sightseeing. Good restaurants nearby.
Directions: *From SH2 (Rotorua - Tauranga) turn at Wilsons Garden Centre, signposted 'Papamoa'. Dickson Road fifth turn right (just after the Papamoa Family Tavern).*

Papamoa Beach

Homestay
Address: 8 Taylor Road, Papamoa
Bay of Plenty
Name: Genyth Harwood
Telephone: (07) 542 0279
Fax: (07) 542 0279
Mobile: (021) 215 1523
Beds: 1 Double, 2 Single (2 bedrooms)
Bathroom: 1 Ensuite,1 Guests Share, 1 Family share.
Tariff: B&B (full) Double $70, Single $40, Children 1/2 price, under 5 free, Dinner $20 p.p. NZ B&B Vouchers accepted
Nearest Town: Tauranga 20km

My beachfront home is situated on the Beach, with beautiful views of Mayor & Motiti Islands. Things to do include swimming, fishing, sunbathing, or beach walks plus, endless interesting excursions round the district. I have a two storeyed home with guest accommodation on the lower level serviced by a shower, toilet and laundry facilities. Continental or cooked breakfast is offered and a home cooked dinner if desired - we also enjoy a barbeque in the warmer weather. Resorts such as Mt Maunganui and Rotorua with its thermal attractions are within easy reach. I invite you to enjoy my home away from home. I have no pets and no children.
Directions: *Turn off State Highway 2 (Tauranga to Rotorua) at "Wilsons Garden Centre", proceed about 2 kms to roundabout at Papamoa Domain, take right turn then about 4 kms to Motiti Road on left and left again into Taylor Road.*

Papamoa
Farmstay
Address: 'Bent Hills Farmstays',
1162 Welcome Bay Rd,
R D 7, Te Puke
Name: Malcolm & Trudie
Telephone: (07) 542 0972
Fax: (07) 542 0972
Mobile: (025) 982 354
Beds: 1 Double (1 Bedrooms)
Bathroom: 1 Ensuite
Tariff: B&B (Full) Double $120.
Nearest Town: 12km Tauranga/Mt Maunganui, 3km Papamoa Beach

Bent Hills farm is part of Papamoa Adventure Park where we offer a large range of activities including a dirt track luge, horse trekking, 4WD bikes, target shooting and grass skiing. It is an animal lovers paradise with approximately 100 pets. The house is built and located in a stunning rural setting. We have 3 boys. Your stay includes either a complimentary horse rise or target shoot. The beach is only 5 minutes away and the city 15 mins. Locally there is a fabulous beach front restaurant and spectacular waterfall. A warm welcome with friendly service is guaranteed.

Papamoa, Mount Maunganui
Bed & Breakfast
Address: 36 Palm Beach Boulevard,
Royal Palm Beach Estate,
Papamoa, Mt Maunganui
Name: "Royal Palm Beach Waters"
Telephone: (07) 575 8395
Fax: (07) 575 8395
Mobile: (021) 510 900
Beds: 2 Queen, 2 Single (3 Bedrooms)
Bathroom: 1 Ensuite, 1 Guests share
Tariff: B&B (Full) Double $95-$125,
Single $75. Not suitable for children. Credit cards accepted.
Nearest Town: Mt Maunganui 10 mins. Tauranga 10 mins.

We invite you to share our award winning home, on the lakeside, with breath-taking sunset views to the Papamoa hills.
Our spacious executive suite has a spa bath and TV. Separate lounge for guests only, has tea making facilities (complimentary), TV and large deck for sun bathing. We are only 300 metres from the surf beach and close to two shopping centres. We are happy to offer airport/business courtesy shuttle.
Directions: *Please phone.*
Your Hosts. Val & Dick Waters

Papamoa, Mount Maunganui
Homestay B&B (semi detached with ensuite)

Address: 118 Tara Road,
Papamoa, RD7, Te Puke
Name: Tara B&B and Homestays
Telephone: (07) 542 3785
Fax: (07) 542 3785
Beds: 1 Queen, 1 Double,
2 Single (3 Bedrooms)
Bathroom: 1 Ensuite,
1 Guests share
Tariff: B&B (Full) Double $80, Single $50,
Dinner $25 (by arrangement), Children $12. Credit cards accepted.
Nearest Town: Palm Beach Mall - Papamoa 2.2 kms

Tara B&B and Homestays. Your hosts Graeme and Rose Wilson.
Situated on Tara Road, Papamoa. Just off the Mt Maunganui - Te Puke State Highway 2, situated on a country road, only 2 km from Palm Beach Shopping Mall, beach and licensed restaurants. Handy to golf, tepid and hot pools. On four acres with extensive gardens, highlighted with objects of old and new and the added interest of their small Emu Farm. Rose and Graeme offer you a friendly relaxed country atmosphere within 15 mins to Tauranga and Mt Maunganui, 7 mins to Bay Fair Mall and 55 mins to Rotorua. We also have a friendly cat.
1 Semi detached queen room with ensuite.
1 Double and 1 twin room with share bathroom.
Continental and cooked breakfast. Evening meals by arrangement.
Directions: *Just off the Mt Maunganui - Te Puke Highway 2. Take the Papamoa turn off then first right on to Tara Rd. A country road only 2km from Palm Beach shopping mall.*

Paengaroa, Te Puke
Homestay+B&B

Address: 'Hafod',
151 Wilson Road South,
Paengaroa, Te Puke
Postal: P O Box 204, Te Puke
Name: Maureen H Oliver
Telephone: (07) 533 1086
Fax: (07) 533 1086
Beds: 4 Single (2 bedrooms)
Bathroom: 2 Ensuite
Tariff: B&B (continental) Double $75, Single $45, Dinner $20-$25,
Children half price, Campervans welcome. NZ B&B Vouchers accepted
Nearest Town: Te Puke 10km, Tauranga 25km. Rotorua 40km,
Whakatane 40km.

Welcome to the HAFOD. Two acres of garden, designed on a Welsh theme, compliments this lovely old country home, part of which are turn of the century. Each bedroom has its own ensuite and the large lounge with piano, library, reading area are available for the use of guests as is the garden room for BBQ. HAFOD, a Welsh name meaning, peace, retreat, is appropriate for this large rambling home and garden that is used extensively for weddings and open to the public.
Travel, tramping, gardening and local promotions are some of your hosts interests together with the family pets. The Te Puke golf course is only 2 mins away, the beach 10. Rotorua and Whakatane 40 mins. Pre dinner drinks can be served and your pets are welcome.
Directions: *Travelling south from Te Puke - Whakatane Highway 2, 1st right passed Te Puke Golf Club, 1st drive right.*

Te Puke
Homestay
Address: 'Lindenhof',
58 Dunlop Rd, Te Puke
Name: Henry & Sandra Sutter
Telephone: (07) 573 4592
Fax: (07) 573 9392
Beds: 1 Double, 4 Single
(3 bedrooms)
Bathroom: 1 Ensuite, 2 Private
Tariff: B&B (full) Double $90, Single $50, Dinner $20.
Credit cards accepted.
NZ B&B Vouchers accepted Same day restrictions.
Nearest Town: Te Puke 2km

New Zealand Association FARM & HOME HOSTS

Lindenhof was built in the kiwifruit boom and is a replica of a mansion. Feature of house is stain glass windows, central stairway and chandelier. House is furnished with period furniture. It is set in semi rural area with landscaped gardens, tennis court and swimming pool. We also offer a spa pool and a full size billiard table. Also available are tours of our area fishing and hunting trips. We are a multi lingual family. I speak English and Swiss, my husband speaks Swiss, French, German and English. Hobbies: Doll making, spinning and vintage cars. No smoking in the house.
Directions: *On reaching Te Puke on SH 2 from Tauranga, Dunlop Rd is on your right by the Gas Centre, 'Lindenhof' is at the end of Dunlop Rd. Phone if you need to be picked up.*

Te Puke
Homestay
Address: 'Mi Casa',
706 No.1 Rd, R.D.2, Te Puke
Name: Peter & Pauline Taylor
Telephone: (07) 573 5284
Fax: (07) 573 5284
Mobile: (025) 450 768
Beds: 1 Queen, 4 Single (3 bedrooms)
Bathroom: 1 Guest share, 2 additional toilets available
Tariff: B&B (special) Double $70, Single $40, Dinner $20. NZ B&B Vouchers accepted
Nearest Town: Te Puke 8km.

Country living, country pace - just what you need for a break.
Arrive to suit yourself, relax in our tranquil interesting garden with swimming pool and spa and an adjacent kiwifruit block guests can wander through. Situated in the heart of the Bay of Plenty, our area offers a wide variety of leisure activities, or allows you to relax in our lovely surrounds. Mt Maunganui, Tauranga only 30 mins to the North, Rotorua 45 mins to the South. Our home has two lounges. Guest bathroom has separate toilet and separate shower. Just 8 mins from Te Puke and 15 mins from the golf course. No smoking please. Dinner by arrangement.
Enjoy your own pace and time, without the worry of meals, housework and timetables. Come for a night - come for a week.
Directions: *No.1 Road leaves State Highway 2, south end of Te Puke at Country Lodge. Travel up No.1 Rd 7km to 706 on your right.*

Maketu - Te Puke
Homestay - B&B

Address: 'Blue Tides' 7 Te Awhe Road.
Please phone for reservations and details
Name: Tricia & Tony
Telephone: (07) 533 2023
Freephone: 0800 359 191
Fax: (07) 533 2023
Mobile: (025) 261 3077
Email: bluetides@tepuke.co.nz
Website: tepuke.co.nz/bluetides
Beds: 2 Queen, 3 Single (3 Bedrooms)
Bathroom: 3 Ensuites. 1 Guests share spa bath
Tariff: B&B (Full) Double $80-$120, Single $50-$65 (seasonal).
Dinner $15-$25 pp, Children welcome. Campervans x 2 welcome.
Vouchers accepted with seasonal surcharges. Credit cards accepted.
Nearest Town: Te Puke 10 mins, Mt Maunganui/Tauranga 30 mins, Rotorua 40 mins.

We searched the world and settled here, come and see why!
* On the waters edge * Wow! views * Central to all tourist attractions
* Ancient history * Bird sanctuary   * Local private open gardens * Elegant, warm and cosy
* Subtropical climate * Amazing sunsets * Magnificent night skies * Multicultural village
* Restaurants nearby * Walks, swims or golf * Boat ramp, hunting * Off street parking *
Laundry available * Piano *BBQ * Cafe on the beach · * Yummy home cooking   * Resident
*cat * Easy to find * Pick ups by arrangement   * Smoke free indoors * **Many** great choices**
NEW, EXCLUSIVE and AFFORDABLE. "Lovers of Life' the world over, know the seductive
appeal of sun and sea!, Come and enjoy our great hospitality!"

Pukehina Beach
Homestay

Address: 217 Pukehina Parade, Pukehina Beach, RD9, Te Puke
Name: Alison & Paul Carter
Telephone: (07) 533 3988
Fax: (07) 533 3988
Mobile: (025) 276 7305
Email: p.a.carter@xtra.co.nz
Beds: 2 Double (2 bedrooms)
Bathroom: 1 Guests share
Tariff: B&B (continental) Double $90, Single $60, Children half price, Dinner $25, Campervans $25. Credit cards.
Nearest Town: Te Puke 21k's.

Welcome to our absolute Beachfront home at Pukehina Beach, situated on the Pacific Ocean. Our two storey home includes two double bedrooms with a bathroom/shower, toilet, T.V./Leisure Lounge with Coffee, Tea and Fridge facilities. Extra beds and laundry facilities available. Your accommodation is situated downstairs, allowing complete privacy if you so wish. Also, you have your own beach access with a spacious Sun Deck, overlooking the Ocean and White Island Volcano. Cast your rod off the beach (rods available), swim, surf, enjoy beach walks or just relax and enjoy our occasional visits from the friendly dolphins. We are 13k's from the Te Puke Golf Course and a 30-40 minute drive from Tauranga, Mount Maunganui, Whakatane and Rotorua. Pukehina Beach has two Restaurants, but we welcome you to dine with us by prior arrangement please. Fishing and Diving Charters are also available. We invite you to enjoy our 'Unique Paradise'.

Matata/Pikowai

Farmstay
Address: 'Pohutukawa Farmhouse',
State Highway 2, R.D 4. Whakatane
Name: Susanne & Jörg Prinz
Telephone: (07) 322 2182
Fax: (07) 322 2182
Email: pohutukawa@prinztours.co.nz
Beds: 2 Queen, 2 Single (3 bedrooms)
Bathroom: 2 Ensuite, 1 Private
Tariff: B&B (continental) Double $90,
Single from $55, Dinner $20, Children by arrangment.
Credit Cards (VISA/Mastercard). NZ B&B Vouchers accepted
Nearest Town: Whakatane 30km, Te Puke 34km

Pohutukawa Farmhouse is set in a picturesque location on the Pacific Coast Highway offering outstanding ocean views. Glance up from the breakfast table and see active volcano White Island. Some times dolphins and whales pass by. Susanne and Jorg and their two well travelled charming sons enjoy meeting you and will make you feel welcome in their family home. The Farmhouse is the base of our tour company "Prinz Tours". We are specialists for guided tours and offer day-tours (tramping, sightseeing) in the area and personalised itineraries for New Zealand-wide holidays. We encourage visitiors to stay several days (discounts available). There is so much to see and do in the Bay of Plenty region. Or simply relax in our garden, by the pool, have a hit on the tennis court or have a 'talk' to our many farm animals. Dinners (with ingredient's from our organic farm) on request. We speak English and German and are looking forward to meet you.
Home Page: http://www.prinztours.co.nz

Whakatane

Homestay on a Farm
Address: Thornton Road, i.e. Whakatane - Tauranga Highway
Name: Jim & Kathleen Law
Telephone: (07) 308 7955
Fax: (07) 308 7955
Email: Kath.law@xtra.co.nz
Beds: 1 Queen, 2 Single (2 bedrooms)
Bathroom: 1 Guests share
Tariff: B&B (continental) Double $60,
Single $35, Dinner $20, Campervans welcome.
Credit Cards (VISA) + Eftpos. NZ B&B Vouchers accepted
Nearest Town: Whakatane 7km

Whakatane is off the beaten tourist track, yet it is the centre for a wide range of activities. The local golf course is nearby. We can arrange sight-seeing trips, including White Island. Ohope Beach is a short drive away. You may wish to relax in peaceful surroundings or watch the activities in our Red Barn Country Kitchen and Craftshop which promotes over 270 Bay of Plenty artisans. We have lived on this farm for 49 years. Two 50/50 sharemilkers milk over 400 cows. We also grow citrus and feijoas and breed black and coloured and spotted sheep. We have travelled extensively overseas and enjoy meeting people of all ages. As "young oldies" we enjoy bowls, Lions Club, genealogy, organic gardening and ballroom dancing - not necessarily in that order. Vegetarian and special diets catered for. The Kiwihost concept motivates us. A warm welcome awaits. We have one cat.
Directions: *Thornton Road - 9km west of Whakatane P.O. (the old State Highway 2).* **Home Page**: http://www.nzhomestay.co.nz/law.html.

Thornton, Whakatane
Farm-Beach Homestay
Address: Postal: P. O. Box 295,
Whakatane,
Rural: 1012 Thornton Road,
Whakatane
Name: 'T' Tree Lodge
Mieke & Max van Batenburg
Telephone: (07) 322 2295
Email: mmbtnbrk@wave.co.nz *Dutch, German & French spoken.
Beds: 2 Super King (or 4 singles), 1 Single (3 bedrooms)
Bathroom: 1 Private with shower, 1 Guests share with spa bath.
Tariff: B&B (special/continental) Double $90, Single $65.
Vouchers accepted $20 surcharge for Double room.
Nearest Town: Whakatane 17 km (west), Matata 8km (east).

Do you wish to "taste" Paradise? Enjoy magnificent sunrises, sunsets, seaviews? On a moonlit night, watch the silvery Pacific from our wooden deck, walk on our secluded beach only four minutes away, laze in a hammock, breathing the silence, get pampered with a scrumptious breakfast..... then this is the place for you. We live a few minutes drive from the main Pacific Coast Highway, on a 9ha lifestyle block, surrounded by a unique Kanuka forest. Our cosy smoke free home is built of mainly native timbers. A warm welcome awaits those who look for a complete rest in tranquil surroundings with only the sounds of the birds, and the symphony of the ocean waves.   There are many unique attractions like visiting an active volcano, swimming with dolphins and many more. Our interests are wide and varied, such as art, reading, music, history. We have a friendly Labrador and two amiable cats. **Directions**: *Please phone for directions.* **Home Page**: http://www.freeyellow.com/members3/ttreelodge*

Whakatane
Farmstay
Address: 'Rakaunui',
Western Drain Road, R.D. 3, Whakatane
Name: Lois & Tony Ranson
Telephone: (07) 304 9292
Fax: (07) 304 9292
Mobile: (025) 246 6077
Email: ranson@wave.co.nz
Beds: 1 Queen, 1 Double, 2 single (3 bedrooms)
Bathroom: 1 Ensuite, 1 Private, 1 Family share
Tariff: B&B (full) Double $70, Single $40, Children half price, Dinner $25,
Campervans welcome.   Credit cards.   Vouchers accepted $10 surcharge
Nearest Town: 12km west of Whakatane

Enjoy warm and friendly hospitality in our comfortable home set in extensive gardens where the peace and tranquillity of rural life can be truly appreciated. You are within easy distance of superb coastal beaches, hot water springs, lakes, rivers, native forests and the tourist attractions of Rotorua. Check our kiwifruit orchard, feed guinea fowl, doves, hens, or talk to the calves. Whakatane is only 12 km away so indulge in some 'retail therapy', visit a live volcano, swim with the dolphins. Lois is the gardener (camellias and roses are her favourites) as well as collector of antiques, quiltmaker, and embroiderer. Examples of her handiwork abound. Tony is the "background support force" and provides those essential services such as cork pulling. Guests have private bath and shower, heated throughout. Tea making facilities in bedroom. If dining out is your choice, excellent restaurants in the vicinity. Continental or cooked breakfast (egg courtesy of the household flock).
Directions: *1.8 kms from SH2 between Awakeri and Edgecumbe.*

Whakatane
Farmstay
Address: Paul Road,
R.D.2, Whakatane
Name: Jill & John Needham
Telephone: (07) 322 8399
Fax: (07) 322 8399
Beds: 1 Queen, 1 King (2 bedrooms)
(You will be the only guests)
Bathroom: 1 Ensuite, 1 Private
Tariff: B&B (full) Double $80, Single $40, Dinner $25 with wine.
Nearest Town: Whakatane 18km

We invite you to stay with us on our deer farm where we also grow avocados and hydrangeas for export. Our children have flown the nest and left us a large home which we enjoy sharing. You will be the only guests so you have a luxurious private wing with your own bathroom and deck where you may enjoy the wondrous views. We have a pool room and spa pool or there are thermal pools five minutes away. Your evening meal will be 'Special' - venison, lamb or fresh seafood with organic vegetables (we make superb coffee). Breakfast can be special too. We dive, fish, tramp, ski, golf and travel. A 6 m boat is available for fishing trips. We have a very friendly chocolate Labrador and a Burmese cat. Laundry facilities available.
Directions: *18 kms from Whakatane on State Highway 30. Please phone/fax for bookings.*

Whakatane
Homestay
Address: "Travellers Rest",
28 Henderson St, Whakatane
Name: "Travellers Rest"
Jeff & Karen Winterson
Telephone: (07) 307 1015
Mobile: (025) 276 6449
Email: travrest@wave.co.nz
Beds: 1 King, 2 Single (2 bedrooms)
Bathroom: 1 Guest Share, Separate Toilet
Tariff: B&B (continental) Double $70-$80, Single $35-$40. Light dinner by arrangement $15. Campervans welcome, Credit Cards.
NZ B&B Vouchers accepted $10 Surcharge
Nearest Town: Whakatane - Ohope 10 mins.

Jeff and Karen welcome you to their smokefree brick home, situated on a back section in a quiet tree lined street overlooking the Whakatane River. Enjoy a swim or scenic river walk. We have some disability aids. Off-street parking available. Handy to shops, restaurants, hospital. Short drive to Ohope beach, airport, golf course. Enjoy a relaxed breakfast overlooking our garden with roses, native trees and shrubs. All beds have wool underlays, electric blankets, and feather duvets. We have a friendly dog and cat. Interests include church activities, pen and stamp collecting, photography, cottage gardens, massage, visitors.
KiwiHost hospitality is assured.

Whakatane

Homestay, Private cottage
Address: 54 Waiewe St, Whakatane
Name: Annette and David Pamment,
BRIAR ROSE
Telephone: (07) 308 0314
Fax: (07) 308 0317 **Mobile**: (025) 942 589
Beds: 1 Queen, 1 Double, 1 Single (2 bedrooms)
Bathroom: 1 Ensuite, 1 Family share
Tariff: B&B (Special, Continental) Double $75, Single $50, Children negotiable,
Dinner $25 by arrangement, Off street parking.
NZ B&B Vouchers accepted
Nearest Town: Whakatane - 1 1/2km walking distance. Ohope 5
minutes.

On the hilltop above the township, Briar Rose and Cottage are nestled in a peaceful cove of native bush where you can relax on the wagon wheel seat and watch and listen to the birdlife. You can also enjoy our beautiful Cottage garden specialising in old fashioned roses. Annette and David have a vast knowledge of the region which boasts many attractions. Active volcano, White Island, Deep sea fishing, boating, diving, Dolphin excursions, Hunting & Fishing, Jet boating, white water rafting, Golf, Mt Tarawera and waterfall, Ohope beach sun and surf. Many walking tracks nearby. There is a good selection of cafes, bars, brasseries and restaurants. But alternatively you can dine with us and enjoy fresh wild game meals or something to your taste. You will be assured of a warm and friendly atmosphere, you will leave with a basket full of memories.

Whakatane

Homestay & Self Contained Accommodation
Address: 'Bakers', Butler Road, RD 2, Whakatane.
Name: Lynne and Bruce Baker
Telephone: (07) 307 0368
Fax: (07) 307 0368
Mobile: (025) 284 6996
Email: bakers.homestay@clear.net.nz
Beds: Home: 1 Queen, 2 Single/Superking
(2 bedrooms). SC Cottage: 1 Queen, 2 Singles (2 bedrooms)
Bathroom: Home: 2 Ensuites. SC Cottage: 1
Tariff: Home: B&B (Full/Continental) Double $100-$110, Single $60. SC
Cottage: Double $80, Single $50. Dinner $25 (by arrangement). Not suitable
for children. Extended stays, at discounted rates, by negotiation. NZ B&B
Vouchers accepted $30 surcharge
Nearest Town: Whakatane 10 kms

Welcome. Enjoy country charm in our modern attractively appointed homestay, or be independent in your own self contained cottage. Share the peace and tranquillity of our park like property with quail, tui, wild pigeon and doves. Use our full size croquet lawn and, if you wish learn the game, Bruce is a qualified coach. Enjoy our beautiful evenings relaxing with a spa, or if you prefer evening privacy, your own lounge. Fishing! Entered in a tournament! There is parking for your boat. Day trip and enjoy our fantastic deep water or land base fishing. Your fish will be well kept in a walk in chiller. By negotiation Bruce will even smoke them for you. Fishing trips can be arranged. Lynne loves her garden, enjoy it with us. Sightseeing! This is the location, be it sea, coast, bush, river or mountain - it is all here. **Directions**: *Please phone for reservations and directions.*

Whakatane
Bed & Breakfast & Self Contained Accommodation
Address: "Clifton Manor",
5 Clifton Road, Whakatane
Name: Leo and Lenore Malone
Telephone: (07) 307 2145
Fax: (07) 307 2145
Freephone: (0800) 307 2714
Mobile: (025) 249 8767
Beds: S/C Units, 2 Queen, 1 Double,
2 Single (3 Bedrooms)
Bathroom: 2 Private in units, 2 Guests share B&B
Tariff: B&B (Full or Continental) Units, Double from $78-$98, Single from $58.
Children $15. Credit cards: Visa/Mastercard
Nearest Town: Whakatane 2 mins walk

We have a lovely old stately home, 2 minutes walk to the centre of town and restaurants, and just 8 minutes drive to Ohope Beach. Only a short stroll to Whakatane's wharf and harbour. Facilities include: Guests only, large, sunny lounge/dining room. Kitchen with fridge, microwave, complimentary tea & coffee available at any time. Electric blankets, heaters, hair drier and robe in all bedrooms. Guest laundry available. Large filtered swimming pool in lovely sheltered garden setting. Off-street parking. Things to do: Tramping - we have many beautiful bush walks and only 1/2 hour to breathtaking Urewera National Park. We also have numerous walking tracks close by. Fishing - great choice of trips available - swimming with dolphins - trips to White Island, our very own active volcano - golf and horse trekking - jet boating. Lenore and Leo look forward to welcoming you and making your stay a happy one.

Whakatane
Homestay
Address: Crestwood Homestay,
2 Crestwood Rise,
Whakatane, Bay of Plenty
Name: Jan and Peter Mckechnie
Telephone: (07) 308 7554
Fax: (07) 308 7551
Beds: 1 Queen, 2 Single (2 Bedrooms)
Bathroom: 1 Private
Tariff: B&B (Continental) Double $70, Single $50, Dinner $20.
Nearest Town: Whakatane 1 1/2 km

WHERE: Hill top location with panoramic views of bush, coastal plains, sea and volcanic island.
WHY: to reciprocate hospitality extended to us in our travels.
US: Retired, professional financial careers, fifties, designed and built home. We have time to spend with you.
INTERESTS: Trout and sea fishing in our boat, water skiing, camping, rugby, surf casting, driving, antique china.
ATTRACTIONS: Volcanic activity, beaches, scenic walks, hot pools, lake and river fishing. World renowned Rotorua one hour away.
ACCOMMODATION: Entire upstairs exclusively for guests. Cosy living room with phone, TV, writing desk, 2 spacious warm bedrooms, separate toilet, vanity and shower. Fridge, coffee/tea area. All rooms have superb views with one bedroom and living room opening onto sunny deck. Excellent parking, campervans etc. Laundry facilities available.

Whale Island and *Volcanic White Island*
as seen from *The Rafters*

Ohope Beach

Homestay, Deluxe, self- contained, beachfront suite
Address: 'The Rafters',
261A Pohutukawa Avenue,
Ohope Beach
Name: Mavis & Pat Rafter
Telephone: (07) 312 4856
Fax: (07)312 4856
Mobile: (025) 283 3276
Beds: 1 King, 1 Single (2 bedrooms)
Bathroom: Ensuite (bath and shower), hair-drier.
Tariff: B&B (Special) Double $90,
Single $80, extra adult $20 (limit 1), Children (1) $10, Infant free. Haute cuisine six course dinner $45 each; 4 course $35; 3 course $30; 2 course $25; 1 course $20, all served with Premium Cantabilay wines. Recommended Mains: Roast dinner (Lamb, Beef, Pork, Chicken); Spicy Persian or Spanish Chicken Casserole; Seafood Fillets; Mixed Grill; Porterhouse Steak; Lamb Medallions; Chinese Stirfry Pork, Beef or Chicken; Vegetarian. Variety of Soups, Entrees, Desserts. Guests may dine by candle light in suite or with Hosts. Complimentary pre-dinner drinks with hosts. NZ B&B Vouchers accepted $30 Surcharge
Nearest Town: Whakatane 8km, Rotorua 80km, Tauranga 90km.

Panoramic seaviews: White, Whale islands, East Coast. Safe swimming, surfing in front of suite. Many interesting walks in the vicinity. Golf (clubs r.h. available free), tennis, bowls, all within minutes. Licensed Chartered Club opposite. Trips to White Island, fishing (deep-sea and trout), jet boating, diving, swimming with dolphins arranged. Full cooking facilities, fridge, microwave; laundry, drier; private entrance, sunken garden, BBQ. Complimentary: tea, coffee, biscuits, fruit, newspaper, personal laundry service.
Mavis, experienced cook, interests: nursing, bowls, art, tramping. Pat, interests: wines, golf, bowls, music, literature, History, tramping.
Courtesy car available. House trained dogs, cats, welcome.
We look forward to your company and we assure you unique hospitality, cuisine and Cantabilay wines.
Directions: *On reaching Ohope turn right, proceed 2 km to 261a (beach-side). Illuminated house   Number on footpath, name "Rafters" on a brick letterbox, with illuminated B&B sign.*

Ohope Beach

Homestay+Self-contained   Accom.
Address: "Shiloah",
27 Westend, Ohope Beach
Name: Pat & Brian Tolley
Telephone: (07) 312 4401
Fax: (07) 312 4401
Beds: 1 Twin, 1 Double, 4 Single (3 bedrooms)
Bathroom: 2 Private (total wet areas), 1 Guest share.
Tariff: B&B (full/continental) Double $66-$80, Single $35-$45,
Children half price, Dinner $18-$25.
Nearest Town: Whakatane 6 km

We have retired to Ohope Beach and built a new home in a tranquil setting and hope to offer hospitality. Disabled guests are welcome in home as we have a lift and two total wet area bathrooms.
Homestay: 1 Double and three single beds with tea/coffee facilities. 1 Twin room, 1 Single room. Tariff: Double $66-$80, Single $35-$45.
Self Contained Unit: 1 Twin room, 1 Single with bed settee if required in main room. Tariff: $25-$35 own bedding, $37-$40 supplied.
Access to beach across road. Fishing, swimming, surfing, bush walks, classic car enthusiasts, well travelled.
Directions: *On reaching Ohope Beach from Whakatane turn left down Westend approx. 1km.*

Ohope Beach

Self-contained   Accom.
Address: "Henton's",
295 Pohutukawa Ave, Ohope Beach
Name: Marion & Graham Henton
Telephone: (07) 312 5095
Fax: 07 312 5095
Mobile: (025) 260 5097
Email: hentons@xtra.co.nz
Beds: 1 Double, 1 Single (1 bedroom)
Bathroom: 1 Private
Tariff: B&B (continental) Double $70-$100, Single $60-$80, Dinner $20pp by arrangement. Credit cards.
Nearest Town: Whakatane 8km

In our guest suite you can be totally private (own entrance, full cooking and laundry facilities) or if you choose, be involved with our family of six, who will give you a warm welcome.   It is spacious and extremely comfortable "Home away from Home". (TV, video, microwave, electric blanket, wool underlay.etc) Private courtyard with outdoor seating. BBQ available. Non smoking inside residence. Situated 150m from the beach and walking distance to a licensed Chartered Club. (Cafe, craft market, churches, bowling club, golf course and incredible coastal bush walks are all handy.) We have plenty of parking space and room for your boat. Graham is an enthusiastic fisherman (trout and sea fishing), who will smoke your "catch of the day" for you. Marion plays the guitar. Special rates for longer term stays.
Directions: *On reaching Ohope turn right, proceed 2.5km until you see our sign (on left).*

Ohope Beach
Bed & Breakfast

Address: "Turneys Bed & Breakfast",
28 Pohutukawa Ave,Ohope Beach
Name: Marilyn and Em Turney
Telephone: 07-312 5040
Freephone: 0800 266 269
Fax: 07-312 5040 **Mobile**: 025-960 894 **Email**: turneys@xtra.co.nz
Beds: 1 King, 1 Queen, 2 Single (3 bedrooms)
Bathroom: 2 Ensuites, 1 Private
Tariff: B&B (full) Double $100-$110, Single $50, Dinner $25 (by prior arrangement).
Not suitable for children. Off season and extended stays discounted rates. NZ B&B
Vouchers accepted $20 surcharge.
Nearest Town: Whakatane 5 kms.

Base yourselves with us and stay refreshed and focused for the Eastbay experience. We are located within a comfortable distance from all the excitement - geysers, erupting White Island, white water rafting, fishing, dolphin swimming, to mention a few. Let us advise and arrange. Our home is multi-level capturing magnificent views. Treat yourself to the special "Blue Room" which opens on to a private deck overlooking the Pacific Ocean: equipped with fridge, phone, television, continuous tea and coffee and other treats. The "Garden Room" opening onto a patio also with sea views, TV, phone, coffee etc. The Twin Room has its own bathroom. Served for your pleasure are generous breakfasts plus trimmings including freshly brewed coffee and home-made bread. You are welcome to share our addictions of golf and tennis - gear provided. We have been hosts for many years and promise you wont be disappointed. **Directions**: *Upon reaching Ohope, turn right and we are opposite the shops, restaurant and beach.* **Home Page**: http://www.nzweb.net/turneys/

Haurere Point, Opotiki
Farmstay+Self-contained   Accom.

Address: Corals B&B,
Morice's Bay,
Highway 35,
R.D.1, Opotiki
Name: Coral Parkinson
Telephone: (07) 315 8052 / 0800-258 575
Fax: (07) 315 8052
LAND-ROVER Daimler & Lanchester OWNERS
Beds: 1 King/Queen, 1 Double, 2 Single (2 bedrooms) **Bathroom**: 2 Private
Tariff: B&B (continental) Double $70-$110, Single $40-$65, Children $15, Dinner $30.
May to October stay two nights or more and get one free.
Nearest Town: 18km to Opotiki

Signposted on Highway 35, 18 km from Opotiki and halfway between Opape and Torere our stained glass windowed rustic cottage provides the opportunity to drift back to the peace of a bygone era. There are no house rules once settled you may decide, as others have not to venture beyond our small farms boundary. Explore the stoney bed creek, check out the glow worms and the swimming hole, enjoy the bush and bird life. We have a collection of classic English vehicles and memorabilia. Beyond our gate a easy walk takes you to secluded Morices Bay, ramble over the rocks, laze on the sandy beach, explore the caves, surf, safe swimming, fish from the rocks. Our smaller unit part of our garage complex is fully equipped with full kitchen. All beds have woollen underlays and feather duvets. We make our own bread and conserves. Free range eggs. Smoking outdoors would be appreciated. Under cover parking. **Directions**: *Call, write or fax.*

Wairata, Opotiki

Farmstay
Address: Wairata,
Waioeka Gorge, Opotiki
Name: Bob & Mary Redpath
Telephone: (07) 315 7761
Fax: (07) 315 7761
Mobile: 025 203 9918
Email: rl.redpath@xtra.co.nz
Beds: 1 Double, 4 Single (2 bedrooms)
Bathroom: 1 Private
Tariff: B&B (full) Double $80, Single $50, Dinner $20, Children $20.
NZ B&B Vouchers accepted
Nearest Town: 50km south of Opotiki on State Highway 2.

Come and join us in the heart of the scenic Waioeka Gorge on our 1900 hectare hill country farm retreat. We farm cattle, sheep, deer and goats and our valley is surrounded by native bush with a host of activities for you to enjoy. There are numerous tracks to walk, streams to meander alongside, glow worms and a crystal clear river at your doorstep for trout fishing, eeling, swimming or tubing. We can take guests on 4WD farm excursions and there is hunting available for the more adventurous. We serve hearty home baked meals and encourage guests to join the family for meals. Guest accomodation is separate but adjoins the main house, we have a pretty garden, and outside cat, and four children two of whom still live with us. We always welcome guests to our home and look forward to meeting you.
Directions: *Please phone.*

Maraenui, East Coast, Opotiki

Farmstay+Self-contained   Accom.
Address: Maraenui Beach, near Motu River
(Postal: Oariki Farmhouse, Box 486, Opotiki)
Name: Chris Stone
Telephone: (07) 325 2678
Fax: (07) 325 2678 **Email**: Oariki@clear.net.nz
Beds: 1 King, 2 Queen, 1 Double, Singles as required (3 bedrooms)
Bathroom: 1 Ensuite, 1 Private
Tariff: B&B (full) Double $95, Single $50. School children half price, Dinner $30, Credit Cards Visa/Mastercard. Self contained cottage sleeps 3 $90/night or sleep up to 7 $140/night. Vouchers accepted Surcharge $20.
Nearest Town: Opotiki. 40km 25 mins, 2 1/2 hrs from Rotorua, Gisborne (via gorge) and Tauranga. On some maps Maraenui is shown as Houpoto.

Our small subsistence farm is on the beach, surrounded by bush, close to the mighty Motu River mouth. We provide you with comfort, company or solitude, organically grown food and fresh fish from the sea whenever possible. Nature provides native birds song, pristine wilderness, boundless sunshine and views of our active volcano "Whakaari" out at sea. A natural paradise. The cottage is set in the orchard; is self contained on two levels with its own private terrace and balcony. The farmhouse guest room has its own luxury ensuite, pool table and reading area, with huge king bed and wing chairs. Each has sea and garden views. Our dog and the cat love to join you for your walk on the beach. For long stay guests we have activities locally which we can arrange for you. We like to enjoy your conversation as our guests, and prefer non-smokers. Please phone for directions as Oariki Farmhouse is in a very secluded location.

Te Kaha, East Coast, Opotiki

Homestay
Address: Tui Lodge,
Copenhagen Road,
Te Kaha, East Coast
Name: Tui Lodge. Joyce, Rex & Peter
Telephone: (07) 325 2922
Fax: (07) 325 2922
Beds: 3 Queen, 4 Single
(6 Bedrooms incl family suite with lounge)
Bathroom: 3 Ensuites, 1 Private
Tariff: B&B (Full) Double $95, Single $75, Dinner $25 pp, Children 1yr-11yrs $25, Pets free.   Credit Cards: Visa/Mastercard
Nearest Town: Opotiki, 66 kms east from Opotiki, 2 kms from Te Kaha Hotel.

Our naturally timbered home stands in what has been described as one of the most idyllic situations on the East coast. Nestled in 3 acres of gardens, Tui Lodge offers warm hospitality, tranquillity and comfort. The new day is heralded by the dawn chorus of birds who reside in our bush surrounds. Our garden produces organically grown vegetables and fruit and our days start with breakfast featuring the freshest Kaimoana (seafood) and eggs from our free ranging hens. "The Lodge" opened on the 26/12/98 and comments in our visitors book include: "The Lodge is a dream, I could stay for life". Horst Kersten, Germany. "On a par with paradise, a glorious setting & great hosts". A&S Goss, Napier. "Congratulations, you have set a new standard". Malcolm McCowan, Hawera. "A fantastic find & wonderful hospitality, thank you". Janice & David Thomson, Montreal.   "We were so lucky to find you, glorious setting and wonderful hosts". Jim & Pat Roy, UK.

Waihau Bay, Opotiki

Homestay+Self-contained   Accom.
Address: State Highway 35,
Waihau Bay via Opotiki, East Coast
Name: Noelene & Merv Topia
Telephone: (07) 325 3674
Fax: (07) 325-3679
Email: n.Topia@clear.net.nz
Beds: 2 Double, 2 Single (3 bedrooms)
Bathroom: 1 Ensuite, 1 Private
Tariff: B&B (continental) Double $80, Single $40,
Children half price, Dinner $25, Campervans welcome.
Credit Cards.   NZ B&B Vouchers accepted
Nearest Town: 112km to Opotiki

You are invited to share our seaside lifestyle. We have a sunny Lockwood home with magnificent views and wonderful sunsets.
We have a small self contained unit with one twin bedroom and sofa bed in lounge, bathroom with disabled facilities, laundry, kitchen and TV. Our guest room has its own entrance with 1 double bed and ensuite with full disabled facilities. Our interests are fishing, meeting people, theatre, music and sports. Come and be as relaxed or as active as you like, we have kayaks and boats and can set you off on a horse trek, jet boat ride or fishing trip. Big game fishing is a feature of Waihau Bay, Dec to March. We have a cat called Wiskey and a wonderful dog called Meg. NZ meals of fish and crayfish (in season) our speciality.
Directions: *Please phone for reservations and directions.*

Ngongotaha, Rotorua
Homestay/Rural B&B
Address: R.D. 2, Rotorua
Name: Roslyn & John Livingstone
Telephone: (07) 357 2368
Fax: (07) 357 2369
Beds: 1 King, 1 Double
(2 bedrooms)
Bathroom: 2 Private
Tariff: B&B (full) Double $70,
Single $45, Credit cards NZ B&B Vouchers accepted
Nearest Town: Rotorua - 12 minutes to city

We warmly invite you to visit our spacious farmhouse (with panoramic rural, lake and volcanic views), just off Highway 5 (Auckland-Rotorua). John and I are "originals" in the NZ B&B book. Therefore we have fine-tuned our hosting skills for thirteen years; and realise the need for rooms with private facilities, TV, tea and coffee making trays, cookie jars, in-room refrigerators, adequate heating/cooling. The breakfast served is as hearty as you require.
Please note:
1. This is a "no smoking" house.
2. Pet cats do come into the house.
3. Bookings - use Bookin 0508-266 546, Toll Free, and reserve a room with us.

Rotorua
Farmstay
Address: Please phone
Name: Maureen & John Hunt
Telephone: (07) 348 1352
Beds: 2 Double, 2 Single (4 bedrooms)
Bathroom: 1 Private, 1 Family share
Tariff: B&B (full) Double $75,
Single $50, Children under 12 half price,
Campervans facilities available.
NZ B&B Vouchers accepted Surcharge $7.50
Nearest Town: Rotorua 4 km (10 minutes by car)

Guests will be warmly welcomed to our large, modern home on the city outskirts. Superb views of the lake, city, forest and surrounding country-side. Enjoy our garden and swimming pool. We farm 150 acres running deer, beef and sheep. Scenic farm tours available. Our adult family of five have now sought pastures new allowing us to offer an attractive suite of rooms consisting of one double bedroom, two single bedrooms and a small sunroom. Underfloor heating, innersprung mattresses, plenty of room for cars, campervans and luggage storage. Non-smokers preferred. Be sure and allow a few days stay so you have time to rest as well as enjoy the many nearby world renowned attractions. We enjoy gardening, water-skiing, tramping and travelling and look forward to sharing our home and farm with you. We have no pets or children.

Ngongotaha, Rotorua
Farmstay+Self-Contained Accom.
Address: 255 Jackson Road, Kaharoa (PO Box 22), Ngongotaha, Rotorua
Name: 'Deer Pine Lodge'(John & Betty Insch)
Telephone: (07) 332 3458
Fax: (07) 332 3458
Mobile: (025) 261 9965
Email: deerpine@xtra.co.nz
Beds: 3 King, 1 Queen, 4 Single (5 bedrooms)
Bathroom: 5 Ensuite
Tariff: B&B (continental) Double $85-$95, Single $70-$75, Extra person $25, Children 1yr-11yrs half price, Dinner $25 (Children $15). Discount from 3rd night or longer. Cooked breakfast extra $5 pp.
Credit Cards Visa/MC NZ B&B Vouchers accepted $20 surcharge
Nearest Town: Rotorua 16km

Welcome to Deer Pine Lodge. Enjoy the panoramic views of Lake Rotorua, Mt Tarawera and Mokoia Island. We farm deer, our property surrounded with trees planted by the New Zealand Forest Research as experimental shelter belts on our accredited deer farm.
The nearby city of Rotorua is fast becoming New Zealand's most popular tourist destination offering all sorts of entertainment. We have a cat and a Boxer (Jake), very gentle. Our four children have grown up and left the nest. Our bed/breakfast units are private, own bathroom, TV, radio, fridge, microwave, electric blankets all beds, coffee/tea making facilities, heaters. Heaters and hair dryers also in all bathrooms.
Our two bedroom fully self contained units, designed by prominent Rotorua architect Gerald Stock, each having private balcony, carport, sundeck, ensuite, spacious lounge, kitchen, also laundry facilities, TV, radio, heater etc. Cot and highchair available. Security arms fitted on all windows, smoke detectors installed in all bedrooms and lounges, fire extinguisher installed in all kitchens.
Holding NZ certificate in food hygiene ensuring high standards of food preparation and serving - lodge has Qualmark 3 Star rating.
Guests are free to do the conducted tour and observe the different species of deer and get first hand knowledge of all aspects of deer farming after breakfast. If interested please inform host on arrival. Three course meal of beef, lamb, or venison by prior arrangement, pre dinner drinks. Hosts John and Betty, originally from Scotland have travelled extensively overseas and have many years experience in hosting look forward to your stay with us. Prefer guests to smoke outside.
Directions: *Please phone, or write for brochure.*

Ngakuru, Rotorua
Farmstay

Address: 'Te Ana' Farmstay, Poutakataka Road,
Ngakuru, R.D.1, Rotorua.   Please phone
Name: Heather & Brian Oberer
Telephone: (07) 333 2720
Fax: (07) 333 2720 **Mobile**: (025) 828 151
Email: teanafarmstay@xtra.co.nz
Beds: 2 Queen, 5 Single + Cot (4 bedrooms)
Bathroom: 2 Ensuite, 1 Family share
Tariff: B&B (special) Double from $90, Single $75, Children $25-$35. Dinner
$35 adults $15 children. Discount from 3rd night. Visa/Master
NZ B&B Vouchers accepted $25 surcharge
Nearest Town: Rotorua 20 miles (NB) Te Ana is 20 miles South of Rotorua.

*Bounded by beautiful Lake Ohakuri, "Te Ana", a 569 acre dairy, sheep, and deer farm, offers
privacy, peace and tranquillity in a spacious country garden setting with panoramic views of
lake, volcanically formed hills and lush farmland. Enjoy farm walks, 4-wheel drive tour,
observe milking and calf rearing in season, or use canoe and fishing rod (licence required).
Discover the luxuries of farm hospitality - healthy 3 course gourmet meals with an abundance
of fresh produce; TV, tea-making facilities, cookies, fairy down duvets, wool underlays, electric
blankets and heaters, fresh flowers and reading material in your room. ACCOMMODATION
a small two roomed cottage with ensuite, sleeps 4; Two homestead bedrooms, one with ensuite,
both adjacent to TV lounge. Relax in front of log fire, on full-length verandah or in our sunny
garden. IDEAL BASE to enjoy thermal parks and swimming pools, golf courses, trout fishing,
lakes, rivers and forests and Rotorua and Taupo attractions.* **Directions**: *Please phone, fax,
e-mail or correspond.* **Home Page**: http://nz.com/webnz/bbnz/teana.htm

Rotorua
Homestay

Address: 3 Raukura Place,
Rotorua
Name: Ursula & Lindsay Prince
Telephone: (07) 347 0140
or Freephone 0800 223 624
Fax: (07) 347 0107
Beds: 1 Queen with 1 single,
2 Single (2 bedrooms)
Bathroom: 1 Ensuite, 1 Private
Tariff: B&B (special) Double $80,
(Surcharge $5 for one night only);
Nearest Town: Rotorua city centre 2 kms

*We warmly invite you to share our spacious modern home at Rotorua's lakefront; quiet,
secluded, 5 minutes drive from downtown. Both spacious guestrooms are well appointed and
have private bathrooms. We are an active retired couple who have lived and travelled overseas,
take an interest in world affairs and cherish the natural environment. Home-hosting has been
an enjoyable part of our lives since 1988. We hope to give you, too, the feeling of being with
friends. Conversations over breakfast which includes home-made specialities are often a
highlight for guests and hosts. Use our extensive library and local knowledge to get the most
from your stay. We'll be happy to arrange your local bookings. Enjoy the tranquil lake and
mountain scene, watch the waterbirds, paddle our Canadian canoe. No smoking please.*
Directions: *Lake Road into Bennetts Road, left Koutu Road, first right Karenga Street, right
Haumoana Street, Raukura Place on left.*
Home Page: www.nzhomestay.co.nz/prince.htm

Rotorua
Homestay
Address: 20 Stanley Drive, Lynmore, Rotorua
Name: Dulcie & Selwyn Collins
Telephone: (07) 345 5778
Mobile: (025) 239 4803
Beds: 1 Double, 2 Single (2 bedrooms)
Bathroom: 2, Guests have private bathroom
Tariff: B&B (continental) Double $75, Single $50, Dinner $20, Children up to 12 years half price. Credit Cards accepted. NZ B&B Vouchers accepted $10 surcharge for 1 night stay.
Nearest Town: Rotorua

We live in a very quiet street close to the Redwood Forest with its many walks. Our new home is centrally heated.
Selwyn's bowling club is at the end of the road. I enjoy my golf, gardening and trying out new recipes. We have a great outdoor area for relaxing, in writing those cards home or just smelling the roses. There are two lounges where you can relax or join us. We enjoy talking with our "new friends". We want them to feel comfortable and relax and enjoy their stay in our lovely city with all its lakes, walks and golf courses. There are so many interesting things to do in Rotorua so come and stay with us. We look forward to meeting you.
Directions: *Tauranga / Whakatane Highway. Turn right into Isles Rd, third left into Warwick Drive, third right into Stanley Drive.*

Rotorua
Homestay
Address: 9 Henare Place,
Tihi-o-tonga, Rotorua
Name: Brian & Kate Gore
Telephone: (07) 347 9385
Fax: (07) 349 2214
Mobile: (024) 944 270
Email: b.gore@clear.net.nz
Beds: 1 Double, 2 Single (2 bedrooms)
Bathroom: 1 Private
Tariff: B&B (full) Double $85, Single $50, Children under 12 years half price, Dinner $25. NZ B&B Vouchers accepted $15 surcharge. Credits Cards (Visa M/C).
Nearest Town: Rotorua

If you are looking to stay with a friendly, lively, middle aged couple in Rotorua's quietest, prettiest suburb - you are almost there!
Our home is large, modern, very comfortable and you are free to use it as your own. Your bedrooms and bathroom are completely private. Breakfast is as you wish: fresh fruit, cereal, toast, tea/percolated coffee, muffins, or fully cooked to set you up for your day. Dinner may be with us or we can arrange a good restaurant.
We have travelled extensively overseas, plus travelled, tramped and lived thru'out NZ, so will happily advice you on places not to be missed, while in our lovely country.
Having hosted people like you for over 15 years we feel we know your needs. Rotorua has so much to offer and we would like to share so much more to make your stay totally memorable.
Directions: *Please phone*

Rotorua

Homestay

Address: Heather's Homestay,
5A Marguerita Street, Rotorua
Name: Heather Radford
Telephone: (07) 349 4303
Beds: 1 Double, 2 Single (2 bedrooms)
Bathroom: 2 Private
Tariff: B&B (full) Double/Twin $70,
Single $40, Children half price. 3 nights or more 10% discount off cash
payments only. Credit Cards. NZ B&B Vouchers accepted
Nearest Town: Rotorua city 2km

*Haeremai. Welcome. If you wish to be close to where 'it's all happening' stay
with me in my comfortable home in the heart of the thermal area, minutes
from the city centre, yet quiet and private. Walk to Whakarewarewa to see
the geysers, mud pools and Maori Arts & Crafts Institute; to the beautiful
Redwood Forest; to a traditional Maori Concert and hangi (feast) in the
evening; play a round of golf on Arikikapakapa Golf Course just down the
road, and take your pick of the many excellent restaurants nearby.
Whether walking or driving you are only minutes away from the weird and
wonderful sights that make Rotorua City so unique. Rotorua born and
bred, I am proud of my City and Maori heritage and enjoy sharing what
knowledge I have with my guests. I am currently teaching part time at a
local College.*
Directions: *Just off Fenton Street, turn at Devonwood Manor. First house
on right.*

Ngongotaha, Rotorua

Homestay

Address: 'Waiteti Lakeside Lodge',
2 Arnold Street, (off Waiteti Rd),
Ngongotaha, Rotorua
Name: Val & Brian Blewett
Telephone: (07) 357 2311
Fax: (07) 357 2311
Beds: 4 Queen, 2 Single (5 bedrooms)
Bathroom: 3 Ensuite, 2 Guests share
Tariff: B&B (full) Double $115-$165, Single $100-$150, Children over 12
welcome, Credit cards (VISA/MC). Vouchers accepted plus surcharge $45-$95
Nearest Town: Rotorua 10km

*The Lodge stands in what has to be the most idyllic location in the region with the
advantage of a picturesque trout stream running on its southern boundary and
magnificent views across the crystal clear waters of Lake Rotorua. Your hosts
Brian & Val built this impressive home of cedar and stone with its private guests
floor. The guests lounge has Sky TV and video, pool table, fridge and tea and
coffee making facilities. Each room has been tastefully decorated, inspired by the
tranquil beauty of the lodge's surroundings. Brian is a member of Rotorua
Professional Trout Fishing Guides Association and skippers his own charters boat,
taking guests on the lakes or to remote streams by 4 wheel drive. Fishing packages
arranged.* **Directions**: *Take Highway 5 from Rotorua, straight on at the
Roundabout through Ngongotaha main town centre and across the railway line
then 2nd turn right in to Waiteti Road. At the end turn right in to Arnold Street
and the Lodge on the left at the end of the street next to the foot bridge.*

Rotorua
Country Stay

Address: Woodbery,
10 Atkins Lane,
R.D. 2 Rotorua
Name: Shirley & Neville Mann
Telephone: (07) 332 2921
Fax: (07) 357 5701
Mobile: (025) 790 238
Email: The_Manns@xtra.co.nz
Beds: 2 Queen, 1 Single (2 bedrooms) **Bathroom**: 2 Ensuite
Tariff: B&B (full) Double $125-$145, Single $100, Children under 12 negotiable,
Cot available. Dinner $25-$40.
Nearest Town: Rotorua (12 km)

We welcome guests to our new spacious home set amongst lovely gardens with extensive views. Enjoy a stroll amongst our sheep, and aviary birds, or relax and enjoy the peaceful setting. We have two pedigree Tibetan terriers and 2 pet Alpacas. Our guests rooms have electric blankets and ensuite. Our home is centrally heated. Enjoy an evening 3 course dinner with us or visit a Maori Hangi. Rotorua is a tourist mecca, and NZ only spa city. 7 mins from Agrodome, Rainbow springs and Paradise Game Park and can help plan an exciting few days sightseeing. Our adult family live away from home. Our interests include gardening, art and building. Being involved in Education, hospitality industry and travelled we enjoy sharing our home with guests. **Directions**: *Please phone.*

Rotorua
Farmstay & Homestay

Address: 'Peppertree Farm',   25 Cookson Road,
R.D. 4, Rotorua
Name: Deane & Elma Balme
Telephone: (07) 345 3718
Fax: (07) 345 3718 **Email**: peppertree.farm@xtra.co.nz
Beds: 1 Queen, 2 Twin (3 bedrooms)
Bathroom: 1 Ensuite, 1 Private or 1 Guests share (if more than 4 people)
Tariff: B&B (full) Double $90, Single $60, Dinner $25pp, Children under 12 half price,
Campervans $25. Discounts for 3 nights or more. Credit cards NZ B&B Vouchers
accepted Surcharge $12 per person
Nearest Town: Rotorua 10 minutes.   Off S.H.30.

Just ten minutes from the central city and handy to airport our charming Lockwood Home, in it's quiet rural tree clad setting overlooking Lake Rotorua, will provide you with a friendly welcome and homely atmosphere. Upon your arrival you may care to enjoy a stroll around our small farm where you will see goats, sheep, cows, calves, horses, working dogs and chickens. Before dinner, you may choose to enjoy your hosts' hospitality while relaxing on the verandah taking in the spectacular views. There is an excellent cuisine using fresh garden produce and served with complimentary New Zealand wine or we can arrange a visit to a Maori Hangi and Concert. Our guest accommodation consist of two twin bedded rooms and one Queensize room all with electric blankets and private bathroom facilities. Horse riding and trout fishing can be arranged. Your hosts are fourth generation New Zealanders with a love of animals and the land, who wish to share the beauty of their surroundings with you. Two pets: 'Lucy' Fox Terrier and 'Edie' the cat. Pet lambs in season. Children welcome.
Home Page: http://members.xoom.com/peppertreefm

Owhata, Rotorua

Homestay & Self-contained Accommodation

Address: 13 Glenfield Road, Owhata, Rotorua
Name: Colleen & Isaac (Ike) Walker
Telephone: (07) 345 3882 (after 5pm or leave message)
Fax: (07) 345 3856 **Mobile**: (025) 289 5003
Email: colleen.walker@clear.net.nz
Beds: S.C.Unit: 1 Double, 2 Single (2 bedrooms/1 Fold Down Sofa in lounge)
Home: 1 Double, 1 Single (1 bedroom)
Bathroom: 1 Private (SC Unit), 1 Ensuite (house)
Tariff: B&B (continental) Double $65, Single $35, Dinner extra, Children half price, Unit: $65 2 persons & $15 extra persons.   NZ B&B Vouchers accepted
Nearest Town: Rotorua - 5km from city centre

Situated in a quiet suburb only 10 minutes drive from Rotorua's city centre, 5 mins from Airport. The unit is private and fully self contained with one double and one twin bedroom, separate lounge, bathroom, laundry and kitchen. The house has a comfortable homely atmosphere with one double bed and one single bed available with ensuite. Light breakfast included. Guests have the opportunity of becoming one of the family. Colleen is a tutor at the local Waiariki Polytechnic. Ike has experience in farming and the paper industry. He is a keen fisherman and golfer. They have hosted many visitors and have travelled extensively themselves both within New Zealand and abroad. They enjoy meeting new friends and helping them make the most of their stay in New Zealand by arranging fishing, golfing, sightseeing and cultural experiences if required. Hosts own two small dachshund dogs. To avoid disappointment and to enable the best service to be offered 24 hours notice would be appreciated, especially if meal is required.

Okere-Falls, Rotorua

Countryhome Lake Stay

Address: 'Waitui', Private Bag,
Okere-Falls Post Office, Rotorua
Name: Waituii'
Telephone: (07) 362 4751
Beds: 1 Double, 2 Single
(2 bedrooms)
Bathroom: 2 Ensuite
Tariff: B&B (full) Double
$80, Single $40,
Children under 12yrs half price, Dinner $25.
NZ B&B Vouchers accepted Surcharge $12
Nearest Town: Rotorua 19km (12 miles)

Come and enjoy our warm and comfortable home in a rural setting. We live in a farmland environment because we are retired hill country sheep and cattle farmers. Our home overlooks magnificent Lake Rotoiti and beautiful farmland from three quarters. We are situated 10 minutes from Rotorua airport on Highway 33 towards Tauranga and 20 minutes from Rotorua city. Experience the peace and tranquillity in a countryhome atmosphere on a bush-clad elevated peninsula with superb lake views and alluring native birds amongst our garden. We have a spacious and comfortable traditional style home. The locality offers beautiful bush walks near spectacular Okere-Falls on the Kaituna River, where there is white water rafting, fishing and local store. Telephone bookings are essential.
Directions: *Please phone.*

Ngakuru, Rotorua
Farmstay

Address: 'Lakehill',
1149 Whirinaki Valley Road,
Ngakuru, R.D.1, Rotorua
Name: John & Susan Shaw
Telephone: (07) 333 2829
Fax: (07) 333 2029
Email: johnshaw@voyager.co.nz
Beds: 1 Queen, 3 Single (2 bedrooms, Triple and Twin)
Bathroom: 1 Ensuite, 1 Private
Tariff: B&B (full) Double $120-$140, Single $90,
Dinner $35. Credit Cards (MC/VISA).
Nearest Town: Ngakuru is 28km south of Rotorua off SH5 or SH30

After eight years of hosting, our enthusiasm for having you to stay at our large comfortable farmhouse remains as strong as ever. We both very much enjoy combining good humour and good conversation with excellent food and wine. Our home interior features New Zealand native timbers, creating a warm and inviting atmosphere. We have several pets, some sheep, cattle, and a commercial chestnut orchard. The farm bounds lake Ohakuri offering excellent views and birdwatching. We are ideally situated between Rorotua and Taupo with relaxing hot thermal pools and a country golf course with sheep manicured fairways only ten minutes away. We challenge you to play a par round on our 4 hole golf course. Success earns a free meal and your name on the Lakehill honours board. Our extensively landscaped grounds also include a mini golf course, grass tennis court and swimming pool. Other interests include Rotary, reading and gardening.
Home Page: babs.co.nz/lakehill

Westbrook, Rotorua
Homestay

Address: 378 Malfroy Rd,
Rotorua
Name: Brian & Judy Bain
Telephone: (07) 347 8073
Beds: 4 Single (2 Bedrooms)
Bathroom: Family share
Tariff: B&B (continental)
Double $65, Single $45,
Children 12 yrs and under half price,
Dinner $25pp (complimentary NZ wine). NZ B&B Vouchers accepted
Nearest Town: Rotorua 3km

We are retired farmers, of farming stock - live on city outskirts, yet only 3km from city centre. We live in a warm comfortable Colonial style home with pleasant grounds. Having been for many years participating in farmstay and currently homestay, our interests include meeting the people, farming, politics (of a mild nature), current affairs etc. Brian is a member of Rotorua Host Lions and Judy's interests extend to all aspects of home making. Both guestrooms are well appointed with comfortable beds and electric blankets.
As well as the friendly welcome at the front door much time can be spent over the meal table chatting with our guests.
Our motto is "Home away from home"!
There is much to do in Rotorua and surrounds and we are happy to assist with your plans for "Things to do and see"! Transport available to and from "Tourist Centre". We look forward to your arrival.

Rotorua
Farmstay
Address: 89 Fryer Road, Off Hamurana Rd, Ngongotaha
Name: Enid & John Brinkler
Telephone: (07) 332 3306
Beds: 1 Queen, 3 Single (2 bedroom)
Bathroom: 1 Private (we only take one party at a time)
Tariff: B&B (full) Double $75, Single $40, Children $20, Dinner $15.
NZ B&B Vouchers accepted
Nearest Town: Rotorua 14km, Ngongotaha 6km

We invite you to enjoy a little of our 'good life' at our hillside homestay. With magnificent lake and rural views, our spacious comfortable home is situated in 10 acres.

We are in our 50s. John is involved in education and enjoys relaxing in our peaceful rural environment which we share with 2 cats, 30 sheep, 2 dogs and several chickens. Our hobbies are fishing, local history, walking, theatre, gardening and travel. We love to meet fellow travellers.

Major tourist attractions are easily accessible from our property. Hamurana Golf Course, trout fishing and horse-riding are close-by.

You will find us 1km up Fryer Road, off Hamurana Road, on the route around Lake Rotorua. Fryer Road is well sign-posted, 15 to 20 minutes from Rotorua city. Please telephone in advance of arrival.

Rotorua
Homestay/Bed & Breakfast
Address: 10 Henare Place,
Tihi-o-tonga, Rotorua
Name: Lorraine & Basil Carter
Telephone: (07) 347 9967
Beds: 1 Queen,
2 Single (2 Bedrooms)
Bathroom: 1 Guests share
Tariff: B&B (continental)
Double $60, Single $35, Children half price,
Dinner by arrangement $25. All beds have electric blankets and TV.
NZ B&B Vouchers accepted
Nearest Town: Rotorua

Welcome to our home, "Woodhall" which is located in a quiet suburb of Rotorua. We have extensive and marvellous views of city, lake and geothermal activities. Only 4 km from the city centre and close to golf courses, tourist attractions, forest walks and restaurants. We enjoy travelling ourselves and love to meet and talk with fellow travellers. Basil is a trained masseur and what better than a relaxing therapeutic massage to complete your busy day ($30/hour). Dine out or have dinner with us, the choice is yours. If you require an evening meal, advance notice is appreciated. Ours is a non-smoking home and ask that guests not smoke in it. We look forward to meeting you and making your stay an enjoyable one.

Directions: *Please phone.*

270

Hamurana, Rotorua
Farmstay
Address: 269 Te Waerenga Road,
R.D. 2, Rotorua
Name: Daniel Farmstay
Telephone: (07) 332 3560
Fax: (07) 332 3560
Mobile: (025) 775 341
Beds: 1 Queen, 1 Double,
3 Single (3 bedrooms)
Bathroom: 1 Guests share + 1 Private 1/2 bath (toilet and vanity)
Tariff: B&B (full) Double $85, Single $60, Dinner $25, 3 course. NZ
B&B Vouchers accepted Surcharge $10
Nearest Town: 20km north of Rotorua, 12km from Ngongotaha

Come and enjoy the peaceful setting of our deer farm and home with its panoramic views over Rotorua lake and city. Guests are welcome to a farm tour with an opportunity to feed a few friendly hinds. You will be assured of a friendly greeting from our dog who stays outdoors. Our modern home has an upstairs area, which is for the exclusive use of guests, with 2 bedrooms, 1 Triple with balcony (Queen & Single bed), 1 Double, games room and bathroom. Downstairs there is a twin guest room with a private toilet and vanity. Being non-smokers we thank our guests for not smoking inside our home. We are well situated to take advantage of the many renowned tourist attractions, thermal activities, Agrodome, Maori hangi and concert, trout fishing in the area. Rod is a keen trout fisherman. Dianne is a teacher and we wish to extend our hospitality to you.
Directions: *Please phone, fax or write for booking and directions.*

Rotorua
Homestay
Address: 10 Iles Rd, Rotorua
Name: Patricia & Ron Heydon
Telephone: (07) 345 6451
or 0800 317 153
Fax: (07) 345 6452
Mobile: 021 273 2974
Email: rhvpnz@clear.net.nz
Beds: 1 King, 2 Single or 4 Single beds (2 bedrooms)
Bathroom: 1 Guests share
Tariff: B&B (continental) Double $60, Single $35, Children under 12yrs half price, Dinner $20 (Vegetarian available with notice). Credit cards (Visa/MC/BC). NZ B&B Vouchers accepted
Nearest Town: Rotorua - 5km East

RELAX in your "Home away from Home" you are welcome to share our relaxed and friendly home with us, (including our laundry, kitchen, lounge). We're easy to find, 4 minutes drive from the city, 10 minutes from the airport, close to Whakarewarewa forest with lovely walks. Enjoy delicious home made muesli, muffins, bread, and preserves, filtered water and herbal teas are available. Electric blankets, heaters, radio in each room. Relax in our heated spa pool, in summer cool off in our swimming pool. We're in our 40's, have lived in Rotorua most of our lives, and enjoy meeting people, walking, sailing, windsurfing, sand yachting, Patricia is a nurse and Ron is involved with video production, photography, computer graphics and teaching. We are happy to help you plan your stay in our beautiful and interesting area. Inside is smoke free.

271

Ngongotaha, Rotorua

Homestay, Bed & Breakfast
Address: 124 Leonard Road, PO box 14, Ngongotaha
Name: Alrae's Lakeview Bed & Breakfast.
Telephone: (07) 357 4913 or 0800 RAEMAS
Fax: (07) 357 4513 **Mobile**: 025 275 0113 **Email**: alraes@xtra.co.nz
Beds: 1 King/twin, 1 Queen, 1 Double (3 Bedrooms)
Bathroom: 1 Ensuite, 1 Private, 1 Guest share.
Tariff: B&B from $95/$120 per night per double,
$70/$90 Single, per night. Dinner by arrangement $25-$30 per person. Visa/Mastercard
accepted. Vouchers accepted $35 Surcharge. **Nearest Town**: Rotorua, 8 Kms

*Welcome to our HOMESTAY/BED & BREAKFAST WITH THE MILLION DOLLAR
VIEW and our two acre lifestyle block with the black sheep and friendly atmosphere where
your comfort is our priority. We are 10 mins from Rotorua City, handy to Skyline Skyrides,
Agrodome, Rainbow Springs, Horse riding, kayaking, Golf, Hangi and Maori concert and
walking distance to Lake Rotorua and Waiteti Stream where you can fly fish and then smoke
your catch in our smoker. We can arrange any other sightseeing you wish to do .... be it Bungy
Jumping or White water rafting or just taking a ramble through some of our beautiful bush
and Redwood groves in the surrounding lake district. Breakfast on scrumptious homemade
food in the conservatory while you enjoy the stunning 200 degree plus view of Lake Rotorua,
Mounts Tarawera and Ngongotaha and surrounding country side. You will have the choice
of three bedrooms, guaranteed to give you a restful nights sleep with comfortable innerspring
mattresses and electric blankets. Bedroom one has King/twin bed, and ensuite with Jacuzzi
(Spa bath), heated towel rail and toilet. Bedroom two has queen bed, private bathroom with
shower and full bath, separate toilet, Bedroom three has a double bed, is tastefully decorated
and has the above amenities. All bedrooms have a pleasant outlook over the garden. Enjoy
our company or the privacy of our location with the guest lounge and conservatory overlooking
the stunning peaceful lake views and the atmosphere of our garden from the terrace and
gazebo. There are no sulphur fumes and traffic noises out here in the country air. The guest
lounge has CTV with teletext, stereo/radio, books and magazines with a relaxing outlook over
the garden and in the conservatory there is tea/coffee making facilities and cookies (biscuits)
available 24 hours for your convenience. If you wish you can enjoy a drink on the sunny garden
patio and listen to the Tuis and Bellbirds. Laundry is available. Dinner is an option but prior
notice please. We have secure off street parking and mobile homes can be accommodated. Meet
and greet service. Your hosts have been hosting for many years and enjoy the wonderful
experience of meeting people from all over the world. Our interests include, Lions, Music,
Masonry, gardening, walking, yachting, trout fishing, ocean surfcasting and boating. Alf is
a retired commercial builder and we have travelled extensively. Our accommodation is smoke
free. We look foward to meeting you.*
Guests comments:
"Warm welcome. Good food & excellent accommodation. Thank you".
"The scenery was beautiful, but your hospitality exceeded it all".
Directions: *To find the BED & BREAKFAST WITH THE MILLION DOLLAR VIEW ,
Please phone/fax/e-mail/write for reservations.*

272

Dec 2-3

Rotorua
Homestay
Address: 24 Mark Place, Lynmore, Rotorua 3201
Name: Kairuri Lodge: Hosts: Anne & Don Speedy
Telephone: (07) 345 5385
Fax: (07) 345 7119   **Mobile**: (025) 929 254
Email: dspeedy@clear.net.nz
Beds: 1 Queen, 1 Superking/Twin (2 bedrooms)
Bathroom: Queen with en-suite,
Superking/Twin with private bathroom
Tariff: B&B (full) Double $120, Single $70, Dinner by arrangement
($30 to $40 pp), Credit Cards Visa, Mastercard, Bankcard, JCB.
Nearest Town: Rotorua 6 km

We offer smoke-free accommodation, ideal for a family group; a private, second floor, two bedroom suite, with TV lounge, featuring panoramic views of Lake Rotorua, Rotorua City and Whakarewarewa Forest. Complimentary refreshments are provided and the use of spa pool and modern laundry facilities is available. Relax in our private rural retreat, explore our extensive landscaped garden with our cat Foxy, or come for an evening stroll in the forest to see the glow worms and hear the moreporks. Your experienced hosts welcome opportunities to offer hospitality by sharing their love of fine food and good wine. Anne works part-time, is a creative cook and keen gardener. A semi-retired surveyor, Don enjoys sailing, music, tennis and can arrange personalised tours with our own tour company for a unique Maori cultural experience, sightseeing, and fishing. Don can provide information on local attractions and help plan your NZ tour if you wish. **Home Page:** www.friars.co.nz/hosts/kairuri.html>

Rotorua
Bed & Breakfast
Address: 3 Toko Street,
Rotorua
Name: Tresco Bed & Breakfast
Telephone: (07) 348 9611
Fax: (07) 348 9611
Beds: 1 Queen, 4 Double,
2 Single (7 bedrooms)
Bathroom: 2 Guests share
Tariff: B&B (full) Double $75, Single $50,
Credit cards (MC/VISA). NZ B&B Vouchers accepted
Nearest Town: Rotorua City Centre (2 blocks)

Owners Gay and Barrie Fenton offer home style Bed and Breakfast hospitality. You will be welcomed into our home as our special guest, with a warm friendly greeting. Star attraction of our thermally heated, non smoking home, is the Hot Mineral pool, which is ideal for travel weary visitors. Our resident chef will start your day with a substantial continental and cooked breakfast. Tea and coffee making facilities are available 24 hours in our cosy TV lounge. We have ample off street parking. Laundry facilities in our thermally heated drying room are available for guests. We are happy to advise on and arrange tours, to ensure you get value for your dollar. We also take pride as Kiwi Hosts in guiding you through New Zealand on a top class Bed and Breakfast trail. With our 2 resident felines: Sybil (of Fawlty Towers) and Mini, we look forward to making our home your home.
Home Page: http://www.leisureplan-live.com

Okere Falls, Lake Rotoiti, Rotorua

B&B, Self-contained Accom.

Address: Please phone for directions
Name: Namaste Point
Telephone: (07) 362 4804
Fax: (07) 362 4060
Mobile: (025) 971 092
Email: namaste.point@xtra.co.nz
Beds: 2 King, 1 Double, 4 Single
Bathroom: 2 Ensuite, 1 Private
Tariff: B&B (Deluxe continental)
$110 - $200.
Self catered kitchen in units.
Credit Cards (VISA/MC).
Nearest Town: Rotorua 19km

Our Guests Words .....

"The setting is superb and the bed definitely the best."
"We have been overwhelmed with the beauty of Namaste Point and the hospitality of our hostess."
"Perfect spot for a romantic weekend."
"Just what we needed. The accommodations are first class, the location fantastic."
"The flora, the fauna, the peace and serenity ..... exactly what we were looking for!!"
"Wonderful luxury with perfect privacy. Excellent weekend!"
A GENUINE KIWI HOSTESS - SECLUSION & PRIVACY - REAL COFFEE - HEATED - SMOKE FREE.
You'd be pushed to find a bed and breakfast in New Zealand which offers such top-class facilities in such a picturesque setting as Namaste Point.
Only 15 minutes drive from Rotorua, our home is on the tip of the Te Akau Peninsula in Lake Rotoiti, surrounded by lake and scenic bush reserve. "Namaste Point" offers modern, first-class self contained accommodation. - A large bedroom with a choice of king or twin beds with electric blankets - view TV and enjoy real brewed coffee in bed - an ensuite bathroom with a hair dryer - a lounge with skylight and two loveseats (convert into single beds), Tibetan floor rugs, TV, stereo, fridge (stocked with delicious breakfast goodies), microwave, oven, coffee perc, kettle, full cutlery and china. - Flowers, fresh fruit, biscuits (cookies), books and magazines. - Private patios with BBQ's, a Jacuzzi spa pool and swimming towels. A paddleboat, dinghy and Coleman Canadian canoe are for our guests use and enjoyment. Our beach is a safe swimming area. Bring your own boat and use our jetty. Use our fly rods to fish in Lake Rotoiti. We are happy to arrange guided trout fishing trips. Enjoy our rose gardens and scenic bush reserve or relax with friends and family on the large lakefront lawn. Our

waterfront is a haven for native birds. Nearby, raft the world famous Okere Falls and enjoy thermal areas, rhododendron gardens, bush walks, two nine hole golf course, and famous fly fishing spots at the Ohau Channel and the Kaituna river trout pools. I have travelled extensively and have chosen this idyllic spot to settle with my pets - Lhasa apsos and a cat. Our accommodation is SMOKE FREE. Telephone booking is essential.
Home Page: http://mysite.xtra.co.nz/~Namaste Point

274

Holdens Bay, Rotorua
Lakeside Retreat
Address: 'Studio 21',
21a Holden Ave, Holdens Bay, Rotorua
Name: Terry Wood & Daphne Frizzell
Telephone: (07) 345 5587
Fax: (07) 345 9621
Beds: Large Studio Unit: 1 Queen+ 1 Single
(sitting area, tea making facilities, fridge)
Bathroom: 1 Private (Studio Unit)
Tariff: B&B (full) Double $80,
Extra person share Studio Unit $20, Single $50, Dinner $25pp by arrangement.
NZ B&B Vouchers accepted $12 surcharge
Nearest Town: Rotorua city centre 10 mins, Airport 3 mins. 2 1/2 hr
scenic drive from Auckland Airport.

Welcome to Studio 21: experience the tranquillity of staying by Lake Rotorua. Waken to birdsong, stroll along the shores of the lake, yet only to 10 minutes from the heart of Rotorua. Your hosts Terry and Daphne love to share their knowledge of camping, fishing, surrounding lakes and bush, local theatre and attractions. Choose from sightseeing or shopping, Maori cultural experience, fishing, tramping, windsurfing, soaking in hot pools, great dining options - or simply relaxing. Our home is spacious, clean and hospitable: even the cats and our Labrador Grace love guests. The large comfortable studio unit has its own private patio and bathroom. You can breakfast in bed, on the deck or by our cosy fire - you choose! Fresh healthy food - our menus are flexible. Dinner, BBQ or spa pool by prior arrangement. Brochures available.

Rotorua
Lakeview Country Homestay + Self-contained Accommodation
Address: 983 Hamurana Rd, Wilsons Bay, R.D. 2, Rotorua
Name: Lakeview Country Homestay
Telephone: (07) 332 2445 **Fax**: (07) 332 2445
Mobile: (025) 467 121
Email: lakeview@xtra.co.nz
Beds: 1 King/Twin, 2 Queen (3 bedrooms)
Bathroom: 1 Ensuite, 1 Private, 1 Guest share,
Tariff: B&B (full) Double $90-$120, Single $70-$90, Dinner $25pp. Suitable for children over 12 years. Credit Cards: Visa/Mastercard.
NZ B&B Vouchers accepted $10-$30 surcharge
Nearest Town: Ngongotaha 8 mins. Rotorua 15-20 mins.

Lakeview is situated on the northern shores of Lake Rotorua, nestled in a picturesque rural setting. IMAGINE....waking up to 180 degrees of spectacular panoramic views of Lake Rotorua, Mt Tarawera, Rotorua's steaming thermal area and the city beyond. A peaceful relaxing rural area surrounded by friendly farm animals, free roaming chickens and a pet turkey that loves to be stroked. Guest rooms are well appointed with large picture windows capturing the spectacular Lake and rural views. Bernie has 38 years catering experience in the airline, cruise shipping and restaurant areas and is well known for his reputation for excellent home brewed (pure spring-water) ale!! Major tourist attractions, trout streams, horse-riding, whitewater-rafting, golf course and Hamurana Springs are easily accessible from our home. We look forward to meeting you. Smoking designated areas.
ARRIVE AS A TOURIST, LEAVE AS OUR FRIEND. **Directions**: *Please phone.*
Home Page: http://nz.com/webnz/bbnz/lakeview.htm or http://mysite.xtra.co.nz/~lakeview

Rotorua City
"Innercity Homestay"
Address: 1126 Whakaue Street, Rotorua
Name: Irvine & Susan Munro
Telephone: (07) 348 8594
Fax: (07) 348 8594
Beds: 1 Double, 2 Single, 1 cot available (2 bedrooms)
Bathroom: 1 Guests share, 1 separate toilet with handbasin.
Tariff: B&B (full/continental) Double $75,
Single $40, Children under 12 yrs 1/2 price,
Dinner up to $30. NZ B&B Vouchers accepted $10 Surcharge
Nearest Town: Rotorua. 200 metres from Tourism Centre towards lakefront.

Our parkside "Innercity Homestay" is in the heart of Rotorua close to mainstreet, restaurants, and many of the star attractions our city offers.
Within a short walking distance you can enjoy scenic walks around the lake edge, thermal activity, the Maori village of Ohinemutu with famous historic church, Kuirau park, Government Gardens, Museum and Art Gallery, Orchid Gardens and Polynesian Spa. Our home is comfortable, spacious and thermally heated. Breakfast is of your choice, either cooked or continental with the emphasis on good quality home-made and fresh produce. Available for guest's use are outdoor thermal pool, bath robes, laundry service for a small charge, off street parking, brochures. "Mieko" our calico cat shares our home. We ask smokers to use the balcony or garden - thank you.
Directions: *Turn left into Whakaue Street two blocks towards Lake from Tourist Centre. We are 50m from the corner, overlooking park and lake.*

Lake Rotorua
Homestay/Self-contained   Accommodation
Address: Lake Edge, 8 Parkcliff Rd., R.D.4, Rotorua
Name: Paul & Glenda Norman
Telephone: (07) 345 9328
Fax: (07) 345-9328
Mobile: 025 758 750
Beds: 1 King, 2 Single (2 bedrooms)
Bathroom: 1 Ensuite
Tariff: B&B (continental) Double $85, Single $65. Dinner $25pp by arrangement.
Nearest Town: Rotorua. 5 minutes from Rotorua Airport

Lake edge home of professional fishing guide with the most productive rainbow trout fishing at the front doorstep. You can go fishing, charter a cruise with special half day rates for guests or simply enjoy the tranquillity of the lakeside lifestyle and be only 10 minutes from all the attractions of Rotorua.
Your accommodation has a separate entrance, cooking facilities, Sky TV, electric blankets, tea and coffee, own private ensuite and can be as self-contained or catered for as you request.
We can help you arrange sight seeing, golf, rafting and of course trout fishing, or simply relax and join us and our Siamese and Burmese cats to watch the sun set over Lake Rotorua.
Directions: *From Rotorua City past Airport on Rotorua-Tauranga Highway.*

Ngongotaha, Rotorua

Homestay
Address: "Ngongotaha Lakeside Lodge",
41 Operiana St, Ngongotaha, Rotorua
Name: Ann and Gordon Thompson
Telephone: (07) 357 4020
Fax: (07) 357 4020
Email: lake.edge@xtra.co.nz

Beds: 2 Queen with single beds, 2 Single (3 bedrooms)
Bathroom: 3 Ensuite
Tariff: B&B (full) Double $95-$125, Single $80-$100, Dinner $35.
Children over 10 welcome. Credit Cards (VISA/MC). NZ B&B Vouchers
accepted $20-$45 surcharge
Nearest Town: Rotorua 10km

*Our lodge, on the shores of beautiful **Lake Rotorua**, commands panoramic views of the lake and surrounding mountains of New Zealand's central North Island. From our conservatory you can sit and watch local fisherman try their luck for fighting **Rainbow** and wily **Brown** trout at the mouth of the Waiteti Stream. The upper level of this two-storied home is exclusively for guests with three **ensuite bedrooms** and **guest lounge** opening on to the **conservatory** which overlooks the lake. We offer friendly service and excellent accommodation at affordable prices. Your room will be serviced daily and a laundry service is available upon request. A full **English breakfast** is served every morning while we help you plan your day using our complimentary map and knowledge of the region. Canoes, golf clubs and fishing rods are free for guests, plus we'll cook your catch for you... Our guest lounge is equipped with stereo with CD player, TV, Sky TV and video. We also offer a comprehensive range of books and magazines for your reading enjoyment. The guest kitchen provides tea and coffee facilities. Each room has everything you require for a comfortable stay including **TV, electric blankets, hairdryers, heated towel rails and central heating**. We will arrange Maori Hangi or concerts, guided fishing tours and horse riding. We have ample off street parking. The city of Rotorua is 10km away - close enough to its many attractions - but far enough away for peace and quiet, and sulphur free! These attractions include thermal reserves, hot pools, fine restaurants and cultural shows by local Maori. We look forward to hearing from you and hope you join us soon for a wonderful holiday.*
Directions: *Take State Highway 5 to Ngongotaha. Drive through the village. After railway crossing turn right into Wikaraka Road, left into Okona Crescent and left into Operiana Street and the lodge is on the right.*

Waikite Valley, Rotorua
Farmstay
Address: "Puaiti", Puaiti Rd., R.D.1,
Rotorua. Phone for directions.
Name: Barb & Philip Hawken
Telephone: (07) 333 1540
Fax: (07) 333 1501
Mobile: (025) 854 258
Beds: 1 Double, 4 Single (3 bedrooms)
Bathroom: 1 Guests share (Separate bath, shower, toilet)
Tariff: B&B (special) Double $90, Single $70, Children $25-$35, Dinner $30, Children's dinner $10-$15.
Nearest Town: Rotorua 35 mins.

A 1200 acre property farming 2000 deer, 2000 sheep, 300 cattle with 100 acres of wood lot, 35 minutes south of Rotorua. The unique setting of our modern warm home with spectacular views over the property, surrounding volcanic country side and Lake Ohakuri, our friendly hospitality and delicious food, much from the garden, make this a special place to stay. Play tennis on our court, croquet on the lawn, wander around our 2 acre garden, tour the property by 4 wheel drive or relax and enjoy the view, the privacy, peace and tranquillity, without seeing another house or a road for miles. As our guests have said "Paradise is right here".
Interests include gardening, cooking, needlework, patchwork, music, golf, fishing, tennis. Trout fishing 10 minutes away, thermal pools, golf course 20 minutes, Taupo 1 hour.
Home Page: http://www.bbchannel.com

Rotorua
Homestay
Address: 367 Old Taupo Road, Rotorua
Name: "Thermal Stay"
Wendy & Rod Davenhill
Telephone: (07) 349 1605
Fax: (07) 349 1641
Mobile: (025) 377 122
Email: davenhill@clear.net.nz
Beds: 2 King/Queen, 3 Single (3 bedrooms)
Bathroom: 2 Guests share, 1 Family share
Tariff: B&B (full) Double $95, Single $55, Children under 12 half price, Dinner $25pp. Credit cards. NZ B&B Vouchers accepted $15 surcharge
Nearest Town: Rotorua 3km (1/2 hour walk)

Comfortable, thermally heated two storeyed home, private gardens surround, large thermally heated pool, BBQ. Centrally located, very quiet, no sulphur fumes, off-street parking. Close to two golf courses, shopping centres, city centre and scenic attractions. Queen bedroom upstairs with adjoining TV lounge and private deck overlooking gardens. Downstairs, a triple bedroom and a twin/king bedroom, large lounge with log fire. We have both travelled and worked in the hospitality industry, Wendy as chef. We enjoy good food, wines, music and conversation. Privacy or our company - we respect your wishes. We know that our home and facilities are special and will fill you with a sense of serenity and give you a taste of Rotorua's thermal charm. Let us spoil you and share our loved home and city. No smoking inside. Pets 'candy', a large, friendly tabby cat - our guests love her! **Directions**: *Please phone, fax or write.*

Ngongotaha, Rotorua
Countrystay
Address: Clover Downs Estate, 175 Jackson Road, RD2, Rotorua
Name: Lyn and Lloyd Ferris
Telephone: (07) 332 2366
Fax: (07) 332 2367
Mobile: (025) 712 866
Email: ferris@cloverdowns.co.nz
Beds: 2 King, 2 Superking/twin (4 Bedrooms)
Bathroom: 4 Ensuite
Tariff: B&B (special) Double $150-$210, Single $140-$195,
Credit Cards (VISA/MC/DINERS/AMEX).
Nearest Town: 18km North of Rotorua City centre (15 minutes drive).

'A UNIQUE PLACE TO STAY'
For the discerning, a place to unwind and rediscover the simple pleasures in life. Luxurious Deer & Ostrich farm retreat set amidst 35 acres of green pasture, just 15 minutes drive from the city centre.
We can offer you the Governor's Suite, or one of the three beautifully appointed spacious guestrooms, complete with ensuite bathrooms. Each room has tea & coffee facilities, refrigerator, TV, video and open to outdoor decks with farm or rural and Lake Rotorua views. Rooms are serviced daily and there are laundry facilities available. From the family room you can watch the deer, ostriches and sheep in their paddocks as you enjoy a sumptuous breakfast and plan your day. Take a farm tour on our 4WD bike with Lloyd and our friendly dogs, try a game of petanque, relax in the hot tub or just sit on the deck and enjoy the peace and tranquillity.
There are many things to do and see in Rotorua. Visit our many cultural and scenic tourist attractions, go horse riding, play a round of golf, or try trout fishing with an experienced guide at one of the many lakes or rivers in the area. Rotorua has some wonderful restaurants and cafes, enjoy a Maori hangi & concert. We have extensive overseas and New Zealand travel experience, let us help make your stay in Rotorua relaxing, pleasant and unique.
ARRIVE AS A GUEST - LEAVE AS A FRIEND.
Directions: *Please telephone, fax or write for bookings and directions.*
Home Page: http://babs.co.nz/cloverdowns

Rotorua
Homestay

Address: 144 Fryer Rd, Hamurana
Phone for reservations & directions
Name: "Panorama" (Christine & Dave)
Telephone: (07) 332 2618
Fax: (07) 332 2618
Mobile: 021 610 949   **Email**: panorama@wave.co.nz
Beds: King, Superking/Twin, Queen plus single (3 bedrooms)
Bathroom: 2 Ensuite, 1 Private
Tariff: B&B (continental, full optional extra) Double $125-$145, Single $95,
Dinner $35 (complimentary wine). Not suitable for Children under 12 years.
Credit cards. NZ B&B Vouchers accepted $20 surcharge per person
Nearest Town: Rotorua 15km

*This is an ideal base to stay whilst visiting Rotorua. Our relaxed lifestyle and
country hospitality will ensure your stay with us is memorable. The architecturally
designed cedar and brick home takes full advantage of the panoramic views of
Lake Rorotua and surrounding countryside. Furnished to a luxury standard, the
guest wing with private entrance, has spacious bedrooms and fresh flowers. Be
as formal or relaxed as you wish. Enjoy music or a book in front of the open fire
or laze in the heated massage spa pool. Play tennis or go for walks to local
Hamurana Springs, beside the lake or farm. Friendly sheep and working dogs are
just waiting for a pat and piece of bread. There are plenty of areas within the
landscaped garden where you can escape. Dinner is available on request before
4pm. The emphasis on meals is fresh home-grown, home-made, or local produce.
Discount for over two nights.*
Home Page: http://nz.com/webnz/bbnz/panorama.htm

Rotorua
Guest House

Address: "Dudley House",
1024 Rangiuru Street, Rotorua
Name: "Dudley House" B&B
Telephone: (07) 347 9894
Beds: 1 Queen, 1 Double, 1 Twin,
1 Single (4 bedrooms)
Bathroom: 2 Guests share
Tariff: B&B (full) Double $60-$65,
Twin $65, Single $40.   Payment by NZ Travellers Cheques or cash.   Tea
& coffee facilities and transport to and from local passenger services
available free.   NZ B&B Vouchers accepted
Nearest Town: Rotorua - 5 mins walk to city centre

*"Dudley House" is a typical English Tudor style house built in the 1930's,
with rimu doors and trims and matai polished floors. The house is tastefully
and warmly decorated, with thermal heating. The dining room is adorned
with military and police memorabilia. Non-smoking.*
*Your hosts are happy to sit and chat about the numerous attractions around
Rotorua, some within walking distance. Restaurants, cafes or bars, shops
and banks are 5 minutes walk, also a 2 minute walk to lake front and village
green. We welcome your inquiry.*

Rotorua - Ngakuru
Country Homestay
Address: Salanga, Ngakuru,
RD 1, Rotorua 3221
Name: Mrs Jo Trent
Telephone: (07) 333 2235
Fax: (07) 333 2235
Beds: 4 Single (2 bedrooms)
Bathroom: 1 Ensuite,
1 Private, Separate toilet
Tariff: B&B Double $85, Single $45, Children over 8,
Dinner $20 by arrangement.
NZ B&B Vouchers accepted $12 surcharge from 1 Oct to 31 March
Nearest Town: Rotorua 29.8km

A warm welcome awaits you at Salanga in a tranquil setting on Lake Ohakuri. Your well travelled and worldwise hosts ex dairy and deer farmers and oriental short-hair cat offer hearty country cuisine, comfort and conversation. Both guest bedrooms offer twin beds with electric blankets, a choice of blankets or duvets and either ensuite or private bathrooms. Heaters and fans supplied seasonally. Play carpet bowls inside, petanque outside, flyfish from the garden, amble over picturesque farmland or visit neighbours cowshed to see milking. Soak in Waikite Valley Hot Pools (10km) or play golf and squash (10km). Rotorua with its many tourist attractions is just under 30km away. Taupo approximately 70km. Help and advice with itineraries a speciality.
Directions: *Please telephone.*

Rotorua
Eucalyptus Tree Country Homestay
Address: 66 State Highway 33,
RD 4, Rotorua
Name: M & I Fischer
Telephone: (07) 345 5325
Fax: (07) 345 5325
Mobile: (025) 261 6142
Beds: 2 Queen, 1 Double (3 bedrooms)
Bathroom: 1 Guests share, 1 Family share
Tariff: B&B Double $80, Single $55, Dinner $25, Campervan $25. Plenty of boat parking. No credit cards.
Nearest Town: Rotorua 12 minutes. Airport 3 minutes.

Welcome to our newly built high quality country home. On our lifestyle block situated between Lake Rotorua and Lake Rotoiti, we have cows, sheep, chickens, rabbits and honey bees. We organically grow vegetables, medicinal herbs and flowers like camomile, lemon balm, mint and more. In minutes a native bush drive to beautiful Lake Okataina in clear deep trophy trout fishing lake with beautiful native bush walks. Hells Gate - Rhododendron Gardens just around the corner, other thermal activities and maori culture, farm shows just minutes away. We can plan your day and book attractions. Our hobbies are: Trout fishing from boat and fly fishing in close by lakes, fly fishing in rivers like Rangitaiki Whirinaki, bush walking, shooting and hunting in Kaingaroa and Whirinaki Forest Park. We have considerable experience and can give advice. We have travelled the World and lived in the USA, Canada, Indonesia, Mexico and Germany and speak their languages.

Lake Rotorua
Homestay and B&B

Address: The Lake House, 6 Cooper Avenue, Holdens Bay, Rotorua
Name: Susan and Warwick Kay
Telephone: (07) 345 3313
Fax: (07) 345 3310
Email: SusanK@xtra.co.nz
Beds: 2 Queen, 2 Bunks (3 bedrooms)
Bathroom: 1 Ensuite, 1 Private
Tariff: B&B (full) Double $90-$110, Single $65-$80,
Dinner $30 by arrangement, Children $35 each. Credit Cards
NZ B&B Vouchers accepted $25 surcharge for ensuite room.
Nearest Town: Rotorua 7km. Airport 2 km

You will be happy with good food and good company in beautiful, peaceful surroundings at The Lake House - a home chosen to give guests the best beach front location at Lake Rotorua. Just relax on the wide sunny verandah, go for a stroll along the shore, paddle a kayak, sail a catamaran or windsurfer or have a swim. Your room will have a wonderful view of the lake, with dawn, sunset and moonlight adding their enchantment. The morning view of the lake is a delightful backdrop to enjoying a full cooked breakfast. Other fine home cooked meals may be arranged, all at times to suit you. We will gladly help with information on the many cultural, sporting and fun activities in Rotorua. Free laundry facilities. Telephone and email available. There is a sheltered area outdoors for smokers. **Directions**: *Holdens Bay is down Robinson Avenue off Te Ngae Road (SH30). Cooper Avenue is right off Robinson Avenue. The Lake House is 200m on left*
Home Page: http://www.friars.co.nz/hosts/thelakehouse.html

Rotorua
Homestay

Address: The Towers Homestay, 373 Malfroy Road, Rotorua
Name: Des and Doreen Towers
Telephone: 07 347 6254
Free phone 0800 261 040
Email: ddtowers@xtra.co.nz
Beds: 1 Double (1 bedroom)
Bathroom: 1 Private
Tariff: B&B (continental) Double $65, Single $40, Dinner $17.50-$25.00 (by arrangement). Credit Cards (VISA/MC). NZ B&B Vouchers accepted
Nearest Town: Rotorua City Centre 4km.

We are average New Zealanders and our lifestyle enables us to spend time, if required, with our guests. Our home is elevated with views over Rotorua and has a very private garden. The guest accommodation is downstairs with private facilities, and upstairs you can relax in our spacious lounge. Our family has grown up and married, giving us time to enjoy visitors to our smoke free home. We offer free pick up from your bus, train or plane, and off street parking is available. Des has many years experience with a national organisation providing both local and New Zealand touring information to the Rotorua visitor. His hobbies are Amiga computes and DIY projects. He is also an ex member of Jaycees and Lions. Doreen originally from South Wales enjoys gardening, is an avid reader and enjoys meeting people. WE LOOK FORWARD TO YOUR VISIT AND GUARANTEE YOU A WARM WELCOME! **Home Page**: www.mist.co.uk/

Rotorua

Homestay and 2 B&B
Address: 155G Okere Road,
Lake Rotoiti, RD4 Rotorua
Name: Laurice and Bill Unwin
Telephone: 07 362 4288
Fax: 07 362 4288
Mobile: 025 521 483
Email: tengae.physio@xtra.co.nz
Beds: 1 King, 2 Queen or 2 single (3 bedrooms)
Bathroom: 2 Ensuites, 1 Private
Tariff: B&B (Full, Continental) Double $80, Single $50, Dinner $20-$25
pp. Children welcome.   NZ B&B Vouchers accepted
Nearest Town: Rotorua 15 minutes.

We have a lovely home in a beautiful setting beside Lake Rotoiti. Within a short walking distance there are bush walks, waterfalls, white water rafting, kayaking, river and lake fishing. Our bed and breakfasts are centrally heated and each has its own ensuite, TV, refrigerator, tea/coffee making facilities. You can have the choice of either enjoying your own space or joining us in our living areas - smoke free. There are many different things to do in this region so whatever your interest, whether thrill seeking, tramping, fishing, boating, golfing, sight seeing, eating or just relaxing and enjoying yourself - it is all here. Boat mooring available. Laundry facilities, BBQ, Petanque court. Ring, write or fax for information. We are easy to find, just one minute from the Rotorua-Tauranga highway. 24 hours notice would be appreciated, especially if a meal is required.
Directions: *Please ring for directions.*

Rotorua

Country Stay
Address: 351 Dalbeth Road,
RD2, Ngongotaha, Rotorua
Name: Anneke and John Van Der Maat
Telephone: (07) 357 5893
Fax: (07) 357 5893
Mobile: (025) 272 6807
Beds: 4 Queen, 3 Single (5 bedrooms)
Bathroom: 3 Ensuites, 1 Guests share, 1 for special needs
Tariff: B&B (full) Double $120-$135, Single $100-$115, Dinner $30,
Children negotiable.   Credit Cards (VISA/MC)
Nearest Town: Rotorua (12 minutes)

This magnificent Victorian style Villa, built in 1906 in Auckland, was transported to Rotorua 90 years later, completely renovated and restored incorporating all modern comforts. You'll be welcomed into our "country-villa", where we provide old fashioned hospitality, home cooking and a friendly atmosphere in a rural setting. The views of Lake Rotorua and the city lights are spectacular. The Villa opens onto lovely gardens and after a good nights sleep in one of our tastefully decorated bedrooms, breakfast is served in the breakfast room where the early morning sun streams through the leadlight windows. There is a hot spa pool and on cool evenings we have a cosy log fire in the guest lounge. Close to all major tourist attractions. Smoke free home.
Directions: *From Auckland, travel South on Highway 5. First turn left past "Lakeview golf course", or through Ngongotaha, over the railway line. First turn left.*

Rotorua
Bed & Breakfast
Address: Accolade Lodge,
30-32 Victoria Street, Rotorua
Name: Accolade Lodge
Telephone: (07) 348 2223
Reservations 0800 279 000
Fax: (07) 348 2238
Email: accolade.lodge@clear.net.nz
Beds: 12 Queen, 6 Single (15 Bedrooms)
Bathroom: All Ensuite
Tariff: B&B (Continental) Double $65 (May-October). Double $70 (November-April). Allow additional $2.50 pp for cooked breakfast. Dinner 2 course $18 pp. All credit cards accepted. Two units provide for disabled persons.
Nearest Town: Rotorua (situated in central city)

Accolade Lodge is Rotorua's newest purpose built bed and breakfast accommodation. It is situated central city and just a few minutes walking distance to city shops and restaurants. All units are fitted out in the finest decor and each has a private ensuite. All units are fully furnished with semi easy chairs, table, TV, radio, telephone, refrigerator, and tea and coffee making facilities. The dining room and lounge are fitted out in comfortable furnishings with TV and tea and coffee making facilities. A limited menu provides for an excellent dinner in the evening at a very competitive price. Dinner is by request. Alternatively, there are excellent restaurants and fast food facilities close by. An inside private spa is also provided. Victoria Street is bounded by Fenton and Ranolf Streets. Excellent off street parking.

Rotorua
Homestay
Address: 7 Meade Street, Rotorua
Name: Ascot Villa
Telephone: (07) 348 4895
Fax: (07) 348 8384
Email: ascotvil@ihug.co.nz
Beds: 2 Queen, 2 Single (3 Bedrooms)
Bathroom: 2 Guests share
Tariff: B&B (Full) Double $150, Single $110, Dinner $35 by arrangement. Credit Cards accepted. Rates change October annually.
Nearest Town: Rotorua 2 kms

An historic two storey art-deco style villa built in the 1940's from locally milled timber for a renown Auckland Department Store family, the Courts.
Centrally located and adjacent to the world famous Whakarewarewa thermal area, Ascot Villa is located in a quiet cul-de-sac and set in half an acre of gardens. The house affords views of the city and the lake beyond. Peaceful, restful and yet close to all tourist activities of the region. The golf course is at the end of the street and the redwood forest, with walking paths, is 10 minutes away. We are avid ten pin bowlers and the bowling lanes are a 5 minutes walk. A homely atmosphere awaits you. We have had years of experience in the travel industry and hospitality fields. We enjoy food and entertaining. Dinner can be arranged with prior notice at an additional cost. No smoking inside. Guests rooms upstairs.
Home Page: www.ascotvilla.co.nz

Rotorua
Homestay
Address: 48 Sharp Road, RD 2, Rotorua
Name: Anchorage Estate
Telephone: (07) 332 2996
Fax: (07) 332 2997
Mobile: (025) 931 943
Email: anchorage@xtra.co.nz
Beds: 2 Queen, 2 Double (3 Bedrooms)
Bathroom: 2 Ensuite, 1 Private
Tariff: B&B (Full) Double $125-$150, Single $90-$125. Dinner $30-$50. Children by arrangement.
Nearest Town: Rotorua 15 minutes.

Anchorage Estate has all the requirements for a perfect holiday hideaway and is highly recommended for its exclusive but relaxed ambience and friendly family atmosphere. Bask in an environment of true kiwi hospitality and enjoy the comforts of Ra and Leon's home complimented by magnificent views overlooking the lush farmland and beautiful Lake Rotorua. The luxurious guest suites are private and spacious with facilities including own entry, bathroom, refrigerator, tea/coffee making facilities, integrated Sky TV/video system and use of the heated spa pool/jacuzzi. An ideal destination for those seeking peace and serenity or there are a wealth of activities nearby to awaken your senses, revitalise and inspire you. Anchorage Estate is a perfect base for visiting the many surrounding attractions - only 15 minutes from Rotorua city, the tourist Mecca of New Zealand. The choice is endless ..... and it's yours! REWARD YOURSELF TO A TRULY MEMORABLE EXPERIENCE - A STAY YOU WILL ALWAYS CHERISH!

Rotorua
Homestay
Address: "Honfleur",
31 Walford Drive, Lynmore, Rotorua
Name: Bryan and Erica Jew
Telephone: (07) 345 6170
Fax: (07) 345 6170
Mobile: (025) 233 9741
Beds: 1 Double, 2 Single (2 Bedrooms)
Bathroom: 1 Ensuite, 1 Family Share
Tariff: B&B (Full) Double $90, Single $50, Dinner $30 pp. Not suitable for young children. Credit Cards accepted.
Nearest Town: Rotorua

"Honfleur" is a 3 year old French country-style home in a quiet, private, semi rural setting. Lakes and forest are nearby and the city is 7 minutes drive. Generous hospitality is offered in our warm gracious home which features antiques and memorabilia, with a beautiful garden of roses, shrubs and perennials. The double guest room with ensuite bathroom has a garden terrace and private entrance. The twin bedroom upstairs has lake views and shares family bathroom (separate toilet). We are retired medical professionals with a friendly Labrador dog; have travelled extensively and enjoy entertaining. Interests include travel, gardening, reading, bridge, music, sport, racing and Erica's special interest is embroidery. We are long-term Rotorua residents and can offer excellent advice on tourist attractions and restaurants. You are welcome to join us for an interesting 3 course dinner if pre-arranged. We prefer non smoking guests and the house is not suitable for young children.

Rotorua
Homestay B&B
Address: 7 Parkcliff Road,
RD4, Rotorua
Name: Island View Homestay
Telephone: (07) 345 6770
Fax: (07) 345 6770
Mobile: (025) 867 439
Beds: 1 Twin, 1 Double, 1 Single (3 Bedrooms)
Bathroom: 1 Guests share, separate toilet
Tariff: B&B (Full/Continental) Double $80, Single $60, Dinner $25 by arrangement, Children under 12 years $25. Credit cards accepted. NZ B&B Vouchers accepted $12 surcharge for double
Nearest Town: Rotorua city centre 15 mins. Airport 5 mins.

Mary and Dave invite you to relax and enjoy the friendly atmosphere overlooking Lake Rotorua, Mokoia Island and take tea in the grape covered pergola. We are handy to Redwood Forest walks, Hellsgate thermal area, Okere falls, Haumurana Springs golf course, Sport and Spa complex, Lake Rotoiti (trout fishing) and day trips to Tauranga and Whakatane. Enjoy our view of the setting sun and the city lights flickering across the lake. Our interests include: overseas travel, gardening, walking, lace making and Lions International. We ask you not to smoke indoors but you are welcome to smoke outside perhaps whilst strolling in the garden with our cat Morph. Evening meals using seasonal home-grown vegetables and preserves are available by prior arrangement. We look forward to meeting you - privacy or our company - we respect your wishes. **Directions**: *We are 5 min past the airport on the Rotorua-Tauranga highway. Please contact us for details.*

Rotorua
Homestay
Address: 2 Hilton Rd,
Lynmore, Rotorua
Name: Leonie and Paul Kibblewhite
Telephone: (07) 345 6303
Email: kibble@xtra.co.nz
Beds: 1 Queen, 1 Double
(2 Bedrooms)
Bathroom: 1 Guests share
Tariff: B&B (Full) Double $80, Single $50.
Credit Cards accepted. NZ B&B Vouchers accepted $10 surcharge
Nearest Town: Rotorua 4 km east; Airport 6 kms

Welcome to our special place: a home of real character nestled in the 'heart of Lynmore' beside forest trails and the beautiful Redwood Grove, yet just 5 minutes drive to the city centre and attractions. Use our in-depth knowledge and enthusiasm - we love this remarkable area of lake, forest, volcano, where every feature has a story and whose various cultures enrich the land. Leonie, teacher, now tourism involved, and Paul, scientist, delight in being New Zealanders; are keen travellers and trampers and very aware of what this country has to offer! Et, Leonie parle francais...... Bedrooms are charming and well appointed; the house is warm, welcoming and interestingly individual with a choice of comfortable, sunny and attractive spaces both indoors and out...... good coffee, excellent breakfast of choice (this couple enjoys food), beautiful garden and, of course, Paul's well-mannered, delightful Guide Dog, Toby, a character in himself. Smoke-free inside; laundry available.

Rotorua, Lake Tarawera

Homestay, Self Contained Accommodaiton

Address: 93 Spencer Road,
Lake Tarawera, RD5, Rotorua
Name: Lakeside Lodge
Telephone: (07) 362 8441
Fax: (07) 362 8441
Mobile: (025) 279 9269
Email: lakesidelodge@xtra.co.nz
Beds: 3 Queen, 4 Single (3 Bedrooms)
Bathroom: 3 Ensuite
Tariff: B&B (Full) Double $90, Single $60, Dinner $25 pp, Children half price. Credit cards accepted. NZ B&B Vouchers accepted $10 surcharge
Nearest Town: Rotorua (15 kms)

Lakeside Lodge is located on the shore of scenic Lake Tarawera, 15 minutes drive from Rotorua. The sparkling waters of our lake fringed by native bush at the foot of majestic Mount Tarawera, provide the perfect setting for a unique experience. The lake is world renowned for its trout fishing, but you can enjoy water sports (kayaks available), bush walking, tramping (mountain trekking), hot water beach tour or just relax in peace and tranquillity only 14 km from Rotorua. We offer two well appointed double rooms with ensuites, also a quality self contained four bed apartment. All facilities are available, including laundry. We provide home style breakfast and meals on request and provide a courtesy pick up from Rotorua and the airport. If required we will arrange your tours to experience Rotorua's numerous sights and attractions. Your hosts Lorraine and Graeme are well travelled and enjoy meeting people. **Home Page**: //www.bnb.co.nz/ www.travel.co.nz

Rotorua

Self Contained Accommodation

Address: Whakarewarewa Village,
PO Box 6063, Rotorua
Name: "Te Whare Maika"
Telephone: (07) 349 1039
Fax: (07) 349 1028
Mobile: (021) 896 743
Email: louise@ro.pl.net
Beds: 1 Queen, 2 Single (suitable for children) in Main House
Bathroom: 1 Private, 1 Family Share
Tariff: B&B (Full) Double $150 per night, Single $125. Children negotiable.
Nearest Town: Rotorua 1.5 kms

"Te Whare Maika" is situated in Whakarewarewa Village, the heart of the thermal valley. Built at the turn of the century from native timbers, it is a traditional structure and unique in both style and location. "Te Whare Maika" is tastefully furnished in keeping with the design and surrounding environment and every convenience has been provided. It accommodates 2 adults and 2 children, has a thermal pool, and is close to the city, lakes and the renowned Redwood forest, ideal for walkers and joggers. There is a well stocked fridge to ensure that you can prepare a fully cooked breakfast. Your hosts are local Maori, whose ancestors once occupied the Lake Tarawera area before the eruption of Mount Tarawera in 1886. We therefore have an intimate understanding and knowledge of this area and look forward to sharing our history and this unique place. Te Whare Maika is smokefree.
Directions: *Please contact*

Kinloch, Lake Taupo
Country Village B&B

Address: "Twynham at Kinloch"
84 Marina Terrace,
Kinloch, Lake Taupo
Name: Elizabeth and Paul Whitelock
Telephone: (07) 378 2862
Fax: (07) 378 2868
Mobile: (025) 285 6001
Email: twynham.bnb@xtra.co.nz
Beds: 1 Queen, 2 Single (2 bedrooms) **Bathroom**: 1 Guests share
Tariff: B&B (full) Double $115, Single $90, Dinner $35, Children half price. Visa/Mastercard.Winter and long stay rates available.Vouchers accepted $45 surcharge
Nearest Town: Taupo, 15 mins drive.

Nestled within large private gardens in the picturesque lakeside village of Kinloch - Twynham is a haven for fresh air, good coffee and relaxation and unequalled as a base for exploring the delights of the Taupo region plus the more strenuous delights of golf (adjacent), fishing (five minute stroll), watersports, snow skiing, bush and mountain walks. Hearty breakfasts, wholesome dinners and warm welcomes assure guests of an enjoyable stay. Guest accommodation is a private wing with bedrooms, large bathroom and elegant lounge. Rooms are furnished for comfort and warmth. Laundry, refreshments and home baking always available. Licensed restaurant nearby. Elizabeth has a wide knowledge of the volcanic and geothermal history of the region, gained over a long career in tourism and industry. Paul is a New Zealand Kennel Club Judge, and dog sports, golf, music and travel are family interests. We have two friendly dogs and pets are welcome. Smoke free environment. Courtesy collection from Taupo and Airport. **Directions**: *Please telephone or fax.*

Kinloch, Lake Taupo
Self Contained Accommodation and Guest Room

Address: 34 Angela Place,
Kinloch, Taupo
Name: Trish and Tom Sawyer
Telephone: (07) 377 2551
Fax: (07) 377 2551
Mobile: (025) 764 739
Email: sawyer@reap.org.nz
Beds: 1 King, 4 Single (2 Bedrooms)
Bathroom: 1 Ensuite
Tariff: B&B (Full) Double $95, Single $50,
Dinner $25.
NZ B&B Vouchers accepted $25.50 surcharge Double
Nearest Town: Taupo

Trish and Tom's Kinloch Bed and Breakfast is ideal for active people looking for a holiday break in a friendly atmosphere set in beautiful park-like surroundings and only 15 minutes from Taupo Town. The accommodation is one twin bedroom with share family bathroom, plus self contained with separate ensuite, TV and in winter, there are electric blankets, electric heaters, a woodburner fire, also use of laundry and tea and coffee making facilities. Ample off street parking is right at your door. Hearty breakfasts are served with home-baked bread and home-made jams. Kinloch offers many activities including golf, tennis, rock climbing, mountain biking, trout fishing, sailing and a licensed restaurant is nearby. Tom is a keen fisherman and frequently sails and fishes the Lake and would love to include guests in these activities. Trish and Tom also play golf and are often available for a game - spare sets of clubs available. You can enjoy a Kiwi BBQ with us at days end.

Taupo
Homestay
Address: Yeoman's Lakeview Homestay,
23 Rokino Road, Taupo
Name: Colleen & Bob Yeoman
Telephone: (07) 377 0283
Fax: (07) 377 0283
Beds: 1 Queen, 3 Single (3 bedrooms, cot + highchair available)
Bathroom: 1 Private, 1 Guests share
Tariff: B&B (full) Double $90, Single $45, Children half price, Dinner $30. NZ B&B Vouchers accepted $15 surcharge
Nearest Town: Taupo 2kms

Welcome to "Yeoman's Lakeview Homestay" where we warmly invite you to spend a relaxing time in our restful home situated in the bird area of Taupo. Enjoy the beautiful lake and mountain views from our spacious lounge and sundeck. During winter our log fire burns day and night. Guests attractive bedrooms are superbly comfortable with electric blankets on all beds - always fresh flowers and up to date magazines. We are retired sheep and cattle farmers, Bob has a great knowledge of New Zealand native trees and is a keen golfer. Colleen's interests are cross-stitch, cooking and CWI. Overseas travel has extensively widened our horizons. At breakfast we specialise in home-made jams, marmalade and preserved fruit. Bob is in charge of bacon and eggs. Available for guests use are hairdryers, laundry facilities, scrabble board and billiard table. Two restaurants within walking distance. Excellent off-street parking. Guests can be met off public transport.
Directions: *Turn into Huia Street from lake front, take fourth turn on right into Rokino Road.*

Taupo
Homestay+Self-contained   Accom.
Address: 18 Hawai St., 2 Mile Bay, Taupo
Name: Jeanette & Bryce Jones
Telephone: (07) 377 3242
Fax: (07) 377 3242
Mobile: (025) 234 0558
Email: jeanettej@xtra.co.nz
Beds: 1 Queen, 2 Single (2 bedrooms)
Bathroom: 1 Guests share
Tariff: B&B (full) Double $75, Single $45, Children $20, Dinner $20, Credit Cards. NZ B&B Vouchers accepted
Nearest Town: Taupo 3km

Taupo, is great for holidays any season. Our attractive warm house has wonderful lake views from lounge and deck. The guest bedrooms are downstairs with a shared bathroom - quiet and comfortable. Home-made muesli, preserves, bread and muffins are my breakfast speciality and tea and coffee are available anytime. As I love to cook, you are welcome to an evening meal or we can recommend first-class restaurants nearby. We are 2 minutes walk to the lake which has an excellent walking track. Bryce is ex RAF Pathfinder and my interests include crafts, Probus and Church activities. We enjoy sharing our home with visitors to this very picturesque area of New Zealand. MARMITE COTTAGE - is also situated on our property. It is a true Kiwi bach - complete with 'comfy' mismatched furniture. Self-contained it has 3 bedrooms and a large open-plan lounge with TV, books and games. Great for families. Linen and firewood supplied. Breakfast available on request.

Acacia Bay, Taupo
Homestay
Address: 77A Wakeman Road, Acacia Bay, Taupo
Name: Pariroa Homestay, Joan & Eric Leersnijder
Telephone: (07) 378 3861
Fax: (07) 378 3866
Mobile: 025 530 370
Beds: 1 Queen, 1 Single, 1 Queen singlem, (2 Bedrooms)
Bathroom: 1 Guests share, separate toilet
Tariff: B&B (full) Double $70, Single $45, Children $20, Credit Cards
Visa and Master Card   NZ B&B Vouchers accepted
Nearest Town: Taupo 5km

Views   Views
*Our home is Scandinavian style with a natural wooden interior, situated in
a very quiet area of Acacia Bay, and surrounded by native ferns and plants.
We have magnificent uninterrupted views of Lake Taupo, Mount Tauhara,
and the ranges from the guest bedrooms, living room and sun deck. We are
retired farmers who have travelled extensively and enjoy meeting people.
Eric, in his younger years, lived in several European countries and was a tea
planter in Indonesia before coming to New Zealand in 1952. We are about
5km from Taupo and minutes from the beach. If you enjoy fishing,
tramping, mountaineering, playing golf, or relaxing in hot thermal pools,
it is all in this area.*
Directions: *Vehicular access is the road going down between 95 and 99
Wakeman Road.   We are the last house on this short road.*

Taupo
Homestay
Address: 30 Rokino Road,
Taupo
Name: Betty and Ned Nolan
Telephone: (07) 377 0828
Fax: (07) 377-0828
Mobile: (025) 244 9035
Beds: 4 Single (2 bedrooms,
1 with balcony and ensuite)
Bathroom: 1 Ensuite, 1 Family share
Tariff: B&B (full)
Double with ensuite $85,
Single $50, Dinner $25.
NZ B&B Vouchers accepted $15 surcharge Oct-Apr incl.
Nearest Town: Taupo 2km, Lake 5 mins

*You will find us at the top of a paved tree lined drive with ample parking. Our one level
home offers breathtaking views over mountains, ranges, lake and township. We are
retired sheep and beef cattle farmers and have travelled extensively. Be as busy or
relaxed as you wish. We can direct you to golf courses, fishing, thermal pools and a
variety of walks, with ski fields just one hour away. Two mountain bikes are also
available. Restaurants are within easy walking distance. Betty loves to cook but
dinners are by prior arrangement. This is not just a Bed & Breakfast but a
HOMESTAY!*
Directions: *From lakefront going south take Taharepa Road to Hilltop Shopping
Centre turning left into Rokino Road - No. 30 is on your right just after Waihora Street.*

Taupo

Self-contained Accommodation
Address: Riverway Cottages,
16 Peehi Manini Rd,
Waitahanui R.D.2, Taupo
Name: Joyce & John Johnson
Telephone: (07) 378 8822
Beds: 1 Queen, 1 Double, 1 Single (2 bedrooms)
Bathroom: 1 Private
Tariff: B&B (continental) Double $75, Single $45, Dinner $25pp, Children half price.
Free bottle of wine with three night stay B&B booking.
Nearest Town: Taupo 14 kms (10 mins)

Riverway Cottages are situated 100 yds from the famous Waitahanui River, and 200 yds from beautiful Lake Taupo. They are older-type properties, one John and Joyce live in, and the second, comprises lounge with TV, kitchen with fridge, freezer, microwave, and conventional ovens, separate dining room, two double bedrooms and bathroom. There is a deck to relax on in summer, and perhaps enjoy a BBQ with us, with complimentary pre-dinner drinks - as evening dinner is optional. In winter there are gas and electric fires, and electric blankets on all beds, for the comfort of our visitors. We have ample parking space, for visitors driving around beautiful New Zealand. For interested fishermen, John has been a successful Trout Fly Fishing Guide for many years, and can take you to some "magic places", and may be booked by the hour or by the day. Joyce is a keen badminton player. Come and visit Waitahanui. We'd love to meet you.
Directions: *Please phone for directions - and we will pick up if needed.*

Lake Taupo

Homestay
Address: 'Pataka House',
8 Pataka Road, Taupo
Name: Raewyn & Neil Alexander
Telephone: (07) 378 5481
Fax: (07) 378 5461
Mobile: 025-473 881
Beds: 2 Queen, 4 Single
(4 Bedrooms)
Bathroom: 1 Private, 1 Guest share, 1 Ensuite.
Tariff: B&B (full) Double $90, Single $60, Garden guest room $100. Children half price. NZ B&B Vouchers accepted $20 surcharge
Nearest Town: Taupo (1km)

Raewyn and Neil extend a warm welcome to Pataka House and enjoy meeting new people and making new friends. You will find us 100 metres from lake Taupo, opposite Mount Ruapehu and very close to restaurants and shops. Our home is off a quiet road up a tree-lined drive way and most privately situated. You are provided with a beautiful environment where you are welcome to wander about the garden. Pataka House is spacious and has a private guest wing of three double bedrooms, which are attractively furnished. We also offer a cosy garden suite with its own bathroom. We are proud of our homestay business which offers hospitality, lounge usage, laundry facilities, swimming pool, barbecue, and roomy car park. We also offer a hearty breakfast whether it be continental or cooked and Neil is adept with his home-baked bread.
Directions: *Please phone or fax. Courtesy car available.*

291

Acacia Bay, Taupo

Lakeside Homestay
Address: Paeroa Lakeside Homestay,
21 Te Kopua St., Acacia Bay, Taupo
Name: Paeroa Lakeside Homestay, Barbara & John Bibby
Telephone: (07) 378 8449
Fax: (07) 378 8446
Mobile: 025 818 829 or 025 828 929
Email: bibby@reap.org.nz
Beds: 2 King/Queen, 2 Single (3 bedrooms)
Bathroom: 1 Ensuite, 1 Private (1 Guests share only in peak times)
Tariff: B&B (full or continental) Double $120-$150, Single $85, Dinner $35, Children under 12 $60. Credit Cards: Visa/Mastercard. NZ B&B Vouchers accepted $20 pp surcharge
Nearest Town: Taupo 5km

Your hosts Barbara & John welcome you to their spacious quality Lakefront Homestay at Acacia Bay, developed on three levels to capture an uninterrupted panoramic view of world famous Lake Taupo and beyond. You are provided with a warm and welcoming environment with comfort, private facilities, spacious lounge areas and outdoor living. Enjoy our delightful gardens, with abundant birdlife leading you to our private beach and boat mooring. We are retired sheep and beef farmers enjoying living in our quiet peaceful and private home beside the beach, just minutes from the centre of town, 3 golf courses, bushwalks, restaurants, shops, boating and all major attractions. Amongst your hosts interests are travel, golf, gardening, fishing. We are 5th Generation New Zealanders.
Guided trout fishing and sightseeing experiences are available with Paeroa's host John in his new 30ft cruiser - we could smoke your trout catch for you or maybe cook it for breakfast. A welcome cup of tea or coffee on arrival if you wish. Tea/coffee facilities in the guest lounge.
Homepage: www.taupohomestay.com

Taupo

Country Homestay
Address: 'Te Awanui',
1506 Poihipi Rd, Taupo
Name: Pam & Martin Bull
Telephone: (07) 377 6040
Fax: (07) 377 6023
Beds: 1 Queen, 2 Single (2 Bedrooms)
Bathroom: 1 Private Bathroom
Tariff: B&B (full) Double $100,
Single $50, Children 5 to 12yrs half price,   Dinner $30.
Nearest Town: Taupo 15 Kms

Te Awanui is set amongst a country garden with magnificent views of the hills and farmland, which grazes sheep, cattle and horses. We are involved with equestrian horses, schooling and students for lessons. Our home is spacious and comfortable with quality accommodation. We welcome you to have with us a delicious three course dinner with complimentary wine, or if you prefer, only Bed and Breakfast. My husband enjoys playing golf, we also love fishing the beautiful Lake Taupo. We have both travelled extensively and enjoy meeting people from other countries. Taupo is a refreshing, lovely place to stay, it has much to offer. We are able to advise or arrange most activities. We are 15km from Taupo and look forward to meeting you, our directions are simple. 1506 Poihipi Road. Please phone (07) 377-6040 We ask guests not to smoke inside our home.

http://www.bnb.co.nz

take a look

Awahuri Lodge, Taupo

Semi-Rural Accommodation close to Taupo town.
Address: Awahuri Lodge, Box 486, Taupo
Name: William & Suzanne Hindmarsh
Telephone: (07) 378 9847 **Fax**: (07) 378 5799 **Freephone**: 0800 426 538
Email: hindmarsh@reap.org.nz
Beds: 1 Queen/Twin, 1 Double/Twin, 1 Queen, 2 Single (5 bedrooms)
Bathrooms: 2 Ensuite, 1 Private
Tariff: B&B Main Room, ensuite: Seasonal rates, per Couple $200-$400, Single $150-$300.. Additional person $55, special arrangements for children. Candle-lit dinners by arrangement $65pp including selected wines and pre-dinner drinks.
Credit Cards: Visa, Mastercard.
Nearest Town: Taupo 1km

William and Suzanne have lived in Taupo for 35 years, in the same secret place beside the Waikato River. Their lodge blends with a tranquil three acre meadow garden which has three 'lakes', a rock waterfall, and amazing bird life amongst mature trees, masses of Camellias, Rhododendrons and Roses etc. Their farmlet has beautiful river and mountain views, yet it's only two minutes by car from town. For them and for you, privacy is the keynote, beauty the pleasure.

Part of the specially-designed accommodation invades the garden. The Main Room includes superb queen-size and single beds, Persian rugs and a lovely double bay-window seat. The ensuite bathroom is off this room, with a single bedroom next door, for that extra person. Inside the house the atmosphere is tasteful and beguiling, with oceans of native timber and oriental carpets. In the colder evenings, a large open fire burns in the house. And Suzanne's meals are just delicious ... you should experience them for yourselves! In the morning, breakfast (cooked if you wish) is served in the dining room at times to suit you.

The Hindmarsh's specialise in providing elegant but uncomplicated ensuite accommodation in a magic environment for up to three couples. Children are welcome and adore the space. The host's interests vary from gardens to music, philosophy, classic cars, current affairs, sports and, of course cooking! A grass tennis court lies beside the river, with Rainbow trout lurking in a tempting manner, ready for smoking in less than 24 hours. Unique river and classic car tours are available. Telephone, Facsimile and Email are there for forward bookings and maintaining personal contact.

Distances: *Taupo town 1km. Lake and fishing guides, 1km. Three golf courses, 3km, including Wairakei International. Arts centres 2km, Snow skiing 100km. William and Suzanne look forward to your company. If you'd like to dine with them, please advise by morning tea. Remember, if it's a comfortable time you need, with good food, conversation and care, a special treat awaits!*

Directions: *Please telephone for enquiries and directions.*

Acacia Bay, Taupo

Lakestay
Address: 'Kooringa',
32 Ewing Grove, Acacia Bay, Taupo
Name: Robin & John Mosley
Telephone: (07) 378 8025
Fax: (07) 378 6085
Mobile: (025) 272 6343 **Email**: kooringa@xtra.co.nz
Beds: Guest Wing 1 Queen, 1 Double, 1 Single (2 Bedrooms)
Bathroom: Ensuite
Tariff: B&B (full) Double $90, Single $60, Credit cards (VISA/MC). NZ B&B Vouchers accepted $10 surcharge per night.
Nearest Town: Taupo 6km

"Kooringa" is situated in sheltered Acacia Bay (2 minutes walk to Lake) surrounded by bush and gardens with magnificent views of Lake Taupo and Mount Tauhara. The guest wing is tastefully furnished with sitting room, TV, tea and coffee making facilities and bathroom. There are 2 bedrooms, one with queen size bed, the other with a double and single bed and your own private deck area. We are a retired professional couple, have travelled extensively with our two sons, lived overseas and now enjoy a relaxed life style in this beautiful area. We are within easy distance of fascinating geothermal activity, famous Huka Falls, bush walks, golf courses, hot pools, restaurants and numerous other attractions. Our interests include gardening, sport, travel, books and hospitality. A generous breakfast with plenty of variety is served in the conservatory overlooking the Lake. We assure you of a warm welcome and comfortable stay.
Directions: *Please phone, fax or Email: kooringa@xtra.co.nz.*
Home Page: www.kooringa.co.nz

Taupo

Homestay
Address: 'Lakeland Homestay',11 Williams Street, Taupo
Name: Lesley & Chris & Pussy cats
Telephone: (07) 378 1952
Fax: (07) 378 1912 **Mobile**: (025) 877 971
Email: lakeland.bb@xtra.co.nz
Beds: 1 Double, 2 Single (2 Bedrooms)
Bathroom: 1 Family share
Tariff: B&B (continental) Double $80, Single $50.
Credit cards: MC/Visa. NZ B&B Vouchers accepted
Nearest Town: Taupo

Nestled in a restful tree-lined street, bursting with birdlife, and a mere five minute stroll from the Lake's edge and Taupo's shopping centre, "Lakeland Homestay" is a cheerful and cosy home that enjoys views of the lake and mountains. Keen gardeners, anglers and golfers Chris and Lesley work and play in an adventure oasis. We can direct you to local attractions and activities. For extra warmth on winter nights all beds have electric blankets and laundry facilities are available if required. A courtesy car is available for coach and airline travellers and there is off-street parking.
Directions: *Travelling from the North turn left into Heu Heu St at the only set of traffic lights, take Heathcote Street on the left and right into Williams St. Travelling from the South turn right into Rifle Range Road (at the Firestation) and left into Williams Street after crossing Heu Heu Street.*
Home Page: babs.co.nz/lakeland/index.html

Taupo
Homestay
Address: 'Tui Glen',
10 Pataka Rd, Taupo
Name: Robbie & Stan Shearer
Telephone: (07) 378 7007
Fax: (07) 378 2412
Mobile: (025) 239 2931
Beds: 1 King, 2 Single (2 Bedrooms)
Bathroom: 1 Private, 1 Ensuite
Tariff: B&B (full) Double 100, Single $65, Dinner with wine and aperitifs by arrangement $35 - $45. Not suitable for children.
Nearest Town: Taupo 1 Km to town centre

WELCOME. Arrive as welcome guests and leave as firm friends. Hospitality is our first priority. Our comfortable home with a meld of modern comfort and a hint of old world charm has evoked many favourable comments. Set in a tranquil garden we are only a few steps from the lakefront beach and an easy stroll to town. Relax in the lounge, wander the garden or siesta on the terrace at your leisure - your choice. Laundry and barbecue facilities available if required. Guest bedrooms are attractive and comfortable with bathroom facilities to match. A tasty breakfast is served in the conservatory amongst the flowers. Cooked breakfast on request at no extra cost. We are a retired couple well versed in hospitality after many years in our award winning lodge and restaurant complex. We will happily advise on local attractions and restaurants or provide a gourmet meal with prior advice. **Directions**: *Please phone - transport available.*

Taupo
Farmstay
Address: 'Ben Lomond', 1434 Poihipi Rd, R.D.1, Taupo
Name: Jack & Mary Weston
Telephone: (07) 377 6033
Fax: (07) 377 6033
Mobile: 025-774080
Email: benlomond@xtra.co.nz
Beds: 1 Double, 2 Single (2 Bedrooms)
Bathroom: 1 Guests share
Tariff: B&B (full) Double $90, Single $45, Children half price. Dinner $25 includes wine, Credit Card. NZ B&B Vouchers accepted
Nearest Town: Taupo 15km west

Ben Lomond is a 500 acre sheep and cattle farm 15km west of Taupo. We have farmed the land for the last 33 years and offer you a pleasant farmstay in our comfortable home. Our interests include equestrian and fishing and we can advise you on the local spots of interest which are wide and varied in the Taupo District. Jack and I have both travelled widely within New Zealand and overseas and enjoy making new friends. Our 3 sons have grown up and virtually left home and we offer you 2 rooms (1 double, 1 twin) and 1 bathroom for guest use only. We have the usual farm animals of which 2 dogs wander in and out. You are welcome to dine with us but please ring and "make a date". We prefer non-smokers.
Directions: *Please phone.*

Taupo
Bed & Breakfast
Address: 115 Shepherd Road, Taupo
Name: Delmont Lodge
Telephone: (07) 378 3304
Fax: (07) 378 3322
Beds: 2 Queen, 2 Single (3 bedrooms)
Bathroom: 2 Ensuite, 1 Private
Tariff: B&B (special) Double $99-$130,
Single $90, Children $15, Dinner $35pp.
Nearest Town: Taupo 3 Kms

A warm welcome awaits you at Delmont Lodge where spoiling, pampering and relaxation abound. Situated adjacent to the Botanical Gardens in half]acre of mature trees, pretty gardens and a large lawn for croquet, this peaceful home commands sweeping views of Lake Taupo and the mountains. The Lodge features a guest wing with 2 Queen bedded rooms with ensuite and 1 bedded room with private bathroom. Your relaxation and comfort are paramount. We Miriam & Bob love living here and would like to help you enjoy Taupo too. Afternoon tea/coffee and home baking greet you upon arrival. Fresh fruit juice start your breakfast and dinner can be arranged to suit your needs. There are many good restaurants only minutes away and we can arrange most tourist activities.
We appreciate guests not smoking in the house.

Taupo
Homestay
Address: 28 Greenwich Street, Taupo
Name: Ann & Dan Hennebry
Telephone: (07) 378 9483
Beds: 1 King, 1 Single (2 bedrooms)
Bathroom: 1 Guests share
Tariff: B&B (full) Double $80, Single $50,
Children half price. Dinner $25, Credit Cards.
NZ B&B Vouchers accepted
Nearest Town: Taupo - 3km from Post Office

We look forward to meeting you, we enjoy having guests in our spacious home overlooking farmland and bordering Taupo's Botanical Gardens. We hope you will join us for dinner (maybe a barbecue in the summer) and complimentary wine in our pleasant dining room. There are many good restaurants in Taupo should you prefer that. Breakfast will also be served here at a time to suit you. Our launch "Bonita" is available if you would like a fishing or sightseeing trip on our beautiful lake - Dan is an excellent skipper. We have lived in and around Taupo for twenty-five years, so can help with advice or arrange most activities in the area. You will find our home warm, comfortable and welcoming.
Directions: Please phone.

Taupo
Country Homestay+Self-contained Cottage
Address: Physical: SH32/Poihipi Rd, Taupo
Postal: South Claragh, RD1, Mangakino
Name: Lesley & Paul Hill "South Claragh"
Telephone: (07) 372 8848
Fax: (07) 372 8047 **Email**: paul.hill@xtra.co.nz
Beds: 1 Queen, 1 Single + extra bed available (2 bedrooms). One party only.
Bathroom: 1 Guest private plus extra W.C.
Tariff: B&B Main guestroom: Single $55, Double $95; Single room with extra bed available: $45, $30 extra bed. Children half price. Dinner $30.
Bird Cottage: 1 Night $75 double, 2 or more nights $65, $20 each additional person, $10 child. Weekly rate negotiable.
Credit Cards. NZ B&B Vouchers accepted (surcharge $15 high season)
Nearest Town: Taupo 34km

Welcome to our comfortable, centrally heated farmhouse set in rambling mature gardens, well situated as a base for exploring the centre of the North Island (tramping, golf, trout fishing, hunting, skiing, thermal parks and sightseeing). Turn into our leafy driveway and relax in a hammock under the wisteria, enjoy the rhododendrons or autumn colours, crack walnuts beside the open fire, play petanque or croquet, join us for a drink on the terrace, meet our gentle donkeys, coloured sheep and outdoor family dog. The spacious and sunny main guest room has a private deck leading into the garden. Meals: Delicious farm breakfast. Home-grown produce and excellent cooking mean that dining is recommended. Bird Cottage is self contained and cosy, perfect for two, but will sleep 4/5. Linen and firewood provided. Self cater or meals by arrangement. Your hosts are well travelled, semi-retired professional people with varied interests. South Claragh is very easy to find - please phone/fax for directions. We ask that our guests not smoke indoors. Members of N.Z. Assn. Farm and Home Hosts.

Taupo
Bed & Breakfast
Address: "Bramham Lodge",
7 Waipahihi Ave, Taupo
Name: John & Julia Bates
Telephone: (07) 378 0064
Fax: (07) 378 0065
Mobile: 025-240 9643
Email: bramham@reap.org.nz
Beds: 1 Double, 3 Single (3 bedrooms)
Bathroom: Private facilities all room.
Tariff: B&B (full) Double $90-$100, Single $50-$60.
NZ B&B Vouchers accepted Surcharge $21-$30
Nearest Town: Taupo

Bramham is situated some 2 minutes walk from the shores of Lake Taupo and offers tremendous views of the lake and mountains to the south.
John and Julia have spent 24 years in the RNZAF including service on exchange with the USAF in Tucson, Arizona and five years running their dairy farm in South Taranaki. We offer you a homely peaceful stay with all mod-cons at your call. We take pride in our business and specialize in good hearty breakfasts of your choice, served with freshly brewed coffee and fruit juice. A continental breakfast is available if you prefer. We include a pick up service from the bus terminal or Airport and offer sightseeing trips or day excursions by arrangement. Being non smokers our dogs ask you not to smoke in our home.

Taupo
Homestay
Address: 55 Grace Crescent, Taupo
Name: Tom & Beverley Catley
Telephone: (07) 378 1403
Fax: (07) 378 1402
Beds: 1 Queen, 1 Double,
2 Single (3 bedrooms)
Bathroom: 1 Private, 1 Family share
Tariff: B&B (full) Double $90, Single $50,
Children half price, Credit Cards.
Nearest Town: Taupo 5km, a few minutes walk to the lake

If you are looking for a quiet place to stay with panoramic views of lake and mountains, breakfasts to remember and warm hospitality, this is the place for you. Our upstairs guest rooms open onto a sheltered sundeck with northerly views across the lake to Taupo town centre, and to the south the snow capped volcanoes. At ground level we have a comfortable self-contained unit with private bathroom and lounge with TV, microwave and tea making facilities. You are welcome to use our laundry. All Taupo's famous attractions are nearby including Huka Falls and hot thermal pools. Our hobbies include floral art, photography and music. With prior notice we can offer an evening meal. We know you will enjoy your stay in this lovely town.

Taupo
Rural Homestay
Address: "Minarapa"
620 Oruanui Road, R.D.1, Taupo
Name: Barbara & Dermot Grainger and pets.
Telephone: (07) 378 1931
Fax: (07) 78 1932
Mobile: 025-272 2367
Email: minarapa@voyager.co.nz
Beds: 2 Queen, 2 Single (3 bedrooms)
Bathroom: 2 Ensuite, 1 Private
Tariff: B&B (full) Double $85-$100, Single $60-$70, Children under 14 half price, 3 course dinner by arrangement $30pp. Credit Cards.
NZ B&B Vouchers accepted $15 surcharge
Nearest Town: Taupo 14km - 2km off State Highway 1

We welcome you along our tree-lined drive to enjoy the peace and tranquility of our 11-acre country retreat just 12 minutes from Taupo, 45 minutes from Rotorua and central to Wairakei and all tourist attractions. Our home is spacious with loads of atmosphere. It has a games room with full-sized billiard table, fridge and TV for guest use and large lounge with feature fireplace. The guestrooms, two with ensuite and balcony, have comfortable beds and individual character. They overlook beautiful park-like grounds where you can relax among mature trees and colourful gardens, play tennis, practise golf or cross the pond and stream to visit our friendly farm animals. Breakfasts, which include homebaking and preserves, may be served indoors or outside on the verandah. We enjoy travel and meeting people. Our interests include gardening, golf, sailing, bridge and the arts. Barbara speaks fluent German.
Directions: *Please phone for directions.* **Home Page**: www.voyager.co.nz/~minarapa/

Taupo

Homestay Farmlet
Address: 466 State Highway 5,
R.D.1, Taupo
Name: "Hereford Lodge"
Keith & Lin Roberts
Telephone: (07) 374 8440
Fax: (07) 374 8460
Mobile: (025) 959 557
Beds: 1 Queen, 1 Double (2 bedrooms)
Bathroom: 1 Private with separate toilet, Separate laundry
Tariff: B&B (full) Double $80, Single $50, Dinner $35 inc wine.
Nearest Town: Taupo 14km

We welcome you to our 17 acre lifestyle property that has been developed to create a tranquil rural setting 8 minutes north of Taupo, 1/2 hour from Rotorua and only 4 minutes from the renowned Wairakei International Golf Course and other scenic attractions of the area. Our guest wing is private, spacious, and beautifully appointed with your every need catered for. The rooms themselves both open out to a large verandah, overlooking garden and swimming pool (heated in summer). We are both very keen golfers and would be only too happy to organise your golfing requirements during your stay with us. We also organise trout fishing excursions for you. We are a younger couple with no children living at home, only one cat and 2 dogs and enjoy good food and entertaining.
Directions: *Please phone for directions. Transport is available if required. Nothing will be too much trouble to make your stay in Taupo memorable.*

Taupo

Bed & Breakfast
Address: 70 Blue Ridge Drive
Name: Ashgrove
Telephone: (07) 378 9851
Fax: (07) 378 9853
Beds: 1 Double, 2 Single
(2 bedrooms)
Bathroom: 1 Guests share
Tariff: B&B (full) Double $90, Single $55.
Nearest Town: Taupo 7km Acacia Bay side

Do you want peace and tranquillity in a glorious setting with easy reach of Taupo's many attractions, then come and share our sunny modern home set in a two acre country garden. Enjoy the magnificent panoramic views of the lake and township while strolling through a garden which is full of surprises and a haven for native birdlife. Our Lockwood home has a conservatory, separate guest wing. laundry available and is smokefree.
We are knowledgable about the region and its attractions, especially the forests, wildlife and gardens. Whatever your interests we can advise on or arrange a wide variety of activities for your enjoyment. Elaine's interests include gardening, floral art, crafts and creative work while Terry's include many sports, tramping, forestry and geography. We both enjoy travelling and meeting people from other countries.
Directions: *Blue Ridge Drive is off the eastern end of Mapara Rd. Please phone for availability.*

Taupo
Bed & Breakfast
Address: 77 Gillies Ave, Taupo
Name: Gerry & Kay English
Telephone: (07) 377 2377
Fax: (07) 377 2377
Email: genglish@reap.org.nz
Beds: 4 Double, 12 Single (9 bedrooms)
Bathroom: 9 Ensuite
Tariff: B&B (full) Double $85, Single $65,
Children under 12 free, Credit Cards.
NZ B&B Vouchers accepted $15 surcharge on Double
Nearest Town: Taupo 1 1/2kms

Gillies Lodge is situated one and a half kilometres from the shopping area and one kilometre from the lake. We are in a quiet residential spot with a small reserve on one boundary. From the upstairs living space (dining, lounge and bar) we have views of the lake. Our twenty four hour licence allows the bar to be open for your convenience. We enjoy sharing our home with visitors and make every effort to make you feel at home at our place. Our six children are scattered around the globe. 'Garp' our cat, has not adapted to visitors. He will remain invisible during your stay. A courtesy car to help you enjoy your stay is available. A variety of activities are available in Taupo including boating, fishing, kayaking, Eco tours. These can be organised for you prior to your visit, or on arrival. Inquire at the Information Office or phone for directions.

Taupo
Homestay
Address: Mountain Views Homestay,
17b Puriri Street, Taupo
Name: Jack & Bridget
Telephone: (07) 378 6136
Fax: (07) 378 6134
Email: ernikemp@reap.org.nz
Beds: 2 Queen, 2 Single
(2 bedrooms)
Bathroom: 1 Guests share
Tariff: B&B (special) Double $70, Single $40,
Children $20 under 10 yrs. Credit cards.
Nearest Town: Taupo 3km

Welcome to our home which is centrally heated and double glazed. Our two guest bedrooms and guest bathroom are upstairs. Both have views of Mount Tauhara. The hilltop shopping centre is five minutes walk away where there are two good reasonably priced restaurants. When you stay two nights or more, Jack will take you onboard his replica steamboat "Ernest Kemp" for a free cruise (conditions apply). We are happy to recommend and book many local activites. You may prefer to just relax in our thermal hot pool and gaze at the stars before betime. We will glady transport you to and from public transport facilites as required. We have off-street parking if you have your own transport. We appreciate guests not smoking in the house. Please phone for directions.

Taupo

Homestay
Address: 32 Harvey Street, Taupo
(PO Box 543, Taupo)
Name: Judi & Barry Thomson
Telephone: (07) 378 4558
Fax: (07) 378 4558
Email: circus@xtra.co.nz
Beds: 1 Queen, 2 Single (1 bedroom)
Bathroom: 1 Private
Tariff: B&B (continental) Double $95, Single $60, Additional guests
same party $40, Cooked breakfast on request,
One party only at one time. Credit cards.
Nearest Town: Taupo 3 kms

Your relaxation and comfort are paramount. We, Judi and Barry, love living here and would like to help you enjoy Taupo too. We have both travelled extensively and enjoy meeting people from other countries. We are happy to offer friendly and comfortable accommodation plus assisting with travel plans and sightseeing. A welcome also from Georgia our Golden Labrador. Our totally private and peaceful facility includes a thermal spa, central heating plus an open fire and television in the living area. A ranchslider provides easy access to lawn and garden with in-ground pool. Two single beds in the living room if required. The lake is only a short stroll away and we can recommend three lakeside restaurants for your evening meal. Judi will serve breakfast at a time to suit you. Ruapehu Skifields are just one and a quarter hours of easy driving and we are very close to three golf courses, fishing and boating, tramping, bush walking and swimming. We request no smoking indoors.

http://www.bnb.co.nz

take a look

Taupo
"Richlyn" Country Homestay. B&B

Address: 1 Mark Wynd,
Bonshaw Park, Taupo
Name: Lyn and Richard James
Telephone: (07) 378 8023
Fax: (07) 378 8023
Mobile: (025) 908 647
Beds: 1 King/ensuite, 2 Queen,
2 Single (4 Bedrooms)
Bathroom: 1 Ensuite, 1 Guests share
Tariff: B&B (full) Double $92-$140, Single $57-$90 (all including GST).
Nearest Town: Taupo, 8 km West

FRIENDLY, PEACEFUL AND VERY COMFORTABLE. Lyn and Richard invite you to share their single story, smoke alarmed, spacious smoke free home, and eight acres of park, trees and gardens, with three toy poodles, two cats and a lovebird. Enjoy the outdoor spa pool, mountain and lake views, the country atmosphere, the gym, comfortable beds, the cup of tea when you arrive, the wonderful cooked breakfasts. Conversation. Walk or rest in the gardens and trees. Stay here, while exploring and experiencing the tourist center of New Zealand, or laze around and rest, it's up to you. Parking's no problem. Groups of eight (4 couples) welcome. Please ring for information and bookings, we don't want to be out entertaining guests if you arrive unexpectedly!
Directions: *From Taupo, up Napier Road 6 km, right into Caroline Drive, 2 km to Mark Wynd on left, first drive on left is Richlyn Homestay. See you soon.*

Taupo
Homestay

Address: 5 Te Hepera Street,
Taupo
Name: Patricia and Russell Jensen
Telephone: 07 378 1888
Fax: 07 378 1888
Mobile: (025) 836 888
Beds: 1 Queen (1 bedroom)
Bathroom: 1 Private
Tariff: B&B (special/full/continental)
Double $95, Single $65, Dinner $35.
Nearest Town: Taupo (1.5 kms on SH1)

Welcome to our sunny home, situated in a quiet cul-de-sac a short walk from the lake and restaurants, within easy reach of all attractions. Guest accommodation is the upstairs level, featuring a sunny bedroom and adjoining guest lounge, both opening onto private balcony with panoramic views of mountains, lake and town. Sky TV and tea/coffee making facilities are provided in lounge. Guest bathroom includes bath and shower. We are retired farmers in our 50's who have travelled extensively and love meeting people. Greta our cat shares our home. Guests can enjoy boating and fishing with us by arrangement and we welcome them to relax in our private thermal pool. You may enjoy a country style evening meal with us by prior arrangement, or breakfast only, if preferred. We ask smokers to use the balcony or garden - thank you.
Directions: *1st right turn up Shepherd Road or phone. We will collect from terminals.*

Taupo
Homestay
Address: 98 Wakeman Rd., Acacia Bay, Taupo
Name: Bob & Marlene Leece
Telephone: (07) 378 6099
Beds: 1 King, 2 Single (2 bedrooms)
Bathroom: 1 Guests share
Tariff: B&B (continental) Double $80, Single $50. NZ B&B Vouchers accepted
Nearest Town: Taupo 6km

Bob and I (and or two Burmese cats) extend a warm welcome to you, and to our large Lockwood home. We are situated 6km from town with panoramic views of lake and mountain. There are many walks nearby around the shores of the lake, and a very interesting one around the block which contains 150 steps (for the energetic ones). The house has two large rooms, one with 2 single beds, the other with a king size bed. Guests have their own toilet, bath, shower, but share if both rooms are full. The guests are welcome to use the decks around the house. You are welcome to smoke, but not in our house.
Directions: *Please phone for directions.*

http://www.bnb.co.nz

take a look

Taupo
Farmstay
Address: 'Brackenhurst',
801 Oruanui Rd., RD 1, Taupo
Name: Margaret and Noel Marson
Telephone: (07) 377 6451
Fax: (07) 377 6451
Beds: 1 Queen, 1 Double, 3 Single (3 bedrooms)
Bathroom: 2 Ensuite
Tariff: B&B (full) Double $90, Single $50, Children half price, Dinner $35. No Credit
Cards. NZ B&B Vouchers accepted $25 surcharge
Nearest Town: 10k past Wairakei on SH1 turn left to Oruanui Road, 3/4k on right.

*Brackenhurst, set among flower gardens on a hillside overlooking picturesque
farmland, offers a warm welcome, wonderful food, peace and tranquillity.
Enjoy the sounds of Tuis and Bellbirds. Watch the Fantail flit from tree to tree.
Practise your pitch and putt on the hillside green. A private guest wing in the
house or a sperate annex offer the ultimate in away from home comfort - fresh
flowers and special touches. Breakfast to suit, healthy, indulgent, or a little of
both. Let us tantalise and spoil you with fine food, freshly brewed coffee, and
selection of teas. Guests are welcome to relax by the fire, on the verandah or
wander over the farm, viewing the animals. We have a house cat and dog (poodle).
Come and enjoy 'Brackenhurst' and share in our warm hospitality. Located close
to the many 'wonders' of the Taupo area. RECOMMENDATIONS: "The Perfect
NZ stay - We loved Lambie and the farm and enjoyed your company and
hospitality" - Craig & Ann - USA. "Lovely home, lovely hosts, super food" - Jean
& Eric - UK.*

Taupo
Farmstay
Address: 'Whitiora Farm'
1281 Mapara Road, RD 1, Taupo.
Name: Judith & Jim McGrath
Telephone: (07) 378 6491
Fax: (07) 378 6491
Mobile: 025 2730879
Email: mcg.whitiora@xtra.co.nz
Beds: 1 Double, 4 Single (3 bedrooms)
Bathroom: 2 Family share
Tariff: B&B (full) Double $100, Single $50, Dinner $30. Children 5 - 12
years of age half price. NZ B&B Vouchers accepted $30 surcharge
Nearest Town: Taupo 12 km.

*3 Course dinner. Breakfast includes fruit, fresh farm eggs, bacon, venison
sausages, tomatoes, home made bread and conserves, coffee, English or herbal
tea. We have a 461 acre farm 10 km north-west of Taupo, grazing sheep, cattle,
deer, goats and thoroughbred horses which we breed and Jim trains and races.
Judith, a food professional takes pride in the large garden, including organic
vegetables. We enjoy sharing our large comfortable home, garden and farm,
travel extensively, enjoy meeting people and making new friends. Local
attractions include: river, stream and lake trout fishing; golf courses for all
abilities, farm, forest and National Park walks; geothermal and volcanic attractions; horse/pony riding and trekking; jet boating and white water rafting; snow
and water skiing; bungy jumping; helicopter and float plane rides; shopping. We
appreciate you not smoking in our home.* **Directions**: *Please phone.*

Taupo

Homestay

Lakeside *Thermal* Homestay

Address: Lakeside Thermal Homestay,
No. 3, 227 Lake Terrace, Taupo
Name: Terri, Bruce, Hayley and Max.
Telephone: (07) 378 1171 (day & eve)
Fax: (07) 378 1101
Mobile: (025) 835 827
Beds: 1 Queen, 2 Double Bunks (2 bedrooms) **Bathroom**: 1 Guests share
Tariff: B&B (special/full/continental) Double $100, Single $60 or $85,
Double Bunks $60 per bunk (2 bunks in one room). Dinner $25 (children's
dinner half price), Children $20 p/child. Vouchers accepted $30 surcharge
Nearest Town: Taupo 2 kms

*This absolute lakeside location, with natural thermal spa and unobstructed views
of the lake and Mt Ruapehu, places you close to town and a menagerie of activities,
i.e. golf, fishing, skiing, water sports, 4-wheel bike riding, bungy jumping, para
gliding etc etc. You are within walking distance to restaurants with a scenic
lakeside walkway out the front door providing a memorable form of exploration
and exercise i.e. thermal steam rising from the ground, hot water streams, superb
sunsets. The homestay motto "your home while you are with us" introduces your
friendly, helpful hosts who can provide a comfortable, pleasant and interesting
stay. They trout fish, tie flies, golf and enjoy wholesome food and your company.
Their small well-behaved dog charms everyone. Stairs to your cosy room are
easy. Children are welcome. We appreciate you not smoking in our home.
Inspections by appointment. We look forward to hearing from you!*
Directions: *Please phone for directions.*

Taupo

Homestay

Address: West Wellow,
39 Mapara Road, Acacia Bay, Taupo
Name: Ian and Mary Smith
Telephone: (07) 378 0435
Fax: (07) 378 0635
Mobile: (021) 455 975
Email: bookings@westwellow.co.nz.
Beds: 3 King/Queen, 2 Single (4 Bedrooms)
Bathroom: 3 Ensuite, 1 Private
Tariff: B&B (Full on request or Continental) Double $180-$200, Single $120.
Credit Cards: Visa/Mastercard. NZ B&B Vouchers accepted
Nearest Town: Taupo 5 km

*Situated above beautiful Acacia Bay, West Wellow was built in the seventies as a
"look-a-like" original colonial home. Genuine components from early New
Zealand buildings were used, giving this home a unique graciousness. Offering
three guest rooms with King or Queen sized beds and ensuites these all open onto a verandah
with wonderful views of the garden and Lake Taupo. A fourth twin "overflow" room with a
private bathroom, can also be made available on request. Widely travelled themselves, your
hosts Ian and Mary love entertaining, gardening, fishing and most of all meeting people. Ian's
involvement with the development of Taupo's thermal energy production, goes back to its very
beginnings ..... Taupo is one of the leisure centres of New Zealand, from hot pools, to golf ....
Taupo is special, West Wellow is special. Let your experienced hosts introduce you to the
wonders of this unique thermal area.*
Directions: *Renovating 1999. Please check availability.*

Te Rangiita, Turangi
Homestay
Address: Raukawa Lodge,
265 SH1, Te Rangiita,
RD 2 Turangi, Postal:
PO Box 195, Turangi
Name: John & Sarah Sage
Telephone: (07) 386 7637
Fax: (07) 386 8137
Email: sages@xtra.co.nz
Beds: 1 Queen, 2 Single (2 bedrooms) **Bathroom**: 1 Private
Tariff: B&B (full) Double $75, Single $45, Children under 10 half price.,
Dinner $25pp, Credit card (VISA). NZ B&B Vouchers accepted
Nearest Town: 12km North of Turangi on SH 1

*Kia Ora - Our home is halfway between Auckland and Wellington on State Highway One - close to the mountains but closer to the lake with a rural outlook reaching to the Kaimanawa Ranges. We are minutes to the Tauranga-Taupo River for trout fishing, and surrounded by beautiful walking treks. Whatever your interest the Central Plateau can ably cater for all tastes in all seasons. We accommodate one party at a time and offer comfortable beds with electric blankets and duvets; your own tea making, laundry and toilet facilities; conservatory with wood burner in the games room. We serve simple New Zealand fare with plenty of fresh fruit, vegetables and homemade bread. We have travelled extensively at home and abroad, are keen golfers, fishers,gardeners - and ... followers of rugby. Our Old English Sheepdog, Sophia, always welcomes new faces. **Directions**: Please phone for directions and availability.*
Home Page: http://members.tripod.com/Raukawa

Tauranga Taupo
Lodge
Address: Rusty's Retreat,
35 Heu Heu Parade, Tauranga - Taupo,
RD 2 Turangi, Central North Island
Name: Lynda Gibson and Graham Bell
Telephone: (07) 386 0123
Fax: (07) 386 0122
Mobile: (025) 848 747
Email: rustysretreat@xtra.co.nz
Beds: 3 Queen, 3 Single (4 bedrooms)
Bathroom: 2 Ensuites, 1 Guests share, 1 Family share
Tariff: B&B double $120, Single $80, Dinner from $35, Children half price.
Nearest Town: Turangi 11 km, Taupo 38 km

Situated in the central North Island, on the banks of the Tauranga Taupo River and only 200 meters from the lake, Rusty's Retreat is an idyllic escape.
We offer full accommodation or bed and breakfast for your next holiday, sporting adventure or business meeting. Trout for breakfast, venison for dinner........ it's tough to take. Stay in our guest rooms which accommodate up to nine people, with ensuite.... step across the road to fish for trout, down the road to swim Lake Taupo, or hit the ski slopes, 45 mins away.... or simply do absolutely nothing and enjoy the hospitality and beautiful surrounds of this district.
Graham is a jeweller and trout fishing guide and Lynda a communications consultant. We have an eight year old son and one friendly dog.

Turangi

Homestay & Self-contained Cottage

Address: 3 Poto Street, Turangi
Name: Jack & Betty Anderson
Telephone: (07) 386 8272
Fax: (07) 386 8272
Beds: Home: 2 Queen,
1 Single (2 bedrooms) Cottage:
1 Queen, 2 Single (2 bedrooms)
Bathroom: Home: 2 Ensuite Cottage: 1 Private
Tariff: Home or Cottage: B&B (full) Double $80, Single $50, Children price negotiable, Dinner $25pp (by prior arrangement). Cottage: Self-catering: Double $65, Extra adult $20pp, Children half price.
VISA/MC Accepted. NZ B&B Vouchers accepted $15 Surcharge.
Nearest Town: Turangi - 35 minutes south of Taupo SH1

Welcome to our relaxed lifestyle beside the Tongariro River, extremely quiet, away from traffic, with bush walks and fishing pools nearby. Maps available. With ensuites for privacy, are two bedrooms: one has a queen bed and one a double and single bed. Electric blankets. Laundry facilities. Off street parking. No smoking inside please. Our self-contained 2 bedroom cottage is adjacent, for travellers preferring independence. Breakfast, leisurely, of your choice. Meals contain fresh vegetables in season. Vegetarians catered for. With both children away, join us in the lounge to share our interest in flying, golfing, skiing and trout fishing. From our central North Island location enjoy trips to Tongariro National Park, Taupo, Rotorua, Napier and Waitomo. Thermal pools are nearby. Scenic flights, guided rafting, horse treks, river and boat fishing arranged. We can meet your bus.

Turangi

Self Contained Accom

Address: "Dyden", Old Mill Lane,
Grace Road, Turangi
Name: Anita & Graham Pyatt
Telephone: (07) 386 6032
Fax: (07) 386 6312
Email: grahampyatt@fishnhunt.co.nz
Beds: 2 Singles (1 bedroom)
Bathroom: 1 Ensuite
Tariff: B&B (continental) Double $70, Single $45, Dinner $30pp by arrangement. Credit Cards (VISA/MC) NZ B&B Vouchers accepted $20 Surcharge
Nearest Town: Turangi 3 kms

Welcome to "DYDEN" in the trout fishing capital of the world situated a few minutes stroll away from the mighty Tongariro River. Guest accommodation is set in 5 acres of quiet relaxing gardens affording great views of Lake Taupo, the surrounding mountains and farmland. Our home is adjacent and as our guests you are welcome to join us in the evening for a chat, a drink or for dinner. We have a friendly cat, dog and budgie. For visiting anglers, Graham, a professional fishing guide can be "booked" to take you to some of those "Special" places on our world famous rivers and lakes. Let us help you to share the magic of our beautiful area which has every outdoor activity imaginable close by. Cooked breakfast is available on request. We look forward to meeting you. **Directions**: *Please phone.*
Home Page: http://www.fishnhunt.co.nz/trout/pyatt.htm

Turangi
Self-contained Cottage
Address: "Akepiro",
169 Taupahi Road, Turangi
Name: John & Jenny Wilcox
Telephone: (07) 386 7384
Fax: (07) 386 6838
Email: jwilcox@voyager.co.nz/jennywilcox@xtra.co.nz
Beds: 1 Queen, 1Double, 2 Single (2 bedrooms)
1 cot and highchair available
Bathroom: 1 Private
Tariff: B&B (continental) Double $65, Single $45, Extra Adult $35, Children up to 12 $15, 4 adults $120, Continental breakfast on request $5pp.
Nearest Town: Turangi - 54km south of Taupo on SH1

Our cottage is set in half an acre of trees and woodland garden, featuring rhododendrons and a wide variety of native plants. The garden attracts many species of birds and their song mingles with the murmur of the Tongariro River which is just through the garden gate. These idyllic surroundings, far from traffic noise, make a perfect retreat for that restful break. Direct access to the river walkway and fine fishing pools. Excellent, challenging scenic golf course 4 minutes by car (clubs available). Relax in the Tokaanu hot pools just 10 minutes away. Our home and award-winning garden is adjacent but allowing the cottage every privacy. Come, share this corner of nature's paradise with us. Enjoy the many outdoor pursuits and activities the region offers. Fishing guides can be arranged. Full, modern kitchen, full laundry facilities, all linen supplied. A warm welcome awaits you at "Akepiro".

Motuoapa, Turangi
Homestay/B&B
Address: "Meredith House",
45 Kahotea Place, Motuoapa, RD2, Turangi
Name: Frances and Ian Meredith
Telephone: (07) 386 5266
Fax: (07) 386 5270
Email: meredith.house@xtra.co.nz
Beds: 1 Queen, 2 Single (2 Bedrooms)
Bathroom: 1 Guests share
Tariff: B&B (Full/Continental) Double $80, Single $50, Dinner $25 pp, Light snacks $10 pp. Credit Cards: Visa/Mastercard. NZ B&B Vouchers accepted $15 Surcharge. Excludes Public/School Holidays.
Nearest Town: Turangi - 10km South. Taupo - 45km North on SH1.

*STOP and ENJOY THIS PIECE OF PARADISE. Just off SH1, our comfortable two storey home, with fantastic views of Lake Taupo and Kaimanawas, has ground-floor self-contained guest accommodation with fully equipped Kitchen (tea, coffee etc provided), Dining room, Lounge (with bed-settee and divan if needed). Two cozy bedrooms with TV. Laundry facilities. MEALS: Guests may self-cater/ or join us for convivial chat and meals, or have meals served in guests' quarters. Vehicle/Boat off-street parking. Minutes to Marina. Excellent river fishing nearby. Also delightful bush walks. 45 minutes to Mount Ruapehu ski field. Our association with Tongariro/Taupo area spans over 30 years, through work and outdoor pursuits. Ian, an engineer, and Frances, an ex Tour Guide, will take pleasure in sharing their passion for this magnificent area with you. We have one small, friendly dog - Keiller. **Directions**: Turn off SH1 at Motuoapa International B&B sign and follow signage up hill.*

Turangi

Self-contained Cottage
Address: 21A Koura Street, Turangi
Name: 'River Birches',
Gill & Peter Osborne
Telephone: (07) 386 5348
Fax: (07) 386 5948
Email: gillo@voyager.co.nz
Beds: 1 King/2 single, 2 Single (2 bedrooms)
Bathroom: 1 Private
Tariff: B&B (full) Double $150, Single $90. Children under 5 years free. Credit Cards: Bankcard/Visa.
Nearest Town: Turangi. Taupo 40 minutes north on SH1.

Experience the tranquillity of our completely private self-contained cottage in its secluded garden setting right on the banks of the Tongariro River.
A fully equipped kitchen with coffee plunger to champagne flutes. Quality crockery and cutlery, games, books and magazines, heated towel rails, electric blankets, duvets, hair drier, robes, TV and a potbelly ensure your comfort. Enjoy a special breakfast at your leisure in the cottage. Later, join us for complimentary pre-dinner drinks. Fish in the world famous Major Jones or Breakfast Pools adjacent to our boundary, or spend a rewarding day with professional guide Kerry Simpson. It's a forty minutes drive to National Park to tramp in the summer or ski Whakapapa in the winter. Closeby are hot pools, bush walks and golf, or just relax with a book in our beautiful garden. We have travelled extensively and enjoy meeting people. We are enthusiastic gardeners, "helped" by our dachshounds, Minnie and Darcy.

Turangi

Homestay
Address: 8 Arahori Street, Turangi
Name: Gwenethley Homestay -
John and Ailsa Twigg
Telephone: (07) 386 7428
Fax: (07) 386 7428
Mobile: (025) 379 019
Beds: 1 Double, 4 Single (3 Bedrooms)
Bathroom: 1 Private, 1 Family share
Tariff: B&B (Continental) Double $60, Single $40,
Dinner by arrangement.
Nearest Town: Turangi 35 mins south of Taupo on SH1.

Welcome to Gwenethley. We offer modern, comfortable, smokefree accommodation. Our rooms are cleaned daily, bedrooms have alarm radios, heaters, comfortable beds with electric blankets and duvets. TV with tea and coffee making facilities, cookies are provided. Laundry facilities and a drying room for ski equipment plus off road parking. Gwenethley is only 4 minutes walk from Turangi Shopping Centre, restaurants, take-away, bakery, Visitor Centre, bus stop and the Tangariro trout fishing and river walks. The Taupo / Turangi area caters for all interests, skiing, thermal pools, guided lake and river fishing, hunting, 4WD motorbike tours, horse trekking, kayaking, tramping, golf, bowls, scenic flights, sky diving, mountainbike hire, self drive boats, jet boat trips, rafting, bird watching, trout hatchery and much more, or just relax by Lake Taupo. Inspection invited. We aim to please.
Directions: *"Arahori Street" is opposite "Burger King" on SH 1.*

Upper Pukawa Bay, Lake Taupo
Self Contained Cottage

Address: "Paratiho Cottage"
Kowhai Drive, Upper Pukawa Bay.
Postal: PO Box 76, Turangi
Name: John and Valda Milner
Telephone: (07) 386 6318
Fax: (07) 386 6418
Email: john milner@xtra.co.nz
Beds: 2 Kingsize doubles
(converts to 4 Kingsize singles) (2 Bedrooms)
Bathroom: 1 Private. Paraplegic with separate shower and toilet
Tariff: Single party bookings.
Double $100. Two bedrooms $150. Long stay discounts. Children welcome. Pets by arrangement. On request - in cottage Continental breakfast basket $10ea.
In homestead: full breakfast $17.50 each. Dinner $30 each. Credit cards:Visa/Mastercard
Nearest Town: Turangi 13 kms (Omori store 2 kms)

"Paratiho Cottage" built 1996 as a modern holiday cottage with wonderful panoramic day views of Lake Taupo and the magical reflected night lights of Taupo township. Cosy timber lined, large lounge, TV, log fire, French doors onto a large sundeck with outdoor table, lounging chairs and gas BBQ. Equipped for all seasons with full laundry and drier, attached garage and total privacy in a native tree lined section. We are only minutes drive from beautiful safe swimming beaches, boat launching ramps, thermal hot pools, world famous Tongariro River fishing (your host is a retired fly-fishing guide), the many walks of Tongariro National park and Whakapapa Ski field. We provide, on request cooked breakfasts and three course evening dinners in our "Paratiho" homestead, 100 metres from the cottage.
Directions: *Please telephone, fax or e-mail for reservations and directions.*

http://www.bnb.co.nz

take a look

Gisborne and District

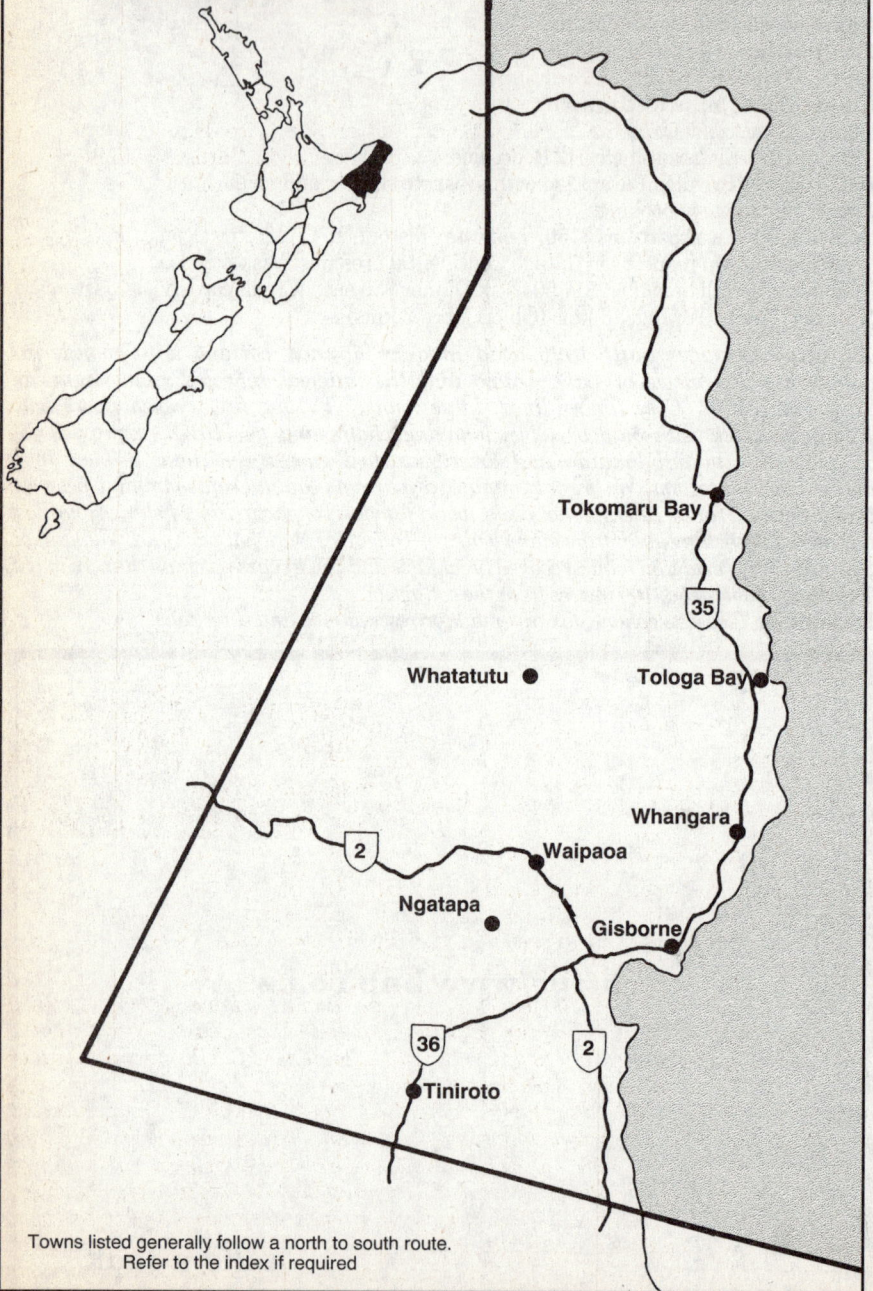

Tokomaru Bay

35

Whatatutu ●

Tologa Bay ●

Whangara ●

2

Waipaoa ●

Ngatapa ●

Gisborne ●

36

2

● Tiniroto

Towns listed generally follow a north to south route.
Refer to the index if required

Tokomaru Bay
Farmstay
Address: 'Tironui', Mata Road, Tokomaru Bay
Name: David & Caroline Jefferd
Telephone: (06) 864 5619
Fax: (06) 864 5620
Email: d.jefferd@xtra.co.nz
Beds: 1 Queen, 1 Single (1 bedroom)
Bathroom: 1 Family share
Tariff: B&B (full) Double $75, Single $50, Children half price. Dinner $25pp, Campervans welcome.   NZ B&B Vouchers accepted. Credit Cards: Visa/M.C.
Nearest Town: 11km from Tokomaru Bay, 84km north of Gisborne

We and our two children live on an 830 hectare sheep and cattle property 12km from the Tokomaru Bay village and beach. The peaceful surroundings and views over the valley and out to sea are a welcome relief to the busy traveller. We have numerous pets and farmyard animals and where possible we will endeavour to show our visitors farm activities that are of particular interest to them.
Tokomaru Bay is a typical East Coast village renowned for its Maori culture and crafts and the wonderful golden sandy beach is still relatively quiet during our long hot summers.
We have a grass tennis court and a swimming pool which guests are welcome to use and who are encouraged to treat their stay as a "home away from home". No smoking inside please.
Directions: *Please phone.*

Tokomaru Bay
Homestay, Farmstay
Address: "Rahiri", 263 Mata Road, Tokomaru Bay, East Coast
Name: Meg and Bill Busby
Telephone: Freephone: 0800-347 411
Fax: (06) 864 5817
Mobile: (025) 246 2619
Email: Info@Rahiri.Com
Beds: 1 Queen, 2 Double, 2 Single (3 Bedrooms)
Bathroom: 1 Ensuite, 1 Private
Tariff: B&B (Full, Special, Continental) Double $120, Single $80, Children welcome 1/2 price, Dinner $40 per head. Credit cards accepted: Visa/M.C.
Nearest Town: Tokomaru Bay 7km. Gisborne 80km.

Welcome to "Rahiri" a gracious 100 year old Homestead situated on Pauariki Station, a 5000 acre sheep and cattle station 7km from Tokomaru Bay on the East Coast of New Zealand's North Island. During the school year you will be hosted by Meg and Bill Busby and their Jack Russell "Sparkey". During school holidays our four children join us. We offer spacious relaxing accommodation for those wanting a break away from a busy stressful life. Enjoy pleasant peaceful surroundings situated amongst mature trees and gardens, with swimming pool, tennis court and wonderful views of Mt Hikurangi, the first landmark to catch the sun rays each new day. Just 5 minutes from the beach in Tokomaru Bay. Fishing trips organised, golf and tramping within easy reach. Open fire places in five rooms including one bedroom, flowers, antique furniture, Alfresco dining in summer, morning tea and / or breakfast in bed a speciality. Dinner includes aperitifs, three course meal, wine included. Laundry facilities available. **Directions**: *Please phone 0800 347 411* **Home Page**: www.rahiri.com

Tolaga Bay
Homestay
Address: 34 Bank Street, Tolaga Bay
Name: "Puketea" Bob & Del
Telephone: (06) 862 6772
Fax: (06) 862 6772
Beds: 2 Double,
3 Single (3 bedrooms)
Bathroom: 2 Guests share
Tariff: B&B (continental)
Double $70, Single $45.
NZ B&B Vouchers accepted
Nearest Town: Gisborne 55 kms

Welcome to our home. Hosts are retired farmers. My wife is a keen gardener and I do part time Real Estate. "Puketea" is a spacious comfortable home built in the 20's high Rimu ceilings are a special feature. You will enjoy our lovely gardens. Our home overlooks the golf course with a peep of the sea. Places of interest are the Cashmere Knitting Co, good fishing with charter boat hire, longest wharf in NZ. Walkway to historic Cooks Cove, walkway to lookout on cliff overlooking Bay and countryside. 5 minutes walk to restaurants, take-aways and hotel. A warm country welcom is assured.
Please phone for reservations. Millenium rates on request. 25.12.99 - 5.1.2000.

Mangatuna, Tolaga Bay
Farmstay/B&B
Address: "Willowflat", Tolaga Bay, SH 35.
Name: June & Allan Hall
Telephone: (06) 862 6341/(06) 862 6848
Fax: (06) 862 6371
Mobile: (025) 923 903
Beds: 1 Double (1 bedroom) - Exta beds by arrangement
Bathroom: 2 Family share (sometimes)
Tariff: B&B (full) Double $75, Single $40, Children half price, Dinner $20,
Campervans $12 (2 people), $16 (4 people).
Nearest Town: Tolaga Bay 12km

"Willowflat" is at Mangatuna on SH35 (the Pacific Coast Highway!) 12km north of Tolaga Bay, an hour's easy drive north of Gisborne.
We have a 200 hectare mixed sheep, cattle and cropping unit including the King Spencer Reserve. Our home is on a rise in spacious grounds, has a conservatory with spa pool (in winter), and set back 100 yards from the Uawa River where there is a good swimming hole.
Our family at home often consists of a son, his daughter and 1 cat.
Within 12km we have 4 beaches (including beautiful Anaura Bay where we own a quiet beachfront section with 2 power points), scenic reserves, Cooks Cove and Anaura Bay Walkways, "Half-Mile Wharf" and the "Hole in the Wall". The village of Tolaga Bay with old English Inn, golf course, bowling green, restaurant, 2 of the 4 beaches, etc., is also within this distance.
Please phone.

Whangara, Gisborne
Farmstay+Self-contained Accom.
Address: Mataurangi Station, Panikau Road, Whangara
Name: Anna & Nick Reed
Telephone: (06) 862 2858
Fax: (06) 862 2857
Email: mataurangi@extra.co.nz
Beds: Cottage: 1 Double, 1 Single (1 bedroom) House: 1 Double, 1 Single (2 bedrooms)
Bathroom: Cottage: 1 Private/House: 1 Private
Tariff: B&B (continental) Double $70, Single $50, Children reduced rate, Dinner $25 pp. Minimum charge for cottage $70. Prices valid to 30/6/00. NZ B&B Vouchers accepted
Nearest Town: Gisborne 50kms

This farmstay is not your ten acre block five minutes from the Central Business District. Mataurangi is a 607 hectare hill country sheep and cattle station situated 14 km up Panikau Road off the Pacific Coast Highway (SH35), between Tolaga Bay and Gisborne.We invite you to come and learn first hand about New Zealand largest industry and enjoy the peace and seclusion of station life. You will stay in "The Roost"; a fully refurbished self contained shepherds cottage (full kitchen facilities, BBQ, sun deck and small garden) where you can prepare your own meals or, if you prefer, walk up through our extensive garden to enjoy a three course, farm fresh dinner with us. While we may be slightly off the beaten track, we know you will enjoy the experience and look forward to meeting you and sharing our corner of New Zealand with you.
Directions: *Please telephone or visit our website.*
Home Page: http://mysite.xtra.co.nz/~mataurangi

Whatatutu, Gisborne
Farmstay
Address: 332 Te Hau Station Road, Whatatutu, via Te Karaka, Gisborne
Name: Chris and Jenny Meban
Telephone: (06) 862 1822
Fax: (06) 862 1997
Mobile: (025) 844 574
Beds: 1 Queen, 1 Double, 2 Single (3 Bedrooms)
Bathroom: 1 Guests share

TE HAU STATION FARMSTAY

Tariff: B&B (Full) Double $80, Single $50, Dinner $25 pp, School-age children half price. Subject to tariff increase. Vouchers accepted $20 surcharge. Credit Cards accepted.
Nearest Town: Gisborne 50 km

Our colonial farmhouse is an easy 40 minute drive from Gisborne, off SH 2 North, on a very good road. We run sheep and Hereford cattle on 4000 acres of hill country, where horses are still used extensively. Riding is available. 4 Wheel drive motor bikes are a great way of seeing our countryside. Walking, clay-bird shooting and hunting are all options, while those who choose to just relax can view our gardens, use our pool, grass tennis court, croquet or petanque. We have a collection of pets and poultry, making this a marvellous experience for children. Our two young sons take pleasure in showing guests around. A nine-hole country golf course, sightseeing to the Tarndale Slip and Marae visits can be arranged. Laundry facilities, Sky TV and a private sitting room with an open fire, are available. No smoking in house please. We welcome you to contact us for enquires and directions.

Waipaoa, Gisborne

Farmstay
Address: 'The Willows' Waipaoa, R.D. 1, Gisborne
Name: Rosemary and Graham Johnson
Telephone: (06) 862 5605
Fax: (06) 862 5601
Mobile: (025) 837 365
Beds: 1 King, 2 Single
(2 Bedrooms)
Bathroom: 1 Guests share
Tariff: B&B (full or continental) Double
$70, Single $50, School children 10% discount,
Dinner $30. NZ B&B Vouchers accepted
Nearest Town: Gisborne 20km

Our home is probably best described in the American Colonial Style with a panelled entry and dining room of our own oak timber milled from trees of which we have some lovely specimens planted by our forefathers. We enjoy the amenities available in the city and also the country life on our 440 acre property involving deer, cattle, sheep, grapes and cropping.We enjoy meeting people and look forward to your visit. We welcome you to have dinner with us, or if you prefer only Bed & Breakfast.We would appreciate if you could ring prior to your arrival. This being the millennium and Gisborne being so strategically advantaged, we are fully booked from the 23rd December 1999 to 5th January 2000.
Directions: *We are situated 20km north of Gisborne on SH2 through to Opotiki and the Bay of Plenty. We have a sign "The Willows" at the end of our driveway above the letter box with the number 1809 close by. A good landmark is the curved Kaiteratahi Bridge and we are 1 km north of that. Our house is white with a black tiled roof situated on a hill overlooking the Waipaoa River.*

Gisborne

Homestay
Address: 159 The Esplanade, Gisborne
Name: Alec & Barbara Thomson
Telephone: (06) 868 9675 or 0800 370 505
Fax: (06) 868 9675
Beds: 1 Double, 2 Single (2 bedrooms)
Bathroom: 1 Guest share - 2 Separate toilets
Tariff: B&B (full) Double $70, Single $50, Dinner $20. (Tariff of 10% discount for any bowlers staying with us when participating in local tournaments). NZ B&B Vouchers accepted
Nearest Town: Gisborne 3-4 mins walk.

Our home is situated overlooking the Waimata River, with river views from each guest room.
We are also a short and pleasant walking distance from the city shopping area, Museum and Art Centre and Lawson Field Theatre, where Gisborne stages many entertaining productions.
Alec and I enjoy meeting people and we look forward to welcoming all who wish to spend time with us.
Off street parking is available.
We are both active members of lawn and indoor bowling clubs.
We also enjoy a game of bridge.

Gisborne
Homestay
Address: 'Fawnridge',
29 Richardson Ave, Gisborne
Name: Kathlyn & Bryan Thompson
Telephone: (06) 868 8823
Fax: (06) 867 6902
Beds: 1 Queen, 2 Single (2 bedrooms)
Bathroom: 1 Ensuite, 1 Private
Tariff: B&B (continental) Double $100-$120,
Single $95, Dinner by prior arrangement.
NZ B&B Vouchers accepted Surcharge $35
Nearest Town: Gisborne 2km

Welcome to Fawnridge set on a private semi rural hill site with sweeping views of Young Nicks Head and City (an easy walk to) but with the tranquillity of country living. We are a working couple with one cat.
Twin bedroom opens onto a private garden deck and each adjoining lounge with TV is exclusively for our guests who are welcome to refreshments at any time.
We are happy to offer an evening meal (venison specialty) by prior arrangement although we can recommend several excellent restaurants nearby.
After your arrival relax in our indoor spa, enjoy the view or take a short walk to view the deer. Brochures on our beautiful area are provided. A must to see is Eastwood Hill Aboretum approx. 20 mins drive.
Our home is smokefree and we request you phone the evening prior to your arrival. Bryan and I look forward to meeting you.

Gisborne
Farmstay
Address: 'Wairakaia Farmstay",
1894 State Highway 2 (South), Gisborne
Name: Rodney & Sarah Faulkner
Telephone: (06) 862 8607
Freephone: 0800 329 060
Fax: (06) 862 8607
Beds: 1 King/Twin,
1 Queen (2 bedrooms)
Bathroom: 1 Ensuite, 1 Private
Tariff: B&B (special) Double $90,
Single $60, Children half price,
Dinner $30. Credit cards
Nearest Town: Gisborne North 25km,
Wairoa South 75km.

We are a semi-retired couple whose interests include travelling, cooking, reading, music, woodworking and gardening. Our home has been the centre of farm and family life since it was built by Rodney's Grandparents in 1905. It is surrounded by a large and ever expanding informal garden. We live on a 1600 acre sheep, beef and forestry farm. Rodney has a wealth of knowledge on the ecology and history of the area which he is happy to share with you.
Breakfast is SPECIAL and is served in the sunporch overlooking the bay. Join us for an evening meal and enjoy our excellent home grown produce and the local award winning cheeses. Relax in our comfortable home. Meet our two cats and Lewis the corgi who will give you a warm but noisy welcome. We are all non smokers. Laundry facilities are available as is our tennis court. Families welcome.

317

Gisborne

Farmstay
Address: Hihiroroa Rd, Ngatapa, Gisborne
Name: Sally & Andrew Jefferd
Telephone: (06) 867 1313
Beds: 1 Double (1bedroom)
Bathroom: 1 Ensuite
Tariff: B&B (full) Double $70, Single $40, Dinner $20. NZ B&B Vouchers accepted
Nearest Town: Gisborne 40 Kms west of Gisborne

We live 5 minutes drive from the famous Eastwood Hill Arboretum. Eastwood Hill is internationally recognized comprising 65 hectares of numerous varieties of trees and shrubs, it is a rewarding experience at any time of the year. We have a 1000 acre hill country property, farming sheep and cattle. We offer our guests separate accommodation with ensuite just a few metres from the main house, giving them the privacy they may desire. We have a tennis court and a swimming pool which the guests are welcome to use. Golf is easily arranged with two courses nearby. We love meeting people and you can be assured of warm and generous hospitality. Reservations:
Free phone 0800 469 4401313
Directions: *Please phone for directions.*

Gisborne

Homestay
Address: "Sea View",
68 Salisbury Road, Gisborne
Name: Raewyn & Gary Robinson
Telephone: (06) 867 3879
Fax: (06) 867 5879
Email: raewyn@regaleggs.co.nz
Beds: 2 Double, 1 Single (2 bedrooms)
Bathroom: 2 Private
Tariff: B&B (continental) Double $85,
Single $60, Children under 12 half price,
under 5 free.
Nearest Town: Gisborne City 1.3km (2 minutes by car)

We welcome you to our modern beachfront home situated 50 metres from the waters edge, offering safe swimming, surfing and beautiful beaches. Our home is 4 mins by car from the City Centre, 2 golf courses and Tepid Olympic Pool. It is 5 mins walk to the Information Centre and bus depot.
We offer two double bedrooms, one with an extra single bed, TV and kitchenette facilities. All beds have electric blankets. Both bedrooms have their own private bathrooms. A babies cot and highchair are available.
We have both travelled extensively overseas and get great pleasure in meeting people. We look forward to you enjoying our hospitality and home comforts. Our home is smoke free.

Gisborne
Beachstay
Address: 111 Wairere Road,
Wainui Beach, Gisborne
Name: Peter & Dorothy Rouse
Telephone: (06) 868 8111
or (06) 864 7748
Fax: (06) 868 8162
Mobile: (025) 794 929
Beds: 1 Queen, 2 Double,
2 Single (2 bedrooms)
Bathroom: 1 Ensuite, 1 Private
Tariff: B&B (full) Double $70, Single $45,
Children $10, Dinner $20pp,
Campervans facilities.
NZ B&B Vouchers accepted
Nearest Town: Gisborne 5km

We live 5km out of Gisborne, "worlds first city to see the sun".
We welcome you to our home which is situated right on the beach front at Wainui.
The steps from the lawn lead down to the beach, which is renowned for its lovely clean sand, surf, pleasant walking and good swimming.
Gisborne can also offer a host of entertainment including golf on one of NZ's finest golf courses, charter fishing trips, wine trails, Eastwood Hill Arboretum, horse trekking etc. Or you may wish to relax on the beach for the day with light luncheon provided.

Gisborne
Self Contained Accommodation
Address: "All Seasons near the Sea",
4 Roberts Road, Gisborne
Name: Jan Ewart and Marie Burgess
Telephone: (06) 862 7505
Fax: (06) 862 7580
Mobile: (025) 419 424
Email: meb@clear.net.nz
Beds: 1 Queen, 1 Double, 2 Single (3 bedrooms)
Bathroom: 1 Guests share
Tariff: B&B (provisions provided) $150-$200 per night,
weekly by arrangemen. (increased rates over millenium period)
Nearest Town: Gisborne, 1.5km to Post Office

THE HOME: All Seasons near the sea is a 3 bedroom fully furnished, self contained home ideal for a family holiday or sharing with friends. Amenities include a deck with outdoor furniture, gas barbecue and a double garage. Inside a cosy Kent woodburning fire, TV/Video and CD player. Complimentary breakfast provisions and a sample of our local products are provided. The nearest store is 5 minutes walk away.
THE AREA: All Seasons near the sea is 2 minutes walk from Waikanae Beach, and close to golf courses, Olympic Pool, Museum and Art Gallery, restaurants and cafes, shops, rivers, parks and swimming and surfing beaches. Gisborne has many interesting places to visit in close proximity including Eastwood Hill Arboretum, East Coast beaches, marae, gardens, wineries and picnic spots Whatever the season, whatever the reason you are very welcome to stay at All Seasons.

Gisborne

Farmstay/SC Accom
Address: 457 Pehiri Road, Gisborne
Name: Waikoke Country Walks & Farmstay
Telephone: (06) 863 7069
Fax: (06) 863 7006
Mobile: (021) 315 215
Beds: 1 Double, 3 Single (4 bedrooms).
Also S/C Lodge sleeps up to 10 people.
Bathroom: 1 Guests share
Tariff: B&B (full) Double $60,
Single $45, Children $30, Dinner $30 pp.
NZ B&B Vouchers accepted
Nearest Town: Gisborne 30 minutes

We warmly welcome visitors to our family home. Alfresco eating tennis, farm activities or total relaxing is the order of the day.
Easy driving into Gisborne city, the beaches, wineries, fishing and local culture with the famous Eastwood Hill Aboretum a twenty minute drive away. Since that last edition of the NZ Bed & Breakfast book we have renovated a ten bed, self contained accommodation premises and created a two day walk to Eastwood Hill, with an overnight stay in their brand new accommodation block. The walk takes you over four farms to Eastwood Hill and a different route returning the next day. All meals and bedding provided if desired. Please do not hesitate to contact us for more information. We welcome children who will get a lot of pleasure form our pets. Kennel available for your own pet.

Gisborne

Homestay & Gallery
Address: 'Studio 4',
4 Heta Road, Gisborne
Name: Judy and Gavin Smith
Telephone: (06) 868 1571
Fax: (06) 868 1457
Beds: 1 Queen, 3 Single (2 bedrooms)
Bathroom: 1 Family Share,
1 Guests Share
Tariff: B&B (continental) Double $75
Single $55, Dinner $25 pp.
Credit Cards accepted.
Nearest Town: Gisborne (8 minutes walk)

Welcome to our American-style character home set amongst old English trees in peaceful surroundings, backing on to Gisborne's most beautiful park and river. We are situated just a very short walk (approximately 8 minutes) to the Central shopping area, the Museum and Arts Centre, the 'Wharf' area and most of Gisborne's highly recommended restaurants. Off street parking is available.
Gavin is a well-known local artist and we have a small gallery where original local and other paintings, prints and cards may be viewed or purchased at your leisure.
We have travelled widely ourselves and enjoy meeting and sharing our home with others.
Directions: *Please ring if possible prior to arrival for directions.*

Gisborne
Exclusive Accommodation
Address: 9 Cleary Road,
Wainui Beach, Gisborne
Name: Big Tree Hideaway
Telephone: (06) 868 5867
Fax: (06) 868 5857
Email: glen.kim@bigtree.co.nz
Beds: 1 King, 1 Queen (2 Bedrooms)
Bathroom: 2 Ensuite
Tariff: B&B (Special) Double $160/$140,
Single $120, Credit cards Visa/Mastercard
Nearest Town: Gisborne 5 mins.

5 minutes North of Gisborne on Eastland's scenic Pacific Coast Highway (SH35), the road meets beautiful Wainui Beach. Here you will find Big Tree Hideaway, accommodation in a renovated historic shearer's cottage, affectionately called "The Shearertin". A mature garden setting, with the Big Tree as a focal point, under which guests can enjoy the hot spa. Each room is tastefully furnished with country furniture and has a fridge, stereo, tea and coffee making facilities including a coffee plunger and biscuits. (TV and phone available by request.) Fresh flowers, chocolates and books in guests rooms. "Shearers" special breakfast served in guests' room, on verandah or with us. Picnic baskets available for champagne sunrise breakfast or lunches. Walk along the beach, visit the lighthouse, swim, surf, play tennis on the adjacent courts, horse trekking or just relax and enjoy the all day sun. Visit local working artists and crafts people or stroll down the road to the cafe/bar.

Gisborne
Self Contained Accommodation
Address: Richardson's Bed & Breakfast
519 Nelson Road, Gisborne
Name: Karen and Vance Richardson
Telephone: (06) 867 2441
Fax: (06) 867 4841
Mobile: (025) 268 5945
Beds: 1 Queen, 2 Single (2 Bedrooms)
Bathroom: 1 Guests Share.
Tariff: B&B (Full) Double $85, Single $55,
Dinner $25pp if convenient,
Children under 12 years half price.
Credit Cards accepted: Visa/Mastercard.
NZ B&B Vouchers accepted $25 surcharge
Nearest Town: Gisborne

Our home is on the outskirts of Gisborne. We enjoy country life, with the central city five minutes drive away. We offer casual, private, self-contained accommodation, plenty of parking, sunny gardens to relax in, pool in summer, open fire in winter. Breakfast is self-catering. Dinner can either be served in your suite, you may join our family or we can recommend a cafe or restaurant.
Gisborne has many attractions, we can suggest what may appeal and help to organise tours etc. Vance is a keen golfer and trout fisherman. We also have various other interests. Our three children are at various stages of leaving home, we also have a dog and cat. Children are welcome, we have a cot and highchair available.
No smoking inside please.

Gisborne
Homestay
Address: 36 Sirrah Street,
Wainui Beach, Gisborne
Name: Roger and Morag Shanks
Telephone: (06) 867 0806
Fax: (06) 868 7706
Beds: 1 Double,
3 Single (2 Bedrooms)
Bathroom: 1 Private,
1 Guests share
Tariff: B&B (full/continental)
Double $100, Single $50,
Dinner $20pp by prior arrangment.
Credit Cards accepted.
Nearest Town: Gisborne 8 km

Our home is 1/2 km off Highway 35 at the northern end of Wainui Beach, with beautiful sea and sunrise views, surrounded by farmland and handy to bush and coastal walkway. We have travelled overseas so enjoy the company of others. Gisborne city and outlying areas have a host of activities. Horse trekking, fishing trips, country excursions by arrangement. We have one friendly small dog not allowed indoors.

Ngatapa, Gisborne
Homestay
Address: 'Manurere',
1405 Main Ngatapa Road, Ngatapa
Name: John and Joanne Sherratt
Telephone: (06) 863 9852
Fax: (06) 863 9842
Email: john.sherratt@xtra.co.nz
Beds: 1 Queen, 1 Single (1 bedroom)
Bathroom: 1 Ensuite
Tariff: B&B (full) Double $80, Single $50,
Dinner $20 pp. Credit Cards accepted +
surcharge of 5%.
NZ B&B Vouchers accepted $12 surcharge
Nearest Town: Gisborne (24km)

We have a lovely old villa in a peaceful setting in an old established country garden only 20 minutes away from the city centre and beaches.
We have a tennis court and swimming pool available for use in season. John runs our sheep and beef farm and we enjoy meeting people and regard homestaying as a wonderful way of achieving this by sharing our home and hospitality with others. Come and enjoy the Ngatapa Valley. Experience our famous 'Eastwoodhill Aboretum" 5 minutes away, and also craft barn, local artists, woodcraft and furniture makers. Reservations by appointment only.

Tiniroto, Gisborne
Farmstay/Self-contained Home
Address: Rongoio Farm Stay,
Ruakaka Rd, Tiniroto, Gisborne
Name: Matt & Jude Stock
Telephone: (06) 867 4065
Fax: (06) 863 7018
Email: patstock at clear.net.nz
Beds: 1 King, 1 Queen, 2 Single (3 bedrooms)
Bathroom: 1 Private
Tariff: B&B (full) Double $100, Single $80,
Children $20, Dinner $30.
Surcharge for 1 night $10.
NZ B&B Vouchers accepted $25 surcharge
Nearest Town: 60km between Gisborne/Wairoa appox 50 mins

Join us on our 440 hectare hill country sheep and beef property and enjoy all that rural NZ life offers. Very close to the homestead but secluded by established trees is a three bedroom totally self contained home that sleeps up to six guests. From this cosy home feel the remote peace and tranquillity along with the magnificent views of the trout filled Hangaroa River and waterfall. At Rangoio we encourage guests to participate in rural activities inc. fishing, wild game shooting, horse and motor bike riding, possum shooting and eeling. Within our small Tiniroto Community is the Hackfalls Arboretum renowned for its huge selection of Mexican Oak Trees. Guides tours available Lake Waikaremoana 3/4 hr drive away. Guests are welcome to enjoy the very best of home cuisine, locally grown cheese and wine. Warm friendly back country hospitality is our specialty.
Directions: *Please phone for bookings along with directions.*
Home Page: http://members.tripod.com/~tony-ford/

http://www.bnb.co.nz

take a look

Taranaki, Wanganui Rangitikei

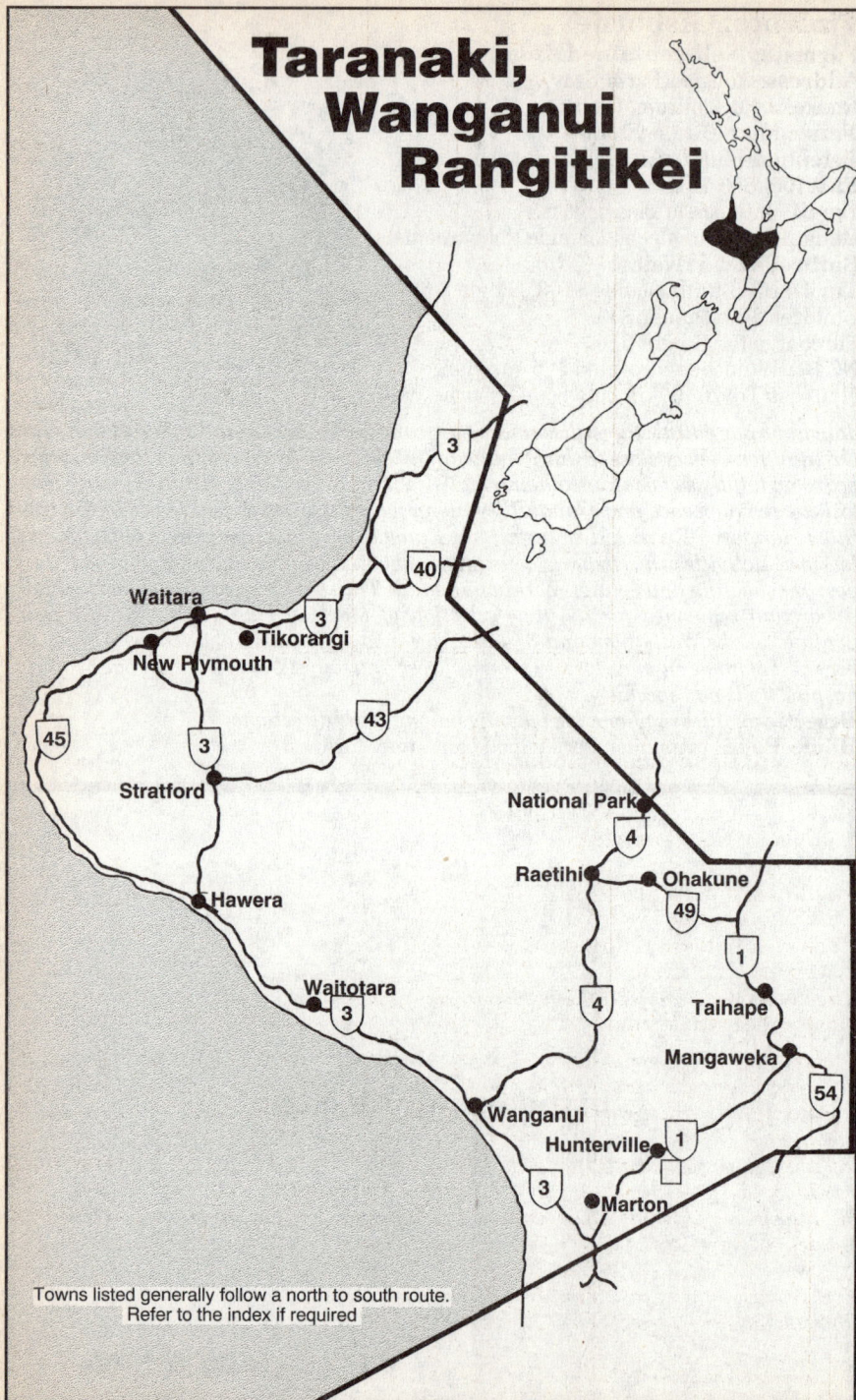

3

40

Waitara

3

Tikorangi

New Plymouth

45

43

3

Stratford

National Park

4

Raetihi

Ohakune

49

Hawera

1

Waitotara

4

Taihape

3

Mangaweka

54

Wanganui

Hunterville

1

3

Marton

Towns listed generally follow a north to south route.
Refer to the index if required

Waitara

Farmstay
Address: 31 Tikorangi Road West, 43 R.D. Waitara
Name: John & Anne Megaw
Telephone: (06) 754 6768
Beds: 1 Double, 2 Single (2 bedrooms)
Bathroom: 1 Guests share
Tariff: B&B (full) Double $60, Single $40, Dinner $15. NZ B&B Vouchers accepted
Nearest Town: Waitara 8 Kms, New Plymouth 20 minutes

Our three bedroomed cosy brick house is situated on a hill with panoramic views of Mt Egmont, the Waitara River Valley farmlands and a glimpse of the sea and is 8 kilometres from Highway 3 turnoff. We live on a dairy farm where we milk 180 cows, and have shade houses for begonias and ferns. Visitors are welcome to participate in any farm activities, or wander to the river or up on the hills if they wish. Taranaki has much to offer scenically with parks and gardens, the mountain and coastline plus numerous walkways. The McKee Energy Field, Waitara Petrolgas, and Motonui Synfuel Plants are all close to Waitara.
Directions: *Travel on Highway 3 to Waitara, turn inland to Tikorangi on Princess St to Ngatimaru Road. Continue to very end of Ngatimaru Road, 8 kms from turnoff Highway 3 and turn right on no exit road. Our house is No. 31.*

Tikorangi/New Plymouth

Self Contained Accommodation
Address: Tikorangi Road, RD 43, Waitara
Name: Paul and Shelley Carrington
Telephone: (06) 754 4282
Fax: (06) 754 4282
Mobile: (025) 970 814
Email: pcarrington.rmy.co.nz
Beds: Self Contained Cottage: 1 Double (1 Bedroom)
Bathroom: 1 Private
Tariff: Double $50 NZ B&B Vouchers accepted
Nearest Town: Waitara

"Ashby Cottage" set in six acres of park-like grounds is a self contained cottage with bedroom / lounge, separate kitchen and bathroom. The cottage provides total privacy and seclusion with a large deck opening into the garden which is surrounded by farmland.
We live 15 minutes drive from New Plymouth with an excellent golf course within 2 minutes.
We have two garden nurseries within walking distance and the famous Duncan & Davies Nursery down the road.

Feel free to use the grass tennis court in the garden.
We look forward to your visit.

New Plymouth
Homestay
Address: 30 Heta Road,
Highlands Park,
New Plymouth
Name: Gerry & Beryl Paulin
Telephone: (06) 758 2900
Beds: 1 Double, 2 Single
 (2 bedrooms)
Bathroom: 1 Guests share
Tariff: B&B (full) Double $60, Single $40,
Dinner $20pp. NZ B&B Vouchers accepted
Nearest Town: New Plymouth City centre 5km

Welcome to our home! We are a cheerful outgoing retired couple with time to look after you. Our comfortable, modern, sunny home in a quiet suburb, has mountain, sea and rural views. We have been hosting with "the Book" since 1988 and have enjoyed meeting people from many countries. We love to hear about your journeys and your home country while relaxing with a glass of wine and a leisurely dinner. We have travelled extensively overseas and know New Zealand well from Cape Reinga to Stewart Island. As retired cut flower growers our interests are gardens, horticulture generally and our own garden. Gerry has a special interest in Pukeiti Rhododendron Trust Gardens and he relaxes on the golf course. Beryl enjoys needlework, porcelain painting, flower arranging and cooking. She is also a Kiwi host.
We look forward to sharing our home with you.
Directions: *Please phone*

New Plymouth
Homestay
Address: 'Blacksmith's Rest',
481 Mangorei Road, New Plymouth
Name: Evelyn & Laurie Cockerill
Telephone: (06) 758 6090
Fax: (06) 758 6078
Mobile: 025-375880
Beds: 2 Queen, 2 Single (2 bedrooms)
Bathroom: 1 Ensuite, 1 Guest share
Tariff: B&B (Full) Double $60-$65, Single $40, Dinner $20.
NZ B&B Vouchers accepted
Nearest Town: New Plymouth centre 6km

New Zealand Association FARM & HOME HOSTS

Welcome to New Plymouth. Our home is situated next to Tupare Gardens which is owned and operated by the Queen Elizabeth II Trust.
From our spacious home you can enjoy glorious sunsets and panoramic rural views although we are just five minutes drive from New Plymouth City.
Each guest room has a Queen and Single bed with an ensuite in the upstairs bedroom and a separate bathroom downstairs.
We enjoy meeting travellers from far and wide, sharing experieces and having a laugh together in a relaxed atmosphere.
We have a large garden, some sheep and a friendly dog called Bill who lives outside. We are a retired couple with a grown up family.
There is plenty of off street parking.
Mangorei Road can be easily found when approaching New Plymouth from north or south off SH 3.

New Plymouth
Homestay
Address: Brooklands Bed & Breakfast,
39 Plympton Street, Brooklands,
New Plymouth
Name: Neal Spragg
Telephone: (06) 753 2265
Beds: 1 Queen, 2 Single (2 bedrooms)
Bathroom: 1 Private
Tariff: B&B (continental) Double $60,
Single $35. NZ B&B Vouchers accepted
Nearest Town: New Plymouth centre 2km

My home is located in a peaceful and tranquil setting overlooking a bush clad walkway leading to the renowned Pukekura and Brooklands Parks. The guest wing consists of bathroom and toilet facilities, two bedrooms, one queen size and the other a twin room. I request no smoking in the house.
Being only minutes from central city you may choose to spend time at our museum, art gallery or library or perhaps take in a movie at the cinema complex. Also nearby and worthy of a visit are the sports stadium, aquatic centre, harbour and beaches.
Taranaki offers a unique diversity of attractions and landscapes, the picturesque Mount Egmont, expansive views of the Tasman Sea, beautiful parks, rhododendron gardens, rich dairy farmlands and energy fields.
I enjoy sharing my comfortable home with visitors from abroad and New Zealand travellers. I offer you a warm and friendly welcome and a relaxed stay in New Plymouth.

New Plymouth
Homestay
Address: 11 Tamati Place,
Merrilands, New Plymouth
Name: Evelyn & Ashley Howan
Telephone: (06) 758 8932
Beds: 1 Double, 4 Single (3 bedrooms)
Bathroom: 1 Guests share,
Tariff: B&B (continental)
Double + Twin $60,
Single $35. Credit cards. NZ B&B Vouchers accepted
Nearest Town: New Plymouth 4km

We warmly welcome you to our comfortable modern home. Situated in a quiet cul-de-sac, it is easily found from both Northern and Southern approaches to New Plymouth, via Mangorei Road. We are an active retired couple who enjoy meeting people and making new friends. A refreshing cup of tea / coffee is always available, and we really aim to make you feel comfortable and 'at home'. We also have a policy of 'No Smoking' in the house.
Mt Egmont / Taranaki dominates the landscape and forms a majestic and beautiful backdrop to the city, and our home.
Within the city boundary and district, attractions include pleasant coastal and riverside walks, parks, garden tours, art galleries, museums, a very popular Aquatic Centre, great surfing, big game fishing, mountain climbing, walks and skiing, and the renowned Pukeiti Rhododendron gardens.
Evening meals can be enjoyed at a variety of good restaurants, including several ethnic options.

New Plymouth
Farmstay
Address: 1602 Carrington Road,
R.D. 1, New Plymouth
Name: Mountain Dew Farm
Telephone: (06) 753 5123
Mobile: (025) 423 789
Email: m_g.rivers@clear.net.nz
Beds: 2 Queen, 2 Single (2 bedrooms)
Bathroom: Separate Guest with Bath/Shower, Laundry available.
Tariff: B&B (full) Double $75, Single $45, Children N/A, Dinner $20pp.
NZ B&B Vouchers accepted Vouchers not accepted between 20 October-1 December
Nearest Town: New Plymouth 16km.

*If you're looking for a place to spread out and rest or meditate in picturesque, peaceful surroundings, ours is your place. Our accommodation on our dairy farm is situated upstairs. From our large home one gets panoramic views south to Mt Taranaki, north towards the city and Tasman sea, and on a clear day east to Mt Ruapehu National Park. Accommodation includes large sunny lounge, TV and self contained kitchen with microwave. Near Pukeiti Rhododendron park (10 day Festival held end October yearly), private zoo, 18 hole golf course. Only 15 minute pleasant drive to New Plymouth city. Come and explore 'the Best in the West'. Walk on a mountain trail and within the hour paddle in the Tasman Sea. Huggable cats Epo, Jasmine and Dixie the poodle share our home and we have an ever-friendly cattle dog called Danny. Active, well travelled, outdoor hosts, non smokers. Adults only please. **Directions**: Please phone for reservations and directions*

New Plymouth
Bed & Breakfast
Address: 161 Powderham Street,
New Plymouth
Name: Balconies
Telephone: (06) 757 8866
Fax: (06) 759-9366
Mobile: (025) 423 789
Beds: 3 Queen,
2 Single (3 bedrooms)
Bathroom: 1 Guest share
Tariff: B&B (special)
Double $70, Single $50,
Credit cards. NZ B&B Vouchers accepted
Nearest Town: Short walking distance to City centre

Vivien & Trevor invite you to stay with them in New Plymouth.
Balconies is nestled amongst mature trees and lovely gardens in the heart of the city, just 5 min walk to city centre. Our warm, comfortable 110 year old character-style home, offers three tastefully decorated guest rooms, large guest bathroom with claw-foot bath, separate toilet facilities and spacious guest lounge with tea & coffee making facilities. Heated guest rooms are downstairs, beds are queen size and have electric blankets. We ask guests not to smoke indoors. Laundry facilities, courtesy transport and off street parking available. Within walking distance are the art gallery, library and museum, Heritage walkways, indoor pool complex and beautiful Pukekura and Brooklands Park. Unwind in the peaceful surroundings of Balconies, we will ensure you have a comfortable night's rest. You will be served a generous fully cooked breakfast.

New Plymouth
Bed & Breakfast Inn
Address: 'Henwood House',
314 Henwood Road, R.D.2 New Plymouth
Name: Lynne & Graeme Axten
Telephone: (06) 755 1212
Fax: (06) 755 1212
Mobile: (025) 248 4051
Email: henwood.house@xtra.co.nz
Beds: 3 Queen, 4 Single (5 Bedrooms)
Bathroom: 3 Ensuite, 1 Guests share

Henwood House - Built 1890 -

Tariff: B&B (full) Double $95-$120, Single $80-$105, Dinner $30, Credit cards
(VISA/MC/AMEX). NZ B&B Vouchers accepted $25 surcharge
Nearest Town: 5km north of New Plymouth.

Henwood House nestles in 2 acres of landscaped grounds. We have extensively restored our homestead to a very high standard with all modern conveniences, yet retaining the romantic charm of the late Victorian era.
Relax in our grand guest lounge with high ceilings, wooden floors, panelling and open fires. Tall French doors open onto wide verandahs which overlook the gardens.
Upstairs are five spacious elegantly furnished bedrooms with quality beds and antique furniture. The Fitzroy Suite features its own fireplace and balcony with views over the countryside to the sea. Guests have their own tea and coffee making facilities. A variety of delicious breakfasts are served in our large country kitchen.
We share our home with our teenage daughter Lauren, Basil a Golden Retriever and Smokey the cat. We ask guests not to smoke indoors.
Directions: *3km up Henwood Road off SH3 from Bell Block, phone for further directions.*

New Plymouth
Homestay - "Kirkstall House"
Address: 8 Baring Terrace,
New Plymouth
Name: Ian Hay & Lindy MacDiarmid
Telephone: (06) 758 3222
Fax: (06) 758 3224
Email: kirkstall@xtra.co.nz
Beds: 2 Queen, 1 Twin, 1 Single (4 bedrooms)
Bathroom: 1 Ensuite, 1 Private , 1 Guest Share.
Tariff: B&B (full) Ensuite: Double $90, Single $70.
Private Bathroom: Double $80, Single $60.
Bathroom Shared: Double $70, Single $50. Dinner $25 pp.
NZ B&B Vouchers accepted plus additional $10 per night,Credit Cards: Visa/M.C.
Nearest Town: City Centre 1 km

"Kirkstall House" invites you to experience its old world beauty and comfort, in an atmosphere of easy hospitality and relaxed surroundings. Only minutes from New Plymouth's central business and shopping area, "Kirkstall House" offers the quiet serenity of its superb views, its rambling English Garden running down to the Te Henui River and the attractive walkways to the beach.
Ian, your host, has a wealth of knowledge in the travel industry and now operates a small tour business specialising in local tours. With his friendly relaxed manner, his help is invaluable to guests. Lindy loves her home and garden and enjoys producing the individual touches that make "Kirkstall House" a home to share with you. Lindy is also a practising physiotherapist. "The warmth of an open fire in the winter, a family cat sprawled in the sun - "Kirkstall House" really is a home away from home.

Omata, New Plymouth
Bed & Breakfast
Address: Rangitui Orchard, Waireka Rd,
R.D.4, Omata, New Plymouth
Name: Tony & Therese Waghorn
Telephone: (06) 751 2979
Email: twaghorn@taranaki.ac.nz
Beds: 1 Queen, 2 Single (2 bedrooms)
Bathroom: 1 Ensuite, 1 Private
Tariff: B&B (full)
Chalet:Double $70, Single $65;
House: Double $50, Single $45. Dinner $30 by arrangement.
Credit Cards Mastercard/Visa NZ B&B Vouchers accepted
Nearest Town: New Plymouth 10 mins

Come and stay with us on an established Macadamia nut orchard, only 10 minutes from New Plymouth city. Accommodation consists of a chalet, with ensuite, Queen bed, TV and balcony overlooking bush and sea (separate from the house) and a twin room with guest facilities in our house. We serve continental or cooked breakfasts of your choice (except kippers!) in your room or in our kitchen. Depending on orchard commitments we can offer guests dinner with wine ($30 per head) or perhaps recommend a suitable restaurant. Enjoy bush or orchard walks, and perhaps a swim in our pool, or visit some of the local attractions nearby; e.g. climbing or walking on beautiful Mt. Taranaki; some of the best surf in the world; famous gardens; art gallery and museum; historic Maori sites and excellent golf courses. We have travelled extensively, and enjoy returning some of the wonderful hospitality we have experienced all over the world. "RANGITUI" - Country peace so close to the city!
Directions: *Please telephone for reservations and directions.*

New Plymouth
Homestay/Farmlet
Address: Birdhaven, 26 Pararewa Drive,
New Plymouth
Name: Ann & John Butler and Cedric our cat.
Telephone: (06) 751 0432
FREEPHONE 0800 306449 (bookings)
Fax: (06) 751 3475
Beds: 1 Queen, 2 Singles (2 bedrooms)
Bathroom: 1 Guests share
Tariff: B&B (special) Double $80,
Single $55-$60, Dinner by arrangement.
10% discount 2 or more nights (by direct booking and cash payment).
Credit cards accepted. NZ B&B Vouchers accepted
Nearest Town: 5.5km to city.

We have lived in England, South Africa and New Zealand and love to travel. We really enjoy welcoming different people to Birdhaven and endeavouring to exceed their varying expectations. Ensuring your comfort and pleasure is most important to us. This is reflected in the quality furnishings in the inviting guest rooms and throughout the house, the complimentary refreshments and the special breakfast of fresh seasonal and home-made temptations. Come and share the tranquillity and space of our comfortable, tastefully refurbished home. Relax in the gardens, in the sun room or on one of the patios overlooking the flight paths of numerous birds as they flit amongst the trees. Stroll down to the duck pond and delight in the native bush, marsh and woodlands within our three acre farmlet. We want you to feel at home, relax and share our appreciation of beautiful Taranaki and our spectacular view of Mt Egmont.
Directions: *Please phone (we will collect you if required).*

New Plymouth
Farmstay
Address: 248 Junction Road,
RD1, New Plymouth
Name: Oak Valley Manor
Telephone: (06) 7581501
Fax: (06) 7581052
Mobile: (025) 420 325
Email: KAURI.HOLDINGS@XTRA.CO.NZ
Beds: 2 Queen, 1 Single (2 bedrooms)
Bathroom: 2 Ensuite
Tariff: B&B (full) Double $95.00 to $125.00,
Single $65, Children half price. Dinner $30.
Credit cards. Pets welcome. Vouchers accepted Surcharge $30
Nearest Town: New Plymouth centre 6km.

Your hosts, Pat and Paul, two warm and friendly people with a wealth of experience in the hospitality industry, invite you to a unique romantic bed and breakfast in their beautifully appointed home with views from each room of the Tasman Sea or Mount Egmont. These beautiful views make an impression which will be everlasting. We have a five acre farmlet with animals for you to enjoy - ostriches, donkeys, deer and several species of wildfowl. We offer guests the use of our family room, lounge and library and newly developed garden with many exciting features. Only a short distance from the world famous Tupare Gardens, Branch Road Winery and 5 minutes away from Pukekura Park, Brooklands Bowl, Westown Golf Course and New Plymouth's lovely garden facilities. Also several beautiful beaches are close at hand. We look forward to meeting you and enjoying your company. Guests are asked not to smoke indoors.

New Plymouth
Heritage Homestay
Address: Hirst Cottage
Name: Daphne
Telephone: (06) 757 9667
Fax: (06) 757 9667
Beds: 1 King, 1 Double,
1 Twin (3 bedrooms)
Bathroom: 1 Private, 1 Guest share
Tariff: B&B (full/continental) Private bathroom: King $80, Double $75, Single $45, Dinner $25 pp, Share bathroom: Double $70, Twin $75.
NZ B&B Vouchers accepted $10 surcharge
Nearest Town: New Plymouth , walking distance 5- 10 minutes.

Hirst Cottage is one of New Plymouth's historic homes. Built in 1862, it is situated in tranquil parklike surroundings, close to the city centre & Pukekura Park. The house is being extensively renovated and offers a comfortable and relaxing stay.
We have large sunny bedrooms with private bathroom and use of our lounge. Our breakfast includes homemade bread, cereal, yoghurt etc, and is served at a time to suit you. We have many interests and cooking is one of my hobbies. I would be happy to cook dinner for you. Prior notice please.
We share our smoke free environment with our old dachshund and two cats and they will make you most welcome.
We look forward to welcoming you and offering you a memorable stay.
Directions: *For reservations and detailed directions, please phone. Ample off street parking and easy access.*

331

New Plymouth
Self-contained Accommodation
Address: Cottage by the Sea
66 Lower Turangi Road, Motunui
Name: Nancy & Hugh Mills
Telephone: (06) 754 7915
Fax: (06) 754 4544
Email: nancy.mills@taranaki.ac.nz
Beds: 2 Double (bedroom, 1 lounge)
Bathroom: 1 Ensuite
Tariff: B&B (continental) Double $95 ($80 excluding breakfast), Single $75.
Each additional person $35 ($27 excluding breakfast). Children negotiable.
Nearest Town: New Plymouth - 25km north of NP, 1k off State Hway 3.

Cottage by the Sea
Go to sleep with the sound of the waves - wake with the birds. This lovely, peaceful cottage is nestled amongst landscaped gardens and lawns.
It offers complete privacy and is self-sufficient with one bedroom (double bed), ensuite and fully equipped kitchen. The comfortable sofa bed in the lounge can sleep two additional guests.
A 2 minute bushwalk down 100 steps takes you to the beach for a leisurely stroll. Enjoy a fun game of tennis on the grass court, request a private tour of our small commercial flower business, relax on the veranda looking out to spectacular and ever-changing sea views, or bring your surfcasting gear. Breakfast includes seasonal fruit, and a choice of homemade scones and muffins or cereals, or you may provide your own.
Ten minutes drive to/from grocery store. Laundry facilities available for small charge.
A non-smoking accommodation. Our family dog may greet you.
Please ring for bookings and directions.

New Plymouth
Bed & Breakfast Inn
Address: 60 Pendarves Street,
Central City, New Plymouth
Name: Alice Jane House
Telephone: (06) 758 1440
Fax: (06) 758 1430
Beds: 1 Queen, 1 Twin
(converts to Californian King),
1 Single (3 Bedrooms)
Bathroom: 1 Guests share
Tariff: B&B (special/full/continental) Double $75, Single $55.
Visa/Mastercard/Amex/Diners Club.
Nearest Town: New Plymouth (5 mins walk to City Centre)

Warmth and welcome abounds in our tastefully decorated sunny central city 1915 villa, where you can relax and be pampered. Our spacious newly renovated character home offers a charm and ambience of yesteryear. Crisp white linen, large luxurious towels and fresh flowers await you with those extra trimmings that make your stay memorable. Enjoy the warmth of a fire in winter or just relax in front of the TV in one of our two guest lounges. A cappuccino/espresso machine is available 24 hours as part of our guests facilities. Gracious breakfast settings of crystal and silver enhance the sumptuous breakfasts served.
Our joys include wood carving, people, laughter and writing. Our family consists of 1 child, two cats and one dog.
Off-street parking and courtesy car available. Our home is smoke free. Five minutes walk to city centre and all that it offers. Pukekura Park is just around the corner.

New Plymouth

Homestay
Address: "The Grange",
44B Victoria Road, New Plymouth
Name: Cathy Thurston and John Smith
Telephone: 06-758 1540
Fax: 06-758 1539
Mobile: 025-244 2639
Email: cathyt@clear.net.nz
Beds: 1 Double, 1 King,
2 Single (2 bedrooms)
Bathroom: 2 Ensuites
Tariff: B&B Double $90, Single $70, Dinner $25.
All Credit Cards accepted. NZ B&B Vouchers accepted $20 surcharge
Nearest Town: New Plymouth - 5 minutes walk to city centre.

Come and stay at our brand new architecturally designed award winning home built with your privacy and comfort in mind. Our home is tastefully appointed and has been designed to take full advantage of the sun.
Each bedroom has its own en-suite,TV, electric blankets, hair dryers and complimentary tea and coffee are provided. One bedroom has a double bed with French doors opening to a covered tiled courtyard. The other bedroom has two single beds convertible to a king-size bed. Our home is centrally heated, security controlled and located adjacent to the well known Pukekura Park and Bowl of Brooklands and is five minutes walk from the city centre. Breakfast is provided with freshly baked bread and espresso coffee, either in the formal dining area, al fresco on the tiled deck, or in the designer kitchen. Cathy and John have travelled extensively overseas and understand and appreciate true hospitality. Non smokers preferred.
Home Page: http://nz.com/webnz/bbnz/grange.htm

New Plymouth
Bed & Breakfast
Address: 32 Carrington Street,
New Plymouth
Name: McMillan's Bed & Breakfast
Telephone: (06) 758 2375
Fax: (06) 758 2375
Beds: 2 Queen,
3 Single (4 Bedrooms)
Bathroom: 1 Guests share
Tariff: B&B (continental) Double $60,
Single $40, Children price by arrangement.
Credit cards, NZ B&B Vouchers accepted
Nearest Town: 2 minutes walk to New Plymouth City.

McMillan's B&B, built in 1857, is situated only a few minutes walk to downtown shops, restaurants, theatres, Information Centre, Pukekura Park and Bowl of Brooklands.
A warm welcome is assured by Ian, Linda, Christie and their two cuddly cats.
We offer guests smoke-free TV lounge with 24 hour tea/coffee facilities. Laundry facilities for small fee. Clean, comfortable rooms.
Off-street parking. Free pick up from bus depot.

New Plymouth
Homestay
Address: 93 "By the Sea" Buller Street,
New Plymouth.
Name: 93 By the Sea
Telephone: (06) 758 6555
Mobile: (025) 230 3887
Email: pabron@xtra.co.nz
Beds: 1 King/Twin,
1 Double fold-out (1 Bedroom)
Bathroom: 1 Private
Tariff: B&B (Full) Double $75,
Single $50, Dinner by prior arrangement.
Credit cards accepted. NZ B&B Vouchers accepted $10 surcharge
Nearest Town: New Plymouth

93 BY THE SEA: a totally renovated and re-decorated 1930's bungalow. Guests park their vehicle off the road by the front door and have exclusive use of the downstairs lounge, bedroom, bathroom and laundry. These facilities are for one party/group only, with a maximum of 4 persons. We call it a "boutique bed and breakfast".
LOCATION, LOCATION, LOCATION: share breakfast with us and reflect on the sights, sounds and feel of the gardens, the surf and the ocean. Take only a few minutes to wander to beaches, walkways and restaurants. 1500 metres will see you in the city centre with all its attractions.
QUOTATIONS FROM THE VISITORS BOOK: "A wonderful relaxing stay, with a beautiful view. It complimented our wedding day". "Loved the warm hospitality, the cleanliness and comfort of the home, and all the little extras".

Stratford

Homestay
Address: 'Woodhill' 15 Taylor Road
(off SH 3), R.D.23, Stratford
Name: John & Elaine Nicholls
Telephone: (06) 765 5497
Beds: 1 Double, 4 Single
(3 bedrooms)
Bathroom: 1 Guests share
Tariff: B&B (full)
Double $80, Single $60,
Dinner $30, Credit Cards (VISA/MC).
NZ B&B Vouchers accepted
Nearest Town: Stratford - 3km south off SH 3

Come and enjoy the tranquillity and beauty of the countryside in the heart of Taranaki. Our home is nestled in two acres of old English gardens and is over a hundred years old. Each bedroom opens out onto the gardens and comfortably appointed.
We offer you warmth, hospitality and a haven from the stresses of everyday life. After a generous, leisurely breakfast enjoy a walk in the gardens or a swim in our large outdoor pool. We have an "upper room" suitable for retreats, small seminars and functions, or for just relaxing. In the evenings guests are invited to enjoy a three course dinner with complimentary wine, or if you prefer there are restaurants in Stratford. Stratford offers a wide range of activities including a picturesque golf course and all types of mountain sports. For garden enthusiasts there is the Taranaki trail of gardens.

Stratford

Farmstay Bed & Breakfast
Address: Stallard Farm, SH 3,
Stratford Nth, 24 R.D.
Name: Billie Anne & Corb Stallard
Telephone: (06) 765 8324
Fax: (06) 765 8324
Mobile: 025-240 2677
Beds: Comfortable Double, Twin,
Triple and Single rooms,
T.V. Electric blankets. (1 bedroom sleeps 4).
Bathroom: 4 Ensuite, 1 Guests share
Tariff: B&B (full) Double $65, Twin $70,
Single $40, Triple $75, 4 Bedroom $80,
Cooking facilities, Credit Cards (VISA/MC/AMEX), NZ B&B Vouchers accepted
Nearest Town: Stratford 1 km

° °
° KIWI °
COUNTRY
COMFORT
° °

Built 1900, this elegant old house, with its extensive gardens and farm walks, offers genuine "Upstairs Downstairs" B&B. Be private if desired, making use of cooking facilities, or settle in as a home away from home. 1km restaurants, taverns, shops. Interests, travel, gemstones, art and people. The Aga cooker in the main kitchen ensures a warm glow throughout the house in winter, and provides a hearty cooked breakfast, or a light breakfast may be chosen. Complimentary tea and coffee, biscuits etc (continuous self-service). Laundry (small charge). TV in bedrooms, Pooltable, Separate lounge, BBQ. Paddle on the lake. Go tramping or skiing on Mt Egmont 15 mins. Trout fishing. Walkways. Museums. Famous gardens. Helicopter sightseeing. Shopping in Stratford or New Plymouth or just lazing. Family all grown.
Directions: *Stratford, north on State Highway 3.*
Home Page: www.nz-travel.com

Stratford, Egmont National Park

Farm and Homestay
Address: 922 Pembroke Road,
P.O. Box 303, Stratford,
Mount Egmont/Taranaki
Name: Anderson's Alpine Residence
Telephone: (06) 765 6620
(if no reply ph/fax (06) 765 6100)
Fax: (06) 765 6100 **Mobile**: (025) 412 372
Email: MOUNTAINHOUSE@XTRA.CO.NZ
Beds: 2 King/Queen, 2 Single (3 bedrooms)
Bathroom: 3 Ensuite
Tariff: B&B (full) Double $95/120, Single $95/120.
Credit Cards. NZ B&B Vouchers accepted Surcharge for $95 room $20 & $120 room $45.
Nearest Town: Stratford 9km

Our Swiss Chalet rests in five acres of native bush. Views of Mount Egmont / Taranaki on our doorstep. The Egmont National Park starts opposite our front gate. Five kilometres from the Mountain House and its internationally famed restaurant and a further three kilometres to the Stratford Plateau and skifields. The National Park offers family tramps, round-the-mountain trek, summit climbs (guides available) and snow skiing. Trout stream, gardens, museums and scenic drives nearby. Private helicopter for summit scenic flights. We have pet sheep, pig, ducks etc. Kiwi Keith and Swiss Berta Anderson owned mountain lodges for 25 years. Won many tourist and hospitality awards. Keith is noted Taranaki Artist specialising in landscape and mountain scenes. Pets welcome. Not suitable for children. All Credit Cards.
Directions: *922 Pembroke Road opposite Egmont National Park, nine kilometres west of Stratford - Please phone reservations. If no reply phone or fax (06) 765 6100).*
Home Page: HTTP://WWWMOUNTAINHOUSE.CO.NZ

Stratford

Country Retreat
Address: "Sarsen House", Te Popo Gardens,
636 Stanley Road, RD 24, Stratford
Name: Bruce & Lorri Ellis
Telephone: (06) 762 8775
Fax: (06) 762 8775
Email: tepopo@clear.net.nz
Beds: 2 Queen, 1 King/Twin, (3 bedrooms)
Bathroom: 3 Ensuite
Tariff: B&B (full) Double $90-$110,
Single $90, Dinner $20- $30.Credit Cards,
NZ B&B Vouchers accepted $30 surcharge
Nearest Town: Stratford 15 km

Sarsen House is set in Te Popo Gardens (34 acres); nestled in the hills 30km east of Mount Taranaki. A peaceful retreat of great beauty in all seasons: stroll in the woodland gardens; explore the unique native-clad gorges and streams; enjoy the abundant birdlife; relax in the comfort of your suite, curled up before your own woodburning fire in colder weather; or venture further afield to enjoy the riches of Taranaki. Our guest wing provides private, quality accommodation in a garden setting. Share the facilities of our formal lounge and dining room, and breakfast in the sun filled conservatory. We would enjoy serving you dinner, however if you wish to self cater, full kitchen facilities are available. We ask guests not to smoke indoors. Our dogs, Sargeant and Pepper are the resident possum hunters.
Directions: *From Midhurst on SH3 travel east on Beaconsfield Road for 5.8km then north on Stanley Road for 6.5km.* **Home Page**: http://friars.co.nz/hosts/tepopo.html

Stratford

Farmstay
Address: Toko Road, RD 22, Stratford
Name: Heather and Peter Savage
Telephone: (06) 762 2840
Fax: (06) 762 2880
Mobile: (025) 284 3820
Email: savage.toko@xtra.co.nz
Beds: 1 Double (1 bedroom)
Bathroom: 1 Ensuite, 1 Family share
Tariff: B&B (full) Double $90, Single $45, Dinner $15, Children $20. NZ B&B Vouchers accepted $20 surcharge
Nearest Town: Stratford 17 kms

"WOODLEIGH" TOKO TARANAKI
We have a large, modern home and garden. It is extremely private and quiet with a truly magnificent view of Mt Egmont. The guest room has separate bathroom facilities and provides guests with the opportunity to relax in private or join in with family activities. We have a delightful house dog called Brandy, a daughter of 10 and a son of 13, and would welcome children but they would have to share facilities with our children.
Our farm is 1150 acres and we run dairy cows, Angus beef cattle and Romney ewes. The farm is approx 15 km east of Stratford, 50 mins by car from New Plymouth and about half an hour from Mt Egmont which has beautiful scenery and bush walks. We offer a quiet, relaxed stay in a rural setting with the opportunity to see and participate in a working farm or maybe even go possum shooting at night!
Directions: *Please phone for directions.*

Hawera

Bed & Breakfast Inn
Address: Cnr Puawai Street - South Road, Hawera
Name: Tairoa Lodge
Telephone: (06) 278 8603
Fax: (06) 278 8603
Mobile: (025) 243 5782
Email: tairoa.lodge@xtra.co.nz
Beds: 2 Queen (2 Bedrooms)
Bathroom: 2 Ensuite
Tariff: B&B (Full) Double $95-$110, Single $75, Dinner by arrangement.
Credit Cards accepted. NZ B&B Vouchers accepted $25-$39 surcharge
Nearest Town: Hawera

Originally built in 1875 our Kauri villa has been renovated to its former Victorian glory. The character of the polished original Kauri floors adds a golden glow to each of the tastefully decorated rooms, whilst the spacious bedrooms each with ensuite, fresh flowers and quality linen, have delightful views over the woodland garden and swimming pool.
Sumptuous full breakfasts are served either in the formal dining room, on the verandah or privately upstairs on the balcony of the master suite.
Tairoa Lodge, Maori for "linger - stay longer" is nestled amongst established grounds with protected Kauri trees, Copper Beech, NZ natives, Rhododendrons and Camellias.
Whether you choose to relax by the log fire, discover nature's delights in the garden, swim, partake in petanque or visit South Taranaki's local tourist and nature spots, Linda, Steve and our friendly American Cocker Spaniel (Emma) assure you of a memorable stay at Tairoa Lodge.

Waitotara

+ Self-Contained Accommodation
Address: SH 3, Waitotara,
Wanganui
Name: Ashley Park
Telephone: (06) 346 5917
Fax: (06) 346 5861
Beds: 1 Queen, 4 Single
(3 bedrooms)
Bathroom: 1 Ensuite, 1 Guests share
Tariff: B&B (full) Double $60-$90,
Single $40; Dinner $25; Power points for caravans and campervans with full
facilities; Cabins available; Self-contained unit for 7 people; Two fully equipped
motels, One sleeping 4-6. Double $75.
NZ B&B Vouchers accepted with surcharge
Nearest Town: Wanganui 29 Kms

We are 2 km from Waitotara village and 8 km to the beach. We have a mixed farm, sheep cattle, deer and cropping. We have a large, comfortable home set in an attractive garden with a swimming pool and aviaries with exotic birds and pheasants. Also in the garden is an antique and craft shop which also serves Devonshire teas and sandwiches from 9 am-5 pm daily. Situated 100 metres from the house and garden is a 4-acre park of native and English trees, surrounding a picturesque lake with waterfowl and hand fed animals. We like to serve New Zealand fare and hope you enjoy the tranquillity of the countryside. Guests are welcome to observe farm activities where possible and there are scenic drives locally.
Directions: *We are situated 29 km north of Wanganui and 12 km south of Waverley on State Highway 3.*

Wanganui

Homestay
Address: 156 Great North Road,
Wanganui
Name: Janet Dick
Telephone: (06) 345 8951
Mobile: (025) 235 2733
Beds: 2 Single (1 Bedroom)
Bathroom: 1 Private
Tariff: B&B (continental)
Double $60, Single $40,
Dinner by special arrangement,
Cooked breakfast on request.
NZ B&B Vouchers accepted
Nearest Town: Wanganui 2 Kms

Our home is a modern Lockwood set amongst mature trees, two kilometres from the centre of Wanganui on the main Wanganui / New Plymouth Highway. We have travelled extensively overseas and enjoy meeting and conversing with people from all countries. We have a small flower growing business and our many interests include sport, tramping, gardening, bridge and travel. Wanganui has many attractions including excellent golf courses and sporting facilities, the Regional Museum and superb Serjeant Art Gallery and the scenic Wanganui River which offers something for everyone from sedate paddle steamers cruises to kayaking the rapids. Or take a day trip by jet boat to see the famous Bridge to Nowhere, the Drop Scene and the Settlement of Jerusalem. Wanganui also has a good variety of restaurants, both licensed and BYO. We look forward to meeting you.
Directions: *2km up SH 3 from Wanganui towards New Plymouth,*

Wanganui

Homestay/Self Contained Accommodation/Conference Centre

Address: "ARLES" 50 Riverbank Road, RD 3   State Highway 4, Wanganui
Name: Peter & Margaret McAra
Telephone: (06) 343 6557 **Fax**: (06) 343 6557 **Mobile**: (025) 507 295
Email: arles@xtra.co.nz
Beds: Homestead: 1 King, 1 Queen, 1 Double, 2 Single (4 bedrooms).
Self Contained Flat: 1 Queen, 2 Singles (2 Bedrooms)
Bathroom: Homestead: 2 Ensuites, 1 Guests share.
Self Contained Flat: Full bathroom facilities
Tariff: B&B (full) Double $95-$115, Single $80-$95, Special arrangements for families, small groups and stays of more than 2 nights. NZ B&B Vouchers accepted $30 surcharge
Nearest Town: Wanganui - 3km north on SH4.

Welcome to "ARLES"
We would like to share our lovely, late 19th Century home with 2 acres of native trees, including New Zealand's most southern Queensland kauri, plus maples, oaks, camellias, rhododendrons, azaleas, kowhai and ferns, citrus grove and numerous other fruit trees including an indoor grape vine. Meet Davy our corgi, and our cat Tiger.
We are situated on State Highway 4 on the road to National Park above the Wanganui River and only 5 minutes from Wanganui City.
Each bedroom contains electric blankets, reading lamps and tea making facilities. Guests are welcome to share the lounge which opens up to an outside verandah and use of a large library. A kitchen is available for guests to use together with laundry facilities.
Our new flat offers spacious self contained, fully furnished 2 bedroom accommodation. Enjoy the peace and tranquillity of the Arles' woodlands and gardens. Breakfast is served in the morning sunshine looking out onto the gardens. Outside facilities include a swimming pool, barbeque and children's play area. Spa available in winter. Nearby are established gardens, art gallery, museum, arts and crafts. We are close to Mount Ruapehu snowfields, mountain and bushwalks and activities on the Whanganui River.
We have six children and seven grandchildren. Margaret is a nurse and enjoys flower arranging, needlework, cake decoration and gardening, when she finds time. Peter enjoys tramping, cycling, photography, and family history. No smoking indoors please.
Directions: *From Wellington & New Plymouth: Take SH 3 to Wanganui. Travel 3km North on Anzac Parade along SH 4. Cross white concrete bridge over Mateongaonga stream and take second driveway on right to Arles.*
From Auckland & Taupo: Travel past National Park and Raetihi on State Highway 4. "ARLES" is 4km South of the small village of Upokongaro, 150m before the Mateongaonga Stream. Please phone for reservations.

Wanganui
Farmstay
Address: Operiki, River Road,
641, R.D.6, Wanganui
Name: Trissa & Peter McIntyre
Telephone: (06) 342 8159
Beds: 1 Double,
2 Single (2 bedrooms)
Bathroom: Family share
Tariff: B&B (full) $35 per adult,
Children $15,
Dinner adult $20/children $10,
Campervans $15. NZ B&B Vouchers accepted
Nearest Town: Wanganui 45 Kms

*Farmstay overlooking the Whanganui River - en route to the Bridge to Nowhere - sheep,
cattle and deer farming. Pottery and macadamia nuts and cat. Enjoy a country picnic
or bush walk. Other activities along the river can be arranged: canoeing, jet boat rides,
horse riding, mountain bike riding, Marae visit and farm activities according to
season.*
45km north from Wanganui turn off SH4.

Wanganui
Homestay
Address: 'Bradgate', 7 Somme Parade,
Wanganui
Name: Frances
Telephone: (06) 345 3634
Fax: (06) 345 3634
Beds: 1 Queen, 1 Double,
2 Single (3 bedrooms)
Bathroom: 1 Guests share
Tariff: B&B (full) Double $70,
Single $40, Dinner $25.
Nearest Town: Wanganui town centre 5 mins

*We welcome you to "Bradgate". This gracious superior, 2 storey home built in 1901.
Comfortable furnished, central heating and river-view from all windows, a most
relaxing place for the traveller wanting homestay accommodation. "Bradgate" has a
beautiful entrance hall with carved rimu staircase, which has been restored to reflect
the original character and gracefulness of this house.*
*I am a qualified chef-caterer, with a grown-up family. 25 years ago my husband and
I came to New Zealand to own and operate Shangri-La Restaurant by Virginia Lake,
Wanganui. After 20 years we retired and decided to welcome guests into our beautiful
old home.*
My mother lives next-door, we share her pet dog Bounce.
We are 8 mins walk to town centre and all amenities.
I play golf, enjoy gardening and love meeting people.
If you can't find me at home, check the garden.
Non-smoking home, Dinner by arrangement.

Wanganui
Guest House
Address: 2 Plymouth Street, Wanganui
Name: Riverside Inn
Telephone: (06) 347 2529
Fax: (06) 347 2529
Beds: 4 Double, 8 Single (8 bedrooms)
Bathroom: 3 Guests share
Tariff: B&B (continental) Double $80,
Single $50,
Campervans parking (No power),
Credit Cards (VISA/MC/BC).
Nearest Town: Wanganui - 10 mins walk to main street

Our homestead, built 1895, has been restored to retain its "old world charm". It is not a modern hotel, you will share facilities, but you will have the homely atmosphere of how New Zealand used to be.

Guest rooms are located on the ground floor, a wing which was added when the original home became a private hospital in 1911. The hospital, named "Braemar", closed in 1976 after which is was converted to a tourist inn.

We are walking distance to Town Centre, museum, art gallery and cafes. A laundry and fully equipped self service kitchen are available.

If you choose to stay with us we will give you our personal attention to ensure your visit is as comfortable as possible.

We request that you do not smoke on the premises and step over "Casper" our cat whose habit is sleeping on the front door mat.

Wanganui
Homestay
Address: "Arlesford House",
State Highway 3,
Westmere, Wanganui
Name: June and George Loibl
Telephone: (06) 347 7751
Fax: (06) 347 7561
Mobile: (025) 852 922
Beds: 4 Queen, 5 Single (4 Bedrooms)
Bathroom: 3 Ensuites, 1 Private
Tariff: B&B (Special/Full) Double $150-$210, Single $80-$120.
Credit cards accepted.
Nearest Town: Wanganui 7 kms

Arlesford House

"Arlesford House" is a stately country home set on 6 acres. We have a lovely garden to explore with expansive lawns dotted with specimen trees, dozens of old and modern roses and interesting plants. Enjoy the solar heated pool, play tennis (flood-lit), croquet, or petanque. Relax in our spacious home, with open fires in the drawing room and den. Leisurely breakfast served in sunroom, formal dining room, poolside or in room if preferred.

Upstairs 3 large guest rooms including for that special occasion super-king room with open fire, spa bath and sunroom. Downstairs double / twin semi-detached poolside room. Heated towel rail and hair driers all rooms. Complimentary laundry, tea / coffee / juice / fruit / snacks. No smoking in house. We have 3 outside cats and 1 outside dog. Interests include travelling, horse breeding and racing, sports, home and garden. Enquire about special rates and packages golf / canoeing etc and many attraction of the Wanganui area.

341

Wanganui

Homestay

Address: "Kembali", 26 Taranaki Street,
St Johns Hill, Wanganui
Name: Wes and Marylyn Palmer
Telephone: (06) 347 1727
Mobile: (025) 270 1879
Email: wespalmer@xtra.co.nz
Beds: 1 Queen, 1 Twin (2 Bedrooms)
Bathroom: 1 Private
Tariff: B&B (full) Double $65, Single $40, Triple $90. Children by arrangement. (We only have one party at a time in the guest accommodation.) Credit cards accepted. NZ B&B Vouchers accepted
Nearest Town: Wanganui (2kms from City Centre on SH3)

Welcome to our modern home. "Kembali" is at the end of a quiet cul-de-sac, overlooking trees, gardens and wetlands. The sunny guest rooms including private lounge with tea and coffee facilities and TV are upstairs. Off street parking is provided and laundry facilities are available. Our family (all married) have left home, our cat is middle aged and so a restful stay is assured. The house is a smoke-free zone.

We have many interests which include travel, house renovation, recreational gardening, reading and of course people.

Wanganui offers many attractions. We are within walking distance of lovely Virginia Lake - a public reserve with fountain, walks, gardens and bird life. Our historic town has an excellent museum, art gallery, attractive shopping, craft shops and many river activities eg. historic paddle steamer, jet boating and canoeing.

Directions: *2kms from City Centre. Phone for full directions.*

National Park

Farmstay or Self Contained Accommodation

Address: Mountain Heights Lodge,
PO Box 43, National Park.
Name: Wendy and Chris Howard
Telephone: (07) 892 2833
Fax: (07) 892 2833
Beds: 2 Double, 2 Single (3 Bedrooms)
Bathroom: 2 Guests share
Tariff: B&B (Full) Double $80*,
Single $45*, Dinner $25, Children half price.
Credit cards accepted. * Winter rates apply.
Nearest Town: national Park 2 km north.

Chris, Wendy and their two children welcome you to Mountain Heights, our small family run farm and lodge.

Adjacent to Tongariro National Park, walk the famous Tongariro Crossing or ski Ruapehu. We are ideally situated for the main activities available in the area and can arrange canoeing on the mighty Wanganui River, horse trekking the Central Plateau and scenic flights across the mountains and volcanoes. One hours drive away is Lake Taupo - famous for its trout fishing.

Alternatively relax in our lodge with views to the mountains and across farmland to native bush. Accommodation is in double or single rooms. Relax in our spa bath - ideal after a days walk or skiing. Our self contained units sleep four with private bathroom, TV and kitchen.

Good food and company assured. We look forward to meeting you.

Raetihi

Homestay, Farmstay
Address: Pipiriki Road, Raetihi
Name: Ken & Sonia Robb
Telephone: (06) 385 4581
Fax: (06) 385 4581
Email: ken.sonia@xtra.co.nz
Beds: 1 Queen, 2 Single (2 bedrooms)
Bathroom: 1 Ensuite, 1 Family share
Tariff: B&B (full) Double $80, Single $50, Children 1/2 price, Dinner $25pp incl wine. NZ B&B Vouchers accepted
Nearest Town: Raetihi 6km

Our 1,000 acres of hill country farm is in the quiet, picturesque Mangaeturoa Valley just 10 minutes drive from Raetihi. Ken farms Romney sheep and Simmental cattle. Our home is set in a spacious garden visited frequently by a large variety of birds throughout the year.
Our interests include family, gardening, travel and photography. Local activities available include skifields, jetboat tours on the Wanganui River, trout fishing, Bush walks in the National Park and canoeing (all within an hours drive) a golf course nearby or a farm tour with Ken. A cot is available and guests are welcome to use the laundry facilities.
Directions: *We are 6 1/2 km from Raetihi on the right hand side of Pipiriki Road*

Raetihi

Homestay+Self-contained Accom. No kitchen.
Address: Log Lodge, 5 Ranfurly Tce, Raetihi
Name: Jan & Bob Lamb
Telephone: (06) 385 4135
Fax: (06) 385 4135
Email: Lamb.Log-Lodge@Xtra.co.nz
Beds: 2 Double, 5 Single
(large mezzanine) + 1 room.
Bathroom: 2 Private
Tariff: B&B (full) Double $90, Single $48, Children $35, Credit Cards.
Nearest Town: Raetihi - on edge of town

A unique opportunity to stay in a modern authentic log home sited high on 7 acres on the edge of town. Completely private accommodation with own bathroom. Sleeping on mezzanine floor with room for 6, your own lounge with wood fire, snooker table, TV/ video and stereo and dining area, opening onto large verandah. Your private area is 1500 square feet. Panoramic views across river and farmlands to the Tongariro National Park and Mts. Ruapehu, Ngauruhoe and Tongariro, just 14km away. We are keen skiers and specialize in winter accommodation for those who share our love of skiing. You can be in the snow with your skis on in 30 minutes. We have a pool, solar heated in summer and a secluded spa. Summer visitors have a full range of recreational activities in the national park and we have mountain bikes for hire to explore the many scenic rides in the district.
We have 2 Persian cats. There is an extra charge for the spa.
We request "no smoking".

343

Ohakune

Homestay/Farmstay
Address: 'Mitredale', Smiths Road, Ohakune
Name: Audrey & Diane Pritt
Telephone: (06) 385 8016
Fax: (06) 385 8016
Mobile: (025) 531 916
Beds: 1 Double, 2 Single (2 bedrooms)
Bathroom: 1 Family share
Tariff: B&B (continental) Double $70,
Single $40, Children 12 and under $20;
Dinner $20, Credit Cards. Vouchers accepted
Nearest Town: Ohakune 6 km, Raetihi 9 km

We are farmers who farm sheep and bull beef and run a boarding kennel in a beautiful peaceful valley with magnificent views of Mt Ruapehu. The Waimarino is an excellent area for holidaying summer or winter. Tongariro National Park offers excellent walks, opportunities for photography and great skiing at Turoa and Whakapapa. The rivers offer good sport for fishermen and an excellent 18-hole golf course 3 km from our door. We are keen members of the Conservation body Ducks Unlimited, and our local Wine Club. We have two Labradors and one large cat. We have two guest-rooms - one with two single beds, the other a double bed. All equipped with electric blankets. The home is heated with a log-fire and open fire - excellent for drying gear after a day's skiing, a comfortable, cosy atmosphere to relax in. We offer dinner with the traditional farmhouse fare or just breakfast - gives you the opportunity to sample our excellent homemade jams. We enjoy sharing our lifestyle with others so come and spend some time on the farm. **Directions**: Take the Raetihi Road at Ohakune Hotel corner / BP Service Station, travel 4 km to Smiths Road, second side road on the left. We are the last house 2 km at the end of the road.

Ohakune

Homestay
Address: Villa Mangawhero,
 60B Burns St, Ohakune
Name: Patricia Mountfort
Telephone: (06) 385 8076
 Beds: 1 Queen, 1 Double,
5 Single (4 bedrooms)
Bathroom: 1 Ensuite,
2 Guests , 1 Private
Tariff: B&B (full) Double $70*, Single $40*, Children negotiable, *Tariff different rates ski season. No Smoking. Credit cards.
NZ B&B Vouchers accepted December to May
Nearest Town: Ohakune 500m approx.

Situated in Ohakune village Villa Mangawhero, built in 1914, has been extensively renovated but still retains many original features. Pressed steel ceilings, antique kauri fire surrounds, rimu tongue and groove wall linings and coloured glass windows and doors. Guests have exclusive use of two lounges one with TV. Bedsitting rooms have tea and coffee making facilities and heating. Ohakune halfway between Auckland and Wellington, 17km from Turoa ski field and 42 from Whakapapa offers fishing, tramping, skiing and other outdoor activities plus sightseeing in national park where some lifts operate all year. Also local shops for browsing, restaurants and cafes a picture theatre and a disco. Patricia Mountfort an artist has paintings for sale. Her house which is furnished with antique kauri furniture has featured in February 95 NZ Womens Weekly open home series under the title of 'Olde World Charm'. Patricia looks forward to sharing this 'charm' with you.

344

Ohakune
Homestay
Address: 1011 Raetihi Road, Ohakune
Name: Bruce & Nita Wilde & cat 'Shah'
Telephone: (06) 385 8026 Please phone
Beds: 1 Queen, 3 Single (3 bedrooms)
Bathroom: 1 Private, 1 Family share
Tariff: B&B (full) Double $80,
Single $45,Children $15, Dinner $20.
Our home is smokefree. NZ B&B Vouchers accepted
Nearest Town: Ohakune 1km

Kohinoor

Named 'Kohinoor' (a gem of rare beauty) our home is a warm and cosy place from where you can enjoy the attractions of the Tongariro National Park and the Turoa skifields. 'Kohinoor' is set in 3 acres of tranquil gardens of special note with an exceptional view of Mt Ruapehu across our lake, rural farmland and native bush.
Our interests include gardening, photography, local trout fishing, skiing and alpine walking.
We are just 20 mins drive from Turoa ski resort and 40 minutes from Whakapapa skifields. In the ski season Ohakune has many exciting bars and restaurants. The beautiful Waimarino Golf Course is only 5 minutes away.One hour's drive gets you to Lake Taupo and the world famous Tongariro trout fishing River.
Directions: *Exactly 1km from Ohakune on the west side of the road to Raetihi.*

Taihape
Homestay
Address: 'Korirata', 25 Pukeko Street, Taihape
Name: Patricia & Noel Gilbert
Telephone: (06) 388 0315
Fax: (06) 388 0315
Email: korirata@xtra.co.nz
Beds: 4 Single (2 bedrooms, electric blankets on every bed)
Bathroom: 1 Guests only share
Tariff: B&B (full or continental) Double $65, Single $40, Primary children half price, Dinner $22, Campervans facilities available, Credit cards NZ B&B Vouchers accepted
Nearest Town: Taihape - 1/2km from Post Office

A warm welcome to Taihape, where we are situated on top of the hill with panoramic views of Mt. Ruapehu, the Ruahines and extensive farming country.
Warmth and comfort is a feature in tranquil surroundings for instant relaxation. The entire section - three-quarters-of-an-acre - has been landscaped with shrubs, hydroponic and orchid houses, and a large area planted in chrysanthemums.
Dinner and lunch are available on request and almost all types of meals are available. Meals with hosts using our home grown produce - cooking is a hobby.
Separate toilet and bathroom available for guests. Farm visits, tramping, rafting, fishing, bunjee jumping and jet boating can be arranged and most are within 1/2 hour. One hour to Ruapehu (skiing), one hour to Lake Taupo, 2 1/2 hours to Rotorua or Wellington, 40 minutes to Titoki Point and other well known gardens.
Noel has retired from the farm to horticulture and Pat teaches.
Directions: *Please phone.*

Taihape
Farmstay

Address: Utiku South Road, Utiku, Taihape
Name: Blair & Dot McLeod
Telephone/Fax: (06) 388 0439
Beds: 1 Double, 1 Single (2 bedrooms)
Bathroom: 1 Private
Tariff: B&B (full) Double $80, Single $45,
Dinner $25. Vouchers accepted $10 surcharge
Nearest Town: Taihape 11 kms

For a relaxing, peaceful stopover with really beautiful mountain and rural views on a genuine NZ farm.
We are: Conveniently situated between Taupo and Wellington.
Just one kilometre off State Highway 1.
Sheep / cattle farmers of 500 hectares of hill country.
Interested in breeding and training sheepdogs, spinning and woolcraft, gardening, travelling and meeting people.
We offer: A warm, sunny, cozy, smoke-free home.
Very comfortable, warm beds. A relaxing, tranquil stopover
Delicious meals with home-baking and farm produce
Complimentary morning or afternoon tea. Kiwi hospitality - Dot is a Kiwi Host
You can: Relax and unwind in a very peaceful locality.
Roam the farm and experience farm life (with a packed lunch if required)
Wander in the garden, listen and watch native birds. Sit and absorb the views
To help our preparations to make your stay most pleasurable, we would prefer a letter or phone call in advance. No dogs please! We have one cat.

Taihape
Fishingstay/Farmstay. A Rangitikei River Holiday

Address: Tarata Fishaway, Mokai Road, RD 3, Taihape
Name: Stephen & Trudi Mattock
Telephone: (06) 388 0354 **Fax**: (06) 388 0954
Email: fishaway@xtra.co.nz
Beds: Homestead: 1 Queen waterbed, 1 Queen, 2 Single
(2 bedrooms). The Cottage: 1 Double, 1 Single (1 Bedroom, kitchen and bathroom)
Bathroom: Guests share 2
Tariff: B&B (continental) $55 per person Children under 12yrs 1/2 price, Dinner $25.
Family concessions available and approved pets welcome. Lunch available (extra).
Credit Cards accepted.NZ B&B Vouchers accepted $30 surcharge
Nearest Town: We are 26 scenic Kms from Taihape, only 6km past Mokai Bungy jump
bridge. Transport available.

*We are very lucky to have a piece of New Zealand's natural beauty. Situated in the remote Mokai Valley where the picturesque Rangitikei River meets the rugged Ruahine Ranges. We spend lots of quality time with our daughters down at the river or tending to our many family pets. Unique trout fishing oportunities are right at our doorstep and we offer guided or unguided fishing and rafting experiences. Our spacious home offers guests private space to unwind and relax. Whether it's by the pool on a hot summer day or spending a cosy winter night with a good wine in front of our open fire. Tarata is a great place for time out for the whole family with donkey rides for the children, milking the house cow, spot light safaris, bush walking or eeling. Words cannot express the feeling we have living here but we would love to share it with you. **Directions**: Turn off S/H 1, 6 kms south of Taihape at the Bungy and Ohotu turn-off. Follow the Bungy and Tarata Fishaway signs, we are 6km past Bungy bridge on Mokai Road. **Home Page**: www.tarata.co.nz*

Taihape

Homestay
Address: "Harmony",
State Highway One,
RD 5, Taihape
Name: Christine and John Tarrant
Telephone: (06) 388 1117
Fax: (06) 388 1117
Beds: 1 Double, 2 single (2 bedrooms)
Bathroom: 1Guests share,
separate shower
Tariff: B&B (full) Double $70, Single $40,
Children half price. NZ B&B Vouchers accepted
Nearest Town: Taihape 10 km

Situated on State Highway One 10 km north of Taihape and 20 km south of Waiouru, our farm homestead offers roomy comfort. Now that our children have left home we have two guest bedrooms and separate lounge available with tea/coffee making facilities. The double room also has a single divan bed. Experience country living amongst the real Taihape hills on a 270 hectare farm with stud Romney sheep, Angus cattle, deer and horses - not to mention the resident two cats and dog.
Taihape is the ideal stop over for travellers being halfway between Rotorua and Wellington. The township itself boasts a promising array of restaurants and cafes. It is the gateway to the alpine world of skiing (Turoa one hour), tramping (accompanied trips by arrangement) and horse trekking. Local rivers offer fishing, rafting, kayaking, and bungy jumping. There are many local gardens open to the public to explore and a golf course 5 km away.

Mangaweka, Rangitikei

Farmstay/Self-contained Accom.
Address: Kawhatau Valley, RD 7, Mangaweka
Name: Jim & Ruth Rainey
Telephone: (06) 382 5507
Fax: (06) 382 5504
Mobile: (025) 549 507
Beds: 2 Single (1 bedroom)
Bathroom: 1 Ensuite
Tariff: B&B (full) Double $80, Single $40, Dinner $20, Baby free.
Nearest Town: Taihape 25km and Mangaweka 15km

Come and enjoy a stay with a typical New Zealand farming family offering fun and conviviality (plus 2500 sheep and cattle, 1 cat, 5 farm dogs, 6 hens, 1 house cow and four children aged between 10 and 15 years.
Ethanbrae is a 350 hectare hill country farm situated in the beautiful Kawhatau Valley with the homestead being set in a pleasant gardens with magnificent views up the valley.
Accommodation is in a detached room featuring a private verandah with a lovely view. Twin beds with own shower and toilet; tea, coffee and toast-making facilities; homemade biscuits; bread etc supplied and laundry done on request.
Join us on the farm or wander down for a swim in the refreshing Kawhatau River. Jim is also a fishing guide for Rangitikei Anglers and can offer either a half day rafted fishing trip on the beautiful Rangitikei River or streamside guiding. Ideal for district visitors seeking a guided fly fishing experience with minimum commitment.

Mangaweka

Farmstay/Self-contained Accom.
Address: 'Mairenui Rural Retreat',
Ruahine Road, Mangaweka 5456
Name: Sue & David Sweet
Telephone: (06) 382 5564
Fax: (06) 382 5885
Mobile: (025) 517 545
Email: mairenui@xtra.co.nz
Beds: 1 Queen, 5 Double, 9 Single (11 bedrooms)
Bathroom: 2 Ensuite, 3 Guest Share
Tariff: B&B (special) Farmstay:
Double $110-$194, Single $75-$97,
Self Contained Accom: Double $50-$80, Single $25-$40, Dinner $35.
Credit Cards: (VISA/MC). NZ B&B Vouchers accepted $30 Surcharge
Nearest Town: Mangaweka 12 km

"Mairenui" is a farmstay complex comprising two self-contained houses as well as in-house accommodation. Situated on a scenic through route from Mangaweka to Palmerston North, it offers overnight and longer stay accommodation in the spectacular Rangitikei hill country. The 320 hectare property has sheep, cattle, horses, farm dogs, two cats, and Benji, the lovable cockerspaniel. "The Homestead" has two ensuite bedrooms, (one with a sunken bath) with their own verandahs and tea and coffee making facilities. "The Retreat", a three and a half storey architect-designed house set in seven hundred year old native trees, sleeps six in three bedrooms with a shared bathroom. The kitchen amenities are modern, and all linen is provided. Evening meals and breakfasts are available at the Homestead. Tariff - $80 double, $20 each extra person. Breakfasts $10-$12.00.

"The Colonial Villa" is a completely restored hundred year old home which sleeps ten - three doubles, one twin, two singles, with two shared bathrooms. It also has modern kitchen amenities, all linen is provided, and meals can be obtained at the Homestead. Tariff - $25 per person, minimum $60. On-farm amenities include a concrete tennis court, fishing, river swimming, farm walks and 4WD farm tours, also petanque and croquet courts. Available locally are river activities, garden visits, four golf courses, an architectural house tour, and scenic flights. Guided fishing can be booked with a world-renowned guide.

Fine food and wine are provided, with the dinner tariff including a pre-dinner drink and a glass of house wine, and as we have an in-house liquor licence, further drinks may be purchased. A commercial coffee machine ensures perfect espresso, cappucino, or latte! French and German are spoken.

Directions: *The farm is situated 12 km from Mangaweka and 84 km from Palmerston North on Ruahine Road, three easy hours from Rotorua or Wellington.*
Home Page: http://www.mairenui.co.nz

348

Hunterville

Farmstay
Address: Vennell's Farmstay,
Mangapipi Road, Rewa, R.D.
Name: Phil & Oriel Vennell
Telephone: (06) 328 6780,
free phone 0800-220 172 PIN 1837
Fax: (06) 328 6780
Mobile: 025-407164
Beds: 1 Queen, 4 Single (3 bedrooms)
Bathroom: 2 Private
Tariff: B&B (full) Double $100 Single $50, Dinner $25.
NZ B&B Vouchers accepted $10 pp surcharge
Nearest Town: Hunterville 13 km

Vennell's **FARM STAY** HOMESTEAD ACCOMMODATION

New Zealand Association FARM & HOME HOSTS

We are fifth generation farmers on a 1200 acre sheep and cattle hill country farm. Our spacious home is in a tranquil setting of mature trees and garden with swimming pool. We have a family room with billiard table and cosy living room with a large open fire. Beautiful rural views can be seen from our home and surrounding hills. Enjoy great farm walks or drive to "Stormy Point Lookout" for a view unique in the world. We are situated just off State Highway One near Hunterville on the scenic route to Feilding and in the centre of Rangitikei Private Gardens and golf courses. We are 3 hours drive from Rotorua, 1 1/2 hours from Mt Ruapehu skifields, 2 1/2 hours from Wellington and 30 minutes from Manfield motor sports and Fielddays. Trout fishing, jet boating, bungy jumping can all be enjoyed on the nearby Rangitikei river. Interests: farming, fishing, flowers, food & fun. We have two outdoor cats. Laundry facilities available. **Directions**: *Please phone for directions.*

http://www.bnb.co.nz

take a look

Hunterville

Homestay/Farmstay
Address: Brick 'n' Birches, 48 Ongo Road,
Hunterville
Name: Shona and John Kilsby
Telephone: (06) 322 8442
Fax: (06) 322 8442
Mobile: (025) 279 8890
Email: bricknb@manawatu.gen.nz
Beds: 1 King, 4 Singles (3 bedrooms)
Bathroom: 3 Ensuite
Tariff: B&B (full) Double $100-$110, Single $60, Dinner by arrangement $25 pp,
Credit Cards. Children welcome. NZ B&B Vouchers accepted $10 surcharge p.p.
Nearest Town: We are within Hunterville town. 1.7 km to SH1 intersection

*Guests at the Brick n' Birches enjoy rural views from spacious upstairs bedrooms (each with
ensuite), relaxing dining and lounge rooms with wood burner and open fire ensuring cosy
winter comfort. Our home started life as a two storeyed colonial cottage in the 1890's.
Subsequent additions and improvements now provide excellent facilities for total guest
comfort. Established trees and gardens provide park-like surroundings enhancing the
completely relaxing atmosphere. Texel sheep from our farm property (five minutes away)
usually graze the six acres adjoining our home. Hunterville is a typically friendly New
Zealand village approximately halfway between Taupo and Wellington. Bungy jumping, jet
boating, rafting and trout fishing are Rangitikei River activities close at hand. magnificent
gardens, bush walks, top country golf courses and typical New Zealand scenery complement
an excellent range of activities. Our friendly courteous hospitality and the wonderful
Rangitikei district ensure our visitors of a most memorable experience.*
Directions: *Directions and enquiries - please phone.*

Marton

Farmstay
Address: 'Tataramoa',
Howie Road, R.D. 2, Marton
Name: Janice & Des Gower
Telephone: (06) 327 8778
Beds: 1 Double, 6 Single (4 bedrooms)
Bathroom: 2 Guests share.
Tariff: B&B (continental) $45 per person,
Children welcome, Dinner $20 per person BYO,
Light snack on request. Picnic table.
NZ B&B Vouchers accepted $10 surcharge
Nearest Town: Marton - 9 mins drive (6 miles)

*Tataramoa is a 140 year colonial wooden homestead set in peaceful landscaped gardens,
surrounded by spacious beautiful mature New Zealand bush filled by many native birds. We
have 1000 acres on which we run sheep, cattle and cropping paddocks. There are great
opportunities for interesting walks around the flats, hills and valleys. Centre of garden and
heritage home visits. Near Palmerston North and Wanganui. A friendly and homely
atmosphere with welcome cosy open log fires. Traditional New Zealand farm meal with
private lounge if preferred. We really enjoy opening our home to both Kiwis and visitors from
all over the world. Ample verandah space for you to relax and unwind.*
Directions: *From Marton township turn at Westpac Bank roundabout to Wanganui for 3
miles. Turn right at Fern Flats Road, proceed and turn left to Waimutu Road. Drive until
'Tataramoa" and Howie Road signpost. Farm at end of road through avenue of trees.*

Rangitikei

Historic Home, Farmstay, Guest House, Conference Centre
Address: 'Maungaraupi', Leedstown Road, R.D. 1, Marton
Name: Kaylene Rose
Telephone: (06) 327 7820
Fax: (06) 327-8619
Beds: 5 Double, 5 Single (8 bedrooms)
Bathroom: 3 Ensuite, 1 Guests share
Tariff: B&B (full) Double $120-$160,
Single $90. Dinner $30.
Eftpos and all Credit Cards.
NZ B&B Vouchers accepted $15 surcharge
Nearest Town: Marton or Hunterville. On State Highway One. 10 minutes.

Let Historical Maungaraupi take you back to an era when life was enjoyed in good style.
We invite you to come and experience a unique lifestyle of a 10,000 square foot two storey tudor
style home set in five acres of native bush, extensive lawns and lovely gardens. Enjoy the
romantic touch of strutting peacocks and abundant native bird life, savour the extensive view
of the Ruahine Ranges and rolling farm land, relax in front of one of the open fireplaces, and
dine in style at a 16 seat antique five legged Kauri table.

The guest rooms are sunny and attractive with electric blankets on all beds. Three double
rooms have ensuite bathrooms, and two have a private balcony.

The atmosphere at Maungaraupi is friendly, relax about the house, take a bush or farm walk,
play billiards, tennis or croquet or travel a short distance to play golf, visit well-known gardens,
or trout fish, white water raft or jetboat on the scenic Rangitikei River. Mount Ruapehu's Turoa
Skifield is 1.5 hours drive away, Wanganui 30 minutes, Palmerston North 40 minutes, and
Marton or Hunterville 10 minutes.

http://www.bnb.co.nz

take a look

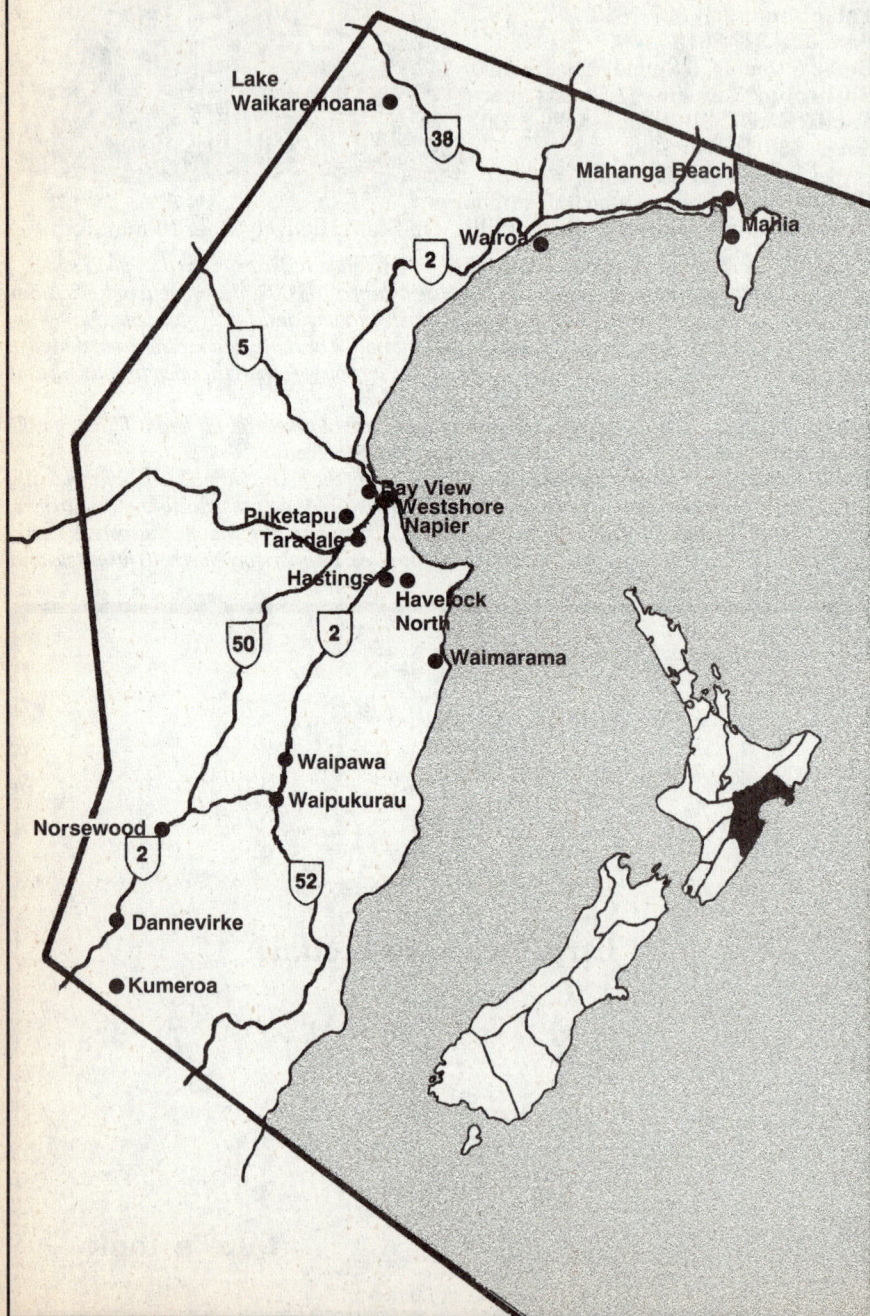

Hawkes Bay

Lake Waikaremoana ●

38

Mahanga Beach ●

Wairoa ●

2

Mahia ●

5

Bay View ●
Westshore
Puketapu ● Napier
Taradale ●

Hastings ● ● Havelock
North

50

2

● Waimarama

● Waipawa

● Waipukurau

Norsewood ●

2

52

● Dannevirke

● Kumeroa

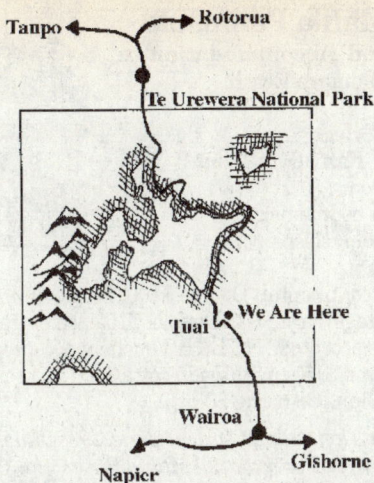

Lake Waikaremoana, Te Urewera National Park

Homestay
Address: 9 Rotten Row, Tuai village, Highway 38.
Name: Waikaremoana Homestay
Telephone: (06) 837 3701
Fax: (06) 837 3709
Beds: 1 Queen, 2 Single (2 bedrooms)
Bathroom: 1 Family Share
Tariff: B&B (full) Double $70, Single $45, Dinner $20.
Credit Cards accepted. NZ B&B Vouchers accepted $5 Surcharge
Nearest Town: Wairoa 55kms

Lake Waikaremoana is a spectacular and unique Native Forest wilderness area on the Eastern boundary of Te Urewera National Park.

Our homestay, set in the picturesque village of Tuai, is the ideal base for a bush-walking, trout fishing, or boating holiday. Tuai Village is the gateway to Waikaremoana and nestles around Lake Whakamarino (Tuai Lake) - part of the Waikaremoana Hydro Electricity Scheme. We are 10 minutes drive from The Panekiri Bluff entrance to the lake Waikaremoana Track one of New Zealand's "Great Walks".

The house, although 70 years old, has been modernised for open living, is smokefree and extremely comfortable.

From the verandah you look out to Tuai Lake, observe native birdlife in the well developed reserve of mature Trees across the road, watch the mist swirling from the bush-clad slopes of the Ngamoko Range, and enjoy the signs of the a rise from elusive brown or rainbow trout as they outwit the fly-fisherman keen to catch a "big one" from this little lake with the trophy reputation.

Excellent homecooking is a speciality of the house, using local produce from garden and district.

As we love to share the peace and unspoilt beauty of our surroundings, let us assist you to explore this awesome area. Sometimes I can even accompany you.

A fishing dinghy is available free for guest's use. Also picnic meals, BBQ's, to your convenience or use of kitchen facilities by arrangement.

Meals are at times to suit your activities, cars can be left at our house and minded by Dusky, the cat, while you walk the local tracks. Please ring for directions as Tuai Village is 1km off Highway 38 and not clearly signposted. We look forward to welcoming you to our relaxed lifestyle in the safe and friendly village of Tuai.

Mahanga Beach, Mahia Peninsula

Farmstay+Self-contained Accommodation.

Address: Postal: R D 8, Mahanga Beach,
Nuhaka, Hawkes Bay
Name: Nicholas & Louise Schick
Telephone: (06) 837 5898 **Fax**: (06) 837 5990
Email: mschick@hotmail.com
Beds: 2 Double, 2 Single (4 bedrooms).
Cottage: 2 Double,1 Bathroom (sleeps 4).
Bathroom: 2 Private
Tariff: "Reomoana" B&B: (continental) Double $100, Single $60, Children under 12yrs
half price, Dinner $30. Cottage Tariff: $75 Double, $15 each extra person. Discount for
weekly rental. Credit Cards accepted. NZ B&B Vouchers accepted $40 surcharge for
Double in main residence, and $15 surcharge in cottage.
Nearest Town: Wairoa 50km, Gisborne 80km

*Featured in the New Zealand Homes and Gardens June, 1999 issue. "Reomoana" - The voice
of the sea. Pacific Ocean-front farm at beautiful Mahia Peninsula. Our spacious rustic home
with cathedral ceilings, hand carved furniture overlooks the Pacific with breathtaking views.
A few steps to bush walks, native bird watching, mustering sheep and cattle. Outside pets,
golden labrador and cat. Louise enjoys painting in her art studio and the area is an artist's
paradise. Swimming, surfing, fishing, shell-fishing, horse back riding on miles of white sandy
beaches or play golf, visit the Mahia reserve, Morere hot pools and thermal swimming pool.
Fishing excursions possible. The host is fluent in German, Italian and Hungarian. We have
both travelled extensively and particularly enjoy meeting overseas visitors. Cottage in avocado
orchard: 2 minutes walk to beach. Self contained unit. Breakfast and dinner not included.
Please telephone / fax for reservations, directions. Nick and Louise Schick, R.D.8, Mahanga
Beach, Nuhaka, Hawkes Bay. Telephone: 06 837 5898 Fax: 06 837 5990.*

Bayview, Napier

Beach Homestay
Address: 'Kilbirnie' 84 Le Quesne Road,
Bay View, Napier
Name: Jill & John Grant
Telephone: (06) 836 6929
Email: jill.john@xtra.co.nz
Mobile: (025) 234 7363
Beds: 1 firm Queen, 1 Double (2 bedrooms)
Bathroom: 1 Ensuite, 1 Private (shower/spa)
Tariff: B&B (full) Double $70, Single $50,
Dinner $20pp, Not suitable for children. Credit Cards. NZ B&B Vouchers accepted
Nearest Town: Napier 12km.

*Three years ago we moved with our pets to Bayview on an unspoiled fishing beach, attracted
by its beauty and position away from traffic noise but only 15 minutes from main attractions.
We now also enjoy the proximity of surrounding vineyards, restaurants, walks and gardens.
Kilbirnie has off road parking and is easy to find adjacent to the Taupo turn-off and Pacific
Highway to Gisborne. Upstairs, guest rooms have restful views of the Pacific Ocean one side,
vineyards on the other, private bathrooms, excellent showers, abundant hot water, comfort-
able firm beds. We invite you to share our local knowledge, imaginative meals, real coffee, fresh
juice, and books while relaxing enjoying friendly hospitality in modern surroundings.*
Directions: *From Taupo first left after intersection Highways Two / Five Franklin Road to
Le Quesne, proceed to far end beachfront. From Napier first right after Bayview "Mobil"
Station.*

Bayview, Napier

Farmstay and Self Contained Lodge
Address: "The Grange", 263 Hill Road,
Eskdale, Hawkes Bay
Name: Roslyn and Don Bird
Telephone: (06) 836 6666
Fax: (06) 836 6456
Mobile: (025) 281 5738
Email: stay_at_the_grange@xtra.co.nz
Beds: Farmstay: 1 King or Twin.
Lodge: 1 King or Twin, 1 Double, 2 Singles (2 Bedrooms) (Cot etc.)
Bathroom: Farmstay: 1 Family Share plus private toilet. Lodge: 1 Private.
Tariff: Farmstay: B&B (full) Double $70, Single $50. Lodge: Double $75,
Single $50, $20 per extra person. Breakfast Provision $7.50 pp (optional),
Dinner $25 pp. Credit Cards accepted.
Nearest Town: Napier 12 minutes South, Bay View 3 minutes.

*In the heart of a thriving wine region overlooking the picturesque Esk Valley is "**The Grange**",
a quiet, delightful self contained lodge. Private, spacious accommodation, relaxing peaceful
surrounds with spectacular rural, coastal and city views. Sample the farmbaking, tempting
snacks and preserve. You may like to join us for dinner? We're an out-going family of five who
enjoy making new friends, travel, hiking, fishing, gardening and all sports. Don a wine maker
and partner of nearby Wishart Estate Winery can give you that personal tour! Roslyn, Drew
(dog) and Sparkie (cat) manage the farmstay and farm, Saanan dairy goats, sheep, cows, pigs
and chickens. There's lots to see and do around here, or unwind on the deck with the soothing
chorus of native birds in the surrounding gardens and trees. Share our home with us or retreat
in the lodge. Our place is your place!*
Directions: *1km off SH5 Eskdale or 2km off SH2 at Bay View.*

Bayview, Napier

Self Contained Accommodation
Address: Beachfront Homestay,
20A Le Quesne Road, Bay View, Napier
Name: Jim and Christine Howard
Telephone: (06) 836 6530
Fax: (06) 836 6531
Mobile: (025) 204 3393
Beds: 1 Double, 2 Single (2 Bedrooms)
Bathroom: 1 Guests share
Tariff: B&B (Full) Double $75, Single $50,
Dinner $25 pp, Children under 12 years half price.
Nearest Town: Napier 12 kms

*Jim, Christine and Sarcha (Jack Russel) will welcome you to their new
beachfront home, with breathtaking views of Hawkes Bay. You are welcome to
their home where they offer guests very comfortable self contained accommodation. Dining, lounge with TV, kitchen facilities and laundry available. Jim a
local stock agent and Christine works at a local winery, both enjoy meeting
people and their interests are fishing, and the outdoor life. The beach offers
good surfcasting and they enjoy setting up the kontiki in the hope of fresh fish
breakfast, you are welcome to join them. Jim and Christine have extensive
local knowledge and are happy to make arrangements to make your stay with
them as pleasant as possible. Beachfront Homestay is just 5 minutes south of
the Napier - Taupo turnoff and 12 minutes from Napier's Marine Parade
activities and cafes.*

Taradale, Napier

Homestay
Address: 'Victoria Lodge',
50 Puketapu Road, Taradale
Name: Don & Sheila Copas
Telephone: (06) 844 2182
Beds: 1 Double, 3 Single (3 bdrms)
Bathroom: 1 Guests share
Tariff: B&B (full) Double $60, Single $30,
Children half price; Dinner $20. NZ B&B Vouchers accepted
Nearest Town: Napier 10 km

Our home is situated in an attractive and interesting one acre garden with sheep in the orchard, a putting green and a swimming pool contributing to its unique rural atmosphere although it is only five minutes walk from the town of Taradale and ten minutes drive from Napier.

The climate of Hawkes Bay justifies the title of "Sunny Napier" and the area in and around the city has much to offer of interest and activity, i.e. sailing, fishing, windsurfing, bush walks, wine trail etc.

Napier is also well endowed with tourist attractions - museums, aquarium, Marineland and can lay a claim to being the 'Art Deco' centre of the world.

We love to entertain and you will be assured of a warm welcome at our comfortable family home from us and our dog and cat.

Directions: *10 km west from Napier. Area maps are available from the Information Centre on Marine Parade or the A.A. Centre in Dickens Street, Napier or phone us for directions.*

http://www.bnb.co.nz

take a look

Napier

Homestay
Address: 19 Alamein Crescent, Napier
Name: Pam & Bill McCulloch
Telephone: (06) 843 6744
Fax: (06) 843 6729
Beds: 1 King, 4 Single + Cot
(3 bedrooms)
Bathroom: 1 Guests share,
1 Family share
Tariff: B&B (continental) Double $75, Single $40, Dinner $20,
Children under 12 half price. NZ B&B Vouchers accepted
Nearest Town: Napier 3km

We are retired and for many years have enjoyed sharing our home and lives with an ever-increasing circle of friends who enjoy real homestay hospitality.
Bill attends Rotary and Probus, and our interests include gardening, travel and crafts. Guest rooms have a comfortable King-size bed or single beds, with electric blankets. Bathroom facilities shared. Children welcome. Cot available.
We have a well-kept garden and swimming-pool for your enjoyment, and one handsome cat! Our generous continental breakfast served at a time to suit you may include freshly squeezed juice, local fruit, cereals, yoghurt, home-made preserves, toast, tea or coffee. There are many restaurants within 10 minutes by car. Dinner is available at home by prior arrangement, and you are welcome to relax with us in our lounge.
Napier is famous for its Art-Deco architecture and surrounding vineyards, Gannet Beach safari (in season) and plenty of sunshine.
Off-street parking. Please - no smoking in the house.

Napier

Homestay
Address: 17 Cobden Road, Napier
Name: Kay & Stewart Spence
Telephone: (06) 835 9454
Fax: (06) 835 9454
Beds: 2 Queen, 2 Single (2 bedrooms)
Bathroom: 2 Ensuites
Tariff: B&B (full) Double $90, Single $65,
Credit Cards Visa M/C
NZ B&B Vouchers accepted $10 Surcharge.
Nearest Town: Napier 1 Km

Our early colonial 1880, two-storeyed home with comfortable and modern facilities is pleasantly situated in a sunny position on Napier Hill. The home is set in attractive grounds spread over almost an acre, in quiet area - just a 10 to 15 minute walk from Napier City Centre. Two guest rooms include a Queen bed and a single bed and ensuite bathrooms, one suite also includes lounge. All rooms are spacious with lounge chairs and tea making facilities and TV's. Beds have electric blankets and woollen underlays.
We have been welcomed into private homes in New Zealand and overseas and wish to extend a warm welcome to you to share our home in the Art Deco city in sunny Hawkes Bay.
We will be happy to meet you at the Hawkes Bay Airport, Napier Railway Station or City bus depot.
Directions: *Port end Marine Parade, Coote Road, right Thompson Road, left Cobden Road*

Napier

Homestay
Address: 7 Charles Street,
Westshore, Napier
Name: Sheila & Rob Comrie
Telephone: (06) 835 9679
Email: robcom@clear.net.nz
Beds: 2 Queen, 2 Single (2 bedrooms)
Bathroom: 1 Guests share
Tariff: B&B (full) Double $70, Single $45,
Dinner $25pp. NZ B&B Vouchers accepted
Nearest Town: Napier 4 Kms

We have retired from farming life and having travelled overseas and enjoyed B & Bs, we would be pleased to share our comfortable modern home with people who enjoy a homely atmosphere. From the house you step out on to a pleasant, safe beach and are only 5 minutes drive from central Napier or the Airport. Hastings, Taradale and Havelock North are all within a 30 minute drive. Accommodation, on the ground floor, consists of lounge, dining room, two double bedrooms, guest bathroom and separate toilet. Kitchen available for tea making. Laundry available. Restaurants handy or dinner by arrangement. We sleep upstairs. All local attractions available including beach walks, windsurfing and sailing almost on the doorstep. Off street parking. Fax and email available to guests - Toll charges.
Directions: *Please phone. Pick-up from Airport, Station or Bus depot if required.*

Napier

Homestay
Address: 9 Milton Terrace, Napier
Name: Helen & Robert McGregor
Telephone: (06) 835 7434
Fax: (06) 835 1912
Email: artdeco@hb.co.nz
Beds: 1 Double (1 bedroom)
Bathroom: 1 Private (bath & shower)
Tariff: B&B (full or continental) Double $80, Single $50. Credit cards.
Nearest Town: Napier 1.3km

A room with a view! When visiting Napier, you are welcome to stay in our modern two-storeyed home, in an old garden on the sunny side of Napier's beautiful hill. The fully-appointed guest-room, has a fine view over Hawke Bay and has a private bathroom. We are a 15 minute walk from downtown or from historic Port Ahuriri, both with excellent restaurants. Cooked or continental breakfast provided. We will be happy to collect you from your arrival point. We ask guests not to smoke in the house. Laundry facilities available at a small charge.

Having experienced home hosting overseas, we are firm believers in its advantages and we enjoy giving our guests true Kiwi home hospitality. Our interests are travel, gardening, the arts, local history and the preservation of Napier's Art Deco architecture. (Robert is the Executive Director of the Art Deco Trust). Please telephone or write beforehand.

Napier
Homestay
Address: 'Hillcrest', 4 George Street,
Hospital Hill, Napier.
Name: Noel & Nancy Lyons
Telephone: (06) 835 1812
Beds: 1 Double, 2 Single (2 bedrooms)
Bathroom: 1 Guests share
Tariff: B&B (continental) Double $70,
Single $45, Dinner by arrangement $25pp.
Credit Cards accepted. NZ B&B Vouchers accepted
Nearest Town: Napier 1km.

A warm welcome awaits you in our comfortable modern, smoke-free home, with panoramic views of Hawke Bay and the hills. All rooms open onto spacious decks where chairs invite you to relax in peace and enjoy the garden. The two guest rooms are downstairs with an adjacent lounge, colour TV and the use of your own telephone. The beds have duvets and electric blankets. Laundry facilities are available. A feature of our home is the beautiful native Rimu timber used throughout. We have travelled extensively and welcome the opportunity of meeting visitors and sharing our knowledge of this area with you. Our interests are travel, gardening, woodturning, embroidery and live theatre. Off street parking is available. Our holiday home, on the foreshore at Mahia Beach is available for a relaxing holiday.
Directions: *Please phone. Pick-up from Airport, Bus or Train if required.*

Napier
Accommodation
Address: 'Anleigh Heights',
115 Chaucer Road North, Napier
Name: Allan & Anne Tolley
Telephone: (06) 835 1188
Fax: (06) 835-1032
Beds: 1 KIng, 1 Queen, 1 Double 4 Poster
Bathroom: 3 Ensuite
Tariff: B&B (special) Double $135-$160.
Single $95, Children welcome. Dinner $45 pp.
Credit cards. NZ B&B Vouchers accepted
Nearest Town: Napier 5 mins.

New Zealand Association
FARM & HOME
HOSTS

Experience the character and charm of a bygone era. Anleigh Heights offers quality accommodation in Napier's grandest historic home. Situated high on the Napier hill, next to the hospital, our home has commanding views over Hawkes Bay.
We have recreated the cossetted lifestyle of the Edwardian House Party for our guests;
- you are greeted at the door by your hosts or family dog
- your rooms are named not numbered
- tea and coffee is served on a silver tray, in fine china, with tea strainers and silver pots
- open fires, flowers, antique furniture and personal possessions all make you feel as if you're part of the household
- breakfast is a house speciality with a varied menu and is served in the elegant dining room.
For reasons of historic preservation and good health there is no smoking in the house. Off-street parking is available, or we can collect you.

Napier City
Bed & Breakfast
Address: Madeira Bed & Breakfast
6 Madeira Road, Napier
Name: Eric & Julie Ball
Telephone: (06) 835 5185
Email: julieball@clear.net.nz
Beds: 1 Queen (1 bedroom)
Bathroom: 1 Family share
Tariff: B&B (full) Double $75, Single $50,
Children by arrangement. NZ B&B Vouchers accepted
Nearest Town: Napier - 3 minute walk

Our home, rebuilt after the 1931 earthquake, commands outstanding views over Hawke Bay and Napier City. As local residents of many years, we can assist you to fill in your days, whether it be sightseeing, wine tasting, golf or dining out, and with parking on site, a 3 minute walk takes you into the city. Your double room has a Queen size bed and ajoining toilet and handbasin. Also tea making facilities. Breakfast may be served on our veranda in the morning sun or in the dining room. We provide good healthy foods and fresh fruit when available. We have an old, small dog and a cat. Testimony to our popularity can be seen in our visitors book "What a gorgeous place and great hospitality," U.S.A. "The highlight of our trip," England. "We felt most welcome and enjoyed our stay."
Directions: *Please phone.*

Greenmeadows, Napier
Homestay
Address: 7 Forward St,
Greenmeadows, Napier
Name: Bill & Jenny Hoffman
Telephone: (06) 844 9630
Fax: (06) 844 1450
Mobile: (025) 932 874
Beds: 1 King, 1 Queen,
2 Single (3 bedrooms)
Bathroom: 1 Ensuite (mobility), 1 Guest share
Tariff: B&B (full) Double $80-$90, Single $50.
Credit cards. NZ B&B Vouchers accepted $20.
Nearest Town: Napier - 8 mins away.

Set in tranquil gardens, close to tourist attractions, shops and wineries, we invite our guests to share the warmth and comfort of home.
Our large rooms offer independent heating, tea / coffee facilities, colour TV, and electric blankets.
For our guests who prefer the ease of a mobility suite, we offer full wheelchair access for their convenience. laundry facilities are also available.
Your day with us will begin with a scrumptious breakfast in our sun-filled dining room, and a chat to help plan your days activities. Maps and brochures are available for you.
After touring the history rich twin cities of Napier and Hastings, relax in our private spa or sparkling pool, or view our antique doll collection.
Our two dogs, Hogan and Tess, and Tabitha the cat also wait to welcome you, too.
Directions: *Head towards Taradale, turn right into Avenue Rd after Greenmeadows shops, then 1st left into Forward Street.*

360

Bluff Hill - Napier

Homestay
Address: "Treeways",
1 Lighthouse Road,
Bluff Hill, Napier
Name: Maurie & Cheryl Keeling
Telephone: (06) 835 6567
Fax: (06) 835 6567
Email: mckeeling@clear.net.nz
Beds: 1 Double, 2 Singles (2 bedrooms)
Bathroom: 1 Guest share
Tariff: B&B (full)
Double $80, Single $55, Dinner $20. NZ B&B Vouchers accepted $15 surcharge
Nearest Town: Napier central city 1km

Peaceful, private, 15 minutes walk to the city centre or Bluff Hill lookout, and set amongst bush and gardens with pleasant views over the sea and northern coastline. A large sunny terrace with tables and chairs, flower garden and lilly pond provide a relaxing atmosphere for people and native birds. Our home with spacious living areas, rimu timber floors and comfortable furnishings is warm and friendly and yours to enjoy. Two double bedrooms, one with double bed, one with Kingsize convertible to two singles have electric blankets, bedside lights, heating and writing desk and chair. Home grown fruits and vegetables are a speciality with meals and we offer complimentary local wine with dinner. We have travelled extensively, enjoy theatre, the outdoors and conversation. We have a Jack Russel dog named Digby.
Directions: *Tourist Drive 11 to Bluff Hill Lookout.*
Webpage: www.napieronline.co.nz.accommodation / treeways

Napier

Homestay
Address: "Snug Harbour" 147 Harold Holt Ave., Napier
Name: Don & Ruth McLeod
Telephone: (06) 843 2521
Fax: (06) 843 2520
Email: donmcld@clear.net.nz
Beds: 1 Queen in studio with ensuite. Twin and Single (2 bedrooms)
Bathroom: 1 Ensuite in studio, 1 Family share
Tariff: B&B (full) Queen Ensuite $80, Twin $70, Single $45.
Credit Cards. NZ B&B Vouchers accepted
Nearest Town: Napier 5km

Our home is situated on the outskirts of Napier City. It has a rural outlook and is in close proximity to local orchards market gardens and wineries. It is 8 minutes by car to many tourist attractions around the centre of Napier City and 5 minutes by car to Taradale shopping centre.
Our home is designed for outdoor living with an attractive private patio to make the most of the sunny Hawkes Bay climate.
We have enjoyed the comforts and friendliness of Bed & Breakfast homes in New Zealand and overseas and look forward to sharing our home with travellers.
Our interests include travel, gardening including orchid growing and keeping in touch with family and friends in New Zealand and overseas. We both have a background in teaching.
We ask guests not to smoke in the house. We will collect you from airport bus or train if required. Members of NZ Association Farm & Home Hosts Inc.
Directions: *Please phone or write for directions.*
Home Page: www.nzhomestay.co.nz/mcleod.htm

Napier

Homestay
Address: "Ourhome",
4 Hospital Terrace, Napier
Name: N&N Hamlin
Telephone: (06) 835 7358
Fax: (06) 835 7355
Mobile: (025) 852 304
Email: ourhomeb&b@xtra.co.nz
Beds: 2 Single (1 bedroom) +
1 Double bed-settee available in guest lounge.
Bathroom: 1 Private
Tariff: B&B (continental) Double $75, Single $50.
NZ B&B Vouchers accepted $5 surcharge
Nearest Town: Napier 1km

Wonderful views of sea and hills from every room (and the private sunny patio) in our very attractive guest suite. We offer accommodation for up to four in one group, the bedroom having two single beds, guest lounge a double bed-settee. Private separate entry. Tea/coffee making facilities; TV, fridge. Laundry available. No smoking, please! A three minute drive takes you to the heart of our famous Art Deco city and Marine Parade, catering for a wide range of interests. Noted Hawkes' Bay wineries (several offering great food too!), popular craft outlets, Hastings City, Havelock North and Clifton (the start of tours to the gannets at Cape Kidnappers) are all within a thirty-minute drive. Off street parking available.
We will be happy to collect you from public transport, and look forward to your company.
Homepage: napieronline.co.nz/accomodation/ourhome

Napier

Boutique Guest Establishment
Address: The "Large" House,
4 Hadfield Terrace, Napier Hill, Napier
Name: The "Large" House, Judith & John
Telephone: (06) 835 0000
Fax: (06) 835 2244
Mobile: (025) 245 2870
Email: large@xtra.co.nz>
Beds: 1 Super King (1 Twin), 1 King, 1 Queen, (3 bedrooms)
Bathroom: 2 Ensuite, 1 Private
Tariff: B&B (special) Double $175, Single $135. Smoke free inside.
Credit Cards (VISA/MC/AMEX/DINERS). Tariff applies 1.9.99-31.8.2000
Nearest Town: A five minute stroll to central Napier City.

Choose to step back in time ..... to a world of character and courtesy, to where today's needs blend with the charm of yesteryear. Circa 1858, The "Large" House takes its name from the original owner James Stanibridge Large Esquire. Share with us one of Napier's earliest landmarks. Discretely nestled in a picturesque setting of cascading gardens, this historic homestead offers an idyllic private environment with a backdrop of breathtaking views of bush surrounds and seascape. The exquisite Grape, Chardonnay and Champagne bedrooms have charming individual features, sumptuous bed furnishings and classical bathrooms. Relax in elegant comfort in the Guest Lounge and watch the ships go by. Breakfast on the gracious balcony or in the stunning conservatory, each with captivating views and the sounds of birdlife, waterfall and waves breaking on the shore. Romantic retreat, business haven .... perfect for the discerning traveller. Enjoy your Hawke's Bay experience in The "Large" House.
Directions: *Kindly telephone for directions.*
Home Page: http://www.friars.co.nz/hosts/largehouse/html

Napier
Bed & Breakfast

Address: "Turangi",
1 Hukarere Road,
Bluff Hill, Napier
Name: Joan & David Donaldson
Telephone: (06) 835 7795
Fax: (06) 835 7096
Mobile: (025) 748 218
Beds: 1 Queen, 2 Single (2 bedrooms)
Bathroom: 1 Ensuite, 1 Private
Tariff: B&B (full) Double Suite $90,
Single Suite $70, Treble $115.
Credit Cards. "Bookin" accepted.
Nearest Town: Napier 0.7km

Turangi "From a High Place" a classic two storey 1930's house, our home is set in a Mediterranean garden with lawn and mature trees and has incomparable views of Hawkes Bay and Napier city. Level access, off street parking. Private guest suite observes the sunrise over the pacific ocean and the lights of Art Deco Napier, which has been called "Nice of the South Pacific". Elegant suite comprises Queen and Single beds with quality linen, own sitting room, tea making, TV, refrigerator. Ensuite bathroom has separate bath and shower, adjoining single bedroom with toilet. Five minutes walk to Napier by picturesque heritage trail, yet only sound is of birds and sea. Breakfast of seasonal produce served in sunny dining room overlooking garden. Comfortably furnished with art and antiques, open fires, garden flowers. Non smoking. Pick-up from terminals.
Directions: *Corner of Clyde and Hukarere Roads, past Girls High School.*

Napier
Guest House

Address: 471 Marine Parade, Napier
Name: Blue Water Lodge
Telephone: 06-835 8929
Fax: 06-835 8929
Mobile: 025-500 192
Email: bobbrown@voyager.co.nz
Beds: 6 Double, 9 Single
(9 bedrooms)
Bathroom: 1 Ensuite, 2 Guests share
Tariff: B&B (continental) Double with ensuite $80,
Double $70 - $80, Single $40, Children under 14 years $10.
All credit cards accepted. (Not open during winter months)
Nearest Town: Napier

Blue Water Lodge is on the beach front opposite the Aquarium car park on Napier's popular Marine Parade.
Close to all local tourist attractions and within walking distance to the city centre, information centre, family restaurants, RSA and Cosmopolitan Club.
Owner operated.

Napier

Self Contained Accommodation
Address: "The Coach-House",
9 Gladstone Road, Napier
Name: Jan Chalmers
Telephone: (06) 835 6126
Beds: 1 Queen, 2 Single
(2 bedrooms)
Bathroom: 1 Private
Tariff: B&B (full)
Double $100, Single $60.
Four people $160. Dinner $20 (by arrangement).
Children school age $25, little chilren free.
NZ B&B Vouchers accepted $30 surcharge
Nearest Town: Napier (5 minutes walk to centre)

The Coach-House built of kauri in the late 1800's, the Coach-house is tastefully renovated and totally self-contained. A lovely Mediterranean style garden on the hill surrounds the Coach-house, and is within sight and sound of the sea. Inside there are two bedrooms (one upstairs) sleeping four people, open plan kitchen / dining / living room. Bathroom adjacent with separate toilet. The fridge will be full of breakfast 'goodies' including "treats". Fresh flowers in the bedrooms. TV, radio and glossy magazines are also included. There are private outdoor living areas including a sunny deck for all fresco dining. Off-street parking and easy access complete the picture. If privacy and relaxation is what you want in an attractive and comfortable home-away-from-home, then the Coach-house is for you. I am also happy to be a 'taxi driver' and do your washing.

Napier

Homestay B&B
Address: No 11, 11 Sealy Road, Napier
Name: Phyllida and Bryan Isles
Telephone: (06) 834 4372
Mobile: (025) 246 3968
Email: phyllbry@xtra.co.nz
Beds: 1 Queen, 2 Singles
(2 bedrooms)
Bathroom: 1 Guests share
Tariff: B&B (special)
Double $90, Single $60.
Seasonal variations may apply.
NZ B&B Vouchers accepted $30 surcharge
Nearest Town: Napier 0.5 km

New Zealand Association
FARM & HOME HOSTS

The name says it all!
You will score our home more than 10 for comfort, convenience, and conviviality.
***Comfort**: Spacious, sunny, quality rooms - each with TV, Tea making facilities, electric blankets, good linen, heater, hairdryer and writing table. Separate guest toilet and large bathroom across hall. **Convenience**: New hill villa, level access, off street parking, great views. An easy walk to city, cafes, Ahuriri and Napier attractions. Drive or bus to Hawkes Bay's many wineries or gannets. **Conviviality**: A friendly welcome and all the help you need to make your stay enjoyable. A selection of special breakfasts are offered and while you sit enjoying them and the view, you can plan your day or Bryan will share with you some of Napier's history. Petanque available. We have travelled ourselves and enjoy meeting others. We look forward to meeting you. Please no smoking indoors. We have a cat and a dog. Please telephone or write beforehand.*

Napier

Self Contained Accommodation B&B
Address: 3 Cameron Terrace, Napier
Name: Inglenook
Telephone: (06) 834 2922
Mobile: (025) 414 992
Beds: 2 Double, 2 Single (twin) (3 bedrooms)
Bathroom: 2 Ensuites, 1 Guests share
Tariff: B&B (special) Double $75, Single $50,
Children on application. No credit cards.
NZ B&B Vouchers accepted $10 surcharge
Nearest Town: Napier

Inglenook is situated on the Hill in a peaceful garden setting and offers expansive views of the City Centre across Marine Parade and the sea to Cape Kidnappers. It is only five minutes walk to shops and restaurants.

Inglenook offers privacy and a quiet, restful atmosphere to visitors. It is immaculately presented and serviced, and has quality chattels and linen. Guest suites are self-contained and independent of the owner's living area, with their own separate entrances and keys. Each has its own outdoor living area set in an expanse of cottage garden, overlooked by trees which provide a home to a range of native birds.

A special breakfast including fresh Hawkes Bay fruit or home baking is served to guests each morning at a pre-arranged time, which can be enjoyed outdoors or in guests' rooms as required. Tea and coffee making facilities are available in each suite and a barbecue area is provided.

Napier, Westshore

B&B/Family Stay
Address: Airport Gardens B&B/Family Stay,
90 Main North Road, Westshore, Napier
Name: Ted and Diane Cunningham
Telephone: (06) 835 6490
Fax: (06) 835 4672
Mobile: (021) 922 271
Email: Airport.Gardens@xtra.co.nz
Beds: 2 Queen, 2 single (2 Bedrooms)
Bathrooms 2: 1 Guests share, 1 Family Share.
Tariff: B&B (Continental) Double $85, Single $65 or as self contained unit $125.
Dinner $20 by arrangement, Children $10 + $1 per year of age up to 12 years. Credit Cards: Visa/Mastercard. Eftpos. NZ B&B Vouchers accepted $15 surcharge
Nearest Town: Napier (5 mins drive)

A warm welcome awaits you in our character "Louis Hay' design home. Built in 1930 before the Napier Earthquake. Situated opposite Napier Airport, just a five minute drive from the city. Just a short stroll from Westshore Beach, handy to local vineyards, recreational areas and many restaurants. We offer you: Choice of 2 lovely rooms with own TV (each furnished with 1 Queen and 1 Single bed); cosy lounge to relax in; fully equipped kitchen; separate bathroom and toilet; laundry facilities; continental breakfast or cooked by arrangement, dinners available if required $20 pp. Guests have own entrance & key. Transport available to and from city, bus, train and airport terminals; local tours by arrangement. Eftpos and credit cards (Mastercard / Visa). Accommodation also available as self contained family unit, sleeps 5. Our interests are gardening, motorcycle touring and entertaining our guests. We and our pets, Pet the dog and Midnight the cat, look forward to sharing our home with you, and making your stay in Napier a memorable one. **Directions**: *250 m from Napier Airport gate on Main North Road into Napier. Please phone for more details.*
Home Page: Airport Garden@xtra.co.nz

Taradale, Napier

Homestay
Address: "Greenwood", 62 Avondale Road, Taradale
Name: Ann and Peter Green
Telephone: (06) 845 1246
Fax: (06) 845 1246
Mobile: (025) 795 403
Email: greenwood@clear.net.nz
Beds: 2 Queen, 2 single (3 Bedrooms)
Bathroom: 3 Ensuite
Tariff: B&B (Full) Double $80,
Single $55, Dinner $20 pp. Credit cards: Visa/Mastercard.
Nearest Town: Napier, 8 minutes drive.

* Delight in birdsong on spring and summer mornings.
* Relax on the deck as the Gleditsia tree filters the afternoon sun.
* Nibble home grown pecan nuts.
* Savour the taste of homemade preserves and chutneys.
* Drool over Ann's superb eggs Benedict (and many other breakfast delights).
* Enjoy some of New Zealand's favourite roast dinners (some people think they are!) by arrangement.
* Put the world to rights as we discuss the follies of presidents and kings.
* Laugh (or cry) as Peter tries to converse in German and French.
* Our interests are history, art, education, computers and golf. Our loves are family, entertaining, and aviation.
A short walk takes you to Taradale shops, restaurants and wineries. Tourist attractions and golf courses are within easy driving distance.
Directions: Please phone, write or visit our home page.
Home Page: http://home.clear.net.nz/pages/greenwood

http://www.bnb.co.nz

take a look

Napier/Hastings

Orchard Homestay/SC Accom/own kitchen, large lounge.

Copperfields

Address: c/- Pakowhai Store, Pakowhai Road, Napier, Hawkes Bay
Name: Copperfields
Telephone: (06) 876 9710 **Fax**: (06) 876 9710
Mobile: (021) 256 7590 **Email**: rich.pam@clear.net.nz
Beds: 1 Double, 2 Single (2 bedrooms)
Bathroom: 1 Private, 1 Family share (laundry facilities available)
Tariff: B&B (full) Double $85, Single $65, Children under 12yrs half price, Dinner $25 pp (3 courses) by arrangement (can be served privately in cottage), Credit Card (VISA). Weekly rates negotiable. NZ B&B Vouchers accepted $10 surcharge
Nearest Town: Midway Napier and Hastings (about 10 km to each)

Welcome to Hawkes Bay. 'Copperfields' is a small mixed apple orchard and lifestyle block on the main road between Napier (famous for its Art Deco buildings) and its 'twin city' of Hastings situated in the rich soil of the Heretaunga Plains. Wineries, craft trails and scenic attractions are readily accessible. We recommend the spectacular view from Te Mata Peak. We are a non smoking married couple with grown up family living away from home. A friendly Labrador dog keeps us company at home. Pam is a weaver and interested in craft work generally. Richard makes and restores furniture and is interested in antiques and curiosities. We both like good food and meeting people from other countries and places. We hope to offer you a friendly and comfortable base from which to enjoy your stay in Hawkes Bay. Guests stay in 'Glen Cottage' a self-contained two bedroom dwelling with large lounge and log fire, attached to our house. It is the original orchard house and enables guests to be totally private if they wish. A continental breakfast is provided in the cottage for those guests wishing to sleep late. Dogs welcome (conditions apply).

Puketapu

Homestay
Address: Silverford, Dartmoor Road, Puketapu, Hawkes Bay.
Name: William and Chris Orme-Wright
Telephone: (06) 844 5600
Fax: (06) 844 4423
Email: homestay@iconz.co.nz
Beds: 1 King, 1 Queen, 1 Double (3 bedrooms)
Bathroom: 1 Ensuite, 1 Guests share
Tariff: B&B (full) Double $135-$155, Single $105. Dinner $35 by arrangement. Credit cards: Visa/Amex
Nearest Town: Napier/Hastings 20 minutes

Situated on the Wine, Trail "Silverford" - one of Hawkes Bay's most gracious Homesteads - is spaciously set in 17 acres of farmland, established trees and gardens. Drive through our half a kilometre long gorgeous Oak lined avenue to the sweeping lawns, bright flower gardens and ponds surrounding our elegant home designed by Natusch at the turn of the century. We are relaxed and friendly and offer a warm ambience in private, comfortable and tranquil surroundings - a romantic haven with tastefully furnished bedrooms, charming guest sitting room and a courtyard to dream in. Silverford is an idyllic welcoming haven for a private, peaceful and cosy stay whilst at the same time being close to all the amenities and attractions that Hawkes Bay has to offer. Friendly deer, cow, pigeons, ducks and dogs. Central Heating. Swimming Pool. We are smokefree and regret the property is unsuitable for children. Some French and German spoken.

Napier/Hastings
Homestay/Farmstay
Address: Charlton Road, R.D.2,
Hastings, H.B.
Name: Mr and Mrs B Shaw
Telephone: (06) 875 0177
Fax: (06) 825 0525
Beds: 4 Single (2 bedrooms)
Bathroom: 1 Ensuite, 1 Family share
Tariff: B&B (special) Double $100,
Single $100, Dinner extra. Campervans welcome.
Nearest Town: Napier - Hastings

Te Awanga is a picturesque coastal village situated fifteen minutes drive from both Napier and Hastings and right next door to the gannets at Cape Kidnappers and one of Hawkes Bay's leading winery restaurants. Charlton Road is the first on your right after passing through Te Awanga and leads to a large and comfortable homestead where you can enjoy space, tranquillity and fine hospitality while receiving every assistance to make your stay in our area as interesting and enjoyable as possible. You will have your own private entrance so can come and go as you please while enjoying the many attractions Hawkes Bay has to offer. For the benefit of those seeking the real New Zealand, ours is a genuine country residence and not a transplant from the city as is sometimes the case. We have a couple of Jack Russell dogs.
Directions: *Please phone Bill or Heather for directions on how to find us and to learn more about what we have to offer.*

Napier/Hastings
Self Contained Accommodation
Address: 524 State Highway 2, Hastings North
Name: Riverbank House
Telephone: (06) 870 0759
Fax: (06) 870 0528
Mobile: (025) 870 0759)
Beds: 2 Double, 3 Single (3 bedrooms)
Bathroom: All ensuite.
Tariff: B&B (full) Double $75, Single $45, Dinner by arrangement.
Children welcome. Credit Cards: Visa/Mastercard. NZ B&B Vouchers accepted
Nearest Town: Napier 8 kms. Hastings 5 kms.

Riverbank House is set on 1 1/2 acres of tranquil garden bordering the Clive Rive. We offer the friendliness of a homestay combined with the privacy of your own cottage both with TV, tea and coffee facilities. We have an in-ground pool and hot spa. Our 2 children enjoy the company of other kids on the move and we are well equipped to amuse them with a trampoline, swings etc.
Our small dog Scruff also enjoys the odd dog to stay. Breakfast is served in the main house or in your cottage. We have all travelled locally and abroad and look forward to helping you enjoy your Hawkes Bay experience. Disabled access and facilities in front cottage.
Directions: *From Napier travel along State Highway 2 along sea front, through Clive village. Look for our sign on the right.*

Hastings

Homestay
Address: 115A Frederick St,
Hastings, Hawkes Bay
Name: Doug & Barbara McConchie
Telephone: (06) 878 4576
Beds: 1 Queen, 2 Single (2 Bedrooms)
Bathroom: 1 Guests share
Tariff: B&B (special) Double $75, Single $40,
Children half price, Dinner $20. Credit Cards.
NZ B&B Vouchers accepted.
Nearest Town: We live in Hastings city, Napier is 20km north.

We are a retired couple with no children, just a Siamese cat. Our home is modern, attractive and peaceful, being in a back garden setting away from traffic noises. It has a guest wing with ranchslider entry. A short walk takes you to the city centre or to parks. A fifteen minute drive takes you to golf courses or up Te Mata Peak to wonderful views. A gannet sanctuary at Cape Kidnappers is a great trip. Wineries, orchards, gardens or walks abound. A five minute drive takes you to the picturesque village of Havelock North. We enjoy meeting people and judging by the letters we get, people enjoy being with us. We give you your choice of breakfast. Continental, cooked or special. Long stays discounted. No smoking inside please. Married couples with or without children and single, separate bedroom folk are extremely welcome.
Directions: *Coming from Napier Marine Parade take SH2 via Clive and Karamu Rd to Hastings. At first set of lights turn right into Frederick St. Coming from Napier airport turn off SH2 into SH50, follow signposts to Hastings. Frederick St is 2nd turning on left off Pakawhai Rd. This way 115a is just past 2nd intersection beyond the lights and down a driveway. Turn into first gateway. Coming from Wellington ring for directions. Arriving by bus or train ring and we will meet you.*

Hastings

Self-contained Accom. B&B
Address: 79 Carrick Rd, Twyford, Hastings
(Postal) Box 2116, Hastings
Name: Anne & Peter Wilkinson
Telephone: (06) 879 9357
Fax: (06) 879 9357
Mobile: (025) 417 807
Email: ph-aawilkinson@clear.net.nz
Beds: 2 Single (1 bedroom)
Bathroom: 1 Private
Tariff: B&B (full) Double $80, Single $60,
Dinner $25pp. NZ B&B Vouchers accepted
Nearest Town: Hastings 8km

We are situated in the country 10 minutes west of Hastings city in a wine growing and orcharding area called Twyford, and our sister city Napier is 20 minutes away. A warm welcome is extended to our visitors. The Ngaruroro River is very close for good trout fishing during the season, and we are within easy reach of a variety of other rivers and lakes. Guided fishing is offered by Peter. Hawkes Bay offers a wide variety of attractions. Wineries, good restaurants, gardens to visit, jet boating, tramping, Heritage & Art Deco walks, golf courses, Cape Kidnappers gannet colony, hot air ballooning are but a few of them. Our accommodation is a self contained Lockwood cottage situated in our garden looking towards the Kaweka ranges, comprising a bedroom with two single beds, bathroom, small kitchen and living room. Non-smoking accommodation and does not cater for children.
Directions: *Please phone.*

Hastings
Homestay

Address: 'Woodbine Cottage',
1279 Louie Street, Hastings
Name: Ngaire & Jim Shand
Telephone: (06) 876 9388
Fax: (06) 876 9666
Mobile: 025-529 522
Email: nshand@xtra.co.nz
Beds: 1 Double, 1 Twin (2 bedrooms).
Bathroom: 1 Guests share.
Tariff: B&B (continental) Double $90, Single $50, Dinner on request $25pp,
Full breakfast $7.50 pp extra. Visa/Mastercard/Bank card accepted
NZ B&B Vouchers accepted $20 Surcharge
Nearest Town: Hastings 2.5 Kms

Our home is set in half an acre of cottage garden on the Hastings boundary. We have a swimming pool and tennis court for you to enjoy in the summer months and a spa bath to relax in at the end of the day. Hastings City Centre is 5 minutes by car, as is Havelock North. "Splash Planet" with its water features and hot pools, is 2 minutes away. We have travelled extensively and really enjoy meeting people. Our home-made bread and jams have been popular items on the breakfast table. Laundry facilities are available. We are most happy to help you with your itinerary while you are with us. No smoking in the house please. We look forward to your company and can assure you of a comfortable and relaxing stay.

Hastings
Farm Orchard Homestay

Address: 808 River Road.
"Waiwhenua", RD9, Hastings, Hawkes Bay.
Name: Kirsty and David Hill
Telephone: (06) 874 2435
Fax: (06) 874 2465
Mobile: (025) 759 369
Email: kirsty.hill@xtra.co.nz
Beds: 2 Double, 3 Single (2 bedrooms)
Bathroom: 1 Guests share, 1 Family shower share.
Tariff: B&B (full/continental) Double $65, Single $35, Dinner $25pp.
Family concessions available. Lunch available too. Children accommodation full,
Meals half price. Campervans welcome for secluded river section. Transportation
available. NZ B&B Vouchers accepted
Nearest Town: Hastings/Napier 50km (40 mins). Taihape 100km (Napier/Taihape Rd)

The perfect place to experience country life, specialty meals of home grown produce, and rural hospitality at our 120 year old historic homestead, farm and orchard. Come and join us on our 440 ha sheep, beef and deer farm and apple and pear orchard. We encourage guests to participate in guided tours and farm activities including horse and bike riding, wild game shooting and fishing in our trout filled Tutikuri River. Our young family (and pet Foxy Becky) and home offers guests a friendly family environment catering for individuals or families interested in the outdoor life with an unrestricted length of stay. While we both work on our property, we enjoy meeting people and sharing our relaxing lifestyle and home with guests and families. Your stay would be enriched by including outdoor attractions and activities at our backdoor including hunting, fishing, bush and farm walks, garden tours, golf, jet boating and extensive mountain hikes. **Directions**: *Please phone in advance. Campervans also welcome at our secluded river section (power point included)*

Hastings
Self Contained Accommodation, B&B
Address: 26 Wellwood Road,
Hastings
Name: Raureka
Telephone: (06) 878 9715
Fax: (06) 878 9715
Email: r.t.ormond@xtra.co.nz
Beds: 1 Queen (1 bedroom)
Bathroom: 1 Ensuite
Tariff: B&B (full/continental)
Double $80, Single $60,
Dinner $20, Not suitable for children.
NZ B&B Vouchers accepted $10 surcharge
Nearest Town: Hastings

We welcome you to our home situated in a quiet rural setting. "Raureka" is an apple orchard only 3 kms from town, close to restaurants, golf courses and boutique wineries. We have an attractive, tastefully decorated detached studio with a queen size bed, ensuite, TV and tea and coffee making facilities. We have a swimming pool, tennis court and barbecue area set in an attractive garden and grounds, with a view out to 100 year old oak trees. We are both keen golfers and would be only too happy to organise your golfing requirements. We offer you a relaxed friendly stay with delicious continental or full cooked breakfast served in the main house or in the garden. We have travelled overseas and enjoy sharing our experiences with fellow travellers.

Hastings/Havelock North
Homestay/Farmstay
Address: 'Peak View' Farm,
92 Middle Rd., Havelock North
Name: Dianne & Keith Taylor
Telephone: (06) 877 7408
Fax: (06) 877 7410
Beds: 1 Double, 2 Single plus cot
& highchair (2 bedrooms)
Bathroom: 1 Family share
Tariff: B&B (full) Double $65, Single $40,
Dinner $20pp (2 course $15), Children half price.
Credit Cards (VISA/ MC/BC). NZ B&B Vouchers accepted
Nearest Town: Havelock North 1 km, Hastings 5km

New Zealand
Association
FARM & HOME
HOSTS

*Welcome to our century old home on horticulture land. Relax in our large tranquil gardens and lawns. We enjoy meeting people and after twelve years of "Happy Hosting" we have an ever increasing circle of friends. We invite you to sample our caring and personal attention in a friendly and relaxed atmosphere. We offer comfortable accommodation. Firm beds, all with electric blankets. Generous breakfast cooked or continental with home baking and preserves. Dinners consist of fresh country cuisine. Interests are bushwalks, fishing, gardening and genealogy. Can also advise on travel throughout New Zealand from own experiences. Handy to many wineries. Splash Planet and Hastings 4 kms. Napier Art Deco capital 20 kms. Panoramic views from Te Mata Peak 10 minutes. Lovely boutique shops and restaurants in Havelock North just a short walk away. Dianne has certificate in Farm / Homestay management. No smoking inside please. Laundry facilities available. Enjoy tea or coffee and home-made biscuits on your arrival. **Home Page**: http://nz.com/webnz/bbnz/peakview.htm*

371

Hastings/Havelock North

Homestay
Address: 134 Kopanga Road, Havelock North
Name: Jill & Jock Taylor
Telephone: (06) 877 8797
Fax: (06) 877 2335
Beds: 1 Double (1 bedroom) plus one outside unit with 2 beds, shower and toilet.
Bathroom: 1 Guests own
Tariff: B&B Double $75, single $45, Dinner $15 by prior arrangement.
Cooked breakfast $5 pp extra.
Nearest Town: Hastings 15 minutes, Havelock North 5 minutes.

Our new wooden home is comfortable and welcomes you. Situated in quiet rural surroundings with extensive views, we are only 5 minutes from Havelock North, Hastings and Napier approximately 15 minutes.
We are gardeners and golfers and what better place to be both than Hawkes Bay, with four excellent golf courses, superb gardens and many reputable wineries. Our family of four have grown and gone but we have two friendly black cats. There is a double bed with guests' own bathroom in the house and an outside unit with two single beds, shower, toilet and tea and coffee making facilities.
No smoking please.
Directions: *Please phone.*

Hastings/Havelock North

Homestay/Farmstay
Address: Wharehau,
R.D. 11, Hastings
Name: Ros Phillips
Telephone: (06) 877 4111
Fax: (06) 877 4111
Beds: 1 Double, 5 Single
(4 bedrooms)
Bathroom: 2 Guests share,
1 Family share.
Tariff: B&B (full)
Double $70, Single $35,
Children half price, Dinner $25.
NZ B&B Vouchers accepted. Credit cards accepted.
Nearest Town: Hastings, Havelock North 16 kms

20 minutes from Hastings, Havelock North or Waipawa a welcome awaits. You can enjoy the space and peace of a beautiful Hawkes Bay farm or use the home as a base for the many local attractions.
We have a Hereford and Romney stud. Farm tours are available with fabulous views of Hawkes Bay. There is also 50 acres of native bush and an excellent fishing river, the Tukituki, nearby.
Ros is actively involved in the day to day running of the farm, enjoys gardening and is a keen cook. The farmhouse has three bedrooms and guest bathroom upstairs, and one guestroom downstairs with shared facilities.
Children welcome.

Havelock North

Homestay
Address: 'Overcliff',
Waimarama Road, R.D.12,
Havelock North
Name: Joan & Nigel Sutton
Telephone: (06) 877 6852
Fax: (06) 877 6852
Beds: 1 Double, 3 Single
(3 bedrooms)
Bathroom: 1 Private
(we only host one group at a time)
Tariff: B&B (full) Double $75,
Single $50. Dinner $25. NZ B&B Vouchers accepted
Nearest Town: Havelock North 4 Kms

Our comfortable family home is set in ten acres of rolling hill country running down to the Tukituki river close to Te Mata peak, yet only five minutes from Havelock North, ten minutes from Hastings and fifteen minutes from Napier. We have a number of friendly animals, three dogs, kunekune pigs, a small flock of coloured sheep, horses, cats and homing pigeons. You can take a stroll with us to the river, meeting and feeding the animals on the way, swim or laze by the pool, play tennis on the grass court, or fish for rainbow trout in the river. Our other interests include theatre, modern jazz, spinning, horse riding and flying. Dinner served with local wine is a pleasant time to get to know one another. Enjoy breakfast by the pool on those special Hawkes Bay days. Being non smokers we would appreciate you not smoking indoors.

Hastings/Havelock North

Homestay
Address: 57c Iona Rd, Havelock North
Name: Colleen & Bruce Hastie
Telephone: (06) 877 4640
Fax: (06) 877 4640
Mobile: 025-407 255
Beds: 1 Queen, 2 Single (2 bedrooms)
Bathroom: 2 Private
Tariff: B&B (continental) Double $70,
Single $40, Dinner $20, Children $10, Credit cards.
NZ B&B Vouchers accepted
Nearest Town: Havelock North 1km, Hastings 6km, Napier 20km.

We invite you to join us in our comfortable modern home, which is situated on a rear section, with country views enjoying peaceful surroundings.
The beautiful picturesque Havelock North village is only 3 minutes away and offers a variety of specialist shops and many excellent restaurants, and an Irish pub in the village. There are interesting walks, good rivers to fish and wonderful picnic spots (we could prepare a lunch for you). The area is well known for orchards, wineries and apiaries.
Bedrooms are one upstairs, one down, with their own bathrooms, tastefully furnished with comfortable beds and electric blankets. We also have a separate spa room, which you are welcome to use. Laundry facilities are available.
You will find us a friendly couple who enjoy meeting people, you can be assured of a relaxed atmosphere in our home. We offer a continental or cooked breakfast.
No smoking in house. Please phone or fax for directions. Looking forward to meeting you and have you stay with us.

Havelock North

Boutique Bed and Breakfast
Address: 'Weldon', 98 Te Mata Road,
P.O. Box 8170, Havelock North
Name: Pracilla Hay
Telephone: (0800)206 499
(06) 877 7551
Fax: (06) 877 7051
Mobile: (025) 303 569
Beds: Queen, Double, Single (5 Bdrms)
Bathroom: 2 Guests share, 1 Private
Tariff: B&B (special) Double $90-$110, Single $50-$60.
Dinner $20pp by prior arrangement.. Children $45. Credit Cards accepted.
NZ B&B Vouchers accepted $20 surcharge.
Nearest Town: Havelock North 1/2 kilometre, Hastings 5km

WELDON was built in 1906 and retains the country elegance of the time. Situated in a quiet, picturesque cottage garden at the end of a lavender lined drive, WELDON offers comfort and quality with olde world charm.

Restaurants, cafes and an Irish pub give ambience to our uniquely beautiful village which is only five minutes walk away.

Havelock North is nestled under the hills of Te Mata Peak and is central to many wineries. The twin cities of Hastings and Napier are close by.

Accommodation at WELDON offers single, twin and double rooms (one has a divan) with open fires, fine bed linen, fluffy towels, fresh flowers, television and tea / coffee making facilities. The rooms are decorated in the country cottage style. A full breakfast is offered and is served outdoors in warm weather. We have two toy poodles (James and Thomas) to welcome you.

http://www.bnb.co.nz

take a look

Havelock North

Homestay
Address: "Belvedere",
51 Lucknow Road, Havelock North
Name: Shirley & Mervyn Pethybridge
Telephone: (06) 877 4551
Beds: 1 Queen, 1 Double,
2 Single (3 bdrms)
Bathroom: 1 Ensuite, 1 Private
Tariff: B&B (full) Double $70,
Single $45, Dinner $20.
Nearest Town: Hastings 5km

Belvedere is a large 2 storeyed Southern style home set in half an acre of well kept lawns and gardens.
The elegant rooms with balconies have views over town and distant ranges. There is an in-ground saline pool and spa for you to relax in.
Our home is a short walk to Havelock North where there are a great variety of shops and restaurants.
Hawkes Bay is a well known tourist resort with so much to fill in your day, visiting local vineyards, orchards, golfing on any of the 5 golf courses. The Gannet Sanctuary or maybe a leisurely drive through to Napier, the Art Deco capital of the world.
We have travelled extensively both in New Zealand and overseas and have enjoyed the hospitality of many homestays and are pleased to be able to offer the same in return. Please phone or write.
Transfer transport available.

Havelock North

Homestay
Address: Matangi,
90 Simla Avenue, Havelock North
Name: Geoff Hubbard
Telephone: (06) 877 4916
Fax: (06) 877 4926
Mobile: (025) 495 078
Email: geoff@inhb.co.nz
Beds: 1 Double,
3 Single (3 Bedrooms)
Bathroom: 1 Ensuite,
1 Guests Share, 1 Family Share
Tariff: B&B (Continental) Double $90, Single $50,
Children under 15 years $30. Credit Cards / EFTPOS accepted. $20 surcharge.
NZ B&B Vouchers accepted. Website www.matangi.inhb.co.nz
Nearest Town: Havelock North

Having been left on my own I do want to extend a real B&B Homestay welcome to anyone who might like to share my home on the hill in Havelock North. I do want guests to share the kitchen because although I am a great cook they are always encouraged to make tea, coffee etc and try some of my great home cooking and to enjoy the TV lounge and conservatory and the TV/smoking/billiard/office, fax/e-mail/hotmail room. Outside I have a secluded pool and the sheltered cobblestone, pot-planted, pergola surrounded, barbecue, afternoon tea area.
We are a non smoking household.

Havelock North

Homestay
Address: 98A Te Mata Road,
Havelock North
Name: Pauline and Ian Mason
Telephone: (06) 877 5796
Mobile: (025) 297 5886
Email: karla@voyager.co.nz
Beds: 1 Queen, 1 Double (2 Bedrooms)
Bathroom: 1 Guests share
Tariff: B&B (Special) Double $80, Single $50. Not suitable
for small children. NZ B&B Vouchers accepted $15 surcharge
Nearest Town: Havelock North

Valley Garden

Escape from life's pressures amidst the tranquil park-like grounds of VALLEY GARDEN. Enjoy our lovely home-made breakfast on the decking with bird life attracted by many large trees and shrubs.
VALLEY GARDEN is planted to create a foliage effect which is forever changing with the seasons.
15 minutes by car will take you to the top of Te Mata Peak (giving superb views) local wineries / beaches / rivers / rural country / Cape Kidnappers Gannet Colony / Splash Planet.
Havelock North village has several Restaurants - Cafes - Wine Bars and an Irish Pub. We welcome you to our garden and Homestay which is comfortable and cosy (log fire plus underfloor heating in winter). Laundry facilities are available. Handmade and restoration of Teddy Bears takes up much of our spare time. (Overnight accommodation on 500 acres with optional sea fishing also available.) No smoking inside.

Waimarama Beach

Homestay
Address: 68 Harper Road, Waimarama
Name: Murray & Rita Webb
Telephone: (06) 874 6795
Beds: 2 Double (2 bedrooms)
Bathroom: 1 Separate bathroom and toilet for guests.
Tariff: B&B (full) Double $70, Single $45,
Children half price, Dinner $20. NZ B&B Vouchers accepted
Nearest Town: Hastings 30 mins drive.

Come and stay a night or three at the lovely Hawkes Bay beach resort of Waimarama, which has facilities for surfing, diving, fishing trips, horse trekking, bush walks etc. Our house is situated five minutes walk from the beach with lovely views of the sea, local park and farmlands. A 9 hole golf course and restaurant is located nearby (15 mins drive).
Havelock North is the nearest shopping area, 20 minutes drive away, with Hastings and Napier 30 and 40 minutes respectively. We have two double bedrooms available and dinner will be provided if required, also a spa pool for guests' use.
Laundry facilities also provided. No smoking inside please.
Please phone for reservations - 06-874-6795. Vouchers accepted.
Pets: One dog, two cats (friendly).

Waipawa

Homestay
Address: Corgarff,
104 Great North Road,
Waipawa
Name: Neil and Judy McHardy
Telephone: (06) 857 7828
Fax: (06) 857 7055
Beds: 5 Single (3 bedrooms)
Bathroom: 1 Guests share,
1 Family share
Tariff: B&B (full) Double $70,
Single $45, Dinner $20.
NZ B&B Vouchers accepted $10 surcharge
Nearest Town: 2.5km north of Waipawa clock

We welcome you to Corgarff, our comfortable and sunny home on the northern outskirts of Waipawa. We are a farming couple, now retired to 13 acres, with a fox terrier, two cats, and some Texel sheep; also various black sheep kept for spinning fleeces. Within half an hours drive are 5 safe sandy beaches, 4 golf courses, excellent trout fishing and a choice of many wineries. Our guest wing has a separate entrance, also a private sitting room with TV and terrace. These facilities are suitable for disabled persons. We enjoy meeting people and our interests include books, gardening, music, art and travel, also croquet on the lawn.
Directions: *An old elm tree drive. Rapid number 1306 on SH2.*

http://www.bnb.co.nz

take a look

Waipukurau
Farmstay
Address: 'Tukipo Terraces', P O Box 114, Takapau 4176, Hawkes Bay
Name: Bay & Shona de Lautour
Telephone: (06) 855 6827
Freephone: 0800 301 696
Fax: (06) 855 6808
Mobile: (025) 928 908
Beds: 2 Double, 2 Single
(2 large, beautifully appointed suites, each opening to garden)
Bathroom: 2 Ensuite
Tariff: Bed & Breakfast: Double $210, Single $115; Dinner $45pp,
Children by arrangement, Lunch Extra, Credit cards (VISA/MC).
Nearest Town: Waipukurau 20 km, Takapau Village 8kms

Tukipo Terraces is a unique riverstone and timber home on a sheep, deer and cropping farm in the heart of sunny Hawkes Bay within easy reach of all Hawkes Bay's tourist attractions. Built in 1986 on terraces above the Tukipo trout stream it combines the ambience of an elegant, spacious country home with its homestay facilities designed specifically for the enjoyment and privacy of guests. It has two suites both with double and single bed and sitting area, each independent of the other, opening onto extensive garden with mountain views. Three golf courses, bush walks and river swimming nearby. Pre dinner drinks, delicious three course dinner with Hawkes Bay wine shared with hosts in a warm and friendly atmosphere. Shona and Bay have travelled widely, Shona enjoys golf, gardening and music. Bay, as well as farming, has interests in business, politics and is a private pilot. 'Alice', friendly fox terrier.
Directions: *From south on Highway 2, 30 kms north of Dannevirke turn left onto Highway 50, travel 5 kms, on right just at end of long line of mature pines.*
From north, on Highway 50, 22 kms from Tikokino, first on left over Tukipo stream. 2581 on entrance railings.

Waipukurau
Farmstay
Address: Hinerangi Station, R.D. 1, Waipukurau
Name: Caroline & Dan von Dadelszen
Telephone: (06) 855 8273
Fax: (06) 855 8273
Email: caro.vond@amcom.co.nz
Beds: 1 Queen, 2 Single
(2 bedrooms)
Bathroom: 1 Guests share
Tariff: B&B (Full) Double $100-$120, Single $60, Dinner $25pp.
Campervans welcome. NZ B&B Vouchers accepted $30 Surcharge
Nearest Town: Waipukurau 20km, Takapau 11km

Hinerangi is an 1800 acre sheep, cattle and deer station set amongst the rolling hills of Central Hawkes Bay. There are magnificent views to be seen from the Ruahine ranges to the sea. We are happy to show guests what is happening on the farm while you are here. Our domestic animals include one small terrier and a cat. Our large 1920 homestead, designed by architect Louis Hay of Napier Art Deco fame, has a full sized billiard table and there is a swimming pool and tennis court for guests to enjoy. Our home is spacious and comfortable with a private entrance for guests. You are welcome to join us for dinner and an evening by the fire. There are beaches, bush walks and trout fishing streams and golf courses within a short drive. Hot air ballooning is based nearby. We are 8km off State Highway 2.
Directions: *Please phone.*

Waipukurau

Farmstay
Address: 'Mynthurst',
912 Lindsay Road,
R.D.3, Waipukurau
Name: David & Annabelle Hamilton
Telephone: (06) 857 8093
Fax: (06) 857 8093
Beds: 1 King, 3 Single,
1 Cot (3 bedrooms) Extra space for families.
Bathroom: 1 Private (We only host one group at a time).
Tariff: B&B (full) $50pp, Children under 12 half price. Dinner $25
NZ B&B Vouchers accepted $25 surcharge
Nearest Town: Waipawa/Waipukurau 9 km, Hastings 40km SH2

Welcome and relax on our sheep and bull-beef rearing farm. We have been hosting for 15 years, enjoying the company of many NZ and international guests. The homestead is large overlooking the garden and farm, with magnificent views of Ruahine Ranges. Sample local produce with delicious home cooked meals. Sleep peacefully in beds provided with electric blankets. Everyone is welcome to observe the farming activities or pause beside the pool. The energetic may use the tennis court, trampoline or fish the trout streams nearby. Hawkes Bay vineyards and excellent attractions of Hastings and Napier are within easy reach. A 30 minutes drive to wonderful mountain walks or picnics beside the sea. Many guests find that our location is excellent when travelling both North and South. Children welcome. Please phone ahead for bookings to avoid disappointment. We have two friendly cats.
Directions: *Please phone.*

Waipukurau

Homestay
Address: "Airlie Mount",
South Service Lane -
off Porangahau Road,
PO Box 368, Waipukurau
Name: Aart & Rashida van Saarloos
Telephone: (06) 858 7601
Fax: (06) 858 7609
Mobile: (025) 249-9726
Beds: 1 Queen, 2 Single (2 bedrooms)
Bathroom: 1 Ensuite, 1 Family share
Tariff: B&B (full) Double $90, Single $60,
Children 12 & under half price. NZ B&B Vouchers accepted $20 surcharge
Nearest Town: Waipukurau centre 50 m

Historic fully restored "Airlie Mount", built in the 1870's, is situated in the exact centre of Waipukurau, a few steps away from shops, restaurants and railway station - yet it's an island of tranquillity and surrounded by cottage gardens and native bush. The comfortable (non-smoking) homestead further offers verandahs, billiard room and swimming pool. The guest wing, which is very private and large enough for 2 adults and 2 children, has its own bathroom, sitting room, TV and outside courtyard. Your hosts, Rashida and Aart, have travelled extensively and have two young children, a Labrador and fat cat who all enjoy meeting new guests. Waipukurau is 1/2 hour drive away from historic Onga Onga, Norsewear and the beaches and vineyards of Hawke's Bay which makes "Airlie Mount" your perfect base to stay and relax. **Directions**: *Immediately behind Public Trust Building, Ruataniwha Street.*

Waipukurau

Homestay/Farmstay
Address: 415 Mangatarata Road, Waipukurau
Name: Donald & Judy Macdonald
Telephone: (06) 858 8275
Fax: (06) 858 8270
Mobile: (025) 480 769 (025) 478 180
Email: mangatarata@xtra.co.nz
Beds: 2 Queen, 1 Double, 2 Single (3 Bedrooms)
Bathroom: 1 Private, 1 Shared
Tariff: B&B (including cooked breakfast) Double $100 & $110,
Single $65. Children under 12 years half price.
We offer a 3 course dinner $30 per person.
Lunches and dinner by prior arrangement.
Groups for morning and afternoon teas welcome.
NZ B&B Vouchers accepted $35 surcharge
Nearest Town: Waipukurau 7km, Hastings 1/2 hour, Napier 1 hour (we are on
the way to Wellington)

*Mangatarata Station Homestead is a beautiful old home, now 101 years old. Built of
the native wood totara that was milled locally.   It is well situated on a rise with a
beautiful view across a pond and in the centre of a well-established garden. There is
a great deal of history here as Mangatarata was the 2nd sheep station to be established
in this entire province. d[in 1851].*
*Guests enjoy walking on the farm and in the garden. We have a solar heated swimming
pool that is in use many months of the year.*
*Donald is a commercial pilot and is available for scenic flights in an open cockpit Tiger
Moth or to wilderness areas in 4 seater fixed wing.*
*Judy and Donald have been hosting for many years and have done some travelling
themselves.*
Home Page: www.napieronline.co.nz/accommodation/mangatarata

Norsewood

Farmstay
Address: Arthur Road,
RD, Norsewood
Name: 'The Hermytage'
Hosts: Wayne & Helen Hermansen
Telephone: (06) 374 0735
Fax: (06) 374 0735
Mobile: 025-248 7988
Beds: 1 Double, 1 Single (1 Bdrm)
Bathroom: 1 Private
Tariff: B&B (full) Double $75, Dinner $15pp
BYO if required. Credit Cards. NZ B&B Vouchers accepted
Nearest Town: Norsewood

Guests will be warmly welcome to our spacious home where you can relax and enjoy the peace of the country and the view of the Ruahine Ranges, or be included in the family and farm activities. We live on a dairy heifer grazing block and have a Town Supply Dairy farm. We are only 2km from Norsewood, which is a one hour drive to either Palmerston North or Hastings on SH 2. Our district is steeped in Scandinavian History with a very interesting museum. Tours of Norsewear Woollen Mills can be arranged. The golf course is just around the corner, or you can do a day tramp up the Ranges. The men run a hay contracting business and you are welcome to watch the harvesting if you wish. Interests include gardening, reading, machinery, travel. We enjoy people, love entertaining and a good game of cards, especially 500. No pets, no smoking please.
Directions: *Please phone.*

http://www.bnb.co.nz

take a look

Manawatu, Horowhenua

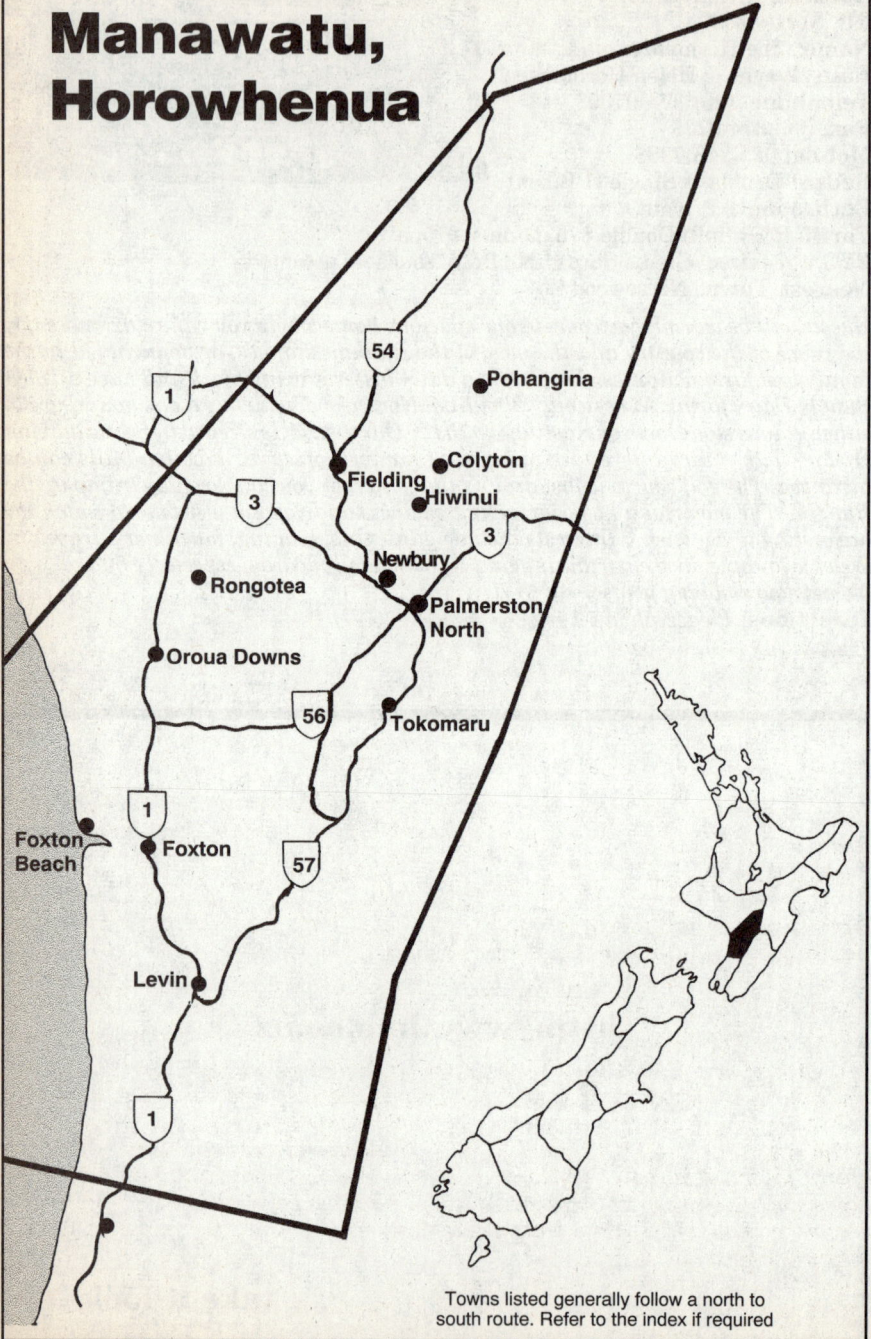

54

1

Pohangina

Colyton

Fielding

Hiwinui

3

3

Newbury

Rongotea

Palmerston North

Oroua Downs

56

Tokomaru

Foxton Beach

1

Foxton

57

Levin

1

Towns listed generally follow a north to south route. Refer to the index if required

Pohangina Valley
Homestay
Address: "Jeneve",
608 West Road, Pohangina
Name: Steve and Jennifer Sinnott
Telephone: (06) 329 4009
Mobile: (025) 907 122
Beds: 1 Queen,
1 Double (2 Bedrooms)
Bathroom: 1 Guests share
Tariff: B&B (Full) Double $95, Single $70,
Dinner by arrangement. Not suitable for children.
Nearest Town: Ashhurst (10 mins)

If a quiet retreat is what you are looking for, 'Jeneve' Homestay is for you. With a breathtaking view of the River Valley and Ruahine Ranges it is ideal for a mid-week or weekend stopover. Our two storeyed home is nestled amongst 20 year old gum trees and sits on an acre of secluded grounds with a wooded garden which the tuis and woodpigeons enjoy. For fun and recreation mountain bikes are available and Beehive Creek walkway is just down the road. Take a drive around the valley and visit some of the local attractions - Pilgrims Rest, Totara Treasures, White Pine Museum. Waterford's cafe and bar is five minutes drive away for evening meals with an Irish theme. They are open seven days and is also a popular stop for afternoon teas. We can provided meals on request. We have not pets, no children. For more information please give us a call. Bookings are essential.

Colyton
Farmstay
Address: 'Hiamoe'
Waiata, Colyton, Feilding
Name: Toos & John Cousins
Telephone: (06) 328 7713
Fax: (06) 328 7787
Email: johnhiamoe@clear.net.nz.
Beds: 1 Queen, 1 Double,
1 Single (2 bedrooms)
Bathroom: 1 Ensuite with spa bath.
Tariff: B&B (full) Double $70, Single $40,
pre school children free, school age half price,
Dinner $15. Credit Cards NZ B&B Vouchers accepted
Nearest Town: Feilding 15 minutes, Palmerston North 25 minutes.

New Zealand Association
FARM & HOME HOSTS

Toos and John, with our 3 young boys, look forward to giving you a warm welcome to "Hiamoe" and during your stay, it is our aim that you experience a home away from home. We are the 3rd generation, farming our sheep, cattle and deer property and live in a 100-year-old colonial home. We have many interests and as Holland is Toos original homeland we are quite accustomed to travel and hosting visitors of all nationalities. There is a pool for the summer months and enjoy the ambience of the open fire combined with central heating during the winter.
Directions: *Details when booking.*

Feilding
Homestay
Address: 5 Wellington Street, Feilding
Name: Beryl Walker
Telephone: (06) 323 4409
Beds: 1 Double, 2 Single or can be 4 Single (2 bedrooms)
Bathroom: 1 Ensuite, 1 Guests share
Tariff: B&B (full) Ensuite Double $70, Twin $65, Single $45,
Children half price. Credit cards. NZ B&B Vouchers accepted
Nearest Town: Feilding 1.3 km from town centre

A comfortable and sunny family home with open fires in winter. Guests should feel free to use all family rooms and facilities as family members. A chance to catch up with your laundry. A choice of breakfast timed to suit your travel arrangements.
Feilding, only 15 minutes from Highway 1 from Sanson if travelling south or through Rongatea, Feilding is the centre of a prosperous farming area with many places of natural beauty within reach. It has easy access to the East Coast and is only 15 minutes from the city of Palmerston North. Manfield Racecourse is situated at Feilding.
Feilding has an interesting shopping area and several good restaurants, licensed and unlicensed.
Directions: *For further directions please ring.*

Feilding
Farmstay, Self contained accom.
Address: Phone for directions
Name: Robert & Ann Campbell
Telephone: (06) 323 4601
Fax: (06) 323 4020
Mobile: (025) 244 7792
Beds: 1 Queen, 1 Double,
3 Single (3 bedrooms)
Bathroom: 1 Private, 1 Guests share
Tariff: B&B (continental) Double $75, Single $45, Dinner $20 pp.
Self contained cottage Sleeps 4, $75 double, $15 per extra person, continental breakfast included. One cottage with Queen bed + Bed settee (double), Ensuite bathroom, Lounge. Meals by arrangement.
NZ B&B Vouchers accepted
Nearest Town: Feilding 5km. Palmerston North 10km.

A warm welcome to our home and farm.
Our 1900 homestead is surrounded by two large gardens which you are welcome to explore. The farm is one of continual activity, with sheep/lambs, beef (including a Red Poll stud and Highland cows, plus cropping).
Our interests are many, from our grandchildren and family, local government politics, the Lions Clubs, voluntary work, travel and of course, people.
Our guest bedrooms are warm and cozy. Electric blankets provided.
We are centrally located between Feilding and Palmerston North, at Taonui. Ten minutes from Palmerston North airport, Manfield Auto Course and the Fielddays, two hours from Wellington and three hours to Lake Taupo and the ski fields. We have 4 farm dogs and 2 cats. For directions please ring, we look forward to meeting you. Non smokers only please.

Feilding
Homestay
Address: 12 Freyberg Street, Feilding
Name: Margaret Hickmott
Telephone: (06) 323 4699
Beds: 1 Queen, 2 Single (2 bedrooms)
Bathroom: 1 Ensuite, 1 Family share
Tariff: B&B (full) Double $70, Single $40, Dinner $20 (by arrangement) NZ B&B Vouchers accepted
Nearest Town: Feilding

Enjoy a break in friendly Feilding, 8 times winner of New Zealand's most beautiful town award. Stay in a comfortable home in an attractive garden setting within easy walking distance of town centre, pool complex and parks. Feilding is 15 minutes by car from Palmerston North.
Each well appointed bedroom has garden views and the double room with en suite has its own entrance. Guests are invited to use all family facilities, including laundry, and covered off street parking is available for your car.
Our interests are music, both classical and easy listening, gardening, cooking, travel and meeting people.
You are assured of a warm welcome and a comfortable stay in a smoke free environment.
Directions: *For further directions, please phone. Connections with public transport can be arranged if you wish.*

Feilding, Palmerston North
Country Stay
Address: "Puketawa", Colyton Road, RD 5, Feilding
Name: Nelson & Phyllis Whitelock
Telephone: (06) 328 7819
Fax: (06) 328 7919
Email: lwhitelock@clear.net.nz
Beds: 1 Queen, 2 Single (2 bedrooms)
Bathroom: 1 Ensuite, 1 Private
Tariff: B&B (full) Double $90, Single $50, Children half price, Dinner $25.
Credit cards accepted: Visa/Mastercard. NZ B&B Vouchers accepted $10 surcharge
Nearest Town: Equal distance to Feilding and Palmerston North (15 mins)

Discover "Puketawa" for yourself and delight in truly tranquil surrounds.
Our lovely modern home, which won a national award in 1996 is situated well back from the road beside 10 acres of native bush. Sheep and beef cattle graze the adjacent family farm. Wander at your leisure through bush and farmland or just relax on the deck overlooking a bush grove which is flood lit at dark. A four wheel drive tour of the property is available. This takes in panoramic views of the Manawatu and beyond. Our interests include our family and grandchildren, camping and tramping around New Zealand, music, floral art, embroidery and of course creating gardens in harmony with the native surroundings.
We offer: Warm, friendly hospitality and delicious meals prepared from fresh home grown produce all in a smoke free environment. Situation: Handy to Feilding, Palmerston North, the Manawatu Gorge and beautiful Pohangina Valley.
Directions: *Please phone for details. Pick up service available.*
Home Page: www.homestaysnz.co.nz/puketawa.htm

385

Palmerston North
Homestay

Address: "Huntbridge", 7 Kings Court,
590 Featherston Street,
Palmerston North
Name: Christine and Ray Lough
Telephone: (06) 357 7705
Fax: (06) 357 7704
Beds: 1 Queen and 1 Single
in each bedroom (2 Bedrooms)
Bathroom: 1 Guests share
Tariff: B&B (Full) Double $70, Single $50,
Dinner by arrangement. Not suitable for children under 12 years.
NZ B&B Vouchers accepted $5 surcharge
Nearest Town: Palmerston North city centre 3 km

Situated in a quiet court, our home offers separate downstairs accommodation including a guest lounge. Being modern, spacious and smoke free it is suitable for short term studying, conference attendance or holidaying.
We offer, with our Labrador, a friendly homely atmosphere and a relaxed base with laundry facilities if required. Having travelled extensively we can, if requested, assist with developing your ongoing itinerary to cover your interests.
For the weary, studio services operating within the NZ Association of Therapeutic Massage Practitioners (NZATMP) are also available.

Newbury, Palmerston North
Homestay/Farmstay/SC accommodation

Address: "Grinton"
Rangitikei Line,
5 R.D., Palmerston North
Name: Keith & Margaret Morriss
Telephone: (06) 354 8961
Fax: (06) 354 8961
Beds: 2 Queen, 1 Single
(2 bedrooms, all with electric blankets).
1 Self contained detached flat (sleeps 4).
Bathroom: 1 Ensuite, 1 Private
Tariff: B&B (full) Double $80, Single $45, Children half price,
Dinner $25. Credit Cards.
Also self contained detached flat, sleeps 4: one double bed, and two bunks.
Suitable for family $80 double, $15 per extra person. Breakfast included. NZ
B&B Vouchers accepted $10 surcharge
Nearest Town: Palmerston North (5 minutes) on State Highway 3

Just a short distance from Palmerston North, friendly hospitality awaits you at "Grinton", its namesake in Yorkshire, England having early family connections. We offer guests a comfortable relaxing stay in our character home with pleasant garden surroundings and rural views. We welcome the stimulation of overseas and Kiwi guests, having travelled extensively ourselves. Farming operations consist of beef fattening and cropping. Visits to large scale dairying, deer farming, equestrian centre can be arranged. Enjoy the many attractions in the area - Massey University, The Victoria Esplanade, the Palmerston North Science Museum - a night at Centrepoint Theatre, the recently refurbished Regent Theatre, or dining at "Grinton" in our Sunset room. Our interests include grandchildren, music, dancing, Lions Club, trout fishing, golf, woodturning and floral art. We look forward to your visit.

Hokowhitu, Palmerston North

Homestay
Address: "Glenfyne",
413 Albert Street,
Hokowhitu, Palmerston North
Name: Jillian & Alex McRobert
Telephone: (06) 358 1626
Fax: (06) 358 1626
Beds: 1 Double, 2 Single
(2 bedrooms)
Bathroom: 1 Guests share (large)
Tariff: B&B (full) Double $70, Single $45, Children half price.
NZ B&B Vouchers accepted, Credit Cards accepted
Nearest Town: Palmeston North city centre 3 kms

A warm welcome awaits you in our comfortable home. After many years of staying Bed & Breakfast in Britain, we would now like to return the hospitality shown to us on our travels. We are a retired, non-smoking couple, with varied interests, including meeting people, travel, gardening, cooking and golf. Our home is close to Massey University, College of Education and within walking distance of the Manawatu Golf Club. There are some interesting walkways nearby, and two minutes walk will take you to the Hokowhitu Village. (Post Office, Pharmacy, Restaurants etc.) In summer, guests can relax in the tranquility of our back garden, enjoy a drink or a barbecue. Jillian is a KiwiHost. Guests are welcome to use our laundry facilities. Tea / coffee always available. We are happy to meet public transport. Covered off-street parking available. Please phone for reservations and directions.

Palmerston North

Bed & Breakfast Hotel
Address: "The Gables",
179 Fitzherbert Avenue,
Palmerston North
Name: Paul & Monica Stichbury
Telephone: (06) 358 3209
Fax: (06) 358 3209
Mobile: (021) 217 5348
Beds: 3 Queen, 1 Twin share, 1 Single (3 bedrooms)
Bathroom: 1 Private, 2 Guests share
Tariff: B&B (continental) Double $80-$110, Single $60-$80,
Dinner by arrangement $15. Credit cards.
Nearest Town: Palmerston North

New Zealand Association
FARM & HOME HOSTS

Situated 800 metres from the Square and 150 metres from the nearest of many restaurants and cafes, the Gables is a classic English two storeyed 1920's home set in a magnificent mature garden. The main house has been totally restored and a character New England barn style apartment has been built behind the main house. Both have been furnished with antiques and in the country style. Garaging is available for that special car if requested. The apartment is completely private and is popular with honeymoon couples. We do not usually host small children and smoking is not permitted in the buildings. We offer a discount for repeat business and have special rates for Senior citizens and mature students.
The Gables is conveniently located on the main route to Massey University. Monica speaks both Mandarin and Cantonese. We welcome you to experience our hospitality.
Home Page: http://www.friars.co.nz/hosts/gables.html

Palmerston North
Self-contained Accommodation
Address: "Iti Mara Homestay",
3 Peters Avenue, Cloverlea,
Palmerston North
Name: Dixie & Neil Signal
Telephone: (06) 354 2666
Fax: (06) 354 2666
Mobile: (025) 231 2446

Iti Mara

Beds: 1 Double, 2 Single (1 bedroom, 1 bedsit)
Bathroom: 1 Ensuite (we only host one group at a time)
Tariff: Unit: Double $70, Single $50, Extra persons $15.00pp, Dinner $20. Breakfast $5.00pp Full or Continental. NON SMOKING INSIDE. NZ B&B Vouchers accepted $10 surcharge
Nearest Town: Palmerston North 3km from city centre

"Iti Mara" (Little Garden) situated in northwest Palmerston North, on local bus route and easily accessible from all main highways - off road lock up parking. When our children left home we converted the rooms above the garage into a sunny self-contained flat. This comprises one double bedroom, with ensuite, spacious living area with two divan beds (extra sofa bed available) - laundry downstairs. We rented the house and using the flat as a base travelled the lower North Island 'oddjobbing' - a wonderful way to meet people. Now retired, the flat enables us to still enjoy meeting people. Our guests can be totally independent; join us for meals, or have meals provided in the flat. We are totally flexible - we do appreciate prior notice for dinner. We enjoy gardening and look forward to sharing our pleasant cottage garden with you. We are able to meet public transport.

Palmerston North
Homestay
Address: 21 Woburn Place,
Palmerston North
Name: Ainslie and Geoff Grey
Telephone: (06) 354 0490
Fax: (06) 354 0490
Email: a-ggrey@xtra.co.nz.
Beds: 2 Single, 1 Bedroom
Bathroom: 1 Guests share

Tariff: B&B (full) Double $75, Single $45, Dinner $20.
Children half price. NZ B&B Vouchers accepted $15 surcharge
Nearest Town: Palmerston North centre 3 kms.

Ainslie & Geoff, along with our small dog, enjoy meeting people and sharing our home with visitors from far and near.
Our interests include meeting people, cooking, gardening, travel and walking.
Our home is situated about 5 mins from both the Square and the Airport, with the Railway Station and the Manawatu Sports Stadium Complex being even closer. We are able to provide transport to and from Public Transport. The Massey University campus is about 15-20 mins away.
Our warm, modern home would ideally suit reasonably active guests as the guest bedroom and bathroom are located upstairs and are not suitable for a wheelchair. Guests are most welcome to make use of our laundry facilities. A welcome is cordially extended to you to come and share our hospitality.

Palmerston North
Homestay
Address: "Karaka House",
473 College Street, Palmerston North
Name: Karaka House.
Lynn and David Whitburn
Telephone: (06) 358 8684
Fax: (06) 358 8685
Mobile: (025) 245 2765
Beds: 2 Queen, 2 Single (3 bedrooms)
Bathroom: 1 Guests share
Tariff: B&B (full) Double $85, Single $60, Dinner by arrangement.
NZ B&B Vouchers accepted $15 surcharge
Nearest Town: Palmerston North, 1km to City Square

Lynn and David offer you a warm welcome to "Karaka House". We are a friendly couple who enjoy meeting people in the relaxed atmosphere of our home. Our spacious home is in a tree lined street in Palmerston North's most beautiful suburb of Hokowhitu within easy walk of the city centre restaurants, theatres and shopping, The College of Education, Polytech, Massey and recreation facilities are within easy reach. The tiled front entrance opens to a wide hall with a rimu staircase leading to the large sunny bedrooms, which have been designed with your comfort in mind and have electric blankets, cotton sheets, duvets, remote TV's and radio. Tea, coffee, laundry facilities are provided and a large guest lounge is fully equipped for your pleasure. Off street parking is available. We look forward to meeting you and having you stay with us. **Directions**: *Please phone. We are happy to meet public transport.*

Palmerston North
Homestay
Address: 52B Ihaka Street Palmerston North
Name: "Arcadia"
Trish and Mike Boland
Telephone: (06) 357 0496
Fax: (06) 357 9378 **Mobile**: (025) 242 8778
Email: mikeb@xtra.co.nz
Beds: 2 Queen (2 Bedrooms)
Bathroom: 1 Guests Share
Tariff: B&B (Full)
Double $75-$85, Single $55-$65.
Not suitable for children.   Credit Cards: Visa/MC.
Dinner available on arrangement. NZ B&B Vouchers accepted $15 surcharge
Nearest Town: Palmerston North - City Centre 3 kms.

New Zealand Association
FARM & HOME HOSTS

Trish and Mike and our two cats welcome you to Arcadia.
"Away from it all in the middle of town", Arcadia is a retreat from the bustle of the city, located in the heart of Hokowhitu suburb in Palmerston North. We are two minutes' walk from Hokowhitu Village, yet in our tranquil, tree-lined garden the main noise you will hear is birdsong. Our accommodation features: The "Jade Room", with a muted oriental flavour and the "Garden Room" featuring indoor-outdoor living, with French doors onto our garden terrace. Our gardens are a mixture of traditional, native and water gardens. Other amenities include a separate guest lounge, a small gymnasium, laundry facilities and off-street parking. Dinner is available by arrangement, with us; or on your own - your choice! Our interests include: travel, gardens, photography, food and wine, books, music. We can meet public transport by arrangement or please phone for directions. We look forward to your visit. No smoking indoors. **Home Page**: http://home.xtra.co.nz/hosts/Arcadia

Palmerston North

Homestay
Address: "Miranui",
148 Russell Street, Palmerston North.
Name: Miranui, Grant and Robyn Powell
Telephone: (06) 355 1772
Fax: (06) 355 1772
Mobile: (025) 285 3643
Email: miranui@xtra.co.nz
Beds: 2 Queen, (2 Bedrooms)
Bathroom: 1 Ensuite, 1 Private
Tariff: B&B (Continental) Double $85, Single $60, Dinner $25.
Children negotiable. NZ B&B Vouchers accepted $15 surcharge.
Credit cards accepted: Visa/Mastercard.
Nearest Town: Palmerston North City Centre 1.2 km

A warm friendly welcome awaits you at Miranui. Our 1906 spacious and beautifully restored villa is situated 1.2 kilometres from the city centre. Unique features of our home are the magnificent stained glasswork in the front entry door (which has been recorded by the Alexander Turnbull Library, Wellington), the heptagonal turret where guests can join us for dinner and the large conservatory, a place to soak up the afternoon sun. We offer 2 bedrooms with queensize beds, one with ensuite, one with separate bathroom and each with own lounge / dining area equipped with TV, fridge, tea and coffee making facilities - or we are happy for you to join us in the family room if you prefer. Miranui is situated in close proximity to UCOL, shops, hospitals, golf courses and the airport. Laundry facilities and off street parking available. Local tours are available if required. Non smoking.

Rongotea

Farmstay
Address: "Andellen", RD3,
Palmerston North.
Name: Kay and Warren Nitschke
Telephone: (06) 324 8359 (after 6 pm)
or **(025) 448 444** (anytime)
Mobile: (025) 244 1393
Email: nitschkek@agriquality.co.nz
Beds: 1 Queen, 2 Single (2 Bedrooms)
Bathroom: 1 Ensuite, 1 Guests share,
Tariff: B&B (Full) Double $80, Single $40, Dinner $25 pp by request. Children half price (cot and high chair available). We have a pet fox terrier dog.
NZ B&B Vouchers accepted $15 surcharge
Nearest Town: Rongntea (5 mins) **Nearest City**: Palmerston North (15 mins).

Kay, Warren and Libby (3 1/2 yearold) invite you to stay at "Andellen", a lovely large 90 year old farm home set on 42 acres with extensive lawn, garden and orchard. We are only 2 kms off State Highway 1. "Andellen" offers guests the opportunity to relax in a lovely tranquil setting with views of the Ruahine and Tararua Ranges. Guests are welcome to enjoy our garden and seasonal farm activities.
We love company and welcome you into our home to share our friendly, relaxed farm life and country living. Children are very welcome, cot and highchair available. Beach 12 minutes away.
***Directions**: We are situated 11 kms south of Sanson or 11 kms north of Himitangi intersection. Off State Highway 1 turn into Kaimatarau Road and travel across the first intersection. We are next gate on LEFT - farm no. 221. Name on gate.*

Tokomaru

Self Contained Cabin
Address: Hi-Da-Way Lodge
21 Albert Road, Tokomaru
Name: Sue & Trevor Palmer
Telephone: (06) 329 8731
Fax: (06) 329 8732
Beds: 1 Double (1 Bedsit)
Bathroom: 1 Private
Tariff: B&B (Full/Continental)
Double $85, Single $60, Children $15. Dinner $20.
NZ B&B Vouchers accepted $15 surcharge
Nearest Town: Palmerston North approx. 20 km

We welcome you to hide away in the country with us. Your own fully self-contained rustic cabin has TV, kitchen facilities and its own spa pool. Although a separate building, it is handy to the Homestead, which is one of the oldest still standing in the Tokomaru area. Guests may enjoy croquet, volley ball, trampoline, BBQ, share swimming pool in season, meander around our 6.5 hectare property which is surrounded by trees or generally relax. Just minutes down the road is Massey University, Tokomaru Steam Engine Museum and Horseshoe Bend - a popular picnic area.
Our interests include fishing, boating, vintage cars and farming. We have four children of which the eldest has left home. We also have a pet dog. No smoking in cabin. Why not come and share our lifestyle.
Directions: *Just off State Highway 57, 2km south of Tokomaru Dairy*

Oroua Downs

Farmstay
Address: Omanuka Road, RD 11, Foxton
Name: Bev & Ian Wilson
Telephone: (06) 329 9859
Fax: (06) 329 9859
Mobile: (025) 986 023
Beds: 1 Double, 3 Single (3 bedrooms)
Bathroom: 1 Guests share
Tariff: B&B (full) Double $70, Single $40,
Children half price, Dinner $20 pp.
NZ B&B Vouchers accepted
Nearest Town: Foxton 14km, Palmerston North 35km

We would like to welcome you to our comfortable two storey home with 1 double bed downstairs and 3 single beds upstairs. Our home is situated 2 km off State Highway One, amongst Manawatu's dairy farming. We have 5 acres of land, 1 acre of gardens to walk around, listening to the bird life and to relax. We are situated 1 1/2 hours north of Wellington and 1/2 hours west of Palmerston North. Our region contains a sheepskin tannery, a giftware shop and an antique shop, it also has a childrens play park and wine shop with restaurant. A beach is only 15 mins away. We are self-employed with a wooden toy manufacturing business operating from our property. As we are non-smokers we request no smoking indoors. We look forward to sharing our home and cat with you and making your stay an enjoyable one. **Directions**: *Turn off at Bed & Breakfast sign on State Highway 1, 13 km north of Foxton and 16 km south of Sanson. Travel 2 km down Omanuka Road.*

391

Foxton
Farmstay
Address: Karnak Stud,
Ridge Road, Foxton
Name: Margaret Barbour
Telephone: (06) 363 7764
Fax: (06) 363 8941
Beds: 1 Double, 2 Single
(2 Bedrooms)
Bathroom: 1 Ensuite, 1 Private
Tariff: B&B (Full) Double $80, Single $45, Dinner $25 each. Children under 5 free
(2 folding beds available), Campervans welcome. Dogs welcome. Horse accommodation: Yard $12, Box $20. Credit Cards.
NZ B&B Vouchers accepted $12 surcharge
Nearest Town: Foxton, 18km to Levin

In the country yet so easy to find, Karnak Stud is a mini farm, full of character and so tranquil - linger awhile. An ideal stopover 1 1/2 hours drive from the Interisland Ferry Terminal. Friendly animals are the main feature, enjoy them while strolling through our sixteen acres of pasture and woodland - we even have a race track! Listen to a fascinating talk on "How Horses Think". Besides keeping thoroughbred mares and their foals, we have placid heifers, a farm dog, Meg, a farm cat, Mousie, and a small aviary. Our guests find their stay relaxing and comment on the excellent meals - organic farmhouse food, locally grown, and home-reared beef. Also we have table tennis, darts, children's toys and a guests' library. Foxton has many attractions including a superb beach. **Directions**: *Follow Farmstay arrow on State Highway One up Purcell St, over white bridge, we are next on your left.*

http://www.bnb.co.nz

take a look

Levin
Bed & Breakfast Homestay
Address: 'Annandale',
108 Arapaepae Rd., Levin (SH 57)
Name: Cheryl & Wayne Strong
Telephone: (06) 368 5476
Beds: 1 Queen,
2 Double (3 bedrooms)
Bathroom: 1 Guests share
Tariff: B&B (full) Queen or Double $95,
Single $60, Vouchers accepted $20 surcharge.
Nearest Town: Levin 3 km

We will make you most welcome at "Annandale".
Our two storeyed old English style home, built in 1917, is set in an acre of trees and gardens, with a further 4 acres of feijoas, marketed from April to July. We offer our guests a peaceful retreat - whether you are just passing through, or wish to get away from it all for a few days. Horowhenua has a number of attractions, mountains, beaches, golf links and bush walks; or you may choose just to potter around in our orchard and talk to our animals, which include two dogs, cats, kunekune pigs, a sulphur crested cockatoo, chooks, ducks and aviary birds. Levin has a number of reasonably priced restaurants for dinner. We are a non smoking household.
Directions: *We are on State Highway 57, 1km north of the Queen St, Arapaepae Rd (SH57) intersection, on the right hand (eastern) side of the road (sign at gate).*

Levin
Farmstay
Address: "Lynn Beau Ley",
Queen Street East, R.D. 1, Levin
Name: Beverley & Peter Lynn
Telephone: (06) 368 0310
Fax: (06) 368 0310
Beds: 1 Double, 2 Single
(2 bedrooms)
Bathroom: 1 Ensuite, 1 Private
Tariff: B&B (full) Double $75,
Single $45, Dinner by arrangement $20.
Credit Cards NZ B&B Vouchers accepted
Nearest Town: Levin - 3.4km east of Levin

10 tranquil rural acres 5 mins from town centre - pastoral retreat. Levin a large horticulture / floriculture centre comfortable distance for Ferry and Air Travel. Activities, tramping / hunting (Tararuas), bush / scenic reserves, golf courses, arts / crafts. Our home is spacious ranch-style with warm aspect. Situated in 1 acre of lawns and gardens. Tastefully appointed guest rooms, 'picture postcard views', delicious breakfasts. Evening dining by arrangement, can by enjoyed with us or visit local restaurants / cafes. We enjoy meeting and entertaining people and have travelled extensively in NZ using B&B accommodation. Beverley has many years experience in the hospitality business. Peter has been involved in Management of Financial Sevices A Jaycee International Senator. Interests / hobbies coloured sheep breeding, handcraft, oilpainting, gardening, debating travel and Beau our cat. Members Small Farmers and Black and Coloured Sheep Breeders Assn.
Directions: *Turn east off State Highway 1 at Post Office into Queen Street East we are 3.4km on left. Sign at gate.*

Levin

B&B/ Homestay/Self Containe Accommodation
Address: "The Fantails",
40 MacArthur Street, Levin
Name: Heather and Peter
Telephone: (06) 368 9011
or 368 9279
Fax: (06) 368 9279
Email: fantails@xtra.co.nz
Beds: 1 Queen, 2 Double,
2 Single, (4 bedrooms)
Bathroom: 3 Ensuite
Tariff: B&B (special) Double $90, Single $60,
Self Contained Cottages $100-$170, Dinner $35,
Children negotiable. Credit Cards.
NZ B&B Vouchers accepted $20 surcharge
Nearest Town: Levin, 5 minutes to town centre

Organic Food a Specialty

As you enter The Fantails you will feel the tranquility and marvel at the lovely surroundings with its English trees, native bush and bird-life.
Enjoy the English style home with your hosts Heather and Peter, our Homestay will provide you with every comfort and standard you require and a quiet night's restful sleep. All bedrooms have a delightful outlook plus T.V's and videos. Enjoy a fantails special breakfast and garden view. We can offer an evening meal with organic food and N.Z. wines.
Levin is situated 1 1/2 hours from Wellington and 1/2 hour from Palmerston North. Levin with its excellent climate and tourist attractions is a great place to spend those extra days. We can provide an appetising picnic basket and assist with planning your stay and onward travel.
We also offer self-contained retreat cottages in our one acre of garden. (They sleep two or four). These are wheelchair friendly and smoke free. Laundry facilities available.
Directions: *Please phone for directions.*

Levin
B&B Homestay
Address: "The Walnut Tree Cottage",
38 Kawiu Road, Levin
Name: Marilyn Kerr
Telephone: (06) 368 1513
Mobile: (025) 238 3934
Beds: 2 Single (1 bedroom)
Bathroom: 1 Ensuite,
Tariff: B&B (full)
Double $75, Single $45, Dinner $25.
Credit Cards. NZ B&B Vouchers accepted
Nearest Town: Levin 1km north of Levin Post Office.

A convenient, tranquil retreat to break your journey, being only 1.5 hours drive from Wellington and two minutes drive from SH 1. Our home is colonial style, comfortable and secluded with rural view, an elevated outlook of the beautiful Tararuas and Kapiti Island in the distance, set among mature trees and attractive garden views.
We offer quality beds with electric blankets, in a comfortable and attractively decorated room, with beverage making facilities, and TV. You will enjoy a delicious breakfast. In summer guests relax on the deck, in winter in a cosy sitting room. Dinner is available by arrangement.
We enjoy meeting people, We are a keen travellers and look forward to offering you warm and generous hospitality in our smoke-free home, shared by Princess, a good natured wheaten dog.
Directions: *Please phone.*

Levin
Farmstay
Address: Buttercup Acres,
55 Florida Road,
Ohau, Levin
Name: Ivan and Pat Keating
Telephone: 06-368 0557
Fax: 06-368 0557
Beds: 1 Double, 2 Single
(2 bedrooms)
Bathroom: 1 Ensuite, 1 Private
Tariff: B&B (Special) Double $90, Single $45,Dinner $20.
Credit Cards accepted. NZ B&B Vouchers accepted $20 surcharge
Nearest Town: Levin, 9 km

Buttercup Acres is a small tranquil rural property situated 9 km SE of Levin at the foothills of the Tararua Ranges. We specialise in breeding Miniature horses and Alpacas. Our home is surrounded by 3 acres of beautiful gardens and a large pond. Guests can feed the animals and explore the garden at their leisure. In the evenings you can relax in the lounge - learn to spin, weave in our weaving studio or view the stars through our telescope. Our model railway layout will fascinate visitors.
The surrounding district offers many interesting walks, beaches, craft shops and gardens. We have two friendly dogs that live in the weaving studio which is adjacent to the house. We requests guests do not smoke inside. Dinner is available by arrangement and we serve a country style breakfast. Meal times are flexible to suit guests.
Directions: *Levin Information Centre or telephone.*

Wairarapa

Kumeroa
Woodville

2

52

Eketahuna

Tinui

Masterton

Whareama

Carterton
Gladestone
Greytown

2

Featherston

Martinborough

Flat Point

2

Western Lake

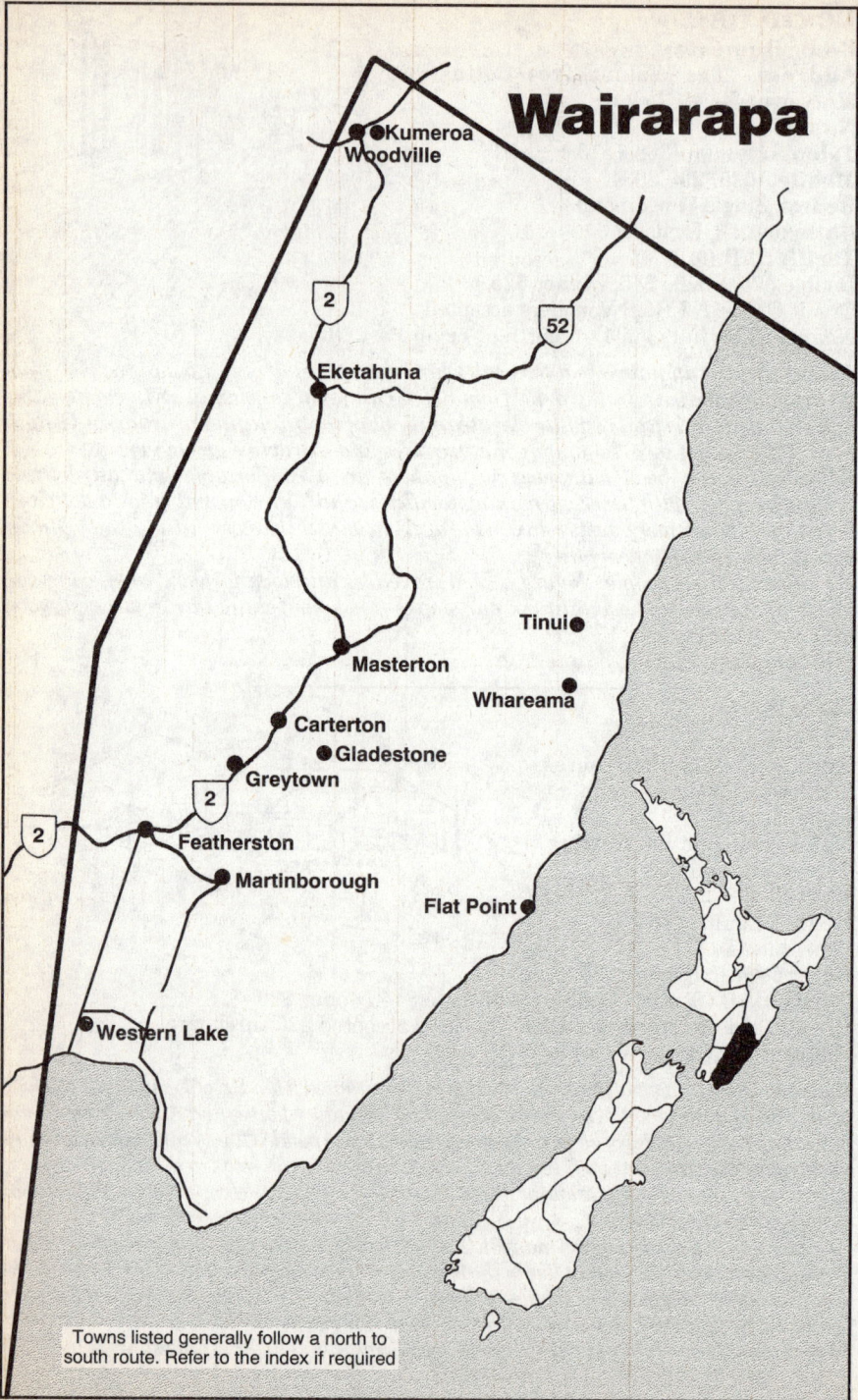

Towns listed generally follow a north to
south route. Refer to the index if required

Woodville
Farmstay/Self-contained   accomm
Address: 370 River Road, Hopelands, Woodville R.D.1
Name: Chris & Jo Coats
Telephone: (06) 376 4521
Email: jo.coats@clear.net.nz
Beds: 1 Double, 2 Single (2 bedrooms)
Bathroom: 1 Family share
Tariff: B&B (full) Double $70, Single $35, Children half price; Dinner $20.   NZ B&B Vouchers accepted
Nearest Town: 12 km North East of Woodville off SH 2

We are sheep and cattle farmers on a hill country farm beside the beautiful Manawatu River renowned for its trout fishing. Fishing tackle and day licence extra. The family have fled the nest but return from time to time, seeking quiet from their busy lives. Depending on the time of year, farming activities of possible interest to tourists may be in progress, i.e. mustering, shearing, etc. and you will be very welcome to participate. The self-contained double bed unit has its own toilet and handbasin. Guests share bathroom facilities if requiring a shower.
Directions: *If approaching via Pahiatua please ring for directions and so avoid Woodville. If travelling between Woodville and Dannevirke - follow the Hopelands Road to cross the high bridge over Manawatu River, turn right heading towards Pahiatua and the fourth house (blue) is where 'Welcome' is on the mat.*

Kumeroa
Country Homestay
Address: "OTAWA LODGE",
Otawhao Road, Kumeroa, RD 1
Name: Del & Sue Trew
Telephone: (06) 376 4603
Fax: (06) 376 5042
Email: OTAWA.LODGE@xtra.co.nz
Beds: 1 King, 1 Queen,
2 King Single (2 Bedrooms)
Bathroom: 1 Guests share
Tariff: B&B (special) Double $120, Single $80,
Children by arrangement, Dinner on request.
Nearest Town: Woodville 15 mins, Dannevirke 20 mins

Rest ... relax ... rejuvenate in our magnificent home set on 80 acres of beautiful hills with spectacular views of the Ruahine Ranges. Be enchanted by the Edwardian elegance preserved in the wood panelling, stunning leadlights, art nouveau plasterwork and authentic period furniture.
Take a walk through native bush, fish for trout in the nearby Manawatu River, wander past the walnut grove to the stream, listen to the tuis or simply read in our unique octagonal library. Dine on fresh local produce with a healthy emphasis on fish and organic cuisine. At the end of the day, sleep in luxurious beds made with pure cotton sheets and enjoy the comfort of bathrobes and complementary toiletries. We are originally from England, have travelled widely and our interests include antiques, music and the theatre. Joss, our small son, is a delightful host. We request guests not to smoke in the house.
Directions: *10 mins off State Highway 2. Please phone*

Eketahuna

Farmstay
Address: 'Mount Donald', Newman, R.D.4, Eketahuna
Name: Jim & Lynne Sutherland
Telephone: (06) 375 8315
Fax: (06) 375 8391
Email: mountdonald@xtra.co.nz
Beds: 1 Double, 2 Single (2 bedrooms)
Bathroom: 2 Private
Tariff: B&B (full) Double $90, Single $60, Dinner $25.
Credit cards (Visa, M/C). NZ B&B Vouchers accepted $20 surcharge
Nearest Town: Eketahuna. We are 5km north SH2.

Our Homestead is set back from the road and is surrounded by large grounds. We are keen gardeners, love to play golf, interested in wildlife and conservation and especially enjoy talking to our guests whilst sharing an evening meal. Our guest accommodation is spacious, warm and comfortable with a large upstairs lounge with TV, pool table and complimentary tea coffee facilities. Enjoy the peace and tranquillity of the countryside. Visit The Mount Bruce National Wildlife Centre, local gardens, trout fish and kayak on our river, play Eketahuna's popular 18 hole golf course nearby. Join Jim for a tour of our 1200 acre sheep and cattle property with magnificent views of this green lush part of New Zealand. We are a good stop over before and after Inter Island Ferry Travel being only 1.5 hours from Wellington. The Palmerston North International / Domestic Airport is 45 minutes drive.

Directions: *We are easy to find, look for our sign on State Highway 2. The Homestead is 68 (2n house on the right) Central Mangaone Road. Mount Donald is written at the entrance.*

http://www.bnb.co.nz

take a look

Masterton
Small Farmstay + Self-Contained accommodation
Address: Harefield,
147 Upper Plain Road, Masterton
Name: Robert & Marion Ahearn
Telephone: (06) 377 4070
Beds: 1 Double, 1 Single (1 bedroom).
Bathroom: 1 Private.
Tariff: B&B (full) Double $70, Single $45, Children half price.
Dinner $20. Detached fully equipped S/C flat $55 for two people, $5.00 each
extra bed (1 Double bed and 1 Single bed in bedroom, and 1 fold down
double in living room. 1 Bathroom private, cot and highchair and baby
bath.)NZ B&B Vouchers accepted
Nearest Town: Masterton 4kms - 1km from Bypass.

*We are retired farmers whose children have left home. Our cedar house has all
modern comforts, including electric blankets on all beds. It is cited on 13 acres,
4kms from town, 1km from By Pass. A cottage garden surrounds house and flat.
We are 200 metres back from road. We look out onto Tararua Mountains and
paddocks with sheep, cattle and deer. We have been homestay guests in New
Zealand, Europe, USA and Australia. Our interests include travel, reading, the
Arts, tramping, gardening, Rose Society and Probus. We are 1 1/2 hours drive
from Inter Island Ferry, half hour to Martinborough's vineyards, half hour to
National Wild Life Centre. Convenient for showgrounds and tramping and
schools. If you stay fin the flat, you can be self catering or arrange breakfast in
our warm dining room. Dinner by arrangement. Excellent restaurants 6 minutes
away. No inside pets. We do not smoke.*

Masterton
Small Farm Farmstay
Address: 'Tidsfordriv',
4 Cootes Road, R.D. 8,
Matahiwi, Masterton
Name: Glenys Hansen
Telephone: (06) 378 9967
Fax: (06)_ 378 9957
Beds: 1 Double,
2 Single (2 bedrooms)
Bathroom: 1 Guests share
Tariff: B&B Double $70,
Single $40, Children half price, Dinner $20,
Campervans $25 . Credit cards. NZ B&B Vouchers accepted
Nearest Town: Masterton 10 km

*Divert off the main highway and visit "Tidsfordriv" where a warm welcome awaits you. A
comfortable new home set in park-like surroundings overlooks wetland habitat which attracts
many species of wetland birds. Take a walk around the large gardens that have recently been
developed and enjoy birdwatching with ease. Sheep and cattle graze the fields on this 64 acre
farmlet. Glenys has home-hosted for 13 years and invites you to join her for dinner.
Conservation and gardening are her interests. Many Wairarapa tourist attractions are within
a short journey-National Wildlife Centre, gardens, crafts, vineyards to name a few.
Friendly cat and a Labrador dog are the family pets.*
Directions: *Please phone for directions. 7km from main Bypass route.*
Home Page: http:/wairarapa.co.nz/accommodation

Masterton
Guest House, Bed & Breakfast

Address: 'Victoria House',
15 Victoria Street,
Masterton
Name: Grant & Jan Beaumont
Telephone: (06) 377 0186
Fax: (06) 377 0186
 Beds: 3 Double,
4 Single (6 bedrooms)
Bathroom: 2 Guests share
Tariff: B&B (full)
Double $65, Single $42,
Not suitable children under 12,
Credit Cards. NZ B&B Vouchers accepted
Nearest Town: 100km north of Wellington on State Highway 2

Welcome to Victoria House. We are forty and have three sons. Our home is a beautiful colonial two storey house built pre 1886. We have renovated the guests' accommodation, keeping the character of the house, while retaining home comforts. (We even stripped light fittings back to the brass and wood). The guests' bedrooms are like your own room away from home. Furnished colonial style and decorated in soft tonings to create a peaceful atmosphere. All rooms equipped with heaters. Some have handbasins. There are two guests bathrooms, tea, coffee, milo available at all times. There is a comfortable TV lounge where smoking is permitted (No smoking in bedrooms). Our tariff includes a continental breakfast but cooked can happily be arranged. We aim for quality accommodation that's warm and friendly. Set in a quiet location we are 2 minutes walk from the town centre and many excellent facilities. No pets.

Whareama, Masterton (close to Castlepoint and Riversdale Beaches)
Farmstay

Address: 'Alderford',
R.D.12, Masterton
Name: Carol & Les Ross
Telephone: (06) 372 3705
Beds: 1 Double (1 Bedroom)
Bathroom: 1 Ensuite
Tariff: B&B (continental - full $7.50pp extra)
Double $75, Single $45, Dinner $25pp (3 course).
Vouchers accepted, Credit cards: Visa/M.C.
Nearest Town: Masterton 40km 1/2 hour, Wellington 2 hours

Les, Carol, Barney the labrador and Dougal the cat, offer you a warm friendly welcome to "Alderford". Stay in our tastefully decorated warm cottage room with ensuite, away from the main homestead. Cosy double bed, electric blanket, feather duvet, radio, TV, 2 easy chairs. Also tea, coffee, Milo and homemade biscuits. Your breakfast served in the cottage, in our dining room or in the garden. Picnic lunches available. Dinner served in our dining room with open fire. Homemade country meals with our homemade jam, bottled fruit, fresh veges from garden, free range eggs. Alderford is a 200 acre sheep, cattle and deer farm. You are very welcome to enjoy the beauty of our farm and our country garden. We are 10 minutes to the beautiful Riversdale Beach with lovely 9 hole golf course, swimming, fishing etc. We are 10 minutes to the well known Tinui pub, craft shop, open gardens and 25 mins to the beauty of Castlepoint Beach. "Alderford" is a 30 min picturesque drive from Masterton.

Masterton

Bed & Breakfast Homestay
Address: Essex House,
29 Essex St, Masterton
Name: Marion & Rick Long
Telephone: (06) 378 6252
Fax: (06) 378 6252
Email: rlong@voyager.co.nz
Beds: 1 King, 1 Queen, 2 Single (3 bedrooms)
Bathroom: 1 Ensuite, 1 Guest share
Tariff: B&B (full) Double $95,
Single $65, Credit Cards (VISA/MC)
Nearest Town: Masterton centre 500m

Essex House was built at the turn of the century and is situated in a quiet tree lined street on Masterton's West side just a few hundred yards from the centre of town and within walking distance of a fine selection of restaurants. Centrally situated for the many interesting outings available in the wonderful Wairarapa. Three bedrooms are available for guests; one twin with ensuite (downstairs), one kingsize double amd one queen size double (upstairs) both sharing a guest bathroom. The kingsize room has its own separate sitting room. There is a large lounge, with an open fireplace, T.V., and tea making facilities set aside exclusively for homestayers. Essex house is centrally heated in winter with a wood stove feeding seven radiators. For Wairarapa sweltering summers relax in the tranquil garden or cool off in the swimming pool. Offstreet parking; Smokefree.

http://www.bnb.co.nz

take a look

Masterton

Homestay, Self Contained Accommodation
Address: Ngahape Road, RD 10,
Masterton, Wairarapa
Name: Emily and Noah
Telephone: (06) 372 2772
Fax: (06) 372 2773
Mobile: (025) 289 0137
Beds: 2 Queen, 8 Single (3 bedrooms)
Bathroom: 1 Guests share
Tariff: B&B (full) Double $55, Single $30, Dinner $24.
Children half price. Credit cards accepted. NZ B&B Vouchers accepted
Nearest Town: Masterton (41 km South East of Masterton)

Guests have pointed out that most B&B's emphasize "tranquillity" and "getting away". They suggest that we need to make the point that we frequently take them on 1 1/2 hr guided walks in a process of getting to know each other as well as getting to know the area, and we enjoy having extended discussions over breakfast. Noah is a professional artist. Emily is a teacher with hobbies in art and music. Ours is an 80 year old homestead on 40 acres of reserve through which the Kaiwhata river meanders. Guests bedrooms, bathroom and "snack" room are in converted shearers' quarters and a purpose-built cottage. We have good scenic hill walks with safe water-holes to cool in. Our extended family includes 2 wonderfully natured dogs and a dozen cheeky hens. We would be pleased to pick you up from the bus depot/railway station in Masterton. Stays of 2-3 days are recommended for the complete country experience. **Directions**: *Our valley at Ngahape is at the end of a No Exit Rd. From Masterton we drive through Wainuioru. Phone for reservations and further directions.*

Masterton

Homestay
Address: "LLandaff",
Fire No. 155 Upper Plain Road,
RD 8, Masterton
Name: Liz Tennet
Telephone: (06) 378 6628
Fax: (06) 378 6612
Beds: 2 Queen,
2 Single (King) (3 bedrooms)
Bathroom: 2 Guests share
Tariff: B&B (full) Double $100, Single $60, Dinner $25,
Children - dollar amount the same as their age.
Nearest Town: Masterton, 5 mins from Masterton Post Office

LLandaff is an historic 1880's Wairarapa homestead providing rural elegance, tranquillity and beauty. Elegantly restored, the homestead boasts beautiful original New Zealand timbers throughout, including polished floors; old pull-handle toilets; a "coffin" bath; open fire places (also in bedrooms); and a cosy wood burning kitchen stove. Guests are invited to enjoy the beautiful large garden beneath 100 year old trees, and to wander the farm and feed the animals. There is also bike riding, cricket, croquet, petanque, and cappuccino coffee. Children are very welcome, and their company is enjoyed by our 11 year old son, and house pets. LLandaff gives peace and tranquillity to the visitor, yet is close enough to a huge range of Wairarapa pursuits - river and sea fishing; canoeing and swimming; bush and farm walks; horse riding; garden visits; wine tasting (35 minutes to Martinborough); antiques; crafts; historic places; and the National Wildlife Centre. Come and enjoy.

Masterton
Homestay
Address: "Mas des Saules",
9a Pokohiwi Road,
Homebush, Masterton
Name: Mary and Steve Blakemore
Telephone: (06) 377 2577
Fax: (06) 377 2578
Beds: 1 Queen, 1 Double (2 Bedrooms)
Bathroom: 1 Guests share
Tariff: B&B (Full) Double $80, Single $50, Dinner $25, Children up to 12 years
half price. NZ B&B Vouchers accepted $12 surcharge
Nearest Town: Masterton 1km from Borough Boundary

*Down a lane, amongst apple orchards, discover our French Provencal farmhouse.
Set for full sun on six hectares, with a stream, water fowl, and petanque court.
Nearby river gives opportunities for walks, fishing, and swimming. Upstairs are
two guest rooms and a guest bathroom with shower and bath. Downstairs is a
large separate guest sitting room. Open fire plus radiators in all rooms, centrally
heated from a wood burning stove. In summer the house is delightfully cool. Our
children have departed, leaving us with a cat, two small dogs and fifteen cattle.
We are a well travelled couple who enjoy meeting people and know the Wairarapa
very well. We can help you plan your stay to include your special interests.
Enjoy farmhouse cooking with fresh vegetables from our large country garden.
Barbecues and picnic lunches by arrangement. Smokefree.*
Directions: *Phone for details, we will direct you from Masterton.*

Tinui, Masterton
Country Homestay/Retreat
Address: Fresh Egg Retreat,
Bute Road, RD 9, Masterton
Name: Danny and Randall
Telephone: (06) 372 3506
Fax: (06) 372 3505
Email: Hosts@Freshegg.co.nz
Beds: 2 Queen,
2 Single (3 Bedrooms)
Bathroom: 2 Ensuites, 1 Private
Tariff: B&B (Special) Double $120, Single $70, Dinner $30 pp.
Not recommended for children. NZ B&B Vouchers accepted
Nearest Town: Masterton 40km.

*Relax in style at our secluded Wairarapa bush retreat! Set in an established garden on six
acres surrounded by willow and pine forest, Fresh Egg will provide you with utter peace and
tranquillity. Although we have no live chickens here, we do offer gourmet, five-course
international dinners with exotic cuisine such as Cajun, Italian, and Jewish, and our
formidable breakfasts include anything from home-made bagels and blintzes to Belgian
waffles, omelettes, or traditional Kiwi fare. For your relaxation, we have a Finnish sauna and
swimming pool, plus a small home gym; indoors are Sky TV, video library, piano, and lots
of games. Nearby activities include Castlepoint and Riversdale beaches, golf, mountain trails,
wineries, and local crafts. Our newly renovated farmhouse has a separate guest entrance for
your privacy. Come and experience our unique combination of hospitality and know-how!*
Directions: *Please phone.* **Home Page**: www.freshegg.co.nz

Masterton
Farmstay
Address: Apple Source Orchard Stay,
Castlepoint Rd, RD6, Masterton
Name: Niel and Raewyn Groombridge
Telephone: (06) 377 0820
Fax: (06) 370 9401
Mobile: (021) 667 092
Email: raeg@voyager.co.nz
Beds: 2 Queen, 1 Double (2 Bedrooms)
Bathroom: 2 Ensuites
Tariff: B&B (Optional full/continental/special) Double $100, Single $60,
Dinner $25, Children half price. No smoking. NZ B&B Vouchers accepted
Nearest Town: Masterton

TRY AN EXPERIENCE THAT'S A LITTLE DIFFERENT
Our homestead is set in the heart of an operating apple orchard surrounded by trees and gardens. Colonial in style and built with ease of living and comfort in mind, the house has a separate guest wing with entrance, deck, lounge along with the two bedrooms each with ensuites. You are welcome to share dinner or a country breakfast with us in the main house and enjoy the ambience of stanley range based cooking along with relaxing by the open fire in winter or on the rose clad deck in summer. There are walks to explore in the orchard and the garden is a haven for pleasant relaxation. Watch the daily orchard activities happen around you and pick some fruit in season. We help with information and assistance on the many activities available from vineyard visits, mountain walks, local beaches and fishing.

Gladstone
Bed & Breakfast
Address: "Hinana Cottage", Admiral Road, RD3, Masterton
Name: Louise Walker (and George & Jessa, the Schnauzers)
Telephone: (06) 372 7667 **Fax**: (06) 372 7667
Email: hinanacottage@xtra.co.nz
Beds: 1 Queen with ensuite, 1 Single
Bathroom: 1 Ensuite, 1 Family Share
Tariff: B&B (full)
Double $120, Single $60.
Full 3 course dinner with wine and aperitifs
by prior arrangement $38 per person. Mastercard/Visa accepted.
Nearest Town: Carterton/Masterton

*Leave the stress and strain, the hustle and bustle of everyday life and experience the peace and tranquility of Hinana Cottage, a delightfully restored 1930's farm cottage nestling on 2 1/2 acres with spectacular views centrally located in the hills overlooking the Gladstone wine district. Just 15 minutes from Masterton, Carterton and Greytown and an easy 20 minutes from Martinborough, smokefree Hinana Cottage is ideally situated for the exploration of the many local attractions including walkways, rivers and vineyards or even for a round of golf after a hearty country breakfast. Totara and matai floors and ornate plaster ceilings combined with fine china and beautiful linen give a gracious, leisured feeling of a bygone era. Play petanque, relax with a pre-dinner drink in the spa pool or by the fire or simply sink into a cane settee on the verandah and take in the ever-changing wonderful views of the Tararuas and Wairarapa valley. **Directions**: Please phone - pick up from Airport, Station or Bus depot by arrangement.*

Flat Point Area/Coastal Wairarapa
Farmstay/Self Contained Accommodation
"Shepherds House"
Address: 'Waimoana Station',
Glenburn Road, R.D.3, Masterton
Name: Lynne & Bill Thompson
Telephone: (06) 372 7732
Fax: (06) 372 7782
Beds: "Shepherds House"
1 Queen, 1 Double, 2 Single (3 bedrooms)
Bathroom: 1 Private.
Tariff: Accomodation Only: Double $90 each extra person $20, Children netotiable
rates, Optional Breakfast on request $10pp. Houses smoke free.
Nearest Town: Carterton and Masterton 55kms, Wellington two hours.

We offer a getaway from the city to relax and enjoy nature, for couples or families staying on 1,000 hectare "Waimoana Station' in the Shepherds House, a modern sunny cottage with wood burner. Sited 400 metres from the Pacific Ocean with garden and fenced lawns for boules, croquet and deck to sit and enjoy ocean to east, hills to west. Adjacent but not in view, the 2 acre homestead garden offers guests native birds, free ranging hens, peacocks, guinea fowl, doves, duckpond, pet pigs, children's play area, proposed astro grass tennis courts for 2000.
3km beach rockpools, swimming, surf casting, snorkelling, tracked hills to 1300 for walking, mountain biking, native bush, great sea views. Pre European historic sites. Nearby DOC walkway to seal colony, honeycomb rock. Fishing charters weather permitting. No phone, TV aerial. Bring own if required. **Directions**: *Please phone or fax for information sheet giving details and directions.*

Flat Point/Coast
Coastal Farmstay/Self Contained Accommodation
Address: Caledonia Station, RD3, Masterton
Name: Wenda and Paul Kerr
Telephone: (06) 372 7553
Fax: (06) 372 7553
Email: wendakerr@xtra.co.nz
Beds: 4 Queen, 2 Single (5 bedrooms)
Bathroom: 1 Ensuite, 2 Private, 1 Guests share
Tariff: B&B Suites Double $125, Single $90, Children $10.
Cottage Double $150 each extra person $15.
NZ B&B Vouchers accepted $40 surchar
Nearest Town: 60 km from Masterton or Carterton

Come experience the ultimate retreat! We are a young Kiwi/Canadian couple with 2 young sons, on an 1880 acre sheep and cattle station on the Wairarapa coast, approximately 2 hours from Wellington or Palmerston North. Our self contained luxury accommodation consists of a fully renovated 3 bedroom, 2 bathroom farm cottage and 2 Queen sized suites, newly built in traditional New Zealand style. Each has its own cooking facilities, fireplace, electric blankets and sea view.
Enjoy walking the beach, through our extensive gardens, exploring the farm or just curl up with a book. There is a 3 hour public walk nearby, providing sights such as a seal colony, ship wreck and honeycomb rock. Special winter and midweek rates available except for public/school holidays.
Please feel free to contact us for further information and directions.
Wheelchair access.

Waiohine Gorge - Carterton/Greytown

Farmstay
Address: Waiohine Farm, Waiohine Gorge Road,
Fire No. 21, RD 1, Carterton
Name: Jenni and Trevor Berthold
Telephone: (06) 379 6716
Fax: (06) 379 6716
Mobile: (025) 523 839
Email: waiohine@xtra.co.nz
Beds: 1 Double,
1 Single foldaway (sleep-out available)
Bathroom: 1 Private
Tariff: B&B (full) Double $80, Single $50, Dinner $20,
children half price. Campervans $20. Credit Cards. Vouchers accepted $10 surcharge
Nearest Town: Carterton and Greytown both 15 minutes away.

Nestled in the foothills of the Tararua Ranges, alongside the Waiohine River, our 100 acre farm offers tranquillity, comfort and variety. A spacious home with fire, guest lounge, spa bath and BBQ area. A touch of the past, our double bedroom is charmingly decorated with oak furniture. Port-a-cot available. We are from professional backgrounds, in mid forties and well travelled. The farm runs a Santa-Gertrudis cattle stud, with sheep, horses, dogs, cats, chickens, ducks and a goat! We are establishing a commercial 'Koura' Farm (NZ freshwater crayfish) You are welcome to wander through farmland, river flats, native bush, wetlands; enjoy the scenery and native bird life. The river is popular for trout, swimming, rafting and within minutes is the forest park for abseiling, hunting or tramping.
Directions: *Only 10 minutes from State Highway 2, between Carterton and Greytown. Please write or phone.* **Website**: www.waiohine.co.nz

Greytown

The Ambers Homestay
Address: 78 Kuratawhiti Street,
Greytown
Name: Marilla & Steve Davis
Telephone: (06) 304 8588
Fax: (06) 304 8590
Mobile: (025) 994 394
Beds: 1 King, 1 Queen,
1 Single (2 bedrooms)
Bathroom: 1 Guests share
Tariff: B&B (continental) Double $90,
Single $55, Children $20. Credit Cards.
Nearest Town: Masterton 40km/Wellington 80km

From the moment you enter "The Ambers" tree lined driveway you begin to experience the "olde worlde" charm of our gracious home. Built in the late 1800's by Mr Hawkins, one of Greytown's first carpenters as his family home, the original totara facade and many interior features are still intact. We have two acres of garden with many beautiful old trees for you to wander and soak up the country atmosphere. Sit in our gazebo and watch the birds bathe in the fountain or enjoy refreshments on your verandah. For anyone wanting to relax, enjoy life and experience historic Greytown, you are minutes from cafes, restaurants, antique shops; ten minutes from Martinborough's vineyards and golf course.
We offer guests luxurious bedrooms, one with king-size and single beds, one with queen-size, guest bathroom, elegant lounge with open fire, spa pool, sunny verandah; delicious breakfast of muesli, fresh fruit and home-made muffins.

406

Greytown
Homestay
Address: 182 West Street, Greytown
Name: Southey Manor
Telephone: (06) 304 9367
Fax: (06) 304 9789
Mobile: (025) 424 035
Beds: 3 Double, 2 Single (4 bedrooms)
Bathroom: 1 Ensuite, 1 Guests share
Tariff: B&B (continental) Double $70-$80.
NZ B&B Vouchers accepted
Nearest Town: Greytown

Spacious relaxed accommodation within easy walking distance of restaurants, cafes and village shops. Double bedroom - ensuite. Twin bedroom, two double bedrooms - share guest bathroom. Group bookings available. Sky, TV, tea/coffee outdoor pool and barbecue facilities provided.
Continental breakfast $70, Double $80 ensuite. Easy to find - follow B&B signs.

Greytown
Homestay
Address: "Westwood",
82 West Street, Greytown
Name: Jill and Peter Kemp
Telephone: (06) 304 8510
Fax: (06) 304 8610
Mobile: (025) 530 154
Email: westwood.kemp@xtra.co.nz
Beds: 2 King, 3 Single (3 Bedrooms)
Bathroom: 2 Ensuite, 1 Private
Tariff: B&B (Full) Double $120, single $90.
Nearest Town: Greytown 500 metres, Wellington 1 hour.

We look forward to welcoming you to our nine acre country retreat set right in the heart of historic Greytown and only a few minutes walk to fine cafes and shops. "Westwood" has been architecturally designed (finalist - NZ House of the Year) to blend into its picturesque surroundings - a tranquil stream, magnificent trees and mountain views. It enjoys the best of both worlds - stylish comfort combined with an old fashioned ambience. You can relax in your own spacious room - complete with ensuite, large dressing room, tea/coffee making facilities and television - or spill out onto the adjoining verandah. And you're welcome to join us for breakfast by the pool.
You can play petanque or croquet, wander through our large herb garden and olive grove, pick raspberries in season, - or simply curl up by the fire with a book. We run a few sheep, and keep hens and bees on the property - this surely is "The Good Life"!
We're close to vineyards, golf courses, tennis courts, mountains for hiking and river walks and we can arrange horse trekking, garden visits, adventure sports etc. We are happy to meet you off the train and bus.
Home page: http://westwood.greytown.co.nz

Greytown
Homestay
Address: 40 Kuratawhiti Street, Greytown
Name: Sue and Fujio Kano
Telephone: (06) 304 9942
Fax: (06) 304 9942
Beds: 1 King, 1 Queen,
2 Single (3 Bedrooms)
Bathroom: 1 Ensuite,
1 Private, 1 Guests share
Tariff: B&B (Full) Double ensuite $110,
Double shared bathroom $100, Single $90, Children $30.
Nearest Town: Wellington

*Rated best B&B in the region by "North and South" magazine (Jan 99 edition),
Summerfield is one of Greytown's most beautiful historic homes. Set in
spacious grounds, which feature protected beeches, this substantial Victorian
villa enables guests to enjoy elegant accommodation in an ambience of tranquillity. We offer fireside breakfasts in winter. Our three guestrooms have
their own entrances leading onto sunny verandahs and the popular outdoor
spa. Summerfield is ideally located opposite the park, pool and tennis courts.
Cafes and galleries are only a short walk away. Enjoy golf, cycling,
bushwalks, or wine tasting or simply collapse into a garden chair and admire
the ever-changing delights of each season. Keen travellers, readers, music
makers and supporters of the Arts will feel particularly feel at home here.
French, German and Japanese spoken.* **Directions**: *Please write or phone.*

Western Lake
Homestay
Address: Tarawai,
Western Lake Road,
RD 3, Featherston
Name: Maria Wallace & Ron Allan
Telephone: (06) 307 7660
Fax: (06) 307 7661
Mobile: 025 962 470
Email: tarawai@xtra.co.nz
Beds: 2 King (both can convert to singles),
1 Queen (3 bedrooms)
Bathroom: 3 Ensuite
Tariff: B&B (full) $270 per couple, Single $180, include dinner and breakfast.
Nearest Town: Martinborough or Featherston (approx 35km from either)

*We enjoy welcoming people to our home which is situated in the Western Lake area of
Palliser Bay. We have 20 hectares of native bush close to Lake Wairarapa, Rimutaka
Forest Park, Lake Onoke and Ocean Beach. We love to share our spectacular views of
the bay, river, lakes and mountain ranges. The house is designed for space, comfort
and warmth. We have large bedrooms, a sauna and a smoke free environment.
We enjoy cooking and sharing delicious meals of fresh, healthy foods. We have
travelled, have wide ranging interests and thoroughly enjoy the company of friends,
old and new. Our region offers many attractions including wetlands, the national
wildlife centre, hunting, tramping, duck shooting, trout and sea fishing, bush and
beach walks, seal colony, vineyards, beautiful gardens, crafts people and many
antique shops.
We accept Mastercard & Visa*

Featherston
Bed & Breakfast
Address: 47 Watt Street,
Featherston,Wairarapa
Name: Woodland Holt Bed & Breakfast
Telephone: (06) 308 9927
Mobile: (025) 291 2774
Beds: 1 Queen, 1 Double,
2 single (4 bedrooms)
Bathroom: 1 Ensuite, 1 Guests share.
Tariff: B&B (continental)
Double $100-$120, Single $60-$65.
Dinner by arrangement. NZ B&B Vouchers accepted Surcharge applies.
Nearest Town: Featherston (located on edge of town)

Judi Adams and her Burmese cats welcome you. We enjoy meeting people and providing friendly hospitality. Our interests include travelling (Spanish is spoken), gardening, books, collecting and cross-stitch. Our home is set in a secluded garden containing native, exotic and rare plants. We offer warm, luxury accommodation with off street parking. For breakfast enjoy home made treats including home preserved fruit and fresh juice. During the day explore beautiful Wairarapa or relax in comfort. In the evening dine at a local restaurant or by prior arrangement join me for an evening meal. Picnic hampers are available (additional charge). Smoking outdoors only please. We look forward to your company and making your stay enjoyable.
Directions: *At Featherston, travelling north, turn left (right if southbound) off main road into Wakefield St and follow the B & B signs to Woodland Holt. Go up the driveway.*

Martinborough
Country Homestay
Address: 'Shadyvale',
Hinakura Road, R.D.4,
Martinborough
Name: Peter & Robyn Taylor
Telephone: (06) 306 9374
Fax: (06) 306 9374
Mobile: (025) 291 7711
Beds: 1 Queen,
1 Double (2 Bedrooms)
Bathroom: 1 Ensuite, 1 Private
Tariff: B&B (full) Double $90-$120,
Single $60-$110, Credit Cards (VISA/MC).
Nearest Town: 3km from Martinborough, and only 1 1/4 hours from central Wellington.

Set amidst an extensive garden and orchard, Shadyvale has breathtaking views to the Tararua ranges across 44 acres of farmland. Enjoy a peaceful stroll around the property, swim or fish in the river, or simply relax around the solar-heated swimming pool. In winter, curl up by the open fire with a good book or join your hosts for a chat in the cosy farmhouse kitchen. All rooms open onto the spacious verandah, beds have electric blankets, and the woodstove provides central heating throughout the house. Our farm style breakfast, featuring eggs from our free range hens, is served in the kitchen or on the verandah, depending on the season. Shadyvale is within walking distance of Martinborough's vineyards and golf course, and we can arrange quad bike rides, kayaking etc. Martinborough is also renowned for its fine restaurants, and we are happy to make bookings for you.

Martinborough

Homestay/Farmstay/SC Accom/House/Cottage
Address: "Glendoon",
Longbush Road, RD 4, Martinborough
Name: Glendoon and Stonemead Cottage
Telephone: (06) 372 7779
Fax: (06) 372 7599
Mobile: (025) 776 968
Beds: 1 Double, 1 Queen and 2 Singles (3 bedrooms)
Bathroom: 2 Private
Tariff: B&B (full) Double $120, Each extra $50, Single $120,
Children negotiable. 1 Double, Divan couch.
Nearest Town: 10 mins to Martinborough, 75 mins to Wellington

Experience country comfort in a private, self contained, three bedroom, traditional NZ country home in tranquil surroundings and set in oaks. "GLENDOON" has lovely views, wildfowl, trout, and National Trust bush. Stroll, picnic, relax in the garden, BBQ, feed the doves or horses, enjoy the books, or simply retreat. Glendoon offers all amenities, TV, music system, video, laundry, woodburners (farm kitchen and dining room), open fire, vintage bath, and master bedroom onto the front verandah with ensuite and shower. Also available is "STONEMEAD COTTAGE," a cozy and comfortable self contained, modern two bedroomed cottage, in a private picturesque setting on Glendoon with English trees, claw bath, shower, fire, TV, music system, gas BBQ, all amenities and front verandah, with lovely valley views. Both provide breakfast foods, heating, garaging, full bedding and home provisions. You do not share. Maps and personal advice on the district, wineries and restaurants available.
Home Page: http://sendme.to/glendoon

http://www.bnb.co.nz

take a look

410

Martinborough

Homestay
Address: "Ross Glyn",
1 Grey St, Martinborough
Name: Ken and Odette Trigg
Telephone: (06) 306 9967
Fax: (06) 306 8267
Beds: 1 Double, 2 Single (2 bedrooms)
Bathroom: 1 Private, 1 Guests share
Tariff: B&B (full) Double $80,
Single $45, Children $25, Dinner $20+. Credit cards.
Nearest Town: Martinborough 5 minutes

Recent retirement has released us to pursue our joint passions of meeting people and developing our 5 acre garden. Our homestay offers absolute peace and privacy, and yet is only 10 minutes away from the town square, vineyards, picturesque golf course, or trout fishing in the Ruamahunga River.

Guests may enjoy discovering peaceful corners of the garden, - the Summer House to Camellia Walk, Woodland area, enclosed circular Rose Gardens and potager Herb and Vegetable garden, fish spotting beside the Lily Ponds, feeding the Fantail, Pigeons, Doves and playing Petanque or Croquet, all possibilities at Ross Glyn. Guests are welcome to relax with us and our small dog and cat in our large cosy (woodburner heated) lounge. Each guest room has French doors, providing private access and opening onto a sunny verandah and garden.

Breakfast includes fresh croissants, home made jams, jellies, preserved fruit. Cooked breakfast on request, and dinner by arrangement.

Martinborough

Homestay
Address: "Oak House",
45 Kitchener Street, Martinborough
Name: Polly & Chris Buring
Telephone: (06) 306 9198
Fax: (06) 306 8198
Email: chrispolly.oakhouse@xtra.co.nz
Beds: 1 Queen, 2 Single (2 bedrooms)
Bathroom: 1 Guests share
Tariff: B&B (special) Double $90,
Single $45, Children by arrangement,
Dinner by arrangement.

Oak House

Nearest Town: Martinborough 5 mins walk

Our characterful seventy year old Californian bungalow offers gracious accommodation only minutes away from Martinborough's renowned vineyards and restaurants. Chris, your host, is a winemaker, and our spacious, cosy guest lounge with ornate ceiling, large bay window and wood burner fire, provides a relaxed setting for sampling Chris's wonderful wines. Breakfast, served in the dining room (or on the verandah when weather permits) features freshly baked croissants, home preserved local fruits and home made conserves. Polly enjoys cooking creatively and dinner, which includes local wild game matched to Chris's wine, is available by arrangement. Our guest wing has its own entrance, bathroom (with large bath and roomy shower) and separate WC and handbasin. Both bedrooms enjoy afternoon sun and garden views. A stately pin oak provides shade in summer and a backdrop for Polly's rose gardens. Our pets include famous artistic cats, chickens and two kunekune piggies.

411

Martinborough
Homestay
Address: 87 Dublin Street,
Martinborough
Name: Swan House
Telephone: (06) 306 9057
Fax: (06) 306 9054
Email: swanhouse@xtra.co.nz
Beds: 3 Queen, 2 Single (3 bedrooms)
Bathroom: 3 Ensuite.
Tariff: B&B (Full/Continental) Double $90,
Single $70, Dinner on request, Children $25.
Credit cards: Visa/Mastercard/Amex
Nearest Town: Featherston/Greytown

Your hosts Margaret and George welcome you to their home to experience their "Scottish & Kiwi" hospitality. Our pleasant home is within easy walking distance of the "Square" around which can be found some fine restaurants and the newly refurbished hotel. The popular vineyards, only minutes away, feature some charming cafes and also nearby are golf, squash and tennis facilities. The wild Palliser Coast with its lighthouse and seal colony is an easy and pleasant drive away. Our home is set back form the road on a 1/2 acre section making it very peaceful and private. The highlight of our garden is a grand old Willow tree which is just perfect for relaxing under. Each of the three large bed sitting rooms have their own entrances and ensuites, all have Queen beds (two of the rooms also have a single bed), electric blankets, TV, tea/coffee making facilities. Ample parking.
Home Page: http://sendme.to/swanhouse

Martinborough
Country Homestay
Address: 'Alder Hey',
Hinakura Road,
Martinborough RD 4.
Name: Sheryll Wilkinson and John Lett
Telephone: (06) 306 9599
Fax: (06) 306 9598
Mobile: (025) 247 5012
Email: ffp.alderhey@xtra.co.nz
Beds: 2 Queen (2 Bedrooms)
Bathroom: 1 Ensuite, 1 Private
Tariff: B&B (Full) Double $100-$120, Single $80,
Children by arrangement. Credit Cards accepted.
Nearest Town: 4 km east of Martinborough, just past the golf course.

Hullo, Welcome to Alder Hey.
Nestled in a pretty valley five minutes drive east of Martinborough, we are close to the wine trail and golf course. Our spacious and comfortable guest accommodation with its own entrance is in a separate wing of our home. The guest lounge cum library has a beautiful view over our olive grove and farm paddocks that lead down to the trout stream on our boundary. A great place to get away from it all, you'll love to curl up with a book or relax on the deck by the pond. Or go fishing or take a country walk. We serve a hearty country breakfast, with eggs from our free-range hens, in our farmhouse kitchen or on the deck on a lovely Wairarapa morning. You'll receive a warm welcome from our farm dogs Ben and Jack, cats Mac and TK and from Sheryll and John.

Martinborough

B&B Homestay, Self Contained Accommodation
Address: Beatsons Of Martinborough
Harrington, 9A Cologne Street, Martinborough
Name: Karin Beatson and John Cooper
Telephone: (06) 306 8242
Fax: (06) 306 8243
Mobile: (025) 499 827
Email: beatsons@wise.net.nz
Beds: 4 Queen (4 bedrooms)
Bathroom: 4 Ensuites
Tariff: B&B (special) Double $120, Single $100,
Dinner by arrangement. Visa/Mastercard.
Nearest Town: Martinborough

Beatson's Of Martinborough's "Harrington" is a 1905 villa ,five minutes walk from Martinborough Square. Carefully restored as a Boutique Bed and Breakfast, it is furnished comfortably in a country style, featuring antique furniture and original work by New Zealand Artists. Harrington offers polished Matai floors, high ceilings and spacious bedrooms with modern ensuites. Overlooking the garden the large open plan kitchen dining and living areas open out to a deck, veranda and courtyard.
Breakfast includes seasonal local produce, home made breads and preserves.
Beatson's of Martinborough's "Heriot Cottage" sits in the garden of Harrington. It is a one bedroom self contained comfortable colonial cottage featuring an original clawfoot bath and veranda.
Beatson's Of Martinborough's "Rothesay" offers three bedrooms, can sleep eight. Suitable for self catering families or groups. The garden has large trees, great outdoor spaces and boasts Martinborough's smallest Vineyard.
All Beatson's Of Martinborough's accommodation are only an hours drive from Wellington and five minutes walk from the Martinborough Square, cafes, restaurants vineyards and specialty shops.

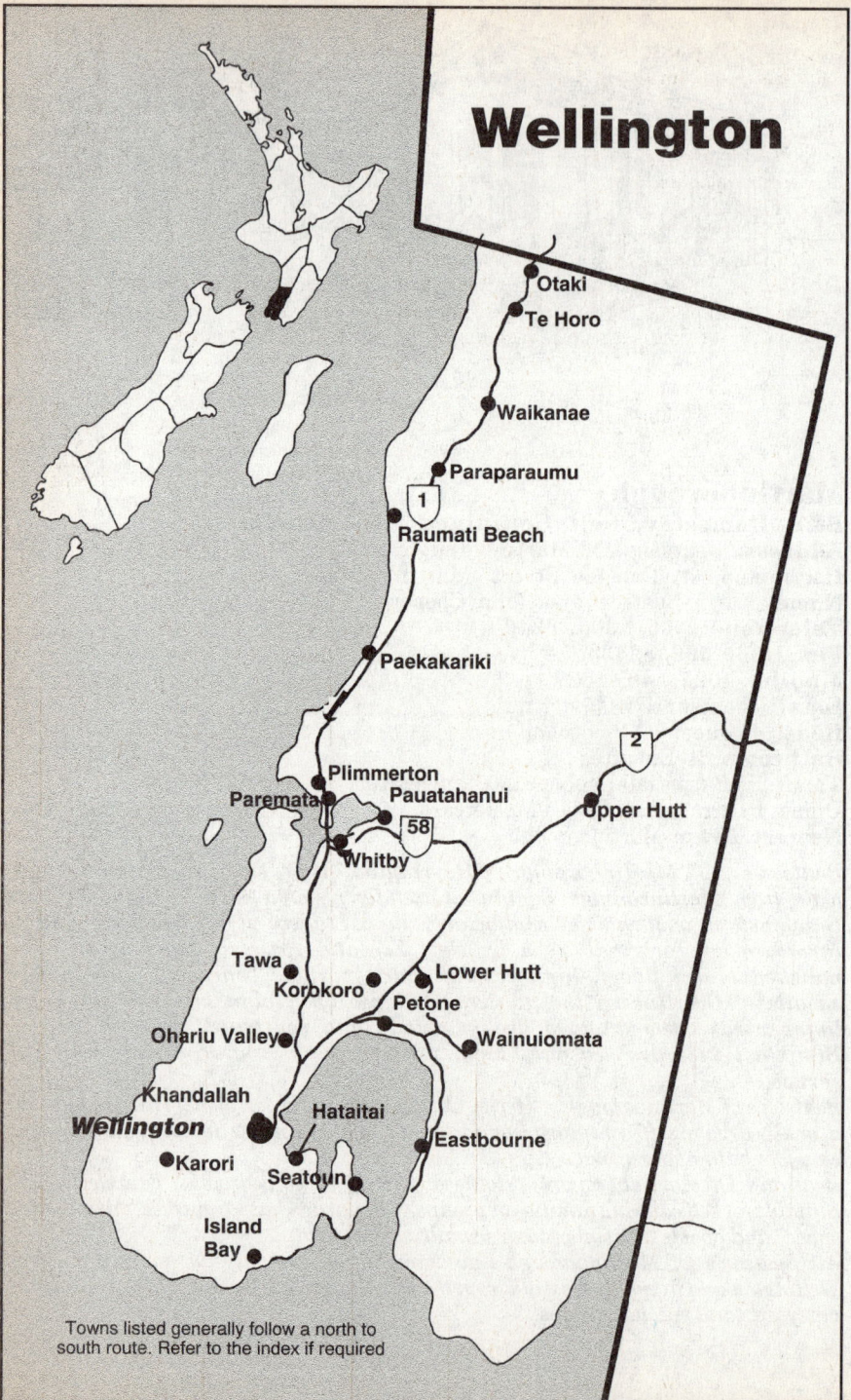

Wellington

Otaki

Te Horo

Waikanae

Paraparaumu

1

Raumati Beach

Paekakariki

Plimmerton

Paremata

Pauatahanui

2

Whitby

58

Upper Hutt

Tawa

Korokoro

Lower Hutt

Petone

Ohariu Valley

Wainuiomata

Khandallah

Wellington

Hataitai

Karori

Eastbourne

Seatoun

Island Bay

Towns listed generally follow a north to south route. Refer to the index if required

Otaki

Country Garden Homestay
Address: Waitohu Lodge,
294 State Highway 1 North, Otaki
Name: Keith & Mary Oldham
Telephone: (06) 364 5389
Freephone 0800 364 239
Fax: (06) 364 5350
Beds: 1 Queen, 3 Single (3 bedrooms) Guest lounge
Bathroom: 1 Guests share, 1 Family share
Tariff: B&B (full) Double/Twin $75, Single $50, Children $25, Dinner by arrangement
$25pp. Credit Cards. NZ B&B Vouchers accepted $5 Surcharge
Nearest Town: 74km North of Wellington city and 16km South of Levin on State
Highway 1

*Welcome to Waitohu Lodge in sunny Otaki. Ideally located, we are only 55 mins drive to
Wellington city and the Picton ferry. Easy to find we are set well back from the highway in an
acre of trees and gardens, with secure onsite parking. At Waitohu Lodge we offer you warm
friendly Kiwi hospitality and top quality accommodation and amenities. We serve wholesome
tasty meals, featuring fresh fruit and vegetables from our garden and homemade preserves
at breakfast. Guests appreciate their luxury bathroom with spa bath and shower, comfortable
rooms with garden views, own private entrance and guest lounge with TV and tea/coffee
making facilities.*
WAITOHU LODGE IS A 'QUALITY AWARD' WINNING HOMESTAY.
*Retired early, Keith was a Geography teacher and Mary a City Councillor. Our interests
include travel, the arts, wine tasting, gardening and Mary enjoys painting water colours. We
and our Burmese cat Raj look forward to welcoming you into our smoke free home.*

Otaki

Country Garden B&B Homestay
Address: 'Glenmore', Rahui Road, Otaki
Name: Jack & Heather Bellaney
Telephone: (06) 364 7319
Fax: (06) 364 7630
Mobile: (025) 213 8876
Beds: 1 King, 2 Single (2 bedrooms),
Guests lounge.
Bathroom: 1 Guests share. Spabath
Tariff: B&B (continental) Double/Twin $75, Single $50. Cooked breakfast on
request. Out-of-season discounts. NZ B&B Vouchers accepted
Nearest Town: Levin/Paraparaumu 15 mins, Wellington/Palmerston North 55 mins.

*Close to Wellfington but in the Country - our bush lined driveway takes you to our hideaway
where peace and tranquillity abounds. Relax and enjoy superb views and warm hospitality
in our modern home overlooking the Racecourse and Kapiti Island. Smoke-free inside.
Sunsets can be quite spectacular. Our five acre farmlet features extensive gardens and
lagoons, native bush/birds and even glow worms. Able to arrange visits to gardens, farms,
Kapiti Island, etc.   We enjoy the outdoors, gardening, travel and hosting our many guests.
Jack is keen on fishing and woodturning.*
*Sash our golden Labrador lives outside but loves to welcome visitors as does our cat Katie.
Forest Park, Vintage Car Museum, Tourist Farm, Bird Sanctuary, Outdoor Pursuits Centre
all close by. Within minutes of shops, restaurants, beach and river.*
*Guests comments: TOPS IN HOSPITALITY - HOME AWAY FROM HOME - LUCKY TO
FIND YOU - MAGIC - QUIET AND SO RELAXING.*
Directions: *1 1/2km from SH1.*

Te Horo, Otaki

Separate Accommodation
Address: 'Stone Pine Creek',
123 Settlement Road, Te Horo, Otaki RD1
Name: Lorraine & Kerry Hoggard
Telephone: (06) 364 3140
Fax: (06) 364 3468
Email: stonepinecreek@clear.net.nz
Beds: 1 Queen (1 bedroom) Separate Accommodation
Bathroom: 1 Private
Tariff: B&B (special/continental) Double $120. Credit Cards accepted: Visa/Mastercard
NZ B&B Vouchers accepted On weekdays Mon-Thurs + $40 Surcharge
Nearest Town: Otaki - 1hr drive from Wellington

Our Italian style farmhouse and separate accommodation are set in a lavender farm with a backdrop of rolling hills and panoramic seaviews. You will wake in the gatehouse to views over the lavender and grapes to Kapiti Island. The gatehouse contains a mezzanine sleeping area, ground floor living area and your own bathroom. A special continental breakfast basket will be waiting for you to have, in privacy, at your leisure. We have a lavender farm in full production and a large garden with a meandering stream. These plus the swimming pool, which is within the walled courtyard, are available to our guests. We sell lavender products made from our oil (distilled on the property) and lavender plants. Our interests include people, books, gardening, music, art, theatre and travel. We also have a few coloured sheep, cows, ducks, cats and two friendly dogs.

Within short distances you may walk in the bush or by the sea, investigate craft places, pick berries, play tennis, golf or just enjoy the peace. We can assure you of a warm welcome and an interesting stay. Non smokers please. **Directions**: *Please write or phone.*

Te Horo

Country Homestay
Address: Shepreth, Te Hapua Rd,
Te Horo, R.D. 1, Otaki
Name: Lorraine & Warren Birch
Telephone: (06) 364 2130
Fax: (06) 364 2134 **Mobile**: (025) 441 088
Beds: 1 Double, 3 Single
(2 bedrooms/1 bedroom has double + single bed, other has 2 singles)
Bathroom: 1 Private plus extra toilet.
(only one party of guests taken at a time)
Tariff: B&B (full) Double $85, Single $45, Dinner $30,
Credit cards accepted. NZ B&B Vouchers accepted $20 surcharge
Nearest Town: Waikanae 6km south, Otaki 8km north

Relax in the country, close to the capital. Shepreth is a small farm north of Waikanae just off State Highway 1, and 45 minutes drive north of Wellington. We graze angora goats, cattle and sheep, and have a cat called Gruffyd. Our home is sheltered, sunny and spacious. Among the many places to visit in the area are Southwards Car Museum, Lindale Agricultural Centre, the Nga Manu Bird Sanctuary and the Paraparaumu Shopping Mall. Golf courses, beaches and open gardens are close by. We have a wide range of interests - including vintage and classic motoring and family history. We have travelled in New Zealand and overseas, and enjoy meeting both New Zealanders and people visiting our country. A generous breakfast with plenty of variety is provided. The area has a selection of restaurants available for dinner, or you are welcome to have dinner with us by arrangement. For the comfort of guests our house is smoke-free. We offer friendly, Kiwi country hospitality at Shepreth.
Directions: *Please phone.*

Te Horo

Te Horo Country Homestay
Address: 109 Arcus Road,
Te Horo, Kapiti Coast
Name: Craig Garner
Telephone: 0800 4 Te Horo
(483 467) or (06) 364 3393
Fax: (06) 364 3323
Mobile: (025) 306 009
Email: TeHoro.Lodge@xtra.co.nz
Beds: Three luxurious bedrooms
(double/twin). One Master-suite
(one queen, one single).
Bathroom: 4 Ensuites
Tariff: B&B (full) Double $150-$185,
Single $125, Dinner $40 (by arrangement).
Not suitable for children. Major Credit Cards accepted.
Nearest Town: Otaki, 8km North, Waikanae 7km South,65 km North of Wellington

Let us pamper you in our purpose built luxurious Country Lodge. Set next to five acres of native bush with a rural outlook, Te Horo Lodge offers a relaxing, tranquil environment. The three bedrooms downstairs open out to a veranda and expansive lawns. The upstairs "master-suite" has a lounge area with intimate bush views. The decor and furnishings throughout consist of strong vibrant colours. The feature fireplace anchors our stunning lounge. It is crafted by a local stone artist and is perfect for those cold winter nights. The dining-room has a striking recycled timber table. Te Horo Lodge also offers a "picture perfect" pool area. It includes a secluded in-ground swimming pool and luxury spa pool. The pool area is surrounded by manicured lawns and gardens. It features a gazebo - our summer dining room - an ideal spot to linger over a scrumptious BBQ dinner. Te Horo Lodge is not suitable for children. For the comfort of our guests the Lodge is smokefree. There are no pets. A generous cooked country breakfast is provided, including fruit locally grown. The Kapiti region has some fine restaurants or you are most welcome to dine with me at the Lodge by prior arrangement. Te Horo Lodge is an ideal escape from the pressures of the city, whether you are looking at just relaxing or exploring this unique part of the countryside. You can even wander around our ten acre property, including a walk through our native bush. Local attractions include: Golf courses, the "World Class" Southwards Car Museum, Kapiti Cheeses, gardens, nature reserve, bushwalks, arts and crafts and our rugged West Coast beaches. For the more active try: Fly by Wire, local kayaking, rafting, abseiling or take a tour to Kapiti Island. We will be happy to assist you in planning your local activities. How to find us: Te Horo Lodge is located just 3 km off State Highway 1, turn across the railway opposite the Te Horo Store, onto School Road, then left into Arcus Road. You'll find us at the end of the road.
Directions: *Please telephone for further directions. I look forward to welcoming you into my home.*

Te Horo - Kapiti Coast

Homestay
Address: "Hautere Lodge"
139 Old Hautere Road,
Te Horo, Kapiti Coast
Name: Rod & Jacqui Guild
Telephone: (06) 364 2411
Fax: (06) 364 2411
Mobile: (021) 608 022
Email: hautere.lodge@xtra.co.nz
Beds: 3 Queen, 1 Single (3 Bedrooms)
Bathroom: 3 Ensuite
Tariff: B&B (Full) Double $95-$120, Single $75, Children $25, Dinner $35. NZ
B&B Vouchers accepted $20 surcharge
Nearest Town: 5 km south of Otaki. 10 km north of Waikanae.

Hautere Lodge is a character home, an original farmhouse, renovated to reflect the nineties, while retaining its character. Beautiful equipped bedrooms with ensuites. A fully cooked breakfast is served either on your private patio or in our dining room, with eggs coming from our free range hens. There is a tennis court, croquet lawn, a large solar heated swimming pool and bicycles available for use. Hautere Lodge is perfect for a getaway weekend or an overnight stop. Dinner is by arrangement. The Kapiti Coast offers many attractions - Kayaking, golf, bush walks, interesting cafes and of course the wonderful beaches or a trip to Kapiti Island.
Directions: *Old Hautere Rd is off SH 1 (on the right going North), just North of the Te Horo Winery.*

Waikanae

Homestay
Address: 'Waimoana',
63 Kakariki Grove, Waikanae
Name: Ian & Phyllis Stewart
Telephone: (04) 293 7158
Fax: (04) 293 7156
Email: waimoana@nzhomestay.co.nz
Beds: 3 bedrooms, two with 1 Queen
and 1 Single bed each, one with two singles and outside entrance.
Bathrooms: 3 Ensuite
Tariff: B&B Double $195 or $120, Single $140 or $85. Credit Cards. Tariffs valid
to 30/9/2000. NZ B&B Vouchers accepted $115 or $48 Surcharge.
Nearest Town: Waikanae 1km. 58km north of Wellington on State Highway 1

At "Waimoana", the generous use of glass invites the outside inside, without compromising privacy. The decor is restful. Expect fresh flowers, warm fluffy towels and balconies to admire the spectacular view. The living quarters radiate from a glass-roofed atrium containing a swimming pool, an indoor garden and a waterfall.
Nearby Kapiti Island is a major bird sanctuary - visits need to be booked well ahead. The Southward Museum houses a huge collection of vintage cars. Paraparaumu Beach Golf Course is nearby. Or try "Fly-byWire". Day trips to Wellington are easy, too.
"Waimoana" is not suitable for children and is smoke-free. There are no pets. First-class restaurants are nearby. 45 minutes north of inter-island ferries at Wellington. Check in is from 3p.m. on. Check out is 10a.m.
Cancellations may incur a fee - details when booking. Please phone for directions.
Home Page: http://nz.com/webnz/bbnz/waimoana.htm

Waikanae

Homestay
Address: 'Allenby',
12 Te Maku Grove, Waikanae
Name: Quintin & Meg Hogg
Telephone: (04) 293 2428,
Freephone 0800 11 00 82
Fax: (04) 293 2428
Beds: 2 Single (1 Bedroom)
Bathroom: 1 Ensuite
Tariff: B&B (full) Double $75,
Single $45, Dinner $20-$25.
NZ B&B Vouchers accepted $10 Surcharge
Nearest Town: Waikanae 1Km

We offer a warm comfortable self-contained twin bed unit which opens onto a sunny terrace and conservatory. Ensuite, private shower, basin and toilet. Laundry facilities also available. Guests will be provided with continental or cooked breakfast as desired. Tea and coffee making facilities and refrigerator in room. Dinner can be provided given reasonable notice or we can recommend excellent restaurants in Waikanae or nearby Paraparaumu Waikanae has a temperate climate, good beaches, wildlife sanctuaries, bush walks, golf course, arts and crafts, and is close to world famous Southwards Vintage Car Museum and Lindale Farm complex. We are handy to Wellington and the Interisland Ferry Terminal (45 minutes by car). We are keen gardeners and have travelled widely in New Zealand and overseas in Australia, U.S.A., U.K. and Europe. Interests include music, embroidery, trout fishing, and meeting people. We welcome non smokers. **Directions**: Please phone for directions (1km off SH1) or will meet travellers arriving by train or bus.

Waikanae Beach

Homestay
Address: 115 Tutere St, Waikanae
Name: Pauline & Allan Jones
Telephone: (04) 293 6532
Fax: (04) 293 6543
Mobile: 025 300 785
Email: albeach@paradise.net.nz
Beds: 2 Queen, 1 Single (2 bedrooms). Twin bedroom available for family or larger party willing to share private bathroom.
Bathroom: 1 Ensuite, 1 Private
Tariff: B&B (full) Double $85, Single $50, Children $20, Children under 8 years $10, Credit Cards. Long stays negotiable.
NZ B&B Vouchers accepted $15 surcharge
Nearest Town: Waikanae, 4km

Pauline and Allan invite you to enjoy the comfort of their warm and sunny open plan home with panoramic views of Kapiti Island, the Tasman Sea, and the Tararua Ranges. An ideal location to break your journey or just to relax. We have a direct access to a sandy beach where you may walk, swim and enjoy the scenery. Tea and coffee making facilities are available in each guest room, laundry and ironing facilities are also available. We have travelled extensively overseas and look forward to offering warm and friendly hospitality to visitors from home and abroad. Our interests include music and crafts. Local attractions include Lindale Tourist Centre, Southwards Car Museum, a golf course, Nga Manu Native Reserve and Kapiti Island Nature Reserve for which a landing permit must be arranged with the Department of Conservation.
Directions: Please phone. Recommended by Frommers.

419

Waikanae Beach

Self-contained Accommodation
Address: Konini Cottage,
26 Konini Crescent, Waikanae Beach
Name: Maggie and Bob Smith
Telephone: (04) 293 6610
Fax: (04) 293 6610
Mobile: (025) 260 6492
Beds: 1 Double, 2 Single (2 bedrooms)
Bathroom: 1 Private
Tariff: Accomodation only: Double $65
plus $10 each extra person.
Optional breakfast (full) $10 per person   NZ B&B Vouchers accepted
Nearest Town: Waikanae 5 Kms

Imagine a long walk on an endless beach, perhaps a round of golf on the adjoining links, or just lazing on the verandah enjoying the tranquillity of our semi rural setting. This is all possible when you stay in our two bedroom Lockwood cottage, with fully equipped kitchen for self catering, laundry and bathroom facilities and comfortable lounge. As we only take one party of guests at a time all this is for your private use.

Whether overseas visitors or fellow Kiwis you will appreciate the spaciousness and quality of our cottage. You can join us in our home for a lingering breakfast or you may choose to have it served in the cottage.

We are a forty something couple with two teenage sons. Bob is a cabinetmaker who restores antiques and makes furniture in his home workshop and Maggie is the inspiration in the landscaping of our large grounds.

Waikanae Beach

Homestay
Address: 36 Fieldway, Waikanae Beach
Name: Jan& Dick Holloway
Telephone: (04) 904 3431
Fax: (04) 902 3793
Beds: 2 Single (1 bedroom)
Bathroom: 1 Private
Tariff: B&B (full) Double $70,
Single $40.
NZ B&B Vouchers accepted
Nearest Town: Waikanae 5km.

We are a retired couple who would like to share their comfortable home with guests. The accommodation is a sunny room with private bathroom. Adjoining this is a garden room and paved garden courtyard. Own tea and coffee making facilities. Continental or cooked breakfast and there are several excellent restaurants nearby. Our home that we share with Jessie our gentle dog is only minutes from lovely Waikanae beach that we both enjoy for swimming and walking. There are several golf courses nearby and we too enjoy a game of golf, we also enjoy pottering in our garden.

Our district has many attractions including gardens, galleries, Lindale Tourist Farm, Southwards Car Museum and Bird Sanctuaries. Waikanae is approx. 1 hour from Wellington and 10 minutes from Coastlands shopping town at Paraparaumu.

We are non smokers.
Directions: *Please telephone.*

Waikanae
Self-contained Accommodation
Address: "Country Patch"
18 Kea Street, Waikanae
Name: Brian and Sue Wilson
Telephone: (04) 293 5165
Fax: (04) 293 5164
Mobile: 025-578 421
Email: wilbri@freemail.co.nz
Beds: 1 King/Queen, 2 Single
(1 bedrooms + mezzanine)
Bathroom: 1 Ensuite
Tariff: B&B (continental)
Double $85, each extra person $30,
Single $60, Children $20, under 5 free.
BC/VISA NZ B&B Vouchers accepted $10 surcharge
Nearest Town: Paraparaumu 12 Kms

"Country Patch" is 2 1/2 acres nestled under the bush line of the foothills of Waikanae. It gets panoramic views along the coast to Kapiti Island and beyond.
Comfortable self-contained accommodation for up to 5 people with own kitchen facilities.
Waikanae is the heart of the garden area on the Kapiti Coast and we are 45 mins from Wellington with bush walks, good beaches and excellent restaurants nearby.
We will gladly meet the bus or train and warmly invite you to share our patch of country. We have two children Kate (14 years) and Simon (12 years) and a friendly golden labrador (Holly). Families welcome . We are strictly smoke free. Please phone or write.
Home Page: www.nzhomestay.hn.pl.net

Waikanae, Kapiti Coast
Homestay
Address: "Millrest",
57 Park Ave, Waikanae
Name: Colleen and Gordon Butchers
Telephone: (04) 904 2424
Fax: (04) 904 2424
Email: pg.cr.butchers@paradise.net.nz
Beds: 1 Queen, (addtl Twin room available)
Bathroom: 1 Private
Tariff: B&b (Full) Double $80, Single $60, Dinner $20 pp, Children $20.
Credit cards : BC/Visa. NZ B&B vouchers accepted $10 surcharge.
Nearest Town: Wellington 45 mins drive

Millrest offers you all that is best in warm Kiwi hospitality. We look forward to sharing our spacious home set in park-like surroundings with you and know that you will enjoy the friendly and informal lifestyle.
We are an active semi-retired couple who have travelled extensively overseas and within New Zealand and enjoy meeting new friends. Our interests include bowls, classic cars, spinning and weaving, music and gardening. Numerous attractions on the Kapiti Coast include Southwards Car Museum, Lindale Farm Complex, a bird sanctuary together with excellent restaurants and shops.
Millrest is a peaceful haven only 45 minutes from the Interisland Ferry Terminal. To ensure our guests are totally relaxed and feel "at home" we host only one party at a time. Buffy our laid back Beagle cross dog shares our smoke free environment.
Directions: *please write or phone in advance.*

Waikanae

**Homestay or
S/C Accommodation**
Address: "Sudbury",
39 Manu Grove, Waikanae
Name: Brian and Glenys Daw
Telephone/Fax: (04) 293 3813
Beds: 2 Queen (2 Bedrooms)
Bathroom: 1 Ensuite,
1 Family share
Tariff: B&B (Continental)
Double $90, Single $60, Visa/MC Credit cards accepted.
NZ B&B Vouchers accepted $20 surcharge

Hear the dawn chorus! The birds are here, only you are missing. When you enter the sweeping driveway you will discover hospitality and tranquillity beyond expectation along with a choice of a new self-contained guesthouse or traditional homestay accommodation. A garden of 2 1/2 acres with over 200 roses, a lily pond, and natural bush with Tui, Woodpigeon and Bellbird create a very peaceful environment where guests may relax while contemplating tomorrow's travel. You can also enjoy a spa bath before retiring. Attractions include the world-class Southwards car museum, crafts, golf courses and bird sanctuary. Paraparaumu is 8 kms to the south and Wellington 60 kms. We can meet and assist if required. Dinner, at a modest cost, can be provided by special arrangement. We enjoy food, travelling and meeting people. We have no children at home and no pets. We prefer guests do not smoke inside the dwellings. Not suitable for children under 10 years.
Directions: *Please phone or fax.*

Waikanae

**Rural Homestay,
Self Contained Accommodation**
Address: RiverStone Garden
111 Ngatiawa Road
Waikanae (Please phone, evenings)
Name: Paul and Eppie Murton
Telephone: (04) 293 1936
Fax: (04) 293 1936
Email: riverstone@paradise.net.nz
Beds: 1 Queen, 1 Single (2 bedrooms) in self-contained studio,
Bathroom: 1 Private
Tariff: B&B (Full) Double $90, Single $60. Not suitable for children. Credit Cards. NZ B&B Vouchers accepted $21 surcharge for Double.
Nearest Town: Waikanae 7km

The local cafe, pottery and birdpark has bush and river walks. The studio is where you can paint with Eppie, and Paul is an engineer and writer. There are more restaurants in Waikanae village, and the Nga Manu bird sanctuary is six minutes drive away. Paraparaumu is ten minutes towards Wellington and on the way is the Southward Vintage car museum. Paraparaumu has craft shops and boutiques at Lindale and general shopping in town. There are beaches in both centres. The capital city Wellington is 45 minutes away and has the airport, inter-island ferries, modern shops, art galleries and the Te Papa museum. Our guests are welcome to join us and use the garden and five hectares of paddocks, trees and rivers reserve for their enjoyment. We can give simple instructions from the traffic lights on SH1 at Waikanae or collect you from the bus or train at Paraparaumu. Our home and accommodation is smoke-free. Laundry facilities available.

Paraparaumu

Homestay
Address: 72 Bluegum
Road, Paraparaumu
Name: Vic & Jude Young
Telephone: (04) 902-0199
Beds: 1 Double,
1 Single (2 bedrooms)
Bathroom: 1 Private,
1 Family share
Tariff: B&B (full) Double $70,
Single $40, Dinner $20.
Children half price.
Vouchers accepted
Nearest Town: Paraparaumu

Our 1950's beach house has excellent hill, island and sea views, and is situated just two blocks back from Marine Parade and the sea. Shops, golf course, airport, cafés and excellent restaurants are a 1 km walk away. Off-street parking is provided and we will meet bus or train. Guests may borrow our bicycles. Jude is, with prior notice, pleased to prepare meals for those on special diets, and packed lunches can be provided for day trips (to Kapiti Island for example). We love walking, food, music, Citroens and meeting travellers from all countries. Non smokers preferred. We have a cat.
Directions: *Watch for yellow letterbox on seaward corner of Bluegum & Rua Roads.*

Paraparaumu

Self-contained Accommodation
Address: 60A Ratanui Rd,
Otaihanga/Paraparaumu
Name: Marius & Sytske Kruiniger
Telephone: (04) 299 8098 work,
(04) 297 3447 home
Fax: (04) 297 3447
Beds: 1 Queen,
2 Single (2 bedrooms)
Bathroom: Private
Tariff: Accommodation only:
Double $65, Single $50, Extra person $10,
Children under 5 $5. Continental breakfast
optional $5 pp. Credit Cards. NZ B&B Vouchers accepted
Nearest Town: Paraparaumu, 55km north of Wellington

Our self-contained lodge offers privacy and tranquillity, with a view of a small lake, full with wildlife. It contains a well equipped kitchen, a cosy lounge with TV, books and some games; spacious bathroom with laundry facilities. We are situated only a few minutes drive from Coastlands Shopping Centre and beaches. Indoor and outdoor attractions, as well as excellent restaurants are within easy reach. Information about these are available in the lodge. No dogs please and guests are asked not to smoke indoors. Please phone or fax for bookings and directions. We look forward meeting you.

423

Paraparaumu Beach

Homestay
Address: 17 Takahe Drive,
Kotuku Park, Paraparaumu Beach
Name: Ernie and Rhoda Stevenson
Telephone: (04) 298 7342
Mobile: (025) 232 5106
Beds: 1 Double, 2 Single (2 bedrooms)
Bathroom: 1 Private
Tariff: B&B (continental)
Double $70, Single $45,
Dinner $25 (by arrangement),
Children under 12 years half price.   Credit Cards.   Vouchers accepted
Nearest Town: Paraparaumu (10 mins drive)

Enjoy warm friendly hospitality in our modern new home, set in peaceful surroundings next to the Waikanae river estuary and Paraparaumu beach. We have panoramic views of the sea, Kapiti Island, a small lake and hills beyond. There are many lovely coastal and river walks, with an abundance of bird life. Paraparaumu is 45 minutes north of Wellington, the centre of Kapiti Coast's many varied tourist attractions, including trips to Kapiti Island's bird sanctuary, and world-ranking Paraparaumu Beach Golf Course - only 5 minutes from our home. We are a semi-retired couple who enjoy meeting people, offering hospitality and sharing our love of NZ scenery, bush and mountain walking. Guests are welcome to share our spacious lounge, use laundry facilities, enjoy dinner with us by prior arrangement, in a relaxing smoke-free environment. Ideal Ferry Stop-over.
Directions: *Please phone for directions.*

Paekakariki

Homestay
Address: Phone for details.
Name: Frances Cherry
Telephone: (04) 292 8534
Fax: (04) 292 7001
Beds: 1 Queen (1 ensuite)
Bathroom: 1 Ensuite
Tariff: B&B (continental) Double $70, Single $45, Dinner $15.
NZ B&B Vouchers accepted
Nearest Town: Paraparaumu (10 mins drive north)

I am a novelist and short story writer and teach writing courses. I love meeting people from overseas and New Zealand. I am interested in politics, human behaviour, and all the arts. My colourful open-plan home is perched on a hilltop and has wonderful views of the sea and Kapiti Island. It takes two minutes to walk to the beach where you can swim, or walk for miles along the sand and through Queen Elizabeth Park. We are a non-smoking household. Paekakariki, on State Highway One, half an hours drive from Wellington (regular train service) is the home of many well known creative people. It has two cafes, a pub, the famous Fly By Wire, is close to craft shops, restaurants, the world-class Southward Car Museum and Nga Manu Bird Sanctuary.
Directions: *Phone for directions.*

Plimmerton

Homestay
Address: 131 Pope Street, Camborne,
Plimmerton, Wellington
Name: Joan & Denis Sawkins
Telephone: (04) 233 9444
Fax: (04) 233 9515 **Mobile**: (025) 461 495
Email: sawkins@xtra.co.nz
Beds: 1 Queen (1 bedroom)
Bathroom: 1 Private
Tariff: B&B (full) Double $90,
Single $70, Dinner $30 pp. Vouchers accepted $20 surcharge
Nearest Town: Wellington 20 mins, Porirua 5 mins

We extend a warm welcome to all guests and offer you:
* *Million dollar views of beach, sea and the South Island*
* *Easy access off State Highway 1, just 200 metres*
* *Off street parking*
* *Easy connections to and from Interisland Ferries and Airport*
* *Modern home with sun and views from every room*
* *Private spacious guest bedroom with queen size bed*
* *Own bathroom with bath and shower   • Dinner by prior request*
* *Relaxing atmosphere - catch up on your e-mail or laundry*
* *Friendly hosts who have travelled extensively*
* *Attractive coastal garden with Pohutakawas and outdoor areas*
* *Walking distance to beach and railway station*
* *Close to Wellington - capital city of New Zealand and Te Papa*
Directions: *Please telephone*

Plimmerton

Homestay
Address: 57 Pope St,
Plimmerton, Wellington
Name: Plimmerton Homestay,
Jill & Ned Pattle
Telephone: (04) 233 8329
Beds: 1 King/Queen,1 Single
(1 Bedroom)
Bathroom: 1 Family share
Tariff: B&B (full and continental)
Double $65, Single $50,   Children half price,
Dinner by arrangement, Credit Cards. NZ B&B Vouchers accepted
Nearest Town: Wellington 20 mins, Porirua 5 mins.

Our comfortable home has beautiful harbour views and glimpses of the South Island. We are easy to find as Pope Street runs off State Highway 1. Guests are welcomed with a cup of tea or coffee. Driving time is 20 minutes to the inter-island ferries.
The large, sunny guest room, in a separate wing, has tea/coffee making facilities and a sitting area. For breakfast we serve fresh fruit and home-made bread. The bathroom, toilet and shower are separate rooms. Cafes, restaurants and beaches for walking or swimming are 1 minute by car.
We have travelled (French, German and Italian dictionaries available) and many of our guests have appreciated our suggestions for touring New Zealand, as we have lots of photographs and we know the walking tracks. Our interests are geology, botany, music and walking. There is off-street parking. Guests may smoke on our deck.

425

Plimmerton
Homestay
Address: 43 Bayview Road,
Paremata, Wellington
Name: "Bayview", Jocelyn and Tony
Telephone: (04) 233 2575
or 233 9431
Fax: (04) 233 9414
Mobile: (025) 492 183
Email: relax@bayview.co.nz
Beds: 1 Double, 1 Single (Futon), (2 Bedrooms)
Bathroom: 1 Guests share.
Tariff: B&B (Full/Continental) Double $85, Single $50. Not suitable for children. Dinner $35-$40. NZ B&B Vouchers accepted $15 surcharge.
Credit cards accepted
Nearest Town: Wellington 20 mins, Porirua 5 mins.

Bayview Homestay is a large, modern, sunny home situated two minutes from Paremata Bridge on State Highway 1. Relax on the sundeck or by the log fire, taking in the spectacular views across Paremata Harbour and out to sea. Join us for dinner. Your hostess, Jocelyn, is a professional caterer who will provide meals to your taste using fresh seasonal produce. Jocelyn is also trained in therapeutic massage should you wish to unwind. Our interests include gardening, music, sport, travel, food and wine. Laundry and drying facilities available. Off street parking. Unsuitable for children and pets. Non smoking inside. Ideally situated to access the attractions of Wellington. Two minutes to trains. Pick up and drop off service available to airport, ferry, bus or train.
Directions: *Please phone, fax or write.*

Whitby
Homestay
Address: 22 Musket Lane, Whitby
Name: Elaine and John Oldfield
Telephone: (04) 234 1002
Beds: 2 Queen (2 Bedrooms)
Bathroom: 1 Guests Share
Tariff: B&B (Continental)
Cooked Breakfast on request.
Double $75, Single $45,
Dinner $25 pp.
Nearest Town: Porirua 10kms.
Wellington, Hutt Valley
and Kapitia Coast 25 mins.

Our home is situated in a quiet cul-de-sac street, with large decks overlooking garden and bush. As our family are now living overseas and we are on our own with our two pet cats, we would really enjoy the company of New Zealand and overseas visitors. We have travelled and lived overseas so are always interested in other peoples experiences. Elaine enjoys cooking, ten-pin bowling, badminton, and gardening. John's interests are soccer, motor sports and international affairs. We are ten minutes Plimmerton train station and main high-way, and only 25 minutes to Wellington City.
We assure you of a very warm welcome, and memorable stay with us.
Laundry facilities available. House smoke-free.
Directions: *Please phone or write.*

Pauatahanui

Rural Homestay
Address: 'Braebyre', Flightys Road,
Pauatahanui (R.D.1 Porirua)
Name: Randall & Jenny Shaw
Telephone: (04) 235 9311
Freephone: 0800 369 311
Fax: (04) 235 9345
Email: braebyre@paradise.net.nz
Beds: 3 Superking/Twin (3 bedrooms)
Bathroom: 3 Ensuite, 1 Guests share
Tariff: B&B (special) From 1/10/99:
Double $100-$150, Single $90-$140, Children under 15 years $20-35, Dinner $ 40. Credit cards: Visa/MC, Vouchers accepted $20-$40 surcharge
Nearest Town: Lower Hutt 15 km, Porirua 12 km

Are you looking for something special and restful away from city noise yet easily accessible on major highways? Located closer to the mid-city than many suburbs "Braebyre", one of Wellington's fine country homes, surrounded by four acres of landscaped gardens, is nestled in a beautiful rural environment on a mohair goat farm. You will love the peace and tranquillity. Jenny and Randall, born and bred Wellingtonians, have travelled extensively and have been hosting for many years and enjoy the experiences of hearing about guests' travels and life's adventures. The guest wing (with separate entrance) includes a recreation room with table tennis table, log fire and indoor spa pool. Evening dinner with your hosts, featuring homegrown produce, is available on request. Laundry facilities are available at $5. Our smoke free home welcomes family groups.
Directions: *Please phone or write.*

Judgeford/Pauatahanui

Homestay
Address: "Kumbelin",
Mulherns Road, RD, Porirua
Name: Joan & Paul
Telephone: (04) 235 7610
Fax: (04) 235 7612
Beds: 4 Single (2 bedrooms)
Bathroom: 1 Guests, 1 Family share
Tariff: B&B Double $70, Single $50,
Dinner by arrangement,
Licensed restaurant handy.
Credit cards. NZ B&B Vouchers accepted
Nearest Town: Lower Hutt 15km, Porirua 12km, Upper Hutt 14km, 20 mins to the ferry and Wellington city.

We welcome you to our spacious family home, where we invite you to feel at home, relax, enjoy and share with us the large open plan living areas. Guests are free to mix with the pet sheep, take comfortable walks near the adjacent 18 hole golf course, enjoy our peaceful garden settings and views or relax and enjoy our place during your stay. Guests are welcome to use our facilities including the laundry and the floodlit half-size tennis court. "Kumbelin" is a 5 acre farmlet, set 200m off SH58 in the beautiful Judgeford basin and is extensively planted with trees, shrubs and Rhododendrons. We offer you a quiet rural retreat handy to the ferry services, central to the region's cities and an ideal base to enjoy the many scenic drives the region offers.

Pauatahanui
Rural Homestay
Address: Huntaway Lodge,
Flightys Road, Pauatahanui
(RD1, Porirua)
Name: Paul and Dianne Boyack
Telephone: (04) 234 1428
Fax: (04) 234 1429
Mobile: (025) 261 8230
Email: huntaway-lodge@xtra.co.nz
Beds: 2 Queen, 2 Single (3 Bedrooms)
Bathroom: 1 Guests Share
Tariff: B&B (Full) Double $120, Single $60, Dinner $30 (adult), $15 (children).
Credit Cards: Visa/Mastercard
Nearest Town: Lower Hutt 17 km, Porirua 14 km, Wellington 31 km.

We've all dreamt of living in a log home, being nestled on a sofa watching the flames flicker on an open fire. Huntaway Lodge is a large log home built using traditional methods set in an idyllic rural setting of 12.5 acres. We along with our two young children enjoy entertaining guests on our farmlet. We have cattle and sheep, along with Jack (Rooster), his 6 hens, Kimba (Golden Labrador) and Raro (Cat). Your children and pets are welcome. From surnrise to sunset the elevation of Huntaway Lodge allows you to enjoy exquisite views over rolling farmland - from Porirua Harbour through to Mana Island and the South Island.
We are well sign posted 1.7 km up Flightys Road on the right hand side off SH58, we are centrally located for all activities. Welcome to Huntaway Lodge.
Directions: *Please phone, email, or visit our website.*
Home Page: www.huntawaylodge.co.nz

Tawa - Wellington
Homestay
Address: 17 Mascot Street,
Tawa, Wellington
Name: Alf & Jeannette Levick
Telephone: (04) 232 5989
Fax: (04) 232 5987
Beds: 1 Queen, 1 Single (2 bedrooms)
Bathroom: Family share
Tariff: B&B (full) Double $70,
Single $40. Dinner $20pp (3 course meal).
Credit cards: Visa/M.C. NZ B&B Vouchers.
Nearest Town: Wellington 15km.

Our home is in a quiet street in the suburb of Tawa. 15 kilometres (15 minutes drive or train) from the central city. We are nestled on the side of the valley with views over farmland. Two bedrooms available for guests, one with a queen sized bed and the other with a single bed. We live in a comfortable family home with a wood burner fire, separate bath and shower and two toilets. You are welcome to use our laundry facilities and swimming pool. We know New Zealand well and enjoy having people share our home. Freshly ground coffee a speciality, breakfast of your choice - continental or full cooked meal. Enjoy a New Zealand style dinner with us in the evening. JEANNETTE'S INTERESTS ARE: Ikebana, embroidery, knitting, dressmaking, tennis, learning to play golf and the piano, tennis, Japanese language and gardening. ALF'S INTERESTS ARE: Lions International, amateur radio, woodwork, ToastmastersInternational and - being allowed to help in the garden!!
Directions: *Please phone.*

Tawa

Homestay
Address: 5 Fyvie Avenue,
Linden, Tawa
Name: Jocelyn and David Perry
Telephone: (04) 232 7664
Beds: 1 Double,
3 Single (3 Bedrooms)
Bathroom: 1 Guests share,
1 Family share
Tariff: B&B (Full)
Double $65, Single $40
Children half price. Dinner $20 pp (by arrangement)
Nearest Town: Wellington (15 kms)

David has recently retired, Jocelyn has always enjoyed being at home. Together we welcome you to stay with us, and our cat. We are 15 kms from Wellington city. A five minute walk to the suburban rail station with half hourly service to the city (15 mins) and north to the Kapiti Coast.
Alternatively, you can drive north to the Coast enjoying sea and rural views before sampling tourist attractions in this area. We are happy to provide transport to and from the Inter Island Ferry. We are a smoke free household.
Directions: *Please phone.*

Te Marua - Upper Hutt

Homestay
Address: 108a Plateau Rd,
Te Marua, Upper Hutt
Name: Sheryl & Lloyd Homer
Telephone: (04) 526 7851
Freephone 0800 110 851
Fax: (04) 526 7866
Mobile: (025) 501 679
Email: sheryl.lloyd@clear.net.nz
Beds: 1 Queen, 1 Double
(2 bedrooms)
Bathroom: 1 Private
Tariff: B&B (continental) Double $70,
Single $45. Dinner $25 (3 course), Credit Cards. Vouchers accepted
Nearest Town: Upper Hutt 7.4km

Our home is situated in a secluded, private bush setting. Guests may choose to relax on one of our large decks and view the native bird life, read books from our extensive library, soak in our outdoor bath or just sit around a cosy fire. For the more energetic there are bush walks, a golf course, mountain bike trails, trout fishing and swimming areas within walking distance and a shooting range and gliding club nearby. The guest wing has private facilities, a TV, microwave and provision for making tea and coffee. Lloyd is a photographer with over 30 years experience photographing the New Zealand landscape. He would enjoy taking guests on local photographic or tramping tours. Sheryl is a teacher. Travel, entertaining, tramping, skiing, photography and music are some of the interests we enjoy together and look forward to sharing with our guests. - We ask that guests do not smoke indoors. - Dinner available on request.
Directions: *Please phone or fax for bookings and directions.*

Upper Hutt

Farmstay

Address: Whispering Pines,
207 Colletts Road, RD 1 Mangaroa,
Upper Htt
Name: Graham & Ruth Ockwell
Telephone: (04) 526 7785
Fax: (04) 526 7785
Beds: 1 Queen, 2 Single (2 bedrooms)
Bathroom: 1 Ensuite, 1 Guests share
Tariff: B&B (full) Double $90, Single $50,
Dinner $25. NZ B&B Vouchers accepted $20 surcharge,
Credit Cards: Visa/Mastercard
Nearest Town: Upper Hutt 8km

A country welcome awaits you at Whispering Pines, where the air is fresh and clean, and the views are picturesque. Our spacious Swiss Chalet style home, has a Douglas Fir theme, and is set in 67 acres of elevated farmland.

Backing onto native bush, we share the land with native birds, pedigree Hereford cattle, Angora goats, coloured sheep, hens, bees, 2 collie dogs and 1 cat.

Whispering Pines is an ideal stopover on your way to, or from the Wellington Ferry, Airport or while visiting the Trentham races.

Ruth: Education Manager for a Budgeting Service, enjoys hobbies of spinning, knitting and sewing.

Graham: A Semi-retired builder, is interested in agriculture, fishing and shooting. Joint interests are, entertaining people, travel, gardening and local Church.

We would appreciate you not smoking in the house.

Please phone or fax to make a booking and receive directions as we are 6km from SH2.

http://www.bnb.co.nz

take a look

Upper Hutt
Homestay
Address: "Tranquillity",
136 Akatarawa Road, Birchville, Upper Hutt
Name: Elaine, Alice & Alan
Telephone: (04) 526 6948, Freephone 0800 270 787
Fax: (04) 526 6968 **Mobile**: (025) 405 962
Email: tranquility@xtra.co.nz
Beds: 1 Queen, 2 Single (3 bedrooms)
Bathroom: 1 Ensuite with spa bath, 2 Family share
Tariff: B&B (continental) Queen with ensuite Double $85 or Single $55,
Children negotiable, Dinner $20 (2 course) by prior arrangement,
Cooked breakfast $5pp extra, Credit Cards welcomed. We will meet you to/from
Wellington Airport/Ferry/Rail by prior arrangement at an extra minimal cost.
NZ B&B Vouchers accepted $10 surcharge
Nearest Town: Upper Hutt 3 mins, Lower Hutt 20 mins, Wellington 35 mins,
Wairarapa 30 mins.

Executive Timeout/Homestay
Escape from the stress of City Life just approx 40 minutes from Wellington off SH 2.Close to Upper Hutt - Restaurants, Cinema, Golf, Racecourse, Leisure Centre (swimming), Bush Walks etc. We are near the confluence of the Hutt and Akatarawa Rivers which is noted for its fishing. 13km to Staglands. Country setting, relax and listen to the New Zealand Tuis and watch the fantails or Wood Pigeons, or just simple relax and read.
Our home is situated on approx 1 acre and is nestled amongst native and planted trees, shrubs with lawn and garden. Comfortable and warm and friendly hospitality, Good New Zealand style food. Outside barbecue if preferred, weather permits. We enjoy meeting people of all cultures and invite you to come and stay in our tranquillity settings. Tea and Coffee facilities available at any time. Laundry facilities. Pets allowed by prior arrangements. As we are non smokers we request you do not smoke inside. TV in room. Guests lounge. We have 2 cats as a pet.
Directions: *Just off SH2/motorway - Akatarawa turn off, 1.3km down Akatarawa Road. Approx 200 metres pass Dairy, on the right (White Gate).*

Kaitoke, Upper Hutt

Homestay "Twin Lakes Bed & Breakfast"
Address: 1280A State Highway 2,
Kaitoke
Name: Keith & Lee White
Telephone: (04) 526 5077
Email: cduncan@clear.net.nz
Beds: 1 Queen, 1 Single (2 Bedrooms)
Bathroom: 1 Family Share
Tariff: B&B (continental) Double $80,
Single $60, Dinner $25 per person
(by prior arrangement).
Nearest Town: Upper Hutt, 10 minutes by car.

We offer you a warm welcome to our home, which is located just off State Highway 2 on an 10 acre rural lifestyle block. You can experience the rural lifestyle from our home which takes in the views of the "Twin Lakes" and the surrounding Rimutaka Ranges. In the evening you can relax in the family room in front of the log fire or test yourself with pool or darts in the game room. If you are feeling energetic, or just fancy a wander you may walk around the farm and view the pine plantation and our farm animals which include 6 sheep, a goat, 6 chooks, dog, cat and white rabbit. Kaitoke and our home is a restful and informal environment and we hope to make your stay with us a pleasant and memorable one.
We request that guests not smoke inside the house.
Directions: *Please telephone*

Lower Hutt - Korokoro

Homestay
Address: 'Western Rise'
10 Stanhope Grove, Korokoro,
Lower Hutt
Name: Virginia & Maurice Gibbens
Telephone: (04) 589 1872
Fax: (04) 589 1873
Mobile: 025 438 316
Beds: 1 Double, 2 Single (2 bedrooms)
Bathroom: 1 Guests share
Tariff: B&B (special) Double $80,
single $50, Dinner $25
NZ B&B Vouchers accepted $12 surcharge
Nearest Town: Petone 1km, Lower Hutt 5km, Wellington 12km

Want a restful setting and still in the centre of things? Just off State Highway 2 (highway to the Wairarapa) you can view Wellington's magnificent Harbour. Watch the planes and boats as you relax over a meal either indoors or out. We have a large family home which we share with a corgi/fox terrier, Prince. We are in our 50's and do not smoke, therefore request our guests not to smoke indoors. Our interests include travel, boating and crafts. Maurice works for the New Zealand Police as a finger print expert and Virginia has always wanted to be involved with home stay so looks forward to sharing time with you. Laundry Service free for persons staying 2 consecutive nights. We are very handy to all that you wish to see and do. A special feature, being the many native bush walks in the area. 10-15 mins to Picton Ferry. Restaurants, many.
Directions: *Please telephone.*

Lower Hutt
Homestay
Address: 11 Ngaio Crescent,
Woburn, Lower Hutt 6009
Name: Judy & Bob Vine
Telephone: (04) 566 1192
Fax: (04) 566 0483 **Mobile**: (025) 500 682
Email: Bob_Vine@compuserve.com
Beds: 1 Double, 2 Single (2 Bedrooms)
Bathroom: 1 Guests share
Tariff: B&B (full) $40 per person, Dinner $25 by arrangement.
Credit cards. Vouchers accepted $12 surcharge
Nearest Town: Lower Hutt 1km, Wellington 15km

Our home is situated plumb in the centre of Woburn, a picturesque central city suburb of Lower Hutt, known for its generous sized houses and beautiful gardens. We offer a warm welcome to our home, based on many enjoyable experiences with bed and breakfast hosts in the United Kingdom, Europe and USA and delight in the opportunity to reciprocate some of the hospitality we have been afforded on our own overseas jaunts. We are within walking distance of the Lower Hutt downtown; only 15 minutes drive from central Wellington and the Railway Station and Ferry Terminal; Airport 25 minutes, 3 minutes walk from Woburn rail station. Our facilities include a separate lounge with TV for the comfort and enjoyment of our guests should they wish to take some time out to themselves. Alternatively, we love to entertain and would be delighted to have our guests join us for some hearty Kiwi style cooking with good New Zealand wine. Laundry facilities. **Directions**: *Please phone, fax, email or write. Transfer transport available.*

Hutt City
Self Contained Accommodation
Address: CASA BIANCA
10 Damian Grove, Lower Hutt
Name: Casa Bianca.
Jo and Dave Comparini
Telephone: (04) 569 7859
Fax: (04) 569 7859
Email: dcompi@mz.co.nz
Beds: 1 King, 1 Single
Bathroom: 1 Private

Tariff: B&B (continental) Double $90,
Single $55. Credit Cards accepted. Vouchers accepted $21 surcharge
Nearest Town: Lower Hutt

Our comfortable house is situated in the Eastern Hills of Hutt City. The idyllic surroundings make this a great place to enjoy a quiet, peaceful holiday. We are within easy reach of four golf courses, city centre, cinemas, good restaurants and a host of other entertainment. Wellington is 15 minutes by train, or 20 minutes by car on SH1. Our interests include: meeting people, walking and tramping, theatre, sports, travel, and dining out. We have a self contained apartment with bedroom (double), bathroom, large lounge and fully equipped kitchen. Breakfast provisions provided in apartment. One extra single bed in lounge. Off street parking and use of lock-up garage is available. We aim to provide guests with time to relax at their leisure, and enjoy our special hospitality. We can assist you with your travelling plans. We prefer no smoking in the house. **Directions**: *Please phone for directions* **Home Page**: compo@voyager.co.nz

Lower Hutt
Homestay
Address: 'Dungarvin',
25 Hinau Street, Woburn,
Lower Hutt
Name: Beryl and Trevor Cudby
Telephone: (04) 569 2125
Email: t.b.cudby@clear.net.nz
Beds: 2 Single (1 bedroom)
Bathroom: 1 Private
Tariff: B&B (full) Double $80,
Single $50, Dinner $25 (by arrangement).
Credit Cards accepted. NZ B&B Vouchers accepted $12 surcharge
Nearest Town: Lower Hutt (2 minutes), Wellington (15 minutes)

Our 70 year old character cottage has been fully refurbished while retaining its original charm. It is two minutes from the Lower Hutt shops, 15 minutes from the Ferry terminal, and 20 minutes from the new Museum of NZ "Te Papa". We have a secluded property landscaped for quiet living, with ample off-street parking. Our home is centrally heated and has space for you to relax, read, listen to music from our CD collection or watch television. The sunny guest bedroom has windows opening over our well established garden and petanque court which you are welcome to use, and the beds have electric blankets and down duvets. Vegetarians are catered for, and laundry facilities are available. Our main interests are travel, music, gardening and shows. We also enjoy entertaining and sampling New Zealand wines. We will help you plan local trips and make the most of your stay in this lovely area. We appreciate our guests not smoking in the house.

Lower Hutt
Homestay
Address: 236 Stratton Street,
Normandale, Lower Hutt
Name: Black Fir Lodge
Telephone: (04) 586 6466
Mobile: (025) 397 614
Email: i.perry@xtra.co.nz
Beds: 1 Queen, 2 Single (2 bedrooms)
Bathroom: 1 Guests Share
Tariff: B&B (full) Double $80, Single $45. NZ B&B Vouchers accepted

Nearest Town: Petone 10 minutes, Wellington 20 minutes.

Our modern, spacious, single-storey home is a tranquil haven from the noise and bustle of Wellington, although only 20 minutes drive away. Animals on our 12 hectare property include sheep and chooks, and we share our home with two friendly dogs (a Newfoundland and Labrador) and Splotch the cat. The guest lounge is an ideal place to relax with a book, or simply enjoy the view of neighbouring Belmont Regional Park. If serious unwinding is required, how about a soak in the bath (and still enjoy the view). The Regional Park is a popular place for walking and mountain biking. We are also handy to the museums, cafes and other attractions of Wellington and Lower Hutt. Our interests include dogs, travel and natural history. Non-smokers please. Bookings recommended. **Directions**: *Take Maungaraki turn-off from SH2. Turn into Stratton St at big sign for St Aidens on the Hill church.*

Lower Hutt

Homestay B&B
Address: 70A Hautana Street,
Lower Hutt
Name: "Rose Cottage" Homestay B&B
Telephone: (04) 566 7755
Fax: (04) 566 7755
Mobile: (025) 481 732
Email: G.G.Gellen, 100406.1025@compuserve.com
Beds: 1 Queen, 1 Single (2 Bedrooms)
Bathroom: 1 Ensuite, 1 Family share
Tariff: B&B (full) Double $85, Single $50, Credit Cards Mastercard/Visa. NZ
B&B Vouchers accepted $12 surcharge
Nearest Town: Lower Hutt CBD 1/2 km, Wellington 15 km

Relax in the comfort of our cosy home which is just a five minute walk to the Hutt City Centre. Originally built in 1910 the house has been fully renovated and extended with an eye-catching "turret" recently added to totally blend into its surroundings. Maureen has been in the Travel Industry for 25 years, and we have both travelled extensively throughout Europe, UK, USA, Australia and NZ. Our interests include Travel, Gardening, Cottage Crafts, Woodwork, Sports and live Theatre.
As well as TV in Guest room there's also Coffee and Tea-making facilities. Our generous breakfast may include freshly squeezed juice, fresh fruit, choice of cereals and yoghurts, home made bread, muffins and preserves; and a traditional cooked English breakfast served in our Dining Room at your convenience.
As we are non-smokers we request no smoking indoors, also no pets.
Maureen & Gordon look forward to welcoming you into their home.

Wainuiomata

Homestay
Address: 22 Kaponga Street,
 Wainuiomata
Name: Kaponga House
Telephone: (04) 564 3495 (after 5pm)
Fax: (04) 564 3495
Beds: 1 Queen (1 bedroom)
Bathroom: 1 Private
Tariff: B&B (continental)
Double $70, Single $45.
NZ B&B Vouchers accepted
Nearest Town: Lower Hutt 6 kms

Wainuiomata Wonderland (just 20 minutes by car from Wellington City). Hilary and Neville offer you top quality accommodation at an affordable price. We live in a lovely, quiet bush setting, and enjoy a relaxed lifestyle. We love entertaining and meeting people. With this in mind, we have made our ground floor available to homestay guests. The apartment includes one double bedroom, private bathroom with heated towel rail, laundry, spacious lounge/living room with gas heating, TV, tea/coffee making facilities and a fridge. We have neither children nor pets at home and we are smokefree. Nearby attractions include the Rimutaka Forest Park, seal colony and an 18 hole golf course. We enjoy gardening, golf, tennis and travel, and we look forward to welcoming you to our home. Come and relax in our peaceful surroundings. Genuine "kiwi" hospitality guaranteed.

Petone
Homestay
Address: 1 Bolton Street, Petone
Name: Anne & Reg Cotter
Telephone: (04) 568 6960
Fax: (04) 568 6956
Beds: 1 Double, 2 Single (2 bedrooms)
Bathroom: 1 Family share
Tariff: B&B (full) Double $60, Single $30,
Children half price, Dinner $15 per person.
Credit cards. NZ B&B Vouchers accepted
Nearest Town: Lower Hutt 5 km, Wellington 15 km

We have an older type home by the beach which we have modernised. It has three bedrooms, a large lounge, dining room, kitchen, bathroom with shower and bath. We are two minutes from the museum on the beach, two minutes from the shops and the bus route into the city. A restaurant is nearby. We offer one double bed in one room, two single beds in another room with room for an extra bed or a child's cot which is available. Children are very welcome. Laundry facilities available. We are ten minutes by road to the Picton ferry. Off street parking available. Reg is a keen amateur ornithologist and he goes to the Chatham Islands with an expedition trying to find the nesting place of the Taiko - a rare sea bird which is on the endangered list. We are keen to show any folk interested in birds the local places of interest. Member of the genealogy society.

Korokoro, Petone
Homestay
Address: 100 Korokoro Road,
Korokoro, Petone
Name: Bridget & Jim Austin
Telephone: (04) 589 1678
Fax: (04) 589 1678
Mobile: (025) 260 4948
Email: jaustin@clear.net.nz
Beds: 1 Double, 1 Twin (2 bedrooms)
Bathroom: 1 Guests share
Tariff: B&B (continental) Double $80, Single $45, Dinner with wine $30.
Credit cards
NZ B&B Vouchers accepted $10 surcharge
Nearest Town: Petone 3km, Lower Hutt 7km, Wellington 12km

In a quiet locality our peaceful property has a large country-style garden with harbour views, bush walk and croquet lawn. Conveniently placed, 12 minutes to ferries and Wellington, we are also easily found - no suburbs to negotiate! We are 1.7 kms from the junction of SH2 and Korokoro Road traffic lights.
Originally from England (40 years ago!) we enjoy travelling and meeting people. Bridget is a teacher and still works part-time. Jim's background is in agricultural and earth-moving machinery and is now a desultory woodworker, 'fix-it' man and indispensable gardener's mate to Bridget, who is a keen gardener and also a weaver and felt-maker. We live in an as environmentally friendly way as possible, a non-smoking house with spacious bedrooms. We enjoy all visual arts, theatre, cinema, classical music and books.

Eastbourne

Homestay
Address: Bush House,
12 Waitohu Road, York Bay,
Eastbourne
Name: Belinda Cattermole
Telephone: (04) 568 5250
Fax: (04) 568 5250
Beds: 1 Double, 1 Single (2 bedrooms)
Bathroom: 1 Private, 1 Family share
Tariff: B&B (full) Double $90,
Single $60, Dinner $35.
NZ B&B Vouchers accepted $15 surcharge
Nearest Town: Wellington City 20 minutes

Come and enjoy the peace and tranquillity of the Eastern Bays. You will be hosted in a beautifully restored 1920's settler cottage nestled amongst native bush and looking seawards to the Kaikoura mountains of the South Island. My love of cordon-bleu cooking and the pleasures of the table are satisfied through the use of my country kitchen and dining room. Other attractions: - Outdoor spa and a Devon Rex cat. Eastbourne is a small seaside village across the harbour from Wellington city with several craft shops, restaurants, a range of other attractions and a good beach. Wellington - 20 minutes: Lower Hutt - 10 minutes: Eastbourne - 5 minutes by car. Non-smokers preferred.

Eastbourne

Homestay
Address: 15 Marine Dr., York Bay, Eastbourne
Name: Barry & Bev
Telephone: (04) 568 7104
Fax: (04) 568 7104
Mobile: (021) 214 9690
Email: bevlaybourn@xtra.co.nz
Beds: 2 Single (1 bedroom)
Bathroom: 1 Private
Tariff: B&B (continental) Double $70, Single $50. Dinner $35 only by previous arrangement. Credit Card NZ B&B Vouchers accepted
Nearest Town: Lower Hutt 10 mins

A breath of fresh air, 20 mins from Wellington City. Quiet, relaxed, nestled between native bush and the beach. Wake to the dawn chorus. Steps to the house allow a spectacular panorama of Hutt Valley, Wellington City, Harbour and the Kaikouras. Cosy woodburner for the winter. Garage parking for 1 car. Laundry and drying facilities available. Tourist attractions: Harbour ferry from Days Bay to City centre. Bus transport to Lower Hutt and Wellington leaves from our front gate. Golf course. Indoor & outdoor swimming pools. Restaurants. All within a few minutes drive. Interests: Dog Shows, Obedience & Agility, we have 2 Belgian Shepherds, which we show and work, NZ wines, our Children and Grandchildren. Barry a Retired Sales Consultant is now a professional Dog Trainer and Bev formerly a School Dental Nurse, is now a Counsellor and kennel maid. Specials: Vegetarian food only, Special diets catered for (vegan, dairy free) Transport can be arranged. Non smokers preferred.

Eastbourne
Self-contained Accommodation
Address: "Treetops",
7 Huia Rd (off Moana Road),
Days Bay, Eastbourne
Name: Robyn & Roger Cooper
Telephone: (04) 562 7692
Fax: (04) 562 7690
Email: r.cooper@gns.cri.nz
Beds: 1 Double (1 bedroom). (1 Double + 1 Single divan in lounge)
Bathroom: 1 Private
Tariff: B&B (continental) Double $85, Single $65, Extra person $20, Children
$15. Credit Cards. Laundry and drying facilities by arrangement. NZ B&B
Vouchers accepted
Nearest Town: Wellington City 20 minutes, Eastbourne Village 3 minutes

*Welcome to our home nestled high in the bush above Wellington harbour - a
secluded peaceful retreat. Take our private cable car, with seating for two, for a
stately scenic two-minute ride up the hillside to the front door or wander up
through beech trees and native bush. The warm attractive guest accommodation
is fully self-contained with bedroom, lounge, kitchenette, bathroom and
downstairs entrance. Wake to the sounds of the bellbird; breakfast on your
private garden patio (provisions supplied in apartment); relax indoors with a
variety of books, puzzles and games, TV and radio. We are a three-minute walk
to a picturesque swimming beach, sailboat hire, tennis courts, bush walks,
interesting restaurants, bus routes and the ferry to central Wellington (20 minute
ride). Our interests include geology, music, writing, orchid-growing, travel.*

Eastbourne
Homestay
Address: 35 Cheviot Rd,
Lowry Bay, Eastbourne
Name: Forde & Pam Clarke
Telephone: (04) 568 4407
Fax: (04) 568 2474
Email: forde.clarke@xtra.co.nz
Beds: 1 King, 2 Single (2 bedrooms)
Bathroom: 1 Private (separate toilet)
Tariff: B&B (full) Double $95, Single $70, Children half price, Credit Cards.
Laundry and drying facilities. NZ B&B Vouchers accepted
Nearest Town: Wellington City 20 minutes, Lower Hutt 10 minutes

*Enjoy your stay in our sunny, warm, friendly family home in sheltered Lowry Bay. Centrally
heated and attractively decorated our bedrooms have their own tea and coffee facilities and
windows overlooking gardens and our sealed tennis court. You may enjoy a sail on our 28 foot
yacht, which is berthed in a local marina, a 5 minutes stroll to the beach or a bush walk (which
could take 15 minutes to a full day!). Within a ten minute drive we have heated swimming
pools, golf courses, Hutt City and the village of Eastbourne with specialty shops, art galleries
and restaurants. We are 20 to 30 minutes from the Inter-island ferries and the airport. There
is an excellent bus service to Eastbourne, Hutt City and Wellington and a ferry service from
Days Bay to Somes Island and Wellington. We enjoy travelling (both in NZ and internationally), sailing, skiing, tennis and gardening. We are strictly non-smoking. With our
two daughters, Isabella (16) and Kirsty (10) and our cat, we live in one of the nicest
places in New Zealand. We will love sharing it with you.*
Directions: *From State Highway 2 follow signs for Seaview then Eastbourne.*

WELLINGTON

Eastbourne
Homestay
Address: Eastern Bays Marine Drive,
Sorrento Bay, Eastbourne
Name: Jennifer and Ken
Telephone: (04) 568 4817
Fax: (04) 568 4817
Mobile: (025) 500 670
Email: kjackson@pop.ihug.co.nz
Beds: 1 Double, 1 Single (2 Bedrooms)
Bathroom: 1 Guests share
Tariff: B&B (Full) Double $75, Single $45, Dinner $25 pp by arrangement.
NZ B&B Vouchers accepted $10 surcharge. Credit cards accepted
Nearest Town: Wellington 17 km (20 mins drive), Lower Hutt 7 km (10 mins
drive)

*Jennifer, Ken and our friendly cat Tuppence look forward to giving you a warm
welcome to our home. It is nestled amongst native bush by the beach. Share with us
the magical views of Wellington harbour and the city. You may wish to join us on the
deck in summer and in front of a cosy fire in winter. You may even wish to arrange to
join us for dinner. Feel free to help yourselves to complimentary tea and coffee. Our
laundry is available for use. Off-street parking is available, or for a modest fee we can
arrange to meet the ferry, bus, plan or train. As non-smokers we appreciate no
smoking inside. At any time we would be pleased to assist you with your stay. We
hope to make your visit a memorable one.*
Directions: *Please phone, fax or email us for directions.*
Home Page: http://homepages.ihug.co.nz/~kjackson

Seatoun, Wellington
Homestay
Address: 10 Monro Street,
Seatoun, Wellington 6003
Name: Frances Drewell
Telephone: (04) 388 6719
Fax: (04) 388 6719
Mobile: 025-241 4089
Beds: 1 Double, 2 Single (2 bedrooms)
Bathroom: 1 Guests share
Tariff: B&B (continental)
Double $80, Single $50, Children $25, Dinner $25, Full breakfast on request,
Credit Cards. NZ B&B Vouchers accepted Accepted all year
Nearest Town: Wellington 9km

*Handy to Wellington Airport our modern home is located in a quiet seaside village. A
unique 'Fairy Shop' is a must to visit. Enjoy a NZ style dinner or dine at nearby
restaurants. A warm welcome awaits those who want a home away from home.
Interests mainly in travel and sport and I play golf regularly. Laundry facilities
available.*
Directions: *Entering Wellington from the North or off the Interisland Ferry follow
the signs to the Airport and following the signs to Seatoun. Monro Street is the second
street on the left after the shops. From the Airport take the first turn right and then
as above. Flat off street parking. One minute walk to bus stop. Travel around
Wellington 'The City of a Thousand Views' on a $5 DAYTRIPPER TICKET. Discover
New Zealand History by visiting 'TePapa' Wellington's new unique Museum.*

W T BISHOP '98

Wellington City
Homestay
Address: "Villa Alexandra"
16 Roxburgh Street,
Mount Victoria, Wellington
Name: Sheridan & Warwick Bishop
Telephone: (04) 802 5850
Fax: (04) 802 5851
Mobile: (021) 420 165
Email: sheridan@artlabels.co.nz
Beds: 1 Queen, (1 bedroom)
Bathroom: 1 Private
Tariff: B&B (full) Double $110, Single $85, Dinner $30. Credit Cards Visa/Mastercard. Waikanae 3 bedroom Beachfront cottage
also available for rent. Please enquire.
Nearest Town: Wellington 500 m - Courtenay Place 2 min walk.

CLOSEST HOMESTAY TO "TE PAPA" - MUSEUM OF NEW ZEALAND.
Our beautiful villa was built in 1906 and has been redecorated in the 90's so we can offer the best of both eras. Park your car in our garage and discover Wellington on foot. We are just a short walk from the centre of the restaurant and theatre district. Within a ten to fifteen minute stroll you have "Te Papa", the Civic Centre, the CBD, many movie and live theatres, the shops, over 50 restaurants of all ethnic persuasions and the excitement of New Zealand's capital city. The botanical Gardens and Parliament are just a few more minutes away. The Airport, the Railway Station and the Inter-Island Ferry terminal are all within a 10- minute drive. We have gas and electric heating so the house is always warm. The Queen room is upstairs away from any road noise with a private bathroom alongside. With the morning sun you have a good view of our small city garden and the many gorgeous old wooden houses on the gentle slopes of Mount Victoria. There are electric blankets, a feather duvet, a TV and tea/coffee making facilities in your room. You are also welcome to make use of our laundry. Please feel free to sit in the garden, on the sunny terrace or use our lounge to read, listen to music or watch TV. We know our country well and delight in meeting fellow travellers either from overseas or around New Zealand while sharing a scrumptious home-made breakfast with you. Sherry enjoys gardening, cooking and sewing while Wawick is an engineer who is interested in painting, photography ,and comput-ing. We both enjoy travel, films and shows. We request that guests do not smoke in the house. **Directions**: *Please Phone, Fax, Write or E-mail to make a booking or seek directions.* **Home Page**: http://www.artlabels.co.nz

Karori, Wellington

Homestay
Address: 83 Campbell Street,
Karori, Wellington
Name: Murray & Elaine Campbell
Telephone: (04) 476 6110
Fax: (04) 476-6593
Mobile: 025-535 080
Email: ctool@ihug.co.nz
Beds: 1 Queen, 3 Single (3 bedrooms)
Bathroom: 1 Guests share
Tariff: B&B (continental) Double $80, Single $50, Dinner $25pp,
Children half price, NZ B&B Vouchers welcomed. Credit cards.
Nearest Town: Wellington (10 minutes from city.)

*Welcome to our home. We enjoy the company of families, groups, long stay and business people.
Our three guest rooms are: 1) Large Queen, 2) Twin, 3) Single, all share one guest shower,
toilet, and separate bathroom. We have an old cat and a very well behaved young
Border Collie dog; enjoy sailing, skiing, boatbuilding, travel and running our
garden tool making business from home. Feel free to join us for pre-dinner drinks,
dine with us, or make use of our laundry/drying facilities, large garden and patio.
Whilst very handy to bus stops, whenever possible we will provide transport to
ensure you enjoy your stay in our wonderful city.* **Directions**: *Telephone and
we will meet you at the ferry/train/bus/air terminals. Driving down State
Highway 1 via the Motorway take the Hawkestone Exit and follow signs to Karori.
From Interisland Ferry terminal take exit to the city and pick up Karori signs. Look out for
our Bed & Breakfast sign on the lamp post at the bottom of the drive and park at the top.*

Ngaio, Wellington

Homestay+Self-contained Accom.
Address: 56 Fox Street, Ngaio, Wellington
Name: Brian & Jennifer Timmings
Telephone: (04) 479 5325   **Fax**: (04) 479 4325
Mobile: (025) 276 9437   **Email**: jennifer.timmings@clear.net.nz
Beds: 2 Double, 2 Single (3 bedrooms). 2 Self contained units-one with double
bed, one with twin beds, kitchen/lounge, bath & shower and laundry facilities.
Bathroom: 3 Ensuite, 1 Private
Tariff: B&B (continental) Double $90 Ensuite, Single $60, Children by arrange-
ment, Dinner $20. SC Accom: Double $95, extra persons $25pp. Each unit can
sleep up to 4 persons, Credit Cards (VISA/MC). Vouchers accepted $20 surcharge
Nearest Town: Wellington city 7 km

*We love our city of Wellington with its beautiful harbour, dramatic hills and spectacular
scenery, and we would enjoy having you as our guests and sharing your "Wellington
Experience" with us. We live 10 minutes from Wellington Railway Station and Ferry
Terminal, in the suburb of Ngaio, surrounded by bush and hills. (We could meet/deliver
guests from any central point.) We have an open plan home, but guests using the ensuite double
room would have their own privacy with French doors opening onto a deck and sunny quiet
garden. The two fully furnished units are separate from the house giving guests their own
space and independence; perfect for corporate stays, extended vacations, sabbatical visitors,
honeymooners or job relocations. Dinner is optional. In the evening guests may like to relax
in our music room as we are a music oriented family. We also enjoy art and the outdoors. Off-
street parking is available. Non smokers only, thank you. Hospitality guaranteed.* **Directions**: *Please phone, preferably before 11am or after 3pm, or fax or write or Email.*
Home Page: http://www.travelwise.co.nz/NIB&B/HSWgtn/index.htm

Ohariu Valley - Wellington
Farmstay
Address: Mill Cottage, Papanui Station, Boom Rock Road, Ohariu Valley,
Wellington
Name: Cliff & Bev Inglis
Telephone: (04) 478 8926
Beds: 1 Double, 1 Twin (2 Bedrooms)
Bathroom: 1 Guests share
Tariff: B&B (full) Double $76, Single $38, Children under 12 half price,
Dinner $28. NZ B&B Vouchers accepted
Nearest Town: Johnsonville 10 minutes

*As the name suggests, Mill Cottage is a cosy and intimate home of Bev and Cliff. We
would like to invite you to experience a stay on a hill country sheep and cattle station
only 25 minutes from Wellington City.*
*Pre-arranged transport is available. Entering Ohariu Valley opens the gateway to
some of the most rugged coastline around the North Island and the ever changing
waters of Cook Strait with mountain views of the North and South Islands. Wellington's highest point Colonial Knob 1500 ft is at the North End of Papanui Station and
at the south end is Boomrock with its vast collection of sea life and bird life, a tour of
Papanui with us to experience the magic viewed daily will make your stay with us
unforgettable. During your stay our home is your home with unique surroundings and
home hospitality. Assured an extreme location within the city of Wellington.*
Directions: *Phone for bookings and directions - (04) 478 8926 available 24 hours.*

Island Bay, Wellington
Self-Contained Accommodation
Address: 326 The Esplanade, Island Bay,
Wellington
Name: The Lighthouse
Telephone: (04) 472 4177 **Fax**: (04) 472 4177
Mobile: (025) 425 555
Email: bruce@sportwork.co.nz
Beds: 1 or 2 Double (1 or 2 bedrooms)
Bathroom: 1 Private
Tariff: B&B (special) Double $180 Friday
and Saturday, $150 Sunday - Thursday.
Nearest Town: Wellington -
Central Wellington 10 mins

*The lighthouse looks out over Island Bay which is 10 minutes from the airport or the central
city. The vista encompasses the fishing boats in the bay the ships steaming in and out of
Wellington harbour, the rocky coast the island with its wheeling seagulls and a view of the
South Island. There are shops and restaurants a few hundred metres around the corner as
well as few hundred metres around the corner as well as the bus terminal. There are three floors
comprising: Kitchen and bathroom; bedroom / sitting room; top floor of studio with bed-settee
and balcony. The bed settees each take two. Whether winter or summer, on holiday, business
or passing through, this is a unique accommodation opportunity not to be missed. Walk the
beach, explore the rocks or walk to the seal colony. Bed and special breakfast rate is $180 or
$150 per night for two people. Bookings to (04) 4724177, (025) 425555 or The Lighthouse, PO
Box 11-275 Wellington.*

Wellington, City

Serviced Apartment
Address: "Talavera"
7 Talavera Terrace, Wellington 6001
Name: Bobbie Littlejohn
Telephone: (04) 471 0555
Fax: (04) 471 0551
Beds: 1 Queen, 2 Single (2 bedrooms)
Bathroom: 1 Private
Tariff: B&B (full) Double $150
($15 surcharge when both rooms in use), Single $125, Additional Guest $35.
Not suitable for children. Credit cards (VISA/MC).
Nearest Town:
Wellington city centre 3 minutes walk

*A **NO SHARE** apartment with its own entrance via a staircase, offering comfort and privacy. 'Talavera', an inner city villa in a quiet terrace, offers spacious modern accommodation. The two bedrooms are light and airy with firm beds and fine cotton linen. The bathroom has a deep claw foot bath with shower over, a heated towel rail, with thick towels and quality toiletries. The spacious living room has Sky TV, magazines, heating, built in refrigerator , with tea/coffee making facilities. The Apartment's verandah overlooks the garden with views of the city, harbour and ranges beyond; at night - quite beautiful! Wellington's historic cable car stops by 'Talavera' with the Botanic Gardens, Victoria University, Parliament and Te Papa Museum close by. Breakfast downstairs with Bobbie and David; antiques, pictures, sliver and flowers. Freshly squeezed orange juice, seasonal fruit platter, home baked honey granola, omelettes, croissants/breads, espresso coffee a speciality! Parking available.*
Directions: *For directions please phone Bobbie.*
WE REQUEST THAT GUESTS DO NOT SMOKE AT TALAVERA

Wellington City
Bed & Breakfast
Address: Holdsworth, 292 Tinakori Road, Thorndon, Wellington
Name: Miriam Pennington
Telephone: (04) 473 4986
Fax: 04 473 9566
Mobile: 025 512 502
Email: miriam@holdsworth.nzl.com
Beds: 1 Queen, 1 Double   (2 bedrooms)
Bathroom: 1 Ensuite, 1 Private
Tariff: B&B (Special) Double $130-$180,
Single $100-$150.   Credit Cards (Visa/MC/BC).
Nearest Town: Wellington CBD 500m

HOLDSWORTH is an 1890's Heritage listed house situated in the heart of Tinakori Road, Thorndon, Wellington's most historic area. Tinakori Road is bound by Botanic Gardens at one end, Katherine Mansfield's birthplace at the other and provides a unique collection of houses (including the Prime Minister's residence), shops, galleries, restaurants and cafes. Parliament and the city shops are only a few minutes walk. HOLDSWORTH offers luxuriously decorated spacious rooms, well appointed and with a welcoming atmosphere. Guests also have their own elegant sitting room with open fire for their relaxation. Complimentary tea, coffee, port, fruit, chocolates are provided. Enjoy a gourmet breakfast of freshly squeezed fruit juice, seasonal fruits, a variety of delicious muffins and breads with homemade preserves and a range of specialty cooked breakfasts. Off street parking is available. I request that guests do not smoke indoors.
Home Page: www.holdsworth.nzl.com

Wellington City
Bed & Breakfast
Address: Dunrobin House,
89 Austin Street   (Cnr Derby St),
Mt Victoria, Wellington City
Name: Carol & John Sutherland
Telephone: (04) 385 0335
Fax: (04) 385-0336
Mobile: (025) 525 952
Beds: 3 Queen, 1 Single
(3 bedrooms, room with luxury ensuite has large dressing room with single bed)
Bathroom: 2 Ensuite, 1 Private
Tariff: B&B (special) Double $125-$165,
Single $115-$135. $30 extra person. Credit cards (VISA/MC).
Nearest Town: Wellington Central 500 m

Dunrobin House is an elegant, romantic two-story Victorian Villa which is centrally situated in sunny, quiet Mt Victoria, a 5-10 minute easy walk to the city's cafes / excellent restaurants, Te Papa Museum of NZ, theatres, art galleries, convention centres, shopping and waterfront. 8 minutes drive to airport and ferry terminal. An excellent location to explore our lovely City. Enjoy the luxury of our three spacious guest rooms which have comfortable beds, fluffy duvets, feather pillows, cotton bed linen, fresh flowers and lovely city views from 2 of the rooms. Relax in our sunny courtyards or elegant lounge with complimentary coffee / tea or Port. Enjoy a gourmet breakfast of orange juice, fresh fruit, home-made muesli, yoghurt, freshly baked muffins and a choice of specialty cooked dishes, including Belgium waffles. Freshly brewed coffee (expresso / cappuccino) and a selection of teas. We are pleased to help you plan your stay in a city we both enjoy and would love to share with you. Parking available.

Tawa, Wellington

Homestay
Address: 3 Kiwi Place, Tawa, Wellington
Name: Joy & Bill Chaplin
Telephone: (04) 232 5547
Fax: (04) 232 5547
Mobile: (025) 349 078
Email: chapta@xtra.co.nz
Beds: 1 Double, 1 Single (2 bedrooms)
Bathroom: 1 Guests share
Tariff: B&B (full)
Double $70, Single $40,
Dinner $20pp,
Campervans (Sml/Med) facilities.
NZ B&B Vouchers accepted $10 surcharge
Nearest Town: Wellington 15 kms

Guests are most welcome at No. 3, which is situated in a quiet street 7 minutes by car and rail from Porirua City and 15 minutes from Wellington and the Interisland Ferry Terminal. Our rooms are warm and comfortable. Tea/coffee making facilities and TV available also an extra bedroom downstairs with single bed or cot if required at reduced rate of $15. Spa, telephone/fax, laundry facilities and off-street parking also available.
The house is wheelchair friendly and suitable for elderly and young alike with areas indoors and out for relaxing. Tawa is close to beaches, ten-pin bowling, roller skating rink, 1/2 size Olympic Swimming Pool and fine walks. Our house is "smokefree"   Dinner by arrangement.

Wellington

Homestay
Address: 22 Lohia Street,
Khandallah, Wellington
Name: Ted & Sue Clothier
Telephone: (04) 479 1180
Fax: (04) 479 2717
Beds: 1 Twin with electric blankets (1 bedroom)
Bathroom: 1 Ensuite
Tariff: B&B (full) Double $100, Single $70,
Dinner $30 by arrangement.   Credit Cards
Nearest Town: Wellington 7km

This is a lovely, sunny, warm open plan home with glorious harbour and city views. We enjoy sharing our home with guests.
We are situated in a quiet easily accessible street just ten minutes from the city and five minutes from the ferry. We are five minutes from the Khandallah Village and the local 'Posties Whistle" which is the nearest thing to an English pub out of England. Excellent food, wine and bar service.   We are a non smoking household.   Another family member is an aristocratic white cat called Dali.
Dinner by arrangement.
Directions: *Please phone or fax.*

Seatoun, Wellington
Homestay
Address: "Edge Water Homestay",
459 Karaka Bay Road, Karaka Bay,
Seatoun, Wellington
Name: Stella & Colin Lovering
Telephone: (04) 388 4446
Fax: (04) 388 4446 or 388 4649
Mobile: (021) 613 357
Email: edgewaterwellington@xtra.co.nz
Beds: 2 Queen, 1 Double, Single twin (4 bedrooms)
Bathroom: 2 Ensuite, 1 Guests share
Tariff: B&B (full) Double $100-$140, Single $80, Dinner from $45. Lunch $30. Credit
Cards (VISA,M/C, Bartercard) NZ B&B Vouchers accepted Plus surcharge
Nearest Town: Wellington

Edge Water Homestay is situated on the sea front at Karaka Bay, Seatoun. Seatoun is a quiet historic seaside village where waterfront houses were originally built as convalescent and holiday homes. Edge Water offers attractive, spacious rooms with a warm and welcoming atmosphere. Complimentary tea, coffee, chocolates and ports are available and guests can relax and take in the expansive seaside views. Enjoy gourmet breakfast of freshly squeezed orange juice, local fruits, homemade breads and preserves and a range of cooked breakfasts a speciality. Lunches and dinners are prepared by Stella, ex Wellington restaurateur (Marbles Restaurant), using fresh vegetables and meats and sometimes shellfish and seafoods caught in Karaka Bay. Swimming, fishing, snorkelling, cycling and walking are all available. We have a small scruffy dog. Edge Water is 10 mins from the City and 5 mins. from the Airport. Bus stop is outside the front door. Off street parking available.
Directions: *Call for directions.*

Hataitai, Wellington
Homestay
Address: "Top o' T'ill", 2 Waitoa Road,
Hataitai, Wellington 6003
Name: Dennis & Cathryn Riley
Telephone: (04) 386 2718
Fax: (04) 386 2719
Mobile: (025) 495 410
Email: top.o.hill@xtra.co.nz
Beds: 1 Queen (s/c studio), 1 Double,
1 Twin, 1 Single (3 bedrooms)
Bathroom: 2 Ensuites, 1 Guests share
Tariff: B&B (full) Studio $90-$120, Double (ensuite) $90,
Twin $85, Single $55. Credit Cards: (Visa,M/C,Bartercard)
NZ B&B & TAN vouchers accepted (studio - not applicable)
Nearest Town: Wellington 3.2km

Hataitai ('breath of the ocean') is situated in the eastern suburbs of Wellington, midway between Airport and City. A homely atmosphere is provided for guests in our comfortable 1919 two storey home, which has been in our family for 60 years. From the bedrooms there are views of Evans Bay, Hataitai Village and Mount Victoria. We enjoy the beauty of our harbour city, including its range of superb restaurants.
Te Papa Tongarewa (National Museum), sports venues, airport and ferry, CBD and the cultural life of Wellington are 5 - 10 minutes by bus or car. We have travelled widely overseas and in New Zealand, and share interests in music and the arts, historic places and meeting people. Our home is smoke-free inside and not suitable for children under 14 years.
Directions: *Please phone, write or fax.* **Home Page**: http://www.homestaysnz.co.nz

Wellington City

Bed & Breakfast
Address: No 11, 11 Hay Street,
Oriental Bay, Wellington
Name: Virginia Barton-Chapple
Telephone: (04) 801 9290
Fax: (04) 801 9295
Beds: 1 King convertible to twin (1 bedroom)
Bathroom: Guest share (with 1 other person)
Tariff: B&B (special) Double $95, Single $77.
Credit Cards.
Nearest Town: Wellington City 2 minutes drive

Oriental Bay is perhaps the finest location in Wellington. Take the opportunity to stay in this inner city area which is within strolling distance of Te Papa: the Museum of New Zealand and the art galleries. The major theatres, cinemas, great restaurants and cafes. No 11 has an intimate view of the city and Virginia has extensive knowledge of what's going on, and where to go. You may be so captivated by the location that you wish only to promenade along the Parade. Or in summer to swim or take a harbour cruise. The accommodation is in a comfortable room for one or two, with the bathroom adjacent. Electric blankets, bathrobes, hairdryer, tea and coffee facilities are provided. Smoking outside would be appreciated. Cat in residence.

Wellington

Serviced/Self Contained B & B
Address: 8 Parliament Street,
Thorndon, Wellington
Name: Eight Parliament Street
Telephone: 0064 (04) 499-0808
Fax: (04) 479 6705
Mobile: (025) 280 6739
Email: grasenack@xtra.co.nz
Beds: 3 Queen (3 bedrooms)
Bathroom: 1 Ensuite, 1 Guests share
Tariff: B&B (full) Double $118-$140, Single $95-$118.
Children over 12 years only. Visa/Mastercard.
Nearest Town: Wellington 5 minutes walk to City

From the outside a house in the traditional Thorndon character. From the inside a stylish artistic home. Eight Parliament located in a quiet street in Wellington's historical part of town, Thorndon is in walking distance to attractions like Parliament Buildings, Botanical Gardens, shops and restaurants. The house features three bedrooms (one ensuite) with contemporary interior and changing artwork. A courtyard offers outdoor relaxation and privacy. There is a modern kitchen / dining area for entertainment and a cup of espresso after a long day of sightseeing. Eight Parliament Street is a serviced self contained B&B where guests are treated with a breakfast of their choice served inside or al fresco in the courtyard. Eight Parliament caters for the traveller and busy executive alike who prefer personal ambience. Smoking is possible in the courtyard only. Laundry service available (extra charge). Please phone prior to arrival. German spoken.
Home Page: http://www.boutique-bb.co.nz

Wellington

Homestay

Address: Newtown Homestay,
85 Rintoul Street, Wellington.
Name: Keith and Gail
Telephone: (04) 389 0416
Fax: (04) 380 0416
Beds: 1 Queen,
3 single (3 bedrooms)
Bathroom: 1 Guests share
Tariff: B&B (full) Double $79-$89,
Single $49-$55.
Nearest Town: Wellington 2km

Newtown Homestay is a quiet spacious refurbished Victorian villa centrally situated 10 minutes from both the CBD and airport with pleasant views over picturesque Newtown. It is only a quick ride to Courtenay Place cafes, theatres, and Te Papa New Zealand national museum, via trolley buses regularly passing our gate. A short stroll takes you to village shops, restaurants, public and private hospitals yet we offer a quiet secure haven from the busy city. Complimentary tea and coffee making facilities are available in the TV lounge which guests can access at any time. All our bedrooms have electric blankets and heaters. We offer a smoke free house however, there is a delightful private back garden for those who wish to smoke. We are a mature couple with previous guest house experience and offer you unobtrusive but friendly hospitality. Our children have long since left home and we have no pets.

http://www.bnb.co.nz

take a look

Palmer Head, Wellington

Homestay
Address: Birkhall House, 14 Birkhall Grove,
Palmer Head, Wellington 6003.
Name: Jocelyn Scown
Telephone: 04-388 2881
Fax: 04-388 2833
Mobile: 025-762 870
Beds: 1 King, 2 Single
(2 bedrooms)
Bathroom: 1 Guests share
Tariff: B&B (continental/full on request)
$85 per room, Dinner $35 (by request).
Nearest Town: Wellington 10 minutes by car

New Zealand Association
FARM & HOME HOSTS

Relax in my lovely sunny home and enjoy the finest views in Wellington. Palmer Head is a new suburb situated on a hill with views from the South Island to Wellington Harbour. I am only 5 minutes drive from Wellington Airport and 10 mins drive to Wellington City with all its many attractions, including the world acclaimed Te Papa Museum. Enjoy a continental breakfast (cooked on request) on the deck, and with notice I am also happy to serve dinner with the finest NZ wines. For those who have energy to burn, there are several walk tracks nearby, and for the sports minded I overlook the golf course, and are five minutes from the aquatic Centre. I would be delighted to have you as my guest and have no objection to house trained dogs and kids. Baby's cot, pushchair and car seat available on request. Complimentary: Tea, Coffee, Juice and biscuits. Smokefree inside, Centrally heated, laundry facilities available.
Directions: *Please phone, fax or write for directions.*

Wellington, Inner City

Homestay
Address: The Cherry Tree,
9 MacFarlane Street, Mt Victoria,
Wellington
Name: Margaret and Frits Bergman
Telephone: (04) 801 5080
Fax: (04) 801 5252
Beds: 1 Queen (1 Bedroom)
Bathroom: 1 Private
Tariff: B&B (Full/Continental)
Double $120, Single $100.
Nearest Town: Wellington City (5 min stroll)

Our comfortable and gracious Victorian home is just a 5 min stroll to Courtnay Place, with all its cafes, theatres and galleries, and is even closer to Te Papa, our National Museum and lovely Oriental Bay.
Our large guest room is upstairs and includes a queen and a single bed, private bathroom and a verandah alongside, comfortable chairs and table, plus a desk and TV, and tea making facilities. Robes are provided.
Our street is very quiet in contrast to all the excitement of Courtnay Place.
We have travelled widely ourselves and lived in different European countries. We share interests in art, architecture and all that our beautiful harbour city offers. Frits will enjoy helping you to plan your stay. Margaret will enjoy spoiling you at the breakfast table. Fiji, our cat, will be a detached observer. Our children have left the nest. (We request that guests do not smoke in the house).

449

Wadestown, Wellington

Homestay
Address: 72 Wilton Road,
Wadestown
Name: Julie Foley
Telephone: (04) 499 6602
Mobile: (025) 203 2228
Beds: 1 Twin, 1 Single
(2 Bedrooms)
Bathroom: 1 Guests share
Tariff: B&B (Continental)
Double &80,
Single $40.
Nearest Town: Wellington 10 mins.

A comfortable quiet home in a lovely bush setting, just a short walk from Otari Native Botanic Gardens. The bus from the door will take you direct to the central city in 10 minutes. A separate lounge is available for those wanting privacy, two bedrooms, one twin, shared guests bathroom, all on a separate floor. Electric blankets and heaters ensure you will be cosy. Laundry facilities available. We enjoy meeting people, sharing the fireside and music in the evening. My interests are gardening, embroidery, playing the cello, attending some of the many and varied cultural activities in the city and playing mahjong. We share the house with a friendly Persian cat. My part-time work enables me to be available to collect visitors form the ferry etc. Parking on the street only.
Directions: *Please phone.*

http://www.bnb.co.nz

take a look

Thorndon, Wellington

Self Contained Accommodation
Address: 37 Newman Terrace,
Thorndon, Wellington
Name: Thorndon Views
Telephone: (04) 938 0783
Fax: (04) 938 0784
Mobile: (025) 284 7996
Email: jmgrady@xtra.co.nz
Beds: 1 Queen, 1 (fold-out)
Double (1 Bedroom)
Bathroom: 1 Private
Tariff: B&B (Continental)
Double $125, Single $100.
Children $15.
Nearest Town: Wellington

Overlooking Wellington harbour and city, Thorndon Views offers character accommodation with the comfort and privacy of your own home. A newly constructed, self-contained studio has been designed to blend in with the architecture of one of Wellington's most characterful districts and is well appointed. Parliament, the newly constructed Westpac Trust Stadium and Katherine Mansfield's birth place are all within ten minute walks. Te Papa National Museum and the Courtenay Place nightlife area are just a short bus trip. Thorndon Views is surrounded by a peaceful bush and garden setting. Cable television and a spa are available. Breakfast is brought to the studio and consists of freshly baked croissants, fresh fruit and brewed coffee. Your hosts are Janelle, David, Fergus (13 years old), Alex (11 years old) and Daisy, our Golden Retriever. **Home Page**: http://mysite.xtra.co.nz/~thorndonviews

Brooklyn (city end), Wellington

Homestay
Address: "Karepa", 56 Karepa Street,
Brooklyn, Wellington
Name: Ann and Tom Hodgson
Telephone: (04) 384 4193
Fax: (04) 384 4180
Email: golf@xtra.co.nz
Beds: 1 King, 1 Queen,
1 Single (2 Bedrooms)
Bathroom: 1 Luxury Guests share
Tariff: B&B (Full) Double $95-$125,
Single $75-$95. Extra person $25.
Dinner from $25 pp.
Nearest Town: Wellington 3 kms.

Stay with us at 'Karepa', our friendly, sunny, spacious home overlooking the city, harbour and mountains. The secluded garden and BBQ at the rear, look onto native bush. City restaurants, shops, theatres, sporting venues, beaches, airport and ferry - all within 10-15 minutes. Private guest rooms have tea/coffee facilities and TV (Sky TV in lounge), single bed in King room. Evening meal by arrangement. Parking on site. Bus at door. Laundry facilities. Originally from the UK, we are much-travelled and enjoy many of the capital's events and activities. Both play golf and tennis (happy to play anytime) and Ann is a keen gardener. Tom prefers to watch her from his deckchair. Sorry, no smokers or pets, and not suitable for really young children. **Directions**: *Please phone/fax for directions.*

Mount Victoria, Wellington
Homestay
Address: 6 Hawker Street,
Mt Victoria,
Wellington
Name: Annette and Logan Russell
Telephone: (04) 801 5761
Fax: (04) 801 5762
Beds: 1 Double (1 Bedroom)
Bathroom: 1 Private
Tariff: B&B (Full) Double $95,
Single $80, Dinner $25 by arrangement.
Credit Cards accepted.
Nearest Town: Central Wellington

Warm and cosy Villa Victoria is in the heart of the city, just up from Courtenay Place. It's a short walk to restaurants, theatres, major shopping, conference centres, Te Papa Museum of New Zealand, Wellington's waterfront, Cable Car, Parliament. Old St Pauls and Wellington Stadium are within walking distance.

A comfortable guest bedroom with TV, tea and coffee making facilities, adjoining sitting room opening on to a balcony with city views. Complimentary port and sherry. A full breakfast of seasonal fruits, juices, breads with speciality cooked dishes. Breakfast is served in our Italian styled dining room. On sunny mornings dine Al Fresco in our courtyard.

We enjoy entertaining and have travelled extensively ourselves. Our interests include cooking, floral design, current affairs, travel and sport. We are a non-smoking household. Laundry available. Pick up by arrangement. Our cat is Nicky.

Directions: *Phone, write or fax.*

Roseneath, Wellington
Homestay B&B
Address: Harbourview Homestay and B&B
125 Te Anau Road, Roseneath, Wellington
Name: Hilda and Geoff Stedman
Telephone: (04) 386 1043
Email: hildastedman@clear.net.nz
Beds: 1 Double, 2 Single (2 Bedrooms)
Bathrooms: 2 Private
Tariff: B&B (Full/Continental) Double $100-$115, Twin $65, Dinner from $35.
Nearest Town: Wellington City

This boutique guesthouse is 5 minutes drive from Wellington city and 10 minutes from the airport, on the No. 14 bus route. The house offers comfortable hospitality and elegance. Each bedroom opens on to a wide deck, offering expansive views of Wellington harbour. Pleasantly decorated rooms feature quality beds and linen. There is a choice of a double bedroom and/ or share twin room, separate guest's bathroom with shower and spa bath. Harbourview is situated in a peaceful setting close to the city, catering for Businesspeople, Tourists and Honeymooners.
We offer:
* Free pick up
* Cooked / Continental breakfast included
* Dinner by arrangement
* Non Smoking Environment
* Laundry facilities available
* Reasonable rates   * Payment by cash or cheque
We can arrange private chauffeured sightseeing tours in a Vintage car or even a Rolls Royce!

Island Bay, Wellington

Homestay

Address: 52 High Street,
Island Bay, Wellington 6002
Name: Theresa & Jack Stokes
Telephone: (04) 970 3353
Free Phone: 0800 33 53 83
Fax: (04) 970 3353
Email: tandj@actrix.gen.nz
Beds: 2 Double or 1 Double
& 1 Twin (2 bedrooms)
Bathroom: 2 Private
Tariff: B&B (full)
Double/Twin $70, Single $45.
NZ B&B Vouchers accepted
Nearest Town: Wellington - 10 minutes drive

A modern Lockwood house in a very private three acre section. Wonderful view over the Cook Strait etc. Ten minutes drive to Town - 10 minutes walk to Bus Terminal. No children under 14 please. We have a small dog and a moggy. WE MAY WELL BE CLOSED JANUARY, FEBRUARY & MARCH.

Directions: *From North take the Aotea Quay turnoff. (from Ferry take City exit). Follow main road to T junction (Oriental Parade). Turn right into Kent Terrace . Right hand lane before going round the Cricket Ground into Adelaide Road. STRAIGHT UP THE HILL - keep going and the road becomes The Parade. On reaching the sea, SHARP right into Beach Street, left and left again into High Street. Straight up Private Road at end - plenty of parking. From Airport, exit via Cargo Area, turn right and follow coast road for ten minutes - Beach Street is on the right.*

http://www.bnb.co.nz

take a look

Chatham Islands

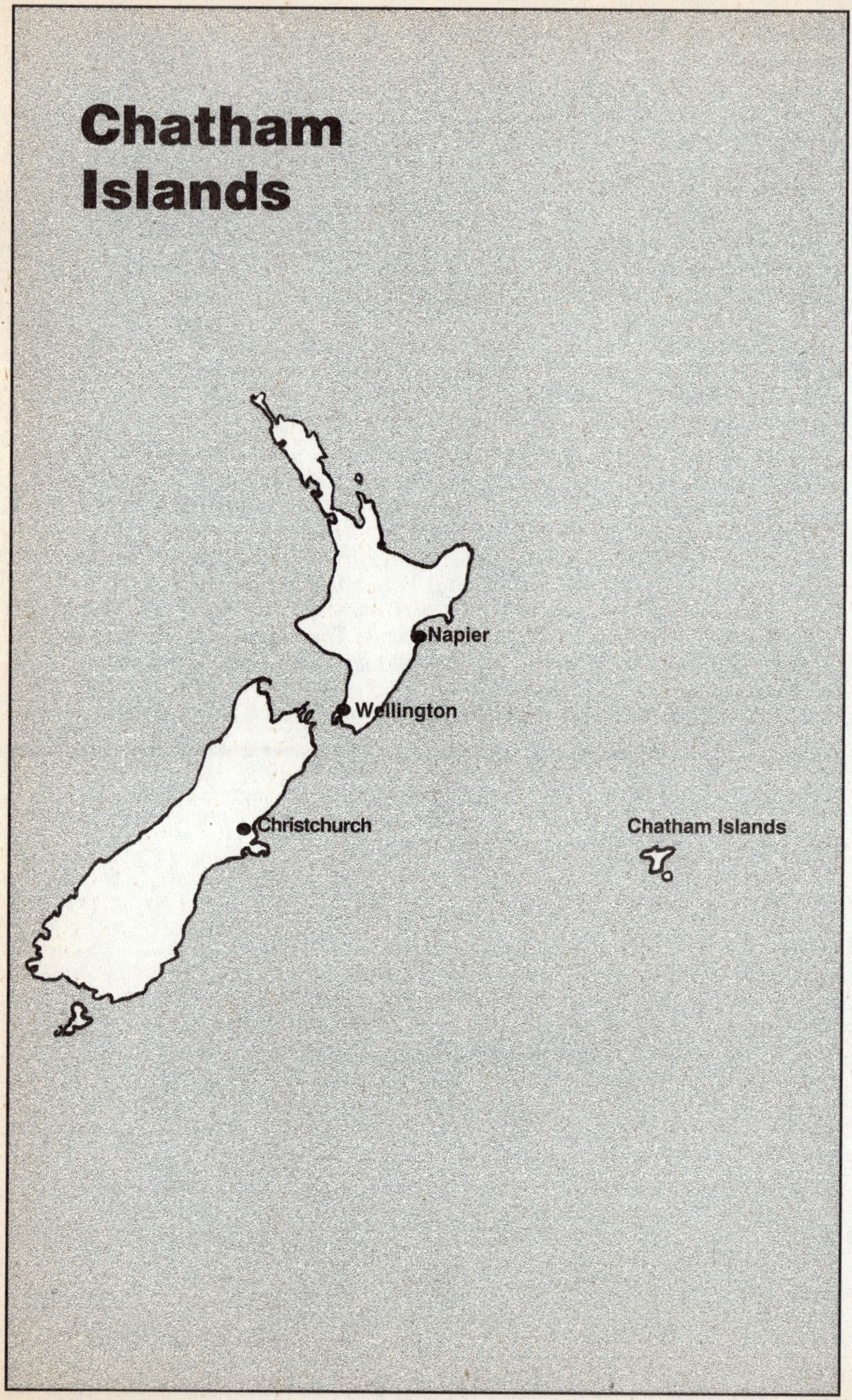

Napier

Wellington

Christchurch

Chatham Islands

Chatham Islands

Farmstay
Address: Te Matarae,
Chatham Islands
Name: Pat & Wendy Smith
Telephone: (03) 305 0144
Fax: (03) 305-0144
Beds: 2 Queen, 2 Single (3 bedrooms)
Bathroom: 2 Ensuite, 1 Family share
Tariff: B&B (continental) Double $85,
Single $73, Dinner $25.
Nearest Town: Waitangi (Chatham Islands)

Relax in our natural wood home which is situated in eighty acres of bush on lagoon edge with mown walkways throughout. The lagoon is ideal for swimming and fishing and has nice sandy beaches. Farm activities and kayaks available. Farm is eleven hundred acres and includes four other bush reserves.

Guests may meal with family or in separate dining room. Bedrooms are separated from main house by covered swimming pool and home gym area.

We are a non smoking household; so request guests to refrain from doing so in our home.

Most meal ingredients are home produced. We have two cats and a host of domestic farm animals.

Air travel exit points are Christchurch and Wellington. Rental car with guide available.

Free pick up and deliver to airport.

The Chatham Islands situated 800km east of Mainland New Zealand, are Islands of Mystery. A place where volcanic cones rise from the mist and sea. Due to isolation and recent history of colonisation, many plants and animals are unique.

Marlborough

Rai Valley

Anakiwa

Picton

Port Underwood

Linkwater

6

Havelock

Koromiko

Canvastown

Pelorus Bridge

Blenheim

1

Henwick

Seddon

Waihopai Valley

63

Awatere Valley

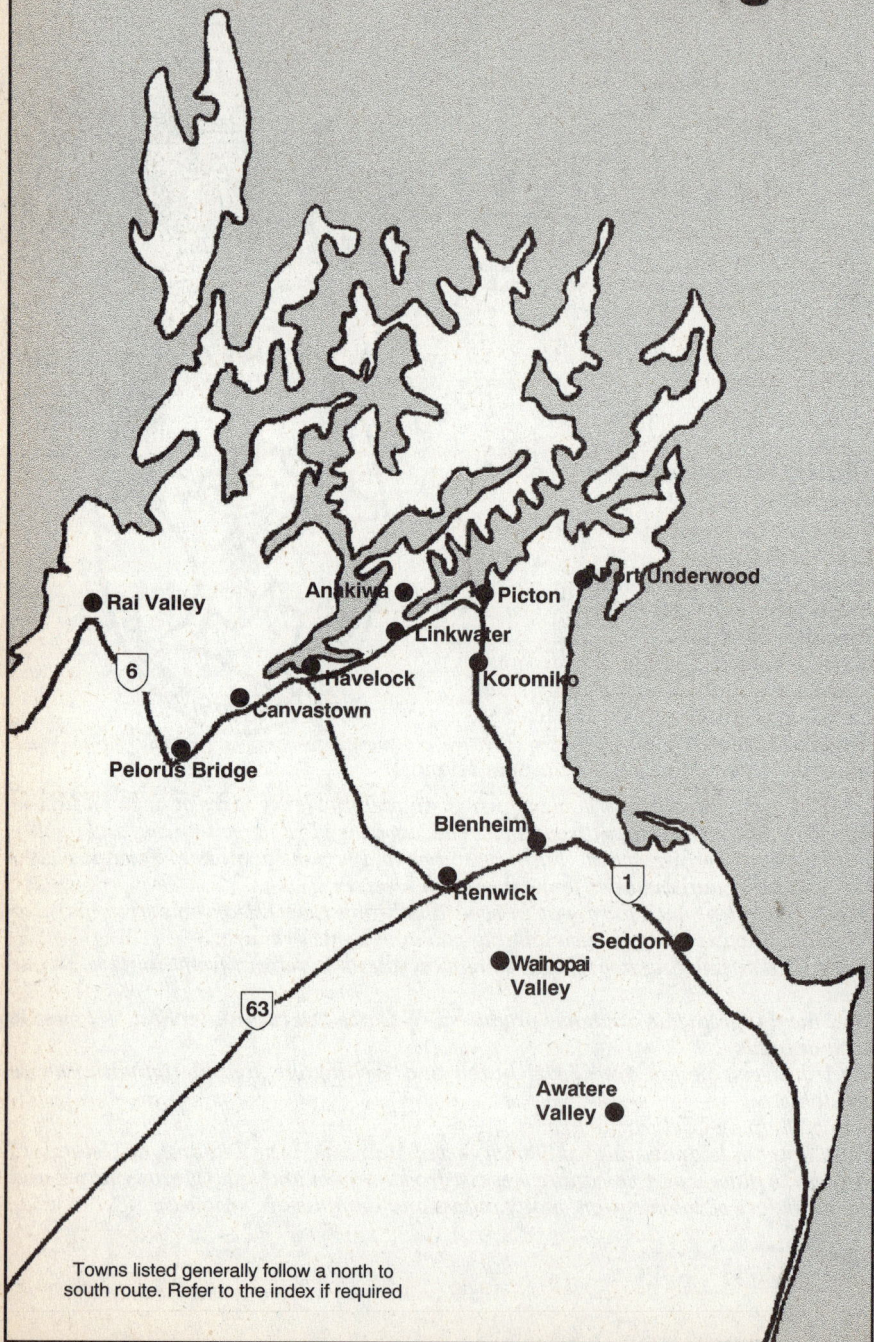

Towns listed generally follow a north to
south route. Refer to the index if required

Waikawa, Picton

Bed & Breakfast Homestay
Address: 'Rainbird Inn' Tom Canes Bay,
Port Underwood Road, PO Box 41, Waikawa.
Name: Raelene & Bill (Former Owners of Green Gables)
Telephone: (03) 579 9155, Freephone 0800 273050
Fax: (03) 579 9155
Beds: 2 King, (2 bedrooms)
Bathroom: 2 Ensuite
Tariff: B&B (full) Double $85, Single $50, Dinner $25, Not suitable for children
NZ B&B Vouchers accepted $15 Surcharge
Nearest Town: Picton 40 minutes, 23 km South of Picton via Port Underwood Road.

Relax and enjoy peace and tranquillity of one of the most charming parts of the Marlborough Sounds. Just 40 minutes form the ferry terminal at Picton. "Rainbird Inn" is nestled into bush covered hills of Tom Canes Bay in Port Underwood.
Guest Accommodation comprises of two comfortable bedrooms both with king-size beds and ensuite bathrooms, tea and coffee making facilities are available with home made cookies. You are invited to use the laundry. Dinner is available by arrangement and features traditional New Zealand cuisine including freshly caught fish, served with a complimentary drink.
For breakfast choose either a full country style cooked breakfast or a light continental breakfast or if you prefer, a delectable combination of both, served with delicious home made jams and preserves. A two minute stroll to a sheltered beach that offers safe swimming, excellent fishing and diving in crystal clear water. An easy walking track leads from the house to a picturesque waterfall and placid rock pools enclosed by native bush. All around bell birds chime fantails flit from branch to branch. Ideal for sea activities, fishing by arrangement of bring your own boat. Bruce our friendly golden cockerspaniel would love to share this delightful spot with you.
Directions: *Follow the Port Underwood Road from Waikawa, don't turn left at Hakahaka. Keep going South to Blenheim, Tom Canes Bay sign on the right.*
Home Page: http://marlborough.co.nz/rainbird/

Picton

Bed & Breakfast Homestay
Address: 'The Gables', 20 Waikawa Road, Picton
Name: Annette and Peter Gardiner
Telephone: (03) 573 6772
Fax: (03) 573 8860
Mobile: (025) 220 5786
Email: gables@mlb.planet.gen.nz
Beds: 2 Queen, 1 Double, 2 Single (3 bedrooms)
Bathroom: 2 Ensuite, 1 Private
Tariff: B&B (special) Double $90-$125, Single $70.
Not suitable for children. Credit cards: Visa/Mastercard.
Nearest Town: Picton 1 block

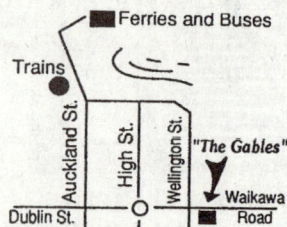

A warm welcome awaits you at "THE GABLES" in Picton, your destination in the Marlborough district, well known for the Queen Charlotte Walkway, kayaking, eco tours, sailing, fishing activities and wineries. "THE GABLES", built in 1924 and purchased by Annette and Peter especially to share with guests, is situated within 1 block of the town centre and the beautiful harbour foreshore. Award-winning restaurants and cafes are all within easy walking distance, most within 2 blocks. Ferry, bus, train and other facilities are within 5 minutes walk of "THE GABLES". Our guest rooms are upstairs, and have been named to recognise the previous families who have owned "THE GABLES". The large "Townshend" room (previous Mayor of Picton) has tea and coffee making facilities, small pink tiled fireplace, an ensuite bathroom and firm queen size bed. The large "Thomson" room has a firm queen size bed and two single beds, private bathroom across the hallway, and tea and coffee making facilities. The "Findlater" room is comfortable with a double size bed and ensuite bathroom, tea & coffee making facilities. Breakfasts are special at "THE GABLES" - after fruit juice, fruit platters, cereal, home-made muesli, you will be offered a choice of our legendary bluecod and smoked salmon crepes, banana pancakes with maple syrup, or traditional bacon and eggs. Delicious home made muffins are baked fresh every morning, to be enjoyed with freshly brewed coffee or a selection of teas. The lounge, with open fire, TV, piano, reading material, tea and coffee making facilities, is where we enjoy a pre-dinner drink with our guests.
You are likely to be met by our very friendly black spaniel, Blackie, or Penelope the cat. Off street parking. Smoking area on front porch.
Tariff: Townshend Room: $125 Double
Thomson Room: $115 Double orTwin, extra person $25
Findlater Room: $90 Double, $70 Single
Home Page: http://www.picton.co.nz/gables

458

Whatamango Bay, Picton

Homestay+SC Apartments
Address: 424 Port Underwood Rd,
Whatamango Bay, Queen Charlotte Sound,
PO Box 261, Picton
Name: 'Seaview', Pam & John
Telephone: (03) 573 7783
Fax: (03) 573 7783
Email: seaview@powerglobe.de
Beds: Apartments: 2 Double
Homestay: 2 Single (1 bedroom)
Bathroom: Apartments: 2 Private   Homestay: 1 Private
Tariff: B&B (full) Double $70, Single $40, Dinner $25,
Self-contained apartment: Double $60.
Nearest Town: Picton 9km

'Seaview' is set in peaceful surroundings only 10 minutes by road from Ferry Terminal.   Our apartments are quiet, clean, comfortable and private with extensive views over Queen Charlotte Sound, forest and distant mountains to the north. Walk in our large garden which abounds with native birds, hike the forest trail behind our home, or take the 1km walk to the historic Maori storage pits. You may see Dolphins in the bay. Take our small boat and try your luck fishing or relax and watch the shipping pass by. Join us in the morning when a full breakfast is served including our own free range eggs. **Directions**: *Follow the Port Underwood Road from Waikawa for 4km. Sign at bottom of drive. 'Seaview' No. 424. Dinner by arrangement.* **Home Page**: http://www.powerglobe.de/New Zealand/bb/seaview/e-seaview.htm

Anakiwa, Picton

Homestay-S.C. Apartment
Address: 'Crafters',
Anakiwa Road,
Queen Charlotte Sound,
R.D. 1, Picton
Name: Ross & Leslie Close
Telephone: (03) 574 2547
Fax: (03) 574 2547
Mobile: (025) 231 2245
Beds: 2 Single (1 bedroom)
Bathroom: 1 Private
Tariff: B&B (NZ style) Double $75, Single $45,
Dinner $25. Credit cards. NZ B&B Vouchers accepted
Nearest Town: Picton 22 Kms, Havelock 18 Kms

Our home at the head of Queen Charlotte Sound has a magnificent 25 mile long sea view and is in a tranquil and peaceful area, noted for its bush walks and variety of bird life. It is only a short walk to New Zealand's Cobham Outward Bound School, and the start of the Queen Charlotte Walkway, a wonderful scenic route from Anakiwa to Ship Cove. Our warm and comfortable guest area has one bedroom with twin beds, a sunny lounge with TV and a large double sofa bed if required, a fully equipped kitchen and private bathroom. Ross is a woodturner and Leslie is a potter and both are happy to demonstrate their skills and their Gallery is open every day. Other interests we enjoy are sea fishing in our motor launch and walking our Jack Russell terrier.   Transport to and from local departure points can be provided by arrangement. **Directions**: *Please phone.*

Whatamango Bay, Picton

Homestay, Self-contained Accommodation.
Laundry facility on request
Address: 418 Port Underwood Road,
Whatamango Bay, Picton
Name: Waipuna Lodge.
Bill and Esther Phillips.
Telephone: (03) 573 8071
Fax: (03) 573 8071
Mobile: (025)232 6600
Beds: 1 Queen (1 bedroom)
Bathroom: 1 Ensuite
Tariff: B&B (full) Double $120, Single $85.
Dinner $25pp (on request).
Nearest Town: Picton - Blenheim

We would like to welcome you to our home, 9km from Picton, commanding a million dollar view of the fabulous 'Queen Charlotte Sounds'.
From your balcony, take in the breathtaking view of scenery, bush clad hills or listen to the songs of tuis and bellbirds. From time to time watch for the odd seal or school of dolphin that frequent our bay. Watch ships glide in and out of the Sounds or simply daydream as flotilla's of yachts with sails full make their way in the breeze. A minutes stroll through the bush, to the beach, where you have the use of a dingly or canoe.
A short walk to Karaka Point where (Kai Pits) used by early Maori to store their food are sited. Minutes away from bush walks, fishing, diving, sightseeing and the world renown "Queen Charlotte Walkway" which commands some of this country's most spectacular scenery.
Directions: *Please phone evening prior. Booking essential.*

Linkwater, Picton

Lodge with Licenced Restaurant
Address: Linkwater Lodge,
Queen Charlotte Scenic Drive, R.D.1, Picton
Name: John Smart
Telephone: (03) 574 2507
Fax: (03) 574 2517
Beds: 2 Queen, 2 Twin (4 bedrooms)
Bathroom: 2 Guests share
Tariff: B&B (continental) Double $75,
Single $45, Children half price,
Dinner - meal in restaurant. Credit cards (VISA/MC).
NZ B&B Vouchers accepted
Nearest Town: Havelock 12km, Picton 22km

Country Base for Marlborough Sounds Experience

Linkwater Lodge is approximately 30 minutes (22 kilometres) drive from Picton Ferry Terminal along beautiful Queen Charlotte Drive. This old homestead, built of native timbers in 1926, is surrounded by farmlands and is centrally located in the Marlborough Sounds. Guests can walk from the Lodge to historic Cullensville Goldfields (1888). All Sounds' attractions, including the Queen Charlotte Walkway, are only a short drive. Upstairs rooms provide comfortable beds and peaceful farmland views. A small restaurant serves home-cooked food ranging from tasty soups and sandwiches to tender steaks and succulent seafood. Nearby Havelock is the green-lipped mussel capital of the world. Marlborough tap beer and wines are served at a magnificent bar milled from a walnut tree standing 90 years on the farm. Enjoy the goldfields atmosphere and learn about this exciting district from friendly locals. Your host, John, is a former outback worker and university professor, now glasswasher and philosopher.

460

Picton

Historic Homestay

Address: 'House of Glenora',
22 Broadway cnr Wellington St's
Picton
Name: Birgite Armstrong
Telephone: (03) 573 6966
Fax: (03) 573 7735
Mobile: (025) 229 0594
Email: glenora.house@clear.net.nz
Beds: 3 Queen, 3 Double, 6 Single (6 bedrooms)
Bathroom: 2 Ensuite, 1 Private, 1 Guests share
Tariff: B&B (continental) Double $85-$120, Triple $95, Twin $75, Single $55-$85,
Children not suitable. Credit cards. Vouchers Accepted. NZ B&B Vouchers
accepted Surcharge Double $25
Nearest Town: Picton Post Office, 50 m

Welcome to the House of Glenora, one of Marlborough Sounds historical homes. Built in 1860 and surrounded by a sprawling garden it is situated in the heart of Picton, yet very secluded and peaceful. Scandinavian creativity and NZ hospitality is blended into a colourful and vibrant home with a difference. As Birgite is a Masterweaver, House of Glenora incorporates the International Weaving School, studio and gallery. The large bedrooms, extensive living areas, wide sunny verandas and patios are decorated with a stunning mixture of antiques and contemporary pieces. Enjoy the magnificent views of Picton harbour and relax in the delightful garden with its 140 year old English oak tree. Central heating, laundry facilities and of course, the Swedish style "smorgasbord" breakfast together with the warm and vivacious feeling of House of Glenora and the beauty of Marlborough Sounds will surely make your stay here a memorable experience. We wish you welcome. Winners of the Marlborough Awards 1993 and 1997.0.

http://www.bnb.co.nz

take a look

Picton

Homestay
Address: 'Retreat Inn',
20 Lincoln Street, Picton
Name: Alison & Geoff
Telephone: (03) 573 8160/
Fax: (03) 573 7799
Mobile: 025-222 5062
Email: elliott.orchard@xtra.co.nz
Beds: 1 Queen, 2 Single (2 bedrooms).
Bathroom: 1 Guests share upstairs. (2nd guest bathroom available downstairs)
Tariff: B&B (full) Double $85, Single $60. Dinner by arrangement $25 pp.
Credit cards (VISA/MC/Bankcard).
NZ B&B Vouchers accepted $20 surcharge 1 May - 30 Sept.
Nearest Town: A 3 minute drive to Picton's main street.

New Zealand Association FARM & HOME HOSTS

Welcome - come share some time with us and our cute cat Morris. Set on a wooded hillside, 'RETREAT INN', which we built ourselves, is peaceful, warm and very private. Your cosy bedrooms are upstairs, facing the sun, and beds have firm mattresses with electric blankets. Two guest bathrooms are available, one upstairs, one down. Our living room, where we have memorable and fun times with guests, has a wonderful woodfire for cooler days, while the outdoor patio area 'beckons' during warmer months.... and for outdoor dinners! 'RETREAT INN' breakfasts are special - fruit juice, fruit platters, choice of cereals - with home-made muesli and yoghurt, fresh jams and croissants, teas, and freshly brewed coffee. Cooked course also available. Transport provided locally; laundry facilities; secure flat, off-street parking. Sorry, no smoking in the house. Safe travelling.
Directions: *For directions, please phone.*
Home Page: www.nzhomestay.co.nz/retreatinn.htm

Picton

Self-contained Apartment
Address: 'Grandvue',
19 Otago Street, Picton
Name: Russell & Rosalie Mathews
Telephone: (03) 573 8553
Fax: (03) 573 8556
Email: grandvue-mathews@clear.net.nz
Beds: 1 Queen
Bathroom: 1 Ensuite
Tariff: B&B (full) Double $75, Single $55, Children $15,
Dinner optional extra. NZ B&B Vouchers accepted $7.50 surcharge
Nearest Town: Picton 2mins walk

Nestled on the hills overlooking Picton, Grandvue offers sweeping panoramic views of the township and port looking out onto Queen Charlotte Sound. Situated at the end of a cul-de-sac, Grandvue is a quiet haven with a secluded garden, only five minutes walk from the main shopping area of Picton with its assortment of restaurants, and only ten minutes walk from the Inter-Island Ferry Terminal. Grandvue offers accommodation in a comfortable and warm self-contained apartment with its own kitchen and ensuite. A television and video is also available as is access to a private barbeque area. Feast on panoramic views from our conservatory upstairs while enjoying a delicious continental or cooked breakfast. If required a portable cot and high chair are also available. Your hosts, Russell and Rosalie will provide courtesy transport to and from the Ferry Terminal, Railway Station or Airport.

Picton
Homestay
Address: 21 Otago Street, Picton
Name: Panorama View
Telephone: (03) 573 6362
Fax: (03) 573 6362
Beds: 1 Double, 2 Single (2 bedrooms)
Bathroom: 1 Ensuite, 1 Private
Tariff: B&B (full)
Double $75, Single $50.
NZ B&B Vouchers accepted
Nearest Town: Picton 2 minutes

We would like to invite you in our sunny-spacious home in Picton, The Diamond of the South Island, where we have a breathtaking view over the city and the harbour, with a 5 minutes walk to the foreshore, shops, boating facilities, mini-golf, Ferry terminal, restaurants etc.
You might like to join us for a 'cuppa' on the balcony and watch the ferry and activities on the water.
The bedrooms have coffee and tea facilities, radio/clock, colour TV, fridge, electric blankets etc.
A warm welcome awaits you at "Panorama View" including a generous breakfast.
We are looking forwards to meeting you. Courtesy car available.
Your Hosts Colin and Din.

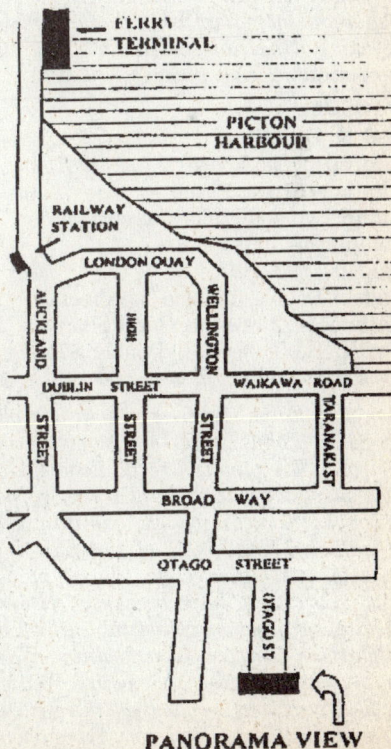

463

Queen Charlotte Sounds - Picton

Homestay+Self-contained Accom.
Address: 'Tirimoana House',
Anakiwa Road, Picton R.D.1,
Queen Charlotte Sounds, Marlborough
Name: Peter & Robyn Churchill
Telephone: (03) 574 2627
Fax: (03) 574 2647
Mobile: (025) 248 7627
Beds: Homestay: 1 King, 1 Queen,
1 Twin (2 bdrms) SC Unit: 1 Double, 3 Single
Bathroom: Homestay: 1 Guests share (incl spa bath and sep shower)
SC Unit: Private bathroom, kitchen, laundry
Tariff: B&B (full) Double $85-$105, Single $60, Dinner $25pp.
Self-contained Unit: Double $75, $12.50 each extra person.
Nearest Town: Picton 22km, Havelock 18km

'SOUNDS MAGIC'
Come and share a slice of Heaven: Set in beautiful grounds of native and exotic plants at the head of Queen Charlotte Sound, enjoy panoramic views of the Sounds and surrounding bush clad hills from all rooms, terraces and swimming pool. Our large waterfront home overlooks Okiwa Bay, the Cobham Outward Bound School and the start/finish of the beautiful Queen Charlotte Track. For your enjoyment we offer hospitality, orthopaedic beds, extensive sun decks, fernery spa pool, barbeque on marble terrace, good food, dawn chorus, billiard table, underfloor heating, convivial glass, log fire, interesting conversation and friendly cat 'Merp''. We respect your wish to laze, gaze and watch the swans go by but will happily encourage you to share our interests of fishing in our launch, boating, golf, bush walks, music. We can arrange kayaking, wine trails, mountain biking, etc. Courtesy car available by arrangement.
Directions: *Please phone.*

Picton

Bed & Breakfast
Address: Echo Lodge,
5 Rutland Street, Picton
Name: Lyn and Eddie Thoroughgood
Telephone: (03) 573 6367
Fax: (03) 573 6387
Beds: 1 Double, 3 Single (3 bedrooms)
Bathroom: 2 Ensuite, Guest Share
Tariff: B&B (special) Double $75, Single $40.   Credit Cards.
Nearest Town: Picton 800 m

Lyn and Eddie welcome you to our older style home named after the ship in our harbour "Echo". We invite you to share a cup of tea, coffee, wine or juice on arrival. The atmosphere at Echo Lodge is friendly and relaxed. Enjoy our lovely spacious lounge with its Turkish carpets and cozy log fire for cold winter nights. Through the arch way to our dining room, where you will be served our special breakfast. The smell of hot baked bread, special pancakes, bacon and eggs, omelets, percolated coffee, home made jams, yoghurt, fruit, muesli awaits you. You may like to have breakfast on our patio. Our Twin and Double rooms have ensuite bathrooms, comfortable firm beds and tea/coffee making facilities. Our single room has washbasin facilities. We are 5 mins walk from shops, restaurants, busses, ferries, with a courtesy car available. We are happy to help you with your travel arrangements. Come stay with us. you will not regret it. A warm Picton welcome awaits you. **Directions**: *800m up Waikawa Road from round about in town. Rutland Street on your right.*

Kenepuru Sound

Farmstay

Address: The Nikaus
Country Garden & Farmstay,
Waitaria bay, RD 2, Picton
Name: Alison and Robin Bowron.
Telephone: (03) 573 4432
Fax: (03) 573 4432
Mobile: (025) 544 712
Beds: 1 Double, 2 Single (2 bedrooms)
Bathroom: 1 Guests share
Tariff: B&B (full) Double $75, Single $45, Children 12 & under half price,
Dinner $20, Credit Cards.NZ B&B Vouchers accepted $7.50 surcharge.
All year round
Nearest Town: Blenheim 110km, Havelock 80km, Picton 80km

The Nikaus is a Sounds sheep & cattle farm situated in Waitaria Bay Kenepuru Sound, 2 hours drive from Blenheim or Picton. We offer friendly personal service in our comfortable spacious home. The large gardens (in AA Garden Book) contain many rhododendrons, roses, camellias, lilies and prennials, with big sloping lawns and views out to sea. A swimming pool is available for guests use. We have 3 aldult children (1 boarding at home). A non-smoking household with interests in farming, boating, fishing and gardening. We have 2 dogs Sam (corgie) and Minnie (foxy x). Other animals include the farm dogs, donkeys, pet wild pigs, "Miss Piggy", turkeys, hens and peacocks. Good hearty country meals, home grown produce and home made ice cream a speciality, thanks to "Muggles" our friendly house cow. We are happy to arrange local fishing trips, launch charters and water taxis for visitors.
Directions: *Please phone.*

Mahau Sound, Picton

Homestay

Address: "Kairangi", Moetapu Bay,
Mahau Sound, RD 2, Picton
Name: Pauline & Gary Graham
Telephone: (03) 574 2548
Freephone:0800 1699 14
Fax: (03) 574 2548
Email: soundswise@xtra.co.nz
Beds: 4 Single, 1 set of bunks (3 bedrooms)
Bathroom: Private (1 party only at a time)
Tariff: B&B (continental) Double $70, Single $40, Children under 12 half price,
Dinner $25, Credit Cards. NZ B&B Vouchers accepted
Nearest Town: Havelock 22km, Picton 32km

We are located just moments off the Queen Charlotte Scenic Drive, within an hour of Picton. Our home is situated to make the most of majestic views of the Inner Sounds (Pelorus and Mahau) and yet enjoy the concealment and quietness of the surrounding bush, where numerous native birds make their homes. All rooms have their own access to decks - where meals can be taken - and you can enjoy the panoramic views. Guests can also relax in our recreation room. We have a large, friendly dog. Our interests include sailing (boats and instruction can be made available if required), gardening, meeting people, overseas travel and if you're looking for a quiet, peaceful, idyllic retreat - this is it. Transport can be provided to, and / or from the Anakiwa end of the Queen Charlotte Walkway, vehicles can be left with us, undercover, for safe-keeping. Our home is smoke-free.
Directions: *Please contact us for directions.*

Picton

Homestay/B&B
Address: "Palm Haven",
5 Newgate St, Picton
Name: Peter & Damian (Dae) Robertson
Telephone: (03) 573 5644
Fax: (03) 573 5645
Mobile: (025) 275 0860
Email: palmhaven@xtra.co.nz
Beds: 2 Queen, 3 Single (3 bedrooms)
Bathroom: 1 Ensuite, 1 Guests share
Tariff: B&B (continental)
Double $60, Single $40,
Children under 12yrs $20, Dinner $25.
NZ B&B Vouchers accepted $15 surcharge for ensuite
Nearest Town: Picton 500m

"Palm Haven" is set in a hillside garden featuring paths, seating and birdlife, all in a quiet cul-de-sac. We have three guest rooms: one en-suite queen; one twin; one with queen and single beds. Latter rooms share guest-only bathroom and separate toilet. Families can be very suitably accommodated and we enjoy children. We provide cot and highchair. We also welcome single travellers at a single rate. Our laundry and evening child-minding services are popular - so are our breakfast muffins! An easy 5-minute walk takes guests to town and our lovely foreshore. And while there's plenty to do in Picton itself, "Palm Haven" provides a great homebase while guests explore the whole of the top of the South. We are keen outdoor bowlers and dabble also in fishing, writing and machine quilting. Our cats, Toby and Bijou, are people-friendly.

Picton

Homestay and Self Contained Accommodation
Address: Ngakura Bay Homestay,
Manuka Drive, RD1 Ngakuta Bay, Picton
Name: Eve Dawson
Telephone: (03) 573 8853
Fax: (03) 573 8385
Beds: 1 Double, 2 Twin (3 Bedrooms)
Bathroom: 1 Ensuite, 1 Guests share
Tariff: B&B (Continental) Double $90,
Single $70, Dinner $30 by arrangement.
Not suitable for children.
Credit cards accepted.
Nearest Town: Picton 11 km

Ngakuta Bay Homestay is 11 km from Picton and 21 km from Havelock on the scenic queen Charlotte Drive with access to beautiful bays.
The homestay is built in NZ larch and set in 1/2 acre of bush with large verandahs and magnificent views over Ngakuta Bay. From this setting guests can go walking the world renowned Queen Charlotte Walkway, sailing, kayaking, fishing, dolphin watching, or a day out by boat to the far reaches of the stunning Marlborough Sounds. Eve, whose pastimes include sailing, horse riding, walking, with a background in he hotel and restaurant business in London and the South of England, continuing an interest in good food and wine, will gladly point you in the right direction, in any or all of these pursuits and make sure your stay is a comfortable, enjoyable and a memorable one in this quite magical place the Marlborough Sounds.
Sky TV, tea and coffee making facilities.

Picton

Homestay
Address: The White House,114 High Street, Picton
Name: Gwen Stevenson
Telephone: (03) 573 6767
Fax: (03) 573 8871
Beds: 2 Double, 3 Single (4 bedrooms)
Bathroom: 2 Guests share (1 Downstairs)
Tariff: B&B (Continental) Double $55, Single $35.
Cooked breakfast extra. Not suitable for children.
Nearest Town: Picton (opposite the Police Station)

The White House in Pictons main street offers affordable luxury - just ask any previous guest - in a friendly, quiet, warm home environment. It nestles on a sunny 1/4 acre, surrounded by mature trees and gardens, and is just a minutes walk to Picton's fabulous cafes and restaurants for your evening meal.

Located conveniently in the middle of town, this delightful 70 year old home is filled with Gwen's porcelain doll collection and numerous 'old worlde' touches. It has been immaculately maintained throughout with all refurbishments reflecting the era in which it was built.

Guest bedrooms are upstairs, all of which have quality beds to ensure a good nights sleep. Also on the same floor is the guest lounge which affords panoramic views over Picton to the harbour and hills beyond. However, if they prefer, guests are most welcome to share the downstairs lounge with their host.

Gwen's long association with the hospitality industry has made her aware that some of the things people miss when travelling is being able to pop into the kitchen and make a pot of tea or a cup of coffee when they like. White House guests are invited to do just that. The laundry facilities are also available for guests.

We look forward to making our guests' Picton visit an enjoyable and memorable one. And while The White House is a non-smoking residence, guests are most welcome to smoke on the front verandah or the back deck areas. We regret our home is unsuitable for children.

Picton

Self-Contained Accommodation
Address: 'Bridgend Cottage',
36 York Street, Picton
Name: Steve & Mila Burke
Telephone: (03) 573 6734
Fax: (03) 573 8323
Email: STEVEJB@VOYAGER.CO.NZ
Beds: 1 King, 1 Double,
2 Single - Disabled access (3 bedrooms)
Bathroom: 2 Ensuite.
All beds with 'Slumbertime' mattresses
Tariff: B&B (special) Double $80, Single $50, Children $20, Dinner $25,
Credit cards Visa/Mastercard. Ask us to quote special rates for families
& small groups. NZ B&B Vouchers accepted Surcharge $10
Nearest Town: Picton

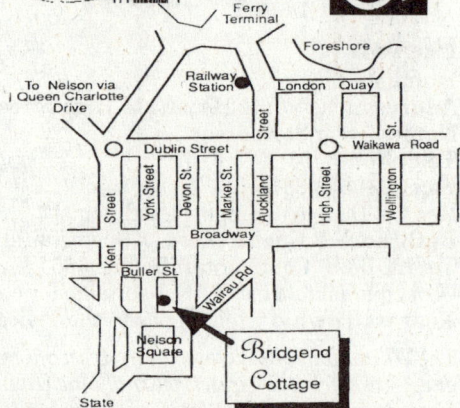

*We welcome you to Picton and our property, which is situated within easy walking
distance of all activities in Picton. The accommodation is self contained and warm
including colour TV, tea/coffee making facilities, a lavish breakfast with freshly
brewed coffee or tea that caters for all tastes and diets and sets you up for the day.
Breakfast arranged for early inter-island ferry passengers. Dinner is a gourmet
meal featuring specialities of our region. Safe and secure off street parking, sun deck, transport
provided from buses, train or inter-island ferry. Our hobbies are walking, gardening, gourmet
cooking, and reading. Mila enjoys sewing, embroidery and art. Steve is interested in all sport.
He has worked in the Travel/Industry and we can assist you with onward travel if required.
We also speak French. Laundry facilities available. We are a non smoking household, you are
most welcome to smoke on the deck or verandah. Member of New Zealand Association of Farm
& Home Hosts. "We enjoy making new friends."*
Home Page: NZHOMESTAY.CO.NZ/BRIDGEND.HTM

Picton, Queen Charlotte Sounds

Self Contained Accommodation, B&B
Address: Tanglewood, Queen Charlotte Drive, The Grove, RD 1, Picton
Name: Stephen and Linda Hearn
Telephone: (03) 574 2080
Fax: (03) 574 2044
Mobile: (025) 814 388
Beds: 2 Super King/Twin (2 Bedrooms)
Bathroom: 2 Ensuite
Tariff: B&B (Full) Double $80, Single $55, Dinner $25.
Credit Cards: Visa/Mastercard.
Nearest Town: Picton 16km, Havelock 16 km.

Snuggled amongst native ferns - yet only 4 minutes stroll to swimming beach and jetty. Tanglewood has a private separate guest wing with lounge, kitchenette and barbecue area for self catering meals. Use us as a stopping-off spot to kayak around the bays, take a fishing trip or enjoy local bush walks, including Queen Charlotte Walkway. Sample some of New Zealand's best wines on the wine trail, visit local arts and crafts. Take a trip to watch or swim with the dolphins and observe some rare and endangered birds.
Relax and listen to the sounds of birds and our stream or take a walk with us to view the glow worms. Our super king or twin beds are of unsurpassed comfort. We both share interest in boating, fishing, swimming, water sports, gardening, walking and meeting people.
We look forward to making you welcome.

Picton, Ngakuta Bay

Homestay, Self Contained Accommodation B&B
Address: Bayswater,
15 Manuka Drive, Ngakuta Bay,
Queen Charlotte Sound,
Picton RD1
Name: Paul and Judy Mann
Telephone: (03) 573 5966
Fax: (03) 573 5966
Beds: 1 Queen, 2 Single (2 Bedrooms)
Bathroom: 1 Ensuite, 1 Private
Tariff: B&B (Continental)
Double $80, Single $45,
NZ B&B Vouchers accepted $10 surcharge
Nearest Town: Picton 11 km, Havelock 24 km

Havelock 24km
Queen Charlotte Dr
Phillips Rd
Picton 11km
15 Manuka Dr
Brough Pl
Bays Water
B&B

Let us introduce you to marvellous Marlborough with its wineries, craft shops, sea kayaking, sailing, Sounds cruises and Queen Charlotte Walkway. Our modern home has extensive views over Ngakuta Bay and surrounding bush. We offer continental breakfast or self catering in a self contained apartment with 2 double bedrooms, kitchen, lounge, dining and laundry. Beautiful views from your own private balcony. Ngakuta Bay offers safe swimming, bush walks, birds chorus and spectacular scenery. Complimentary transport available for Picton ferry, buses or train and to Queen Charlotte Walkway at Anakiwa 13 km. Please phone. Mini tours by arrangement. A warm welcome and relaxed stay awaits you in our little piece of paradise. Inspection invited.
Directions: *Ngakuta Bay on Queen Charlotte Drive. Turn into Phillips Road then right then left into Manuka Drive. up the drive at Bayswater B&B sign.*

469

Moenui Bay, Havelock, Pelorus Sound
Bed & Breakfast/Homestay
Address: Moenui Bay, Queen Charlotte Drive,
R.D.1 Picton (Near Havelock)
Name: "The Devonshires"
Telephone: (03) 574 2930
Fax: (03) 574 2930
Mobile: 025-463 118
Email: devs.1@clear.net.nz
Beds: 1 Queen, 2 Twin (2 bedrooms)
Bathroom: 1 Private Guests share
Tariff: B&B (full) Queen $80, Twin $70, Single $45, Children not suitable, except by arrangement. Dinner $20-$25 each. Special winter rates. Credit cards. NZ B&B Vouchers accepted $20 surcharge ensures exclusive use of guest facilities
Nearest Town: Blenheim 32km, Picton 32km

The Devonshires invite you to share with them the peaceful sounds of forest, bird and sea. Visit Moenui Bay, just ten minutes from Havelock along the scenic Queen Charlotte Drive and forty minutes from the Ferry. Enjoy warm hospitality and sample Marlborough's harvest from orchard, farm, vineyard and sea. Brian, an educator, American Football buff and keen fisherman, has a good working knowledge of South Island wines. Susan enjoys painting, gardening, craftwork and practising her culinary skills. Your guest bathroom is adjacent to the well appointed bedrooms. Enjoy spacious living areas with expansive sea views. Guests can choose to enjoy the garden and listen to the birds or use our home as a base for exploring Marlborough. Our meals, served with pride, feature home-baking and preserves, herbs, fresh seafood, fruit, local cheeses and flavoursome egg dishes. Please - no smoking in the house. Longer visits welcomed. Water and vineyard tours arranged.
P.S. Lucy and Mindy are the resident cats.

Port Underwood Sound
Country Homestay
Address: 'Ocean Ridge',
Ocean Bay, Private Bag, Blenheim
Name: Ken & Sara Roush
Telephone: (03) 579 9474
Fax: (03) 579 9474
Email: roush@nmb.quik.co.nz
Beds: 2 Queen, 1 Double, 1 Single (3 bdrms)
Bathroom: 3 Ensuite
Tariff: B&B (continental) Double $95/$125, Single $70/$95.
Dinner by arrangement $30pp. Not suitable for children. Credit Cards Visa/Mastercard
Nearest Town: 35km (45 mins)Nth of Blenheim, 35km (60 min)Sth of Picton via Port Underwood Rd.

Fifty acres of solitude from Clifftops to shore line with magnificent views of Port Underwood Sound, Pacific Ocean, snow-capped mountains and rocky coastline, a perfect place to break your journey for several days. Sara and Ken invite you to share this beautiful, peaceful area with them, their cats, and friendly dog. For the active there is fishing, diving and beach combing nearby, and several steep, rugged nature tracks to the water's edge on the property. A hot spa pool is available for those wishing to relax. You might see orcas, dolphins or seals playfully swimming in the waters just below our home, watch Ken and Sara create their unique pewter sculptures and jewellery, or at night, star gaze with Ken and his telescope. The separate guest area has three large bedrooms (each with its own bathroom) and a kitchen, dining, lounge area for the exclusive use of our guests. All rooms have water views.
Home Page: http://www.nmb.quik.co.nz/roush

Blenheim
Farmstay
Address: 'Rhododendron Lodge', State Highway 1,
St Andrews, R.D.4, Blenheim
Name: Charlie & Audrey Chambers
Telephone: (03) 578 1145
Fax: (03) 578 1145
Beds: 2 Queen, 2 Single (2 bedrooms + 1 Suite)
Bathroom: 1 Ensuite, 1 Private
Tariff: B&B (full) Double $70,
Single $50, Suite $90. 10% discount 3 days or more.
NZ B&B Vouchers accepted Suite $10 surcharge
Nearest Town: Blenheim 1.5km

Welcome to previous guests and new ones. We have retired to an attractive small farm in Blenheim, where we provide quality accommodation in our spacious home. Excellent beds with Woolrest underlays and electric blankets. Bacon, eggs and tomatoes all produced on our farm make a delicious breakfast. Our executive suite has a "Bechstein" piano in it. A private courtyard with tree ferns and gardens surrounds a large swimming pool. Extensive lawns and gardens with rhododendrons, roses and many trees. We are close to Blenheim's gourmet restaurants and have available a selection of their menus. Marlborough has much to offer - beautiful parks, wine trails, scenic Marlborough Sounds and walkways. Visitors travelling by train or bus will be collected in Blenheim. Laundry available and courtesy phone call for next homestay. Purified water available for guests.
Directions: *1.5 km south from town centre on SH 1. Large sign at gate. We are 20 minutes from Picton ferry - "Happy Holidays".*

Blenheim
Homestay
Address: "Hillsview" - Please phone
Name: Adrienne & Rex Handley
Telephone: (03) 578 9562
Fax: (03) 578 9562
Beds: 1 King, 1 Double, 5 Single (4 bdrms)
- 1 double, 2 twin (1 converts Kingsize) 1 single (4 Bdrms)
Bathroom: 2 Private
Tariff: B&B (Full) Kingsize $75, Double/Twin $70, Single $45,
(Tariff less 10% if prebooked by night before), Dinner by arrangement.
NZ B&B Vouchers accepted
Nearest Town: Blenheim 3km from Town Centre

Welcome to our warm and spacious 1970's era home situated in a quiet southern suburb with its mature trees, flowering shrubs, sundeck, outdoor pool, ample off road parking and no pets. Two renovated private bathrooms (one per party) serve the four heated guest rooms. All beds have quality mattresses, electric blankets and wool overlays. Your hosts are a non smoking married couple with a grown up family and enjoy sharing mutual travel experiences. Rex, a retired airline pilot, has interests in all aspects of aviation from models to home builts and gliding - also builds miniature steam locomotives. Adrienne enjoys cooking, spinning and woolcraft hobbies. We offer our vintage model A Ford soft top tourer for hood down rides or to be photographed in, and sightseeing flights around Marlborough can also be arranged. Comments from our guest book suggest our home has a warm and friendly atmosphere. We invite you to sample this along with our caring personal attention and complimentary beverages.

Blenheim

Homestay
Address: 'Mirfield', 722 Severne Street, Blenheim
Name: Pam & Charles Hamilton
Telephone: (03) 578 8220
Freephone: 0800 395 720
Fax: (03) 578 8220
Mobile: 025 2845912
Beds: 2 Queen, 2 Single (3 bedrooms)
Bathroom: 2 Private, 1 Family share
Tariff: B&B (continental, cooked breakfast $5 extra pp) Double $70, Single $40,
Children half price up to 12 years, Dinner (by arrangement) $17.50.
NZ B&B Vouchers accepted
Nearest Town: Blenheim Town Centre: 3km

Welcome to Marlborough and our spacious family home that offers two private TV lounges, comfortable beds and homely hospitality. If you haven't tried B&B before - try us, as we cater for individuals, couples or small groups. We enjoy meeting people having hosted for eleven years, and will be sensitive to your needs. Our interests include commercial flower growing, sports, hand knits, and we offer organically grown produce for your enjoyment. "Mirfield" is handy to wineries, Rainbow Skifield and the Sounds with its walkways and sea activities. It is a stopping place for those using the ferries, airport, or en route elsewhere. Our rates should entice you to stay longer. By arrangement, transport could be provided to and from departure points. Make your destination Marlborough and stay with us.
Directions: *Highway 6 from Blenheim to Nelson. Turn first left after the Shell Service Station. Opposite the last street light.*

Blenheim

Farmstay
Address: Maxwell Pass,
PO Box 269, Blenheim
Name: Jean & John Leslie
Telephone: (03) 578 1941
Fax: (03) 578 1941
Beds: 1 Double,
3 Single (3 bedrooms)
Bathroom: 1 Private, 1 Family share
Tariff: B&B (full) Double $75, Single $40,
Dinner by arrangement. Children half price. Credit cards.
Nearest Town: Blenheim 8 km

We live 8 km from Blenheim on a 750 acre hill country property running beef cattle. Our home is two-storeyed in a quiet valley with spacious grounds and lots of native birds. All beds have woollen overlays and electric blankets. Laundry available. Now that our family are all married we enjoy spending time with guests. Marlborough is a major grape growing area with several wineries plus horticulture, agriculture and livestock farming from high country to the coast. Marlborough Sounds is nearby either by sea or road. Trout fishing is also close at hand and there is a skifield 1 1/2 hours drive. Blenheim has a golf course, croquet green and hard and grass tennis court as well as beautiful gardens. Horse trekking 5 mins drive. No pets.
Directions: *Please phone.*

Blenheim
Vineyard Homestay+Self-catering Accommodation
Address: Thainstone, Giffords Road., R.D. 3, Blenheim
Name: Jim & Vivienne Murray
Telephone: (03) 572 8823
Fax: (03) 572 8623
Mobile: (021) 283 1484
Email: thainsto@voyager.co.nz
Beds: 1 King, 1 Queen, 1 Double, 1 Single (3 bdrms).
Self contained house: 1 Queen, 2 Single (2 bdrms)
Bathroom: 1 Ensuite, 1 Guests share; Self contained house: 1 bathroom
Tariff: B&B (full) Double $95, Single $55, Dinner $25. Accommodation only in self-catering house $90-150 (2 to 4 people), Credit Cards (VISA/MC/BC/American Express).
NZ B&B Vouchers accepted $20 surcharge, same day restriction.
Nearest Town: 12km NW of Blenheim off Rapaura Rd, a Picton-Nelson through route.

We have a very large comfortable home set in our own vineyard and surrounded by neighbouring vineyards and orchards. We have our own wine labels, Thainstone Sauvignon Blanc and Chardonnay and our winery on Rapaura Road. We are central to most other Marlborough wineries, only a few minutes from the airport, and 30 minutes from the ferry. Our home has a guest wing that includes three spacious bedrooms, a lounge, dining room, 2 bathrooms and also tea/coffee making facilities. The self-catering house, set back from our home with its own driveway, is fully equipped with a modern kitchen, bathroom, two bedrooms and lounge. We have a swimming pool in our BBQ area. We are widely travelled and have many interests including woodworking, tramping, card playing and trout fishing. Our family have left home and we have no pets, but enjoy bird watching and the outdoor life. Our evening meals, by prior arrangement, are served with Marlborough wines.
Home Page: http://www.voyager.co.nz/~thainsto/

Blenheim
Homestay+Self-contained units
Address: Chardonnay Lodge,
Rapaura, R.D.3, Blenheim
Name: Lorraine & Alan Hopkins
Telephone: (03) 570 5194
Fax: (03) 570 5194
Beds: 3 Queen, 5 Single (4 bedrooms)
Bathroom: 1 Ensuite. 1 Private
Tariff: B&B (continental) Double Accommodation $89 in Units plus
$20 each extra person. Homestay: Double $89, Twin room $89, Single $89.
NZ B&B Vouchers accepted &25 surcharge
Nearest Town: Blenheim 5 mins

"A VERY SPECIAL PLACE OUR OWN MINI RESORT", comments made by delighted guests and they keep coming back!! Nestled amongst lovely mature trees, beautiful park-like gardens in a country locality, we offer excellent accommodation, modest prices, a sheltered, secluded, large heated swimming pool, spa, top class tennis court and petanque. We are situated on he doorstep of Marlborough's "exciting wine region", close to superb vineyard restaurants, trout fishing rivers, and walks AND still only 6 minutes to Blenheim, 20 mins to Picton. We provide 'in house' B&B accommodation with own ensuites or modern very high standard self contained units, where you can cook for yourself or dine out. OVER TO US -we have travelled extensively, love fishing and golf, have lived beside the sea in the "Sounds" for 19 years and we really enjoy people. Situated on Rapaura Road. Spring Creek turn off. Courtesy vehicle for ferry and airport pick ups.

Blenheim

Country Retreat
Address: 'The Sentinel', Wrekin Road,
R.D.2, Fairhall, Blenheim
Name: Neil & Lyn Berry
Telephone: (03) 572 9143
Fax: (03) 572 9143
Email: The Sentinel@xtra.Co.NZ
Beds: 2 Queen, 2 Single (2 Bedrooms)
Bathroom: 2 Ensuite
Tariff: B&B (special) Double $100, Single $65. Dinner $30pp,
Credit Cards. NZ B&B Vouchers accepted March to October
Nearest Town: Blenheim 15km

*Your hosts Neil and Lyn and their Labrador "Rusty" welcome you to "The Sentinel",
a 35 acre (14ha) property situated 15km west of Blenheim, in the Brancott Valley
beside Marlborough's famous wine trail. We overlook vineyards in the area and the
Lower Wairau Valley to the sea.*
*Our two upstairs guest bedrooms, each containing
a queen and a single bed, have their own private
ensuites. A farm style breakfast is provided.
Dinner is additional by arrangement. All meat,
vegetables and fruit organically grown.Our interests
are pottery, sports, fishing, painting. We can help you
plan, wine trail visit, golf, skiing, tours of
Marlborough, to name just a few. Transport can
be provided to and from Blenheim and the airport.*
Directions: *See Marlborough's Wine Trail map.*

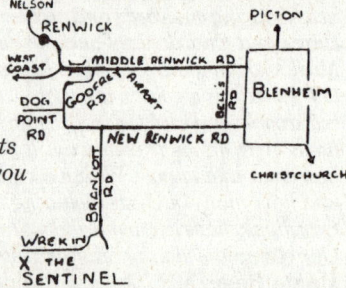

Blenheim

Homestay+Self-contained Accom.
Address: Beaver Bed & Breakfast,
60 Beaver Road,
Blenheim, Marlborough
Name: Jennie & Russell Hopkins
Telephone: (03) 578 8401
Fax: (03) 578 8401
Mobile: (021) 626 151
Email: jhopkins@voyager.co.nz
Beds: 1 Queen (1bedroom)
Bathroom: 1 Ensuite
Tariff: B&B (continental - self serve)
Double $70, Single $50.
Credit cards. NZ B&B Vouchers accepted
Nearest Town: Blenheim 1 Km

*Our self-contained unit can accommodate one couple and is a modern addition to our 90 year
old home. Features include your own entrance, queen size bed, mini kitchen, bathroom - large
bath, shower and a separate toilet. Use of our laundry can be made upon request. Two cats
and a bird live with us in a quiet street. We have off-street parking. We are within ten minutes
walk from central Blenheim and many excellent restaurants. We have a broad local
knowledge and are happy to assist you in exploring Marlborough. Please phone before 8 am
or after 4.30 pm during the working week. If no response, Jennie can be contacted via her cell
phone or fax us anytime.*
Home Page: http://marlborough.co.nz/beaver

Blenheim
Farmstay Retreat
Address: 'Charmwood',
415 Murrays Rd, R.D.3, Blenheim
Name: Bill & Ann Betts
Telephone: (03) 570 5409
Fax: (03) 570 5110
Beds: 2 Queen, 2 Single (3 bedrooms)
Bathroom: 1 Ensuite, 2 Private
Tariff: B&B (full) Double $95-$110, Single $60.
Credit cards. NZ B&B Vouchers accepted Surcharge applies
Nearest Town: Blenheim 5 mins, Picton ferry 20 mins, Airport 10 mins.

Charmwood is comfortably furnished with country charm and touch of luxury and surrounded by large trees and garden areas overlooking paddocks containing stud cattle and sheep. Stroll with our two corgis through the home orchard and aviary area, enjoy game of tennis or swim in pool. Start the day with our special country fare breakfast where we would be happy to help with your itinerary. Close to ferry and airport and conveniently placed at start of wine, craft, garden trails also handy to excellent restaurants and golf courses, trout fishing streams. We are ideally sited to enjoy the boating trips, fishing, visiting green mussel or salmon farms in Marlborough Sounds or taking outback safari. We have enjoyed overseas travel to many countries, have extensive interests and members of Lions service club, non-smokers and welcome guests to our home.

Blenheim
Homestay
Address: 'Wycoller',
106a Maxwell Road,
Blenheim, Marlborough
Name: Valerie & Terry McCormick
Telephone: (03) 578 8522
Beds: 1 Double,
1 Twin (2 bedrooms)
Bathroom: 1 Ensuite, 1 Private
Tariff: B&B (full/continental)
Double $90, Twin $80, Single $60.
Nearest Town: Blenheim 10 minutes walk.

Set amongst tall trees and an expanse of fragrant garden, "Wycoller" has been architecturally designed to blend into its surroundings. Less than an 10 minute stroll into town, Wycoller enjoys the best of both worlds - old fashioned tranquillity and modern convenience. We have a separate guest wing, including tea/coffee making facilities. Relax totally in your own spacious guest wing, or join us to "chat".... as you wish. Your own private patio is there for you to enjoy the garden. Soak up the atmosphere of Wycoller. A short walk away, the town centre offers a diversity of restaurants and excellent cuisine. We are a retired couple, with four grown children, all who have travelled extensively. We enjoy meeting people from all walks of life and would like to extend our warmest hospitality. Modern elegance, tranquillity and exceptional location all give Wycoller a special feel. We welcome you to our home. Please phone first.

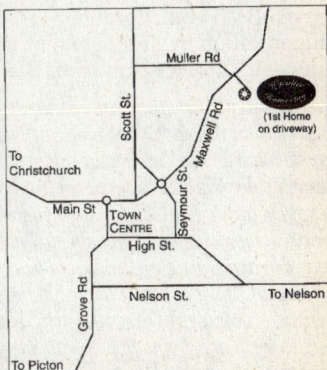

Blenheim
Homestay
Address: 'Philmar Lodge',
6 Gaylee Place, Blenheim
Name: Lex & Wynnis
Telephone: (03) 577 7788
Fax: (03) 577 7788
Beds: 3 Queen, 2 Single
(3 bedrooms)
Bathroom: 1 Ensuite, 1 Guests share
Tariff: B&B (continental) Double $65, Single $45, Children half price.
Dinner $20. Bedroom with ensuite $75.
Nearest Town: Blenheim 2 Kms

Welcome. Our modern home is just 2km from the town centre and has three guest bedrooms, with Queen or Single beds. Guests share bathroom and toilet facilities, one bedroom with ensuite. The TV and tea/coffee area open to a large balcony where you are welcome to smoke as we don't encourage smoking indoors. But to sit with us in our very large formal lounge would be our pleasure. Both members of the Lions organisation. Our other interests include woodturning and all handcrafts. We are also keen TV sports persons. Blenheim is an ideal base from which to visit Nelson, whale watch, wine trails and many other places of interest. Originally from the far South with many years of hosting we enjoy meeting people from most parts of the world. We have 2 cats, Snookie and Cuddles share our home. Just phone from airport, train or bus to be picked up.

Blenheim
Vineyard Homestay
Address: 'Stonehaven',
445A Rapaura Road, R.D.3, Blenheim
Name: David & Jocelyn Wilson
Telephone: (03) 572 9730
Fax: (03) 572 9730
Mobile: 025-222 1656
Email: dgwilson@voyager.co.nz
Beds: 1 King, 1 Queen, 1 Single (3 bedrooms)
Bathroom: 1 Ensuite, 2 Private
Tariff: B&B (full) Double $110-$120, Single $80.
Dinner $40pp by arrangement (with selected wines) .
Nearest Town: 12km from Blenheim. 4km from airport. Transport available.

Our recently built stone and cedar home is surrounded by gardens and 17 acres of Sauvignon Blanc vines. Closeby are some of NZ's most outstanding wineries which we can arrange for you to visit. We have the space, comfort, and privacy to make your stay relaxing and memorable. We like to serve an interesting breakfast in the 'Pavilion' overlooking the pool with its spacious surrounds for summer relaxing. In winter you many enjoy the comfort of an open fire and a good book. Our special interests include travel, books, music, gardening and good food. We are skiing enthusiasts and in winter can introduce you to Marlborough's Rainbow Ski-area. Closer to home we can teach you to play P'etanque on the lawn or arrange golf, tennis, fishing or voyages of discovery in Marlborough's Sounds. Blenheim has a number of excellent restaurants or, if you prefer you may dine with us.
We have a friendly Burmese cat, and are non-smokers.
Home Page: www.voyager.co.nz/~dgwilson/

Blenheim
Vineyard Homestay
Address: 'Black Birch Lodge',
Jeffries Rd, R.D.3, Blenheim
Name: Black Birch Lodge
Telephone: (03) 572 8876
Fax: (03) 572 8806
Email: barnsley@ihug.co.nz
Beds: 2 Queen, 3 Single (3 bedrooms)
Bathroom: 2 Ensuite
Tariff: B&B (full) Double $90-$105, Single $75, Children under 15 half price,
Dinner by arrangement $30 (3 course), Credit Cards (VISA/MC).
NZ B&B Vouchers accepted Surcharge applies
Nearest Town: Blenheim 10 mins, Renwick 5 mins

Black Birch Lodge

Black Birch Lodge is ideally situated for exploring the Marlborough wine trail. Just off Rapaura Road, Black Birch is within ten minutes drive of most of Marlborough's wineries some of which are within easy walking distance. Your hosts David and Margaret Barnsley have been involved in the local wine industry since 1981, both as grape growers and David as editor of "Winepress". They can help you plan your wine trail itinerary or if preferred David offers personally conducted winery tours. In the evening you will return to your ensuite bedroom overlooking our Pinot Noir vineyard. We offer two separate guest lounges; an extensive library; tennis court; swimming pool; petanque and barbecue areas. Mountain bikes are available. Our breakfasts feature freshly baked bread, local preserves, conserves, honey and fruit. Cooked breakfasts available on request. Reduced tariffs for more than two night stays.
Directions: *Please phone, write or fax.*

Blenheim
Homestay
Address: 28 Elisha Drive,
Blenheim
Name: Brian & Kathy Baxter
Telephone: (03) 578 3753
Fax: (03) 578 3796
Beds: 1 Double, 2 Single
(2 bedrooms)
Bathroom: 1 Private, 1 Guests share
Tariff: B&B (full) Double $85-$95,
Single $65-$85, Dinner $25pp.

Our modern comfortable home is in a quiet cul-de-sac with magnificent views over Blenheim and across Cook Strait to the North Island. Guests are able to enjoy their privacy as all the top level of our home is solely allocated to them, including a sheltered deck with outstanding views. A perfect spot to relax and enjoy a coffee or a local wine. Brian is a well known New Zealand artist with home studio/gallery for viewing original paintings i.e. New Zealand landscapes (including local scenes), flowers etc. Our landscaped colourful gardens which have been selected for "Garden Marlborough" tours include special deciduous trees, roses, rhododendrons, camellias, perennials etc. Walks up the Wither Hills behind our home are great exercise and also offer spectacular views. We can arrange tours to wineries, gardens, ski field etc. for our guests. Our interests are: music, fishing, ski-ing, travel, gardens and meeting people.

477

Blenheim
Olive Grove Homestay B&B
Address: "Creekside" Homestay,
774 Rapaura Rd., R.D.3, Blenheim
Name: Libby Fulton & Ken Prain
Telephone: (03) 570 5372
Fax: (03) 570 5650
Email: Ken.creekside@xtra.co.nz
Beds: 2 Queen, 2 Single (2 bedrooms)
Bathroom: 2 Ensuite
Tariff: B&B (continental) Twin $135, Single $90,
Credit Cards welcome (VISA/MC/BC).
Nearest Town: Blenheim 10 mins

"Creekside" Homestay is superbly located on the banks of Spring Creek in the heart of the grape growing area of Blenheim. Our house and attached units are new and modern. The outlook from the house and units is beautifully rural and private down to trees and the creek. We have a 500 tree Olive Grove and 15 acres of grapes. Your rooms are particularly comfortable with queen size beds, underfloor heating, ensuite bathrooms and individual coffee and tea making facilities. We are ideally situated in a rural location close to Blenheim 10 mins, the airport 10 mins, and Picton 20 mins. Vineyard restaurants are close by for lunches and dinner. We are also located adjacent to 6 grass tennis courts for those who want to play tennis. We have a very friendly small dog called VITA who loves chasing tennis balls. Please phone, fax or email for bookings and directions.

Blenheim
Vineyard Stay
Address: De Gyffarde Vineyard,
Giffords Road, Rapaura, Blenheim
Name: Rod & Di Lofthouse
Telephone: (03) 572 8189
Fax: (03) 572 8178
Mobile: (021) 362 777
Email: dgwinz@xtra.co.nz
Beds: 1 Queen and second bedroom available
Bathroom: 1 Ensuite + separate toilet
Tariff: B&B (continental) Double $120, Single $100.
Credit Cards (Visa, M/C) accepted. Discount for more than 2 nights.
Nearest Town: 15km west of Blenheim

De Gyffarde Vineyard in the heart of Marlborough's world renowned wine region is the setting for our pine built home, a few minutes walk from the Wairau river. Sheltered raised decks and paved patios lead to the gardens and solar heated pool. Guest bedroom with views over the vineyard has a Queen size bed and en-suite. Complimentary welcome platter served to guests on arrival, together with De Gyffarde wine made at our Rapaura Road Winery.

Your hosts Rod & Di Lofthouse, originally from England, have both been involved in the film and TV industry for many years and have travelled extensively and enjoy sailing, skiing, and riding.

Wine trails can be arranged for you and vineyard restaurants are close by for lunch and dinner. Together with their golden retriever, Brix, and burmese cat, Sizi, Rod and Di look forward to meeting new friends in their smoke-free home.

Laundry facilities available. Wooldrest and duvet.

478

Blenheim
Farmstay
Address: "Windmill Farm", 908B Main Rd, Riverlands, Blenheim
Name: Millie Amos
Telephone: (03) 577 7853
Fax: (03) 577 7853
Beds: 1 Double, 2 Single (2 bedrooms)
Bathroom: 1 Ensuite, 1 Private
Tariff: B&B (continental) Double $80, Single $50. Credit cards.
Nearest Town: Blenheim 5km

Only 5km south of Blenheim on SH1, you will find Windmill Farm, a spacious and modern home in close proximity to the golf driving range and to Montana Winery. Comfortably appointed spacious twin bedroom with private ensuite and one double bedroom with private bathroom and spa. We have travelled to many countries overseas and aim to make our guests feel welcome and relaxed. We are non smokers who enjoy gardens, travel and meeting people. We welcome you to our home. Please phone first.

Blenheim
Homestay
Address: "Opawa Lodge"
143A Budge Street, Blenheim.

Name: Brian & Cindy Pratt
Telephone: (03) 577 9989
Fax: (03) 577 9949
Mobile: (025) 411 214
Email: b.pratt@xtra.co.nz
Beds: 1 Queen, 1 Double, 2 Single (3 bedrooms)
Bathroom: 1 Ensuite, 1 Guests share
Tariff: B&B (full) Double $100-$130, Single $80,
Dinner by arrangement $35, Campervans facilities, Credit Cards (VISA/MC).
Nearest Town: Blenheim C.P.O. 2 kms

Our home overlooks the Opawa River with stunning rural views of Marlborough. Enjoy breakfast in your private conservatory, with gardens rolling down to the river where you can try your hand at trout fishing or rowing our boat, maybe just feed the ducks. This tranquil setting offers a superb opportunity for relaxation. Opawa Lodge offers outstanding comfortable accommodation with close proximity to the town with its excellent restaurants. However dinner is available by arrangement. The guest lounge has tea and coffee facilities and television, there is also a swimming pool for your enjoyment. Blenheim is ideally situated to visit the world renowned Marlborough Sounds, Vineyards and Rainbow Skifield. Courtesy transport can be provided from airport or ferry, we would be delighted to help with your itinerary. Brian and Cindy's interests included travel, gardening, music and a 1935 vintage sports car. We and our golden retriever "Fenton" look forward to making your stay memorable.
Home Page: http://marlborough.co.nz/opawa/

Blenheim

Bed & Breakfast/Homestay
Address: "GROVE BANK", 362c SH 1,
Grovetown, Blenheim, Marlborough.
Name: Pauline & Peter Pickering
Telephone: 0800 422 632 (0800 4 B and B)
Fax: (03) 578 8407
Email: grovebank@xtra.co.nz
Beds: 4 Queen, 2 Single (4 bedrooms). Plus Family
Unit 3 bedrooms, 2 Private bathroom (sleeps up to 6)
Bathroom: 2 Ensuite, 2 Private
Tariff: B&B (full and continental) Double $65-$75, Single $45, Dinner $25pp.
3 nights 10%, Winter rate 20% discount. Family Unit: from $75 (includes full
breakfast). Credit cards. NZ B&B Vouchers accepted $5 surcharge
Nearest Town: 1 1/2km from Blenheim town centre

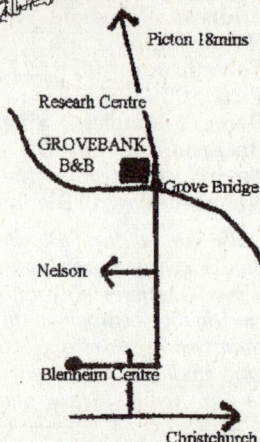

Pauline and Peter invite you to stay at our 8 acre olive grove and vineyard, which is located conveniently on SH1 on the northern boundary of Blenheim. We offer 4 double bedrooms with bathrooms plus bedroom and bathroom appliances and free laundry facilities. Our home is designed especially with homestay guests in mind. Spacious guest lounges (with televisions) opening onto large balconies, offer panoramic views of the plains ranges and river. After a day of sightseeing and enjoying the delights of the "Gourmet Province", cool off in the swimming pool, relax in the spa, take a stroll in Pauline's gardens the olive grove/vineyard. Courtesy transport is available for evening wining and dining. We offer continental and cooked breakfast and meals as requested. A former restaurateur and butcher, Peter's breakfasts are legendary. Evening meals may consist of meats and fresh vegetables or fish caught by Peter from the Marlborough Sounds, rivers and lakes. If you feel like dining out, Marlborough's finest Italian Restaurant (best pasta in the world - "Cuisine"), the Whitehaven winery and cafe and local bar and bistro are within 5 minutes walking distance. We are happy to share our extensive local knowledge and contacts which will enable you to personalise and optimise your stay in the "Gourmet Province".
Directions: *North of Blenheim on SH1 turn left into entrance 100 metres past Grove Road bridge. Travelling south 20 mins/25 kms from Picton, 100 metres before Grove Rd bridge, turn right at Marlborough Research Centre (multi-signed) entrance, then hard left and follow gravel drive.*

Blenheim

Homestay
Address: Uno Più,
75 Murphy's Road, Blenheim
Name: Gino & Heather Rocco
Telephone: (03) 578 2235
Fax: (03) 578 2235
Mobile: (025) 241 4493
Email: unopiu@iname.com
Beds: 2 King, 2 Single (3 bedrooms)
Bathroom: 2 Ensuite, 1 Private
Tariff: B&B (special) Double $125, Single $85,
Extra person $40pp, Dinner $40pp, Credit Cards.
Nearest Town: Blenheim 3km from town centre

Uno Piu' is set in 4 acres and offers comfort, relaxation and Italian hospitality within close proximity of the wineries. Our elegant 1917 homestead is surrounded with established trees and gardens; outdoor furniture awaits on the camomile lawn beside the 10 metre swimming pool. The bedrooms have quality linen, TV, tea/coffee facilities, fridge with complimentary drinks, iron and hairdryer. The European style bathrooms are luxurious and a sauna room is on site. A baby grand piano, open fire, good books and music are for your enjoyment in the guest lounge. Breakfast includes an Italian platter, hot rolls, pancakes, maple syrup, berries and cream served with Italian coffee or a choice of teas, dinner is by arrangement, fresh home made pasta is a speciality. Gino an Italian and Heather a New Zealander enjoy welcoming guests and have interests in wine, food, opera, sea fishing and gardens. We have a friendly collie and 2 cats.
Home Page: http://www.geocities.com/TheTropics/Shores/3129

Blenheim

Bed & Breakfast
Address: 28 Henry Street,
Blenheim, Marlborough
Name: Henry Maxwell's B&B
Telephone: (03) 578 8086
Fax: (03) 578 8089
Mobile: (021) 460 826
Reservation Freephone: (0800) 436 796
Email: b&b@mlb.planet.gen.nz
Beds: 2 Queen, 1 Double, 3 Single (4 bdrms)
Bathroom: 2 Ensuite, 1 Private, 1 Guests share
Tariff: B&B (full) Double/Twin $70-$90, Single $50. Credit Cards.
Nearest Town: In Central Blenheim

"A very special world within your walls" wrote a guest from Geneva when he signed our visitors' wallquilt. Our gracious home is off Maxwell Road, 1 block from shops, cinemas, churches and 11 restaurants. Upstairs is dedicated to guests, offering spacious quiet bedrooms each with TV and comfortable chairs. Complimentary hot and cold drinks are available at any time. Downstairs the sitting room, decorated with maps and charts, provides deep couches in which to read or meet friends. The traditional or lifestyle breakfast features home baking and real coffee served in an elegant dining room or to your bedroom. Relax in the large garden or outdoor spa...... Ample off-street parking, courtesy bikes and laundry facilities provided. Ken & Christy are warm and informal hosts, have wide interests and are microlight enthusiasts. They network with aviators, quilters, Warbirds, golfers, artists, boating, horticulture and wineries. Air, Bus and Rail pickups are available.

Blenheim

Homestay
Address: Maxwell House,
82 Maxwell Road, Blenheim
Name: Gary and Jeanette Tee
Telephone: (03) 577 7545
Fax: (03) 577 7545
Mobile: (025) 234 9977
Beds: 1 Queen, 2 single (2 bedrooms)
Bathroom: 2 Ensuites
Tariff: B&B (full) Double $115, Single $90.
Credit Cards accepted.
Nearest Town: Blenheim (800 metres)

Welcome to Marlborough. Make your stay memorable by staying at Maxwell House, a grand old Victorian residence. Built in the 1880's, our home has been elegantly restored and is classified with the Historic Places Trust.
Our large guest rooms are individually appointed with ensuite, lounge area and television. Breakfast will be a memorable experience. Served either in your room, on the verandah or around our original 1880's kauri table. Make breakfast as formal or informal as you desire. An assortment of teas and coffee are available at any time.
Set on a large established property with ample parking, Maxwell House is an easy ten minute walk to the town centre with its many fine restaurants, bars and cafes.
Your hosts, Gary and Jeanette, love travel. Having travelled extensively throughout the world we will enjoy sharing your experiences with ours. We have a non smoking home. Inspection invited.
Directions: *Please phone or write.*

Blenheim

Vineyard Homestay
Address: "Glenavy", SH 63,
RD1, Blenheim
Name: Jackie and Trevor McGarry
Telephone: (03) 572 9562
Fax: (03) 572 9567
Beds: 1 Queen, 2 Single (2 Bedrooms).
Plus 1 Self Contained Apartment
Bathroom: 1 Private
Tariff: B&B (Full) Double $110, Single $80.
Self Contained Apartment: $160 for 2 people,
Full breakfast included. Dinner $30 pp by arrangement.
Nearest Town: Blenheim, 20 kms west of Blenheim on SH 63

A warm welcome awaits you to our recently built dream home situated in the Wairau Valley overlooking the Wairau River. We offer guests an upstairs self contained apartment with a queen bedroom and full facilities. Guests may choose from the 2 bedrooms in our house. Only one group of visitors at any one time in our home. Tea and coffee making facilities available anytime, guests are welcome to use our laundry. All rooms open onto a verandah and have spectacular views of the Richmond Range and the Wairau River - just 5 minutes walk. Breakfasts are hearty with a choice of full or continental. Evening meals are available by prior arrangement and include fine Marlborough wines. We are situated on a 60 acre developing vineyard, the first vines planted in 1999. We have a black Labrador "Banner" and "Twiggy" the cat. We are a no smoking home. Phone bookings are essential.

Blenheim
Country Homestay
Address: "Green Gables", SH1, St Andrews, RD 4, Blenheim
Name: Ben and Jeannine Van Straaten
Telephone: (03) 577 9205
Fax: (03) 577 9206 **Mobile**: (025) 547 520
Email: linknz@voyager.co.nz
Beds: 1 Queen, 3 Double, 1 Single (3 Bedrooms)
Bathroom: 2 Ensuites.
Tariff: B&B (Continental - cooked breakfast $5 extra pp) Double $85,
Single $40-$60, Dinner $25. 10% discount 3 days or more. Credit cards accepted.
Nearest Town: 2km from Blenheim town centre.

Enjoy your stay at our exceptionally spacious two storey home located in rural Blenheim. Only 2km from the town centre, Green Gables is set in a beautiful, one acre landscaped garden.

Guest accommodation comprises of two large double bedrooms, both with en-suite bathroom. The Blue Room has a queen-size bed and a double bed; the Apricot Room has two double beds. Both rooms are fully equipped with electric blankets, clock radios, hair dryers and room heating and have glass doors opening onto private balconies affording panoramic views of the area. An adjoining guest lounge has a small library and television set, and an additional TV set is available for use in either room. Tea and coffee making facilities are available and you are invited to use the laundry, fax and email facilities if required.

For breakfast choose either a full, country-style, cooked breakfast or a light continental breakfast or if you prefer a delectable combination of both, served with delicious home made jams and preserves. Dinner is available by arrangement and features traditional New Zealand cuisine served with a complimentary drink.

We are horticulturists and grow fresh vegetables and flowers in our green houses. Green Gables backs onto the picturesque Opawa River. In season this gentle river offers trout fishing, eeling and whitebaiting. A small rowing boat is available for your use at no extra charge. Our ginger cat Sharky is visitor friendly and lives outside. An additional courtesy, we would be pleased to help you with the on-booking of your bed and breakfast accommodation. Let us phone ahead for you and you'll make valuable savings on your phone card.

Directions: *On SH1, 2 km south of Blenheim town, gate number 859A. 20 minutes from Picton ferry. Green Gables sign at drive entrance.*
Home Page: http://marlborough.co.nz/green_gables

Blenheim
B&B/Homestay
Address: "Close In Bed & Breakfast",
109 Charles Street, Blenheim
Name: Warren and Sylvia Minogue
Telephone: (03) 578 2761
Fax: (03) 578 2761
Mobile: (021) 251 6311
Email: close-in@xtra.co.nz
Beds: 1 Queen, 5 Single
(3 Bedrooms)
Bathroom: 1 Guests share
Tariff: B&B (Continental) Double $70, Single $40,
Dinner $20 by arrangement. Credit Cards: Visa, Vouchers accepted.
Nearest Town: Blenheim (3 mins walk to town centre).

If you need a place to lay back and catch your breath, or just a place to touch down at, our comfortable home is just what's needed. We are a very relaxed and easy going couple that enjoy having guests in our home. Being only 3 minutes walk from the town centre it makes most places accessible by foot. We can help you plan your stay in our beautiful town. Warren is a keen outdoor bowler and a TV sports viewer, Sylv enjoys a wide variety of crafts. Free pre-arranged pick up from airport, bus stops and train available. Wine trail mini bus does pick up and drop off at our door. Good bicycles for free use. Laundry facilities on request. Diabetics catered for. Off street parking. And most of all a warm welcome at Close In where 'nothing is a problem'.

Koromiko, Blenheim
Homestay
Address: SH 1, Koromiko
RD 3, Blenheim
Name: Koro Park Lodge
Telephone: (03) 573 5542
Fax: (03) 573 5548
Beds: 2 Queen, 3 Single
(3 Bedrooms)
Bathroom: 1 Ensuite (spa), 1 Private
Tariff: B&B (Special/Continental)
Queen $110/$150, Single $70, Dinner $35 pp.
Credit Cards: Visa/Mastercard.
Nearest Town: Picton, 5 mins.

Welcome to our little slice of heaven, set in 1 hectare of gardens, nestled in a rural valley, 9km from Picton ferry terminal, gateway to fishing, wineries and beautiful scenery. Golf course 1km away.
We offer warm, homely hospitality, breakfast to delight, and use of the laundry, plus all the comforts of home. Tom has a wealth of talent with wood, producing lots of fine furniture in his workshop for our home. I, Vonnie, love gardening and have a keen interest in crafts.
Our main aim is to make your stay with us a memorable one and a taste of winding ng down on your holiday, taking time to smell the flowers.
Situated on SH1, we are easy to find in Koromiko.

Renwick

Homestay
Address: "Devonia", 2A Nelson Place,
Renwick, Marlborough
Name: Maurie & Marg Beuth
Telephone: (03) 572 9593
Fax: (03) 572 7293
Beds: 1 Queen, 2 Single (2 bedrooms)
Bathroom: 2 Private
Tariff: B&B (full) Double $75-$85,
Single $55. Credit cards.
Nearest Town: Blenheim 10km

Our colonial style home is set in 1/2 acre of lovely private grounds, in the very heart of vineyard country. We overlook orchards and out to the Richmond Range.
In summer, relax under the trees with tea, coffee or a local wine - or by a glowing fire in winter.
Visit our quaint local English country pub or dine at one of the many vineyard or village restaurants.
We are within "stroll and taste" distance of a number of prestigious vineyards.
Our interests are many and varied. In early married life we farmed and later chartered our 38' sloop. We have four adult children - all now flown the nest.
For a number of years we have been well known in the hospitality industry and are suitably equipped to meet all your needs.
A warm welcome definitely awaits you at "Devonia"
10km from Blenheim, on Highway 6 to Nelson.

Renwick

Garden Homestay
Address:
Name: "Broomfield"
Telephone: (03) 572 8162
Mobile: (021) 226 1769
Beds: 1 King (1 bedroom)
Bathroom: 1 Ensuite
Tariff: B&B (full) Double $120.
Nearest Town: Blenheim 12 Kms

Broomfield is our two storeyed rammed earth house set beside a nectarine orchard in the heart of Renwick wine country.
The house decor is very country as befits its earthy origins. We have a spacious upstairs bedroom for you with excellent bedding, a sitting area, and TV. The bedroom overlooks our charmingly laid out gardens with an interesting potager. Our garden is very much a feature of our home and guests are most welcome to wander through. The house is warmed throughout by radiators from a wood and coal range.
We are 15 mins from Blenheim and 5 mins from the airport. Around us within 5-10 mins are 16 wineries (8 with restaurants) plus country gardens, an olive grove, a pottery and wonderful fruit orchards. Transport around the wineries can be arranged (for the hirage) by horse and cart or bicycle. Breakfast is special. We have one cat. We look forward to meeting you. Please phone if possible.
Directions: *Off High Street Renwick into Inkerman Street, 1st house on L past old hotel on corner. Signposted.*

Renwick - Blenheim

Vineyard Stay+Self-contained Accommodation
Address: LeGrys Vineyard, Conders Bend Road,
Renwick, Marlborough
Name: John & Jennifer Joslin
Telephone: (03) 572 9490
Fax: (03) 572 9491 **Mobile**: (021) 313 208
Email: legrys@voyager.co.nz
Beds: 1 Queen (1 bedroom) Self-contained:1 Queen, 2 Single (2 bedrooms)
Bathroom: 1 Private. Self-contained: 1 bathroom, lounge, cooking & dining facilities
Tariff: B&B (full) Double $120, S/C: $170 for two, $35 each extra person.Visa/MC.
Nearest Town: Blenheim. 12 kms. Picton 25 mins

LeGrys vineyard "Homestay" and "Water-fall Lodge" separate-secluded, self-contained accommodation, offer you the chance to stay on a vineyard in either a unique cottage or home both built of Mud-blocks. The two bedroom Lodge offers peace, tranquillity and seclusion beside a trickling stream amongst the vines. House and Lodge both offer rustic charm with complementary furnishings, warm comfortable beds, luxury bathroom, gas BBQ available. Lodge is a one group situation and is ideal for honeymooners. Heated indoor pool available for guests. Stunning views - Richmond ranges and vineyard. We are ideally situated for winery visits, many with restaurants. River walks, trout fishing, country gardens, olive-groves, Sounds cruising, and the delightful town of Blenheim only 10 mins drive. "LeGrys" own label wines are available with complimentary tastings and snacks on arrival to welcome you. John and Jennifer cruised the world in their yacht, enjoy meeting people and look forward to making your stay memorable. We have a springer spaniel, Pippin who is part of our family.
Home Page: http://nz.com/webnz/bbnz/legrys.htm

Blenheim - Waihopai Valley

Farmstay & S.C. Cottage
Address: "Netherwood",
Waihopai Valley Road, 6 RD Blenheim 7321
Name: Nola & Bruce Dick
Telephone: (03) 572 4044
Fax: (03) 572 4043
Beds: 1 Queen, 2 Single (2 bedrooms)
Bathroom: 1 Private (per single party booking)
Tariff: B&B (full/continental) Double $140, Single $120.
Each extra person $50. Dinner $30 pp, Lunch available. Campervans $30.
Credit Cards NZ B&B vouchers accepted - $40 surcharge.
Nearest Town: Blenheim 50km

We invite you to share our home and lifestyle in an idyllic setting on Netherwood, our 3000 acre property in the beautiful Waihopai Valley. Only one hour to Picton, 45 minutes to Blenheim on sealed road. Closer to wine trail. Delicious country-style meals (lamb a speciality) using home-grown and Marlborough 'gourmet province' produce, with wine included. Congenial non-smoking hosts, family away from home, one indoor cat. You are welcome to smoke on the verandahs. On farm experiences - the garden, swimming, walking in the valleys, tramping the hills, farm activities and animals. Guest annexe has woolrests and electric blankets on the beds, heaters in rooms. We take only one booking per night. Laundry facilities. Also available - self contained cottage. **Directions**: *From Blenheim - SH6 to West Coast Road, then SH63 for 3 km. Turn left at Grove Mill Winery into Waihopai Valley. Follow this sealed road 40 km to number 1114. Please phone for availability.*

Awatere Valley, Blenheim

Farmstay
Address: "Duntroon", Awatere Valley Rd,
Private Bag, Blenheim
Name: Trish & Robert Oswald
Telephone: (03) 575 7374
Fax: (03) 575 7374
Mobile: (025) 865 223
Email: oswald@xtra.co.nz
Beds: 1 Double, 6 Single (4 bedrooms)
Bathroom: 1 Guests share, 1 Family share
Tariff: B&B (full) Double from $90, Single $65, Children under 15 half price,
Lunch $15, Dinner $30 (three course), Credit Cards.
Nearest Town: Blenheim 63km, Oak Tree Cottage 42km

We welcome you to our character villa built in 1917, set in lovely established grounds with pool and tennis court. Our home has been renovated and centrally heated, the bedrooms are spacious with comfortable beds, electric blankets and guest shared bathroom. Laundry available. Lunch and dinner by arrangement. "Duntroon" a 3500 acre property has been in the Oswald family for three generations, and carried 4500 Merino sheep and 300 Angus cattle. It is located in the high country of the picturesque Awatere Valley. We have three sons, all away from home at present, our family also includes 2 cats, our interests include clay target shooting, boating, tennis, skiing, sewing, fishing. We enjoy meeting people and invite you to share high country life with us for a night or longer. Farm tours by arrangement. Over the summer the Awatere Valley Road is open through Molesworth Station to Hanmer Springs. Some of the Awatere Valley road is gravel, but it is very lovely and well worth the drive.
Directions: *Please phone ahead as bookings are necessary.*

Rai Valley

2 Self-contained Chalets
Address: Bulford Lodge,
Bulford Road, RD 2, Rai Valley
Name: Iris & Helmut
Telephone: (03) 571 6049
Fax: (03) 571 6049
Mobile: 025- 2414 498
Beds: 2 Queen, 1 Double,
4 Single (3 bedrooms).
Bathroom: 2 Private
Tariff: Double $75-$100, Single $65. Breakfast (continental) $8 pp extra.
Dinner $30 by arrangement. NZ B&B Vouchers accepted $31 surcharge
Nearest Town: Halfway between Blenheim and Nelson 76km

Bulford Lodge offers a unique combination of European style accommodation with warm hospitality of their 125 acre property. Guests will enjoy the comfort of their own chalet with kitchen and bathroom. Chalet 2 has its own dishwasher. The chalet nestled amongst the trees on the hills overlooks the lush pastureland of Rai Valley. Bulford Lodge is ideally situated to take advantage of all recreational and cultural activities of Marlborough and Nelson. Walking, fishing and hunting in nearby Mount Richmond Forest Park and Rai River. Boat and fishing tours in the Marlborough Sounds. Explore the historic Maungatapu track and Wakamarina goldfields. Alternatively you may relax on the terrace and enjoy the flower garden or choose to walk around the property and listen to the birds. Homemade bread a speciality. Foot reflexology massage available on request. Wirfreuen uns auf Ihren Besuch. Iris and Helmut speak English, German and French.

Nelson, Golden Bay

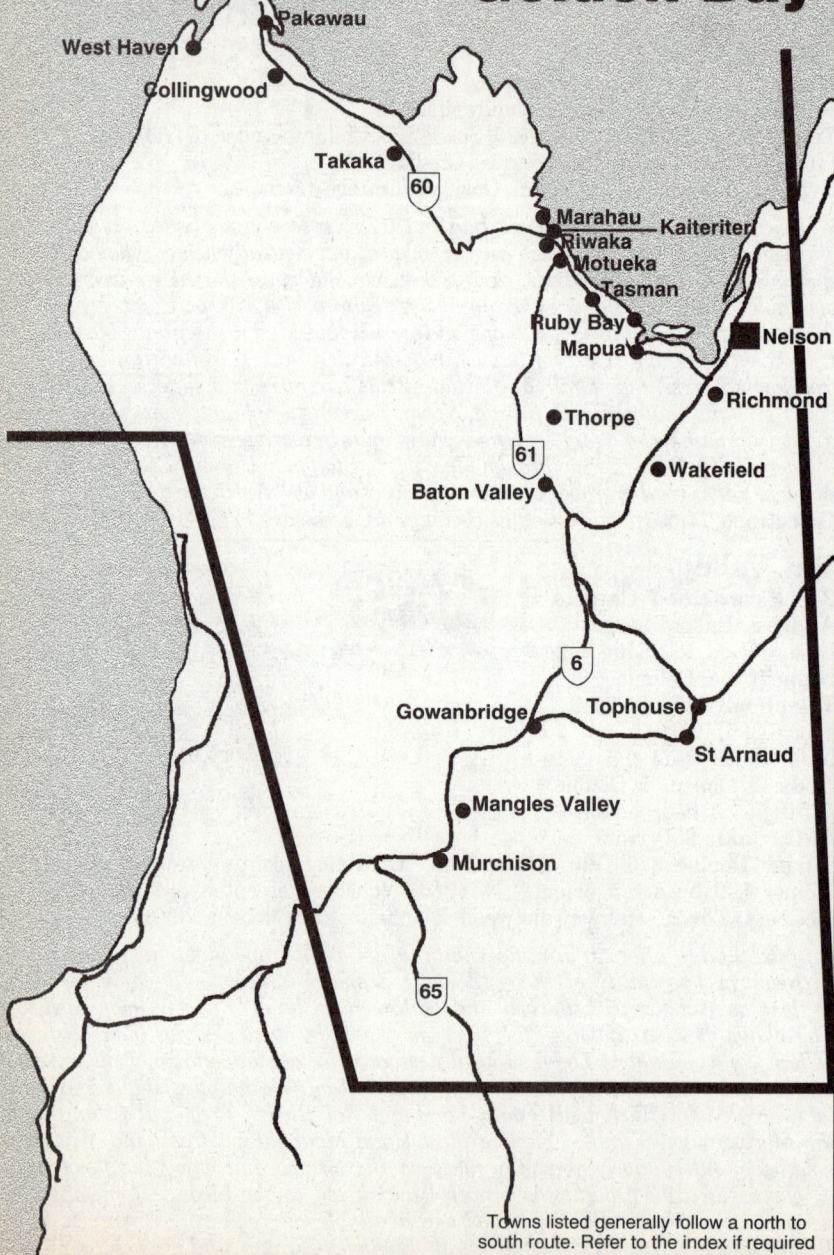

West Haven •

Pakawau •

Collingwood •

Takaka •

60

Marahau •
Riwaka •
Motueka •
Tasman •
Ruby Bay •
Mapua •

Kaiteriteri

■ Nelson

• Richmond

Thorpe •

61

• Wakefield

Baton Valley •

6

Gowanbridge •

Tophouse •

St Arnaud •

Mangles Valley •

Murchison •

65

Towns listed generally follow a north to
south route. Refer to the index if required

488

Nelson
Heritage Inn
Address: 'California House Inn'
29 Collingwood Street, Nelson
Name: Neil and Shelley Johnstone
Telephone: (03) 548 4173
Fax: (03) 548 4173
Email: calhouse@tasman.net
Beds: 4 Queen, 1 Double, 1 Twin, 1 Triple (5 bedrooms)
Bathroom: 5 Ensuite
Tariff: B&B (Special) Double $150-$185, Single $125-$140.
Credit cards (MC, Visa) NZ B&B Vouchers accepted $90 surcharge
Nearest Town: Nelson - 3 blocks from town centre.

*CALIFORNIA HOUSE is set back from the street in a quiet residential area yet is handily located within 5 minutes walk from the town centre. This beautifully preserved example of Victorian architecture built in 1893 is classified by the NZ Historic Places Trust and features wide, sunny verandahs overlooking established gardens, English oak panelling, art nouveau stained glass windows, open fires and spacious rooms. Our guest accommodation includes sitting room and library with games and morning / afternoon tea facilities and 5 individually decorated guest rooms, each with ensuite bathroom. The house is furnished throughout with colonial oak furniture, antiques, Persian rugs, memorabilia and fresh flowers from the garden. Guests enjoy leisurely home-baked Californian breakfasts in our sunny dining room. These may include Finnish pancakes with strawberries, asparagus frittata, baked French toast, ham and sour cream omelette and fresh juices, muffins, coffee and teas.
No smoking inside the house please.*
Home Page: http://www.californiahouse.co.nz

CALIFORNIA HOUSE

1893

Tahunanui, Nelson
Homestay
Address: 'Bagust Retreat',
201 Annesbrook Drive, Nelson
Name: Junie Bagust
Telephone: (03) 548 5868
Mobile: 025 243 1280
Beds: 1 Queen, 1 Queen Postupaedic, 1 Single (2 bedrooms)
Bathroom: 2 Ensuite
Tariff: B&B (continental)
Double $60 & $65, Single $50,
Children $12, NZ B&B Vouchers accepted
Nearest Town: Tahunanui, Nelson 4 km

WE ARE HERE

Drive up our private drive from Highway 6 to our peaceful home in a quiet sunny bush setting with views. Each delightful bedsit has its own separate entrance with some covered parking, ensuite, TV, fridge, electric blankets, hair dryer, heating, table and chairs, tea and toast facilities, microwave, also homemade extras. Telephone available. Our ancestors came to Nelson in 1842 and we feel very proud of our city and district with its many tourist attractions. We have toured extensively throughout N.Z. Also overseas and we delight to return the hospitality we have received from both our overseas and NZ friends. We extend a warm welcome to anyone visiting our city. Near Tahuna beach, golf course and airport we are only 4 kilometres to the city centre on a main bus route. Our nicest compliment is that all our guests want to return. Reasonably priced restaurants near. Look for the lime green letterbox!!

Nelson

Homestay
Address: Harbour View Homestay, 11 Fifeshire Crescent, Nelson
Name: Judy Black
Telephone: (03) 548 8567
Fax: (03) 548 8667
Mobile: (025) 247 4445
Beds: 2 Queen, 2 Single (3 bedrooms)
Bathroom: 2 Ensuite, 1 Private
Tariff: B&B (full or continental) Double $110-$115, Single $65-$80, Children by arrangement. Credit cards (VISA/MC).
NZ B&B Vouchers accepted $35-$40 surcharge for double
Nearest Town: Midway between Tahunanui Beach and Nelson City via the waterfront.

Our home is above the harbour entrance with huge windows and decks to capture the spectacular views of beautiful Tasman Bay, Haulashore Island, Tahunanui Beach, and across the sea to Abel Tasman National Park and mountains. You can observe from the decks, dining-room, or BBQ, ships and pleasure craft cruising by as they enter and leave the harbour.

If you can tear yourself away from our magnificent view, within walking distance along the waterfront there are excellent cafes and restaurants. A few more minutes will take you to our popular swimming beach or city centre for shopping.

We want our guests to completely relax therefore all our bedrooms have private bathrooms, electric blankets and central heating in winter. We thank you for not smoking inside, outside is fine. Judy, your host, offers you a warm welcome and a memorable stay.

Directions: *We would be happy to meet you at the airport or bus or if directions are required please phone.*

Nelson

Homestay
Address: 4 Seaton Street, Atawhai, Nelson
Name: Mike Cooper & Lennane Kent
Telephone: (03) 545 1671
Fax: (03) 545 1671
Beds: 1 Double, 2 Single (2 bedrooms)
Bathroom: 2 Ensuites
Tariff: B&B (full) Double $65, Single $40, Three persons $90, Dinner $25pp, Credit Cards. NZ B&B Vouchers accepted No surcharge.
Nearest Town: 6km from Nelson close to main Picton & Blenheim Road

Only five minutes from Nelson city centre we offer you quiet, comfortable, safe accommodation with superb views across Tasman Bay to the mountains beyond.

Widely travelled ourselves we know the importance of a hot shower, a clean comfortable bed and helpful service. Although our guest accommodation is virtually self contained on the ground floor of our two level home, you are welcome to join us for the evening or be as independent as you wish. The garden and verandah deck are also available for your enjoyment. The small guest lounge houses part of our large collection of books among which you are welcome to browse. Tea and coffee making facilities, a microwave oven and a washing machine are available for your use.

Our interests include education, sea fishing and boating, veterans class running and canine obedience with our beautiful and friendly schnauzer dog.

We are a non-smoking household.

Directions: *We can give you simple directions or meet you in town or at the airport.*

NELSON WATERFRONT

SPINNAKER HOMESTAY

Margaret & George

Nelson Central
Homestay
Address: 'Spinnaker Homestay', 7 Victoria Road, Nelson
Name: George & Margaret Collins
Telephone: (03) 548 8669 **Fax**: (03) 548 8663 **Mobile**: (025) 487 603
Beds: Queen, Twin & Single accommodation available.
Bathroom: Guest rooms have private bathrooms.
Tariff: B&B (full) Double $85, Single $60.
MEALS: Home-style meals available by arrangement.
NZ B&B Vouchers accepted $15 surcharge
Nearest Town: Nelson city centre 2.5 kms, Tahunanui Beach 2kms.

Spinnaker Homestay offers all that is best in warm Kiwi hospitality. Margaret and George have a friendly, informal private home - a very comfortable, peaceful, convenient environment. It has extensive views of harbour, Tasman Bay and mountain ranges.

The colourful waterfront area is just a few steps away; the centre of Nelson City is a few minutes drive or a pleasant flat walk; beautiful Tahunanui Beach is within an easy distance; and the airport is about 10 minutes away. This is an ideal stepping off point for your Nelson-Golden Bay experience.

We are a hospitable couple, keen trampers and much travelled. We enjoy exchanging "travellers tales" with congenial company.

Complimentary pick-up and delivery of guests for airport and other local terminals.

THIS IS A SMOKE FREE ZONE.
000000000000000

ASK ABOUT MARGARET'S "SPINNAKER KNITS"
Hand knitted garments for adults and children are available from stock or to order at knitter to buyer prices.

Directions: *WE'RE EASY TO FIND!*
Victoria Road is easy to find. It is about half-way between the City and Tahunanui, on the waterfront drive South of the City. You'll see the Boatshed Cafe on Wakefield Quay. Victoria Road is almost directly opposite. Spinnaker Homestay is just four houses up on the left ... look for our sign.

Nelson

Inner-city Bed & Breakfast
Address: 'Borogove',
27 Grove St, Nelson
Name: Bill & Judy Hiener
Telephone: (03) 548 9442
Email: hiener.fam@xtra.co.nz
Beds: 2 Queen,
1 Single (3 Bedrooms).
Separate laundry available.
Bathroom: 3 Ensuite
Tariff: B&B (Full) Double $85/Twin $90, Single $65.
Nearest Town: 3 Blocks from town centre.

Borogove is under 5 minutes' stroll from the Information Centre, Post Office, shops and restaurants. Set within a secluded and fragrant English garden, our elegant 1907 Edwardian villa is of authentic New Zealand design, with the characteristic high ceilings, glowing rimu woodwork and spaciousness of that era. Period furnishings and antiques contribute to its unique charm. Each self-contained bedroom is delightfully decorated and has its own ensuite bathroom. Relaxing arm-chairs, tea/coffee, heaters, electric blankets, reading lights, TV and writing table ensure your comfort. A generous cooked breakfast is served in our Victorian Dining room, warmed by an open fire in winter. Nelsonians for many years, we are familiar with its many attractions and we look forward to welcoming you to our heritage home. Our interests include historical research and genealogy. Arrangements made for Abel Tasman bus collection from our door. Off-street parking available. No smokers please.

Tahunanui, Nelson

Homestay
Address: 'Treetops',
 156 Moana Avenue,
Tahunanui, Nelson
Name: Jim & Jill Mills
Telephone: (03) 548 5831
Fax: (03) 548 5831
Beds: 1 Double,
2 Single (2 bedrooms)
Bathroom: 1 Guests share *Rooms with a View*
Tariff: B&B (full) Double $80, Single $55,
Dinner by arrangement $25. NZ B&B Vouchers accepted $10 surcharge
Nearest Town: Nelson 3 Kms

We warmly welcome visitors to our hillside home above Tahunanui Beach. Panoramic views from the house and deck of Tasman Bay and the Mount Arthur Range are part of our life, as are the frequent magnificent sunsets. Alternatively we have a secluded patio with herb garden for sitting and relaxing. Downstairs, between the modern, comfortable guest rooms, is a sitting room with TV, books, writing area, tea/coffee facilities and a deck if you wish to be on your own. Our house is a few minutes drive from the airport, beautiful beach, city centre, many excellent restaurants, golf course and tennis courts. Having travelled extensively ourselves, we love to meet visitors from all parts. Our interests include sailing, gardening, walking, tennis, golf, cooking, fly and sea fishing, and we can usually arrange these and other activities for our guests. **Directions**: *Please ring for directions or we can pick you up from the city or airport.*

Nelson

Self-contained Homestay Units
Address: 'Arapiki', 21 Arapiki Road, Stoke, Nelson
Name: Kay & Geoff Gudsell
Telephone: (03) 547 3741
Fax: (03) 547 3742
Mobile: (025) 517 131
Email: arapiki@nelson.planet.org.nz
Beds: 1 Queen, 1 Double, 1 Single (2 bedrooms)
Bathroom: 2 Private
Tariff: Unit: 1 Single $60, Double $75; Unit 2: Single $55, Double $65 (ask about reductions for longer stays), Continental Breakfast $5, Dinner $20 pp. Credit Cards accepted. NZ B&B Vouchers accepted $15 surcharge for Unit 1. Same day restriction.
Nearest Town: Stoke Shopping Centre 1km, Nelson/Richmond 7km

The two units in our large home offer you comfort and privacy and are also very suitable for longer stays. You need at least two days to enjoy the attractive Nelson area. Unit 1 which is larger is in a pleasant and private garden setting. A ranchslider opens out to a new deck with outdoor furniture for your use. It has an Electric Stove, Microwave, TV, Auto Washing Machine and Phone available. 2 beds in private 'Sunroom' could sleep additional family members. Unit 2 has a balcony setting with seating to enjoy sea and mountain views. It has TV, Microwave, and Phone available. We have 2 cats and an elderly Labrador dog. Offstreet parking is provided. We are very centrally located in the Nelson area. Meals are by arrangement. Quiet, Friendly and Comfortable. Both units are 'SMOKEFREE'.
Home Page: www.ts.co.nz/brochures/arapiki/

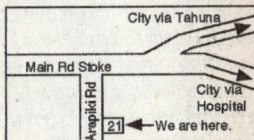

Stoke, Nelson

Homestay
Address: 'Tarata Homestay' 5 Tarata St, Stoke, Nelson
Name: Mercia and John Hoskin
Telephone: (03) 547 3426 Freephone 0800 107 308
Fax: (03) 547 3640
Email: john.mercia@xtra.co.nz
Beds: 1 Double, 2 Single (2 bedrooms)
Bathroom: 1 Private
Tariff: B&B (continental) Double $80, Single $60.
Credit cards accepted. NZ B&B Vouchers accepted
Nearest Town: Nelson or Richmond 6 km

In a quiet cul-de-sac away from the busy main road, surrounded by gardens and mature trees, our family style home captures the best of the Nelson sun. We offer quality accommodation for up to four in one group so that guests have exclusive use of the facilities. These include a comfortable lounge with TV, video and tea / coffee making facilities. Ample off street parking is provided. Centrally located between Nelson and Richmond, Tarata Homestay makes an ideal base for exploring the Tasman Bay area. Use our local knowledge to help you plan your sightseeing and activities, or for that evening meal let us help you select one of Nelson's fine restaurants. In the morning enjoy our delicious continental breakfast. Leisure interests include travel, sailing, social dancing and our garden. Our very friendly Labrador dog lives outside, but loves the opportunity to socialise with guests. We requests no smoking indoors.
Directions: *From Main Road Stoke turn into Maitland Ave. Take the third turn right then the next turn left.*
Home Page: www.infobahn.co.nz/taratahomestay/

Nelson Central

Homestay
Address: Jubilee House, 107 Quebec Road, Nelson
Name: Jubilee House. Sheridan & Patsy Parris
Telephone: (03) 548 8511
Fax: (03) 548-8511
Mobile: (025) 487 767
Beds: 2 Double, 2 Single (4 bedrooms)
Bathroom: 1 Guests share
Tariff: B&B (special) Double $80, Single $50, Children 12+. Dinner $25.
Credit cards Visa, Mastercard, Bankcard.
NZ B&B Vouchers accepted $10 surcharge
Nearest Town: Nelson 2km

We offer probably the best views you will experience in any homestay in New Zealand, one hundred and twenty five metres high, almost a 360 degree view, of the environs. You are encouraged to come upstairs to view the panorama from our lounge, and soak in the scenery, Tasman Bay, mountains, harbour entrance, and all of Nelson city the other side, three minutes by car, twelve walking. Even our bedrooms have splendid views. It's been our privilege to host many folk, from all over the world, we want you feeling at home when you visit us. Breakfasts are SPECIAL, a choice of home-made muesli, yoghurt, preserves, in season fruit, waffles with maple syrup fruit, and bacon to make your mouth water. No matter what you choose our breakfasts will give you the start needed to explore our region. Our home is smoke free. Complimentary pick-up from airport and bus depot. **Directions**: *Please phone or fax for bookings and directions.*

Nelson City Centre

Bed & Breakfast Inn
Address: 369 Trafalgar St South, Nelson
Name: Cathedral Inn
Telephone: (03) 548 7369
Free Phone 0800 88 33 77
Fax: (03) 548 0369
Email: cathedral.inn@clear.net.nz
Beds: 4 Queen/King, 3 Double, 4 Single (7 bdrms)
Bathroom: 7 Ensuite
Tariff: B&B (Special/Fullt) Double $150-$190, Single $130-$150. All credit cards accepted.
Nearest Town: Nelson city.

Superbly located in the heart of Nelson, the Cathedral Inn is set on a rise two doors behind the Cathedral. Surrounded by trees, sunny and quiet, this c1870's spacious manor is beautifully renovated, retaining charm and character ye offering every amenity. Bedrooms include TV, phone, desk, tea/coffee, robes, toiletries, hairdryer and heated towel rails. Breakfast is served in the grand dining room with open fire and comfortable living area. The secluded sunny verandah and a gracious lounge entice guests to relax or socialise.
• Complimentary refreshments, glossy magazines. • Convenient "snug" with kitchen/ironing facilities • Internet/email/fax available • All accommodation upstairs • Off-street parking • Laundry service available• Luggage hoist• Suited to children 9 years +.
At the Cathedral Inn we delight in providing guests with the warm relaxed ambience and personal attention that ensures their comfort. We enjoy advising on restaurants and the variety of excursions/activities for which nelson is renowned.
Home Page: http://nz.com/webnz/bbnz/cathdral.htm

Nelson
Bed & Breakfast
Address: 455 Rocks Rd Nelson
Name: Waterfront Bed & Breakfast
Telephone: (03) 548 3431
Fax: (03) 548 3743
Mobile: (025) 363 600
Beds: 2 Queen (2 Bedrooms)
Bathroom: 2 Ensuites.
Tariff: B&B (full) Double $100/$110,
Single $75, Credit Cards.
Nearest Town: Nelson City 2.5km

Waterfront Bed & Breakfast provides wonderful sea and mountain views of Tasman Bay. Sit out on the verandah and enjoy the panoramic views or stroll down to the beach, go fishing or swimming. Ideally situated to walk to waterfront quality fish restaurants and stroll back along the promenade to enjoy the sunset or take an evening walk along the beach. 2.5km to Nelson town centre, ten minutes drive from the Airport and Bus Station. Nelson is renowned for the arts, pottery, quality wines and of course its sunshine!
We provide comfortable bedrooms with ensuites, TV and Fridge, with sea views. Cooked or continental breakfast, freshly brewed coffee; all local fresh produce used. Non-smoking environment, off-street parking. Regretfully no children under 12. Come and enjoy our paradise.
Directions: *Highway 6 south, left turn at Fireshire Rock you will see the yellow sign "Water Front B&B".*

Nelson
Homestay
Address: 23 Brougham St, Nelson
Name: Leanne & Lenard Dillimore
Telephone: (03) 545 6494
Fax: (03) 545 6494
Mobile: (025) 248 2798
Beds: 2 Queen (2 bedrooms)
Bathroom: 1 Ensuite, 1 Guests share
Tariff: B&B (full) Double $100, Single $85,
Children $20. Credit cards.
NZ B&B Vouchers accepted $25 surcharge
Nearest Town: Nelson 4 blocks.

Brougham Bed & Breakfast offers all that is best in warm Kiwi hospitality. Leanne and Lenard have been in the hospitality industry for several years. Leanne being a Kiwi Host and Lenard a chef. Brougham B&B is just 5 minutes walk from the downtown shopping centre. Set in lovely bush surroundings with a swimming pool and spa for that relaxing time after a busy day. All guest services are separate with TV, video, library, kitchenette and conservatory available for your pleasure, along with phone and fax facilities.
Leanne, Lenard, young family (twins) and two delightful cats would love to share their home with you. Non smokers preferred.

Nelson

Homestay
Address: "Wainui Villa",
5 Wainui Street, Nelson
Name: Carolynn & Kevin Hannah
Telephone: (03) 545 7062
Mobile: (025) 248 2441
Beds: 1 Queen, 1 Double (2 Bedrooms)
Bathroom: 1 Ensuite, 1 Guests share.
Tariff: B&B (special) Double $85-$95,
Single $65, Credit Cards.
NZ B&B Vouchers accepted $25 surcharge
Nearest Town: Nelson centre 500m

Wainui Villa

Our home is a recently restored villa (c 1904) combining the charm and character of the past with modern comforts, only minutes walk from the city centre. Your spacious guestroom is warm, sunny and attractively decorated. It includes a comfortable bed, TV/video, complimentary tea and coffee, antique furnishings and homely touches to make your stay memorable. Our luxurious spa pool is also available for your relaxation. A special breakfast may include home-made muffins or bread and other treats. Your hosts have over ten years experience in the hospitality industry and along with Darrell (5) you can be assured of friendly, personal attention. Feel free to join us and our friendly labrador, Paddy, or relax in your room or cosy guest lounge with an inviting fire in winter and a wisteria covered verandah in summer. Our home is smoke free. Mr Frisky and Diesel are resident cats.

Nelson

Homestay/Bed & Breakfast
Address: "Walmer",
7 Richardson St, Nelson
Name: Bob & Janet Hart
Telephone: (03) 548 3858
Fax: (03) 548 3857
Beds: 1 Queen, 1 Single (2 bedrooms)
Bathroom: 1 Private
Tariff: B&B (full) Double $120, Single $85,
Not suitable for children under 12.
Credit Cards: Visa, MC, BC. NZ B&B Vouchers accepted $45 surcharge
Nearest Town: Nelson city centre 2.4km, Tahunanui Beach 1.4km

"Walmer" is a spacious, sunny, colonial house superbly situated opposite the harbour entrance, close to the sea, beach and city. Three seaside restaurants are within easy walking distance.
You have your own lounge and sunroom with stunning and immediate views of the harbour and Tasman Bay. Harbour views are also gained from the main bedroom. There is also a private bathroom, kitchenette, single bedroom and laundry. The upstairs suite of rooms with an external staircase can be fully self-contained using the kitchenette for self-catering.
A private and relaxing stay is assured as we cater for single party bookings only. Two Labrador dogs complete the household. A full, cooked, New Zealand breakfast is offered. Our home is an excellent base for exploring Abel Tasman National Park with its beautiful beaches, as well as Nelson's arts and wine trails.
"Walmer" is easy to find and has off-street parking. Smokefree.

Nelson

Bed & Breakfast Inn
Address: "Muritai Manor",
48 Wakapuaka Road, Nelson
Name: Jan & Stan Holt
Telephone: (03) 545 1189
Reservations: Freephone: 0800 260 662
Fax: (03) 545 0740 **Mobile**: (025) 370 622
Email: muritai.manor@xtra.co.nz
Beds: 2 Super King/Twin, 2 Queen, 1 Double (5 bdrms)
Bathroom: 5 Ensuite
Tariff: B&B (special) Double $150-$170, Single $115- $125,
Children by arrangement, Credit Cards (MC/VISA/Amex).
Off season rates available. NZ B&B Vouchers accepted $90 surcharge
Nearest Town: 6km north of Nelson on State Highway 6, five mins by car to Nelson
city centre.

*Built in 1903, for the local archdeacon, relax in an elegant country atmosphere, with superb
views of Nelson Haven and the Western Ranges across Tasman Bay.*
*Our Edwardian home combines colonial charm with modern facilities and timeless decor.
Relax in the hot spa or in the lounge by a cosy fire in winter. Cool down on summer evenings
by dipping in the swimming pool, or enjoying the sunset from the verandahs. All rooms have
ensuites with tea/coffee making facilities, T.V., radio, irons, electric blankets, toiletries and
candies. Breakfast can be tailor made to your needs. A full cooked breakfast, freshly squeezed
juices, homemade preserves, yoghurt, fruit, muesli, with fresh ground coffee and selection of
teas. A good start to days of sightseeing, sailing, tramping, kayaking or just relaxing! We are
a non-smoking home with one thirteen year old daughter and two friendly dogs. .*
Directions: *Muritai Manor is 6 kms north of Nelson city on State Highway 6 towards
Blenheim, 1/2 km beyong Clifton Terrace School on right.*
Home Page: http://MuritaiManor.webnz.co.nz

Nelson

Homestay
Address: 106 Brooklands Road, Atawhai, Nelson
Name: Lorraine & Barry Signal
Telephone: (03) 545 1423
Beds: 1 Double, 2 Single (2 bedrooms)
Bathroom: 1 Guests share
Tariff: B&B (full) Double $85, Single $55,
Dinner $25. Credit Cards accepted.
NZ B&B Vouchers accepted $15 surcharge
Nearest Town: Nelson 3km

*We have a spacious luxurious 4 level home with superb views of Tasman Bay, the Boulder
Bank and nearby ranges. Guests have exclusive use of one level. The extra large guest bathroom
has shower, tiled floors and walls, marble vanity and spa bath for two. There are 2 dining
rooms, 2 lounges and several outdoor living areas. The main outdoor patio is private, sunny
and sheltered.*
*Lorraine has a keen interest in crafts and makes porcelain dolls and teddy bears. Her other
interests include gardening, walking and cooking. We both enjoy sports, running and the
outdoors. We have no family left at home.*
*We are close to all the attractions of Nelson and the surrounding areas including its beaches,
wine and craft trails, national parks, rivers, lakes, mountains and skifields.*
*We enjoy meeting people and making new friends. We are non smokers. Courtesy transport
available.*

Nelson

Historic & Exclusive Inner-city B&B
Address: 'Sussex House', 238 Bridge Street, Nelson
Name: Carol Palmer and Stephen Rose
Telephone: (03) 548 9972
Fax: (03) 548 9972
Mobile: (025) 784 846
Email: sussex@xtra.co.nz
Beds: 4 Queen, 2 Single (4 bedrooms)
Bathroom: 3 Ensuite, 1 Private
Tariff: B&B (full) Double/Twin $120-$130, Single $100-$110,
Credit cards Visa/Mastercard. NZ B&B Vouchers accepted $40 surcharge
Nearest Town: Nelson city centre 1/2 km

Experience the peace and charm of yesteryear in our fully restored c1890 B&B, one of Nelson's original family homes. Situated beside the beautiful Maitai River, Sussex House has retained all the original character and romantic ambience of the era. It is only minutes walk from central Nelson's award winning restaurants and cafes, the Queens Gardens, Suter Art Gallery and Botanical Hill (The Centre Of NZ) and many good walks, river and bush. The four sunny bedrooms all have TV's and are spacious and charmingly furnished. All rooms have access to the verandahs and complimentary tea & coffee facilities are provided. Enjoy the swimming pool in summer or just relax in the tranquil surroundings. In winter time, sip your complimentary port by the roaring fire before bed. This is a musicians house and travelling musicians can enjoy the use of our instruments including guitars, fiddles, mandolins, player piano, double bass and more. Breakfast includes lots of seasonal fruits, muffins and croissants baked fresh every morning, homemade yoghurts or a cooked breakfast on request. Sussex House provides a smoke-free environment and all foods, to the best of our knowledge, are free from genetically modified ingredients.
NELSON EXPLORER TOURS: Arrange your tour of the region with our tour company. We have standard tours available which include Wine & Craft Trails, Trout Fishing, Lakes District and Golden Bay or you can design your own tour to suit.
OTHER FACILITIES INCLUDE: Email/Internet access; Fax; Courtesy phone; Laundry; Bicycle hire; Separate lounge for guest entertaining; Complimentary Port; Very sociable cat (Riley); Bread to feed the ducks.
Your hosts, Carol Palmer and Stephen Rose.

Nelson
Bed & Breakfast
Address: Collingwood House,
174 Collingwood Street, Nelson
Name: Emmy & Lane van Wessel
Telephone: (03) 548 4481
Fax: (03) 548 4481
Beds: 2x2 King/Queen, 3 Double,
2 Single (4 bdrms)
Bathroom: 3 Ensuite, 1 Private
Tariff: B&B (full)
Double $85, Single $70,
Credit Cards Visa, Bankcard, Mastercard.
NZ B&B Vouchers accepted $16.50 surcharge.
Nearest Town: Nelson 3 mins walk to city centre.

Our centrally located Bed & Breakfast is a character family home. Having lived in many parts of the world we know how to make a guest at ease. Spacious bedrooms have excellent beds, comfortable chairs, duvets, woolrests, fresh flowers, TV, coffee & tea compliments. We'll welcome you with refreshments. Breakfast at Collingwood house is a real feature. A hearty continental of cereals, yoghurt, fruits, or traditional breakfast farm fresh eggs, bacon, tomatoes, fine teas and freshly ground coffee.
Our house is located three minutes walk to many fine restaurants, Queens Garden and Nelson Cathedral. We have no pets. No smoking please. We have two boys aged 14 and 11. They are involved in classical music. We are a minute walk to the School of Music.

Nelson Central
Bed and Breakfast
Address: 70 Tasman Street, Nelson
Name: Sunflower Cottage,
Marion and Chris Burton
Telephone: (03) 548 1588
Email: sunflower@netaccess.co.nz
Beds: 1 Super King, 2 Single
(2 bedrooms)
Bathroom: 2 Ensuites
Tariff: B&B (continental)
Double $75, Single $50, Dinner $25.
NZ B&B Vouchers accepted $5 surcharge
Nearest Town: Nelson, five minutes walk

We would like to welcome you to Nelson, giving you a relaxing stay in our sunny home on the banks of the Maitai River. Our freshly decorated large bedrooms, with fully tiled ensuite bathrooms, are serviced daily with fresh flowers, complimentary basket of fruit, homemade bread and jams. Both rooms contain TV, microwave, fridge, tea/coffee making facilities, and toaster. Our continental breakfast is self-service. Queen's Gardens and the Suter Art Gallery are nearby. We overlook the Botanical Hill, where you can take a shady walk to the Centre of New Zealand, to experience wonderful views over Tasman Bay and Nelson township. We enjoy meeting people and making new friends, as does our friendly Border Collie. Our hobbies are gardening in our cottage garden, cooking, travelling, sailing and the Internet. We are happy to collect you from the airport or bus depot. We are non-smokers and appreciate no smoking inside.
Home Page: http://SunflowerBandB.webnz.co.nz/

Nelson

Bed & Breakfast
Address: 51 Domett Street, Nelson
Name: Baywick Inn,
Janet Southwick and Tim Bayley
Telephone: (03) 545 6514
Fax: (03) 545 6514
Mobile: (025) 545 823
Email: baywicks@iconz.co.nz
Beds: 2 Queen, 1 Single (2 bedrooms)
Bathroom: 2 Ensuite.
Tariff: B&B (full) double $120-$140, Single $90. Dinner by arrangement.
Not suitable for children. Credit Cards: Visa/Mastercard.
Winter & Business rates available.
Nearest Town: Nelson - 5 minutes stroll to down town.

Overlooking the Maitai Rover and Brook Stream, the Baywick Inn is an elegantly restored 1885 Victorian 2 story villa. Here a warm New Zealand-Canadian welcome awaits you as you're greeted by their lively wire haired fox terrier, who will want to join you (but isn't allowed to) for afternoon tea or cappuccino served in the Brookside garden.

Guest rooms are luxuriously appointed with comfortable beds, down duvets, antique furnishings, ensuites (one with the original 'claw' foot tub and a shower) and with a sunroom or an open air deck. Relax in the sitting room with its cozy fire place and enjoy a conversation with Tim about his classic MG's or wine cellaring systems. Janet, a cook by profession, makes breakfasts to order, healthy or indulgent, cooked or continental, but always a treat served in the sunny dinning room. Private off street parking is provided. Non smoking.
Home Page: http://friars.co.nz/hosts/baywick.html

Nelson

Homestay Bed & Breakfast
Address: Grove Villa,
41 Grove Street, Nelson
Name: Lynne Harrison-Greening
Telephone: (03) 548 8895
Fax: (03) 548 8856
Mobile: (025) 260 5173
Email:amtec@clear.net.nz
Beds: 1 Queen, 2 Single (2 Bedrooms)
Bathroom: 1 Private, 1 Guests share
Tariff: B&B (Full) Double $80, Single $60, Dinner by arrangement $25.
Off season and business rates available. Credit cards: Visa/Mastercard
Nearest Town: Nelson 5 minutes walk.

Grove villa is 5 minutes from Visitor Information Centre and City Centre, with off street parking and flat access. Built in 1909, tastefully restored, furnished with interesting furniture and set in a delightful private garden. While a guest in our home you may be as private and independent as you choose - we are happy to answer your questions and assist with itinerary. Each room is most comfortable with electric blankets, heaters, reading lights, radio alarm clocks, TV, hairdriers, writing tables, chairs and good quality beds. Complimentary tea, coffee. Comfortable sitting room available for guest use. Pick up from bus or airport when possible. No smoking inside. We have travelled extensively in New Zealand and overseas and are keen to provide a comfortable friendly affordable base for our visitors, to explore this wonderfully exciting region or for a quick restful stopover. We also offer selected collectible treasures for sale - if this interests you please do ask. We have no family or pets.

Nelson

Bed & Breakfast
Address: "Rockhaven 437",
437 Rocks Road, Nelson
Name: Barbara and Jack Harte
Telephone: (03) 548 3822
Fax: (03) 548 3822
Email: roy.pip.dwason@xtra.co.nz
Beds: 2 Queen, 2 Single
(2 Bedrooms -1 Queen + 1 Single in each room)
Bathroom: Private facilities for each bedroom
Tariff: B&B (Full or Continental) Double $110, Single $80.
Vouchers accepted $25 surcharge.
Nearest Town: Nelson City Centre, 1.5 km.

As we are right on Nelson's exclusive waterfront our guests can enjoy close-up views overlooking Haulashore Island, the Harbour Entrance and through to Nelson's busy port. This entrance to the harbour is a man-made cut trough a 12.5 km long natural boulder bank which gives Nelson City considerable protection from the sea and prevailing northerly - norwesterly weather patterns. Enjoy these fascinating views form our lovely home that offers a large degree of guest privacy, warmth, convenience and ample off street parking (just drive up behind our house 437). Interesting restaurants and Tahunanui Beach are but a short distance away and can be visited either by car or a comfortable stroll. Your hosts Barbara & Jack Harte have had 11 years experience in the Hospitality Industry and have extensive knowledge of the Nelson, Golden Bay and Sounds areas can assist you with your day trips or suggestions for your next port of call. Peppy our minature Fox Terrier is our family pet.

Nelson

Homestay
Address: Roevyn Homestay
- 32 Atawahi Drive, Nelson
Name: Rose and Merv Hosie
Telephone: (03) 548 8756
Freephone:0800 763 896 (0800-Roevyn)
Fax: (03) 548 8756
Mobile: (025) 302 700
Email: rhosie@xtra.co.nz
Beds: 1 Queen, 1 Double, 1 single (2 Bedrooms)
Bathroom: 1 Ensuite, 1 Family share
Tariff: B&B (Full) Double $85-$120, Single $75-$90. Meals $25pp by arrangement. Credit Cards accepted. Winter/Business rates available.
Laundry/fax/email available to guests/Sky TV.
Nearest Town: Nelson 2 minutes

Our home is modern and spacious, with a warm, friendly relaxed atmosphere. We enjoy meeting people and making new friends and welcome you to enjoy our home as your own. The ensuite room has its own private access with TV, T & C making facility, off street parking. We are an excellent base for exploring the Nelson District. Founders Park, Miyazu Gardens, and Central City are all within a few minutes of our place. We will happily provide information and make arrangements as required. We offer a complimentary pickup / delivery to transport services. Breakfast includes seasonal fruit / berries, home made bread, jams and preserves. Cooked breakfast available on request. You can join us for an evening or be as independent as you wish, we'll endeavour to make your stay both enjoyable and memorable. Join us and cat, for sunsets and views over Nelson to the mountains.

501

Nelson

Inner-city Bed & Breakfast
Address: "Redwood Lodge",
126 Nile Street,
Nelson
Name: Judith and Jim Lambie
Telephone: (03) 546 6629
Fax: (03) 546 6613
Mobile: (025) 309 137
Beds: 1 King/Twin, 2 Queen
Bathroom: 2 Ensuite, 1 Private
Tariff: B&B (Full or Continental)
Double $115-$145, Single $100.
Credit cards accepted. NZ B&B Vouchers accepted $25 surcharge
Nearest Town: Nelson city cente 1/2 km.

A warm welcome awaits you at Redwood Lodge, so named after the huge protected redwood tree at our front gate. The quiet location provides easy walking access to shops, restaurants, cafes, parks and the nationally-renown Nelson Saturday Craft market. We are also close to a golf course and several walkways. Laundry service is available. Our luxurious affordable guest accommodation includes a large sitting-room, and continuous tea/coffee making facilities with off-street parking provided. Our adult children have left home and we are left with "Scruffy" the cat. PS: Our home is smoke-free.

Nelson

Bed & Breakfast
Address: Magic Sunset
90 Glen Road, RD 1, Nelson
Name: Liselotte Seckler
Telephone: (03) 545 1413
Fax: (03) 545 1167
Mobile: (021) 256 3373
Beds: 1 Double, 2 Single (3 Bedrooms)
Bathroom: 1 Guests share, 1 Family share
Tariff: B&B (Continental) Double $100, Single $55, dinner $25 pp, Children half price.
Nearest Town: Nelson 12 km.

WELCOME TO MAGIC SUNSET, our hillside home! 1 acre of enchanting organic gardens with breathtaking views of Tasman Bay and mountain ranges. Delightful guest accommodation on separate level features private entrance, garden setting; all rooms facing panoramic views. High quality beds (Lattoflex) with head- and feet elevation to ensure you a comfortable stay. Non-smoking.

Only 12 minutes North of Nelson this is the perfect retreat for those who value privacy and nature. Wander through the garden, meet the lovable Golden Labrador and 2 pet sheep and relax in the peaceful atmosphere. We are 2 minutes drive to the beach and 3 minutes to tennis courts in rural setting.

Devonshire teas/espressos and dinner served by arrangement. We also offer guided native bush walks and flower arranging courses. Having travelled extensively in this beautiful country, we look forward to meeting you. Wir sprechen "Schwyzerdutsch".
Directions: *Exit "The Glen" (enroute to Picton).*
Please phone/fax for reservations and details.

Richmond, Nelson
Homestay
Address: 46 Rochfort Drive, Richmond, Nelson
Name: Jean & Jack Anderson
Telephone: (03) 544 2175
Fax: (03) 544 2175
Mobile: 025-440 530
Beds: 1 Double, 2 Single (2 bedrooms)
Bathroom: 1 Guest share
Tariff: B&B (full) Double $55, Single $30, Children half price,
Dinner $12.50, Credit Cards. NZ B&B Vouchers accepted
Nearest Town: Richmond 1/2km, Nelson 11km

We are a couple who like meeting people. We live in a modern comfortable home just minutes from the Richmond Shopping area. Near by are lovely gardens, many crafts, such as Pottery, Glass Blowing, Dried Flowers, Weaving and Wood Turning. Beaches at Tahuna and Rabbit Island are only 10 minutes away by car. A two minute walk will take you to a bus to go to Nelson city. We are situated in an area which is very central for travellers going South or North or into the lovely Golden Bay and Tasman areas. We are happy to meet planes or buses and trust that we can make your stay enjoyable. Enjoy Kiwi hospitality in Richmond. A phone call or letter would be appreciated before arrival.
Directions: *At round-about on Queen Street Richmond, continue on Queen Street toward the hills, first turn right, Washbourn Drive, first turn left, Farnham Drive, second turn right, Rochfort Drive.*

Richmond, Nelson
B&B+Self-contained Accom.
Address: 'Bayview', 37 Kihilla Road,
Richmond, Nelson
Name: Ray & Janice O'Loughlin
Telephone: (03) 544 6541
Fax: (03) 544 6541
Email: bayview@ts.co.nz
Beds: 1 Super King, 2 Queen (3 bedrooms)
Bathroom: 1 Ensuite, 1 Guests share
Tariff: B&B (full or continental) Double $85-$100, Single $65, Dinner $25 pp,
Credit Cards: Visa/Mastercard. NZ B&B Vouchers accepted $15 surcharge
Nearest Town: Richmond 1 km. Nelson 10 km

Bayview is a modern, spacious home built on the hills above Richmond township, with spectacular views of Tasman Bay and mountain ranges.
We offer rooms that are quiet, private and immaculately furnished with your complete comfort in mind. A large guest bathroom has shower and spa bath. The lounge opens onto a sheltered deck where you can relax, enjoy a drink or sit and chat.
The self-contained suite with private entrance, off-street parking, kitchen, bathroom / laundry, lounge area and Queen bed offers privacy and all home comforts.
We have two miniature Schnauzer dogs, a variety of birds in a large aviary, tend our colourful garden and enjoy meeting people from New Zealand and overseas.
By car Bayview is 15 minutes from Nelson, 2 minutes from Richmond and award-winning restaurants, close to National parks, beaches, vineyards and crafts.
Be assured of warm, friendly hospitality and a happy stay in our smokefree home.
Home Page: http://nz.com/webnz/bbnz/bayview.htm

Richmond

Country Homestay B&B
Address: 87 Main Rd, Hope, Nelson
Name: Alison & Murray Nicholls
Telephone: (03) 544 8026
Fax: (03) 544 8026
Beds: 1 Queen, 1 Double,
2 Single (3 bdrms)
Bathroom: 1 Guests share,
1 Family share
Tariff: B&B (full or continental)
Double $70, Single $40,
Dinner by arrangement $12.50pp.   NZ B&B Vouchers accepted
Nearest Town: Richmond 2km, Nelson 17km

Our home is situated on a kiwifruit and apple orchard, on State Highway 6 2km south of Richmond. A lengthy driveway ensures quiet surroundings in a lovely garden setting. Guests may enjoy a stroll through the orchard, or swim in our pool. We are centrally situated placing Nelson's many attractions within easy reach. We will happily provide information about these and make arrangements as required. Complimentary tea or coffee is available to guests upon arrival. Full or continental breakfast is included, and dinner is provided by arrangement. A phone call before arrival would be appreciated.Ours is a non smoking home.

Richmond

Exclusive Bed & Breakfast

althorpe
THE BED & BREAKFAST ESTABLISHMENT

Address: "Althorpe", 13 Dorset St,
Richmond, Nelson
Name: Bob & Jenny
Telephone: (03) 544 8117
0800 258467 (0800 Althorpe)
Fax: (03) 544 8117
Email: rworley@voyager.co.nz
Beds: 1 Double,
2 Single/King (2 bedrooms)
Bathroom: 1 Ensuite, 1 Private
Tariff: B&B (full) Double $110-$120, Single $90-$100, Dinner $40.
Credit cards: Visa/Mastercard. NZ B&B Vouchers accepted $30 Surcharge
Nearest Town: Richmond - 5 mins walk

Call us out of this world if you will. But with just two intimate guest rooms, ALTHORPE provides warm old fashioned fuss and care that defines the art of hospitality. An ensuite serves our double bedroom while a private bathroom is provided for the twin / king suite. Guests are afforded the quiet luxury of two relaxing lounge rooms while outside spacious gardens with their own swimming pool and spa invite a casual stroll or a dip in summer. Among the services that have our guests reluctant to leave us you'll find a delightful, tasty gourmet breakfast. By arrangement guests may also enjoy an evening dinner complemented by a vintage wine from the cellar. And it all comes within walls and grounds that carry the echoes of bygone colonial years. At the end of the day's journey you deserve nothing but a little pampering, personal attention and all the comforts of home. We have a friendly tabby cat called Tackles.
Directions: *Please phone for details. Smoking outside please.*

Richmond, Nelson

Farmstay
Address: Redwood Vly Rd,
Richmond R.D. 1, Nelson
Name: Cecelia Miller
Telephone: (03) 544 0801
Fax: (03) 544 0801
Beds: 1 King/Queen,
3 Single (3 bedrooms)
Bathroom: 1 Ensuite,
1 Guests share
Tariff: B&B (full) Double $85, Single $55, Children same,
Dinner $25, Campervans welcome. Credit cards.
NZ B&B Vouchers accepted same day restriction
Nearest Town: Richmond 10km, Nelson 28km

Experience the warm hospitality of our good food and well presented gardens and lawns. The farm is set on 38 acre with Hereford cattle and breeding ewes. You are welcome to enjoy a conducted tour of the property. All bedrooms are very well appointed with panoramic views of rolling hills and open green tree studded valley. Within the Nelson region there is a large variety of activities including fishing, skiing, boating, trekking, tramping, golf, conducted wine trails, pottery trails, glass blowing. You are welcome to enjoy a dinner (3 course) including fresh garden vegetables and fruit of your choice. Relax with a game of snooker/pool in the large games room. Your welcome and comfortable stay is assured. **Directions**: *Please phone or write.*

Richmond, Nelson

Homestay B&B
Address: Chester Le House,
39 Washbourn Drive,
Richmond, Nelson
Name: Noelene and Mike Smith
Telephone: (03) 544 7279
Fax: (03) 544 7279
Email: n.smith@xtra.co.nz
Beds: 1 Queen,
4 Single (3 bedrooms)
Bathroom: 1 Ensuite, 1 Guests share, 1 Family share
Tariff: B&B (full) Double $80-$90, Single $50, Dinner $25,
Major Credit Cards. NZ B&B Vouchers accepted $20 surcharge
Nearest Town: Richmond 1/2km, Nelson 10km

If you are looking for something special and restful away from city noise yet conveniently located to Nelson City and Abel Tasman National Park then Chester Le House beckons. Our lovely modern home has rural and sea views with safe walkways for evening strolls just a few steps away. Evening dinner featuring fine NZ wines or a typical Kiwi barbecue is available on request. Our out-door living area is relaxing and welcoming for a memorable evening of New Zealand hospitality. Our guest rooms are spacious combining charm with modern facilities, warmth and comfort. Locked garaging, laundry facilities and a drier are available for your convenience.
It is a pleasure to share our home with both business and leisure travellers with courtesy car for pick-up available. Why not spoil yourself, extend your stay to relax and explore our beautiful province. A friendly and relaxed place to stay.

505

Richmond, Nelson

Homestay
Address: "Hunterville",
30 Hunter Avenue, Richmond, Nelson
Name: Cecile & Alan Strang
Telephone: (03) 544 5852.
Toll Free: 0800 372220
Fax: (03) 544 5852
Beds: 1 King Extra Large, 3 Single (2 Bdrms)
Bathroom: 1 Private, 1 Family share
Tariff: B&B (special) Double $70, Single $50, Dinner $20.
Credit cards NZ B&B Vouchers accepted
Nearest Town: 2 Blocks up Queen Street, off Main Highway.

When you are travelling south or the Able Tasman Park Area, don't stop in busy Nelson City, but come a little further to Richmond where you will be welcomed with tea or coffee or pre-dinner drinks. Having recently travelled several months on a budget in Europe, we appreciate the needs of travellers. Our guest rooms are spacious, sunny, and have views over Tasman Bay, and our Laundry is available. Our special breakfast caters for all tastes with homemade muesli, fresh fruit, and muffins or a cooked selection. Join us for dinner and share our enjoyment of good food, wine and travellers tales, or we will recommend the regions best restaurants close by. Our interests are music, bridge, bowls and you will be surrounded by books. We look forward to sharing with you our private garden, our friendly Dalmation, "Co,Co", ample parking, and our beautiful countryside by the sea.

Richmond, Nelson

Boutique Accommodation
Address: Kershaw House,
10 Wensley Road,
Richmond, Nelson 7002
Name: Deidre and Ashley Marshall
Telephone: (03) 544 0957
Fax: (03) 544 0950
Mobile: 025-389 347
Beds: 1 King, 1Queen, 1 Single, (Twin)
Bathroom: 3 Ensuite
Tariff: B&B (full) Double $125-$165, Single $110-$125,
Credit Cards accepted
Nearest Town: Richmond 5 mins walk, Nelson 13km

We invite you to experience the genuine warmth of Kiwi hospitality in our elegant (1929) home.
You are welcome to enjoy our comfortable, character residence which is both restful and relaxing, and yet only 3 minutes walk to the Richmond shopping centre and its excellent restaurants.
"Gateway to the Nelson Region", the Abel Tasman National Park, Golden Bay and Nelson Lakes, Richmond is but a short drive to many of areas renowned attractions. Off-street parking is available and for our guests' comfort we are a "smoke free" home. We enjoy meeting people and will make every endeavour to ensure that your stay with us is both enjoyable and memorable.
The resident dog is Henry (a mini Dachshund).
Directions: *Please phone or fax for reservations or directions. A courtesy car is available.*

Richmond, Nelson
Guest House
Address: Surrey Road, Richmond,
Nelson (1/4 hr drive south of Nelson)
Name: Antiquarian Guest House
Telephone: (03) 544 0253 or 544 0723
Fax: (03) 544 0253
Mobile: (025) 417 504
Beds: 1 King, 1 Queen,
1 Twin (3 bdrms)
Bathroom: 1 Ensuite, 1 Guest share
Tariff: B&B (full) Double $95, Single $75, Credit Cards.
NZ B&B Vouchers accepted $25.50 surcharge on Double, $16.50 on Single.
Nearest Town: 11km south of Nelson

Bob and Joanne Such and family (teenage son left at home) welcome you to their peaceful quality home only 2 mins from Richmond and 1/4 hr drive south of Nelson. You are invited to relax in our lovely private, treed garden, beside the swimming pool, or in the large TV/guest lounge. Tea and coffee making facilities with home baking are provided. Breakfast includes local seasonal fruits, freshly baked bread and muesli, coffee, tea etc, and we are happy to cook you an English breakfast, if desired. Our family cat is called Zoe. Richmond is an excellent base for exploring the Nelson region close to Abel Tasman Park, Golden Bay, Nelson Lakes and Rainbow Skifield. We are also owners of a local antique shop and know the area well. You are assured of a warm welcome and a discount is offered to guests staying 3 nights or more. We thank you for not smoking inside.

Richmond, Nelson
Homestay Bed & Breakfast
Address: 'Idesia',
14 Idesia Grove, Richmond
Name: Jenny and Barry McKee
Telephone: (03) 544 0409
Reservations: 0800 361 845
Fax: (03) 544 0402
Email: idesian@xtra.co.nz
Beds: 1 Queen, 2 Single (2 Bedrooms)
Bathroom: 1 Private (one party per night)
Tariff: B&B (Special) Double $85, Single $60, Children negotiable. Dinner by arrangement. Credit Cards: Visa/MC. NZ B&B Vouchers accepted $15 surcharge
Nearest Town: Richmond 1 km, Nelson 12 km

Jenny and Barry wish to welcome you to Richmond, the gateway to the south and west. We can introduce you to many crafts, wineries and the Abel Tasman National Park.
Our modern, elevated home is close to the country, yet the quiet cul de sac is within walking distance of the township. The energy efficient house is comfortable all year and allows for indoor outdoor living. Jenny has interests in education for the deaf and Barry computer consultancy. Breakfast to suit your taste includes seasonal fruits, yoghurt and a selection of cereals or, a more substantial cooked breakfast. We would be delighted if you dined with us, or if you wished for a special meal we can cater for your requirements. We enjoy food and wine and particularly enjoy sharing a meal with friends. Our aim is to specialise in providing tasteful and attractive
meals complemented by local wine.
Home Page: http://mysite.xtra.co.nz/~IdesiaBB

Richmond
Kiwi Hospitality
Address: 11 Crescent Street, Richmond, Nelson
Name: Roy and Dorita
Telephone: Freephone: 0800 229 868
Fax: (03) 544 4892
Email: baytours@ts.co.nz
Beds: 1 or 2 King or 4 Single (2 Bedrooms)
Bathroom: Ensuite
Tariff: B&B (Full) Double $95, Single $65, Children under 5 free.
Dinner by arrangement. Credit Cards: Visa/Mastercard
NZ B&B Vouchers accepted $24 surcharge
Nearest Town: Richmond/Nelson

"YOU WON'T FIND US ON THE MAIN ROAD"
We guarantee our guests a warm, relaxing, peaceful stay in our friendly, well appointed home, with sea and mountain views from every room. Large decks and BBQ areas, for you to enjoy, overlooking 3 acres of serene gardens. 2 minutes walk to Shopping Centre and Award Winning Restaurants. We nave a nice cat and smoking outside is ok. We own and operate a Tour Company, "0800 BAY TOURS" which specialises in QUALITY WINE TOURS, Arts / Craft / Scenery and Guided Trout Fishing. You may like to take advantage of a tour with us (Discount for guests). Our LOCAL KNOWLEDGE is invaluable to maximise your stay in "NELSON". Laundry and off street parking available. Courtesy coach between airport or bus depot. Guest comment: "We can't pay you a higher compliment other than, we'll never forget our stay & tour".
Directions: *FREE-PHONE 0800 229 868*
Home Page: http://webnz.co.nz/baytours/

Wakefield, Nelson
Homestay, Self Contained Accommodation
Address: 'Serenity Gardens',
72A Eighty-Eight Valley Road, Wakefield, Nelson
Name: Barbara and Graham
Telephone: 03 541 8895 **Fax**: 03 541 8895
Beds: 1 Double, 1 Single (1 bedroom) + 1 additional bed available
Bathroom: 1 Ensuite
Tariff: B&B (continental) Double $80, Single $50. Additional adults $20,
Children reduced rates, Discount 3+ nights. Dinner $25. No pets.
Nearest Town: Richmond, 14 km on SH6

* *Welcome to separate, but attached accommodation situated on 4 acres in a tranquil valley with complete privacy and quietness.*
* *Bordering idyllic stream setting with mature trees and extensive gardens of shrubs (native / exotic), plus roses, camellias, rhododendrons etc.*
* *Homestay unit adjoins main homestead with modern Kitchenette, microwave, TV and video and comfortable dining area. Laundry facilities available. Ample off-road parking.*
* *Guests welcome to share evening meal with us. Farmstyle meals using our organically grown fresh vegetables. Wine or beer served with meals.*
* *Complimentary tea / coffee and home made baking upon arrival. Home baked bread for breakfast.*
* *We appreciate your support for our smoke-free home. Smoke alarms for your protection.*
* *Much loved companions, small dog, Candy and 2 cats live outside.*
* *Positioning ideally centrally located for exploring Nelson - Golden Bay - Nelson Lakes.*
Directions: *Please phone or fax. Homestay, South of Wakefield, 500 metres from main road on 88 Valley Road.*

Thorpe, Nelson

Accommodation
Address: Rerenga Farm, Thorpe,
Dovedale-Woodstock Road, Nelson
Name: Robert & Joan Panzer
Telephone: (03) 543 3825
Fax: (03) 543-3640
Mobile: (025) 243 1284
Email: Tailored@ts.co.nz
Beds: 1 Double (1 bedroom).
Bathroom: 1 Ensuite.
Tariff: B&B (special) Double $95, Single $65, Dinner $25.
Nearest Town: Upper Moutere 25 mins.

New Zealand Association
FARM & HOME
HOSTS

We regard our guests as visiting friends; not as commercial clients.
Thorpe is halfway between Nelson and Motueka, with plenty of nearby options for tramping
(Abel Tasman and Kahurangi National Parks); fishing (Motueka River 3 minutes away); or
the local crafts and vineyards. We offer a peaceful, rural retreat with the sunny
Nelson climate, view of Mt Arthur, good food, and international hosts. Our 85
year old homestead surrounded by rolling hills, forests and situated along the
Dove River, is in the middle of 20 acres of planted fruit and nut trees, plus sheep,
pigs, chooks, cats and a dog. You can arrive at our door by foot crossing over our
own swingbridge or by driving over a vehicle bridge. Robert is from the
Netherlands and Joan from the United States. We have two children (6 and 8
years) who are real "Kiwi's". E-mail and fax facilities available for you to use.
Note: We also operate Tailored Travel: Personal custom tours (6 max) tailored
to specific requirements and dates. **Home Page**: http://webnz.co.nz/nzct

Wakefield, Nelson

Bed & Breakfast + Self-Contained Accommodation
Address: Pigeon Valley Road, RD 2, Wakefield
Name: Peter & Alison Warren
Telephone: (03) 541 8500/(0800 347 208)
Fax: (03) 541 8500
Email: pigeon@iconz.co.nz
Beds: 1 Queen, 2 Single (2 bedrooms)
Bathroom: 2 Ensuite
Tariff: B&B (full) Double $140, Single $120,
Extra adult $40, Extra Child $10, Dinner $30, Credit Cards.
Nearest Town: Wakefield 2 mins, Richmond 10 mins

Pigeon
Valley
Lodge

Imagine waking to the sound of native birdsong. After a day on the road, perhaps the thought
of a refreshing dip in our swimming pool appeals.
At Pigeon Valley Lodge you will be our special guests (single party booking). Our contemporary
lodge with warm timber interior offers all facilities for your relaxation and comfort, in a
secluded hillside setting. Both bedrooms have ensuite bathrooms with lovely rural views.
A brief stroll leads you to our historic homestead, where we provide country style hospitality,
including a gourmet breakfast and optional dinner. Our family includes four children and
two friendly dogs. Just 2km from Wakefield, the lodge is within easy reach of
wineries, arts and craft studios, National Parks and skifields. Totaradale Golf
Course is a minute away and we have golf clubs. If you would like to go fly fishing,
your in-house guide, Peter, is on hand.
Home Page: http://webnz.co.nz/pigeon

Mapua, Nelson

Country Accommodation

Address: "Atholwood Country Accommodation",
Bronte Rd East, R.D.1,
Upper Moutere, Nelson
Name: Robyn & Grahame Williams
Telephone: (03) 540 2925
Fax: (03) 540 2925
Mobile: (025) 310 309
Beds: 2 Queen, 1 Single (2 bedrooms)
Bathroom: 2 Ensuite
Tariff: B&B (full) Double $145-$165,
Single $120-$145.
Dinner by arrangement. Credit cards.
Nearest Town: Nelson (25 mins) and Motueka (20 mins)

Our home is set well back from the road, within two acres of landscaped gardens. Bordered by the Waimea Inlet, abundant with birdlife, you can enjoy peace and total privacy. Within the gardens are a swimming pool, spa, croquet lawn, secret garden paths and a Gazebo for your pleasure.

The interior decor of natural rimu adds to the casual and country atmosphere. Two well appointed guest rooms, each with adjoining ensuites have extensive views. The upstairs guest wing has a separate lounge with tea and coffee making facilities.

Breakfast at "Atholwood" is arranged to suit your timetable and is wholesome and filling, taking advantage of local fresh fruit and produce. Evening meals and lunches are available by prior arrangement, and local restaurants are close and excellent.

At "Atholwood" you can be assured of our personal attention in a relaxed and informal atmosphere. Our household is also shared with Martha our aged faithful Spaniel and our 3 legged cat Lucy.

http://www.bnb.co.nz

take a look

Mapua Village, Nelson
Coastal Village Accommodation

Address: "Hartridge", 103 Aranui Road,
Mapua Village, Nelson
Name: Sue & Dennis Brillard
Telephone: (03) 540 2079
Fax: (03) 540 2079
Mobile: (025) 247 4854
Email: hartridge@mapua.gen.nz
Beds: 1 Super King/Twin, 1 Queen (2 bedrooms)
Bathroom: 2 Ensuite
Tariff: B&B (special) Double $155, Single $115,
Dinner by arrangement $35, Not suitable for children.
Credit Cards (MC/VISA). Tariff applies fromn 1 November 1999.
Nearest Town: Richmond or Motueka (Either is 20 mins).

*Set on a rise in mature gardens Hartridge offers friendly hospitality and 1915
ambience. Upstairs guest accommodation, (a later addition), is spacious and sunny
with quality beds, crisp linen, comfortable seating, fresh garden flowers, tea, coffee and
biscuits. Each ensuite provides robes, toiletries, luxurious towels and heated towel
rail. Your gourmet breakfast includes fresh fruit, home made toasted muesli and
yoghurt, home baked bread and special cooked dishes using hot-smoked fish, free-
range eggs or chicken. It is served in the antique-furnished guest lounge overlooking
the rose garden, or on the sunny porch among ferns, orchids and passionflower. Walk
to beach, award-winning cafes / bars. Nearby are wineries, arts and crafts, golf, trout
fishing and national parks. Smoke-free house, friendly dog, Jack, vintage Morgan,
ample, easy private parking. Light meals always available- $12p.p.*
Home Page: http://nz.com/webnz/bbnz/hrtridge.htm

Ruby Bay, Nelson
Bed & Breakfast

Address: 42 Broadsea Avenue, Ruby Bay, Nelson
Name: Broadsea Bed & Breakfast (Rae and John)
Telephone: (03) 540 3511
Fax: (03) 540 3511
Beds: 1 Double (1 Bedroom)
Bathroom: 1 Private
Tariff: B&B (Full) Double $100, Single $60. Not suitable for children.
Nearest Town: Richmond, travel 20 mins along the Coastal Highway and turn
off at Tait street.

*Beach front accommodation, new home. Bedroom with sea view, own bathroom and
toilet facilities. Lovely walks on beach and reserve. Cafes, tavern, wineries and
restaurants in close vicinity. Fifteen minutes from Richmond and Motueka, thirty
minutes from Nelson.*
*Beaches; Rabbit Island, Kaiteriteri and Tahuna in close proximity. Near Gateway to
Abel Tasman National Park.*
*We have just started our Bed & Breakfast and wish to make guests feel at home and
enjoy their stay, with privacy if wanted, while we are here to help in any way.*
*Our accommodation is one double room, own facilities. Not suitable for children.
Breakfast arranged to suit, cooked or continental. Plenty of places to see and things
to do, or just be lazy on a beach with no maddening crowds.*
Smoking outside only. Broadsea Bed & Breakfast, Ruby Bay.
*Your hosts - Rae & John plus the Birman cat and Sally our Labrador will greet you
outside.*

Tasman

Farmstay
Address: Permin Road Tasman R.D.1, Upper Moutere
Name: "Aporo Orchard" Marian & Mike Day
Telephone: (03) 526 6858
Fax: (03) 526 6258
Mobile: 025 240 3757
Email: aporo@xtra.co.nz
Beds: 1 Queen, 1 King/Twin (2 bedrooms)
Bathroom: 2 Ensuite
Tariff: B&B (full) Double $130, Single $105, Dinner by arrangement $40.
Credit Cards: Master Card/Visa. NZ B&B Vouchers accepted $60 surcharge
Nearest Town: Motueka 11km, Nelson 40km

Our comfortable secluded home, with grape and hop clad verandahs, is set in a colourful garden which attracts many birds and is enthusiastically maintained by Marian. It overlooks our apple orchard, with magnificent views of Tasman Bay to D'Urville Island and the Kahurangi ranges to the west. Guests can enjoy the swimming pool, relax in the garden, compete on the petanque court or croquet lawn, stroll through the orchard to the beach (5 mins) or woodland walk. Or simply enjoy a complimentary glass of our own grape wine or cider.

We are centrally situated in the heart of Nelson's fruit growing region, only 200 m off Coastal Highway 60 between Nelson / Motueka enabling travellers to explore the best of the Nelson Province, Golden Bay, Abel Tasman and Kahurangi National parks. Beautiful safe swimming beaches and walks are nearby, as are two golf courses, award winning wineries, trout fishing rivers, art and craft trails and great restaurants in nearby Mapua on the water's edge.

The Nelson region, arguably NZ's sunniest spot, offers a wealth of activities to warrant a 2-3 days stay. An ideal area to relax away from the pleasures of long driving days.

We offer two spacious well appointed, purpose built double bedrooms each with TV, refrigerator, coffee / tea making facilities, home made biscuits, fresh fruit and flowers.

Delicious home baked breakfast is served in our farmhouse kitchen or sunny deck outside. Picnic lunches and 3 course diners are available by arrangement featuring fresh, seasonal local produce, organically home grown vegetables and local wine.

Cat and farm dog.

Tasman, Motueka

Holiday & Health Retreat

Address: "Kina Colada", Kina Peninsula,
RD 1, Tasman/Upper Moutere
Name: Dr Hans & Susanne Brutscher
Telephone: (03) 526 6700
Fax: (03) 526 6770
Email: mani@cactus-soft.co.nz
Beds: 3 King, 3 Single (3 bedrooms)
Bathroom: 3 Ensuite, with underfloor heating.
Tariff: B&B (special) Double $175/suite, $130/apartment, Single $95-$130,
extra person $50, Dinner $30, Credit Cards (VISA/MC).
Nearest Town: Motueka 7km, Nelson 40km

Kina Colada - a healthy cocktail for body and soul! Our Mediterranean home offers more than just charming suites with excellent sea and mountain views plus scrumptious breakfasts! Spend all or part of your holidays amid uniquely beautiful surroundings on our 8 ha property adjoining estuary and Tasman Bay, directly above Kina Beach. Located on lovely and tranquil Kina Peninsula with its own golf course we are in the centre of many activities. Our area offers something exciting to every seeker! After a good night's sleep in our great European beds let your eyes do the walking from Abel Tasman to Kahurangi National Park, Rainbow Skifield, Richmond Ranges to the Marlborough Sounds. Nearby you find famous beaches with a variety of watersports, excellent fishing, inviting vineyards, arts and crafts. Is your understanding of the true 'dolce vita" more like total relaxation? Perfect - enjoy quiet days on the peninsula! After a yummy breakfast take the 5 minutes private bushwalk down to the beach, watch the large variety of birds, enjoy long walks. Our stunning pool invites you to float for ages! Shape up in the fitness room or relax in the sauna with a book and your favourite music from our library! The cosy suites are equipped with stylish ensuites, tea making facilities, fridge, TV, phone and private balcony. Meals can be served by prior arrangement in the Mediterranean courtyard, the charming guest lounge with fireplace or ... by the pool in romantic setting.

For recharging your batteries we recommend the traditional German "Cure" spa treatments in our in-house clinic; enjoy the lasting effects of Moor-mud, loampacks, medical baths, oxygen therapy, Kneipp-water-treatments and massages. Prices $9-$30. We welcome children above 10 years; exceptions during off-seasons can be arranged. During the last 14 years we have been working with tourists and patients in a German Spa Resort, and we enjoy to spoil you with our experience!

Our children are 11 and 21 years; a friendly family dog lives with us. Tariff includes great breakfast, tea and coffees, sauna and pick-up service from Motueka or Nelson airport. Special winter tariff available!

Doone Cottage

Motueka Valley

Country Homestay
Address: "Doone Cottage",
Motueka Valley Highway, R.D.1, Motueka
Name: Glen & Stan Davenport
Telephone: (03) 526 8740
Fax: (03) 526 8740
Mobile: (021) 707 055
Email: doone-cottage@xtra.co.nz
Beds: 1 King/Twin, 1 Double, 1 Single (2 bedrooms).
Garden Chalet: 1 Double, 1 Single
Bathroom: 3 Ensuite
Tariff: B&B (full) Double $110-$130, Single $80-$95, Dinner by arrangement, Not
suitable for children, Credit cards. (Please check tariff for new season end 2000) NZ B&B
Vouchers accepted $25-$30 surcharge per person.
Nearest Town: Motueka (28 km), Nelson (64 km)

New Zealand Association
FARM & HOME HOSTS

*Homely hospitality, peace and tranquility, trout fishing, beautiful garden and bush setting,
native birds, household pets, goats, sheep, chickens, ducks and donkeys, weaving studio - all
abound at Doone Cottage. A lovely 100 year old home, comfortably furnished cottage style in
an attractive 4 acre setting of garden, native trees and ferns, lawns and shrubs, with a beautiful
outlook across the Motueka Valley to the Mt Arthur Range. King, Double and Twin
accommodation available each with own private verandah. Meals are country style with fresh
natural food. Home-made breads, fresh garden vegetables, free range eggs etc. Your hostess
spins wool from the raw fleece and has her own weaving studio where you can see the finished
garments, blankets, wallhangings, rugs etc. There is much to interest the tourist and
fisherman. The Motueka River is at the gate, with several others closeby, providing the
opportunity to fish some of the best brown trout rivers in the South Island. Fishing licences
are sold here, and a local guide can be arranged. Advance bookings are advisable. Horse
Trekking and Golf Courses are also nearby. Excellent day trips include 3 National Parks,
(Abel Tasman, Nelson Lakes and Kahurangi), Kaiteriteri beaches, Golden Bay and Nelson.
Your hosts will gladly help guests needing assistance with bookings/information on any
activities in the area. This is one of New Zealand's main fruit producing regions where the
sun shines over 2,400 hours annually. The region is rich in crafts of all descriptions. We are
very fortunate to live in this beautiful corner of New Zealand and have enjoyed sharing our
family home and surroundings with visitors from all over the world for many years.*
Directions: *Entering Motueka on SH60 turn left at Clock Tower next to Caltex Service Stn,
we are 28K along the Motueka Valley H'way (old SH61), heading South. From Murchison
and the South, turn left off SH6 at Kohatu Hotel Motupiko, we are 28K from this junction on
Motueka Valley H'way (old SH61).*
Home Page: http:/nz.com/webnz/bbnz/doone.htm

Motueka Valley
Country Homestay
Address: "The Kahurangi Brown Trout"
Westbank road, Pokororo, Motueka, R.D. 1
Name: Heather Lindsay & David Davies
Telephone: (03) 526 8736
Fax: (03) 526 8736
Email: katselig@xtra.co.nz
Beds: 2 Super King/Twin, 1 Single (2 bedrooms)
Bathroom: 2 Ensuite
Tariff: B&B (continental) Double $95, Single $70,
Children under 12 half price, Dinner $25. NZ B&B Vouchers accepted
Nearest Town: Motueka (26km), Nelson (66km)

Beside the Motueka River and close to 3 National Parks, trout fishing, scenic walks, river rafting, sea kayaking, horse trekking ....
We have friendly pets. Smoking outdoors.
Comments from our visitors book say the rest:
"Heaven on Earth". "NZ is trout heaven and this is B&B heaven". "Just the most glorious heavenly spot". "Absolutely fantastic - couldn't fault the hospitality". "Thanks for making us feel so at home". "Superb location". "We like houses with character. You have it". "Excellent breakfast". "Delicious meals". "The (organic) home grown veges and fruit were incredible". "Highly therapeutic. Can recommend the hill walk". "So glad I stayed, for the (inner tube) trip down the river". "Our room, bed and facilities were the most comfortable yet". "We'll be back to the Garden of Eden and the special hot bath under the stars". "We had a fantastic stay and will be back for more".
Directions: *2nd house downstream from Pearse River- Motueka River confluence. Approx. halfway (26km) between Motueka and Tapawera on the west bank of the Motueka River.*

Motueka Valley
Farmstay & Self-contained Accommodation
Address: 'Mountain View Cottage',
Waiwhero Road, R.D.1, Motueka
Name: Veronica & Alan Hall
Telephone: (03) 526 8857
Beds: Cottage: 1 Double (1 bedroom),
Homestead: 1 Twin (1 bedroom)
Bathroom: 1 Private, 1 Ensuite
Tariff: B&B Double $65-$75, Single $45,
Dinner $20pp. Credit cards.
NZ B&B Vouchers accepted
Nearest Town: Motueka 18km

We own a 14.2 hectare property, 18km from Motueka off Highway 61. An ideal base for outdoor pursuits or just relaxing. The area is renown for Arts & Craft and ideally situated for anglers. We live in a new homestead on the property and run a small herd of cattle; we have organic gardens and a farm walkway. Your accommodation will be either the one bedroom farm cottage - completely self-contained with own driveway, gardens, cooking / laundry facilities and colour TV; or the self-contained, twin accommodation attached to our homestead - you can be fully independent or join us for meals and refreshments. We are happy to share vegetarian and non-vegetarian cuisine, using a variety of home and local produce; whilst breakfast includes homemade bread, pancakes, jams and muesli. We really enjoy meeting people, have travelled extensively and our interests include outdoor pursuits, board games and cards.

R. Nairn

Motueka

Boutique Accommodation
Address: Weka Road, Mariri, RD 2, Upper Moutere, Nelson
Name: Wairepo House
Telephone: (03) 526 6865
Fax: (03) 526 6101 **Mobile**: 025 357 902
Email: wairepo@xtra.co.nz
Beds: 5 Super King, 2 Single (5 bedrooms), Top suite sleeps 2-4.
Bathroom: 2 Ensuite, 1 Private
Tariff: B&B (special/full) Double $185-$350, Single $155-$250, valid to
1st Nov 2001, Dinner $45pp by special arrangement only, Children under 12yrs
half price, Children under 5 no charge, each extra person $45, cot provided.
Credit Cards (VISA & M/C).
Nearest Town: Motueka 6km

*Wairepo House is an exclusive country homestead blended into the orchard hills
overlooking the tranquil waters of Tasman Bay, set in large woodland gardens with
summerhouse and pond. Offering warm hospitality, superb comfort, delicious food
with country ambience, native timbers, antique furnishings, New Zealand and local
art work.*

*Upstairs suite comprises two bedrooms, double spa overlooking native fernery,
kitchenette, private lounge with library, open fire, balconies off master bedroom and
lounge with magnificent views.*

*Other suites all have Super King rooms, private lounge, heated tiled bathrooms,
double spa and conventional bath, kitchenette, French doors opening to pool and
garden area. Full special al fresco breakfast served at times of guests choosing on deck
overlooking pool. Cobbled paths lead thru established garden which attracts numerous native birds, to tennis court. Garden suite has wheelchair access and facilities.
Complimentary platters, alcoholic beverages and laundry.*

*Adjacent are 40 hectares of apple and pear orchard, 7000 Paeonie tubers which flower
from October - December.*

*We are only minutes form some of Nelson's beautiful beaches for swimming, walking
and windsurfing. Two hours from Picton ferry.*

*Centrally placed to visit Abel Tasman and Kahurangi National Park, kayaking, wine
and craft trails. Excellent trout fishing, guides available.*

Directions: *On State Highway 60 Coastal Route to Motueka 40kms from Nelson,
first stone entrance right Weka Rd, 3kms from Tasman Township.*
Home Page: http://nz.com/webnz/bbnz/wairepo.htm

Motueka

Homestay B&B
Address: 15 North St, Motueka
Name: The Blue House
Telephone: (03) 528 6296
Beds: 1 Double, 2 Single (2 bedrooms)
Bathroom: 1 Guest share, 1 Family share
Tariff: B&B (full) Double $60, Single $40, Children age plus $1,
over 12 adult price, Dinner $15. Credit cards. NZ B&B Vouchers accepted
Nearest Town: Motueka 2km

Our house, shared with one cat, is located on the beach in a quiet locality, with safe swimming, beautiful walks and an estuary which is a bird-watchers paradise, all within minutes of our gate. Secure off-street parking. Guest accommodation is an annexe comprising lounge, bathroom, two bedrooms and a private courtyard. Tea / coffee making facilities. Breakfast is shared with us in our house. No smoking inside. There are heaps of things to do in this area close to two national parks, catering for all interests. Explore this beautiful place by car, foot, kayak, horse-back etc or enjoy the magic of golden beaches, sea and a myriad birds while we provide a comfortable friendly base for you. We have travelled widely ourselves and thoroughly enjoy meeting people from near or far away.
Directions: *At the southern roundabout in High St, turn into Wharf Road, continue straight into Everett St, at the end turn left into North St.*

Motueka

An Artist's Home.
Address: 240 Thorp Street, Motueka
Name: Copper Beech Gallery.
John and Carol Gatenby
Telephone: (03) 528 7456
Fax: (03) 528 7456
Beds: 1 Queen, 2 Single
(2 bedrooms)
Bathroom: 2 Ensuite
Tariff: B&B (Special) Double $130,
Single $90, Credit Cards (MC/BC/VISA).
NZ B&B Vouchers accepted $55 double surcharge,
$20 single surcharge, May-Oct
Nearest Town: Motueka 1km

Treat yourself to a stay at the home of John R Gatenby, one of New Zealand's leading landscape artists. Light, space and tranquillity await you in John and Carol's smoke-free contemporary home set in two acres of garden designed by the artist and his wife. Share the environment that provides John's inspiration. Experience beautiful coastal Abel Tasman and mountainous Kahurangi National Parks with easy access to a full range of outdoor activities. From spacious living areas browse through the interior gallery, leading to separate guest accommodation which opens onto sun-drenched patios overlooking a bird and waterfowl sanctuary. Indulge in Carol's stunning breakfasts - culinary and visual delights - enjoy surprise complimentary touches provided by unobtrusively attentive Kiwi hosts and share in their rich local knowledge. As an optional extra take painting tuition at the on-site gallery. John, Carol and their outdoor golden Labrador, Abbi, take pleasure in the art of hospitality.

Motueka

Bed & Breakfast
Address: 259 Riwaka- Kaiteriteri Rd,
R.D. 2, Motueka, Nelson
Name: "Seaview B&B"
Jackie & Tig McNab
Telephone: (03) 528 9341
Fax: (03) 528 9341
Beds: 1 Queen, 1 Double, 1 Single (2 bdrms)
Bathroom: 1 Guests share
Tariff: B&B (continental) Double $85, Single $55.
Credit Cards: Visa/Mastercard. NZ B&B Vouchers accepted $20 surcharge
Nearest Town: Motueka 9km

Ideally located Jackie and Tig's coastal property is just 5 minutes to Kaiteriteri beach and handy to the Abel Tasman and Kahurangi National Parks. Set against a large area of private native bush with abundant bird life, we offer panoramic views of Tasman Bay with breathtaking sunrises and sunsets not to be missed. A secluded beach is a short stroll from the guest rooms. Guest lounge with seaviews and complimentary tea/coffee making facilities. At your convenience a leisurely continental breakfast is served in the house dining room. Activities available: boat trips, sea kayaking, seal swim, bush walks. With a lifetime of farming experience in this district we can provide a unique insight into local history and opportunities to explore the region. We welcome you with New Zealand hospitality and clean, comfortable accommodation. Bar and restaurant 4 mins.
Directions: *9 kms north of Motueka on Riwaka-Kaiteriteri Road. "Seaview B&B" sign on left at entrance.*

Motueka

Bed & Breakfast
Address: "Rosewood",
48 Woodlands Avenue, Motueka
Name: Barbara & Jerry Leary
Telephone: (03) 528 6750
Mobile: (021) 251 0131
Email: Barbara.Leary.Rosewood@xtra.co.nz
Beds: 1 Double, 2 Single (2 bedrooms)
Bathroom: 1 Ensuite, 1 Family share
Tariff: B&B (full) Double $80, Single $45,
Children half price. Credit Cards accepted.
Nearest Town: Motueka - 5 minute walk

Hi, welcome to Rosewood, where our home is your home, a home away from home offering a warm and friendly atmosphere in private, peaceful surroundings, a short stroll to the town centre, cafes, shops, estuary and 20 minutes drive to the beautiful Abel Tasman National Park. Both bedrooms are tastefully decorated to meet your needs. The upstairs double bedroom and ensuite has adjacent lounge to relax in with TV, offering magnificent views of the surrounding bush-clad mountains. You will be treated to a delicious breakfast offering the best seasonal specialities. Interests include roses, travel, golfing, fishing, or just enjoying a friendly chat with our guests over a cuppa or a complimentary glass of sherry. Jasper our cat will be around to welcome you. Motueka District has a myriad of attractions, beautiful Kaiteriteri Beach, arts and crafts, local wines, golf, canoeing, trout fishing, sea kayaking and beautiful swimming beaches. Come indulge yourself.
Directions: *Take second turning on right after the Clock Tower.*

Motueka

Self Contained Accommodation
Address: 430 High Street, Motueka
Name: Ashley Troubadour.
John and Coral Horton
Telephone: (03) 528 7318
Fax: (03) 528 7318
Beds: 2 Queen, 2 Double, 2 Single (4 bedrooms)
Bathroom: 2 Ensuite, 2 Guests share
Tariff: B&B (continental) Double $70, Single $52,
Ensuites Self Contained $78-$85, Children $10. Mastercard/Visa
NZ B&B Vouchers accepted Share bathroom facilities only with $10 surcharge.
Nearest Town: Motueka (Town Centre 1km)

Ashley Troubadour used to be a nunnery! Nowadays it is used as an "ADVENTURE BASE" for the Abel Tasman and the Kahurangi National Parks and also all the other numerous outdoor pursuits on hand in the Motueka area. Tramping, water taxi cruising, sea kayaking, swimming with the seals, sunbathing, horse riding, fishing, sky-diving, 4x4 bus safaris to Farewell Spit, wine trails, terrific restaurants and shopping. You name it, we've got it! And John and Coral, your friendly Ashley Troubadour hosts will gladly arrange all bookings etc. for these local activities. Nothing is too much trouble for us to make your stay a pleasure. Laundry facilities, undercover drying area for tents etc. "security room" for valuables and excess luggage and ample off-street parking are all available for your peace of mind. Our ensuite rooms are near new with a sunny verandah overlooking a lovely quiet garden. They contain Queensize beds, TV, microwaves and tea/coffee making facilities. And we would love to meet you!

Motueka

Homestay
Address: Tri-angle Inn,
142 Thorp Street, Motueka
Name: Daniel and Lesley
Telephone: 03-528 7756
Mobile: 025-484 778
Email: Daniel.hdt@xtra.co.nz
Beds: 2 King, 1 Double, 4 Single (3 bedrooms)
Bathroom: 2 Ensuite
Tariff: B&B (special, continental) Double $125,
Single $75. Children half price.
Nearest Town: Motueka 1 km.

The Tri-Angle Inn is set in 1 acre of garden, has magnificent views of the Mt Arthur ranges and yet is only 5 mins. walk from local restaurants, cafes, an 18 hole golf course and the sea. Our rooms are large, with very comfortable king size beds. Each room has its own private entrance, ensuite, tea making facilities, TV and Fridge.
We pride ourselves in providing a large healthy, wholesome breakfast.
Our family, which includes Liam our son and our 2 dogs, are "outdoors" people who actively participate in the multitude of sport and recreational facilities available in the area.
Daniel is a part time local trout guide, he can take you to some "magic places" and can be booked by the hour, equipment may also be hired and licenses arranged. We are on the doorstep to all local attractions and look forward to sharing them with you.
Regrettably not suitable for children under 5.
NO SMOKING INSIDE.

Motueka
Bed & Breakfast
Address: Bracken Hill B&B,
265 Riwaka Kaiteriteri Road,
RD 2, Motueka, Nelson
Name: Bracken Hill B&B.
Grace and Tom Turner
Telephone: (03) 528 9629
Fax: (03) 528 9629
Beds: 1 Queen, 1 Twin (2 bedrooms)
Bathroom: 2 Guests share.
Tariff: B&B (continental) Double $90, Single $60.
Visa/Mastercard/Bank Card.
Nearest Town: Motueka 10 kms

We welcome you to enjoy and experience our modern home with marvellous views over Tasman Bay from D'Urville Island to Nelson and St Arnaud Range. The guest TV lounge and dining room (with tea / coffee making facilities) and two bedrooms have native bush, lagoon, and sea views. In the evening when the moon shines on the sea you would think you are half-way to heaven!! We are a few minutes from Tapu Bay, Stephens Bay, beautiful Kaiteriteri Beach and close to Kaharangi and Abel Tasman National Park. We would share with you our extensive knowledge of the Nelson, Golden Bay area, which has a diverse range of attractions to experience. From the guest lounge a large sun deck leads you to a natural rock garden for your relaxation and enjoyment, BBQ available. Our home is non smoking. We have a friendly Golden Labrador Jake, who will greet you on arrival.
Directions: *2.65 kms from Cook Corner on Riwaka Kaiteriteri Road.*

Motueka
Homestay
Address: 184 Thorp Street, Motueka
Name: Ian and Rebecca Williams
Telephone: (03) 528 9385
Fax: (03) 528 9385
Mobile: (025) 480 466
Beds: 2 Queen,
2 Single (2 bedrooms)
Bathroom: 2 Ensuite
Tariff: B&B (full) Double $60-$70, Single $40,
Children $15, Dinner by arrangement.
Nearest Town: 50 km West of Nelson City.

Children are welcome to our home set on a two acre block with plenty of room to roam or spend time in the swimming pool. We are 1.4 km to shopping centre and 1.2 km to a 18 hole golf course. We have two bedrooms for guests, one upstairs has one queen size and one single bed with own ensuite and lounge. Downstairs one queen and one single bed with own ensuite Motueka is the stop over place for visitors to explore Abel Tasman and Kahurangi National Parks, Golden Bay and Kaiteriteri golden sands beach is 10 km away. Local attractions include Alpine and coastal walks, trout and sea fishing, boating and many interesting crafts and wine trails. Guided tours can be arranged. Motueka has New Zealand's best climate. No Smoking inside please. We have "Major", the friendly family cat and Bunge the spoodle dog.

MOUNTAIN VIEW & WATERFRONT

Motueka

Homestay B&B
Address: "Grey Heron", 110 Trewavas Street, Motueka
Name: Sandro and Laura
Telephone: (03) 528 0472
Fax: (03) 528 0473
Email: S1369@TravelSite.co.nz
Beds: 1 King, 2 Queen, 1 Single King, 1 Single (4 bedrooms)
Bathroom: 1 Ensuite, 1 Guest Share
Tariff: B&B (Special) Ensuite $100, King $80, Queen $70, Single $40, Twin $60, Babies in cots free, Dinner $30 pp.
Nearest Town: Motueka town centre 2km

We are a couple recently moved from the North of Italy to the South of New Zealand, much travelled and keen on tramping and mountaineering. Our beautiful garden faces the Moutere River Estuary: you will enjoy our breakfast (traditional English and Italian specialities) overlooking a superb tidal view of the Kahurangi National Park mountain range (Mt Arthur). You will appreciate our Mediterranean atmosphere in the heart of New Zealand nature, among native trees and lovely singing birds. Depending on the season, you will have the chance to see the spectacular White Herons and Royal Spoonbills feeding in the Estuary.

Sandro is a registered "Mountaineering and Outdoor" Instructor and Italian Language teacher: you can book courses of rock-climbing and ice-climbing. If you prefer tramping, Sandro can be your Guide along the tracks of the surrounding National Parks. We offer to our clients the opportunity to know better the Italian culture, arranging lessons of Italian language and cooking (ideal for weekly staying).

Our house is close to the beach: you can have a jog or a quiet walk along the Quay, safe wind-surfing, boating and swimming just across the road. The 18 hole golf course is 15 min. walking. The ensuite bedroom includes a private driveway and entrance if you want to feel more comfortable. On request we prepare delicious recipes of our Italian Cuisine, famous all around the world, using fresh herbs and vegetables from our garden. You can enjoy dinner with us, overlooking wonderful sunsets beyond the mountains. Coffee, tea, laundry facilities. No smoking in the house. Secure off-street parking. Links with kayaking and trout fishing companies for booking tours. Benvenuti tutti gli amici italiani.

Directions: *At the southern roundabout in High Street (coming from Nelson) turn right into Wharf road towards Port Motueka, then turn left into Trewavas Street. Look for our sign on the left side of the street.*
Home Page: http://www.TravelSite.co.nz

Motueka

Self Contained & Homestay B&B

Address: 27 Fearon Street, Motueka
Name: Rowan Cottage,
Renee Alleyne and Trish McGee
Telephone: (03) 528 6492 or (03) 528 6442
Email: trish-renee@clear.net.nz
Beds: King or 2 Single (2 Bedrooms)
Bathroom: 1 Ensuite,
1 Family share
Tariff: B&B (Full) $5 extra cooked breakfast p.p
Double $80, extra person $20, children under 12 $10.
Homestay single room $35. Dinner $15 by arrangement.
NZ B&B Vouchers accepted $20 surcharge
Nearest Town: Motueka, less than 1 km

We welcome you to our home. Beside the cottage, we have a sunny separate newly-built studio for your accommodation, situated on our 1/2 acre organic property - fruit trees, flowers, vege garden and chickens. We know you'll find your stay tranquil. We also have a modest room in our cottage for the budget conscious traveller, where you can experience the joy of a home away from home. Our family includes a large, friendly Newfoundland X dog, who will bark to let us know that you have arrived. Children are welcome, but will generally need to share your bed/living room, although sometimes we can offer a single room in our house.
Town is only a 10 minute walk and our local beach which boasts a breeding colony of spoonbills is 15 minutes walk. Motueka is not more than 1 hours drive form Abel Tasman National Park, Golden Bay, Mt Arthur & Kahurangi National Park and only 20 minutes form beautiful Kaiteriteri beach. Smoking outside only please.

Riwaka, Motueka

Homestay

Address: 'Bridge House', 274 Main Road,
Riwaka, R.D.3, Motueka
Name: Alwynne & Joe Farrow
Telephone: (03) 528 6217 **Fax**: (03) 528 6217
Email: JoeFarrow@xtra.co.nz
Beds: 1 Double, 3 Single (3 bedrooms)
Bathroom: 1 Guests share, 1 Family share
Tariff: B&B (full) Double $70, Single $40,
Children 50%, Credit Cards. NZ B&B Vouchers accepted
Nearest Town: 3km north of Motueka

We warmly welcome guests to our beautiful area and enjoy sharing with them our local knowledge and discoveries. We are situated on State Highway 60, midway between Nelson and Takaka and adjacent to the Motueke River - a popular trout fishing and whitebaiting venue. Our home is centrally located for wineries, local artists and crafts people. There is easy access to both Kahurangi and Abel Tasman National Parks, and a 10 km drive to Kaiteriteri Beach. We have a comfortable family home - without period furniture or chandeliers - and our tariff is reasonable. Our own interests include music, quilting, gardening, exploring, woodturning and woodworking. We provide good cooked or continental breakfasts (at any time to suit) and can personally recommend excellent nearby restaurants for eveing dining out. Our home is a non-smoking zone, but smokers are welcome to use the covered veranda, off the lounge. We have no children or animals but do offer laundry facilities.
Directions: *3km north of Motueka township, first house on right across the Motueka River Bridge on State Highway 60. (Watch for following traffic as you slow to turn in!)*
Home Page: members.tripod.com/BridgeHouseBanB

Motueka
Self Contained Accommodation
Address: 'Sea Haven', 43 Green Tree Road,
Riwaka RD3, Motueka
Name: Barbara and Tim Robson
Telephone: (03) 528 8892
Beds: 1 Double, 2 Single (1 Bedroom)
Bathroom: 1 Private
Tariff: B&B (Continental) Double $85,
Single $70, $15 each additional person.
NZ B&B Vouchers accepted. Credit cards accepted
Nearest Town: Motueka 5 km

Welcome to Sea Haven.
Enjoy the serenity of the Riwaka Estuary while using us as your base to explore the beauty of Tasman and Golden Bay.
Sit on the jetty and take in the rustic fishing village charm and changing moods of the estuary. Swim on he high tide or wander the beach on the low and enjoy the panoramic view and the bird life.
Start your day with freshly baked croissants on the patio and in the evenings sit in our private garden and relax.
We have travelled, tramped and cycle-toured extensively both overseas and throughout New Zealand and are happy to help you plan your visits in our area.
A non smoker household with two teenage children, we welcome families. Laundry available.
Directions: *Head north from Motueka on Kaiteriteri Rd, cross Motueka River Bridge and take 1st right into Lodders Lane, then left into School Rd and right into Green Tree Rd.*

Kaiteriteri Beach, Nelson Bays
Bed & Breakfast
Address: Bayview B&B, Kaiteriteri Heights, RD2 Motueka.
Name: Aileen and Tim Rich
Telephone: (03) 527 8090
Fax: (03) 527 8090 **Mobile**: (025) 545 835
Email: kaiteri.bayview@xtra.co.nz
Beds: 1 Twin, 1King (2 bedrooms)
Bathroom: 2 Private
Tariff: B&B (special) Double $120, Single $90,
Dinner by arrangement. Credit cards accepted.
Nearest Town: Motueka (10 mins by car) Nelson 60kms

We welcome you to share our lovely new home at the sunniest and most beautiful area in New Zealand. Bayview overlooks the sparkling blue waters and golden sand of Kaiteriteri, the gateway to the Abel Tasman National Park. We can arrange Park excursions, kayaking, trout fishing the Riwaka, only 5 minutes away. Visit craft people and wineries, play golf, horse ride, take a day trip to Golden Bay or simply make the most of our 3 beautiful beaches. Your rooms are large with extensive views from private terraces. They are beautifully decorated, have comfortable sitting area, ensuite with heated towel rail and hair dryer, fridge, tea/coffee facilities and TV. Laundry, phone, fax and e-mail available. A full breakfast is served at your convenience on your terrace or in dining room. Walk to beach, launches and water taxis, and 2 restaurants. A variety of cafes within 5-10 minutes drive. Packed lunch, dinner or barbecue by arrangement.
Directions: *Turn off 3 kms along Kaiteriteri Road at the Blue Bed sign on Cederman Drive corner. Our sign is at the gate. Map on Homepage.*
Home Page: bayviewbandb.webnz.co.nz

Kaiteriteri Tasman District

Holiday & Health Resort
Address: Martin Farm Road, Kaiteriteri Beach, Tasman.
Name: Kimi Ora Holiday & Health Resort /Owner Dietmar Glaser
Telephone: (03) 527 8027 **Freephone**: 0800 222 999
Fax: (03) 527 8134 **Email**: info@kimiora.co.nz
Beds: 18 Queen, 9 Double, 43 Single (22 Bedrooms)
Bathroom: 22 Private
Tariff: B&B (Continental) from $55-$99 per person per night. Studio Units up to 3 people. Family Units 4-7 people. Family or Honeymoon suite up to 4 people. Dinner available during summer. Credit cards accepted.
Nearest Town: Kaiteriteri

Take time out - Relax, Recharge, Get Healthy. Kimi Ora offers: A wide range of health therapies, including massage, yoga, counselling, reflexology, beauty care and herbal baths. Our fully qualified professional staff will help you get the balance back into your life. Enjoy contemporary chalet comfort, in peaceful surroundings. Watch the sun rise over the sea in the morning and enjoy stunning coastal views from your chalet balcony or conservatory. Each unit has tea making facilities - some have cooking facilities. Kimi Ora also has full conference facilities. Indulge in our resort facilities: heated swimming pool, spa pool, sauna, tennis courts, gymnasium, fitness trail, lounge and superb whole food restaurant which is open during summer. Adventure into nature's best known scenic playground with the Abel Tasman National Park at your backdoor - you can go kayaking, fishing, horse trekking, tramping, gold penning, golfing and much more.
Directions: *Well sign posted from Kaiteriteri. Arrangements for collection from Motueka airport of bus terminal can be made.*
Home Page: www.kimiora.co.nz

Marahau, Abel Tasman National Park

Homestay+Self-contained Accom.
Address: 'Abel Tasman Stables' Marahau Valley Road, R.D. 2 Motueka
Name: George Bloomfield
Telephone: (03) 527 8181 **Fax**: (03) 527 8181
Email: abel.tasman.stables.accom@xtra.co.nz
Beds: Homestay: 1 Queen, 2 Single (2 bedrooms)
SC Cottage: 1 Double, 2 Single (2 bedrooms).
Bathroom: Homestay: 1 Ensuite, 1 Family share SC Cottage: 1 Private.
Tariff: Homestay B&B: Double $80 to $90, Single $55 includes continental breakfast. Self contained cottage: $85 two persons, $10 each additional person. Continental breakfast $7 per person. Continental breakfast $7 per person. Cooked breakfast $5 extra. Dinner $25 by arrangement. Credit Cards (Visa/MC). NZ B&B Vouchers accepted $10 surcharge Dec-Apr.
Nearest Town: Motueka 18 Kms

Abel Tasman Stables accommodation situated alongside the very beautiful and popular Abel Tasman National Park offers a variety of accommodation, friendly NZ hospitality in extensive garden setting only five minutes walk to beach and Abel Tasman coastal track.
The house situated on elevated site gives magnificent views of Tasman Bay and Marahau valley. Activities available in Marahau include sea kayaking, boat trips, swimming with seals, tramping or walking in the national park, fishing and gathering shellfish. Meals available at the licensed Park Cafe at the start of the coastal track or by arrangement with host.
Directions: *From Motueka travel north 18km following signs to Abel Tasman National Park Marahau. Marahau Valley Road is well signposted. The homestay property is up the first drive on the left.*

Marahau, Abel Tasman National Park

Self-contained Accommodation

Address: Beach Rd, Marahau, RD2 Motueka
Name: Robert Palzer
Telephone: (03) 527 8232 **Fax**: (03) 527-8211
Email: o.v.ch@xtra.co.nz
Beds: 8 Queen (8 bedrooms)
Bathroom: 8 Ensuite
Tariff: B&B (full) Double $111-$128, Children $17. Accommodation only: $88-$105.
Credit cards accepted.   NZ B&B Vouchers accepted surcharge for Chalet with B&B $43.
Chalet only: $20. Studio with B&B $26. Studio Only no surcharge.
Nearest Town: 15km north of Motueka on SH60. Signposted to: Abel Tasman
National Park-Marahau.

*Your hosts Robert and Constanca Palzer welcome you to the OCEAN VIEW CHALETS - right
at the entrance to that beautiful ABEL TASMAN NATIONAL PARK. Located on a 20 ha
coastal farm, slightly elevated you will find the natural timber Chalets, fully self-contained,
with excellent panoramic views towards Tasman Bay, Fisherman Island, Marlborough
Sounds, Durville Island and onto rural farm land. Each Chalet has a kitchen, ensuite
bathroom, spacious living area, bedroom with view, balcony, TV phone, radio / clock. We offer
also two double studio bedrooms with panoramic views, ensuite bathroom, coffee / tea making,
phone, balcony. We will serve you a delicious and healthy breakfast (continental or cooked)
at our sunny main building or alternatively you can provide your own breakfast. Within
walking distance you will find: Park Cafe-Restaurant, sea kayaking, water taxi, swim with
seals and Marahau beach, Abel Taman Coastal Walkway. We are looking forward to
welcoming you at sunny Marahau.*
Home Page: http://abel.tasman.chalets.webnz.co.nz/

Takaka Hill, Motueka

Farmstay+Self-Contained Accom.

Address: Kairuru State Highway 60, Takaka Hill, Motueka
Name: David & Wendy Henderson
Telephone: (03) 528 8091/Freephone 0800-524 787
Fax: (03) 528 8091 **Mobile**: (025) 337 457
Email: kairuru@xtra.co.nz
Beds: Homestead: 1 Dble,1 Twn(2 bdrms):
Kea Cttge:1 Queen,1 Twin/Superking,
1 Attic twin (3 bdrms) **Pipit Cttge**:1Qun,1Twn(2bdrm)
Bathroom: Homestead: 1 Private. Cottages: Each has private bathroom.
Tariff: B&B (Full) Double $100, Extra person $20, Children under 5 free; Dinner $30
adult, Children $10; Selfcatering: $80 - 2 people - $10 extra
person. Credit cards, Vouchers accepted $15 Surcharge
Nearest Town: Motueka 17km

*Kairuru is a working hill country sheep and cattle farm of 4000 acres, nestled high on the
unique Marble Mountain. Guests accommodation is offered in two fully equipped private two
bedroom cottages, exclusively yours. Both cottages have wonderful sea views overlooking the
Abel Tasman National Park. We are ideally situated to explore both Golden Bay and the Abel
Tasman National Park. The wooden cottages are modern and comfortable with sitting room,
telephone, TV, electric blankets, kitchen and laundry. A good selection for breakfast is supplied
and made by yourselves. Our home is set in an established attractive garden with swimming
pool and many native birds. You are welcome to join in on farming activities or to stroll around
the farm. We look forward to your company and we will do our very best to ensure your stay
is enjoyable.* **Directions**: *From Motueka take the road to Takaka (S / H 60). Kairuru is 17km
from Motueka on the right hand side of the road.* **Home Page**: http://webnz.co.nz/kairuru

Patons Rock, Takaka

Farmstay
Address: Patons Rock Road, Takaka
Name: Patondale
Telephone: (03) 525 8262
Toll Free: 0800 306 697
Mobile: (025) 936 891
Fax: (03) 525 8262
Beds: 1 Double,
2 Single (2 bedrooms)
Bathroom: 1 Private
(we take one party at a time).
Tariff: B&B (full) Double $100, Single $70, Children $20, Dinner $20.
Nearest Town: Takaka 10km, Collingwood 17km

A BAY BEAUTY.
IMAGINE! Waking to the sounds of the waves breaking on the beach below, enjoy a leisurely stroll along our long sandy beach and then taste a "real farmers" breakfast with us using farm fresh produce. We are CENTRALLY situated for all Golden Bay attractions. Our architecturally designed home nestled above Patons Rock beach offers "SIMPLY MAGIC" 360 degree views and is well appointed for your comfort. Our 200 acre Dairyfarm allows you the chance to see a modern dairying operation in action. We have interests in travel, gardening and local government and are non smokers. David, Vicki and Hayden INVITE YOU to be our guest at "Patondale" where we offer genuine Kiwi hospitality, peace and tranquillity.
Directions: *Turn off at Patons Rock sign on SH60, 10km from Takaka township enroute to Collingwood. E.S. No 197*

Takaka

Self-contained Accommodation
Address: 'Amanzi', Rangihaeata Road,
R.D.2, Takaka
Name: Barbara & John Dunn
Telephone: (03) 525 9615
Fax: (03) 525 9678
Mobile: 025-247 0378
Beds: 2 Single,
Divan bed in living area (1 bedroom)
Bathroom: 1 Private
Tariff: B&B (full) Double $75, Single $45.
Credit cards accepted. NZ B&B Vouchers accepted
Nearest Town: Takaka 6 kms

Our two-acre property is situated above the Takaka Estuary where we are privileged to enjoy one of the most spectacular views in Golden Bay. We enjoy travel but love to return here to our cat, our garden and our seaside lifestyle. For our guests we have a self-contained wing-bedroom, bathroom and living room with a well-equipped kitchen area with rangette. This gives the option of preparing light meals as an alternative to going out each night to one of Takaka's wide range of eating places, and allows a total self-catering option (Discount tariff). We aim to provide a comfortable base for guests while they explore Golden Bay: beautiful wild beaches, walking tracks, limestone caves, boat trips, restaurants in remote places, art and craft trails. Weary guests can sit on the deck and gaze at the view! Breakfast full or continental as requested. No smoking inside, please.
Directions: *Please phone.*

Takaka
Bed & Breakfast and Self contained accommodation
Address: "Rose Cottage", Hamama Rd,
R.D.1, Takaka, Golden Bay
Name: Phil & Margaret Baker
Telephone: (03) 525 9048
Beds: 1 King/Queen, 2 Single (2 bedrooms)
Bathroom: 1 Guests share
Tariff: B&B (continental) Double $70,
Single $45. Self contained Double $85-$100,
$15 extra person. Credit Cards.
Nearest Town: Takaka 5km

Rose Cottage, much loved home of Phil and Margaret is situated in the beautiful Takaka Valley 103km from Nelson and 5km before Takaka township. Set on 2 1/2 acres amongst mature totara trees with bush and mountain views, the perfect place from which to explore this peaceful area of New Zealand. The two room Bed & breakfast was refurbished last year, the furniture being made by Phil in his craft workshop. The three self contained units which are separate from Rose Cottage have full kitchens, quality furnishings and private sun decks.
The 12 metre indoor solar heated swimming pool is available to all guests.
Phil and Margaret have travelled extensively on photographic and mountaineering expeditions around the world, other interests include natural history, gardening, arts & crafts, and helping to make their guests stay a memorable one.

Takaka, Golden Bay
Homestay
Address: 177 Commercial Street, Takaka
Name: "Haven House"
Telephone: (03) 525 9554
Fax: (03) 525 8720
Beds: 1 Queen, 3 Single (2 bedrooms)
Bathroom: 1 Guests share, 1 Family share
Tariff: B&B (special) Double $70-$85,
Single $50, Triple $95,
(off season rates May to October)
Dinner $18pp on request, Credit Cards.
NZ B&B Vouchers accepted
Nearest Town: Takaka - 400m from township

New Zealand Association
FARM & HOME HOSTS

Haven House, centrally located in quiet area, off street parking, situated 10 minutes walk from shops / cafes and all amenities, has been our home and 'haven' for many years. Our grown family are now away enjoying life elsewhere. We have always loved travelling and meeting new people and have decided to share with you the tranquillity and comforts of our home for your pleasure. The guest lounge (TV) and dining room overlooks the large established secluded garden. A barbeque area, (crockery etc supplied) Laundry facility is available. Enjoy grapefuit from our trees and other 'home' goodies for your breakfast. Complimentary afternoon teas in the garden. (Winter time in front of a cosy fire. Bedrooms have electric heating. Golden Bay enjoys moderate winter temperatures.) A courtesy vehicle pick up service to aerodrome and bus depot is available. Notification and bookings for accommodation recommended. My aim is personal service and hospitality, endeavouring to make your stay a memorable one. Looking forward to meeting you.
Your Host
       Pam Peacock

Takaka
Homestay
Address: "Halcyon Homestay",
Rangihaeata Rd, PO Box 21, Takaka
Name: Bev & Jock Harrison
Telephone: (03) 525 8125
Fax: (03) 525 8127
Beds: 1 Queen, 1 Single (2 bedrooms)
Bathroom: 1 Private
(we take one party at a time)
Tariff: B&B (full/continental) Double $70,
Single $45, Children half price. Credit Cards
NZ B&B Vouchers accepted
Nearest Town: Takaka 5 kms

Our 10 acre water-front property overlooks the Bay with views of the estuary and up the Takaka river. Its central location brings Abel Tasman and Kahurangi National Parks as well as the West Coast and Farewell Spit within easy travelling distances. The township is just 10 minutes away by car As we only take one booking at a time you have a choice of rooms-one with a queen sized bed, the other with an extra long single bed. There is a TV, radio and tea and coffee making facilities in your own sitting area with a private entrance from a spacious sun deck. Our interests include travel, tramping, photography and weaving and we are happy to suggest how to make the best use of your time in the Bay. No smoking please.
Directions: *Rangihaeata Road, emergency No. 44. Phone for detailed directions.*

Takaka
Homestay
Address: Croxfords Homestay
Dodson Road, RD 1 Takaka
Name: Pam and John Croxford
Telephone: (03) 525 7177
Freephone 0800 264 156
Fax: (03) 525 7177
Email: CROXFORDS@xtra.co.nz
Beds: 2 Bedrooms, 1 with 1 Double and 1 Single,
1 with 2 Single (fully accessible).
Bathroom: 2 Ensuites (1 fully accessible)
Tariff: B&B (full) Double $90, Single $70. Children under 10 free. Dinner $20pp.
Credit Cards: Visa/Mastercard/Bankcard.
Nearest Town: Takaka 2 km

Pam and John welcome you to our spacious modern home in a peaceful rural setting only 2 minutes from Takaka. The view overlooking the Kahurangi National Park is spectacular. Pam loves cooking and her evening meals are special, using produce from our garden. She enjoys catering for special diets. Our substantial breakfasts include home made bread, muesli, yoghurt and preserves. In summer we often have evening barbecues. Golden Bay offers many activities and crafts and we enjoy assisting visitors make the most of their time here. We are close to the beautiful beaches of the Bay and our two magnificent National Parks, Kahurangi and Abel Tasman. Our library has many New Zealand books for browsing. We have no children at home, nor pets. We ask guests not to smoke inside. We also operate KAHURANGI GUIDED WALKS specialising in walks for all ages and levels of fitness. See more about both Homestay and Walks at www//KahurangiWalks.webnz.co.nz.
Directions: *Turn left at the 1st or 2nd junction (both Dodson Rd) after Paynes Ford bridge, 2 km before Takaka* **Home Page**: www//KahurangiWalks.webnz.co.nz

Takaka

Homestay
Address: Central Takaka Road, RD 1, Takaka
Name: Baytime Manor
Telephone: (03) 525 8551
Beds: 1 Queen (1 bedroom)
Bathroom: 1 Private
Tariff: B&B (full)
Double $105 (November 1 - April 30).
Double $80 (May 1-October 31).
VISA and Mastercard Accepted.
Nearest Town: Takaka (2.5 kms).

We look forward to welcoming you to our home and helping you switch to 'baytime'! Our beautiful 1880's homestead has been lovingly renovated and we offer our upper living area being a large comfortable double room and private bathroom. Baytime Manor is set in a lovely developing garden which includes a huge variety of fruit trees which we hope you will enjoy. A swim in the pool or a game of Petanque on the lawn are great ways to end the day. We are close to Takaka township and are centrally located to many of Golden Bay's pleasures including stunning scenery, great walks, arts and crafts, fishing, golden sand beaches and freshwater swimming holes. Joe, Dee, Sarah (aged 7 years), and Darmah the cat will be happy to help you discover the best the Bay has to offer and make your stay special. Sorry but there's no smoking in the Manor.
Directions: *After crossing Paynes Ford bridge on your way into Takaka turn right at 1st junction by the Community Hospital on the Central Takaka road and we are 200 metres up on the left.*

Takaka, Golden Bay

Beachfront Bed & Breakfast
Address: "The Beach House",
Patons Rock Beach,
Takaka, Golden Bay
Name: Lesley & Murray McIver,
& Iain (aged 13 yrs)
Telephone: 03-525 8133
Mobile: 025-302 729
Beds: 1 Super King or 2 Single
(1 bedroom)
Bathroom: 1 Ensuite
Tariff: B&B (full) Double $100-120, Single $80-100.
Nearest Town: Takaka 11 km, Collingwood 18 km.

Patons Rock is a north facing beach within the beautiful sheltered waters of Golden Bay. Great for swimming, walking, fishing, beach combing or just sitting in the sun on your own terrace. Your room is well appointed, right on the beach, with space to relax and have the kind of holiday you would usually have to travel overseas for. Sit in bed and watch the tide come and go, or the moon reflecting on the water - this is truly a magic place. We offer peace and privacy in quality surroundings. We enjoy a wide variety of interests including gardening, embroidery and handcrafts, kayaking, walking, fishing, and share our home with our three beautiful cats. Breakfast is served in your own generous room or on the terrace, you choose the time and place. Lesley and Murray both enjoy cooking and will provide a full and varied breakfast menu. Guests are welcome to smoke outside. We are happy to collect you from the airport or bus station.

Takaka and Collingwood

Homestay, Self Contained Accommodation
Address: Tukurua RD 2, Takaka
Name: Golden Bay Lodge and Garden.
Ray and Mary Nelson
Telephone: (03) 525 9275
Fax: (03) 525 9275
Email: goldenbaylodge@xtra.co.nz
Beds: 4 Queen, 4 Single (4 bedrooms)
Bathroom: 4 Private
Tariff: B&B (full)
Double $110-$130, Single $80, Self Contained $105.
Dinner $30 by arrangement, Children $25. No pets. Credit Cards accepted.
Nearest Town: Collingwood 10 km, Takaka 18 km.

We are pleased to welcome you to "Golden Bay Lodge and Garden".
We offer you 10 acres of piece and tranquillity with the best views of Golden Bay taking in Fairwell Spit to Separation Point and Durville Island. Quality self contained and B&B accommodation is available with panoramic views from well appointed and comfortable cliff top units, twenty metres from the beach front. Walk down the pathway to the sandy beach and enjoy all that Golden Bay has to offer or spend time strolling among acres of magnificent rhododendrons, azaleas and camellias in the company of Tuis and other native birds. 100 old fashion roses have recently been added to the garden. We are handy to all of Golden Bay's many attractions and are happy to help with any tourist information you may require.
We look forward to your visit, where we are sure your expectations will be exceeded.
Non smokers preferred. Kayaks available.
Home Page: http://GoldenBayLodge.webnz.co.nz

Collingwood (Village)

Homestay
Address: Collingwood Homestead,
Elizabeth Street,
Collingwood, Golden Bay
Name: Adrian & Maggie Veenvliet
Telephone: (03) 524 8079
Fax: (03) 524 8979
Email: Maggie@CollingwoodHomestead.co.nz
Beds: 2 King, 1 Queen, 2 Single (4 bedrooms)
Bathroom: 3 Ensuite, 1 Private
Tariff: B&B (special)
Double $150-$165, Single $125,
Dinner $35 includes pre-dinner drink & wine,
Credit Cards (VISA/Mastercard/Bankcard).
Nearest Town: Collingwood (we are in the village)

Collingwood
Homestead

Welcome to Collingwood Homestead.
At the top of our drive you will find our "Slice of Paradise". Our beautifully renovated colonial style home is situated in an unbeatable location, overlooking the Aorere River Estuary and mountain range. Enjoy the ever-changing views from an easy chair! Enjoy the romance and elegance, with good food, candle light, an open fire, antiques and flowers everywhere. We aim to recapture the gracious lifestyle that most people have forgotten. So come and stay and let us pamper you.
We regret our home is not suitable for children.
Home Page: CollingwoodHomestead.co.nz

Collingwood
Bed & Breakfast
Address: Hakea Hill House, Para Para, Collingwood, Golden Bay
Postal: P O Box 35, Collingwood, Golden Bay
Name: Vic & Liza Eastman
Telephone: (03) 524 8487. From USA: 011-64-3-524 8487
Fax: (03) 524 8487
Email: vic.eastman@clear.net.nz
Beds: 2 Double, 6 Singles (3 bedrooms).
Bathroom: 1 Guests share
Tariff: B&B (special) Double $100, Single $75, Children $35 each.
Nearest Town: Takaka 20Kms /Collingwood 10 Kms

Hakea Hill House, built above an estuary behind Para Para Beach, has views that encompass Para Para Peak and the Wakamarama Ranges to the South, Farewell Spit to D'Urville Island beyond Separation Point over Golden Bay, and to Mount Taranaki on the North Island. The house is modern and spacious with a hint of Southwest and New Mexico style. Two guest rooms have large balconies. Both American and New Zealand electric outlets are installed. Television and tea or coffee in guest rooms and telephone and Fax and modem access are available at all times. Vic is a practising physician specialising in Family Practice and Emergency Medicine. His hobbies include astronomy; guests are welcome to explore the magnificent Southern skies with Questar 3.5 and Odyssey 17.5 inch telescopes weather permitting. Liza, besides homemaker, community activist, and expert cook, is interested in sailing, horse riding, machine quilting and wearable art. We have three adult children, five computers, two outdoor dogs, and thirty five hectares of hills and trails. Golden Bay is well worth the effort of a visit. The best weather is late summer and autumn. One may fly from Wellington for the weekend with Takaka Valley Air Services (Telephone 0800 501 901) or drive from Nelson (two hours) to explore Farewell Spit, Kaihoka Lakes, Aorere gold fields, limestone caves, Waikoropupu Springs, Settlers' Museums, pottery and craft outlets, wild West Coast or serene Bay beaches, mudflats and estuaries, scenic light plane flights, pony trekking, golf, Bay and estuary sailing, canoeing, river rafting, fishing, scalloping and whitebaiting in season, bush walks.
No smoking in the house please.
Directions: *Reservations are necessary. Please telephone in person for reservations and detailed directions.*

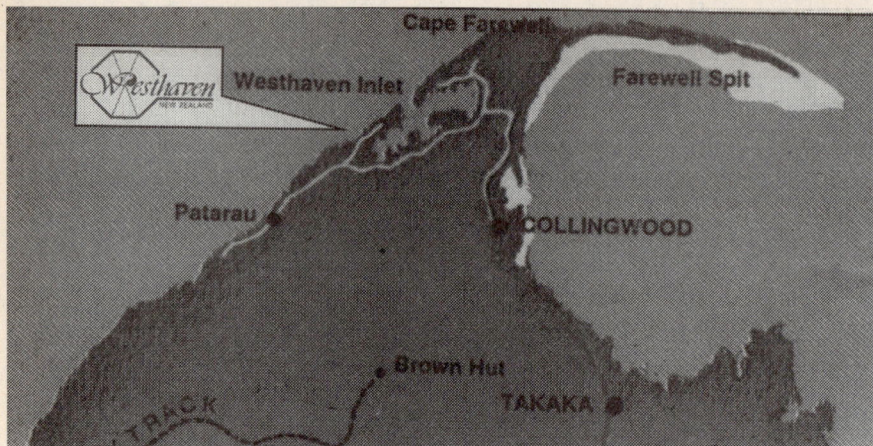

Westhaven

Retreat
Address: Te Hapu Road, Collingwood
Name: Westhaven Retreat
Telephone: (03) 524 8354
Fax: (03) 524 8354
Mobile: (025) 220 3941
Email: Westhaven.Retreat@xtra.co.nz
Beds: 4 Queen, 4 Single (5 bedrooms)
Bathroom: 2 Ensuite, 1 Guests share, 1 Family share
Tariff: B&B (full) Double $118-$140, Single $45-$85,
Dinner by arrangement. Credit Cards.
Nearest Town: Collingwood 30km

Westhaven Retreat invites you to take a break and relax on our Peninsula. Overlooking the Tasman Sea and the complete Westhaven Inlet, which is the second largest estuary in the South Island there are 800 acres of unspoiled wilderness for you to explore to leave you breathless. Take a stroll on the beach, swim, fish or discover beautiful rock formations, caves, palm groves and rainforests. Watch the bird life and look out for seals and dolphins. Westhaven is a very special place of outstanding ecological valves. Enjoy a guided eco-tour in total comfort with our gentle llamas or you may spend some quality time with them.
It is a place of complete relaxation in a brand new house with an ever-changing view. Tranquillity and peace with a variety of delicious meals make you forget the stress of daily life.
Bruno and Monika will do their utmost to make you feel at home. For friendly and old fashioned European hospitality you have come to the right place.
Directions: *Please phone, fax or email for reservations. Pick up can be arranged.*

Pakawau Beach, Collingwood
Homestay+Self-contained Accom.
Address: Pakawau Beach, Collingwood R.D. Golden Bay
Name: Val & Graham Williams
Telephone: (03) 524 8168
Fax: (03) 524 8168
Beds: 1 Double, 1 Single (1 bedroom)
Bathroom: 1 Family share, Spa available.
Tariff: B&B (full) Double $75, Single $60, Dinner $20.
NZ B&B Vouchers accepted All year.
Nearest Town: Collingwood 12km

We are the northern most bed and breakfast accommodation in the South Island, 9km from Farewell Spit. We are on the beachfront with views from Separation Point to Farewell Spit with a safe swimming beach only metres from our front door. We offer self contained accommodation with a base rate of $70 per night.
We are keen gardeners and grow most of our vegetables. Local seafoods available eg. whitebait, scallops, cockles. We have lived here for fifteen years and can advise or guide you to the 'Beauties of the Bay'.
The Farewell Spit Safari and Westhaven Mail Scenic Run will pick you up from our gate. We are handy to Wharariki Beach, Kaihoke Lakes, Te Anaroa Caves, Heaphy Track and Pupu Springs. A licensed cafe and tennis court are within walking distance. We are non smokers who enjoy walking, biking and swimming. Our two children have left home but not our cats. We look forward to meeting people and sharing our lifestyle.

Baton Valley, Motueka
Self Contained Farmstay Lodge
Address: River Island Lodge,
Baton Valley Road, Woodstock,
RD1, Motueka
Name: Carol Mckeever & Alistair Webber

RIVER ISLAND LODGE

Telephone: (03) 543 3844
Fax: (03) 543 3844
Email: riverfarm@ts.co.nz
Beds: 4 Queen, 4 Single (4 Bedrooms)
Bathroom: 4 Ensuite.
Tariff: B&B: Double $80(accommodation only). Special rates for children.
Breakfast (continental with home baking) $8 per person.
Dinner: several options available.
Credit cards: Visa/Mastercard
Nearest Town: Motueka 35 mins drive. Tapawera Village 20 mins drive.

At River Island Lodge we offer our guests a unique experience of the Nelson Backcountry. The lodge is part of our farm which is situated where the Baton river flows into the Motueka river (well known for its brown trout). You can fish for trout in pristine conditions, swim in clear deep pools, take a gentle kayak trip or go horse trekking in the mountains. The Lodge is self contained and has a stylish and comfortable country atmosphere. There are two well equipped country style kitchens for your use, a guest laundry, gas BBQ and a large lounge with lots of books and board games. You can enjoy the peaceful privacy of our remote location or become involved in the day to day activities of our farming family which includes our two school age children, two dogs, horses, cattle, chickens and ducks. River Island Lodge is 35 minutes from Motueka, one hour from Nelson and an easy drive to the Kahurangi, Abel Tasman and Nelson Lakes National parks. Wine, craft and garden trails are close by.
Website: http://www.riverislandlodge.co.nz

Tophouse

Historic, Farmstay and Self Contained cottages
Address: Tophouse, R.D.2, Nelson
Name: Melody & Mike Nicholls
Telephone: Freephone/fax 0800 Tophouse (867468)
Fax: (03) 521 1848
Email: tophouse@clearn.net.nz
Beds: 4 Cottages: 1 Double, 2/3 Singles (2 Bedrooms).
Homestay: 1 Queen, 1 Double, 6 Single (4 Bedrooms).
Bathroom: Cottages: Private. Homestay: 3 Guests share
Tariff: B&B (continental) $35/Adult, Dinner $20, Children double age plus $10.
Cottages $80/2 Adults plus $10/Extra, $8/Child. Credit cards.
Nearest Town: Blenheim 98km, Murchison 57km, Nelson 72km, St Arnaud 9km.

We, Melody and Mike Nicholls, with our young sons and two cats, invite you to share our unique home with its huge open fires, lovely setting and homely atmosphere.

Tophouse, a cob (mud) building, dating from the 1880's when it was a hotel, and reopened in 1989 as a Farm Guest House, has that 'good old days' feel about it. Situated on a golf course on 300 ha (730 acres) of picturesque high country farm running cattle, with much native bush and an abundance of bird life, a popular holiday spot for its peace and beauty, bush walks, fishing, and in the winter serves the two local ski fields. Tophouse is only 9 km from St Arnaud, gateway to Nelson Lakes National Park.

A typical farmhouse dinner is taken with the family and since the fire's going, 'real' toast for breakfast.

Cottages are 2 bedroom, fully self contained, with great views of the surrounding mountains.

Directions: *Just off State Highway 63 between Blenheim and Murchison and 9 km from St Arnaud is Tophouse, that's us! The area took its name from the building. If travelling from Nelson, leave State Highway 6 at Belgrove and travel towards St Arnaud, we're signposted from the main road and looking forward to your visit.*

St Arnaud, Nelson Lakes
Homestay
Address: St Arnaud Homestay,
Counter Post, St Arnaud, Nelson 7150
Name: Colin & Jill Clarke
Telephone: (03) 521 1028
Fax: (03) 521 1028
Email: c-clarke@st-arnaud.co.nz
Beds: 3 Queen, 2 Single (3 bedrooms)
Bathroom: 2 Ensuite, 1 Private
Tariff: B&B (full) Double $105, Single $65.
Dinner $25 (by prior arrangement). Credit cards.
Nearest Town: Blenheim and Nelson each about 1 hour travelling.

Our beautiful timbered home, warm and private, is set amidst native forest with a 3 minute walk to Lake Rotoiti (one of NZ's most beautiful and unspoiled lakes), Nelson Lakes National Park. The home affords lovely views of surrounding forests and mountains. Native birds abound. We offer superior accommodation and varied cuisine. Game meats (Colin is the hunter) may be served with quality NZ wines. Vegetarians also catered for. Guests may simply relax in comfort, enjoy the Park, or select one of Colin's highly acclaimed eco-activities and adventures. Colin operates St Arnaud Eco-Activities and Adventures. As a former ecologist, well versed in natural history, he has an extensive local knowledge. His 4WD alpine flora and fauna tours provide unparalleled access to the mountain summits, for any age or ability. A range of guided activities include nature walks, treks, historical and scenic 4WD tours (e.g. Molesworth), and gold prospecting. We warmly welcome you to our lifestyle hideaway.
Directions: *At St Arnaud, turn off at Black Valley Stream Bridge, into Bridge Street. We are at the first intersection.* **Home Page**: http://www.ts.co.nz./~c-clarke

St Arnaud, Nelson Lakes
Homestay
Address: State Highway 63, RD2, Nelson
Name: Merv and Gay Patch
Telephone: (03) 521 1191
Fax: (03) 521 1191
Email: Home@Tasman.net
Beds: 1 Queen, 2 Single (2 Bedrooms)
Bathroom: 2 Ensuite
Tariff: B&B (Full) Double $85, Single $50,
Dinner $20 pp.
Credit cards: Visa/Mastercard.
Nearest Town: Nelson 85 km; Blenheim 100 km; St Arnaud 4 km.

Enjoy the luxury and comfort of our one level purpose built home, nestled in a sunny 1 1/2 ha garden on the foot hills of the St Arnaud mountain range.
We are just 4 km from Lake Rotoiti and St Arnaud township - gateway to Nelson Lakes National Park, with its fishing, boating, tramping, white water rafting and 2 ski fields or just enjoy the beech forest and bird song. We are still developing our native plant gardens but the house - finished March 1999 - is fully developed for your comfort and enjoyment, with magnificent views from every window. Our spacious lounge is comfortably furnished, tea, coffee and cookies are available at all times. There is garaging for your vehicle with internal access and laundry facilities for your use. At the end of an exciting, energetic or relaxing day, share our delicious evening meal and friendly relaxed atmosphere. We are a non smoking household with a small shy cat. **Directions**: *State Highway 63 - 200 metres towards St Arnaud from the Nelson intersection. Please phone for direction.*

Mangles Valley, Murchison
Farmstay+Self-contained Accom.
Address: 'Green Hills Farm',
Mangles Valley, Murchison
Name: Margaret & Henry Rouse
Telephone: (03) 523 9067
Beds: 4 Single (2 bedrooms)
Bathroom: 1 Private (Cottage),
1 Family share (separate shower)
Tariff: B&B (continental)
Double $80, Single $50,
Dinner $20pp. NZ B&B Vouchers accepted $10 Surcharge
Nearest Town: 5kms North Murchison SH6. 7kms up Mangles Valley on sealed
Road.

We welcome you to our hill country sheep and beef farm set in the beautiful Mangles Valley. We have hosted overseas and New Zealand visitors for many years and all have appreciated the beauty and relaxed atmosphere. There is excellent trout fishing, and gold-panning in the Mangles River below the house. We are within close proximity of a nine-hole golf course (clubs available), horse trekking, white water rafting and kayaking. We are surrounded by native bush, beautiful rivers and peaceful bush walks. We are still actively farming, have travelled overseas several times, love meeting people and welcoming them to our home and lovely garden. We are involved in community affairs - Lions, W.D.F.F. and S.P.E.L.D. teaching. Breakfast includes home-made muesli, fresh fruits from the garden, local honey, home-made marmalade and farm eggs if wanted.. All vegetables home grown. A very comfortable self-contained cottage (can sleep 4) is also available - includes colour TV, wood-burner. This is ideal for a longer stay or overnight privacy. **Directions**: *Please phone.*

Gowanbridge, Murchison
Homestay
Address: Dizzy's Corner,
Gowanbridge, R.D.3, Murchison
Name: Heather Davis & Gordon Trotter
Telephone: (03) 523 9678
Fax: (03) 523 9678
Email: dizzycorner@xtra.co.nz
Beds: 1 Queen, 1 Double, 1 Single (3 bedrooms)
Bathroom: 1 Guests share
Tariff: B&B (full) Double $100, Single $55, Children negotiable, Dinner $30pp.
NZ B&B Vouchers accepted $30 surcharge (double)
Nearest Town: Murchison, 30km south on SH6

Share with us the beauty and tranquility of our farmlet nestled amongst the hills and surrounded by the magnificent native bush and the Buller River. Local activities include world-class trout fishing and hunting (guides available), tramps in the nearby National Parks (Kahurangi and Nelson Lakes, rafting, kayaking and gold-panning, or, just en route to or from the West Coast or Christchurch. Our home is solid and warm with a comfortable country charm. Guest bedrooms, bathroom and separate lounge are upstairs, or you can join us downstairs if you wish. Smoking outdoors only please. Delicious breakfasts and evening meals (wine included if wanted) are tastefully prepared from fresh local foods, some of which are home grown. Our interests include yachting, car racing, cooking, gardening, golf and travelling. We keep sheep and have ducks and hens as well as Kea, our fox terrier and Jess our bearded collie.
Directions: *Please phone.*

Murchison

Farmstay
Address: 'Awapiriti', Highway 65,
Maruia Valley, Murchison
Name: Irene & David Free
Telephone: (03) 523 9466
Fax: (03) 523 9777
Mobile: (025) 220 4466
Beds: 1 Queen, 1 Double,
2 Single (3 bedrooms)
Bathroom: 2 Ensuite, 1 Private
Tariff: B&B (continental/full) Double $100, Single $70, Dinner by arrangement.
Not suitable for children.
Nearest Town: Murchison 17km

Awapiriti is nestled in the beautiful Maruia Valley and occupies its own unique position accessed by a large bridge. Here we farm Elk, Deer, Cattle, Sheep and a friendly Bison family along with a few other farm pets. The comfortable Homestead is complimented by extensive lawns, gardens and pond. We have a special interest in our native birds and enjoy sharing this with our visitors. Guests are welcome to take a casual bush or farm walk or perhaps just relax in the garden. The Maruia river which bounds the farm offers trout fishing and swimming. the guests bedrooms are sunny and attractively decorated in colonial style with ensuites for comfort. Dinner is by arrangement and mostly consists of home-grown produce providing healthy country style meals. Breakfast is full or continental with seasonal fresh fruit and homemade jams and bread. Awapiriti is a haven for adults, unsuitable for children.
Directions: *Please phone or fax for a reservation.*

NELSON, GOLDEN BAY

http://www.bnb.co.nz

take a look

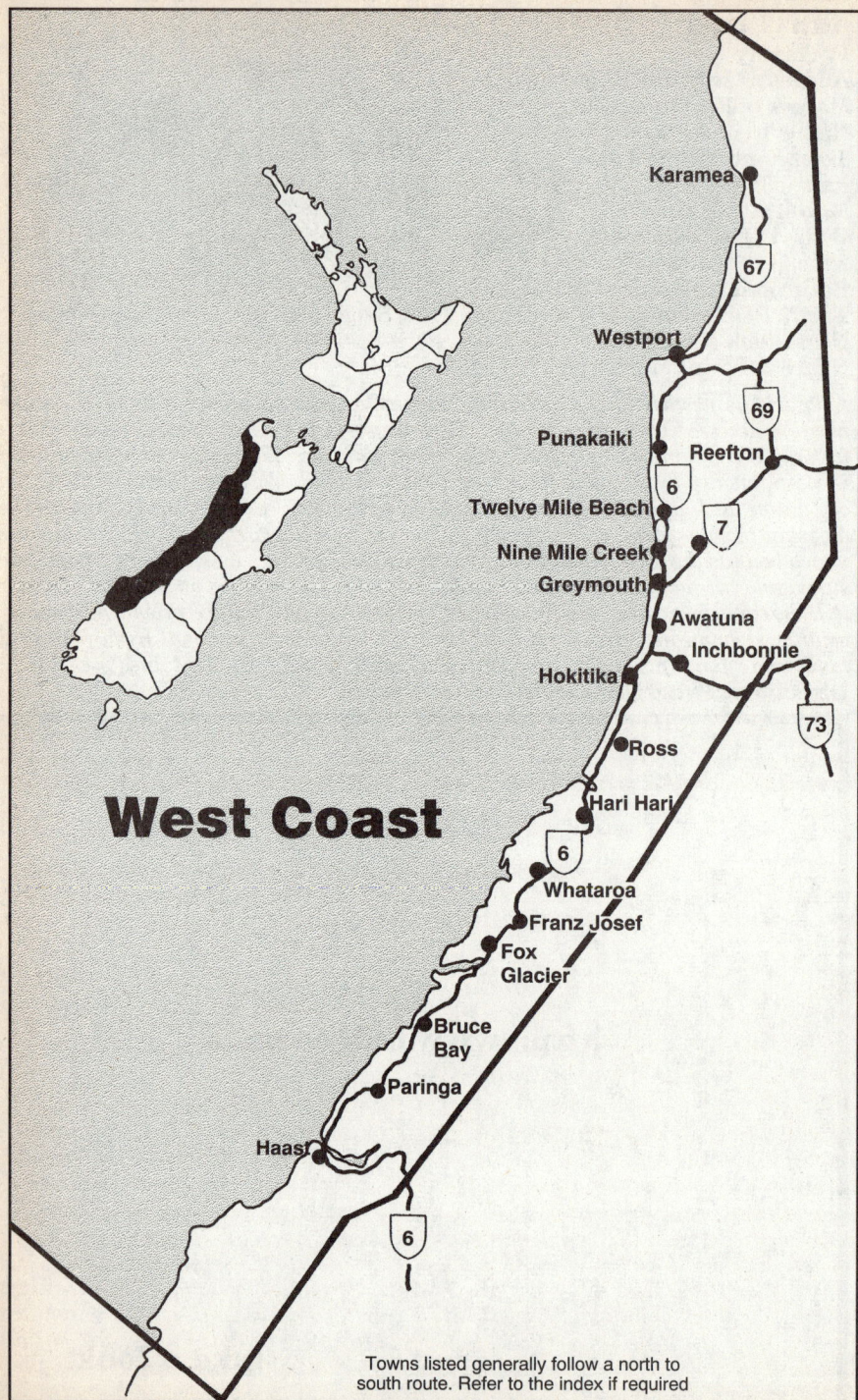

West Coast

Karamea

67

Westport

69

Punakaiki   Reefton

6

Twelve Mile Beach

7

Nine Mile Creek

Greymouth

Awatuna

Inchbonnie

Hokitika

73

Ross

Hari Hari

6

Whataroa

Franz Josef

Fox Glacier

Bruce Bay

Paringa

Haast

6

Towns listed generally follow a north to
south route. Refer to the index if required

Karamea
Farmstay
Address: "Beachfront Farmstay",
Karamea, RD 1, Westport
Name: Dianne & Russell Anderson
Telephone: (03) 782 6762
Fax: (03) 782 6762
Mobile: (025) 222 1755
Email: farmstay@xtra.co.nz
Beds: 1 Queen, 3 Single (3 bedrooms)
Bathroom: 1 Family share, 1 Ensuite
Tariff: B&B (full) Double $90, Single $60,
Children $20, Dinner $25pp, Credit cards. No smoking inside.
NZ B&B Vouchers accepted $20 surcharge
Nearest Town: 84km north of Westport on H67.

New Zealand Association FARM & HOME HOSTS

Our home is 2 mins walk from a sandy beach, you can walk for 8 kms and seldom see another person. I enjoy cooking, delicious home made shortbread and carrot cake is complimentary with tea and filter coffee at any time. Breakfasts are generous with juice, fresh fruit, yoghurt, cereals, fresh baked bread and pan fried fish straight from the sea (if the tide is right). We own a secluded valley, 8 kms long and it runs into the Kahurangi National park, it is bounded by native forest and to hear and see the native birds is a delight. Karamea offers the spectacular limestone arch and caves, trout fishing, golf course, walking tracks including the Heaphy and Wangapeka tracks. Children welcome (portacot and highchair).
Directions: *3km north of Little Wanganui on H67.*
Home Page: http://nz.com/webnz/bbnz/karamea.htm

Karamea
Farmstay, Self Contained Accommodation
Address: Bridge Street, Karamea,
No 1 RD, Westport
Name: Bridge Farm
(Rosalie and Peter Sampson)
Telephone: (03) 782 6955
0800 527 263 (0800 Karamea)
Fax: (03) 782 6748
Email: brdgfarm@voyager.co.nz
Beds: 4 Queen, 8 Single (8 Bedrooms)
Bathroom: 6 Private
Tariff: B&B (Continental) Double $80-$90. Children $8, Credit cards accepted.
Nearest Town: Karamea 500 m.

Since relinquishing their dairy farm to daughter Caroline and son-in-law Bevan, Rosalie and Peter have purpose built on their farm accommodation that neatly bridges the gap between motel and farm stay. Rosalie is now free to develop and tend her extensive flower garden and Peter is enjoying the transition from farmer to host. Both have an extensive knowledge of their district, its people and environment and are happy to direct guests to the many short walks that Karamea offers. We have time to converse with guests and are happy to do so. Each suite is self contained and has a private lounge that overlooks the farm to Kahurangi National Park beyond and features comfortable settees and elegant solid rimu tables and chairs. A small mob of deer graze nearby. A hearty continental breakfast is offered that includes fresh home baked croissants and nearby Karamea provides a choice of restaurants.

Westport

Boutique Country Lodge
Address: SH6, Lower Buller Gorge,
Westport Riverview Lodge.
Name: Noeline Biddulph
Telephone: (03) 789 6037
Free phone 0800 184 656
Fax: (03) 789 6037
Mobile: (025) 249 1286
Beds: 3 Queen, 1 Twin,
1 Double (4 bedrooms)
Bathroom: 4 Ensuite
Tariff: B&B (Full) Double $130, Single $97, Children under 12 $10, Dinner (3 course) $30pp, Credit Cards (VISA/MC).
Nearest Town: Westport 7km

Our lodge is a peaceful retreat overlooking the Buller River, 10 min from Westport on the main road from Picton to the West Coast. It is set on 35 acres farming deer and sheep. The suites are private tastefuly decorated, luxuriously appointed with ensuites. Large verandahs for outside meals if required. All amid the glory of a large flower garden and lawns. Activities close by include jet boating, horse trekking, underworld rafting, golf course, visit the seals. We also have a good selection of restaurants and cafes close by. We serve breakfast continental or full in your suite or our dinning room. Lunch and dinner by arrangement. Laundry facilities available. We have one small dog, very friendly. Smoking outside only. Unsuitable for pets. Reservations are recommended. Tariff changes end October 1999 to October 2000. Ample parking space. **Home Page**: http://friars.co.nz/host/riverview.html

Westport

"Steeples" Homestay
Address: Lighthouse Road,
RD 2, Cape Foulwind
Name: Pauline & Bruce Cargill
Telephone: (03) 789 7876
Mobile: 025-291 7665
Beds: 1 Queen,
2 Single (2 bedrooms)
Bathroom: 1 Private,
1 Family share
Tariff: B&B (full) Double $70,
Single $40, Children $15, Children under 5 free.
Nearest Town: Westport 11kms

We are in a peaceful rural area with beautiful views of the Tasman Sea and coastline, surrounded by beaches great for swimming, surfing, diving, fishing, walking. We are 3 mins walk from the end of the very popular Cape Foulwind Seal Colony Walkway. Tourist attractions in our area are white water rafting, jetboating, horse-riding, underworld rafting, golf links, scenic bush walks and Coal Town Museum. We are 5km from Tauranga Bay and the very popular Bayhouse Restaurant Café overlooking the sea. Guests have full use of laundry, kitchen, BBQ, outdoor living facilities and off street parking. Westport is a historic town with a good selection of restaurants, cafés and bars, also 500 metres from our home is a friendly country tavern. We are keen gardeners, enjoy all sports, and whitebaiting. We hope to be able to offer our guests an evening meal of whitebait at $15 a head, depending how good the season was. We have a Jack Russell dog and a cat.

540

Westport

Beachside Homestay and Detached Self Contained Accommodation

Address: "Chrystal Lodge", Crn Craddock Dr. & Derby St.,
PO Box 128, Westport.
Name: Ann and Bill Blythe
Telephone: 03 789 8617
Reservations: 0800 259 953
Fax: 03 789 8617   **Email**: chrystal@clear.net.nz
Beds: Homestay: 1 Double, 2 Single (2 bedrooms).
Units (2): 1 Queen and double settee. 3 Single and double settee
Bathroom: Homestay: 1 Guests share (spa bath, separate toilet). Units: 2 ensuite.
Tariff: Homestay: B&B (special continental) - full $3 extra. Double $70, Single $45.
Units: Double $70, Single $55, Extra adults $10. Children half price. Breakfast optional
$7.50. Discounts after 2 nights and off season rates. Credit Cards: Visa, Mastercard,
Bankcard.   **Nearest Town**: Wesport Town centre 2 km.

We are a friendly semi-retired couple enjoying the extra time we have to provide hospitality and promote our unique region with its many attractions. Our modern home built on 20 acres is beside the beach used for fishing, surfing and swimming in a quiet setting near race course and sporting venues. We are midway between two whitebaiting rivers with nets available during the season. All guest beds have electric blankets. The near new units are fully equipped with stove, microwave, fridge / freezer and heating. Phone, barbecue and video available on request. Complimentary bicycles and pony. Free guest laundry. Household guests are free to help themselves to drinks and biscuits any time and relax in our sunny lounge, conservatory and outdoor verandah. Continental breakfast includes home-made bread, croissants, muffins and fresh yoghurt. We have two cats. Smoking outside please.
Directions: *Turn right at Post Office and continue down Brougham Street, turn left at Derby Street until at end of street.*

Westport

Homestay
Address: 76 Queen Street,
Westport.
Name: Havenlee
Telephone: (03) 789 8543
(after 3 pm) or 0800 673 619 PIN1950
Fax: (03) 789 8502
Beds: 1 Queen, 1 Double, 1 Twin (3 bedrooms)
Bathroom: 1 Private, 1 Guests share, Plus separate shower room.
Tariff: B&B (Continental plus) Double $80, Single $50, Children negotiable.
Nearest Town: Nelson - north 3 hours. Greymouth - south 1 1/4 hours.
Chirstchurch - east 4 1/2 hours.

Ian and Jan welcome you to Havenlee. We are both born and bred West Coasters, where hospitality is part of our heritage. We offer the perfect spot for those seeking peaceful central location in our modern spacious home situated just 300 metres from the town centre. Havenlee is set amongst an array of native and exotic trees and shrubs in an area that boasts some of the most beautiful scenery in the world, as well as some of the most thrilling adventure experiences. We are situated approx 49 kms from the Punakaki Pancake Rocks and 14 kms from the Tauranga Bay Seal Colony, both attractions a must for any itinerary. We offer our guests a continental plus breakfast, warm and comfortable beds, full laundry facilities, restaurant and cafe recommendations (within walking distance of our home) lots of local knowledge in a friendly, relaxed smoke free environment, with one cat residing.
Directions: *Turn right at Wakefield Street, left at Queen Street (first house)*

Westport, Cape Foulwind
Homestay
Address: "Clifftop Homestay",
Cape Foulwind, RD2, Westport
Name: Paddy and Gail Alexander
Telephone: (03) 789 5472
Beds: 1 Double, 2 Single (2 Bedrooms)
Bathroom: 1 Private, 1 Family Share
Tariff: B&B (Full) Double $70,
Single $50, Children under 15 $15.
Credit Cards. NZ B&B Vouchers accepted $10 surcharge
Nearest Town: Westport (10 mins drive) 11 km

Born and bred Coasters proud of our unique unspoilt Buller district we wish to share with you the "MAGIC" that is "The Cape".
Time out at our new "Clifftop Homestay" in its tranquil coastal setting will massage your soul.
Unrestricted close up views of the Tasman Sea and The Steeples - everchanging skies and glorious sunsets - rugged coastal walks - secluded beaches - we have it all!
5 kms to Tauranga Bay (surfing, seal colony, Bay House cafe) and Carters Beach (golf links, mini golf), 11 kms to Westport (Coaltown Museum, Adventure Tours).
To relax and unwind we have spacious decks and balcony, spa bath and a friendly country "pub" within walking distance. Laundry and tea and coffee available any time. Smoking outside please.
We, our teenage son and "Murphy the Beagle" look forward to hosting an unforgettable stay.
Directions: *Turn first right past "Star Tavern", then right again at beach car park.*

Westport
Bed & Breakfast
Address: 118 Derby Street,
Westport
Name: Derby Street Bed & Breakfast
Telephone: (03) 789 7757
Beds: 1 Queen, 2 Double, 2 single
(3 Bedrooms)
Bathroom: 2 Ensuite, 1 Private
Tariff: B&B (Full + Continental)
Double $70, Single $55,
Dinner $12 pp. Children by arrangement.
Nearest Town: Westport

Derby Street Bed & Breakfast offers quality accommodation in turn of the century villa with original pressed steel ceilings and decor. We have two ensuite bedrooms, one with shower (double or twin) and one with double spa bath (queen) plus one bedroom (1 double or twin) with private bathroom. Tea and coffee is served as required and we have a comfortable guest lounge with open fireplace and TV, in which to relax. We hope you will take the opportunity to dine in our pleasant dining room on your choice of menu. We utilise fresh produce from our garden and whitebait is available in season. We are only 5 mins from town centre and offer you a warm and friendly welcome. Basic laundry done free of charge and facilities provided for smokers.
Directions: *Entering Westport on main road (Palmerston Street) turn right at Mill Street, then left in Derby Street.*

Westport

Homestay
Address: 32 Lighthouse Road,
Cape Foulwind
Name: Helen Jenkins and Derek Parsons
Telephone: (03) 789 7942 Freephone
0800 22 73 22 (Cape BB)
Fax: (03) 789 7942
Email: derek.parsons@xtra.co.nz
Beds: 2 Queen, 2 Single (3 Bedrooms)
Bathroom: 1 Ensuite, 1 Guests share
Tariff: B&B (Continental)
Double with ensuite $80, Double share bathroom $70, Single $40,
Children $15. Dinner by arrangement $25.
Nearest Town: Westport 10 km

*Enjoy the soothing tranquillity of an amazing sea view from your bedroom / patio.
Short walk to the impressive Cape Foulwind Walkway with its seals and captivating
coastline, ending at The Bayhouse, a magic little restaurant overlooking Tauranga
Bay. Activities in the area include: sightseeing and nature tours, whitewater and
underworld rafting, caving, rock climbing, swimming, surfing, fishing, diving, horse
riding, jetboating, or a game of tennis, or round of golf at the local links.*
*We can take you kayaking, windsurfing, mountain biking, bush walking, or flounder-
ing at the lagoon.*
Relaxing beach walks below the cliffs, or a beach barbecue.
Friendly local country pub short walk away.
Laundry facilities available for guests. Smoking outside only please.

Reefton

Dinner Bed & Breakfast
Address: 78 Sheil St, Reefton,
West Coast
Name: Marie & Ray Armstong
Telephone: (03) 732 8383
Freephone: 0800 302 725
Fax: (03) 732 8383
Email: nzbandb@river.net.au
Beds: 1 Queen, 1 King, 2 Single (3 bedrooms)
Bathroom: 2 Ensuite, 1 Private, 1 Guests share
Tariff: B&B (special/full/continental) Double from $70,
Single from $35, Children half price. Dinner from $20.
All credit cards. Off peak tariff: Double $60.
Nearest Town: Reefton - 1 hr from Greymouth, 1 hr from Westport

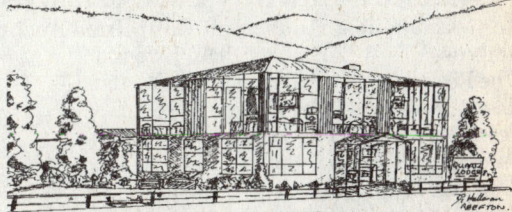

*Marie and Ray invite you to experience "Quartz Lodge" nestled within Victoria Forest Park
and in the heart of the West Coast quartz gold / coal mining country. We consider ourselves very
lucky to own a lovely large modern two storeyed centrally heated lodge with sun all day and
the "Best View In Town" from huge picture windows in every room, a fantastic location only
one block from the town centre close to all activities yet quite tranquil. * Spacious sunny guests
only lounge / dining / TV room * Guests own entrance * Luxurious beds * Self-service tea, coffee,
biscuits * Original paintings and crafts * Marie's breakfast and dinners have become famous
and are always available * Latest newspapers * Laundry facilities Our central location makes
us an ideal stopover as we are: 3 1/2 hours from Christchurch and Franz Josef Glacier 2 1/
2 hours from Nelson 4 hours from Picton Ferry and Kaikoura 1 hour from Greymouth and
Westport We are always open and looking forward to meeting you.*

543

Reefton
Bed & Breakfast/Self-contained Accommodation
Address: "Reef Cottage Bed & Breakfast Inn",
51-55 Broadway, Reefton
Name: Susan & Ronnie Standfield
Telephone: (03) 732 8440 **Fax**: (03) 732 8440
Mobile: 025-262 3855 **Freephone**: 0800 770 440
Email: reefton@clear.net.nz
Beds: 1 King/twin, 2 Queen,
1 Double, 1 Single (4 bedrooms)
Bathroom: 2 Ensuite, 2 Private, 1 Guests share
Tariff: B&B (special) Double $60-$140, Single $49-$90,
Children half price. Dinner $10-$35, Credit cards. As self contained cottage - tariff $70-$225 NZ B&B Vouchers accepted $10 - $60 surcharge
Nearest Town: Reefton (central), Greymouth - 1 hour, Westport - 1 hour. Glaciers 4 hours. Kaikoura 4 hours

The ideal stopover between attractions
Reef Cottage takes its name from the discovery of Gold Bearing 'Reefs' last century. Built from local native Rimu in 1887, this colonial cottage was transformed into a quality bed and breakfast in 1995 adding ensuite, bathroom / laundry and full kitchen in harmony with the existing style. French doors open from the lounge on to a private courtyard and riverbed garden backed by wooded hills. An enchanting cottage, featuring high ceilings, Rimu panelling, antique furnishings and a superb breakfast combining to produce fine hospitality, the hallmark of the Reef Cottage experience. Susan, Ronnie and family live next door close enough to provide personal attention yet separate to ensure guests total privacy. Cafes, restaurants and shops within one minutes stroll. Full disabled facilities: Single party bookings.

Punakaiki (halfway between Wesport and Greymouth)
Homestay/Guest House/Self Contained Accommodation/B&B
Address: No. 3 Hartmount Place Extension.
"The Rocks", PO Box 16, Punakaiki, Westland
Name: Kevin and Peg Piper
Telephone: (03) 731 1141
Freephone 0800 272 164
Fax: (03) 731 1142
Email: therocks@minidata.co.nz
Beds: 2 Queen, 2 Single (3 bedrooms)
Bathroom: 1 Ensuite, 1 Private, 1 Family Share
Tariff: B&B (Continental. Cooked-extra cost) Double $95-$130, Single $75.
Evening meal $30. Children welcome by arrangement. Credit cards accepted.
Nearest Town: Punakaiki - halfway between Greymouth and Westport.

We are a semi-retired couple who welcome you to share our home and surrounds. We have recently built "The Rocks Homestay" in a unique wilderness setting at Punakaiki.
Guests enjoy exclusive panoramic views encompassing the Pancake Rocks, the Tasman Sea coast, the limestone cliffs and the rainforest of the Paparoa National Park. Sunsets are magnificent. We offer warm hospitality, evening meals and wine. Our home has comfort and modern amenities including email. We enjoy taking guests on eco-tours of the superb rainforest, limestone landscapes and beaches while sharing our interests in photography and the outdoors. We can arrange a wide variety of other activities. Guests can refer to our extensive library of New Zealand books. Also available: new self-catering bush haven house. Both smoke free. Children welcome. No pets. **Directions**: *Turn off SH6 at the Hartmount Place blue bed sign, 3km North of Punakaiki Visitors Centre. Drive 400 metres towards the coast.*

Twelve Mile
Self-contained Accom.
Address: 'Tasman Beach'
Bed & Breakfast, Twelve Mile,
1R.D., Runanga, Westland
Name: Tasman Beach
Telephone: (03) 731 1886
Fax: (03) 731 1886
Beds: Cottage : 1 Double,
1 Single (2 bedrooms).
Cottage 2: 1 Queen, 1 Double,
1 Single (2 bedrooms).
Bathroom: Both cottages private facilities
Tariff: B&B (continental) Double $90.
NZ B&B Vouchers accepted
Nearest Town: Greymouth 21km

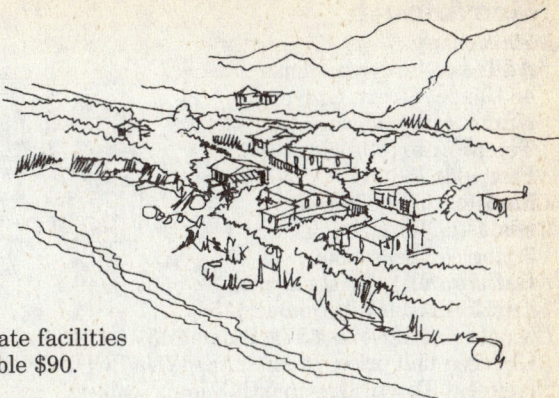

Two self-contained beach cottages in a stunning location, giving garden access to the rocky shoreline plus a wondrous backdrop of bush clad slopes and views of Mt. Cook. Sea views from bedrooms. Bountiful soft mountain water. Organic vegetable garden for guests wishing to self cater. Your stay will be full of discoveries perhaps of gold and greenstone. The Cottages are well placed for visitors to walk in the National park. Breakfast supplied - evening meal - self cater or enjoy the restaurant 5 mins away. Families children and pets enjoyed and welcome here.
Directions: *23 kms north of Greymouth. 22 km south of Punakaiki.*

Nine Mile Creek, Greymouth
Homestay
Address: 'The Breakers'
Nine Mile Creek, Greymouth,
Highway 6,
Coast Road, Westland
Name: Dot & Bill Dee/
Barbara & Frank Ash
Telephone: (03) 762 7743
Freephone 0800-350 590 Bookings
Fax: (03) 762 7733
Email: breakers@minidata.co.nz
Beds: 2 Queen, 1 Double, 2 Single (3 Bedrooms).
Bathroom: 3 Ensuite.
Tariff: B&B (full) Double $125-$165, Single $100-$140,
Dinner $30 by prior arrangement. Visa/Mastercard
Nearest Town: 14 kms north of Greymouth on SH6

Stunning. Is the only way to describe the ocean views from our two acre, landscaped beach front property. Lie in bed and listen to the surf and then next morning pull the drapes and watch the ocean for ever changing. After a good breakfast use our private access and walk along the beach fossicking for greenstone (Jade), pretty stones and shells. You'll probably want to stay another night and enjoy our home cooked dinner and Kiwi hospitality, which is the second thing that our guests write glowingly about in our comments book. Being just 14kms north of Greymouth and 35 kms south of the Pancake Rocks, we are central to all north Westland's tourist attractions and we would be happy to offer advice on what to see and do. "The Breakers" is non smoking indoors. Local tours arranged.
Home Page: www.minidata.co.nz/breakers

Greymouth
Homestay
Address: 'Ardwyn House'
48 Chapel Street, Greymouth
Name: Mary Owen
Telephone: (03) 768 6107
Fax: (03) 768 5177
Mobile: (025) 376 027
Beds: 2 Queen,
3 Single (3 bedrooms)
Bathroom: 1 Guests share
Tariff: B&B (Full) Double $75,
(Continental) Double $70, Single $45,
Children half price, Credit cards (Visa/BC)   NZ B&B Vouchers accepted
Nearest Town: Greymouth 3 mins walk

Ardwyn House is three minutes walk from the town centre in a quiet garden setting of two acres offering sea, river and town views.
The house was built in the 1920s and is a fine example of an imposing residence with fine woodwork and leadlight windows, whilst being a comfortable and friendly home shared with possibly one small elderly dog.
We are ideally situated for travellers touring the west coast as Greymouth is central and a popular stopover with a good choice of restaurants.
We offer a courtesy car service to and from local travel centres and also provide off-street parking.

Greymouth
Homestay
Address: 5 Stanton Crescent,
Greymouth
Name: Tony and Ib Pupich
Telephone: (03) 768 4348
Fax: (03) 768 4348
Beds: 1 King or 2 Single
(1 Bedroom)
Bathroom:
1 Private toilet and hand basin,
1 family share shower (guest-first option)
Tariff: B&B (Full) Double $80, Single $50, Dinner $25 pp.
Nearest Town: Greymouth 3 km

We are retired farmers offering warm hospitality in our lovely home, nestled on a hillside overlooking the Tasman Sea and the coastline south to Glacier Country and Mount Cook and Tasman. Tony and I have home-hosted for many years, firstly farmstays and then at a beautiful coastal property north of Greymouth, so you can be assured of a relaxed stay in this quiet street only five minutes walk from the beach.
Belying its name, Greymouth has many wonderful features, the Grey River and Floodwall, colourful Fishing Harbour, lovely walks close by, a Lagoon with water fowl, golf course and, for the fishermen, trout and salmon in the rivers and lakes.
We offer you complimentary pre-dinner drinks while watching the unbelievably beautiful sunsets and just maybe the atmospheric phenomenon, (The Green Flash).
Directions: *Please phone.*

Greymouth
Bed Breakfast Rural Homestay
Address: 'Oak Lodge',
Coal Creek, Greymouth
Name: Zelda Anderson
Telephone: (03) 768 6832
Fax: (03) 768 4362
Beds: 2 Double, 1 Single (3 bedrooms)
Bathroom: 3 Ensuite
Tariff: B&B (full) Double $95-$130,
Single $90, Credit cards (VISA/MC).
10% Discount on two night stay only on direct bookings. Winter rates from May until September applicable. NZ B&B Vouchers accepted $50 surcharge
Nearest Town: Greymouth. Centre of the West coast and natureally amazing. Deserves two nights.

OAK Lodge is set in rural surroundings 3km North from Greymouth, State Highway 6 and is centrally situated to visit Shantytown, Punakiki, The Paparoa National Park with good fishing rivers and lakes nearby. Antique furniture and many interesting curio's will fascinate you in what was an old farmhouse built in 1901. While the gardens are an outdoor treat, especially in early spring when the rhododendrons, azaleas and bulbs are in full bloom.
We have lived in Greymouth much of our life and can share our knowledge of the area particularly the lovely bushwalks. The 20 acre hobby farm supports sheep and Scottish Belted Galloway cows. Delicious breakfasts of your choice are offered at your leisure. Percolated coffee and herbal teas. Try the freshly baked bread. There are a choice of excellent restaurants in Greymouth. On the premises are a spa, sauna, swimming pool, and tennis court available for guests.
Homepage: http://www.nz.travel.co.nz *or* www.minidata.co.nz/greymouthbnb/

Greymouth
Homestay
Address: 20 Stanton Crescent, Greymouth
Name: Bev & Graham Piner
Telephone: (03) 768 5397
Fax: (03) 768 5397
Beds: 4 Single (2 Bedrooms)
Bathroom: 1 Private, 1 Guests share
Tariff: B&B (special) Double $80, Single $55, Children negotiable, Dinner $25.
Credit Cards accepted. NZ B&B Vouchers accepted
Nearest Town: Greymouth 3 Kms

West Coasters are famous world wide for their hospitality and as born and bred Coasters, your hosts Bev and Graham offer you a visit you will long remember. Many of our guests return again just for the food.
We offer luxury at an affordable price, your every comfort catered for plus a few surprises - lovely sunsets, sea views, just cross the road to the seaside. We are nestled in the bush and plenty of bird life abounds.
Until recently Graham was gold mining for 10 years and has a wealth of knowledge about the subject. He also enjoys fishing. Bev enjoys reading the many books in their home and is a real "foodie", so cooking great meals is no problem. Interior decorating and antiques are other interests and of course we both love meeting people. We have two very spoiled "children" (our cats) sharing our home.
Guests are welcome to smoke out on our terrace. Special diets are no problem - Vegetarian, Diabetic etc. We have a courtesy pick up from Busses or TraNz Alpine.
Directions: *Please phone.* **Homepage:** www.homestaysnz.co.nz/piners.htm

Greymouth
Homestay
Address: 345 Main South Road, Greymouth
Name: Paroa Homestay
(formerly Pam's Homestay)
Telephone: (03) 762 6769
Fax: (03) 762 6765
Mobile: (025) 208 7293
Beds: 2 Super King, 1 Single (3 bedrooms) **Bathroom**: 1 Guests share
Tariff: B&B (cooked or continental/special) Double $79, Single $60, Children under 12yrs$20. Credit cards: Visa/Mastercard. NZ B&B Vouchers accepted $15 surcharge (continental only)
Nearest Town: Greymouth

"Unbelievable sunsets", "Home away from Home", "Wonderful super-kingsize beds", "superb breakfast" - most quoted comments during past five years from guests.   Enjoy the amazing seaview from the twin terraces of our modern, spacious home. Established shrubs and Pohutukawa trees surround our home, enhancing its lovely setting. Guest facilities include off-street parking and luxurious lounge, TV, bath robes, hair dryers, irons and ironing boards in bedrooms for your convenience.   Centrally situated, six minutes from Shantytown and excellent eating establishments in Greymouth. My interests are meeting people, baking, cooking, antiques and walking Ruby, our friendly dog (who lives outside). Being Westcoast born, my local knowledge and contacts are an asset in assisting with itinerary suggestions. Bush walks, fishing tours can be arranged. Will meet bus or Transalpine. Bookings not always essential, but recommended to ensure availability. Smoking outside. Home hosting is such a pleasure! (Host has food safety and hygiene certificates also Tourist Awareness certificate). **Home Page**: http://nz.com/webnz/paroa.htm

Greymouth
Lodge
Address: 58 Herd Street, Dunollie
(12km north of Greymouth
and 2km off Highway 6)
Name: Graeme
Telephone: (03) 762 7077
Fax: (03) 762 7077
Email: kereru.lodge@xtra.co.nz
Beds: 2 Queen, 1 King,
1 Twin (4 bedrooms)
Bathroom: 1 Ensuite, 3 Private or Share
Tariff: B&B (continental) Queen $90-$120, Children negotiable, Dinner $20-$25. All Credit Cards.   NZ B&B Vouchers accepted $5-$50 surcharge depending on room requirements
Nearest Town: Greymouth

KERERU LODGE is located at the head of a quiet, sleepy valley, surrounded by native bush and birds. This is the centre of Westland. You can use KERERU LODGE to "take a holiday from your holiday" and try some of the lesser demanding activities in the area like easy walks of 1-2 hours, lazy canoeing, black-water rafting, dolphin and seal watching, bird watching - or our favourite - putting your feet up and relaxing. If you're into collecting high-adrenalin rushes then use KERERU as a base for New Zealand's least known, but arguably its best, adventure area. 2-4 day tramps, horse trekking, wild deer and pig hunting, fantastic fishing, white-water rafting, jet-boating - it's all here. Good music. Great traditional food. Cottage gardens. Peaceful streams. Large beds. Warm fires. Good coffee. This is KERERU LODGE - A haven for the discerning Traveller and Adventurer.

Greymouth
Homestay
Address: Maryglen Homestay, 20 Weenink Rd,
Karoro, Greymouth
Name: Glen & Allison Palmer
Telephone: (03) 768 0706 **Fax**: (03) 768 0599
Mobile: (025) 380 479
Email: maryglen@minidata.co.nz
Beds: 1 Queen, 1 King/Twin, 3 Singles (3 bedrooms)
Bathroom: 2 Ensuites, 1 Host Share
Tariff: B&B (continental) till 31/12/99: Double $65-$80, Single $40-$50. From 1/1/00
Double $70-$80, single $45-60.. Dinner $17.50 pp. Children welcome. Credit Cards
accepted. NZ B&B Vouchers accepted $10 Surcharge. Winter rates May-Oct.
Nearest Town: Greymouth - 2.5km south of town (off the main road)

*A warm welcome awaits you at our home which is situated in the bush and overlooking the
Tasman Sea. From the two downstairs rooms (which have ensuites) you can step out onto our
large deck and relax in the beauty and quietness and in the evening enjoy many beautiful
sunsets. Spa pool available $5 pp). Our family is now grown up, so our only resident family
is a very friendly dog "Lady". For over 30 years now we have enjoyed having guests in our home.
Alison enjoys gardening, hospitality being a grandma and playing bridge. Glen enjoys
restoring furniture, large jigsaws and reading. If there are guests who like playing cards or
games we would be willing starters. We also have Cable / Sky TV plus some videos of the West
coast that are available to guests. We are happy to collect guests from the Trans Alpine train
or buses. We can take those without transport to the beautiful attractions of our area (for a
moderate cost). Laundry and Internet facilities available (charge). Our home is smoke free.*
Directions: *2.5km south of Greymouth business area, off Main Road.*
Home Page: http://nz.com/webnz/bbnz/maryglen.htm

Greymouth
Bed & Breakfast
Address: Rosewood,
20 High Street, Greymouth.
Name: Ian and Margaret
Telephone: (03) 768 4674
Freephone: 0800 185 748
Fax: (03) 768 4694
Mobile: 025-220 3525
Email: rosewoodnz@xtra.co.nz
Beds: 3 Queen/King, 4 Single (5 Bedrooms)
Bathroom: 3 Ensuite, 1 Guest Share
Tariff: B&B (full) Double $85-$110, Single $60-$80, Children under 15, $20.
Credit Cards. NZ B&B Vouchers accepted $25 surcharge.
Nearest Town: Greymouth 1 km

*Rosewood B&B is one of Greymouth's finest old character homes. Built in the 1920's and
recently restored, it is situated a few minutes walk from the town centre and restaurants. Guest
rooms feature quality beds (incl king and queen size), telephones and several have TV.
Laundry service available, as is complimentary courtesy transport to bus, train or restaurants.
Rosewood is an excellent home from which to experience several national parks, the
internationally acclaimed Punakaiki rock formations and Glaciers, as well as the wide range
of recreational opportunities our region offers, especially for guests who are to stay for 2 or more
nights. Margaret is a trained social worker, while Ian operates a personalised tour service
(4WD vehicle). A polite 10 year old Trent, and a friendly cat 'Mischief' add to the experience.
A smoke free house with secure off street parking. Inspection will impress.*

Greymouth
Rural Homestay/Bed and Breakfast
Address: "Chapel Hill",
Rutherglen Road, Marsden, Greymouth
Name: Lynette and Bill
Telephone: (03) 762 6821 **Fax**: (03) 762 6470
Email: menzies2@xtra.co.nz
Beds: 1 Double, 4 single (3 bedrooms)
Bathroom: 1Ensuite, 1 Guests share
Tariff: B&B (continental) Double $80, Single $45, Children under 12 half price, Dinner $25 by prior arrangement. NZ B&B Vouchers, Visa and Mastercard accepted
Nearest Town: Greymouth 17km, Hokitika 40 km

Bill and I invite you to share our comfortable, peaceful home built with the history of our area in mind - old church doors, windows, recycled staircases, furniture, and filled with old relics of the past. A home of interest! Would you believe all of this is nestled in amongst our West Coast rain forest - tuis, bellbirds, pigeons, wekas and native trees.

We are both much travelled - Bill the carpenter, Lynette the teacher and have four adult children. Passionate organic gardeners we are! Guests love the peace and cosiness of our home. Staying with us you have the best of both worlds, 30 minutes to Hokitika, 15 minutes to Greymouth, 4 minutes to Shantytown. Come visit the Woods Creek Track, Punakaiki, Glaciers, Shantytown and beautiful Arthurs Pass. We promise you a wonderfully, peaceful time! Come that extra distance for that extra difference. We are "Simply the Best!"

Directions: *From Greymouth or Hokitika. Turn at the Paroa turnoff to Shantytown. continue 4.8 km past the Shantytown Gates. Sign posted "Chapel Hill" on the left.*
Home Page: www.minidata.co.nz/chapelhill/

Inchbonnie
Self-Contained Accom. Farmstay
Address: 'Whispering Pines',
Inchbonnie, R.D.1, Kumara, Westland 7871
Name: Russell & Jean Adams
Telephone: (03) 738 0153
Fax: (03) 738 0353
Beds: 1 Double, 4 Single (2 bedrooms)
Bathroom: 1 Private
Tariff: B&B (full) Double $80, Single $60,
Children under 12 $15, Dinner by arrangement $25 adults. Campervan facilities $25, Credit Cards (VISA/MC). NZ B&B Vouchers accepted
Nearest Town: Arthurs Pass apprx 30 km (East) Hokitika or Greymouth approx 70km (West)

An opportunity to stay in an authentic sawmiller's cottage built in the 1930's restored and refurbished in the 1970's. The cottage 1km from the homestead is simply furnished in 70's style, comfortable and clean with all "mod cons" except TV and phone. The original rough sawn exterior cladding and interior hand planed window and door frames have been retained keeping the original charm. This is a great place to relax and "catch up" - with reading, letters, fishing in nearby lakes and rivers, bird watching or walking in clear country air. Inchbonnie is a small farming community - no shops - so fill up with petrol etc. before arriving. We farm sheep, beef and deer. Russell being the farmer, while Jean cares for inside the "garden gate" and also handspins, handknits garments to sell. Our two cats share the garden and sometimes the house. A true West Coast welcome awaits all our guests.

Directions: *Turn over Taramakau River at Stillwater-Greymouth sign near Jacksons (S.H. 73) onto Lake Brunner Road, continue straight on to Mitchells Road. We are on the left. "Whispering Pines" at gate. Approx. 8.5 km from S.H. 73*

Hokitika
Bed & Breakfast
Address: 20 Hamilton Street, Hokitika
Name: Teichelmann's Bed & Breakfast
Telephone: (03) 755 8232, Reservations: Freephone 0800 743742
Fax: (03) 755 8239
Email: teichel@xtra.co.nz
Beds: 3 King/Twin, 2 Double, 2 Single (7 bedrooms)
Bathroom: 4 Ensuite, 3 Guests share
Tariff: B&B King/Twin $105-$115, Double/Twin $85-$115, Single $60-$85,
Credit Cards. NZ B&B Vouchers accepted Up to $30 surcharge
Nearest Town: Located adjacent to Hokitika business area.

At Teichelmann's we pride ourselves in offering friendly, informal hospitality with the comforts of a warm character home, and the opportunity to relax after an eventful day. Teichelmann's is a large home giving our guests the freedom to come and go as they please. Our comfortable guests lounge enables you to interact with others if desired. Teichelmann's has been recently refurbished including new beds, quality furnishings and modern bathroom facilities.

Moments away by foot from our central, yet quiet location, is a comprehensive range of services, shopping, museum, excellent restaurants, beach and river. We will be pleased to assist you in getting the most from your stay, including local attractions, excellent day trips to National Parks including the Glaciers, Punakaiki Pancake Rocks, and the dramatic Arthurs Pass. We have a non smoking environment and are suitable for children 10 years old and over.

Directions: *Turn left at Town Clock into Sewell Street, then take first street to right into Hamilton Street.*
Home Page: http://nz.com/webnz/bbnz/teichel.htm

Hokitika
Homestay
Address: 'Rossendale',
234 Gibson Quay, Hokitika
Name:
Vi & Arthur Haworth
Telephone: (03) 755 6620
Fax: (03) 755 6620
Email:Rossendale.Homestay@xtra.co.nz
Beds: 1 Queen, 2 Single (2 bedrooms)
Bathroom: 1 Guests share.
Tariff: B&B (Full) Double $75, Single $50, Dinner $20,
Children under 12 half price.   NZ B&B Vouchers accepted
Nearest Town: Hokitika

Welcome to Rossendale - We are a semi retired couple with a grown up family who are now married. We have travelled extensively both within NZ and overseas and enjoy meeting people from other countries, also fellow New Zealanders. We offer hospitality in a spacious home situated at the edge of town on the banks of the Hokitika River and are 1 km from the centre of town with full view of the Southern Alps and with off street parking. We have two guest bedrooms, one double with H & C, and one twin. All beds have electric blankets and wool rests. Guests have their own bathroom. We offer a full cooked breakfast or a continental, whichever you prefer. Dinner by arrangement. Our hobbies are gardening, fishing, bush walks, gold panning and meeting people. Hokitika is within easy reach of all 'West Coast' main attractions, from the beaches to the Alps, together with pleasant bush walks, and scenic drives. We will meet the plane or bus.

Hokitika
Homestay
Address: 70 Tudor Street,
Hokitika
Name: Brian & Berna McCarthy
Telephone: (03) 755 7599
Freephone: 0800 622 278
Beds: 1 Double, 2 Single
(2 bedrooms)
Bathroom: 1 Guests share
Tariff: B&B (Kiwi continental)
Double $75, Single $50.
NZ B&B Vouchers accepted Off season
Nearest Town: Hokitika 1km from town centre

We are both fourth generation West Coasters who have retired to Hokitika from South Westland and have been home hosting for 14 years. We enjoy meeting people, are proud of our region and are only too keen to tell you of it's attractions. Our interests are Rugby, Lions, gold prospecting, West Coast history, we both play lawn bowls as well as fishing for whitebait in season. Guest's comments returned all say Home away from Home. The glow worm dell is only 5 minutes walk away. Hokitika has three greenstone shops where you can watch the artifacts being made, a paua jewellery, a gold room, museum, excellent craft shops, and 2 glass blowing studios.
Directions: *When travelling from North take the first turn on your left. Our two storied brick home is the third house on the left. Travelling from South take the last turn on your right (Tudor Street) third house on your left. Turn off SH6 at airport sign from either direction.*

Awatuna, Hokitika

Farmstay/Homestay
Address: 'Gold and Green',
Awatuna, SH6,   Hokitika
Name: Helen & John Hadland
Telephone: (03) 755 7070
Fax: (03) 755-7070
Email: gold&green@xtra.co.nz
Beds: 1 Queen, 1 Double,
2 Single (3 Bedrooms)
Bathroom: 1 Guests share,
1 Family share
Tariff: B&B (special/continental) Double $80, Single $60, Children half price.
NZ B&B Vouchers accepted $15 surcharge
Nearest Town: Hokitika SH 6 (8 mins south), Greymouth SH6 (25mins)

Welcome to our comfortable, modern, rural, family home perched high above the road on a bushclad terrace overlooking the driftwood strewn coast of the Tasman Sea with fantastic sea views. Explore the native bush of our 160 acre farm, with sheep and cattle. Feed the pigs and goats and enjoy our farm dogs. Perhaps stroll the beach. John and I have in the past fostered scores of children but now welcome the opportunity to share genuine West Coast hospitality. John's work is in conservation enjoying fishing and gold-panning while my interests are centred around the home and gardens. We offer FREE evening guided trips to nearby glowworm dells and their historic abandoned mines and day trips, fishing or goldpanning should they stay a day or two. Large covered hot spa and outdoor swimming pool. Children welcome. Directions: 15km north of Hokitika on SH6 or 7km south of Kumara Junction roundabout. Look for the Gold and Green signs.

Hokitika

Homestay
Address:
Terrace View Homestays
24 Whitcombe Terrace, Hokitika
Name: Dianne and Chris Ward
Telephone: (03) 755 7357
Fax: (03) 755 8760
Mobile: (025) 371 254
Email: c.ward@minidata.co.nz
Beds: 1 Queen, 2 Single (2 bedrooms)
Bathroom: 1 Guests share
Tariff: B&B (full) Double $80, Single $65. Dinner $25pp.
Credit cards.   NZ B&B Vouchers accepted
Nearest Town: Hokitika 1 Km (to town centre)

We invite guests to share our spacious, warm home with 2 comfortable guest bedrooms. Views from the mountains to the sea from our upstairs lounge. Complimentary night tour to the glow-worms. Chris runs his own Property Consultanting business, is keen on golf and fishing and is also a Rotarian, (meetings Monday evenings). Dianne, a Reading Teacher enjoys handcrafts, ceramic dolls and cooking. We both enjoy sharing time and conversation with our guests. We are centrally situated to the Coast's many attractions and can assist you in making the most of your time. We have lived in several NZ locations and have a good knowledge of local and national features. We have a Labrador and a cat.
Directions: *Meet us by turning into Tudor Street from the main highway; take the next turn left into Bonar Drive, which will take you up the hill. At the top, turn left into Whitcombe Terrace.*

553

Hokitika

Boutique Lodge
Address: "Villa Polenza",
Brickfield Road, Hokitika
Name: Russell & Trina Diedrichs
Telephone: (03) 755 7801,
Reservations: 0800 241 801
Fax: (03) 755 7901
Mobile: (025) 477 123
Email: villapolenza@xtra.co.nz
Beds: 1 King, 1 Queen,
2 Single (3 bedrooms)
Bathroom: 2 Ensuite, 1 Private
Tariff: B&B (full) Double $160-$240, Single $120. Credit cards.
Nearest Town: Hokitika 4 mins

Our home is new, modern Italian, situated high on the top terrace overlooking Hokitika with each bedroom providing breathtaking views of Mts Cook and Tasman to the south, and to the west, the wonderful sea sunsets. The area is very quiet except for the birdlife in the adjacent native bush. The guest lounge features a telescope, chessboard and a bounteous supply of the latest magazines. The bedrooms, all with underfloor water heating have large french doors opening to a patio while the beds have feather/down duvets. We have one daughter at home, a Persian cat called Oscar and a German roller canary with a voice surpassed only by Pavaroti. Continental or cooked breakfast is available with freshly squeezed orange juice, home-made bread, jams and yoghurt. Dinner is by arrangment. Villa Polenza is smoke-free and not suitable for children under 13. **Directions**: *For reservations and directions, please phone.*
Home Page: http://www.friars.co.nz/hosts/polenza.html

Hokitika

Farmstay
Address: Kowhaioak Farmstay,
Johnston Road, RD 1, Hokitika
Name: Elaine and John Fuller
Telephone: (03) 755 7933
Fax: (03) 755 7933
Beds: 2 Queen (2 bedrooms)
Bathroom: 1 Family Share
Tariff: B&B (full) Double $80, Single $50, Children 12 and under half price,
Dinner $25pp by prior arrangement. Credit Cards (VISA,M/C)
Nearest Town: Hokitika 30km East to Kowhitirangi

We offer true kiwi hospitality on our 130 cow Dairy Farm set in against the Southern Alps near the picturesque Hokitika Gorge. Relax in our warm comfortable open plan home with large conservatory and timber decking over looking the lush tranquil Kowhitirangi Valley enjoying nature at its very best. Help with milking or feed the calves, ducks, hen and two house cats. Try our many rivers for a brown trout. Perhaps a day or two hunting or walk some of the native bush tracks enjoying the songs of the bird life. A game of pool and a pint or two at the local. Elaine born in Wales, enjoys handicrafts and home hosting. John enjoys pool, hunting, fishing and people. As dinner is by prior arrangement, your early booking would be appreciated. Thank you for not smoking in our house.
Directions: *From SH6 turn at the Central Hotel into Stafford Street and follow all signs to Kokatahi. Then follow signs to Hokitika Gorge until Staion Road on left. Turn right at end of Station Road onto Johnston Road. Second house on right up the hill.*

Hokitika

Semi Rural Homestay-close to Hokitika Town.
Address: 'Prospect House', Blue Spur, RD2, Hokitika
Name: Danielle & Lindsay Smith
Telephone: (03) 755 8043
Fax: (03) 755 6787
Mobile: (025) 221 2779
Email: prospect@minidata.co.nz
Beds: 1 King, 1 Queen, 1 Double, 1 Single (3 Bedrooms)
Bathroom: 2 Ensuites, 1 Private
Tariff: B&B (full) Double $125-$135, Single $75-$80, Dinner by arrangement, Children half price, Credit Cards.
Nearest Town: Hokitika 4km

Prospect House is situated on the outskirts of Hokitika on an ancient river terrace property of some 10 acres.
This lovely colonial style family home commands sweeping views of the Southern Alps, has beautiful gardens and trees and is owned by a caring, friendly family. Our guest books are full of accolades as to the space and luxurious comfort of our home, the friendliness of the host family as well as the fine food and wines that we provide thus ensuring a truly relaxing stopover. All say that they wish they had arranged their trip so that they could stay longer.
This spacious home features native rimu timbers, central heating, large deck and BBQ facilities, piped music throughout and office facilities too.
The main suite contains a King size double bed and full ensuite plus tea and coffee making facilities as well.
Adjoining this is a separate bedroom with a double and single bed.
The second suite has a Queen size bed and ensuite.
We enjoy catering by arrangement for our guests and provide full 3 course meals. Breakfast can be either continental or a full cooked breakfast.
Our interests vary from the garden to music, current affairs, sport flying and yes .... catering for guests.
We can arrange scenic flights for you to the Glaciers or to the historic goldtown port of Okarito or to other interesting destinations. We can also assist to arrange other adventures for you.
We have three dogs, a Westie, a Scotty and a Lab. We also have two cats.
Directions: *To find us, if travelling from North turn left into Hampden Street, continue on for 3KM without turning again.*

Hokitika

Country Lodge+Self-contained Cottage
Address: Chesterfield Rd, S/Hway 6, Kapitea Creek, RD 2, Hokitika, Westland
Name: Kapitea Ridge Country Lodge & Cottage
Telephone: (03) 755 6805 Freephone: 0800 186 805
Fax: (03) 755 6895 **Mobile**: (025) 223 4905
Email: Kapitea@minidata.co.nz
Beds: Country Lodge: 2 King/Twin, 2 Queen, 1 Double, 2 Single (6 bedrooms). Cottage: 1 Queen, 2 Single, 1 Sofabed (2 bedrooms)
Bathroom: Country Lodge: 6 ensuites. Cottage: 1 private
Tariff: Country Lodge: B&B (special) $145-$220 Dbl. Kapitea Cottage: $125 (1 Bedroom, 1-2 persons) $20 per additional person. Sleeps 6. Dinner $40 pp. Credit Cards.
Nearest Town: Hokitika 17km, Greymouth 23km

Hospitality and comfort Within Nature. Experience superior contemporary rural accommodation in our architecturally designed lodge, completed 1998, situated on our authentically farmed coastal property. A spacious retreat with commanding views of surf, sunsets, wild storms and distant mountains. Breakfast and evening summertime dining in conservatory. Garden spa. Country fare, dinner is by prior arrangement. Enjoy country living in laid back luxury suitable for children over 12 years. Kapitea cottage is our self contained accommodation designated especially for families and folks seeking an independent stay. Charming interior decor, full facility kitchen. French doors lead to a covered deck and developing cottage garden. Gas BBQ. Single party bookings only. Surrounding area offers, native birds/bush, sheep and cattle. Gumboots and gold pans, pentaque, clay bird shooting, walking distance to beach. Golf. Jade and Gold Artisans, Historic Gold fields, fishing lakes and rivers within 20 minutes drive. **Directions**: *On S/Hway 6, 17km north of Hokitika, 5km south of Kumara junction. Signposted 'Lodge 2 km' at Chesterfield Road.* **Home Page**: *www.kapitea.co.nz*

http://www.bnb.co.nz

take a look

Hokitika
Homestay
Address: Alpine Vista Homestay,
38 Bonar Drive, Hokitika
Name: Rayleine and Jon Olson
Telephone: (03) 755 8732 **Fax**: (03) 755 8732
Email: jolson@minidata.co.nz
Beds: 2 Queen (2 bedrooms)
Bathroom: 1 Ensuite
Tariff: B&B (full) Double $85, Single $55, Children $25. Credit Cards accepted.
NZ B&B Vouchers accepted $15 surcharge
Nearest Town: Hokitika, town centre: 1 km

We look forward to meeting you and welcoming you to our comfortable home situated on a terrace overlooking Hokitika, affording us unsurpassed views of Mount Cook, Southern Alps, Tasman Sea and brilliant sunsets. There is a private entrance to the guest rooms which include one queen size bedroom with ensuite and a small sitting area with TV (Sky). Adjoining this is a Queen bedded room so it is especially suitable for one or two couples. There are tea and coffee making facilities and guests are welcomed with home baking. Credit cards accepted, off street parking and laundry provided. We have travelled widely and invite guests to share a drink with us in the evening as we enjoy listening to your experiences. Jon is a fourth generation West Coaster with an abundant knowledge of the area.
Directions: *Please turn into Tudor Street towards the Airport from the main highway then first left into Bonar Drive and up the hill into the cul-de-sac.*
Home Page: http://www.minidata.co.nz/wdc/nztour/alpinev.htm

Hokitika
Homestay
Address: 261 Revell Street,
Hokitika, Westland
Name: Russell and Alison Alldridge
Telephone: (03) 755 7025
Fax: (03) 755 7025
Beds: 2 Queen, 2 Single (2 Bedrooms)
Bathroom: 1 Family share
Tariff: B&b (Continental) Double $75,
Single $50. NZ B&B Vouchers accepted $10 surcharge
Nearest Town: Hokitika (1 km from town centre)

Welcome to 'Montezuma' by the sea. So named after a ship that was wrecked here in 1865.
Alison was born in Queensland and Russell is a genuine West Coaster.
Our children have grown up and moved on and we now have space in our comfortable home which we would like to share with you. We have plenty of parking space.
While staying with us take in the spectacular views of the mountains and the Tasman Sea. Enjoy a leisurely walk along the beach and watch the breathtaking sunsets. In the evening take the three minute stroll to the glow worm dell, relax and take time out to enjoy our West Coast hospitality.
Directions: *When travelling to Hokitika from north take first turn to your right (Richards Drive). We are the last house on the street. When travelling from South turn left at the last street out of town.*

Hokitika

Rural Homestay

Address: "Meadowbank"
Takutai, RD 3, Hokitika
Name: Tom and Alison Muir
Telephone: (03) 755 6723
Beds: 1 Double,
2 Single (2 Bedrooms)
Bathroom: 1 Family Share,
separate shower.
Tariff: B&B (Full) Double $75,
Single $50, Dinner $25,
Children under 12 years half price.
NZ B&B Vouchers accepted
Nearest Town: Hokitika 3 kms North on SH6

Tom and Alison welcome you to their lifestyle property, situated just 5 minutes south of Hokitika. The property carries mainly deer, with just a few young cattle. Our home is modern, sunny and warm. We enjoy meeting people and would like to have you stay with us. As our 3 daughters have left home, our large house has plenty of room for visitors. All beds have electric blankets. Cot and high-chair available. A large, tranquil garden surrounds our home, and in summer, there is a large, colourful Dahlia garden, which guests are welcome to browse around. Nearby we have the beach, an excellent golf course, an old gold-mine, river, and of course Hokitika with all its attractions. Laundry facilities available if required. Dinner by arrangement. Smoking outside please.

Directions: *Travel south 2 kms from south end of Hokitika Bridge on SH6, then turn right - second drive on right. North-bound traffic- look for sign about 1km north of Golf Links.*

http://www.bnb.co.nz

take a look

Ross, Westland
Homestay+Self-contained Accom.
Address: Bellbird Bush, 4 Sale Street, Ross, Westland
Name: Peter & Vicky Bennett
Telephone: (03) 755 4058
Fax: (03) 755 4064
Mobile: (025) 314 819
Beds: 1 Queen + bed settee, 2 Single (2 bedrooms)
Bathroom: 1 Private, 1 Family share
Tariff: B&B (continental) Double $70, Single $40, Children under 12 $15.
Nearest Town: 30km south of Hokitika on SH6

Welcome to our comfortable and secluded home overlooking the historic gold town of Ross, site of the largest gold nugget ever discovered in NZ. Located at the base of the pine forested Mont D'Or (Mountain of Gold) with beautiful views of the Tasman Sea and Alps our home, set in 5 acres, enjoys a quiet privacy but within easy walking distance of the town's goldfield, walkways and historic sites. We offer the choice of a self-contained unit (new) or accommodation in our home. Coming from rural Welsh and Welsh border background we consider ourselves very fortunate to live in such a beautiful and rugged part of NZ and we are very keen to share our West Coast hospitality with you.
Directions: *If travelling south turn/left (right if northbound) off SH6 at Goldfields Garage/City Hotel intersection and go straight ahead 400m turning right into driveway at road end.*

Ross
Self Contained Accommodation
Address: Dahlia Cottage, 47 Aylmer Street, Ross, Westland
Name: Dianne and Bill Johnston
Telephone: 03 755 4160
Fax: 03 755 4160
Mobile: 025 296 5934
Beds: 1 Queen, 3 Single (3 bedrooms)
Bathroom: 1 Private
Tariff: B&B (Full/Continental) Double $70, Single $40, Dinner $20, Children $20. NZ B&B Vouchers accepted
Nearest Town: Hokitika 20 mins

Dianne and Bill welcome you to Dahlia Cottage. We are situated on the main North South Highway second house on your right travelling from North. A 20 minute drive from Hokitika and 1 1/2 hours scenic drive to the Glacier. This makes an ideal stopover. We offer a cosy, peaceful, self contained cottage next to our home with private parking. We offer a delicious evening meal with the traditional pavalova dessert by arrangement.
We have a 16 year old son Danny.
Ross is very pretty with the native bush surrounds with the Tasman Sea, Totara River and Historic Walkways you can enjoy at your leisure. Trout fishing, hunting, gold panning a guided walk to the glowworms, walkways and our Dahlia Garden.
A traditional West Coast welcome awaits you at Dahlia Cottage.
We look forward to meeting you and will make your stay a memorable one.

Hari Hari

Country Lodge/Farmstay
Address: State Highway 6,
Hari Hari, South Westland
Name: Wapiti Park Homestead
Telephone: (03) 753 3074
International 64 3 753 3074
Fax: (03) 753 3074   **Email**: wapitipark@minidata.co.nz
Beds: 2 King, 2 Queen, 1 Double, 3 Single (5 bedrooms)
Bathroom: 3 Ensuite, 2 Private (5 bathrooms)
Tariff: B&B (special, continental) Double $110-$165, Single $90-$125, Dinner $30.
Credit cards (VISA/MC). Children by arrangement only.
Nearest Town: Hari Hari 1/2km north. Hokitika 75km north.

"A real tonic for weary travellers, food, facilities excellent. Hosting incomparable!" (R.J. USA)
"Absolutely Superb - Hosts, food, room - Best stay 5 weeks in NZ" (GH. UK) Hosts Bev & Grant Muir invite you to discover the unique experience of staying at South Westlands premier hosted establishment for the discerning traveller. Enjoy a special combination of elegance and warm hospitality. Relax in complete comfort and affordable luxury. Extensive indoor / outdoor living areas, trophy / games room., large spacious bedrooms with superior comfort beds and private facilities are complimented by bountiful traditional country-style meals. Set in tranquil surroundings, our modern colonial style lodge overlooks the farm which specialises in breeding Wapiti (Rocky Mountain Elk). Join the 6pm tour to learn about and handfeed the Wapiti. Our location on SH6 makes the ideal midway stopover between Nelson, Christchurch and Wanaka, Queenstown area, or to explore this scenic wonderland at leisure. Guided hunting and trout fishing available. **Directions**: *Reservations: Freephone 0800 Wapiti*
Home Page: http://minidata.co.nz/wapitihomestead/

Hari Hari

Self Contained Accommodation, Country Stay
Address: Carrickfergus B&B,
Haddock Road, RD 1, Hari Hari, South Westland
Name: Catherine Healy and Lindsay Grenfell
Telephone: 03 753 3124 **Fax**: 03 753 3124
Beds: Homestay: 1 Queen, 2 Single (2 bedrooms).
 2 Units: Double, and Double Settees
Bathroom: 1 Guests share.   Units - Private
Tariff: B&B (continental) Double $100, Single $65,
Dinner $25 pp (by arrangement).
Credit Cards: Visa and Mastercards.
Nearest Town: Hari Hari 6 km (50 minutes from Hokitika). Blue signage on SH6 1.5km Nth Hari Hari, Robertson Road.

Our modern home and new studio units are north facing, set in landscaped grounds which adjoin our 32 acre sheep and Highland cattle farmlet affording extensive mountain and rural views. You are welcome to stroll around our property which enjoys native trees and birds. If you choose to stay in a unit, which have mini-kitchen and private facilities , you may breakfast at your leisure or join us in our home.
It is our endeavour to make your stay comfortable , enjoy our gardens, meet Fillip our retired Basset Hound, or browse our West Coast book collection.
Allow time to explore our coastal walkway "from start to finish, the Hari Hari coastal walkway is a delight, a two to three hour feast for the senses" (Dept. Cons. pamphlet). Or test your skills against brown trout in springfed streams, especially noted La Fontaine. Leave time for a visit to Glaciers and White Herons. A welcome midway destination between Christchurch and Wanaka or Nelson and Queenstown.

Whataroa, South Westland

Farmhouse
Address: 'Matai Lodge' Whataroa, South Westland
Name: Jim & Glenice Purcell
Telephone: (03) 753 4156
Fax: (03) 753 4156
Email: jpurcell@xtra.co.nz
Beds: 2 Queen, 2 Single(3 bedrooms)
Bathroom: 2 Private
Tariff: B&B (full) Double $120, Single $70 person, Dinner $25
Nearest Town: Franz Josef 20 mins (south), Hokitika 1 hour 30 mins (north) SH6.

New Zealand Association
FARM & HOME
HOSTS

You are warmly welcomed to share with us our tranquil rural retreat 5 mins from the main highway, on a 400 acre farm of sheep, cows, horse and sheep dog, only 20 mins from the Franz Josef Glacier.

Our spacious modern home has been designed for farmstay guests, with large lounge and dining area downstairs, looking out over farmland to the spectacular views of the Southern Alps and the world Heritage Park.

Upstairs our guests have their own suite of two bedrooms one Queensize and one twin with lounge, conservatory and private bathroom, or downstairs Queensize room with ensuite.

Enjoy delicious three course home cooked dinners, in a relaxed atmosphere where we can share interesting and entertaining conversations. As we have travelled overseas and enjoyed meeting people, we find this an ideal way to extend that pleasure, and our motto is; "A Stranger is a Friend we have yet to meet". I speak Japanese and have taught felting spinning and weaving in Japan, Jim and I play golf and tennis, there is a very picturesque golf course nearby. Now our family has left home we look forward to sharing our home and knowledge of this beautiful scenic area with our guest.

Activities in the area: Horseriding, Kayaking (Okarito Lagoon) 15 mins drive; Fishing salmon and trout Lake Mapourika and Waitangi river can be arranged; Golf course (clubs available); White heron bird Sanctuary by jet boat, from November to February; Gold panning in natural riverbed and bush valley.

Driving Time:
Christchurch - Whataroa 5 hours
Queenstown - Whataroa 6 hours
Greymouth   - Whataroa 2 hours
Nelson   - Whataroa 6 hours

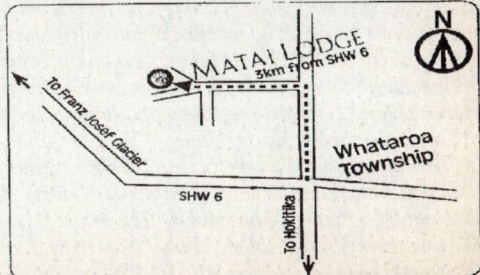

Whataroa, South Westland

Bed & Breakfast /Farmstay

Address: Sleepy Hollow, State Highway 6, Whataroa, South Westland
Name: Carolyn and Colin Dodunski
Telephone: FREEPHONE: 0800 575 243 (NZ) or 0064 3753-4139
Fax: (03) 753 4079
Email: hollow@xtra.co.nz
Beds: 3 Queen, 1 Single. Self contained accommodation: 1 Queen, 1 Single + sofabed/portacot available.
Bathroom: Homestead: 1 Guests share   S.C. Unit: 1 Ensuite
Tariff: B&B (continental) Double $90-$100, Single $60. Credit Cards: Visa/MC/Amex//Diners. NZ B&B Vouchers accepted $20-$30 surcharge
Nearest Town: Franz Josef 20 mins south, Hokitika 1 1/2 hours north

Heading to the glaciers?   Stay a night or two at Sleepy Hollow, your Ideal base in glacier country. We are just 20 minutes drive North of the Franz Josef Glacier!! Here you can relax, away from the sometimes hectic pace of travel and take time to unwind whilst admiring the breathtaking scenery of dramatic mountain views (even from your room!).

The homestead accommodation is on the top floor with guest share bathroom.   Each beautifully decorated bedroom has queen sized beds and big fluffy towels, tea / coffee facilities, heater, electric blankets and television, enabling you to relax in privacy if you wish, or feel free to pop downstairs for a chat, but be warned! the jolly and relaxing atmosphere at Sleepy Hollow is contagious.   The self contained unit is a real little gem and excellent for guests with children, with your own bathroom, lounge, dining & kitchen area, microwave, electric frypan and television, this is your own little home away from home.   Telephone, fax, email and laundry are available.

Our 400 acre dairy farm milks 200 friesian cows, we have 3 horses and some sheep. Mint Sauce our pet sheep loves being fed a slice or two of bread and is eagerly awaiting your arrival. We have one house cat, Angus the friendly fox terrier (who lives outside!!) and 2 farm dogs Waite and Buff. A short bush walk takes you to the farm lane where you can view and feed our peacocks, pheasants, ducks etc in the bird enclosure or take a leisurely stroll over the farm. The area has lots to offer with breathtaking views of the glacier to be had via a helicopter or fixed wing ski-plane flight both of which we would be happy to provide details or make your reservations for you. At Okarito (20 mins drive) you can kayak on the Lagoon, and take some excellent walks, view beautiful sunsets on the beach. Whataroa has a population of around 300 people, there is a 9 hole golf course, excellent fishing and tours to New Zealand's only White Heron Colony, Gold prospecting is available on the Whataroa riverbed. Casual evening meals are available in Whataroa Village. Nearest banks are Hokitika and Wanaka. Credit cards are welcome here. We look forward to sharing our little slice of paradise and some laughter with you!! Distances: Picton-Whataroa: 6 hours. Hokitika-Whataroa: 1.5 hours. Whataroa-Wanaka: 4.5 hours. Whataroa-Queenstown: 6 hours. Christchurch - Whataroa: 5 hours

Directions: *Sleepy Hollow is very easy to find, we are on State Highway 6, 1km north of Whataroa village.* **Home Page**: http://nz.com/webnz/bbnz/sleepyh.htm

Franz Josef Glacier
Boutique Country Stay

Address: Waiho Stables Country Stay,
Docherty Creek, Franz Josef Glacier
Name: Alex and Suzy Miller
Telephone: (03) 752 0747
Fax: (03) 752 0786
Email: waiho@minidata.co.nz
Beds: 2 Queen, 1 Double,
2 Single (3 bedrooms)
Bathroom: 2 Ensuite, 1 Host share
Tariff: B&B (special) From 1st October Double $188, Single $170, Children by
arrangement. Dinner: ethnic vegetarian byo. Credit cards. Min. two nights' stay
Nov - Mar. NZ B&B Vouchers accepted 3 double.
Nearest Town: Franz Josef village 6km

*The South-West World Heritage Area is a vast reservoir of wilderness. Its 2.6 million
hectares, including four national parks, contain towering peaks, majestic glaciers,
temperate forests and rugged coastlines. In the heart of the World Heritage Area at
Franz Josef Glacier, guests at Waiho Stables Country Stay can sojourn on the edge of
wilderness. Here, guests sleep soundly, intoxicated by the pure air and the pleasant
pursuits of the day, and they can be as indolent or as active as they wish.*
*At breakfast, which is flexitime, a resplendent panorama of the Alps may be viewed
while sampling an array of delicious breakfast selections and concoctions.*
*The vastness of wilderness, plus a thin veneer of civilisation, combine at Waiho Stables
Country Stay, to provide a respite from schedules and a tonic for the senses.*
Home Page: http://www.waiho.co.nz

Franz Josef Glacier
Bed & Breakfast

Address: Knightswood Bed & Breakfast
SH6, Franz Josef Glacier
Name: Jackie and Rusty Knight
Telephone: (03) 752 0059
Fax: (03) 752 0061
Beds: 2 King/Twin (2 Bedrooms)
Bathroom: 2 Ensuite
Tariff: B&B (Full) Double $110-$140.
Children by arrangement. Credit Cards accepted. Special winter rates.
Nearest Town: 3 km South of Franz Josef Village

Jackie and Rusty would like to welcome you to Franz Josef.
*Our house was built from local material in true pioneering spirit. Rusty, a carpenter
by trade, played a major part in its planning and construction during 1998.*
*Knightswood is situated on 250 acres, nestled in native bush, which attracts prolific
tuneful and chatty native birdlife. Spectacular views of the Southern Alps can be
enjoyed whilst having breakfast in your well appointed room. Jackie, originally from
England, is a paediatric nurse who worked at Gt Ormond Street Hospital, more
recently in Christchurch, prior to their B&B venture. She also works part-time at the
DOC Information Centre. Rusty is a local helicopter pilot of 10 years and keen deer
farmer. At present 200 deer have been bred on the property - deer farm tours at your
request.*
*We look forward to helping you discover the magical qualities of the West Coast.
Smoking outside only.*

563

Fox Glacier
Farm Bed & Breakfast
Address: 'The Homestead',
Cook Flat Road, Fox Glacier
(Postal: P.O. Box 25, Fox Glacier)
Name: Noeleen & Kevin Williams
Telephone: (03) 751 0835
Fax: (03) 751 0805
Beds: 2 Queen,
2 Single (3 bedrooms)
Bathroom: 2 Ensuite, 1 Private
Tariff: B&B (continental, full $5.00 pp extra). Double $95-$115, Single $75-$85.
Travellers cheques accepted.
Nearest Town: Fox Glacier 1/2 km, Hokitika SH6 (North) 160 km.

*Kevin, Noeleen and Chancy our friendly Corgi welcome you to our 2,800 acre beef-cattle and sheep farm. Beautiful native forest-clad mountains surround on three sides, and we enjoy a view of Mt Cook. Our spacious character home, built for Kevin's grandparents in the mid 1890's, has fine examples of stained glass windows. A guest lounge, with open fire for late autumn nights, is provided in our smoke-free home. Beds have Woolrests and are firm and very comfortable. hairdryers supplied. Breakfast includes muesli, home-made yoghurt, preserves and marmalades with cooked if required. We feel our lovely old home has the best of both worlds, having no immediate neighbours, yet within walking distance of village and tourist facilities (Glacier walks, helicopters, restaurants) 6 km to glacier, 4 km to world famous Lake Matheson with its mirror reflection. **Directions**: On Cook Flat Rd (road to Lake Matheson), 5th house on right, before Church.*

Fox Glacier
Homestay
Address: Roaring Billy Lodge,
PO Box 16, Fox Glacier
Name: Billy & Kathy's Place
Telephone: (03) 751 0815
Freephone: 0800 352 121
Fax: (03) 751 0815
Email: billy@xtra.co.nz
Beds: 1 Double, 3 Single
(2 bedrooms)
Bathroom: 1 Guests share, robes available
Tariff: B&B (special, cooked) Double $80-$90, Single $65-$75 (from 1st Oct).
Unsuitable for children.
Nearest Town: 2 minute walk to Fox Glacier township. Hokitika (North) 2
hours (160 km) SH6

"Fox Glacier Experience"
Guest wanted no experience needed! Climb it, hike it, fly over, or view it from afar...whichever way you experience Fox Glacier it'll leave you wanting more. We're only two minutes walk from the action in the town centre and can make any bookings you need. Try our legendary cooked breakfast and then wear yourself out on the glacier and surrounding walks. Relax in the comfort and warmth of our renovated farmhouse. Our living area is lined with local timbers and enjoys 360 degree views of the glacier valley, mountains, farms and township.Billy, a seasoned bushman and guide, will take you on a complimentary evening bushwalk to learn about the rainforest and its animals. If you visit us in April you might be lucky enough to hear the stags roaring. They're the clue to our name. We have one cat and hunting dog!

Fox Glacier
Homestay
Address: Reflection Lodge
Cook Flat Road, Fox Glacier
PO Box 46
Name: Raelene Tuck
Telephone: (03) 751 0707
Beds: 1 Queen, 2 Single
(2 bedrooms)
Bathroom: 1 Ensuite, 1 Host share
Tariff: B&B (continental) Queen $95-$110,
Twin $90-$100, Single $65-75, Children $35.
Nearest Town: North Hokitika 2 hours. South Wanaka 3 hours.

Welcome to Fox Glacier. We are a middle aged couple with our children away at boarding school, and we have a little dog called Fe Fe.
Our modern home is surrounded by lovely gardens, and offers panoramic views of New Zealand's two highest peaks, reflecting in our own private pond directly outside the dining room, or you can sit back and relax in the lounge and enjoy the ever changing moods of the mountains (sunsets are a must). Fox Glacier offers many activities, all within easy distance from home. Evening dining can be enjoyed at either of the local restaurants or hotels. We can assist with any sightseeing activities you would like to do, eg. helicopter flights, glacier walks, to name a few. We look forward to seeing you and sharing our wonderful piece of paradise Smoke free.
Directions: *1 1/2 km down Cook Flat Road sign at gate. Drive up drive until you come through trees. Welcome you have found me.*

Fox Glacier
Lodge/Self Contained Accommodation
Address: Fox Glacier Lodge,
Main Highway 6, Fox Glacier
(Postal: PO Box 22, Fox Glacier)
Name: Fran and Laurie Buckton
Telephone: (03) 751 0888
Reserv. freephone 0800 369 800
Fax: (03) 751 0888
Beds: 5 Queen (5 bedrooms)
Bathroom: 5 Ensuites
Tariff: B&B (continental) Double $78-$160.
Special winter rates. Not suitable for children.
Credit cards: Vsa/Mastercard/Eftpos
Nearest Town: Hokitika 2 hours North, Wanaka 3 hours South.

Fox Glacier Lodge is nestled in a pristine forest setting with mountain backdrop, yet is right in the heart of Fox Glacier village itself. The recently completed solid timber lodge is clean, warm and welcoming. Bathrooms are private ensuite. Two have private double spa baths. The country kitchen is fully equipped and well stocked with supplies for self-serve continental breakfasts. Also available: coin laundry. "Glow-worm forest walk" is right here: a short stroll after dark to the grotto. Very close to restaurants, cafes, shops. Walk to the Glacier, around Lake Matheson, or enjoy the magnificent views of Mt Cook and Tasman. Also available: Heli-hikes, kayaking, bird watching, scenic flights, fishing, hunting, biking, information. Lodge is smoke free. Reservations recommended.
Directions: *On the southern fringe of Fox Village (opposite BP) you'll see our home/office. The lodge is beyond, hidden from view.*

Bruce Bay
Farmstay
Address: Mulvaney Farm Stay,
Condons Road, Bruce Bay, South Westland
Name: Peter & Malai Millar
Telephone: (03) 751 0865
Fax: (03) 751 0865
Email: mulvaney@xtra.co.nz
Beds: 1 Double, 1 Twin (2 bedrooms)
Bathroom: Family share
Tariff: B&B (full) Double $75, Single $50, Children $20, Dinner $20 pp. No smoking inside.
Nearest Town: Fox Glacier

Welcome to Mulvaney Farmstays! The Mulvaneys were Irish and my great grandfather settled in this valley 130 years ago. Our home was built in the 1920's by my great uncle for his wife to be, but she never arrived. So he lived there by himself until 1971 raising Hereford cattle. We have lived here with our children (who are all away at school) for 19 years. Our home has been fully renovated into a comfortable home. We offer an evening meal - Malai your hostess offers you European or Thai dinners (with bookings).

We are close to the sea, lakes and rivers which are ideal for fishing, walking or just relaxing. We are only 30 minutes from Fox Glacier and can arrange helicopter flights and glacier walks, or you can just relax with us enjoying our surrounding scenery. We have two cats and you shall be heartily greeted by our friendly dog Monty!
Directions: *1km off SH6 on Condons Rd. Well sign posted.*

Paringa
Farmstay
Address: State Highway 6,
Paringa,
South Westland
Name: Glynis and Tony Condon
Telephone: (03) 751 0895
Fax: (03) 751 0001
Beds: 1 Double, 4 Single (3 bedrooms)
Bathroom: 1 Family Share
Tariff: B&B (full) Double $75, Single $40,
Dinner $20, Children $20 + $1 per year of age. No Credit Cards.
Nearest Town: Fox Glacier (45 mins north), Haast (45 mins south)

New Zealand Association FARM & HOME HOSTS

We run a 4th generation working beef farm, with a few sheep. We enjoy meeting people. Our interests include hunting, jet boating, fishing, spinning, knitting and reading. Our farm is nestled beneath the bush-clad foothills of the Southern Alps, close to Lake Paringa and the Paringa river. We have three adult children and one grandson, two living in New Zealand, one overseas. We have travelled to America, England, Scotland, some parts of Europe, Kenya and Australia. We live only three quarters of an hour from Fox Glacier, four hours from Queenstown and we are quite happy to arrange helicopter flights etc. at Fox Glacier. We are Kiwi Hosts and belong to the NZ Association Farm & Home Hosts and Tourist Industries Association. We have two house cats and a small dog.
Directions: *70 kms south of Fox Glacier, 50 kms north of Haast on State Highway 6. 4 kms from South Westland Salmon Farm Cafe.*

Haast

Homestay Bed & Breakfast

Address: "Okuru Beach", Okuru, Haast
PO Box 59, Haast
Name: Derek & Marian
Telephone: (03) 750 0719
Fax: (03) 750 0722
Email: maryglen@minidata.co.nz
Beds: 2 Double, 2 Single (3 bedrooms).
Bathroom: 1 Guests share/1 Ensuite.
Tariff: B&B (continental) $65-$70, Single $35, Children $20, Dinner $15 BYO.
Credit Cards Visa/Mastercard. NZ B&B Vouchers accepted
Nearest Town: Haast 16km.

"Okuru Beach" gives you the opportunity to stay in a unique part of our country, where time moves slowly.

Enjoy the coastal beaches with interesting driftwood and shells, also experience walks among the rainforest where a variety of native birds can be viewed. In the season, Fiordland Crested Penguins can be seen, within walking distance along a rocky beach near Jackson's Bay, a 30 min drive away. We and our friendly Labrador dog enjoy sharing our comfortable home and local knowledge of the area. With prior notice we can serve dinner (BYO), vegetarian available. Our interests are our handcraft shop, photography, fishing, shooting and tramping.

We enjoy the chance to meet new people both New Zealanders and overseas. Complimentary tea or coffee on arrival. Laundry facilities available (minimal charge).

Directions: *From Highway 6 turn into Jackson's Bay Rd. Drive 14km south and turn Right into Okuro. Look for the B&B sign.*

Home Page: http://www.minidata.co.nz/maryglen/okuru.htm

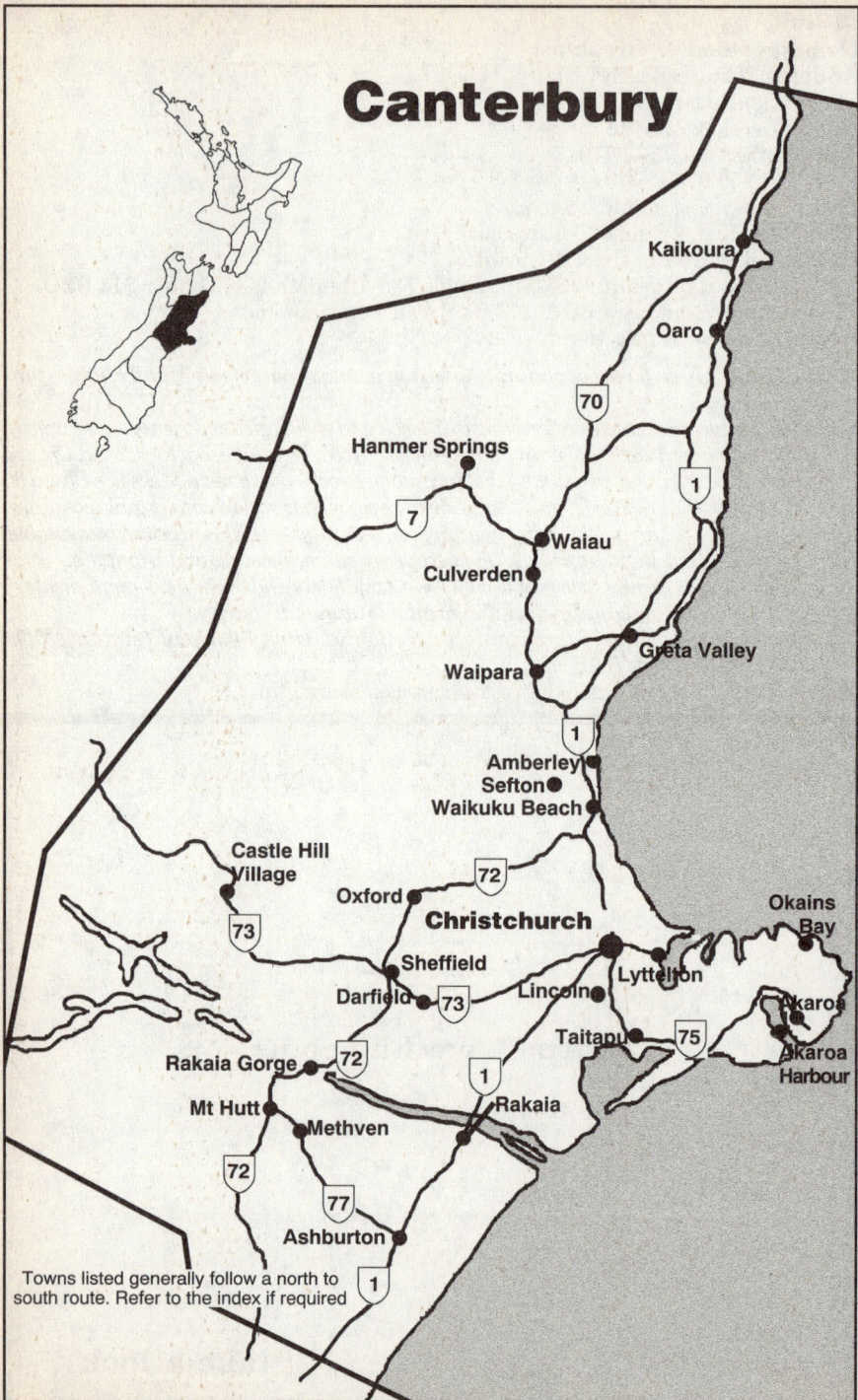

Canterbury

Kaikoura

Oaro

70

1

Hanmer Springs

7

Waiau

Culverden

Greta Valley

Waipara

1

Amberley
Sefton
Waikuku Beach

Castle Hill
Village

72

Oxford

Christchurch

Okains
Bay

73

Sheffield

Lyttelton

Darfield

73

Lincoln

Akaroa

Rakaia Gorge

72

Taitapu

75

Akaroa
Harbour

Mt Hutt

1

Methven

Rakaia

72

77

Ashburton

Towns listed generally follow a north to
south route. Refer to the index if required

1

Christchurch City

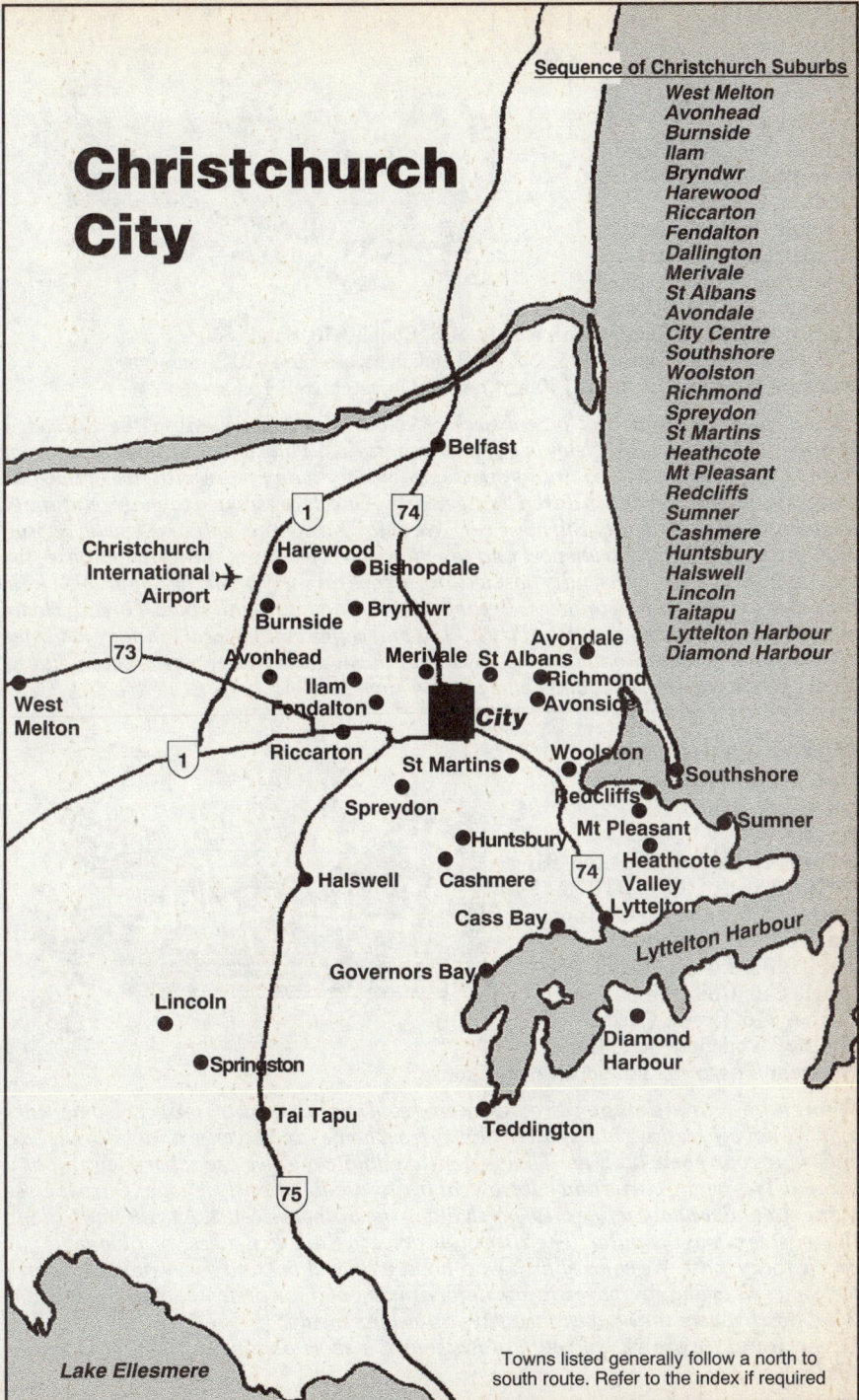

Sequence of Christchurch Suburbs

West Melton
Avonhead
Burnside
Ilam
Bryndwr
Harewood
Riccarton
Fendalton
Dallington
Merivale
St Albans
Avondale
City Centre
Southshore
Woolston
Richmond
Spreydon
St Martins
Heathcote
Mt Pleasant
Redcliffs
Sumner
Cashmere
Huntsbury
Halswell
Lincoln
Taitapu
Lyttelton Harbour
Diamond Harbour

Belfast

1

74

Christchurch International Airport

Harewood

Bishopdale

Bryndwr

73

Burnside

Avonhead

Merivale

Avondale

St Albans

1

Ilam

Fendalton

Richmond

Avonside

West Melton

City

Riccarton

Woolston

St Martins

Southshore

Spreydon

Redcliffs

Mt Pleasant

Sumner

Huntsbury

74

Halswell

Cashmere

Heathcote Valley

Cass Bay

Lyttelton

Governors Bay

Lyttelton Harbour

Lincoln

Springston

Diamond Harbour

Tai Tapu

75

Teddington

Lake Ellesmere

Towns listed generally follow a north to south route. Refer to the index if required

Kaikoura

Homestay
Address: 'Bay-View',
296 Scarborough Street,
Kaikoura
Name: Margaret Woodill
Telephone: (03) 319 5480
Beds: 2 Double,
2 Single (3 bedrooms)
Bathroom: 1 Ensuite,
1 bathroom Guests share,
1 shower + toilet Guests share.
Tariff: B&B (full) Double with ensuite $75, Double $70, Single $50,
Children half price, Dinner $25. NZ B&B Vouchers accepted $10 Surcharge
Nearest Town: Blenheim 130 km north, Christchurch 183 km south

"Bay-view" a peaceful spot on an acre of colourful garden high on the Kaikoura Peninsula with splendid views of sea and mountains. Only a few minutes drive from town. Our family has lived in this spacious home for many years with two of the four children and seven grandchildren living nearby. Guests are invited to share our family life including our friendly Burmese cat. We enjoy gardening, golf and bowls, sewing and ceramics. We offer transport and are happy to book any of the local activities for you. Margaret is a very friendly host willing to cook an early breakfast for dawn whale watchers and dolphin swimmers. Breakfast include traditionally baked bread, Home made muesli and home preserved fruit. Tea and coffee making and laundry facilities are available. Scarborough Street, is just off the main highway on the south side of town. While you are here, our home is your home.

Oaro, Kaikoura

Country Homestay
Address: Oaro, R.D.2,
Kaikoura
Name: Kathleen & Peter King
Telephone: (03) 319 5494
Beds: 2 Single (1 bedroom)
Bathroom: 1 Private
Tariff: B&B (full) Double $65,
Single $40, Children half price;
Dinner $15, Credit Cards.
NZ B&B Vouchers accepted
Nearest Town: 22 km south of Kaikoura

We are semi-retired living on 48 acres having sold our hill-country property some years ago. We have three daughters - all live away from home - and seven grandchildren. Two cats share our home with us. This is a mild climate and we are experimenting in a small way growing citrus and subtropical fruits, predominantly feijoas. Oaro is close to the sea and we have a fine view north along the Kaikoura coast. A walk south along the coast is always popular. The 20 minute drive to Kaikoura takes you alongside our scenic rocky coast. We enjoy sharing our home with visitors and assure you of a warm welcome. We are happy for you to join us for dinner but if you prefer there is a restaurant 2 km north where they have takeaways as well as meals.
Directions: *We are 22 km south of Kaikoura, a short distance off the main north-south highway.*

Kaikoura
Bed & Breakfast
Address: 'Bevron',
196 Esplanade, Kaikoura
Name: Bev & Ron Barr
Telephone: (03) 319 5432
Beds: 2 Double,
2 Single (2 bedrooms)
Bathroom: Ensuites
Tariff: B&B (full) Double $80, Single $60,
Children under 12 half price. NZ B&B Vouchers accepted $15 surcharge.
Nearest Town: 130 km south of Blenheim, 183 km north of Christchurch.

We are a friendly, active retired couple who enjoy meeting new people and sharing the delights of our wonderful two storeyed home on the Kaikoura beachfront. The view from our balcony is breathtaking, giving an unobstructed panorama of the sea and mountains. We offer two very comfortable guest rooms (each with double and twin beds). We have a private guest TV lounge, games room, off street parking, and a spacious private garden. There is a safe swimming beach opposite the house with children's playing area, BBQ and swimming pool.
Kaikoura is well endowed with tourist attractions and we are able to offer local advice to help make the most of your stay. We are willing to make Whale Watch bookings for you prior to your arrival. Our home is centrally located, being a short walk to restaurants, galleries and many scenic attractions.

Kaikoura
Bed & Breakfast Inn
Address: The Old Convent ,
Cnr Mt Fyffe & Mill Road, Kaikoura
Name: Marc & Wendy Launay
Telephone: (03) 319 6603
Fax: (03) 319 6690 **Free Phone**: (0800) 365 603
Mobile: (025) 353 954 **Email**: o.convent@xtra.co.nz
Beds: 3 Queen, 7 Double,5 Twin, 2 Single
(17 bedrooms/4 rooms suitable for family, Double/Twin with bathroom)
Bathroom: 14 Ensuite, 2 Private Facilities
Tariff: B&B Queen $135, Family Unit $185, Double/Twin Ensuite $110, Single $70, Dinner $45, Visa, American Express, M/C and EFTpos available. Above prices held until 30th September 2000.   Please add $10 per room effective 1st October 2000.
Nearest Town: Kaikoura town centre - 3.6km.

THE OLD CONVENT
B & B   KAIKOURA

Experience the atmosphere in our beautifully preserved homestead built in 1911. Owned by French Architect Marc and his New Zealand wife Wendy you will find personal service, charm, French Cuisine and a relaxed setting amongst a quiet and peaceful environment. Kaikoura has some of the most incredible marine and land attractions in the world, and we will assist you to visit these wonderful experiences. In the morning enjoy home baked Breads and Croissants, home made yoghurt and muesli and our French Brioche with freshly brewed coffees. In the evening meet Marc in the kitchen where his passion for French cooking will overwhelm you. William is 9 years old and loves other children, Jack the Labrador and our two cats are very friendly. Laundry facilities are available at a minimal charge. Fully licensed. Coffee, tea, bicycles and courtesy car complimentary. Spanish and French spoken.
Directions: *At the North edge of town turn west off SH 1 and travel down Mill Road for 1.5km and we are on the right hand side.*
Home Page: http://nz.com/webnz/bbnz/convent.htm

Kaikoura
Bed & Breakfast and Self Contained Accommodation
Address: Ardara Lodge, Schoolhouse Road, Kaikoura (formerly The Gums)
Name: Ian & Alison Boyd
Telephone: (03) 319 5736,
Freephone   0800-226164
Fax: (03) 319 5732
Email: aemboyd@xtra.co.nz
Beds: 5 Queen, 3 Single (5 Bedrooms)
Bathroom: 4 Ensuites/Spa Bath
Tariff: House: B&B (continental) Double $85-$90, Single $60.
Cottage: Double $110, 4 Persons $180. Families welcome.
Credit cards (VISA/MC). NZ B&B Vouchers accepted $10 surcharge
Nearest Town: Kaikoura 5km

You will enjoy a relaxed and peaceful stay in a beautiful rural setting near the magnificent Kaikoura mountains. Relax on our deck and enjoy Alison's colourful garden which completes the panoramic view. Ian's Great, Great, Uncle Jim left "Ardara", Ireland in 1876. He bought our land here in Kaikoura in 1883 and milked cows. He established an orchard and planted Macrocarpa trees for shelter. One macrocarpa tree was milled and used to build the cottage which was designed and built by Ian in 1998.
The cottage has an upstairs bedroom with a queen and two single beds. Downstairs there is a bedroom with a queen bed, a bathroom with a shower, and a lounge, kitchen, dining room. The deck is private with a great view of the mountains. It has been very popular with groups, families and honeymoon couples.
The house has ensuite bedrooms with queen beds, tv, fridge, settee and coffee/tea facilities. You have your own private entrance and you can come and go as you please. We offer laundry facilities, off street parking, courtesy car from bus/train. Booking for local tourist attractions, restaurants and farm tours can be arranged. Ian's brother Murray, has Donegal House, an Irish Garden Bar and Restaurant, which is within walking distance.
Ian is a retired teacher and Alison a Librarian. Our hobbies are tennis, golf, designing and building houses, gardening, handcrafts, spinning and we like to travel. No smoking indoors please.
We look forward to your company.
Directions: *Driving north, 4km from Kaikoura on SH 1, turn left, 1.5km along Schoolhouse Road.*
Home Page: http://www.kaikoura.co.nz/ardara

Kaikoura
Farmstay
Address: 'The Kahutara',
Dairy Farm Road, Kaikoura
Name: John & Nikki Smith
Telephone: (03) 319 5580
Fax: (03) 319-5580
Beds: 1 Queen,
4 Single (3 Bedrooms)
Bathroom: 1 Luxury Ensuite, 1 Private, 1 Guest share
Tariff: B&B (full) Double $130-$150, Single $80, Dinner $35pp wine served. NZ
B&B Vouchers accepted $30 surcharge
Nearest Town: 20km from Kaikoura township on inland Waiau route -
183km north of Christchurch, 130km south of Blenheim.

The Kahutara is a haven in the hills. Situated 20km from Kaikoura on Highway 70. Our comfortable country home is nestled among the hills in a tranquil garden setting. We operate a 2000 acre beef cattle and sheep farm with a small thoroughbred stud. The Kahutara river runs through our property with the nearby Lake Rotoroa providing a sanctuary for the unique cormorant colony. Enjoy quality homestead accommodation and experience country hospitality. Guests can take a pleasant walk to explore the surrounding valleys, including the bridle path used as the early mail route over the hills to avoid the rocky coastline; or enjoy lawn croquet. Our well appointed guest rooms include one single room and one twin room with private bathroom; and one Queen bedroom with Luxury Ensuite. We are 40 minutes to the popular Mt Lyford Skifield. We can book you on a Whale Watch, swim with the dolphins. **Directions**: *Please phone or fax.*

Kaikoura
Self-contained B&B
Address: 'Churchill Park Lodge',
34 Churchill St, Kaikoura
Name: Moira & Stan Paul
Telephone: (03) 319 5526
Freephone: 0800 36 36 90
Fax: (03) 319 5526
Email: churchill.park@xtra.co.nz
Beds: 2 Double, 1 Single (2 bedrooms)
Bathroom: 2 Ensuite
Tariff: B&B (continental)
Double $80, Single $55,
Credit Cards (VISA/MC). NZ B&B Vouchers accepted $15 surcharge
Nearest Town: Blenheim 130kms

Wanting superior bed & breakfast accommodation?
Stay with us in one of our luxurious upstairs guest rooms, fully self contained with private entrance and carparking facilities. Relax on your balcony and soak up the sun and most stunning mountain, coastline and sea views offered in Kaikoura. If you can drag yourself away from this, stroll along the waterfront to our popular swimming beach and excellent selection of cafes, restaurants and shops. Delicious continental breakfast is served in your room. Our home is smoke free and is designed to guarantee your stay with us will be the most comfortable and enjoyable you have had. Use our guest laundry. Access family and friends on our Internet facility. Allow us to book your local Tours. Enjoy our two friendly and welcoming cats and most of all, our hospitality. Call us free now (0800 36 36 90), we look forward to hearing from you. **Home Page**: http://www.canterburypages.co.nz/churchillpark

573

Kaikoura

B&B Lodge
Address: "Carrickfin Lodge", Mill Road, Kaikoura
Name: Roger Boyd
Telephone: (03) 319 5165, Freephone 0800 265 963
Fax: (03) 319 5162
Beds: 5 Queen, 5 Single (6 bedrooms)
Bathroom: 6 Ensuite
Tariff: B&B (continental) Double $85, Single $60, Credit Cards.
This property is not suitable for children.
NZ B&B Vouchers accepted $20 surcharge
Nearest Town: Kaikoura 3km

WELCOME TO KAIKOURA (Kai = Food, Koura = Crayfish)
My name is Roger and I'm the fourth generation "BOYD" to own and farm "Carrickfin". It is an ancient Irish name from where my Great Grandfather originated. He bought and settled this land in 1867 for 100 Gold Sovereigns.
The Lodge is a Colonial home built on 100 acres adjoining the Kaikoura township. It is a large and spacious place with an open fire, and guest bar, two outdoor areas with seating and barbecue facilities. It was built well back from the road amidst two acres of lawn and shrubs to give complete privacy. There are breathtaking views from all rooms, looking directly at the "Seaward Kaikouras" a spectacular mountain range which rises to 8500ft. These mountains are home to a unique variety of wild life including the giant weta, rare ghekos, keas, falcons, deer, pig and most native birds. This is also the habitat of the Hutton Shearwaters, an artic petrel which returns ever year from the Northern Hemisphere and nests in burrows high in these mountains.
As well as fattening cattle I am a professional Woolclasser, and have worked in Shearing Sheds throughout the South Island High Country.
In keeping with Irish hospitality, Complimentary drinks with local cheese is served in the evening.
I am 3kms from Whale Watch, Dolphin Encounter and some of the best Seafood Restaurants in the South Island.
Directions: *At North End of town, turn West off SH1 into Mill Road, drive 1km and I'm there on the left.*

Kaikoura (on the Peninsula)
Homestay+Self-contained   Accom.
Address: "Austin Heights",
19 Austin Street, Kaikoura
Name: Margaret & Kevin Knowles
Telephone: (03) 319 5836
Fax: (03) 319 6836
Mobile: (025) 233 8528
Beds: 1 Queen, 1 Double, 2 Single (3 bedrooms)
Bathroom: 1 Ensuite, 1 Family share
Tariff: B&B (full) Queen Ensuite $ 75, Double $65, Single $40,
Children half price. NZ B&B Vouchers accepted $5 - $15 Surcharge
Nearest Town: 130km south of Blenheim, 183km north of Christchurch

*We are friendly semi-retired grandparents having lived in Kaikoura for 26
yrs and enjoy lawn bowls, tramping, walks, gardening and patchwork. We
look forward to welcoming you into our comfortable modern home set on
half an acre of gardens and lawns on the Kaikoura Peninsula, just a few
minutes from shops and restaurants. We offer peaceful private comfortable
surroundings, sea and mountain views, tea and coffee making facilities and
a delicious breakfast. Our accommodation consists of a queen with own
private facilities, a double and two singles with private lounge and family
share bathroom. We are happy to make bookings for the many tourist
attractions and offer transport for guests to and from terminals. Austin St
is the second turn left off Scarborough St, which is off the main highway on
the south side of town. We have a friendly Persian cat and are a non smoking
household.*

Kaikoura
Farmstay
Address: "Okarahia Downs",
Private Bag, Kaikoura
Name: Richard & Hillary Watherston
Telephone: (03) 319 5187
Fax: (03) 319 5187
Mobile: (025) 338 051
Beds: 1 Queen, 1 Double,
2 Single (2 bedrooms)
Bathroom: 1 Ensuite, 1 Family share
Tariff: B&B (full) Double $60-$80, Single $40, Children under 15 half price.
Nearest Town: Kaikoura 25 mins.

*Okarahia Downs is a 4500 acre sheep, cattle and deer farm running from the coast to
very steep hills with large native bush gullies which allow excellent bush walks.*
*We are situated on State Highway 1, 1/2 hour north of Cheviot and 25 mins south of
Kaikoura.*
Our home is a large comfortable recently renovated homestead.
*We offer a guest room with Queen bed and ensuite, and also tea/coffee
making facilities. Extra beds are available with shared facilities. Children
very welcome.*
*We run commercial farm tours, jet boating, fishing and hunting trips are
available by arrangement. Meals available.*

Kaikoura
Licenced Rest & accommodation
Address: Donegal House,
Shcoolhouse Road, Kaikoura
Name: Mimi and Murray Boyd
Telephone: 03 319 5083
Fax: 03 319 5083
Beds: 10 Queens, 2 Single (10 bedrooms)
Bathroom: 10 Ensuite
Tariff: B&B (full/continental) Double $95, Single $55,
Dinner $19 (main), Children half price. Credit Cards, Eftpos.
NZ B&B Vouchers accepted $20 Surcharge
Nearest Town: Kaikoura 5.5 km Large Transit sign on main road.
Just North of township, 5 minutes drive.

"One Hundred Thousand Welcomes" - "Donegal House", the little Irish Pub in the country, brimming with warmth and hospitality, open fires and accordion music. Set on an historical dairy farm which has been farmed by the Boyd family since their arrival from Donegal, Ireland in 1865, "Donegal House" offers, accommodation, full bar facilities and a public licensed restaurant. The a-la-carte menu, specialising in Kaikoura's famous crayfish and seafood, plus locally farmed beef. NZ beers, Kilkenny and Guinness are on tap along with a good selection of Marlborough wines. Two spring fed lakes, home to Chinook salmon, Mute and Black Swans, Blue Teal, Paradise and Mallard ducks, are feature in the extensive lawns and gardens which surround "Donegal House". the towering Kaikoura Mountains make a perfect backdrop to this unique setting.

The Restaurant and Bar facilities at "Donegal House" have become a very popular place for visitors staying at the nearby Carrick-finn Lodge, Ardara Lodge, The Old Convent and Dylans Country Stay, to meet the Kaikoura locals and enjoy the rural hospitality in a unique Irish atmosphere. We book whale watching, dolphin and seal swimming and horse trekking etc. Approved Wheelchair facilities available.

"Even if you're not Irish-this is the place for you!" "A home away from home!"

Directions: *Driving North 4kms from Kaikoura on SH1 turn left at Large transit signs, 1.6km along Schoolhouse Road.*

Kaikoura
Farmstay+Self-contained Accom.
Address: "Clematis Grove",
Blue Duck Valley, RD 1, Kaikoura
Name: Ken & Margaret Hamilton
Telephone: (03) 319 5264
Fax: (03) 319 5278
Email: clematisgrove@xtra.co.nz
Beds: 1 Double,
2 Single can be made into a king (2 bedrooms)
Bathroom: 1 Private or Family Share
Tariff: B&B (continental) Double $80,
extra adults $35 each, Single $55, Children half price, Dinner by arrangement $25pp.
Winter rates apply. Credit cards. NZ B&B Vouchers accepted $20 surcharge
Nearest Town: Kaikoura

Clematis Grove, B&B and Farmstay. Your hosts Ken & Margaret Hamilton welcome you to stay in our modern self-contained unit situated in a lovely bush clad valley a short distance north of Kaikoura. Our unit is large of a superior quality incorporating one double bedroom and one twin room. The kitchen is modern with every convenience you have your own shower room. The lounge and dining area are modern and comfortable. Also available for guests a large lounge upstairs with full size pool table and great views. Come and enjoy a peaceful setting in rural NZ enjoy the bush and birdlife. Shearing demonstration and Tours to 800 metres with incredible views of sea and mountains can be arranged. Also transport from and to K.K. charges for these extra activities by arrangement with your hosts. Continental breakfast supplied, Full breakfast and other meals by arrangment - or you can prepare these yourself. Our motto Come as a stranger go as a friend. We are smoke free. **Directions**: *Please phone or fax for directions.* **Home Page:** http://www.kaikoura.co.nz/clematisgrove*

Kaikoura
Guest House, B&B Inn
Address: 53 Deal Street, Kaikoura
Name: Nikau - the inn with the view
Telephone: (03) 319 6973
Fax: (03) 319 6973
Mobile: (025) 247 6691
Email: jhughey@xtra.co.nz
Beds: 2 Queen, 2 Double, 3 Twin
6 Single (6 bedrooms)
Bathroom: 5 Ensuites, 1 Private
Tariff: B&B (special) Double $65-$85, Single $50-$60.
Nearest Town: Blenheim 1hour 45mins North

Dear Traveller,
I am sure you will enjoy your stay at Nikau.
Start the day with home-baked bread, fresh fruit salad, muffins, yoghurt, etc at a giant rimu table - 4.2m long. It's appropriate that the former council meeting table is at Nikau as my great, great uncle Frank Monk was a long-serving chairman from 1908. The Monk's were among the first European-settlers in Kaikoura in the 1850's. Nikau was built in 1925. It is only a short stroll from shops, etc and has stunning views over a colourful garden and park to the sea and mountains.
See you soon, Judith
P.S. Tea and coffee always available, laundry also.
Directions: *Easy to find, just off SH1, near the hospital, south side of town centre.*
Home Page: http://www.kaikoura.co.nz

Peketa, Kaikoura

Bed & Breakfast

Coastal Retreat
Bed & Breakfast

Address: Cnr Rakanui & Bullens Road, Peketa, RD2, Kaikoura
Name: Eileen and Kim
Telephone: (03) 319 6960
Fax: (03) 319 6964
Email: the_prestons@xtra.co.nz
Beds: 2 Queen, 2 Singles (3 bedrooms)
Bathroom: 1 Ensuite,
Family share
Tariff: B&B (Full) Double $75-$65, Single $50.
Nearest Town: Located 8 km south of Kaikoura on SH 1

Welcome to the Coastal Retreat "Where the mountains meet the sea". Relax in our tranquil garden and enjoy the native birds singing. Experience the spectacular mountain views from our patio or take advantage of the beach & river walks on our doorstep. What better way to start your day than with a delicious cooked breakfast made from local produce? A home cooked evening meal and picnic lunches are available. You are welcome to join us for a traditional Kiwi barbecue in our garden on those long summer nights. Enjoy the many attractions Kaikoura has to offer including whale watching both air & sea, diving, surfing, fishing, seals, dolphins, bush walks, horse treks, skiing & snowboarding (Mt Lyford one hours drive). The golf course and airport are near by. We can arrange your activities and sight seeing for you.
A WARM WELCOME AND COMFORTABLE STAY GUARANTEED!

Waiau

Farmstay/Homestay
Address: Mason Hills, Inland Kaikoura Rd, Waiau R.D., North Canterbury
Name: Averil & Robert Leckey
Telephone: (03) 315 6611
Freephone: 0800 101 961
Fax: (03) 315 6611
Mobile: (025) 285 1333
Email: mason_hills@xtra.co.nz
Beds: 1 Queen, 2 Single (2 bedrooms)
Bathroom: 1 Ensuite, 1 Private
Tariff: B&B (full) Double $90, Single $50, Dinner $25.
Credit Cards. NZ B&B Vouchers accepted $20 surcharge
Nearest Town: Kaikoura 1 hour, Hanmer Springs 1 hour, Christchurch 1 hour & 45 mins.

Welcome to Mason Hills, a hill country beef and sheep farm. We are situated on the inland route from Kaikoura to Hanmer Springs. Our lovely character homestead looks directly at Mount Lyford ski area which is only 8km away.
We can offer a four wheel drive adventure as an extra. See the Coast from Kaikoura to Banks Peninsula and the Southern Alps spreading away into the distance. Visit the unique "potholes" and stand on top of the "Battery". See sheep and cattle grazing in picturesque surroundings. Or you can stroll along the Mason river, visit native bush or relax on our verandah and listen to the bellbirds. We are centrally situated to visit the Whales at Kaikoura or swim at Hanmer's hot springs. A home cooked meal is available in the evenings and we would welcome you company by the open fire. We share our home with 2 cats and a friendly Labrador.
Home Page: http://www.destination-nzcom/masonhills/

Hanmer Springs
Homestay
Address: Champagne Flat
Hanmer Springs
Name: Chris & Virginia Parsons
Telephone: (03) 315 7413
Fax: (03) 315 7412
Beds: 1 Queen,1 Double, 1 Single (3 Bedrooms)
Bathroom: 1 Guests share
Tariff: B&B (full) Double $45pp, Single $60pp, Children under 12 half price,
Dinner $25pp. Credit cards. NZ B&B Vouchers accepted Surcharge $20.
Nearest Town: Hanmer Springs 6km

Champagne Flat is a small farmlet situated just 6 kilometres from the tiny township of Hanmer Springs. Its history is closely tied in with the building of the Ferry Bridge in 1887 and we are only 2 minutes from this historic construction which is now used for bungy jumping. Our home is a modern two-storeyed farm house with its own facilities for guests. Each guest room has its own outstanding views - wake up to a spectacular view of the snow-capped mountains and the braided Waiau River. You will have warm, spacious surroundings and share our enjoyment of the peace and tranquillity of the Hanmer Valley. We are a friendly, outgoing couple - husband a school principal, wife a 'retired' social worker dabbling in art, gardening and Tai chi. We have one independent cat and a gentle Springer Spaniel dog. We specialise in scrumptious full English breakfasts and you may join us for dinner if you wish. Participate in local activities - thermal pools, trout fishing, forest walks, golf, skiing, jet-boating. **Directions**: *1 1/2 hours easy drive north from Christchurch. SH 7 Hanmer turn off. 4 hours south from the Picton Ferry via Kaikoura inland.*

Hanmer Springs
Country Homestay
Address: 'Mira Monte',
324 Woodbank Road,
Hanmer Springs
Name: Anna & Theo van de Wiel
Telephone: (03) 315 7604
Fax: (03) 315 7604
Mobile: (025) 220 3487
Email: VDWIEL@XTRA.CO.NZ
Beds: 2 King/Queen (2 Bedrooms)
Bathroom: 2 Ensuites
Tariff: B&B (Special/Full)
Double $100, Single $85, Dinner $25.
Credit Cards: Visa/Mastercard. NZ B&B Vouchers accepted $20 surcharge
Nearest Town: Hanmer Springs 5 km.

Wake up to the song of the birds, the view of the mountain and a scrumptious breakfast. Our house is nestled at the foot of the mountains overlooking pastures with grazing sheep, cattle and deer. Our new guest rooms are very comfortable, lovely decorated and have en-suites, heating, electric blankets, hairdryers and TV's. Withdraw to your own sitting room or join us in a glass of wine or listen to some music. We have an extensive CD collection. There is a grand piano for the budding Mozart or the full fledged Bach. Our big garden has a swimming pool, where you can exercise those wary bones or just cool off in our summer heat.

We are retired chefs, travelled widely and speak Dutch and German. An elderly Labrador and a young Jack Russell are part of the family. We are a non-smoking household. We love to have you stay with us. **Home Page**: http://nz.com/infocus

Hanmer Springs
Bed & Breakfast
Address: 13 Cheltenham Street,
Hanmer Springs
Name: Len & Maree Earl
Telephone: (03) 315 7545
Fax: (03) 315 7645
Email: cheltenham@xtra.co.nz
Beds: 4 Queen, 2 Single (in house suites),
2 Queen (Garden Suite). (6 Bedrooms)
Bathroom: 5 Ensuite, 1 Private
Tariff: B&B (special) Double $130-$140, Single $100,
Credit Cards (VISA/MC/BC). NZ B&B Vouchers accepted 2 Vouchers
Nearest Town: Located in centre of Hanmer Springs

Cheltenham House offers luxury accommodation 200 m from Hanmer Springs unique Thermal Pools, shops and restaurants, including the award winning "Old Post office". We renovated this gracious 1930's villa with the traveller's comfort paramount. Four sunny, spacious, tastefully decorated suites in the house and two cottage suites in the extensive garden, offer a tranquil environment. The house is centrally heated. All suites provide superior quality bedding, tea and coffee making facilities, TV, hairdryer and comfortable seating and dining areas. Socialise in the original billiard room, with its full size table, piano and open fire. In the morning enjoy a substantial breakfast, served in your own suite, at your leisure. Hanmer Springs is a picturesque alpine resort providing activities for the most adventurous tourist to the most relaxed. Along with our gentle Labrador and sociable Siamese, we love to meet people and share our gracious home with them.
Home Page: http://www.cheltenham.co.nz

Hanmer Springs
Bed & Breakfast + Luxury Suites
Address: Glenalvon Lodge & Motels
29 Amuri Avenue, Hamner Springs
Name: Trish and John Burrin
Telephone: (03) 315 7475
Fax: (03) 315 7361
Email: glenalvon@xtra.co.nz
Beds: 6 Queen, 6 Double, 7 Single (10 Bedrooms)
Bathroom: 9 Ensuite, 1 Private
Tariff: B&B (Continental) Double $80 + $85, Suites $79-$125
(Breakfast optional extra). Single from $60. All credit cards accepted.
NZ B&B Vouchers accepted $15 - $20 surcharge
Nearest Town: In town centre.

ACCOMMODATION & RELAXATION RECIPE Take a 90 year old colonial house, beautifully restore it, fit one bedroom with ensuite and another with private facilities. Place in a cottage garden, locate in the heart of Hanmer Springs on the tree lined avenue, opposite the thermal pools and handy to shops, restaurants and adjacent to a cafe/wine bar. In the grounds at the rear add 8 luxury suites - construct the suites with extra sound proofing and insulation to ensure a quiet environment. Make them spacious, tastefully decorate and fit them out with TV, phone, bar fridge and mini kitchens. Provide special continental and cooked breakfasts, serve in the dining room in the house, with time to mingle and chat with other guests or in the units if required. Obtain a 4 STAR Qualmark rating and provide assistance with bookings for local attractions. Blend with friendly hosts and you have a recipe for a unique accommodation package.
Homepage: http://www.nzholiday.co.nz/hamner.springs/glenalvon

Hanmer Springs
Bed & Breakfast
(formerly 'Merlins')

Albergo Hanmer

Address:
Rippingale Road,
Hanmer Springs

Name: Bascha and Beat Blattner

Telephone/Fax: 0064 (0) 3 315 7428.
Freephone: 0800 342 313 (bookings only)
Email: albergohanmer@hotmail.com
Beds: 2 Super King/Twin,
1 King (3 Bedrooms)
Bathroom: 3 Ensuites (1 with spa bath),
Tariff: B&B (full/special/continental)
Double $110-$140, Single $90.
Credit Cards: (Visa/Mastercard),
NZ B&B Vouchers accepted
$30-$60 surcharge

Nearest Town: Town centre 1.5 km

Swiss Brunch-style Breakfast

Fruit Juice

Fresh fruit platter
or
Swiss Birchermuesli

Choice of cereals &
home-made yoghurt

Your choice of a hot main:
◇ Akaroa Salmon
◇ Albergo Special: Eggs Benedict
◇ Soufflé Omelettes, savoury or sweet
◇ Traditional English Breakfast
◇ French Toast with fruit compote

Freshly brewed italian coffee or teas

Seasonal changes!

Experience true hospitality without compromise, in a unique alpine setting!
Albergo Hanmer has all the comforts of European styling: double glazing, underfloor heating, spacious guestrooms - styled for privacy - each with in-room TV. Enjoy your own lounge with french doors leading to the sunny conservatory.
Albergo Hanmer offers uninterrupted panoramic mountain & rural views, all day sun, situated next to 18 hole Golf Course.
WE ARE PASSIONATE ABOUT BREAKFASTS AND SERVING NZ & EUROPEAN DINNERS!
Experience our 'Cuisine du Marché' dinners... Prime tenderloin fillet beef, Racks of baby Lamb, fresh Ocean Salmon, tempting Swiss Desserts, prepared by Beat and beautifully food-styled by Bascha using the freshest of produce. We are a younger couple with two young cats, just back from 10 years in Europe in hospitality. Bascha's background is in Fashion, Teaching and Communications (NLP). Beat is a Tourism Expert and Desktop Publisher. We speak English, Swiss German, German, French, some Spanish & Italian. Come and view our collection of Seahorse Memorabilia.
QUOTES: 'Wow we love this place. This is our second visit and we are already planning our third.' Paula & John Hunt, Wellington.
"This place is a tonic for the body & soul. Unbeatable hospitality, mouthwatering breakfasts.' Julie Haggie, Wellington.
'What gracious hosts, fabulous dinners. We'll certainly recommend it to our friends.'Helen & Steve Schlosser, USA.
'The highlight of our holiday! Total comfort and relaxation, not to mention the most scrumptious of breakfasts.' Amanda & Graeme Bassett, Rakaia.
Directions: *At junction before main village, 300m past Shell Garage, take ARGELINS RD (Centre branch), go past Hanmer Golf Club, take first road on left RIPPINGALE RD (no Exit). Albergo Hanmer is 700m down, at the very end of this country lane.*
Home Page: *www.albergohanmer.com*

Hanmer Springs
Bed & Breakfast
Address: 'Hanmer View', 8 Oregon Heights,
Hanmer Springs, Nth Canterbury
Name: Will and Helen Lawson
Telephone: Reserv: 0800-92 0800
(03) 315 7947 **Fax**: (03) 315 7958
Mobile: (025) 22 109 22
Email: lawsurv@xtra.co.nz
Beds: 1 Queen, 1 Double, 2 Single (3 Bedrooms)
Bathroom: 3 Ensuites
Tariff: B&B (Full) Double $100-$110, Single $70-$80,
Children negotiable. Dinner $25 pp by arrangement. Credit Cards: Visa/Mastercard
Nearest Town: Hanmer Springs

A warm welcome awaits you at 'Hanmer View'. Our new home, on the lower slopes of Conical Hill has been built with the comfort of our guests in mind. Our home nestles into the hillside and is surrounded by beautiful bush and breathtaking alpine views. Each room opens onto a wide deck with spectacular panoramic views of the countryside and mountains. We offer warm, spacious bedrooms with wool duvets and handmade quilts. Each room has its own ensuite and TV. Tea, coffee and home baking are always available, and a generous breakfast is provided. You won't go away hungry. 'Hanmer View' is only a short stroll from the Hot Thermal Pools, new Hydroslide Complex, Mini golf courses, Mountain biking and Horse trekking and a short drive to the picturesque 18 hole Golf Course, Bungy jumping, Jet boating, Rafting and Kayaking. Hanmer Ski Area, only 35 minutes drive away. **Directions**: *Oregon Heights turns left off the top of Conical Hill Road. Proceed up the hill to the end of Oregon Heights. Turn up the private road at the RIGHT of the cul de sac. 'Hanmer View' is on the right at the end of the private road.*

Culverden
Farmstay
Address: 'Ballindalloch', Culverden, North Canterbury
Name: Diane & Dougal Norrie
Telephone: (03) 315 8220
Fax: (03) 315 8220
Mobile: (025) 373 184
Beds: 1 Queen, 2 Single (2 bedrooms)
Bathroom: 1 Guests share
Tariff: B&B (full) Double $105, Single $55,
Children under 14 $30. Dinner $30pp.
NZ B&B Vouchers accepted
Nearest Town: Culverden - 3km south of Culverden

Welcome to "Ballindalloch" a 2090 acre dairy and sheep irrigated property 3km south of Culverden. We milk 1060 cows in 2 floating rotary dairies', a concept unique to New Zealand. We run a top Corriedale sheep stud and 600 sheep. Our German daughter-in-law has recently introduced emus to our farming scene. Our newly refurbished home is set amongst lawns and gardens and a swimming pool. Panoramic views of the hills and mountains surround us. Our home is centrally heated in winter and has a log fire. Dinner with wine by arrangment. Culverden is situated between 2 excellent fishing rivers. There is a local golf course; nearby Mt Lyford ski village. Hanmer Springs is 30 minutes from here with its famous thermal pools and full range of outdoor activities. Kaikoura whale watch being 1 1/2 hours away. We have travelled extensively overseas and appreciate relaxing in a homely atmosphere. This we extend to all guests. Complementary farm tour. We have one cat Thomas, guests are welcome to smoke outdoors. **Directions**: *Please phone or fax for directions.*

Culverden, North Canterbury
Farmstay
Address: "Pahau Pastures",
St. Leonards Road, Culverden,
North Canterbury
Name: Di Bethell
Telephone: (03) 315 8023
Fax: (03) 315 8966
Mobile: (025) 362 530
Email: Pahua.Pastures@xtra.co.nz
Beds: 1 Double, 4 Single (3 bedrooms)
Bathroom: 1 Ensuite, 1 Private
Tariff: B&B (full) Double $110, Single $55, Children under 12 half price, Dinner $35 (includes wine). Credit Cards. NZ B&B Vouchers accepted $30 surcharge
Nearest Town: Culverden 4.5km. Christchurch 100 kms.

Pahau Pastures is a sheep and cattle property of 3500 acres, with border-dyke irrigation, and has been in our family for 120 years. Our large rambling historic kauri homestead has been restored, as has our garden with mature trees, sweeping lawns, stunning views, and acres of daffodils which are a feature late September. New areas are planted in roses, paeonies, perennials, irises, lavender and rhododendron. Tour the farm or relax on our huge verandah or by a warming fire in winter. Dinner is by arrangement, with local wine complimentary. Local activities available are hot thermal pools, bungy jumping, fishing, ski-ing, golf, jet boating, Maori rock art, whale watching, bush walks and local wineries. We have a Labrador and a cat, and you are welcome to smoke outdoors. We have travelled a lot and enjoy meeting new people.
Directions: *Please ring for details.*

Gore Bay, North Canterbury
Homestay
Address: Elliotts Garden
249 Cathedral Road,
Gore Bay, RD 3, Cheviot
Name: Bette and Murray Elliott
Telephone: (03) 319 8139
Fax: (03) 319 8139
Beds: 1 Queen,
1 Double (2 Bedrooms)
Bathroom: 2 Ensuites, 1 Private
Tariff: B&B (Continental)
Double $120, Single $80.
Nearest Town: Cheviot (9 kms)

This new house has been architecturally designed for Bed and Breakfast with spacious accommodation. It is situated in a very private and pleasant coastal setting encompassing magnificent views of the coast line and rolling pastural country. A developing garden surrounds the house and consists of large new plantings - Rhododendrons, Camellias, Magnolias, Proteas and many others, with walking tracks and ponds throughout.
Bette and Murray, the hosts, can guide you to all the local activities, i.e. two salmon fishing rivers, sea-fishing, coastal walks, swimming in one of New Zealand's safest surfing beaches - all within 15 minutes of your accommodation. Also day trips to Christchurch, Hanmer Hot Pools, Kaikoura whale watch and Waipara wine trail.
Tea and coffee facilities, television, fridge are available in your room. The entire house is centrally heated. Spa bath by request. No smoking.

Waikari

Historic home & Farmstay
Address: 'Waituna', Waikari,
North Canterbury
Name: David & Joanna Cameron
Telephone: (03) 314 4575
(best before 8.30am or after 5pm)
Fax: (03) 314-4575
Email: waitunawaikari@hotmail.com
Beds: 1 King/Twin, 1 Queen, 4 Single (4 Bedrooms)
Bathroom: 1 Ensuite, 1 Private, 1 Guests Share
Tariff: B&B (continental) Double $110-$120, Single $55,
Dinner includes wine $40pp by arrangement.   Credit cards.
NZ B&B Vouchers accepted $30 surcharge per double
Nearest Town: Waikari 5km, 76km north of Christchurch,
under 1 hour from Christchurch airport.

'Waituna' is a sheep and cattle farm situated 2.5km off Highway 7, halfway between Christchurch and Hanmer Springs. The homestead, one of the largest and oldest in this area, is listed with the Historic Places Trust, the original part, built of limestone in 1879 and the last addition with extensive use of kauri, was completed in 1905. Nearby are well known wineries, golf courses, horse treks and good fishing rivers, while in Hanmer (45 mins) there are thermal pools, forest walks, skiing, bungy jumping, jet boating etc. Whale Watching at Kaikoura is only 2 hours away. We enjoy all sports, meeting people and travelling, being drawn mainly to the United Kingdom and Ireland, where we lived until 1972. (David is English and Jo a New Zealander.) We look forward to welcoming you to our gracious old home. **Directions**: *Please phone, fax or write for bookings and directions.*

Waipara

Cottage Bed & Breakfast
Address: Winery Cottage,
9 Johnson Street,
Waipara, North Canterbury
Name: Julian Ball
Telephone: (03) 314 6909
Fax: (03) 314 6909
Mobile: 025 288 6849
Beds: 2 Queen (2 bedrooms)
Bathroom: 2 Ensuite
Tariff: B&B (full, continental) Double $110,
Credit Cards VISA. NZ B&B Vouchers accepted $30 surcharge
Nearest Town: 12km north Amberley

Situated on the northern edge of Waipara village, Winery Cottage offers you the ideal location to experience the many attractions that make our area unique. Base yourself in a cosy cottage with warm, spacious bedrooms and your very own modern ensuite bathroom. In the morning take a relaxed hearty breakfast with freshly baked breads, home-made muesli, fruit juice, hot porridge and filling cooked breakfast. Evening meal available upon request Within walking distance, the Weka Pass Railway will take you on a steam train excursion. Through the hills to Frog rock - a spectacular limestone outcrop. Colmonel Horse Treks provides wagon rides through the vineyards, Glenmark church and nearby wineries. Smoke Free.

Amberley
Homestay/Farmstay
Address: Bredon Downs, Amberley RD 1,
North Canterbury
Name: Bob & Veronica Lucy
Telephone: (03) 314 9356
Fax: (03) 314 8994
Mobile: (025) 224 4061
Email: lucy.lucy@xtra.co.nz
Beds: 1 Queen, 3 Single (3 bedrooms)
Bathroom: 1 Ensuite, 1 Private
Tariff: B&B (full) Double $100-110, Single $60, Dinner $25, Credit Cards (VISA/MC). NZ B&B Vouchers accepted $15 surcharge for "doubles".
Nearest Town: 1km South of Amberley township

Our old farmhouse is off the road and surrounded by an English style garden with swimming pool and lawn tennis court. We breed ostriches and we are only too pleased to show these to anyone interested. Bob and I have lived abroad and travelled extensively and very much look forward to the company of local and overseas visitors and to entertaining them in our home. Bredon Downs is on SH1 and conveniently on the way to or from the inter-island ferry - just 48km north of Christchurch, and will appeal to those who prefer seeking country accommodation rather than the hustle and bustle of a city. The well known Waipara Wine Trail starts just north of Amberley, offering a wide selection of tasting and excellent lunches. The beach is only 2km away and there is an attractive Golf Course. We share our lives with 3 geriatric donkeys, a friendly Newfoundland dog, an ancient Labrador and Rupert the cat.

Waikuku Beach
Homestay
Address: 74 Waikuku Beach Road,
Waikuku Beach
Name: Graeme & Pauline Barr
Telephone: (03) 312 2292
Fax: (03) 312 2235
Mobile: 03 3122292
Beds: 1 Double, 2 Single
(2 bedrooms). 1 Self Contained Unit: 1 Double
Bathroom: 1 Private, 1 Family share
Tariff: B&B (continental) Double $60, Single $40, Children half price. NZ B&B Vouchers accepted. Credit Cards accepted.
Nearest Town: Rangiora 10 mins, Christchurch 30 mins.

Nestled amongst pine trees in a rural atmosphere at a quiet beach settlement, and not far from the main highway, we are just 30 minutes drive north of Christchurch city and International Airport. We offer a friendly bed and breakfast service with off-street parking in our modern two storeyed comfortable accommodation. Guests can relax on spacious decks or in a comfortable fireside lounge.
Tea and coffee-making facilities are available at all times. Laundry facilities available. Enjoy a continental breakfast before exploring the nearby beach, bird life (sanctuary), lavender fields and potteries. Mt Grey and Mt Thomas, with their numerous walking tracks, are a short drive away. We are keen trampers (trekkers) and have first hand experience of many of the well-known tracks in the South Island. We have a friendly Labrador dog which lives outside.
Our home is smoke-free, peaceful and warm.

Oxford

Homestay + Self-Contained Acco
Address: 137 High Street, Oxford
Name: Norton & Helen Dunn
Telephone: (03) 312 4167
Beds: 3 Double bedrooms,
(one brm has guest shower, toilet,
sitting room, kitchen facilities, verandah ent)
Bathroom: Other bathrooms are handy
Tariff: B&B (full)
Self-contained unit Double $70, Single $40,
Homestay B&B (full) Double $60, Single $35,
Dinner $20 by arrangement, Children 5-13yrs $12, under 5 no charge.
Nearest Town: Walking distance to the shops, 55 km from Christchurch

Our house is 80 years old and has a spacious garden – warm and sunny. We are a contented married couple with a family of three grown-up sons. We retired from Dunedin to live in Oxford – a charming, restful town and a friendly community. Oxford offers scenic walks, horse treks, homecrafts, pottery and home spun hand-knitted garments, bowls, tennis, squash, restaurant, golf and bridge club handy.
Directions: *High Street is off the Main Road – left – sign outside the gate.*

Oxford

Homestay
Address: 'Glenariff',
136 High St, Oxford
Name: John and Beth Minns
Telephone: (03) 312 4678
Beds: 1 Double,
2 Single (2 bedrooms)
Bathroom: 1 Guests share
Tariff: B&B (full) Double $60, Single $30, Children half price. Dinner $20 by arrangement. NZ B&B Vouchers accepted
Nearest Town: Oxford - town centre 500m

Your hosts John and Beth came to Oxford leaving the hustle and bustle of the city to sample the 'good-life' in the country. Along the way acquiring sheep, hens plus a handsome goat named 'Walter'. We would like you to share our hospitality and enjoy a taste of country life. A leisurely breakfast, candle-light dinner or a Devonshire Tea served on the verandah.
'Glenariff' is a 2 storey character home (circa 1886) operated as a Devonshire Tea Rooms, set in 1 1/4 acres of lawns with mature trees and a paddock for Walter and friends. Oxford caters for most sports including tennis, squash and bowls with golf, fishing, horse riding, and jet boating close by. There are walks and tramps to suit all levels of interest and fitness.
We enjoy meeting people and as Beth's forte is cooking we guarantee you'll leave well fed and rested.

Oxford
Farmstay+B&B
Address: 345 Woodside Rd,
Coopers Creek, Oxford,
North Canterbury
Name: Don and Anne Manera
Telephone: (03) 312 4964
Beds: 1 Double, 1 Twin, 1 Single (3 bedrooms)
Bathroom: Family share
Tariff: B&B (continental) $40 per person,
Double $75, Children $20, Dinner $20pp. NZ B&B Vouchers accepted
Nearest Town: Oxford 3km, Rangiora 25km, Christchurch 40km.

Welcome to Twin Bridge Farm our home set amidst tranquil situated on rolling farm land with views of the Southern Alps. Our farm of 116 acres has sheep, cattle, 3 farm dogs. A short walk to a pond has wild life in different seasons. Oxford area featues many walks casual or for more experienced trampers through forest reserve, native bush and birds. 2 local rivers for fishing, jetboating, golf course, horseriding tuition trecking hourly or day within 10 min. Approx. 45 minutes away to ski fields in the Southern Alps. 1 double, 1 twin and 1 single bedrooms, shared bathroom with hosts. Large combine dining-lounge room with featured open fire, Evening meal consists of local meat and produce. We are 3.7km west of Oxford Township watch for sign. 45 minutes from Christchurch. Dinner $20 per person. Ph. 03-312-4964. No smoking.

Oxford
Homestay
Address: 74 Bush Road, Oxford
Name: Hielan' House,
Shirley and John Farrell
Telephone: (03) 312 4382
Booking Freephone: 0800 279 382
Fax: (03) 312 4382 **Mobile**: (025) 359 435
Email: meg29@1hug.co.nz
Beds: 1 Queen, 2 Single/King (2 Bedrooms), bedsettee in lounge
Bathroom: 1 Private, 1 Ensuite
Tariff: B&B (full/Special) Double $90-$110, Single $50, Children
negotiable, Dinner $25 pp 3 course. Credit Cards: Visa/Mastercard.
NZ B&B Vouchers accepted $20 on double
Nearest Town: Oxford 1km, Christchurch Airport 40 minutes.

Welcome to our two storied home which is set in the heart of the country, an ideal place to relax before tackling the rest of the South Island or to have a peaceful break. Your hosts Shirley and John invite you to join them for their generous menu breakfasts; delicious three course evening meals available. Slightly elevated on 6 acres (inground swimming pool) enjoy lovely surroundings, with rural views to the mountains. Homestay apartment offers all comforts: electric blankets / heaters, lounge, tea / coffee making facilities, TV, private entrance. Laundry facilities available. Our welcome includes tea / coffee, delicious home baking and friendly greetings from our two dogs and cat. Golf course, jetboating, superb fishing, bush walks and Darfield Railway Station to the TransAlpine Express, all within easy reach. A gateway to the West Coast, Mid Canterbury, North Canterbury, yet Christchurch Airport only 40 minutes away. Non smoking, but there's a big ashtray outside! **Directions**: *Turn into Bay Road (off Main Street) first left into Bush Road. Our signposted entrance is on right, 740 metres along road. A phone call would be appreciated to ensure your booking.*

Darfield

Homestay
Address: 'Knockdolian',
Deans Road,
RD 1, Darfield
Name: Steve and Michelle Lassche
Telephone: (03) 318 3636
Fax: (03) 318 3636
Beds: 1 Queen (1 Bedroom)
Bathroom: 1 Ensuite
Tariff: B&B (Continental)
Double $90, Single $80, Dinner $20.
Credit cards accepted.
Nearest Town: Sheffield 2 km, Christchurch 35 mins, Airport 30 mins.

Knockdolian is situated 35 mins from Christchurch (30 mins from the Airport), just off SH73 to Arthurs Pass, nestled up to the Canterbury foothills. We offer a private quiet homestay surrounded by a large mature sheltered garden , which we encourage our guests to enjoy. The house is of interesting character and comfortable for weary travellers. We are a very relaxed family, keen to meeting people and share some good old fashioned Kiwi hospitality, with an emphasis on making you as welcome and comfortable as possible. You are welcome to join us for an evening meal, or maybe we can suggest a local restaurant. We can also arrange a number of day time adventures, or maybe you'll just be passing through. Ideal location for travellers wanting rural accommodation near to Christchurch. To avoid disappointment, bookings are strongly advised. Sorry, no smoking indoors.

West Melton, Christchurch

Farmstay
Address: "Hopesgate",
Hoskyns Road, RD5, Christchurch
Name: Yvonne & Robert Overton
Telephone: (03) 347 8330
Fax: (03) 347 8330
Beds: 1 Queen, 2 Single
(usually only look after one couple
unless party of four travelling together, therefore bathroom private)
Bathroom: 1 Guests share
Tariff: B&B (full) Double $80, Single $45,
Dinner by arrangement - from $15 pp.
Nearest Town: Christchurch city 30 kms.

We have a 50 hectare property where we farm sheep, and are situated between State Highway 1 and State Highway 73, 15 minutes from Christchurch Airport, close to all the city amenities, but with a quiet rural setting with magnificent views of the mountains. (2 hours to the skifields.) Many day trips can be taken from our home - why not make it your base. We have enjoyed entertaining folk from many parts of the world and look forward to meeting and caring for many more. We have a cat.
Ours is a relaxed and warm atmosphere where guests can socialise with us, or alternatively rest in their own rooms after making a cuppa in their own mini-kitchen. If you choose to have dinner with us it will be real farmhouse fare. Fresh home grown meat and vegetables. We would love to help you make your holiday a memorable one. Smoke free home.

West Melton, Christchurch

Homestay & Self Contained Accommodation
Address: 'Bramasole", Genesis Drive,
West Melton, RD1, Christchurch
Name: David and Sally Macdonald
Telephone: (03) 318 1688
Fax: (03) 318 1338
Email: samacd@xtra.co.nz
Beds: 1 Queen, 2 Single (2 Bedrooms)
Bathroom: 1 Guests share
Tariff: B&B (Full) Double $100, Single $60, Dinner $25.
Nearest Town: Christchurch 30 mins to city centre.

"A home away from home for the weary traveller".
Having recently moved from England, we created Bramasole with friends'
visits in mind, and would now like to extend our excellent hospitality to
others. Our peaceful rural location is easily found, just 1/2 km from
Highway 73, 15 mins from Christchurch airport, and 30 mins from the city
centre. There are several wineries nearby, and Mt Hutt ski-field is 1 1/2
hours away. Guests can relax in the privacy of the self contained guest wing,
or join the family in the house, or garden with the swimming pool, tennis
court and croquet lawn. David is always happy to advise or accompany keen
fishermen to local venues - the Waimakariri is just 5 mins away.
Sally enjoys gardening and is an enthusiastic cook, happy to cater for
special diets. We have two young teenagers, two friendly puppies, a cat and
chickens. Laundry facilities are available.
A non-smoking home.

Old West Coast Road, Christchurch

Homestay
Address: Cherry Grove
431 Old West Coast Road,
No. 6 RD, Christchurch
Name: Jan & Kirwan Berry
Telephone: (03) 342 8629
Fax: (03) 342 4321
Beds: 1 Queen, 1 Twin
(2 Bedrooms)
Bathroom: 1 Ensuite, 1 Private
Tariff: B&B (Continental) Double $90,
Twin $80, Single $65.
NZ B&B Vouchers accepted
Nearest Town: Christchurch (20 mins to city centre)

Relax and enjoy the best of both worlds in a lovely rural setting on the edge of the city.
You are welcome to wander in our spacious garden and grounds, feed the ducks and
breathe our clear country air. Daily discoveries include a 20 minute drive to
Christchurch city centre with all its olde English charm and many attractions. A 10
minute drive to the Christchurch International Airport and Antarctic Centre. Five
local vineyards/restaurants and 4 golf courses within 15 minutes. Canterbury
beaches are only 40 minutes drive away. Our modern facilities offer 1 Queen room with
ensuite, television, fridge and patio, and 1 Twin room with television and private
bathroom. Continental breakfast is standard fare with farm fresh eggs available on
request. We are on the direct route to the West Coast and many ski fields. You are
assured of a very warm welcome and friendly hospitality.

Avonhead, Christchurch

Homestay
Address: 67 Toorak Avenue,
Avonhead,
Christchurch 4
Name: Fleur Lodge
(Beverley & Harry)
Telephone: (03) 342 5473
Beds: 1 Double, 2 Single (2 bedrooms)
Bathroom: 1 Guests share, 1 Family share
Tariff: B&B (full) Double $80, Single $60, Dinner $25.
NZ B&B Vouchers accepted $12 Surcharge
Nearest Town: Christchurch 8km

In a quiet residential street, our home attracts the warm rays of the days sun, with a cosy log burner for added warmth. An attractive visual setting has been created from our passion for gardening which we mix with travel, lawn bowls and membership of several clubs. Guest bedrooms offer bright, comfortable firm beds complete with electric blankets while the adjacent guest bathroom houses a luxurious spa-bath. Tea, coffee and homemade cookies always available and as we enjoy good food, we invite you to sample our three course dinner using local grown produce - prior notice advisable. A delightful selection of breakfast dishes are available together with freshly made muffins - special requests catered for. Our home is a smoke free zone. A handy location to airport (4km) city centre (9km), well served by regular buses, or with free pickup for sightseeing trips. A warm welcome awaits you at Fleur Lodge. We share our home with two burmese cats.

Avonhead, Christchurch

Homestay
Address: 101A Yaldhurst Road,
Avonhead, Christchurch 4
Name: "Yaldhurst Homestay"
Peter & Penny Davies
Telephone: (03) 348 9977
Fax: (03) 348 9585 **Mobile**: (025) 320 146
Email: p.p.davies@clear.net.nz
Beds: 2 Queen, 2 Single (2 Bedrooms)
Bathroom: 2 Ensuites
Tariff: B&B (full) Double $100, Single $70,
Credit cards accepted. NZ B&B Vouchers accepted $20 surcharge
Nearest Town: Christchurch 6 mins by car.

A warm Kiwi welcome awaits you when you arrive at our family home.
We are in our early forties. We enjoy meeting people and are happy to assist with your travel plans. Our hobbies include gardening, crafts, golf, fishing, tennis and tramping. Our accommodation offers two spacious bedrooms, firm comfortable beds, each room having a double and single bed, ensuite bathroom, television, iron, ironing board, hairdryer, heater and electric blankets. There is a separate guest lounge with fridge and tea / coffee making facilities. Restaurants close by. Laundry services available.
Directions: *We are situated on the main road west (Highway 73), halfway between the airport and the city (6 km each way) and 2 mins from Highway. We live on a quiet rear section with off street parking (please drive in). City buses leave outside the gate.*

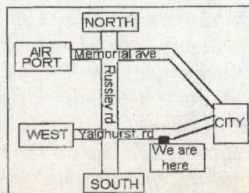

Avonhead, Christchurch
Homestay
Address: Avonhead, Christchurch 4
Name: Sally's Homestay
Telephone: (03) 342 8172 **Fax**: (03) 342 8905
Mobile: (025) 288 2366
Beds: 3 Single (2 bedrooms)
Bathroom: 1 Family share
Tariff: B&B (continental) Double $60, Single $40,
Dinner $20. NZ B&B Vouchers accepted
Nearest Town: Christchurch 10 minutes drive.

Please come and share my attractive comfortable home. The very best in New Zealand hospitality awaits you. A twin bedroom and a single are available for guests. I also have a second living room in which you may may entertain your friends, or you may join me in my family room. I have travelled extensively throughout New Zealand and would be happy to help you with your stay while you are here. Situated 2km from Christchurch International Airport, also 1km from the Riccarton Racecourse and easy access to the North South and West Highways. Bus stop two houses away, 10 minutes to Christchurch city centre, and handy to restaurants.
I belong to numerous organisations and really enjoy people and assure you of a warm welcome. On arrival I will serve you delicious home baked scones or bran muffins on my terrace or in one of my two sunny living rooms.
Directions: *Please phone. I am always home before 9.30am, if not home a message on my answerphone will get a prompt reply.*

Avonhead, Christchurch
Bed & Breakfast
Address: 302 Russley Rd.,
Christchurch
Name: "Russley 302"
Telephone: (03) 358 6543
Fax: (03) 358 6553
Mobile: (025) 224 3752
Email: carpsrussley302@clear.net.nz
Beds: 1 Queen, 3 Single (3 bedrooms)
Bathroom: 1 Ensuite, 1 Private, 1 Share.
Tariff: B&B (full) Double $95-$100, Single $55-$70,
Credit Cards (Visa/Mastercard)
NZ B&B Vouchers accepted $25 surcharge
Nearest Town: Christchurch City 15 minutes.

A warm welcome awaits you at "Russley 302" home of Sally and Brian Carpenter. We have recently retired from sheep farming and now live on 10 acres and farm a flock of black / coloured sheep. The wool from these sheep form the basis of Sally's involvement in the handcraft industry. Brian's interests include Rotary and sport. We are situated 2 minutes from Christchurch International Airport, an ideal first or last night stay. Our modern home offers electric blankets, hair dryers, refrigerators, tea / coffee, laundry and fax facilities. We have enjoyed many years of farm hosting and invite you to share this experience with us.
  Directions: *Refer to map.*

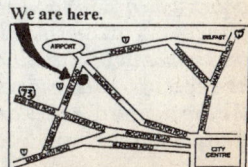

591

Burnside, Christchurch

Bed & Breakfast
Address: 31 O'Connor Place,
Burnside,
Christchurch 8005
Name: 'Burnside Bed and Breakfast'
Elaine & Neil Roberts
Telephone: (03) 358 7671
Fax: (03) 358 7761
Email: elaine.neil.roberts@xtra.co.nz
Beds: 4 Single (2 bedrooms)
Bathroom: 1 Guests share
Tariff: B&B (continental) Double $75, Single $45.
NZ B&B Vouchers accepted $20 Surcharge
Nearest Town: Christchurch centre, 15 minutes drive

Elaine and Neil welcome you to their comfortable modern home situated in a quiet street 5 minutes from Christchurch Airport. Our home is close to the Antarctic Centre, Russley Golf Course and hotel restaurants. We are near Memorial Avenue with frequent buses and an easy 15 minute drive to the city centre. A generous continental breakfast is included in the tariff. Tea and coffee are available at all times. Guests are welcome to relax in the garden or in the living room with books or television. We are a non-smoking family with one friendly cat. Our interests include golf, gardening, local history, bush walks and reading. We enjoy having guests and look forward to meeting you. **Directions**: *Please phone (03) 358 7671 for reservations and directions. Transport available.*

Ilam, Christchurch

Homestay
Address: Waimairi Lodge,
58 Waimairi Road,
Ilam, Christchurch
Name: Stewart & Gaynor Rutherford
Telephone: (03) 343 2269
Fax: (03) 343 2269
Mobile: (025) 358 707
Email: Christchurch
Beds: 3 Double, 1 Single (4 bedrooms)
Bathroom: 2 Ensuites, 1 Family shae.
Tariff: B&B ($5 extra full) Ensuite Double $85, Double $70, Single $55, Children negotiable, cot available. Dinner $30 pp, Credit cards (no American Express). NZ B&B Vouchers accepted $20 surcharge Dec to March
Nearest Town: Christchurch (Approximately 6km to centre of Christchurch)

Nestled amongst established trees and shrubs we believe our garden setting to be well worth your visit. Past prize winner Canterbury Horticultural Garden Society competition. Weekly garden tours. Situated close to University in Illam 10 minutes from Airport and only 2 blocks from Bush Inn Mall and restaurants. A drive through Hagley Park will take you into the heart of the city. Taxi and bus stops only a short walk away, however if available we can show you the highlights of Christchurch. Christchurch is a beautiful city and we pride ourselves to be part of it. To be able to pass on some of its attributes to our visitors is our pleasure. We assure you of a very warm welcome and a relaxing stay. A Kiwi dinner available but require prior notice.

Ilam, Christchurch
Homestay
Address: 7 Westmont St, Ilam, Christchurch 8004
Name: Anne & Tony Fogarty
Telephone: (03) 358 2762
Fax: (03) 358 2767
Email: tony.fogarty@xtra.co.nz
Beds: 4 Single (2 Bedrooms)
Bathroom: 1 Guests share
Tariff: B&B (continental)
Double $75, Single $45, Dinner $25.
Credit Cards. NZ B&B Vouchers accepted
Nearest Town: Christchurch 7 kms

Our home is in the beautiful suburb of Ilam, ideally situated close to Christchurch Airport (7 mins by car), the Railway Station (10 mins) and the central city (10 mins). Adjacent to the city bus route, we are very accessible to Christchurch's many attractions. We look forward to sharing our New Zealand hospitality as well as our local knowledge. We would be happy to collect visitors from the Airport or Railway for a small additional charge. We serve dinner by arrangement (extra charge). Complimentary cups of tea available. Guests are welcome to use our laundry. As parents of four young adults, all of whom have attended nearby Canterbury University, we enjoy a broad understanding of people. We are interested in sport, travel, politics, gardening and happy to chat about almost anything!! We look forward to helping make your stay in Christchurch a special time.

Bryndwr, Christchurch
Homestay
Address: 'Allisford',
1/61 Aorangi Road (off Ilam Rd),
Bryndwr, Christchurch
Name: Allison Crawford
Telephone: (03) 351 7742
Fax: (03) 351 6451
Mobile: (025) 229 2486
Email: saint@clear.net.nz
Beds: 2 Single (1 bedroom)
Bathroom: share with Allison
Tariff: B&B (special, continental)
Double $60-$70, Single $40. NZ B&B Vouchers accepted
Nearest Town: Christchurch city centre 10 mins by bus or car.
Airport 10 mins

A warm welcome awaits you in my comfortable home which I enjoy sharing with guests. My hobbies are gardening, walking, travel, some clubs, and meeting people. I am easily reached from North, South and West Highways or drive down memorial Avenue from the Airport turn left into Ilam Road, past Aqualand and you are in Aorangi Road. Golf courses are close by and Race courses are an easy drive away. Beds have electric blankets, there are heaters in your bedroom and bathroom, laundry and ironing facilities are available. You are assured of no waiting for the bathroom and are welcome to make tea or coffee any time. Excellent licensed restaurants are ten minutes pleasant walk or you are welcome to bring home take-aways. The bus stop is three minutes walk away and passes the Gardens, Arts Centre and Tourist Information Centre on the way to the City. **Directions**: *Please phone. If I am out, the answer phone will direct you.*

Harewood, Christchurch

B&B/Homestay

Address: 411 Sawyers Arms Road,
Harewood, Christchurch
North west area by airport
Name: Fairleigh Garden
Guest House
Telephone: (03) 359 3538
or freephone 0800 611 411
Fax: (03) 359 3548
Mobile: (025) 224 3746
Email: fairleighgardenbb@xtra.co.nz
Beds: 2 Queen, 2 Super Single,
1 Single (3 bedrooms)
Bathroom: 3 Ensuite,
1 double spa bath (1 wheelchair access)
Tariff: B&B (special/full) Double $130-$150, Single $80-$100,
Dinner $30 - $45 pp by arrangement. Credit Cards (Visa/Diners/Amex/Bankcard)
Nearest Town: Christchurch 10 mins. Airport 4 mins.

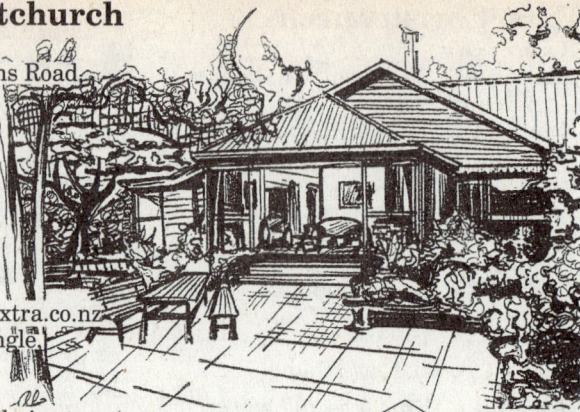

A wonderful atmosphere of complete relaxation awaits you at Fairleigh Garden Guest House, "CHRISTCHURCH'S BEST KEPT SECRET".

Our country style cedar-wood house has native heart rimu throughout with quality furnishings and native timber antique dressers.

The honeymoon suite, garden room and sunshine room all have their own ensuite, luxury bedding, warm woollen underlays, feather duvets, cotton bed linen, aromatherapy oils, fresh flowers, lovely garden views plus TV, telephone, heaters, hairdryers and door keys.

Relax in our comfortable lounge or conservatories and enjoy listening to music, playing chess, reading or perhaps planning your holiday. We are happy to help you with any queries you may have. Fax and e-mail are available to you.

Your breakfast is served at anytime you choose and will be delicious fresh fruits in season, juice, home-made muesli and yoghurt or porridge, brown sugar and cream. Home-made breads, jams and NZ butter with freshly brewed coffee or tea. A cooked breakfast of farm bacon, fresh eggs, local tomatoes and mushrooms will be cooked any way you wish - the choice is yours! Homebaking, juice, tea and coffee are freely available anytime. Dinner of tender Canterbury lamb or freshly caught fish are popular choices enhanced by the use of local produce - fruit, vegetables, herbs - and Valerie's enjoyment of cooking make this a truly unique experience.

A large urban garden gives all year round vistas of many varied plantings - spring bulbs, magnolias, camellias, roses, flowering cherry trees, vegetables, herbs and many more. The petanque and croquet lawns plus barbecue areas provide a quiet environment on the outskirts of the city and close to the airport. We have bicycles for guests that wish to explore the local countryside.

COME AND ENJOY GENUINE NZ HOSPITALITY AT ITS BEST WITH 4TH GENERATION NEW ZEALANDERS - YOU WILL NEVER FORGET THIS WONDERFUL EXPERIENCE.

4 mins to the airport - 10 mins to city - free transfers to and from airport - laundry available - ample off street parking - no smoking indoors - come and meet our lovable cat "Zambie".
Directions: *800 metres off major bypass - Johns Road.*
Home Page: http://www.friars.co.nz/hosts/fairleigh.html

Riccarton, Christchurch
Homestay
Address: 70A Puriri Street, Riccarton, Christchurch.
Name: Caroline and Keith Curry
Telephone: (03) 348 4081
Fax: (03) 348 4081
Email: curryc@xtra.co.nz
Beds: 4 Single (2 Bedrooms)
Bathroom: 1 Guests share
Tariff: B&B (Continental) Double $80, Single $40. Not suitable for children. Credit cards accepted.
Nearest Town: City Centre 8 minutes by car.

Our home is a comfortable modern two storied townhouse situated in a quiet street near the University and Riccarton House and midway between the airport and the city centre. We have a small private garden and courtyard for outdoor relaxation. Facilities for guests are two spacious upstairs twin bedrooms and a bathroom with a separate toilet. The laundry is available for guest use. Keith enjoys the outdoors, including white water rafting. Caroline is interested in local history and embroidery. Having travelled overseas and throughout New Zealand we are sympathetic to the requirements of travellers and offer you a warm welcome. We are a pet free home and don't mind if you smoke outside. If necessary we offer a pickup service from the airport, railway station or city centre. Otherwise please phone for directions.

Fendalton, Christchurch
Homestay
Address: 'Fendalton House', 50 Clifford Avenue, Fendalton, Christchurch 1.
Name: Pam Rattray
Telephone: (03) 355 4298 or 0800 37 4298
Fax: (03) 355 0959
Email: fendaltonhouse@xtra.co.nz
Beds: 1 Super King/Twin, 1 King, 1 Queen, 1 Single (3 bedrooms)
Bathroom: 3 Ensuite
Tariff: B&B (special) Double $145-$165, Single $135-$155, Credit Cards.
Nearest Town: Driving, Airport 10 minutes, City Centre 5 minutes

Enjoy warm relaxed hospitality staying with us right in the middle of one of Christchurch's most beautiful suburbs with large trees and lovely gardens. Being central it's a pleasant walk into town through Hagley Park or Mona Vale. You can sit under the grape vine in the big conservatory that warms the whole house or wander down past the swimming pool to feed the wild ducks in the clear stream at the bottom of the garden. Eat your large home cooked breakfast (may include waffles with berry sauce, pancakes etc.) in the sunny dining room which has a small New Zealand art collection. Each room has large beds, an ensuite bathroom, colour TV and tea making facilities. The spa (jacuzzi) is usually hot but it's worth ringing 24 hrs in advance if you are really keen. Laundry facilities available. Major credit cards accepted. We are a non-smoking household with a small friendly cat.
Home Page: http://nz.com/webnz/bbnz/fendalt.htm

Fendalton

Homestay
Address: 23A Jeffrey's Road,
Fendalton, Christchurch 5
Name: Mary & Gerald
Telephone: (03) 351 7330
Fax: (03) 351 8967
Beds: 3 Single (2 bedrooms)
Bathroom: 1 Private,
1 Family share
Tariff: B&B (full)
Double $100, Single $80.
Credit Cards. NZ B&B Vouchers accepted $40 Surcharge.
Nearest Town: Christchurch, 10 mins drive to city centre

Our spacious Colonial property is situated in a very private, tranquil garden setting. We are midway between the Airport and City centre, 10 minutes from either by car. A large sunny twin bedroom is available with private bathroom for guests plus one single room. Mary embroiders and sculpts when time permits. We both enjoy gardening, music, good food, books, travel, and meeting people. Our elderly house minder is a little Dachshund dog. A fine breakfast is served in a charming dining room. You are welcome to smoke but please do so outdoors. Off street parking.
Please phone for reservations and directions.

Dallington, Christchurch

Homestay + Self Contained Accommodation
Address: Killarney,
27 Dallington Terrace,
Dallington, Christchurch
Name: Russell and Lynne Haigh
Telephone: (03) 381 7449
Fax: (03) 381 7449
Email: haigh.killarney@xtra.co.nz
Beds: 2 Double,
1 Single (3 bedrooms)
Bathroom: 1 Ensuite,
1 Guests share, 2 Family share
Tariff: B&B (full) Double $85, Single $60
NZ B&B Vouchers accepted $10 surcharge
Nearest Town: Chirstchurch City Centre: 6 minutes

Peace and tranquillity and a cottage garden set on the banks of the Avon River. You can walk the river banks or borrow our dinghy and row. The self-contained double ensuite accommodation is detached from the house, with its own private garden. Other accommodation is in the house with great views. We are only 6 minutes by car to the City Centre, and also close to The Palms Shopping Mall, golf courses and beaches. Buses 11 and 29 stop nearby. Tea, coffee and home baking are always available, and Russell's breakfasts are great. You can join us for dinner if you wish ($20 max. pp) but please give us warning. Laundry service available - please enquire.
Directions: *Phone for directions. We will collect you from the airport, train or bus station if required. Both of us, as well as our cats and bearded collie Mac, look forward to meeting you.*

Merivale, Christchurch
Bed & Breakfast Inn
Address: The Lane,
27 Holly Road,
Christchurch 1
Name: "Villa Victoria" Kate McNeill
Telephone: (03) 355 7977
Fax: (03) 355 7977
Mobile: 025-397 376
Beds: 2 Double,
1 Single (3 bedrooms)
Bathroom: 3 Ensuite
Tariff: B&B (special) Double $160, Single $110, Credit cards (VISA/BC/MC).
Nearest Town: Christchurch. 5 minutes from City. 20 minutes walk

A warm welcome awaits you at "Villa Victoria". Built from native kauri this 98 year old villa has been authentically restored by its owner Kate and reflects all the elegance and charm of a world gone by. Furnishings are appropriate to the late Victorian / Edwardian era with lace curtains / bedspreads, brass / iron beds, antiques and collectables. This tranquil haven has been designed to be a home away from home - it is small and intimate. Each bedroom is completely private with its own ensuite. Delectable breakfasts are speciality served in the formal dining room or during summer on the verandah overlooking the picturesque private garden. "Villa Victoria" is ideally situated within walking distance for all city activities, excellent restaurants, boutique shopping. Complimentary NZ wine / cheese or a port / coffee after dining. Please phone for reservations and directions. No smoking. Off-street parking. Not suitable for children. **Home Page**: http://nz.com/heritageinns/villa victoria

Merivale, Christchurch
Homestay
Address: 'Aldeburgh',
12 Holly Road, Christchurch 1
Name: Sue and Eric Jackson
Telephone: (03) 355 2557
Fax: (03) 355 2537
Mobile: (025) 327 515
Email: ej@cashbuys.co.nz
Beds: 2 King, 1 Queen, 1 Single (2 bedrooms)
Bathroom: 1 Ensuite, 1 Private
Tariff: B&B (full) Large Suite $120, Double $100, Single $70, Children $25, Credit Cards (VISA/MC). NZ B&B Vouchers accepted $45 surcharge for Aldeburgh Suite, $30 for Holly Room.
Nearest Town: Christchurch City Centre (3 minutes by car)

Sue and Eric welcome you to Aldeburgh, a gracious Victorian residence Circa 1880, located in the 'golden mile' for tourist accommodation close to the city's attractions. Our home is furnished with antiques and fine art in keeping with its heritage, with all the comforts and facilities of the new millennium (e-mail, internet, fax). A beautiful fretwork verandah surrounds the property, an ideal place to relax on a summers day, in a private garden setting. The spacious elegant Aldeburgh Suite features a new gas fire and has a dressing room and ensuite. The Holly Room has delightful leadlight windows and a private outlook. The guest rooms have TV, tea / coffee facilities, excellent beds and fresh flowers. There is an in-house remedial massage service, perfect for the travel weary. The household comprises of ourselves and our daughter Jessica (12). We offer a complimentary pickup from the Airport, Railway or Bus. Laundry service is available. Secure off street parking. **Home Page**: http://canterypages.co.nz.aldeburgh/

Merivale, Christchurch

Bed & Breakfast Inn
Address: 'Elm Tree House',
236 Papanui Rd,
Merivale, Christchurch
Name: Karen & Allan Scott
Telephone: (03) 355 9731
Fax: (03) 355 9753
Mobile: 025-794 016
Email: elmtreeb.b@clear.net.nz
Beds: 2 King, 3 Queen,
5 Single (5 bedrooms)
Bathrooms: 5 Ensuites
Tariff: B&B (full/continental)
Double $100-$175, Single $100-$145,
Dinner $35. Triple and family room available $145-$195.
Credit Cards (VISA/MC/American Express/Bartercard). Seasonal rates apply.
NZ B&B Vouchers accepted $45 Surcharge April-October. 2 Vouchers Nov-March
Nearest Town: City Centre 5 minutes drive

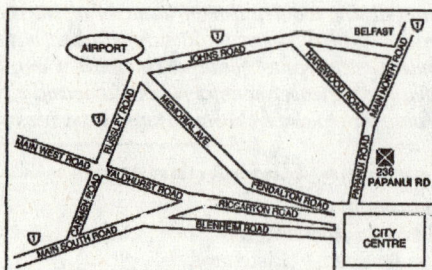

'Elm Tree House' is a spacious Historic listed home situated in the heart of Merivale, an area known for its fine homes, restaurants and boutique shops and mall. Comfort and style is the theme of this gracious home built in 1920, with carefully chosen King and Queen beds for a peaceful nights sleep complimented by our large guest lounge and dining room with its Wurlitzer Jukebox, or relax by the solar heated pool in our garden setting. Just 10 minutes by car to the airport and Trans Alpine Rail Station, or a 20 minute stroll takes you to the city centre's many attractions from beautiful Hagley Park and gardens, the Arts Centre and Gallery to punting on the Avon or trying your luck at the Casino. Start each day with the breakfast of your choice and then sample the fine restaurants close by or enjoy an evening dinner with us, by prior arrangement please. Karen and Allan, daughters Martina and Courtney and Summer our cat wish you a happy and enjoyable stay in our beautiful city.
Close to St Georges Hospital, laundry service, smoking in the garden please. Our home is fitted with a full sprinkler and smoke alarm fire system.
Home Page: http://www.elmtreehouse.co.nz

Merivale, Christchurch
Homestay
Address: 121 Winchester Street, Christchurch
Name: Villa 121
Telephone: 03 355 8128
Fax: 03 355 8126
Beds: 1 King, 1 Queen, 2 Single (3 bedrooms)
Bathroom: 1 Guests share, 1 Family share.
Tariff: B&B (full) Double $95, Single $80, Dinner $20, Children half price. Credit Cards.
Nearest Town: Christchurch - 4 km

We are well travelled, fun loving and really enjoy meeting people. We provide a relaxing atmosphere and look forward to making your stay happy and memorable. "Villa 121" is a tastefully and stylishly restored villa set in a lovely old world garden. Delicious continental and/or cooked breakfast is available at a time to suit you, and complimentary tea/coffee and home-baking is available at any time.

Your hosts are Trish (school teacher), Barry (consultant surveyor) and Melanie (4th year Fine Arts student). We are very keen sports people, especially tennis, golf and skiing and happy to help you organise your sporting activities. The closest golf course and tennis courts are only 3 minutes away.

Relax in the sun on the wisteria and vine clad verandah in summer or enjoy the open fire in winter.

http://www.bnb.co.nz

take a look

Merivale, Christchurch
Homestay/Bed & Breakfast
Address: 34B Leinster Road,
Merivale, Christchurch
Name: "Leinster Homestay"
Kay and Brian Smith
Telephone: (03) 355 6176
Fax: (03) 355 6176
Mobile: (025) 330 771
Email: brian.kay@xtra.co.nz
Beds: 1 Queen, 1 Double (2 Bedrooms)
Bathroom: 1 Ensuite, 1 Private
Tariff: B&B (Full/Continental) Double $100-$110, Single $70.
Children negotiable. Credit card facilities.
Nearest Town: Driving, Airport 10 mins - City Centre 5 mins

New Zealand Association FARM & HOME HOSTS

Kay and Brian invite you to their sunny modern townhouse situated in the heart of Merivale, one of Christchurch's most beautiful suburbs with established trees and gardens and only a short stroll to the exclusive Merivale shopping centre and many top class cafes and wine bars. Hagley Park, the Arts Centre, Museum, Botanical Gardens and Casino are all within a 10 minute drive. At the end of an enjoyable day exploring our wonderful city you are welcome to relax in our courtyard garden or inside by the fire in our warm inviting lounge. Guests bedrooms are comfortably appointed with electric blankets and duvets. Tea and coffee available at all times, laundry and ironing facilities. Along with our friendly dog Jake and Max the cat, we look forward to welcoming you to our home. Easy to find off a main arterial Road. No smoking indoors. Mt Hutt and other skifields: 1 - 1 1/2 hours drive.

St Albans, Christchurch
Homestay
Address: 23 Eversleigh Street,
St Albans, Christchurch 1.
"Eversleigh"
Name: Karen and John Law
Telephone: (03) 365 6779
Fax: (03) 352 5617
Email: kjlaw@xtra.co.nz
Beds: 1 Queen (1 bedroom)
Bathroom: 1 Ensuite
Tariff: B&B (continental) Double $80, Single $60, dinner by arrangement.
Not suitable for children. NZ B&B Vouchers accepted $20 surcharge
Nearest Town: Christchurch City.

"Eversleigh", just 15 minutes walk from Cathedral Square, the botanical gardens, the arts centre and art gallery, is a large, two storey home built around the turn of the century. Surrounded by a beautiful garden containing huge trees, the house stands on a tranquil three quarter acre section. Our guest room has French doors opening to a balcony overlooking the garden, a queen size bed with electric blanket, a private ensuite and separate toilet. We are a young couple who love meeting people and look forward to welcoming you into our home. Among our interests are travel, dining out and theatre. We are non-smokers but you are welcome to smoke outdoors. Dinner is available on request (at extra cost) or we could guide your choice of one of Christchurch's many restaurants. Tourist information is available. We enjoy having guests and look forward to meeting you.
Directions: *Please phone.*

St Albans, Christchurch

Homestay
Address: Barrich House
82 Caledonian Road,
St Albans, Christchurch 1
Name: Barbara and Richard
Telephone: (03) 365 3985
Email: exti066@its.canterbury.ac.nz
Beds: 1 Queen, 2 Single (2 Bedrooms)
Bathroom: 1 Ensuite, 1 Family share.
Tariff: B&B (Full) Double $80-$90, Single $50-$65,
Children under 12 years half price. Dinner $25 by prior arrangement.
NZ B&B Vouchers accepted $20 surcharge (queen)
Nearest Town: Christchurch, 20 mins easy walk to city centre.

Our home is startlingly alive and loves company. It is modern, well designed and furnished with strong but tasteful interior colours and has a sunny courtyard garden. In a quiet street, very handy to buses, shops, city centre, casino, restaurants and Southern Cross Hospital. The queen suite is a beautiful spacious room with its own facilities and a lovely outlook. The bedrooms have fresh flowers, comfortable beds, good linen, electric blankets, heaters and TV. Help yourselves to tea, coffee and cookies, and the use of the laundry, piano, high chair and cot. Complimentary pickup transport available. We have no resident children or pets, and request no smoking indoors, please. Choose breakfast from our menu. Reduced rates for longer stays; Christchurch is worth it. We look forward to welcoming you and helping you enjoy this lovely city and our home. Please phone in advance.

Avondale, Christchurch

Bed & Breakfast
Address: Hulverstone Lodge,
18 Hulverstone Drive,
Avondale, Christchurch
Name: Ian & Diane Ross
Telephone: (03) 388 6505
Fax: (03) 388 6025
Mobile: (025) 433 830
Email: hulverstone@caverock.net.nz
Beds: 1 Queen, 2 King or twin, 1 Single (4 bedrooms)
Bathroom: 1 Ensuite, 1 Private, 1 Guests share
Tariff: B&B (full) Double $80-$110, Single $60-$80, Credit Cards welcome (VISA/MC).
NZ B&B Vouchers accepted $0-$40 surcharge
Nearest Town: Christchurch - 15 mins from city centre

A stately Tudor-style house, Hulverstone Lodge overlooks the Avon River.
Watch the sun rise over the river, enjoy views of the Port Hills or catch glimpses of the Southern Alps. Delightful walks pass the door while other nearby recreational facilities beckon. A leisurely stroll brings you to New Brighton's restaurants, sandy Pacific Ocean beach and pier. Hulverstone Lodge is an ideal base for skiing or other leisure activities in the Canterbury region. The ski-fields, Akaroa, Hanmer Springs and Kaikoura are all within a couple of hours' drive. Buses passing close by offer a frequent, fast, friendly ride to the city. Hulverstone Lodge provides convenient access to all parts of Christchurch City, the airport and railway station, as well as main routes north and south, yet it offers a tranquil riverside haven. We, and our cat, look forward to sharing it with you. Complimentary pick-up from plane, train or bus available.
Home Page: www.canterburypages.co.nz/hulverstone

Christchurch - City Centre

Private Hotel

Address: 52 Armagh Street, Christchurch
Name: Windsor Private Hotel
Telephone: (03) 366 1503 or 366 2707
Fax: (03) 366 9796
Email: reservations@windsorhotel.co.nz
Beds: 40 bedrooms
Bathroom: Guests share
Tariff: B&B (full) Double $98, Single $66, Children under 12 years $15. Credit cards/Eftpos. Quote this book for 10% discount.
Nearest Town: Christchurch City

"The Windsor", originally named Warwick House, was built at the turn of the century. Situated in the quiet northwest situation of Cranmer Square, we are centrally located on the tourist tram route and within easy walking distance of the Art Centre, museum, gardens, theatre, convention centre, Casino and Cathedral Square (our city centre), with its banks, buses, shopping arcades and excellent restaurants.

Guests are greeted on arrival and shown around our charming colonial style home. Our nicely furnished bedrooms all with a small posie of flowers, and an original water colour by local artist Denise McCulloch, lend charm to the warm and cosy bedrooms which are all individually heated. The shared bathroom facilities are all conveniently appointed for guests comfort with bathrobes provided on request. The dining room where our generous morning menu includes juice, fresh fruit and cereals, followed by a choice of bacon and eggs, sausages, tomatoes, toast and marmalade. The lounge where we serve tea, coffee and biscuits each evening at 9.00 pm is where everyone gathers to watch television and have a chat. There are 24 hour tea, coffee and laundry facilities along with off-street parking for the motorist. For the comfort and convenience of our guests we encourage non-smoking. "The Windsor" is family owned and operated.

Home Page: www.windsorhotel.co.nz

TURRETHOUSE

R.F.H. '96

Christchurch - City Centre
Bed & Breakfast
Address: Turret House
Céad Mile Fáilte
435 Durham Street North, Christchurch
Name: Justine & Paddy Dougherty
Telephone: (03) 365 3900/0800 488 773 (0800 4 Turret)
Fax: (03) 365 5601
Email: turretb.bchch@xtra.co.nz
Beds: 1 King, 5 Queen, 1 Twin, 1 Single (7 bedrooms)
Bathroom: 7 Ensuite
Tariff: B&B (continental) Double $85-$110, Single $65.
Major Credit cards accepted. NZ B&B Vouchers accepted $20 surcharge
Nearest Town: Christchurch centre 10 mins walk

'Céad Míle Fáilte'
(One hundred thousand welcomes)
Turret House is a gracious superior Bed & Breakfast accommodation located in downtown Christchurch. It is within easy walking distance of Cathedral Square, the Botanical Gardens, Museum, Art Gallery, the Arts Centre and Hagley Park 18 hole golf course. Also Casino, new Convention Centre, Town Hall. Built around 1900 this historic residence is one of only three in the area protected by the New Zealand Historic Places Trust. It has been restored to capture the original character and charm. Situated within the grounds is one of Christchurch's best examples of our native kauri tree. Attractively decorated bedrooms with heaters and electric blankets combine comfort and old world elegance, with private bathrooms, some with bath and shower, all offering a totally relaxed and comfortable environment. Tea, coffee and biscuits available 24 hrs. Cots and highchairs are also available. Family room sleeps 4. If you're looking for a place to stay where the accommodation is superior and the atmosphere friendly - experience Turret House.
Non smoking policy.
Directions: *Just 15 minutes from Christchurch Airport. Situated on the corner of Bealey Ave and Durham Street. (Off-street parking).*
Home Page: www.turrethouse.co.nz

Christchurch - City Centre

Bed & Breakfast/Homestay/Apartment

Address: 'Riverview Lodge'
361 Cambridge Terrace, Christchurch
Name: Ernst & Sabine
Telephone: (03) 365 2860
Fax: (03) 365 2845
Email: riverview.lodge@xtra.co.nz
Beds: 3 King/Queen, 2 Double, 1 Single
(3 bedrooms, 2 Suites)
Bathroom: 4 Ensuite, 1 Private
Tariff: B&B (special) Double $135-$195, Single $80-$120, Children neg.
Credit cards.
Nearest Town: 10 min river walk into city.

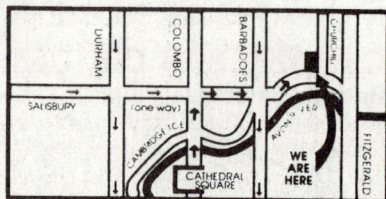

Listed in FODOR'S as "pick of the B&B accommodation in Christchurch".
If you like quality accommodation in a relaxed and quiet atmosphere, still just minutes walking away from the centre of an exciting city: this is the place to stay. Our house is a restored Edwardian residence that reflects the grace and style of the period with some fine carved Kauri and Rimu features. It is ideally situated on the banks of the Avon River in a tranquil setting surrounded by an old English garden with mature trees. Guest rooms are elegant, combining modern facilities with colonial furnishings. All rooms have ensuite/private facilities, colour TV and heating, balconies provide a superb river view. Tea and coffee making facilities are available at all times. Breakfast is a house speciality with a wide choice of cooked and continental fare. In the Edwardian townhouse next door there are two very spacious (90m2) apartments for a very private stay. Guests find antiques and quality furniture, a fully equipped kitchen, television, private telephone and a lovely formal yard which backs onto the city park. For full breakfast we invite guests into the lodge or if requested supply a self service breakfast in the apartment Kayaks, bicycles and golfclubs are available for guests to use. As experienced travellers and tour operators we'll be happy to provide you with all the information that will make your stay in Christchurch and New Zealand unforgettable. German, Spanish, Dutch, French is spoken. For cancellations 48 hrs prior to arrival we charge the full amount of one night.
Directions: *RIVERVIEW LODGE is located on the corner of Cambridge Terrace and Churchill Street.*
Home Page: http://www.superiorinns.co.nz

Christchurch - City Centre
Guest House
Address: 56 Armagh Street, Christchurch
Name: The Grange
Telephone: (03) 366 2850
Fax: (03) 374 2470
Mobile: (021) 366 608
Email: info@the grange.co.nz
Beds: 2 King/Twin, 2 Queen,
3 Double, 1 Single (8 Bedrooms)
Bathroom: 6 Ensuite, 1 Guests share
Tariff: B&B (full) Summer: Double $110, Twin $110,
Single $95. Extra Adult $35, Children under 12 years $15. Shared Bathroom:
Double $98, Single $85. NZ B&B Vouchers accepted 1st April to 30th September.
Nearest Town: We are in Christchurch centre

At The Grange Guesthouse you will enjoy your visit in this tastefully "renovated" Victorian mansion with wood panelling and a magnificent wooden feature staircase, you can relax in the guest lounge or in the garden. The Grange Guesthouse is situated within walking distance to most of Christchurch's favourite spots including; Cathedral Square, the Arts Centre, Art Gallery and Museum also the Botanic Gardens, Hagley Park and Mona Vale. During your stay at The Grange you will be treated to superior accommodation, complimentary tea and coffee, off-street parking, laundry service and sightseeing tours and onward travel can be arranged. If you wish to stay indoors there is a TV. Non-smoking is encouraged. Banks, shops, restaurants, night clubs and the Art Centre are all easy walking distance. Paul and Marie Simpson are a mother and son team whose hospitality will ensure your stay is a pleasurable and pleasant one. **Home Page**: http://www.thegrange.co.nz

Christchurch - City Centre
Bed & Breakfast Hotel
Address: 63 Armagh Street, Christchurch
Name: Croydon House
Bed & Breakfast Hotel
Telephone: (03) 366 5111
or 0800-276 936
Fax: (03) 377 6110
Email: b&bcroydonhouse@xtra.co.nz
Beds: 12 Bedrooms
Bathroom: 6 Guests share, 6 Ensuite
Tariff: B&B (full) Credit Cards (MC/VISA)
Guest Share facilities: Single $70.00, Double/Twin $95.00.
Private facilities: Single $90.00, Double/Twin $120.00.
Nearest Town: Christchurch City Centre 5 minutes walk

Croydon House is an attractive, small, personal Hotel that offers charming accommodation in the Heart of New Zealand's Garden City. We have a range of Guestrooms - with either Guest share or private ensuite facilities in the Hotel, or Garden rooms in our tranquil adjoining cottage. Start your day with our scrumptious breakfast buffet including cooked dishes, before exploring - perhaps a ride on the tram that passes by Croydon House's front door, or a punt on the nearby Avon River. Major attractions, great Restaurants, conference venues and the famous Botanical Garden are within easy walking distance. For more information visit our Home Page on the Internet. Your hosts Nita and Siegfried Herbst. **Home Page**: www.croydon.co.nz

Christchurch - City Centre

Bed & Breakfast Inn
Address: 'Hambledon',
103 Bealey Avenue, Christchurch
Name: Jo & Calvin Floyd
Telephone: (03) 379 0723
Fax: (03) 379 0758
Email: hambledon@clear.net.nz
Beds: Victorian Cottage and Coach house
5 King/Queen, 1 Double, 5 Single (6 bedrooms incl. 2 2-bedroom suites)
Bathroom: 8 Ensuite
Tariff: B&B (special, full) Double $155-$230, Single $135-$185.
Credit cards: Visa/ Mastercard/Amex. NZ B&B Vouchers accepted Surcharge
Nearest Town: Christchurch City Central

*Jo and Calvin welcome you to Hambledon, a gracious Historic Mansion built as a home for the prominent city father George Gould. Once again guests can enjoy the warmth and ambience of a grand family home. Relax in one of six charming character rooms or suites that offer privacy, the elegance of antique furnishings, crisp linen, flowers, comfort and convenience with ensuite bathrooms. Start the day with a wonderful breakfast in the magnificent dining room with its Lancaster Sideboard and NZ Art. Later read the paper and relax in the elegant guest lounge with its oriental rugs, in the conservatory, or on the wisteria clad verandahs. Enjoy the tranquil cottage gardens with the box hedges, brick paths, hollyhocks and roses, or stroll to restaurants, Hagley park or Cathedral Square. Ample off street parking and a guest laundry. For reasons of safety and the health of others we ask you not to smoke indoors. It will be our please to ensure your stay at Hambledon is memorable. Member Surperio Inns of NZ. **Home Page**: www.hambledon.co.nz*

Christchurch - City Centre

Guest House
Address: "Armagh Lodge",
257 Armagh St., Christchurch
Name: Armagh Lodge
Telephone: (03) 366 0744
Fax: (03) 374 6359
Mobile: 025-317 026
Beds: 6 Double, 11 Single
(10 bedrooms)
Bathroom: 3 Ensuite, 3 Guests share
Tariff: B&B (full) Double $75, Single $50, Children half price, free in parents room, Dinner $10. Credit Cards. NZ B&B Vouchers accepted
Nearest Town: 5-10 mins walk to central city.

Armagh Lodge is a charming Edwardian Villa with the original ornate plaster ceilings and lead light windows. It is spacious, warm and comfortable with a large garden area. Situated in the inner city residential area, it has the advantages of a short (5-10 min) walk to shops, restaurants etc. with none of the bustle and noise of the city at the end of the day. We have off-street parking or the number 11 bus will drop you at the gate. The large lounge has a TV, and coffee and tea is available 24 hours, or sit in the conservatory and watch the garden grow or the cats trying to catch the birds. In the morning a generous full breakfast will be served. No smoking indoors please.

Christchurch - City Centre
Bed & Breakfast
Address: The Worcester of Christchurch,
No. 15 Worcester Boulevard,
Central Christchurch
Name: Maree Ritchie & Tony Taylor
Telephone: (03) 365 0936 Freephone: 0800 365 015
Fax: (03) 364 6299
Email: the.worcester@clear.net.nz
Beds: 1 Super King/Twin, 2 Queen (3 bedrooms)
Bathroom: 3 Ensuite
Tariff: B&B(full) Double $195-$250, Credit Cards (VISA/BC/AMEX/DINERS).
Nearest Town: 5 minutes walk to Cathedral Square, Christchurch

*The Worcester
of Christchurch*

The Worcester of Christchurch is a beautifully preserved colonial mansion built in 1893 for the Chief Constable of Lyttelton decorated in classic Victorian style with antiques and art. Uniquely situated in Worcester Boulevard, just a walk across the road to the Arts Centre, Botanic Gardens, Museum, wine bars and cafes, and a five minute walk to Cathedral Square and central city shopping. The Worcester Suite features super king antique bed, dressing room and ensuite, Rolleston and Gloucester Rooms are queen size with ensuites. All rooms have Sky television, direct dial telephones, electric blankets, irons, ironing boards, hair dryers. A full breakfast is served in the elegant dining room. Maree also has her fine art business at Worcester, where guests can experience the rich history of New Zealand art, while enjoying the warm hospitality and unique surroundings of the Worcester. Off street parking court. We have a small black poodle "Joe". **Directions**: *Follow Hagley Park into Park Terrace and Rolleston Avenue, turn into Worcester Boulevard opposite Museum.* **Home Page**: http://www.intermart.co.nz/worcester.*

Christchurch - City Centre
Home Lea B&B

Home Lea B&B
Address: 195 Bealey Ave
Christchurch
Name: Graham and Glenda Weavers
Telephone: (03) 379 9977
Fax: (03) 379 4099
Email: homelea@xtra.co.nz
Beds: 1 King, 2 Queen,
5 Single (5 Bedrooms)
Bathroom: 2 Ensuite, 2 Guests share.
Tariff: B&B (Continental) Double $85-$110, Single $50-$65. Children $10 each.
All credit cards accepted.
NZ B&B Vouchers accepted $20 surcharge (not Nov-31 Mar)
Nearest Town: Christchurch

Friendly warm hospitality is offered to guests in our charming character home built in 1904. We are very easy to find and close to the City Centre, good restaurants, Botanical Gardens, Museum, Casino and all tourist attractions.
Our guest bedrooms are roomy and elegantly furnished for comfort, and are all individually heated. Relax in the large guest lounge, with tea and coffee available at all times. Enjoy an extensive continental buffet breakfast in the morning to start your day. We have safe off street parking. For guests comfort no smoking is allowed indoors. We look forward to meeting you and will endeavour to make your stay an enjoyable and memorable one. Inspection welcome.
Home Page: http://nz.com/webnz/bbnz/homelea.htm

Christchurch - City Centre

Bed and Breakfast
Address:
88 Chester Street East,
Christchurch
Name: "Crighton"
Telephone: (03) 366 2557
Fax: (03) 366 2557
Email: anna.crighton@xtra.co.nz
Beds: 1 Double, 1 Single (2 Bedrooms)
Bathroom: 1 Ensuite
Tariff: B&B (Full/Continental)
Double $130-$150, Single $120,
Not suitable for children. Credit cards accepted.
Nearest Town: Christchurch Central 2 mins walk

CRIGHTON

You are offered a great stay at "Crighton" a listed heritage townhouse only 2 minutes walk from the central city. Built in 1894 for William Widdowson this gracious house has seen many changes. From family home, student hostel, offices, and apartments to a recently decorated and converted select bed and breakfast. You will have privacy and comfort with a double bedroom and en suite and a single bedroom, together catering for up to three guests. Your own lounge with TV and telephone where you can relax and enjoy a unique view over the Avon River. A short stroll along the river takes you to an excellent selection of restaurants, cafes, theatres, Town Hall, Convention Centre, Museum, Art Gallery plus all the shopping a busy city offers. Off street parking. Laundrette nearby. Rooms are upstairs and not suitable for disabled or children.

http://www.bnb.co.nz

take a look

Christchurch - City Centre

Bed & Breakfast
Address: 62 Park Terrace, Christchurch 8001
Name: The Weston House
Telephone: (03) 366 0234 **Fax**: (03) 366 5254
Mobile: (025) 381 927
Email: weston.house@xtra.co.nz
Beds: 1 Super King/Twin, 1 Queen (2 Bedrooms)
Bathroom: 2 Ensuite
Tariff: B&B (Full) Double $250, Single $225. Children by arrangement.
Credit Cards Amex/Diners/Visa/Mastercard/Eftpos
Nearest Town: Less than 500m from CBD.

THE WESTON HOUSE, a well known Christchurch landmark, was designed by Cecil Woods and has been described in respected publications as the finest Neo-Georgian building in New Zealand. Extensively restored in 1998/99, Len and Stephanie invite you to enjoy luxurious accommodation in a Category 1, listed historic house. * CENTRALLY LOCATED on prestigious Park Terrace the Weston House is a short walk to the CBD and its shopping precincts, historic arts centre, galleries and museum.* SPORTING ACTIVITIES, FITNESS TRAINING & GOLF opposite in Hagley Park. * FINE FOOD, LIVE THEATRE - CASINO, a few minutes walk. Two luxury suites are furnished with antiques and each has TV, fridge, electric blankets, hair dryer, robes, plus COMPLIMENTARY SHERRY, COFFEE, TEA BISCUITS, FRUIT & CHOCOLATES. A FULL, COOKED OR CONTINENTAL BREAKFAST IS INCLUDED IN YOUR TARRIF AND EACH EVENING WE SERVE FINE NEW ZEALAND WINES & HORS D'OEUVRES.*Courtesy vehicle to/from airport
Directions: *Opposite Hagley Park - on direct city route form airport.*
Home Page: www.nz.com/heritageinns *or* www.westonhouse.co.nz

---

Christrchurch - City Centre

Bed & Breakfast Lodge
Address: 69 Armagh Street,
Christchurch
Name: Devon Travel Lodge
Telephone: (03) 366 0398
Fax: (03) 366 0398
Email: bernieh@xtra.co.nz
Beds: 9 Queen, 6 Double
(15 Bedrooms)
Bathroom: 4 Ensuites, 2 Guests share.
Tariff: B&B (Full/Continental)
Double $78-$95, Single $55-$66.
Children under 12 years half price. All credit cards accepted.
NZ B&B Vouchers accepted
Nearest Town: Christchurch City Central

The Devon is a small personal lodge offering a warm, friendly atmosphere in homely accommodation in the quiet, historic part of Christchurch near Hagley Park. Very central. On the circle route with a tram stop only 100 yards from our door. Just 5 minutes walk to Cathedral Square, the Casino, Convention Centre, Botanic Gardens, Arts Centre, Town Hall, Public Library and restaurants. Writing room, ironing facilities, TV lounge, tea and coffee making facilities with microwave. Our many repeat guests both national and international are our best testimonial. Off-street parking, microwave and car hire.

Southshore, Christchurch

Homestay
Address: 71A Rockinghorse Road,
Southshore
Name: Jan & Graham Pluck
Telephone: (03) 388 4067
Beds: 1 Queen, 2 Single
(2 Bedrooms)
Bathroom: 1 Ensuite, 1 Family share
Tariff: B&B (full) Double $80,
Single $50, Dinner $25pp.
NZ B&B Vouchers accepted $10 surcharge
Nearest Town: Christchurch centre 20 mins drive

Share with us an environment unique to Christchurch - Southshore.
Only 20 minutes from the city, Southshore is situated between the ocean and the estuary of the Avon River. This seaside enclave offers walkways to enjoy the open water views of the estuary and its varied bird-life, or miles of sandy beach for strolling or swimming.
Our house is situated down a private driveway with access to the beach. A large double room with ensuite and a smaller twin room are available to guests. Both rooms are warm and welcoming and overlook the dunes wilderness. We are in our sixties and together enjoy antiques, gardening and music. Jan is a keen embroiderer and Graham a member of the Vintage Car Club. We are non-smokers, including Jaffa the cat.
Directions: *Please phone for reservations and directions. City and Airport pick up if required.*

Woolston, Christchurch

Homestay
Address: "Treeview",
6 Lomond Place,
Woolston, Christchurch
Name: Kathy & Laurence Carr
Telephone: (03) 384 2352
Beds: 1 Double, 2 Single
(2 bedrooms)
Bathroom: 1 Guests share
Tariff: B&B (continental)
Double $65, Single $45,
Children half price, Dinner $20. NZ B&B Vouchers accepted
Nearest Town: Christchurch 10 minutes

Welcome to "Kathy's Place", 10 mins drive from City. We offer Friendly Kiwi hospitality. Enjoyed many years of hosting. Smoke Free home, no stairs. Guests Carport. Guests delighted at the quiet relaxed atmosphere. Lounge and dining room have Cathedral Ceilings and Log fire for warmth, are away from guest bedrooms. Remarks:- Comfortable beds, generous breakfasts, central position. 10 mins drive to Beaches, Brighton Pier, Tower Bungy, Sumner, Port Hills, Para Gliding, 5 mins walk to buses, Restaurant. Probus Members.
Directions: *From Cathedral Square take Gloucester Street to Roundabout at Linwood Avenue, turn Right, pass Eastgate Mall to traffic lights end of Avenue of trees. Right into Hargood Street, First Left into Clydesdale Street, first Left Lomond Place. Cul-de-sac, no 6 on right. Alternative: Ferry Road Woolston to traffic lights Hargood Street. 4th Street on right is Clydesdale. First Left is Lomond Place. Courtesy Transport from Railway or Coach Depot. Super Shuttle from Airport. Please phone (03) 384 2352.*

Willow Lodge

Richmond, Christchurch City
Homestay, Bed & Breakfast
Address: 'Willow Lodge', 71 River Road, Richmond, Christchurch 1
Name: Grania McKenzie
Telephone: 0064 (03) 389 9395
Email: willow@inet.net.nz
Fax: 0064 (03) 381 5395

Willow Lodge

Beds: 1 King, 1 Queen, 3 Single (2 bedrooms incl. 2 room family suite)
Bathroom: 1 Ensuite, 1 Private
Tariff: B&B (full) Double $95-$120, Single $70, Childrenby arrangement. Credit cards. Longer stays welcome. NZ B&B Vouchers accepted $30 surcharge/double
Nearest Town: 20 mins walk - central city, Lancaster Park, Convention Centre (5 minutes by car)

THE SETTING is wonderful, a feel of country near the heart of the city. We overlook the Avon River, lined with large trees and only 5 minutes drive to the central city. There you will find much to enjoy - Cathedrals, Museum, Art Galleries, Botanical Gardens, Hagley Park, The Arts Centre with its weekend market, good shopping and vibrant cafe scene.

THE HOUSE retains plenty of original 1920's character - leadlight windows and lovely rimu doors and robes.

THE GUEST ROOMS are spacious, King and Queen beds, ensuite or private bathrooms and river and tree views, 1920/30's furniture and china combine with contemporary art and books.

THE BREAKFAST is fresh and generous, organic breads, fresh fruit and cereals, B+E, good teas and coffee.

OUR AIM is to provide fine quality accommodation in a friendly homestyle atmosphere. Use our extensive local knowledge to help make your trip more memorable. We have an elderly Labrador - downstairs and/or outside only. LASTLY! Guest phone, fax, TV's, mountain bikes, off street parking and laundry available.

Directions: *Booking recommended. Shuttle service from Railway/Airport or phone for directions.*

Spreydon, Christchurch

Self-contained Accommodation
Address: 105 Lyttelton Street, Christchurch
Name: Bev & Kerry Bloomfield
Telephone: (03) 332 5360
Fax: (03) 332 5362
Beds: 1 Queen, 2 Single (2 bedrooms)
Bathroom: 1 Private
Tariff: B&B (continental)
Double $75, $10 each extra person.
Children welcome, Campervans welcome.
NZ B&B Vouchers accepted

If you would like peace and quiet in our lovely city our modern two bedroom apartment is ideal. Our apartment adjoining our home has a large lounge and fully self-contained kitchen, washing facilities, phone and TV.
For your privacy and enjoyment you have your own front lawn to sit and relax on. If we can be of any assistance to make your holiday more enjoyable we are only to pleased to help. Children are welcome and there is a cat and highchair available if needed. We are close to the Railway Station, Addington Raceway, Westpac Trust Centre. Walking distance, Shopping Mall and an Indoor Swimming Pool at the Pioneer Stadium, and by car 5 mins from the centre of the city. We provide a comprehensive sytle continental breakfast. This is prepared and placed in your apartment so you can breakfast at your leisure. If you prefer you may do your own catering (discount tariff)

St Martins, Christchurch

Homestay & Self-Contained Accommodation
Address: "KLEYNBOS", 59 Ngaio Street, St Martins,Christchurch
Name: Gerda de Kleyne and Hans van den Bos
Telephone: (03) 332 2896
Fax: (03) 332 2896
Mobile: 025-223 4144
Email: lucien.dol@xtra.co.nz
Beds: 1 Queen, 1 Double, 1 Single (2 bedrooms)
Bathroom: 1 Ensuite, 1 Guest share
Tariff: B&B (continental)
Double $65-$85, Single $40-$60, Studio Room $80 (only $60 when full self catering).
Credit Cards accepted. NZ B&B Vouchers accepted $00-$10 surcharge
Nearest Town: City Centre only 4km, Railway Station 6km, Airport 15km.

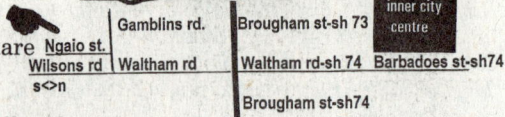

ESPECIALLY FOR YOU, QUALITY ACCOMMODATION WITH A PERSONAL TOUCH. Our love for wooden floors and oil paintings brings atmosphere to life, it facilitates feeling at home. Away from the 'hustle and bustle', close to the city centre, in an easy to find tree-laned street, that's us! As travelling is rather wearing on your body and mind, your room is generous in size and very important has a comfortable bed. The studio room is artistic with full kitchen facilities and TV. Hans and Gerda are in their forties, the children 7 and 10. Gerda works in the mental health field. We have enjoyed the privilege to live in New Zealand for over 10 years and having guests is a little like having family come to stay.
Home Page: http://www.nzhomestay.hn.pl.net/chch/chch1.htm

St Martins, Christchurch City

Self catering Apartment/Homestay

Address: 'Locarno Gardens',
25 Locarno Street, St Martins,   Christchurch 8002
Name: Aileen & David Davies
Telephone: (03) 332 9987
Fax: (03) 332 9687
Mobile: (025) 399 747
Beds: 1 King, 1 Queen, 1 Single (2 bedrooms)
Bathroom: 1 Ensuite, 1 Private
Tariff: Villa B&B (continental) Double $95, Single $75. Self-catering
STUDIO apartment $85 double. Self-catering superior STAND-ALONE 1
bedroom apartment $95 double.
(Breakfast optional extra for self-catering guests.)
NZ B&B Vouchers accepted $25 surcharge.
Nearest Town: 5 minutes drive from Cathedral Square, Christchurch
City Centre

Aileen and David invite you to relax in their fine 70 year old character slate-roofed villa with stained glass windows, surrounded by mature trees and established gardens, full of beautiful birdlife (fantails etc). Located in a quiet, tree-lined street, shops and popular attractions such as the Gondola, Lyttelton Harbour and Jade Stadium are just a short drive away.

A spacious bedroom within the villa offers tea and coffee making facilities and TV.   The STUDIO apartment, with private veranda entrance, has a King bed, plus a single, TV, microwave and fridge. The STAND-ALONE apartment has a separate lounge, Queen bed, bedsettee, TV, microwave, fridge and telephone. (Private brick courtyard, garden chairs.) A friendly smokefree atmosphere allows guests to relax in the delightful garden setting by the fish pond. Lovely river walks and a tennis court are close by. Aileen's knowledge of restaurants is extensive; David enjoys diving and tramping.
Directions: *Locarno Street is opposite St Mark's Anglican church in Opawa Road. Bus stop 3 minutes walk. Taxi from city centre approx $8. Laundry facilities available.*

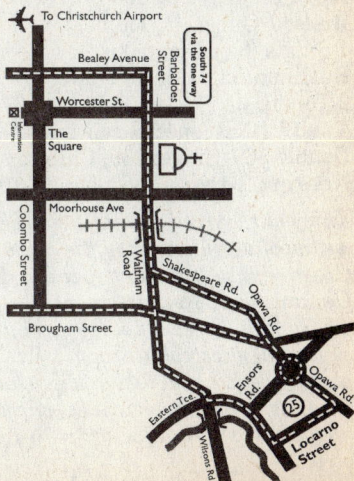

613

Heathcote Valley, Christchurch
Homestay
Address: Bloomfield House,
146 Bridle Path Road,
Heathcote Valley, Christchurch 2
Name: Jean and William Cumming
Telephone: (03) 384 9217 **Fax**: (03) 384 9267
Mobile: (025) 293 6809
Email: cumming_bloomfield@clear.net.nz
Beds: 2 King/Twin, 2 Single (3 bedrooms)
Bathroom: 1 Ensuite, 1 Guests share (spa bath and shower),
2 separate toilets with hand basins.
Tariff: B&B (special) Double $130 (sole use of bathroom $160),
Single $90, Dinner $40 pp, Visa/Bankcard/Mastercard.
Nearest Town: Christchurch (13mins drive)

You may have seen Bloomfield House and Garden on TV or in a Gardening magazine. Bloomfield House is nestled in historic Heathcote Valley, a unique rural corner of the city surrounded by the distinctive Port Hills. Experience peace and tranquillity in beautiful surroundings only 13 minutes easy drive from central Christchurch. Our interesting modern home was architecturally designed and the garden was designed by William. William, an artist and Art School Tutor has exhibited in Australia, USA and Japan, and is represented in major New Zealand public collections. Jean is a musician and experienced choral director having had successful choir tours to Australia, Russia and USA. Our interests include garden design, art collection, travel, cooking, mountain trekking, music, antiques and reading, (and our Westie pup). There are many activities within easy reach, some within walking distance, the Gondola & restaurant, Lytttleton Harbour, Ferrymead Historic Park, horse riding, wind surfing, Port Hills walks and beautiful beaches.

Mt Pleasant, Christchurch
Homestay
Address: 2 Plains View
Name: Peter & Robyn
Telephone: (03) 384 5558
Fax: (03) 384 5558
Mobile: (025) 211 3606
Beds: 1 Queen, 1 Double,
1 Single (3 bedrooms)
Bathroom: 1 Guests share,
2 Toilets
Tariff: B&B (special continental)
Double $69, Single $39, Children negotiable.
Nearest Town: Christchurch 10-15 min drive

Enjoy our warm hospitality in the comfort of our modern home, spacious and sunny with wonderful views of the city and Southern Alps.
Close by is Sumner beach, Ferrymead Historical Park, Mt Cavendish, Gondola and a variety of restaurants.
There are three guest bedrooms, one queen, one double, one single, and a separate guests bathrooms. We are in our 40's with a 9 year old daughter, our travels have taken us throughout New Zealand and we would be happy to share our experiences with you. We provide laundry facilities, complimentary tea and coffee, we are a non smoking household. Please phone for directions.

Redcliffs, Christchurch

Homestay
Address: "Redcliffs on Sea",
125 Main Rd., Redcliffs, Chch 8
Name: Cynthia & Lyndsey Ebert
Telephone: (03) 384 9792
Fax: (03) 384 9703
Beds: 1 Double, 1 Single (1 bedroom).
1 Twin (1 bedroom)
Bathroom: 1 Ensuite, 1 Family share
Tariff: B&B (continental) $50 pp.
Credit Cards accepted,
NZ B&B Vouchers accepted $25 surcharge
Nearest Town: Christchurch 8kms

Relax and enjoy our comfortable home by the sea. Situated approximately 15 minutes from the city centre, our home is "absolute waterfront" on the Christchurch Estuary, with magnificent views of the sea, birds and boating. What more could you wish for? Nearby is the Sumner beach, Christchurch Gondola, and lovely walkways with hills and beaches to explore. We are non-smoking and our guest facilities include a sunny double and single bed bedroom with ensuite, plus a twin bedroom with family share bathroom. Guests are welcome to enjoy the tranquil garden and seaside surroundings. Kayaks are available for exploring the estuary.Local restaurants offer a wide choice of cuisine. A generous continental breakfast is included in the tariff, laundry facilities and off street parking are available. We have no pets or children.
Please phone (03) 384-9792 or fax (03) 384-9703 before calling.

Sumner, Christchurch

Homestay
Address: Panorama Road,
Clifton Hill
Name: Jo & Derek
Telephone: (03) 326 5755
Fax: (03) 326 5701
Email: PANORAMAhomestay@xtra.co.nz
Beds: 1 Double
Bathroom: 1 Private
Tariff: B&B (continental) Double $85,
Single $55, Dinner by arrangement.
Nearest Town: Christchurch 20 mins drive to city centre.

When you stay with us you will be our only guests. Your bedroom and lounge have superb views to the ocean, the estuary, the city and across the plains to the mountains. The three decks and terraced garden make the most of the all day sun, and you can take a quiet country walk on the Port Hills within minutes of the house. We are about 20 minutes drive east of the city centre and three minutes drive from Sumner Village and its popular beach, cafes and restaurants. There are just two of us at home now and our interests centre around the outdoors, gardening, sport and music. We are both well travelled and are always delighted to meet the many interesting people who choose to stay with us, but if you want some private time, there is a comfortable guest lounge with TV and a separate deck for your use.

Sumner, Christchurch

Homestay
Address: 'Villa Alexandra',
Clifton Hill
Name: Wendy & Bob
Telephone: (03) 326 6291
Fax: (03) 326 6096
Beds: 1 Queen, 1 Double, 1 Twin (3 bedrooms)
Bathroom: 1 Ensuite, 2 Private
Tariff: B&B (full) Double/Twin $75, Single $60. Dinner $25.
The Loft Apartment $95 for two adults (queen & single bed,
private facilities and separate entrance).
NZ B&B Vouchers accepted $20 surcharge for Loft Apartment.
Nearest Town: Christchurch 12km.

Enjoy the warmest hospitality in our spacious turn of the century villa overlooking Sumner Bay. Our home retains the graciousness of a by-gone era while offering all the comforts of modern living. In cold weather enjoy the open fires, hot baths and cosiness of our farmhouse-style kitchen where all meals are cooked in the coal-range. On sunny days, relaxing on the verandah or in our enchanting turret is a delight. Spectacular sea views extend from Sumner beach to the Kaikoura mountains. Good food is a speciality, with home grown vegetables and our own free range eggs. Our interests are food, wine, music, gardening, tramping and travel. We have 3 children, all grown some flown; 2 cats and 4 hens. We are 20 minutes from the city centre; 5 minutes from Sumner beach and close to many attractions. Off-street parking; laundry facilities available.
Please phone for directions.

Sumner Beach

Bed & Breakfast Guest House
Address: 'Cave Rock Guest House',
16 Esplanade, Sumner,
Christchurch 8
Name: Gayle & Norm Eade
Telephone: (03) 326 6844/326 5600
Fax: (03) 326 5600
Mobile: (025) 360 212
Email: eade@chch.planet.org.nz
Beds: 2 Double (2 bedrooms)
Bathroom: 2 Ensuite
Tariff: B&B (continental self-serve) Double $75-$95, Credit Cards.
Nearest Town: Christchurch City - 15 minutes

The Cave Rock Guest House is Christchurch's only seafront accommodation, directly opposite Sumner's famous "Cave Rock". Your hosts Gayle and Norm Eade have been in the hospitality industry for 10 years and enjoy meeting people from overseas and within NZ. Our large double rooms have lovely seaviews from every window. Both rooms have ensuites and colour TV, and can sleep up to 4 people. Full kitchen facilities are available. Cooked breakfast available if required. Sumner Village is the ideal location being 5 minutes walking distance to top restaurants and cafe/bars, shops and movie theatre. Scenic hill walks offer magnificent views over the city and mountains to Kaikoura. Christchurch city is only 15 minutes from Sumner and the Gondola only 5 mins away. Buses to the city run every half hour. We have an ancient cat and Dalmatian dog. We look forward to welcoming you to Sumner.

C·R·BULL '93.

Cashmere, Christchurch

Homestay
Address: 3 Lucknow Place, Cashmere 2, Christchurch
Name: 'Burford Manor' Kathleen & David Burford
Telephone: (03) 337 1905
Fax: (03) 337 1916
Email: burfords@xtra.co.nz
Beds: 2 Queen, 2 Single (3 bedrooms)
Bathroom: 1 Ensuite, 2 Private
Tariff: B&B (full) Double $110-$120, Single $90, 10% discount for 2 or more nights (only by direct booking & cash payment). Credit Cards (M/C & Visa).
Nearest Town: Christchurch (5 mins drive)

Our ten year old home is the ultimate in luxury, built in Halswell Quarry Stone, it incorporates the charm of yesteryear plus all the conveniences of a modern home, spacious and warm with private and ensuite bathrooms. Five minutes drive from city centre and conveniently located to excellent public transport. Prize-winning cottage garden. Million dollar views of rural Canterbury and the Southern Alps. Easy flat access and parking. Home-made patchwork quilts abound in each room. Quiet and peaceful. Your hosts David and Kathleen have three adult children and are an informal couple who love meeting people. We have travelled extensively in New Zealand and overseas and are happy to offer assistance with travel plans. Third generation Cantabrians our local knowledge and contacts are an asset to guests particular interests.

Our hobbies include Rotary, travel, tramping, skiing, gardening, stamp collecting, embroidery and patchwork. Breakfast - the choice and time is flexible - try our home-made bread. Guests are welcome to share in all the facilities of our home. No smoking in the house. Tim, our friendly cat also offers a special welcome.

Directions: *Please telephone anytime. The map may be of assistance.*
HomePage: http://nz.com/webnz/bbnz/burford.htm

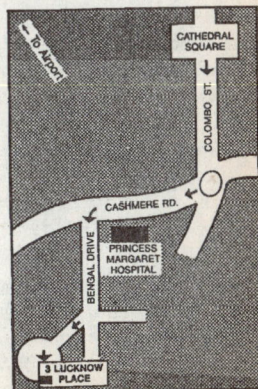

617

Cashmere Heights, Christchurch
Homestay

Address: Cashmere Heights B&B, 6 Allom Lane,
Cashmere Heights, Christchurch 2.
Name: Karen and Barry Newman
Telephone: (03) 332 1778 **Fax**: (03) 332 9399 **Mobile**: (025) 241 0911
Email: rover@iconz.co.nz
Beds: 3 Super King, 6 Single (3 bedrooms)
Bathroom: 1 Guests share
Tariff: B&B (Special/Full/Continental) Double $150-$165, Single $90. Dinner by
arrangement. Not suitable for children. Major credit cards accepted.
Nearest Town: Christchurch City approx 10 minutes

*Cashmere Heights - where a warm friendly welcome awaits you in a home where you
can relax in comfort and quiet elegance. This is our near new home on two levels in
an exclusive suburb of Christchurch. Nestled high on the Port Hills amongst other
high quality homes and 220 metres above sea level, Cashmere Heights captures the
"Million dollar views" with 180 degrees unobstructed panorama from the Pacific
Ocean, across the city and the Canterbury Plains to the playground of the South
Island, the Southern Alps.*

*Our guest accommodation is located on a separate level of our home thereby ensuring
total privacy and relaxation. All bedrooms are large and individually decorated in
bold bright colours to enhance our desire to create and maintain a relaxing holiday
and homely environment. All bedrooms are located to ensure all take advantage of the
views. We have a separate guest lounge which is large and offers tea / coffee facilities,
home theatre entertainment system, reading area, computer station, phone and fax.
Adjoining this lounge is a sun deck with outdoor furniture, barbecue and a spa pool.
A leisurely breakfast may be selected from the wide choices available and may be taken
in the cafe style eatery, or weather permitting, al fresco on the sun deck or on the garden
patio.*

*We are only 400 metres from the Historic "Sign of the Takahe Restaurant" and there
are several other good restaurants close by. Also close by are numerous scenic walking
trails. We are aged in our early forties and have travelled extensively. We enjoy meeting
people and welcoming guests into our home. Our home is a non smoking home, which
we share with our cat. You may also wish to take advantage of our Tour service, Rover
Tours NZ, which specialise in luxury customised tours. These are personally guided
tours for a maximum of four persons anywhere in the South Island.*

Directions: *Please phone.*
Home Page: http://nz-holiday.co.nz/cashmere

Huntsbury Hill, Christchurch
Homestay
Address: Huntsbury House,
16 Huntsbury Avenue,
Huntsbury Hill, Christchurch 2
Name: Anthea & Paul
Telephone: (03) 332 1020
Fax: (03) 337 0666
Mobile: (025) 353 880
Email: huntbnb@voyager.co.nz
Beds: 1 King, 3 Single (2 bedrooms)
Bathroom: 2 Ensuite
Tariff: B&B (full) Double $90-$100, Single $60-$75, Credit Cards(VISA/MC).
Nearest Town: City centre 5 minutes drive

Welcome to our spacious, elegantly restored, 1920's style Port Hills home with magnificent city / mountain views - a great starting point for Banks Peninsula travels and city exploration. City centre, Casino, Jade Stadium, Gondola 5-10 mins drive, airport 20 mins. Walking tracks and excellent restaurants close by. Off-street parking. Bus at gate. Downstairs accommodation offers large rooms with tea / coffee facilities. Delicious breakfasts are served in the dining room with its stunning view or by the pool. Try home-made preserves, yoghurt, muesli, fruit compote, freshly brewed coffee and choice of teas, as well as a cooked selection. Paul's special porridge and herbed eggs are favourites. Relax in the lounge with TV and fire, in the pool, romantic garden or BBQ area. Laundry facilities. We have a wide range of interests and enjoy listening to travellers' tales. We would love to meet you and help plan your stay in our delightful city. **Directions**: *Please phone.* **Home Page**: http://www.voyager.co.nz/~huntbnb

Halswell, Christchurch
Guest House
Address: Halswell Old Vicarage,
335 Halswell Road,
Christchurch 3
Name: Rosemary & Tom
Telephone: (03) 322 6282
Fax: (03) 322 6582
Email: mcconnel@voyager.co.nz
Beds: 2 Queen, 1 Single (3 bedrooms)
Bathroom: 2 Private
Tariff: B&B (continental) Double $90, Single $50.
NZ B&B Vouchers accepted $20 surcharge
Nearest Town: Christchurch 6 Kms

We offer a comfortable home in a rural setting just 10 minutes drive from central Christchurch on Highway 75 to Akaroa. Originally St. Mary's Vicarage the house was built 100 years ago and stands in a garden of almost an acre. We have 2 friendly sheep, a small dog and cat. Guest rooms have new beds, duvets and electric blankets. There is a guest lounge with television. Breakfast is served in the sunny conservatory. There are many places nearby for those interested in walking, gardening, pottery, flowers or vineyards. Across the road is a shopping centre including family restaurant and bar. It is a 5 minute drive to the racecourses at Addington or Riccarton and another few minutes to central Christchurch. Our interests include computers and the Internet, gardening, company and conversation. You will be welcome whether you become part of the household or prefer privacy and independence. Please phone ahead.

Halswell, Christchurch
Homestay+Self-contained Accom.
Address: "Overton",
241 Kennedys Bush Road, Christchurch 3
Name: Judi & Joe
Telephone: (03) 322 8326 **Fax**: (03) 322 8350
Email: brizzell.accom@xtra.co.nz
Beds: 1 Queen, 4 Single (3 bedrooms)
Bathroom: 1 Private, 1 Family share
Tariff: "Garden Lodge": B&B (full) Double $80 ,min of 2 persons Extra person $30,
Children $15. Self-Catering: Double $70, min. of 2 persons, Extra person $20.
Home: B&B (full) Twin or Single $35 per person. Dinner from $20.
Credit cards Visa/MCBankcard Vouchers accepted $12 Surcharge
Nearest Town: Christchurch City, Airport 20 mins.

Best of all worlds ....Only 20 mins from Christchurch Cathedral Square and near the Akaroa Highway, our 1/2 acre landscaped garden on the Port Hills overlooks the rural setting of the Canterbury Plains to the Southern Alps. Tranquil, cosy and convenient! Choose the completely self-contained "Garden Lodge", yours for exclusive use, with one double bedroom and one twin, toilet, shower, TV and cooking facilities, or, share the very comfortable home with a New Zealand family experienced in tourist requirements. Fibre Arts, gardening and walking Cass (our friendly Golden Retriever) are some of Judi's many interests. And she is happy to provide New Zealand cuisine featuring homegrown and local produce. Joe enjoys sharing his love of angling at local rivers and lakes (although admittedly, not always successful!). He is also a keen debater and gardener with an interest in history. Smoking acceptable outdoors. **Directions**: *Please phone anytime.*
Home Page: http://www.canterburypages.co.nz/overton/

Lincoln, Christchurch
Country Homestay
Address: 'Menteith', Springs Road, R.D.6,
Christchurch 8021
Name: Fay & Stephen Graham
Telephone: (03) 325 2395
Fax: (03) 325 2395
Email: menteith@clear.net.nz
Beds: 1 King/Twin, 1 Queen (3 bedrooms)
Bathroom: 1 Ensuite, 1 Private
Tariff: B&B (full)
Ensuite Double $95, Double $85,
Single $60, Children negotiable, Dinner $30,
3 night discount. Credit cards: Visa/Mastercard
Vouchers accepted Surcharge $15,
Nearest Town: Christchurch/Airport, 15 mins

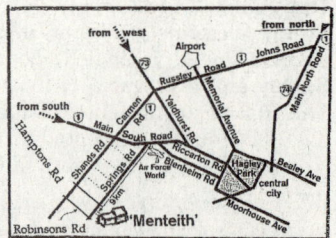

'Menteith', a 10 acre farmlet is nestled among mature trees with spectacular mountain views and country tranquillity. After a busy day sightseeing relax in the warm indoor spa / swimming pool conservatory. Your spacious guest bedrooms offer tea / coffee making facilities and cookies, electric blankets, heating, clock radios, hair dryers and cosy firm beds with duvets. Laundry available. We share our non-smoking home with our 2 cats, offering warm hospitality and home grown produce. Breakfast - the choice and time is flexible. Delightful reasonably priced restaurants nearby. Lincoln golf course and University 3km. Our retirement interests are Rotary, skiing, golf, tramping, genealogy and travel. Fay is a keen spinner - you're welcome to try your hand! **Directions**: *9kms along Springs Road from SH1 at Wigram / Hornby.***Home Page**: http://nz.com/webnz/bbnz/menteith.htm

620

Tai Tapu, Christchurch
Farmstay+Self-contained   Accom.
Address: "Ballymoney", Wardstay Road,
R D 2,   Christchurch
Name: Merrilies & Peter Rebbeck
Telephone: (03) 329 6706
Fax: (03) 329 6709
Mobile: (021) 468 378
Email: rebbeckpandm@hotmail.com
Beds: 1 Twin/King, 2 Double, 1 Single (3 Bedrooms)
Bathroom: 1 Ensuite, 1 Guest share or Private.
Tariff: B&B (special) Double $90/$130, Single $90, Children under 12 half price if
sharing with parents, Dinner $25, Campervans welcome. Credit cards. NZ B&B
Vouchers accepted $40 surcharge
Nearest Town: Christchurch 20 km, Lincoln and Tai Tapu 5 km

*"Ballymoney" is situated on a quiet road. The character farmhouse, surrounded by a two acre
rambling garden. Guest accommodation includes a self-contained flat with a double and
single bed and ensuite bathroom overlooking the spa and separated from the house by a
courtyard. In the house is a large twin / king room opening onto a private veranda. Also a small
room with a double bed. All rooms have heating, tea and coffee making facilities, hairdryers,
TV and lots of extras. Relax in spacious surroundings, enjoy Irish-Kiwi hospitality and
gourmet meals including our home-grown vegetables, fruit, meat, and free range eggs.Masses
of animals include horses, a donkey, cattle, sheep, pigs, hens and friendly dogs and cats. The
large pond hosts many ducks, geese, guinea fowl, peacocks, pheasants etc. Play croquet, boules
or ride the bicycles. Twenty four hour full farmstay includes three meals, a farm tour feeding
the animals and horse riding. **Directions**: Please phone.*

Lyttelton, Christchurch
Homestay+Self-contained   Accom.
Address: Randolph House, 49 Sumner Road,
Lyttelton, Christchurch
Name: Judy & Jonathan Elworthy
Telephone: (03) 328 8877 **Fax**: (03) 328 8779
Mobile: (025) 356 309
Email: randolph@netaccess.co.nz
Beds: 2 Double, 2 Single (3 bedrooms)
Bathroom: 1 Ensuite, 1 Guests share
Tariff: B&B (full) Double $100-$120,
Single $80-$100, Credit cards, Vouchers accepted $30 surcharge
Nearest Town: Christchurch 10km

*Enjoy a village atmosphere with great little restaurants, late night music at the Wunderbar
and yet be within fifteen minutes from the centre of Christchurch! Lyttelton is a fun place to
be. Our Victorian villa overlooks the harbour. In summer we enjoy a glass of wine outdoors
as the sun sets in the west. Spectacular! We enjoy meeting interesting people and have very
happy memories of our many guests. Jonathan is a former member of Parliament, who is
actively involved in community organisations, and enjoys lively conversation. I am an Interior
Designer and Real Estate Consultant, and enjoy choral singing and playing the viola. We have
travelled extensively, have three married children, including a German daughter-in-law and
several grandchildren. Dougal a labrador lives here. Accommodation: Studio: En suite, twin
beds, feather duvets, kitchenette, private balcony, breakfast served in studio, or in the dining
room. Garaging for car. House: Historic, comfortable, double attic bedrooms with guest
bathroom downstairs. Commode and bathrobes.*
Home Page: http://nz.com/webnz/bbnz/ randolph.htm

Christchurch - Lyttelton
Guest House (B&B)
Address: Shonagh O'Hagan's Guest House,
Dalcroy House,
16 Godley Quay, Lyttelton
Name: Shonagh O'Hagan
Telephone: (03) 328 8577
Mobile: (025) 346 351 between 9.30am & 4.40pm
Beds: 1 King (or 2 Single), 2 Queen, 1 Single (3 bedrooms)
Bathroom: 1 Guests share, 2 shared with hosts. Robes provided
Tariff: B&B Double $100, Single $75, Breakfast caters to all tastes,
Dinner by arrangement (additional charge), Children welcome.
Nearest Town: Christchurch 9 kms, 15 mins, Akaroa 80kms, 1 1/4 hours

PARKING AND ACCESS: Good on street parking and access
DALCROY HOUSE: Established 1859 has served as a:
- Private residence
- Boarding and Day School for boys
- Boarding and Guest House
- Rental Property for Sea Captains
- Hostel for female naval ratings
SHONAGH O'HAGAN Your hostess is a cook, Nurse, Educator, Health
Manager and mother with a keen interest in old houses. Have a good
night's sleep in pleasant historic surroundings with a clear view of
Lyttelton Harbour and the port hills, only five minutes' walk from the
centre of Lyttelton. Shonagh and her young son will ensure your stay is
comfortable and memorable.

Cass Bay-Lyttelton (Christchurch)
Homestay & Self-contained Townhouse
Address: 'Harbour View Homestay',
3 Harbour View Tce., Cass Bay, Lyttelton
Name: Susi & Hank Boots
Telephone: (03) 328 7250 **Fax**: (03) 328 7251
Mobile: (025) 226 2633
Email: harbourview.homestay@clear.net.nz
Beds: 1 King, 1 Queen, 3 Single (3 bedrooms)
Bathroom: 1 Guests share, 1 Family share
Tariff: B&B (full) Double $90-$100, Single $60, 10%
discount from 3 nights, 15% from 1 week
(discounts only with direct booking). Self-contained facilities $100-$120 double, $25 for
each further person/bed. Discount applies as above. Credit cards (Visa/Mastercard)
welcome. NZ B&B Vouchers accepted $30 surcharge
Nearest Town: Christchurch Centre 12km, Lyttelton 3km

Cass Bay, nestled in the Porthills, is only a short drive away from Christchurch and offers easy
access to all city amenities. The beautiful and tranquil area around the harbour has walking
tracks, nature reserves, several swimming beaches, a golf course, horse track facilities and the
harbour provides for sailing and steam-boat trips. Our home is an ideal base for day-trips to
Akaroa and other tourist attractions. It incorporates warmth and luxury with comfort, has
a relaxed atmosphere, an open fireplace, a lovely garden setting with a solar-heated swimming
pool and breathtaking views. Separate lounge area also available. Our beds are very
comfortable and extra long. The fully tiled bathrooms have a massage-shower which
everybody loves. Gymnasium free to use. Sauna available at small cost. For guests' comfort
no smoking indoors please. Wir sprechen Deutsch und Schweizerdeutsch. Nous parlons
Français en spreken Nederlands.

Governor's Bay, Christchurch

Homestay
Address: 'Orchard House',
Governor's Bay
Name: Neil & Judy
Telephone: (03) 329 9622
Beds: 1 Double (1 bedroom)
Bathroom: 1 Ensuite
Tariff: B&B (continental)
Double $85, Single $60.
NZ B&B Vouchers accepted $15 surcharge
Nearest Town: Christchurch 13km, Lyttelton 8km

Governor's Bay is one of the many scenic bays surrounding Lyttelton Harbour, and is only a short drive over the Port Hills from Christchurch. Our hillside home is situated to take full advantage of the spectacular views over the bay. The area is noted for its beautiful gardens and walking tracks, and is ideally situated for exploring Banks Peninsula. A wide range of cuisine is offered by local restaurants.
Our separate guest wing has a large sunny bedroom with ensuite and French doors which open to a private balcony. The room has a TV and tea/coffee making facilities. We have two daughters, one still living at home, and Suzy the cat. We are a non-smoking home. We look forward to meeting you.
Directions: *Please phone.*

Banks Peninsula - Governor's Bay

Homestay
Address: The Anchorage,
Governor's Bay.
Name: Kim and Mark Soltero
Telephone: (03) 329 9051
Beds: 1 Queen (1 Bedroom)
Bathroom: 1 Private
Tariff: B&B (Continental)
Double $90, Single $60,
Dinner $25 pp by prior arrangement.
Nearest Town: Christchurch 13 km, Lyttelton 8 km.

Nestled in Governor's Bay, The Anchorage looks East, out to the headlands and Lyttelton Harbour. The upper deck is private and warm, offering 180 degree views of the bay. Upstairs guests enjoy a large private non smoking room with modern facilities, including a jacuzzi bath. Table-tennis is also available on the front patio. Kim and Mark, with their son (3) Raphael, warmly welcome you. We are both practising artists with a passion for culture and entertaining. Governor's Bay is a delightful retreat 15 to 20 minutes drive over the hill from Christchurch. Many native birds, such as bellbirds, fantails and wood pigeons share our garden. Within walking distance from our home is a modern cafe/wine bar, or you are welcome to dine with us. Several bush and shore walks, and further afield, the many lovely features of Banks Peninsula.
Directions: *Please phone for directions.*

Teddington, Lyttelton Harbour

Farmstay

Address: Bergli Hill Farmstay,
RD 1, Lyttelton
Name: Rowena and Max Dorfliger
Telephone: (03) 329 9118
Fax: (03) 329 9118
Mobile: (025) 829 410
Email: bergli@ihug.co.nz
Beds: 2 Queen, 4 Single (2 bedrooms).
Self Contained Unit: 1 Queen, 3 Singles
Bathroom: 1 Family Share,
Self Contained Unit: 1 Ensuite
Tariff: B&B (full) Twin/Double $70, Single $45, Triple $35, Dinner $25, Children half price. Self Contained Unit: $75 per night. Vouchers accepted. Credit cards accepted.
Nearest Town: Lyttelton (20 minutes), Christchurch (35 minutes)

Lyttelton harbour and the Port Hills create a dynamic panorama, superb for sunsets and stargazing. Our 100 acre farm on the sunny slopes of Mt Herbert is near a comprehensive net of walking tracks, boating, swimming and golf course. Our smoke-free home has two guest rooms with a double and two single beds in each, and we have a pet cat. We are both self-employed (woodworker and shadow puppeteer) and able to take time out for a day sail on our yacht or a guided Peninsula tour. We have a wealth of stories from experiences of living 27 years in Japan (Rowena speaks fluent Japanese) and around the world sailing and mountain climbing by Max who is a German speaking Swiss. Whether relaxing on the veranda at Max's hand-crafted table or sipping wine in the spa bath, we are sure you will take away good memories of your visit. **Home Page**: http://homepages.ihug.co.nz/~mr_chops/bergli*

Church Bay, Diamond Harbour

Bed and Breakfast

Address: Kai-o-ruru Bed & Breakfast,
32 James Drive, Church Bay,
Lyttelton RD1.
Name: Robin and Philip Manger
Telephone: 03 329 4788
Fax: 03 329 4788
Email: manger@xtra.co.nz
Beds: 2 Single (1 bedroom)
Bathroom: 1 Ensuite
Tariff: B&B (special)
Double $80, Single $50, Dinner $25.
Nearest Town: Christchurch approximately 40 minutes

Church Bay is the ideal base for those wishing to explore Banks Peninsula.
In our separate, ensuite unit, you will wake up to bellbirds and a view across the harbour to Quail Island. The room is cosy, has electric blankets, TV, books, games and a tea / coffee tray with home-made biscuits. Our timber house commands marvellous views; our coastal garden is there for you to explore or sit in, or if you're energetic, a scramble down the bank will take you to a fascinating volcanic shore. We are a non-smoking household and have an unobtrusive cat. Philip and I are travelled, retired teachers with wide interests who enjoy meeting people and making them welcome to our wonderful area. languages: German, Dutch (some Spanish and Italian).
Directions: *Will meet ferry. Call us.*

Church Bay, Diamond Harbour

Homestay
Address: Island View Homestay,
11 Emerson Crescent, Church Bay,
Diamond Harbour, Lyttelton RD 1
Name: Alex & Sally Alexander
Telephone/Fax: (03) 329 4272
Freephone 0800 367 321
Beds: 1 SuperKing/Twin, 1 Single
(2 Room Suite).
ONE PARTY BOOKINGS
Bathroom: 1 Private
Tariff: B&B Full (special) Double $100, 3 guests $145.
Quality Menu Dinners (essential to book by 10 am) $35 pp.
Also gourmet suppers $20 pp.
Credit cards: Visa/MC, Vouchers accepted $25 surcharge double
Nearest Town: Christchurch 40 minutes. Lyttelton 20 minutes.

Until recently, we hosted at "MERLINS" Hanmer Springs, and our FINE CUISINE was acknowledged internationally. Now at ISLAND VIEW, we continue our tradition of CARE, COMFORT, LOVELY FOOD and WONDERFUL SCENERY. The heated Guest Suite has armchairs, TV, tea/coffee, electric blankets, books. Our spacious sitting/dining room has BEAUTIFUL everchanging HARBOUR VIEWS, which you can enjoy with your MEMORABLE MENU BREAKFAST. (Choice of 7 hot dishes). If you choose to have our delicious 3 course DINNER (You May bring Your own Wine)we can offer N.Z's Best: Fillet Steak, Lamb Racks, Fresh Salmon, Seafood, Duckling etc. The harbour offers Cruises, Golf, Lovely Walks, Places to dine. Tranquillity, yet Christchurch a 40 minute scenic drive. Airport 45 minutes. Akaroa 55 minutes. Easy Access and Parking. We're non-smoking, so is KIS, our Abbysinian cat! Easy Directions when you book.

Church Bay, Diamond Harbour (Lyttelton Harbour)

Homestay
Address: 'Otamahua', Athol Place,
Church Bay, R.D. 1, Lyttelton
Name: Alison Gibbs
Telephone: (03) 329 4728
Mobile: (025) 288 8294
Email: a.gibbs@ext.canterbury.ac.nz
Beds: 1 Queen, 2 Single (2 bedrooms)
Bathroom: 2 Ensuite
Tariff: B&B (full) Double $90, Single $50,
Dinner $25, Credit cards (VISA/MC). NZ B&B Vouchers accepted $15 Surcharge
Nearest Town: Christchurch approx 40 minutes

Relax in the peace and quiet of "Otamahua" and enjoy the magnificent views of Lyttelton Harbour and the surrounding hills from all rooms. Local activities include walks, golf, boating, horse trekking and tennis, or explore Banks Peninsula, a fascinating and lovely part of Canterbury. The two attractive, downstairs guest bedrooms offer complete privacy. There are heaters, electric blankets, TV, tea making facilities, and books in both rooms. The house is comfortable and relaxed whether you wish to doze in the sun on the balcony, or by the fire in winter. Breakfast includes fresh juice, fruit, cereal, a cooked dish, and home made bread. Dinner by arrangement. No smoking inside, please. I have travelled extensively and my interests include people, food, walking, gardening, local history and NZ literature - and my cat, Tigger. **Directions**: *Phone for directions – or to be collected.*
Home Page: http://nz.com/webnz/bbnz/otamahua.htm

Barrys Bay, Akaroa

Homestay/Farmstay
Address: Rosslyn Estate, Barrys Bay, Akaroa
(formerly Oihitu Estate)
Name: Ross and Lynette Curry
Telephone: (03) 304 5804
Fax: (03) 304 5804
Email: Rosslyn@xtra.co.nz
Beds: 2 Queen (2 bedrooms)
Bathroom: 2 Ensuite
Tariff: B&B (Special) Double $100, Single $70, Dinner $25,
Children negotiable. Credit cards (Visa/MC). Laundry no charge.
NZ B&B Vouchers accepted $30 surcharge
Nearest Town: Akaroa 12 km, Christchurch 70km

We are fortunate to live in one of the larger historic homes in the county, built in the 1860's, set amid the rolling hills of Banks Peninsula with views of the Akaroa Harbour.

Our 150 cow dairy farm still has many native bush lined streams abundant with bird life. Besides twice aday milking we also run 80 red deer and 130 fattening pigs, and a few much loved pets most of whom live outside.

Our children Kirsten (7) and Mathew (5) are fourth generation to this home and lifestyle which we enjoy sharing with others.

We have converted two of the larger rooms to accommodate you in comfort. Each room has ensuite bathroom, firm queen sized bed, central heating and antiques of the period.

A selection of teas and freshly ground coffee together with home baking are offered upon your arrival and are always available by request.

It is a pleasure for us to share our evening meal, served in the farm style kitchen at the family table. The traditional Kiwi roast with home grown vegetables being one of our favourites.

For breakfast enjoy smoke cured bacon, eggs fresh from our own hens and toast cooked on the embers of the wood burning stove, topped with a selection of home made jams. Also fruit from our own orchard, together with fresh treats still warm from baking.

We have both travelled and try to offer our guests facilities such as the use of our laundry, spacious bedrooms and the privacy that we value as travellers. We enjoy meeting people whether it be relaxing in front of the open fire, on the large verandah or strolling though the informal gardens.

Directions: *Our front entrance is conveniently situated on the Akaroa Highway (SH75) with our sign "Rosslyn Estate" behind a white picket fence on the harbours edge (on the left travelling to Akaroa). The homestead is set well off the road.*

Lavaud House

Akaroa

Homestay B&B
Address: 'Lavaud House', 83 Rue Lavaud, Akaroa
Name: Francis & Frances Gallagher
Telephone: (03) 304 7121
Fax: (03) 304 7121
Beds: 2 Queen, 1 King, 1 Twin (4 bedrooms)
Bathroom: 2 Ensuite, 1 Guests share
Tariff: B&B (continental) Double $80-$100, Single $60.
  Credit cards (Visa/MC). NZ B&B Vouchers accepted $20-$30 surcharge
Nearest Town: Christchurch 80 kms

Our historic French designed 2 storied home overlooks the main beach and harbour and is within 2 mins walk of restaurants, galleries and shops.
All rooms have fresh flowers, heaters and harbour or rural views plus television and electric blankets.
The ensuite bedroom upstairs has a king sized bed and harbour views.
The ensuite room downstairs has a queen sized bed and a woodland view with a glimpse of the harbour. Both twin and queen rooms upstairs have rural views.
The sunny guest sitting room has books, television, piano, and superb harbour outlook.
Enjoy our lovely antique furniture. Full continental breakfast is served in the dining room around our old dining table.
Tea and coffee are available.
Spend time in our large and colourful garden, enjoy the birds and harbour views.
Retired farmers, well travelled, we enjoy meeting people.
You will love this area as much as we do. Plan to stay awhile.
Directions: *Centrally situated in the main street, opposite the war memorial.*

Akaroa
Farmstay
Address: Paua Bay
Postal: c/- 113 Beach Road, Akaroa
Name: Murray & Sue Johns
Telephone: (03) 304 8511
Fax: (03) 304 8511
Email: paua_bay@hotmail.com
Beds: 1 Double,
1 Twin (2 bedrooms)
Bathroom: Guests share
Tariff: B&B (full)
Double $80, Single $50, Dinner $25.
NZ B&B Vouchers accepted Accepted all year round,
same day restrictions Nov to March.
Nearest Town: Akaroa 15 kms

We are a family of four, William and Kate attend boarding school. We have a sheep, cattle and deer farm of 900 acres at Paua Bay, surrounded by coast-line with valleys of native bush and streams. Those interested in taking a stroll can enjoy the unique scenery including seal and penguin colonies which are a 30 minute walk from the house. You would be most welcome to participate in any farm activity that occurs during your stay. Qualified riding instruction available. Our cosy colonial home is nestled against native bush surrounded by a large cottage garden including a swimming pool and spectacular views over the Pacific. The farm is a twenty minute drive from picturesque Akaroa, a French-style harbour village. We love meeting people and making new friends.
Directions: *Please phone. Evening if possible.*

Takamatua, Akaroa
Bed & Breakfast
Address: "The Barn", Akaroa Main Road
(Highway 75), Takamatua (Akaroa)
Name: Jeanine De Kraker
Telephone: (03) 304 7277
Fax: (03) 304 7277 **Mobile**: (025) 227 7775
Beds: 1 King, 2 Queen,
1 Single, 1 Twin (5 bedrooms)
Bathroom: 1 Ensuite, 1 Guests share
Tariff: B&B (full) Double Ensuite $125,
Double $95, Single $65, Twin $95,
Dinner on request, 10% discount from 3 nights, Children welcome.
Nearest Town: Akaroa 3km

The "Barn" is a rustic home surrounded by 3 acres of beautiful gardens, an orchard, tennis court and stream boundary offering peace and tranquillity. We are less than five minutes away from Takamatua's peaceful bay which is a good fishing spot with many opportunities to launch a boat. Akaroa is close by; thus, if you want to visit a beautiful and historical township, it offers art galleries, interesting shops, licensed restaurants, the pier, a swimming beach, sailing trips, swimming with the dolphins or just watching them. It's a trampers paradise with several tracks to choose from. Jeanine is a bubbly and outgoing personality, speaks five languages, worked and travelled internationally as a general nurse and enjoys caring for people. She loves tennis, skiing and surfing. Weather permitting, breakfast will be served in the lovely garden setting. A warm welcome, peace and tranquillity await you.

Okains Bay, Akaroa

Farmstay
Address: 'Kawatea', Okains Bay, Banks Peninsula
Name: Judy & Kerry Thacker
Telephone: (03) 304 8621
Fax: (03) 304 8621
Beds: 2 Queen, 1 Double, 2 Single (3 bedrooms)
Bathroom: 1 Ensuite, 1 Guest Bathroom
Tariff: B&B (full) Double $100, Single $60,
Children negotiable. Dinner $25. VISA & M/C accepted.
NZ B&B Vouchers accepted $30 Surcharge
Nearest Town: Akaroa 20km.

Do you enjoy fine dining and stimulating conversation? Do you want to revel in the peace of country life, but still be close to sights and activities? Then escape to 'Kawatea', an historic Edwardian homestead set in spacious gardens, that has been in our family for four generations. Built in 1900 from native timbers 'Kawatea' has been carefully renovated to add light and space without losing its old world charm. Elegantly decorated, the house features original stained glass windows, handcrafted furniture, and NZ artwork. Linger over breakfast of your choice in the sunny conservatory with speciality teas and freshly ground plunger and expresso coffee. Join us for summer barbecues on the expansive verandah, savouring seafood from the Bay, and fresh produce from our garden and farm. Participate in farm activities such as moving stock, feeding our pet sheep, lambing, calving or shearing. Wander our hillside farm, climbing to enjoy a breathtaking panoramic view of Banks Peninsula. Relax or swim at Okains Bay, observe the birdlife on the estuary, or walk along the scenic coastline to secluded beaches and a seal colony. Learn about Maori culture and the life of early NZ settlers at the acclaimed Okains Bay Museum. Explore the township of Akaroa, with its strong French influence. Visit art galleries and craft shops; play golf or go horse riding, sample local wines and watch traditional cheeses being made. Take a harbour cruise, even swim with the rare and fascinating Hector's dolphin.

We have been providing farmstays since 1988, and we pride ourselves on thoughtful personal service. We enjoy getting to know our guests and love to learn from their experiences, while sharing our own, whether its farming, travel, world events, or life in NZ. We hope you will come as a visitor and leave as a friend.

Directions: *Take Highway 75 from Christchurch. Follow the signposts to top of Okains Bay. We are 6km down hill on the right hand side.*

Akaroa
Bed & Breakfast
Address: 113 Rue Jolie, Akaroa, Banks Peninsula
Name: "La Belle Villa"
Telephone: (03) 304 7084
Fax: (03) 304 7084
Beds: 1 King, 2 Queen, 1 Twin (4 bedrooms)
Bathroom: 1 Ensuite, 2 Private, 1 Guest share
Tariff: B&B (special) Double $85/$100, Single $60.
Nearest Town: Christchurch approx. 80km

A warm welcome awaits you. Relax in the comfort of a bygone era, and appreciate the antiques in our picturesque historic villa. Built in the 1870's for a prominent business man it became one of the 1st doctor's surgeries in Akaroa and is now established on approx. 1/2 acre of beautiful, mature grounds, surrounded by rolling hills and lush scenery. Enjoy the indoor/outdoor living, large private swimming pool and gently trickling stream. We offer warm, spacious bedrooms, large guest lounge, fabulous fires in winter, breakfast 'Al Fresco' in the summer if you choose with the birds and trees. We offer to make your stay with us special. It will be a pleasure to book you on to any cruises, fishing trips, swim with the dolphins, horse treks etc that you may require. Being centrally situated, restaurants, cafes, and wine bars are all walking distance. So too, you will find, are the majority of galleries, shops and excursions available in New Zealand's most charming, quaint and quintessential French township.

Takamatua, Akaroa
Farmstay
Address: Takamatua Valley Road. Postal: PO Box 4, Akaroa
Name: Hanne & Paul Lelievre
Telephone: (03) 304 7255 (before 8.30 am or after 6 pm)
Fax: (03) 304 7255
Email: Double.L@Xtra.co.nz
Beds: 1 Double, 1 Single (1 bedroom)
Bathroom: 1 Ensuite
Tariff: B&B (full) Double $80, Single $45, Children negotiable.
Dinner optional $20 pp. Campervans welcome.
NZ B&B Vouchers accepted plus $15 surcharge
Nearest Town: Akaroa 5km

Your hosts farm approximately 800 acres, running sheep, cattleand deer. Our home possesses a native bush outlook, and is situated some 1.5km up the picturesque Takamatua Valley, and only 5km from the lovely French village of Akaroa. From here you are only 20 minutes drive from most of the spectacular beaches, bays and walks of Banks Peninsula.
We have a number of pets, and would recommed personalised horse riding instruction, or a trip on our "Seal Colony Safari", as optional extras.
Hanne is of Danish origin and speaks that language fluently, whilst we have both worked and lived in Australia for more than 10 years.
We offer spacious, yet cosy accommodation, in a sheltered position, and invite you to enjoy some good old fashioned country hospitality.

Akaroa Harbour
Farmstay
Address: 'Bossu', Wainui,
Akaroa R.D.2, Banks Peninsula
Name: Rana & Garry Simes
Telephone: (03) 304 8421
Fax: (03) 304 8421
Email: bossu@pop. 3.xtra.co.nz
Beds: 1 Queen, 3 Single (3 bedrooms)
Bathroom: 1 Private, 1 Guests share
Tariff: B&B (full) Double $80, Single $50, Dinner $25
Nearest Town: Akaroa 20 km

"Bossu" farm is situated on the edge of Akaroa Harbour with magnificent panoramic views to the picturesque French village of Akaroa. We are in our 50's with three adult children. We live in a modern sunny homestead and farm 100 acres of forestry, sheep, a small vineyard and cattle. It is situated on 2km of coastline nestled amongst bush, planted trees and shrubs in a garden including a well used grass tennis court. We have a power boat and can offer fishing and the viewing of hector dolphins, penguins and nesting sea birds. Enjoy our fresh fish and homegrown lamb vegetables with a selection of pre-dinner drinks and wine. Breakfast includes homegrown bacon and marmalade. Rana and Garry have travelled extensively and interests include bridge, spinning, golf and tramping. We look forward to your visit and offer you a very warm welcome.
Directions: *"Bossu" accommodation sign is on State Highway 75 at the commencement of Barrys Bay. Follow coastal road to Wainui 8km. Farm is located through Wainui first property on seaward side.*

Akaroa
Boutique B&B
Address: Mill Cottage,
Rue Grehan, Akaroa
Name: Joan & John Galt
Telephone: (03) 304 8007
Fax: (03) 304-8007
Beds: 1 Double,
2 Single (3 bedrooms)
Bathroom: 1 Private
Tariff: B&B (continental)
Double $120, Each extra person $40,
Single $100. Credit Cards (VISA/MC)
Nearest Town: Christchurch 80km

Enjoy the unique experience of staying in a fully restored, listed historic pioneer cottage, in a tranquil rural setting. Wake to the dawn chorus, the sound of the nearby stream, and a generous breakfast hamper on your doorstep. Wander around the secluded two acre garden, relax on the wide verandah, or explore the attractions of the picturesque township of Akaroa, with its enchanting streets and waterfront cafes. In restoring the cottage, care has been taken to retain as much as possible of its original form and character, while providing all essential amenities for guest comfort. The privacy of the cottage, and its historical charm, provide an ideal atmosphere for tho se seeking a romantic setting for a special holiday break. The cottage is exclusively yours during your stay. **Directions**: *800 metres up Rue Grehan. (We ask our guests to refrain from smoking)* **Home Page**: http://nz-holiday.co.nz/akaroa

Akaroa - Banks Peninsula
B&B and self-contained cottage
Address: Bells Road,
Takamatua, R.D. 1, Akaroa
Name: David & Sue Thurston
Telephone: (03) 304 7499
Fax: (03) 304 7499
Email: takamatua@xtra.co.nz
Beds: 3 Queen (2 bedrooms).
1 Semi detached barn loft room.
Bathroom: 1 Private, 2 Ensuite
Tariff: B&B (continental) Double $130-$150, Single $100,
Children welcome. Credit Cards (Visa/Mastercard)
Nearest Town: Akaroa 4km

This is New Zealand at its best. A picturesque and easy 1 1/2 hour drive from Christchurch brings you to this spacious colonial home set amongst century old walnut trees, bounded by creeks and bush teeming with birdlife. Enjoy the tranquil garden with its roses, croquet lawn and swimming pool or the seaside resort of Akaroa is 5 mins away. Guest rooms are situated in a separate wing with rooms opening onto the verandah and are centrally heated by radiators from a wood-burning range, complemented by two open fires. David is a nationally recognised furniture maker and the house features many fine examples of his work and his studio is open for viewing. The family have many farm animals including tame eels, pet rabbits, sheep and ponies. Sumptuous breakfast includes fresh fruit from the orchard, farm eggs, croissants, home-made preserves and freshly ground coffee. A 3 bedroom self contained cottage in its private garden is an ideal retreat. **Home Page**: http://www.welcome.co.nz/takamatua/

Akaroa

Homestay B&B and self contained Cottage
Address: "Blythcliffe", 37 Rue Balguerie, Akaroa 8161
Name: Rosealie & Jan Shuttleworth
Telephone: (03) 304 7003
Freephone: 0800 393 877
Fax: (03) 304 7003
Email: blythcliffe@xtra.co.nz
Beds: 2 Queen, (2 bedrooms).
Self cotained cottage 1 Queen (1 bedroom)
Bathroom: 1 Ensuite, 1 Private. Self contained cottage 1 Private.
Tariff: B&B (continental) Double $125, Single $100. Self contained cottage $150.
Hamper breakfast extra. Multiple night rates available.
Unsuitable for children. Credit Cards (Visa/MC)
Nearest Town: Central Akaroa

Saunter 200 metres from the town centre to Blythcliffe our historic home (circa 1857) set against a hillside of native bush with a chattering stream dividing the bush from the semi formal garden, croquet lawn and petanque terrain. Jan, Rose and Garfield the moggy, (the three grown up kids have transplanted themselves to other places), warmly welcome our guests to share the history of this unique piece of NZ family heritage. Upstairs we have two double bedrooms each with its own bathroom as well as a modern self contained, intimate cottage for two at the bottom of the garden. Play billiards on our full sized table, tinkle the ivories in the parlour. Breakfast is served in our cosy country kitchen or al fresco during the summer. Jan supplements the family income with his woodturning. Smoke free zone in the house.
Directions: *200 metres up Rue Balguerie on the left. Please phone.*
Home Page: http://www.nz-holiday.co.nz/blythcliffe

Akaroa

Bed & Breakfast
Address: Maison de la Mer,
1 Rue Benoit, Akaroa
Name: Jill and Barry Walker
Telephone: (03) 304 8907
Fax: (03) 304 8907
Mobile: (025) 373 940
Email: maisondelamer@xtra.co.nz
Beds: 3 Queen (3 Bedrooms)
Bathroom: 3 Ensuite
Tariff: B&B (Special) Double $100-$130. Credit cards Visa/Mastercard.
Nearest Town: Akaroa 1 min. Christchurch 80km

Built in 1910 for a local merchant, Maison de la Mer is a two-storey villa sited directly opposite the beach and one minute from the Information Centre. Guests can easily walk to the village shops, restaurants, and cafes. Two of the rooms have gorgeous harbour views, one with a double spa bath and dressing room and another with a private sitting room. All the rooms are elegantly furnished and have television and tea and coffee facilities. A spacious lounge with an open fire and panoramic sea views is also available for guest use. A full breakfast is served in the dining room or on the lawn during summer if desired. It is our aim to provide a warm welcome and excellent hospitality, and we can assure you of a very enjoyable stay. Note that we share our home with our cocker spaniel, Bessie.
Home Page: www.welcome.co.nz/maisondelamer

Akaroa Harbour

Country Retreat + Llama Farm
Address: "Kahikatea", Wainui, RD 2, Akaroa, Banks Peninsula
Name: Jane & Joe Yates
Telephone: (03) 304 7400 **Fax**: (03) 304 7430 **Email**: landsendllamas@xtra.co.nz
Beds: 3 King/Queen, 1 Double (3 Bedrooms)
Bathroom: 2 Private
Tariff: B&B (Special) Single party bookings only. Homestead Double $155, Single $130, Dinner $40pp. Cottage: Double $245, Extra person $35 each. (Special rates available for cottage). Not suitable for children under 12. Credit Cards (VISA/MC). Deposit required.
Nearest Town: Akaroa - 22km along spectacular harbour drive

High on the slopes of Banks Peninsula overlooking Wainui Valley and the impossibly blue Akaroa Harbour lies "Kahikatea", our beautiful colonial homestead and the home of Lands End Llamas. Featured in both US (Sept '92) and NZ (June '98) editions of House and Garden Magazine, our historic 1860's home has been faithfully renovated with French doors leading to large verandas, English flower gardens, and dazzling views. The house has been meticulously designed with cathedral ceilings, native Rimu wood furniture and staircases, English and American antiques, and art collected from world-wide travels. Central heating has been installed for year-round comfort. The luxurious two story accommodation in the homestead has a beautifully furnished living room with library and a second floor queen bedroom with a sunny balcony overlooking the llama paddocks and sea. Delicious cooked breakfasts are served on the veranda or dining room and, by prior arrangement, three-course dinners with hors d'oeuvres and NZ wines can be enjoyed, "Te Rangi", our recently built cottage, offers deluxe accommodation and total privacy with its superb location and separate driveway. Ideal for honeymooners and those seeking a quiet respite from the world, Te Rangi is nestled in a llama paddock with panoramic views of the mountains and dazzling South Pacific. Totally self-contained with a full kitchen (and BBQ for summer nights), the cottage has a large queen bedroom, living room with sleep sofa and cozy sleeping nook and can accommodate up to 5 people. The Italian-tiled bathroom offers a large double tub and separate shower. Full breakfast provisions are supplied. Antiques, Persian rugs, original NZ art, beautiful fabrics, and a stone fireplace all contribute to making Te Rangi a special romantic getaway.

Enjoy the privacy of our 20 acres including large gardens, duckpond, and rushing stream bordered by lush native bush. Our menagerie includes a growing herd of llamas, pet sheep, miniature horses, cats and dogs. We can help organise activities such as golf, tennis, sea kayaking, fishing, boating, or a swim with the dolphins. Guests have called Kahikatea "truly breathtaking", "heaven on earth", and "the prettiest spot in NZ". Come experience the magic and leave knowing why our llamas hum so contentedly.

Directions: *Please phone. Advance bookings only.*
Home Page: http://www.friars.co.nz/hosts/kahikatea.html

Akaroa
Self Contained Accommodation, B&B and Country Cottages
Address: 'Loch Hill' Country Cottages Motel, Main Highway, Akaroa
Name: Donna and David Kingan
Telephone: 03-304 7195
Freephone: 0800 456 244
Fax: 03-304 7672
Email: lochhill@xtra.co.nz
Beds: 8 King/Queen, 4 Single (11 bedrooms)
Bathroom: 5 Ensuite, 2 Private, 3 Spa
Tariff: B&B (Continental) Double $110, Single $75. Self contained cottages: Double $90-$140, each extra person $18. Credit Cards: Visa/Mastercard
Nearest Town: Akaroa 1 km, Christchurch 81 km

"Loch Hill" our thirty-five acre property, is set in a rural situation overlooking Akaroa Harbour. Our large, new stone cottages, nestled in the surrounding native bush, provide luxury accommodation for those who appreciate privacy, attractive park and garden setting, magnificent views and tranquillity. Whether your are staying in our self-catering, secluded one bedroom bush cottages, our 2 or 3 bedroom luxury self-contained cottages, or B&B studio unit with antique decor, we would like to extend the hospitality of "Loch Hill". Here you will find a warm welcome, cottages with their own individual design and character, large rooms, some air-conditioned, some with cozy log fires, and country theme furnishings. Your hosts David and Donna Kingan, are well-travelled, semi retired business people. Interests include gardening, vintage and classic vehicles and antiques. Our cluster of private, tastefully appointed cottage motels, on the outskirts of the historic village of Akaroa, with its early French history, are ideal for the perfect holiday retreat, or the smaller business conference, or wedding group. **Directions**: *On Akaroa Main State Highway 75, well signposted, on the right. One km north of Akaroa.*

Akaroa Harbour
Country Bed & Breakfast
Address: RD 1, Akaroa
Name: Cabbage Tree Corner
Host: Prue Billings
Telephone: (03) 304 5155
Mobile: (021) 655 862
Email: prueb@xtra.co.nz
Beds: 1 Double, 2 Single (2 Bedrooms)
Bathroom: 2 Ensuite
Tariff: B&B (Full) Double/Twin $85, Single $60. Credit Cards (VISA/MC)
Nearest Town: Akaroa 7 km

This newly restored 1920's farmhouse "Cabbage Tree Corner" is superbly sited at the north end of beautiful Akaroa Harbour. It's the ideal starting point for enjoying the full recreational possibilities of Banks Peninsula.
A 7 minute drive takes you to the picturesque and historic village of Akaroa with its many fine shops, galleries and restaurants. You can explore the peninsula by foot, cycle, sea kayak or fishing boat - and even swim with dolphins! Along with Toby the retiring tabby, I will ensure that you are well cared for during your stay. Expect all the comforts of a friendly, cosy and smoke-free home, with views to die for.
Directions: *The Akaroa / Christchurch shuttle bus will drop you at the gate, otherwise, just phone for directions.*

Barrys Bay, Akaroa

Self Contained Accommodation
Address: The Honey House,
Barrys Bay, RD2, Akaroa
Name: Jennifer and Kevin Wilson
Telephone: (03) 304 7186
Fax: (03) 304 7186
Beds: 1 Queen, 2 Single (2 Bedrooms)
Bathroom: 1 Private
Tariff: B&B (Special Continental, other by request)
Double $100, Single $70, Children negotiable.
Nearest Town: Akaroa 12 km, Christchurch 60 km

Get away from the hustle and bustle of daily life and enjoy a more relaxed pace at the Honey House in Barrys Bay, Akaroa. A leisurely hour from Christchurch, the Honey House is sited on five acres of rolling farmland. Modern loft style accommodation, built in keeping with the owners' historic cottage, offers outstanding and uninterrupted views of Onawe Peninsula and across to the Akaroa heads. Breakfast is creative and all home-made from the breads to the preserves and honey delivered to your door each morning. While away your day with a relaxing winery lunch, a game of golf at Duvauchelle (2 km away), or perhaps your idea of relaxation is a good book and unsurpassed views. The picturesque French village of Akaroa just 15 minutes away offers many attractions. Privacy and seclusion are guaranteed. All information is available form your hosts Jennifer and Kevin Wilson.

Directions: *Well signposted two kilometres past the Barrys Bay Cheese Factory on the Akaroa Main State Highway 75. Smoke free home.*

Sheffield

Homestay
Address: Pine House, Waddington Corner,
and Waimakariri Gorge Roads Corner,
Waddington, Sheffield, Canterbury
Name: Graeme & Debra Short
Telephone: (03) 318 3762
Beds: 2 Double, 3 Single (4 bedrooms)
Bathroom: 1 Guests share
Tariff: B&B (full) Double $90,
Single $50, Dinner $25.
NZ B&B Vouchers accepted $20 surcharge
Nearest Town: Darfield 12km east.

Pine House is a 2 storeyed character home built 1875, set in a large country garden, where guests can enjoy a leisurely stroll, and afternoon tea surrounded by our favourite roses and Rhododendrons. Our Guest Bedrooms are warm, cosy and comfortable. A Hearty breakfast is served in the guests sitting room. Our family is 2, Graeme a chef and Debra a Housewife with varied interest. Both are keen gardeners and have enjoyed travelling extensively. We enjoy entertaining both overseas visitors and New Zealand travellers alike. Situated close by the intersection of Highway 72, the scenic southern inland road, and Highway 73, the main road to the West Coast. The Tranz Alpine Express passes Waddington and can by boarded nearby. The nearest ski fields are 25 mins away, Central Christchurch is a pleasant 45 minutes drive, while the Airport can be reached in 30 minutes. We look forward to your visit. No smoking inside the house.

Directions: *Pine House is on Highway 72, just north of the intersection with Highway 73 to the West Coast, and 12km west of Darfield.*

Castle Hill Village
Homestay
Address: 11 Torlesse Place,
Castle Hill Village
(Rural Bag 55037),
Christchurch
Name: The Burn
Telephone: (03) 318 7559
Fax: (03) 318 7558
Beds: 3 Double, 2 Single (4 bedrooms)
Bathroom: 1 Guests share, 1 Family share
Tariff: B&B (continental) Double $90, Single $60,
Dinner $25, Children half price.
Nearest Town: Springfield (33 km)

A carefree atmosphere prevails at "The Burn" nestled in the heart of the Southern Alps and arguably New Zealand's highest B&B. We have designed and built our alpine lodge to maximise mountain vistas. A great place to return after a days activity or just relax on the huge deck. There are a host of outdoor sports on hand e.g. hiking, mountain biking, tennis, rock climbing, caving, children's playground, alpine golf, ski touring, ski / snowboarding (7 areas), High Country fly fishing, salmon fishing (5 lakes and rivers). Professional guiding for fishing and alpine sports available in house. POA. Your hosts Bob Edge & Phil Stephenson are active friendly informative and well travelled. As we are often out enjoying the great outdoors we recommend advanced bookings so we can be on hand to meet you. This is preferred but not essential. A home cooked evening meal is available by arrangement if required. No smoking indoors please. **Directions**: *State Hway 73, 33 km West of Springfield.*

Rakaia Gorge: Windwhistle
Self-contained   Accommodation
Address: 'Birchview',
Darfield RD2,
Canterbury
Name: Tom & Jenny McElrea
Telephone: (03) 318 6813
Fax: (03) 318 6813
Beds: 1 Double,
4 Single (3 bedrooms)
Bathroom: 1 Private
Tariff: B&B (full) $45 per person,
Children half price, Dinner $30 with wine.
Nearest Town: Methven 23km, Darfield 30km

Do you need a place to stay while you ski Mt Hutt or ski Porter Heights or Mt Cheeseman or Broken River or Craigieburn or for the foolhardy Mt Olympus? Do you need a place to stay while you fish the Rakaia River for salmon or fish for trout in Lake Coleridge or Lake Selfe or Lake Georgia or Lake Lyndon? Do you need a base while golfing the Hororata, Methven or Terrace Downs golf courses. Or alternatively just a place to rest up during your travels? Our self-contained chalet is only 80 kilometres from Christchurch on the inland scenic route heading south West and is situated in the middle of our sheep cattle and deer property. Ideal first stop when arriving in Canterbury. There is also a fascinating canyon to explore for those who want to stretch their legs. Guests do enjoy having their own self contained privacy. **Directions**: *We are 23km northwest of Methven or 30km west of Darfield. Please phone for details.*

Mt Hutt, Rakaia Gorge, Methven

Farmstay & Countrystay
Address: 'Tyrone Deer Farm',
Mt Hutt Station Rd, No.12 R.D.,
Rakaia, Mid Canterbury
Name: Pam & Roger Callaghan
Telephone: (03) 302 8096 **Fax**: (03) 302 8099
Beds: 2 Double, 3 Single (3 bedrooms) (Max. 5 people)
Bathroom: 2 Ensuites, 1 Private
Tariff: B&B (full) Double $95, Single $65, Children by arrangement,
Dinner $25pp. NZ B&B Vouchers accepted Surcharge $25.
Nearest Town: Methven 8km

"Tyrone" Deer Farm is centrally situated in the Methven, Mt Hutt, Rakaia Gorge area. One hour from Christchurch international airport and in the centre of the South Island, which makes it an ideal place to stop over when either going south to Queenstown etc or north to Picton/Nelson, we are handy to Highway 73 which goes to Arthur's Pass and the West Coast and only 5km from the Inland Tourist Route H/W 72. The farm consists of 300 acres running deer, cattle and a few sheep. Our home is situated on the farm to take advantage of the mountain views (Mt Hutt) this forms the back drop for the deer grazing a few metres away. As our family have left home we now have 3 spare bedrooms which we like to share with guests. There are electric blankets on the beds, heaters and hairdryers in the rooms, open fire in the lounge, with Sky TV, tea and coffee making facilities, guest fridge and swimming pool. Come and meet Guz our pet deer, her daughter $$ and cat called 10.30. A three course evening meal is available. For the visitor the surrounding area provides adventures and sporting activities ie skiing (Mt Hutt), Heliskiing (remote ranges), Jet Boating (Rakaia River), Ballooning, Tramping, Horse-riding, Guides are available for Hunting (Tahr, Chamois, Red Deer etc) also Trout and Salmon fishing (seasonal). Golf at Methven one of New Zealand's best 18 hole country courses. Numerous walks: scenic, bush, garden or alpine and each year in April, Methven hosts New Zealand's only walking festival. **Directions**: *8 km from Methven on the alternative Rakaia Gorge Route, 10 km from Rakaia Gorge Bridges. Please refer to map.*

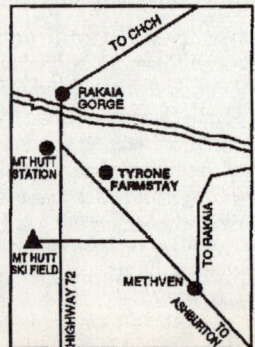

Mt Hutt, Methven

Farmstay+Self-contained Accom.
Address: Hart Rd, HW 72, Methven   Postal: 'Glenview', R.D. 12, Rakaia
Name: Andrew & Karen Hart
Telephone: (03) 302 8620
Fax: (03) 302 8650 **Mobile**: (025) 335 136   **Email**: ahart@voyager.co.nz
Beds: 1 Queen, 1 Double, 3 Single + Cot (3 bedrooms)
Bathroom: 1 Ensuite, 1 Private, 1 Family share
Tariff: B&B (continental - full on request) Double $80,
Single $45, Children half price, under 2 meals only, Dinner $25, Campervan power point
available. NZ B&B Vouchers accepted $10 surcharge
Nearest Town: Methven 10km

Our family invites you to sample their warm hospitality and come and join us on our large sheep and beef farm (1200 acres/480 hectares) at the top of the Canterbury Plains. Our spacious, modern farmhouse at 1500ft/450m above sea level; is built to enjoy views of our animals grazing on the farm, to see more than 50 miles/80km out across the plains to Christchurch, or to look directly up into Mt Hutt Skifield and along the Southern Alps. Our farm is situated on the Inland Scenic highway 72 between Christchurch and southern destinations. You are welcome to relax and enjoy the beautiful scenery, or take the opportunity to experience a large, working sheep and beef farm. Let Andrew take you for a tour. Go and observe the farming activities. There is always something to see and do on a working farm. There are many optional activities for you to experience. A choice of walks, horse riding, skiing, salmon and trout fishing, jet boating, golfing, parachuting and ballooning are all within 10 minutes drive. Enjoy the comfort of our spacious guest areas. Family accommodation consists of 2 bedrooms sleeping 2-5. Also available is a self-contained unit (double) situated in a garden next to the house. Both areas have separate access, good heating, comfortable beds with electric blankets, and private facilities. Meals are good quality NZ fare. Come and enjoy our warm, relaxed hospitality. Andrew enjoys computing. Karen teaches and is a Marriage Celebrant. Jonathan (16) loves farming, and Renee (13) loves animals. Hartley (small, white fluffy dog) loves meeting people. Our home is your home away from home. **Directions**: *Christchurch or Timaru - 1 hour. Geraldine, Ashburton - 30 mins. Rakaia Gorge, Methven - 10 mins. Hart Road with our Farmhouse Accommodation signs, is on Highway 72 between Pudding Hill and the Mt Hutt Skifield Road.*

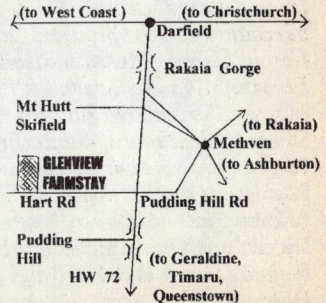

Mt Hutt - Methven
Farmstay

Address: 'Green Gables Deer Farm', S/H 77, Waimarama Road, Methven
Name: Roger & Colleen Mehrtens
Telephone: (03) 302 8308 **Fax**: (03) 302 8309 **Email**: greengables@xtra.co.nz
Beds: 3 Super King (3 Bedrooms)
Bathroom: 2 Ensuite, 1 Private with bath
Tariff: B&B (full) Double $95-$110, Single $70, Children half price.,
Dinner $30, Credit cards. NZ B&B Vouchers accepted $30 surcharge
Nearest Town: Methven - Mt Hutt Village 4km

A warm welcome awaits you at Green Gables which is minutes from Methven-Mt Hutt, a beautiful picturesque village, which has an impressvie range of both summer and winter activities. This is an area of freshness, adventure and enjoyment situated 1 hour from Christchurch the garden city of New Zealand and its International Airport. Queenstown 5 hours.

Relax in our peaceful farmhouse. The tastefully appointed guest wing is complete with ensuite facilities, super-king beds, wool underlays, electric blankets, heaters, hair dryers and clock radios. French doors opening from all bedrooms provide private access to all the guests bedrooms. Green Gables presents magnificent views of Mt Hutt and the surrounding mountains Hand feed pet deer "Lucy" and her lovely fawn in a tranquil setting with white doves, Royal Danish White Deer. Meet "Max" the golden Labrador and "Henry" the marmalade cat. Dine in the evening with delicious New Zealand country cuisine and wine. Relax with an open fire and TV in our comfortable sitting room. We delight in sharing our knowledge of this fascinating area, its history and its wide range of all seasons activities.

* *Salmon Fishing - Rakaia River*
* *Fishing Guides*
* *Skiing - Mt Hutt - Transport from gate*
* *Hot Air Ballooning*
* *Scenic Bush Walks*
* *Horse Riding*
* *Breakfast served to suit your schedule*
* *Trout Fishing - Lakes & Rivers*
* *Hunting - Guides Available*
* *Closest Farm Stay - Ski Area*
* *Golf - 18 hole course - Club Hire*
* *Open Gardens to Visit*
* *Jet Boating*
* *Restaurants nearby*

Directions: *Green Gables is on SH77, 4 kms North West of Methven - Village or from Scenic Route 72 turn into SH 77 travel 5 kms towards Methven - Village Green Gables on right.*
Home Page: http://www.nzhomestay.co.nz/mehrten.htm

Methven - Mt Hutt Village
Farmstay
Address: Methven Chertsey Road,
Methven, Postal: 12 RD, Rakaia.
Name: Pagey's Farmstay
- Gene and Shirley Pagey
Telephone: (03) 302 1713
Fax: (03) 302 1714
Beds: 1 Queen, 1 Double,
2 Single (3 bedrooms)
Bathroom: 1 Guests share
Tariff: B&B (full) Double $80, Single $50,
Children under 12 half price, Dinner $25,
Nearest Town: Methven 6km, Christchurch 1 hour, Ashburton 35km

If you want great hospitality, mountain views experience the peace and tranquillity of a NZ Romney Sheep Stud Farm of 400 acres close to Mt Hutt, then welcome to the Pagey's. Our very spacious home set amidst old trees and rose garden has high ceilings, beautiful carpet and large well equipped bedrooms each with woollen underlays, electric blankets, quality pillows and feather and down duvets. Treat your palate to some good old fashioned cooking made up of home grown meat and veges and a pot full of conversation. You are welcome to participate in the feeding out of sheep and watch the dogs working or relax in the house with Sky TV. Within minutes of the farm you could be skiing, jet boating, horse riding, ballooning, bush walking, lawn bowling or golfing on our magnificent 18 hole country course. Laundry facilities available. Courtesy car if required to Methven. **Directions**: *From Methven town centre. Turn at the Medical Centre down Methven Chertsey Road 6km on left.*

Mt Hutt - Methven
Homestay
Address: Airdrie House,
134 Forest Drive, Methven
Name: Margaret and Norman Riddle
Telephone: (03) 302 8827
Fax: (03) 302 8802
Beds: 2 Queen, 2 Single
(3 bedrooms) Maximum 5 people
Bathroom: 1 Ensuite, 1 Guests share
Tariff: B&B (full) Double $98, $90.
Single $60. Credit Cards accepted.
NZ B&B Vouchers accepted Oct-June only $25 surcharge.
Nearest Town: Ashburton 34 kms.

We are a retired couple who moved to Methven and live in a warm and comfortable home with wonderful views of the mountains. We have heaters, electric blankets and TV in each room. A lovely upstairs sitting area where the sun pours in in winter. Tea / coffee facilities available. Methven is the base for the Mt Hutt ski field and is one hour from Christchurch. There is a very good golf course available, trout and salmon fishing, jet boating, horse trekking and tramping. Methven is also on the interesting route travelling from Christchurch or further north to Geraldine, Fairlie, Tekapo, Mt Cook or further south to Queenstown and Wanaka. We have drying and storage facilities available. Being non smokers we appreciate you not smoking indoors. We have one cat and a small dog. We look forward to welcoming you.

Rakaia

Guest House
Address: 'St Ita's Guesthouse' Barrhill/Methven Rd, Rakaia
Name: Ken & Miriam Cutforth
Telephone: (03) 302 7546
Fax: (03) 302-7546
Mobile: (025) 233 4670
Email: st.itas_rakaia@xtra.co.nz
Beds: 2 Double, 4 Single
(3 Bedrooms / 2 Double +1 Twin bedroom with ensuites)
Bathroom: 3 Ensuite
Tariff: B&B (full) Double $90, Single $60, School Children $30, Dinner $25, Hamper lunch $10. Tariff includes complimentary morning or afternoon teas.
Credit Cards. NZ B&B Vouchers accepted $20 surcharge
Nearest Town: Rakaia 2 minutes walking distance

A warm welcome is assured at St Ita's. Built in 1912, this former Convent is full of charm. The spacious home is set in more than an acre of grounds and is located on the western fringe of Rakaia township opposite the Domain. Rakaia is 50 kilometres south of Christchurch, with its river famous for salmon fishing. Jetboating, horse trekking, golf and visiting the local pubs are popular pastimes in Rakaia. Within 30 minutes you can be at Mt Hutt Skifield, on the Transalpine Railway or a Scenic Walkway. St Ita's meals are based on local produce - fresh vegetables and fruit (mainly from our garden); lamb, beef, venison or salmon. Espresso coffee or tea is complimentary to wash down home baking. Cooked or continental breakfasts are served. Many guests choose St Ita's for its tranquillity - relax in front of an open fire with our cat and golden retriever; watch Sky Television; play tennis or pool. **Home Page**: www.ashburton.co.nz/stitas

Ashburton

Homestay
Address: 1 Sudbury Street, Ashburton
Name: Pat & Dave Weir
Telephone: (03) 308 3534
Beds: 1 Double, 2 Single (2 bedrooms)
Bathroom: 1 Family share
Tariff: B&B (full) Double $60, Single $30, Dinner $15,
Children under 13 half price. NZ B&B Vouchers accepted
Nearest Town: Ashburton is apprx 80 km south of Christchurch

We are 10-15 minutes walk from town, our comfortable home is situated in a quiet street and we have the added enjoyment of looking out onto a rural scene. The guest accommodation is comfortable. Your hosts are nearing retirement and have a variety of interests. We welcome the opportunity to meet and greet visitors and wish to make your stay a happy one. We do request visitors not to smoke in our home.
Vegetarian or additional meals to bed and breakfast available on request. We are a few minutes walk away from Ashburton River Walkway and Riding for Disabled grounds.
Laundry facilities are available to guests.

Ashburton

Farmstay
Address: 'Carradale Farm'
Ferriman's Road, Lagmhor, No 8 R.D.,   Ashburton
Name: Jim & Karen McIntyre
Telephone: (03) 308 6577
Fax: (03) 308 6548 **Mobile**: (025) 338 044
Beds: 4 Single (2 bedrooms)
Bathroom: 1 Private, 1 Family share
Tariff: B&B (full,continental)   Double $80, Single $50, Dinner $25,
Children under 12 half price, Campervans & caravan power point $25.
Spa pool. Credit Cards.   NZ B&B Vouchers accepted
Nearest Town: Ashburton - 8 km West of Ashburton; 1 hour Christchurch
International Airport.

Our homestead which captures the sun in all rooms is cosy and inviting. It is situated in a sheltered garden where you can enjoy peace, tranquility and fresh country air or indulge in a game of tennis. Both guest rooms have comfortable twin beds, electric blankets, reading lamps and tea making facilities. Breakfast may be served either in dining room or conservatory. Laundry and ironing facilities available. We offer home grown meat and vegetables. We have a 225 hectare irrigated sheep and cattle farm. You may like to join in farm activities or be taken for a farm tour; sheep shearing demonstration available (in season). Our 3 adult children have left home. As we have both travelled extensively in New Zealand, Australia, United Kingdom and Europe we would like to offer hospitality to fellow travellers. Our hobbies include meeting people, travel, reading, photography, gardening, sewing, cake decorating, rugby, cricket, Jim belongs to Masonic Lodge and Karen is involved in Community Affairs. **Directions**: *Turn off State Highway 1 and cross the railway line at Tinwald Tavern, heading west onto Lagmhor Road driving past Tinwald Golf Course. The road then becomes Frasers Road. Travel 6 km to 5 crossroads. Make a left turn onto Ferriman's Road. Our home is the only house on the right side of the road.*

Ashburton

Homestay B&B
Address: 'Weatherly House', 359 West St, (S.H.1) Ashburton
Name: Helen Thomson
Telephone: (03) 308 9949
Beds: 1 Double, 2 Single (2 bedrooms)
Bathroom: 1 Guest share
Tariff: B&B (continental) Double $65, Single $35, Children by negotiation, Dinner $20, Full breakfast extra, Campervans welcome (No power).
Credit cards.   NZ B&B Vouchers accepted
Nearest Town: Ashburton (In town)

Weatherly House is a charming turn of the century villa set in an attractive and private garden and with off-street parking. There is an inviting spa pool which is very relaxing after a long day travelling or on the slopes, and Weatherly House is particularly suitable for the not so able as there is ramp access and hand rails on the toilet and shower We are situated about 5 minutes walk from Ashford's Craft Village and from the lovely Ashburton Domain. A 15 minutes walk will take you to the town centre or the hospital. Christchurch and Timaru are both 1 hours drive away and mid-Canterbury has much to offer the travellers. Your comfort is our aim, a courtesy car is available, hot drinks and home made goodies available at any time. Dinner is by arrangement and there is a cosy open fire in the colder weather.

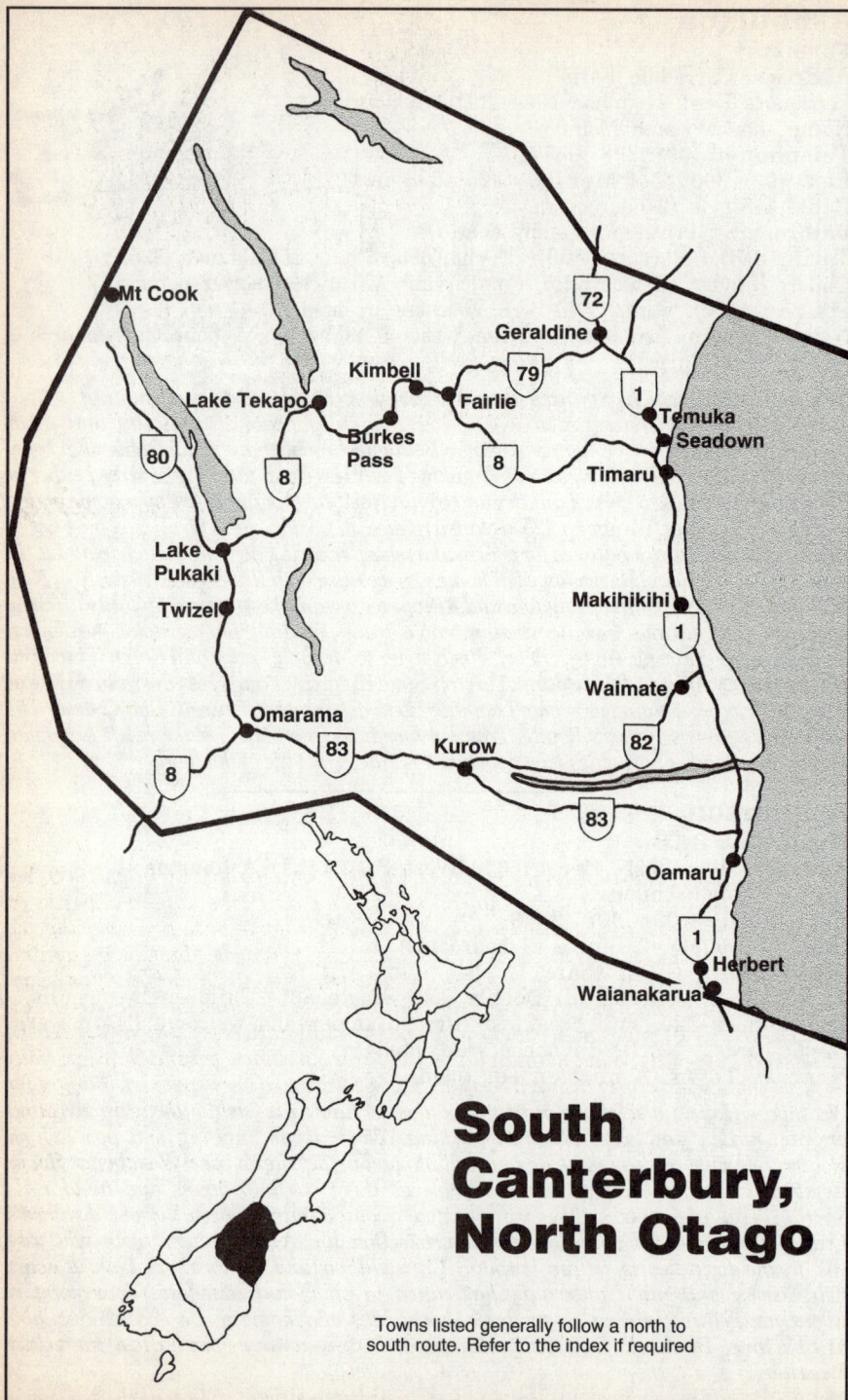

Mt Cook

72

Geraldine

Kimbell

79

Lake Tekapo

Fairlie

Burkes
Pass

1

Temuka
Seadown

80

8

Timaru

8

Lake
Pukaki

Makihikihi

1

Twizel

Waimate

82

Omarama

83

Kurow

8

83

Oamaru

1

Herbert

Waianakarua

South Canterbury, North Otago

Towns listed generally follow a north to
south route. Refer to the index if required

The Crossing

Geraldine
Guest Lodge
Address: 'The Crossing', Woodbury Rd, R.D.21, Geraldine
Name: The Crossing
Telephone: (03) 693 9689
Fax: (03) 693 9789
Email: srelax@xtra.co.nz
Beds: 2 Queen, 1 Double, 1 Single (3 bedrooms)
Bathroom: 2 Ensuite, 1 Private
Tariff: B&B (full) Double $120-$160, Single $100-$120, extra person $20;
Dinner a la carte. Suitable for children over 12 years. Credit Cards.
Nearest Town: Geraldine 2 kms.

The Crossing is a beautifully restored old English style manor house built in 1908. We are situated on 37 peaceful acres near the base of the Four Peaks range and bordered by the Upper Waihi River. Our location is ideal as a home base for exploring the features of the area such as Tekapo, Mt Cook, Akaroa, Oamaru, MacKenzie country, and Mt Hutt, or a day trip through Arthur's Pass on the Tranz Scenic alpine railway. You can enjoy a game of golf in either of the two local golf clubs, fish for salmon or trout, explore Peel Forest or go white water rafting on the Rangitata river. Upon your return at the end of the day, relax with a glass of wine on our shady verandah before your evening meal in our fully licensed restaurant. We have two very spacious lounges for reading, enjoying a selection of board games, or having a yarn with us or our other guests.

For complete relaxation, enjoy a game of croquet or petanque in our lovely garden or just read a book in peaceful surroundings.

We are located 1 km off SH72/79, the Inland Scenic Route between Christchurch and Queenstown, Mount Cook, and Dunedin. Approaching on SH1 from the north, take SH79 at Rangitata. Approaching on SH1 from the south, take SH72 at Winchester. The Crossing is smoke free inside the house. suitable for children over twelve years. Member Heritage Inns.

Directions: *Signposted on SH72/79 approx. 1km north of Geraldine. Turn into Woodbury Road, then 1km on right hand side.*

Home Page: http://www.heritageinns.co.nz/the.crossing

Geraldine

Farmstay + Backpackers
Address: 90 Main North Road,
Postal: 21R.D. Geraldine,
South Canterbury
Name: Raukapuka Roost -
Hilary Muir Slater
Telephone: 0064 (03) 693 7665
Fax: 0064 (03) 693-7665
Email: roost90@hotmail.com
Beds: 1 Double, 1 Single sunroom (2 bedrooms)
Bathroom: 1 Ensuite, 1 Guests Share (with bath)
Tariff: B&B (continental) Double $80, Single $40,
Dinner $20 (by arrangement), Children under 14 yrs $10,
Babies no charge. NZ B&B Vouchers accepted $10 surcharge
Nearest Town: Geraldine - on SH72/79 'The Roost' is 2 km from Geraldine.
Mt Cook - 2 hrs; Lake Tekapo - 1 hr; Christchurch Airport 1 1/2 hrs.

Sheltered and sunny rural location. A home away form home where Drysdale sheep are bred. Farmyard animals live beside the Raukapuka Stream. "Buttercup" a ewe will eat from your hand and "Puppit" a working sheep dog will greet you.
"The Roost" is a short drive to Waihi Gorge for picnicking and swimming; a pleasant drive to Peel Forest's native trees and walks; the Rangitata River is also handy for fishing and rafting. Relax outdoors and enjoy the morning sunrise and morning and evening bird song. Interests: Golf, community, amateur theatre and the environment. I have hosted since 1993 - a warm welcome is assured.
Directions: *"Geraldine" township sign is directly outside the property. A sign is at the gate.*

Geraldine

Bed & Breakfast
Address: 'Oak Grove',
26 Main North Road, Geraldine
Name: John & Ngaire Davis
Telephone: (03) 693 9830
Fax: (03) 693 9830
Beds: 3 Queen, 2 Single (4 bedrooms)
Bathroom: 1 Ensuite, 1 Guests share
Tariff: B&B (full) Double $90-$125,
 Single $60. Dinner $35pp, Booking essential.
Credit Cards: Visa/Mastercard.
Nearest Town: Geraldine. We are 1.5 km north of Geraldine on S.H. 79.

"Oak Grove," our fully restored 1907 home, is set amongst 5 acres of hundred year old English trees. The setting, the food, the warm hospitality, make this a special "B&B", with a reputation we are proud of. Light, airy bedrooms have the luxury of crisp white linen, fluffy towels and firm beds. Our honeymoon suite is perfect for that romantic weekend. Scrumptious breakfasts are served in the country-style breakfast room, warmed by the adjacent coal range. French doors open to a lovely garden. Dinner is served in the intimate dining room, where antiques and open fireplace complete the scene. Guests welcomed with complimentary refreshments on arrival. Laundry service available. Ngaire is a retired Home Economics teacher, and John handmakes gold and silver jewellery and special wooden toys. Our home is smokefree, and unsuitalbe for children.
Directions: *1.5 hours from Christchurch on S.H. 79, main route to Mt. Cook and Queenstown.*

Geraldine
Farmstay
Address: "Camberdown",
State Highway 79, Geraldine
Name: Colin & Susan Sinclair
Telephone: (03) 697 4849
Fax: (03) 697 4849
Beds: 1 Queen, 2 Single (2 bedrooms)
Bathroom: 2 Guests share
Tariff: B&B (full) Double $100,
Single $70, Dinner $25pp, Credit Cards.
NZ B&B Vouchers accepted $30 surcharge
Nearest Town: Geraldine 22km and Fairlie 24km -

Camberdown Homestead is situated on State Highway 79 between Geraldine and Fairlie, only two hours from Christchurch. The 430 acre farm is situated in lush green rolling country with mountain views. Bird life abounds in small areas of native bush. Relax on our sunny verandah with our cat or enjoy taking part in daily running of our sheep and cattle farm.
Nearby are wineries, golf courses, skifields, trout and salmon fishing and bush walking. Susan enjoys patchwork, needlework and runs a flock of coloured sheep. Colin is a member of the Lions and enjoys trout fishing. Where possible we offer our guests home grown fruit and vegetables. Home made bread, jam, preserves are part of our delicious meals. Non-smoking household.

Geraldine
Farmstay
Address: "The Woolshed",
211 Main North Road, Geraldine
Name: Sue and Colin Matthews
Telephone: 03-693 9394
Fax: 03-693 9394
Email: csmatthews@hotmail.com
Beds: 1 Queen, 2 Single (2 bedrooms)
Bathroom: 1 Guests share
Tariff: B&B (full/continental)
Double $75, Single $40, Dinner $25,
Children under 12 half price.
NZ B&B Vouchers accepted $15 Surcharge
Nearest Town: Geraldine 2 kms.

Our small farm is in a lovely setting with river boundary, expansive views of Mt Peel and Four Peaks and handily located on the main State Highway. Our main emphasis is black and coloured sheep of special interest to spinners and weavers, and we also operate a worm breeding farm. We keep the usual array of domestic farm animals. A wool, art and craft gallery is situated on the farm. We run a clean and relaxed home. Guests have a separate bathroom and the choice of a separate lounge (with TV) or may share our lounge. We have computer facilities with Internet access, and fax. Sue is interested in horticulture (herbs, flowers and organically grown vegetables), art (painting sculpture and photography), and plays tennis. Colin plays squash and is interested in computing and writing. Both enjoy travel and have worked overseas. Both are non smokers. Guests are welcome to join in farm activities.

Temuka
Homestay B&B
Address: "Ashfield", 71 Cass Street, Temuka
Name: Ann & Martin Bosman
Telephone: (03) 615 6157
Fax: (03) 615 9062
Beds: 2 King/Queen, 1 Double,
2 Single (4 bedrooms)
Bathroom: 1 Guests share.
Single party bookings accepted.
Tariff: B&B (special) Double $88, Single $50,
Children half price, Credit Cards (VISA/MC/Amex/Diners).
Nearest Town: Timaru 10 minutes, Christchurch 90 minutes

"Ashfield" is set on 4 acres of woodlands, situated inside the Temuka boundary. We are only a 10 minutes walk from the shops and restaurants. Our house was built around 1883 and features marble fireplaces and spectacular gilt mirrors. A warm welcome awaits you. Join us for a drink in the evening or maybe you would like to challenge Martin to a game of snooker on the full size table in the summer house. Two of our bedrooms open up to a balcony with beautiful views of the mountains in the distance. Several skifields are within one to one and a half hour drive. Lake Tekapo is one hour away. If salmon and trout fishing is your thing then this is the place to come to. So come and join us and our 2 dogs and 2 cats for a wonderful stay in a lovely setting. Guests are welcome to use our laundry facilities.

Timaru
Rural Homestay
Address: 'Mountain View',
Talbots Road, Kingsdown,
No 1 R.D., Timaru
Name: Mary & Graeme Bell
Telephone: (03) 688 1070
Fax: (03) 688 1069
Email: mvhomestay@xtra.co.nz
Beds: 1 Double, 4 Single (3 bedrooms)
Bathroom: 2 Private, 1 Family share
Tariff: B&B (full) Double $75, Single $50, Children under 12 half price;
Dinner $20; Campervans $6 per person with power. Credit cards accepted.
NZ B&B Vouchers accepted
Nearest Town: Timaru 3kms from Southern boundary.

'Mountain View' is a farmlet on Talbots Road 200 metres from State Highway 1, just 3 kms from the southern boundary of Timaru. Blue and white Bed & Breakfast signs are on State Highway 1 north and south of the turn off into Talbots Road. Your hosts offer warm Kiwi hospitality and are semi-retired farmers who have hosted on their farm for 10 years. We still have a few deer and sheep. Our home is situated in a tranquil sheltered garden overlooking farmland and a wonderful view of the mountains. Electric blankets on all beds, two private bathrooms for guests and laundry facilities available. Breakfast of your choice is served at your requested time and an evening meal is available with prior notice. Our interests include gardening, spinning and engineering. Nearby fishing, golf courses, swimming both at beach and heated swimming pool and a walk on the sea coast to the lighthouse. Day trips can be comfortably taken to Mt Cook, Hydro Lakes and Ski Fields. One hour drive in the evening to visit the Penguins.

Timaru

Homestay
Address: 16 Selwyn Street, Timaru
Name: Margaret & Nevis Jones
Telephone: (03) 688 1400
Fax: (03) 688 1400
Beds: 2 Double, 2 Single (3 bedrooms)
Bathroom: 2 Ensuites, 1 Guests share
Tariff: B&B (full) Double $80, Single $40,
Children half price. NZ B&B Vouchers accepted
Nearest Town: Timaru

Our home is a spacious, comfortable, two-storeyed brick house with a grass tennis court in use from October until March. Situated in central Timaru – 5 minutes walk from the beach and 15 minutes from town, our home is set back from the road in a private garden surrounded by trees.
We have travelled and worked overseas in numerous countries - namely the UK, South Africa and the Middle East. We therefore feel we have an appreciation of what it is like to be a visitor in a foreign country and share this enjoyment of meeting people from other countries. Our main interests are music and the theatre in which we are both actively involved. We also play tennis and golf. We enjoy making use of the many walks and opportunities to get into the mountains which are so accessible from Timaru.
Directions: *Please phone.*

Seadown, Timaru

A Country Homestay
Address: Seadown, R.D.3, Timaru
Name: Margaret & Ross Paterson
Telephone: (03) 688 2468
Fax: (03) 688 2468
Beds: 1 Double, 2 Single, can put up extra day bed if nesessary. (3 bedrooms)
Bathroom: 1 Guests share
Tariff: B&B (full/continental) Double $70, Single $45, Children half price,
under 5 years no charge for meals. Dinner $20
Credit Cards. NZ B&B Vouchers accepted
Nearest Town: Timaru 4.8 kms from northern Boundry on Seadown Rd

We welcome you to our homestay at Seadown which is approx 10 minutes north of Timaru. Situated 4.8 kms on the Seadown Road which is off State Highway 1, at Washdyke, second house on the left past the Pharlap statue. Your hosts are semi-retired farmers who have hosted on their farm for 11 years. We have a country farmlet which has enabled us to bring some of our farm animals with us. Our home is in the centre of a farming community with wonderful views of farmland and mountains. Guests can comfortably take day trips to Mt Cook, Hydro Lakes and ski fields. Fishing and Golf course a few minutes away. Electric blankets on all guests beds. Laundry facilities are available. Our interests are gardening, spinning and overseas travel. You are welcome to have your meals with us and a warm welcome awaits overseas and New Zealand visitors alike.

Timaru

Homestay
Address: 264 Pages Rd, Timaru
Name: Carol Angland & Ross Carrick
Telephone: (03) 686 0323 (h)
or (03) 688 4628 (w)
Fax: (03) 686 0272
Beds: 1 Queen, 1 Double,
2 Single (2 bdrms)
Bathroom: 1 Ensuite, 1 Private
Tariff: B&B (full) Double $85, Single $60, Dinner $25, Children half price,
Under 5 no charge, Credit cards.   NZ B&B Vouchers accepted $20 surcharge
Nearest Town: Centre Timaru 4km

Our spacious, sunny, comfortable home set on 1 acre in Timaru city, looks out over farmland to the mountains. The extensive garden features established trees, 100 roses and a tennis court. You can also relax on the sheltered terrace or play petanque or croquet. The queen bedroom has an adjoining sunroom / childrens room. A cot and high chair are available. Laundry facilities. Dinner by arrangement. Breakfasts are tempting, healthy and generous. Many extras. Smoke-free home.

We enjoy an informal lifestyle; theatre, literature, food, travel, sport and our grown-up family of five, three grandchildren and Harry-our (outdoors only) Labrador.

To find us - from Christchurch (150km north) turn right at Washdyke at the Mobil Truck stop and road sign to Gleniti and Pages Road. From Dunedin (230km south) left at Otipua Rd (Mobil garage), left at Wai-iti Rd, right at Morgans Rd and left into Pages Rd.

Timaru

Garden Homestay
Address: Ethridge Gardens,
10 Sealy Street, Timaru
Name: Nan & Wynne Raymond
Telephone: (03) 684 4910
Fax: (03) 684 4910
Beds: 1 Queen, 3 Single (3 bedrooms)
Bathroom: 1 Private, 1 Guests share,
Spa bath by arrangement
Tariff: B&B (full) Double $120, Single $90,
Dinner (3 course with wine) $40pp,
Casual meals also provided $20-$30, Lunch $15pp.
Laundry service available. Credit Cards, Vouchers accepted $60 Double, $30 Single
Nearest Town: Timaru

Ethridge Gardens is a beautiful two storey red brick house built in 1911. High brick walls divide the romantic English-style garden into several garden rooms. Iron gates and rose-covered archways lead through to exciting vistas, each one differing in style, colour and design. To stay here is to enjoy the very best in hospitality. Guests are welcome to relax in a spacious sitting room that opens out onto the terrace and garden with   heated swimming pool. Tea, coffee, fruit and fresh flowers in the bedrooms. T.V in the main bedroom. A three course dinner with wine, flowers and candlelight can be served in the formal dining room, or enjoy alfresco in the gazebo during summer and a casual meal beside the fire in winter. Delicious breakfasts range from traditional to European. Good licensed restaurants nearby and transport can be easily arranged. Wynne is presently Mayor of Timaru District and Nan is a renowned New Zealand gardener.

Timaru

Homestay
Address: 15 Bidwill Street, Timaru
Name: Dorothy & Ron White
Telephone: (03) 688 5856
Fax: (03) 688 5870
Beds: 4 Single (2 bedrooms)
Bathroom: 1 Private
(we only take one party at a time)
Tariff: B&B (continental) Double $80,
Single $60, Children half price,
Dinner $15/$25pp.
NZ B&B Vouchers accepted $20 Surcharge
Nearest Town: Timaru

We are recently retired from farming and offer superior homestay in a classic two storeyed home with a delightful garden situated in a quiet street in central Timaru - 5 minutes walk to the town centre and Caroline Bay. The main guest bedroom has two single beds with electric blankets and own bathroom. There is also a smaller bedroom with two single beds. Laundry facilities are available also a courtesy car for arrival pickups.
Timaru is central to the many attractions of South Canterbury, and as we are licensed to transport passengers, we can, if required, undertake day trips and longer guided tours anywhere in the South Island. These services are at a separate cost.
We both have many interests including gardening and travel and look forward to meeting and offering our hospitality to people who prefer homestays.
Directions: *Please phone.*

Timaru

Rural Self-contained Accommodation
Address: Otipua, No. 2 R.D., Timaru
Name: Lorraine & Wayne Calvert
Telephone: (03) 686 4874
Fax: (03) 686 4874
Beds: 1 Queen (1 bedroom)
Bathroom: 1 Ensuite
Tariff: B&B (continental) Double $85,
Single $75, Dinner $25pp. Credit cards.
Nearest Town: Timaru 8km

"Beaconsfield Lodge"

We welcome visitors to our home with surrounding flower garden and lawns. We offer you a self-contained private detached unit with bed, living area and ensuite. A comfortable queen size bed with wool underlay and electric blanket, TV, microwave, refrigerator, toaster and tea making facilities. A continental breakfast is placed in your unit to enjoy at your leisure. An evening meal is available with prior notice. Our property is used for market gardening. Lorraine's interests include flower gardening, sewing and children's smocking. Wayne enjoys corresponding with overseas pen-friends. We both enjoy meeting people and travel. Two Country golf Courses, Maori Rock drawings, and bush walks near by. We are within easy travelling to Christchurch, Dunedin, Mt Cook and Queenstown. Non-smoking self contained accommodation.
Directions: *Take first turn right on Southern boundary of Timaru, Beaconsfield Road. We are situated 8km from the main highway, 10 minutes from Timaru. We are on the right hand side of road (cross roads on top of hill). Name on mail box. Please phone in advance if possible.*

Timaru

Homestay B&B
Address: Ballyagan, SH8 Levels, RD 4, Timaru
Name: Gail and Bill Clarke
Telephone: (03) 614 8221
Fax: (03) 614 8221
Beds: 1 Double, 4 Single (3 Bedrooms)
Bathroom: 1 Guests share, 1 Family share
Tariff: B&B (Full), Double $70, Single $35, Children half price. Dinner $20.
Vouchers accepted.
Nearest Town: Pleasant Point 5 km, Tiomaru 12 km.

Welcome to Ballyagan, where a warm welcome awaits. We are semi-retired sheep and grain farmers enjoying the friendliness of the South Canterbury people. Our home is set among trees and gardens with the sound of native birds, also with a walk around our small farm. Bedrooms have electric blankets and bedside lamps. Laundry facilities are available. You are welcome to dine with the family. Restaurants are 5 min away to Pleasant Point, which also has vintage train and golf course, 5 min to airport and Levels motor race way. 15 min to Timaru with walks through the Botanic Gardens and beach walks.
Mt Cook, skifields and fishing are all within 2 hours travel.
We have two pets, a cat and a dog.
Directions: *We are on SH8 approx 7 km from Washdyke, 5 km to Pleasant Point. B&B homestay sign at gate.*

Timaru

Homestay B&B
Address: 11 Wai-iti Road, Timaru
Name: Okare Leisure Stop
Telephone: (03) 688 0316
Fax: (03) 688 0316
Mobile: (025) 229 7301
Email: okare@xtra.co.nz
Beds: 1 King, 1 Queen, 1 Double,
4 Single (5 Bedrooms)

Bathroom: 1 Ensuite, 1 Private, 1 Guests share
Tariff: B&b (Full) Double $95, single $70, Dinner by prior arrangement.
Children half price $35. Cot and highchair available. Credit Cards accepted.
(Tariffs reviewed annually 1st Oct) Laundry facilities available.
NZ B&B Vouchers accepted $25 surcharge
Nearest Town: Timaru

Welcome to the Timaru District and the greater Aoraki region which extends to Mt Cook. Shelley and I own a local restaurant and considered homestay a natural extension of our business, as we love entertaining visitors from out of town. OKARE is a substantial Edwardian brick residence built in 1909 and offers discerning travellers and small families comfortable accommodation with warm welcoming hospitality. Okare's ground floor offers sunny living spaces, also a disabled access Queen accommodation. Up the Rimu staircase a landing leads to four guestrooms. A super King, a Double with ensuite and a bunkroom as well as a sunroom with two day beds and the guest share bathroom. A lovely spot for breakfast is the substantial patio with views over Caroline Bay, here you can watch the antics of Anna(stasia) and Tsar(ervich) our two Siberian Huskies. Five minute walk leads to Caroline Bay, a selection of restaurant and the town center. The first on your stroll into town, Boudicca's Cafe and Wine bar is our own where there is charge back facilities for your convenience. Enjoy your stay - Malcolm and Shelley.

Fairlie
Farmstay/Homestay
Address: 'Fontmell',
Nixons Road, No 17 R.D. Fairlie
Name: Anne & Norman McConnell
Telephone: (03) 685 8379
Fax: (03) 685 8379
Beds: 2 Double, 4 Single (3 bedrooms)
Bathroom: 1 Guests share
Tariff: B&B (full) Double $70-$90, Single $45,
Children $25, Dinner $20. NZ B&B Vouchers accepted
Nearest Town: Fairlie 3km

Our farm consists of 400 acres producing fat lambs, cattle and deer, with numerous other animals and bird life. The house is situated in a large English style garden with many large mature trees in tranquil setting.
In the area are two skifields, golf courses, walkways and scenic drives. Informative farm tours available. Our interests include golf, gardening and music.
Directions: *Travel 1 km from town centre, along Tekapo highway, then turn left into Nixon's Road when two more kilometers will bring you to the "Fontmell" entrance.*

Fairlie
Lodge with 6 Units
Address: 16 School Rd, Fairlie
Name: Keith & Janya McCulloch
Telephone: (03) 685 8452
Freephone: (0800) 685 845
(Reservations only)
Fax: (03) 685 8452
Mobile: 025 206 0883
Beds: 3 Double, 4 Single (5 bedrooms)
Bathroom: Private, Guests share
Tariff: B&B (full) Double $70, Single $35,
Children $10. Dinner $15. Under cover car parks.
Nearest Town: Fairlie

Fairlie is a beautiful town, it has a indoor swimming pool, golf, squash, tennis, boating, fishing, shopping, its all five minutes walk or just relax and enjoy the peaceful life of Fairlie.
We are a family of five, with three young children. We have transport to the skifields or sightseeing and we have a sauna, spa to relax in after meal or a drink.
Fairlie To: Christchurch 2 1/4 hours; Mt Dobson 40 mins; Timaru 50 mins; Queenstown 3 hours; Dunedin 3 1/4 hours; Mt Hutt 1 1/2 hours; Tekapo 30 mins.
We have TV in all the rooms. There are 6 units with showers, toilets in each. Asian food can be cooked for you in the evenings or just a Kiwi meal.
A new lake with good boating and fishing has been built ten minuites from Fairlie.
Directions: *Signposted: its up the road form Fairlie Hotel.*

Fairlie

Countrystay
Address: "Braelea", SHwy 79,
Fairlie, Sth Canterbury
Name: Les, Sandra & Gerry Riddle
Telephone: (03) 685 8366
Fax: (03) 685 8943
Mobile: (025) 234 8384
Beds: 1 Super/King which
unzips, and 2 singles (2 bedrooms)
Bathroom: 2 Private
Tariff: B&B (full) Double $80, Single $60, Dinner $25 by arrangement,
Children $10 plus $1 for each year. Campervans welcome, Credit Cards.
NZ B&B Vouchers accepted $12 Surcharge
Nearest Town: Fairlie 3km.

Welcome to the Mackenzie Country. Relax in our new centrally heated home, and enjoy the panoramic mountain view. We are situated 2 hours south of Christchurch and 4 hours north of Queenstown, on the main highway. You may like to enjoy the privacy of your own guest lounge with its tea making facilities or join us in the family area. We are on a 50 acre country block with sheep, calves and hens, which you are welcome to help tend. Our resident puss is called Snoopy. We are 4 minutes east of Fairlie township, where there are diverse eating facilities, golf, squash, indoor summer swimming and beauty parlour. We enjoy our countryside and are happy to help you do the same, by providing a short sightseeing tour, and providing information about local hunting, fishing, flying, walking , hiking and tramping.

Kimbell, Fairlie

Country Homestay
Address: Rivendell Lodge,
Stanton Rd, Kimbell, RD 17, Fairlie
Name: Joan & Kevin
Telephone: (03) 685 8833
Fax: (03) 685 8825
Mobile: (025) 819 189
Email: Rivendell.lodge@xtra.co.nz
Beds: 1Queen, 1 Double, 3 Single (3 Bedrooms)
Bathroom: 2 Private, Spa bath available
Tariff: B&B (full) Double $90, Single $50, Children negotiable,
Dinner $25pp, Campervans welcome, Credit Cards (VISA/MC/Bankcard).
NZ B&B Vouchers accepted $20 surcharge
Nearest Town: Fairlie 8km, Tekapo 33km, skifield 5km. Lake Opuha 12 kms.

"They stayed long in Rivendell and found it hard to leave. The house was perfect whether you liked sleep, or work, or storytelling, or singing, or just sitting and thinking best, or a pleasant mixture of all them all. Everyone grew refreshed and strong in a few days there. Merely to be there was a cure for weariness, fear and sadness." – Tolkien
Joan is a writer who shares a passion for mountains with Kevin, a keen hunter and fisherman. Our home is set in a large garden complete with stream and two cats.
Discover peaceful Kimbell on the Christchurch-Queenstown road, close to Mt Dobson skifield. Book two nights and come fishing, hunting, play golf (clubs available), ski, or try our awesome alpine experience.
Complimentary beverages and homebaking on arrival. Laundry facilities available. Rivendell Lodge is 100 metres up Stanton Rd at Kimbell on SH 8.
Home Page: http://homestay.cjb.net/

Kimbell, Fairlie
Homestay/Farmstay
Address: "Poplar Downs",
Mount Cook Road, Kimbell, RD 17, Fairlie
Name: Shirley & Robin Sinclair
Telephone: (03) 685 8170
Fax: (03) 685 8210
Email: bigred@es.co.nz
Beds: 1 King (or 2 Single),
1 Double (2 bedrooms)
Bathroom: 1 Ensuite, 1 Private
Tariff: B&B (full) Double $90, Single $60, Children negotiable, Dinner $25,
Credit Cards (VISA/MC/BC). NZ B&B Vouchers accepted $20 surcharge
Nearest Town: Fairlie 7km, Tekapo 30km, Skifield 6km

Our homestead is an elegant early 1900's villa tastefully restored with the comfort of modern amenities. Heated rooms open onto the verandah overlooking the garden to the mountains. Take a stroll over our farmland and take in some splendid views of the surrounding basin and mountains, explore the turn of the century Loafing Barn used then to house a large team of Clydesdales, or just wander around our spacious garden where there are numerous quiet spots to sit and relax and admire the many and varied birdlife. We have the usual menagerie of farm animals including pet lambs, hens, mares and foals, sheepdog and cocker spaniel as well as the household moggy. Kimbell is a quiet rural village with beautiful trees and fresh clear air. Locally there is skiing, golf, fishing and tramping. Maori rock drawing, craft and art outlets, a colonial museum and excellent eateries from licensed to fast foods. **Directions**: *On State Highway 8 from Fairlie to Mt Cook (7km). Sign at gate. Our home is smoke free with children most welcome.*

Burkes Pass
Country Homestay
Address: Dobson Lodge, Burkes Pass,
RD17 Mackenzie Country
Name: Keith & Margaret Walter
Telephone: (03) 685 8316
Fax: (03) 685 8316
Email: dobson_lodge@xtra.co.nz
Beds: 2 Queen, 1 Double,
2 Single (3 bdrms)
Bathroom: 2 Ensuite, 1 Family share
Tariff: B&B (continental) Double $85, $95, $120, Single $60,
Children negotiable. Dinner by arrangement $20pp. Winter rates apply.
Credit Cards. NZ B&B Vouchers accepted $25 surcharge
Nearest Town: Lake Tekapo or Fairlie - Apx 19km to Fairlie, 23km from Lake Tekapo

Come and share with us our unique stone homestead with exceptional character set in 15 acres. We are nestled in a picturesque valley, with views of Mount Dobson and close to Lake Tekapo. We are on the main tourist route between Christchurch, Queenstown and Te Anau, which makes us an ideal halfway stop. The entrance to Mount Dobson ski-field road is approximately 5 minutes away. Only one kilometre from the settlement of Burkes Pass, with a Kiwi restaurant and craft shop. Our house is something special, built from glacier stones, exterior walls 700 mm thick with cedar shingled roof, and large stone open fireplace. A welcoming aroma of rough sawn timber from the ceiling pervades the whole home. You will not forget your stay with us. We have a daughter aged 14. Our interests include photography, crafts, travel and animals. We have one cat, a friendly collie and pet sheep. No smoking indoors. **Directions**: *Watch for Dobson Lodge east of Burkes Pass village.*

Lake Tekapo

Homestay Lodge
Address: Lake Tekapo Lodge,
24 Aorangi Crescent, Lake Tekapo
Name: Lake Tekapo Lodge,
John & Lynda
Telephone: (03) 680 6566 / 0800 525 383 Lake Tekapo
Fax: (03) 680 6599   **Mobile**: (025) 332 597   **Email**: lake.tekapo.lodge@xtra.co.nz
Beds: 2 King Zippers, 1 Queen, 2 Single (just in case a group of 6
single were wanting accommodation we can split our King size beds)
Bathroom: 4 Ensuite. 1 With wheelchair acccess, 1 with spa bath.
Tariff: B&B (full) Double $160, Dinner $35 pp. Credit Cards accepted.
Nearest Town: Lake Tekapo - Fairlie 30 minutes by car/bus.

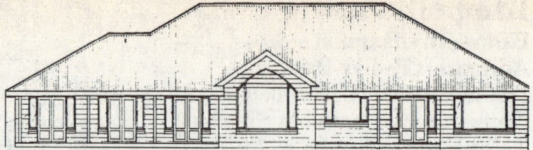

*Lake Tekapo Lodge - purpose built bed and breakfast lodge in the village of Lake Tekapo, across road from restaurants, shops, post shop. Two minutes walk to church of Good Shepherd, lake edge. Beautiful views of mountains and lake from lodge where John and Lynda welcome you. Our adobe earth block home has antique entrance doors, guest dining and entrance clad in earth block with open fire. Separate lounge with gas fire, piano, books, chess set, tea / coffee making facilities, star watch window. Guest laundry. Fishing / hunting guides available. Golf, skiing, horse riding, walking, mountain biking, scenic flights over lakes, mountains (including Mount Cook), glaciers. All available from Lake Tekapo Lodge (built 1998). We have enjoyed home hosting since 1983 and hope you will come and spend some time with us in the beautiful area of Lake Tekapo as you travel from Christchurch to Queenstown on SH 8. **Directions**: Turn into Aorangi Crescent opposite Lake Tekapo Tavern, off Highway 8. Follow to end of Crescent - Lake Tekapo Lodge if on your right - No. 24. **Home Page**: www.laketekapolodge.co.nz*

Lake Tekapo

Self-contained Farmstay
Address: 'Holbrook',
State Hwy 8 between
Burkes Pass & Lake Tekapo.
12km east of Tekapo.
Name: Lesley & Alister France
Telephone: (03) 685 8535
Fax: (03) 685 8534
Mobile: (025) 387 974
Email: lesley@holbrook.co.nz
Beds: 1 Queen, 6 Single (3 bedrooms)
Bathroom: 1 Private
Tariff: (Accommodation only) Double & Single $80 plus $15 per extra person.
Breakfast: Continental $8 pp, Full $12 pp.   NZ B&B Vouchers accepted $25 Surcharge
Nearest Town: Lake Tekapo 12 kms

*Holbrook is part of a high county sheep station of 14,000 hectares (35,000 acres) situated on the main tourist route (State Highway 8) between Burkes Pass and Lake Tekapo. Our cottage is close to our homestead, is fully self contained and is warm, spacious and comfortable. We provide electric blankets, feather duvets, wood for the log fire, telephone, TV, automatic washing machine and everything necessary to make your stay with us an enjoyable experience. You will be most welcome to explore our property and view any activities that are going on during your visit. There is a small lake available for trout fishing near our cottage. We look forward to sharing our way of life with you over breakfast in the homestead and if you make a prior arrangement with us, we would be happy to prepare and share an evening meal with you. **Home Page**: http://www.kiwi-nz.com/*

Lake Tekapo
Bed & Breakfast
Address: 'Creel House',
36 Murray Place, Lake Tekapo
Name: Grant & Rosemary Brown
Telephone: (03) 680 6516 **Fax**: (03) 680 6659
Email: creelhouse.l.tek@xtra.co.nz
Beds: 2 Queen, 2 Single (3 bedrooms)
Bathroom: 2 Private, 1 Ensuite
Tariff: B&B (special) Double/Twin $125-$135, Single $70.
Off season rate $95 double/twin May - September.
Credit cards (Visa/MC/BC). NZ B&B Vouchers accepted $35 surcharge May-Sept
Nearest Town: Fairlie 35 mins, Twizel 45 mins, Mt Cook 75 mins

Your Hosts
Grant &
Rosemary Brown

36 Murray Place
Lake Tekapo
NEW ZEALAND
Ph 03 6806 - 516

Our home built by Grant is three storeyed with expansive balconies and panoramic views of the Southern Alps, Mt John, Lake Tekapo and surrounding mountains. We have two primary school girls, 2 cats and we live on the ground floor, our living quarters thus separate from our guests accommodation. All rooms are spacious and comfortable, with guest lounge and separate guest entrance. A native garden adds an attractive feature. Grant is a flyfishing guide (trout / salmon) inquiries welcome. Lake Tekapo is an ideal place to stay for those day trips to Mt Cook, for fishing, or to rest and relax along your journey and enjoy the local walks and views of our turquoise blue lake, scenic drives or a Scenic Flight. Restaurants in township. No smoking indoors.
Directions: *From SH 8 turn at Greig Street, 100ms east from bridge, follow road round to top of hill and turn right. 200ms on left, signposted.*
Home Page: http://www.friars.co.nz/hosts/creel.html

Lake Tekapo
Bed & Breakfast
Address: 'Freda Du Faur House',
1 Esther Hope St, Lake Tekapo
Name: Dawn and Barry Clark
Telephone: (03) 680 6513
Beds: 1 Queen, 1 Double,
2 Single (3 bdrms)
Bathroom: 1 Guest share
Tariff: B&B (Continental)
Double $90, Single $60.
Credit Cards accepted, Full breakfast extra $9.
NZ B&B Vouchers accepted $25 surcharge
Nearest Town: Timaru

SOUTH CANT'
NORTH OTAGO

Experience tranquillity and a touch of mountain magic at Lake Tekapo. You can be sure of a warm and friendly welcome. Our comfortable home has lovely mountain and lake views. Guests admire the rimu panelling, heart timber furniture and attractive decor that blends with the Mackenzie Country. Guest bedrooms, bathroom and separate toilet are in a private wing - all the rooms overlooking the garden with two opening onto the terrace. Relax with tea / coffee on the patio surrounded by roses or enjoy the ever changing panorama from the lounge. Guests are most welcome to swim in our private pool. Several walkways are nearby and Mount Cook is just over an hours scenic drive away. (Smoke-free).We have views of nearest ski field from our bay windows. Our cat "Missy" welcomes all our guests. 5 min walk to shops and restaurants. **Directions**: *From SH8 turn into Lakeview Heights and follow the green B&B sign into Barbara Hay Street. At the end of this street turn right to see our Freda Du Faur sign.*

Lake Tekapo

B&B/Homestay
Address: "Charford House",
14 Murray Place,
 Lakeview Heights, Lake Tekapo
Name: Lorraine & Winston Swan
Telephone: (03) 680 6888
Fax: (03) 680 6888
Beds: 1 Queen, 1 Double,
3 Single (3 bedrooms)
Bathroom: 2 Private, 1 Guests share
Tariff: B&B (continental) Queen $110, Double $90-$100, Single $90-$100. Credit Cards (VISA/MC). Not suitable for children.
Nearest Town: Fairlie 40 km E, Twizel 56 km W

Relax in the peace and tranquillity at Charford House, and enjoy the magnificent views of the mountains, lake and the Church of the Good Shepherd. From the ground floor bedrooms you step out onto a patio where the views are spectacular, and can enjoy Alfresco dining. The large upstairs Queen room has a private bathroom, TV and tea-making. You look down on the river and Mt John. Breakfast is served with views of our flower garden. We enjoy meeting people and like to make visitors welcome, a Home away from Home atmosphere. We have 2 family cats, and a smokefree environment. You can park your car on site and take in many of our walks, or go into the village, shops and restaurants. Charford House is not suitable for children. We have a large lounge where guests can watch TV or take in the views.
Directions: *Turn from SH8, 100 m east of bridge into Lakeview Heights, follow road up hill, turn first right into Scott Street, then left into Murray Place, signposted on right side of street.*

Lake Pukaki/Mt Cook

Homestay
Address: 'Rhoborough Downs', Lake Pukaki, P.B. Fairlie
Name: Roberta Preston
Telephone: (03) 435 0509
Free phone: (0800) 420 007
Fax: (03) 435 0509
Email: mtdb@mtcook.org.nz
Beds: 1 Double, 3 Single (3 bedrooms)
Bathroom: 1 guests share, with bath, 2 toilets.
Tariff: B&B (full) Double $90, Single $50, Dinner $25pp
Nearest Town: Twizel 10 minute drive

A wonderful quiet place to stop a night or two approximately halfway between Christchurch and Queenstown.
It is a 40 minute drive to Mt Cook National Park and Church of the good Shepherd Lake Tekapo.
The 18,000 acre property has been in our family since 1919 where merino sheep graze the high mountains to 6000 feet. We also have a cat and a dog. Wonderful views of the southern sky.
The homestead is set in quiet, tranquil surroundings. Roberta is a Kiwi Host. Dinner can be served by prior arrangement. Afternnon tea and drinks served on the veranda. Twizel is 10 minutes away has a bank, doctor, hairdresser, shops etc, golf tennis and several restaurants. Smoking not permitted in lounge or bedrooms.
Directions: *Please phone a day before or preferably earlier as bookings are necessary.*
Home Page: http://www.mtcook.org.nz

Lake Pukaki / Mount Cook
Farmstay
Address: 'Tasman Downs Station',
Lake Tekapo
Name: Linda, Bruce & Ian Hayman
Telephone: (03) 680 6841
Fax: (03) 680 6851
Beds: 1 Double, 2 Single
(2 bedrooms)
Bathroom: 1 Private,
1 Family share
Tariff: B&B (full) Double $100,
Single $60, Dinner $30.
Nearest Town: Lake Tekapo 27kms.

"A place of unsurpassed beauty" Perfectly located on the shores of Lake Pukaki, behind which are magnificent views of Mount Cook and the Southern Alps. Our modern, local stone home, blends in with the natural surrounds. We have a 9-hole mini golf course, and peaceful surrounds to relax in. Your host, who is an ex RAF Pilot, and whose family have farmed this property since 1914, has rich pioneering, and surprisingly wide experiences. This high-country farm runs mainly cattle with crops grown for self-sufficiency. Informative farm tours are available by arrangement. This is your great opportunity to experience true New Zealand farm life, with friendly hosts and good natured pets Charles the Corgi and Tom Kitten.

Twizel/Mt Cook
Homestay
Address: "Aoraki Lodge",
32 Mackenzie Drive, Twizel
Name: Kerry & Steve Carey
Telephone: (03) 435 0300
Fax: (03) 435 0305
Email: aorakilodge@xtra.co.nz
Beds: 1 Queen, 2 Double,
4 Single (4 bedrooms)
Bathroom: 4 Ensuite, 1 Family share
Tariff: B&B (Full) Double $110-$130,
Single $70, Dinner $30, Credit Card (VISA).
NZ B&B Vouchers accepted $20 surcharge
Nearest Town: Twizel - 2 min walk to Twizel Village

Haere Mai Ki Aoraki (Welcome to Mt Cook / Mackenzie Country).
If you prefer a casual informal atmosphere with friendly genuine "Kiwi" hosts then Aoraki Lodge is the place for you. Relax in our warm, sunny home at the end of your day, and enjoy our private garden.
Kerry is of Maori descent and would love to share with you her knowledge of Maori culture and history. Steve is a flyfishing guide and can offer helpful advice and information on all the attractions and activities in the area. Breakfast time (Kerry's homemade goodies) is flexible and a great time to talk over travel plans and arrangements. Dinner is available with prior notice or there are a variety of excellent restaurants within easy walking distance.
Directions: *Turn left Twizel Service Station, travel 200 metres, look for Aoraki Lodge sign on your left.*

Twizel/Mt Cook

Bed and Breakfast
Address: 33 North West Arch,Twizel
Name: Artemis Bed and Breakfast
Telephone: (03) 435 0388
Fax: (03) 435 0377
Mobile: (021) 211 2000
Email: connieh@xtra.co.nz
Beds: 1 Queen, 1 Single (1 Bedroom)
Bathroom: 1 Private
Tariff: B&B (Continental) Double $90,
Single $60, Children $30.
Nearest Town: Twizel

Welcome to the awe inspiring Mackenzie Country. Relax in our friendly, comfortable home. Enjoy mountain views from our green, rose-scented garden. Only 60 kilometres from magnificent Aoraki/Mt Cook and five minutes to cafes, restaurants and bars. Well appointed guest room sleeps three and has a separate, private bathroom (shower and bath) and toilet. No smoking in our home please.
Tranquillity, privacy and a friendly welcome are assured from your host, Connie, her 10 year old son and two cats.
Directions: *From State Highway 8 at Twizel bridge, turn onto Glen Lyon Road, then 2 km to North West Arch on left, then 2 km to Artemis Bed and Breakfast on left.*

Twizel

Homestay, Self Contained Accommodation, Small Conference Centre
Address: "Lake View", Lake Pukaki,
Private Bag, Fairlie
Name: Rusty and Wendy Houston
Telephone: (03) 435 0567
Fax: (03) 435 0568
Mobile: (025) 238 5334
Beds: 4 Queen, 4 Single (6 Bedrooms)
Bathroom: 1 Guests share, 1 Family share
Tariff: B&B (Full) Double $90-$125,
Single $65, Dinner $25 pp.
Nearest Town: Twizel 10 mins drive. 40 km to Mt Cook SH80.

Come and enjoy yourself in he deep heart of the MacKenzie Country, the peace and privacy of Lake View Homestay overlooking Lake Pukaki, with a magnificent view of Mt Cook ant the Southern Alps.
We are a two hour drive to Queenstown via Arrowtown and 40 minutes to Mt cook. Your visit to this part of New Zealand gives you endless opportunities.
Relax in our humble abode or by the pool away from the hustle and bustle of city life.
Directions: *Sign posted Turn off SH.8 onto SH.80. Mt Cook. Glentanners Rd approx 3km on right hand side.*

Twizel

Homestay
Address: 19 North West Arch, Twizel
Name: Heartland Lodge
Telephone: (03) 435 0008 or **Bus**: (03) 435 0386
Fax: (03) 435 0387 **Mobile**: (025) 927 778
Email: european@xtra.co.nz
Beds: 2 King Zipper (2 Bedrooms)
Bathroom: 2 Ensuites
Tariff: B&B (Full) Double $120, Single $80, Dinner $35 with wine. Credit cards.
Nearest Town: Twizel - 15 mins walk

Welcome to our new, large, comfortable, purpose-built homestay lodge in the heart of the beautiful and awesome Mackenzie Country. We are only 45 mins from Mt Cook National Park, in the midst of spectacular turquoise lakes, rivers and canals. Fishing and hunting are major activities around Twizel and we can arrange guides to help you snare your choice of game. Pre-booking is essential.

Our aim is to make your stay with us as comfortable and relaxed as possible. Our upstairs smoke-free guest rooms offer beautiful views of the Southern Alps and are luxuriously appointed with king-zipper beds, electric blankets, feather duvets, ensuites with spa baths and hair driers. Adjacent ironing room has tea / coffee making facilities or join us for tea / coffee and home baking. Complimentary laundry.

Downstairs our home is heated with a cosy wood cooker in the kitchen and wood fire in the living room. Our black Labrador, Megan, will also extend a warm welcome. Guests are invited to join us for a complimentary pre-dinner drink before sharing a delicious 3 course dinner complemented by New Zealand wine (by prior arrangement) or dining at one of several nearby restaurants. A scrumptious breakfast is served at your convenience in either the dining room or out on the sunny patio.

Sightseeing, horse-trekking and farm visits can be arranged and other local activities include skiing, boating, tramping and golf.

"The Loft" - we also have a large self-contained loft above our garage which can sleep up to 6 people - more if necessary. Own kitchen facilities, shower, toilet, laundry and wood fire to keep you warm and cosy in winter. Available for short or long term stays. Minimum charge $60 or $15 per person.

Directions: *From State Highway 8, (north of Twizel at Bridge) turn into Glen Lyon Rd, then 2 km to North West Arch on left, then approx 2 km to Heartland Lodge on left.*

Omarama/Lindis Pass

Farmstay+Self-contained Accom.
Address: Dunstan Downs,
Omarama
Name: Tim & Geva Innes
Telephone: (03) 438 9862
Fax: (03) 438 9517
Mobile: (025) 353 211
Email: tim.innes@xtra.co.nz.
Beds: 1 Queen, 5 Single (3 bedrooms)
Bathroom: 1 Ensuite, 1 Guests share, 1 Family share
Tariff: B&B (full) Double $90, Single $45,
Budget $12 Single, Children 1/2 price, Dinner $35 wine served,
Campervans $25, Credit Cards. NZ B&B Vouchers accepted Surcharge $15
Nearest Town: Omarama: Dunstan Downs is 17 km west of Omarama on State
Highwy 8.

*Dunstan Downs is a Merino sheep, cattle and deer station in the heart of the South Island high
country. We have two adult children seldom home. Our home is full of country warmth and
you are welcome to join us for dinner (wine served) or bed and breakfast. The Ahuriri River
is at our back door, fishing guides can be arranged. The Ahuriri Valley and surrounding
mountains and valleys are an adventure playground: tramping, mountain biking, kayaking
(bring your own), and of course farming activities, or maybe just lazing around soaking up
the peace and tranquillity. If you would like to fend for youselves we have Budget Accommodation available: self-contained: - 9 singles and 1 double in 5 rooms with kitchen and
bathroom / laundry facilities.*

Omarama

Country Homestay
Address: 'The Briars',
Ahuriri Heights,
Omarama, SH8
Name: Marylou & Don Blue
Telephone: (03) 438 9615
Fax: (03) 438 9655
Email: info@mtcook.org.nz
Beds: 1 queen, 2 single (2 Bedrooms)
Bathroom: 1 Guests share
Tariff: B&B (continental) Double $75, Single $40. NZ B&B Vouchers accepted
Nearest Town: 2km north of Omarama on State Highway 8

A perfect mountain location to overnight in the Mount Cook area.
*"The Briars", a comfortable drive to Mt Cook, is approximately halfway between
Christchurch and Queenstown. This quality homestay is also on the main turn off to
Dunedin and overlooks two important fishing rivers. The Ahuriri River and the
Omarama Stream. "Great Fishing". Marylou and Don graciously welcome guests to
their charming hilltop home created with lovely antiques, paintings, embroideries and
impressive porcelain collection. Beautiful formal country gardens blend into the
countryside. The attractive guests quarters are on a separate level where the bedrooms
have electric blankets and heaters. Tea making facilities available. Return from your
evening meal, at one of Omarama's quality restaurants, in time to share supper with
your congenial hosts. Next morning enjoy an elegantly served breakfast while viewing
unsurpassed panoramic mountain landscapes. Phone or just arrive.*
Home Page: http://mtcook.org.nz/briars

Omarama
Farmstay
Address: 'Omarama Station',
Omarama, North Otago
Name: Beth & Dick Wardell
Telephone: (03) 438 9821
Fax: (03) 438 9822
Email: subtil@voyager.co.nz
Beds: 2 Queen, 2 Single
(3 bedrooms)
Bathroom: 1 Ensuite, 1 Guest share
Tariff: B&B (full) Double $90, Single $55,
Dinner $30. NZ B&B Vouchers accepted $20 surcharge.
Nearest Town: Omarama 1km

Experience a stay on a busy high country sheep station. Omarama Station is a merino sheep and beef cattle property adjacent to the Omarama township. The 100 year old homestead is nestled in a small valley in a tranquil parklike setting of willows, poplars and a fast flowing stream (good fly fishing), pleasant walking environs, an interesting historical perspective to the high country as this was the original station in the area. Swimming pool and a pleasant garden. An opportunity to experience day to day farming activities. We have travelled extensively overseas and enjoy meeting and entertaining our guests. Dinner by arrangement. Please phone in advance.

Omarama
Rural Homestay.
Address: "Glenburn Park", SH 83,
Lake Benmore, Omarama
Name: Alan & Marie Campbell
Telephone: (03) 438 9624
Fax: (03) 438 9624
Email: glenburn.park@xtra.co.nz
Beds: 1 Queen, 2 Single (2 bedrooms)
Bathroom: 1 PRIVATE
Tariff: B&B (full) Double $70, Single $40, Dinner $30, Campervans $10 per person, Self-contained Accom. from $15 per person, Credit Cards (VISA/MC).
Nearest Town: Omarama 7km

GLENBURN PARK
FLY FISHING and ACCOMMODATION

Glenburn is a "retired" high country sheep station now specializing in friendly rural accommodation. In addition to the homestead, with its open fires and sleep-maker mattresses, there is also the choice of 3 tourist flats, an ensuite cabin and special campervan facilities with private ablutions.
*We are situated at the head of Lake Benmore, home to swans, geese, ducks etc and only 1/2 hours walk to the world renown Ahuriri River giving us a brilliant fishing location. Try your hand at tying your own trout fly or cast to a cruising brown trout only 50 metres from the homestead. Your host is a registered member of the NZ Professional Fishing Guides Association. Fishing tackle is available including personally tied flies. Other activities include hill or lakeshore walks, and the French game of petanque. Our interests also include gardening, boating and golf. Fluent French spoken. Please book in advance to avoid disappointment. No smoking please. Discount for 2 or more nights. **Directions**: 7km east of Omarama on SH83. We will be happy to collect you if you are travelling by bus*
Home Page: http://www.griffler.co.nz/glenburn

Makikihi - Waimate
Farmstay
Address: 'Alford Farm',
Lower Hook Road,
Waimate R.D.8
Name: June & Ken McAuley
Telephone: (03) 689 5778
Fax: (03) 689 5779
Beds: 1 Double, 2 Single (2 bedrooms)
Bathroom: 1 Family share
Tariff: B&B (Continental) Double $70,
Single $50, Dinner $20, Campervans $10 pp.
Credit cards. NZ B&B Vouchers accepted
Nearest Town: Makikihi 6km, Timaru 35km, Oamaru 50km

Welcome to 'Alford Farm' Conveniently situated approximately halfway between Christchurch and Dunedin, 2km from SH1. Your hosts offer warm Kiwi hospitality, comfortable beds with electric blankets, delicious meals and relaxed atmosphere in smoke free home. Our modern home is situated in a peaceful / sheltered garden with a variety of roses, trees, and birds with views of farm and hills. If time permits enjoy a complementary farm tour and see our farm dog performing. No household pets.
We raise deer and cattle and run a few sheep at times. Visitors are welcome to view or join farm activities. Our interests are American Square Dancing, gardening and farm related activities. Our family have flown the nest. Please feel free to call in. Often we are outside and don't hear the phone.
Directions: *4km south of Makikihi turn inland into Lower Hook Road. "Alford Farm" is 2nd on right (2km).*

Waimate
Farmstay B&B
Address: "The Hills",
Hodges Road, RD 7,
Waimate, South Canterbury
Name: Daphne and Fred
Telephone: (03) 689 8747
Email: Bookings@nzfarmstays.com
Beds: 2 Queen, 1 Single (3 bedrooms)
Bathroom: 1 Private, 1 Family share
Tariff: B&B (Full/Continental) $40 per person.
Dinner $20, Children $15. Credit Cards NZ B&B Vouchers accepted
Nearest Town: Waimate 2 minutes. Timaru 46 km, Oamaru 46 km

A warm welcome awaits the tired traveller to our renovated character homestead tucked away on the foothills overlooking Waimate on 31 acres. Whether you want to participate in the feeding of the farm animals or just lay back and listen to Fred's tales of Goldmining on the West Coast, your Hosts will ensure your stay is a memorable one. With comfortable beds, electric blankets, excellent home cooked meals, tea, coffee available anytime you will enjoy the relaxed atmosphere in a mature garden setting. We share our surroundings with Bellbirds, Calves, Lambs, Ostriches, Emus and an old farm dog. We also have a Cattery on the property. Local activities include, golf, fishing, walks, country club and lakes 1 hour drive. E-Mail, laundry facilities available. Smoking allowed (not in bedrooms). Can meet bus (Waimate). It's worth the 8km drive off SH1.
Directions: *Halfway between Timaru and Oamaru go 8km inland to Waimate, down Queen Street, past gardens, through ford, right into Hodges Road, first driveway on left.*
Home page: http://nzfarmstays.com

Kurow – Oamaru

Farmstay+Self-contained Accom.
Address: 'Glenmac', 7K R.D., Oamaru
Name: Kaye & Keith Dennison
Telephone: (03) 436 0200
Fax: (03) 436 0202
Mobile: 025 222 1119
Email: glenmac@xtra.co.nz
Beds: 1 Queen, 1 Double,
4 Single (4 bedrooms)
Bathroom: 1 Family share
Tariff: B&B (full) Double $70, Single $35, Children under 13 half price, Dinner
$20, Campervans $15 (2 people). Credit cards.
NZ B&B Vouchers accepted $10 surcharge
Nearest Town: Oamaru 60 km East, Kurow 13 km West

Welcome to Glenmac Farm - the perfect place for those wanting to get away from traffic noises,
enjoy delicious home cooked meals, have a comfortable bed and relax and be treated as one
of the family. Our 4000 acre high country farm has merino sheep and beef cattle. On farm
activities are horse riding, a four wheel drive farm trip, walking/tramping or daily farm
activities which are seasonal. Nearby are trout and salmon fishing rivers (guide available)
and a nine hole golf course. Also available - comfortable Budget accommodation - self
contained, sleeps 9 - specially suitable for families and backpackers. $15 per person (includes
linen). Meals available by arrangement. Please feel free to call in. We are not always near
the phone. **Directions**: *We are 5km off Highway 83 which is a direct link to and from Mt*
Cook. Situated at end of Gards Road which is 4th road on right after Kurow or 4th road on
left after Duntroon. **Home Page**: http://www.nzcentre.co.nz/glenmac/

Oamaru

Homestay
Address: 'Wallfield',
126 Reservoir Road, Oamaru
Name: Pat and Bill Bews
Telephone: (03) 437 0368
Mobile: (025) 284 7303
Beds: 1 Queen,
2 single (2 bedrooms)
Bathroom: 1 Guests share
Tariff: B&B (continental) Double $60,
Single $35. NZ B&B Vouchers accepted
Nearest Town: 5 mins to town.

Our modern home is situated high above the North end of Oamaru with superb views
to the east and the mountains in the west. We have four children, all happily married,
and an ever increasing number of grand children. We have been home hosting for the
last eight years and although recently retired from farming, still enjoy the buzz of
meeting new friends. Our interests include gardening and tramping.

Oamaru

Rural Homestay
Address: 'Tara', Springhill Road,
3. 0.R.D. Oamaru
Name: Marianne Smith
Telephone: (03) 434 8187
Fax: (03) 434 8187
Email: smith.tara@xtra.co.nz
Beds: 2 Single (1 Bedroom)
Bathroom: 1 Private
Tariff: B&B (full) Double $80, Single $50,
Dinner $25 by arrangement. Credit Cards
Nearest Town: Oamaru - 8 minutes away

Want to be pampered? "Tara" is the place for you. Enjoy the comfort and luxuries of our character Oamaru stone home. "Tara" boasts all day sun and the privacy to soak up the country atmosphere. Nestled amongst six acres of roses, mature trees and rural farmland, "Tara" is the perfect place to unwind. Our livestock include Alpacas, coloured sheep, donkeys and an aviary. We also have a Burmese cat and a Lassie collie. My husband Baxter and I will ensure your visit is an enjoyable experience.
Directions: *Turn off SH1 at Oamaru southern boundary drive to Weston. Turn left at supermarket into Weston Ngapara Road. Take first left into Kia Ora Road. Second left is Springhill Road, Tara 50 yds up Springhill Road on right.*

Oamaru

Homestay
Address: 11 Stour St,
South Hill, Oamaru
Name: Jenny & Gerald
Telephone: (03) 434 9628
Beds: 1 Double, 2 Single
(2 bedrooms)
Bathroom: 1 Private, 1 Family share
Tariff: B&B (continental) Double $90,
Single $65. Dinner $25pp.
NZ B&B Vouchers accepted $10 surcharge
Nearest Town: Oamaru

We have a charming, two storey, character home surrounded by gardens and easily located in a quiet street near the main highway. Our guest bedrooms are attractive and well appointed. Tea or coffee is available on arrival. Dinner - by arrangement if required - is a leisurely meal with New Zealand wine, preceded by drinks beside the fire. We are a middle-aged couple who have travelled, and enjoy meeting people, especially visitors to New Zealand . We share our home with one rather timid family cat.
Oamaru has many fine, stone, Victorian buildings and we are involved with the Historic Precinct and the Victorian Town at Work Programme. Our many interests include gardening and the vintage car club. Time permitting, you might enjoy one of Oamaru's many lovely walks, the attractive public gardens, or a visit to our art gallery, museum or penguin colony. A warm welcome awaits you. Non smokers preferred.
Directions: *Phone first if possible, and use front gate - not driveway please.*

Waianakarua, Oamaru

Homestay
Address: Glen Foulis,
39 Middle Ridge Road,
Waianakarua Postal:
O.R.D. 9, Oamaru 8921
Name: John & Margaret Munro
Telephone: (03) 439 5559
Fax: (03) 439 5220
Mobile: (021) 940 777
Email: hjm@clear.net.nz
Beds: 1 King or 4 Single (2 bedrooms).
Bathroom: 1 Guests share, 1 Family share.
Tariff: B&B (full) Double $80, Single $50, Children half price, Dinner $25,
Children $25. Credit Cards. Campervans $25 up to 4 people. Vouchers accepted
Nearest Town: 20 mins south Oamaru, 1 hour north Dunedin

Glen Foulis, a modern, well heated home accented by efficient open fireplaces, elegantly styled with Oamaru Stone, surrounded by acres of green lawns, tall beech, birch, weeping willows, maples. Beautiful vistas, up to the huge Herbert Forest, over bushy glades, looking down a unique river valley. Two wisteria and rose-clad terraces catch the sun and view. The song of native birds, only metres away. If you plan more than one night here, we can show you the hidden treasures of North Otago from our tough but comfortable 4 wheel drive. Margaret enjoys cooking with enough notice and a 5 star restaurant is minutes away in a picturesque, restored Mill House by the river. We both enjoy working at Energy related businesses here. Our two outdoor, well-trained Golden Retrievers are always very friendly, as is our matching ginger pussycat. Larger parties welcome, together with Glen Dendron on the opposite hill.
Directions: *Please phone for directions.*

Oamaru

Homestay
Address: Innwoodleigh,
39 Forth Street,
Oamaru, North Otago
Name: Howard Bradley
Telephone: (03) 437 0829
Fax: (03) 437 0829
Beds: 1 Double, 2 Single
(2 bedrooms)
Bathroom: 1 Private
Tariff: B&B (continental) $55 pp.
Nearest Town: In Oamaru township - in Borough

A unique private Pole House nestled into the side of a hill with panoramic views of the town and ocean. Allow yourself the luxury of star gazing at night and a spectacular sun rise in the morning on your own exclusive private level that accommodates up to 4 people. Bookings essential. Catering for Honeymooners - Business Executives - Independent Free Travellers . I specialise in Charter Deep Sea Fishing on my own boat the 'Dolphin'. Local interests are: Penguin Viewing, Whitestone Buildings.
Directions: *North of the town off SHW1 - highlighted by Blue B&B sign. Top of street left hand side.*

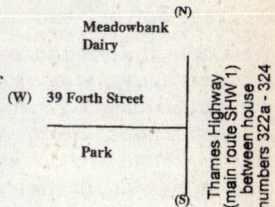

(N)

Meadowbank
Dairy

(W) 39 Forth Street

Park

Thames Highway
(main route SHW1)
between house
numbers 322a - 324

(S)

Herbert - Oamaru

Farmstay
Address: Herbert,
12.O.R.D. Oamaru
Name: Dorothy & Duncan McKenzie
Telephone: (03) 439 5614
Fax: (03) 4395814
Beds: 1 Double, 3 Single (3 bedrooms)
Bathroom: 1 Guests share
Tariff: B&B (full) Double $70,
Single $40, Dinner $25, light meal $15.
Children half price. No pets. Credit cards. NZ B&B Vouchers accepted
Nearest Town: Oamaru 20km north of Herbert Township

We are a semi-retired couple living on a small sheep and cattle farm set in a beautiful area of rolling downland between SH 1 and the Pacific Ocean.
We have been involved in home hosting for the past 18 years and enjoy meeting guests from all parts of the world. Our large retirement house set in one acre of garden was built with home hosting in mind. We are close to rivers, beaches and bush walks with the Moeraki Boulders the chief local attraction. Both yellow-eyed and little blue penguins may be seen at Moeraki or Oamaru. Oamaru, our nearest shopping centre, is famous for its early white stone buildings. The Oamaru stone quarries may be visited. Evening meal by arrangement; cooked breakfast.
Directions: *Please phone.*

Waianakarua-Oamaru

Farmstay
Address: "Glen Dendron",
284 Breakneck Road,
Waianakarua
Name: Anne & John Mackay
Telephone: (03) 439 5288
Fax: (03) 439 5288
Mobile: 021-615 287
Email: anne.john.mackay@xtra.co.nz
Beds: 1 Queen, 4 Single (3 bedrooms).
Larger groups catered for in combination with 'Glen Foulis'
Bathroom: 2 Guests share
Tariff: B&B (full) Double $80, Single $50, Children $25, Dinner $25. Credit cards. NZ B&B Vouchers accepted
Nearest Town: 30km south of Oamaru, 95km north of Dunedin.

We look forward to sharing our recently completed, spacious home with you. It is ideally suited for homestay comfort with sunny, warm, stylish facilities, panoramic views of our developing garden, the Waianakarua river and the sea. Enjoy our riverside walks, native bush, waterfalls and native birds. Nearby are the famous Moeraki Boulders, seal and penguin colonies, beaches, fishing, forest walks in the neighbouring Herbert forest, and the historic whitestone buildings of Oamaru. We can plan customised day tours of the area's many attractions and arrange access to a private family golf course. Recently retired to this small sheep farm we can share our lifetime knowledge of farming and forestry. Enthusiastic gardeners with our own nursery we enjoy reading and overseas travel. Anne is a floral designer. Arrange to join us for dinner. Do allow time to enjoy this tranquil area with caring hosts - we don't mind short notice! **Directions**: *3km off Highway One. Phone for directions.*

http://www.bnb.co.nz

take a look

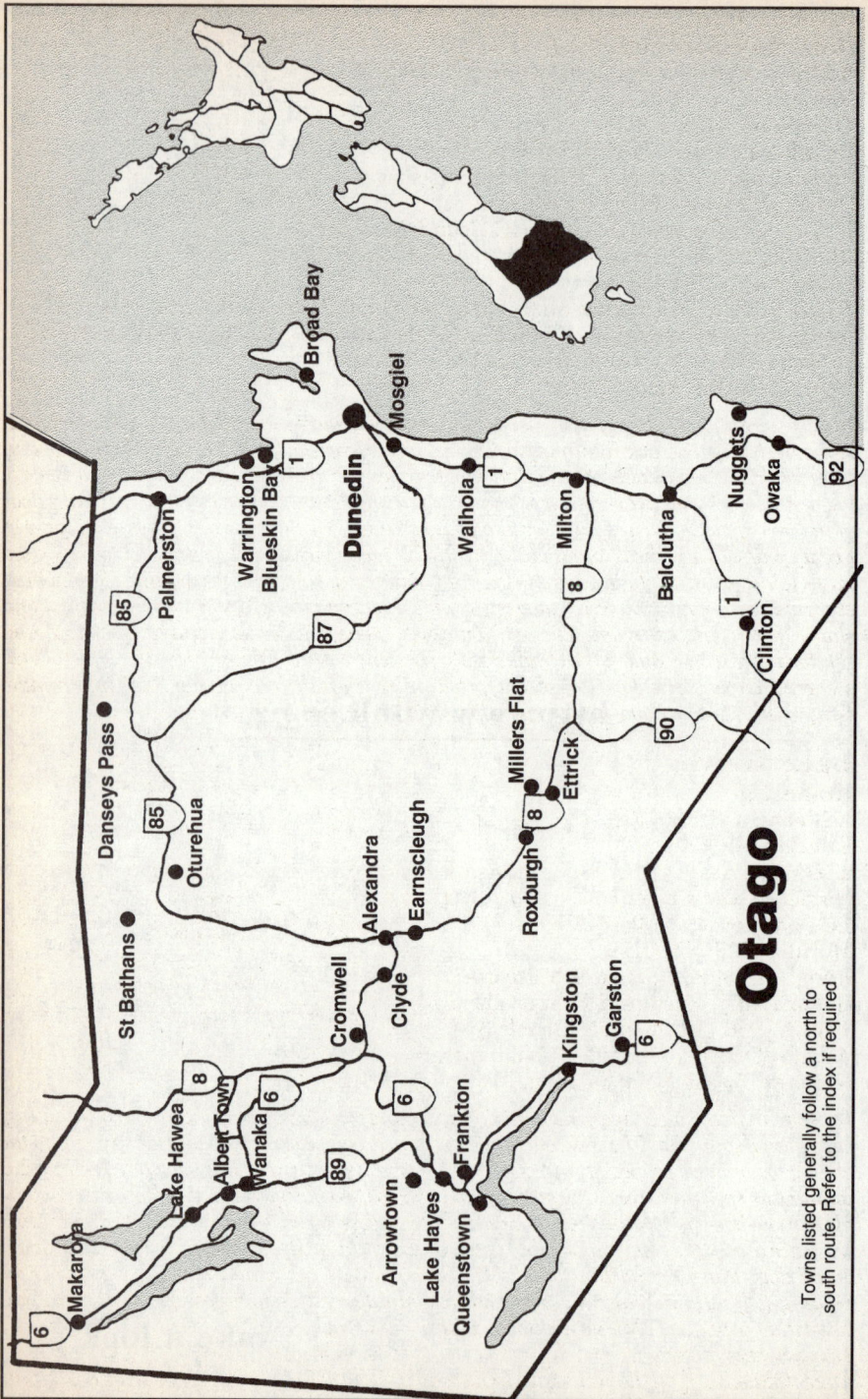

Otago

Broad Bay
Mosgiel
Warrington
Blueskin Bay
Dunedin
Palmerston
Waihola
Milton
Balclutha
Nuggets
Owaka
Clinton

Danseys Pass
Oturehua
Millers Flat
Ettrick
St Bathans
Alexandra
Earnscleugh
Roxburgh

Cromwell
Clyde
Kingston
Garston

Makarora
Lake Hawea
Albert Town
Wanaka
Arrowtown
Lake Hayes
Frankton
Queenstown

Towns listed generally follow a north to
south route. Refer to the index if required

Makarora

Homestay+Self-contained Accomm
Address: Makarora, via Wanaka (State Highway 6)
Name: Larrivee Homestay
Telephone: (03) 443 9177
Email: andrea_larrivee@hotmail.com
Beds: Homestay: 2 Double, 1 Single (2 bedrooms).
Cottage: 1 Double, 2 Single (2 bedrooms)
+ 2 Divans and double fold out couch in lounge if needed.
Bathroom: Homestay: ensuite, guests share if second
bedroom used. Cottage: private
Tariff: B&B (full) Homestay: $100 Couple, $70 Single. Dinner $30. Cottage $90 for 2
people, $20 each extra adult. Children under 12 half price. Breakfast and dinner
available. NZ B&B Vouchers accepted $30 surcharge
Nearest Town: Wanaka 65km

Nestled in native bush, my home is secluded. Only a short walk down the drive are a Mt Aspiring National Park Information Centre and a tearooms/shop where jet boating and scenic flights are available. A ten minute walk takes you to the Makarora River and some of the best trout fishing in the country. Two walks in the National Park begin out my back door with others nearby. Originally from the United States, We have lived in Makarora for over twenty years. Our home is a unique, two storied octagon built mostly with local and recycled materials. The upper storey contains the open living area with mountain and bush views out every window making it a bird watcher's delight. The guest rooms are on the ground floor and share their own bathroom. The self-contained stone and cedar cottage is quaint and comfortable. Come and enjoy Makarora's relaxed, casual atmosphere and spectacular scenery. **Directions**: *Last house on a private drive next to the National Park Information Centre. Please telephone in advance, if possible.*

Lake Hawea

Homestay
Address: 4 Bodkin Street,
Lake Hawea, Otago
2RD Wanaka
Name: Sylvan Chalet
Telephone: (03) 443 1343
Mobile: (025) 224 9192
Beds: 1 Double, 2 Single (2 bedrooms)
Bathroom: 1 Ensuite, 1 Family share
Tariff: B&B (continental) Double $70,
Single $38, Children under 12 half price.
Nearest Town: Wanaka 15km

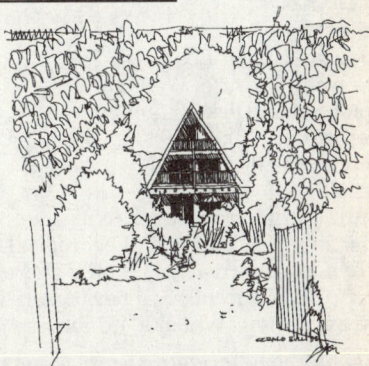

I am a retired teacher actively involved in craft dyeing of silks. My other interests are tramping, skiing and spinning. I have frequently entertained overseas visitors and always enjoy the chance to meet new people. My three-storied A frame is set in an extensive sheltered compound with many specimen trees. One guest room opens onto a balcony with a mountain view; the other room has a mountain view and an ensuite. Access to both via a circular staircase. Over the fence are tennis courts, a bowling green and a children's playground. I have a cat and a small dog. Washing machine available. Lake Hawea - two minutes walk - is popular for boating, fishing and swimming. Wanaka - ten minutes drive - offers good food, shopping and adventure activities. Three skifields are within easy reach.
Non-smokers preferred.

Directions: *Turn off the Wanaka - Haast road at Hawea Dam. Drive up past the hotel to the store and you will see 'the A-frame through the Archway'.*

Lake Hawea

HILLKIRK HOUSE

Homestay
Address: 117 Noema Terrace,
Lake Hawea, Central Otago
Name: Mike & Doreen Allen
at Hillkirk House
Telephone: (03) 443 1655
Fax: (03) 443 1655
Beds: 1 King, 4 Single (2 bedrooms)
Bathroom: 1 Ensuite, 1 Family share
Tariff: B&B (full) Ensuite $85, Double $80,
Single $50, Children under 12yrs half price, Dinner by arrangement $25.
NZ B&B Vouchers accepted Surcharge: Dble $15, ensuite $20.
Nearest Town: Wanaka 15km

We are a congenial retired English couple, well travelled and actively involved in outdoor pursuits, who enjoy sharing our home and lifestyle. Our main interests are fly fishing, tramping and skiing, but the immediate area offers most outdoor sports imaginable. We happily share our local knowledge and contacts to help guests maximise this potential. Strategically located at the eastern foot of Haast Pass, within easy reach of Mt. Aspiring National Park and local ski fields, our comfortable modern Ridgecrest home offers impressive mountain views. A pleasant sundeck overlooks secluded garden. Lakeshore, 5 minutes stroll. Doreen boasts,"last all day breakfasts" - fresh fruit and percolated coffee - with dinner and lunch by arrangement, using home produce. 'All inclusive' stays negotiated to individual requirements. Mike regularly hosts famous overseas anglers. Quality hire gear, books, videos and fly tying facilities 'in house'. One twin (or king) with ensuite. Second bathroom, separate toilet and shower. **Directions**: *Over Hawea Dam up past hotel, on past store, first right, first left, sign on right before bend.*

Wanaka

Homestay
Address: Rippon Lea B&B,
15 Norman Terrace, Wanaka
Name: Sue & Dick Williman
Telephone: (03) 443 9333,
Freephone 0800 169 674
Fax: (03) 443 9343
Email: williman@voyager.co.nz
Beds: 2 Queen, 3 Single (3 bedrooms)
Bathroom: 1 Private, 1 Family share
Tariff: B&B (special) $40 per person, Children $20. NZ B&B Vouchers accepted
Nearest Town: Wanaka 1.5 km

Our family home includes a warm visitors flat with twin and queen bedrooms, living room with colour TV, dinette with tea making facilities. It is particularly suitable for families. Our lavish continental breakfast, served for you to eat at your leisure, has been a point of commendation by many guests. Our home is less than 100m from Lake Wanaka. There is easy access to it and to pleasant lakeside walks through the trees of Wanaka Station Park. We have travelled extensively overseas ourselves and take a special delight in welcoming overseas visitors as well as New Zealanders. Wanaka is a holiday centre with appeal to those who like scenic grandeur. We look forward to advising you on the many fine summer and winter activities. Laundry facilities and garage space available. We request visitors not smoke in our home. Single travellers welcome. **Directions**: *From the town centre follow west around the lake towards Glendhu Bay. Take the second on the right (Sargood Drive) into Rippon Lea. Norman Terrace is the first road on the right. Follow around the dog leg, ours is a back section on the left.* **Home Page**: http://www.voyager.co.nz/~williman/

Wanaka

Homestay
Address: 75 Tenby Street, Wanaka
Name: Betty & Bill Miller
Telephone: (03) 443 7369
Fax: (03) 443 7800
Beds: 1 Double, 2 Single (2 bedrooms)
Bathroom: 1 Private, 1 Family share (Spa Bath)
Tariff: B&B (continental) Double $100, Single $50, Twin $80 NZ B&B Vouchers accepted $30 surcharge Double, $10 Twin
Nearest Town: Wanaka

Our spacious apartment for guests is on the ground floor of our modern 2-level home in Wanaka, close to the town centre, churches, bowling green and Wanaka's beautiful golf course. The apartment has a private entrance, lounge with TV, tea / coffee making facilities in a small kitchen which is also equipped with fridge, crockery and cutlery. You have double bedroom, bathroom and toilet.
Guests in our twin room share hosts' bathroom and toilet.
We are both retired, have travelled extensively and are interested in meeting visitors from both N.Z. and overseas. We can advise about things to do and see around Wanaka including walks, drives, trout fishing, lake cruises and scenic flights and are happy to help our guests organise their leisure time.
As an ex fighter pilot Bill is involved with the NZ Fighter Pilots' Museum, Wanaka. Smoke free. Please phone.

Wanaka

Homestay
Address: Lake Wanaka Homestay, 85 Warren St, Wanaka
Name: Peter & Gailie Cooke
Telephone: 03 443 7995, Freephone 0800 443799
Fax: (03) 443 7945
Beds: 1 Double, 2 Single (2 bedrooms)
Bathroom: 1 Guests share, 1 Family share
Tariff: B&B (full) Double $85, Single $50, Dinner by arrangement, Children negotiable. Vouchers accepted $15 surcharge
Nearest Town: Wanaka, Centre of Wanaka

Relax with us in our warm comfortable home ideally situated in the centre of Wanaka with magnificent views of Lake and surrounding mountains.
Wanaka has an excellent choice of restaurants and shops all within 5 minutes walk of our home. We both enjoy skiing; golf; boating and outdoor activities. Peter - retired farmer - now in Real Estate is a keen fly fisherman - happy to show guests his favourite fishing spots with 'Kim' our frienly Labrador. Guests are welcome to tea or coffee at anytime and enjoy a homemade muffin or biscuit from 'Cookie' Jar. Our comfortable beds all have electric blankets. Hair dryers in bedrooms. We have met so many wonderful people over the years - we assure you of a warm welcome. We are happy to meet public transport. Smoke-free home.
Directions: *Turn left Lakefront into Helwick St., 4 blocks right into Warren St., 2nd block 4th house on right opposite school. FOR RESERVATIONS FREEPHONE 0800 443799*
Home Page: http:www.accommodat@co.nz/bbc/lakewa.htm

Wanaka

Bed & Breakfast Luxury Lodge

Address: Te Wanaka Lodge, 23 Brownston St, Wanaka
Name: Nora, Rowland and Robyn
Telephone: (03) 443 9224 Reservation Freephone: 0800 926252
Fax: (03) 443 9246
Email: tewanakalodge@xtra.co.nz
Beds: 9 Queen, 9 Single (12 bedrooms), plus Self Contained Cottage
Bathroom: All Ensuite
Tariff: B&B (special) Double/Single $115-$160,
Single $105-$120. Credit Cards Visa/Amex..
Nearest Town: Wanaka - centre of town

The unique design and use of local materials and craftsmanship, give Te Wanaka Lodge a contemporary yet warm and welcoming atmosphere. A place to relax in that you'll never forget! Start the day with freshly brewed coffee, home-made croissants, a buffet of cereals and fruits, juice, yoghurt, cold meats and cheeses - the choice is yours. The comfortable guest lounges, tea kitchen and breakfast room are all there for your use, with the added attraction of a collection of international art and artefacts. Nestling close to the heart of Wanaka, the lodge is located within a short walk of restaurants, shops, the beach and golf course.

On a hot summer's day, relax under the walnut tree, enjoy the mountain views from your balcony, or stroll to the lake shore for a swim. Shake off winter's chill by the log fire or wallow in the garden hot tub. Have a chat with your fellow travellers, or write all those overdue postcards. For the safety and comfort of all our guests we provide a non-smoking environment.

Your hosts Rowland and Nora lived and worked in Asia for many years and have travelled world-wide in pursuit of their passion for fly fishing, golf and the great outdoors. They will be more than happy to share their experiences with you, advise on a favourite restaurant, accompany you on a fishing trip, or join you in round of golf. You only have to ask.

If you enjoy adventure and the outdoor life in an unspoiled, pristine environment there is virtually nothing that Wanaka cannot provide. Why choose more commercialised destinations when you can access it all from the convivial and stimulating surroundings of TE WANAKA LODGE.

Parapenting, fishing, jetboating, tramping, skiing, scenic flights to Mount Cook and Milford Sound or just browsing in the shops and galleries; with all that Wanaka has to offer we suggest that you plan on staying for a few days.

Directions: *Turn left at the Caltex Service Station, we are 150 metres down on the right.*
Home Page: www.tewanaka.co.nz

Wanaka

Homestay
Address: Aspiring Images Homestay,
26 Norman Tce, Wanaka
Name: Betty & George Russell
Telephone: (03) 443 8358
Fax: (03) 443 8327
Email: grussell@xtra.co.nz
Beds: 1 King/Twin,
1 Double (2 bedrooms)
Bathroom: 1 Ensuite, 1 Private, 1 Guests share
Tariff: B&B (full) Double $85-$95, Single $50-$65, Children under 12 $25.
Dinner by arrangement $25, Credit cards (VISA/MC). NZ B&B Vouchers
accepted $10-$20 Surcharge
Nearest Town: In Wanaka township.

*Wanaka's beauty is compelling. We have vitality and tranquillity here, scenery grand and
intimate, activities challenging and restful, mountain light ever changing.*
*Our welcome is genuine. We enjoy extensive lake and mountain views, a quiet parkside
location and easy lakeshore access, while the house features the rich restfulness of heart Rimu
timber, sunny rooms and sheltered patios. We'll help with travel plans - we've travelled widely,
been involved in education, played and coached many sports and sung in a lifetime of choirs.
We offer free mountain bikes, and discounts on our photography / 4WD sightseeing ecotours
to encourage understanding of Wanaka's dramatic scenery, diverse ecology, varied history
and distinctive climate. We're less than an hour from Mt Aspiring Park's marvellous walks,
less than an hour from Milford Sound - by awesome flight - and only an hour, but a world
away, from Queenstown. We love Wanaka, and understand why visitors say "We'll be back!"*
Home Page: www.nzhomestay.co.nz/russell.html

Wanaka

Homestay Bed & Breakfast
Address: 'The Cedars',
7 Riverbank Road, Wanaka
Name: Brian & Jessie Anderson
Telephone: (03) 443 7933
Fax: (03) 443 7931
Beds: 1 Queen, 1 Double,
1 Single (2 Bedrooms)
Bathroom: 1 Private, 1 Family share
Tariff: B&B (full) Double $110, Single $80, Children $25, Credit cards. NZ B&B
Vouchers accepted $20 surcharge. No vouchers Jan, Feb and March.
Nearest Town: Wanaka 2 km

*We welcome you to our spacious home with breathtaking mountain views from every
window. We are only two minutes from our tranquil, beautiful town and lake. There
are many restaurants to choose from and a great choice of activities to help you enjoy
your stay. We can guide you with fishing, boating, golfing, warbirds museum,
tramping, 3 ski fields, scenic flights etc.*
*Our property is 12 acres, planted in many varieties of attractive trees, sheep, cattles and
if you care to look over the garden wall, "Moses" and "Zachariah" (two adorable
donkeys) will come and talk to you - especially if you have an apple or carrot to offer!
We have tea and coffee facilities, spa bath, TV in your bedroom, laundry (at a small
cost) and a delicious breakfast to last you all day. And of course "Edgar" our large cat
will help you remember our friendly hospitality. Prior bookings are preferred.*

Wanaka
Country Stay
Address:
'Wanaka Sky Lodge',
Studholme Road.
Name:
Claudia & Ron McAulay
Telephone: (03) 443 9349
Fax: (03) 443 9349
Email: wanaka-sky-lodge@xtra.co.nz
Beds: 3 Queen (3 bedrooms)
Bathroom: 3 Private Ensuites
Tariff: B&B Double $120, Credit Cards. Neg. 3 days or more.
NZ B&B Vouchers accepted to bring it to our charge.
Nearest Town: From Wanaka (Queenstown: 1 hour)

'Welcome' to our farm home. Expansive view of farmland and mountains provide a tranquil setting on 90 acres. Guests are invited to relax in a rural environment yet to be within 3km from Wanaka's township with many tourist and recreational activities - skiing - heli-skiing - fishing - tramping - scenic flight, not to mention the number of cafes and restaurants. Accommodation is spacious and comfortable with own ensuites, large living areas with open fire. Coffee and tea always available. Ron is an airline pilot, hobbies being light aircraft and gliding which is operated of our property. Claudia is a keen gardener and cook, enjoys anything creative along with looking after or should say running after their two sons 14 and 17 years of age. Dutch is spoken. Home away from home!

Wanaka
Homestay
Address: 'Tirohanga',
(House With A View)
102 Lismore Street, Lake Wanaka
Name: Ken & Noeleen McDiarmid
Telephone: (03) 443 8302
Fax: (03) 443 8702
Mobile: (025) 314 066
Beds: 1 King, 2 Single (2 bedrooms)
Bathroom: 2 Ensuites
Tariff: B&B (continental) Double $90, Single $55, Dinner $30. NZ B&B Vouchers accepted $20 surcharge
Nearest Town: Wanaka 400 metres

Without exception our guests acclaim our panoramic view to be the best in Wanaka. This glorious and grand stand action scene from lounge and bedrooms would equal any spectacular mountain vista in New Zealand. Our modern home overlooks the lake and boat harbour, being very central, five minutes walk to Post Office, garages, shops, restaurants, schools and heated swimming pool. We have one double unit and one twin room both with separate ensuites. Ken and Noeleen are semi-retired business people who have travelled widely and enjoy golf, the outdoors, boating, fishing, music and entertaining. It is their wish to help and advise with any requests in order to make your stay a happy and exciting one. We have plenty of on-site parking and we have no animals.
Directions: *Turn up Little Street opposite Post Office, first turn left and continue along Lismore Street to 102, Green letter box opposite pine tree.*

Wanaka
Homestay B&B, Self Contained Unit.
Address: "Gold Ridge", 191 Anderson Road, Wanaka (PO Box 6)
Name: Diana & Dan Pinckney
Telephone: (03) 443 1253
Fax: (03) 443 1254
Mobile: 025 354 847
Beds: 1 Queen, 2 Single (2 bedrooms/unit)
Bathroom: 1 Private
Tariff: B&B (continental) Double $80, Single $45, Dinner $25, Children $20. NZ B&B Vouchers accepted $10 Surcharge
Nearest Town: Wanaka (2 1/2km to 191 Anderson Road)

Our new comfortable spacious home with 10 acres of land is situated on the outskirts of Wanaka. Expansive views of farmland and mountains together with large cottage gardens, trees, lawns and tennis court. Very private and tranquil setting. Some of our many interests include cooking, gardening, flyfishing, boating, forestry, real estate, our children and grandchildren. We enjoy having our guests for dinner and helping them plan their stay. The cottage style unit is spacious, sunny with breathtaking views, log burner, bathroom, TV and microwave. We are very flexible and enjoy the company of guests.
Directions: *On entering Wanaka, 1st right passed the "Maze", Anderson Road. Travel to T section, turn right 600 metres on left, 191 Anderson Road.*

Wanaka

Farmstay+Self-contained Accom.
Address: Maxwell Road,
Mt Barker, R.D. Wanaka
Name: 'Willow Cottage'
Kate & Roy Summers
Telephone: (03) 443 8856
Fax: (03) 443 8856
Mobile: (025) 228 1982
Email: willowcottage@xtra.co.nz
Beds: 1 Double, 2 Single (2 bedrooms)
Bathroom: 1 Private
Tariff: B&B (full) Double $145 (complete cottage) + $40 extra person, Dinner $45.
Nearest Town: Wanaka

Less than 5 minutes drive from Wanaka is our charming 120 year old cob and stone cottage complete with its own old fashioned garden.
Step back in time and relax in the peace and tranquillity of our historic cottage with its stunning mountain views. The completely self contained character filled cottage is furnished with antique furniture and collectibles but has all mod cons including a washing machine and dryer. Join Kate and Roy for breakfast at the homestead or enjoy breakfast at leisure from fresh ingredients provided in the cottage pantry. We offer guests original charm and furnishing, great home cooked breakfasts, fresh flowers, lovely old-fashioned linen, a huge old bath for that luxurious soak and friendly warm hospitality. The historically listed cottage is exclusively yours during your stay.
Nearby an original 1890 Stone Stables houses an Antique and Gift Gallery.
Home Page: http//nz.com/heritage inns/willow cottage

Wanaka

Homestay
Address: 'Becklee',
28 Upton Street, Wanaka
Name: John & Yvonne Gale
Telephone: (03) 443 8908
Freephone: 0800 207 099.
Fax: (03) 443 8908
Email: J&Y.GALE@XTRA.Co.NZ
Beds: 1 Queen, 2 Single (2 bedrooms)
Bathroom: 1 Ensuite, 1 Private
Tariff: B&B (full) Double $100 Single $60. No cost laundry facilities with 2 or more nights stay. NZ B&B Vouchers accepted $30 Surcharge
Nearest Town: In Wanaka township.

We invite you to share with us the comfort of our new and spacious home nestling in the mature trees at the end of a quiet cul-de-sac right in the centre of Wanaka township, with lake and mountain views. Enjoy the privacy of our loft, with ensuite, queen size bed, TV, tea making. Or choose between a spacious queen or twin room with private facilities and garden access. Leave your transport behind as a short stroll takes you to shops, restaurants, golf course and the lake. In the winter, enjoy a large open fire, ski drying facilities. Ski transport can be arranged to pick you up from the door. We have a good knowledge of the many activities offered in the area including fishing, walking, skiing, climbing, rafting, boating. We look forward to entertaining you in our home.FOR RESERVATIONS FREEPHONE 0800 207 099.
Directions: *Entering into Wanaka on SH8, turn left at Caltex service station, turn 3rd left - Helwick Street, turn 1st left - Upton Street, we are at the end.*

Wanaka
Country Home
Address: 'Champagne Heights',
P.O. Box 41, Wanaka
Name: John & Karen Hallum
Telephone: (03) 443 8280
Fax: (03) 443 8281
Mobile: (025) 366 589
Beds: 1 Queen, 2 Single (2 bedrooms)
Bathroom: 2 Private
Tariff: B&B (full) Double $125,
Single $65, Children under 12 half price
Credit cards. NZ B&B Vouchers accepted $30 Surcharge
Nearest Town: Wanaka 3 Kms

Are you looking for amazing Lake and Mountain Views, Warm Luxury accommodation, Peace and Quiet? Welcome to "Champagne Heights". Experience Hospitality at its best!
Our large modern home, set on 10 acres is situated just 3km from Wanaka township, on the road to Mt Aspiring National Park and Treble Cone skifield.
Join our family of four (ex farmers), along with our pet sheep, cows and pony, for an interesting "typical Kiwi" country home stay. Guest bedrooms are warm and spacious, each with magnificent lake and mountain views and opening out onto balconies. Our hobbies and interests include sports, wine tasting and over the last few years home hosting.
Wanaka has much to offer visitors, skiing, tramping, jet boating, fishing, golf and great restaurants. Our family welcomes you to your "Home away from home".
Laundry available. **Directions**: *Please phone.*

Wanaka
Homestay
Address: 95 McDougall St, Wanaka
Name: Harper's
Telephone: (03) 443 8894
Fax: (03) 443 8834
Email: harpers@xtra.co.nz
Beds: 5 Single (3 bedrooms)
Bathroom: 1 Guests share (bath + shower)
Tariff: B&B (special) Double $85, Single $50.
Credit cards accepted.
NZ B&B Vouchers accepted Surcharge $15
Nearest Town: Wanaka 1 Km

'Harpers' is a homestay where friendliness, comfort and visitors needs are a priority. Your hosts, Jo and Ian have travelled and lived in various parts of the world. We have been home hosting for several years and gain a lot of pleasure from sharing our home and garden..
*Ian is: * a semi-retired builder who purpose built our house for home hosting.*
*Jo is: * a retired schoolteacher and more recently retired office worker. Wanaka is a resort township and is noted for: * a wide variety of very good restaurants * adventure activity, * fishing the local rivers and lake.* a top class scenic golf course *walks around the lake and tramps into the Mt Aspiring National Park. *A Fighter Pilots museum of World War 2 planes. * flights to Milford Sound, Mt Cook and Mt Aspiring *3 top class skifields, which can be easily accessed. Also cater for skiers in the winter. Black cat Bo completes the household. We are a smokefree home.* **Directions**: *Drive along the lake to the Queenstown / Cardrona turn off. Drive up this road - Highway 89 - for 4 blocks and look for our sign just past the 3 tall Redwood trees.* **Home Page**: www.nzhomestay.co.nz

Wanaka

Self-contained Accommodation
Address: The Stone Cottage, Dublin Bay, 2 R.D. Wanaka
Name: Belinda Wilson
Telephone: (03) 443 1878
Fax: (03) 443 1276
Email: stonecottage@xtra.co.nz
Beds: 1 King, 2 Double, 2 Single (2 bedrooms)
Bathroom: 2 Private
Tariff: B&B (full) Double $155-$175, Single $140, Children under 12 half price.
Dinner from $40. Credit cards (VISA/MC).
Nearest Town: 10km from Wanaka

Fifty years ago, a spectacular garden was created at Dublin Bay on the tranquil shores of Lake Wanaka. The Stone Cottage nestles in a beautiful garden with the South Island's Majestic Southern Alps as a backdrop.

Accommodation is private, comfortable and elegantly decorated. The Stone Cottage offers two self-contained loft apartments with breathtaking views over Lake Wanaka to snow clad Alps beyond. Featuring your own bathroom, bedroom, kitchen, living room and private entrance.

Enjoy breakfast at leisure, made from fresh ingredients from your well stocked fully equipped kitchen. Pre dinner drinks, delicious 3 course dinner and NZ wines or a gourmet picnic hamper by arrangement.

Walk along the sandy beach just 4 minutes from the Stone Cottage or wander in the enchanting garden. Guests can experience trout fishing, nature walks, golf, boating, horse riding, wine tasting and ski fields nearby.

Only 10 minutes from Wanaka, this is the perfect retreat for those who value privacy and the unique beauty of this area.

Relax in the magic atmosphere at the Stone Cottage and awake to the dawn bird chorus of native bellbirds and fantails.
Home Page: http://nz.com.travel/stonecottage

Wanaka
Lodge
Address: Cameron Creek Lodge,
State Highway 6, Wanaka
Name: Grant & Angie Longman
Telephone: (03) 443 8784
Fax: (03) 443 1262
Beds: 2 Queen,
2 Single (3 bedrooms)
Bathroom: 1 Ensuite, 1 Guests share
Tariff: B&B (full) Double $95-$110, Single $55, Children half price,
Dinner from $25, Credit Cards (VISA/MC).
Nearest Town: Wanaka 3km

Welcome, when you are looking for that special holiday in a relaxed atmosphere Cameron Creek Lodge has it all; Angie and I have had extensive involvement in the hospitality trade and are now channelling our talents into the Lodge. The Lodge is built from 60 tons of natural rock and native timber milled from the surrounding 20 acre property. Rooms are centrally heated and situated with mountain vistas which can be viewed from the sweeping verandahs. The hub of the Lodge is based around the warm hearth of the living area; and the domain of Angie's culinary delights - the kitchen; Angie creates superb meals using fresh New Zealand fare and home grown produce. Horses and mountain bikes are available to explore the stunning surrounding terrain or hitch up Cedric the donkey to a cart for a more humorous alternative; we also have two cats, Bubble and Squeek.
Directions: *Phone or fax us today.*

Wanaka
Rural Homestay
Address: Halliday Lane, Wanaka
Name: "Stonehaven"
Dennis & Deirdre
Telephone: (03) 443 9516
Fax: (03) 443 9513
Beds: 1 Double, 1 Queen, 2 Single
(2 bedrooms)
Bathroom: 1 Private, 1 Ensuite.
Tariff: B&B (full) Double $80,
Single $50, Children negotiated according to requirements,
Dinner $25. NZ B&B Vouchers accepted $10 Surcharge
Nearest Town: Wanaka 4km away

Our home is set in a largely undeveloped two acres about five minutes drive from Wanaka. All beds have electric blankets and tea and coffee is freely available. We have extensive views of the mountains surrounding Wanaka. We have an adjacent ten acres planted as an arboretum. The accent is on Autumn colour and the collection includes about 150 Genus. The best represented are Rowans (nationally significant collection), Maples, Pines and crab-apples. Deirdre is a children's nurse and we have the appropriate toys and furniture including trampoline. Children welcome. Child care by arrangement. Dennis is interested in the region, conservation and trees / gardening. Dennis is familiar with Mt Aspiring National Park. Guided trips by arrangement. Organic fruit both in season and preserved. We have twin 10 year old girls, a small dog and three cats. Laundry facilities available. No smoking inside please. Please phone for directions.

Wanaka

B&B, Homestay, Self-contained Apartment
Address: Temasek House, 7 Huchan Lane, Wanaka
Name: David & Poh Choo Turner
Telephone: (03) 443 1288
Fax: (03) 443 1288 **Mobile**: (025) 277 9594
Email: temasek.house@xtra.co.nz
Beds: 1 Queen, 1 Double, 1 Single (3 bedrooms)
Bathroom: 1 Ensuite, 1 Guests share
Tariff: B&B (continental) Double $80-$90, Single $55, Children under 12 half
price. Credit cards. Vouchers accepted $5 surcharge
Nearest Town: Wanaka.

Why not pamper yourself? - take in the truly amazing views of the surrounding mountain ranges from our sun deck. Temasek House offers you everything you associate with your own home plus more. The separate upper floor guest area is equipped with TV, stereo, extensive literature collection, coffee and tea making facilities, small kitchenette and most importantly for travellers - a washing machine and dryer (small additional charge). For the brave - why not venture downstairs into our living quarters and let our two young children entertain you? They organise everything and everybody - but when it all gets too much, we can lock them away with the cat. Our interest in fitness persists - you can join us for a run, bike or personal fitness workout. Temasek House is a non-smoking home with smoke alarms, heaters and electric blankets in all bedrooms. We also offer ample off-street private parking. Our home, including the name of the house, reflects our travels and lengthy spell in SE Asia and we have many artefacts from that part of the world. **Directions**: *Take the Mt. Aspiring Road out of Wanaka and turn right into Sargood Drive, Rippon Lea (opp Edgewater sign). First left into Huchan Lane and we are to be found down the driveway between the 2nd and 3rd houses on the left.*

http://www.bnb.co.nz

take a look

Wanaka

Homestay
Address: 56 Manuka Crescent, Wanaka
Name: "Hunts Homestay"
Bill & Ruth Hunt
Telephone: (03) 443 1053
Fax: (03) 443 1355
Beds: 1 Double,
2 Single (2 bedrooms)
Bathroom: 1 Guests share
Tariff: B&B (continental) Double $90, Single $55, Children half price,
Dinner $30 by arrangement. Credit Cards.
Nearest Town: Wanaka: 15m walk, 5 min car to centre.

We would like to welcome you to our new home in Wanaka. After retiring from our farm near Wanaka in 1995 we built our house overlooking the mountains and lake on a half acre section. Our interests are gardening, golf, travel and meeting people. Having lived in the Wanaka Districts virtually all our lives we have an extensive knowledge of the area and its attractions. Bill is a volunteer at the Wanaka Visitor Centre and a Kiwi Host and so keeps informed of the local tourist ventures and conditions. For those interested farm visits can be arranged.

We will welcome you with a cup of tea or coffee in our smoke-free home and settle you into our spacious ground floor accommodation. Free laundry facilities area available. We have no pets or children.

Directions: *Follow Beacon Point Road, turn right into Manuka Cres. We are opposite the motels.*

Wanaka

Self Contained Accommodation
Address: 76 Golf Course Road, Wanaka
Name: Johanna and Wolfram Gessler
Telephone: (03) 443 1210
Fax: (03) 443 1255
Email: olive@xtra.co.nz
Beds: 1 Queen, 1 King,
1 Bunkbed (2 bedrooms)
Bathroom: 1 Guests share
Tariff: B&B (continental)
Double $70, Single $50,
Children $20 each. Dinner in our restaurant 10% discount.
Credit Cards and Eftpos. NZ B&B Vouchers accepted
Nearest Town: Wanaka walking distance from town.

We invite you to stay with us in a rural setting above Wanaka (walking distance from town), the golf Course is just across the road. The unit is a fully self-contained cottage: two bedrooms, bathroom, kitchenette, living-dining. Originally from Germany we have lived in Italy, France and West Africa and found Wanaka the place to be. As a family of seven, a friendly Newfoundland dog, and two cats, we are now well settled here and would enjoy having you as our guests. Wolfram is running a Tuscan Restaurant on our property with in and outdoor dining, where you can enjoy the beauty and grandeur of Lake Wanaka and the mountains, while having a good Italian meal (for our B&B Guests 10% discount on lunch and dinner). Share our solar heated swimming pool with us in summer. **Directions**: *Please use the common entrance with the Restaurant to the House which is 150 meters back from the road.*

Wanaka

Lodge/Homestay
Address: "Anubis Lodge",
264 Beacon Point Road, Wanaka
Name: Michelle and Bob Mercer
Telephone: 03-443 7807
Fax: 03-443 7803
Mobile: 025-221 7387
Email: m.b.mercer@xra.co.nz
Beds: 1 Super King, 2 Queen, 4 Single (4 bedrooms)
Bathroom: 3 Ensuites, 1 Private
Tariff: B&B (full) Double $100-$120, Single $80, Dinner $25 (2 courses), Children $60. Special rates over quiet times. NZ B&B Vouchers accepted $20 surcharge
Nearest Town: Wanaka 1.8km

Recently completed our Oamaru Stone home is purpose built for Bed and Breakfast accommodation, with every consideration given to privacy and comfort for our visitors. Rooms are large and have their own dressing rooms and ensuite bathrooms. Beds are luxuriously fitted with quality linen, feather duvets and electric blankets. Native timber accents the decor throughout with touches of fresh flowers, Italian art, Belgium rugs, Scottish leather and English linens. The views are unobscured to lake and mountains, looking directly Northwest onto Treble Cone Ski field. a two minute walk brings you to the lake edge for fishing, swimming or secluded relaxation. The house is centrally heated plus two fireplaces.

Breakfast is varied and generous, special requests or dietary requirements need only be advised. Our purpose is to enjoy every person we meet and our aim is to help them have their best holiday ever.

We look forward to welcoming you ....

Wanaka

Homestay
Address: 'Glens of Roy',
Mt Aspiring Road, Wanaka
Name: Kate and Trevor Norman
Telephone: (03) 443 7392
Fax: (03) 443 7848
Mobile: (025) 201 0593
Beds: 1 Queen, 2 Single (2 bedrooms)
Bathroom: 1 Ensuite, 1 Private
Tariff: B&B (full) Double $100,
Single $75. Credit cards accepted.
Nearest Town: Wanaka 4 km

Glens of Roy
Rural Bed and Breakfast

Welcome to "Glens of Roy" our rural homestay property, overlooking Lake Wanaka with spectacular lake and mountain views. Our spacious modern home offers guests the choice of queen or single beds, both bedrooms have electric blankets and TV with private or ensuite bathrooms. Laundry facilities available.

Living and dining areas with native timber and stone fireplace provides guests with a homely comfortable stay.

Situated on Mt Aspiring - Glendhu Bay Road "Glens of Roy" is within close proximity to three major skifields, Mt Aspiring National Park, a walkers paradise, also a world heritage area and world famous brown trout fishing at Lake Wanaka's Paddock Bay, yet only five minutes drive from Wanaka's shops and restaurants. With a lifetime of local knlwledge and history, we, our (outdoor) character Corgi dog George look forward to meeting you.

Directions: *Travel West along Mt Aspiring - Glendhu Bay Road, 4 km from State Highway 89, Glens of Roy is sign posted on the left.*

Wanaka

Homestay
Address: 19 Bill's Way,
Rippon Lea, Wanaka
Name: Lake Wanaka Home Hosting
Telephone: (03) 443 9060
Fax: (03) 443 1626
Mobile: (025) 228 9160
Beds: 1 King, 1 Double,
2 Single (3 bedrooms)
Bathroom: 2 Private
Tariff: B&B (Special/full/continental) King $125, Double $100, Single $50.
Dinner available. Children welcome.
NZ B&B Vouchers accepted $25 surcharge for Double, $35 surcharge for King
Nearest Town: Wanaka 2 1/2 km to Post Office.

We welcome visitors to Wanaka and enjoy sharing our natural surroundings with others. We have a large peaceful home where our guests can experience not only the austerity of the lake and mountains around them, but also experience the ambience of Wanaka itself. The picturesque walk around the lake to Wanaka town is 20 to 30 minutes is well worth while. Our guests room with a super king size bed has a joining lounge with tea and coffee making facilities, TV, a sofa that will convert into a bed, private bathroom. Our double room has private bathroom also. Our home has smoke alarms, central heating and all beds have electric blankets. Good laundry facilities. We have no children living at home, and no pets. Our interests are sport, gardening, boating, farming and good cuisine. We wish your stay in Wanaka will be a very happy one. **Directions**: *Please ring for directions (025) 228 9160 or 443 9060*

Wanaka

Homestay
Address: 11 Botting Place,
Wanaka
Name: Northridge
Telephone: (03) 443 8835
Fax: (03) 443 1835
Mobile: (025) 950 436
Email: s.atkinson@xtra.co.nz
Beds: 2 Queen,
2 Single (3 Bedrooms)
Bathroom: 2 Guests Share
Tariff: B&B (Continental)
Double $100-$120,
Single $80. NZ B&B Vouchers accepted $20 surcharge. Credit cards: Visa/MC.
Nearest Town: Wanaka within walking distance

Welcome to beautiful Wanaka, where we invite you to stay in our quality 2 storey, 4 bedroom home built of stone and natural timbers. We have 180 degrees unobstructed breath-taking views of the lake and Alps from every window with the Golf Course literally at the back door. The bedrooms are large, all beds are fitted with woollen underlays, electric blankets, feather and down duvets and quality linen. Our house is centrally heated and also has a gas fireplace to ensure warmth and comfort. Your hosts have travelled extensively overseas and look forward to sharing some friendly time with other travellers, where you can relax and take in the awesome views either inside or out. Wanaka offers great fishing, tramping, skiing, jet boating and loads of other recreational activities. We are in walking distance to lake, shops and restaurants. We are smoke free indoors. **Directions**: *Please phone.*

OTAGO

Wanaka

Boutique B&B accommodation
Address: 20 Mt Aspiring road,
Wanaka.
Postal: PO Box 38, Wanaka.
Name: Joan and Rodger Cross
Telephone: (03) 443 8883
Fax: (03) 443 6683
Beds: 1 Queen, 2 Single
(2 Bedrooms)
Bathroom: 1 Private
Tariff: B&B (Full/Continental)
Double $100, Single $60,
Dinner on request. Non smoking.
Nearest Town: Wanaka

Crofthead - named after the family farm - is situated right on the edge of picturesque Lake Wanaka and within easy walking distance of shops and restaurants. Our modern timber and stacked stone home is set in a peaceful cottage garden complete with mature trees and masses of roses. We offer uninterrupted mountain and lake views, secluded courtyard areas for relaxing outdoor living; cosy log fire, spa bath and washing and drying facilities.

Wanaka

Homestay Boutique
Address: "Larchwood",
Dublin Bay Road, Wanaka
Name: Carol and Dan Orbell
Telephone: (03) 443 7914,
Freephone 0800 325 914
Fax: (03) 443 7910
Email: larchwood@xtra.nz
Beds: 3 Queen, 4 Single
(5 Bedrooms)
Bathroom: 5 Ensuites
Tariff: B&B (Full/Continental) Double $125 - $135, Single $100, Dinner $25 pp,
Children $20. Credit Cards: Visa/Mastercard, Bankcard. Animals welcome
Nearest Town: Wanaka, 10 km (off Haast Highway) 1 hour from Queesntown

Why stay with us.... Unless our secret hideaway meandering down to the shores of Lake Wanaka to walk, kayak, swim, fish or relax by, sounds like YOU.
Explore our tranquil gardens, trees framing the majestic mountains, or use the tennis court and mountain bikes, to expend any energy, left over from ski-ing, golfing, tramping or enjoying a good book. Maybe the "oldworlde" rustic charm of the Lodge, wide doors opening to summers heat, or crackling fires on cold winter nights, has appeal.
A choice of five bedrooms, with King sized -zip to single beds, all overlook the Lake and Mountains, and open onto outdoor balconies. TV's are banished to bedrooms, leaving the lounge for soft music, exchanging good yarns and sharing our life in Central Otago with you. Our golden retriever 'Mac' helps form the 'Welcoming Committee', but the cat's more elusive. Your animals are welcome.
Directions: *Free phone available for directions.*

Wanaka
Stone Cottage & Stables
Address: 'Queensberry Inn',
Wanaka Rd, No 3 R.D. Cromwell
Name: Bev & David Belsham
Telephone: (03) 445 0599
Fax: (03) 445 0014
Email: belsham@xtra.co.nz
Beds: 2 Units - Stables & Cottage
Bathroom: 2 Ensuite
Tariff: B&B Cottage: $220,
B&B Stables: $180.
Gourmet dinner in romantic garden setting - by arrangement.
Nearest Town: Wanaka 25 km

"Queensberry Inn" is a romantic restored stone cottage + stables circa 1860 which was originally the grooms quarters and tack room to the Inn. They are fully heated, old style furnished with tea and coffee making facilities. "Queensberry Inn" was an earlier travellers rest for gold miners, and others at the turn of the century. It is situated on a 5 acre property consisting of the farm buildings and amidst trees, gardens and lawn; and in excess of 400 white roses. Ideal for special occassions it is peaceful and relaxing. Also handy to Lakes Wanaka, Dunstan and Hawea which are renowned for their fishing. Centrally situated between four ski fields: Coronet, Remarkables, Cardrona and Treble Cone. Named as one of the best B&B experiences in New Zealand in 1999 (see North and South Magazine January 1999 issue). Family pet - cat called Lucy. **Directions**: *Midway between Wanaka and Cromwell on State Highway 6. 15 minutes to Wanaka.* **Home Page**: www.queensberryinn.co.nz

Cromwell
Orchard Stay
Address: 'Cottage Gardens',
3 Alpha St, cnr. State Highway 8B.
Name: Jill & Colin McColl
Telephone: (03) 445 0628
Fax: (03) 445 0628
Email: eco@xtra.co.nz
Beds: 4 Single (3 bedrooms)
Bathroom: 1 Ensuite, 2 Family share
Tariff: B&B (continental)
Double $70, Single $40/$50,
Dinner $20, Credit Cards.
NZ B&B Vouchers accepted
Nearest Town: Cromwell, 1km to town centre

Come and enjoy Cromwell Central Otago, the centre of attractions and summer fruit bowl of New Zealand. Apricots are our specialty. The Gateway to historic goldfields and high adventure tourism. Three hours Te Anau, Manapouri, Milford. 45 minutes Wanaka and Queenstown. One hour travel to four ski fields. Our home and orchard overlook Lake Dunstan surrounded by snow capped mountains in winter. Visit orchards and vineyards during our hot summers. Our large double guestroom with ensuite has private entrance and verandah, TV, fridge, tea making facilities. We enjoy sharing quiet evenings by the fire in winter or on the verandah in summer with our guests. Colin is a member of Lions International. We both care for our spacious garden. Experience the finest fruit and hospitality at Cottage Gardens, where George (the cat) and Golden Labrador Jessica May will make you feel very welcome. Laundry facilitates. Smoke free. Sorry unsuitable for children.

Cromwell
Bed & Breakfast
Address:
Quartz Reef Creek,
Northburn, State Highway 8, Cromwell
Name: June Boulton
Telephone: (03) 445 0404
Fax: (03) 445 0404
Beds: 1 Queen + 1 Single, 2 Singles (2 bedroom)
Bathroom: 1 Ensuite, 1 Private
Tariff: B&B (continental) Double $90, Single $50.
NZ B&B Vouchers accepted $20 surcharge.
Credit cards accepted
Nearest Town: Cromwell 4km

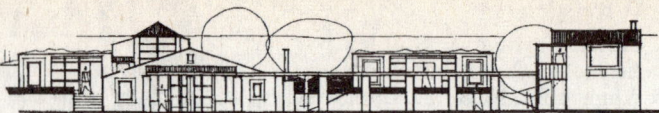

You are invited to stay at my home - an architecturally designed house situated near the lake edge with panoramic views of lake and mountains. There is a boat ramp within 200 metres and fishing spots virtually on the doorstep. Popular ski fields at Wanaka, Queenstown and Cardrona are within easy reach, or enjoy a game of golf, or explore the local gold mining areas.

Your sunny room has total privacy with its own entrance and deck. For your convenience there are tea making facilities, fridge, microwave and TV. Another room with twin beds has a private bathroom. I enjoy making pottery in my studio and supply craft galleries. Guests are welcome to view and purchase - ask for a demonstration if interested. We possess a friendly black cat called Tom (should be Tomasina!).

Directions: *3 1/2 km north of Cromwell Bridge, SH 8, 1st house on lake front.*

Cromwell
Farmstay
Address: Swann Road, Lowburn
RD 2, Cromwell
Name: Claire & Jack Davis
Telephone: 03 445 1291 or
Freephone 0800 205104
Fax: (03) 445 1291
Email: hiburn@xtra.co.nz
Beds: 1 Double, 2 Single (2 bedrooms)
Bathroom: 1 Guests share
Tariff: B&B (full), Double $80,
Children half price, Dinner $15 per person. NZ B&B Vouchers accepted
Nearest Town: Cromwell 10km

Situated at Cromwell the centre of beautiful Central Otago halfway between Wanaka and Queenstown. Farming 400 hectares with merino sheep and deer. Guests are welcome to join in farming activities and farm tour always included with working sheep dogs a speciality. We encourage guests to come for dinner and enjoy time to chat over a meal. Morning and afternoon teas complimentary home produce used as much as possible.

Our joint interests include curling, sports, gardening, sheep dog competitions, handcrafts.

Local attractions: gold mining history, fruit growing area, lakes, rivers and mountains, fishing and walking, 4 ski fields nearby.

Come and relax in our beautiful and peaceful surroundings. Use us as a base to visit the area. Children welcome. We treat our guests as friends.

Please phone for reservations and directions - best time evening or meal times.

Home Page: http://mysite.xtra.co.nz/~farmholiday/

Cromwell
Lodge/Homestay
Address: 'Lake Dunstan Lodge', Northburn, No. 3 RD, Cromwell
Name: Judy & Bill Thornbury
Telephone: (03) 445 1107
Fax: (03) 445 3062
Mobile: (025) 311 415
Beds: 2 Queen, 2 Single (3 bedrooms)
Bathroom: 1 Ensuite, 1 Guests share, separate toilet
Tariff: B&B (full) Double $120, Single $60, Children negotiable, Dinner $20 per person, childten under 12 meals half price. Campervans facilities available. Credit cards accepted. NZ B&B Vouchers accepted $20 surcharge
Nearest Town: Cromwell 6km

We offer friendly hospitality at 'Lake Dunstan Lodge'. Our new spacious home is privately situated on the edge of Lake Dunstan, 6 kilometres from Cromwell. We have recently shifted from a sheep and deer farm in Southland along with our friendly cat "Ollie". Our interests include Lions, fishing, boating, lawnmowing, gardening and crafts. The sunny bedrooms have lake views and attached open balconies, fridge, tea and coffee making facilities available at all times. Guests share our spacious living areas with TV's and make free use of our spa pool and laundry facilities. Local attractions include orchards, vineyards, gold diggings, golf course, fishing, boating, walks, 4 ski fields within easy reach. We welcome you to have an evening meal with us or just bed and continental or full breakfast. No smoking inside please. Come and fish or just relax at the lake edge surrounded by our spacious lawns and gardens.
Directions: *5km from Cromwell Bridge on Tarras/Omarama Highway 8. Sign at gate.*

Arrowtown
Homestay / Bed & Breakfast
Address: 20 Wiltshire St, Arrowtown, Central Otago
Name: Cynthia Balfour
Telephone: (03) 442 1326
Beds: 1 Double, 2 Single (2 bedrooms)
Bathroom: 1 Guests share
Tariff: B&B (special) Double $100, Single $80, Children half price.
NZ B&B Vouchers accepted Surcharge $20
Nearest Town: 19km Queenstown

For more than ten years I have been privileged to host hundreds of wonderful visitors from many parts of the world. They have enjoyed my small intimate garden, pleasant cottage, the beauty of the surrounding mountains and historic Arrowtown. We are perfectly located as a base for your activities - quick and easy access to Queenstown and the Southern Lakes, but removed from the hustle and bustle. Consistently guest rated "Excellent" to "Absolutely Perfect". No effort is spared to make your stay interesting and memorable. Satisfied guests say it best:"Which was the best, the breakfast, garden or hospitality????" "A Charming hostess - feel sorry to leave, every minute was enjoyable" or simply "Brilliant". Comfortable beds are also commented on, as is the breakfast - often! Two house cats. Non-smokers preferred.
Please phone ahead for bookings and directions.
Two minutes from Arrowtown Post Office.

Arrowtown
Homestay/Self-contained Accomm
Address: R24 Butel Road,
Arrowtown
Name: Barry & Ann Bain
Telephone: (03) 442 1252
Fax: (03) 442 1252
Mobile: 025 274 3360
Email: norman@queenstown.co.nz
Beds: 1 Queen, 4 Single (2 bedrooms)
Bathroom: 1 Ensuite, 1 Private
Tariff: B&B (full, continental) Double $80-$90, Single negotiable, Children
negotiable. Credit cards accepted. NZ B&B Vouchers accepted $10 surcharge
Nearest Town: Arrowtown 1 km to town centre. Queenstown 19km

We are retired business couple who have travelled extensively. Our interests include local history, music, gardening, pottery and patchwork. We welcome our guests to a spacious, sunny, self-contained upstairs suite, complete with kitchen. Plenty of space for children, who will love to play with our friendly black Cocker spaniel. Your private balcony commands 360 degree views of the mountains and overlooks our large landscaped garden and orchard, grazing sheep and the famous Millbrook Country Club. Extra continental breakfast with freshly baked bread and Ann's shortbread, jams and preserves is provided in your suite; or alternatively join us in the house for a full breakfast. As booking agents for all local tour operators, we can advise your best options for the many pleasant activities in the surrounding Lakes District and Fiordland. Complimentary laundry, road bikes, gold mining gear, BBQ etc. Our courtesy car is a former Archibishop's rare 1924 Austin drophead coupe.
Home Page: http://www.GoldRiverHomestays.co.nz

Arrowtown
Homestay
Address: 'Rowan Cottage'
9 Thomson St, Arrowtown,
Central Otago
Name:
Elizabeth & Michael Bushell
Telephone: (03) 442 0443
Beds: 1 Double, 2 Single
(2 bedrooms)
Bathroom: 1 Guests share
Tariff: B&B (full) Double $75, Single $50.
Dinner $25pp. NZ B&B Vouchers accepted $10 surcharge
Nearest Town: Arrowtown. Queenstown 19km

Rowan Cottage is situated in a quiet tree lined street with mountain views. We are 10 minutes walk to the town and 20 minutes drive to Queenstown.
We have a lovely cottage garden to relax in and have coffee, tea and homemade goodies. We are well travelled and can advise you on things to see and do in our beautiful part of the country. You will be assured of a friendly and comfortable stay.
"Comments" - Thanks so much for your wonderful hospitality, wonderful breakfasts and such helpfulness in organising our acitivities. We felt so welcome in your relaxed atmosphere. Wish we could have sat in your gorgeous garden for a few days but your country beckons us to see more of its beauty.

Arrowtown
Homestay
Address: 25 Caernarvon St,
Arrowtown
Name: Liz & Steve Daniel
Telephone: (03) 442 1227
Freephone 0800 186 844
Email: daniels@es.co.nz
Beds: 2 Queen (2 bedrooms)
Bathroom: 1 Ensuite, 1 Family share
Tariff: B&B (continental) Double with Ensuite $80; Double $70; Single $50;
Children negotiable. Special rates May - September, and consecutive nights.
Nearest Town: Arrowtown 3 mins walk, Queenstown 19km

Liz and Steve welcome you to our traditional stone built home. It is spacious and comfortable with a sheltered garden, sun-baskers patio, two lounges and an open log fire. The ensuite bedroom is very private with TV, and tea making facilities. The other room has french windows to the tree-lined garden. Three minutes walk to tranquil Arrowtown's main street with its shops, museum, post- office, chinese village and restaurants. Our sunny sheltered climate here and proximity to Queenstown's activities give you the best of both worlds. With extensive knowledge of the hospitality trade our other interests are our highschool and university sons, cat, dog, travelling, skiing, cycling, golfing and fishing. Dine at one of Arrowtown's eateries, 'Millbrook Country Club's' three restaurants, with golf course, gymnasium and pool, 5 minuntes drive, or try busy Queenstown just twenty minutes away with its extensive range of restaurants and cafes. Laundry facilities available. Smoking outside only.

Arrowtown
Homestay
Address: 18 Stafford St,
Arrowtown
Name: Anne & Arthur Gormack
Telephone: (03) 442 1747
Freephone: 0800 184990
Fax: (03) 442 1787
Email: agormack@xtra.co.nz
Beds: 1 King, 2 Single (2 bedrooms)
Bathroom: 2 Private
Tariff: B&B (continental)
Double $90.00, Single $45.00.
NZ B&B Vouchers accepted $20 Surcharge
Nearest Town: Arrowtown - Queenstown 19km

Our spacious home, overlooking Millbrook Country Club and the Wakatipu Basin, offers spectacular views from every window. Although only 5 minutes walk from the town centre, our outlook is totally rural. We have a warm and comfortable home with plenty of space inside and out. Guest rooms have TV, reading lights, electric blankets and heaters. There is also a gym room with exercise equipment for your use. During the Summer, join us for a glass of wine beside our heated swimming pool. During the Winter you can curl up in front of the fire and read our many books on local history, or have a friendly chat. Bread, preserves, muesli and jam all homemade.

Arrowtown

B&B+Self-contained Accom.
Address: 43 Bedford St, Arrowtown
Name: POLLY-ANNA COTTAGE/
Daphne and Bill
Telephone: (03) 442 1347
Fax: (03) 442 1307
Mobile: (025) 220 3974
Beds: 1 Double, 2 Single (2 bedrooms)
Bathroom: 1 Ensuite, 1 Guest share
Tariff: B&B (continental) Double $80, Single $50. Dinner by arrangement $25
pp. Credit Cards. NZ B&B Vouchers accepted surcharge $10
Nearest Town: Queenstown

Daphne and Bill are retired business couple who have restored and renovated a quaint 100 year old cottage from the gold rush days. We recommend a restful and informative stay in historic Arrowtown, and offer our warm hospitality and completely private ensuite facility. Arrowtown is an area of great beauty and serenity the town is 15 mins from Queenstown with superb views and excellent tourist attractions. Features are 18 hole golf course, a superb lakes district museum, shops and restaurants. Three major ski fields are within easy reach. We are 5 mins from Millbrook International Golf Resort. We welcome the opportunity to share our hospitality with overseas and Kiwi visitors. Try Daph's delights, home preserves and fudge. Comments we have received include; "The highlight of our trip", "Came 2 days, stayed 6", "Wonderful experience", "Graciously warm people we shall return", "Thanks for the memory I feel so at home". Why not share historic Arrowtown with us. Can inform on all local attractions.
Directions: *"Polly Anna" sign at front gate on Main Road into Arrowtown*

Arrowtown - Gibbston Valley

Homestay+Self-contained Accom.
Address: Coal Pit Road, Gibbston,
R.D. 1, Queenstown
Name: Claire & Alan Perry
Telephone: (03) 442 5339
Fax: (03) 442 5339
Beds: 1 Queen, 2 Single (2 bedrooms)
Bathroom: 1 Private
Tariff: B&B (continental) Double $85,
Single $50, Children over ten $15. Dinner by arrangement.
Nearest Town: Arrowtown 15km

Nestling among the grape vines in the Gibbston Valley is our stone cottage - offering a comfortable relaxed holiday in the country yet only 1 kilometre from the main Queenstown-Cromwell highway. The cottage is part of Coal Pit - vineyard and has been restored from an historic stable; well over 100 years old. Trees from the era make up the garden of the homestead and cottage. Guests can be self contained or share meals with their hosts.
The area offers beautiful Central Otago scenery and being in the Gibbston area gives easy access to the two local wineries, and is only 10 minutes to Arrowtown with its golf course, historic buildings and many restaurants.
Coronet Peak and the Remarkables ski-fields are within half an hour drive, as is Queenstown and all its exciting activities.
Two twin rooms are available in the homestead with guest bathroom.
Chester (Labrador) and George (JR / Foxterrier) and Jack (Siamese cat) are in residence - awaiting visitors. **Directions**: *Please phone.*

692

Arrowtown

Homestay
Address: 13 Stafford Street, Arrowtown
Name: Wiki & Norman Smith
Telephone: (03) 442 1092
Fax: (03) 442 1092
Email: norman@queenstown.co.nz
Beds: 1 Queen, 2 Single (2 bedrooms)
Bathroom: 1 Guests share
Tariff: B&B (continental) Double $80,
Single $50, Dinner on request $20.
NZ B&B Vouchers accepted Surcharge $10
Nearest Town: Arrowtown (5 mins walk), Queenstown 19km, Frankton Airport 12km.

Arrowtown is one of NZ's most famous old goldmining towns and remains a popular holiday destination because it has - charm and tranquillity - all the adventure attractions of Queenstown (20 mins away) or the more sedate life of golfing - Wine Trails - Art Trails - Historic Tours etc. After 23 years in meat Industry management and 4 years as Moteliers in Arrowtown we have now retired to our architecturally designed home and garden. We have travelled widely and we are keen trampers, and enjoy gardening, golf, computing and helping other people to enjoy the beauty and tranquillity of our historic area. Our breakfasts are generous with homemade jams and yoghurt, freshly baked bread and freshly brewed coffee. Laundry complimentary. Off street parking is provided and we also have a cat named "Timothy George". We look forward to meeting you at our friendly homestay.
Please phone, fax or email for a booking.
Home Page: http://www.dotco.co.nz

http://www.bnb.co.nz

take a look

Arrowtown - Queenstown
Farmstay Bed & Breakfast
Address: 'Golden Hills', Highway 6, 1 RD, Queenstown
Name: Patricia Sew Hoy
Telephone: (03) 442 1427 **Fax**: (03) 4421 427
Mobile: (025) 388 388
Email: goldhill@queenstown.co.nz
Beds: 2 Queen, 1 Double, 3 Single (4 bedrooms)
Bathroom: 3 Ensuite, 1 Private
Tariff: B&B (continental) Double $90-$95, Single $60. Travellers cheques accepted. NZ B&B Vouchers accepted $15 surcharge.
Nearest Town: Arrowtown 4km, Queenstown 18km

Golden Hills is a distinctive, superior home with four large bedrooms, each with their own bathroom. Set in 30 acres, private, quiet, with beautiful mountain views, the home has all the extras one would expect from warm country hospitality in a charming spacious sunfilled house.

Surrounded by a 3 acres award winning garden with private terraces, barbecue, garden walks and ponds, it nestles back from, and is easy to find, on Highway 6. Arrowtown 4 kms away with dining, shops, walks, golf etc. Queenstown is 18 km away.

Free tea and coffee making facilities area available at all times, I enjoy your company. Guests are so welcome to share the spacious conservatory, lounge and terrace areas with me and make free use of book exchange.

Library and laundry facilities and email. Having lived in this beautiful area for over 50 years, I can happily advise about local walks, spectacular viewpoints, and any onwards bookings, itineries etc without charge. Let's discuss this together.

The farmlet is 30 acres surrounding the house and garden (which hosts garden tours) and leases this 30 acres to nearby sheep farmers. Plenty of carparks available. I look forward to meeting you.

Directions: *FROM NORTH: Keep on Highway 6, travel 300 metres past Arrowtown turnoff, stonewall entrance & sign on left. Turn in.*
FROM SOUTH: Reach Frankton turn right onto Highway 6, travel 11 km, stonewall entrance on right. Turn down drive - welcome!

Arrowtown/Queenstown

Guest House
Address: "Willowbrook", Malaghan Road, RD 1, Queenstown
Name: Roy & Tamaki Llewellyn
Telephone: (03) 442 1773
Fax: (03) 442 1773
Mobile: (025) 516 739
Email: wbrook@queenstown.co.nz
Beds: 1 King, 1 Queen, 2 Single (3 bedrooms), (cot available)
Bathroom: 2 Ensuite, 1 Private
Tariff: B&B (continental) Double $95-$105, Single $80-$90, Credit Cards (VISA/AMEX/MC/Diners/JCB). ($15 surcharge applies 20/12/99 to 05/01/00).
Nearest Town: Arrowtown 5 mins, Queenstown 15 mins.

Our little corner of paradise lies at the foot of Coronet Peak in the heart of the beautiful Wakatipu Basin. Behind us to the south are the Remarkables; to the east is Cardrona skifield; to the west, Queenstown, and from our front deck, the peaceful scene of hangliders and parapentes gently drifting downwards.

Our home is an old farmhouse, built in 1914 and now listed as a 'protected feature', which we have renovated and added to. Don't worry, the high ceilings, open fireplaces, T & G floors and wood panelling all remain. A couple of things they didn't have back in 1914 such as central heating and Sky TV, we've taken the liberty of adding. Guests' rooms all contain a bed (or beds) more comfortable than you would find in most hotels and are ensuite or have a private bathroom. The spacious lounge with its open fires and 'help-yourself' tea and coffee, is yours to enjoy, as are the delights of our large, mature garden: patio with BBQ; luxurious spa pool; tennis court and historical outhouses.

Skiers will be in their element here. Coronet Peak is a mere 30 minute drive from our front door, the Remarkables 45 minutes and Cardrona 1 hour. Queenstown is only 15 minutes away and offers a dazzling array of shops, restaurants and nightlife not to mention a range of activities that will quench any adrenalin thirst, appeal to all ages and suit every budget. The quaint gold mining settlement of Arrowtown is just 4km up the road while for golfers, the greens of prestigious Millbrook Resort can be reached in 3 (minutes!)

I'm a Brit and my wife, Tamaki, is Japanese. We have both travelled extensively (including 13 years living in Tokyo) before deciding NZ was the most beautiful country we had seen. We have a young daughter, Jodie, and a nutcase dog. Please call if you can't find us - otherwise feel free to just 'arrive.'

Directions: *We are on Malaghan Road (the 'back' road between Queenstown and Arrowtown). From Queenstown, take Gorge road out through Arthurs Point, make no turns and after about 15 minutes look for our sign on your right. From the north, turn right at Lake Hayes, go 5km and turn left into Malaghan Road. Millbrook Resort is on your left and we are 3km further along the road, also on the left.*
Home Page: www.nz.com/Queenstown/Willowbrook

Arrowtown/Queenstown

Country Bed and Breakfast and/or SC Accommodation

Address: Ferry Hotel Guest House, R. D. 1.
Spence Road, Lower Shotover, Queenstown
Name: Ferry Hotel Guest House
Telephone: 64 3 442 2194 **Fax**: 64 3 442 2190
Mobile: (025) 221 0123 **Email**: info@ferry.co.nz
Beds: 2 Double, 2 Single (3 bedrooms)
Bathroom: 1 Ensuite, 1 Guests share + extra toilet with vanity.
Tariff: B&B (continental-full on request) Double with ensuite $155, Double Share B/R
$125, Twin Share B/R $125. Children under 12 half price. Credit Cards: Visa/MC/AMEX
Nearest Town: 11km from Queenstown & Arrowtown on SH6, 6km from Airport

*The Guesthouse was first built in 1862, burnt down & rebuilt in 1872, and relocated in 1915.
It operated as a Hotel until 1972 and has a fascinating history. "Old World Elegance" aptly
describes the charming interior which consists of guest lounge with enormous wood burning
fire, character country kitchen "granny would have been proud of", 3 bedrooms, 2 bathrooms.
Tea and coffee complimentary, laundry and barbecue facilities. Bathrobes and slippers
provided , rooms individually heated, and all beds have electric blankets. We are 10 minutes
drive from Queenstown & Arrowtown and centrally located for Coronet & Remarkables ski
fields. Hosts accommodation is completely separate allowing privacy when desired, although
we are here to offer local knowledge, assistance and friendship; also from Chester our lovable
Springer Spaniel. We enjoy gardening, fly fishing (Kevin is President - Wakatipu Angling
Club), socialising with guests, assisting with tour / travel arrangements / bookings.   No
smoking indoors (Verandah good for smokers).Airport 5 minutes away FREE pick-up on
request. **Directions**: Turn into Lower Shotover Road from SH6 and immediately turn left
into Spence Road. **Home Page**: www.ferry.co.nz*

Arrowtown - Queenstown

Homestay, Bed & Breakfast

Address: Lake Hayes, No 1 RD,
Queenstown. Rapid No. 712
Name: Noelene and Ron Horrell.
Telephone: (03) 442 1107
Fax: (03) 442 1160
Beds: 2 Queen, 1 Single
Bathroom: 1 Ensuite, 1 Guests share
Tariff: B&B (continental)
Double $125-$150, Single $75. Children half price. Visa/Mastercard
Nearest Town: Arrowtown 6 km.

*This distinctive lakeside retreat, offers luxury accommodation with good old fashioned
hospitality. Perfectly situated in the Historic Arrow basin, with views across beautiful Lake
Hayes, to the Coronet Peak skifield. All guestrooms overlook the lake, mountains, and award
winning garden. The Master bedroom, a honeymoon retreat, with turret tassels and a clawfoot
bath. Enjoy pool in the Games room, put a log on the fire in our romantic little sitting room,
and awake to the aroma of home-made bread. Heaven doesn't come much better than this!
It's a short drive to Queenstown, The Adventure Capital of
the World, with its Smorgasbord of shops and restaurants.
Jetboating and skiing. 6 km to Arrowtown, Born of Gold in
the 1860's with boutique restaurants, bush walks, top rated
museum, gold panning and old worlde atmosphere. Wine
tasting , bungy jumping, golf at Millbrook and Arrowtown.
We love it here. You will too! Noelene, Ron and Burt the
Cat.* **Home Page**: www.welcome.co.nz/turret

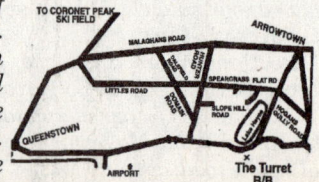

Queenstown
Homestay and Health Retreat
Address: Bush Creek Health Retreat,
21 Bowen Street, Queenstown
Name: Ileen Mutch
Telephone: (03) 442 7260
Fax: (03) 442 7250
Beds: 1 Queen, 3 Single (3 bedrooms)
Bathroom: 2 Guests share
Tariff: B&B (Special) Double $100,
Single $50, Children half price. (2 nights minimum)
NZ B&B Vouchers accepted $10 surcharge
Nearest Town: Queenstown 1 km

3 acres of natural paradise only 10 minutes walk to the centre of town, one of the longest established Health Retreats in New Zealand. Nutritious, organically grown and prepared food.
Ileen Mutch is an internationally recognised natural healing practitioner. One of the longest practising in this part of the globe. Bush Creek Health retreat is pet free and Ileen's family has left the next. Deep tissue massage therapy is available.
Still your soul and revitalise your energies in this renowned magical garden, tuned to native birdsong and cascading waterfall. Rooms fully appointed with all the extras that provide the ultimate in comfort.
Join the list of travellers that return again and again. Exceptional value.
Directions: *From roundabout at top of Shotover St (Main St) follow Gorge Rod approx 1 km to block of Homestores on left and up Bowen St - 2 signposts - for unforgettable dreamy rejuvenating stay.*

Queenstown
Homestay
Address: 'Colston House'
2 Boyes Crescent, Frankton,
Queenstown
Name: Lois & Ivan Lindsay
Telephone: (03) 442 3162
Beds: 1 King, 2 Single
(Twin) (2 Bedrooms). All with hand basin.
Bathroom: 1 Guests share
Tariff: B&B (full) Double $100, Single $60, Children $30,
Dinner by arrangement $25. NZ B&B Vouchers accepted $10 surcharge
Nearest Town: Frankton 1 km, Queenstown 6 km

Our home, which is in a sunny situation overlooking Lake Wakatipu, has guest rooms with handbasins, electric blankets, bedside lamps, and heaters. Guests have exclusive use of bathroom with separate toilet, laundry facilities, and a sunny conservatory overlooking flower gardens. We are retired sheep and grain farmers with a family of six all married. We have been hosting tourists for a number of years and offer warm and friendly hospitality, taking a special pride in our meals which we share with our guests. Full cooked breakfast and tea or coffee on arrival if required. Shopping Centre, airport, coach-stop, golf, tennis, walking tracks, jet-boating, and bungy jumping coach all within 1 km of our home. Guests going to Milford or Doubtful Sound by coach picked up and returned to our gate at night. Bookings arranged for all tours. Personal transport provided from coaches, airport, and to and from Queenstown.
Directions: *Turn into McBride Street at Mobil service station, Frankton. Proceed to where road forks and our home "Colston House", with archway over drive will be seen.*

Queenstown
Country Guest Lodge &SC Accom.
Address: 'Trelawn Place', Arthurs Point, Queenstown Postal: Box 117,Queenstown
Name: Nery Howard & Michael Clark
Telephone: (03) 442 9160
Fax: (03) 442 9160
Email: qvc@xtra.co.nz

Trelawn Place
Bed & Breakfast

Beds: 1 Twin, 2 Queen, 1 King (4 bedrooms)
Bathroom: 4 Ensuite
Tariff: B&B (full) Double $155-$185, Single $110 (from October 1), Credit cards: Visa/Mastercard.
Nearest Town: Queenstown 4 km

Sited dramatically above the shotover river with gardens and lawns sweeping to the cliff edge, Trelawn Place is a superior country lodge only 4 km from busy Queenstown. Four comfortably appointed ensuite rooms furnished with country chintz and antiques. Guest sitting room with open fire, well stocked library, outdoor Jacuzzi / spa, shady vine covered verandas.
Generous cooked breakfast features home made and grown produce. If you are missing your pets, a cat and friendly corgis will make you feel at home. 48 hour cancellation policy.
FLY FISHING GUIDE. Michael, an Orvis Endorsed guide is available for trout fishing trips in the area. We can also help with bookings for all other local activities.
SELF CONTAINED COTTAGE. with its own fireside and roses framing the door, the 2 bedroom stone cottage is a honeymoon hideaway.
Directions: *Take HW 6A into Queenstown, right at 2nd roundabout into Gorge Road, travel 4 km towards Arthurs Point. Trelawn Place sign posted beside gate on right.*
Home Page: http://nz.com/web nz/bbnz/trelawn.htm

Queenstown

Homestay
Address: 'The Stable', 17 Brisbane Street, Queenstown
Name: Isobel & Gordon McIntyre
Telephone: (03) 442 9251
Fax: (03) 442 8293
Email: gimac@queenstown.co.nz
Beds: 1 Double, 1 King or Twin, 1 Single (3 bedrooms)
Bathroom: 1 Ensuite, 1 Private, 1 Guests share
Tariff: B&B (full) Double $120-$140, Single $60-$85, Dinner $35 by prior arrangement, Credit cards.
Nearest Town: Queenstown town centre 3 minutes walk

A 125 year old stone stable, converted for guest accommodation, and listed by the New Zealand Historic Places Trust, shares a private courtyard with our home. The "Garden Room" and "Lake Room" are in the house, all providing convenience and comfort with fantastic lake and mountain views. Our home is in a quiet cul-de-sac and set in a garden abundant with rhododendrons and native birds. It is less than 100 metres from the beach where a small boat and canoe are available for guests' use. The famous Kelvin Heights Golf Course is close and tennis courts, bowling greens and ice skating rink are in the adjacent park. All tourist facilities, shops and restaurants are within easy walking distance, less than 5 minutes stroll on well lit footpaths.

All rooms are well heated with views of garden, lake or mountains. Tea and coffee making facilities are available at all times. Guests share our spacious living areas and make free use of our library and laundry.

A courtesy car is available to and from the bus depots. We can advise about and are booking agents for all sightseeing tours. Do allow an extra day or two for all the activities in the Queenstown region.

When it is convenient for us, and by prior arrangement, guests will enjoy 3 course dinners served with New Zealand wines. The choice includes lamb, venison, fresh fish and chicken. Breakfast is often served in the courtyard. No smoking indoors.

Your hosts, with a farming background, have bred Welsh ponies and now enjoy weaving, cooking, gardening, sailing and the outdoors. We have an interest in a successful vineyard and enjoy drinking and talking about wine. We enjoy meeting people and have travelled extensively overseas.

Directions: *Follow State Highway 6a (Frankton Road) to where it veers right at the Millenium Hotel. Continue straight ahead. Brisbane Street ("no exit") is 2nd on left. Phone if necessary.*

Queenstown
Homestay
Address: 'Remarkable View',
22 Brecon Street, Queenstown
Name: Shirley Jackson
Telephone: (03) 442 9542
Beds: 1 Double, 2 Single
(2 bedrooms)
Bathroom: 1 Family share
Tariff: B&B (full)
Double $75, Single $45,
School age children negotiable. Dinner $20.
Nearest Town: Queenstown - 3 minute stroll to Mall

Our home overlooks the town centre and has a fantastic view of the surrounding area, especially the rugged mountain range - "The Remarkables". Although so close to the centre of a very popular tourist resort we can offer a comfortable and peaceful stay. We offer 2 guest rooms, one with 2 single beds, the other with a double bed. All have electric blankets, warm bedding and are very comfortable. Bathroom facilities shared with hosts. Breakfast either continental or cooked - your choice. We offer a nourishing 3 course dinner with wine. Being a tourist town, Queenstown has seven day shopping and many fine restaurants catering for most tastes. Plenty to do both summer and winter. "Sooty Cat" will be aloof or friendly as you like it.
Directions: *Look for the hill with the gondola's, find the street that takes you there. We are the black house, 2nd on the left.*

Queenstown
Self-contained Accommodation
Address: 'Braemar House',
56 Panorama Terrace,
Queenstown
Name: Ann & Duncan Wilson
Telephone: (03) 442 7385
Fax: (03) 442 4385
Beds: 1 Double, 1 Single
+ 2 divans in lounge (1 bedroom)
Bathroom: 1 Private
Tariff: B&B (continental - plus)
Double $85, Single $60, Children half price,
(enquire other options when booking).
Nearest Town: Queenstown 1.5km from town centre

The apartment on the middle floor of our home is self-contained and private if guests want it that way, but our personal hospitality is always available.
"Braemar House", is situated on a steep hill section but with easy access from roadways, provides magnificent panoramic views of lake and mountains, and as guests will realise, our interest include gardening with many varieties of native trees and plants. Other activities which could interest visitors are tramping (hill walking), skiing, golf, photography and local history. For travellers with their own transport, we have off-street parking, but a courtesy car is available for others. Transport and Guiding services are also available to out-of-town locations. We have travelled extensively at home and overseas, and believe we fully understand the requirements of visitors to Queenstown.
Directions: *Turn up Suburb St off Frankton Rd, then first right into Panorama Tce.*

Queenstown

Homestay
Address: 8 Sunset Lane,
Larchwood Heights,
Queenstown
Name: Robin & Alwyn Rice
Telephone: (03) 442 6567
Beds: 1 Double,
2 Single (2 bedrooms)
Bathroom: 1 Guests share
Tariff: B&B (full)
Double $90, Single $60
Nearest Town: Queenstown 1.5km from town centre

After spending 30 years in business in Invercargill, we moved to Queenstown and built our home in a quiet cul-de-sac with panoramic views of Lake Wakatipu and the surrounding mountains.
Our guest rooms are spacious and comfortable, with electric blankets, TV and private bathroom, as we take just one couple, or a party travelling together.
You can enjoy the magnificent scenery from the deck overlooking the lake, or relax in our private and sunny garden. We have travelled extensively in new Zealand and overseas, and our interests include gardening, golf and skiing.
Directions: *Travelling along Frankton Road towards Queenstown, turn right into Hensman Road, 2nd road on left is Sunset Lane, we are last house on left, or phone if necessary.*

Queenstown

Homestay /Self-contained Accom
Address: 'Birchall House',
118 Panorama Terrace,
Larchwood Heights, Queenstown
Name: Joan & John Blomfield
Telephone: (03) 442 9985
Fax: (03) 442 9980
Mobile: by call divers.
Beds: 1 Double, 2 Single (2 bedrooms)
Bathroom: 1 Private
Tariff: B&B Double $90, $100, $110, Single $75.
NZ B&B Vouchers accepted $25 surcharge

We welcome you to our new home in Queenstown which is within walking distance of town centre, and from where we enjoy magnificent 200 degree views of Lake Wakatipu and surrounding mountains. Our guest accommodation, is completely self-contained, has the same views, separate entrance, is private, spacious, smoke free and centrally heated. Electric blankets on all beds. A continental or full breakfast is available and guests are very welcome to share our table. Before moving to Queenstown, we farmed sheep, cattle and deer in Western Southland where we were also active members of the Western Southland Farm Hosting Group. On a recent visit to U.K. and Europe we enjoyed the B&B experience immensely and feel confident we can make your stay a pleasant one. Our interests include most sports but golf in particular, together with gardening and handcrafts (embroidery, patchwork etc.). Off-street parking is available and courtesy transport to / from terminals is provided. Bookings can be arranged for all tours. **Directions**: *From Frankton Road, turn up Suburb Street, then first right into Panorama Terrace. Access via Sunset Lane.*
Home Page: http://nz.com/Queenstown/Birchall.House

Queenstown
Homestay and Garden Room
Address: Grant Road, 1 R.D.,
Queenstown
Name: Pat & Ron Collins
Telephone: (03) 442 3801
Beds: 2 Queen, 2 Single (3 bedrooms)
Bathroom: 1 Ensuite, 1 Private
Tariff: B&B (full) Double $80,
Single $60. Garden Room $90.
Credit cards.
NZ B&B Vouchers accepted & $10 surcharge.
Nearest Town: Queenstown 10 mins

Pat & Ron offer warm relaxed Kiwi hospitality in a rural environment with lovely mountain views. Our new sunny home with separate guest wing is surrounded by lovely gardens. Bathroom with bath and shower. Rooms with Woolrests, electric blankets, heaters. Laundry facilities no charge. We are 'retired' and interested in travelling, golf, gardening and walking Sam, our outside Golden Labrador. BJ the cat prefers to lie in the sun. Golf clubs, gold pans, fishing rods could be available for your use.
GARDEN ROOM: New warm bedsit.   1 Queen with ensuite, TV, Refrigerator, Microwave, BBQ. Looking forward to meeting you.
Directions: *North: 1 km before Frankton on SH 6. Name on mailbox. Go down Grants Road, first turn left through farm gate to end of road.*
South: turn right at Frankton on SH6 second right Grant Road.

Queenstown
Homestay
Address: 8B Birse Street,
Frankton, Queenstown
Name: Shirley & Pat Paulin
Telephone: (03) 442 3387
Beds: 1 Double, 2 Singles
(2 bedrooms)
Bathroom: 1 guests share
Tariff: B&B (full) Double $90,
Single $50, Children $25, Dinner $25 per person.
Nearest Town: Queenstown 6km

Welcome to "Paulin Place" a homestay where you can enjoy relaxed and friendly hospitality with the hosts in their surrounding.
Our home is situated in sunny Frankton, 6km from the centre of Queenstown in a picturesque garden with views of Lake Wakatipu and the Remarkables. Courtesy transport provided if required.
Pat grew up in the district, so is conversant with the history of the Wakatipu Basin. Our interests are gardening, walking, fishing, gold mining, reading, cooking, embroidery, wine making, entertaining and meeting people from other countries as well as New Zealand.
Explore the wonders through your hosts local knowledge.
Directions: *Please phone for reservations and directions.*

Queenstown
Homestay/B&B
Address: BJ's Place, 36 Lochy Rd,
Fernhill, Queenstown
Name: Berit & John Brown
Telephone: (03) 442 8348
Fax: (03) 442 8348
Beds: 1 Double, 3 Single (2 bedrooms)
Bathroom: 1 Guests share
Tariff: B&B (continental) Double $95,
Single $50, Children under 12 half price.
Credit cards. NZ B&B Vouchers accepted $20 surcharge
Nearest Town: Queenstown 5 min

Welcome to BJ's Place where you are assured of warm and friendly hospitality - A home away from home - with peaceful and relaxed atmosphere in our new modern and spacious home overlooking Lake Wakatipu - Cecil Peak and the Remarkables.
We are an informal semi-retired couple of English / Norwegian origin with 3 children spread around the country and we love meeting people from all walks of life.
Our 2 guestrooms on the lower floor are warm, private and spacious 1 room with a double and a single bed the other with 2 single beds and guests share bathroom facilities.
Continental breakfast with fresh fruit, homemade muesli, yoghurt etc or cooked if you prefer with plenty of brewed coffee or tea.
Make Queenstown your destination which offers a wealth of activities for all ages all the year round. We are "smokefree".
Directions: *Please phone for direction.*

Queenstown
Guest Units B&B
"HIGHVIEW" Guest Units Queentown N.Z.
Address: 'Highview',
17 Wakatipu Heights, Queenstown
Name: Highview
Telephone: (03) 442 9414
Fax: (03) 442 9414
Mobile: (021) 702 705
Beds: 2 Queen,1 Single (3 Bedrooms)
Bathroom: 3 Ensuite
Tariff: B&B (continental) Double $55pp,
Single $76, Share Triple $42pp.   NZ B&B Vouchers accepted Surcharge $39
Nearest Town: Town centre 10 minutes walk or $5 taxi.

Imagine! Floor to ceiling glass with unobstructed panoramic lake and mountain views. The sound of birds. The convenience of your ensuite bathroom. Safe parking, walk to Queenstowns shops including fifty restaurants. Be uplifted for a jet boat safari, Milford, Doubtful Sounds or enjoy the view, alpine air and peaceful environment. Welcome to our home, 100 metres above Lake Wakatipu on the side of Queenstown Hill. Ann, a nurse and Mike, a local government officer home hosted for five years prior to building these especially designed, warm private guests units. Each with separate entrance, ensuite bathroom, TV and tea / coffee facilities. Steps to the units which are secluded among rhododendrons and conifers allow spectacular views of Lake Wakatipu, golf course, yacht club and Remarkable Mountains. Sumptuous breakfast included. **Directions**: *Turn up Suburb Street off Frankton Road. Then first right into Panorama Terrace, second left into Wakatipu Heights.*
"A warm welcome awaits you"

"NUMBER TWELVE"

Queenstown
Bed & Breakfast, Homestay
Address: 12 Brisbane St, Queenstown - "quiet and convenient"
Name: Barbara & Murray Hercus
Telephone: (03) 442 9511
Fax: (03) 442-9755
Email: hercusbb@queenstown.co.nz
Beds: 1 Studio King or Twin, 1 Room King or Twin (2 Bedrooms)
Bathroom: 1 Ensuite, 1 Private with bath and shower.
Tariff: B&B (continental) Double $110, Single $70, Dinner by arrangement $35.
Credit Cards: Visa/Mastercard. NZ B&B Vouchers accepted $30 surcharge per night
Nearest Town: We are only a 3 minute walk to town centre,

We would like you to come and share our quiet convenient home situated in a no exit street. Our home has lake and mountain views. A warm, centrally heated home, all bedrooms have TV and tea/coffee making facilities. Laundry facilities available. We have a solar heated swimming pool (Nov - March), this plus sundeck and BBQ for your use. While we serve a continental breakfast, a cooked breakfast can be provided by arrangement at a small additional charge. There are several walking routes to the town centre - a short one through the Botanical gardens or via the Lake shore if you would like a longer stroll. Once settled with us you will seldom need to use your car. We have both travelled extensively, our interests include classical/choral music. Barbara had a nursing/social work career, Murray a retired chartered accountant. Our Burmese cat will join us in welcoming you to our home. We will be happy to assist you when planning your local activities. E-mail facilities available.
Directions: *Highway 6A into Queenstown becomes Frankton Road. Do not veer right into Stanley Street at the Millenium Hotel corner, carry on straight ahead. Brisbane Street is the second street on your left, a sharp left turn and we are on the left side. Our sign is "Number Twelve".*
Home Page: http://www.qt.co.nz/no12/

Queenstown
Bed & Breakfast
Address: 'Brecman Lodge',
15 Man Street
Name: Pat & Kevin MacDonell
Telephone: (03) 442 8908
Fax: (03) 442 8904
Beds: 1 Double, 5 Single
(3 Bedrooms)
Bathroom: 1 Guests share, 1 Family share
Tariff: B&B (continental) Double $85, Single $60.
Credit Cards. NZ B&B Vouchers accepted $15 surcharge
Nearest Town: Queenstown, 2 minutes walk from the centre of town

Brecman Lodge is homestyle NZ hospitality at its best. Brecman Lodge is situated on the corner of Brecon and Man Streets, opposite the top of the Brecon Street steps, just above Queenstown's town centre. Brecman Lodge is friendly, warm and comfortable with single, twin and family accommodation. Upstairs is a bathroom and two bedrooms; one room has a double bed and the other has two single beds. Downstairs consists of guest lounge, bedroom with two single beds and a guest share bathroom. The warm comfortable guest lounge has a television and a wonderful view of the Queenstown's township, Lake Wakatipu, Walter Peak and The Remarkables. A continental breakfast is served in the lounge. From Brecman Lodge guests have easy walking access to the town centre, Lake Wakatipu and the Gondola. Queenstown's centre has a wide range of quality tourist shops, many restaurants and sporting and adventure opportunities all year round. There is ample and easy off street parking. Do come and stay I'm sure you'll love it.

Queenstown
Guest House
Address: 27 Lomond Crescent,
P O Box 851, Queenstown
Name: 'Scallywags' Guest House
Telephone: (03) 442 7083
Fax: (03) 442 5885
Beds: 3 Double, 3 Twin
(6 bedrooms)
Bathroom: 2 Guests share
Tariff: (Bed only-breakfast available on request)
Double $55, Twin $27.50pp, Children under 5 years free.
Nearest Town: Queenstown 700 metres

A unique New Zealand home for you to share. We are a "B&B with no B". However, bring your own food and use the excellent kitchen and great bbq area. Tea, coffee and milk is complimentary. Linen, towels, duvets and electric blankets are on all beds. Share bathroom facilities. Famously Fantastic views - 180 degrees panorama - sunrise to sunset - lake mountains, valleys. The ambience is casual and informal. Enjoy world class conversation. The house is situated adjacent to a bush reserve with native birdlife and song abundant. A peaceful haven just 10 minutes pleasant walk to village centre. Please don't just view from the road. You are invited to come up and inspect the rooms and views etc. We have one cat called Domino. Resident host / owner offers: personal service, visitor information, local knowledge, free pick-up, smoke free. Reservations recommended.   Service   Ambience   Value

Queenstown
Homestay
Address: 4 Panorama Tce,
Queenstown
Name: Elsie & Pat Monaghan
Telephone: (03) 442 8690
Fax: (03) 442 8620
Mobile: 025-2231 880
Beds: 1 Queen (1 bedroom)
Bathroom: 1 Ensuite
Tariff: B&B (full)
Double $90, Single $70.
NZ B&B Vouchers accepted $20 surcharge
Nearest Town: Queenstown 5 minute walk

Our house is situated close to town with panoramic views of the mountains and Lake Wakatipu. Off-street parking. Our spacious guest room is private with a separate entrance and garden patio. It has a table for letter writing, heater, radio, television, fridge, and tea, coffee and biscuits supplied; Queen bed with electric blanket and you have your own bathroom, shower and toilet. Breakfast at the time that suits you. Queenstown has an excellent variety of restaurants. Our interests include sport, music, pottery, gardening, travelling and meeting people. We will enjoy your company but respect your privacy. We can meet you at the airport or bus depot if required.
Directions: *Turn right up Suburb St. off Frankton Road which is the main road into Queenstown. The first right into Panorama Tce to No.4.*

Queenstown Central
A Small Boutique Hotel
Address: 69 Hallenstein St, Queenstown
Name: Queenstown House
Telephone: (03) 442 9043
Fax: (03) 442-8755 **Mobile**: (025) 324 146
Email: queenstown.house@xtra.co.nz
Beds: 8 King (8 bedrooms)
Bathroom: 8 Ensuite
Tariff: B&B (special) Double $185, Single $165. Dinner by arrangement. Credit cards (VISA/BC/MC/AMEX). NZ B&B Vouchers accepted 2 vouchers required
Nearest Town: Queenstown - 300 metres

In 1994 Louise Kiely transformed one of Queenstown's oldest guest houses into what is now firmly established as the "best small B&B Hotel" in town. Louise has owned 3 successful restaurants, having gained her culinary skills in Euope, and has been catering to the discerning traveller for over 20 years. The 8 rooms all have private bathrooms, king size beds, crisp white linen, European duvets and plenty of plump pillows. Each room is individually decorated and has a "Town and Country" elegance. The elevated position allows every room magnificent lake and mountain views. Off-street parking is available with the town centre only 300 metres away. Breakfast is included and is served in our private lake view dining room. It is hearty and wholesome, using the best local seasonal foods served with aromatic freshly brewed coffee. A selection of beverages are available all day long in the guests' kitchenette. Dinner is on request. Between 6.00 and 7.00pm each evening complimentary New Zealand wine and cheese is served in the cosy fireside sitting room or in the fragrant courtyard, depending on the season. Television, hairdryers and heating are in all rooms. Laundry, valet service and baggage storage is available. We are "smoke free".Because of our size and popularity, 7 days cancellation is required, otherwise full tariff is payable.
Home Page: http://nz.com/Queenstown/House

Queenstown
Self-contained Accommodation
Address: "Anna's Cottage",
67 Thompson Street, Queenstown
Name: Myrna & Ken Sangster
Telephone: (03) 442 8994
Fax: (03) 441 8994
Beds: 1 Queen (1 bedroom)
Bathroom: 1 Private
Tariff: Double $85,
Single $55,
$15 extra per person.
Breakfast available on request $10 extra.
Nearest Town: Queenstown 5minute walk.

A warm welcome to Anna's Cottage.
Myrna a keen gardener and golfer, Ken with a love of fishing.
Enjoy the peaceful garden setting and mountain views at Anna's Cottage. Full kitchen facilities and living room combined. Tastefully decorated throughout, the bedroom is furnished with Sheridan linen. Only a few minutes from the centre of Queenstown. Private drive and parking at cottage. We are smoke-free.
Airport transfers by arrangement.

Queenstown
B&B
Address: "Turner Lodge",
Cnr Turner St. & Gorge Rd,
Queenstown
Name: Hazel Seeto
Telephone: (03) 442 9432
Fax: (03) 442 9409
Email: turnerlodge@xtra.co.nz
Beds: 1 Double, 2 Single
(2 bedrooms)
Bathroom: 2 Ensuites
Tariff: B&B (full)
Double $100, Single $65,
Credit Cards (VISA/BC/MC).
Nearest Town: Queenstown 3 min walk

I offer friendly hospitality in a warm, comfortable home. It is 3 minutes walk to central Queenstown - you don't have to climb any hills but there is still a lovely view. On-site parking and laundry facilities are available. Each room has its own TV and tea / coffee making facilities. The double room has ensuite with bath, shower box, vanity and toilet. I serve a full menu breakfast which is available from 6-9am.
I am happy to help you organise your activities and make local reservations for you. Seasonal rates available.
Home Page: http://www.nz.accommodation.co.nz/stay/turnerlodge

Queenstown
Homestay
Address: 2 Perkins Road,
Queenstown
Name:
Stanley & Isobel Bremner
Telephone: (03) 442 3415
Beds: 1 King,
2 Single (2 bedrooms)
Bathroom: 1 Guests share
Tariff: B&B (continental)
King $85, Single $45,
Children under 12 $25.
Nearest Town: Queenstown

We are situated halfway between Queenstown and Frankton township (satellite to Queenstown). We look directly onto Lake Wakatipu. The Remarkables Mountains, Cecil Peak, Kelvin Heights and the famous Queenstown Golf Course can be seen across the lake. The walkway to Queenstown begins at the bottom of our road at the Marina. A lounge with television and video is available for guests also a pool room for relaxation.

We are retired from a nursing and farming background and have lived here for forty years. Smokers welcome. Electric and continental blankets are on all beds for winter and summer comfort. Heaters and bedside lights in all rooms. Laundry facilities are available and we have a springer spaniel. Excellent off street parking.

Directions: *Proceeding towards Queenstown along main Frankton Road turn off into Perkins Rd., on right, past Marina and Service Station.*
Our house, brown; first on left.

Queenstown
B&B+Self-contained Accom.
Address: 10 Wakatipu Heights,
Queenstown
Name: Ruth & Owen Campbell
Telephone: (03) 442 9190
Fax: (03) 442 4404
Beds: S.C. Unit, 1 Queen, 1 Double,
1 Single (2 Bedrooms)
House: Super King/Twin (1 Bedroom)
Bathroom: 1 Private, 1 Guests share
Tariff: B&B (continental)
Double $100-$120, Single $60-$70. Generous family rates. Credit Cards.
NZ B&B Vouchers accepted $20 surcharge on self contained unit.
Nearest Town: Queenstown - 10 minutes walk

As we have 2 girls at school, children are welcome in our home. Our level section has covered, off street parking and playground. We can also provide child care. Tea, coffee and herbal teas are complimentary. Our tranquil home with one cat is in a quiet garden setting and has outstanding views over Lake Wakatipu and Queenstown. Owen and I have a good knowledge of the area. Our fully self contained 2 bedroom cottage garden unit with BBQ, laundry etc has proven immensely popular with guests - especially those with children! This allows you complete privacy or to mix with us as you wish. A super king or twin bedroom with private bathroom is in the house. Complimentary laundry. There are no stairs as all guest facilities are on ground level. Enjoy a generous continental breakfast including fresh baked bread and real coffee at your leisure. Cooked breakfast $5 per person extra. Guest pick-up is available. We request no smoking inside please. Guests say "Excellent value for money".

Fernhill, Queenstown

B&B+Self-contained Suite
Address: 107 Wynyard Crescent,
Fernhill, Queenstown
Name: "Haus Helga"
(Ed & Helga Coolman)
Telephone: (03) 442 6077
Fax: (03) 442 4957
Email: haushelga@xtra.co.nz
Beds: 2 King/Queen, 1 Double, 2 Single (3 bedrooms)
Bathroom: 3 Ensuite, 1 with Spa Tub, all with hair dryers
Tariff: B&B (special) Rooms $139 to $239.
Credit Cards (MC/Visa/BC) Vouchers accepted $45 Surcharge
Nearest Town: Queenstown 3km, 5 minutes

Haus Helga

Haus Helga overlooks Lake Wakatipu and the Remarkables Mountains and provides the "best view in all of New Zealand!" Our luxurious home has extra large tastefully furnished guest rooms, each with a private deck or terrace. The self-contained suite includes a large kitchen / dining / living room. We offer a lounge with TV and a games room with an octagon bumper pool table for our guests enjoyment. We can provide honeymoon specials, family plans, tour bookings and courtesy transport. We are now in our fourth year of operation and we feel truly fortunate to have made so many great new friends, our wonderful guests. They have been so kind in their comments: "Without a doubt, the Ritz-Carlton of B&B's." "Best bed, best views, wonderful hospitality." "I won't forget your great breakfast, Helga." "Perfect hosts, perfect breakfast, perfect accommodation." Helga speaks fluent German and some Japanese. We are smoke-free inside. **Directions**: *Please call for reservations and directions.*
Home Page: http://nz.com/webnz/bbnz/helga.htm

Queenstown

Homestay
Address: "Windsor Heights"
5 Windsor Place, Queenstown
Name: Diane & Bill Forsyth
Telephone: (03) 442 5949 and
0800 27 16 17 **Fax**: (03) 441 8989
Email: windsor.heights@clear.net.nz
Beds: 1 Queen, 2 Single (2 Bedrooms)
Bathroom: 1 Ensuite, 1 Private
Tariff: B&B (full) Double$120, Single $80. Children under 12 $45.
Credit Cards (VISA/MC/Amex).
Nearest Town: Queenstown - 15 minutes walk to town centre

Our modern home sits high above Queenstown, offering breathtaking views of mountains and lake. The sheltered courtyard provides a relaxed outdoor living style, complete with gas barbecue and large spa / hot tub. On summer evenings this area is a real favourite, before moving to the lounge and watching fabulous sunsets across the lake. We invite our guests to join us for refreshments in the evening before leaving for dinner in one of the many superb restaurants that Queenstown offers. A courtesy car is available to meet guests. As authorised booking agents, we will gladly offer advice and help arrange your Queenstown activities. If walking is your pleasure we have the Queenstown Hill track close by. We have one very shy cat named Zinny who chooses to hide from our guests as a rule, but might be persuaded to say hello to cat lovers! Ours is a non-smoking environment.
Directions: *Pass Quality Resort Terraces on right, then take 2nd street on right (Dublin St). Continue up hill into Edinburgh Drive, then left into Windsor Place - we are No. 5 on left.*
Home Page: www.queenstown-holiday.co.nz

Queenstown
Guest House
Address: 10 Isle St., Queenstown
Name: The Dairy Guesthouse
Telephone: (03) 442 5164
Freephone: 0800 333 393
Fax: (03) 442 5164
Mobile: (025) 204 2585
Email: TheDairy@xtra.co.nz
Beds: 4 Queen,
6 Single/3 King (7 bedrooms)
Bathroom: 7 Ensuite
Tariff: B&B (full) Double $180-$220,
Single $180, Dinner by request. Winter rates available.
Credit Cards accepted.
Nearest Town: Queenstown (2 minute walk)

The Dairy Guesthouse ..... a boutique bed & breakfast located, just 150m from the town centre. The ideal central location from which to explore wonderful Queenstown and the surrounding alpine region. This very special place....has six private rooms all with en-suite, lounge room with a cosy fire, ski storage and off street parking. A relaxing retreat. The Dairy.... once a 1930's general store, now lovingly restored offers the intimate appeal of a traditional setting, where a full breakfast served each morning ensures a great start to the day. The Dairy Guesthouse....surrounded by views of the stunning Remarkables mountain range, Coronet Peak and tranquil Queenstown Bay. Conveniently situated below the Skyline Gondola, on the corner of Brecon and Isle Streets. Reservations are recommended. Your hosts Brian and Sarah welcome you.
Home Page: http://www.thedairy.co.nz

Queenstown
Boutique Hotel
Address: 1 Dublin St, Queenstown
Name: Chalet Queenstown
Telephone: (03) 442 7117
or (03) 441 8821
Fax: (03) 442 7508
Mobile: (025) 330 834
Beds: 6 King/Queen,
14 Single (6 bedrooms)
Bathroom: 6 Ensuite
Tariff: B&B (continental) Single Standard $145,
Double Standard $165, Single Superior $165, Double Superior $185. Family $225.
NZ B&B Vouchers accepted 1 May-30 September
Nearest Town: Queenstown - 500m to town centre

Chalet Queenstown has been selected by "Superior Inns of NZ" for its commitment to providing quality accommodation, hearty breakfasts and gracious hospitality for the discerning traveller. Chalet Queenstown offers 6 rooms, all with private ensuite, and decorated in a town & country elegance, plenty of pillows, feather duvets and fresh flowers to create a feeling of luxury. The elevated position gives each room magnificent lake and mountain views. Enjoy at your leisure a delicious cooked breakfast also home-made cereals, fresh seasonal fruits, croissants, muffins, yoghurt, home-made preserves, juice and freshly brewed tea or coffee. Complimentary drinks are available in the lounge, or courtyard garden from 6/7pm each evening. We are situated in a very sunny and peaceful location only 400 yards easy walk to the town centre.

Queenstown
Bed & Breakfast

Address: PO Box 623, Atley Road,
Arthurs Point, Queenstown
Name: Kerry and Graeme Hastie,
Hollyhock Inn
Telephone: (03) 441 8037
Fax: (03) 441 8058
Email: hollyhock@queenstown.co.nz
Beds: 3 Queen, 2 Single (3 bedrooms)
Bathroom: 3 Ensuite
Tariff: B&B (special) Double $220, Single $195,
Not suitable for children, Credit Cards.
Nearest Town: Queenstown 6km

Discover "Hollyhock Inn", surrounded by its lush acreage of garden only 5 minutes drive from Queenstown. This tranquil homestay has unobstructed views of the spectacular alpine environment - above, the encircling mountains - snowclad in Winter - tussock golden in summer and below the famous gold-bearing Shotover River. Hollyhock Inn's locality enables visitors to choose between Queenstown's myriad adventures, such as dining, walking, skiing and horse riding or to simply relax and contemplate within its beautiful environs. The large and elegantly decorated guest suites are all separate from the main house enabling guests to have their much needed peace and privacy together with panoramic rural alpine views and their own private balconies. Each suite has ensuite bathrooms, queen and single sized beds with electric blankets, quality bathrobes and toiletries, hairdryers, cotton linen, tea and coffee making facilities, televisions, fresh flowers and homemade biscuits. We have one pet cat. Our house is non smoking. **Home Page**: http://www.hollyhockinn.co.nz

---

Queenstown
Self Contained Accommodation/B&B

Address: 13 Panorama Terrace, Queenstown.
Name: Maree Dawson
Telephone: 03-442 9444
Beds: 1 Queen, 1 Single
Bathroom: 1 Private
Tariff: B&B (continental)
$55 pp ($65 pp if one night only).
Dinner $25 per person.
Nearest Town: Queenstown, 8 min. walking , also on Bus route.

Our home in Panorama Terrace is in the dress circle, with fantastic views of Lake Wakatipu and the mountains. We are keen gardeners and have a private sunny courtyard garden for relaxing and outdoor living. Off street parking is provided.
All beds have duvets, electric blankets and reading lamps. Guests may have a private den with TV, VCR or share family living areas. Tea and coffee making facilities are available.
Our interests include overseas travel, education, local history, pottery, embroidery, music, golf and gardening. Help given with organising sight seeing and travel.
Directions: *Turn up Suburb Street, off Frankton Road (State Highway 6), then right into Panorama Terrace.*

Queenstown
Homestay, Bed & Breakfast
Address: Birchwood, Rapid No. 78.
Lower Shotover Road,
RD1, Queenstown
Name: Richard and Lynne Farrar
Telephone: (03) 442 3499.
Reservations 0800 364 550
Fax: (03) 442 3498
Beds: 1 King, 1 Double ,
2 Single (3 Bedrooms)
Bathroom: 1 Ensuite, 1 Private
Tariff: B&B (Continental/Full on request) Double $110-$140, Single $100.
Children under 13 years half price. Credit cards accepted.
Nearest Town: Just off SH6, 11 kms from Queenstown; 5 kms from airport

You are warmly invited to stay with us in our modern, classic style country home set in a sunny, sheltered two acre garden surrounded by farmland. Relax in a private, tranquil setting with mountain views or enjoy a game of tennis on our court.
The house is single storeyed with good access and easy parking. In winter there is underfloor heating, a wood burner / open fire. There is a spacious guest room with ensuite bathroom and its own entrance, and a choice of twin or double bedroom with a bathroom with bath. Children are welcome. Laundry and drying facilities. No smoking indoors.
We are close to cafes and restaurants, wineries, skifields and golf courses. Our interests are gardening, fishing, farming, reading and the outdoors. We look forward to welcoming you and ensuring you have an enjoyable visit in this unique area.
Directions: *Please phone.*

Queenstown
Homestay/B&B
Address: 16 Panners Way,
Goldfields, Queenstown
Name: Maria and Chris Lamens
Telephone: (03) 442 4811
Fax: (03) 441 8882
Email: chris@larchhill.com
Beds: 3 Double, 1 Twin (4 Bedrooms)
Bathroom: 2 Ensuite, 2 Private,
Tariff: B&B (Special)
Double $120-$130, Twin $100, Apartment $140.
Single $75. Dinner $35. Credit cards accepted: Visa/BankCard/Mastercard
Nearest Town: Queenstown

All rooms and sun-deck overlook the blue waters of Lake Wakatipu and surrounding mountains. Situated at Gold-fields, Larch-Hill homestay is only 3 min. drive from Queenstown's Centre. This home provides a feeling of relaxation. A restful theme flows through the bedrooms into the dining room with its library, opening to a sunny courtyard. On arrival you are welcomed with fresh coffee and home made cake. In winter there is a roaring log fire awaiting your return from a days skiing or sightseeing. Having worked as a chef, Maria provides three course dinners by prior arrangement. Breakfast; continental, home made bread and yoghurt, fresh fruit salad. We have pleasure in organising any Queenstown experiences. We speak English, German and Italian. We provide: complimentary pick-up from Queenstown airport or bus-station. Fax and e-mail communication facilities. Smoke free accommodation. **Directions**: *From Highway 6A turn into Goldfield heights at Sherwood Manor. Drive up the hill. Second left is Panners way.* **Home Page**: http://www.larchhill.com

Queenstown
Homestay, Self Contained Acocmmodation, Guest House
Address: 24 Mcmillan Road, Arthurs Point, Queenstown
Name: Ester Jh Yoon
Telephone: (03) 442 5299
Fax: (03) 441 8819
Mobile: (025) 238 8578
Beds: 2 King, 3 Double, 6 Single (7 Bedrooms)
Bathroom: 1 Ensuite, 2 Private, 1 Guests share
Tariff: B&B (Continental) Double ensuite $180 - $150, Double $85, Single $65,
Dinner $35, Children under 12 half price. Credit cards: Visa/Mastercard/Amex.
Free pick up from airport.
Nearest Town: Queenstown (7 km/5 mins)

A warm welcome awaits you at Camelot Lodge, situated at historic Arthurs Point, with splendid rural views over the Shotover River towards Coronet Peak. Dowe steps, our lovely home is spacious and sunny, with attractive guest rooms. The large lounge opens onto generous sundecks: a perfect spot to relax. A three bedroom fully self-contained holiday apartment is also available - sleeps six. We have lived and worked extensively overseas and have been involved with tourism / hospitality for 10 years. We also have a detailed knowledge of this region.
Camelot Lodge is a short drive from Queenstown, and 2 km from the Coronet Peak ski area turn off. Summers in this rural setting are delightful. Activities include golf, walking, tramping, riding and jet boating / rafting on the famous Shotover river. Complimentary tea / coffee available. No smoking indoors please. We look forward to making your stay with us memorable. Your hostess Esther Yoon.

Garston
Homestay
Address: 17 Blackmore Road,
Garston.
Please phone for directions
Name: Bev and Matt Menlove
Telephone: (03) 248 8516
Beds: 1 Double,
2 Single (1 Bedroom)
Bathroom: 1 Ensuite
Tariff: B&B (continental)
Double $70, Single $40, Dinner $20.
NZ B&B Vouchers accepted
Nearest Town: Lumsden 30 km,
Queenstown 50 km

We are organic gardeners and our other interests include lawn bowls, sailing, gliding and alternative energy.
Garston is New Zealand's most inland village with the Mataura River (famous for its fly fishing) flowing through the valley, surrounded by the Hector Range and the Eyre Mountains. A fishing guide is available with advance notice.
For day trips, Garston is central to Queenstown, Te Anau, Milford Sound or Invercargill. We look forward to meeting you.
Directions: *Please phone for directions.*

Kingston/Garston

High Country Station Experience.
Address: "Mataura Valley Station",
Cainard Rd., PO Box 2, Garston, 9660, Southland
Name: Robyn & David Parker
Telephone: (03) 248 8552
Fax: (03) 248 8552
Email: matauravalleystation@nzhomestay.co.nz
Beds: 2 King, 1 Double, 4 Single (5 bedrooms)
Bathroom: 2 Ensuite, 1 Guests share, 2 Family Share
Tariff: B&B (full) Double $100-$120, Single $60, Dinner $30, Children under 12
meals half price. Credit Cards. Family suite: 3 bedrooms, private bathroom $220,
exclusive occupancy $400. NZ B&B Vouchers accepted $10 - $20 Surcharge
Nearest Town: Kingston 20km, Garston 17km, Queenstown 50km

*Welcome to our 19,000 acre sheep and cattle station overlooking the Mataura river, famous
for brown trout fishing. Comfortable modern home with glorious views and sunny site.
Experience Alpine tranquillity 10 km from the Queenstown-Te Anau highway. Only an hours
scenic drive from Queenstown. Enjoy farm activities, go fishing, mountain biking, take a walk,
or soak up the view. Enjoy skylarks, paradise ducks, water birds, hawks and New Zealand
falcons. Farm-style meals with vegetables fresh from David's organic garden. We have 10,000
sheep, 350 cattle, 6 sheep dogs and 2 cats. Fishing guides arranged with advance notice. A
great base for travel to Fiordland or Queenstown. Aerial
trips by arrangement. Complimentary mini-tour of farm,
4-wheel drive mountain tours, 1/2 day (extra cost). Adult
family involved in travel, shearing, massage therapy and
teaching outdoor skills. We aim to make your stay a
special memory. We look forward to meeting you.
Pre-arrival notification please.*

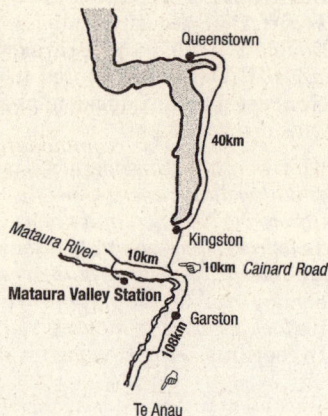

St Bathans Village

Self-contained Accommodation
Address: "The School Teachers (1879) Cottage",
St Bathans, R.D. Oturehua,
Central Otago 9071
Name: Lorraine and Tristan
Telephone: (03) 482-1067 or (03) 447 3624
Beds: 2 Queen (2 double bedrooms),
one fold-down double settee.
Bathroom: 1 Private
Tariff: Self contained: B&B (continental) Double $95 per day, minimum stay two days,
Self Contained Double $80 per day for 3 days and over. Children under 12 free. Discounts negotiable for stays over a week.
Nearest Town: Alexandra 30 minutes, Ranfurly 20 minutes, Queenstown 90 minutes.

*This delightful, 100 year old stone cottage (1879), is nestled in the tranquil, historic, goldmining village of St Bathans, at the foot of Mt St Bathans, Central Otago's highest mountain. Amidst spectacular, tussock covered high country. It is a place where nature holds sway and time is forgotten. Wrapped in snow in winter, gold leafed in autumn, fresh green and lush with wild-flowers in spring, and in summer, swimming in the Blue Lake with its magnificent sculptured cliffs. St Bathans has many heritage buildings, beautiful walks, horse riding, trout fishing, mountain biking and hunting. The cottage provides peace, privacy and comfort. Enjoy a cosy log fire, fresh flowers, and generous breakfast provisions. All modern conveniences are provided for self catering, you can provide your own meals or dine at the historic Vulcan Hotel (1882). Within easy driving distance of Queenstown, Wanaka, the Lakes District, historic Naseby, Clyde, Alexandra and Cromwell. **Directions**: Turn off Highway 85, 90 minutes from Queenstown, Wanaka, 2 hours from Dunedin.*

Earnscleugh - Alexandra

Orchard Stay
Address: 'Iversen',
47 Blackman Road, Earnscleugh,
Alexandra
Name: Robyn & Roger Marshall
Telephone: (03) 449 2520
Fax: (03) 449 2519
Mobile: (025) 384 348
Beds: 2 Queen (2 bedrooms)
Bathroom: 1 Guests share
Tariff: B&B (continental) Double $80,
Single $45, Dinner $25. NZ B&B Vouchers accepted $10 surcharge
Nearest Town: Alexandra 6km, Clyde 8km

Our detached guest accommodation offers you privacy and comfort and combined with a warm welcome into our home, you can share with us, the peaceful and relaxing location of our orchard setting. Around the festive season you can enjoy our cherry harvest. Take in our garden setting, walk the adjoining hills, or just relax. Rooms have tea making facilities, heating, electric blankets, TV and radio. Golfing, fishing, iceskating, vineyards, craft galleries, and museums all within 10 minutes drive. Experience the grandeur and contrasts of the Central Otago landscape by staying an extra night and joining us on a 4WD trip into the mountains, an orchard tour, or a wine trail. (Indicate interest at time of booking - extra cost)
Directions: *From Alexandra or Clyde, travel on Earnscleugh Road, turn into Blackman Road, look for our sign on left. Advance bookings preferred.*

Alexandra
Vineyard Homestay/Bed & Breakfast
Address: Hawkdun Rise Vineyard,
Letts Gully Road, Alexandra RD3
Name: Judy & Roy Faris
Telephone: (03) 448 7782
Fax: (03) 448 7752
Mobile: (025) 337 072
Email: rfaris@clear.net.nz
Beds: 2 Queen, 1 Double (3 bedrooms)
Bathroom: 2 Ensuite, 1 Guests share
Tariff: B&B (special) Double $115, Single $85.
Nearest Town: Alexandra 6 Kms(approx)

Less than five minutes from Alexandra our spacious new home is set in a small developing vineyard and commands expansive views of the Dunstan, Hawkdun and Old Man Ranges. We have designed our home to provide a semi-detached guest accommodation wing with verandahs and deck.
We are a professional couple with grown family and have travelled widely. We share our home with Tess, a small springer spaniel and Rodger, a Burmese cat, all non smokers.
Laundry, tea and coffee making facilities are available.
Complimentary wines and cheeses served early evening.
You can enjoy the privacy, views, a spa and our small underground cellar.
We are able to arrange wine trails, lake fishing and 4WD trips.
If you are looking for privacy, tranquillity accompanied by first class accommodation along with the space to be as sociable as you please - you have found us.
Directions: *Please phone or fax.*

Alexandra
Country Homestay
Address: "Ardshiel",
Letts Gully, Alexandra
Name: Ian & Joan Stewart
Telephone: (03) 448 9136
Fax: (03) 448 9136
Mobile: (025) 732 973
Beds: 1 King, 1 Double,
2 Single (2 bedrooms)
Bathroom: 1 Ensuite, 1 Guests share
Tariff: B&B (full) Double $110,
Single $75, Dinner by arrangement.
Nearest Town: Alexandra 3km

Nestled in a peaceful sheltered valley, our country homestead offers superior accommodation only minutes from Alexandra. A new Cape Cod design house, spacious rooms, an air of elegance, luxurious suite for guests, ensuite, formal dining room, spacious lounge and outdoor spa for total relaxation. Rest, enjoy the crystal clear air and absorb the tranquil atmosphere. Stroll amongst the mature trees and gardens of the old established house site. Meander through the fruit trees, up the thyme covered hill for breathtaking views of Central Otago, or simply put your feet up and relax in our sun drenched private courtyard. We provide a full travel service including guided tours, historic goldfield excursions, ski trips (in season), golf days, pick up and delivery to airports or other tourist destinations. Sample the superb local cuisine, bookings can be arranged at several excellent local restaurants or enjoy a beautiful meal in our own dining room. We enjoy the company of our little dog Ollie.

Alexandra

Homestay
Address: "Duart", Bruce's Hill,
No 3 RD, Alexandra, Highway 85
Name: Mary and Keith McLean
Telephone: (03) 448 9190
Fax: (03) 448 9190
Beds: 1 Double, 1 3/4
2 Single (3 Bedrooms)
Bathroom: 1 Private,
1 Family Share
Tariff: B&B (Continental) Double $70,
Single $35, Dinner $20, Children under 12 years half price.
Nearest Town: Alexandra

Your accredited Kiwi-Hosts, Mary and Keith, welcome you to our secluded home, situated only 5 minutes from Alexandra, where spectacular views from all windows and balcony offer some idea of the grandeur and contrasts to be found here in the heart of Central Otago, a 'Place For All Seasons'.

We are an hour's drive from Queenstown and Wanaka, close to other lakes, dams and rivers. Or you may prefer to climb the hills, especially when the Thyme is flowering; walk the trails; fossick amongst gold-mining ruins; visit a winery, museum, gallery; explore the shops and restaurants; play a sport.

If feeling jaded, you are most welcome to relax on our verandahs, benefiting from our unique Central air, or wander around our extensive garden or 10 acres. Our cat, 'Horse" may accompany you. Laundry facilities are available, and perhaps you would care to share some of our many varied interests after a dinner of traditional Southland/Otago fare.

Roxburgh - Dumbarton

Country Inn
Address: 4760 Roxburgh-Ettrick Road,
SH8, No. 2 R.D., Roxburgh
Name: The Seed Farm
Telephone: (03) 446 6824
Fax: (03) 446 6024
Beds: 3 Queen, 2 Single (4 bedrooms)
Bathroom: 4 Ensuite
Tariff: B&B (continental) Double/Twin $100,
Dinner a la carte, All credit cards.
Nearest Town: Roxburgh 9km

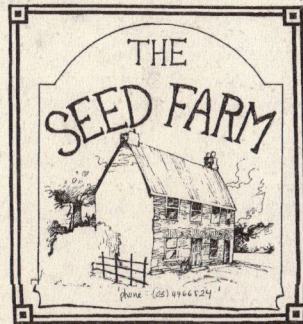

The Seed Farm is one of the oldest properties in the Teviot Valley constructed in 1869 of local schist, it comprises a two storeyed cottage and separate stables set amidst two acres of cottage gardens. The buildings all carry Historic Places Trust 2 classification reflecting their historic significance to the district.

The stables have been refurbished and offer 4 bedrooms (with ensuites), central heating, TV and tea making facilities.

The ground floor of the cottage was converted to a restaurant in 1990 and offers an eclectic menu in an olde world ambience.

The Teviot Valley is the centre of NZ's cherry and apricot growing region and the property is bounded by apple orchards and farms. The Clutha River is minutes away offering salmon and trout fishing in season. Queenstown/Wanaka area 1 1/2 hours drive. A warm country style welcome awaits you at the Seed Farm.

Roxburgh (Coal Creek)

Country Inn
Address: Halfway Inn,
Cnr State Highway 8
& Tamblyn Drive,
Coal Creek, Roxburgh
Name: Danny and Robina
Telephone: (03) 446 8788
Fax: (03) 446 8788 **Mobile**: (025) 374 707   **Email**: robina88@ihug.co.nz
Beds: 2 Queen, 2 Single (3 Bedrooms) **Bathroom**: 2 Ensuite, 1 share.
Tariff: B&B (Full) Double $90-$130 (ensuite), Single $45 (shared). Dinner by
arrangement. Children welcome by arrangement. Credit cards accepted. Laundry facilities available. NZ B&B Vouchers accepted $50 surcharge on ensuite; $20
surcharge on other rooms. **Nearest Town**: Roxburgh 8 km, Alexandra 32 km.

We are positioned on a corner of SH8 approximately halfway between Queenstown and Dunedin. Danny a carpenter/joiner is renovating the old cafe and accommodation using as many natural products as possible. We are planning to open November 1999. Our home has natural timber joinery with timber furniture. We will operate a licensed cafe for daytime meals with a relaxing bar for an evening drink with guests. The Halfway Inn is surrounded by orchards, on 3/4 acre, in a natural environment. We offer the original 'Inn' style accommodation where you can join the Innkeepers family. Evening meals are by arrangement. There is a 3 minute walk to our local restaurant or a 5 minute drive to a selection in Roxburgh. Our small dog has his own yard away from guests. We intend having hens to produce fresh eggs for breakfast. We enjoy looking at the brighter side of life. Our interests include travel and cultures, sailing, alternative medicine, health and music to mention a few. Rooms are all non smoking.

Millers Flat

Self-contained Accommodation
Address: Millers Flat, R.D.2,
Roxburgh, Central Otago
Name: Sheena & Wallace Boag
Telephone: (03) 446 6872
Beds: 2 Single (1 bedroom)
plus double bed settee (upstairs)
Bathroom: 1 Ensuite
Tariff: B&B (continental) Double $65,
Single $40. Children $20. Credit Cards.
NZ B&B Vouchers accepted
Nearest Town: Roxburgh 16 km

An easy 2-hour drive from Dunedin, Wanaka, Queenstown and Invercargill, Millers Flat is an ideal place to break your journey. Originally a goldmining settlement, Millers Flat is an attractive village in farming and fruitgrowing country. It has a strong sense of community and is well equipped with facilities - swimming pool, tennis courts, bowling green, easy access to fishing, walking tracks, gardens to visit, and the well known community-owned general store "Faigan's".
We live on 10 acres in a 110 year-old house of rammed-earth construction and our guest accommodation is a detached 2-storey building of more recent vintage, an interesting composition of space and light, formerly Wallace's architectural studio. Comfortably heated and with tea/coffee making facilities.
Directions: *Turn off SH8 at Millers Flat, then left through the village for 1 km. Turn off to Lake Onslow for 100m. Phone ahead if possible.*

Ettrick, Roxburgh
Farmstay/Self-contained Accom.
Address: 'Clearburn Station', Dalmuir Rd, No 2 R.D., Roxburgh
Name: Ian & Margaret Lambeth
Telephone: (03) 446 6712
Fax: (03) 446 6774
Beds: 2 Single + Bed Settee (1 bedroom)
Bathroom: 1 Ensuite
Tariff: B&B (continental) Double $70, Single $50, Dinner $20.
NZ B&B Vouchers accepted
Nearest Town: Roxburgh 10km

Clearburn Station is a 7000 acre property with a Homestead Block and Hill Country Run stocked with Merino sheep and Cattle. The property is operated as a family partnership with son John and his wife Linda and children living in the main homestead while we, Ian and Margaret, have a smaller house.

Guest accommodation is a detached unit containing twin beds with ensuite and a bed settee in the large lounge. Electric blankets, heaters, tea making facilities, fridge and TV provided. Laundry facilities available.

Guests are very welcome to join in the farm activities occurring on the day which vary from high country mustering to work on the Home Block, or simply feed the hens, pigs and pony. Visits to local places of interest can be arranged - restaurants, golf course and fishing are within 5 mins drive.

Directions: *Please phone. We are 1 3/4 hour drive from Dunedin and only 300 metres from the main road.*

http://www.bnb.co.nz

take a look

Danseys Pass - Maniototo

Farmstay,
Address: Shortlands Station,
Naseby Danseys Pass Road,
RD 2, Ranfurly
Name: Glenis and David Crutchley
Telephone: (03) 444 9621
Fax: (03) 444 9610
Email: d&gcrutchley@xtra.co.nz
Beds: 1 Queen, 3 Single (3 Bedrooms)
Bathroom: 1 Ensuite, 1 Private, 1 Family share
Tariff: B&B (Continental) Double $110,Single $60, Dinner $25,
Family rate by negotiation. NZ B&B Vouchers accepted $30 surcharge
Nearest Town: Naseby 11 km

Shortlands Station, 6007 hectares situated in the Danseys Pass that links Central Otago to North Otago. 16000 stock units consisting of sheep and cattle. Large two storeyed modern home with spacious living area. Come and visit us, enjoy the large garden, swimming pool and tennis court. Just relax or sample the running of the property with a farm tour. We also offer High Country 4WD trips cost $60 per hour per vehicle, carrying up to four passengers. Two vehicles available. Duration 1.5 hour or take a bigger trip of three hours or five hours which includes a complimentary picnic lunch. Glenis enjoys gardening and singing, is a qualified nurse and trained St John's Ambulance officer. David is a keen dog trialist having won and judged New Zealand championships. Friendly farm dogs and Jack Russelll called "Kye". Two adult children and 1 teenager at boarding school.

Palmerston

Homestay (Historic Homestead)
Address: "Centrewood Historic Homestead"
Bobby's Head Road, Goodwood,
Palmerston, Otago
Name: Jane & David Loten
Telephone: 03 465 1977
Fax: (03) 465 1977
Email: centrewood@xtra.co.nz
Beds: 2 Queen, 1 Single (2 bedrooms)
Bathroom: 1 Private
Tariff: B&B (special) Double $120, Single $100, Dinner $30 (includes wine).
Credit cards
Nearest Town: Palmerston (SH 1) 5 minutes, Dunedin 40 minutes.

*Experience the peace and charm of yesteryear in our large colonial homestead, rambling gardens and park-like grounds. Our comfortable private guest suite comprising 2 bedrooms and spacious bathroom has its own entrance and verandah overlooking the croquet lawn. It is available for your exclusive use since only one party is hosted at a time. Breakfast in our large country kitchen includes home-made bread, croissants, fruit, muesli and yoghurt. Scrumptious afternoon tea is served on the verandah, and dinner in the dining room. Adjacent is a penguin reserve and sandy beach with a spectacular cliff top walk allowing easy viewing of seals and penguins and seabirds. On-site attractions include tennis, croquet, native bush walks, bird life and tame farm animals. As Lord Ernest Rutherford's great grand daughter, Jane has set up a corner of Rutherford memorabilia. Nearby attractions are the Moeraki Boulders, Macraes Goldmine and Dunedin City. No Smoking please.***Directions**: *Take SH 1 to Palmerston. Turn East at Warrens Garage into Goodwood Rd. After 10 mins turn left into Bobby's Head Road. Centrewood Homestead is 1 km on the right.*

Warrington
Homestay
Address: 'Sunny Hill Farm',
367 Coast Road, Warrington, Otago
Name: Angela & Maurice Corish
Telephone: (03) 482 2631
Beds: 2 Queen (2 bedrooms)
Bathroom: 2 Ensuite
(1 shower and 1 bath)
Tariff: B&B (full) Double $80, Dinner $25pp.
Not suitable for children.
NZ B&B Vouchers accepted $15 surcharge
Nearest Town: 18km north of Dunedin, off SH1

We live in a 100 year old farmhouse, nestled in a rambling wild garden and orchard. The 25 acre farmlet, with sheep, 2 kune pigs, 1 cat and Jess the sheep dog are worth a visit after breakfast. Enjoy a leisurely cooked breakfast accompanied by freshly brewed coffee and homemade bread, in our large comfortable farmhouse kitchen with wood-burning stove. Your chef host serves innovative, delicious food using fresh organically home grown and local produce. We offer two double rooms, one upstairs with panoramic views of sea and farmland. The other is in detached accommodation, with a private sunny patio fringed with aromatic herbs. Our interests are in country life, antiques, old houses, books, tramping and biking. New Zealand's tallest tree is close by. Warrington beach, Blueskin Bay and the Silverpeaks offer superb walks. World famous Otago Peninsular (albatross, yellow-eyed penguins, seals) is close to Dunedin, which is 25 minutes from Warrington. A large games cupboard. No smoking and no pets please. Not suitable for children.

Warrington
Self Contained Villa
Address: "Montrose"
38 Bay Road, Warrington, Dunedin
Name: Margaret & Paul Harris
Telephone: (03) 477 9413
Fax: (03) 477 3114
Mobile: 025 320 350
Email: polaris@clear.net.nz
Beds: King & Queen (4 bedrooms)
Bathroom: 1 Bathroom, 2 toilets.
Tariff: B&B (Self catering)
$150 per night plus $10 per person. All credit cards welcome.
Nearest Town: Dunedin 20 minutes

Montrose: Barnett Lodge seaside villa- suitable for a group of 1, 2, 3 or 4 couples. Montrose is a seaside villa with a sweeping view over Warrington Beach. It was built following WW1 using original kauri timber salvaged from the historic 1880 military barracks on nearby Taiaroa Head. Located 20 minutes from the centre of Dunedin. 4 large bedrooms. Beautifully restored bathroom. Two toilets. Panelled lounge with logburner. Restored kauri floors. Large sunny verandah. Tennis court. Double garage. Large garden. Self catering or fully serviced including cooked breakfast.
Home Page: www.barnett.co.nz/montrose *or* www.barnett.co.nz

Blueskin Bay

Homestay
Address: 'Ngeratua Farm',
Kilpatrick Road, Waitati
Name: Adrienne & Stuart Heal
Telephone: (03) 482 1152
Fax: (03) 482 1153
Email: heals@es.co.nz
Beds: 1 Double, 2 Single (1 bedroom)
Bathroom: 1 Private
Tariff: B&B (full) Double $90,
Single $60, Children half price. Dinner $35pp.
Credit cards (VISA/MC). NZ B&B Vouchers accepted $10 Surcharge.
Nearest Town: Dunedin, 18km south

Situated 15 minutes north of Dunedin at Blueskin Bay is our lifestyle farm overlooking the Bay and Pacific Ocean. On our property we graze sheep and cattle and are developing an expanding garden, including a commercial flower venture.
Our home offers a large guest room with a double bed and two singles, lounge suite, TV and private bathroom and toilet. Guests are encouraged to join us for an evening meal where we enjoy quality local food and wines. Breakfast on our sunny deck is a relaxing way to start the day. Our home, a non smoking environment, is shared with our pet cat, Whisky. We are located near many bush and hill walks, Dunedin's unique wildlife and architecture, or you may simply enjoy a walk on our property, which is less than one kilometre off State Highway 1. We offer a peaceful environment, minutes from the city.
Directions: *Please phone for details and reservations.*

Otago Peninsula, Dunedin

Homestay
Address: 'Captains Cottage',
422 Portobello Road, R.D.2. Dunedin
Name: Christine & Robert Brown
Telephone: (03) 476 1431
Fax: (03) 476 1431
Mobile: (021) 352 734
Beds: 1 Double, 2 Single (2 bedrooms)
Bathroom: 1 Guests share, 1 Private
Tariff: B&B (continental) Double $95
or with private bathroom $135,
Single $60, Dinner $25.
Nearest Town: Dunedin 9km

An 8km scenic drive from the city centre, the Captains Cottage is located on the waterfront in a bush setting beside the Glenfalloch Gardens, on the beautiful Otago Peninsula, enroute to the Royal Albatross, Penguin and Seal colonies.
Robert is a specialist wildlife cameraman for the BBC and TVNZ who loves to share his interest in wildlife with visitors. Christine has travelled widely and with her wealth of local knowledge and contacts can help you organise an interesting stay.
We have our own sport fishing boat and can take you fishing or explore the unique bird and marine life found in the area.
So if you enjoy great food and hospitality; BBQ's, boating, lying in the sun, relaxing beside the log fire or having a drink as the sun sets on the deck of our boat shed, then let us share our interesting home with you. Our two dogs are Penny and Socrates.

Otago Peninsula, Dunedin

Bed & Breakfast
Address: The Mission, Mission Cove,
Company Bay, Otago Peninsula
Name: Pat & Phillipa Cummings
Telephone: (03) 476 1321
Fax: (03) 476 1028
Mobile: (025) 751 782
Email: cummings@deepsouth.co.nz
Beds: 1 Twin, 1 Double, 4 Single (6 bedrooms)
Bathroom: 3 Guests share
Tariff: B&B (continental) Double $85, Single $45, (Downstairs $35).
Nearest Town: Dunedin 12 Kms

Situated on the picturesque Otago Peninsula, our place is a recently refurbished ex-nurses home (19 bedrooms originally), built in 1948. We have a very pleasant double bedroom and a twin room upstairs with 2 guest bathroom facilities. Downstairs include 4 single rooms and self-contained. We have a large garden and landscaped area which includes a stream, "summer house", expansive patio area and courtyard with established trees, breathtaking harbour views and a chapel with stained glass windows. We are 15 minutes from the centre of Dunedin and about the same from the Royal Albatross Colony, world famous penguins, seals and only 3km from Larnach Castle and Glenfalloch Gardens. A warm welcome is guaranteed from Pat, Phillipa, Daniel (15 year old son), Grace (Weimeraner) and Ruby (Poodle) our "very well mannered people-friendly dogs". **Directions**: *Travelling from Dunedin go 1.1km past Macandrew Bay Store on Portobello Road, turn right into Mission Cove at Company Bay, go straight to the top of the drive. Reservations recommended. Smoke free.* **Home Page**: http://www.visit-dunedin.co.nz

Portobello Village - Otago Peninsula

Homestay
Address: Peninsula Homestay B&B,
4 Allans Beach Road,
Portobello Village,
Otago Peninsula, Dunedin.
Name: Rachel and Mike Kerr
Telephone: (03) 478 0909
Fax: (03) 478 0909
Email: otago_peninsula@hotmail.com
Beds: 2 Queen (2 bedrooms)
Bathroom: 2 Ensuite
Tariff: B&B (continental) double $95, Single $85, Extra person $30.
Credit Cards: Visa/Mastercard.
Nearest Town: Dunedin, city centre 25 mins.

Our lovely home is an historic villa set among an 1/2 acre of beautiful gardens with sea views and rural outlook. We have two LUXURIOUS BEDROOMS EACH WITH A PRIVATE ENSUITE, TV, electric blankets, heating and hairdryers. Tea/coffee and laundry facilities, also off street parking are provided. We are situated in the heart of Portobello Village, overlooking Lathum Bay, opposite the 1908 Cafe, Otago Peninsula's famous restaurant. Portobello is most central to all the attractions on the Otago Peninsula. The Albatross, Seal and Penguin colonies, Larnach Castle and a variety of scenic walks, drives and harbour cruises are all close by. Rachel's family are descendants of the 1st European Settlers in 1838 and have farmed on the Otago Peninsula for 5 generations. We look forward to sharing our home, local and NZ knowledge with you. A WARM WELCOME AWAITS YOU AT PENINSULA HOMESTAY B&B. **Home Page**: http://www.visit-dunedin.co.nz

Broad Bay - Otago Peninsula
Homestay+Self-contained Accom.
Address: 'Chy-an-Dowr'
687 Portobello Road, Broad Bay, Dunedin
Name: Herman & Susan van Velthoven
Telephone: (03) 478 0306 **Fax**: (03) 478 0306
Mobile: 025 270 5533 **Email**: hermanvv@xtra.co.nz
Beds: 1 Queen, 1 Double, 2 Single (3 bedrooms).
SC Cottage: 1 Queen, 1 Bed settee (1 Bedroom)
Bathroom: 1 Guest share or Private. SC Cottage: 1 Private
Tariff: B&B (full) Double $90-$125. Self-contained cottage $95, extra person in cottage
$20. Breakfast in cottage optional. Credit cards. Vouchers accepted $20-$50 surcharge
Nearest Town: Dunedin 16km

"CHY~AN~DOWR" ("House by the Water"), a quality homestay located on scenic Otago Peninsula with panoramic harbour views and situated directly opposite a small beach. The upstairs guestrooms are comfortable and private with heating, electric blankets, bathrobes, hairdryer, tea / coffee making facilities, TV, guest lounge, and sunroom with extensive harbour views. Enjoy a cooked or continental breakfast with our fresh fruit salad, homemade yoghurt and muesli, freshly baked croissants and breads served with a good Dutch coffee or tea of your choice. "SLEEPY HOLLOW", our peaceful, private SELF-CONTAINED COTTAGE has the same home comforts and is situated in Portobello on a quiet country road with rural outlook, a five minute drive from our house. The Otago Peninsula, renowned for its Albatross and Penguin colonies, has many walkways and two good restaurants. We emigrated from Holland in 1981 and we enjoy welcoming people into our home. Our accommodation is smoke-free. We have two cats. **Directions**: *Follow signs Peninsula. Follow Portobello Road along the harbour until you come to Broad Bay, we are on the corner of Portobello Road and Clearwater Street in Broad Bay.* **Home Page**: http://www.visit-dunedin.co.nz/chyandowr.html

Broad Bay – Otago Peninsula
Self-contained Accommodation
Address: 'The Cottage', 748 Portobello Road,
Broad Bay, Dunedin
Postal: 7 Francess St,
Broad Bay, Dunedin.
Name: Lesley, Janet and Leonie
Telephone: (03) 478 0073
Mobile: (025) 381 291
Email: thecottage@xtra.co.nz
Beds: 1 Double (1 bedroom)
Bathroom: 1 Ensuite
Tariff: B&B (special) Double $98. Accommodation without breakfast $80 double. NZ
B&B Vouchers accepted $30 surcharge for B&B..
Nearest Town: Dunedin - 18km from city centre

Our self-contained cottage, built at the turn of the century as a fisherman's retreat, is right on the Otago Harbour. A picket fence encloses a mature native bush garden. Wonderful vignettes of the harbour are enjoyed from the privacy of the verandah and garden. Full of old-world charm, this cosy cottage with original matai floors reflects the nostalgia of a bygone era (No TV!), whilst fresh linen, a comfortable bed and modern conveniences ensure a relaxing stay. Our generous hamper breakfasts are a speciality. Evening meals may be self-catered or taken at one of the fine Peninsula restaurants. Enjoy the freedom to come and go as you please whilst exploring the many Peninsula attractions. "The owners have thought of just about everything" (Gourmet Traveller Magazine). "If you spend only one night at The cottage you'll be sorry you didn't leave more room in your schedule. A few days is best". (Grace Magazine).

724

Dunedin

Homestay
Address: Magnolia House,
18 Grendon Street,
Maori Hill, Dunedin
Name: Joan & George Sutherland
Telephone: (03) 467 5999
Fax: (03) 467 5999
Beds: 1 Queen, 1 Double,
2 Single (3 bedrooms)
Bathroom: 2 Guests share
Tariff: B&B (full)
Double $80, Single $55.
Special full menu of cooked and continental foods.
Nearest Town: Dunedin city centre 2 km

We live in a superior suburb on half an acre of land, one third of which is native bush with wood pigeons, tuis, bellbirds and fantails. The rest is in lawn and attractive gardens. Our 1910 house is spacious with a large dining room and drawing room, and a more intimate sitting room. The Queen room has its own large balcony looking out on lawns and bush. The guest rooms are airy and have antiques. Guests' bathrooms with showers. There is central heating and piano. Two nights in Dunedin is a must. We are very close to Otago Golf Club and can supply clubs and bag. Also nearby is Olveston stately home and Moana Olympic-size swimming pool. The Otago peninsula is a wonderful day's sightseeing. We have two cats, a courtesy car, bus nearby and no smoking. Not suitable children. Prefer non-smokers.
Directions: *Please phone*

Dunedin

Homestay
Address: 'Harbourside Bed & Breakfast', 6 Kiwi Street, St Leonards, Dunedin
Name: Shirley & Don Parsons
Telephone: (03) 471 0690
Fax: (03) 471 0063
Beds: 2 Double, 3 Single (2 bedrooms)
Bathroom: 1 Guests share
Tariff: B&B (full) Double $75, Single $45, Children 4-12yrs $15, Under 4 free
share room; Dinner $20pp. 10% discount 2 or more nights, Credit Cards. NZ B&B
Vouchers accepted
Nearest Town: Dunedin - 7 km to City Centre

We live in a quiet suburb 10 minutes from the city centre. Our home overlooks the lovely Otago Harbour and is within easy reach of many of the local attractions - Larnach Castle, Olveston, the Albatross colony and Disappear-ing Gun, Portobello Aquarium, Harbour Cruises and Taieri Gorge Excursion Train, also Yellow-eyed penguins. Dunedin is a lovely city situated at the head of the Otago harbour with many interesting and historic stone buildings to view. There are also many lovely bush walks within easy reach of the city. We have two rooms available, one with a double and single bed and one with a double and bunks and cot available. Children very welcome and we have a generous amount of living space for you to relax..
Directions: *Driving into City on the one-way system watch for Port Chalmers Highway 88 sign, follow Anzac Avenue onto Ravensbourne Road. Continue down the Harbourside approximately 5 km to St Leonards. Turn left at the Play centre opposite the boatshed into Pukeko Street then left into Kaka Road then straight ahead to Kiwi Street, turn left. Courtesy car available. See you soon.*

Dunedin
Bed and Breakfast

Address: Deacons Court,
342 High Street, Dunedin
Name: Karen & Dene MacKenzie
Telephone: (03) 477 9053
Fax: (03) 477 9058
Mobile: (025) 518 664
Email: Deacons@es.co.nz
Beds: 3 Double, 3 Twin, (3 bedrooms)
Bathroom: 2 Ensuite, 1 Private non share
Tariff: B&B (full) Double $110-$120, Single $70, Credit Cards.
NZ B&B Vouchers accepted $30 surcharge
Nearest Town: Dunedin, city centre 10 min walk from octagon.

Enjoy that special feeling of being a guest in our comfortable private Victorian home which is surrounded by trees and a sheltered rose garden. Guests can relax in one of our three spacious bedrooms or the sunny conservatory. Karen has a diploma in massage and aromatherapy and has those facilities available for guests in our home. We are 1 km to the city centre, the Dunedin art gallery, the visitors centre, the Octagon, and a wide choice of restaurants. our Rose Room has a stunning view across the city to the harbour and the sea while our Garden Room overlooks the rose garden. Our generous breakfast may include fruit juice, fresh fruit, choice of cereals and yoghurt, home-made muffins and a traditional cooked breakfast. Complimentary tea, coffee and home baking on arrival. We have a wide knowledge of Dunedin attractions and can help you with your sightseeing. Family groups welcome. We cater for non smokers and have two children and a cat. **Home Page**: www.visit-dunedin.co.nz/deaconsc.html

Dunedin Central
Bed & Breakfast

Address: 'Castlewood'
240 York Place, Dunedin
Name: Peter & Donna Mitchell
Telephone: (03) 477 0526
Fax: (03) 477 0526
Email: Relax@castlewood.co.nz
Beds: 2 Queen, 1 twin or 1 Single (3 bedrooms)
Bathroom: 1 ensuite, 2 Guests share
Tariff: B&B (Continental) Single $65, Twin $85, Double $95-$125. Visa & Mastercard Credit Cards welcome. NZ B&B Vouchers accepted 2 vouchers required.
Nearest Town: Only 800 metres walking distance to Dunedin's city centre.

Relax at Castlewood and experience the old world charm of our graciously restored Tudor residence. Set on a rise above Dunedin, Castlewood offers expansive views and all day sun yet is only 800 metres, (10 minutes walk) from the best restaurants, live theatre, cafes, shops and attractions such as Olveston, and the Dunedin Art Gallery.Both Peter and Donna are Dunedin born and know New Zealand intimately. They provide useful and friendly advice on local attractions and having travelled internationally, appreciate the requirements of discerning travellers. Peter is a well known artist and his water-colour paintings are displayed throughout Castlewood."For warm hospitality in a beautiful home, the comfiest bed, and best breakfast muffins in NZ(!!) Look no further than Castlewood." Dr Jonathan Williams (U.K.)"A beautiful house, lovely city, and most friendly hosts." Michaela (Germany) "Wonderful and cosy, lovely outlook and brilliant artwork." Steve Amos (Australia) **Directions**: *From the top of the Octagon proceed up Stuart Street, turning left into Cargill Street, then left again into Arthur Street. At the next traffic lights Castlewood can be seen diagonally opposite.* **Home Page**: www.castlewood.co.nz

Dunedin City
Guest House
Address: 3 Peel St,
Mornington, Dunedin
Name: 'Glenfield House'
(Cal & Wendy)
Telephone: (03) 453 5923
Fax: (03) 453 5984
Beds: 2 Queen, 2 Double
(4 bedrooms)
Bathroom: 2 Ensuite, 1 Guests share
Tariff: B&B (special) Double $150, $135,
Single $135, $95, Dinner $40. Credit cards welcome.
Nearest Town: Dunedin City

Glenfield is our restored Victorian residence situated on the edge of the town belt 2 km from the centre city. All of our rooms have heating, electric blankets, feather and down duvets, television, tea and plunger coffee. Our facilities include an original billiard room with 3/4 size table, a congenial lounge with fire, laundry and off-street parking. At the top of our range we offer our blue room with ensuite and adjoining sun room - a suite of rooms where you may dine if you prefer and have your own access to the verandah to enjoy the harbour views and Dunedin's night lights. With notice, a sumptuous 3 course meal, prepared from Otago produce, will be served in the guest dining room. If you are staying more than one night and have a craving for some particular food just let us know. We thank you for not smoking.

Dunedin
Heritage Inn
Address: 'Barnett Lodge', 34 Alva Street, Dunedin
Name: Margi & Paul Harris
Telephone: (03) 477 9413 **Fax**: (03) 477 3114
Mobile: (025) 320 350 **Email**: polaris@clear.net.nz
Beds: 2 King or Twin with Ensuite,
1 Queen plus Single with private bathroom.
Bathroom: 2 Ensuite, 1 Private
Tariff: B&B (full) Double $195 and $225, Single $165 - $195, Credit Cards welcome.
A self contained apt with two queen bedrooms, ensuite and lounge is also available.
Nearest Town: Dunedin central

Barnett Lodge will appeal to the traveller seeking accommodation at the upper end of the range. It is a handsome heritage residence of English Tudor architecture, built of the finest materials for Arthur Barnett, Dunedin's leading retailer, in 1938. It features an original oak panelled and beamed reception area and lounge, furnished elegantly, with accompanying sunroom and dining room on the ground floor. The lodge is centrally heated. Heaters, hairdryers and full range of toiletries in each bedroom. Decor is peaceful and attractive with all facilities completely upgraded in 1993. The atmosphere is sunny and quiet. Beds are top quality. You are assured of a warm, friendly and informative reception and stay. Breakfasts are generous and cater for all tastes. We are strictly non smoking. Our location is within five minutes drive from the city centre in a quiet suburb adjacent to parks and authentic bush walks. Tea, coffee and home baking are available when required. Complimentary pre-dinner drink or nightcap available. Laundry and fax and internet facilities available at a charge. Four excellent restaurants within 2 minutes drive or walking distance.
Home Page: www.barnett.co.nz *or* www.barnett.co.nz/montrose

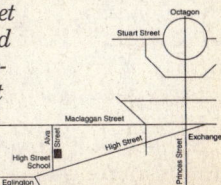

Albatross Inn

Dunedin City
Bed & Breakfast/Private Hotel
Address: 'Albatross Inn', 770 George St, Dunedin
Name: Kerry Kirkland & Nigel Brook
Telephone: (03) 477 2727: Reservations Freephone: 0800 441441
Fax: (03) 477 2108
Email: albatross.inn@xtra.co.nz
Beds: 1 King, 4 Queen, 3 Double, 5 Single (8 bedrooms)
Bathroom: 8 Ensuite
Tariff: B&B (continental) Double $75-$125, Single $65-$85, Children $15 (under 5 years free), Extra adult in room $20. Credit cards. Winter and long stay rates available.
Nearest Town: Dunedin Central.

Welcome to Dunedin! Our family, Nigel, Kerry, Zoe (7), Joanna (5) invite you to stay with us at Albatross Inn. Our Edwardian House is superbly located close to University, gardens, museum and centre city.
Our beautifully decorated bedrooms have ensuite bathrooms, telephone, TV, radio, tea/coffee, warm duvets and electric blankets on modern beds. Extra firm beds available for those with back problems. Very quiet rooms at rear of house.
Several rooms have own kitchenette/cooking facilities and fridge.
Enjoy breakfast in your room or in front of our open fire. We serve freshly baked bread, fresh fruit salad, muffins, yoghurt, juices, cereals, choice of teas, fresh brewed coffee. We are both Dunedin born and have an intimate knowledge of the city and its surrounds. We offer our guests a warm welcome and can recommend great things to do and see and excellent places to eat, laundry service, non smoking, cot and highchair.

What our guests say!
- The convenience of your location is wonderful. You can walk everywhere! Combined with a gorgeous house: Such friendly hosts to make an unbeatable combination. Best B&B in NZ!
Joe & Cathy Wallace, Georgia, USA.
- This is everything a B&B ought to be...our only regret is leaving.... Thank you Kerry and Nigel for organising 3 wonderful days and making our stay so special!
Diana and William McDowell, England.
Home Page: www.albatross.inn.co.nz

Dunedin

Homestay
Address: 'Harbour Lookout', 3 Taupo St, Ravensbourne, Dunedin
Name: Ron & Maire (Moya) Graham
Telephone: (03) 471 0582
Mobile: (025) 263 7244
Beds: 2 Single (1 Bedroom)
Bathroom: 1 Family share
Tariff: B&B Double $65, Single $40, Dinner $20. NZ B&B Vouchers accepted
Nearest Town: Dunedin 3K

Welcome to Dunedin, Edinburgh of the South. We are a retired couple who can assure you of a warm welcome to our comfortable home in Ravensbourne, only 3km from Dunedin's Railway Station and therefore close to all wonderful attractions Dunedin has to offer. To find us follow Port Chalmers Highway 88, along Anzac Ave, continue into Ravensbourne Road, along the harbour side until you reach Adderley Terrace which turns uphill behind Harbour View Hotel. On entering first bend be alert for signpost on your right for Taupo St and Lane, drive in turn right downhill and into our drive with ample off street parking. Your twin bedroom with private toilet adjacent is on this level. No carrying luggage upstairs, however our bathroom and living areas are upstairs and here you can relax with a cuppa and enjoy the wonderful view. Our interests are golf, bowls and gardening. We look forward to meeting you.

Dunedin

Homestay
Address: 'Kincaple', 215 Highgate, Roslyn, Dunedin
Name: Del Cox
Telephone: (03) 477 4384
Freephone 0800 269 384/PIN 4774
Fax: (03) 477 4380
Mobile: (025) 2488 968
Beds: 1 Double, 3 Single (3 bedrooms)
Bathroom: 1 Guests share, 1 Family share
Tariff: B&B (Continental) Double $80, Single $55. $5 surcharge for cooked breakfast. Credit cards welcome.
Nearest Town: Dunedin city centre 2km

"Kincaple" built in 1903, is a gracious home set in a well established suburb. It has been our family home for 26 years, lies well to the sun and is surrounded by an attractive garden. There is off-street parking and the bus stops at the door. The Visitor Centre is 2km and the Roslyn shops, Moana Olympic sized swimming pool and the Belleknowes Golf Club are all a short walk. The stately home, "Olveston", and the Otago Golf Club are 3km distance. Inside this smoke free environment are rooms of generous proportions with open fires and central heating, excellent bedding and plenty of reading material. A great place to relax. We have a short haired dachshund we walk in the green belt.
FOR RESERVATIONS FREEPHONE: 0800 - 269 384 / PIN 4774
Directions: *Please phone*

Dunedin City
Homestay
Address: 'Brownville Lodge',
49 Brownville Cres., Maori Hill,
Dunedin
Name: Gaynor & Neville Dippie
Telephone: (03) 467 5841 (home)
or (03) 477 8733 (work)
Fax: (03) 467-5841
Beds: 2 Queen, 1 Double, 1 Single,
1 Twin room (5 bedrooms)
Bathroom: 1 Private, 1 Guests share,
1 Family share,
Tariff: B&B (special) Double $110-$140,
Single $80, Children $20. Credit cards Visa/Mastercard.
NZ B&B Vouchers accepted Guests pay surcharge
Nearest Town: Dunedin City

A warm welcome awaits the discerning traveller at our modern home situated a few minutes by car from the city centre. Facing the northern hills, the house is sunny. Bedrooms are on a separate level and furnishings and bedding are of a superior quality. We are non smokers who enjoy gardening and travel, and look forward to welcoming guests to our city. Choice of breakfasts. Laundry & dryer available at no charge. Many good restaurants a few minutes drive away. Booking in time after 6 pm or by arrangement.

Dunedin
Homestay
Address: Gowrie House,
7 Gowry Place, Roslyn,
Dunedin
Name: Vivienne & Rod Nye
Telephone: (03) 477 2103
Fax: (03) 471 9169
Beds: 1 Double, 2 Single
(2 bedrooms)
Bathroom: 1 Guests share,
1 Family share
Tariff: B&B (full) Double $80,
Single $50,   NZ B&B Vouchers accepted
Nearest Town: Dunedin

"Gowrie House" is in a quiet suburb, on a sunny west-facing site, with lovely rural views. We are only 20 minutes walk from the city, close to bus routes. A courtesy car is provided, within the city.
Our garden has a cosy cottage atmosphere with all available space occupied by perennial and biennial flowers - regularly picked for rooms. The guests' bedrooms are warm and sunny. The bathroom is handily placed across the hall. All beds have electric blankets. The double room has access to the patio and cottage garden where one can enjoy the floral fragrances. Otago Peninsula is easily accessible, as are bush walks and historic buildings. We will happily provide information about popular attractions. No smoking please.
Directions: *Please phone.*

Dunedin

Bed and Breakfast
Address: Nisbet Cottage,
6a Elliffe Place, Shiel Hill, Dunedin
Name: Hildegard & Ralf Lübcke
Telephone: (03) 454 5169
Fax: (03) 454 5369
Email: nisbet@wingsofkotuku.co.nz
Beds: 2 Queen, 2 Single (3 bedrooms) **Bathroom**: 3 Ensuite
Tariff: B&B (special) Room rate $95-$120,
Credit Cards Visa/MC. Prices valid until 15th October 2000.
Vouchers accepted Surcharge $40. Prior arrangement please.
Nearest Town: Dunedins city centre 7km.

A warm welcome to Nisbet Cottage! We offer character accommodation in a peaceful and quiet environment. Situated near the high road to Otago Peninsula yet close to the city, Nisbet Cottage is the perfect base for your trips to Dunedin and its wildlife. Enjoy panoramic views from the large sun deck or relax in front of the open fireplace in the guest lounge, and meet Basil our cat. Restaurant and bus stop nearby. Ralf works at Dunedin Hospital, Hildegard operates "Wings of Kotuku" nature tours. We can assist in planning your holiday and are happy to arrange necessary bookings. For a taste of real nature join our Sunrise Penguin Walk - a truly magic wildlife adventure! **Directions**: *Turn from Highway 1 into Andersons Bay Road, continue into Musselburgh Rise and Silverton Street, turn left into Highcliff Road, proceed 700m, turn left into Every Street, 1st right Albion Street, 1st left Elliffe Place.*
Home Page: http://www.wingsofkotuku.co.nz

St Claire, Dunedin

A Boutique Lodge. Averleigh Cottage
Address: 7 Coughtrey Street, St Clair, Dunedin
Name: Joanne McKellar
Telephone: (03) 455 8829
Fax: (03) 455 6380
Mobile: (021) 631 725
Email: joanne@averleigh.co.nz
Beds: 1 Queen (with ensuite),
1 Twin (guest bathroom) (2 bedrooms)
Bathroom: 1 Ensuite, 1 Private
Tariff: B&B (special) Room rate Double $175-$195, Single $155-$175.
Credit Cards accepted Visa/Mastercard/Bankcard/American Express/Diners.
Nearest Town: Dunedin 5 kms

• *Welcome to Averleigh Cottage, a classic Edwardian 1910 villa*
• *Original house ornate ceilings - native timbers, antiques.* • *St Clair beach 2 min walk, 10 min drive from City Centre* • *Waterfront cafes at St Clair beach* • *"Tarlton Room" (Queen) with ensuite. Bath robes, hairdryer, toiletries, phone, radio / alarm clock.* • *"Watson Room" (King / Twin) with Victorian open fire, guest bathroom with antique bath. Bath robes, hairdryer, toiletries, phone, radio / alarm clock.* • *Gourmet continental breakfast included* • *Two elegant sitting rooms plus formal dining room, all with open fires* • *Central heating. Fresh flowers, TV in guest bedrooms.* • *Morning Room leads to the courtyard rose gardens* • *Garden rooms include roses, lavenders, rhododendrons, natives* • *Petanque, croquet, complimentary beverages* • *Brunch, picnic hampers, dinners, private guided tours - by arrangement* • *Finbar & Brodie (curly coated retrievers).* • *Averleigh is for animal, art and garden lovers.* • *Reservations essential* **Home Page**: http://www.averleigh.co.nz

Roslyn, Dunedin

Homestay
Address: 33 Littlebourne Road,
Roslyn, Dunedin
Name: Eileen & Wallie Waudby
Telephone: (03) 477 4963
Fax: (03) 477 4965
Mobile: (025) 228 7840
Email: wallie.waudby@xtra.co.nz
Beds: 1 Double, 2 Single
(2 bedrooms)
Bathroom: 1 Guests share
Tariff: B&B (full)
Double $85, Single $50.
Nearest Town: Dunedin City Centre 1 km away.

Eileen and Wallie would like to welcome visitors to Dunedin to their smoke free home situated in a quiet street just off Stuart Street and opposite Roberts Park. We have travelled extensively ourselves and understand how visitors feel when they arrive in a new town. Our home is in short walking distance to Dunedin's stately home "Olveston", the Moana Swimming Complex and just over a kilometre to the town centre. The guest bedrooms situated on the top floor for privacy and quietness are warm and sunny and as a back up all beds have an electric blanket. Tea and coffee making facilities. You are sure of a warm welcome and comfortable stay at No.33.

Dunedin

Homestay
Address: 117 Easther Crescent,
Kew, Dunedin
Name: Bill & Jenny Smith
Telephone: (03) 455 5731
Beds: 1 King, 2 Single (2 bedrooms)
Bathroom: 1 Guests share
Tariff: B&B (full) Double $80,
Twin $75, Single $55,
Dinner $25pp by prior arrangement.
NZ B&B Vouchers accepted $15 surcharge
Nearest Town: Dunedin 3km

Enjoy the relaxed atmosphere of our "Smokefree" Spanish style home with panoramic views over St Clair and St Kilda beaches, the Otago Harbour Basin and the hill suburbs of Dunedin City. The focal point of the House is a centrally situated "Atrium" with fernery, fish pond with fountain and a spa pool for your relaxation. We share our home with a pearly pied cockatiel named Sam. We have travelled extensively and enjoy meeting people from all walks of life. Dunedin has many architecturally significant buildings, an internationally recognised art gallery and museum. Other local attractions include the Otago Peninsula wildlife, Albatross Colony and Larnachs Castle. Sporting facilities within easy reach include golf (hire clubs available), bowls and tennis. The Carisbrook International Rugby / Cricket Ground is within easy walking distance. The house is situated down a quite private drive with off street parking. A warm friendly welcome awaits you.

Dunedin
Homestay Bed & Breakfast
Address: Dalmore Lodge,
9 Falkirk Street, Dalmore, Dunedin
Name: Loraine & Mike
Telephone: (03) 473 6513
Fax: (03) 473 6512
Mobile: (025) 287 1517
Beds: 1 Queen, 1 Twin,
1 Single (3 bedrooms)
Bathroom: 1 Guests share + extra shower/toilet downstairs
Tariff: B&B (continental) Queen $85, Twin $80, Single $55, Dinner N/A, Children under 12 $25, Children under 5 free. Credit Cards accepted.
Nearest Town: Dunedin 3.2 kms to city centre.

Come and enjoy the peaceful setting of Dalmore Lodge whilst at the same time being close to all the amenities and attractions the city of Dunedin has to offer. Our colonial home offers views of the harbour, Pacific Ocean, city lights, Botanical Gardens, hills and rural areas. The balcony leads out onto a sheltered garden where you can relax, read a book or just enjoy watching the native birds along with our cat Teagan.
A three minute drive or a 20 minute walk can take you into the main business and shopping area. Public transport is available at the end of the driveway. We will meet you to/from airport, train, bus by prior arrangement at an extra minimal cost. There is ample off street parking. Guests please no smoking indoors. We look forward to your visit.
Directions: *Please phone/fax for reservations/directions before 9 am or after 5 pm.*

East Taieri, Dunedin
Homestay
Address:
19 Main South Road (SH 1),
East Taieri, Dunedin
Name: Dorothy and Wyn Chirnside
Telephone: (03) 489 5790
Fax: (03) 489 1410
Email: chirnsides@xtra.co.nz
Beds: 1 Queen,
2 Single (2 Bedrooms)
Bathroom: 1 Private
Tariff: B&B (full) Twin $80, Dinner $30 pp, Children half price.
Credit Cards accepted. NZ B&B Vouchers accepted $12 surcharge
Nearest Town: Mosgiel 2 kms

We invite you to share with us our near new spacious home, situated on over 1 acre of developing grounds and having a restful rural outlook over the Taieri Plains.
Our home is located on State Highway One between Dunedin Airport and Dunedin City, with each being approximately 15 minutes away by car.
Our home is a non smoking environment. The generously sized bedrooms are located adjacent to the bathroom which has both a bath and shower, hairdryer etc. All beds have electric blankets.
Guests are most welcome to relax with the family in the evenings for friendship and conversation.

OTAGO

Dunedin

Homestay
Address: 'Harbour Homestay',
19 Finch Street, Burkes, Dunedin
Name: Jill and Warwick Graham
Telephone: 03-471 0027
Beds: 1 Twin, 1 Double (2 bedroom)
Bathroom: 1 Ensuite, 1 Handbasin in room, shower in spa room across hall
Tariff: B&B (continental) Double $70, Single $35. Children under 12 years half price.
Nearest Town: Dunedin 4.5 kms (8 mins)

We live in a quiet suburb 8 minutes from the city centre. Welcome to our interesting home overlooking the beautiful Dunedin harbour.

Our guest room has a comfortable bed with electric blanket, and we also have a full size spa available for your use at no extra charge.

our interests are boating, rugby, crafts, gardening and meeting people. Our cats mainly live outside but are very people friendly.

Directions: *Follow Port Chalmers Highway 88 along Anzac Avenue into Ravensbourne Road. Continue down the harbour side about 4.6 kms. Turn left at the 'Burkes' sign into Finch Street. Continue to top of hill, we are the last house on the left.*

http://www.bnb.co.nz

take a look

Dunedin City

Guest House
Address: 3 Peel St,
Mornington, Dunedin
Name: 'Glenfield House'
(Cal & Wendy)
Telephone: (03) 453 5923
Fax: (03) 453 5984
Beds: 2 Queen,
2 Double (4 bedrooms)
Bathroom: 2 Ensuite, 1 Guests share
Tariff: B&B (special) Double $150, $135,
Single $135, $95, Dinner $40. Credit cards welcome.
Nearest Town: Dunedin City

Glenfield is our restored Victorian residence situated on the edge of the town belt 2 km from the centre city. All of our rooms have heating, electric blankets, feather and down duvets, television, tea and plunger coffee. Our facilities include an original billiard room with 3/4 size table, a congenial lounge with fire, laundry and off-street parking. At the top of our range we offer our blue room with ensuite and adjoining sun room - a suite of rooms where you may dine if you prefer and have your own access to the verandah to enjoy the harbour views and Dunedin's night lights. With notice, a sumptuous 3 course meal, prepared from Otago produce, will be served in the guest dining room. If you are staying more than one night and have a craving for some particular food just let us know. We thank you for not smoking.

Dunedin

Homestay
Address: 65 Every Street, Dunedin
Name: Alloway
Telephone: (03) 454 5384
Fax: (03) 454 5364
Email: alloway@xtra.co.nz
Beds: 1 Queen, 1 Single, 1 Double,
1 Single (2 bedrooms)
Bathroom: 1 Guests share
Tariff: B&B (continental)
Double $90 and $120, Single $85,
Dinner not available. Not suitable for children.
Clothes washing available. NZ B&B Vouchers accepted $20 surcharge
Nearest Town: Dunedin 4.5 kms.

New Zealand Association
FARM & HOME HOSTS

OTAGO

We are situated on the gateway to the Otago Peninsula, which features wildlife, Walking Tracks, Taiaroa Head Albatross Colony, Disappearing Gun, Seal Colonies, Yellow Eyed Penguins, Glenfalloch Gardens, and much more.
We are seven minutes to town centre. Our home is a modern interpretation of a traditional Scottish house, and set in 1 acre of gardens and lawns, with indoor/outdoor living. Awake to the sound of abundant bird life in a quiet and secure neighbourhood. We serve delicious healthy breakfasts. One luxury bedroom complete with one queen and one single bed, plus one luxury bedroom with one double and one single bed, plus one luxury bedroom with 2 single beds. All rooms have tea-making facilities, TV, heaters, electric blankets. Separate facilities with modern guest bathroom. Relax far from the madding crowd.
Businessmen welcome. All non smoking, no pets and not suitable for young children.
Home Page: www.bnb.co.nz

Dunedin
Bed & Breakfast
Address: 52 Tennyson Street, Dunedin
Name: Hulmes Court
Telephone: (03) 477 5319
(Freephone 0800 448 563)
Fax: (03) 477 5310
Mobile: (025) 351 075
Email: normwood@earthlight.co.nz
Beds: 3 Queen, 2 single (5 bedrooms)
Bathroom: 2 Ensuite, 2 Guests share
Tariff: B&B (continental) Ensuite $110, Double $85, Single $55. Visa/Mastercard/ Dinners/Amex/JCB. NZ B&B Vouchers accepted $12 surcharge for Double, $39 surcharge for Ensuite.
Nearest Town: Dunedin (in fact right in the heart)

Hulmes Court Bed and Breakfast is a beautiful 1860's Victorian mansion just 2-3 minutes walk to town. There is plenty of off-street parking. Your host Norman Wood and his staff are frequent travellers around New Zealand and the world. We will provide you with warm, friendly and informative stay in our beautiful city. Norman has an advertising business and is interested in history, geography and has stood for parliament twice. At the same time, Norman at 33 and his staff are youthful and full of energy. Hulmes Court provides guests with a continental breakfast, free tea, coffee and biscuits, complimentary laundry, mountain bikes, email, phone and fax (free for local calls).
Directions: *Drive up Stuart Street from the Octagon, over the Moray Place intersection, then left into Smith Street, then veer to the left, this is Tennyson Street, and Hulmes Court.*
Home Page: http://www.hulmes.co.nz

Dunedin
Self Contained Accommoation B&B
Address: 300 York Place, Dunedin
Name: The Station Master's Cottage
Telephone: Call Free 0800 327 333
Beds: 2 Queen, 2 Single
(3 Bedrooms)
Bathroom: 1 Guests share
Tariff: B&B (Continental) $80-$140.
Visa, M/C, Amex, Diners Club.
Nearest Town: Dunedin Central City, Octagon 850 m easy walking.

"A Scottish Dream...."
Imagine a romantic historic cottage in a tranquil garden in the city, circa 1890. Built for Dunedin's first Station Master, William Popperwell and his wife Elizabeth, extensively renovated and luxuriously furnished with fine linen and dreamy beds. Full central heating and a crackling fire, fresh flowers, and a hearty breakfast.
Ten minutes walk to the best cafes, restaurants, bars, shops, central city Octagon, art gallery and Otago University. Self-contained, serviced accommodation. Beautifully appointed bedrooms, large luxury bathroom, country kitchen, dining room, and lounge-sitting room. Single party bookings welcome.
A delightful boutique bed & breakfast oozing the charm, comfort and ambience of times past......
No smoking.
Directions: *From the Octagon travel up Stuart Street, turn left into Cargill Street, then left into Arthur St. At the traffic signals travel up Yout Place to the Station Master's Cottage.*

Dunedin-Mosgiel

Homestay
Address: 14 Mure Street, Mosgiel
Name: Lois and Lance Woodfield
Telephone: (03) 489 8236
Fax: (03) 489 8236
Email: l.l.woodfield@clear.net.nz
Beds: 1 Queen, 2 Single
(2 bedrooms)
Bathroom: 1 Guests share
Tariff: B&B (full) Double $60-$80,
Single $40. Credit Cards accepted. NZ B&B Vouchers accepted
Nearest Town: Mosgiel (14kms South of Dunedin - 15 minutes drive)

Welcome to "The Old Vicarage", our English-style cottage home, set in a fragrant garden. Originally built by a dentist in the 1920's, it later served as the local vicarage for 46 years, before passing into the hands of various private owners, all of whom made sympathetic restorations and improvements. The outstanding feature is the exquisitely balanced garden with many varieties of rhododendrons, perennials, spring bulbs, and over 70 roses, all laid out in garden 'rooms'. The two upstairs guest rooms and bathroom enjoy a commanding view of the archery lawn and rock garden below, while warm Oregon panelling and unique leadlight windows throughout enhance the atmosphere.
Situated in Mosgiel, close to the Airport on the beautiful Taieri Plains, the property is just 15 minutes drive from central Dunedin. We are a retired Christian couple who have travelled extensively, have a collector's library and enjoy gardening, architecture, tramping, theology and history.

Waihola

Homestay/Self-contained Accomm
Address: Sandown Street,
Waihola, South Otago
Name: Lillian & Trevor Robinson
Telephone: (03) 417 8218
Fax: (03) 417 8287
Beds: 1 Double, 2 Single(2 bedrooms)
Bathroom: 1 Ensuite, 1 Family share
Tariff: B&B (full) Double $60, Single $40,
Dinner by arrangement $20. NZ B&B Vouchers accepted
Nearest Town: 40 km south of Dunedin, 15 min to Dunedin Airport

We have a very comfortable home which is situated in a quiet street with views of mountains, Lake and township.
Our double bedroom has ensuite, tea making facilities, fridge, TV and heater. All beds have electric blankets.
Lake Waihola is very popular for boating, fishing and swimming. There is a bowling green and a golf course within 10 minutes drive.
We enjoy meeting people and ensure you a very pleasant stay.
Dinner by arrangement.
Directions: *Please phone night before where possible.*

Waihola

Lakeside Cottage Homestay

Address: 'Ivy Cottage', 7 SH 1, Waihola, Otago 9055
Name: Bryan & Robin Leckie
Telephone: (03) 417 8946
Fax: 03 4178966
Beds: 1 Double, 2 Single (2 bedrooms)
Bathroom: 1 Private, 1 Guests share
Tariff: B&B (full) Double $65 ($120 for 2 nights - longer stays negotiable), Single $50, Children under 12 $20, Dinner $25 per person (includes wine). Credit cards (MC/BC/VISA).NZ B&B Vouchers accepted
Nearest Town: 40 km South of Dunedin on SH 1 (30 minutes) 15km from Dunedin Airport.

We are situated on "The Southern Scenic Route" with uninterrupted views of Lake Waihola. Visitors find "Ivy Cottage" is an excellent base for day trips. To the north are Dunedin's Albatross, Penguins, Historic buildings, University, Scenic Railway, cafe`s and sporting facilities including "The House of Pain". South is New Zealand's best kept secret "The Catlins", real natural beauty. West is Central Otago with gold history, you can pick fruit in season and choose local wines. East is Taieri Mouth where there are deep sea fishing and river charters available.Waihola offers many attractions, aquatic recreation, heritage, walks, limestone fossils, wetlands, birds, fishing and golf. Our interests include most sports, wildlife and craft work. We are retired restaurateurs and enjoy creative cooking.Our double accommodation is detached. Affectionately known as "The Shed" with bathroom, laundry, TV and heating. We have a friendly Golden Retriever "Bud". We look forward to hosting you. **Directions**: *Please phone. Transport can be arranged from the Airport & Bus / Train terminals.*

Balclutha

Farmstay+Self-contained Accom.

Address: 'Balcairn', Blackburn Road, Hillend No.2 R.D, Balclutha
Name: Ken & Helen Spittle
Telephone: (03) 418 1385
Fax: (03) 418 4385
Email: balcairn@xtra.co.nz
Beds: 1 Double, 2 Single (2 bedrooms)
Bathroom: 1 Guests share
Tariff: B&B (continental) Double $80, Single $40, Children under 14yrs half price. Dinner by arrangement $25pp. Campervans $5 per head. NZ B&B Vouchers accepted
Nearest Town: Balclutha 22km, Milton 25km

Join our family at "Balcairn" a 500 acre sheep, beef and deer working farm and enjoy the quiet, peaceful surroundings of life in the country. You can join in whatever farm activity is happening on the day or enjoy a farm tour. We are located not far from State Highway 1 and 8, just one hour south of Dunedin - an ideal stopover for guests travelling through the beautiful Catlins Scenic Reserve with its wonderful wildlife. The Historic Gold Mining and fruit growing areas of Central Otago are closeby and with prior notice and booking we could arrange a tour of these areas for you.Our home is a modern spacious two storey house with fully self contained guest accommodation all downstairs. All beds have electric blankets and full cooking and laundry facilities are available. Guests arriving by bus or train can be met at Balclutha or Milton, or by plane at Dunedin Airport, 60km. No smoking in our home please. **Directions**: *Please phone.*

Balclutha

Farmstay
Address: Clydevale, Clutha River Road,
No 4 RD, Balclutha
Name: Argyll Farmstay/Trish & Alan May
Telephone: (03) 415 9268
Fax: (03) 415 9268
Mobile: (025) 318 241
Beds: 1 Queen, 2 Single (2 Bedrooms)
Bathroom: 1 Guests Share
Tariff: B&B (Full) Double $70, Single $35,
Children under 12 half price.
Dinner $25. Campervan 2 power points $10 per person.
NZ B&B Vouchers accepted
Nearest Town: Balclutha approx 26 km.

Argyll Farm is situated on the banks of the mighty Clutha River and this provides guests with an unique opportunity to enjoy several recreational pastimes or relax in our large picturesque garden. We farm 530 acres running 800 deer, 150 cattle and 1000 sheep. Guests would be welcome to tour our farm or join the family at their daily farming tasks. Our home is a comfortable four bedroom brick home with a modern kitchen and bathroom facilities.
We are ideally situated for guests travelling through to Dunedin, the Catlins area, the Lakes District eg. Queenstown or Te Anau. Our farm is within a short distance from several very good fishing rivers and we also offer guests an extra option of a Jet Boat Tour or Fishing Trip on the river. Guests could also take the famous Tuapeka Ferry across the river (approx. 5 km away). 2 Campervan power points available.
Directions: *Please phone*

Balclutha

Farmstay, Bed & Breakfast
Address: 'Breadalbane',
293 Freezing Works Road, No 3 RD, Balclutha
Name: Carolynne and Ken Stephens
Telephone: (03) 418 2568
Fax: (03) 418 2591
Beds: 1 Double, 2 Single (2 Bedrooms)
Bathroom: 1 Guests Share
Tariff: B&B (Full) Double $80, Single $45,
Dinner by arrangement $25 pp, Children Primary $20.
Nearest Town: Balclutha 7 mins.

A warm welcome awaits you at Breadalbane, located on 1300 acres of rolling farm land, 7 minutes from the Balclutha Information Centre, recreational facilities and restaurants. Two minutes from the farm gate, you will find the popular Southern Scenic Route, with all the coastal attractions. Nearby Telford Rural Polytechnic and fishing on the Clutha River.
Guests can relax in peaceful surroundings in our large country garden, while enjoying the panoramic views north, south, east and west. We invite you to stroll along the farm lane, where you can view deer, sheep and farm forestry, for which we received a National Award.
Our comfortable home is well heated, all beds have electric blankets. Each room has tea/coffee facilities, with TV in the double room.
complimentary laundry available.
We have a friendly cat and corgi dog, who loves being part of the activities.
Directions: *Please phone.*

Clinton - South Otago

Farmstay
Address: 'Wairuna Bush',
Rural Delivery Clinton,
South Otago.
Situated on Main South Highway 1
Name: LAR & KF Carruthers
Telephone: (03) 415 7222
If no reply ring after 5pm.
Email: kath.carruthers@xtra.co.nz
Beds: 1 King/Queen, 1 Double,
2 Single (3 bedrooms)
Bathroom: 1 Guests share
Tariff: B&B (full) Double $70, Single $40, Dinner $25.
Nearest Town: South/Gore, North/Balclutha both 1/2 hour drive on SH1.

KATHLEEN and ROY CARRUTHERS welcome you to their warm spacious home, set on 45 acres of farmland surrounded by native Podocarp Bush.
Unwind from your travel in peace and tranquillity.
Listen to Bellbirds, fantails and wood pigeons.
Follow newly formed walkways through 5 acres of native flora.
See Kahikatea, Matai, Miro and Totara trees (some being over 500 years old).
If you wish, Roy will be happy to introduce you to their farm dog and thoroughbred horse, sheep, cattle and calves. Or take you for a game of bowls. There is a very challenging 9 hole golf course in Clinton and some extremely good fishing spots close by, or you can just laze around. Please phone or book in advance.

Nuggets (Catlins)

B&B + Self-contained Beachfront.
Address: Nugget Lodge,
Nugget Road, RD1, Balclutha
Name: Noel & Kath Widdowson
Telephone: (03) 412 8783
Fax: (03) 412 8784
Beds: Two self contained private units
with panoramic sea views. Both units

have a separate bedroom with a double bed. One unit will sleep 2 extra in living area
Bathroom: Ensuite each.
Tariff: Units $80 Double, $10 per additional person.
Breakfast $10 each. Credit Cards (VISA/MC/BC).
Nearest Town: Balclutha, Owaka 24km

*Sleep to the roar of the waves and awake to the spectacular views and sunrises as Nugget Lodge is absolutely on the waters edge, situated on the edge of the Nugget Lighthouse Reserve. Home for Fur seals, sealions, Yellow-eyed Penguins, NZ sea birds and in the spring and early summer Elephant Seals and Leoard Seals. After 11 years we are taking a rest from meals, breakfast will still be in our home and our warm hospitallity will still be the same. Units have full facilities, stove, fridge, microwave, central heating and TV. We have an excellent restaurant at Owaka "The Lumberjack" and we will provide meals on their closed nights. Organic vegetables and herbs from our garden are free to our guests. Kath is an Honorary Wildlife Ranger and an expert on the wildlife, a professional photographer and keen walker. Noel is employed in valuation and farm finance. Our children are away from home and our cat and dog respect the privacy of our guests. **Directions**: From Southern Senic Route take signs to Nugget Point we are the only accommodation on road.*

Owaka – (The Catlins)
Farmstay+Self-Contained Cottage (Papatowai Beach)
Address: 'Greenwood', Purakaunui Falls Road, Owaka, South Otago
Name: Alan & Helen-May Burgess
Telephone: (03) 415 8259 (if no reply, phone after 6pm).
Fax: (03) 415 8259   **Mobile**: (025) 384 538
Email: greenwoodfarm@xtra.co.nz
Beds: 1 Queen, 3 Single (3 bedrooms)
Bathroom: 1 Ensuite, 1 Private, 1 Family Share
Tariff: B&B (full/continental) Double $70, Single $45, Children half price, Dinner $25, Lunch if required; Campervans $25; Self contained house at Papatowai beach (sleeps 8) $60 per night (4 persons), $10 each extra person.
NZ B&B Vouchers accepted $10 surcharge
Nearest Town: Owaka 14 km

*We welcome you to our 1900 acre farm in the heart of the Catlins, where our homestead is situated within walking distance from the beautiful Purakaunui Falls. Our home, which is set in a large garden, offers warm, comfortable accommodation for up to five persons. The main guest bedroom which has an ensuite, walks through to a furnished day-room and this opens to the outdoors. Other guest rooms are serviced with a private bathroom. We enjoy providing a three course dinner and dining with our guests in the evenings. Alan enjoys taking people around our sheep, cattle and deer farm. The district features the yellow-eyed penguin and many beautiful, scenic drives and walking tracks through native bush and beaches. Trout and sea fishing may also be enjoyed.*__Directions__*: Take Highway 92 (Southern Scenic route) to Owaka from Balclutha or Invercargill. From Owaka follow the signposts to Purakaunui Falls for 14 km. Our name and farm name is on the gate entrance (just before you reach the falls).*

Owaka – (The Catlins)
Farmstay
Address: 'Tarara Downs', 857 Puaho Rd, R.D.2 Owaka
Name: Ida & John Burgess
Telephone: (03) 415 8293
Fax: (03) 415 8293
Beds: 1 Double, 2 Single (2 bedrooms)
Bathroom: 1 Ensuite, 1 Family share
Tariff: B&B (full) Double $55, Twin with ensuite $70, Single $35, Children half price; Dinner $15 (2 course), Campervans welcome. NZ B&B Vouchers accepted
Nearest Town: Owaka 16 km

Our 2000-acre farm is situated in an area renowned for its bush and coastal scenery, within walking distance of the beautiful Purakaunui Falls. Our farm runs sheep, cattle and deer. As well as seeing normal farm activities, horse riding, bush walks and fishing trips are available in the district. We live in a comfortable New Zealand farmhouse with two cats, as our family have all left home, and enjoy eating our own produce and local delicacies. Children very welcome.
Directions: *Follow State Highway 92 to Owaka from Balclutha or Invercargill. Approximately 1 3/4 hours drive from Dunedin or Invercargill on a scenic road, follow signposts to Purakaunui Falls - we are the closest house to them.*

Owaka – (The Catlins)

Farmstay
Address: Glenomaru, No1 R.D.,
Balclutha
Name: Bruce & Kathryn Wilson
Telephone: (03) 415 8282
Fax: (03) 415 8282
Beds: 1 Double, 4 Single
(3 bedrooms)
Bathroom: 2 Family share
Tariff: B&B (full) Double $60, Single $35,
Children half price; Dinner $15; Campervans $25.
NZ B&B Vouchers accepted
Nearest Town: Balclutha 22 km, Owaka 11 km

We farm a 1500 acre property carrying sheep, cattle and deer.
Guests may be taken on a farm tour, which includes an inspection of a 130 year old home presently being preserved and water wheel. We have a friendly fox terrier called "Boon".
Fishing trips may be arranged. Golf equipment available, 9 hole golf course only ten minutes drive. We are near Kaka Point, renowned for beach, lighthouse and viewing the yellow-eyed penguins and seals. You may have family dinner with us or if preferred bed and breakfast. Guests can be collected off public transport from Balclutha free of charge.
Directions: *Take Highway 92 from Balclutha towards Owaka, first turn right past sawmill. Matuanui Rd No Exit. From Owaka turn left beside Sawmill up gravel road Matuanui Road No Exit.*

Owaka – The Catlins

Homestay/B&B/Separate Unit
Address: 'Kepplestone Park', Surat Bay Road, Newhaven, RD 1, Owaka
Name: Gay & Arch Maley
Telephone: (03) 415 8134 Freephone: 0800 105 134
Fax: (03) 415 8137
Email: gayandarch@hotmail.com
Beds: 1 Queen, 4 Single (3 bedrooms) Separate guest unit, tea/coffee & TV
Bathroom: 2 Ensuite, 1 Family share
Tariff: B&B (special) Double $60/$85, Single $55, Dinner $25. NZ B&B Vouchers accepted Surcharge $25 excess
Nearest Town: Owaka 6km

Having taken early retirement we welcome guests to our home, situated one minute from a beautiful beach, at the confluence of the Catlins and Owaka rivers. For the enthusiasts, unpolluted beach, golf links, clubs available, Hooker seals basking on beach, all within five minutes, or Amateur Radio (Gay ZL4JO.) 9 hole chip & putt on property.
Having travelled extensively we understand the needs of fellow travellers and wish to share with you our homely atmosphere and hospitality. Approximately 20 minutes from Penguins and Purakaunui Falls.
We are both keen gardeners of our two acre property and organically grow our own vegetables. Share an evening meal with us, served with a glass of wine. Choice of menu with prior notice. Bicycles for riding on the beach. Smoking negotiable (being ex smokers we understand the needs of smokers!).
Directions: *At north end of Owaka (at Royal Terrace St) follow signs to Newhaven, at golf course, go "across" bridge, follow signs to Newhaven and Surat Bay. 3km from bridge, first house on left on Surat Bay Road.*

Owaka – The Catlins
Farmstay+Self-contained Accom.
Address: 'Hillview', Rapid no. 161, Hunt Rd, Katea, RD 2, Owaka, South Otago
Name: Kate & Bruce McLachlan
Telephone: (03) 415 8457
Fax: (03) 415 8650
Email: hillviewcatlins@hotmail.com
Beds: Cottage;1 Queen, 3 Single (3 bedrooms) Homestead; 1 Queen 2 Single (2 bedrooms)
Bathroom: Cottage; 1 Guests share. Homestead; 1 Guests share
Tariff: B&B (continental) Double Homestead $65, Cottage $75, Single $40, Dinner $20. Credit Cards: Visa/Mastercard.
NZ B&B Vouchers accepted $10 surcharge
Nearest Town: Owaka 6km, Balclutha 27km

Our 450 acre sheep and cattle grazing unit is situated just off the Southern Scenic Route, 5 mins from the golf course, 15 mins from Nugget Point Lighthouse and wildlife, 10 mins from sealions at Cannibal Bay.We offer you a cosy private cottage in a garden setting adjacent to our home. A "Home away from home", it is self contained with all modern appliances and a log burner. Alternatively enjoy the comfortable relaxed non-smoking atmosphere of our home which we share with our friendly toy poodle and two Burmese cats.
*Bruce's hobbies include breeding and training working farm dogs and driving "Lucky" the Shetland pony. Kate enjoys reading, breeds black sheep, spins their natural wool and participates in a variety of handcrafts. Together we enjoy meeting people, gardening and our grandchildren. Breakfast with us or enjoy a leisurely breakfast provided at the cottage. Evening meals are available by arrangement. Phone bookings essential. Please phone after 4 pm. **Directions**: 27km from Balclutha, 5km north of Owaka. 1.5km from the main highway.Please phone ahead.*

Owaka - Catlins
Bed & Breakfast
Address: Catlins Retreat Bed & Breakfast, 27 Main Road, Owaka, Catlins, South Otago
Name: Catlins Retreat Bed & Breakfast
Telephone: (03) 415 8830
Beds: 3 Queen, 1 Twin (4 bedrooms)
Bathroom: 2 Guests share
Tariff: B&B (full/continental) Double $75, single $40, School children half price, Dinner $25 (3 course).
NZ B&B Vouchers accepted $10 surcharge
Nearest Town: Balclutha

Steve and Melanie, both early thirties and widely travelled, welcome you into their elegantly restored Rimu villa. All rooms are spacious and comfortable, warm with plenty of room to relax. We have no children and offer a relaxed informal home away from home. Ideally situated in the Catlins main town, within an easy stroll to the information centre and amenities. An excellent base to explore the Catlins wildlife, beaches and many walks. We will gladly give advice and directions to get the most out of your stay. After an active day collapse in our hot spa, relax in the large garden, enjoy a scrumptious home cooked meal, bbq or wander to local restaurants.
To find us we are on the Southern Scenic Route, 1 1/2 hours south of Dunedin and 2 1/2 hours north of Invercargill. You can't miss our blue picket fence and signs in Owaka.

Southland

Progress Valley
Waikawa
Tokanui
Fortrose
Wyndham
Edendale
Brydon
Mataura
Pukerau
Waikaka
Gore
Rimu
Invercargill
Bluff
Tussock Creek
Winton
Wendonside
Balfour
Lumsden
Dipton
Otautau
Mossburn
Riverton
Te Anau
Manapouri

1
92
1
6
96
6
6
99
96
94
6
94
94

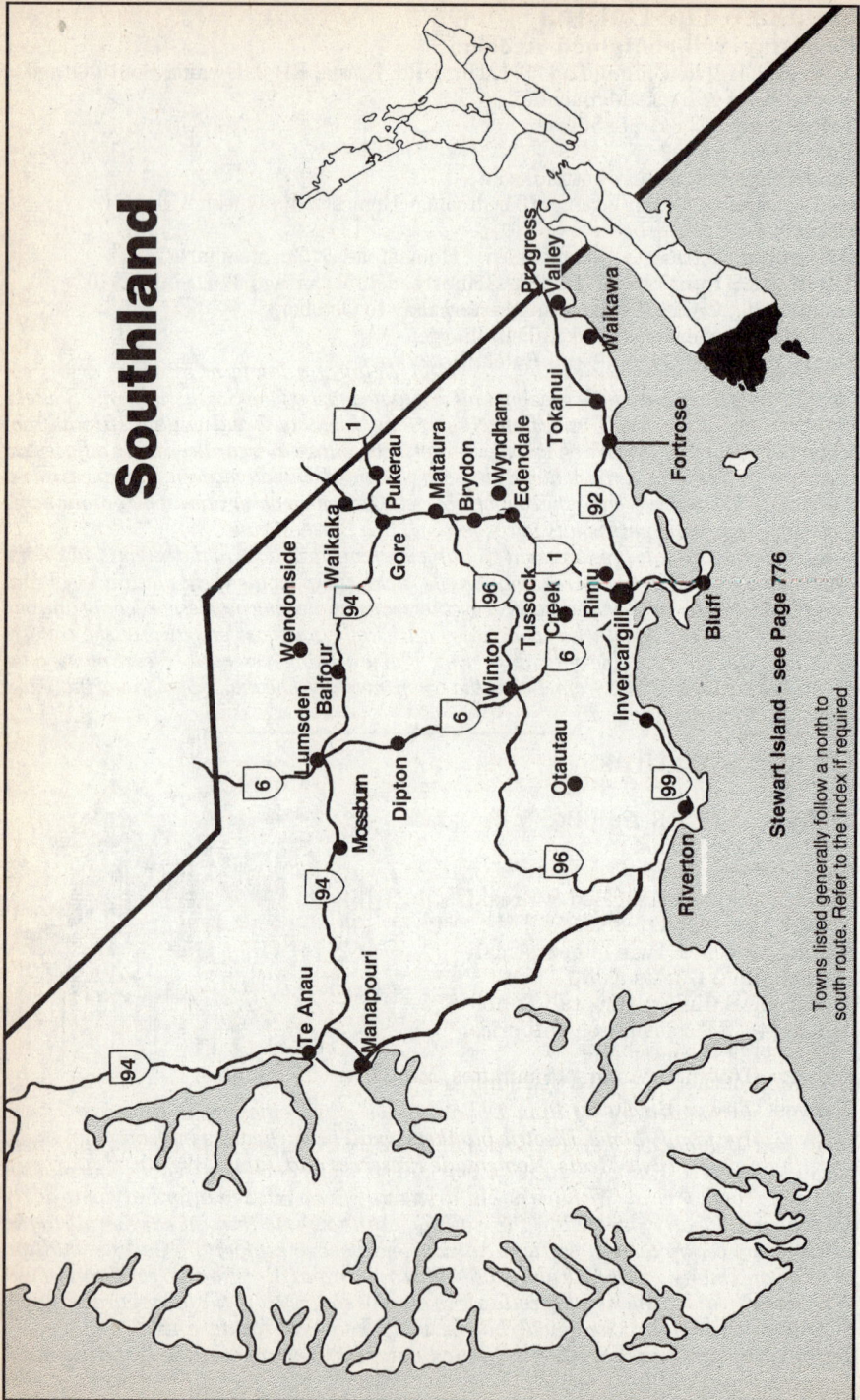

Stewart Island - see Page 776

Towns listed generally follow a north to
south route.. Refer to the index if required

Te Anau
Farmstay
Address: 123 Sinclair Road,
R.D.1, Te Anau
Name: Dave & Teresa Hughes
Telephone: (03) 249 7581
Fax: (03) 249 7589
Mobile: (025) 344 016
Beds: 2 Single (1 bedroom)
Bathroom: 1 Ensuite
Tariff: B&B (continental) Double $70,
Single $50. NZ B&B Vouchers accepted May to October
Nearest Town: Te Anau 5 km

A warm welcome to travellers visiting Fiordland. We live on a deer farm, 5 minutes drive from Te Anau township, just 1 kilometre off the Milford Highway. David, besides farming, works in the Deer Industry, while I teach at the local Primary School. We have three children; all are away from home now. Our pets, a dog and a cat, enjoy meeting our visitors as well. Your accommodation, which has magnificent views of Lake Te Anau and the Kepler and Murchison mountains, is a self-contained bed-sittingroom with ensuite, TV, tea/coffee making facilities and private entrance. We can assist with information and reservations to ensure your stay in Fiordland is memorable. We request guests do not smoke in our home. **Directions**: *Continue through Te Anau on road to Milford Sound for 5 km to Sinclair Road, turn right. We are the second house on the left - our name is on the letterbox.*

Te Anau
Farmstay
Address: 'Tapua' RD 2,
Te Anau
Name: Dorothy & Donald Cromb
Telephone: (03) 249 5805
Fax: (03) 249 5805
Mobile: (025) 201 9109
Email: Tapua.Cromb@xtra.co.nz
Beds: 4 Single (2 bedrooms)
Bathroom: 1 Guests share
Tariff: B&B (full) Double $90, Single $60, Children under 12 half price, Dinner $25pp, Discount for groups of 4 adults, Credit cards (VISA/MC). NZ B&B Vouchers accepted $15 surcharge
Nearest Town: Te Anau - 15 minutes, Manapouri 15 minutes.

You are surrounded by "Million Dollar" views while enjoying the comfort of our modern large family home. Electric blankets on all beds - heaters in bedrooms. Enjoy traditional Farm Style Meals, Homemade Preserves and Jams. We are situated in a very handy position close to the main road, only 15 minutes from Te Anau or Manapouri making an excellent base for your sightseeing trips to magnificent Milford and Doubtful Sounds. We recommend a two night stay so that you can enjoy a relaxing trip to the Sounds, as well as a look over our 348 Hectare (870 acres) farm which carries 3700 sheep and 100 cattle. Some of New Zealand's best fishing rivers within a few minutes drive as are the finest walking tracks in the world, golf courses etc. We are happy helping plan your day trips. We have 2 cats. Personal attention and service assured. Smoke Free home. **Directions**: *Please phone.*
Home Page: http://www.fiordland.org.nz/html/tapua.html

Te Anau

Homestay + Self-contained Acco
Address: 13 Fergus Square, Te Anau
Name: Rob & Nancy Marshall
Telephone: (03) 249 8241
Fax: (03) 249-7397
Mobile: (025) 226 1820
Email: rob.nancy@xtra.co.nz
Beds: 2 King, 2 Single (3 bedrooms)
Bathroom: 1 Ensuite, 1 Guests share
Tariff: B&B (full/continental) Double $80-$100 s.c.,
Single $50 Dinner $35, Credit cards. No smoking. NZ B&B Vouchers accepted
$10 surcharge
Nearest Town: Te Anau 5 minutes walk

*Rob, Nancy & Chardonnay, our Chocolate Burmese cat, welcome you to our quiet and
tranquil home facing a park and only 5 minutes walk from the town and lake.*
*We are a couple retired from farming and are grandparents who enjoy meeting people
from all walks of life. Rob is a member of the Lions Club and involved in community
affairs. Our modern home has two bedrooms, one king and one twin share facilities,
a self-contained suite, sheltered courtyards and gardens. All rooms have tea making
facilities and meals are served in the main dining room.*
*Most excursion tours, including Milford and Doubtful Sounds, can be booked from our
home and guests are picked up at the door. Off-street parking is available and baggage
can be securely stored for those walking the tracks.*
Directions: *Follow Lakeside Drive past town centre turn right into Matai Street then
left into Fergus Square. RESERVATIONS: Please ring, fax or email.*

Te Anau

Farmstay
Address: Perenuka Farm,
R.D. 1, Te Anau
Name: Margaret & Les Simpson
Telephone: (03) 249 7841
Fax: (03) 249 7841
Beds: 2 Queen (2 bedrooms)
Bathroom: 2 Ensuite
Tariff: B&B (continental) Double $85.
Commission extra for Agency Bookings.
Nearest Town: Te Anau 5km

*Our 750 acre sheep and cattle farm is 5 km North of Te Anau, on the highway to Milford
Sound. Our smokefree home and accommodation is situated well back from the road,
on a terrace with panoramic views of the lake and surrounding mountains from all
rooms. Spacious guest rooms are private, individual buildings in a garden setting. We
enjoy guests joining us for breakfast and evenings of friendship and conversation.
Each unit has high quality furnishings, fridge, tea / coffee making, electric blankets,
heating, hair dryer, and full sized ensuite bathroom.*
*We both enjoy the outdoor opportunities of this region, so feel we can offer impartial
information on the areas attractions. We also have a small flock of very friendly pet
sheep.*
Directions: *Follow Milford Sound Highway 5km north of Te Anau. Turn right into
Sinclair Road, and immediately right into our driveway. Second house up the drive.*
Home Page: http://nz.com/webnz/bbnz/perenuka.htm

Te Anau

Guest House
Address: 'Matai Lodge', 42 Mokonui Street, Te Anau
Name: Richard Bevan
Telephone: (03) 249 7360
Fax: (03) 249 7360
Beds: 1 Queen, 2 Double, 9 Single (3 Twin, 1 Triple) (7 bedrooms)
Bathroom: 2 Guests share
Tariff: B&B (full) Double/Twin $76, Single $55, Triple $102,
Credit cards. NZ B&B Vouchers accepted
Nearest Town: Te Anau

The Matai Lodge is ideally located in a quiet residential area just 2 minutes walk from the lake and 5 minutes walk from the town centre. It offers clean, friendly, "homestyle" accommodation in a smoke-free environment. Full (and substantial) breakfasts are served in the dining / lounge area with tea and coffee always available, whilst there is also a separate TV lounge. All rooms are on the ground floor, have hot and cold vanity units, electric blankets and heaters. Te Anau is the hub of Fiordland, a World Heritage National Park. Among the main attractions of the area are Milford Sound, Doubtful Sound and Te Ana-au glowworm caves. World famous walking tracks including the Milford, Kepler, Routeburn and Hollyford all start close to the town. All excursion trips can be booked at the lodge, with bus pick-up at the gate. Off-street parking is available, with vehicles and baggage stored for guests walking the tracks.

Te Anau

Country Homestay
Address: 'The Farmyard',
Charles Nairn Rd, R.D.1, Te Anau 9681
Name: Ray & Helen Willett
Telephone: (03) 249 7833
Fax: (03) 249 7830
Mobile: (025) 289 0939
Beds: 1 Double, 1 Single (1 bedroom)
Bathroom: 1 Ensuite
Tariff: B&B (continental) Double $88
($80 if booking direct), Single $55.
Nearest Town: Te Anau 3km.

THE FARMYARD

Our home is on a 12 acre 'Hobby' farm 3km from Te Anau with spectacular views of mountains and bush. We have lived in Fiordland for many years, and invite you to share our knowledge and enthusiasm of the region with us.
We are ideally situated for excursions to Milford and Doubtful Sounds. As we both drive visitors to Milford, and for many years worked on the Milford Track, we are able to offer the very best advice for your Milford experience.
Our accommodation is a detached, self-contained cottage (microwave, fridge, etc) with privacy assured.
If possible, please phone before 8 am or after 5.30 pm, but we are often available during the day. Our pets - donkey, pony, Kune Kune pig, terriers (2), goats, sheep, will all be delighted to meet you.
Come and enjoy your stay with us. Welcome to Te Anau-Fiordland.

Te Anau
Bed & Breakfast
Address: 2 Lake Front Drive, Te Anau
Name: 'The Cats Whiskers'
Hosts: Irene & Terry
Telephone: (03) 249 8112
Fax: (03) 249 8112
Beds: 1 King, 2 Queen,
4 Single (3 bedrooms)
Bathroom: 3 Ensuite
Tariff: B&B (full) Double $110, Single $65,
Children half price. Credit cards. Off Season rates.
Nearest Town: Te Anau 10 minute walk to centre.

Our home is situated on Te Anau lakefront opposite the Dept of Conservation Park Headquarters. We provide guests with comfort and outside access to all 3 rooms. Two bedrooms have 1 Queen and 1 Single. One large bedroom has 1 King and 2 Single and extra single can be added to the room, ie families. All have TV and tea making facilities. We are happy to provide a courtesy car to any of the variety of restaurants for dinner or as most of these are close by enjoy a walk along the lovely lakefront. We have a good car park and cars and luggage may be left while walking any of our famous tracks. We can book you any of the daily excursions to the famous Milford and Doubtful Sounds trips. We have a much loved Blue Tortie Female Burmese cat called Bianca.
Directions: *To Lakefront Drive turn left off Highway 94 where signposted on edge of town. 1st house on right.*
Home Page: http://nz.com/webnz/bbnz/catwh.htm

Te Anau
Homestay
Address: 'House of Wood',
44 Moana Crescent, Te Anau
Name: Elaine & Trevor Lett
Telephone: (03) 249 8404
Fax: (03) 249 7676
Mobile: 025-220 4356
Beds: 1 Queen, 1 Double,
2 Single (3 Bedrooms)
Bathroom: 1 Ensuite,
1 Guests share
Tariff: B&B (continental)
Double $90,
Queen Ensuite $105, Single $70.
Nearest Town: Te Anau 3 minutes walk.

Welcome to Te Anau. We invite you to join us in our "House of Wood" with natural timber throughout interior. "House of Wood" is a uniquely designed two storey wood house with outside balconies and beautiful views. We are in a quiet residential area with the town centre just a short walk away. We are close to all tourist facilities and Lake. We know the Otago / Southland area extremely well and can help you make the most of your time in this area. Trevor is a builder and now our three daughters have left home we have more time for interests which include wood-turning, tramping and quilting. We offer smokefree friendly Kiwi accommodation. Along with Kaidy our Westhighland Terrier, we welcome you to our home and advise early bookings for our peak period November-March. Please phone for directions.

Te Anau
Farmstay
Address: The Wilderness,
No 1 RD, Te Anau
Name: Phyllis & Wayne Burgess
Telephone: (03) 249 5833
Fax: (03) 249 5833
Beds: 1 Double,
2 Single (2 bedrooms)
Bathroom: Family share
Tariff: B&B (continental) Double
$70, Single $55, Children negotiable,
Dinner $25, Full breakfast $6 extra per person.
Nearest Town: 19km east of Te Anau State Highway 94

Phyllis and Wayne welcome you to their sunny and warm home situated in a quiet garden setting with mountain views. We are a middle aged couple. Wayne combines farming and operating a Balage Contracting business over the summer months, he enjoys hunting, boating, fishing and the outdoor life.
Phyliis interests are gardening and the outdoors also cooking, which include home grown lamb and beef and fresh vegetables from her garden, followed by home made desserts. Breakfasts are according to you needs and range from light to hearty with my bottled fruit and tasty homemade jams. We would be happy to assist you with your planning of day trips around the "Walking capital of the World" and see the splendour and ruggedness of the real New Zealand Fiordland.
Directions: *4km past The Key on State Highway 94, 19km east of Te Anau. Name on mailbox. A friendly and warm welcome awaits you.*

Te Anau
Countrystay
Address: Country Style B&B,
Sinclair Road, R.D.1, Te Anau 9681
Name: Kerri & Stephen James
Telephone: (03) 249 7252
Freephone: 0800 200 865
Fax: (03) 249 7672 **Mobile**: (025) 316 765
Email: CountryStyleBB@xtra.co.
Beds: 1 Queen (1 bedroom) - may make up extra bed.
Bathroom: 1 Family share
Tariff: B&B (continental) Double $80, Single $70, Children $15, Dinner $25, Full breakfast $6 extra per person, Campervans $8pp, Credit Cards (VISA/MC). NZ B&B Vouchers accepted Accepted April-November. $10 Surcharge
Nearest Town: Te Anau 7km

A "Kiwi" welcome awaits you to our home which captures the sun or relax beside our cosy fire in winter. We are situated just off the Milford Sound highway in a garden setting, where you can enjoy peace, tranquillity and fresh country air. Surrounded by impressive sheep and deer farming views and mountains. Our daughters Shelley (12) and Katie (9) along with ourselves enjoy meeting our guests. We have farming backgrounds and enjoy the outdoors. Help feed our pet lambs from September - February and other farm pets throughout the year. Our guest bedroom is tastefully decorated with heating and electric blankets. Tea, coffee and herbal teas always available. Full laundry service. We provide our guests with a smokefree environment indoors. **Directions**: *Continue through Te Anau towards Milford Sounds for 5 km to Sinclair Road, turn right. Travel 2 1/2 km. Our green mail box has our name S.T & K.A. James on it. Mailbox on left. House on right.* **Home Page**: www.homestaysnz.co.nz/countrystyle.htm

Te Anau

Farmstay/S.C. Cottage
Address: 'The Key',
2 R.D., Te Anau
Name: John & Carolyn Klein
Telephone: (03) 249 5807
Fax: (03) 249 5807
Beds: 1 Queen, 3 Single
(2 bedrooms) with adjoining bathroom
Bathroom: 1 Private
Tariff: B&B (continental) Double $75 plus $20 per extra person, Single $55, Children negotiable. Dinner $20pp. Campervans negotiable. Credit cards accepted. NZ B&B Vouchers accepted Winter rates; May-October inclusive $65 double.
Nearest Town: The Key is 32km from Mossburn and 15 minutes out of Te Anau.

We are a family with three children , Chris 18, Alistair 17 and Casey 12 years old and we all enjoy meeting people. We share our home with 2 cats (Joe and Nipper) and Misty the dog who loves to play fetch. We also have a pet lamb over the summer which you are welcome to help bottle feed.

Carolyn is a keen gardener and a superb cook with local venison or fresh Fiordland fish a favourite, she also offers a special "Lobster" menu during our rock lobster season (Prices will vary on availability and size). Nobody has ever left our place hungry! John operates a contracting business in the local farming community. His interests include "winter" squash and he is also an active member of our local Lions Club. His first love though is hunting and fishing in Fiordland so he is well qualified to offer guided fishing on our local rivers for brown or rainbow trout.

We are also available to arrange wilderness fishing or hiking trips whether they be guided or not. We can supply the necessary gear and advice and plan any trips to suit your budget and make them a memorable experience.

Our country property overlooks the scenic Mararoa River which is itself famous for its trout fishing and only a 5 min walk away.

We live at "The Key" a small rural community on the main Queenstown - Te Anau highway (15 min drive to Te Anau). Surrounded by sheep, beef and deer farms and majestic mountains it makes an ideal base to explore Fiordland (Day trips to Milford Sounds and Doubtful Sounds are a must) and get away from the hustle of town. For your convenience we also operate a booking agency for any of the local tourist trips. We also offer free of charge for anyone interested evening bike rides, bushwalks, fishing or small game hunting for those wanting a "country experience".

Your accommodation is a warm, sunny 3 year old self-contained cottage with large bedrooms and adjoining bathroom. The kitchen and lounge have everything you'll need for a comfortable stay.

Your cottage has a beautiful country view and privacy if you prefer, or you are welcome to join us at your leisure for some good old country hospitality - We'd love to see you!

Te Anau

Rural Homestay
Address: William Stephen Road, Te Anau
Name: Kepler Cottage
Telephone: (03) 249 7185
Fax: (03) 249 7186
Mobile: (025) 314 076
Email: kepler@southnet.co.nz
Beds: 1 Queen, 3 Single (3 bedrooms)
Bathroom: 1 Ensuite, 1 Private
Tariff: B&B (full) Queen with ensuite $100, Twin with Private $90, Single $70, Single with ensuite $80. NZ B&B Vouchers accepted From 1 May to 1 November.
Nearest Town: 5km Te Anau

Jeff and Jan Ludemann welcome you to their small lifestyle property, situated on the edge of Fiordland and just five minutes drive from Te Anau. Jeff is an aircraft engineer and Jan works from home as a freelance journalist and marketing consultant. Our hobby farm carries deer and sheep and our family includes two dogs and "Floyd" the cat. We have both travelled widely and in return welcome International and New Zealand visitors to share the magic of Fiordland. We can advise on tours and sightseeing and make bookings where needed. Te Anau is a comfortable base for travellers visiting the world famous Milford or Doubtful Sounds, or for anyone planning to walk one of the many popular walking tracks in the area. There is an excellent golf course nearby and several trout laden rivers, and we have mountain bikes, golf clubs and fishing gear available for your use.
Directions: *Phone (03) 249-7185 for directions.*
Home Page: http://www.fiordland.org.nz/html/kepcot.html

Te Anau

Guest House+Self-contained Acc
Address: "Shakespeare House",
10 Dusky Street, Te Anau
Name: Margaret & Jeff Henderson
Telephone: (03) 249 7349
Fax: (03) 249 7629
Mobile: (025) 392 225
Email: marg.shakespeare.house@xtra.co.nz
Beds: 4 King, 3 Double, 4 Single (7 bedrooms)
Bathroom: 7 Ensuite
Tariff: B&B (full) Double $98-$112,
Single $70-$80, Children phone for price, Credit Cards. (Off season rates). Self-contained: 1 Double, 3 Single (2 bedrooms), TV, lounge, galley kitchen, own bathroom.
Nearest Town: Te Anau, 10 minutes walk to centre.

Shakespeare House is a well established Bed and Breakfast where we keep a home atmosphere with personal service. We are situated in a quiet residential area yet are within walking distance of shops, lake, restaurants and attractions. All our rooms are ground floor and we have a choice of King, double or twin beds. Each room has private facilities, TV and tea / coffee making. Our self-contained two bedroom unit is popular for families. We also have a wheelchair unit. Our rooms open onto a large warm conservatory. Laundry facilities are available and non-smoking is preferred. Our tariff includes the choice of continental or a delicious cooked breakfast. A courtesy car is available. Off street parking. Baggage can be stored for guests walking tracks. A warm welcome awaits you from Margaret and Jeff and our cats Brothersoul and Sleepy.

Te Anau
Farmstay, Gardens
Address: Lynwood Park,
State Highway 94, 8km before Te Anau, on left, signposted
Name: Allan & Trina
Telephone: (03) 249 7990   **Fax**: (03) 249 7990
Email: lynwood.park@xtra.co.nz
Beds: 2 Queen, 3 Single (3 bedrooms)
Bathroom: 2 Ensuite
Tariff: B&B (continental) Double $80, Single $65,
Children $30. Full breakfast by prior arrangement $5 extra.
NZ B&B Vouchers accepted $10 surcharge.
Credit cards: (Visa/MC/Bankcard/Diners/Amex/EFTPOS)
Nearest Town: Te Anau 8km.

Lynwood Park is a developing 6 acre display garden set amidst a 450 acre sheep, cattle and deer farm. Our new home was built to ensure maximum comfort and privacy for guests with semi detached accommodation. Each guest has a private entrance and tea/coffee making facilities. We both have a keen interest in horticulture, growing our own plants for sale and inclusion in 6 acre of gardens. Having built our own home we have a well equipped workshop that is now used to build garden furniture.
We offer the use of our barbecue, laundry facilities, guest fridge, kitchen and children's playground which our children Zach and Daniella look forward to sharing with you. Come and meet our friendly dog named Gunther. We are able to advise or arrange most activities to make your holiday a memorable experience. Wheelchair access and facilities. Come as guests - leave as friends.
Directions: *Lynwood Park, State Highway 94, 8km before Te Anau, on left, 100 metres past Lynwood Homestead. Signposted.*

Te Anau
Rural Homestay
Address: 'Eatons Coach House',
11 Charles Nairn Road,
Te Anau
Name: Pam & Barry Eaton
Telephone: (03) 249 7078
Fax: (03) 249 7078
Beds: 1 Double, 2 Single
(2 bedrooms)
Bathroom: 2 Private
Tariff: B&B (full) $95 ($85 if booking direct),
Single $70, Credit cards (VISA/MC) accepted.
Nearest Town: Te Anau - 3km south off Manapouri Highway

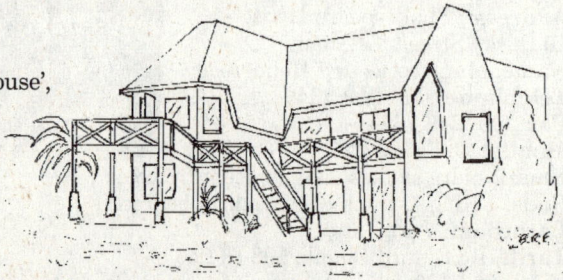

Our farmlet is situated with breathtaking mountain views, and a scenic 18 hole golf course next door. Horses, sheep, hens, ducks and Bob the cat share our life; you choose our self-contained 'Rose Cottage' or in-house twin room. Barry has an intimate knowledge of Fiordland, having spent much of his life hunting and guiding within this unique area. Pam is a horse riding instructress and lessons can be arranged. Te Anau, gateway to Fiordland, has much to offer: tramping, fishing, boating, diving, kayaking, golf and lots more. Discuss your plans with us as we provide extensive and impartial information and bookings can be made for you. We look forward to meeting you and know you will enjoy Fiordland, The Real New Zealand. Phone us direct for personal service.

Te Anau

Bed &Breakfast Guest House
Address: 186 Milford Road, Te Anau
Name: Cosy Kiwi
Telephone: 0063 3 249 7475
Freephone 0800 249700
Fax: 0064 3 249 8471
Email: cosykiwi@teanau.co.nz
Beds: 2 King, 4 Queen, 9 Single (5 bedrooms, 1 family room)
Bathroom: All ensuites
Tariff: B&B (special) Double $80-$95, Single $55-$70, Family room $110-$150.
Children negotiable. Credit Cards accepted.
Nearest Town: Te Anau - 3 mins walk

ALL NEW

Virginia, Gerhard and our 2 children welcome you to our all new Bed & Breakfast House. (We have both worked in Hospitality for over 20 years, we can speak German). A sumptuous breakfast buffet with home-made breads topped with more home-made jams and marmalade, yoghurt, fresh fruit salad, home bottled fruits, choice of juices, brewed coffee, special teas and legendary pancakes with maple syrup. Spacious ensuited rooms with top quality King/Queen beds, TV and relaxing decor, double glazed windows for warmth and sound proofing. We offer off-street parking, safe storage, laundry, telephone, fax, email, upstairs lounge-room and terrace with sun-loungers overlooking the every changing moods of the Murchison Mountains or stroll into town only 3 minutes, to a variety of highly recommended restaurants. We are always able to help book and recommend sightseeing trips, and other information to make your stay in Te Anau memorable. **Directions**: *Main Road to Milford Sound opposite school on right, just look for our sign "COSY KIWI".*
Home Page: nzhomestay.co.nz/hirner.htm

Te Anau

Farmstay, Self Contained Accommodation
Address: Rose n' Reel,
Ben Loch Lane, RD2, Te Anau.
Name: Lyn and Lex Lawrence
Telephone: (03) 249 7582
Fax: (03) 249 7582
Mobile: (025) 545 723
Beds: 1 Queen, 1 Double, 1 Single (3 bedrooms)
Bathroom: 1 Guests share, 1 Private
Tariff: B&B (full) Double $80, Single $50.
Credit Cards accepted.
Nearest Town: Te Anau 3 kms

Genuine Kiwi hospitality in a magic setting. Our small deer farm is only 5 minutes from Te Anau and you will be able to hand feed our tame fallow deer. Two friendly cats and a farm dog complete the menagerie. Our fully self contained cabin has two rooms plus bathroom with 1 Queen and 1 single. Complete with cooking facilities, fridge, microwave and TV. Sit on the veranda and watch the deer with a lake and mountain back drop.
Our modern two storey smoke-free home is set in an extensive garden. Two downstairs guest bedrooms. Laundry available.
Lex is a keen fly fisherman and average golfer, while I love to garden.
Fiordland is a special area and we will do all we can to make your time here memorable. Leave your car and baggage in safety with us while walking tracks etc.
Directions: *Please phone.*

Te Anau

Rural Lifestyle/Self Contained Accommodation

Address: The Croft, Te Anau Milford Sound Rd,
RD 1, Te Anau
Name: Jane and Ross McEwan
Telephone: 03-249 7393
Fax: 03-249 7393
Email: rossjane.mcewan@xtra.co.nz
Beds: 1 Queen, 1 Single (1 bedroom)
Bathroom: 1 Ensuite
Tariff: B&B (continental) Double $85,
Single $60, Children $20.
Nearest Town: Te Anau 3 km

Just 3 km from the centre of Te Anau on the Milford Sound Highway, our detached guest cottage offers you privacy and comfort, in a tranquil setting, combined with a warm welcome into our home. Look across our garden to delightful views of the lake and mountains. The cottage is new, spacious, warm with very comfortable Queen and Single beds, TV. Use the kitchen with the microwave, fridge and hot plates if you wish. We welcome you into our home for breakfast or have it served in your cottage. Ross is a builder and Jane a part-time teacher. We enjoy the rural lifestyle and gardening. Our three teenage children are away during the school year, joining us in the holidays. We have a friendly Jack Russell, two cats, and a small flock of sheep. Laundry service and email available. **Directions**: *Follow Te Anau-Milford Sound Road 3 km north of Te Anau. Rapid No 153. International B&B sign at gate.*
Home Page: http://nz.com/webnz/bbnz/thecroft.htm

Te Anau

Self Contained Accommodation
Address: Fiordland Lodge,
Kakapo Road, RD2, Te Anau
Name: Ron and Robynne Peacock
Telephone: (03) 249 7832
Fax: (03) 249 7832
Email: fiordlandguidesltd@xtra.co.nz
Beds: 1 Queen, 2 Single (2 bedrooms)
Bathroom: 1 Private
Tariff: B&B (continental) Double/Twin
$120 (each extra person $20), Single $100.
Children $15. Visa/Mastercard.
NZ B&B Vouchers accepted $48 surcharge.
May 1 - September 30 no surcharge.
Nearest Town: Te Anau 4 kms.

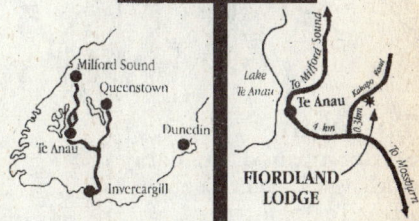

LOCATION MAPS

FIORDLAND LODGE

Fiordland Lodge is our specially designed log cabin which has been built in the traditional method with sun dried logs that have been hand peeled. The interior is completed with recycled New Zealand native timbers. The Lodge is situated on our 80 acre farm, just 5 minutes from the Te Anau township and looks across a large pond to rural farm land, with the mountains of Fiordland National Park beyond. The lodge is fully self-contained and fitted out with a queen sized bed downstairs and two single beds upstairs. We can cater for one extra with a comfortable roller bed for upstairs. The grounds are landscaped with barbecue area. Laundry facilities are available in our house. Other facilities include telephone, facsimile and email. You have all the privacy you need, but we enjoy meeting our guests and welcome you to share our hospitality. Transport can be arranged from Te Anau.

Ron is a licensed professional guide. He specialises in Wilderness fly fishing, with access by fourwheel drive vehicle, boat, floatplane or helicopter. He supplies all the fishing equipment required plus tuition for the less experienced. Ron also provides nature guiding services for birdwatching, natural history and geology. Guided hunting is also available for all species of wild game animals. Two hour, half day, full day or longer trips are available. Ron's expertise is unique. He was a National Park Ranger for 25 years, eighteen of those in Fiordland. His love and knowledge of the area is extensive. Robynne's interests include hiking, reading, travelling and gardening. Together we enjoy the outdoors, both in New Zealand and overseas. We have three teenage children, two dogs, one cat, cows calves, sheep and lambs, ducks and hens. Please phone for directions.

Note that off-season rates for the Lodge apply, May 1st September 30th.
Home Page: http://www.fiordlandguides.co.nz

Te Anau
Self-contained farmstay
Address: Davaar Country Lodge,
RD 2, Te Anau
Name: James and Fiona Macdonald
Telephone: (03) 249 5838
Mobile: (025) 377 297
Beds: 1 Queen, 3 Single (2 Bedrooms)
Bathroom: 1 Private
Tariff: B&B (Continental) Double $75 (+ $20 per extra person), Single $55. NZ
B&B Vouchers accepted $8 surcharge
Nearest Town: Te Anau 26 kms; Mossburn 30 kms.

A unique holiday experience awaits you at Davaar Country Lodge, nestled in the foothills of the Takitimu Mountains near Milford Sound in Fiordland. 'Davaar' is a 2800 acre (1100 hectare) sheep and cattle station, located in an idyllic rural setting on state highway 94, just 20 minutes east of Te Anau, at The Key.
The Lodge is exclusively yours and is fully self-contained with comprehensive kitchen and laundry facilities. A wood-burning log fire and electric blankets on all the beds make Davaar Country Lodge a cozy, warm retreat. We provide a continental style breakfast including fresh farm eggs, which is available in the lodge for you to breakfast at your leisure. The lodge is perfect for tourists, families, mountain-bikers, trampers and hunters, it is also great for anyone just looking for a real Kiwi experience. Located on the Mararoa River, with the Oreti River and Mavora lakes nearby, it is a fisherman's paradise. A fishing guide can be arranged on request.
'Davaar' offers a wonderful combination of country hospitality with the freedom to suit your own special vacation needs. Here you can get off the beaten track and explore some of New Zealand's most spectacular back country.
Your hosts James and Fiona Macdonald look forward to welcoming you.
Directions: *Please phone for directions.*

Manapouri/Te Anau

Farmstay
Address: 'Crown Lea',
Gillespie Road, 1 R.D., Te Anau
Name: Florence & John Pine
Telephone: (03) 249 8598
Fax: (03) 249 8598
Mobile: (025) 22 783 66
Email: crownlea@xtra.co.nz
Beds: (3 bedrooms)
Bathroom: 2 Private
Tariff: B&B (full) Double $90, (continental) Double $80, Single $65, Dinner $25,
Campervans welcome. NZ B&B Vouchers accepted $15 Surcharge
Nearest Town: Manapouri 20 minutes, Te Anau 30 minutes

*Our 900 acre sheep, cattle and deer farm offers you a farm tour at 6pm and the
wonderful views of the whole Te Anau Basin, the beautiful Fiordland mountains and
Lake Manapouri, can be seen from the farm and our home.*
*Two nights are more restful for the traveller, and we are an ideal base for day trips to
Doubtful and Milford Sounds, Te Anau Glow-worm Caves, or hikes on the many
walking tracks in "The Walking Capital of the World".*
*Our grown family of three have "flown the nest", but their pets - sheep, deer and cat
extend their warm welcomes to guests!*
*We have enjoyed hosting and meeting overseas guests and have travelled ourselves to
England, Wales, Scotland, Ireland, Europe and Canada.*
We look forward to welcoming you to our home.
Home Page: http://www.fiordland.org.nz/html/crownlea

Te Anau/Manapouri

Farmstay+Self-contained Accom.
Address: Hillside / Manapouri Road, Te Anau
Name: Murray & Marie Christie
Telephone: (03) 249 6695
(If no reply, phone after 1pm)
Fax: (03) 249 6695
Beds: 1 Double, 2 Single (2 bedrooms)
Bathroom: 1 Private
Tariff: B&B (continental) Double $75,
Single $50, Children negotiable,
Credit Cards (VISA/MC). Winter rates May - September.
NZ B&B Vouchers accepted accepted all year
Nearest Town: Manapouri

*We invite you to spend time in beautiful Fiordland. Murray and I with our two children
live on a sheep / cattle farm 5 minutes from Manapouri and 12 minutes from Te Anau.
We have a delightful, warm, sunny self-contained cottage exclusively yours, with all
facilities. Your tranquil setting overlooks the Mararoa River and the rugged Takitimu
Mountains. This gives you full privacy but you are welcome to join our family at your
leisure. I especially welcome families. Within walking distance the Mararoa River
provides superb trout fishing. Murray, who is a keen fisherman and hunter enjoys
sharing his experience and knowledge. Guided lake / river fishing trips are available.
We love to share our famous Milford and Doubtful Sounds and can advise and help
plan your stay. For your convenience we can make bookings for many of the local
tourist trips. We really look forward to meeting you; travel safely.*

757

Te Anau/Manapouri
Self-contained Farmstay
Address: No. 1 R.D., Te Anau
Name: Carol & Ray McConnell
Telephone: (03) 249 8553
Fax: (03) 249 8333
Email: ray.mcconnell@xtra.co.nz
Beds: 2 Double, 6 Single (3 bedrooms)
Bathroom: 2 Private
Tariff: B&B (continental)
Double $70, $10 each extra person.
Nearest Town: Manapouri 15 mins, Te Anau 25 mins

Our sheep and beef farm is situated at the base of the Takitumu Mountains with magnificent views. Your accommodation is a comfortable fully self contained spacious farmhouse. It has an attractive private setting and is an excellent base for families or groups to explore The Fiordland National Park.
Many visitors return to enjoy another happy holiday.
There are wonderful day trips to doubtful Sound or Milford Sound plus several good walks in Fiordland. The Mararoa - Warau Rivers are popular for fishing.
We look forward to meeting you.

Manapouri
Self-Contained Accommodation
Address: 1 Home Street, Manapouri
Name: Ruth & Lance
Telephone: (03) 249 6600
Fax: (03) 249 6600
Email: eco@xtra.co.nz
Beds: 2 Double, 2 Single (2 1/2 bedrooms)
Bathroom: 2 Ensuite
Tariff: B&B (continental) Double $70,
Single $50. Credit Cards.
NZ B&B Vouchers accepted $10 surcharge
Nearest Town: Manapouri - 3 mins walk

FIORDLAND
ECOLOGY HOLIDAYS

YOU
& ME & NATURE

Lance and I live in a small town on the perimeter of Fiordland National Park, only 3 minutes walk from Lake Manapouri, and 15 minutes drive from Te Anau. We are the gateway to Doubtful Sound.
Our home is a popular Bed & Breakfast stopover for birds as we are surrounded with mature trees. Wake up to the call of the bellbird or tui, and watch the birds feeding while you have breakfast. A warm, homely self-contained flat with an open fire will help make your stay comfortable. You have the option of total privacy or joining us. We both have a keen interest in underwater and natural history photography, sailing, diving and conservation. We run our own business, Fiordland Ecology Holidays. We also run 3, 5 and 10 day live aboard charters in Fiordland throughout the year. Why not join us on board for a few days and learn about our rainforest, be introduced to fur seals and play with dolphins? We feel it is a privilege to be able to share our knowledge and love of this part of the world. Having both travelled widely, we know how important it is to have somewhere that feels like home. We suggest at least a 3 to 4 day stay as there is so much to do off the beaten track, especially if you join us on one of our trips. If we can help plan your holiday, please write to us. We really look forward to meeting you and hope that where ever you come from your travels are safe and happy.
Home Page: www.fiordland.gen.nz

Manapouri
B&B Homestay
Address: 'The Cottage', Waiau St, Manapouri
Name: Don & Joy MacDuff
Telephone: (03) 249 6838 Freephone: 0800 677 866
Fax: (03) 249 6839
Email: don.joymacduff@xtra.co.nz
Beds: 2 Queen, 1 Single (2 bedrooms)
Bathroom: 2 Ensuite
Tariff: B&B (continental) Double $70-$85, Single $55. Full Breakfast $5 extra
pp. Laundry facilities available (small charge). Credit Çards. NZ B&B Vouchers
accepted $16 surcharge
Nearest Town: Manapouri a small peacefull town coveniently close to the
facilities of the larger town of Te Anau.

Charm tranquillity and a warm welcome is assured when you choose to stay with us in our lovely picturesque cottage, situated by the lower Waiau River in the Manapouri township. We are only a few minutes walk to where the boat departs for the magnificent Doubtful Sound Fiord Trip. Our home is surrounded by trees and we offer magnificent views of the mountains, river and lake. Our guestrooms are ensuite with tea and coffee making facilities.   Each bedroom has French doors that open to an English cottage garden. Wander outside and listen to the birds, sit and enjoy the peace and quiet. An ideal stay is 3 nights to enjoy both Milford and Doubtful Sounds and the many walks in the area. Enjoy seafood at our local restaurant or use our gas B.B.Q overlooking the river. We are middle-aged and have enjoyed living in many parts of New Zealand, including the wilderness of Fiordland. We (Don, Joy, Rosie the Skye terrier and Kittie) look forward to meeting you and making our spacious cottage your home away from home. **Home Page**: www.fiordland.org.nz.html/cottage.html

Manapouri
Homestay
Address: PO Box 93, Manapouri
Name: Edith Jones
Telephone: (03) 249 6991
Email: EdithJ@xtra.co.nz
Beds: 1 Double (1 Bedroom)
Bathroom: 1 Private
Tariff: B&B (Continental) Double $90.
Credit cards welcome. Direct booking $80.
Nearest Town: Manapouri

You will feel completely at home here, especially if you enjoy a spectacular view and are garden lovers. The ever changing picture of Lake Manapouri and the Cathedral Mountains fills an entire wall of your room. A balcony leads into the upper glass house with grapes, jasmine, and vegetables growing.
Enjoy the serenity of Manapouri and its unspoiled lake with clean, safe beaches.
I'm a transplanted American who fell in love with the New Zealand culture and this view! My interests include gardening, hiking, sailing, diving, travelling and meeting people, of course. I'll be happy to advise you on all our local activities, including cruise options in Milford and Doubtful Sounds, fishing, kayaking, diving and the many walking tracks in the area. After a long day, a private shower or bath awaits you, followed by a relaxing evening in front of a toasty open fire.
Kitchen facilities are available for self-caterers.
Please call for directions.

Mossburn

Farmstay
Address: No. 1 R.D, Otautau
Name: Joyce & Murray Turner
Telephone: (03) 225 7602
Fax: (03) 225 7602
Email: murray-turner@clear.net.nz
Beds: 1 Double, 4 Single (3 bedrooms)
Bathroom: 1 Guests share
Tariff: B&B (full)
Double $70, Single $40,
Children under 12 half price, Dinner $25.
NZ B&B Vouchers accepted
March to October.
Nearest Town: Mossburn 25 km, Otautau 40 km

Our modern home is on 301 hectares situated approximately halfway between Invercargill and Te Anau which can be reached in an hour. We enjoy meeting people and will provide good quality accommodation and farm fresh food in a welcoming and friendly atmosphere. We winter 3000 sheep and 200 beef cattle. You are welcome to join in on farm activities if you wish, come for a tour of the farm or just relax. Swimming pool is available in summer. Murray is a keen fly fisherman and regulary fishes the Aparima and surrounding rivers (guiding is available). Joyce is a keen gardener and is currently Area Representative for the International Agriculture Exchange Association. You are welcome to join us for an evening meal or bed and breakfast at your discretion. (No pets please)
Directions: *Please write, phone or fax. At least 24 hours notice is advised to avoid possible disappointment.*

Lumsden

Farmstay
Address: R.D. 4, Lumsden
Name: Annette & Bob Menlove
Telephone: (03) 248 7114
Fax: (03) 248 7114
Mobile: (025) 204 9753
Beds: 2 Double, 4 Single (4 bedrooms)
Bathroom: 2 Private, 1 Family share.
Tariff: B&B (full) Double $60,
Single $30, Dinner $20.
Booking thru an agent is extra 10%
NZ B&B Vouchers accepted.
Nearest Town: 9 km south of Lumsden,
Invercargill 80 km

Josephville Gardens

We have a 480 hectare farm which runs sheep cattle and deer. Surrounding our comfortable warm home we have a large garden with a small nursery attached. The garden has a large selection of Rhododendrons, specimen trees, roses and perennials. The golf course is 3 kms away, golf clubs are available, a good fishing river nearby. We have hiked in our mountains a lot and can give advise on where and what to see. If you wish, a four wheel drive trip is available.
We live on State Highway 6 (Rapid sign 824), 9 kms south of Lumsden.

Winton

Self Contained Farmstay Accommodation
Address: 710 Riverside Road,
Centre Bush (nearWinton)
Name: Nethershiel Farm Cottage
Telephone: (03) 236 0791
Fax: (03) 236 0101
Mobile: (025) 340 598
Email: kathieh@southnet.co.nz
Beds: 2 Queen, 2 Single,
Double divan bed plus bunks
Bathroom: 1 Private
Tariff: B&B (Full) Double $75, Single $50,
Children under 12 years of age $20.
Longer stays by negotition. NZ B&B Vouchers accepted
Nearest Town: Winton (10 mins)

Enjoy your own comfortable fully equipped three bedroom house plus separate bunkhouse for energetic children. Set in its own historical garden on a sheep and flower farm in the heart of Southland. Flowers are packed from October to June and you can lend a hand. Tennis court on the property and trout river two minutes away. Excellent 18 hole golf 10 minutes away, only $10 per round! Winton is 10 minutes south and has super markets, banks, three pubs, two take-aways, delightful cafe and frendly Bridge club. The cottage is central to all Southern region activities including Stewart Island, Catlin's, Borland, Lake Hauroko, the Southern Lakes, Fiordland and coastal drives. It's a good area to settle into for a few days and meet the friendly locals. Pets welcome. Allergen friendly.
Home Page: www.nz.homestay.co.nz

Balfour

Farmstay
Address: Longridge North,
No. 6 R.D., Gore
Name: Ivor & Margaret
Telephone: (03) 201 6090
Fax: (03) 201 6090
Beds: 4 Single (2 bedrooms)
Bathroom: Guests share shower
Tariff: B&B (full) Double $70, Single $40, Dinner $20 pp.
Nearest Town: Balfour 5 minutes, Lumsden 15 minutes, Gore 30 min

We live in a beautiful farmland valley surrounded by majestic mountains on the main tourist route to Queenstown, Milford Sounds, Lakes Te Anau and Manapouri, all excellent day trips.
We farm deer, cattle and sheep and are very fortunate to be only ten minutes from one of the most famous trout fishing rivers in the world, the Mataura River, Oreti and Waikaia rivers close by - so, if it is fishing, farming or just relaxing in our tranquil surroundings, we will enjoy sharing it with you.
Directions: *From Lumsden take road to Gore about 4 km, turn left at sign post to Longridge follow tarseal over hill. We are fourth house on right.*
From Gore (30 min) turn right at Balfour crossroads, then second turn left (signpost follow tarseal fourth house on left (5 min)). Please phone early.

Balfour
Farmstay
Address: 'Hillcrest',
206 Old Balfour Road,
No. 1 R.D., Balfour
Name: Ritchie & Liz Clark
Telephone: (03) 201 6165
Fax: (03) 201 6165
Email: clarkrl@esi.co.nz
Beds: 1 Double, (2 single, studio unit)
2 bedrooms. (Fold-up bed + cot available for children)
Bathroom: 1 Private, 1 Family share
Tariff: B&B (full) Double $80, Single $40, Children half price; Dinner $20p.p.
Campervans $20. NZ B&B Vouchers accepted
Nearest Town: Balfour 3 km, Lumsden 16 km, Gore 40 km

We welcome you to join us on our 650 acre sheep and deer farm. We have three school-age children and our interests include handcrafts, gardening, tennis, photography, fishing and our two cats. Enjoy a relaxing dinner with fine food, wine and conversation. Breakfast is served with fresh baked bread, homemade yoghurt, muesli, jams and preserves. Relax in our garden and enjoy the farm and mountain views or a game of tennis on our asphalt court. We are close to the Mataura, Waikaia and Oreti rivers which are great for trout fishing. A fishing guide can be arranged on request. A complimentary farm tour is included. Laundry available for guest use. Our farm is situated 3km from Balfour which is a popular stopover, being on the main tourist route from the lakes to Dunedin via Gore. (S.H.94) Smoke free home.
Directions: *When arriving at Balfour crossroads, take the road to Waikaia, then the first turn to the left Old Balfour Road and travel 2.5km, we are on the right. Please phone, fax.*

Wendonside
Farmstay
Address: 'Ardlamont Farm',
110 Wendonside Church Road North,
Wendonside, No.7 R.D., Gore
Name: Lindsay & Dale Wright
Telephone: (03) 202 7774
Fax: (03) 202 7774
Email: ardlamont@xtra.co.nz
Beds: 1 Double, 2 Single (2 bedrooms)
Bathroom: 1 Private
Tariff: B&B (full) Double $80, Single $40,
Children half price. Dinner $25.
Nearest Town: Riversdale 15 km, Balfour 12 km

Come and experience 'Ardlamont', a 4th generation 1200 acre sheep and beef farm which offers panoramic views of Northern Southland. Gourmet meals are a speciality and will be served with fine New Zealand wines. Our farmstyle breakfasts are another treat - the aroma of freshly baked bread to greet you in the morning. Take a tour of the farm, then return to the comforts of our large recently renovated 90 year old homestead. Having travelled widely and experienced this kind of hospitality in other countries we enjoy welcoming visitors into our home. We have 3 school-age children and welcome family groups. We have a wide range of interests including sport, the arts, Toastmasters, music and restoring our house to its former glory. Two of New Zealands best trout fishing rivers only five minutes away.
We are 15 minutes off S.H.94 - (Queenstown - Dunedin route) and well worth the detour.
Directions: *Please phone or write.*

Waikaka

Farmstay
Address: Blackhills, R.D.3 Gore, Southland
Name: Blackhills Farmstay - Dorothy & Tom Affleck
Telephone: (03) 207 2865
Fax: (03) 207 2865
Beds: 1 Queen, 2 Single (2 bedrooms)
Bathroom: 1 Family share, 1 Guest share
Tariff: B&B (full) Double $80, Single $40, Children under 13 half price; Dinner $25. NZ B&B Vouchers accepted
Nearest Town: Waikaka township 8km, Gore 30km.

Our sixty-year-old home, renovated to give generous comfortable living area, is situated on our 360 ha intensive sheep farm on a ridge above Waikaka River. You may have dinner with us or if you prefer only bed and breakfast. A farm tour is available and as our family becomes more independent we like to share time with guests. Venture off the main road and enjoy warm hospitality, superb views and the refreshment of a quiet rural visit.
Directions: *Turn off State Highway 1 just north of Gore, onto State Highway 90. Turn left at Waikaka Valley corner, marked by church and windmill, follow signposts to Waikaka until T corner (approx 10 km). At T corner turn left, then first right onto gravel Nicolson Road. Proceed 4 km veering right at each intersection. We live on Robertson Road, the last kilometre a steep hill - 20 minutes from State Highway 1.*

Waikaka Valley, Gore

Farmstay
Address: 'Glenellen', Waikaka Valley, No 5 R.D., Gore
Name: Brigette & Donald Morrison
Telephone: (03) 207 1857
Fax: (03) 207 1857
Email: rosedale@esi.co.nz
Beds: 1 Double, 3 Single (2 bedrooms)
Bathroom: 1 Private, 1 Family share
Tariff: B&B (full) Double $75, Single $45, Dinner $25. NZ B&B Vouchers accepted
Nearest Town: 10 km northeast of Gore on SH90

Welcome to "Glenellen" and to Waikaka Valley, a small traditional rural community, 10 km from Gore. We are a young family on a 1,500 acres mixed farm of sheep and arable with our two boys representing the sixth generation on the property. We also maintain a Romney Stud amidst this setting of beautiful green rolling countryside. We are both well travelled and enjoy our sport and outdoor activities. There is fishing on the farm and most other amenities are available locally. Our spacious home secluded by mature gardens offers a warm and relaxed stay and our labrador and spaniel provide a hearty welcome. Verandahs and sunny lounge and open fires accommodate all seasons. You may have dinner with us and enjoy the best of New Zealand cuisine, or if you prefer just bed and breakfast. There is a good range of restaurants in Gore. We prefer no smoking in the dining room and bedrooms.
Directions: *Please phone*

Pukerau, Gore
Country Homestay
Address: 1158 State Highway 1, Pukerau
Name: Dawn & David Connor
Telephone: (03) 205 3896
Fax: (03) 205 3896
Beds: 1 Double, 2 Single (2 bedrooms)
Bathroom: 1 Private, 1 Guests share
Tariff: B&B (full) Double $70,
Single $45, Dinner $25,
Credit Cards.
NZ B&B Vouchers accepted
Nearest Town: Gore 12km

We welcome you to our warm and comfortable home. We have a small private garden with mature trees and shrubs and have a lovely rural outlook. We have two acres where we run a few pet South Suffolk sheep. Growing a variety of Orchids is our main interest and we enjoy sharing these beautiful flowers with others. We are just minutes away from several rivers including the Mataura which is well known for brown trout fishing. All beds have electric blankets. Laundry facilities available. We welcome you to have an evening meal with us, or if you prefer, only Bed and Breakfast, cooked or continental. We are 12km east of Gore on State Highway 1. We prefer guests not to smoke in our home.
Directions: *Please phone for directions and bookings.*
Home Page: ewen@esi.co.nz

Gore
Farmstay
Address: 'Dellmount',
Woolwich Street,
Gore, Southland
Name: Brian & Noelene Ross
Telephone: (03) 208 1771
Fax: (03) 208 1771
Beds: 1 Queen, 2 Single (2 bedrooms)
Bathroom: 1 Private, 1 family share
Tariff: B&B (full) Double $70, Single $45,
Children half price, Dinner $20pp (by prior arrangement).
NZ B&B Vouchers accepted
Nearest Town: Gore 2km

A warm Kiwi welcome awaits you at "Dellmount". We are situated approximately 2km from the town centre, on the banks of the Mataura River, which is famous for brown trout fishing. We have a small farm of 50 acres, where we run our Arabian Horse Stud, plus sheep and cattle also a few hens, two cats and two dogs. Our modern home is warm and comfortable with spacious lounge and dining areas. Being handy to the local golf course, shops and bush walks, we will provide you with a comfortable base from which to explore the delights of the area or a pleasant peaceful overnight haven on your travels. A home cooked meal using local produce is available by prior arrangement if required or just Bed & Breakfast. We, Brian and Noelene, would enjoy meeting and sharing our home with you.

Gore

Homestay
Address: 584 Reaby Road, 7 RD Gore
Name: Irwin's Farmstay
Telephone: (03) 208 6260
Beds: 1 Queen, 4 Single (3 bedrooms)
Bathroom: 1 Guests share, plus 1 extra toilet
Tariff: B&B (full) Double $70, Single $40, Children half price, Dinner $25 pp.
Nearest Town: Gore (10 minutes)

Sandy and Tricia are semi retired having left two sons farming where we did eight years of farmstays. Sandy goes back to lend a hand when necessary. We have 43 acres with native bush covered hills nearby, run sheep and have two sheep dogs and are in the process of building a completely new garden, come and share our joys and frustrations.
Gore is 10 minutes away and we are on the road to Dolamore Park (another 5 minutes) where there are several walks and a playground. Many trout fishing rivers are an easy drive away. We enjoy meeting people having done some overseas travel and other interests include sport, reading, gardening and knitting. Beds have electric blankets, laundry facilities, cot and highchair available. No smoking indoors please. We have a geriatric cat that may get company. Please phone for directions.

Gore

Homestay
Address: 143A Broughton Street, Gore
Name: McRae Homestay
Telephone: (03) 208 0662
Fax: (03) 208 0662
Beds: 1 Double, 2 Single (3 Bedrooms)
Bathroom: 1 Private
Tariff: B&B (full) Double $80, Single $40, Dinner $25 pp, Children half price.
Nearest Town: Gore

David and Jean are from a farming background. David's interests are horse trekking and rugby, while Jean enjoys gardening and golf. Our home is very comfortable with a lovely garden. We are ideally situated, with great fishing and a beautiful golf course a few minutes drive. It is an easy walk to town. Queenstown is 1 1/2 hours and Dunedin 1 3/4 hours drive. We have a Bichon Frise dog "Bobby Mac" who is visitor friendly.
We offer: Bed & Breakfast, Dinner by prior arrangement, use of laundry facilities.

Mataura, Gore
Farmstay
Address: 291 Glendhu Road,
No. 4 R.D., Gore
Name: 'Kowhai Place'
Telephone: (03) 203 8774
Fax: (03) 203 8774
Beds: 1 Queen, 6 Single (4 bedrooms)
Bathroom: 1 Guests share, 1 Private
Tariff: B&B (full) Double $70,
Single $40,
Children half price, Dinner $20pp.
NZ B&B Vouchers accepted
Nearest Town: Mataura 3 kms

John and Helen have a mixed farm of cattle, sheep, deer, goats. We farm at the bottom of the South Island, and have been told, several times by overseas visitors - this area is the most beautiful in the world. We live 5 minutes from one of the best brown trout fishing rivers in the world. Drive one hour south and you are at the seaside. One and a half hours to beautiful lakes district, and ski fields.
We both play golf, enjoy gardening and working on our farm.
15 minutes south of Gore at 291 Glendhu Road. Turning off State Highway 1 opposite the Freezing Works at Mataura. 3 minutes from Mataura. 30 minutes from Invercargill. A warm welcome and a farm style, cooked meal, if orderd in advance, awaits you on arrival. Fishing guide can be booked by prior arrangement.

Wyndham
Farmstay
Address: 365 Wyndham - Mokoreta Rd.
No 2 R.D, Wyndham, Southland.
Name: Smith's Farmstay,
Beverly & Doug Smith
Telephone: (03) 206 4840
Fax: (03) 206 4840
Email: smith'sfarmstay@nzhomestay.co.nz
Beds: 1 King/1 Queen or 4 Single (3 bedrooms)
Bathroom: 1 Ensuite, 1Guests share, one separate toilet
Tariff: B&B (full) Double Ensuite $100, Double $80, Single $50, Children negotiable, Dinner $25. Credit Cards: Visa/Mastercard.
Nearest Town: Wyndham 5km, Edendale 10km

You are assured of a warm welcome to our modern farm house and 172 hectare sheep farm. We are situated on the hills 5km from Wyndham giving a panoramic view of the Southland Plains and the mountains beyond. The Mataura, Mimihau and Wyndham Rivers, renowned for brown trout, are just a short 5km drive away. Doug is a keen and experienced fisherman will only be too happy to share his knowledge of these rivers with you. Beverly, a qualified nurse, enjoys cooking, floral art, gardening and knitting. We have two friendly cats. You will enjoy comfortable and homely surroundings and genuine home cooking including preserved fruits, jams, home grown meat and vegetables. Special diets available. Your are welcome to join us for an evening meal, if required. Please ring the night before. We enjoy meeting people and both are of friendly disposition with a sense of humour. We enjoy travel and have three adult sons. Tours of lovely gardens offered. Long stayers most welcome: - Please book in advance, to avoid disappointment. We are members of New Zealand Association of Farm & Home Hosts. **Directions**: *5km from Wyndham on the Mokoreta Road. Sign at gate.*

Progress Valley, South Catlins

Farmstay
Address: 'Catlins Farmstay' 174 Progress Valley Rd, R.D.1, Tokanui,
Name: June & Murray Stratford
Telephone: (03) 246 8843 **Fax**: (03) 246 8844
Email: catlinsfarmstay@xtra.co.nz
Beds: 1 Queen, 1 Double, 2 Single (3 bedrooms)
Bathroom: 1 Ensuite, 1 Guests share, 1 Family share
Tariff: B&B (full) Double $90-$100, Single $55, Children neg, Dinner $30.
Credit Cards. Vouchers accepted $10 surcharge
Nearest Town: Invercargill 80 km, Dunedin 170 km, Waikawa 6 km.

Welcome to our place in the Catlins situated 6 km from Waikawa and close to the Petrified Forest at Curio Bay and Hectors Dolphins. Our home is centrally heated, plus open fire in lounge and is set in large garden with tennis court. The farm is 1000 acres and runs 3000 sheep, 50 cattle including Dexters and 500 deer along with one eye dog and two huntaways. Our family is grown up and interests include meeting people, music, cooking, gardening and most sports including rugby. Guests are most welcome to join in farm and community activities or walk the hilltops for great views of the coast. Our favourite menus consists of local seafood for entree, followed by home grown meat and fresh veges from the organic garden, followed by home-made desserts. Breakfasts are according to your needs and range from light to hearty with my bottled fruit and home-made jams and jellies hard to resist.
Directions: *From Invercargill follow scenic route and 22 km past Tokanui take right turn to Progress Valley. We are first house on right. Alternative coastal route Invercargill via Curto Bay, 6 kms north Waikawa turn right into Manse Rd, we are 2nd house on the right. From Dunedin go to Balclutha on to scenic route through Owaka and Catlins Forest until sign post to Progress Valley. Turn left, we are first house on right.*
Homepage: http://www.nzhomestay.co.nz/stratford.htm

Tokanui

Farmstay
Address: 'Egilshay', R.D.1, Tokanui
Name: Jean & John McWilliam
Telephone: (03) 246 8703
Fax: (03) 246 8551
Email: jeanmcw@xtra.co.nz
Beds: 1 Double, 3 Single (2 bedrooms)
Bathroom: 1 Guests share
Tariff: B&B (full) Double $80, Single $50, Dinner $25, Children half price,
Campervans welcome. Credit Cards. NZ B&B Vouchers accepted
Nearest Town: Invercargill, 60 km, Dunedin 165 km

Welcome to our home, which is a 640 acre sheep and cattle property on the "Southern Scenic Route" - the Gateway to the Catlins. We have a modern home in attractive surroundings with sunny bedrooms, comfortable beds and electric blankets. Guests have own bathroom and toilet. We have one very talkative cat. Come and see our unique Porpoise Bay with its friendly Hectors' dolphins, and Curio Bay on the rugged south coast of New Zealand. Trout fishing, golf course, bowling green and tennis courts are all nearby. Deep sea trips available. You are welcome to inspect the many seasonal activities on the farm. Join us for dinner, which features our own homegrown produce. Continental and cooked breakfast available. Our interests include cooking, gardening, woolcrafts and service clubs. Come and enjoy our warm Southern Southland hospitality in a relaxed, rural setting. Our home is a smokefree zone.
Directions: *Easy to find. Southern Scenic Route Highway 92, 6km east of Tokanui Rapid No 583.* **Home Page**: http://www.nzhomestay.co.nz/mcwill.htm

SOUTHLAND

Waikawa
Farmstay
Address: 595 Yorke Road, Progress Valley,
No. 1 RD Tokanui, Southland.
Name: Bruce & Alison Yorke
Telephone: (03) 246 8833
Fax: (03) 246 8833
Mobile: (025) 260 9203
Beds: 1 Double, 2 Single (2 bedrooms)
Bathroom: 1 Guests share, 1 family share
Tariff: B&B (full) Double $90,
Single $55, Dinner $25.
NZ B&B Vouchers accepted $15 Surcharge
Nearest Town: Invercargill 85km, Dunedin 175km

A warm welcome awaits you at Bay Farm, your hosts are Bruce and Alison Yorke. Bay Farm is a tranquil retreat situated in native bush overlooking Waikawa Harbour South Catlins. (It is one of Catlins best kept secrets.) We farm sheep and cattle on 1200 acres. Dinner with us includes fresh home grown produce. Opportunities exist for farm tours, fishing, walks on a private beach. Non-smokers preferred.Our interests include tramping, sailing, horticulture, meeting people and golf.
Directions: *From Invercargill take Southern Scenic Route 70km, turn right at Progress Valley turn right into Yorke Road. We are 6km in Yorke Road. From Dunedin take Southern Scenic Route, turn left at Progress Valley, turn right into Yorke Road. Bay Farm 6km.*

Fortrose "Gateway to the Catlins" Southland
Farmstay - Bed & Breakfast
Address: 'Greenbush' 298 Fortrose -
Otara Road,
No. 5 R.D., Invercargill
Name: "Greenbush Farmstay"
Ann & Donald McKenzie
Telephone: (03) 246 9506
Fax: (03) 246 9506
Mobile: (025) 239 5196
Beds: 1 Double, 4 Single (3 bedrooms)
Bathroom: 1 Guests share
Tariff: B&B (full)
Double $90, Single $55,
Children negotiable, Dinner $25. NZ B&B Vouchers accepted $20 surcharge
Nearest Town: Invercargill 50km

Greenbush is situated 4 kms from Fortrose on the "Catlins Coastal Heritage Trail" the ideal place to stay prior to or after you have explored "The Catlins" (the last unspoilt treasure of New Zealand). Our farm is boundaried by Foveaux Strait where we farm sheep, beef cattle. You may like to stroll along a wild beach, watch the bird life on our own lake, and enjoy a farm tour. We are the fourth generation at 'Greenbush'. Our 1920's home is nestled in a well established garden where you may wake up to birdsong or just enjoy our tranquil surroundings. We have a cat and dog that will respect your privacy. You are welcome to join us for an evening meal or just Bed & Breakfast. Please ring the night before to avoid disappointment. Non smokers preferred.
Directions: *Approximately 4 km from Fortrose Garage. 298 on the Fortrose-Otara Road.*

Invercargill on Southern Scenic Route
Farmstay/Self-contained Cottage
Address: 'Fernlea', Mokotua, No 1 R.D., Invercargill
Name: Anne & Brian Perkins
Telephone: (03) 239 5432 or (03) 239 5412
Fax: 03 239-5432   **Mobile**: (025) 313 432
Email: hermanvv@xtra.co.nz, refer to fernlea
Beds: Self-contained Cottage - 1 Double + Double divan in lounge (1 bedroom)
Bathroom: 1 Private
Tariff: B&B (full) Double $90 one night, $160 for two nights. Extra persons $20, Children negotiable, Dinner $25, Breakfast foods provided - self-catering. NZ B&B Vouchers accepted $15 surcharge
Nearest Town: Invercargill 15km

Our family farm on the Southern Scenic route makes an ideal stopover for those travelling, either south via the Southern Coastal route to Stewart Island, Te Anau or Queenstown, or north from these places. Anne's cottage nestles tranquilly in its own olde world garden, lovingly restored as a romantic hideaway, close to the beautiful unspoilt area of the Catlins and Mataura fishing river, it holds particular attraction for those wishing to get away from it all. The cottage is completely self contained with colour TV, electric blankets, microwave in fully equipped kitchen, shower, toilet, and cosy pot belly stove. We milk 160 pedigre Holstein Friesian cows & we are happy to take folk around the farm. Our extensive gardens surround a large in-ground swimming pool and barbecue area which guests are welcome to use. By prior arrangement a farm style 3 course meal awaits you on arrival. City pick-ups can be arranged.
Directions: *From Invercargill follow SH92 to Mokotua Garage (15km) turn left, 4th house on right is Fernlea. From Dunedin on SH1 - 17km from Invercargill - turn left at WOODLANDS BP garage, over railway line turn sharp right to Rimu Church (6km), veer left for 2.4k, at Mokotua sign turn right, Fernlea is on left.*
Home Page: http://www.visit-dunedin.co.nz/fernlea.html

Invercargill
Farmstay
Address: 'Tudor Park', Ryal Bush, RD 6, Invercargill
Name: Joyce & John Robins
Telephone: (03) 221 7150
Fax: (03) 221 7150
Mobile: (025) 310 031
Email: janemckay@xtra.co.nz
Beds: 2 King/Queen, 1 Double, 2 Single (3 bedrooms)
Bathroom: 2 Private
Tariff: B&B (continental) Double $80-$100, Single $40, Dinner $20. Credit Cards. NZ B&B Vouchers accepted
Nearest Town: Winton 12km, Invercargill 14km

If you are garden lovers or travellers looking for a warm comfortable place to stay that is close to all amenities but peaceful with good food, comfortable beds (electric blankets), your own bathroom and always a warm welcome. Tudor Park is for you. We are conveniently situated just off State Highway 6 to Queenstown between Winton and Invercargill close to Southern Scenic Route and Stewart Island connections. Te Anau, Queenstown and Dunedin are an easy drive. We enjoy sharing our large garden with others. As well as gardening our interests include a Simmental Beef Cattle Stud, showing cattle, horse racing, and breeding, art and we have travelled overseas.
Directions: *Please phone preferably after 5pm before 8am or at meal times.*

Rimu, Invercargill

Homestay/Farmstay
Address: Rimu, RD 1, Invercargill
Name: Southern Home Hospitality
Margaret&Alan Thomson
Telephone: (03) 230 4798
Fax: (03) 230 4798
Beds: 1 Queen, 2 Single (2 bedrooms)
Bathroom: 1 Guests share
Tariff: B&B (special/full/continental)
Double $75, Single $45, Children $12, Dinner $25
NZ B&B Vouchers accepted
Nearest Town: Invercargill approx 12 kms.

We welcome you to our comfortable and sunny home, surrounded by colourful gardens, and the farm beyond. We are semi retired and enjoy meeting people, we graze cattle and sheep, and both play golf - several courses are nearby. The beautiful city of Invercargill is 12 km away - interesting museum, housing the pre-historic live Tuatara Lizard, historic buildings and parks. The choice of trips by sea or air easily arranged to wonderful Stewart Island. We are just off the Southern Scenic highway, to the Catlins en route to Fiordland. You may have dinner with us and share an evening of relaxation and friendship. We provide the breakfast of your choice - stay as many nights as you wish - a "welcome" is always assured. Member of NZAFHH.
Directions: *From Invercargill travel approximately 7 km towards Dunedin - turn right at Clapham Road (towards large green building with red roof) - turn left - then right over railway line. Travel straight ahead for 4 km AJ Thomson on mail box - rural number 375.* **Homepage:** www.nzhomestay.co.nz.

Tussock Creek, Invercargill

Farmstay
Address: Sherwood Farm, Channel Road, Tussock Creek, No.1 R.D., Winton
Name: Pat & Derek Turnbull
Telephone: (03) 221 7270
Fax: (03) 221 7270
Email: iere@southnet.co.nz
Beds: 4 Single (2 bedrooms)
Bathroom: 1 Guests share
Tariff: B&B (continental) Double $70, Single $35. Dinner $20; Campervans $25.
Not suitable for toddlers. NZ B&B Vouchers accepted
Nearest Town: 20 mins to Invercargill

If you are looking for an interesting stay in a spacious residence in a peaceful setting then this is it. Native birds are usually present in the garden and the adjacent reserve. We have a grown up family of six (including triplets) and farm 600 acres of river flat with sheep and cattle. Our interests include veteran athletics, tramping, gardening, C.W.I., and genealogy. We have travelled extensively. Derek is a current world record holder in veteran running. We are suitable for a base as all Southern tourist attractions are within easy daily reach. Having 400 acres on Stewart Island helps us to arrange connections and accommodation over there.
Directions: *On Highway 6, coming from Invercargill, turn right into Wilsons Crossing Road 18.5km from the Information Centre, Ingill or turn left 12km from the centre of Winton. Proceed east for 9.3km on bitumen.- and 2.2km on gravel on Channel Road, passing the radio mast, cross the Makarewa River and our gateway is by the bridge. Follow the arrows up drive. Please phone first.*

Invercargill

Country stay + Self-Contained Acco
Address: 352 Lorne–Dacre Road, 6 R.D.,
Lorneville, Invercargill
Name: Bill & Pauline Schuck
Telephone: (03) 235 8031
Fax: (03) 235 8031
Email: lorneville@kiwi-camps.co.nz
Beds: 2 Double, 3 Single, 1 child's cot (3 bedrooms)
Bathroom: 1 Guests share
Tariff: B&B (special) Double $80, Single $45; Dinner $25; Children under 13 half price; Campervans $8.50 per person. Self-contained tourist flat $55 2 Adults, $13 each extra adult (sleeps 7), Cabins, from $15 per person. NZ B&B Vouchers accepted $3 Surcharge
Nearest Town: Invercargill 12 km

We are situated 3 km from the main highway to Queenstown and Te Anau.
We are a family who have moved out of town to enjoy the "good life" on a 17-acre farmlet. We have sheep, hens, cat, dog. Our home has had extensive renovations so that we can provide the most comfortable accommodation possible. All beds have Sleep Well mattresses, electric blankets and sheepskin overlays. You have a private bathroom if requested. You may wish to spend time with us helping with chores or perhaps you want to sit and relax to take time out from your busy itinerary. You may have a family dinner with us or if you prefer only bed and breakfast. All meals are prepared from farm fresh produce and our vegetables come from our own organic garden. I enjoy cooking and can promise you a delightful meal. If you are travelling by bus or plane we are happy to meet you. **Directions**: *Travel north on State Highway 6 from Invercargill city for 8 km. Turn right at Lorneville garage on to State Highway 98 (Lorne-Dacre Road), proceed for 3.5 km.*

Invercargill

Bed and Breakfast Hotel
Address: 240 Spey Street, Invercargill
Name: Montecillo Lodge
Telephone: (03) 218 2503
Fax: (03) 218 2506
Beds: 2 Queen, 3 Double,
6 Single (6 bedrooms)
Bathroom: 6 Ensuites,
6 Guests Share
Tariff: B&B (full)
Double $96, Single $76;
Dinner $25, Children $12.
Most credit cards accepted.
NZ B&B Vouchers accepted $25 Surcharge
Nearest Town: Invercargill - C.B.D

Our Bed & Breakfast Hotel is in a quiet street and close to the centre of town. The main building is almost 100 years old. Bedrooms have ensuite facilities, telephone, tea and coffee, and central heating troughout. We provide a full cooked breakfast up to 9 am, served in the dining room. Marian cooks a three course dinner for our guests during the week, served at 6 pm - please request early. You can walk to the city centre, museum, parks and golf course in ten minutes. We can arrange trips to Stewart Island, and make a free call to your next B&B. We recommend a two night stay to at least find out about Invercargill, Bluff and Stewart Island. Your Host: Marian and Harry Keil

771

Invercargill
Bed & Breakfast
Address: 22 Taiepa Road, Otatara,
No 9 R.D., Invercargill
Name: The Oak Door
Telephone: 64-3-213 0633
Fax: 64-3-213 0633
Email: blstuart@xtra.co.nz
Beds: 1 Double, 1 Queen,
2 Single (3 Bedrooms)
Bathroom: Two Bathrooms
Tariff: B&B (includes full breakfast)
$80 per couple, $60 per single person. Discount for direct guest bookings. Children welcome. Extra costs for in house services of toll calls, faxes, email and laundry facilities. Vouchers accepted
Nearest Town: Invercargill 5 minutes from city centre 2 minutes from airport

THE OAK DOOR takes its name from the front door, which welcomes our guests. A two storey home, built by the present owner, is situated in the scenic native bush and country setting of Otatara, just three minutes from downtown Invercargill, and two minutes from the airport. Our location offers guests the opportunity to visit Invercargill, the world's most southern city, population 57,000, and the gateway to New Zealand's Fiordland, the Catlins and Stewart Island. The tranquil homestyle atmosphere is the courtesy of your hosts, Bill and Lisa. Both have travelled throughout New Zealand and overseas. Lisa a Canadian, has lived in Holland and the USA as well as Canada. Note: No smoking No pets Thank you
Directions: *At Clyde and Tweed St, Take Tweed West at the roundabout, pass the airport, take the first left (Marama Ave South) take the first right (Taiepa Road) enter at the second driveway on the right "The Oak Door" Please call ahead to avoid disappointment.*

Invercargill
Bed & Breakfast
Address: 'Aarden House',
193 North Road, Invercargill
Name: Aarden House
Telephone: (03) 215 8825
Fax: (03) 215 8826
Beds: 1 Queen, 3 Single (2 bedrooms)
Bathroom: 1 Guest share
Tariff: B&B (full) Double $65-75, Single $40-$50.
NZ B&B Vouchers accepted $5 Surcharge
Nearest Town: invercargill centre 2 mins drive

Being retired farmers we enjoy meeting people and wish to make your stay as pleasant and comfortable as possible. Our home is five min's drive from the centre of Invercargill on the main highway (to / from) Queenstown or Te Anau. Bus stops to City Centre close by. Good fishing rivers handy.
There are seven town or country golf courses within 30 mins of Aarden House.
Visits to Stewart Island can be arranged, Catlins Information available.
Aarden House has a comfortable lounge with open fire, tea coffee and TV facilities plus an adjoining conservatory for your use. All beds have electric blankets. Off street parking. Our house is a non smoking zone. We look forward to having you visit us.
Dorothy & Raymond

Invercargill

Farmstay
Address: 154 Oteramika Road,
R.D. 1, Invercargill
Name: The Grove Deer Farm
Telephone: (03) 216 6492
Fax: (03) 216 6492
Beds: 1 Double, 4 Single
(3 bedrooms)
Bathroom: 1 Guests share, 1 Family share
Tariff: B&B (continental or full)
Double $75, Single $45.
Nearest Town: Invercargill 1 Km

Alex and Eileen Henderson hosts.
Bed and Breakfast accommodation on deer farm. Unique quiet rural setting only 1 kilometre from city boundary. Homestyle atmosphere and welcome. See farmed deer and sheep, guests welcome to tours of the farm. We are the gateway to Fiordland-Catlins and major tramping tracks of NZ. Halfway stopover on the Southern scenic route. Air or sea trips to Stewart Island or tour the Aluminium Smelter. Southland is one of the great pastoral farming areas and we offer tours of sheep and cattle farms (a charge for this). Famous trout fishing rivers within easy reach. Alex is a vintage car and farm machinery enthusiast and can arrange good viewing.
Directions: *Find Tweed Street - travel east and cross Rockdale Road - we are then 1 kilometre on right. Look for "The Grove" sign.*

Invercargill

Farmstay/Self Contained Accommodation
Address: Long Acres Farmstay,
Waimatua No. 11 RD, Invercargill
Name: Helen and Graeme Spain
Telephone: (03) 216 4470
Fax: (03) 216 4470
Mobile: 025 228 1308
Beds: 2 Double, 3 Single (4 bedrooms)
Bathroom: 1 Private, 1Family Share
Tariff: B&B (full) Double $80, Single $40,
Children half price, Dinner $25. Campervans welcome.
NZ B&B Vouchers accepted $12 surcharge
Nearest Town: Invercargill 10 kms on SH92

Southland hospitality at its best awaits you at our warm and friendly home. Our farm is 500 acres carrying 2500 Romney sheep and 80 cattle. We are a farming and shearing family. Shearing videos are available to watch. Visitors are welcome to join in day to day farm activities. We enjoy the garden and grow our own vegetables all yearr round. A barbecue area and spa pool are available for guests to use. Our farm makes an ideal stopover to see Bluff and Stewart Island before moving on to the Catlins or Te Anau and Queenstown. Being travellers ourselves, we look forward to sharing our home with visitors from all over the world. Stay as long as you wish. A home cooked meal is always available or if you prefer just B&B. A welcome is assured.
Directions: *From Invercargill follow SH92 till you come to the crossroad - Longbush South Road. Approx 10km (Long Acres Sign on roadside). Turn right, travel to the end of road, turn left, 2nd house on left is Long Acres.*

Invercargill
Homestay
Address: 177 Gala Street, Invercargill
Name: 'Gala Lodge'
Jeanette and Charlie Ireland
Telephone: (03) 218 8884
Fax: (03) 218 9148
Beds: 1 Queen, 3 Single (3 bedrooms)
Bathroom: 1 Guests share, 1 Family share
Tariff: B&B (Full) Double $70, Single $45,
Children under 12 half price,
Dinner $25 by arrangement.
Nearest Town: Invercargill (10 mins walk)

Gala Lodge, frequently photographed because of its appealing character is ideally located, five minutes walk from the Information Centre, Museum and Art Gallery. Queens Park, containing wonderful gardens, playgrounds, magnificent new bird aviary, Japanese Garden, observatory and sports grounds, is immediately across the street. Ten minutes walk to city centre. Gala Lodge is set in extensive grounds. Ample parking. Bedrooms upstairs are spacious, well appointed. Electric blankets provided. Downstairs two guest lounges give privacy - or you may join us for the evening. Laundry facilities available. Forty years hosting includes students from Asia, America and Europe (living as family for up to one year) and casual hosting of travellers. OUR BAKCGROUND: Farming, Education and Training management, Police and gardening. OUR INTERESTS: Travel, cultural appreciation, geneology, reading and handcrafts. OUR COMMITMENT: To provide a relaxing base for guests and to give support in their welfare and travel arrangements. Courtesy car available. You are most welcome.

Invercargill
Homestay
Address: 15 Stoneleigh Lane
Invercargill
Name: Joan and Neville Milne
Telephone: (03) 215 8921
Beds: 1 Queen, 3 Single
(3 Bedrooms)
Bathroom: 1 Guests share
Tariff: B&b (Full) Double $80,
Single $55, Dinner $25.
NZ B&B Vouchers accepted $15 surcharge
Nearest Town: Invercargill

We welcome you to share our new home and gardens, situated 50 mtrs off North Road and 5 mins from the city centre. Our home is warm and comfortable with underfloor heating and electric blankets. Neville owns a wholesale fruit and vegetable market so fresh produce is assured. Joan has been involved for years with catering and enjoys cooking, so we would love to share an evening meal with you. We are keen golfers and members of the Invercargill Golf Club, rated in the top 10 courses in New Zealand.
City and Airport pick-ups can be arranged. Laundry facilities extra. We look forward to welcoming you to our home.
Directions: *Travelling South on SH6, Stoneleigh Lane is 500 mts on your left past the Welcome to Invercargill sign.*

Waianiwa - Invercargill

Country Homestay
Address: Annfield Flowers,
126 Argyle - Otahuti Road,
Waianiwa, RD 4, Invercargill
Name: Mike and Margaret Cockeram
Telephone: (03) 235 2690
Fax: (03) 235 2745
Email: annfield@clear.net.nz
Beds: King/King twin (1 bedroom)
Bathroom: 1 Ensuite
Tariff: B&B (full or continental) Double $70, Dinner $25, Light meals $15.
Visa/Mastercard. NZ B&B Vouchers accepted
Nearest Town: Invercargill 18 km, Riverton 22 km.

Annfield, originally built in 1866, has around 17 acres of ground, of which five acres are being converted to the commercial growing of flowers, mainly gentians and lilacs. The rest is still in pasture with coloured and white sheep and also Dexter cross cattle. The house has recently been renovated, from foundations to roof, with the old character being kept and the convenience of modern facilities added. The garden is still being developed. There are a couple of dogs and cats around but they have only limited access to the house. The children have been away from home for some years.
There is good trout fishing - in season - an easy distance away and we can arrange for a guide if you let us know in advance. We are just over 1 km from the Southern Scenic Route. No smoking please. Complimentary laundry facilities.
We look forward to welcoming you to our home.
Directions: *Please phone for detailed directions.*

Riverton

Farmstay
Address: 124 Otaitai Bush,
No.3 R.D., Riverton
Name: Ian & Elaine Stuart
Telephone: (03) 234 8460
Fax: (03) 234 8460
Beds: 2 Single (1 bedroom)
Bathroom: 1 Private
Tariff: B&B (full) Double $70, Single $40, Dinner $20; Campervans $10 (2 person). Credit cards. NZ B&B Vouchers accepted
Nearest Town: 5 km from Riverton on Southern Scenic Route, Highway 99 40km from Invercargill.

Our 350 acre sheep farm is situated on the Southern Scenic Route 5km from Riverton. Our sunny and well heated house is surrounded by flower and vegetable gardens. The guest room has twin beds with electric blankets. Guest bathroom facilities. View of Foveaux Strait and Stewart Island from lounge window. You may share dinner with us or if you prefer just bed and breakfast.
Riverton is one of the oldest settlements in NZ, a fishing port with safe swimming beaches. A game of golf or squash can be arranged. Laundry facilities available. We enjoy sharing our home and farm with visitors and a friendly stay assured.
Directions: *Please phone.*

SOUTHLAND

Riverton

Bed & Breakfast
Address: 93 Towack Street, Riverton
Name: 93 Towack
Telephone: (03) 234 8732
Fax: (03) 234 8732
Beds: 3 Queen (3 Bedrooms)
Bathroom: 1 Guests Share
Tariff: B&B (Continental)
Double $80, Single $48
Nearest Town: Ivercargill

Relax and enjoy our comfortable home by the sea, situated on the waterfront with 2 of our 3 large double bedrooms opening onto a sunny veranda with peaceful water and garden views. We like to provide a friendly relaxed homestyle stay and enjoy the company of our guests. We are only 20 minutes form Invercargill on the Southern Scenic Route. Enjoy a peaceful walk on the beach and walking tracks. Walking distance to an excellent restaurant. Laundry facilities available. We look forward to meeting you.

Halfmoon Bay, Stewart Island

Homestay
Address: "The Nest", Box 88,
Halfmoon Bay, Stewart Island
Name: Lorraine Squires
Telephone: (03) 219 1310
Fax: (03) 219 1310
Email: thenest@es.co.nz
Beds: 1 Queen, 1 Double (2 bedrooms)
Bathroom: 1 Ensuite, 1 Private
Tariff: B&B (full) Double $160,
Single $80. Credit Cards.
Nearest Town: Invercargill

We are a commercial fishing family and we invite you to share our home as you explore "Rakiura", Isle of the Glowing Skies. Lindsay and Lorraine Squires
"The Nest"
Halfmoon Bay
(03) 219 1310

We are a non smoking household.

Beautiful Island, we know so well
Where freedom, love and peace do dwell
Haven of refuge in time of strife
Heavenly place to enjoy sweet life.
- A. von Tunzelman

Stewart Island
Homestay+Self-contained Accom.

Address: 'Thorfinn Charters', PO Box 43, Halfmoon Bay, Stewart Island
Name: Bruce + BJ
Telephone: (03) 219 1210
Fax: (03) 219 1210
Mobile: (025) 201 1336
Email: thorfinn@southnet.co.nz
Beds: 2 Double, 1 Single (2 bedrooms)
Bathroom: 1 Ensuite, 1 Family share
Tariff: B&B (full) Double $90, Single $65, Dinner up to $25. Credit cards (VISA/MC). Self-contained: $90 per night/2 people + $15 additional people, Family & Weekly Rates available. NZ B&B Vouchers accepted $15 surcharge
Nearest Town: Invercargill

Situated on a sheltered peninsula and only 50 metres from a beautiful beach, our home commands a magnificent sea view. Formerly a hill country farmer, now as charter boat operator, we enjoy meeting people with a love of the outdoors. As Department of Conservation Concessionaires we specialise in photographing/viewing birds and marine wildlife, bush walks and scenic/historic cruises. Our home is modern, comfortable and centrally heated with two double rooms. Both have attached bathroom and toilet, one private, and one family share. Evening meals available by prior arrangement. Two self-contained houses share the setting and provide privacy and independence. They have double and twin bedrooms, well equipped kitchens, bathroom/toilets, lounge/dining rooms, conservatory and central heating. A sleepout is also available. A courtesy transfer on arrival. We shall enjoy showing you Stewart Island's magnificent scenery, wildlife, and interesting history.

Stewart Island
B&B+Self-contained Accom.

Address: "Goomes" B&B, PO Box 36, Halfmoon Bay, Stewart Island
Name: Jeanette & Peter Goomes
Telephone: (03) 219 1057/217 6585
Fax: (03) 219 1057
Beds: 2 Queen, 1 Single (2 Bedrooms)
Bathroom: 2 Ensuite
Tariff: B&B Continental)
Double $140, Single $90.
Self Contained $100/night/2 people
+ $25 additional person. Credit Cards.
Nearest Town: Oban 5 minute walk

Our modern centrally heated home is only five minutes walk to the township, quiet and private on a bush clad point with magnificent views of Halfmoon Bay and the islands beyond. Both rooms have been refurbished, have sea views, ensuites, tea/coffee facilities and television. You can relax and watch the boats coming and going, observe the ever changing moods of the sea. Watch native birds feeding on the balcony. We are a fifth generation Stewart Island family. Peter and I have travelled extensively in New Zealand and overseas, we know how travellers appreciate relaxing in a homely atmosphere. Courtesy transfer.

Our self-contained holiday houses have been completely refurbished, have similar setting and outlook to our B&B. Well equipped, centrally heated and private. They have three star plus Qualmark grading. Courtesy transfers.

PLEASE HELP US
TO KEEP OUR STANDARDS HIGH

To help maintain the high reputation of *The NZ Bed & Breakfast Book* we ask for your comments about your stay. Please post the form in the envelope provided. Every comment form you return will go in the draw for **A weeks free B&B.** See page 6 of *The B&B Book* for details. It will help us if you save your comment forms and return them in one envelope. There are forms at every B&B and at the back of the book.

Name of Host...

Address...

It was (please circle one):
Absolutely Perfect, Excellent, Good, Adequate, Not Satisfactory.

Do you have any comments which could help your host, on such things as breakfast, meals, beds, cleanliness, hospitality, value for money.

Complete this section. It will be detached and entered into the draw for a weeks free B&B before we send your comments to the host.

YOUR NAME...

YOUR ADDRESS...

....

Please post this form to
The New Zealand B&B Book, PO Box 41022, Eastbourne, New Zealand

Index